Essentials of Psychology

Exploration and Application

Fourth Edition

Essentials of Psychology

Exploration and Application

Dennis Coon
Department of Psychology
Santa Barbara City College, California

West Publishing Company
St. Paul   New York   Los Angeles   San Francisco

A study guide has been developed to assist you in mastering the concepts presented in this text. The study guide clarifies concepts by presenting them in concise, condensed form. It reinforces your understanding of terms, concepts, and individuals and also provides a programmed review and self-test questions. The study guide is available from your local bookstore under the title, *Study Guide to Accompany Essentials of Psychology: Exploration and Application*, prepared by Tom Bond.

If you cannot locate this book in the bookstore, ask your bookstore manager to order it for you.

50 W. Kellogg Boulevard
P.O. Box 64526
St. Paul, MN 55164-1003

Printed in the United States of America

96 95 94 93 92 91 90 89 8 7 6 5 4 3

Library of Congress Cataloging-in-Publication Data

Coon, Dennis.
Essentials of psychology: exploration and application / Dennis Coon.—4th ed.
p. cm.
Bibliography: p.
Includes index.
ISBN 0-314-62480-5
1. Psychology. I. Title.
BF121.C624 1988 87-29829
150—dc 19 CIP

Cover: *Lovers* by Yankel Ginzburg reproduced by permission of the artist and S&Y Art, Ltd.

Text illustrations: Barbara Barnett, Heather Preston, Sue Sellars
Anatomical illustrations: Marsha Dohrmann
Photo research: Stuart Kenter
Design: Janet Bollow
Production Coordination: Janet Bollow Associates
Composition: The Clarinda Company

Acknowledgments The author is indebted to the following for permission to reproduce copyrighted materials.

Fig. 1-1 *(upper right)* © Art Sweezy, Stock Boston; *(upper left)* © Bruce Rosenblum, The Picture Cube; *(lower right)* Story Litchfield, Stock Boston; © Susan Van Etten, The Picture Cube.
Fig. 1-3 © Susan Kuklin, Photor Researchers.
Fig. 1-4 Brown Brothers.
Fig. 1-5 Brown Brothers.
Fig. 1-6 Brown Brothers.
Fig. 1-7 United Press International
Fig. 1-8 The Bettmann Archive
Fig. 1-9 © Ted Polumbaum
Fig. 1-11 The Bettmann Archive.

(continued following Index)

Contents in Brief

Part One An Introduction to Psychology and Psychologists 1

Part Two Foundations of Human Consciousness 47

Part Three Learning, Memory, and Thinking 175

Part Four Actions and Reactions 291

Part Five Human Development and Personality 375

Contents

Chapter 5
Perception 110

Chapter 6
States of Consciousness 140

Actions and Reactions 291

Part Four

Chapter 11
Motivation 292

Chapter 12
Emotion 321

Human Development and Personality 375 — Part Five

Chapter 14
Human Development 376

Chapter 20
Psychosis 532

Chapter 21
Insight Therapy 557

Preface

To the Student

Psychology is at once familiar, exotic, commonplace, surprising, and challenging. Most of all, psychology is changing. Indeed, this book can be no more than a "snapshot" of a colorful passing scene. And yet, it is rapid change that makes psychology so fascinating: What, really, could be more intriguing than our evolving understanding of human behavior?

Psychology is about each of us. Psychology asks, "Why do we think, feel, and act as we do? How can we best learn to understand our own behavior? Psychologists believe the answer is "through careful observation, and spirited inquiry." As simple as this may seem, it is the guiding light for everything that follows in this book.

I sincerely hope that you will find psychology as fascinating as I do. In this text, I have done all that I could imagine to make your first encounter with psychology enjoyable and worthwhile. To help you get a good start the Introduction preceding Chapter 1 discusses how to study effectively. The ideas covered there will help you get the most out of this text, class lectures, and your psychology course as a whole. In the remaining pages, I hope that the delight I have found in my own students' curiosity, insights, imagination, and interests will be apparent. Please view this book as a long letter from me to you. It is, in a very real sense, written about you, for you, and to you.

To the Instructor

This book differs from traditional texts in a number of important ways. If you are already familiar with its format, a description of Fourth Edition changes follows shortly. If the text is unfamiliar, a brief account of its design and underlying philosophy is in order.

A Book for Students As an instructor I have learned that selecting a textbook is half the battle in teaching. A good text does much of the work of imparting information to students. This leaves class time free for discussion, and it leaves students asking for more. When a book overwhelms students or cools their interest, teaching becomes an uphill battle. For this reason, I have worked hard to make this a clear, readable, and interesting text.

This book is a concise introduction to psychology. I believe an important question to ask of the introductory course is, "What will students remember next year, or in 10 years?" Consequently, I have tried to give students a clear grasp of major concepts, rather than bury them in details. At the same time, I have tried to show the value of a variety of theoretical perspectives. I think students will find this book full of intellectual challenge, and teachers will find major topics covered to their satisfaction. In addition, I have made a special effort to relate psychology to practical problems of daily life.

A major feature of the book is the Applications section in each chapter. Each of these sections explicitly bridges the gap between psychological theory and practical application. I believe students have every right to ask, "Does this mean anything to me? Can I use it? Why should I learn it if I can't?" No matter how interesting or stimulating it is, a text that fails to show the practical value of adopting new ideas is irrelevant in a basic sense. The Applications sections, therefore, spell out how students can use the principles of psychology. By doing so, they breathe life into its concepts.

A Format for Learning Before this book first appeared, psychology texts made surprisingly little use of learning principles to teach psychology. The extensive use of learning aids herein is based on my belief that students can be guided into more effective study and reading habits while learning psychology. Basically, each chapter is built around the well-known SQ3R study-reading formula. Thus, in addition to helping students learn, the chapter format encourages the development of valuable study skills. Student response to this feature of the text has been very positive, with many students reporting that they transfer the SQ3R technique to their other texts as well.

Each chapter is divided into four major parts: a *Preview*, *Resources*, *Applications*, and a *Chapter Summary*. Chapter Previews are used to arouse reader interest, to give an overview of the chapter, and to focus attention on the task at hand. Each Preview concludes with a series of *Survey Questions* to further orient readers and aid the survey step of the SQ3R method. The Resources section, which follows, presents major concepts of the chapter. Next comes an Applications section that shows how concepts can be applied. After that a Chapter Summary offers a point-by-point review of key ideas.

Throughout each chapter, *guide questions* are used to maintain attention and to make reading an active learning experience. Despite its appearance, this is not just a quesiton-and-answer format. Rather, it takes the form of a dialogue in which student questions and reactions are anticipated. Guide questions cue students to look for important points in the paragraphs that follow, thus fulfilling the *question* part of SQ3R. And, significantly, they also allow clarification of difficult points through a lively give-and-take between questions and responses.

If you glance through the text you will immediately notice the *Learning Checks* that appear throughout. These are short, non-comprehensive quizzes that allow readers to gauge recall and understanding of preceding material. Students who cannot answer Learning Check questions are directed to review the previous section before reading more. Completing Learning Checks also serves as a form of recitation to enhance learning (the fourth step in SQ3R). The last SQ3R step (review) is aided by the detailed Chapter Summary.

To supplement its SQ3R format, *Essentials of Psychology* employs a full array of traditional learning aids. These include: part outlines, boldface type and phonetic pronunciations for important terms, bullet summaries, a running glossary and a complete end-of-book glossary (also with pronunciations), summary tables, a detailed index, and a robust new illustration program.

All chapters have been kept short so they can be read in single sessions. This brevity provides excellent flexibility for the order in which chapters are assigned. It also gives students a sense of closure or completion at the end of each assignment. Finally, and perhaps most importantly, the readability of each chapter has been carefully controlled for maximum student involvement and comprehension.

I sincerely hope that teachers and students will consider this book a refreshing change from the ordinary. Writing and revising it has been quite an adventure. In the pages that follow, I think the reader will find an attractive blend of the theoretical and practical, plus many of the most exciting topics in psychology.

Fourth Edition Changes

The last 3 years have been a fertile and productive period for psychology. Perhaps as never before, researchers are revising long-standing ideas and pioneering new topics of study. Reporting these developments has been stimulating and rewarding: With this revision, *Essentials of Psychology* has become more than ever the text I always dreamed it could be.

Illustrations The most visible change in this edition is the use of color in every chapter. Added color has made it possible to improve almost all drawings, graphs, tables, and photographs so that they present information more clearly and effectively. Beyond this, the text's enhanced visual appeal should have a positive effect on student interest and motivation.

Chapter Format The format for this edition has been fine tuned in two ways. First, is the added use of highlighted boxes in each chapter. These boxes contain brief discussions of high-interest topics and are set off from the main body of the text. Most focus on current research, interesting controversies, or novel viewpoints. I think students will like them very much. A second notable change is that Applications now *precede* each Chapter Summary. This switch was made to more closely tie Applications to core chapter content.

Content Changes This Fourth Edition reflects an extensive updating. Virtually every chapter has been rewritten, reorganized, or improved, with new information evident at every turn of a page, including hundreds of new references (many as recent as 1986). Indeed, the line-by-line updates and content changes are too numerous to describe here. I would, nevertheless, like to give at least a sample of new or revised topics. These include: study skills (Introduction); women in psychology (Chapter 1); split-brain research (Chapter 3); artificial hearing (chapter 4); innate understanding of drawings, ESP research (Chapter 5); hypnosis, drug effects, meditation, behavioral remedies for insomnia (Chapter 6); human conditioning, stimulus control, behavioral self-management (Chapter 7);

CAI, skill learning, TV as a model (Chapter 8); state dependent learning, hypnosis and memory, exceptional memory, (Chapter 9); mental imagery, insight, animal intelligence, intuition (Chapter 10); obesity, circadian rhythms, jet lag, high achievement, anorexia and bulimia, coping with test anxiety (Chapter 11); emotional expression, lie detectors (Chapter 12); burnout, stress and hassles, stress management (Chapter 13); social referencing, birth, enrichment, genetics and reproduction (Chapter 14); parenting styles, "hurried adolescence," biological aging, child abuse (Chapter 15); multiple intelligences, teaching intelligence (Chapter 16); personality traits, self-concept, theories of personality, traits and situations, androgyny, identical twins and personality (Chapter 17); self-reinforcement, characteristics of self-actualizers (Chapter 18); DSM-III-R terminology, sexual deviance, post-traumatic stress disorders, postpartum depression (Chapter 19); DSM-III-R, Alzheimer's disease, biological research on depression and psychosis, the Genain quads (Chapter 20); short-term dynamic therapy, family therapy, large group awareness training, media psychologists (Chapter 21); rapid smoking, cognitive behavior therapy, covert reinforcement (Chapter 22); sexual scripts, AIDS and sexually transmitted diseases, (Chapter 23); attribution theory, selecting a mate, resisting compliance pressures (Chapter 24); anger control, aggression and pornography (Chapter 25). It is worth noting again, that this list is really just a sample of the new information to be found in this edition.

Careers in Psychology Appendix A, Careers in Psychology, is another prominent addition to this edition. Appendix A is designed to help students decide whether an undergraduate major in psychology would be appropriate for them. Employment opportunities at each degree level are described along with projections of future job prospects. Special emphasis is placed on the broad applicability of an undergraduate psychology degree to various careers and occupations. At the same time, the advantages of more advanced training are clearly stated. Appendix A answers many preliminary questions about careers in psychology and provides a general overview of the field. Psychology majors and non-majors alike should find it worth reading.

Study Guide An excellent study guide is again available to accompany *Essentials of Psychology*. To structure learning, Tom Bond's *Study Guide* offers students a thorough review and a chance to practice concepts presented in the text. The *Study Guide* includes a list of important terms and individuals, learning objectives (with space for student responses), two tests ("Do You Know the Information," "Can You Apply the Information"), and a fill-in-the-blanks Chapter Review.

WESTUDY A new microcomputer study program called WESTUDY is available to accompany this edition of the text. WESTUDY poses questions to students in three easy-to-run formats: a multiple-choice review, a race, and a college bowl contest. When used by one or more students, WESTUDY is a motivating and enjoyable study aid.

IM and Test Bank Carol Woodward has done a super job of enlarging and updating the *Instructor's Manual*. The IM includes updated film annotations and resource materials as well as new demonstrations and class exercises created by

Carol Woodward and Bill Titus. For this edition, Bill Dwyer once again brought his talents to bear on the Test Bank. The result is a collection that now contains over 2500 questions, a large percentage of which are new. In his revision Bill made a special effort to include general conceptual items as well as items that test recall of the text. The Test Bank is again available on computer tape or disks.

Transparencies I am very pleased to report that Bill Dwyer also has created a set of transparencies to enliven classroom presentations. Bill's transparencies are on acetate, in color, and ready for use. Trasparency masters that duplicate figures and graphs from the text are also available. Contact your West representative for more information on either of these media aids.

Psychware Another exciting development is the debut of *Psychware*, a CAI package to enrich the introductory course. Robert S. Slotnick and the New York Institute of Technology have developed a stimulating collection of tutorials, simulations, and experiments for use on microcomputers. Each exercise is highly interactive and features engaging graphics. By using *Psychware* students can apply the principles of operant conditioning, they can test their short-term memory, they can explore social behavior or gain insight into Piaget's stages of cognitive development, and much more.

Acknowledgements The effort required to revise this text has grown with each edition. More than ever, it has benefited from the combined efforts of a large number of people. I would like first to thank the many students who sent comments, suggestions, and letters of encouragement. To the professional users/reviewers who gave their time and expertise I extend my sincere thanks. I deeply appreciate the contributions of all those who have, over the years, contributed to this text's evolution. I especially wish to thank those who helped make this edition a reality:

Stuart Appelle
SUNY Brockport

Bruce Cannon
Vincennes University

Thomas G. Comiskey
Long Beach City College

Kathleen M. Dillon
Western New England College

David W. Martin
New Mexico State University

James P. O'Brien
Tidewater Community College

Doug Soderstrom
Wharton Community College

David L. Stritmater
Herkimer County Community College

Sandra Wilcox
CSU Dominguez Hills

In addition, I would like to thank Tom Bond and David Gershaw for their ongoing advice and support. I am also grateful for the contributions of the following individuals, whose work has so obviously enhanced this text and its supporting materials: Tom Bond, Bill Dwyer, George Johnson, Steven Pollock, Bob Slotnick, William Titus, and Carol Woodward. It has been a pleasure working with such talented and inspired psychologists.

Getting a text into print seems almost miraculous at times. With this fact in mind, I would like to thank Jane Fischer and Theresa O'Dell for their editorial support, and to Bill Stryker for translating impulse into action at West. Thanks also to Stuart Kenter for exceptional photographic research, to Maureen Rosener for getting the word out, to Dan and Mariette Francis for photographic excellence, to Marsha Dohrmann for wonderful anatomical art, and to Barbara Barnett for the colorful figures that appear throughout this text. These individuals, and many others at West Publishing Company, share greatly in the credit for this book's final form.

Finally, I would like to express my continuing gratitude to Clyde H. Perlee, Jr., everyone's favorite Editor-in-Chief, for his patience, inspiration, and friendship. This is his book a well as mine. I am equally indebted to Janet Bollow for rising to the challenge once again even though it meant foregoing a plunge to the depths.

Last of all, I would like to thank my wife Sevren, whose emotional support and countless hours of help made this book possible.

Dennis Coon

Introduction

The Psychology of Studying

Do you find learning challenging and rewarding? Or painful and intimidating? The second reaction is common even among bright students, if they lack basic "tools of the trade." Even if you're not one of those students, you may be able to improve your study skills. Would you like to learn more in less time? There is a good chance you can, if you apply the methods described here.

The SQ3R Method—How to Tame a Textbook

Have you ever completed a reading assignment, only to discover afterward that you remembered little of what you read? This problem has plagued students for decades. Fortunately, an excellent solution exists. Over 40 years ago, educator Francis Robinson developed a superb reading technique called the **SQ3R method.**

Robinson's method is simply a way of studying while you read. The symbols S-Q-R-R-R stand for *survey, question, read, recite,* and *review*. Following these five steps can help you understand ideas quickly, remember more, and review effectively for tests (Robinson, 1941):

S = *Survey.* Look ahead through a chapter before you begin reading. As you do, read only topic headings, captions for illustrations, and any chapter summary or review. This step should give you an overall picture of what lies ahead.

Q = *Question.* To focus your attention as you read, turn each topic heading into one or more questions. For example, the heading "Stages of Sleep" could raise questions such as: "Is there more than one stage of sleep?" "What are the stages of sleep?" "How do they differ?" Asking questions will increase your interest, and it will help relate new ideas to what you already know, for better comprehension.

R1 = *Read.* The first *R* in SQ3R refers to *read*. As you read, try to answer the questions you asked. Read in short "bites" from one *topic heading* to the next, then stop. (If the material is very difficult, you may want to read only a paragraph or two at a time.)

R2 = *Recite.* The second *R* stands for *recite*. After you have read a short bite of information, you should stop and recite. That is, try to silently answer your questions or summarize what you've read by writing brief notes. If you can't summarize main ideas in your own words, scan back over the section until you can. Until you can remember what you just read, there's little point to reading more.

After you have completed one section in this way, turn the next topic heading into questions. Then read to the following heading. Again, you should look for answers as you read, and you should recite before moving on. Repeat the question-read-recite cycle until you've read the entire chapter.

R3 = *Review*. When you've finished reading, skim back over the chapter, or read your notes. Then check your memory by reciting and quizzing yourself again. Or better yet, get someone to ask you questions about each topic to see if you can answer in your own words.

Question: Does this method really work?

Experiments show that using the SQ3R method improves both reading comprehension and grades (Boker, 1974; Driskell & Kelly, 1980). Simply reading straight through a chapter often leads to a case of intellectual "indigestion." That's why it's important that you stop often to think, question, recite, review, and "digest" information.

How to Use this Text With practice, you can apply the SQ3R method to any book. However, as you may have guessed, its steps are built into this text to help you use them.

Each chapter opens with a short Preview, followed by Survey Questions to help you get oriented. After you have read these two sections, take a minute or two to make your own survey of the chapter. As you read, questions woven into the text will help clarify ideas and focus your attention. Research shows that this arrangement leads to improved learning and memory (Boker, 1974; Melton, 1978).

Every few pages, Learning Checks allow you to "recite" by testing your memory of important points. (Again, you should also take notes or recite on your own.) Near the end of each chapter a special Applications section on an interesting topic will add to your practical knowledge of psychology. This is followed by a Chapter Summary you can use for review.

As you read, new terms will be defined where they first appear in the text. Key terms are printed in **boldface type** and are often followed by pronunciations. (Capital letters show which syllables are accented.) As a further study aid, a **glossary,** or mini-dictionary, of terms also appears near the end of this book. Perhaps you should take a moment to find it now.

Together, these features should make learning psychology enjoyable and effective, but there is still more you can do on your own.

■ Effective Note Taking—Good Students, Take Note! ■

Question: The SQ3R method may be good for reading, but what about taking notes in class when it's difficult to know what's important?

Effective note taking requires active listening. **Active listeners** know how to control their attention to avoid classroom daydreaming. Here's a listening/note-taking plan that works for many students. The important steps are summarized by the letters in the word **LISAN**, pronounced "listen" (Carman & Adams, 1985).

L = *Lead. Don't follow.* Try to anticipate what the instructor is going to say. As in SQ3R, use questions as guides. Questions can come from the instructor's study guides or the reading assignments.

I = *Ideas.* Every lecture is based on a core of important ideas. Usually an idea is introduced and examples or explanations are given. Ask yourself often, "What is the main idea now? What ideas support it?"

S = *Signal words.* Listen for words that tell you the direction the instructor is taking. For instance, here are some groups of signal words:

There are three reasons why . . .	Here come ideas
Most important is . . .	Main idea
On the contrary . . .	Opposite idea
As an example . . .	Support for main idea
Therefore . . .	Conclusion

A = *Actively listen.* Sit where you can hear and where you can be seen if you need to ask a question. Look at the instructor while he or she talks. Bring questions you want answered from the last lecture or from your reading. Raise your hand at the beginning of class or approach your instructor before the lecture begins. Do anything that helps you be active.

N = *Note taking.* As you listen, write down only key points. Listen to everything, but be selective and don't try to write down everything. If you are too busy writing, you may not grasp what is said. Any gaps in your notes can be filled in immediately after class.

Here is something more you should know. A revealing study (Palkovitz & Lore, 1980) found that most students do make reasonably good notes—and then don't use them! Most students wait until just before exams to review their notes—which have, by then, lost much of their meaning. If you don't want your notes to seem like hieroglyphics or "chicken scratches," it pays to review them *on a regular basis.* And remember, whenever it is important to listen effectively, the letters LISAN are a good guide.

Study Habits—Avoiding the Last-Minute Blues

It is important to realize that virtually every topic is interesting to someone, somewhere. Although I may not be interested in the sex life of the South American tree frog, a biologist might be fascinated. If you wait for your teachers to "make" their courses interesting, you are missing the point. Interest is a matter of *your attitude.* If you bring an inquiring mind and a positive attitude to your studies, you will find learning challenging and interesting. Students and teachers *together* make a class rewarding.

With these thoughts in mind, let's consider a few things you can do to improve your study habits.

Study in a Specific Place It goes almost without saying that you should study in a quiet, well-lighted area that is free of distractions. If possible, you should also have at least one place where you *only study*. Do nothing else at that spot: Keep magazines, radios, friends, pets, posters, games, puzzles, food, lovers, sports cars, elephants, pianos, televisions, hang gliders, kazoos, and other distractions out of the area. In this way, studying will become strongly linked with one specific place (Beneke & Harris, 1972). Then, rather than trying to force yourself to study by "willpower," all you have to do is go to your study area. Once there, you'll find it relatively easy to get started.

Use Spaced Study Sessions It is quite reasonable to review intensely before an exam. However, if you are actually learning information for the first time (cramming), you are asking for trouble. Psychological research suggests that **spaced practice** is a more efficient way to study. **Spaced practice** consists of a large number of relatively short study sessions, rather than one or two long ones (called **massed practice**). (It might be worth remembering that if you "massed up" your studying you probably messed it up too.) Cramming puts a tremendous burden on memory. It is far better to learn small amounts on a daily basis and to review frequently.

Try Mnemonics Students sometimes complain about having to memorize for classes. But learning has to start somewhere, and memorizing is often the first step. Psychologists now know a great deal about how to improve memory. Since many of the most important points are summarized in Chapter 9, let's consider just one technique here.

A **mnemonic** (nee-MON-ik) is a memory aid. Most mnemonics link new information to ideas or images that are easy to remember. For example, imagine you want to remember that the Spanish word for duck is *pato* (pronounced POT-oh). To use a mnemonic, you could picture a duck in a pot or a duck wearing a pot for a hat (Pressley et al., 1980). Obviously, the possibilities for creating mnemonics are numerous. If you would like to learn more, look ahead to Chapter 9.

Test Yourself Many students overlook one of the best ways to improve test scores: When studying, you can arrange to take several practice tests before the real one in class. In other words, studying should include **self-testing** by use of flash cards, Learning Checks, a study guide, or questions you ask yourself. As you study, ask as many questions as you can and be sure you can answer them. Studying without testing yourself is like practicing for a basketball game without shooting any baskets.

Overlearn There is something else to keep in mind when you study: Many students *underprepare* for exams, and most *overestimate* how well they will do on exams (Murray, 1980). A solution to both problems is **overlearning**. To overlearn, you should continue studying beyond bare mastery of a topic. This means that you need to give yourself time for extra study and review *after* you think you are prepared for a test. Another reason for overlearning is provided by the following experiment:

The Perils of Multiple Choice

College students were given 15 minutes to study a passage on human rights. Students were told to expect either an essay, multiple-choice, "memory," or unspecified type of test. In fact, all students took the same test, which included multiple-choice and short-answer questions. Students expecting multiple-choice questions scored *lowest*, even on the multiple-choice questions. (Foos & Clark, 1984)

Before tests, students always ask, "Will it be essay or multiple-choice?" But as the experiment shows, it is probably best to approach all tests as if they were essays. By doing so, you will learn information more completely, so that you will really "know your stuff" when you take the test.

Question: All of these study techniques are fine. But what can I do about procrastination?

Procrastination

A tendency to procrastinate is almost universal among college students. (When campus workshops on procrastination are offered, many students never get around to signing up!) Even when procrastination doesn't lead to failure, it can cause much suffering. Procrastinators put off work until the last possible moment, work only under pressure, skip classes, give false reasons for late work, and feel ashamed of their last-minute efforts (Burka & Yuen, 1983).

Question: Why do so many students procrastinate?

It is fairly natural to put off long-range assignments, at school and elsewhere. However, there are additional reasons for student procrastination. Psychologists Jane Burka and Lenora Yuen observe that many students seem to equate performance in school with their *personal worth*. By procrastinating, students can blame poor work on a late start, rather than a lack of ability—after all, it wasn't their best effort, was it?

Perfectionism is a related problem. If you have high expectations for yourself, you may find it hard to start an assignment. Students with high standards expect the impossible from themselves and end up with all-or-nothing work habits (Burka & Yuen, 1983).

Time Management Burka and Yuen supervise a program for procrastinators at the University of California, Berkeley. Eventually, they say, most procrastinators must face the self-worth conflict, but progress can be made by learning better study skills and more effective time management. Since we have already discussed study skills, let's consider time management.

A **formal time schedule** can do much to prevent procrastination and maintain motivation in school. To prepare your schedule, make a chart showing all of the hours in each day of the week. Then fill in times that are already committed: sleep, meals, classes, work, team practices, lessons, appointments, and so forth. Next, fill in times when you will study for various classes, and label them. Finally, label the remaining hours as open or free times.

The beauty of keeping a schedule is that you know you are making an honest effort to do well in your classes. In addition to getting more done, you will avoid the trap of yearning to play while you work and feeling guilty about not working when you play. The key to time management is to treat your study times as serious commitments, like class meetings or a job, and to respect your free times as well.

Taking Tests—Are You "Test Wise"?

Question: If I have read and studied effectively, is there anything else I can do to improve my grades?

Learning is only a first step. You must then be able to show what you know on a test. Here are some guidelines for improving your test-taking skills.

Objective Tests Objective tests (multiple-choice and true-false items) test your ability to recognize a correct statement among wrong answers or a true statement against a false one. If you are taking an objective test, try this:

1. Read the directions carefully; they may give you good advice or clues. If the directions are not clear, ask the instructor to clarify them.
2. Read *all* of the choices for each question before you make a decision. If you immediately think "a" is correct, for instance, and stop reading, you might miss seeing a last choice like "both a and d" that is a better answer.
3. Read rapidly and skip items you are uncertain about. Later questions may give you "free" information that will help you answer difficult items. Return to skipped items if time allows.
4. Eliminate certain alternatives. With a four-choice-per-item, multiple-choice test, the odds are 1 in 4 that you could guess right. If you can eliminate two alternatives, your guessing odds improve to 50–50. Unless there is a penalty for guessing, be sure to answer every question.
5. There is a bit of folk wisdom that says, "Don't change your answers on a multiple-choice test. Your first choice is usually right." Careful study of this idea has shown it is *false*. Students who switch answers are more likely to change from wrong to right than the reverse (Davis, 1975; Edwards & Marshall, 1977). This is especially true if you feel *very* uncertain of your first answer. ("When in doubt, scratch it out!") When you have strong doubts, your second answer is more likely to be correct (Johnson, 1975).

Essay Tests Essay questions are a weak spot for many students simply because of poor organization, poor support of main ideas, or not writing directly to the question. When you take essay exams, try the following:

1. Read the question carefully. Make sure that you note key words, such as *compare*, *contrast*, *discuss*, *evaluate*, *analyze*, or *describe*. These words all demand a certain emphasis in your answer.
2. Think about your answer before putting words on paper. It's a good idea to make a brief list of the points you want to make. Just list them in any order as

they come to mind. Then rearrange your ideas in the order you want to write them.

3. Don't beat around the bush or pad your answer. Be direct. Make a point and support it. Get your list of ideas into words.
4. Look over your essay for spelling errors, sentence errors, and grammatical errors. Save this step for last. Your *ideas* are of first importance. You can work on spelling and grammar separately if they affect your grades.

A Final Word There is a distinction made in Zen between "live words" and "dead words." Live words come from personal experience, dead words are "about" a subject. This book can only be a collection of dead words without your personal involvement. It is designed to help you learn psychology, but it cannot learn for you. You will find many helpful, useful, and exciting ideas in the pages that follow. To make them yours, you must set out to *actively* learn as much as you can. The ideas presented here should get you off to a good start. Good luck!

For more information, consult any of the following books:

Annis, L. F. *Study Techniques*: Brown, 1983.
Burka, J. B., & L. M. Yuen. *Procrastination: Why You Do It; What to Do about It*. Addison-Wesley, 1983.
Carman, R. A., & W. R. Adams. *Study Skills: A Student's Guide for Survival*. Wiley, 1985.
Deese, J., & E. K. Deese. *How to Study*. McGraw-Hill, 1979.
Ellis, A., & W. J. Knaus. *Overcoming Procrastination*. Rational Living, 1977.

Learning Check

1. The three *Rs* in SQ3R stand for read, recite, and review. T or F?
2. When using the LISAN method, students try to write down as much of a lecture as possible so that their notes are complete. T or F?
3. Spaced study sessions are usually superior to massed practice. T or F?
4. According to recent research, you should almost always stick with your first answer on multiple-choice tests. T or F?
5. To use the technique known as overlearning, you should continue to study after you feel you have begun to master a topic. T or F?
6. Procrastination is related to seeking perfection and equating self-worth with grades. T or F?

Answers: **1.** T **2.** F **3.** T **4.** F **5.** T **6.** T

Part One

An Introduction to Psychology and Psychologists

Chapter 1

An Introduction to Psychology and Psychologists

Psychology: Psyche = Mind; Logos = Knowledge or Study
A Brief History of Psychology's Brief History
Psychologists—Guaranteed Not to Shrink
How to Be a Psychologist—Let Us Count the Ways
Applications: Pseudo-Psychologies—Palms, Planets, and Personality

Chapter 2

Research Methods in Psychology

Scientific Method—Can a Horse Add?
Naturalistic Observation—Psychology Steps Out!
Correlational Studies—In Search of the Perfect Relationship
The Psychology Experiment—Where Cause Meets Effect
Placebo Effects—Sugar Pills and Salt Water
The Clinical Method—Data by the Case
Survey Method—Here, Have a Sample
Applications: Psychology in the News—Notes on Reading the Popular Press

Chapter 1

An Introduction to Psychology and Psychologists

Chapter Preview

Why Study Psychology?

You are a universe, a collection of worlds within worlds. Your brain is possibly the most complicated and amazing device in existence. Through its action you are capable of art, music, science, philosophy, and war. Your capacities for love, compassion, and dedication coexist with your potential for aggression, hatred, and . . . murder? You are the most frustrating riddle ever written, a mystery at times even to yourself. You are at one and the same time a unique event in human history and like everyone who has ever lived. Your thoughts, emotions, and actions, your behavior and conscious experience are the subject of this book.

Look around you. Newspapers, magazines, radio, and television abound with psychological information. Psychology is discussed in homes, schools, businesses, and bars. Psychology is an explosive, exciting, and ever-changing panorama of people and ideas. You can hardly consider yourself "educated" without knowing something about it.

There is another reason for studying psychology. Socrates said, "Know thyself," and although we must envy those who have set foot on the moon or cruised the dreamlike landscapes of the ocean's depths, the ultimate frontier still lies close to home. Psychologist D. O. Hebb put it this way: "What is psychology all about? Psychology is about the mind: the central issue, the great mystery, the toughest problem of all" (Hebb, 1974).

Psychology is a journey into inner space. This book is a travel guide. Psychologists can't claim to have "the answers" to all your questions, but they can show you the contours of the landscape already explored. More importantly, you may find skills in psychology that will aid you in your own search for answers. Ultimately the answers must be your own, but studying psychology is a rich starting point.

Survey Questions What is psychology? What are its goals? How did psychology emerge as a field of knowledge? What are the major specialties in psychology? How does psychology differ from false systems that also claim to explain behavior?

Resources

"The elephant," said the blind man as he felt the elephant's leg, "is very much like a tree."

"Why, how foolish!" said a second blind man (who had hold of the elephant's tail). "The elephant is like a rope."

The third blind man, having encountered the beast's trunk, said, "You're both wrong, the elephant is like a snake."

Psychology: Psyche = Mind; Logos = Knowledge or Study

Question: What is psychology?

Psychology is: memory, stress, psychotherapy, love, persuasion, hypnosis, perception, death, conformity, creativity, conditioning, personality, aging, intelligence, sexuality, emotion, and so many more topics that for a time you may be in a position similar to that of the blind men. Psychology has become such an enormous and colorful beast that no short description can do it justice.

It is important, then, to be open-minded as you begin this course. Consider your introduction to psychology an adventure, and judge after you have seen what it has to offer. By the time you have read this entire book, you will begin to have an overall picture of what psychology is, and what psychologists do. For now, let's just say that **psychology** *is the scientific study of human and animal behavior.* Its goals are to **describe, understand, predict,** and **control** behavior. Beyond this, psychology's ultimate goal, like that of other sciences, is to gather knowledge for the benefit of humanity.

Psychology The scientific study of behavior and conscious experience.

Overt behavior An action or response that is directly observable.

Covert behavior A response that is internal or hidden from view.

Question: What does "behavior" refer to in the definition of psychology?

Behavior Anything you do—eating, sleeping, talking, thinking, or sneezing—is a behavior. So is dreaming, gambling, taking drugs, watching TV, learning Spanish, basket weaving, or reading this book. Notice that the word *behavior*, as used here, includes **covert** (private, internal) processes, such as thinking, as well as **overt** (visible) actions. To a psychologist, even hidden activities, such as thinking or perceiving, are behaviors because they are things that you do.

Much of our overt behavior can be studied by direct observation. But how do we study problem solving, daydreaming, or memory? In such cases we must *infer* what is happening "internally" from what we can observe directly. For example, try answering these questions: "Is a horse bigger than a mouse?" "Is a collie bigger than a German shepherd?" If you are like most people, you answered the first question faster than the second. Why? Most people report forming mental images of the animals to compare their size. A difference in the time it takes to answer,

Empirical evidence Facts or data based on direct observation or experience.

therefore, suggests that comparing images close in size is more difficult (Moyer & Bayer, 1976). Although we couldn't directly observe thinking, we were able to learn something interesting about it just the same.

Question: It seems from this example that psychologists try to be objective in their observations. Is that correct?

Yes. Psychologists have a special respect for **empirical evidence**—that is, information gained by direct observation and measurement, rather than through opinion, argument, or reliance on authority. Would you say it's true, for instance, that "you can't teach an old dog new tricks"? Why argue about it? A psychologist would get 10 "new" dogs, 10 "used" dogs, and 10 "old" dogs and then try to teach them all new tricks to find out!

Empiricism Whenever possible, psychologists settle differences by direct investigation. This allows them to compare what they have observed and draw accurate conclusions. As self-evident as the empirical approach may seem in fields like biology or physics, often in psychology we are tempted to accept what seems reasonable or sensible, rather than what *is*. For example, see if you can tell, on the basis of personal experience or common sense, which of the following statements are true. Then we will compare your answers to answers found empirically.

True or False?

1. If you happened to step on a nail, you would feel it instantly. (Chapter 3)
2. A one-eyed man could not land an airplane. (Chapter 5)
3. The apparent size of the moon is greatly magnified by the atmosphere when the moon is low in the sky. (Chapter 5)
4. When hypnotized, witnesses to crimes can be made to have perfect memory for what they saw. (Chapter 6)
5. Brain activity almost ceases at various times during sleep. (Chapter 6)
6. Punishment is the most effective way to reinforce the learning of new habits. (Chapter 8)
7. All memories are permanent, if only there were some way to retrieve them. (Chapter 9)
8. People who have high IQs are also highly creative in most instances. (Chapter 10)
9. A person facing major surgery would be better off if he or she worried about it as little as possible. (Chapter 12)
10. Stress is almost always bad for you. (Chapter 13)
11. Intelligence is completely inherited from one's parents. (Chapter 16)
12. Those who threaten suicide rarely actually commit suicide. (Chapter 19)
13. Schizophrenics have two or more distinct personalities. (Chapter 20)
14. If your car breaks down, you are more likely to get help from a passerby on a busy highway than on a lightly traveled country road. (Chapter 25)

Scoring this quiz is easy because all of the statements are *false*. (To find out why, you may want to look ahead at the chapters shown in parentheses.) If you missed some questions, don't despair. The point is simply this: Psychology became a science when psychologists began to perform experiments, make observations, and seek evidence, and you will become a better observer of human behavior to the extent that you do the same.

Question: I've heard that psychology isn't scientific. You have said that it is. Is it?

Fig. 1-1 *The variety and complexity of human behavior make psychological investigation challenging.*

Science Psychology has been described by some as an "almost science" because scientific study of some of its topics is not yet possible. But the same is true of almost all sciences. Psychologists, like other scientists, are sometimes unable to answer questions because of moral or practical concerns. What would happen, for instance, if a child were placed in a soundproof, lightproof box for the first 5 years of life? This question will probably never be directly answered. (However, many times an indirect answer can be obtained by studying animals.) In other cases research must await a receptive social climate. Very little was known about human sexual response until William Masters, a gynecologist, and Virginia Johnson, a psychologist, directly recorded physical responses to sexual inter-

Research method A systematic approach to answering scientific questions.

Comparative psychology The study and comparison of the behavior of different species, especially animals.

Anthropomorphic fallacy The error of attributing human thoughts, feelings, or motives to animals.

Animal model In research, an animal whose responses serve as a replica of human behavior.

course. Such research would have been impossible to carry out and publish 30 years ago. Likewise, much of what we know about the psychology of death was learned in the last 10 years, as this once taboo subject has come under study.

More often, psychological questions remain unanswered for lack of a suitable **research method.** For years the reports of people who said they never dream had to be considered accurate. But with an advance in technology, the EEG (electroencephalograph or brain wave machine) was developed. It then became possible to tell objectively when a person is dreaming. People who "never dream," it turns out, dream frequently and remember their dreams vividly when awakened during one. Through use of the EEG, the study of dreaming has become quite scientific. Many people think of scientific research as dull and painstaking. But, as you can see, often it takes a great deal of creativity to find new methods for answering long-standing questions in psychology. Moreover, what we *do* know today adds up to a large and highly useful body of knowledge.

Animals Notice from our definition that psychology includes the study of animals, as well as people. As a group, psychologists are interested in natural laws governing the behavior of *any* living creature—from flatworms to humans. Indeed, specialists known as **comparative** psychologists may spend their entire careers studying rats, cats, dogs, turtles, chimpanzees, or other animals (Fig. 1–3). Comparative psychologists *compare* the behavior of different animals to learn which principles apply to all species, and which are unique to a particular creature. As psychologists study animals, they must be very careful to avoid the **anthropomorphic fallacy** (AN-thro-po-MORE-fik: attributing human thoughts, feelings, or motives to animals).

The temptation to assume that an animal is "angry," "jealous," "bored," or "guilty" can be strong. But this often leads to false conclusions. As an example, let's say I observe gorillas in the wild (where food is plentiful) and conclude that by nature gorillas are not very "greedy." You, on the other hand, place two hungry gorillas in a cage with a banana, stand back to watch the action, and conclude that gorillas are in fact *very* "greedy." Actually, all we have observed is

Fig. 1-2 *The scientific study of dreaming has been made possible by use of the EEG, a device that records the tiny electrical potentials generated by the brain of a sleeping subject. The EEG converts these electrical potentials to a written record of brain activity.*

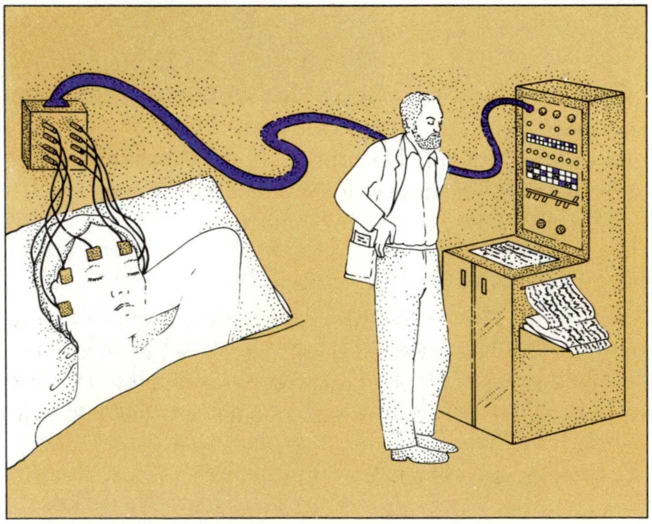

Fig. 1-3 *Some of the most interesting research with animals has focused on attempts to teach primates to communicate. (See Chapter 10 for more information.)*

that competition for food is related to the availability of food. Allowing the human concept of greed into the picture just clouds our understanding of gorilla behavior.

Question: Are comparative psychologists the only ones who study animals?

No. Other research psychologists use animals in experiments to discover principles that help solve human problems. Studies of topics as diverse as obesity, memory, stress, psychosis, therapy, and aging have been enriched by animal research. More importantly, animals sometimes serve as **models,** to provide the *only* information available on a particular subject. For instance, the majority of what is known about the human brain is based on animal research.

Psychological knowledge has also benefited animals. For example, behavioral research has provided ways to avoid the killing of animals, such as coyotes, crows, or deer, that destroy crops or livestock. The successful breeding and raising of endangered species in zoos also relies on behavioral research, as does the training of guide dogs for the blind (Miller, 1985). For these and other reasons, animals are very much a part of psychology.

Goals To conclude this discussion, let's return for a moment to the goals of psychology. What do they mean in practice? Assume that we would like to answer the following questions: What happens when a person has an injury on the right side of the brain? Is there more than one type of memory? How does creative problem solving differ from routine thought? Do autistic children react differently to their parents than to other adults? The answer to each question would require a careful **description** of behavior, the first goal of psychology.

Question: But a description doesn't explain anything, does it?

Right. Useful knowledge in psychology begins with accurate description (naming and classifying). But description fails to answer the important "why" questions. *Why* do more women attempt suicide, and why do more men complete it? *Why* does frustration encourage aggression? *Why* are bystanders often unwilling to help in an emergency?

Psychology's second goal, **understanding** behavior, is satisfied when we can *explain* why a phenomenon occurs or exists. Take the last question as an example.

Psychometrics Specialty that focuses on mental measurement or testing, such as personality and intelligence testing.

Introspection To look within; to examine one's own thoughts, feelings, or sensations.

Experimental self-observation Wilhelm Wundt's technique of combining trained introspection with objective measurement.

Structuralism The school of thought in psychology concerned with analyzing sensations and personal experience into basic elements.

Research on "bystander apathy" has shown that people often fail to help when *other* potential helpers are present. This causes a "diffusion of responsibility" so that no single bystander feels obligated to help. Generally, the larger the number of potential helpers present, the less likely it is that help will be given (Darley & Latane, 1968) (see Chapter 25 for more information).

Psychology's third goal is **prediction.** Notice that the explanation for bystander apathy makes a prediction about the chances of getting help. Anyone who has been stranded by car trouble on a busy freeway will recognize the accuracy of this prediction. Of course, prediction in psychology is rarely as precise as it is in "hard sciences" like physics or chemistry. Just the same, psychological predictions are often quite useful. For example, psychological theory predicted that students high in test-taking anxiety would score higher if given reassurance and advice during testing—a prediction that proved true when tried (Sarason, 1975). Psychological prediction is especially important in the field of **psychometrics.** Specialists in this area use various tests to predict such things as success in school, work, or career (see Chapter 26).

Question: Description, explanation, and prediction seem reasonable, but is control a valid goal for psychology?

Control is a frequently questioned and misunderstood goal of psychology, probably because it sounds like a threat to personal freedom. To most psychologists, however, "control" simply means altering conditions that influence behavior in predictable ways. For example, if a psychologist suggests changes in classroom procedures that help children learn more effectively, the psychologist has exercised control. If the psychologist uses conditioning principles to help a person overcome a crippling fear of heights, control is involved. Control is also present if psychological research is used to design an aircraft instrument panel that reduces pilot errors. Clearly, psychology can provide the means for changing behavior, but it does not say what changes should be made. As is the case with knowledge in other areas, psychological principles must be used wisely and humanely (Kipnis, 1987).

In summary, psychology's goals are a natural outgrowth of our desire to understand behavior. For the many topics studied in psychology, the goals boil down to asking:

What is the nature of this behavior? (description)
Why does it occur? (explanation)
Can we predict when it will occur? (prediction)
What conditions affect it? (control).

Learning Check

To improve your memory of this chapter, see if you can answer these questions. If you miss any, skim over the preceding material before continuing, to make sure you understand what you just read.

1. Psychology is the ___Scientific___ study of the ___behavior___ of organisms.

2. Information gained through direct observation and measurement is called ___~~overt~~ Empirical___ evidence.

3. The ______________ fallacy involves attributing human feelings and motives to animals.

4. Which of the following questions relates most directly to the goal of *understanding* behavior?
a. Do men and women differ in intellectual abilities?
b. Why does a blow to the head cause memory loss?
c. Will productivity in a business office increase if room temperature is raised or lowered?
d. How can test anxiety be prevented?

Answers: **1.** scientific, behavior **2.** empirical **3.** anthropomorphic **4.** *b*

A Brief History of Psychology's Brief History

Psychology has a long past but a short history. Psychology's past is centuries old because it includes **philosophy**, the study of knowledge, reality, and human nature. In contrast, psychology's history began only about 100 years ago. As sciences go, psychology is the new kid on the block: Easily 9 out of 10 persons to ever work in the field are alive today. Of course, to some students this history is still "not short enough!" Yet, the ideas in psychology's past are intimately tied to the present. To understand where psychology is now, let's take a brief look at its short history.

Into the Lab Psychology's history as a science began in 1879 at Leipzig, Germany. There, the father of psychology, **Willhelm Wundt** (VILL-helm Voont), created the first psychological laboratory so that he could study *conscious experience*. How, he wondered, are sensations, images, and feelings formed? To find out, Wundt observed and carefully measured **stimuli*** of various kinds (lights, sounds, weights). He then used **introspection,** or "looking inward," to examine his reactions to them. Wundt called this approach **experimental self-observation** (Blumenthal, 1979). Over the years, he used this approach to study vision, hearing, taste, touch, reaction time, memory, feelings, time perception, and a host of other topics.

Experimental self-observation was a highly developed skill, much like that needed to be a professional wine taster. Wundt's subjects had to make at least 10,000 practice observations before they were allowed to describe their sensations in a real experiment (Lieberman, 1979). With such emphasis on careful observation and measurement, psychology was truly off to a good start.

Structuralism Wundt's ideas were carried to the United States by one of his students, a psychologist named E. B. Titchener (TICH-in-er). There, Titchener and others launched a school of thought called **structuralism.** The structuralists hoped to develop a sort of "mental chemistry" by *analyzing* experience into basic "elements" or "building blocks."

Question: How could they do that? You can't analyze experience like you can a chemical compound, can you?

*Stimulus: singular; stimuli (STIM-you-lie): plural.

Fig. 1-4 *Wilhelm Wundt, 1832–1920.*

Fig. 1-5 *William James, 1842–1910.*

Fig. 1-6 *John B. Watson, 1878–1958.*

Perhaps not, but the structuralists tried, mostly by using introspection. In this approach, a structuralist might heft an apple and then decide that he or she had experienced the elements "hue" (color), "roundness," and "weight." Another example of the kind of question that might have interested a structuralist is, "What elemental tastes mix together to create complex flavors as different as liver, lime, bacon, or burnt-almond fudge?"

It soon became evident that introspection was an ineffective way to answer many kinds of questions. The most troublesome problem was that structuralists frequently *disagreed*. And when they did, introspection provided no method for settling differences. If two structuralists came up with different lists of elementary taste sensations, for example, who was to say which was right? Despite such limitations, "looking inward" is still a part of modern psychology. The study of hypnosis, meditation, drug effects, problem solving, and many other topics would be incomplete without reports of subjective experiences.

Functionalism William James, an American psychologist, agreed with Wundt and the structuralists that psychologists should study the mind. However, he broadened the scope of psychology to include animal behavior, religious experience, abnormal behavior, and a number of other interesting topics.

Question: Did James use introspection?

James and other **functionalists** were willing to use introspection, experimentation, and even a dash of armchair philosophizing to study mental life. The term *functionalism* comes from James' interest in how the mind *functions* to adapt us to our environment. To James, consciousness was an ever-changing *stream* or *flow* of images and sensations—not a collection of lifeless building blocks, as the structuralists claimed.

The functionalists were strongly influenced by Charles Darwin. According to Darwin, organisms evolve, through **natural selection,** in directions that favor their survival. This means that features that help animals adapt to their environment are retained in evolution. Similarly, the functionalists wanted to learn how thought, perception, habits, and emotions aid human adaptation. In short, they wanted to study the mind *in use.*

Question: What effect did functionalism have on modern psychology?

Functionalism brought the study of animals into psychology by linking human and animal adaptation. It also encouraged the development of **educational psychology.** Functionalists stressed that learning improves personal adaptability, and they urged psychologists to help improve education. Today, modern educational psychologists develop tests and conduct research on classroom dynamics, teaching styles, and learning. Functionalism also spurred the growth of **industrial psychology,** a specialty involving the study of people at work. (See Chapter 26.)

Behaviorism: Stimulus-Response Psychology Functionalism was soon challenged by a new school of thought called **behaviorism.** Behaviorist John B. Watson objected to defining psychology as the study of the "mind" or "conscious experience," and he considered introspection unscientific. Watson quickly learned that he could study animals quite effectively even though he couldn't ask them questions or know what they were thinking. He simply observed the relationship between **stimuli** (events in the environment) and an animal's **responses** to them. Why not, he argued, apply the same objectivity to the study of humans?

Watson soon adopted Russian physiologist Ivan Pavlov's (ee-VAHN PAV-lahv) **conditioned response** concept as a way of explaining most behavior. (A conditioned response is a learned reaction to a particular stimulus.) Watson's enthusiasm for conditioning obviously had reached extremes when he proclaimed:

> Give me a dozen healthy infants, well-formed, and my own special world to bring them up in and I'll guarantee to take any one at random and train him to become any type of specialist I might select—doctor, lawyer, artist, merchant-chief, and yes, beggarman and thief. (Watson, 1913)

Question: Would most psychologists agree with Watson's claim?

Today, most would probably consider it an overstatement. Just the same, behaviorism has had a profound effect on modern psychology. One of the best-known and most influential behaviorists, B. F. Skinner, has said,

> The environment is the key causal matrix. . . . In order to understand human behavior we must take into account what the environment does to an organism before and after it responds. Behavior is shaped and maintained by its consequences. (Skinner, 1971)

Skinner, too, has been criticized. Skinner's emphasis on stimulus-response relationships and his tendency to ignore thought and subjective experience have led some observers to charge that Skinnerian psychology has "lost consciousness." Despite such criticisms, a majority of psychologists would probably agree that most human behavior is influenced in one way or another by learning.

The behavioristic approach is responsible for much of what we know today about learning, memory, conditioning, and the effective use of reward and pun-

Functionalism School of psychology concerned with how behavior and mental abilities help people adapt to their environments.

Natural selection Darwin's theory that evolution favors those plants and animals best suited to their living conditions.

Educational psychology The psychological study of learning, teaching, and related topics.

Industrial psychology The application of psychology to work, especially to personnel selection, human relations, and machine design.

Behaviorism School of psychology that emphasizes the study of overt, observable behavior.

Stimulus Any physical energy that has some effect on an organism and that evokes a response.

Response Any muscular action, glandular activity, or other identifiable aspect of behavior.

Conditioned response A reflex response that has become associated with a new stimulus.

Box 1-1

Women in Psychology

Histories of psychology abound in "forefathers" but seldom mention women. This situation exists largely because men dominated academic life in the late 1800s. Women, in fact, were actively discouraged from seeking advanced degrees. Even so, by 1906 in America about 1 psychologist in every 10 was a woman. Who were these "foremothers" of psychology? Several who became prominent in the field were Mary Calkins, Christine Ladd-Franklin, Lillien Martin, and Margaret Washburn.

Christine Ladd-Franklin was the first American woman to complete requirements for the doctorate in psychology, in 1882. However, her degree was not awarded due to a university policy that denied women the doctorate. The first woman to be awarded a Ph.D. in psychology was Margaret Washburn, in 1894. Over the next 15 years many more women followed Washburn's pioneering lead.

Today the number of males and females receiving doctoral degrees in psychology is roughly equal (New female Ph.D.'s actually exceeded males in 1984.) And, in recent years, the number of female psychology graduates at the bachelor's level has far exceeded the number of male psychology graduates. Clearly, psychology has become a profession shared equally by both men and women. (Sources: Furumoto & Scarborough, 1986: Howard et al., 1986)

ishment. A very direct product of behavioristic thought is a type of therapy known as **behavior modification.** In behavior modification, conditioning principles are used to treat problems such as overeating, phobias, and childhood misbehavior. (See Chapter 22 for more information.)

Question: Were all the early psychologists men? So far, no women have been mentioned.

For the most part, men dominated science and academia at the turn of the century. Nevertheless, women were active in psychology from its beginning. Box 1–1 gives some details.

Gestalt Psychology Imagine for a moment that you have just heard a familiar tune such as "Yankee Doodle" played on a tuba. Next it is played on a high-pitched violin. Even though none of the original sounds are used, the melody will still be recognizable—*if* the *relationship* between notes is the same. Now, what if the original notes were played in the correct order, but at a rate of one per hour? What would we have? Nothing. The separated notes would no longer be a melody. The melody is somehow more than the sum of its parts. It was observations such as this that launched the **Gestalt** school of thought in psychology.

The German word *Gestalt* (geh-SHTALT) means form, pattern, or whole. The Gestalt viewpoint, first advanced by the German psychologist Max Wertheimer (VERT-hi-mer), held that it is a mistake to analyze psychological events into pieces or "elements" as the structuralists did. Instead, the Gestaltists tried to study experiences as *wholes*. Their slogan was, "The whole exceeds the sum of its parts."

Like a melody, many other experiences resist analysis into "parts" or "pieces." For this reason, the Gestalt viewpoint remains influential in the study of perception and personality.

Psychoanalytic Psychology As the mainstream of psychology grew more objective, scientific, and experimental, an Austrian physician named Sigmund Freud was developing his own theory of behavior. Freud's point of departure was his belief that mental life is like an iceberg—only a portion is exposed to view. According to Freud, vast areas of **unconscious** thoughts, impulses, and desires, which cannot be known directly, influence our behavior. This idea added a new dimension not only to psychology, but to art, literature, and history as well.

Freud theorized that many unconscious thoughts are of a threatening, sexual, or aggressive nature. Hence, they are *repressed* (actively held out of consciousness). But sometimes, he said, they are revealed by dreams, emotions, or slips of the tongue. ("Freudian slips" are often humorous, as when a student who is tardy for class says, "I'm sorry I couldn't get here any later.") Also notable was Freud's insistence that all thoughts, emotions, and actions are *determined* (nothing is an accident); his emphasis on the importance of childhood in later personality development ("the child is father to the man"); and his creation of a method of therapy called **psychoanalysis.**

Freud had not held sway for very long before some of his students, such as Carl Jung, began to break away from him. (See Table 1-1.) These psychologists advanced their own theories and became known as **neo-Freudians** (*neo* means new or recent). Today, Freud's ideas have been enlarged, altered, revised, and adapted to the point that few strictly psychoanalytic psychologists are left. However, Freud's legacy is still evident in various **psychodynamic** approaches to psychology, which emphasize the interplay of internal forces in the personality.

Humanistic Psychology A fairly recent development in psychology is a point of view known as **humanism.** Humanism is sometimes called the "third force" in psychology. (Psychodynamic psychology and behaviorism are the other two.)

Question: How is the humanistic approach different from other approaches?

Psychologists Carl Rogers, Abraham Maslow, and others offered the humanistic viewpoint as an antidote to the negativity they saw in psychoanalysis and early versions of behaviorism. Humanists reject the Freudian idea that personality is ruled by unconscious forces and the behavioristic idea that we are controlled by the environment. Such views have a strong undercurrent of **determinism.** Determinism is the idea that behavior is largely determined by forces beyond our control. In contrast, the humanists stress the importance of **free will,** the human ability to make choices. Although humanists admit that one's past affects personality, they believe that people can freely choose to live more creative, meaningful, and satisfying lives.

The humanists also brought a new emphasis to psychological needs for love, self-esteem, belonging, self-expression, and creativity. According to the humanists, such needs are as important as biological needs for food and water. For

Behavior modification The application of learning principles to change human behavior, especially maladaptive behavior.

Gestalt psychology The school of psychology emphasizing the study of thinking, learning, and perception in whole units, not by analysis into parts.

Unconscious That part of a person's mind or personality that contains impulses and desires not directly known to the person.

Psychoanalysis A Freudian approach to psychotherapy emphasizing exploration of unconscious conflicts.

Neo-Freudian A personality theorist who accepts the broad features of Freud's theory but has revised the theory to fit his or her own concepts.

Humanism An approach to psychology that focuses on human experience, problems, potentials, and ideals.

Determinism The doctrine that all behavior has prior causes that would completely explain one's choices and actions if all such causes were known.

Free will The doctrine that human beings are capable of freely making choices or decisions.

Table 1-1 The Early Development of Psychology

Approximate Origin	Date	Notable Events
Experimental psychology	1875	First psychology course offered by William James
	1878	First American Ph.D. in psychology awarded
	1879	Wilhelm Wundt establishes first psychology laboratory in Germany
	1883	First American psychology lab founded at Johns Hopkins University
	1886	First American psychology textbook published by John Dewey
Structuralism	1898	Edward Titchener advances psychology based on introspection
Functionalism	1890	James publishes *Principles of Psychology*
	1892	American Psychological Association founded
Psychoanalytic psychology	1895	Sigmund Freud publishes first studies
	1900	Freud publishes *The Interpretation of Dreams*
Behaviorism	1906	Ivan Pavlov reports his research on conditioning
	1913	John Watson presents behavioristic view
Gestalt psychology	1912	Max Wertheimer and others advance Gestalt viewpoint
Neo-Freudianism	1914	Carl Jung breaks with Freud

example, newborn infants who are deprived of human love and warmth may die just as surely as they would if deprived of food.

Question: How scientific is the humanistic approach?

Humanists collect data and seek evidence to support their ideas. But for the most part they tend to be less interested in attempts to treat psychology as a science. Since they are basically interested in solving human problems, humanists show less interest in research with animals or laboratory studies of behavior. Instead, they stress the importance of such *subjective* factors as one's **self-image, self-evaluation,** and **frame of reference.** It is possible, however, to apply scientific methods to humanistic goals, and some humanists do so.

One of the most distinctive contributions of the humanistic approach is Maslow's description of **self-actualization.** Self-actualization is the need to develop one's potential fully, to lead a rich and meaningful life, and to become the best person one can become. According to the humanists, everyone has this potential. The humanists seek ways to allow it to emerge.

Psychology Today At one time schools of thought in psychology were almost like political parties. Loyalty to a particular viewpoint was often fierce, and clashes between schools were common. Today, several of the traditional schools of thought have given way to a blending of ideas and perspectives. Although loyalties and specialties still exist, many psychologists can be described as **eclectic** (ek-LEK-tik: drawing from many sources) in their approach. Even so, five major perspectives are evident in modern psychology. These are the **behavioristic, humanistic,** and **psychodynamic** views, plus the increasingly important **cognitive** and **biological** perspectives.

The value of biological approaches for understanding behavior has risen dramatically in recent years. This is largely due to an explosive growth in knowledge about how the brain works and its relation to thought, feelings, perception, abnormal behavior, and other important topics. A similar trend has occurred for **cognitive psychology.** *Cognition* means thinking or knowing. Cognitive psychologists study thoughts, expectations, language, perception, problem solving, consciousness, creativity, and other mental processes. Some of these topics were neglected for so many years that it may be fair to say that psychology has recently "regained consciousness."

Whatever their theoretical leanings, most modern psychologists prefer facts and principles that have survived rigorous scientific testing. In the next section we will further explore what psychologists do and what some of their specialties are. First, see if you can correctly match the items in the following Learning Check.

Self-image Total subjective perception of oneself, including images of one's body, personality, capabilities, and so forth.

Self-evaluation Positive and negative feelings held toward onself.

Frame of reference A mental and emotional perspective relative to which events are perceived and evaluated.

Self-actualization The full development of personal potential.

Cognitive psychology The area of psychology concerned with thinking, knowing, understanding, and information processing.

Eclectic Selected or chosen from many sources.

Scientific Conducted strictly according to the principles of evidence used in the natural sciences.

Cognition - thinking or knowing
Cognitive ψ - studys thoughts, expectation, language, perception, problem solving ect.

Fig. 1-7 *Max Wertheimer, 1880–1941.*

Fig. 1-8 *Sigmund Freud, 1856–1939.*

Fig. 1-9 *Abraham Maslow, 1908–1970.*

Learning Check

Match:

____ **1.** Philosophy
____ **2.** Wundt
____ **3.** Structuralism
____ **4.** Functionalism
____ **5.** Behaviorism
____ **6.** Gestalt
____ **7.** Psychoanalytic
____ **8.** Humanistic
____ **9.** Cognitive
____ **10.** Washburn

A. Against analysis; studied whole experiences
B. "Mental chemistry" and introspection
C. Emphasizes self-actualization and personal growth
D. Interested in unconscious causes of behavior
E. Gave rise to educational and industrial psychology
F. First woman Ph.D. in psychology
G. Studied stimuli and responses, conditioning
H. Part of psychology's "long past"
I. Concerned with thinking, language, problem solving
J. Used "experimental self-observation"
K. Also known as engineering psychology

Answers: **1.** H **2.** J **3.** B **4.** E **5.** G **6.** A **7.** D **8.** C **9.** I **10.** F

Psychologists—Guaranteed Not to Shrink

Question: What is the difference between a psychologist and a psychiatrist?
Answer: About $20 an hour. (And going up.)

Confusion often exists about the differences among **psychologists, psychiatrists, psychoanalysts, counselors,** and other mental health professionals. It is quite inaccurate to think of them all as "shrinks." Each title reflects distinct differences in training and emphasis.

A psychologist usually has a master's degree or a doctorate in psychology; that is, from 3 to 8 years of specialized postgraduate training in psychological theory and research methods. Depending on their interests, psychologists may teach, do research, administer psychological tests, or serve as consultants to business, industry, government, or the military. (This statement applies to psychiatrists and psychoanalysts too.) Psychologists interested in human emotional problems and their treatment specialize in **clinical** or **counseling psychology** (see Table 1–2).

To enter the profession of psychology today, you would probably find it necessary to have the doctorate (Ph.D., Psy.D., or Ed.D.) in order to be licensed or to qualify or compete for positions. (For more information, see Appendix 1, Careers in Psychology, at the end of the text.) Most clinical psychologists now have a Ph.D. or a Psy.D. (Doctor of Psychology) degree. The Psy.D. is a newly created degree that places emphasis on practical clinical skills rather than on research (McNett, 1982).

Like clinical psychologists, psychiatrists are also interested in human problems, but they are trained differently. A psychiatrist is a medical doctor. After training in general medicine, psychiatrists specialize in abnormal behavior and psychotherapy. Psychiatrists often become "talking doctors" who spend much of their time doing psychotherapy. In practice, then, a major difference between clinical psychologists and psychiatrists is that psychiatrists are trained to treat the physical causes of emotional problems. In the vast majority of cases, they do so by prescribing drugs, something a psychologist cannot do.

To be a psychoanalyst, you must have a moustache and goatee, spectacles, a German accent, and a well-padded couch—or so the TV and movie stereotype goes. Actually, to become an analyst, you must have an M.D. or Ph.D. degree and then receive specialized training in the theory and practice of Freudian psychoanalysis. In other words, either a psychologist or a psychiatrist may become an analyst by completing additional training. Analysts typically undergo psychoanalysis themselves before applying the method to others.

Question: Is psychoanalysis widely used?

The fact that traditional Freudian analysis is expensive and time consuming is gradually making psychoanalysts something of a rare breed. Nowadays, few psychologists or psychiatrists become analysts, and fewer clients seek analysis. In practice many psychotherapists find that a flexible and eclectic approach is most effective.

In many states counselors (such as marriage and family counselors, child counselors, or school counselors) also do mental health work. To be a licensed counselor typically requires a master's degree plus 1 or 2 years of full-time supervised counseling experience. Almost all of a counselor's advanced education is directly related to practical counseling skills, with little emphasis on research.

The practice of counseling was once limited to problems not involving serious mental disorder, such as vocational or educational adjustment. In recent years, however, an increasing number of counseling psychologists have shifted to doing psychotherapy primarily. As a result, differences between counseling and clinical psychology are beginning to fade (Fitzgerald & Osipow, 1986; Watkins et al., 1986).

Question: Do psychologists have to have a license?

Before the American Psychological Association (APA) began a push for licensing and certification, it was possible in many states for almost anyone to purchase an inexpensive license and hang out a shingle as a "psychologist."

Now, however, to be legally called a psychologist, a person must meet rigorous educational requirements. To work as a clinical or counseling psychologist, he or she must have a license issued by a state examining board. However, the law does not prohibit you from calling yourself anything else you choose—Gestalt therapist, primal feeling facilitator, cosmic aura balancer, or Rolfer—or from selling your "services" to anyone willing to pay. Beware of people advertising under such self-proclaimed titles. Even if their intentions are honorable, the training of such individuals is often limited or nonexistent. A fully trained, certified psychologist who chooses to use a particular type of therapy is not the same as someone "trained" solely in that technique.

Unfortunately, psychology, like medicine, has attracted a fringe of opportunists, quacks, and charlatans who seek to profit by taking advantage of human

Psychologist An individual highly trained in the methods, factual knowledge, and theories of psychology.

Psychiatrist A medical doctor with additional training in the diagnosis and treatment of mental illness.

Psychoanalyst A mental health professional (usually a medical doctor) trained to practice psychoanalysis.

Counselor A mental health professional who specializes in problems not involving serious mental disorder; for example, marriage counselors, career counselors, or school counselors.

Clinical psychologist A psychologist who specializes in the treatment of psychological and behavioral disturbances or who does research on such disturbances.

Counseling psychologist A psychologist who specializes in the treatment of milder emotional and behavioral disturbances.

psy clinical counseling

Basic research Scientific study undertaken without concern for immediate practical application.

Applied research Scientific study undertaken to solve immediate practical problems.

Experimental psychologist A psychologist primarily interested in the scientific study of human and animal behavior.

Comparative psychologist A psychologist primarily interested in studying and comparing the behavior of different species, especially animals.

Developmental psychologist A psychologist interested in the course of human growth and development, from birth until death.

needs, fears, and suffering. When the escapades of these "not-really psychologists" make the news, or when a friend or relative has a bad experience with one, psychologists often pay the price in negative public attitudes toward psychology in general. This is indeed unfortunate because psychologists follow a professional code established by the APA that stresses: (1) accurate statement of one's professional qualifications; (2) confidential handling of personal information in teaching, practice, or research; and, above all, (3) protection of the client's welfare. The APA also encourages psychologists to make their services available to anyone who seeks them, regardless of social considerations or ability to pay.

How to Be a Psychologist—Let Us Count the Ways

Question: Do all psychologists do therapy and treat abnormal behavior?

Even when combined, clinical and counseling psychology account for only about 50 percent of psychologists. The rest are found in a large number of other specialties. At present, there are 45 divisions of the APA, each reflecting a special skill area or interest. Some of the major specialties are listed in Table 1–2. (Also see Fig. 1-10.) Roughly 1 psychologist out of every 3 is employed at a college or university. In this setting they teach and may also do research, consultation, or therapy. Those engaged in research may do **basic research,** seeking knowledge for the sake of knowledge, or **applied research,** in which immediate uses are planned for the information gained.

Question: What kinds of research would a typical psychologist at a university do?

Here is a sampling of representative research topics.

Comparative "I have always been interested in basic questions about animal behavior, but my current research is applied. I am investigating ways of preventing abnormalities that result when an animal is kept in social isolation for extended periods of time. My goal is to help the space program. If I can provide a

Fig. 1-10 *(a) Specialties in psychology. Percentages are approximate (from Howard et al., 1986). (b) Where psychologists work. (From Pion, 1986)*

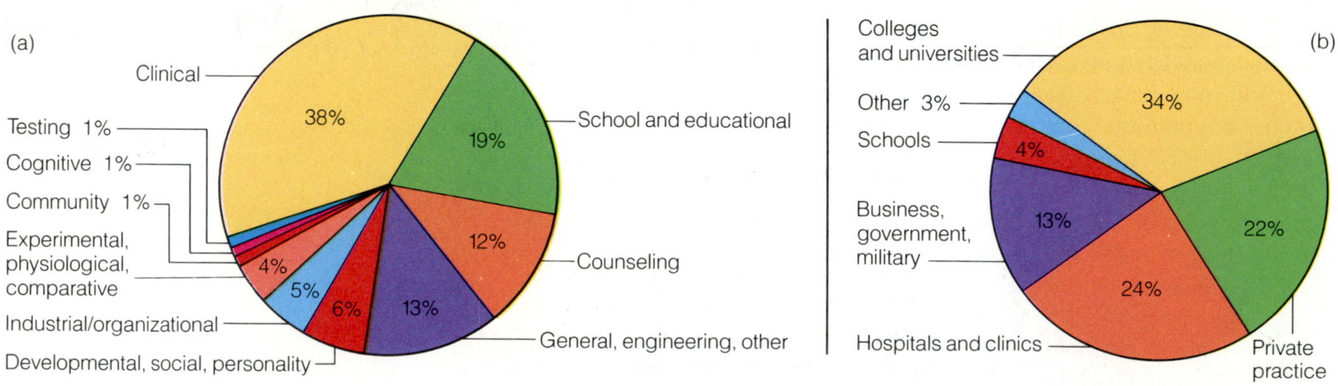

Table 1-2 Kinds of Psychologists and What They Do

Specialty		Typical Activities
Clinical and counseling psychologists	A*	Does psychotherapy and personal counseling, helps with emotional and behavioral problems, researches clinical problems, is involved in community mental health
Industrial psychologist	A	Selects job applicants, does skills analysis, evaluates on-job training, improves work environments and human relations in work setting
Educational psychologist	A	Conducts research on classroom dynamics, teaching styles, and learning variables; develops educational tests, evaluates educational programs, acts as consultant for schools
Consumer psychologist	A	Researches and tests packaging, advertising, and marketing methods; determines characteristics of product users, conducts public opinion polling
School psychologist	A	Does psychological testing, emotional and vocational counseling of students; detects and treats learning disabilities; improves learning and motivation in the classroom
Developmental psychologist	A, B	Carries out basic and applied research on child development, adult developmental trends, and aging; does clinical work with disturbed children; acts as consultant to preschools, programs for the aged, and so forth
Engineering psychologist	A	Does applied research on design of machinery, controls, airplanes, automobiles, and so on for business, industry, and the military
Medical psychologist	A	Studies the relationship between stress, personality, and disease (heart attacks, high blood pressure, ulcers); manages emotional problems associated with illness or disability
Environmental psychologist	A, B	Studies the effects of urban noise pollution, crowding, attitudes toward environment, and human use of space; acts as consultant for design of industrial environments, schools, housing for elderly, and urban architecture
Forensic psychologist	A	Studies problems of crime and crime prevention, rehabilitation programs in prisons, courtroom dynamics, psychology and law; selects candidates for police work
Experimental psychologist	B	Applies scientific research methods to study of human and animal behavior; may conduct research in the areas of comparative animal behavior, learning, sensation/perception, personality, physiology, motivation/emotion, social behavior, or cognition

*Research is typically: applied (A); basic (B); or both.

way to keep animals 'mentally' healthy while in space, the effects of prolonged weightlessness can be studied."

Developmental "I am interested in development from conception until death. I am trying to learn how people grow and change over time. My interests stretch over the whole lifespan, but I am especially interested in early childhood. My colleagues and I seek the principles whereby a child develops the ability to think,

Learning psychologist A psychologist interested in variables affecting learning and in theories of learning.

Personality psychologist A psychologist who studies personality traits and dynamics.

Sensation and perception psychologist A psychologist with expert knowledge on the sense organs and the processes involved in perception.

Physiological psychologist A psychologist who studies the relationship between the nervous system and behavior.

Social psychologist A psychologist particularly interested in the effects of other people on individual behavior.

speak, perceive, and act. Broadly speaking, I am interested in how adult personality and skills emerge from childhood, but my current research is more limited. I am studying the effects of stimulating childhood environments on the development of intelligence."

Learning "I'm also interested in how people get to be the way they are, but in a much more abstract sense. I believe that most human behavior is learned. At any given moment I would describe your behavior as the result of your personal learning history. By studying various kinds of learning, conditioning, and memory in humans and animals, I am helping construct theories about how learning occurs and what factors affect it. My doctoral dissertation was on avoidance learning. I had rats learn to press a bar in order to avoid receiving an electric shock that followed the onset of a signal light. Right now I'm studying the effects of patterns of reinforcement on learning in pigeons."

Personality "In many ways my area is both the most rewarding and the most frustrating. Personality theorists draw on the findings of all other research areas as well as their own in an effort to create as total a picture and understanding of human personality as possible. I concern myself with the structure and dynamics of personality, motivation, and individual differences. I am studying the personality profiles of college students who score high on tests of creativity."

Sensation and Perception "How do we come to know the world? How does information 'get into' our nervous systems? How is it processed and given pattern and meaning? These are my concerns. I am using an information processing theory called signal detection to study the visual perception of random shapes."

Physiological Psychology "The brain and nervous system are my meat . . . so to speak. It is my belief that ultimately all other areas in psychology—learning, perception, even personality and abnormal behavior—will be explained by the action of nerve cells and brain chemicals. I have been doing some exciting research on the role of the hypothalamus in hunger. I find that if I remove part of the hypothalamus in the brain of a rat, the rat will eat and gain weight until it looks like a furry water balloon. If I remove an area just a few millimeters away, the rat will starve to death if not force-fed."

Social Psychology "I study people in a group setting, or under any circumstance in which social factors play a part. Social psychologists in general are interested in attitudes, social influence, riots, conformity, leadership, racism, friendship, and a growing list of other topics. My personal interest is interpersonal attraction. I place two strangers together in a room for a short time and investigate factors that affect their ratings of attraction toward each other."

This small sample should give you some idea of the diversity of psychological research. It also gives a hint of some of the kinds of information covered later in this book.

Learning Check

See if you can answer these questions before continuing.

1. Which of the following can prescribe drugs? Psychologist, psychiatrist, psychoanalyst, counselor?

2. A psychologist who specializes in treating human emotional difficulties is called a ____________________ psychologist.

3. Roughly 40 percent of psychologists specialize in counseling psychology. T or F?

4. Seeking knowledge for the sake of knowledge is called ____________________ research.

Match the following research areas with the topic they cover.

____ **5.** Developmental
____ **6.** Learning
____ **7.** Personality
____ **8.** Sensation and perception
____ **9.** Physiological psychology
____ **10.** Social psychology
____ **11.** Comparative

A. Attitudes, groups, leadership
B. Conditioning, memory
C. The psychology of law
D. Brain and nervous system
E. Child psychology
F. Individual differences, motivation
G. Animal behavior
H. Information processing

12. Who among the following would most likely be involved in the detection and treatment of learning disabilities?
a. consumer psychologist *b.* forensic psychologist
c. experimental psychologist *d.* school psychologist

Answers: **1.** psychiatrist **2.** clinical or counseling **3.** F **4.** basic **5.** E **6.** B **7.** F **8.** H **9.** D **10.** A **11.** G **12.** *d*

Applications

Pseudo-Psychologies—Palms, Planets, and Personality

Pseudo-psychologies (SUE-doe-psychologies) are dubious and unfounded systems superficially resembling psychology. Many pseudo-psychologies offer a highly developed system that gives the appearance of science but is actually false. (*Pseudo* means false.) Let's begin by considering some of the less convincing pseudo-psychologies.

Palmistry Palmistry claims that lines in the hand are indicators of personality and a person's future. Lines that are longer or shorter, more bent or less bent, clear or distinct supposedly predict destiny, fortune, length of life, occupation, and health. The fact that palmistry assumes that the hands tell the story of the whole body is hard enough to swallow, but ignoring the effects of dishwater, manual labor, or hand lotion is inexcusable. Even so, palmists can still be found separating the gullible from their money in many cities.

Phrenology During the nineteenth century, a German anatomy teacher, Franz Gall, popularized the theory that personality is revealed by the shape of the skull. Phrenologists assumed that parts of the brain responsible for various "mental faculties" caused bumps on the head. By feeling these bumps, the phrenologist claimed to read a person's abilities. Phrenology faded rapidly when greater understanding of the brain showed that this is impossible. For instance, the area of the brain that controls hearing was listed on phrenologists' charts as the center for "combativeness" and "destructiveness"!

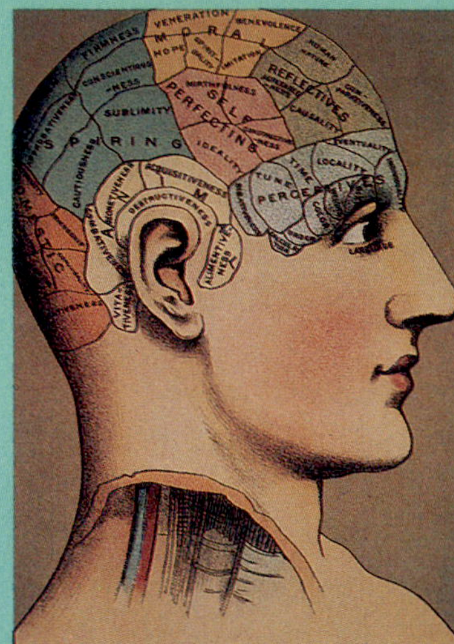

Fig. 1-11 *Phrenology was an attempt to assess personality characteristics by examining various areas of the skull. Phrenologists used charts such as the one shown here as guides.*

Graphology Graphologists believe that personality is revealed by handwriting. Graphology is only moderately popular in the United States, although at least 500 companies in this country use handwriting analysis to evaluate job applicants. In European countries graphology is widely used for job placement and advancement. These uses are somewhat distressing to psychologists because studies show that graphologists score close to zero in tests of accuracy in rating personality (Guilford, 1959). In fact, in one recent study, professional graphologists did no better than untrained college students in rating personality and sales success, based on the handwriting of a group of salespersons (Rafaeli & Klimoski, 1983). (The failure of graphology as a means of personality evaluation should be distinguished from its proven value for the detection of forgeries.)

Question: If the pseudo-psychologies have no scientific basis, how do they survive and why are they popular?

There are several reasons, all of which can be demonstrated with astrology.

Astrology Astrology–probably the most popular pseudo-psychology—is based on the assumption that the position of the stars and planets at the time of a person's birth determines personality characteristics

Applications: Pseudo-Psychologies, continued

and affects behavior. Like other pseudo-psychologies, astrology has repeatedly been shown to have no scientific validity (Jerome, 1975). The objections to astrology are numerous and devastating, as shown by the following:

Problems in the Stars

1. The zodiac has shifted by one full constellation since astrology was first set up. However, few astrologers take this shift into account. (In other words if astrology calls you a Scorpio, you are really a Libra, and so forth.)
2. There is no connection between the "compatibility" of the astrological signs of couples and their marriage and divorce rates.
3. Studies have found no connection between astrological signs and leadership, physical characteristics, career choice, or personality characteristics.
4. The force of gravity exerted by the physician's body at birth is greater than that exerted by the stars. Also, astrology has failed to explain why the moment of birth should be more important than the moment of conception.
5. A study of over 3,000 predictions by famous astrologers found that only a small percentage were fulfilled. These "successful" predictions tended to be vague ("There will be a tragedy somewhere in the eastern United States in the spring") or easily guessed from current events.
(Sources: "Astrology and Astronomy," 1983; Culver & Ianna, 1979; Pasachoff, 1981; Randi, 1980.)

In short, astrology doesn't work.

Question: Then why does it so often seem to work?

Uncritical Acceptance If you have ever had your astrological chart done, you may have been impressed with its seeming accuracy. Careful reading shows many such charts to be made up of a preponderance of flattering traits. Naturally, when your personality is described in *desirable* terms, it is hard to deny that the description has the "ring of truth." How much acceptance would astrology receive if the characteristics of a birth sign read like this:

> **Virgo:** You are the logical type and hate disorder. Your nitpicking is unbearable to your friends. You are cold, unemotional, and usually fall asleep while making love. Virgos make good doorstops.

Positive Instances Even when an astrological description of personality contains a mixture of desirable and undesirable traits, it may seem accurate. To find out why, read the following personality description.

> You have a strong need for other people to like you and for them to admire you. You have a tendency to be critical of yourself. You have a great deal of unused energy which you have not turned to your advantage. While you have some personality weaknesses, you are generally able to compensate for them. Your sexual adjustment has presented some problems for you. Disciplined and controlled on the outside, you tend to be worrisome and insecure inside. At times you have serious doubts as to whether you have made the right decision or done the right thing. You prefer a certain amount of change and variety and become dissatisfied when hemmed in by restrictions and limitations. You pride yourself on being an independent thinker and do not accept other opinions without satisfactory proof. You have found it unwise to be too frank in revealing yourself to others. At times you are extroverted, affable, sociable, while at other times you are introverted, wary, and reserved. Some of your aspirations tend to be pretty unrealistic.*

Does this describe your personality? A psychologist read this summary individually to college students who had taken a personality test. Twenty-nine said it was an "excellent" description of their personality; 30 said it was "good"; 15 said it was "average"; and 5 said it was "poor." Thus, only 5 students out of 79 felt that the description failed to adequately capture their personality.

Reread this description and you will see that it contains both sides of several personality dimensions

*Reprinted with permission of author and publisher from: R. E. Ulrich, T. J. Stachnik, and N. R. Stainton, "Student acceptance of generalized personality interpretations," *Psychological Reports*, 1963, *13*, 831–834.

Applications: Pseudo-Psychologies, continued

("At times you are extroverted . . . while at other times you are introverted . . ."). Its apparent accuracy is an illusion based on the **fallacy of positive instances,** in which a person remembers or notices things that confirm his or her expectations and forgets the rest. The pseudo-psychologies thrive on this effect. For example, you can always find "Leo characteristics" in a Leo. If you looked, however, you could also find "Gemini characteristics," "Scorpio characteristics," or whatever.

The Barnum Effect P. T. Barnum, the famed circus showman, had a formula for success: "Always have a little something for everybody." Like the personality description above, palm readings, fortunes, horoscopes, and other products of pseudo-psychology are stated in such *general* terms that they can hardly miss. There is always "a little something for everybody." If you doubt this, read *all* 12 of the daily horoscopes found in newspapers for several days. You will find that predictions for other signs fit events as well as those for your own sign do.

Question: Couldn't that be because commercial horoscopes don't take into account a person's specific time of birth?

If they did, they would probably not be any more accurate, just more convincing. In a recent experiment people were given standardized horoscopes. Some had provided only their sign; others the year, month, and day of their birth. All received the same personality description, but those who had provided more detailed information considered their horoscope more accurate (Snyder & Schenkel, 1975). Thus, the more hocus-pocus a fortune teller, palmist, or astrologer goes through, the more believable are the results.

A Final Note Astrology's continuing popularity shows the difficulty many people have in separating valid psychology from systems that seem valid but are not. The goal of this discussion, then, has been to make you a more critical observer of human behavior and to clarify what is, and is not, psychology. In Chapter 2, you will get a chance to further sharpen your critical skills as we investigate the research methods used in psychology. In the meantime here is what the "stars" say about your future.

> Emphasis now on education and personal improvement. Learning experience of lasting value awaits you. Take care of scholastic responsibilities before recreation. Research new possibility. The number 2 figures prominently in efforts.

Learning Check

1. ____________________ is the outdated theory that personality is revealed by the shape of the skull. It was popularized by Franz ____________________.

2. The fallacy of positive instances refers to graphology's proven value for the detection of forgeries. T or F?

3. Personality descriptions provided by pseudo-psychologies are stated in general terms, which provide "a little something for everybody." This fact is the basis of the

a. palmist's fallacy
b. uncritical acceptance pattern
c. fallacy of positive instances
d. Barnum effect

4. The more accurate the information given an astrologer concerning a person's time and place of birth, the more accurate the astrological descriptions of personality become. T or F?

Answers: **1.** Phrenology, Gall **2.** F **3.** *d* **4.** F

Chapter Summary

- Psychology is the scientific study of human and animal behavior. Its goals are to *describe*, *understand*, *predict*, and *control* behavior.
- Whenever possible, psychologists seek *empirical* (objective and observable) *evidence*.
- Not all psychological questions are answerable, usually because of moral, practical, technological, or methodological limitations.
- Psychologists study animals as well as people, either out of interest in animals themselves or to use animals as *models* for human behavior. One danger in studying animals is the *anthropomorphic fallacy*, the tendency to treat animals as if they had human characteristics.
- Accurate description is one goal of psychology, but psychologists also seek understanding and the ability to predict and control behavior. Psychologists engage in control when they alter conditions that affect behavior in predictable ways.
- The history of psychology begins with *philosophy*, an "armchair" approach to understanding human behavior.
- The first psychological laboratory was established in Germany by *Wilhelm Wundt*, who tried to apply scientific methods to the study of conscious experience.
- The first school of thought in American psychology was *structuralism*, which was a kind of "mental chemistry" based on the method of *introspection*.
- Structuralism was followed by *functionalism*, *behaviorism*, and *Gestalt* psychology. The *psychoanalytic* approach, which emphasizes unconscious influences on behavior, developed separately. A more recent development is *humanistic* psychology.
- Three main streams of thought that can still be seen in modern psychology are *behaviorism*, *humanism*, and the *psychodynamic* approach, but there is a strong trend toward blending the best features of many viewpoints. Two additional perspectives have grown in importance recently. These are the *biological* viewpoint, which stresses the biological foundations of behavior, and the *cognitive* viewpoint, which emphasizes thinking, knowing, perceiving, and other internal events.
- *Psychologists*, *psychiatrists*, *psychoanalysts*, and *counselors* work in the field of mental health, although their training and methods differ considerably.
- *Clinical* and *counseling* psychologists, who do psychotherapy, represent only one of dozens of specialties in psychology. Other representative areas of specialization are: *industrial*, *educational*, *consumer*, *school*, *developmental*, *engineering*, *medical*, *environmental*, *forensic*, *psychometric*, and *experimental*.
- Psychological research may be *basic* or *applied*. Some common research specialties are: comparative, learning, sensation, perception, personality, physiology, motivation and emotion, social, cognitive, and developmental.
- Many *pseudo-psychologies* have been practiced over the years. Four common examples are palmistry, phrenology, graphology, and astrology. Belief in these false systems is based on *uncritical acceptance* of their claims, the *fallacy of positive instances* (remembering "hits" and forgetting "misses"), and the *Barnum effect* (use of generalities that apply to almost everyone).

Chapter 2

Research Methods in Psychology

Chapter Preview

From Common Sense to Controlled Observation

Comment overheard on campus: "I don't know why he bothers taking psychology classes. Psychology is just common sense." Is psychology common sense? Is common sense a good source of information?

Consider some ***"commonsense" statements:*** *Let's say that your grandfather has gone back to college. What do people say? "Ahh . . . never too old to learn." And what do they say when he loses interest and quits? "Well, you can't teach an old dog new tricks." Let's examine another commonsense statement. It is frequently said that "absence makes the heart grow fonder." Those of us separated from friends and lovers can take comfort in this knowledge—until we remember that it's also "out of sight, out of mind"! Much of what passes for common sense is equally vague and inconsistent. Notice also that these B.S. statements work best after the fact. (B.S., of course, stands for Before Science.)*

Common sense can be a set of blinders that prevents us from seeking better information or seeing the truth. Einstein reportedly said, "Common sense is the layer of prejudice laid down in our minds before we are 18." In the early stages of the scientific revolution, people laughed at the idea that the world is round. Anyone with eyes could see that it wasn't. They laughed at Pasteur when he proposed that microorganisms cause disease. How could creatures too small to be seen kill a healthy human? Certainly, ideas such as these contradicted the common sense of their time. Now, few people argue with the findings of sciences such as chemistry, physics, or biology. But many still write off psychology as "just common sense."

Jab a hat pin into your finger. The sensation of pain seems instantaneous. We can go no further with personal observation. However, by using electrical recorders to measure the speed of nerve impulses, psychologists have found the top speed to be 120 meters per second. This is one-third the speed of sound. That's fast but certainly not instantaneous. Pain from the finger takes at least a hundredth of a second to reach the brain.

As you can see, research psychologists use careful measurement and a number of specialized approaches to improve observation and to avoid the pitfalls of "common sense." Their techniques are the topic of this chapter.

Survey Questions How do psychologists collect information? What are the advantages and disadvantages of each approach? How is an experiment performed? What ethical questions does psychological research raise? How dependable is psychological information found in the popular press?

Scientific Method—Can a Horse Add?

In the United States today it is still possible to find people who believe that the earth is flat. To the "flat-earther" the earth is disk shaped, with the North Pole at the center and the South Pole ringing the outer edge.

Question: How could anyone believe such a thing after seeing the astronauts' photographs of the earth?

Flat-earthers point out that the opposite side of large lakes can be seen through binoculars; therefore, the earth must be a flat surface. Also, a person who jumps up in the air for 1 second does not come down 190 miles away. Surely, they say, this proves that the earth cannot be a rotating globe (McCain & Segal, 1969).

Obviously the flat-earthers have made the wrong observations, in the wrong way, and for the wrong reasons—*if* they are interested in the truth. In many ways psychologists in search of accurate information must avoid the same trap of faulty observation. To do so they use the **scientific method,** which is based on the collection of solid observable evidence, accurate description and measurement, precise definition, controlled observation, and repeatable results. In its ideal form the scientific method has five steps:

1. **Observation**
2. **Defining a problem**
3. **Proposing a hypothesis**
4. **Experimentation**
5. **Theory formulation**

Question: What is a hypothesis?

A **hypothesis** (hi-POTH-eh-sis) is a tentative explanation of an event or observation. In common terms a hypothesis is a clearly stated and *testable* "hunch" or "educated guess" about the causes of behavior. For example, on the basis of your own observation, you might form the hypothesis that "aggression is encouraged by frustration." How would you test this hypothesis? First, you would have to decide how you were going to frustrate people. (This part might be fun.) Then you would have to devise a way of measuring whether they became more aggressive. (Not so fun.) The procedures you chose would provide **operational definitions** of frustration and aggression. Operational definitions state the exact procedures used to represent a concept.

Forming a hypothesis and other steps in the scientific method can be illustrated with the story of Clever Hans, a "wonder horse" (Rosenthal, 1965). Clever Hans seemed to be able to solve math problems, which he answered by tapping his

Resources

Scientific method Testing the truth of a proposition through careful measurement and controlled observation.

Hypothesis The predicted outcome of an experiment or an educated guess about the relationship between variables.

Operational definition Defining a scientific concept by stating the specific procedures used to measure it. For example, "hunger" might be defined as "the number of hours of food deprivation."

foot. If you asked Hans, "What is 12 times 2, minus 18," Hans would tap his foot 6 times. Hans was so astonishing that he attracted the attention of an inquiring scientist who discovered how Hans was able to perform. Assume that you are the scientist and that you are just itching to find out how Hans *really* does his trick.

Your investigation of Hans' mathematical abilities would probably begin with careful **observation** of both horse and owner while Hans was performing. If these observations fail to reveal any obvious cheating the *problem* becomes more clearly **defined**: What signals Hans to start and stop tapping his foot? Your first **hypothesis** might be that the owner is giving Hans a signal. Your proposed test (an **experiment** of sorts) would be to make the owner leave the room. Then someone else could ask Hans questions. Your proposed test would either confirm or deny this possibility and thereby support or eliminate the hypothesis. By changing the conditions under which you observe Hans, you have **controlled** the situation to gain more information from your observations.

Incidentally, Hans could still answer when his owner was out of the room. But a brilliant series of controlled observations revealed Hans' secret. If Hans couldn't see the questioner, he couldn't answer. It seems that questioners always *lowered their heads* (to look at Hans' foot) after asking a question. This was Hans' cue to start tapping. When Hans had tapped the correct number, the questioner would always *look up* to see if Hans was going to stop. This was Hans' cue to stop tapping!

Question: What about theory formulation?

Fig. 2-1 *Applying the scientific method to the study of behavior requires careful observation. Here, a student programs a computer to record a rat's responses in a learning experiment.*

Since Clever Hans' ability to do math was an isolated problem, no theorizing was involved. However, in actual research, theory building is often important. A **theory** allows the results of a large number of observations to be summarized in a way that accounts for existing data, predicts new observations, and guides further research. Theories of forgetting, personality, mental illness, and the like are valuable products of psychological research. Without them psychologists would drown in a sea of seemingly disconnected facts.

In their search for accurate information and useful theories, psychologists study behavior in many ways: They observe behavior as it unfolds in natural settings (**naturalistic observation**); they make measurements to discover relationships between events (**correlational method**); they use the powerful technique of controlled experimentation (**experimental method**); they study unique problems and therapeutic solutions in the psychological clinic (**clinical method**); and they use questionnaires and surveys to poll large groups of people (**survey method**). Let's see how each of these is used to advance psychological knowledge.

Observation Gathering data directly by recognizing and recording facts or events.

Experiment A formal trial undertaken to confirm or disconfirm a fact or principle.

Theory A system designed to interrelate concepts and facts in a way that summarizes existing data and predicts future observations.

Natural setting The environment in which an organism typically lives. For animals the setting is usually a wilderness area. For humans it may be a man-made environment.

Naturalistic Observation—Psychology Steps Out!

Instead of waiting to encounter haphazardly whatever they are interested in, psychologists may set out to **actively observe** subjects in a **natural setting.** A good example of this style of research is the work of Jane Goodall. She and her staff have been observing chimpanzees in Tanzania since 1960. A quote from her book *In the Shadow of Man* captures the excitement of a scientific discovery:

> Quickly focusing my binoculars, I saw that it was a single chimpanzee, and just then he turned in my direction . . . Cautiously I moved around so that I could see what he was doing. He was squatting beside the red earth mound of a termite nest, and as I watched I saw him carefully push a long grass stem down into a hole in the mound. After a moment he withdrew it and picked something from the end with his mouth. I was too far away to make out what he was eating, but it was obvious that he was actually using a grass stem as a tool. (van Lawick-Goodall, 1971)

Notice that naturalistic observation only provides *descriptions* of behavior. To explain what we observe often requires more information from other research methods. Just the same, Goodall's discovery forced many scientists to change their definition of humans. Previously, humans had been regarded as the only tool-making animals.

Question: Chimpanzees in zoos use objects as tools. Doesn't that demonstrate the same thing?

Not necessarily. One of the advantages of naturalistic observation is that the behavior being studied has not been tampered with by outside influences. Only by observing chimps in their natural environment can we tell if they use tools without human interference.

Question: But doesn't the presence of human observers in an animal colony affect their behavior?

Fig. 2-2 *A special moment in Jane Goodall's naturalistic study of chimpanzees—a chimp uses a grass stem to extract a meal from a termite nest.* (Photo by Baron Hugo van Lawick, © National Geographic Society)

Yes. A major problem with naturalistic observation is the **effect of the observer** on the observed. Naturalists studying animal colonies must be very careful to keep their distance and to avoid the temptation to "make friends" with the animals. **Observer bias** is a closely related problem, in which observers see what they *expect* to see, or record only selected details. Despite such problems, naturalistic observation can provide a wealth of useful information (Sommer, 1977). This is particularly true when the observer is *concealed*, and *careful record keeping* is used to minimize biased observation.

Correlational Studies—In Search of the Perfect Relationship

Let's say that a psychologist notes a correspondence between the IQs of children and their parents, between physical attractiveness and social popularity, between anxiety and test performance, or even between riots and weather conditions. In each instance two observations or events are **co-related** (linked together in some orderly fashion). A **correlational study** is one that determines the degree of correlation, or relationship, between two existing traits, behaviors, or events (Myers, 1980). Unlike naturalistic observation, correlational studies can be done either in the lab or in the natural environment. Two factors of interest are measured, and then a statistical technique is used to find their degree of correlation. (See Appendix B for more information.) For example, we could find the correlation between the average number of hours slept each night and daytime anxiety levels. If the correlation is large, knowing the number of hours slept would allow us to predict anxiety level. Likewise, knowing anxiety level would allow prediction of sleep needs.

Question: How is the degree of correlation expressed?

Correlations can be expressed as a **coefficient of correlation,** which is simply a number falling somewhere between +1.00 and −1.00. (See Appendix B.) If the number is zero or close to zero, it indicates a weak or nonexistent relationship. For example, the correlation between shoe size and intelligence is zero. (Sorry, size 12 readers.) If the correlation is +1.00, a **perfect positive relationship** exists; if it is −1.00, a **perfect negative relationship** has been discovered.

Correlations in psychology are rarely perfect. Most fall somewhere between zero and plus or minus one. The closer the correlation coefficient is to +1.00 or −1.00, the stronger the relationship. For example, identical twins are likely to have almost identical IQs, whereas parents and their children have IQs that are only generally similar. The correlation between IQs of parents and children is .35; that between identical twins is .86.

Question: What do the terms "positive" and "negative" correlation mean?

A positive correlation indicates that increases in one measure are matched by increases in the other (or decreases are accompanied by decreases). For example, there is a positive relationship between high school grades and college grades; students who do better in high school tend to do better in college (and the reverse). In a negative correlation *increases* in the first measure are associated with *decreases* in the second. We might observe, for instance, that students who watch many hours of television tend to get lower grades than those who watch few hours. (This is the well-known TV zombie effect.)

Question: Would that show that watching TV too much causes lower grades?

It might seem so, but we cannot be sure of it without performing an experiment. Correlational studies help us discover relationships and make useful predictions, but correlation *does not demonstrate causation.* Just because one thing *appears* to be related to another does not mean that a cause-effect connection exists.

Consider an example of mistaking correlation for causation: What if a psychologist detected a certain chemical in the blood of schizophrenic patients that was not found in the blood of people functioning normally? Would this demonstrate that the chemical **causes** schizophrenia? It may seem so, but schizophrenia could cause the chemical to form. Or, both schizophrenia and the chemical might be caused by some unknown third factor. Just because one thing *appears* to cause another does not *confirm* that it does. This fact can be seen clearly in the case of obviously noncausal relationships. For example, there is a correlation between the number of churches in American cities and the number of bars; the more churches, the more bars. Does this mean that drinking makes you religious? Does it mean that religion makes you thirsty? No one, of course, would leap to such conclusions about cause and effect in this instance. But in more realistic situations it's tempting.

Exactly 9 months after a major power failure in New York State, doctors and nurses in New York hospitals noticed a sharp rise in the birthrate. News reports

Observer effect Changes in a subject's behavior brought about by an awareness of being observed.

Observer bias The tendency to distort observations or perceptions to match one's expectations.

Correlation The existence of a consistent, systematic relationship between two measures or variables.

Correlational study A nonexperimental study designed to assess the degree of relationship (if any) between two or more variables.

Coefficient of correlation A statistical index ranging from −1.00 to +1.00 that indicates the direction and degree of correlation.

Causation The act of causing some effect.

of this event assumed that when the lights and TVs went off, people had nothing better to do, and the result was a "baby boom" 9 months later. A closer look at the birthrate would show that it fluctuates up and down all year. The "baby boom" was but one of dozens of small peaks and therefore not necessarily linked to the power failure at all. The only way to be absolutely certain that a cause-effect relationship exists is to perform a controlled experiment. You'll learn how in the next section.

Learning Check

Before reading on, anwser the following questions about what you just read.

1. Most of psychology can rightfully be called "common sense" because psychologists prefer naturalistic observation to controlled observation. T or F?

2. A hypothesis is any careful observation made in a controlled experiment. T or F?

3. Two problems in naturalistic observation are:
a. getting subjects to cooperate and identifying correlations
b. defining a problem and proposing a hypothesis
c. effects of the observer and observer bias
d. running the experiment and making careful records

4. Correlation does not demonstrate causation. T or F?

5. Which correlation coefficient represents the strongest relationship?
a. -0.86 *b.* $+0.66$ *c.* $+0.10$ *d.* $+0.09$

Answers. **1.** F **2.** F **3.** *c* **4.** T **5.** *a*

The Psychology Experiment—Where Cause Meets Effect

One of the most powerful research tools available is the **experiment.** Research psychologists carefully control conditions in an experiment to gain reliable information and to identify cause-effect relationships. An experiment contains three essential elements, or **variables:**

1. **Independent variables,** which are conditions altered, applied, or varied in known ways by the experimenter. Independent variables are the suspected *causes* in an experiment.

2. **Dependent variables,** which measure the outcome of the experiment. Dependent variable reveal the *effects* of independent variables.

3. **Extraneous variables,** which are conditions the researcher wishes to prevent from affecting the experiment.

The simplest psychological experiment is based on two groups of **subjects** (animals or people). One group is called the **experimental group;** the other becomes the **control group.**

Question: How do these groups differ?

The control group and the experimental group are treated exactly alike except for one condition, the **independent variable.** (For the moment just think of a variable as any condition that can change or vary and that might affect the outcome of the experiment.) Suppose you notice that you study better with background music on. This suggests the hypothesis that music improves learning. We could test this idea experimentally by forming two groups of people. One group studies with music. The other studies without music. Then we could compare their scores on a test. The group exposed to music is the experimental group because the independent variable (music) is present. The group not exposed to music is the control group.

Question: Is a control group really needed? Can't people just study with music on to see if they do better?

Without a control group it would be impossible to tell if music had any effect on learning. The control group provides a *point of reference* to which scores of the experimental group can be compared. If the average test score of the experimental group is higher than that of the control group, it can be concluded that music improves learning efficiency. If the average is lower than the control group, we will know that music hampers learning. If there is no difference, we know that the independent variable had no effect on learning. In this experiment the "amount learned" (indicated by scores on the test) is the **dependent variable.** In an experiment we are asking the question, "Does the independent variable *affect* or influence the dependent variable?" (Does music affect or influence learning?) Another way to think of this is that results of an experiment are measured by the dependent variable, which *depends* on the independent variable. (The amount learned depends on whether music accompanied study.)

Question: How do we know that people in one group aren't more intelligent than those in the other group?

It's true that differences in personal characteristics of subjects might influence the outcome of an experiment. However, these can be eliminated by *randomly* assigning subjects to the two groups. **Random assignment** means that a subject has an equal chance of being a member of either the experimental group or the con-

Variable Any condition that changes or can be made to change; a measure, event, or state that may vary.

Experimental subjects Humans or animals whose behavior is investigated in an experiment.

Experimental group In a controlled experiment, the group of subjects exposed to the independent variable or experimental manipulation.

Control group In a controlled experiment, the group of subjects exposed to all experimental conditions except the independent variable.

Independent variable In an experiment, the condition being investigated as a possible cause of some change in behavior.

Dependent variable In an experiment, the condition (usually a behavior) that reflects the effects of the independent variable.

Random assignment The use of chance (for example, flipping a coin) to assign subjects to experimental and control groups.

Extraneous variables In an experiment, those conditions or factors to be excluded from possible influence on the outcome.

trol group. Even in fairly small groups, this selection method results in few differences in the number of people in each group who are geniuses or dunces, hungry, hung over, Democrat, Republican, tall, music lovers, or whatever.

Other **extraneous,** or outside variables—such as the amount of study time, the sex of subjects, the temperature of the room, the time of day, the amount of light, and so forth—must also be prevented from affecting the outcome of the experiment. But how? Usually by making all conditions except the independent variable *exactly the same* for both groups. If every possible condition is the same for subjects in both groups, *except* the presence or absence of music, and if there is a difference in the average amount learned, then that difference *must* be caused by the music (Fig 2-3).

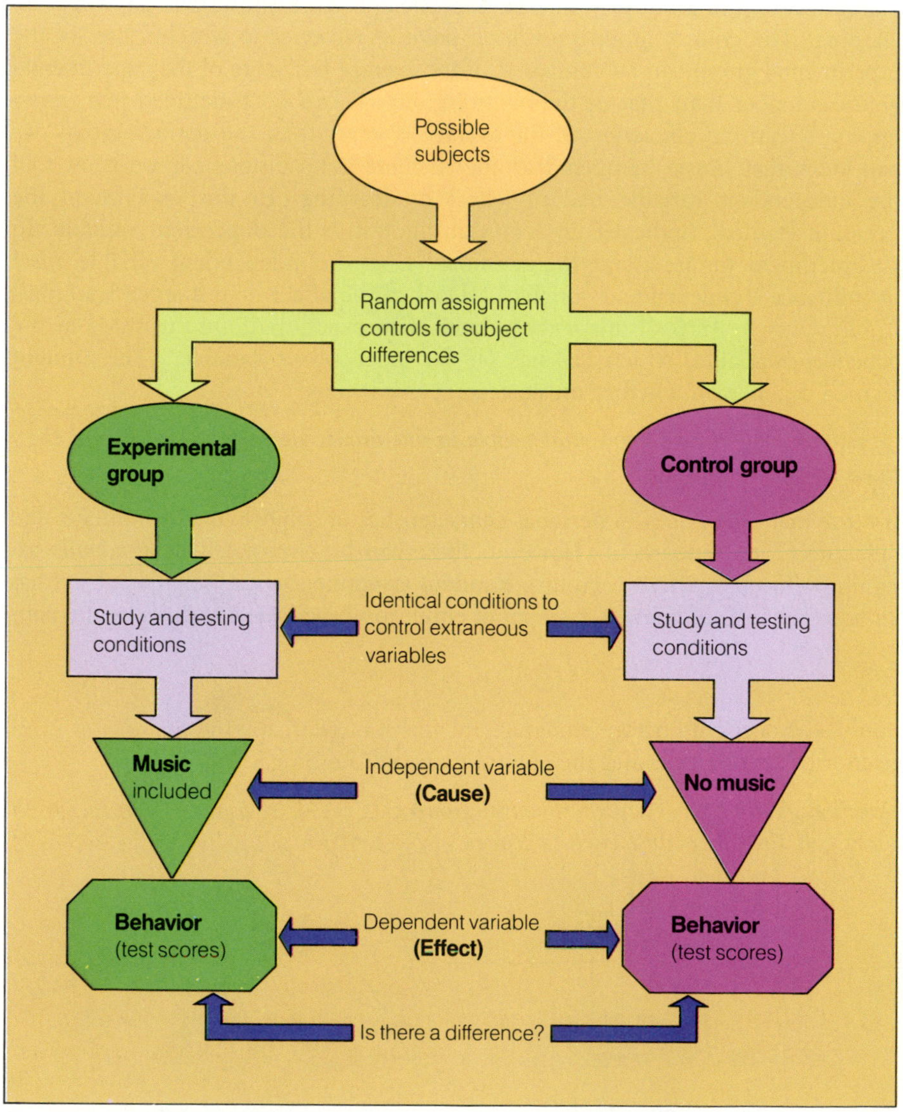

Fig. 2-3 *Elements of a simple psychological experiment to assess the effects of listening to music during study.*

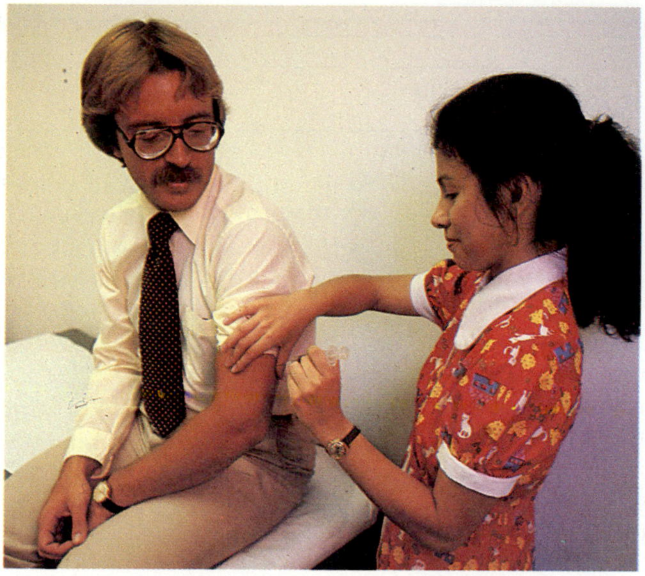

Fig. 2-4 *The placebo effect is a major factor in medical treatments.*

Now let's summarize more formally. In a psychological experiment two or more groups of subjects are treated differently with respect to the independent variable. In all other ways they are treated the same. That is, extraneous variables are identical for all groups in the experiment. This prevents conditions we are not interested in from affecting the results of the experiment. The effect of the independent variable (or variables) on some behavior (the dependent variable) is then measured. In a carefully controlled experiment, differences in the independent variable can be the only possible **cause** for any **effect** noted in the dependent variable. This allows clear cause-and-effect connections to be identified.

Placebo Effects—Sugar Pills and Salt Water

Assume that we want to perform an experiment to see if Dexedrine (a powerful central nervous system stimulant) affects learning. An accurate test of the drug would *not* occur if, before studying, members of the experimental group were given a Dexedrine pill, and the control group got nothing.

Question: Why not? The experimental group gets the drug and the control group doesn't. If there is a difference in learning scores, it must be due to the action of the drug, right?

No, because an error has been made: The experimental group and the control group have been treated differently with respect to more than just the presence or absence of the drug. Members of the experimental group took a pill, and control subjects did not. Without using a **placebo** (plah-SEE-bo), it is impossible to tell if the drug affected learning. It might be that those who swallowed a pill *expected* to do better, and that their expectations affected their performance.

Box 2-1

That's Interesting, But Is It Ethical?

Three areas of ethical concern in psychological research are the use of *deception*, *invasion of privacy*, and the risk of doing *lasting harm* to subjects. The first and third problems are illustrated by a classic experiment, in which subjects thought they were giving painful and dangerous electric shocks to another person (no shocks were actually given) (Milgram, 1974). Belief that they were hurting someone proved extremely stressful for most subjects. Many left the experiment shaken and upset, and some presumably suffered guilt and distress for some time afterward.

Such experiments raise serious ethical questions. Does the information gained justify the emotional costs? Was deception really necessary to answer the researcher's question? As a reply to such questions, the American Psychological Association has adopted guidelines that state in part: "Psychologists must carry out investigations with respect for the people who participate and with concern for their dignity and welfare." To ensure this, most university psychology departments have ethics committees that oversee proposed research. Nevertheless, no easy answers exist for the ethical questions raised by psychology, and debate about specific experiments is likely to continue.

Placebo effect Changes in behavior due to expectations that a drug (or other treatment) will have some effect.

Endorphin A class of brain chemicals similar in structure and effect to opiate drugs such as morphine.

Single-blind experiment An arrangement in which subjects remain unaware of whether they are in the experimental group or the control group.

Double-blind experiment An arrangement in which both subjects and experimenters are unaware of which group subjects are in until the experiment is completed.

Question: What is a placebo?

A placebo is a fake pill or injection. A placebo's beneficial effects come from what it suggests, rather than from what it contains. Sugar pills and saline (saltwater) injections are common placebos.

Although they have little or no direct effect, placebos can have a tremendous *psychological* impact. As an example of how powerful the **placebo effect** can be, one study showed that an injection of saline solution was 70 percent as effective as morphine in reducing pain for hospital patients (Beecher, 1959). This fact is well known to physicians, who for years have prescribed placebos for complaints they feel have no physical basis (Jospe, 1978). Exactly how placebos relieve pain is not fully understood, but experiments suggest that they trigger the release of brain chemicals called **endorphins** (Cohen, 1977; Levine et al., 1979). Endorphins are similar to pain-killing opiate drugs such as morphine. Thus, the placebo effect is not imaginary.

To control for placebo effects, a psychologist doing drug research could use a **single-blind** arrangement. In this approach, *all* subjects get a pill or injection. The experimental group gets the real drug, and the control group gets a placebo. Thus, subjects are *blind* as to whether they received the drug. But this is not enough. Experimenters must also be blind as to whether they are giving the drug or a placebo to a particular subject. The **double-blind** arrangement, as this is called, prevents the experimenter from unconsciously influencing subjects' reactions.

Question: How could the experimenter influence the subject?

The Experimenter Effect Psychological researchers face an interesting problem not shared by physicists and chemists. Human subjects are very sensitive to hints from an experimenter about what is expected of them. The **experimenter effect,** as this is called, can have a powerful impact on a subject's behavior (Rosenthal, 1976).

Experimenter effect Changes in subjects' behavior caused by the unintended influence of an experimenter's actions.

Self-fulfilling prophecy A prediction that, when made, influences the course of events toward fulfilling the prediction.

The experimenter effect even applies outside the laboratory, where expectations have been shown to influence people in interesting ways. Psychologist Robert Rosenthal (1973) reports a typical example: At the U.S. Air Force Academy Preparatory School, 100 airmen were randomly assigned to 1 of 5 math classes. Their teachers were unaware of this random assignment. Instead, the teachers were told that their students were selected for high or low levels of ability. Students in the supposed "high-ability" classes improved much more in math scores than those in "low-ability" classes. Yet, initially, the classes were all of equal ability. Apparently, the teachers subtly communicated their expectations to students. This, in turn, created a **self-fulfilling prophecy** that affected students' performance. That is, students tended to perform as they expected to perform. In short, people sometimes become what we prophesy for them. It is wise to remember that others tend to live *up* to or *down* to our expectations for them.

Learning Check

1. To identify cause and effect, a simple psychological experiment is based on creation of two groups: the ____________ group and the ____________ group.

2. Anything that can change (vary) and that might affect the behavior of subjects is called a ____________.

3. There are three types of variables to consider in an experiment: an ____________ variable (which is manipulated by the experimenter); a ____________ variable (which is a measure of the outcome of the experiment); and ____________ variables (factors not of interest in a particular experiment).

4. A researcher performs an experiment to learn if room temperature affects the amount of aggression displayed by college students under crowded conditions in a simulated prison environment. In this experiment, the independent variable is (circle):

room temperature   the amount of aggression   crowding   the simulated prison environment

5. A procedure used to control both the placebo effect and the experimenter effect in drug experiments is the:
a. correlation method *b.* extraneous prophecy
c. double-blind technique *d.* random assignment of subjects

Answers: **1.** experimental, control **2.** variable **3.** independent, dependent, extraneous **4.** room temperature **5.** c

The Clinical Method—Data by the Case

Many experiments that might be informative or revealing are impractical, immoral, or impossible to perform. In instances such as these, information may be gained from **case studies.** A case study is an in-depth focus on all aspects of a single subject. Case studies are used heavily by clinical psychologists.

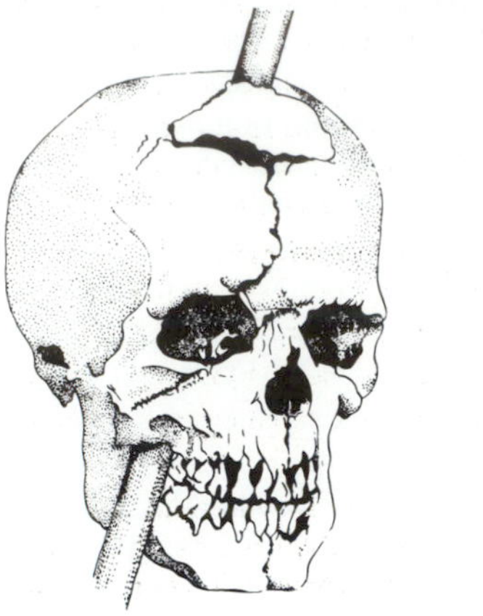

Fig. 2-5 *Some of the earliest information on the effects of damage to frontal areas in the brain came from a case study of the accidental injury of Phineas Gage.*

Case studies may sometimes be thought of as **natural experiments.** Gunshot wounds, brain tumors, accidental poisonings, and similar disasters have provided much information on the functioning of the human brain. One remarkable case from the history of psychology was reported by Dr. J. M. Harlow (1868). Phineas Gage, a young foreman on a work crew, had a 13-pound steel rod blown through the front of his brain by an excavating charge. Amazingly, he survived the accident, but not without undergoing a profound personality change. Dr. Harlow carefully recorded all details of what was perhaps the first well-done case study of an accidental *frontal lobotomy* (the destruction of front brain matter).

Over 120 years later, a Los Angeles carpenter named Michael Melnick was the victim of a similar freakish accident. Melnick fell from the second story of a house and impaled his head on a steel reinforcing rod. Incredibly, he recovered completely, with no sign of lasting ill effects (*Los Angeles Times*, 1981). Melnick's very different reaction to a similar injury shows why psychologists prefer controlled experiments and often use lab animals for studies of the brain. But when a purely psychological problem is under study, the clinical method may be the *only* source of information.

A classic psychological case study is *The Three Faces of Eve* (Thigpen & Cleckley, 1957). Eve White was a mild, restrained, suburban housewife who in the course of psychiatric treatment revealed the existence of a second, separate personality. This second personality, Eve Black, was the antithesis of Eve White. Eve Black was childish, mischievous, and erotically flirtatious. Eve Black knew about Eve White and openly talked about the times she had disobeyed her parents or gotten drunk and then "went into" Eve White. After Eve Black's escapades, Eve White faced her punishment or bore her hangover with bewilderment because she did not know of Eve Black's existence. Eventually, this duality was resolved when a third personality—who called herself Jane—emerged. Jane ultimately separated from Eve White's husband and began a relatively stable new life marked by the slow development of a progression of other personalities.

Now in her 50s, the former Eve White has manifested 21 different personalities over the years. The careful recording of all pertinent facts in cases such as this one is essential to psychology. *Multiple personality* is a rare event and there are no experimental means for producing it. (Multiple personality is discussed further in Chapter 19.)

Survey Method—Here, Have a Sample

Sometimes psychologists would like to ask everyone in the world a few well-chosen questions: "Have you ever smoked marijuana?" "Have you engaged in premarital sexual intercourse?" "What is your marital status now, and were your parents ever separated or divorced?" "Do you favor abortion?" The answers to questions such as these can reveal much about significant psychological events in the lives of large groups of people. But since it is impractical to question everyone, psychologists use the **survey method.** In a survey, people in a **representative sample** are asked a carefully worded series of questions. A representative sample includes the same proportion of men, women, white-collar workers, Republicans, Democrats, blacks, and so on as found in the population as a whole.

A careful survey can provide an accurate picture of how large segments of the general population feel about current issues, even though only a small percentage of people are polled. However, some psychologists have questioned—tongue in cheek—psychology's claim that its conclusions apply to people in general. The distinguished psychologist Edward Tolman once noted that much of American psychology is based on two sets of subjects: rats and college sophomores. Tolman urged his colleagues to remember that rats certainly are not people and that college sophomores may not be!

Question: How accurate is the survey method?

Modern surveys like the Gallup and Harris polls are quite accurate. The Gallup poll has erred in its election predictions by only 1.5 percent since 1954. This level of accuracy has not always been the case. During the 1936 presidential election, a well-known magazine, the *Literary Digest*, predicted that Alfred Landon would defeat Franklin Roosevelt by a large margin. In actuality, Roosevelt defeated Landon by a landslide!

Question: How could the poll have been so wrong?

The answer lies in the way the sample was taken. Most people in the poll were contacted by *telephone*. In 1936, during the Depression, people who had phones were much more wealthy than average, and the wealthy favored Landon. Thus, the sample was biased rather than representative.

Even when questions are carefully stated and the sample is representative, a survey may be limited by another problem. If a psychologist asked you detailed questions about your sexual history and current sexual activities, how accurate would your replies be? Would you be self-conscious and perhaps not completely frank? Or might you have a tendency to exaggerate? Replies to survey questions are not always *accurate* or *truthful*. Many people show a distinct **courtesy bias,** or tendency to give answers that are agreeable and socially acceptable. For example, pollsters working on a 1979 election found that black persons talking to white interviewers were less likely to admit support for a black candidate. Similarly, white persons talking to black interviewers were more likely to claim support for the black candidate (McKean, 1984).

Despite such limitations, surveys frequently produce useful information. For instance, in recent years working women have complained of sexual harassment at their jobs. How widespread is this problem? A recent survey of working men and women conducted by psychologist Barbara Gutek provides an answer. Gutek (1981) found that 53 percent of women but only 37 percent of men had experienced some form of sexual harassment at work. Although such information does not solve the problem of sexual harassment, it is a first step toward understanding it and remedying it.

A Look Ahead To complete our discussion, this chapter's Applications offers a critical look at psychological information reported in the popular press. You should find this section an interesting way to conclude our look at research in psychology.

Case study An intensive investigation of the behavior of a single person.

Natural experiment An accident or other natural occurrence that allows the gathering of data on a psychological phenomenon of interest.

Multiple personality A rare form of psychiatric disturbance in which a person maintains two or more distinct personalities.

Survey method The use of public polling techniques to answer psychological questions.

Representative sample A subset of a larger population of subjects that accurately reflects the characteristics of the population.

Courtesy bias The tendency to give "polite" answers; especially, the tendency to alter answers so as not to hurt an interviewer's feelings.

Learning Check

1. Case studies can often be thought of as natural experiments and are used frequently by clinical psychologists. T or F?

2. For the survey method to be valid, a representative sample of people must be polled. T or F?

3. The phenomenon of multiple personality would most likely be investigated by use of:
a. a representative sample *b.* field experiments *c.* the double-blind procedure *d.* case studies

4. A problem with the survey method is that answers to questions may not always be ____________________ or ____________________.

Answers: **1.** T **2.** T **3.** *d* **4.** accurate, truthful

Applications

Psychology in the News—Notes on Reading the Popular Press

Question: Is so much emphasis on "research" really necessary in psychology?

In a word, yes. As we have seen, "science" is a powerful way of asking questions about the world, a way of getting trustworthy answers. More importantly, we might ask, "What is the alternative to using the scientific method?" In most areas of knowledge, including psychology, wiping out scientific advances would mean a return to the Dark Ages. Awareness of this fact, along with your understanding of psychological research methods, should do much to make you a more critical observer of human behavior. Below are some additional pointers to sharpen your skills.

Notes on Reading the Popular Press

The tremendous popularity of psychology has spurred extensive coverage of psychological research and theories in popular magazines and daily newspapers. Unfortunately, much of what is covered is based on wishful thinking rather than science. Here are some suggestions for telling the difference.

Suggestion 1 Be skeptical. Psychological reports in the popular press tend to be made uncritically and with a definite bias toward the reporting of sensational findings. Remember, saying "That's incredible" means "That's not believable"—which is quite often true.

Example: A few years ago stories appeared in the press reporting research in the Soviet Union and the United States on "dermo-optical perception." According to these stories, people had been found who could identify colors and read print (even under glass) while blindfolded. These feats supposedly were performed using the fingertips and were given as an indication of the existence of a "sixth sense," or "X-ray eyes." Martin Gardner, a scientist whose hobby is magic, suggests that such "abilities" are based on what professional performers call a "nose peek." Gardner says that it is impossible to prepare a blindfold (without doing damage to the eyes) that does not leave a tiny space on each side of the nose through which a person can peek. In accordance with Gardner's criticism, the phenomenal ability of individuals who performed in the first dermo-optical perception experiments disappeared each time the opportunity to peek was controlled (Gardner, 1966).

Here is another indication of the need to be skeptical. Psychologist Philip Zimbardo tells with amusement about his mentioning to a reporter that in the

Applications: Psychology in the News, continued

back wards of two mental hospitals in which he had worked, female patients seemed to use a greater number of obscenities than male patients. Zimbardo emphasizes that this was nothing more than a casual statement and that it was not based on data of any kind. When it was reported in *The New York Times*, however, it became an "observation" that he had "noted" over a long period of time. When *Newsweek* reported the *Times* article to its readers, the relationship that was "noted" became one that had been "found." Ultimately, *Playboy*'s version stated that "a number of psychologists, *The New York Times* reports, have found that women of every social level have become increasingly uninhibited in their use of obscene language" (*Playboy*, 1969). Zimbardo notes that the only authority mentioned to confirm this "fact" was himself (Ruch & Zimbardo, 1971)!

Suggestion 2 Consider the source of information. It should come as no surprise that information given by an individual or a company intent on selling a product often reflects a desire for profit rather than the objective truth. Here is a typical advertising claim: "Government tests prove that no pain reliever is stronger or more effective than Brand X aspirin." A statement like this usually means that there was *no difference* between the product and others tested. No other pain reliever was stronger or more effective, but none was weaker either.

Keep the source in mind when reading the claims of makers of home biofeedback machines, sleep-learning devices, and the like. Remember also that psychological services may be merchandised as well. Expensive courses that promise instant mental health and happiness, increased efficiency, memory, ESP or psychic ability, control of the unconscious mind, an end to the smoking habit, and so on are usually supported by a few testimonials and many unsupported claims.

"Psychic" phenomena should be viewed with special caution. Stage mentalists make their living by deceiving the public. Understandably, they are highly interested in promoting belief in their nonexistent powers. Psychic phenomena when (and if) they do occur are quite unpredictable. It would be impossible for a mentalist to do three shows a night, six nights a week without consistently using deception.

Question: I've seen some amazing things on TV. Could you give an example of how I may have been fooled?

Here is a typical stage mentalist's routine. The mentalist picks a member of the audience "at random" and begins telling him personal things that "he could not possibly know." How does he do it? Easy! One of his many assistants stood in line outside the theater and eavesdropped on the person's conversations before the show. The assistant then made careful note of where the person was seated and passed on the location and information to the mentalist. The mentalist then announces, "You have an aunt . . . Aunt Bessie . . . she has been very ill . . . you were thinking about her earlier this evening . . . you had a flat tire on the way here this evening."

Suggestion 3 Ask yourself, "Was there a control group?" The essential importance of a control group in any experiment is frequently overlooked by the unsophisticated—an error to which you are no longer susceptible! The popular press is full of reports of "experiments" performed without control groups: "Talking to Plants Speeds Growth"; "Special Diet Controls Hyperactivity in Children"; "Food Shows Less Spoilage in Pyramid Chamber"; "Theater Reports Increased Beverage Sales during Showing of *Lawrence of Arabia*."

Consider the last example for a moment. Almost every year it seems a theater somewhere will claim that a movie has had an unusual effect on viewers. If the showing of *Lawrence of Arabia* were accompanied by increased beverage sales, would this indicate that viewers had been influenced by the desert scenery? Actually, they may have been influenced, but since there is no control group (people who watch another movie under identical conditions), it is impossible to tell if the temperature in the theater, the time of year, the kind of crowd attracted, or the movie itself affected beverage consumption.

Applications: Psychology in the News, continued

Suggestion 4 Look for errors in distinguishing between correlation and causation. An earlier discussion should make it clear that it is dangerous to presume that one thing has *caused* another just because there is a correlation between the two. In spite of this, you will encounter numerous claims based on questionable correlations. Recently, a nutritionist was quoted in the news as saying that excessive consumption of milk may cause juvenile deliquency. (This must have been a real hit with the National Dairy Association.) On what did he base this conclusion? Adolescent males who are often in trouble, he said, drink greater than average amounts of milk. Certainly, this correlation is interesting. But, in no way does it demonstrate that milk causes delinquency. The situation could easily be, for instance, that young males who mature early are more likely to be aggressive or get into trouble. Maturing early involves rapid growth. And rapid growth promotes hunger. It is entirely possible that this is the only link between milk and delinquency. Or, perhaps some other unknown factor is involved.

Here's another example of mistaking correlation for causation. Jeanne Dixon, a popular astrologer, once answered a group of prominent scientists—who had declared that there is no scientific foundation for astrology—by saying: "They would do well to check the records at their local police stations, where they will learn that the rate of violent crime rises and falls with lunar cycles" (Dixon, 1975). Dixon, of course, is implying that the moon affects human behavior.

Question: If it is true that violent crime is more frequent at certain times of the month, doesn't this prove her point?

Far from it; increased crime could be due to darker nights, the fact that bills fall due at the first of the month, or any number of similar factors.

Suggestion 5 Be sure to distinguish between observation and inference. If you see a person *crying*, is it correct to assume that he or she is *sad?* Although making this assumption seems reasonable, it is actually quite risky. We can observe objectively that the person is crying, but to *infer* sadness may be in error. It could be that the individual has just peeled 5 pounds of onions or just won a million-dollar lottery or is trying contact lenses for the first time. Psychologists, politicians, physicians, scientists, and other experts often go far beyond the available facts in their claims. This does not mean that their inferences, opinions, and interpretations have no value; the opinion of an expert on the causes of mental illness, criminal behavior, learning problems, or whatever can be very revealing. But be careful to distinguish between fact and opinion. Here is an example that illustrates why this is important.

> A 54-year-old schizophrenic patient was rewarded for holding a broom that was given to her by a ward attendant. If she held the broom after it was handed to her, she was given a cigarette by another attendant. The purpose of this experiment was to determine if rewards should be used to alter the patient's rather listless behavior (she had been hospitalized for 23 years and refused to do anything on the ward). Soon the patient spent much of her time holding the broom. At this point two psychiatrists were invited to observe the patient through a one-way mirror. One psychiatrist's interpretation of the "broom-holding behavior" was that it was a symbolic expression of deep-seated unfulfilled desires. According to him, the broom could be a symbol for:
>
> **1.** "a child that gives her love and she gives him in return her devotion,
> **2.** a phallic symbol,
> **3.** the sceptre of an omnipotent queen." (Ayllon et al., 1965)

The psychiatrist *observed* that the patient spent much of her time holding a broom. He *inferred* that this behavior had deep psychological meaning. In fact she held the broom for one reason: She received cigarettes for doing so!

Suggestion 6 Beware of over-simplifications, especially those motivated by monetary gain. Courses or programs that offer a "new personality in three sessions," "six steps to love and fulfillment in marriage," or newly discovered "secrets of unlocking the powers of the mind" should be immediately suspect.

Applications: Psychology in the News, continued

An excellent example of oversimplification is provided by a brochure entitled, "Dr. Joyce Brothers Asks: How Do You Rate as a 'Superwoman'?" Dr. Brothers, a media psychologist who has no private practice and is not known for research, wrote the brochure as a consultant for the Aerosol Packaging Council of the Chemical Specialties Manufacturing Association. A typical suggestion in this brochure tells how to enhance marriage: "Sweep him off to a weekend hideaway. Tip: When he's not looking, spray a touch of your favorite *aerosol* cologne mist on the bedsheets and pillows" (italics added). Sure, Joyce. . . .

Suggestion 7 Remember, "for example" is no proof. After reading this chapter, you should be sensitive to the danger of selecting single examples. If you read, "Law student passes state bar exam using sleep-learning device," don't rush out to buy one. Systematic research has shown that these devices are of little or no value (Koukkou & Lehmann, 1968).

A key element in the scientific pursuit of truth is the ability to replicate (repeat) observations or experiments. In contrast, a failure to replicate observations is a major failing of parascience (that which resembles science but is not truly scientific). A good example is the idea that plants have feelings. This claim, which received wide media coverage, was largely based on "experiments" performed by Cleve Backster, a polygraph expert. (The polygraph is commonly referred to as a lie detector. See Chapter 12.) Backster claimed that plants wired to a lie detector responded to music, threats (such as lighting a match nearby), and other stimuli. However, when scientists tried to repeat the experiments, using either identical or improved methods, the results were completely negative (Galston & Slayman, 1983). A long list of other purported phenomena—from pyramid power to dowsing to moon madness—likewise have disappeared in the light of careful scrutiny.

Summary Journalist Alvin Toffler and others have suggested that we are in the midst of an "information explosion." Indeed, we are all bombarded daily with such a mass of new information that it is difficult to adequately absorb it. The available knowledge, even in a limited area like psychology, biology, medicine, or contemporary rock music, is so vast that no single person can completely know and comprehend it. With this situation in mind, it becomes increasingly important that you become a critical, selective, and informed consumer of information. And if you think the value of scientific thought is restricted to the laboratory, remember the words of Oliver Wendell Holmes: "All life is an experiment."

Learning Check

1. Newspaper accounts of dermo-optical perception have generally reported only the results of carefully designed psychological experiments. T or F?
2. Stage mentalists and psychics often use deception in their acts. T or F?
3. Blaming variations in the rate of violent crime on changes in the lunar cycle is an example of mistaking correlation for causation. T or F?
4. Psychiatric interpretations of a patient's "broom-holding behavior" (described previously) show the importance of using a control group in experiments. T or F?

Answers: 1. F 2. T 3. T 4. F

Chapter Summary

Many of the important ideas in this chapter are summarized in the accompanying comparison chart. A few additional points to remember follow it.

	Advantages	Disadvantages
Naturalistic observation	Behavior is observed in a natural setting; much information is obtained and hypotheses and questions for additional research are formed.	Little or no control is possible; observed behavior may be altered by the presence of the observer; observations may be biased; causes cannot be conclusively identified.
Correlational method	Demonstrates the existence of relationships; allows prediction; can be used in lab, clinic, or natural settings.	Little or no control is possible; relationships may be coincidental; cause-effect relationships cannot be confirmed.
Experimental method	Clear cause-effect relationships can be identified; powerful controlled observations can be staged; no need to wait for natural event.	May be somewhat artificial; some natural behavior not easily studied in laboratory (field experiments may avoid these objections).
Clinical method	Takes advantage of "natural experiments" and allows investigation of rare or unusual problems or events.	Little control is possible; subjective interpretation is often necessary; a single case may be misleading or unrepresentative.
Survey method	Allows information about large numbers of people to be gathered; can address questions not answered by other approaches.	Obtaining a representative sample is critical and can be difficult to do; answers may be inaccurate; people may not do what they say or say what they do.

- The *scientific method* is used to improve on common sense and avoid the pitfalls of casual observation. Important steps in scientific investigation usually include: *observing*, *defining a problem*, *proposing a hypothesis*, *experimenting*, and *forming a theory*.
- *Naturalistic observation* is a starting place in many investigations. Three problems with this approach are: the effects of the observer on the observed, observer bias, and an inability to explain observed behavior.
- In the *correlational method*, relationships between two traits, responses, or events are measured. Then a *correlation coefficient* is calculated to gage the strength of the relationship. Correlations allow prediction, but they are usually insufficient to demonstrate cause-and-effect connections.
- Cause-effect relationships are best identified by *controlled experiments*. In an experiment, two or more groups of *subjects* are formed. These groups differ only with regard to the *independent variable* (condition of interest as a cause in the experiment). *Effects* on the *dependent variable* are then measured. All other conditions *(extraneous variables)* are held constant.
- In experiments testing drugs, a *placebo* (a fake pill or injection) must be used to control psychological expectations associated with taking a drug. Drug research also frequently employs a *double-blind* procedure so that neither subjects nor experimenters know who is receiving the drug.

- A related problem is the *experimenter effect*. This is the tendency for experimenters to subtly and unconsciously influence the outcome of an experiment. Expectations can create a *self-fulfilling prophecy*, in which a person changes in the direction of the expectation.
- The *clinical method* employs *case studies*, which are in-depth records of a single subject. Case studies provide important information on topics that would not be studied any other way.
- In the *survey method*, people in a *representative sample* are asked a carefully worded series of questions. Responses to these questions provide information on the attitudes and psychological functioning of large groups of people.
- Information in the popular media varies greatly in quality and accuracy. It is wise to approach such information with skepticism and caution. This is especially true with regard to the *source* of information, *uncontrolled observation*, *correlation* and *causation*, *inferences*, *oversimplification*, *single examples*, and *unrepeatable results*.

Part Two

Foundations of Human Consciousness

Chapter 3

The Biology of Behavior

Chapter Preview

Worlds within Worlds within Worlds

Imagine yourself smaller than the period at the end of this sentence. Then join me as we enter a bizarre microscopic world. Surrounding us is a tangle of spidery branches, delicate fibers, and transparent globes. As we watch, pulsing waves of electrical energy flash through the fibers, arriving and scattering in thousands of directions. Meanwhile, all is bathed in a swirling sea of exotic chemicals. We are indeed in a strange realm. Yet there is beauty here, and mind-bending complexity—for we have just stepped into that most amazing of all computers, the human brain.

Crack open the fragile shell of the skull and you find, in the truest sense, "worlds within worlds within worlds." The human brain is a mass of spongy tissue about the size of a large grapefruit. Weighing a little over 3 pounds, it consists of some 100 billion individual nerve cells called **neurons** *(NEW-rons). All human behavior can ultimately be traced to the activity of these tiny cells. Each neuron in the brain's "enchanted loom" is connected to as many as 10,000 others. This network provides an exceedingly large capacity for combining and storing information. Scientists estimate that the number of possible pathways between neurons in a single human brain exceeds the number of atoms in the entire universe!*

Psychologists have long known that the brain is the organ of consciousness and action. But only in recent years has it become possible to demonstrate this directly. To prove the point, researcher José Delgado once entered a bullring with a cape and a radio transmitter. The bull charged. Delgado retreated. At the last possible instant the speeding bull stopped short. Why? Because Delgado's radio activated electrodes implanted deep within the bull's brain. These, in turn, stimulated "control centers" that brought the bull to a halt.

Physiological psychology *is the study of how the brain and nervous system relate to behavior, including the effects of damage to these delicate systems. The physiological psychologist occupies an exotic midground between mind and brain, biology and psychology. Let us enter this fascinating realm for a closer look at our biological heritage and human potential.*

Survey Questions How do nerve cells operate and communicate? What are the functions of major parts of the nervous system? What happens when the brain is injured? How does the glandular system relate to the nervous system? How do right- and left-handed individuals differ?

Neurons—Building a "Biocomputer"

As physiological psychologist Paul MacLean once remarked, the towering question before the world concerns whether humans can master their brains and behavior before they have blown themselves to smithereens through their mastery of physics and chemistry. One of the most powerful keys to understanding the brain is the study of individual nerve cells. Unlike other cells in the body, neurons are specially designed to carry information. They are the basic units of the human "biocomputer."

Question: How do neurons carry information?

Parts of a Neuron If we think of the nervous system as long "chains" of communicating cells, then neurons are the links. No two neurons are exactly alike in size or shape, but most have four basic parts (Fig. 3-1). Notice first the **dendrites** (DEN-drytes), which look like the roots of a tree. The dendrites specialize in receiving information from other neurons. The cell body, or **soma** (SOH-mah), also gathers incoming information, which it collects and combines. Periodically, the soma sends nerve impulses down a long thin fiber called an **axon** (AK-sahn).

Some axons are only about 0.1 millimeter long. (That's about the width of a pencil line.) Other axons stretch up to a meter through the nervous system of an adult. Axons act like tiny cables carrying messages from the sensory organs to the brain, from the brain to muscles or glands, or simply from one nerve cell to the next. Most axons branch at their ends to form an array of **axon terminals.** These branches link the neuron to the dendrites and somas of other nerve cells.

The Nerve Impulse Each neuron can be thought of as a tiny biological battery ready to be discharged. Nerve cells are filled with, and surrounded by, electrically charged molecules called **ions** (EYE-ons), especially sodium and potassium ions (Fig. 3-2). Differing amounts of these ions are found inside and outside the cell. As a result, a tiny difference in electrical charge exists across the cell membrane (or "skin"). In humans this electrical charge, called a **resting potential,** is about minus 70 millivolts (a millivolt is one-thousandth of a volt).

Messages arriving from other neurons alter the resting potential until it reaches a **threshold,** or trigger point, for firing. The threshold for human neurons averages about minus 50 millivolts. (See Fig. 3-2.) When a neuron reaches this point, a nerve impulse, or **action potential,** sweeps down the axon. The threshold for firing makes the action potential an **all-or-nothing** event; an impulse occurs completely or not at all. Thus, you might find it helpful to picture the axon as a fuse. This "fuse" is normally lit at the soma and burns rapidly to the axon terminals.

Resources

Neurons Individual nerve cells that form the basic structure of the nervous system.

Dendrites Branching projections from nerve cell bodies that conduct information from other neurons to the cell body.

Soma The main body of a neuron or other cell.

Axon A thin fiber that conducts information away from the cell body of a neuron.

Resting potential The electrical charge that exists across the cell membrane of a neuron when it is at rest.

Action potential The nerve impulse, which is a rapid change in electrical charge across the cell membrane.

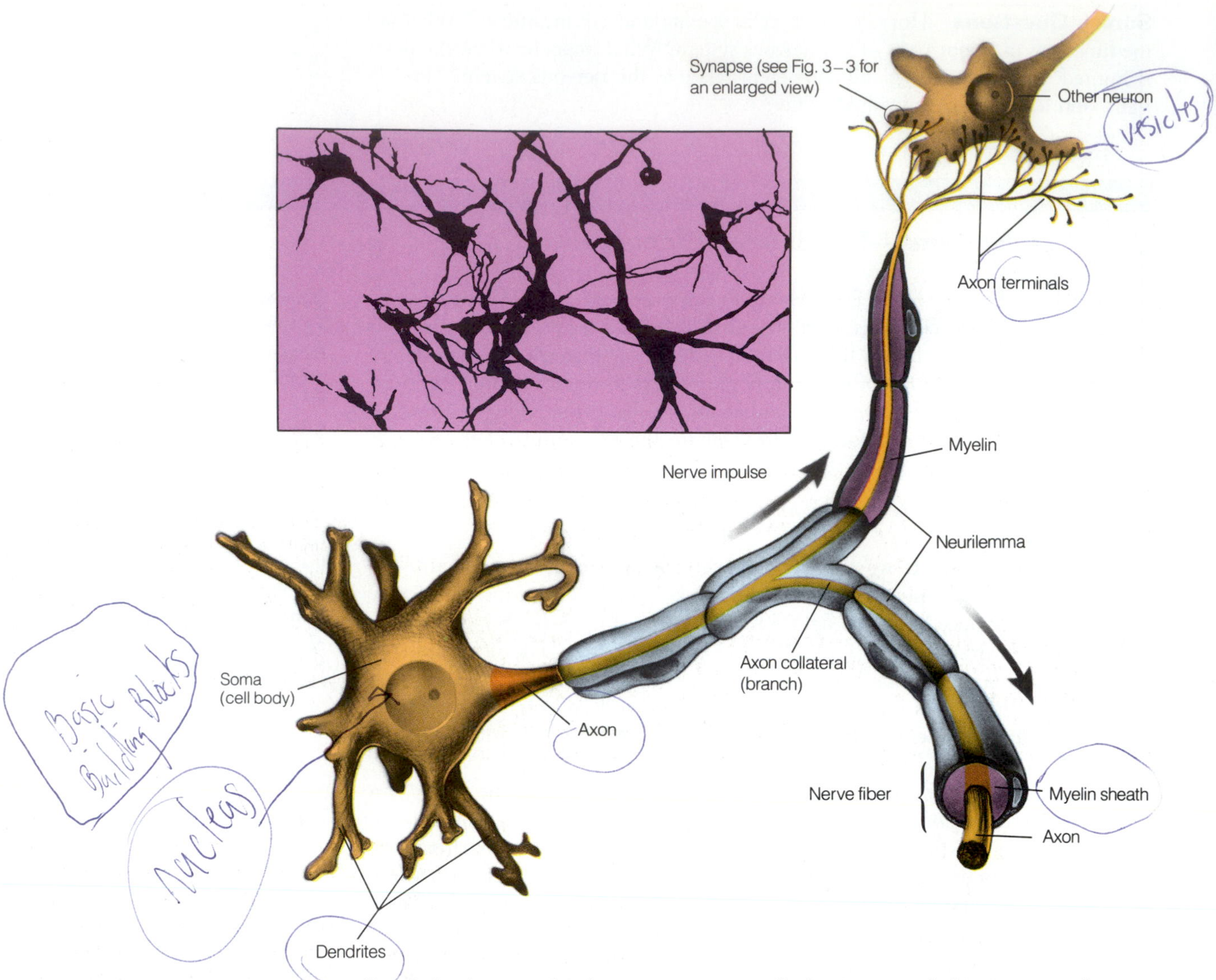

Fig. 3-1 *An example of a neuron, or nerve cell, showing several of its important features. The right foreground shows a nerve fiber in cross section, and the upper left inset gives a more realistic picture of the shape of neurons. The nerve impulse usually travels from the dendrites and soma to the branching ends of the axon. The neuron shown here is a motor neuron. Motor neurons originate in the brain or spinal cord and send their axons to the muscles or glands of the body.*

Neurotransmitter Any of a number of chemical substances secreted by neurons that alter activity in other neurons.

Synapse The microscopic space between two neurons over which neurotransmitters travel.

Question: How is information carried from one neuron to another?

Neurotransmitters We have seen that the nerve impulse is primarily an electrical event. This is why behavior is affected when the brain is stimulated electrically. (A good example is José Delgado's "electronic bullfighting" described in the Chapter Preview.) In contrast, communication between neurons is molecular. A nerve impulse that reaches the tips of the axon terminals causes **neurotransmitters**

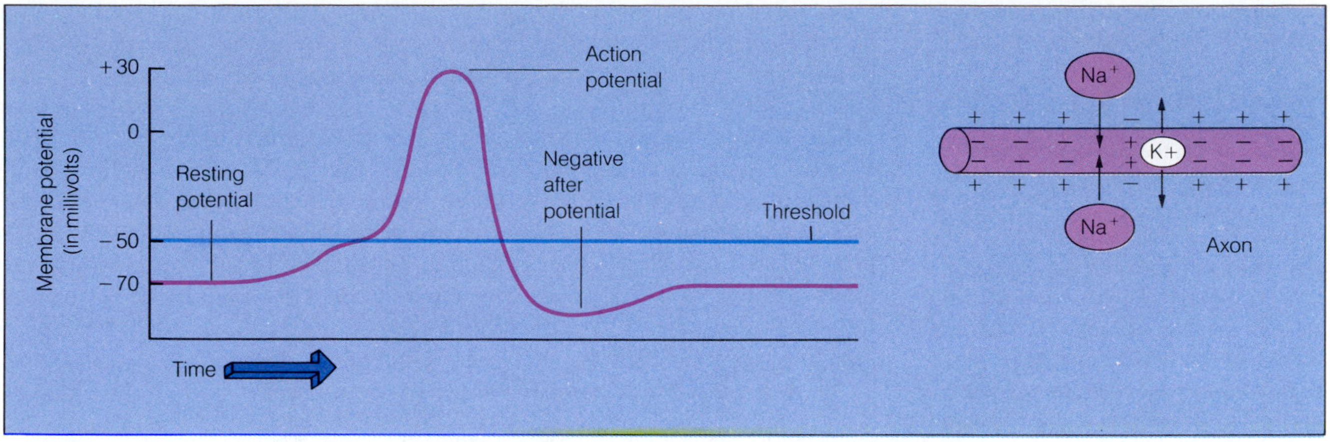

Fig. 3-2 *Electrochemical changes in a nerve cell generate an action potential. When positively charged sodium (Na +) ions rush into the cell, its potential briefly becomes positive. This is the action potential. After the action potential, an outward flow of positive potassium (K +) ions restores the negative charge of the resting potential. (See text for further explanation.)*

(NEW-row-TRANS-mit-ers) to be released. These potent chemicals cross the tiny gap, or **synapse** (SIN-aps), between neurons. Transmitter molecules then attach to special **receptor sites** on the dendrites and soma of the next neuron (Fig. 3-3). (This is also how neurotransmitters activate muscles and glands.)

Question: Does the arrival of a neurotransmitter trigger an action potential in the next neuron?

Not always. Neurotransmitters may *excite* the next neuron (move it closer to firing) or *inhibit* it (make an impulse less likely). At any instant each neuron receives messages from hundreds or thousands of others. If several "exciting" messages arrive close in time, and they are not canceled by "inhibiting" messages, the neuron reaches its threshold for firing. This means that chemical messages are

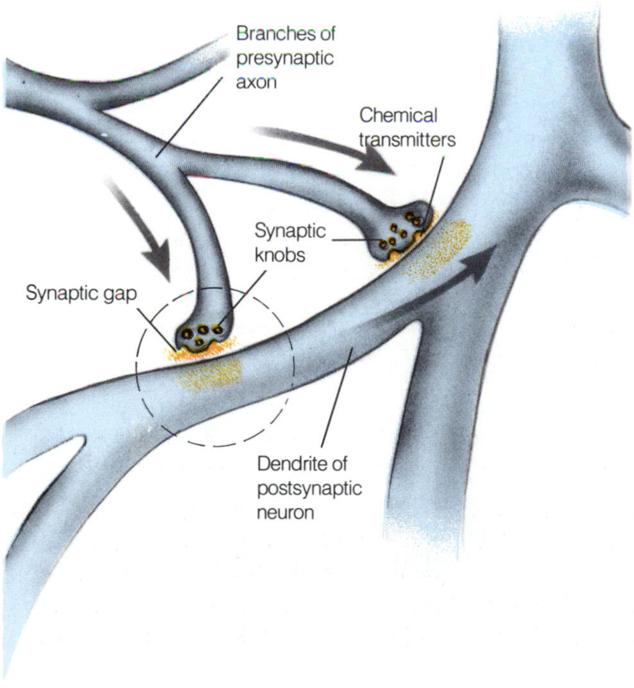

Fig. 3-3 *A highly magnified view of the synapse shown in Fig. 3-1. Transmitter molecules cross the synaptic gap to affect the next neuron. The size of the gap is exaggerated here; it is actually only about one-millionth of an inch. Transmitter molecules vary in their effect: Some excite the next neuron and some inhibit its activity.*

Acetylcholine The neurotransmitter released in the junction between neurons and muscles.

Neuropeptides Newly discovered brain chemicals that influence moods and behavior by modifying the activity of neurons.

Myelin A fatty layer surrounding some axons that increases the rate at which nerve impulses travel along the axon.

Neurilemma A layer of living cells that encircles the axons of many neurons.

Central nervous system The brain and spinal cord as a combined system.

Peripheral nervous system All portions of the nervous system lying outside the brain and spinal cord.

combined before a neuron "decides" to send on its all-or-nothing message. Multiply these events by 100 billion neurons and 100 trillion synapses and you have a computer of astounding capacity—all fit into a space one-half the size of a shoe box.

There are now some 30 known or suspected neurotransmitters in the brain. The large variety of transmitter chemicals is one reason why there are literally thousands of drugs that affect the brain. Many drugs operate by imitating, duplicating, or canceling the actions of neurotransmitters. For example, one of the best known transmitters is **acetylcholine** (ah-SEET-ul-KOH-leen), which normally activates muscles. The drug **curare** (cue-RAH-ree), however, prevents nerve cells from activating muscle cells (Evarts, 1979). As a result, a person or animal given curare will be paralyzed—a fact known to South American Indians of the Amazon River Basin, who use curare as an arrow poison.

Neural Regulators A stunning series of recent discoveries has revealed a new class of brain transmitters called **neuropeptides** (NEW-row-PEP-tides), or, simply, brain peptides. Rather than carrying messages directly, these chemicals seem to *regulate* the activity of other neurons. In doing so, they affect memory, pain, emotion, pleasure, mood, hunger, sexual behavior, and other basic processes (Krieger, 1983). Ultimately, an understanding of brain peptides may help explain depression, schizophrenia, drug addiction, and other puzzling problems.

General Neuroanatomy—Wired for Action

Picture two people playing catch with a Frisbee. To an outside observer this appears to be an interesting but certainly not amazing activity. But consider what is going on inside the body. To launch the Frisbee on its flight, or to anticipate its path for a catch, an incredible amount of information must be sensed, interpreted, and directed to countless muscle fibers. The neural circuits of the body are ablaze with activity. Let us consider in more detail the "wiring diagram" that makes this possible.

Neurons and Nerves

Question: Are neurons the same as nerves?

No. Nerves, which can be seen with the unaided eye, are not single cells; rather, they are bundles of nerve fibers (axons and dendrites). Many nerves have a whitish color because they are made up mainly of axons having a coating of **myelin** (MY-eh-lin). Myelin, which forms a layer of fatty insulation around the axons of some neurons, increases the speed of the action potential. Most nerve fibers outside of the brain and spinal cord also have a thin layer of living cells called the **neurilemma** (NEW-rih-LEM-ah) wrapped around them. (See Fig. 3-1.) The neurilemma is important because it provides a "tunnel" through which damaged nerve fibers can grow when repairing themselves.

The Nervous System

Taken as a whole, the nervous system is a single unified structure, but it may be divided into smaller parts to make it easier to understand. As seen in Fig. 3-4 and Fig. 3-5, a distinction can be made between the **central** and the **peripheral** nervous systems. The central nervous system (CNS) consists of all nervous tissue encased by bone, or more simply, it includes the brain and spinal cord. Fortunately, the CNS is highly protected. CNS neurons lack neurilemma, so regrowth of damaged neurons is impossible. A serious injury to the brain or spinal cord is usually permanent. However, there is growing evidence that damage can sometimes be repaired with grafts of healthy brain cells. In one experiment, for example, the brains of rats were damaged in an area that affects learning. Some of the rats then received implants of healthy brain tissue in the damaged region. Others remained untreated. Next, a maze-learning test was conducted, with encouraging results: Rats that received transplants did significantly better than those left untreated (Labbe et al., 1983).

Obviously, it's a little early to think about seeking a brain graft to get you through final exams. Transplants are highly experimental at present, and it is not known if foreign tissue can be transplanted in humans, as it has been in animals. Just the same, brain grafting has profound implications. By doing transplants, it may become possible to repair some brain and spinal injuries that are now irreversible. Imagine what that could mean to a person confined to a wheelchair or someone suffering the aftereffects of a stroke.

Question: How are the CNS and the peripheral nervous system related?

The Peripheral Nervous System The peripheral system consists of nerves that carry information to and from the CNS. The peripheral system is divided

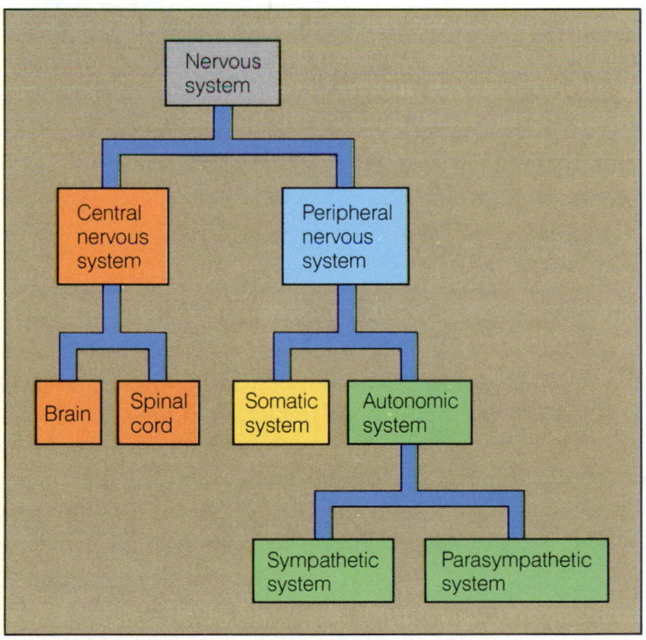

Fig. 3-4 *Subparts of the nervous system.*

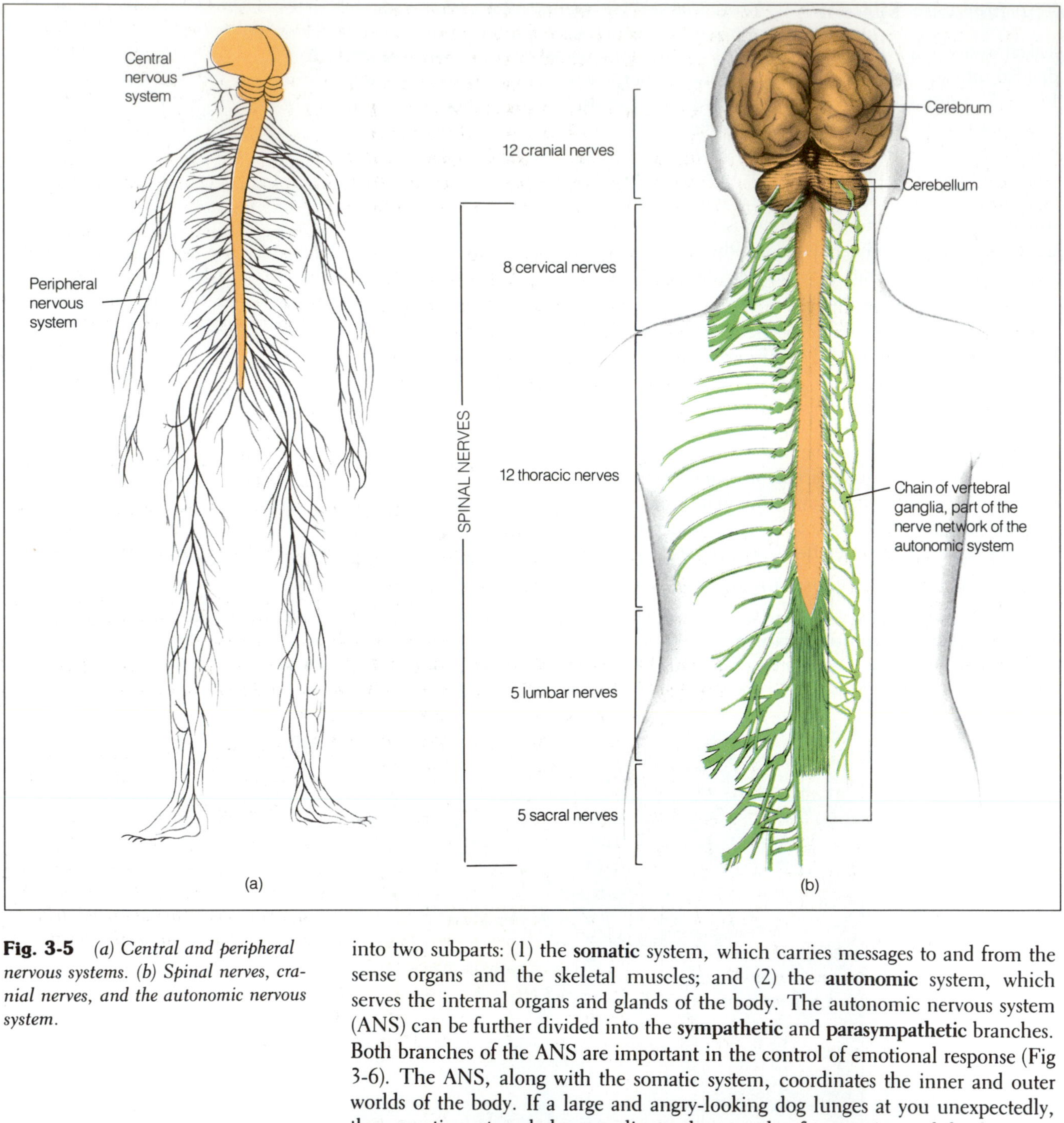

Fig. 3-5 *(a) Central and peripheral nervous systems. (b) Spinal nerves, cranial nerves, and the autonomic nervous system.*

into two subparts: (1) the **somatic** system, which carries messages to and from the sense organs and the skeletal muscles; and (2) the **autonomic** system, which serves the internal organs and glands of the body. The autonomic nervous system (ANS) can be further divided into the **sympathetic** and **parasympathetic** branches. Both branches of the ANS are important in the control of emotional response (Fig 3-6). The ANS, along with the somatic system, coordinates the inner and outer worlds of the body. If a large and angry-looking dog lunges at you unexpectedly, the somatic system helps coordinate the muscles for running, while the autonomic system arranges a rise in blood pressure, quickening of the heart, and so forth.

Question: How do the branches of the autonomic system differ?

The sympathetic branch responds during times of emergency or emotion to perpare the body for "fight or flight." In essence, it mobilizes the body's resources for action. The parasympathetic branch, on the other hand, is most active immediately *after* a stressful or emotional event. Its role is to quiet the body and return it to a lower level of arousal. It also helps maintain vital functions such as heart rate, breathing, and digestion at moderate levels. Of course, both branches of the ANS are active at all times. It is the balance of their activity that determines if the body is aroused or quieted. (See Chapter 12 for more information on the autonomic system.)

The Spinal Cord The spinal cord is an especially important part of the nervous system because it acts like a cable connecting the brain to other parts of the body. If you were to cut through the spinal cord, you would see columns of **white matter**—nerve tissue made up of the axons of neurons that leave the spinal cord at various points to form peripheral nerves. As you can see in Fig. 3-5*b* there are 30 pairs of **spinal nerves** leaving the spinal cord and 1 pair leaving the bottom tip. The 31 pairs, together with an additional 12 nerves that leave the brain directly (the **cranial nerves**), place the entire body in sensory and motor communication with the brain.

Question: How is the spinal cord related to behavior?

Within the spinal cord itself, the simplest behavior pattern (a **reflex arc**) can be carried out without any direct participation from the brain (see Fig. 3-7). Imagine that one of our Frisbee players steps on a thorn. This is detected in the foot by a **sensory neuron**, and a message (in the form of an action potential) is fired off to the spinal cord.

The sensory neuron synapses with a **connector neuron** (or **interneuron**) inside the spinal cord. The connector neuron in turn activates another connector cell

Somatic system The system of nerves that carries information from the body to the spinal cord and commands from the spinal cord to the muscles.

Autonomic system The system of nerves that carries information to and from the internal organs and glands of the body.

Sympathetic system A branch of the autonomic system responsible for activating the body at times of stress.

Parasympathetic system A branch of the autonomic system responsible for quieting the body and conserving energy.

White matter Portions of the nervous system that appear white due to the presence of myelin.

Spinal nerve One of 62 major nerves that channel sensory and motor information in and out of the spinal cord.

Cranial nerve One of 12 major nerves that leave the brain without passing through the spinal cord.

Reflex arc The pathway of nervous activity leading from a stimulus to an automatic or involuntary response, such as an eyeblink or kneejerk.

Sensory neuron A nerve cell that carries information from the senses toward the central nervous system.

Connector neuron A nerve cell that serves as a link between two others.

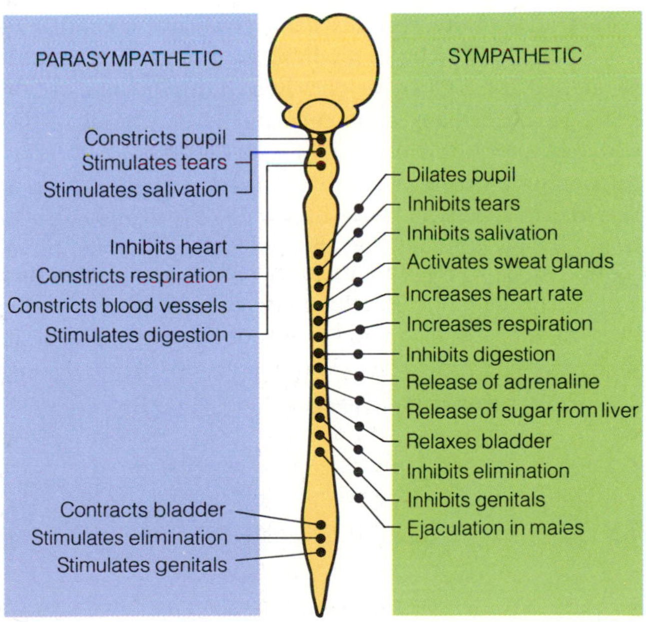

Fig. 3-6 *Sympathetic and parasympathetic branches of the autonomic nervous system. Both branches control involuntary functions. The sympathetic system generally activates the body, whereas the parasympathetic system generally quiets it. The sympathetic branch relays through a chain of ganglia (clusters of cell bodies) outside the spinal cord.*

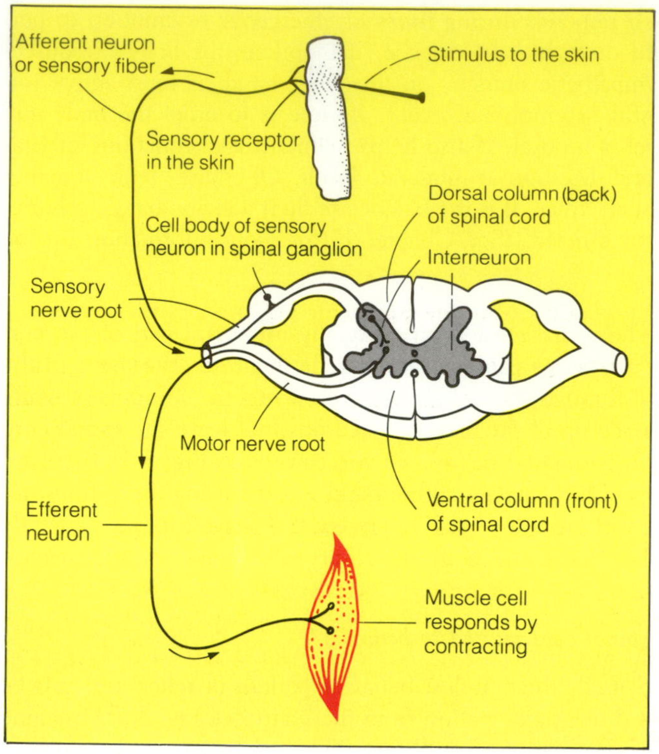

Fig. 3-7 *A simple sensory-motor (reflex) arc. A simple reflex is set in motion by a stimulus to the skin (or other part of the body). The nerve impulse travels to the spinal cord and then back out to a muscle, which contracts. Reflexes provide an "automatic" protective device for the body.*

Motor neuron A nerve cell that carries motor commands from the central nervous system to muscles and glands.

Effector cells Cells in muscles and glands specialized for the production of responses.

(in this case a **motor neuron**) that leads back to muscle fibers. The muscle fibers are made up of **effector cells,** which contract and cause the foot to withdraw. Note that brain activity was not required for a reflex arc. The body can react to protect itself without any help from the brain.

In reality, more complex activity usually accompanies even a simple reflex. For example, muscles of the limb on the opposite side of the body must contract to support the shift in weight. Even this can be carried out by the spinal cord, but it involves many more cells and several levels of the spinal nerves. Perhaps you have already realized how adaptive it is to have a spinal cord capable of responding on its own. Such automatic responses leave the brain of our Frisbee ace free to deal with more important information—such as the whereabouts of trees, lampposts, and attractive onlookers—as he or she makes a grandstand catch.

Learning Check

Before reading further, see if you can answer these questions.

1. The ____________ and ____________ are receiving areas where information from other neurons is accepted.

2. Nerve impulses are carried down the ____________.

3. The point of interchange between two neurons is called a myelin. T or F?

4. The ______________ potential becomes an ______________ potential when a neuron passes the threshold for firing.

5. Neuropeptides are a newly discovered class of transmitter substances that seem to regulate the activity of neurons. T or F?

6. The somatic and autonomic systems are part of the ______________ nervous system.

7. Sodium and potassium ions cross the synapse to trigger a nerve impulse in the receiving neuron. T or F?

8. The simplest behavior sequence is a ______________.

9. The parasympathetic nervous system is most active during times of high emotion. T or F?

Answers: **1.** dendrites, soma **2.** axon **3.** F **4.** resting, action **5.** T **6.** peripheral **7.** F **8.** reflex arc **9.** F

The Cerebral Cortex— My, What a Big Brain You Have!

In many respects humans are pretty unimpressive creatures. Fragile, weak, born naked and helpless, humans are excelled by other animals in almost every category of strength, speed, and sensory sensitivity. The one area in which humans excel is intelligence.

Question: Do humans have the largest brain?

Surprisingly, no. Elephant brains weigh 13 pounds and whale brains, 19 pounds. At 3 pounds the human brain seems puny—until we figure the proportion of brain weight to body weight. We then find that an elephant's brain is 1/1,000 of its weight; the ratio for sperm whales is 1 to 10,000. The ratio for humans is 1 to 60 (Cohen, 1974). If someone says you have a "whale of a brain," be sure to find out if they mean size or ratio!

So, relatively speaking, humans have very highly developed brains. More importantly, as we move from lower to higher animals, there is an ever-increasing proportion of brain tissue devoted to the **cerebral cortex** (SER-eh-brel or seh-REE-brel) (see Fig. 3-8). In humans the cerebral cortex accounts for no less than 70 percent of the neurons in the central nervous system.

Corticalization The cortex covers most of the visible portions of the brain with a mantle of **gray matter** (spongy tissue made up mostly of cell bodies), which looks a little like a giant, wrinkled walnut. The cortex in lower animals is small and smooth; in humans it is the largest brain structure. Human intellectual superiority appears to be related to this **corticalization** (KORE-tih-kal-ih-ZAY-shun), or increase in the size and wrinkling of the cortex.

Cerebral Hemispheres The cortex is composed of two sides, or **hemispheres.** At first glance the hemispheres appear to be mirror images of each other, but they actually differ slightly in shape and wrinkling (Corballis, 1980). The two hemispheres are connected by a thick band of fibers called the **corpus callosum** (KORE-pus kah-LOH-sum). Surprisingly, the two halves control opposite sides of

Cerebral cortex The convoluted mantle of tissue that makes up most of the visible portion of the brain.

Gray matter Areas in the nervous system that have a grayish color due to a high concentration of nerve cell bodies.

Corticalization An increase in the relative size of the cerebral cortex observed as one ascends the biological scale from lower animals to humans.

Cerebral hemispheres The right and left halves of the cerebral cortex.

Corpus callosum The large bundle of fibers connecting the right and left cerebral hemispheres.

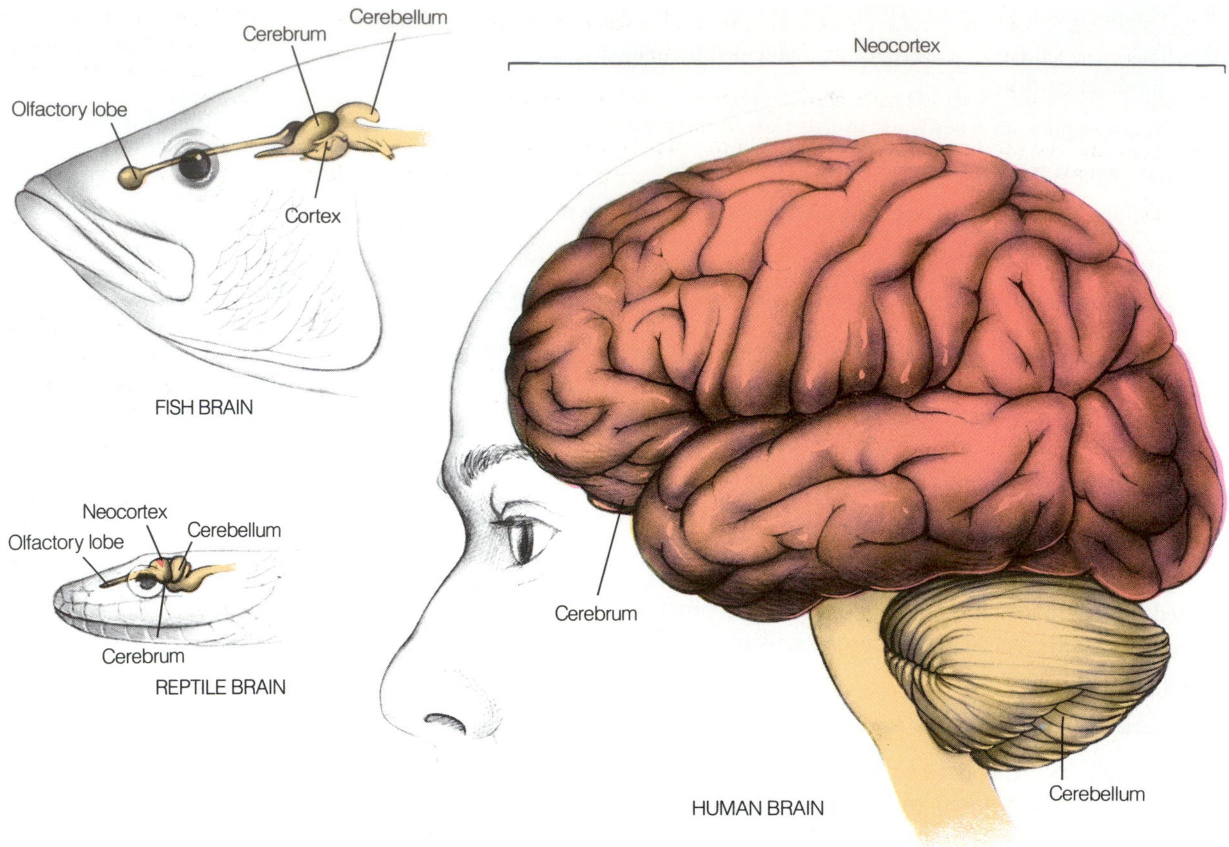

Fig. 3-8 *An illustration showing the increased relative size of the human cerebral cortex, a significant factor in human adaptability and intelligence. Wrinkling of the cerebrum also allows more cortical surface area within the confines of the human skull.*

the body. The left side of the brain mainly controls the right side of the body, and the right half of the brain mainly controls left body areas. Thus, if a person has an injury or a stroke that damages the right hemisphere, we can expect parts of the left side of the body to be paralyzed or to lose sensation.

Hemispheric Specialization

We turn now to some very remarkable findings. In 1981, Roger Sperry of the California Institute of Technology won a Nobel Prize for his work on the special abilities of the cerebral hemispheres. Sperry and other psychologists have shown that the right and left sides of the brain perform differently on tests of language, perception, music, and other capabilities.

Question: How is it possible to test only one side of the brain?

One way is to work with people who have had a type of surgery for epilepsy that literally *disconnects* the brain hemispheres. The result of these "**split-brain**" operations is essentially a person with two brains in one body (Sperry, 1968). After the surgery it is a simple matter to route information to one hemisphere or the other (see Fig. 3-9).

"Split Brains" In both animals and humans, dividing the hemispheres consistently results in a doubling of consciousness. As Sperry (1968) says:

In other words, each hemisphere seems to have its own separate and private sensations; its own perceptions; its own concepts; and its own impulses to act.

Split-brain operation A surgical technique in which the corpus callosum is cut, functionally disconnecting the two cerebral hemispheres.

Question: How does a split-brain person function after the operation?

On occasion, having two "brains" in one body creates quite a dilemma. Another researcher, Michael Gazzaniga, recounts that one of his split-brain patients would:

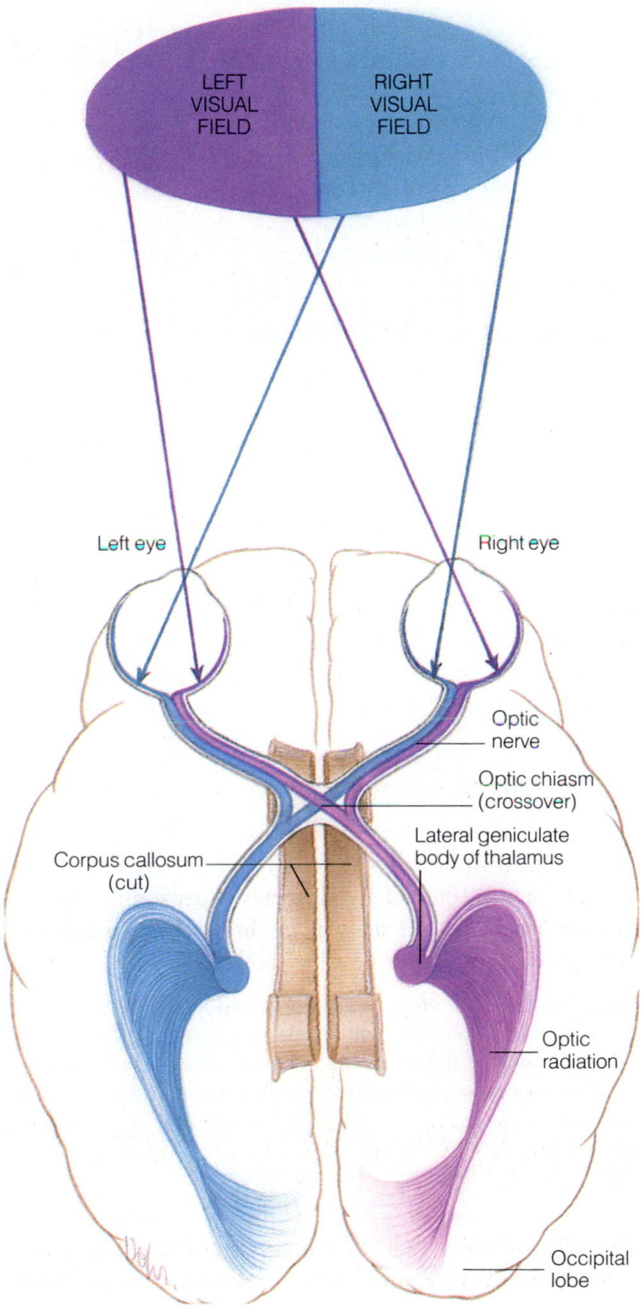

Fig. 3-9 *Basic nerve pathways of vision. Notice that The left portion of each eye connects only to the left half of the brain; likewise, the right portion of each eye connects to the right brain. When the corpus callosum is cut, a "split brain" results. Then visual information can be directed to one hemisphere or the other by flashing it in the right or left visual field as the person stares straight ahead.*

> . . . sometimes find himself pulling his pants down with one hand and pulling them up with the other. Once, he grabbed his wife with his left hand and shook her violently, while with the right trying to come to his wife's aid in bringing the belligerent left hand under control. (Gazzaniga, 1970, p. 107)

It is far more typical, however, for split-brain individuals to act normally in most situations. The reason is that both halves of the brain experience approximately the same thing at the same time. Also, if any conflict arises, one hemisphere tends to override the other. (To find out which of your brain hemispheres is dominant, see the Applications section of this chapter.)

Split-brain effects become most apparent in specialized testing. For example, a dollar sign can be flashed to the right brain and a question mark to the left brain. (Figures 3-9 and 3-10 show how this is possible.) If the person is asked to draw (out of sight) with the left hand what he or she saw, the dollar sign will be drawn. If then asked to point with the right hand to a picture of what the left hand drew, the subject will point to a question mark (Sperry, 1968). In short, for the split-brain person, one hemisphere does not know what is happening in the other. This has to be the ultimate case of the right hand not knowing what the left hand is doing!

Question: Earlier it was stated that the hemispheres differ in abilities. In what ways do they differ?

Right Brain/Left Brain The brain divides up its work in interesting ways. For example, language is a specialty of the left hemisphere. Roughly 95 percent of all adults use the left side of the brain for speaking, writing, and comprehending language. In addition, the left hemisphere is superior at math, judging time and rhythm, and at ordering or coordinating complex movements (especially those needed for speech) (Corballis, 1980). In contrast, the right hemisphere responds to only the simplest elements of language and numbers. Working with the right hemisphere is a little like talking to a child who only understands a dozen words or so. To express itself, the right hemisphere must point to objects or make other nonverbal responses (see Fig. 3-10).

At one time the right brain was regarded as the "minor" hemisphere. But we now know that it has talents of its own. The right hemisphere is superior at perceptual skills such as recognizing patterns, faces, and melodies, and it is involved in detecting and expressing emotion (Geschwind, 1979).

The superiority of the right hemisphere at spatial tasks leads to another intriguing split-brain observation. A common test of spatial ability involves solving a geometric puzzle. On this test the split-brain patient's left hand typically can perform quite well, but the right cannot. Robert Ornstein (1972) reports that:

> Professor Sperry often shows an interesting film clip of the right hand attempting to solve the problem and failing, whereupon the patient's left hand cannot restrain itself and "corrects" the right—as when you know the answer to a problem and watch me making mistakes, and cannot refrain from telling me the answer.

Question: Do people normally solve puzzles with just their right hemisphere? Do they do other things with just the left?

If you were to solve a puzzle like the one mentioned, your spatially oriented right hemisphere would indeed be more active than the left. But at the same time, your left hemisphere would be more active than it was before you started the

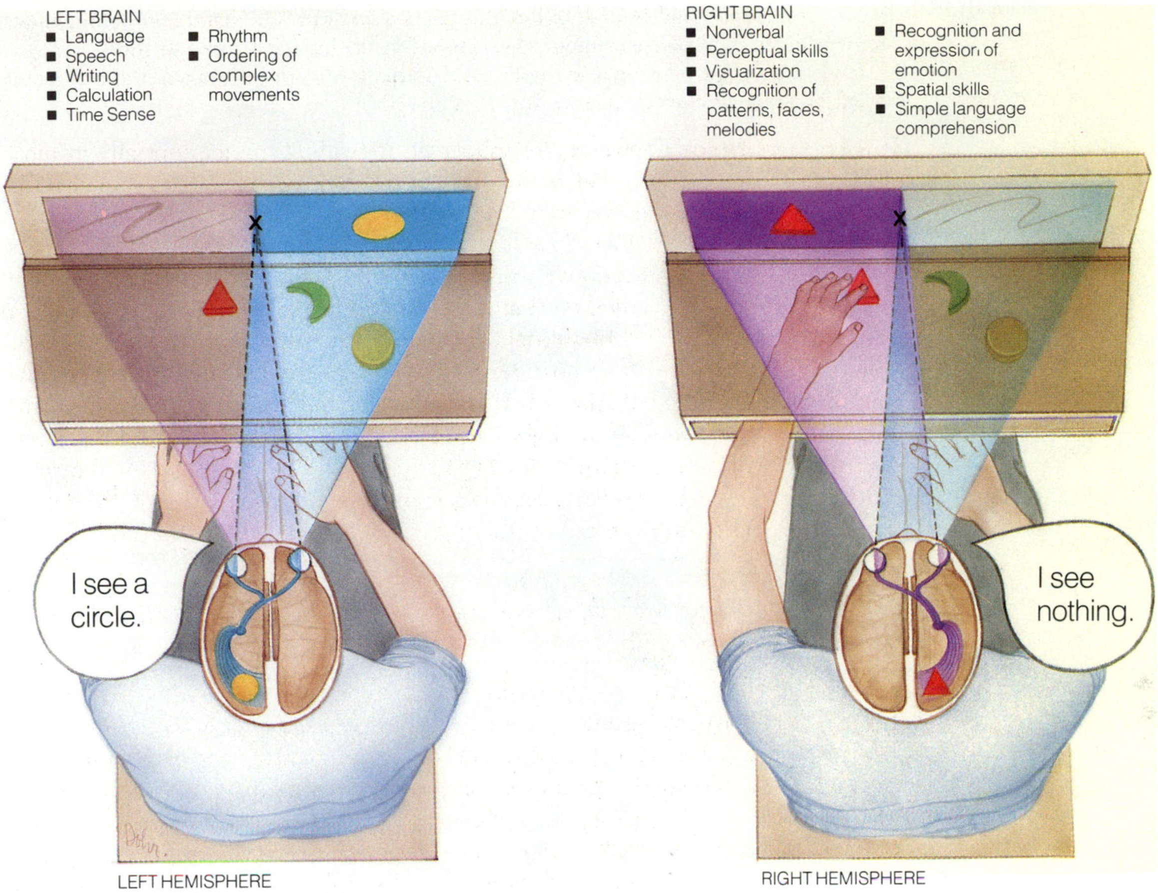

Fig. 3-10 *If a circle is flashed to the left brain and the person is asked to say what he or she saw, the circle is easily named. The person can also pick out the circle by touching shapes with the right hand, out of sight under a tabletop (shown semitransparent in drawing). However, the left hand will be unable to identify the shape. If a triangle is flashed to the right brain, the person cannot say what was seen (speech is controlled by the left hemisphere). The person will also be unable to identify the correct shape by touch with the right hand. Now, however, the left hand will have no difficulty picking out the hidden triangle. Separate testing of each hemisphere reveals distinct specializations, as listed above. (Figure adapted from an illustration by Edward Kasper in McKean, 1985)*

puzzle. Thus, while activity may focus on one hemisphere, the skills of both sides of the brain are *combined* in most activities. Perhaps this is why lawyers, artists, and psychologists showed no differences in a test of right and left hemisphere activity (Arndt & Berger, 1978; Ornstein & Galin, 1976). Such findings also suggest that books purporting to teach you to use the "right brain" to be more creative, and the like, ignore the fact that the entire brain is used at all times.

Lobes of cerebral cortex Areas on the cortex bordered by major fissures or associated with particular functions.

Cerebral Maps of Reality

In addition to the hemispheres, the cerebral cortex can be divided into several smaller areas, or **lobes** (see Fig. 3-11).

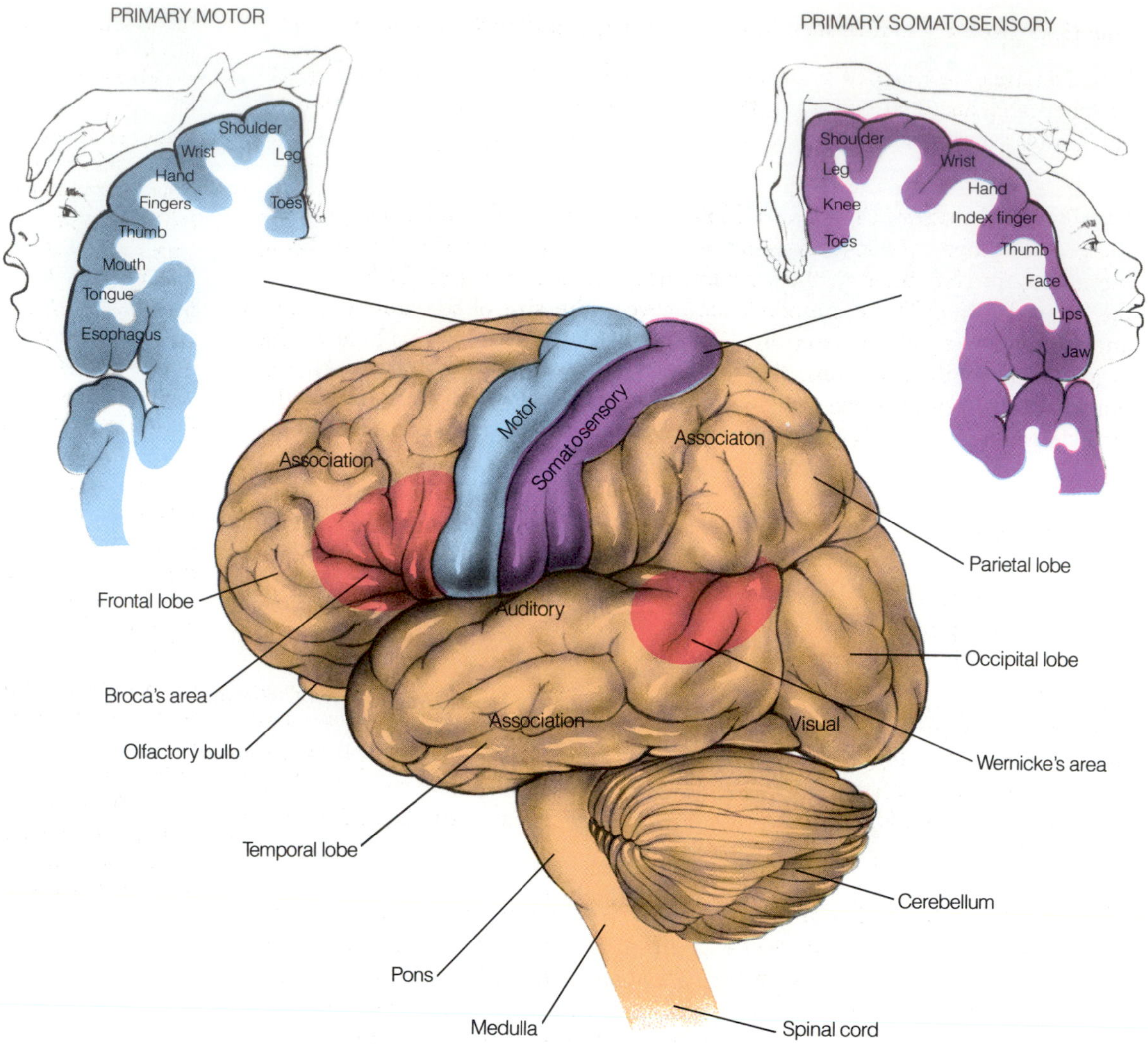

Fig. 3-11 *The drawing shows the lobes of the cerebral cortex and the primary sensory, motor, and association areas on each. The top diagrams show (in cross section) the relative amounts of cortex "assigned" to the sensory and motor control of various parts of the body. (The left cross section, or "slice," is viewed from the back of the brain, the right slice is shown from the front.)*

Question: What is known about the function of the lobes?

The functions of various areas in each of the lobes have been "mapped" by clinical and experimental studies. Experimentally, the surface of the cortex can be activated by touching it with a small electrified needle or wire called an **electrode.** When this is done to a patient undergoing brain surgery—using only local painkillers—the patient can report what effect the stimulation had. The functions of the cortex have also been identified by clinical studies of changes in personality, behavior, or the senses caused by brain diseases or injuries. Let us consider the outcome of such studies.

The Occipital Lobes The occipital lobes (ok-SIP-ih-tal), which are located at the back of the brain, are the primary **visual area** of the cortex. Patients with *tumors* (cell growths that interfere with brain activity) in the occipital lobes experience blind spots in areas of the visual field.

Question: Do the visual areas of the cortex correspond directly to what is seen?

Visual images are mapped onto the surface of the cortex, but the map is greatly stretched and distorted (Carlson, 1981). In other words, visual information creates complex patterns of activity in nerve cells; it does *not* make a TV-like image.

The Parietal Lobes The parietal lobes (puh-RYE-ih-tal) are located just above the occipital lobes. Touch, temperature, pressure, and other somatic, or bodily, sensations are channeled to the **somatosensory areas** (SO-mat-oh-SEN-so-ree) on the parietal lobes. The correspondence between the size of somatosensory areas and body parts is not a perfect one. The distorted body in Fig. 3-11 shows that, as a map of bodily sensations, the cortex represents the *sensitivity* of body areas, not their size. For example, the lips are large in the illustration because of their great sensitivity, while the back and trunk, which are less sensitive, are much smaller.

The Temporal Lobes The temporal lobes are located on each side of the brain and extend below to the underside of the cortex. Auditory information is carried directly to the temporal lobes, making them the site where hearing registers. If we were to stimulate the **primary auditory area** of a temporal lobe, our subject would "hear" a series of sound sensations (Carlson, 1981).

An area called the **hippocampus,** located within the temporal lobes, appears to be important for the storage of long-term memories. Stimulation of the temporal lobe in humans produces memory-like or dream-like experiences. (See Chapter 9 for more information on this point.) Tumors in the temporal lobes can cause seizures, disordered use of language, memory disturbances, and unusual dream states.

The Frontal Lobes The frontal lobes perform a mixture of functions. For one thing, **olfactory** (smell) information registers on the underside of the frontal lobes. Another important area is the **motor cortex,** an arch of tissue running roughly ear-to-ear over the top of the brain. This area directs the body's muscles. If the motor cortex is stimulated with a brief electrical current, muscular twitches will be observed in various parts of the body. Like the somatosensory area, the motor cortex corresponds to the importance of bodily areas, not to their size. The hands, for example, get more area than the feet (see Fig. 3-11).

Also related to the frontal lobes are behavioral functions of a more complex nature. When areas of the frontal lobes other than the motor cortex are removed, animals lose the ability to judge the passage of time, to hold the solution to a problem in mind, or to respond to emotionally unpleasant situations. Damage to the frontal lobes in humans tends to decrease emotionality and ability to perform tasks requiring thinking, reasoning, or planning (Thompson, 1967).

Question: The sensory and motor areas leave a lot of the cortex unaccounted for. What do the remaining areas do?

Associative Areas In the human brain, areas that are specifically sensory or motor in function make up only a small part of the cerebral cortex. All other areas (including parts of all the lobes previously described) have been collectively called the **association cortex.** The association cortex seems to process and com-

Electrode Any device (such as a wire, needle, or metal plate) used to electrically stimulate nerve tissue or to record its activity.

Occipital lobes Portion at the back of the cerebral cortex that includes areas where vision registers in the brain.

Parietal lobes Area at the top of the brain that includes sites where bodily sensations register in the brain.

Somatosensory area The part of the parietal lobes that serves as a receiving area for bodily sensations.

Temporal lobes Areas on each side of the cerebral cortex that include the sites where hearing registers in the brain.

Auditory area Sites on the temporal lobes where auditory information registers.

Frontal lobes Areas at the top front of the cerebral cortex that include sites associated with the control of movement, the processing of smell, and higher mental functions.

Olfactory area Sites on the frontal lobes where information on smell registers.

Motor cortex An area on the top of the brain directly associated with control of voluntary movements.

Association cortex All areas of the cerebral cortex that are not specifically sensory or motor in function.

bine information from the various senses. When stimulated, it yields responses more complex than simple sensations or movements. For example, humans with damage to the associative areas may suffer **aphasias** (ah-FAZE-yahs) or impaired use of language.

One type of aphasia results when there is damage to a "speech center" called **Broca's area** (BRO-cahs), on the left frontal lobe. Persons with damage in Broca's area have great difficulty speaking or writing. Typically, their speech is slow and labored. For example, the person may say "bife" for bike, "seep" for sleep, or "zokaid" for zodiac. Generally the person knows what he or she wants to say, but can't seem to get it into words (Geschwind, 1979).

If damage affects Wernicke's area (VER-nick-ees; see Fig. 3-11), the person has problems with the *meaning* of words, not their pronunciation. Whereas someone with Broca's aphasia might say "tssair" when shown a picture of a chair, a Wernicke's patient might say "stool" (Goodglass, 1980). Similarly, damage to a visual association area would result in an **agnosia** (ah-KNOW-zyah). This condition is sometimes referred to as "mindblindness" because it involves an inability to identify seen objects. If shown a candle, for instance, someone with an agnosia might describe it as a long narrow object tapering at the top, or might draw it accurately, and yet fail to name it. However, if the person is permitted to feel the candle, he or she will name it immediately (Benton, 1980).

In summary, the cerebral cortex is an impressive living assembly of billions of sensitive cells. The bulk of our daily experience and understanding of the world can be traced directly to the sensory, motor, and association areas of the cortex. The human brain is among the most advanced and sophisticated of the brain-bearing species on earth. This, of course, is no guarantee that this marvelous "biocomputer" will be put to full use. Still, we must stand in awe of the potential it represents.

Learning Check

See if you can match the following.

_____ **1.** Corpus callosum
_____ **2.** Occipital lobes
_____ **3.** Parietal lobes
_____ **4.** Temporal lobes
_____ **5.** Frontal lobes
_____ **6.** Association cortex
_____ **7.** Aphasia
_____ **8.** Corticalization
_____ **9.** Left hemisphere
_____ **10.** Right hemisphere
_____ **11.** "Split brain"
_____ **12.** Agnosia

A. Visual area
B. Language, speech, writing
C. Motor cortex and abstract thinking
D. Spatial skills, visualization, pattern recognition
E. Language disturbance
F. Causes sleep
G. Increased ratio of cortex in brain
H. Bodily sensations
I. Treatment for severe epilepsy
J. Inability to identify seen objects
K. Fibers connecting the cerebral hemispheres
L. Cortex that is not sensory or motor in function
M. Hearing

Answers: **1.** K **2.** A **3.** H **4.** M **5.** C **6.** L **7.** E **8.** G **9.** B **10.** D **11.** I **12.** J

The Subcortex—At the Core of the (Brain) Matter

Question: What do brain areas below the cortex do?

A person can lose large portions of the cerebrum and still survive. As a matter of fact, if damage is limited to the less crucial areas of the cortex, little visible change may take place. Not so with the brain areas below the cortex. Most of these are so basic to normal functioning that damage may endanger a person's life.

Question: Why are the lower brain areas so important?

Below the cerebral cortex and completely covered by it are structures that are collectively termed the **subcortex.** The subcortex can be divided into three general areas, called the **brainstem** or **hindbrain,** the **midbrain,** and the **forebrain.** (The forebrain also includes the cerebral cortex, which was discussed earlier because of its size and importance.) For the purpose of this discussion, the midbrain can be viewed primarily as a link between the brain structures above and below it. Therefore, let us focus on the hindbrain and the forebrain to more fully appreciate their importance (see Fig. 3-12).

The Hindbrain

As the spinal cord enters the skull to join the brain, it widens into the brainstem, consisting principally of the **medulla** (meh-DUL-ah) and the **cerebellum** (ser-ah-BEL-um). The *medulla* contains centers important for the reflex control of vital life functions, including heart rate, breathing, swallowing, and the like. For example, the medulla receives information about the carbon dioxide content of the blood and the tension of the muscles that expand the chest for breathing. Combining this information, the medulla *excites* the muscles so that you will inhale, then *inhibits* this excitement to cause exhalation. You can, of course, override this reflex by voluntarily holding your breath; but if you hold your breath long enough to pass out, the higher brain centers relinquish control, and once again you will begin reflex breathing. Various drugs, diseases, or injuries can interrupt the vital functions of the medulla enough to end or endanger life. That's why a karate chop to the back of the neck, like those depicted in movies, can be extremely dangerous.

The *cerebellum,* which looks like a miniature cerebral cortex, lies at the base of the brain. The cerebellum is closely connected to many areas in the brain and spinal cord and functions primarily to regulate posture, muscle tone, and muscular coordination.

Question: What happens if the cerebellum is injured?

Without an intact cerebellum, seemingly simple tasks like walking, running, or playing catch are impossible. The importance of the cerebellum is indicated by the effects of a crippling disease called *spinocerebellar degeneration.* The first symptoms of this disease include tremor, dizziness, and muscular weakness. Soon, affected persons find that they underreach or overreach for objects and have difficulty standing, walking, or even feeding themselves.

Aphasia A speech disturbance resulting from damage to language areas on the temporal lobes of the brain.

Agnosia A disturbance in the ability to perceive the meaning of stimuli, such as words, objects, or pictures.

Subcortex All brain structures below the cerebral cortex.

Brainstem The lowest portions of the brain, including the cerebellum, medulla, and reticular formation.

Midbrain The area of the brain consisting of structures linking the forebrain and the brainstem.

Forebrain The highest brain areas, including the hypothalamus, thalamus, corpus callosum, and cerebrum.

Medulla The enlarged stalk at the base of the brain that connects to the spinal cord and controls vital life functions.

Cerebellum A cauliflower-shaped projection at the base of the brain associated with the control of posture and coordination.

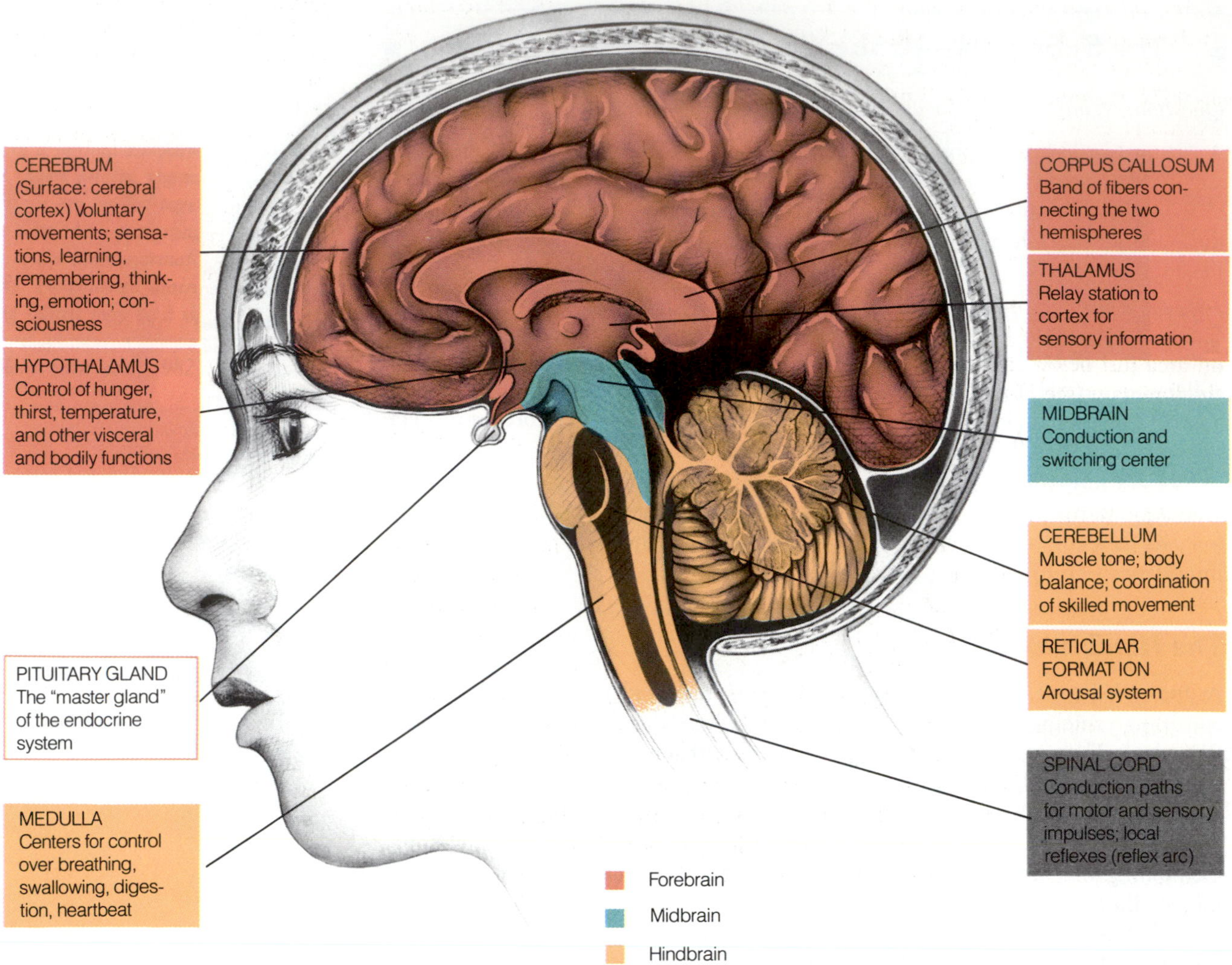

Fig. 3-12 *This simplified drawing shows the main structures of the human brain and describes some of their most important functions.*

Reticular Formation In a space within the medulla and brainstem is a *network* of fibers and cell bodies called the **reticular** (reh-TICK-yuh-ler) **formation** (RF).

Question: What does the reticular formation do?

The RF is important for several reasons. First, it acts as a kind of central clearinghouse for most of the information coming to and from the brain. Second, the reticular formation gives priority to some incoming messages, while excluding others. This is basically what we mean by *attention*. Without the RF, we would be overwhelmed with useless information from the environment. Third, and perhaps most important, the reticular formation is responsible for alertness and wakefulness.

Incoming impulses from the sense organs branch into the reticular formation, where they form a **reticular activating system** (RAS). The RAS bombards the cortex with stimulation, keeping it active and vigilant (Malmo, 1975). Researchers have found that destroying the RAS causes animals to enter a permanent coma resembling sleep. In contrast, electrical stimulation of the same area instantly awakens sleeping animals (Lindsley, Bowden, & Magoun, 1949; Moruzzi & Magoun, 1949). The sleepy driver who snaps to attention when an animal appears in the middle of the road can thank the RAS for arousing the rest of the brain.

Reticular formation A network of fibers within the medulla associated with attention, alertness, and activation of higher brain areas.

Thalamus A structure at the center of the brain that relays sensory information to the cerebral cortex.

Hypothalamus A small area below the thalamus that regulates a large variety of emotional behaviors and motives.

Limbic system A system of interconnected structures in the forebrain that are closely associated with emotional response.

The Forebrain

Like gemstones of nerve tissue, two of the most important parts of the body lie buried deep within the center of the brain. The **thalamus** (THAL-ah-mus) and an area just below it called the **hypothalamus** (HI-po-THAL-ah-mus) are part of the forebrain (see Fig. 3-12).

Question: How could these be any more important than other areas already described?

The thalamus is a football-shaped structure that acts as a final "switching station" for sensory information on its way to the cortex. Not only does information from vision, hearing, taste, and touch relay through the thalamus, it undergoes preliminary processing and analysis there as well. Injury to even small areas of the thalamus can cause deafness, blindness, or loss of any other sense, except smell.

The hypothalamus in the human is about the size of a thumbnail. Yet small as it may be, the hypothalamus is related to the control of behaviors as diverse as sex, rage, temperature control, hormone release, eating and drinking, sleep, waking, and emotion. The hypothalamus is a sort of crossroads that connects with many other areas of the cortex and subcortex. As such, it acts as a final path for many kinds of behavior leaving the brain. You might think of the hypothalamus as the last area in the brain where many behaviors are organized or "decided on." (See Chapter 11 for a discussion of the role of the hypothalamus in hunger and thirst.)

The Limbic System The hypothalamus, parts of the thalamus, and several structures buried within the cortex have been collectively labeled the **limbic system** (Fig. 3-13). Although the specific function of some parts of the limbic system is unclear, as a group these parts share an unmistakable role in the production of *emotion* and motivated behavior. Rage, fear, sexual response, and other instances of intense arousal have all been obtained from various points in the limbic system. For example, cats made aggressive by electrical stimulation of the limbic system will crouch, hiss, expose their claws, lean forward, and tense their muscles—all characteristics of defense or attack.

One of the most exciting discoveries in psychology was the finding that animals will learn to press a lever in order to deliver electrical stimulation to the limbic system as a reward (Olds & Milner, 1954). Since the original discovery, many additional areas of the limbic system have been shown to act as reward or "pleasure" pathways in the brain. Many are found in the hypothalamus, where they overlap with areas associated with drives such as thirst, sex, and hunger (Olds, 1977) (see Chapter 7). In addition, punishment, or "aversive," areas have also been found. When these areas are stimulated, animals show discomfort and will

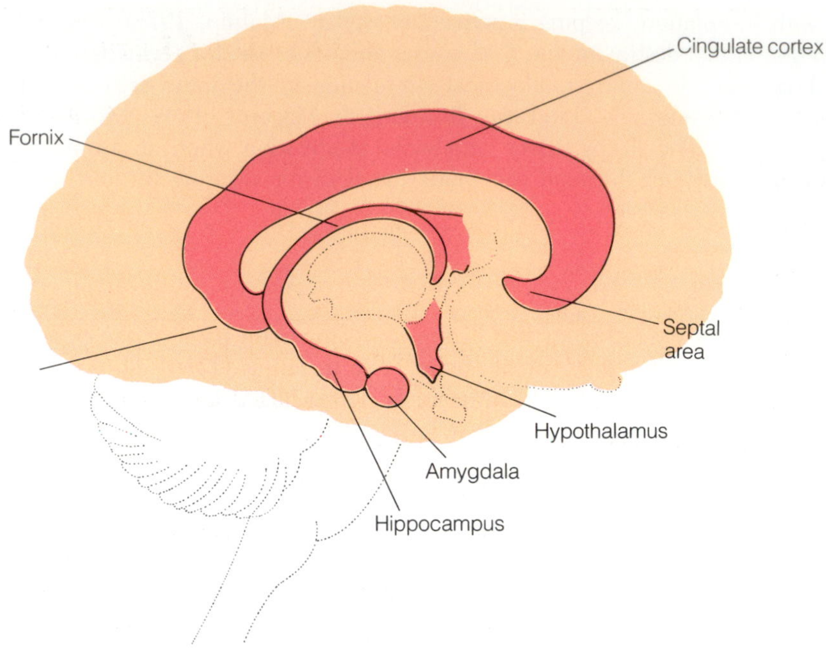

Fig. 3-13 *Parts of the limbic system are shown in this highly simplified drawing. Although it is not apparent in the drawing, the hippocampus and the amygdala extend out into the temporal lobes at each side of the brain. The limbic system is a sort of "primitive core" of the brain strongly associated with emotion.*

work to turn off the stimulation. Since a great deal of human and animal behavior is directed by the pursuit of pleasure and the avoidance of pain, these discoveries continue to fascinate psychologists.

An Overview of the Brain

Given the amount of information covered in our journey through the brain, a short review is in order. We have seen that the brain controls vital bodily functions, keeps track of the external world, issues commands to the muscles and glands, generates complex responses in the light of current needs and past experience, creates the magic of consciousness, and regulates its own behavior—*all* at the same time. Each of these basic needs is met by the action of one or more of the three main brain divisions: Control of vital bodily functions is carried out by the hindbrain (with some assistance from the hypothalamus in the forebrain); gathering sensory information and issuing motor commands takes place at all three levels of the brain; response selection, learning, memory, and higher thought processes are controlled by the forebrain, particularly the cortex and association areas.

A final note of caution is now in order. For the sake of simplicity we have assigned functions to each "part" of the brain as if it were a computer. This is only a half-truth. In reality, the brain always functions as a unit. Incoming information scatters all over the brain and converges again as it goes out to muscles and glands. The overall system acts in ways that go far beyond any view that considers only "parts," or "brain centers" (Nauta & Fiertag, 1979). To say the least, the brain is much, much more complicated than implied here.

Learning Check

Test your comprehension with these questions. If you miss any, skim back over the preceding section.

1. Three major divisions of the brain are the brainstem, or ______________________, the ______________________, and the ______________________.

2. Reflex centers for heartbeat and respiration are found in the (circle one):

cerebellum thalamus medulla RF

3. Portions of the reticular formation serve as an ______________________ system for the cerebral cortex.

a. activating *b.* emotion *c.* adjustment *d.* inhibitory

4. The ______________________ is the final "switching station" for sensory information on its way to the cortex.

5. Damage to the cerebellum would cause a loss of

a. attention *b.* emotion *c.* vision *d.* coordination

6. The limbic system is closely connected to emotion and motivated behavior. T or F?

Answers **1.** hindbrain, midbrain, forebrain **2.** medulla **3.** *a* **4.** thalamus **5.** *d* **6.** T

The Endocrine System—Slow but Sure Messenger Service

The nervous system is not the only communication network in the body. The **endocrine system** (EN-duh-krin) is made up of a number of glands that release chemicals directly into the bloodstream (see Fig. 3-14). These chemicals, called **hormones,** are transported throughout the body, where they affect bodily functioning and behavior.

Endocrine system The bodily system made up of those glands whose secretions pass directly into the bloodstream or lymph system.

Hormone A bodily chemical carried by body fluids that has an effect on bodily functions and behavior.

Pituitary gland The "master gland" at the base of the brain whose hormones influence the output of other endocrine glands.

Question: How do hormones affect behavior?

Although we are seldom aware of them, hormones affect us in a multitude of ways. Here is a brief sample: Hormone output from the adrenal glands rises during stressful situations; androgens ("male" hormones) are related to the sex drive in both males and females; hormones secreted during times of high emotion intensify memory formation; at least some of the emotional turmoil of adolescence is due to elevated hormone levels; different hormones predominate when a person is angry than when he or she is fearful (Hoyenga & Hoyenga, 1984). Since this is just a sample, let's consider some additional effects hormones have on the body and behavior.

The **pituitary** is a small grape-sized structure hanging from the base of the brain (return to Fig. 3-12). One of the pituitary's more important roles is regulation of growth. During childhood, the pituitary secretes a hormone that speeds bodily development. If too little **growth hormone** is released, a person may remain far smaller than average. If this condition is not treated, a child may fall 6 to 12 inches behind age-mates in height. As adults some will be **hypopituitary dwarfs** (HI-po-pih-TU-ih-ter-ee). Such individuals are perfectly proportioned but tiny. Too much growth hormone produces **giantism** (see Fig. 3-15). Secretion of too

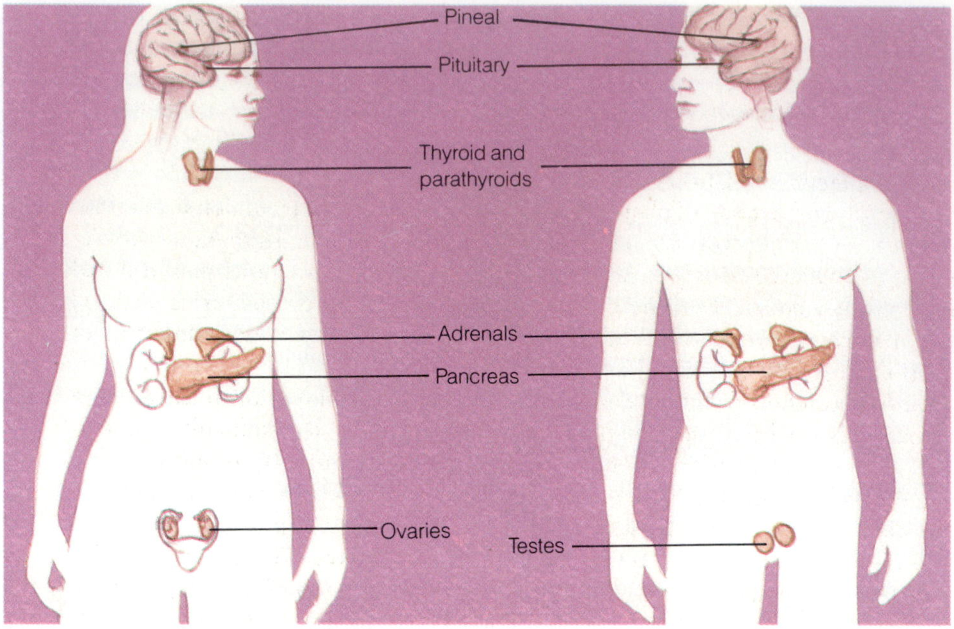

Fig. 3-14 *Locations of the endocrine glands in the male and female.*

Fig. 3-15 *Underactivity of the pituitary gland may produce a dwarf; overactivity, a giant.*

much growth hormone late in the growth period causes the arms, hands, feet, and facial bones to become enlarged. This condition, called **acromegaly** (AK-row-MEG-uh-lee), distorts appearance in a way that some people have turned into successful careers as sideshow entertainers, wrestlers, and the like.

The pituitary also regulates the functioning of other glands (especially the thyroid, adrenal glands, and ovaries or testes). These glands in turn regulate such bodily processes as reproduction, metabolism, and responses to stress. In women the pituitary also controls the production of milk during pregnancy. Because of its many effects, the pituitary is often called the "master gland."

The **thyroid gland** consists of tissue found in the neck on each side of the windpipe. The thyroid regulates **metabolism**—the rate at which energy is produced and expended in the body. As a consequence it can have a sizable effect on personality. A person with an overactive thyroid (termed **hyperthyroidism**) tends to be thin, tense, excitable, and nervous. An underactive thyroid (**hypothyroidism**) in an adult can cause inactivity, sleepiness, slowness, and overweight. In infancy, hypothyroidism limits development of the nervous system and can bring about severe mental retardation (see Chapter 16).

When you are frightened or angry, a number of important changes take place in your body to prepare it for action: Your heartbeat and blood pressure are raised; stored sugar is released into the bloodstream for quick energy; the muscles tense and receive more blood; and the blood is prepared to clot more quickly in the event of injury. These changes are brought about by the hormones **adrenaline** and **noradrenaline,** which are produced by the **adrenal glands.**

The adrenal glands are located just under the back of the rib cage, atop the kidneys. The **adrenal medulla,** or inner core of the adrenal glands, is the source of adrenaline and noradrenaline. The **adrenal cortex,** or outer "bark" of the adrenal glands, produces a second set of important hormones called **corticoids** (KOR-tih-coids). One of their jobs is to regulate salt balance in the body. A deficiency of certain corticoids can evoke a powerful craving for the taste of salt in humans (Beach, 1975). The corticoids also help the body adjust to stress, and they are a secondary source of sex hormones. (For a full discussion of the role of sex glands in development, see Chapter 23.)

Perhaps you have heard about the use of anabolic steroids by athletes who want to "bulk up" or promote muscle growth. These drugs are a synthetic version of one of the male corticoids. Like all of the corticoids, they are quite powerful and therefore dangerous. There is no evidence that they improve performance, and they may cause voice deepening or baldness in women and testicle shrinkage or breast enlargement in men (*Sexual Medicine*, 1980).

An oversecretion of the auxiliary sex hormones can cause **virilism**, in which a woman grows a beard or a man's voice becomes so low it is difficult to understand. Oversecretion in children may cause **premature puberty**, resulting in full sexual development. One of the most remarkable cases on record is that of a 5-year-old Peruvian girl who gave birth to a son (Strange, 1965).

In this brief discussion of the endocrine system, we have considered only a few of the more important glands. Nevertheless, this should give you an appreciation of how your behavior and personality are tied to the ebb and flow of hormones in the body. In the upcoming Applications section, we return to the brain to examine some fascinating links between right- or left-handedness and brain dominance.

Thyroid gland Endocrine gland whose hormones help regulate metabolism (the production and expenditure of energy within the body).

Adrenal glands Endocrine glands whose hormones arouse the body, regulate salt balance, adjust the body to stress, and affect sexual functioning.

Learning Check

Here is a chance to check your memory of the preceding discussion.

1. Giantism, dwarfism, and acromegaly are associated with disorders of the ________________ gland.

2. During adulthood, undersecretion from the thyroid can cause (circle):

dwarfism giantism overweight mental retardation

3. The body's ability to resist stress is related to the action of the adrenal ________________.

4. In infancy an underactive thyroid can cause premature puberty. T or F?

Answers: **1.** pituitary **2.** overweight **3.** cortex **4.** F

Applications

Handedness—If Your Brain Is Right, What's Left?

In the English language, "what's right is right," but what's left may be wrong. We have left-handed compliments, leftovers, people with "two left feet," those who are left behind, left out, and . . . left-handed. On the other hand (so to speak), we have the right way, the right whale, the right angle, the right-hand man (or woman), righteousness, and . . . the right-handed.

The Sinister Hand Left-handedness has a long and undeserved bad reputation. Southpaws have been accused of being clumsy, stubborn (for refusing to use their right hand), and maladjusted. One 1930s psychologist described the left-handed as: "Awkward in the house, and clumsy in their games, they are fumblers and bunglers at whatever they do." But as any lefty will tell you, and modern psychology has confirmed, none of this is true. The supposed clumsiness of lefties is merely a consequence of living in a right-handed world: If it can be gripped, turned, folded, held, or pulled, it's probably designed for the right hand. Even toilet handles are on the right side.

What causes handedness? Why are there more right-handed than left-handed people? How do left-handed and right-handed people differ? Does being left-handed really create problems? Are there any benefits to being left-handed? The answers to most of these questions lead us back to the brain, where handedness begins. Let's see what recent research has revealed about handedness, the brain, and you.

Hand Dominance To begin with, you might find it interesting to compare your hands by copying the accompanying design on a piece of paper, once with your right hand and once with your left. You should notice a definite superiority in the copy done by your dominant hand. The interesting thing about this exercise is that there's no real difference in the strength or dexterity of the hands themselves. The agility of the dominant hand is an outward expression of superior motor control on one side of the brain (Herron, 1980).

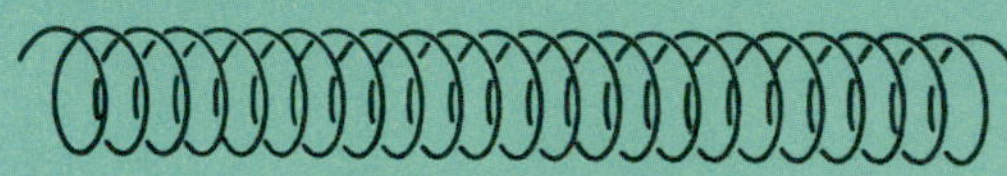

Question: If a person is left-handed, does that mean the right hemisphere is dominant?

Not necessarily. It's true that the right hemisphere controls the left hand, but a left-handed person's language-producing, dominant hemisphere may be on the opposite side of the brain.

Brain Dominance About 97 percent of right-handers process speech in the left hemisphere and are left-brain dominant. A good 60 percent of left-handers produce speech from the left hemisphere, just as right-handed people do. About a quarter of all lefties, and 3 percent of righties, use their right brain for language. And approximately 15 percent of left-handers use *both* sides of the brain for language processing (Corballis, 1980; Herron, 1980).

Question: Is there any way for a person to tell which of his or her hemispheres is dominant?

For a time some psychologists believed that hemispheric dominance could be revealed by eye movements. But recent experiments offer little support for this idea (Erlichman & Weinberger, 1978). A better approach is based on the way you write. Right-handed individuals who write with a straight hand, and lefties who write with a hooked hand, are left-brain dominant for language. Left-handed people who write with their hand below the line, and righties who use a hooked position, are right-brain dominant (Levy & Redd, 1976; Pines, 1980). Are your friends right-brained or left-brained? (See Fig. 3-16.)

Question: How common is left-handedness, and what causes it?

Applications: Handedness, continued

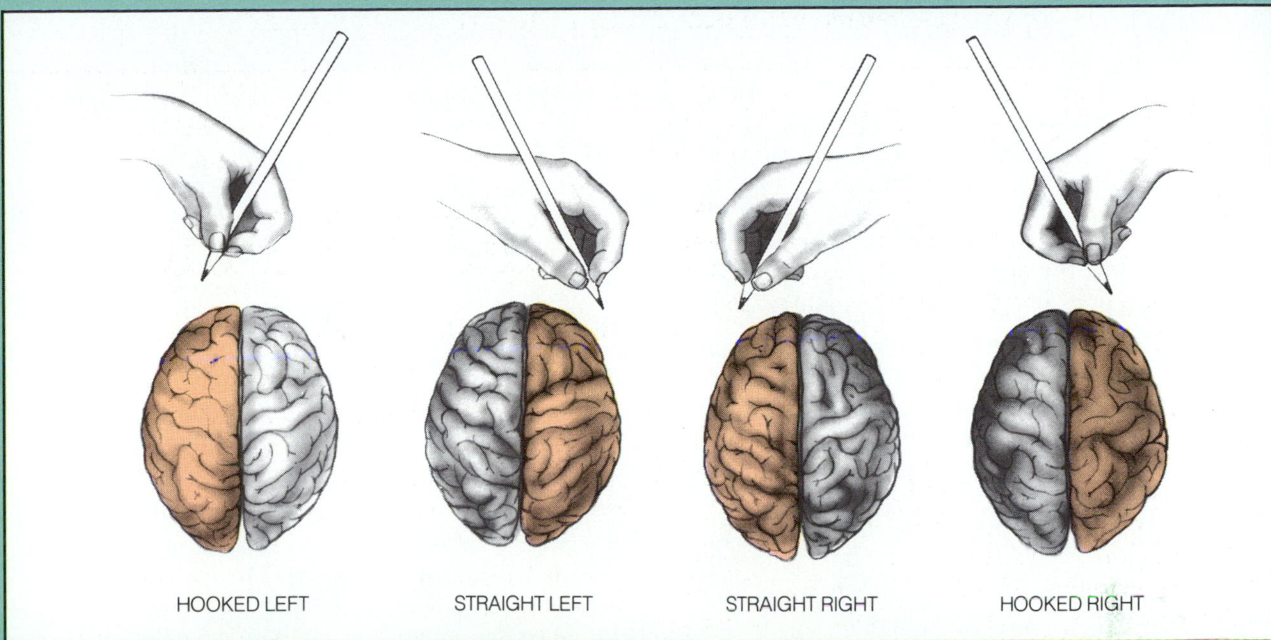

Fig. 3-16 *Recent research suggests that the hand position used in writing indicates which brain hemisphere is used for language. (Redrawn from an illustration by M. E. Challinor)*

Handedness Animals, such as monkeys, show definite hand preferences. However, in most animal groups there is a 50-50 split of right and left "handedness." Among humans the split is about 90-10, with right-handedness being most common. The prevalence of right-handedness in humans probably reflects the left brain's specialization for language production (Corballis, 1980). Evidence exists that the majority of humans have been right-handed for at least 50 centuries (Coren & Porac, 1977).

It was long believed that children don't express clear-cut handedness until they are 4 or 5. But a recent study shows that hand preference for many children is stabilized by 18 months of age or earlier (Gottfried & Bathurst, 1983). Such early preferences underscore the fact that handedness cannot be dictated. Parents should never try to force a left-handed child to use the right hand. To do so may invite speech or reading problems because handedness is hereditary (Herron, 1980).

Question: Are there any drawbacks to being left-handed?

Other than the fact that lefties must live in a right-handed world, there seem to be none. A recent large-scale study of high school students in California found no differences in school achievement between left- and right-handers and no physical or mental defects associated with left-handedness (Hardyck et al., 1976). In fact, there may actually be some advantages to being left-handed.

Advantage Left Throughout history a notable number of artists have been lefties—from Leonardo da Vinci and Michelangelo, to Pablo Picasso and M. C. Escher. Conceivably, since the right hemi-

Applications: Handedness, continued

sphere is superior at imagery and visual abilities, there is some advantage to using the left hand for drawing or painting (Pines, 1980). Whether this is true or not, the left-handed do seem better at putting together verbal and pictorial symbols or ideas—which may be why there are more left-handed architects than would be expected (Herron, 1980).

One striking feature of lefties is that they are generally less **lateralized** than right-handed persons are. This means that there is less distinct specialization in the two sides of their brains. In fact, even the physical size and shape of the cerebral hemispheres are more identical in left-handed persons. If you are a lefty, you can take pride in fact that your brain is less lopsided than the brains of your right-handed friends (Corballis, 1980)! In general, left-handers are more symmetrical on almost everything, including eye dominance, fingerprints—even foot size (Corballis, 1980).

In some situations less lateralization may be a real advantage. For instance, individuals who are moderately left-handed or ambidextrous seem to have better than average pitch memory, which is a basic musical skill (Deutsch, 1978). Correspondingly, more musicians are ambidextrous than would normally be expected. It's not clear, however, if those who are musically gifted were initially less lateralized or if playing music develops both hands, or possibly both sides of the brain (Pines, 1980). The clearest advantage of being left-handed shows up when there is a brain injury. Because of their milder lateralization, left-handed individuals typically experience less language loss after damage to either brain hemisphere, and they recover more easily (Geschwind, 1979). Maybe having "two left feet" isn't so bad after all.

Learning Check

1. About 97 percent of left-handed people process language on the left side of the brain, the same as right-handed people do. T or F?
2. Left-handed individuals who write with their hand below the line are right-brain dominant. T or F?
3. Most animals, like most humans, show a preference for the right limb. T or F?
4. In general, left-handed individuals show less lateralization in the brain and in fact throughout the body. T or F?
5. A recent study of high school students demonstrated that left-handed individuals are superior in school achievement. T or F?

Answers: **1.** F **2.** T **3.** F **4.** T **5.** F

Chapter Summary

- The brain and nervous system are made up of linked nerve cells called *neurons*. Neurons are arranged in long chains and dense networks. They pass information from one to another through *synapses*.
- The basic conducting structures of neurons are *axons*, but *dendrites* (a receiving area), the *soma* (the cell body and also a receiving area), and the *axon terminals* (the branching ends of an axon) are also involved in communication.
- The firing of an *action potential* (nerve impulse) is basically electrical, whereas communication between neurons is molecular. Neurons release chemicals called *neurotransmitters* at the synapse. These cross to *receptor sites* on the receiving cell, causing it to be excited or inhibited. Transmitters called *neuropeptides* appear to regulate activity in the brain.
- Nerves are made of axons and associated tissues. Neurons and nerves in the peripheral nervous system can often *regenerate*; damage in the central nervous system is *permanent*, unless repair is attempted by *implantation* of healthy tissue.
- The nervous system can be divided into the *central nervous system* (the brain and spinal cord) and the *peripheral nervous system*, which includes the *somatic* (bodily) and *autonomic* (involuntary) nervous systems. The autonomic system has two divisions: the *sympathetic* (activating) and the *parasympathetic* (conserving).
- The human brain is marked by advanced *corticalization*, or enlargement of the *cerebral cortex*. The *left cerebral hemisphere* contains speech or language "centers" in most people. It also specializes in writing, calculation, judging time and rhythm, and ordering complex movements. The *right hemisphere* is largely nonverbal. It excels at spatial and perceptual skills, visualization, and recognition of patterns, faces, or melodies.
- "*Split brains*" have been created experimentally in animals, and for medical reasons in humans, by cutting the *corpus callosum*. The split-brain individual shows a remarkable degree of independence between the right and left hemispheres. Under some circumstances the hemispheres function as separate brain units.
- The most basic functions of the *lobes* of the cerebral cortex are: *occipital lobes*—vision; *parietal lobes*—bodily sensation; *temporal lobes*—hearing and language; *frontal lobes*—olfaction, motor control, speech, and abstract thought.
- There are a number of *association* areas on the cortex that are neither sensory nor motor in function. These are related to more complex skills such as language, memory, recognition, and problem solving. Damage to either *Broca's area* or *Wernicke's area* causes speech and language problems known as *aphasias*. Damage in other areas may cause *agnosia*, the inability to identify objects by sight.
- The brain as a whole can be subdivided into three general areas: the *forebrain*, *midbrain*, and *hindbrain*.
- The *subcortex* includes several crucial brain structures. The *medulla* contains centers essential for reflex control of heart rate, breathing, and other "vegetative" functions. The *cerebellum* maintains coordination, posture, and muscle

tone. The *reticular formation* directs sensory and motor messages, and part of it, known as the RAS, acts as an activating system for the brain.

- The *thalamus* carries sensory information to the cortex. The *hypothalamus* exerts powerful control over eating, drinking, sleep cycles, body temperature and other basic motives and behaviors. The *limbic system*, which is made up of several structures, serves as an emotional system in the brain. It also contains distinct reward and punishment areas.
- The *endocrine system* provides *chemical* communication in the body through the release of *hormones* into the bloodstream. Many of the endocrine glands are influenced by the *pituitary* (the "master gland"). The endocrine glands influence behavior, body configuration, and even personality.
- The vast majority of people are right-handed—and therefore left-brain dominant for motor skills. Ninety-seven percent of right-handed persons and 60 percent of left-handed persons also produce speech from the left hemisphere. In general, the left-handed are less strongly lateralized in brain function than the right-handed.

Chapter 4

The Sensory World and Reality

Chapter Preview

Sensation and Reality

At this very moment you are bathed in a swirling kaleidoscope of light, heat, pressure, vibrations, molecules, radiation, mechanical forces, and other physical energies. Without your senses, all of this would seem like a void of darkness and silence. The next time you drink in the beauty of a sunset, a flower, or a friend, remember this: ***Sensation*** *makes it all possible.*

It is apparent that the world as we know it is created from sensory impressions. Less obvious is that what passes for "reality" is shaped by the senses. Our sensory organs can detect only a limited range of physical energies. Thus, events go unrecorded when the senses are not attuned to them. We have, for instance, no receptors for atomic radiation, X rays, or microwaves. For this reason it is possible to be injured by each of these energies without being aware of it.

Yellow Is Amazing but Red Is Best *What would the world be like if new senses could be added—if we could "see" gamma rays, "hear" changes in barometric pressure, or "taste" light? We can only guess. It is far easier to imagine losing or regaining a sensory system. Consider the words of Bob Edens, who had his sight restored at age 51 after being blind since birth:*

> I never would have dreamed that yellow is so. . . so yellow. I don't have the words, I'm amazed by yellow. But red is my favorite color. I just can't believe red. I can't wait to get up each day to see what I can see. And at night I look at the stars in the sky and the flashing lights. You could never know how wonderful everything is. I saw some bees the other day, and they were magnificent. I saw a truck drive by in the rain and throw a spray in the air. It was marvelous. And did I mention, I saw a falling leaf just drifting through the air?

If you are ever tempted to take everyday sensory impressions for granted, remember Bob Edens. As his words show, sensation is our window on the world. All our meaningful behavior, our awareness of physical reality, and our ideas about the universe ultimately spring from the senses. It may be no exaggeration then, to claim that our topic for this chapter is quite . . . sensational.

Survey Questions In general, how do sensory systems function? What are the limits of our sensory sensitivity? How do each of the major senses work, and what causes common sensory problems, such as deafness or color blindness? Why are we more aware of some sensations than others? How can pain be reduced or controlled in everyday situations?

Resources

Sensory Receptors—What you See Is What You Get

We begin with a paradox. On one hand we have the magnificent power of the senses. In one instant you can view a star light-years away, and in the next you can peer into the microscopic universe of a dewdrop. Yet vision, like the other senses, is also carefully limited in sensitivity, so that it acts as a **data reduction system.** That is, our senses routinely "boil down" floods of information into a select stream of useful data. Such selection can be seen in the fact that "light" is only a small slice of a broader range of energies. In addition to visible light, the **electromagnetic spectrum** includes infrared and ultraviolet light, radio frequencies, television broadcasts, gamma rays, and other energies (see Fig. 4-2). If the eyes were not limited to "light" sensitivity, "seeing" would be like getting hundreds of different "channels" at once. The confusion would be overwhelming. Obviously, *selection* of information is important.

Question: How are selection and data reduction accomplished?

Some selection occurs simply because sensory receptors act as biological *transducers*. A **transducer** is a device that converts one kind of energy into another. For example, a phonograph needle converts *vibrations* into electrical signals. Scrape the needle with your finger and the speakers will blast out sound. However, if you shine a light on the needle, or put it in cold water, the system will remain silent. (The owner of the stereo, however, may get quite loud at this point!) Similarly, each sensory organ is most sensitive to a select range of energy, which it most easily translates into nerve impulses.

As they transduce information, many sensory systems analyze the environment into important *features* before sending messages to the brain. This is called **sensory analysis.** For example, frog eyes are especially sensitive to small, dark, moving spots. Researcher Jerome Lettvin (1961) calls sensitivity to this feature a "bug detector." It seems that the frog's eyes are "wired" to detect bugs flying nearby. But, the insect (spot) must be moving. A frog may starve to death surrounded by dead flies.

In addition to selection and analysis, then, sensory systems **code** important features of the world into messages understood by the brain (Hubel & Wiesel, 1979). To see coding at work try this simple demonstration:

> Close your eyes for a moment. Then take your fingertips and press firmly on your eyelids. Apply enough pressure to "squash" your eyes slightly. Do this for about 30 seconds and observe what happens. (Persons with eye problems or contact lenses should not try this.)

If you followed the instructions, you probably saw stars, checkerboards, and flashes of color called **phosphenes** (FOSS-feens). The reason for this is that the receptor cells in the eye, which normally respond to light, are also somewhat sensitive to pressure. Notice, though, that the eye is only prepared to code stimulation—including pressure—into *visual* features. As a result, you experience *light sensations*, not pressure. Also important in producing this effect is **localization of function** in the brain.

Question: What does localization of function mean?

It means that specific brain areas receive messages from each of the senses. Thus, the sensation you experience depends ultimately on which area of the brain is activated.

One practical implication of such localization is that it may be possible to artificially stimulate specific brain areas to restore sight, hearing, or other senses. For example, researchers have already tested a system that uses a miniature television camera to create electrical signals that are applied to the visual cortex of the brain (Dobelle et al., 1974) (see Fig. 4-1). Unfortunately, artificial vision of this type still faces major hurdles. However, artificial hearing is proving more workable—as we will see later.

It is fascinating to realize that experiences such as "seeing" and "hearing" ultimately take place in the brain, not in the eye or ear. Each sense organ is only the first link in a long chain that ends in the vast cell and fiber forest of the brain. Much as we may be tempted to think so, our sensory systems simply do not operate like cameras or tape recorders, sending back "pictures" of the world. Rather, they collect, transduce, analyze, code, and transmit a never-ending flow of data to an active, information-hungry brain. This incoming flow of information is what we refer to as **sensation.** (When the brain organizes sensations into meaningful patterns, we speak of *perception*, which is the topic of Chapter 5.) In a moment we will see how each of the senses operates. But first, let's explore the question of how sensitive we are to our "sensational" world.

Data reduction system Any system that selects, analyzes, or condenses information.

Electromagnetic spectrum The full range of electrical and magnetic wavelengths, including X rays, radio waves, light waves, and so forth.

Transducer A device that converts energy from one system into energy in another.

Sensory analysis The capacity of sensory systems to separate incoming information into important elements.

Sensory coding Various codes used by the sense organs to transmit information to the brain.

Phosphene A visual impression caused by mechanical excitation of the retina, as by pressure on the closed eyelid.

Localization of function The principle stating that sensations are determined by the area of the brain that is activated.

Sensation The immediate neural response in the brain caused by excitation of a sensory organ.

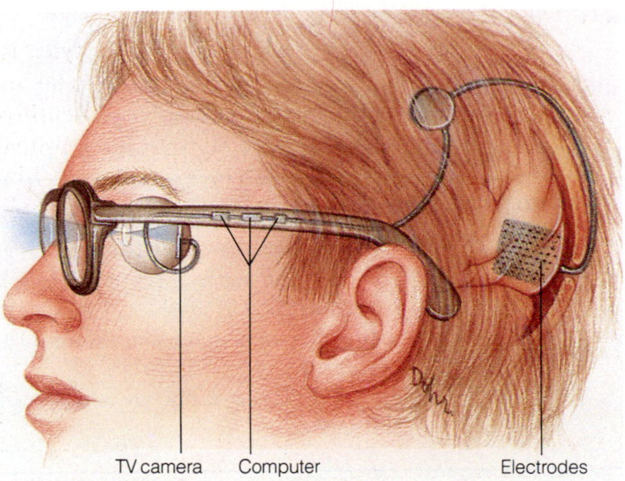

Fig. 4-1 *Artist's concept of an artificial visual system. Images received by an artificial eye would be transmitted to electrodes placed in the visual area of the brain (shown in cutaway view). The artificial eye, which operates like a television camera, might be placed in the eye socket as shown in the drawing. A major barrier to such systems is the brain's tendency to reject implanted electrodes.*

Psychophysics—Taking It to the Limit

Question: What is the quietest sound that can be heard? The weakest light that can be seen? The lightest touch that can be felt?

The sense organs are our link to reality. What are their limits? An approach called **psychophysics** provides some answers. In psychophysics, changes in *physical* stimuli are measured and related to *psychological* sensations, such as loudness, brightness, or taste. A basic question psychophysics asks is, "What is the absolute minimum amount of stimulation necessary for a sensation to occur?" The answer defines the **absolute threshold** for a sensory system.

Testing for absolute thresholds is a good indication of just how sensitive we are. For example, it only takes *three* photons of light striking the retina to produce a sensation. This is the equivalent of being able to see a single candle flame 30 miles away! Table 4-1 gives the approximate absolute thresholds for the five major senses.

Some sensory systems have upper limits as well as lower ones. For example, when the ears are tested for pitch (higher and lower tones), we find that humans can hear sounds down to 20 **hertz** (vibrations per second) and up to about 20,000 hertz. Note that the lower threshold is as low as practical: If the ears could respond to tones below 20 hertz, you would hear the movements of your own muscles (Oster, 1984). Imagine how disturbing it would be to hear your body creak and groan like an old ship each time you moved. The 20,000-hertz upper threshold for human hearing, on the other hand, could easily be higher. Dogs, bats, cats, and other animals can hear sounds well above this limit. That's why a "silent" dog whistle (which may make sounds as high as 40 or 50 thousand hertz) can be heard by dogs but not by humans. For dogs the sound exists. For humans it is beyond awareness. It's easy to see how thresholds define the limits of the sensory world in which we live. (If you want to buy a stereo for your dog, you will have a hard time finding one that reproduces sounds above 20,000 hertz!)

Perceptual Defense and Subliminal Perception

Question: Wouldn't the absolute threshold be different for different people?

Not only do absolute thresholds vary from person to person, they also vary from time to time for a single person. The type of stimulus, the state of one's nervous

Table 4-1 Absolute Thresholds

Sensory Modality	Absolute Threshold
Vision	Candle flame seen at 30 miles on a clear dark night.
Hearing	Tick of a watch under quiet conditions at 20 feet.
Taste	A teaspoon of sugar in 2 gallons of water.
Smell	A drop of perfume diffused into a three-room apartment.
Touch	A bee's wing falling on your cheek from 1 centimeter above.

(From Galanter, 1962)

system, and the costs of false "detections" all make a difference. Emotional factors are also important. Unpleasant stimuli, for example, may *raise* the threshold for recognition. This effect is called **perceptual defense.** It was first demonstrated in experiments on the recognition of "dirty" and "clean" words (McGinnies, 1949). So-called dirty words such as *whore, rape, bitch,* and *penis* were briefly flashed on a screen. These words consistently took longer to recognize than did "clean" words such as *wharf, rope, batch,* and *pencil.*

Question: Couldn't it be that people wanted to be really sure they had seen a word like penis *before saying it?*

Yes. For many years psychologists worried about this and other flaws in the original experiment. But later research that avoided these problems suggests that perceptual defense does occur (Erdelyi, 1974). Apparently, it is possible to process information on more than one level and to resist information that causes anxiety, discomfort, or embarrassment (Dember & Warm, 1979).

Question: Is this "subliminal" perception?

Basically, yes. Anytime information is processed below the normal **limen** (LIE-men: threshold or limit) for awareness, it is subliminal. **Subliminal perception** was recently demonstrated by an experiment in which people saw a series of shapes flashed on a screen for 1/1000 second each. Later, they were allowed to see these shapes, and other "new" shapes, for as long as they wanted. At that time they rated how much they liked each shape. Even though they could not tell "old" shapes from "new," they gave "old" shapes higher ratings (Kunst-Wilson & Zajonc, 1980). Apparently, the "old" shapes had become familiar and thus more "likable"—but at a level below normal awareness.

Question: Could this finding be applied to advertising?

The urge to manipulate shoppers must be strong, since many businesses have tried subliminal advertising over the years. But do subliminal sales pitches actually work? Let's see.

In one early attempt at subliminal advertising, a New Jersey theater flashed the words *Eat popcorn* and *Drink Coca-Cola* on the screen for 1/3000 second every 5 seconds during movies. Since the words were presented so briefly, they were below the normal threshold for awareness. During the 6 weeks the messages ran, the firm claimed an increase of 57.5 percent in popcorn sales and 18.1 percent in Coca-Cola sales.

In the uproar that followed this "experiment," some states rushed to pass laws against the "invisible sell." However, they really had nothing to fear. Subliminal advertising has proved largely ineffective (McBurney & Collings, 1984). Such early "experiments" appeared to succeed only because they didn't take into account weather conditions, time of year, films shown, type of audience, snack bar displays, and so forth.

To summarize, there is evidence that subliminal perception occurs. However, well-controlled laboratory experiments have shown that subliminal stimuli are basically weak stimuli. An advertiser would be better off using the loudest, clearest, most attention-demanding stimulus available—as most do. Despite the evidence, some advertisers still use subliminal messages. Maybe *they* haven't gotten the message.

Psychophysics The study of the relationship between physical stimuli and the sensations they evoke in a human observer.

Absolute threshold The minimum amount of physical energy necessary to produce a sensation.

Perceptual defense The tendency to resist perceiving stimuli that are threatening or disturbing.

Subliminal perception Perception of a stimulus presented below the threshold for conscious recognition.

Learning Check

Before you read more, it might be a good idea to stop for a quick check on some of the ideas we have covered.

1. Sensory receptors are biological ________________, or devices for converting one type of energy to another.

2. Lettvin found that the frog's eyes are especially sensitive to phosphenes. T or F?

3. Important features of the environment are transmitted to the brain through a process known as:
a. phosphenation
b. coding
c. detection
d. programming

4. The minimum amount of stimulation necessary for a sensation to occur defines the ________________ ________________.

5. A stimulus that causes discomfort or embarrassment may have to be viewed longer before it is perceived because of ________________ ________________.

6. Subliminal stimuli have been shown to have a powerful effect on the behavior of viewers, especially when embedded in movies. T or F?

Answers: **1.** transducers **2.** F **3.** *b* **4.** absolute threshold **5.** perceptual defense **6.** F

Vision—Catching Some Rays

Question: Which of the senses is most essential?

There really isn't an answer to this question. Nevertheless, for most people loss of vision is the single most devastating sensory disability. Because of its tremendous importance, we will explore vision in more detail than the other senses. Let's begin with the basic dimensions of light and vision.

Dimensions of Vision Recall that the room in which you are sitting is filled with **electromagnetic radiation,** including light and other energies. The **visible spectrum** is made up of light of various wavelengths. The spectrum starts at wavelengths of 400 nanometers (nan-OM-et-ers). A nanometer (nm) is one-billionth of a meter. Wavelengths at this end of the spectrum produce sensations of purple or violet. Longer wavelengths of light produce sensations of blue, green, yellow, and orange, until red, with a wavelength of 700 nm, is reached (Fig. 4-2).

This physical property of light, its *wavelength,* corresponds to the psychological experience of **hue,** or the specific color of a stimulus. White light is made up of a mixture of frequencies from the entire spectrum. Colors produced by a very *narrow band* of wavelengths are said to be very **saturated,** or "pure." A third dimension of vision, **brightness,** corresponds roughly to the *amplitude* (or "height") of light waves; light of greater amplitude carries more energy and appears brighter.

Visible spectrum That portion of the electromagnetic spectrum to which the eyes are sensitive.

Hue That property of color sensations represented by classification into basic categories of red, orange, yellow, green, blue, indigo, and violet.

Saturation That quality of colors related to their being very pure, free from mixture, or from a concentrated area of the spectrum.

Brightness The intensity of light reflected from or emanating from a surface.

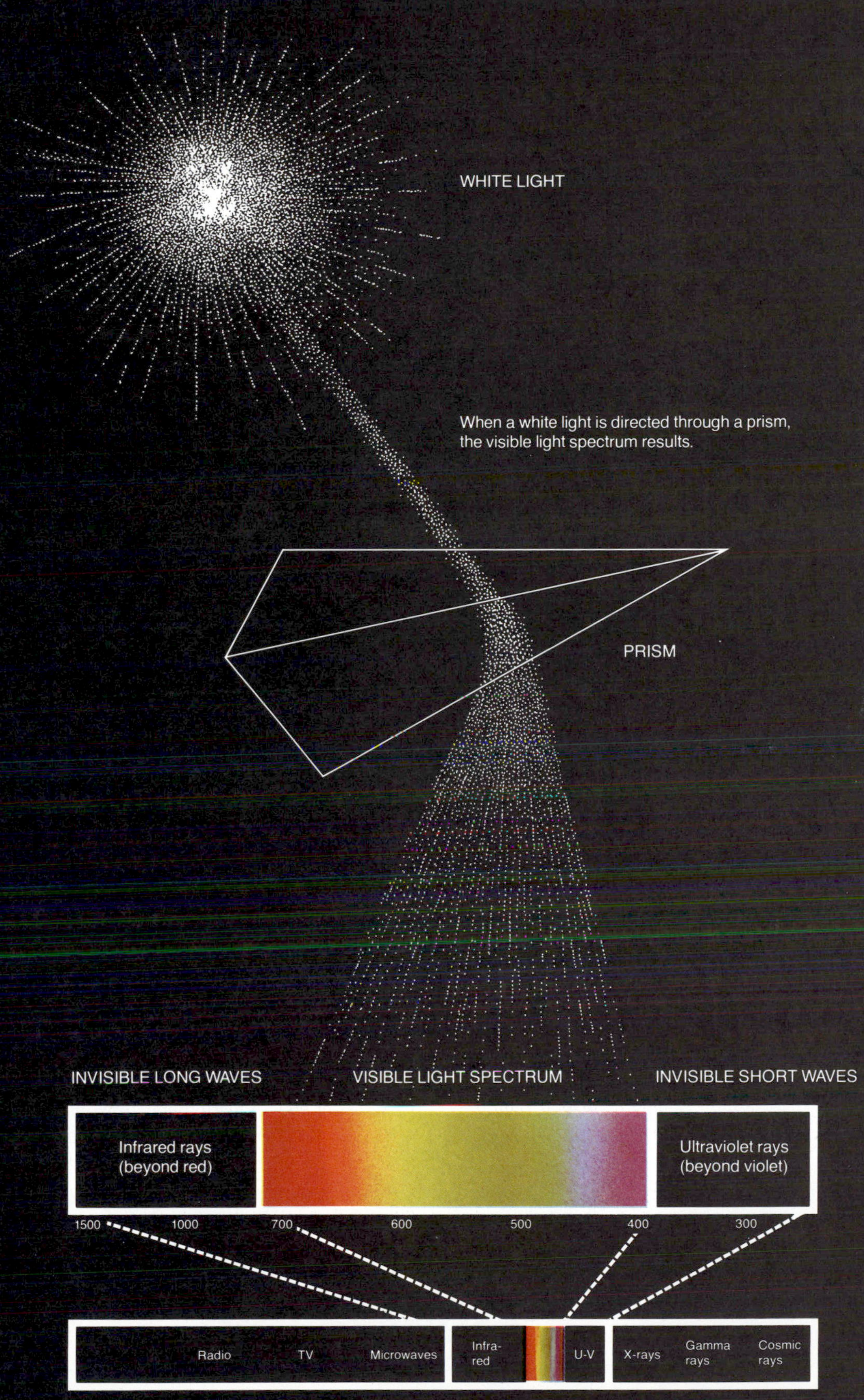

Fig. 4–2 *The visible spectrum.*

Photoreceptor Sensory receptors sensitive to light and specialized for the transduction of light stimuli into neural impulses.

Retina The light-sensitive lining at the back of the eye containing rods and cones.

Accommodation Changes in the shape of the lens of the eye that serve to focus objects at varying distances.

Hyperopia The visual defect commonly known as farsightedness.

Myopia A visual defect that makes it difficult to focus distant objects (nearsightedness).

Astigmatism A defect in the shape of the cornea, lens, or eye as a whole that causes some areas of vision to be out of focus.

Presbyopia Farsightedness caused by a loss of elasticity in the lens due to aging.

Pupil The dark spot at the front of the eye through which light passes.

Structure of the Eye

Question: Is it true that the eye is like a camera?

If we were willing to push the issue a bit, the eye could be used as a camera. When the light-sensitive back surface of the eye is bathed in alum solution, the last image to strike it will appear like a tiny photograph. This fact might make for a great murder mystery, but it's obviously not much of a way to take a photograph. In any case, several basic elements of eyes and cameras are similar. Both have a **lens** that focuses images on a light-sensitive layer at the back of a closed space. In a camera this layer is the film; in the eye it is a layer of **photoreceptors** (light-sensitive cells) about the size and thickness of a postage stamp, called the **retina** (see Fig. 4-3).

Question: How does the eye focus?

Focusing The front of the eye has a clear covering called the **cornea.** The curvature of this transparent "window" bends light rays inward. Next, the lens, which is elastic, is stretched or thickened by a series of muscles, so that more or less additional bending of light occurs. This bending, flattening, and stretching of the lens is called **accommodation.** In cameras, focusing is done more simply—by changing the distance between the lens and the film.

Visual Problems The overall shape of the eye also affects focusing. If the eye is too short, nearby objects cannot be focused, but distant objects are clear. This is *farsightedness,* or **hyperopia** (HI-per-OH-pea-ah). If the eye is too long, the

Fig. 4-3 *The human eye, a simplified view.*

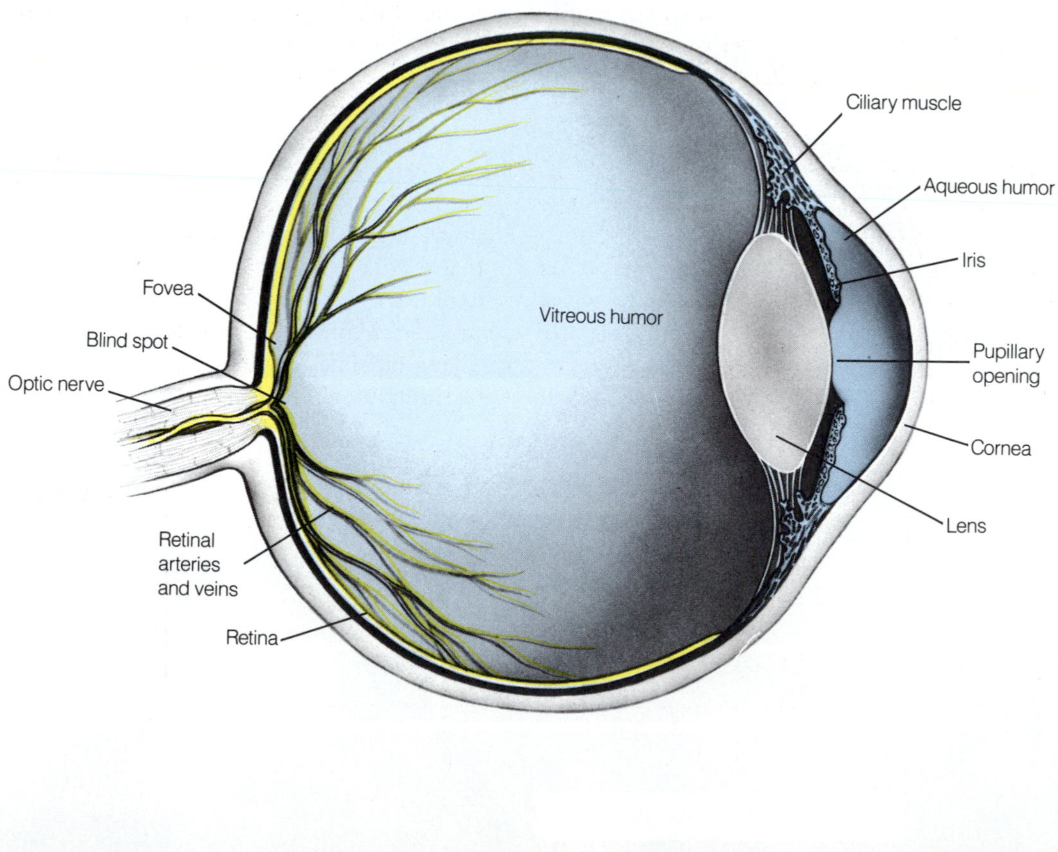

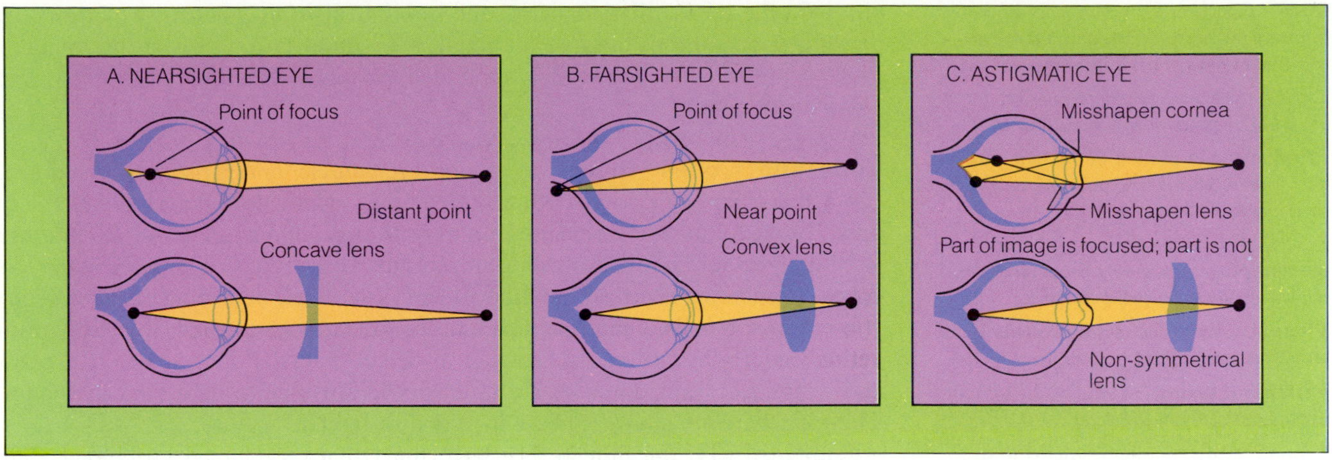

Fig. 4-4 *Visual defects and corrective lenses:* (a) *A myopic (longer than usual) eye. The concave lens spreads light rays just enough to increase the eye's focal length.* (b) *A hyperopic (shorter than usual) eye. The convex lens increases refraction (bending), returning the point of focus to the retina.* (c) *Astigmatic (lens or cornea not symmetrical) eye. In astigmatism parts of vision are sharp and parts are unfocused. Lenses to correct astigmatism are non-symmetrical.*

image falls short of the retina, and distant objects cannot be focused. This condition results in *nearsightedness*, or **myopia** (my-OH-pea-ah). When the cornea or the lens is *misshapen*, some of the visual field will be focused and some will be fuzzy, a problem called **astigmatism** (ah-STIG-mah-tiz-em). All three visual problems can be corrected by placing eyeglasses or contact lenses in front of the eye. These added lenses change the path of incoming light to restore crisp focusing (see Fig. 4-4).

Sometimes, with age, the lens grows less flexible and less able to accommodate. Since the lens must do its greatest bending to focus nearby objects, the result is **presbyopia** (prez-bee-OH-pea-ah, "old vision," or farsightedness due to aging). Perhaps you have seen a grandparent or older friend reading a newspaper at arm's length because of presbyopia. Also, if you now wear glasses for nearsightedness, you may need bifocals as you age. Bifocal lenses correct near vision *and* distance vision.

Light Control There is one more major similarity between the eye and a camera. In front of the lens in both is a mechanism to control the amount of light entering. This mechanism in a camera is the diaphragm, in the eye it is the **iris** (see Fig. 4-5). The iris is a colored circular muscle that expands and contracts to control the size of the **pupil,** or opening at the center of the eye.

The iris is extremely important for normal vision. The retina can adapt to changing light conditions but only very slowly. By making rapid adjustments, the iris allows us to move quickly from darkness to bright sunlight or the reverse. In

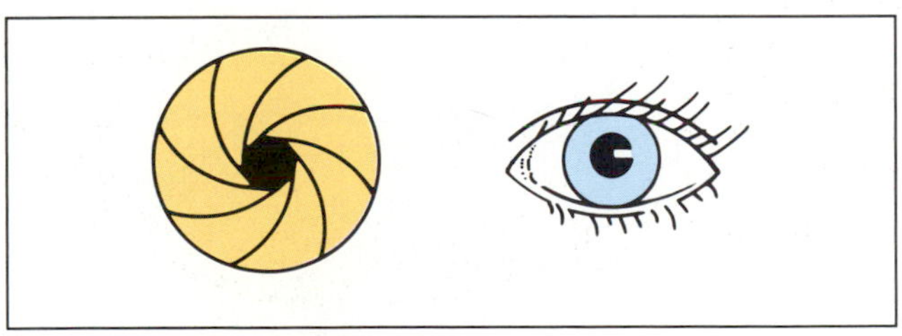

Fig. 4-5 *The diaphragm and iris.*

Rods Visual receptors that are responsive to dim light but produce only black and white sensations.

Cones Visual receptors responsible for color vision and daylight visual acuity.

Blind spot A portion of the retina lacking visual receptors (the point where the optic nerve leaves the eye).

Fovea A small depression at the center of the retina containing only cones and providing the greatest sharpness of vision.

Visual acuity The clarity or sharpness of visual perception.

Peripheral vision Vision at the periphery (edges) of the visual field.

Tunnel vision Vision restricted to the center of the visual field.

dim light the pupils **dilate** (enlarge) and in bright light they **constrict** (narrow). At the largest opening of the iris, the pupil is 17 times larger than at the smallest. Were it not for this, you would be blinded for quite some time on walking into a darkened room.

Rods and Cones At this point our eye-camera comparison breaks down. From the retina on, vision becomes a complex system for analyzing patterns of light. Besides, the eye would make a very strange camera. First of all, the eye has two types of "film," consisting of receptor cells called **rods** and **cones.** The cones, numbering about 6.5 million in each eye, work best in bright light. They also produce *color* sensations and pick up fine details. In contrast, the rods, numbering about 100 million, are unable to detect colors. Pure rod vision is black and white. However, the rods are much more sensitive to light than the cones. The rods therefore allow us to see in very dim light.

Compared with the film in a camera, the visual receptors are backward. The rods and cones point toward the *back* of the eye, away from incoming light (see Fig. 4-6). In addition, the "film" has a hole in it. Each eye has a **blind spot** because there are no receptors where the optic nerve leaves the eye (see Fig. 4-7). And last, the eye is constantly in motion. This would be disastrous for a camera, but as we shall see later, motion is essential for normal vision.

Question: Are there other differences between the rods and cones?

Visual Acuity The cones lie mainly at the center of the eye. In fact there is a small cup-shaped area in the middle of the retina called the **fovea** (FOE-vee-ah) that contains *only* cones—about 50,000 of them. If you look at your thumbnail at arm's length, its image just about covers the fovea. Like a newspaper photograph made of many small dots, the tightly packed cones of the fovea produce

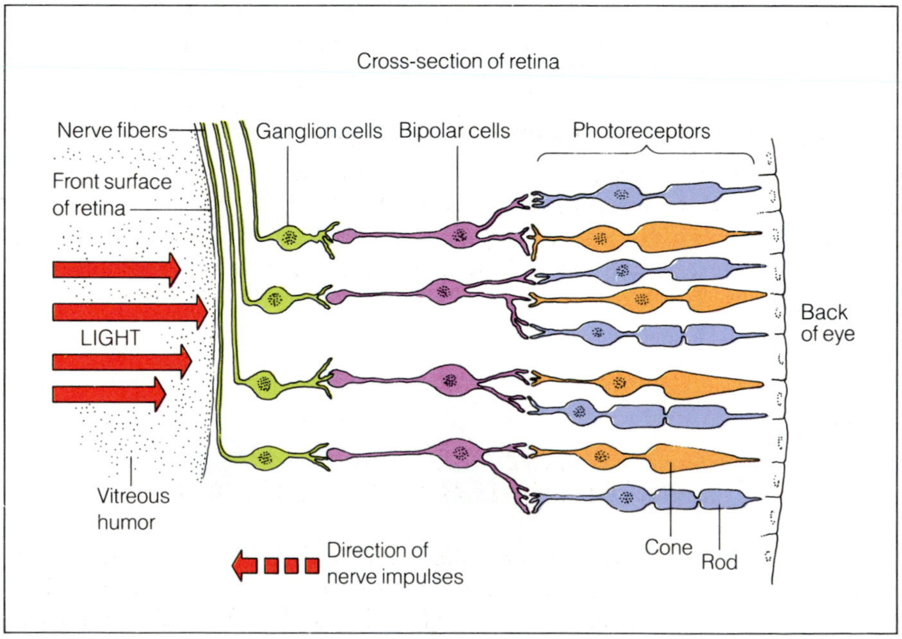

Fig. 4-6 *Anatomy of the retina, light-sensitive element of the eye. Note that light does not fall directly on the rods and cones. It must first pass through the outer layers of the retina. Only about one-half of the light falling on the front of the eye reaches the rods and cones—testimony to the eye's amazing light sensitivity. The rods and cones are much smaller than implied here. The smallest receptors are 1 micron (one-millionth of a meter) wide.*

Fig. 4-7 *Experiencing the blind spot.* (a) *With the right eye closed, stare at the upper right cross. Hold the book about 1 foot from your eye and slowly move it back and forth. You should be able to locate a position that causes the black spot to disappear. When it does, it has fallen on the blind spot.* (b) *Repeat the procedure described but stare at the lower cross. When the white space falls on the blind spot, the black line will appear to be continuous. This may help you understand why you do not usually experience a blind spot in your visual field.*

the greatest **visual acuity,** or sharpness. In other words, vision is sharpest when an image falls on the fovea. It then steadily decreases as images are moved to the edge of the retina.

Figure 4-8 describes a widely used rating system for acuity. If vision can be corrected to no better than 20/200 acuity, a person is considered legally blind. With 20/200 vision the world is nothing but a blur.

Question: What is the purpose of the rest of the retina?

Peripheral Vision Areas outside the fovea also get light, creating a large region of **peripheral** (side) **vision.** The rods are most numerous about 20 degrees from the center of the retina; hence, much peripheral vision is rod vision. Fortunately, the rods are quite sensitive to *movement.* Thus, while the eye gives its best acuity to the center of vision, it maintains a radarlike scan for movement in side vision. Seeing "out of the corner of the eye" is important for sports, driving, and walking down dark alleys. Those who have lost peripheral vision suffer from **tunnel vision,** a condition much like wearing blinders.

Sailors, pilots, astronomers, and military spotters have long made use of another interesting fact about peripheral vision. Although the rods give poor acuity, they are many times more responsive to light than the cones are. Since most rods are 20 degrees to each side of the fovea, the best night vision is obtained by looking *next* to an object you wish to see. Test this yourself some night by looking at, and next to, a very dim star.

Color Vision—There's More to It than Meets the Eye

What would you say is the brightest color? Red? Yellow? Blue? Acutally, there are two answers to this question, one for the rods and one for the cones. The differing *maximal color sensitivity* of the rods and cones has practical importance.

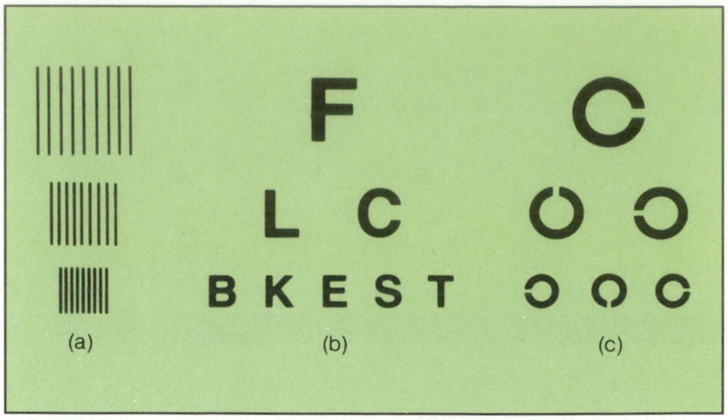

Fig. 4-8 *Tests of visual acuity. Above are some common tests of visual acuity. In* (a) *sharpness is indicated by the smallest grating still seen as individual lines. Part* (b) *requires that you read rows of letters of diminishing size until you can no longer distinguish them. The Landolt rings* (c) *require no familiarity with letters. All that is required is a report of which side has a break in it. Normal acuity is designated as 20/20 vision: At 20 feet in distance you can distinguish what the average person can see at 20 feet. If your vision is 20/40, you can only see at 20 feet what the average person can see at 40 feet. If your vision is 20/200, you need glasses! Vision that is 20/12 would mean that you can see at 20 feet what the average person must be 8 feet nearer to see, indicating better than average acuity. American astronaut Gordon Cooper, who claimed to see railroad lines in northern India from 100 miles above, had 20/12 acuity.*

The cones are most sensitive to the *yellowish green* region of the spectrum. In other words, if all colors are tested in daylight (with each reflecting the same total amount of light), then yellowish green appears *brightest*. The increased use of yellow fire trucks, and of Day-Glo yellow vests worn by roadside work crews, reflects this fact (Fig. 4-9).

Question: To what color are the rods most sensitive?

Remember first that the rods do not produce color. If very dim colored lights are used, no color will be seen, but one light will appear brighter than the others.

Fig. 4-9 *Yellow-green fire trucks are far more visible in daylight because their color matches the cones' sensitivity peak. However, many cities continue to prefer red trucks because of tradition.*

When tested this way, the rods are most sensitive to *blue-green* lights. Thus, at night or in dim light, when rod vision prevails, the brightest-colored light will be one that is blue or blue-green. For this reason, police and highway patrol cars in many states now have blue emergency lights for night work. Also, you may have wondered why the taxiway lights at airports are blue. This may seem like a poor choice, but blue is actually highly visible to pilots.

Trichromatic theory The theory of color vision based on the assumption that there are three types of cones, with peak sensitivity to red, green, or blue.

Opponent-process theory The theory of color vision stating that three coding systems (red or green, yellow or blue, black or white) are used by the visual system to analyze color information.

Afterimage A visual sensation that persists after the stimulus causing it has ceased.

Color Theories

Question: How do the cones record color sensations?

No short answer can do justice to the complexities of color vision, but, briefly, here is the best current explanation. The **trichromatic** (or three-color) **theory** of color vision holds that there are three types of cones, each most sensitive to a specific color: red, green, or blue. Other colors are assumed to result from combinations of these three areas of the spectrum, whereas black and white sensations are produced by the rods.

A basic problem with the trichromatic theory is that four colors seem psychologically primary: red, green, blue, and yellow. A second view, known as the **opponent-process theory,** was developed to explain why you can't have a reddish green or a yellowish blue. According to this theory, the visual system analyzes information into either-or color messages. It is assumed that the visual system can produce messages for either red or green, yellow or blue, black or white. Coding one color in a pair (red, for instance) seems to block the opposite message (green), so a reddish green is impossible, but a yellowish red (orange) can occur. According to the theory, fatigue caused by making one response causes an **afterimage** of the opposite color as the system recovers. To experience an afterimage of this type, see Fig. 4-10 and follow the instructions given there.

Fig. 4-10 *Negative afterimages. Stare at the dot near the middle of the flag for at least 30 seconds. Then look immediately at a plain sheet of white paper or a white wall. You will see the American flag in its normal colors. Reduced sensitivity in yellow, green, and black receptors in the eye, caused by prolonged staring, results in the appearance of complementary colors. Project the afterimage of the flag on other colored surfaces to get additional effects.*

Question: Which color theory is correct?

Both! The three-color theory seems to apply to the retina, where three types of visual pigments have been found, with sensitivity peaks in approximately the red, green, and blue regions. The opponent-process theory seems to explain events recorded in the optic pathways after information leaves the eye. So both appear to be correct at a particular level in the visual system.

Color Blindness and Color Weakness

Do you know anyone who regularly draws hoots of laughter by wearing clothes of wildly clashing colors? Or someone who sheepishly tries to avoid saying what color an object is? If so, you probably know someone who is color blind.

Question: What is it like to be color blind? What causes color blindness?

A person who is completely **color blind** sees the world as if it were a black and white movie. How do we know? In a few rare cases people have been color blind in only one eye and can compare (Hsia & Graham, 1965). Two colors of equal brightness look exactly alike to the color-blind individual. The color-blind person either lacks cones or has cones that do not function normally (Rushton, 1975). Total color blindness is rare. **Color weakness,** or partial color blindness, is more common. Approximately 8 percent of the male population (but less than 1 percent of females) are red-green color blind. (Another form of color weakness, involving yellow and blue, is extremely rare.) Red-green color blindness is a recessive, sex-linked trait. This means that it is carried on the X, or female, chromosome. Women have two X chromosomes, so if they receive only one defective color gene, they still have normal vision. Color-blind men, however, only have one X chromosome, so they can inherit the defect from their mothers (who usually are not color blind themselves). The red-green color-blind individual perceives both reds and greens as the same color, usually a yellowish brown (Rushton, 1975). (See Fig. 4-11.)

Question: Then how can color-blind individuals drive? Don't they have trouble with traffic lights?

(a) (b) (c)

Fig. 4-11 *Color blindness and color weakness. Photograph on left* (a) *illustrates normal color vision. Middle photograph* (b) *is printed in blue and yellow and gives an impression of what a red-green color-blind person sees. Right image* (c) *simulates total color blindness.*

Red-green color-blind individuals have normal vision for yellow and blue, so their main problem is to tell red lights from green. In practice this is not difficult. In the United States the red light is always on top, and the green light is brighter than the red. Also, to help remedy this situation, most modern traffic signals have a "red" light that has a background of yellow light mixed with it and a "green" light that is really blue-green.

Question: How can a person tell if he or she is color blind?

A common test for color blindness and weakness is the **Ishihara** test. In the test, numbers and other designs made up of dots are superimposed on a background also made of dots. The background and the numbers are of different colors (red and green, for example). A person who is color blind sees only a collection of dots. The person with normal color vision can detect the presence of the numbers or designs. Figure 4-12 is a replica of the Ishihara test. You should not consider Fig. 4-12 a true test of color vision, but it may give you some idea of whether you are color blind.

Color blindness A total inability to perceive colors.

Color weakness An inability to fully distinguish some colors from others.

Ishihara test A test for color blindness and color weakness.

Dark adaptation The process by which the eye adapts to low illumination, principally by a shift to rod vision.

Visual pigment A chemical found in the rods and cones that is sensitive to light.

Rhodopsin The photosensitive pigment in the rods.

Dark Adaptation—Let There Be Light!

Question: What happens to the eyes when they adapt to a dark room?

Dark adaptation is the dramatic increase in light sensitivity that occurs after you enter the dark. Consider walking into a theater. If you enter from a brightly lighted lobby, you practically need to be led to your seat. After a short time, however, you can see the entire room in detail (including the couple kissing over in the corner). Studies of dark adaptation show that it takes about 30 to 35 minutes of complete darkness before your eyes reach maximum sensitivity (Fig. 4-13). When dark adaptation is complete, the eye can detect lights 10,000 times weaker than those to which it was originally sensitive.

Question: What causes dark adaptation?

Both the rods and cones contain light-sensitive chemicals known as **visual pigments.** When struck by light, these pigments bleach, or break down chemically. (The afterimages caused by flashbulbs are a direct result of this bleaching.) To restore light sensitivity, the visual pigments must recombine, which takes time. Night vision is due mainly to an increase of the rod pigment, **rhodopsin** (row-DOP-sin). When completely dark-adapted, the human eye is almost as sensitive to light as the eye of an owl.

Before artificial illumination, gradual adaptation at sunset posed few problems. Now we are often caught in temporary semiblindness. Usually this isn't dangerous, but it can be. Even though dark adaptation takes a long time, it can be wiped out by just a few seconds of viewing bright light. Try this demonstration:

> Spend 15 or 20 minutes in a darkened room. At the end of this time, you should be able to see clearly. Now, close your left eye and cover it tightly with your hand. Turn on a bright light for 1 or 2 seconds and look at it with your right eye. With the light off again, compare the vision in your two eyes, first opening one and then the other. You will be completely blinded in your right eye.

This experience should convince you of the wisdom of the oft-repeated warning to avoid looking at the headlights of approaching cars during night driving. Under

ARE YOU COLOR BLIND?

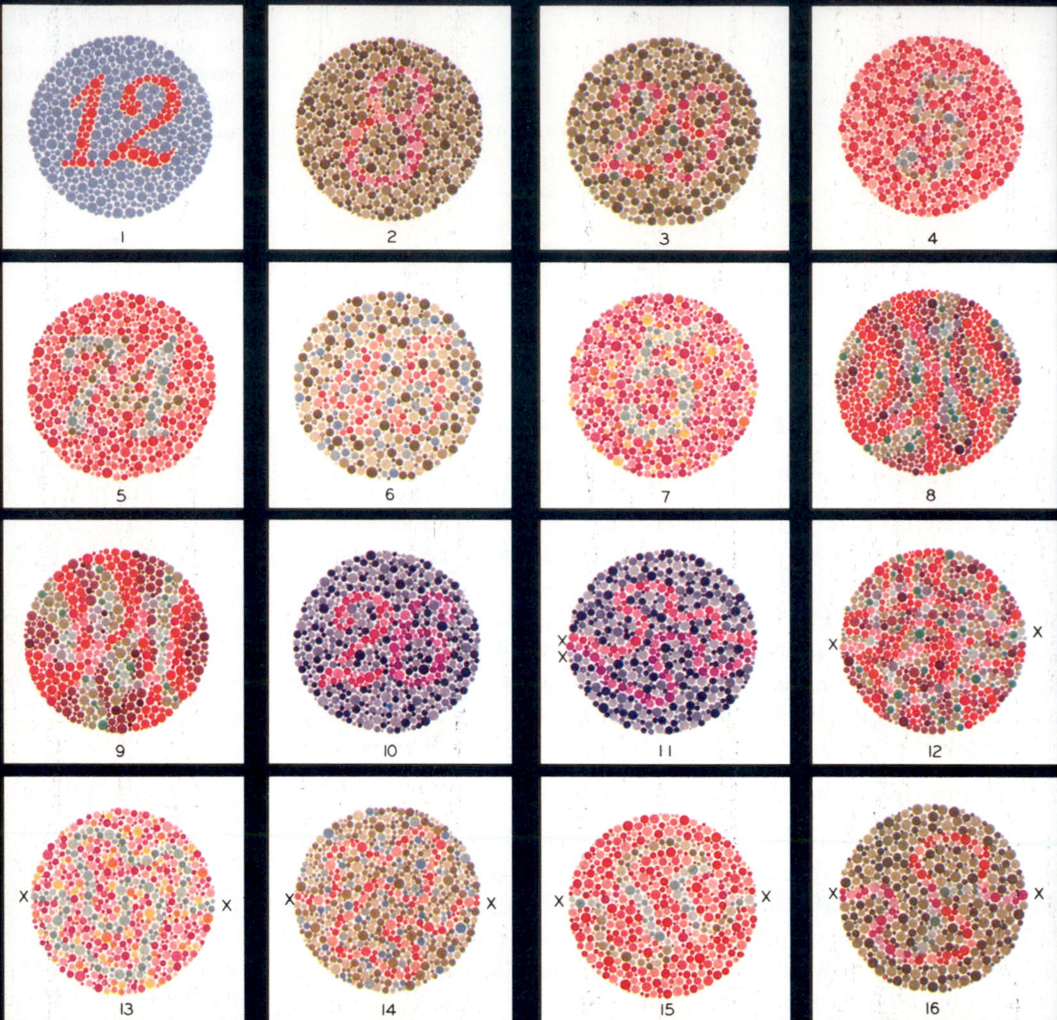

NO.	NORMAL EYE	COLOR BLIND EYE
1	12	12
2	8	3
3	29	70
4	5	2
5	74	21
6	45	NOTHING
7	5	NOTHING
8	NOTHING	5
9	NOTHING	45
10	26	2 OR 6
11	2 LINES X TO X	LINE X TO X
12	NOTHING	LINE X TO X
13	LINE X TO X	NOTHING
14	LINE X TO X	NOTHING
15	LINE X TO X	NOTHING
16	LINE X TO X	LINE X TO X

Fig. 4-12 *Replica of a test for color blindness.*

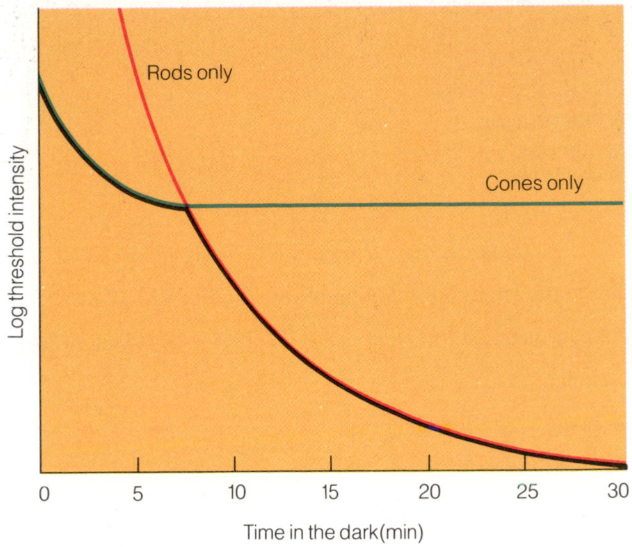

Fig. 4-13 *Time course of dark adaptation. Lowering of the threshold for vision after varying amounts of time in the dark is plotted by the black line. (A lower threshold means that less light is needed for vision.) Colored lines show that the cones adapt first but reach maximum sensitivity quickly. Rods adapt slowly but continue adding to night vision after the cones have adapted.*

normal conditions, glare recovery takes about 20 seconds, plenty of time for an accident. After a few drinks, it may take 30 to 50 percent longer, because alcohol dilates the pupils, allowing more light to enter.

Question: Is there any way to speed up dark adaptation?

The rods are *insensitive* to extremely red light. To take advantage of this lack of sensitivity, submarines and airplane cockpits are illuminated with red light. So are the ready rooms for fighter pilots and ground crews (Fig. 4-14). In each case this allows people to move quickly into the dark without adapting. Since the red light doesn't stimulate the rods, it is as if they had already spent time in the dark.

Question: Can eating carrots really improve vision?

One of the "ingredients" of rhodopsin is **retinal,** which the body makes from vitamin A. When too little vitamin A is available, less rhodopsin is produced. Thus, a person suffering from vitamin A deficiency may develop **night blindness.** In night blindness the person sees normally in bright light while using the cones but becomes totally blind at night when the rods must function. Since carrots are an excellent source of vitamin A, they could improve night vision for someone suffering a deficiency, but not the vision of anyone with an adequate diet (Carlson, 1981).

Fig. 4-14 *Red light allows dark adaptation to occur because it provides little or no stimulation to the rods.*

Learning Check

After such an extended discussion of vision, you may find it helpful to review the following questions.

1. The ______________ ______________ is made up of electromagnetic radiation with wavelengths between 400 nm and 700 nm.

2. Match:

____ Myopia	**A.** Farsightedness
____ Hyperopia	**B.** Elongated eye
____ Presbyopia	**C.** Farsightedness due to aging
____ Astigmatism	**D.** Lack of cones in fovea
	E. Misshapen cornea or lens

3. In dim light, vision depends mainly on the ______________; color and fine detail are produced by the ______________.

4. The fovea has the greatest visual acuity due to the large concentration of rods found there. T or F?

5. The term 20/20 vision means that a person can see at 20 feet what can normally be seen from 20 feet. T or F?

6. For the cones, the most visible color is (circle):

reddish orange blue-green yellow-orange yellowish green

7. The eyes become more sensitive to light at night due to a process known as ______________ ______________.

Answers: **1.** visible spectrum **2.** B, A, C, E **3.** rods, cones **4.** F **5.** T **6.** yellowish green **7.** dark adaptation

Hearing—Good Vibrations

Rock, classical, jazz, country, pop—whatever your musical taste, you have probably been moved or soothed by the riches of sound. Hearing also provides the brain with a wealth of information not available through the other senses, such as the approach of an unseen car or the information imparted by spoken language.

Question: What is the stimulus for hearing?

If you throw a stone into a quiet pond, a circle of waves will spread from it in all directions. In much the same way, sound travels as a series of invisible waves of **compression** (peaks) and **rarefaction** (RARE-eh-fak-shun: valleys) in the air. Any object set in motion—a tuning fork, the string of a musical instrument, or the vocal cords—will produce **sound waves** as it vibrates. The **frequency** of sound waves (the number of waves per second) corresponds to the perceived **pitch** of a sound. The **amplitude,** or physical "height," of a sound wave tells how much energy it contains, so amplitude corresponds to sensed **loudness** (see Fig. 4-15).

Question: How are sounds converted to nerve impulses?

After they are guided into the ear, sound waves collide with the **eardrum,** which is like a tight drumhead within the ear canal. The sound waves set the eardrum in motion, which in turn causes three small bones called the **auditory ossicles** (OSS-ih-kulz) to vibrate (see Fig. 4-16). The third ossicle is attached to a second membrane, or drumhead, called the **oval window.** As the oval window moves back and forth, it makes waves in a fluid within the **cochlea** (KOCK-lee-ah). The cochlea is really the organ of hearing, since it is here that waves in the fluid are detected by tiny **hair cells,** which generate nerve impulses to be sent to the brain.

Retinal A major portion of the chemical compound that makes up rhodopsin.

Night blindness A visual defect in which daylight vision is normal, but blindness occurs under conditions of low illumination.

Sound wave A cyclic compression of air molecules.

Pitch That quality of sound sensations determined by the number of vibrations per second striking the ear.

Loudness The intensity of a sound sensation, which is determined by the amplitude of sound waves (that is, by the amount of energy they carry).

Auditory ossicles The three small bones that link the eardrum to the inner ear.

Cochlea The snail-shaped organ that comprises the inner ear.

Hair cells Receptor cells within the cochlea that transduce vibrations into nerve impulses.

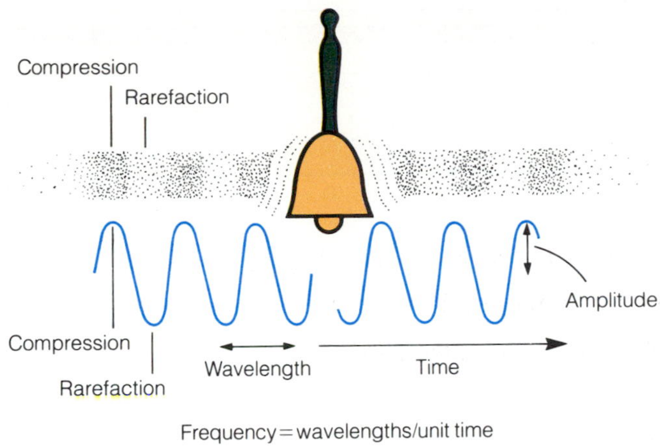

Fig. 4-15 *Waves of compression in the air, or vibrations, are the stimulus for hearing. The frequency of sound waves determines their pitch. The amplitude determines loudness.*

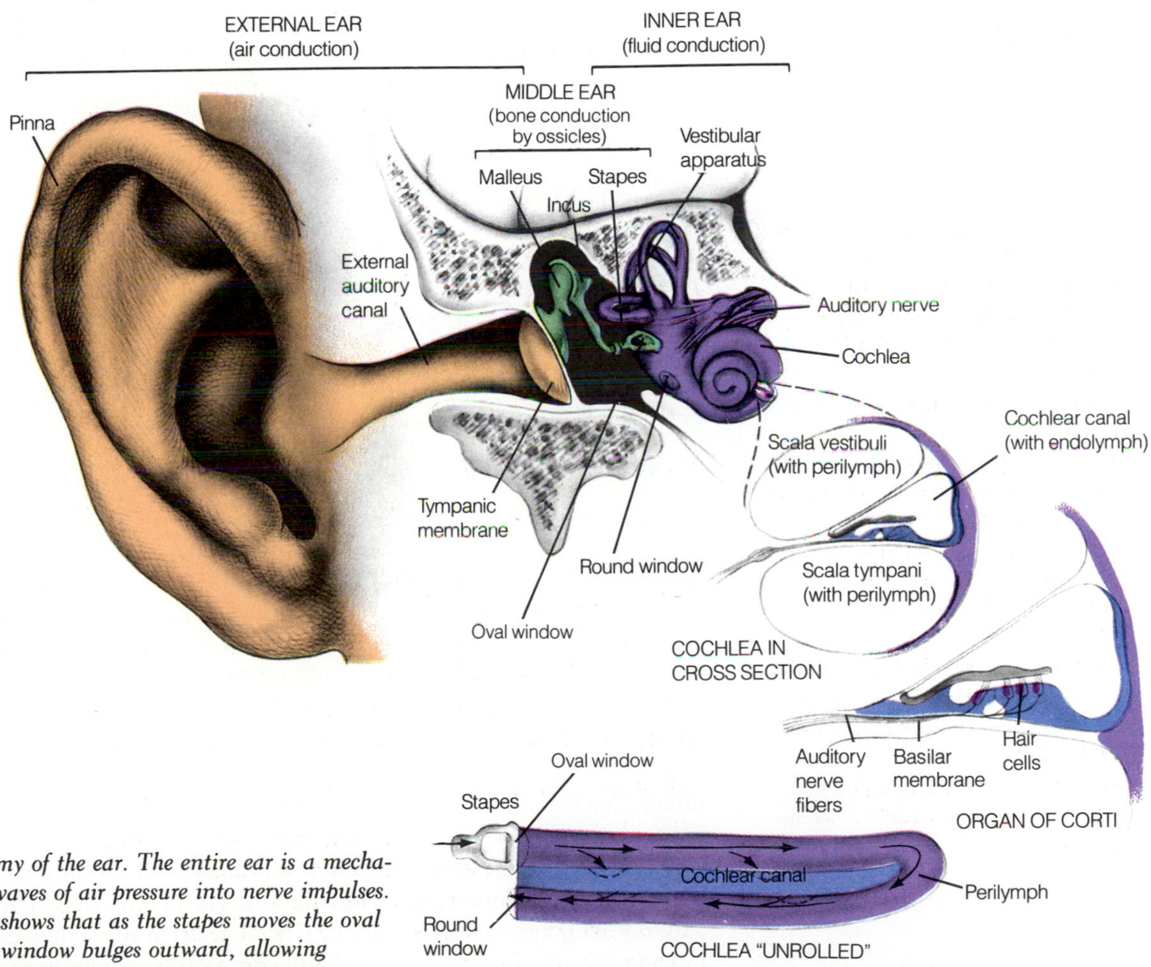

Fig. 4-16 *Anatomy of the ear. The entire ear is a mechanism for changing waves of air pressure into nerve impulses. Inset in foreground shows that as the stapes moves the oval window, the round window bulges outward, allowing waves to ripple through fluid in the cochlea. The waves move membranes near the hair cells, causing the cells to bend. The hair cells then generate nerve impulses carried to the brain. (See enlarged cross sections of cochlea.)*

Box 4-1

Artificial Hearing

Researchers have recently found that in many cases of "nerve" deafness, the nerve is actually intact. This finding has spurred development of **cochlear implants** that bypass hair cells and stimulate the auditory nerves directly (see Fig. 4-17). As you can see, wires from a microphone carry electrical signals to an external coil. A matching coil under the skin picks up the signals and carries them to one or more areas of the cochlea. Early implants allowed recipients to hear only low-frequency sounds, such as a dog's bark or the horn of a speeding car. Now, newer multi-channel models can separate higher and lower tones. This has allowed some formerly deaf persons to hear human voices and other higher frequency sounds (Franklin, 1984).

At present, artificial hearing remains crude. Most implant recipients describe the sound as "like a radio that isn't quite tuned in." In fact, 30 percent of adults who have tried implants have given up on them (Dreyfuss, 1985). But the implants are sure to improve. And even now it is hard to argue with enthusiasts like Kristen Cloud. Shortly after Ms. Cloud received an implant, she was able to hear a siren and thus to avoid being struck by a speeding car (Williams, 1984). She says simply, "The implant saved my life."

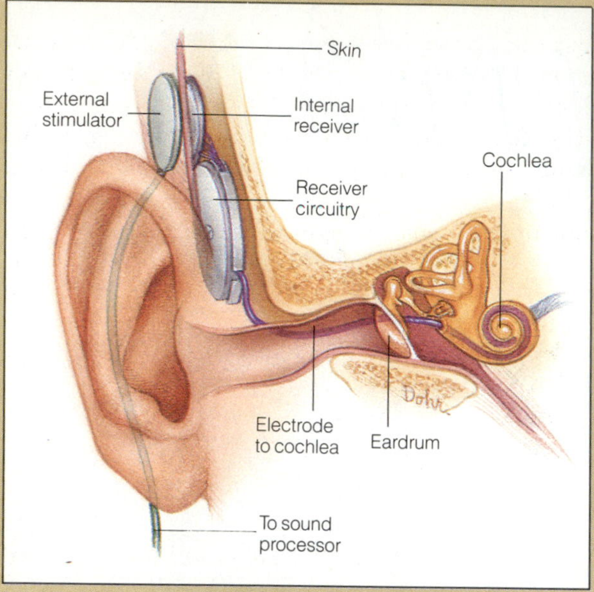

Fig. 4-17 *A cochlear implant, or "artificial ear."*

Question: What causes deafness?

Deafness There are three principal types of deafness. **Conduction deafness** occurs when the eardrums or ossicles are damaged or immobilized by disease or injury. Such damage reduces the transfer of sounds to the inner ear. In many cases conduction deafness can be overcome by a hearing aid, which makes sounds louder and clearer. **Nerve deafness** is a hearing loss resulting from damage to the hair cells or auditory nerve. Hearing aids are of no help in this case, because auditory messages are blocked from reaching the brain. However, a new artificial hearing system is making it possible for some persons with nerve deafness to break through the wall of silence. (See Box 4-1.)

A third problem, called **stimulation deafness,** is of special interest because many jobs, hobbies, and pastimes can cause it. Stimulation deafness occurs when very loud sounds damage hair cells in the cochlea. If you work in a noisy environment, or if you enjoy loud music, motorcycling, snowmobiling, hunting, or similar pursuits, you may be risking stimulation deafness. The hair cells, which are about as thick as a cobweb, are extremely fragile and easily damaged.

Question: How loud must a sound be to be hazardous?

The danger of hearing loss depends on both the loudness of sound and the length of exposure. Daily exposure to 85 decibels or more may cause permanent hearing loss. Short periods of exposure to 120 decibels (a rock concert) may cause a **temporary threshold shift,** or temporary loss of hearing. Even brief exposure to 150 decibels (jet airplane nearby) can cause permanent deafness (Apfel, 1977; Lipscomb, 1974).

You might find it interesting to check the decibel ratings of some of your activities in Fig. 4-18 as a way of estimating hearing risk. Notice that music, as well as noise, can do damage. People who sit directly in front of the speaker columns at highly amplified musical concerts run considerable risk of hearing loss. Walkman-style stereo headphones also present a danger. If the sound from the headset you are wearing can be heard by someone standing next to you, the volume is probably damaging your ears.

Conduction deafness Deafness that occurs when sounds are not fully transferred from the eardrum to the inner ear.

Nerve deafness Deafness caused by damage to the hair cells or auditory nerve.

Stimulation deafness Deafness resulting from damage caused by exposure to excessively loud sounds.

Temporary threshold shift A temporary decrease in sensitivity to sound.

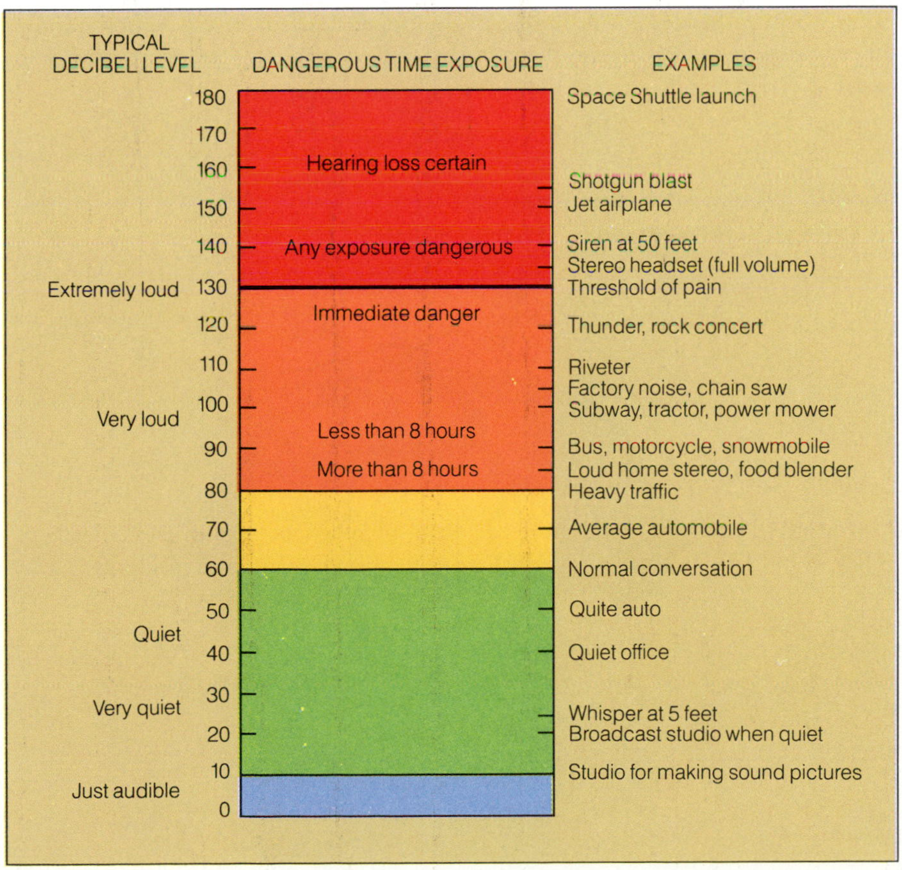

Fig. 4-18 *The loudness of sound is measured in decibels. Zero decibels is the faintest sound most people can hear. Sound in the range of 110 decibels is uncomfortably loud. Prolonged exposure to sounds above 85 decibels may damage the inner ear. Rock music, which may rate 120 decibels, is known to have caused hearing loss in musicians and may affect audiences as well. Sounds of 130 decibels pose an immediate danger to hearing.*

If a ringing sensation known as **tinnitus** (tin-NYE-tus) follows exposure to loud sounds, chances are that hair cells have been damaged (Dunkle, 1982; McFadden & Wightman, 1983). Almost everyone experiences tinnitus at times. But after repeated sounds that produce this warning, you can expect to become permanently hard-of-hearing (Apfel, 1977). The next time you are exposed to an excessively loud sound, remember Figure 4-18 and take precautions against damage. (Remember, too, that for temporary ear protection, fingers are always handy.)

Smell and Taste— The Nose Knows When the Tongue Can't Tell

Unless you are a wine taster, a perfume blender, chef, or gourmet, you may think of **olfaction** (smell) and **gustation** (taste) as least important among the senses. Certainly, a person could survive without these two **chemical senses**. Just the same, the chemical senses occasionally prevent poisonings and daily add pleasure to our lives. Let's see how they operate.

The Sense of Smell The receptors for smell respond primarily to gaseous molecules carried in the air. As air enters the nose, it passes over millions of nerve fibers embedded in the lining of the upper nasal passages. Airborne molecules passing over the exposed fibers trigger nerve signals that are sent to the brain (see Fig. 4-19).

Fig. 4-19 *Receptors for the sense of smell (olfaction). Olfactory nerve fibers respond to gaseous molecules. Receptor cells are shown in cross section at left of part* (a).

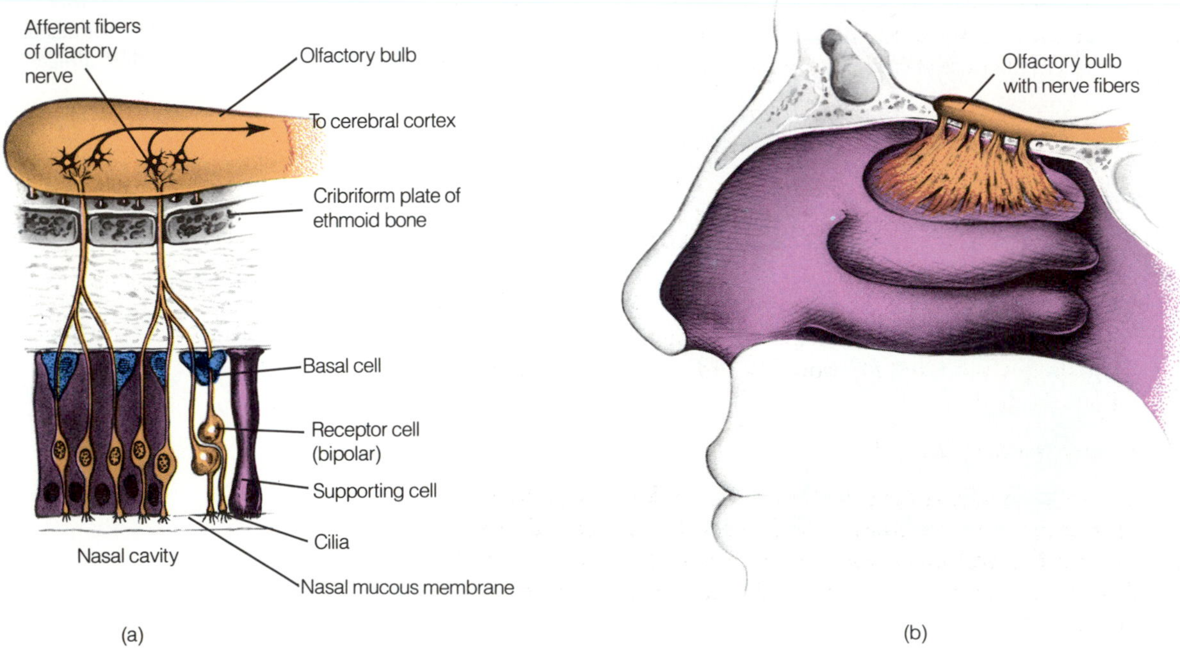

Question: How are different odors produced?

This is still something of a mystery. One hint comes from the fact that it is possible to develop a sort of "smell blindness" for a single odor. This loss, called an **anosmia** (an-NOSE-me-ah), suggests that there are specific receptors for different odors. Indeed, scientists have noticed that molecules having a particular odor are quite similar in shape. Specific shapes have been identified for the following odors: *floral* (flowerlike), *camphoric* (camphorlike), *musky* (Have you ever smelled a sweaty musk ox?), *minty* (mintlike), and *etherish* (like ether or cleaning fluid). Scientists currently believe that there are different shaped "holes," or depressions, on the odor receptors. Like a piece fit in a puzzle, a molecule produces an odor when it matches up with a hole of the same shape. This is called the **lock and key theory**. Although there are some exceptions, the theory seems to explain many odors.

Taste There are at least four basic taste sensations: sweet, salt, sour, and bitter. We are most sensitive to bitter, next to sour, less sensitive to salt, and least sensitive to sweet. This order may have helped prevent poisonings during earlier times when humans foraged for food, because bitter and sour foods are more likely to be inedible.

Question: If there are only four tastes, how can there be so many different flavors?

Flavors seem more varied than suggested by the four taste qualities because we tend to include sensations of texture, temperature, smell, and even pain ("hot" chili peppers) along with taste. Smell is particularly important in determining flavor. Small bits of apple, potato, and onion "taste" almost exactly alike when the nose is plugged. It is probably no exaggeration to say that subjective flavor is one-half smell. This is why food loses its "taste" when you have a cold.

The four primary tastes are detected by **taste buds** located mainly on the top of the tongue but also at other points inside the mouth (see Fig. 4-20). As food is chewed, it dissolves and enters the taste buds, where it sets off nerve impulses to the brain. As you can see in Fig. 4-20, taste receptors are not equally distributed: Some areas of the tongue are more sensitive to certain tastes than others.

The Somesthetic Senses—Flying by the Seat of Your Pants

A gymnast "flying" through a routine on the uneven bars may rely as much on the **somesthetic senses** as on vision. Even the most routine activities, such as walking, running, or passing a sobriety test, would be impossible without somesthetic information from the body.

Question: What are the somesthetic senses?

The somesthetic senses (*soma*: body; *esthetic*: feel) include the **skin senses** (touch), the **kinesthetic senses** (receptors in the muscles and joints that detect body position and movement), and the **vestibular senses** (receptors in the inner ear that signal balance—and contribute to motion sickness). Because of their importance, let us focus on the skin senses.

Tinnitus A ringing or buzzing sensation in the ears not caused by an external stimulus.

Olfaction The sense of smell.

Gustation The sense of taste.

Chemical senses Senses responsive to the presence of chemical stimuli (smell and taste).

Anosmia Loss or impairment of the sense of smell.

Lock and key theory The theory of olfaction which holds that odors are related to the shapes of chemical molecules.

Taste bud The receptor organ for taste.

Somesthetic sense Pertaining to sensations produced by the skin, muscles, joints, viscera, and organs of balance.

Skin senses The senses of touch, pressure, pain, heat, and cold.

Kinesthetic senses The senses whose organs lie in the muscles, tendons, and joints; the muscle senses.

Vestibular senses The senses of balance, body position, and acceleration.

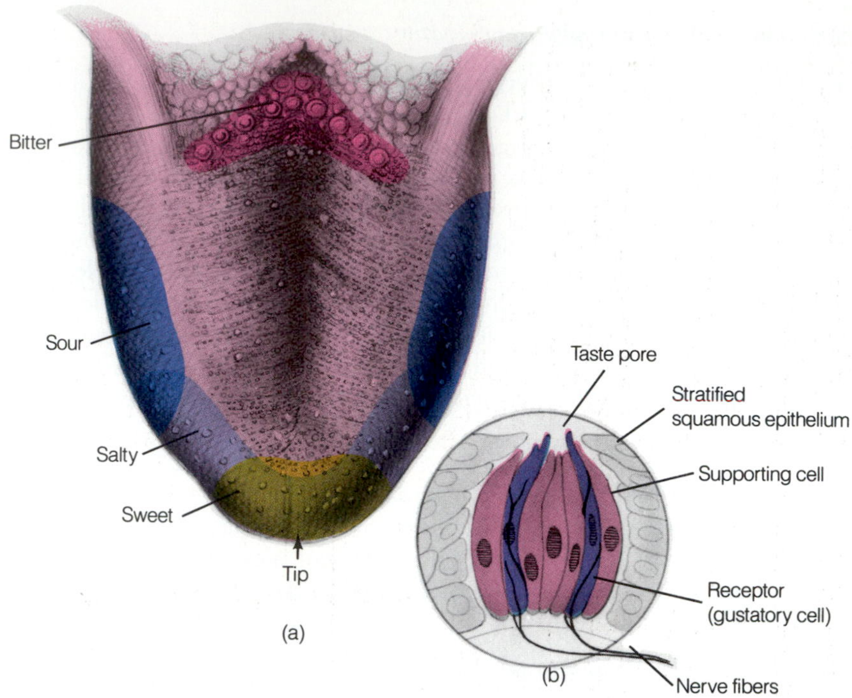

Fig. 4-20 *Receptors for taste:* (a) *Position of receptors (taste buds) especially sensitive to four taste qualities.* (b) *Detail of a taste bud within the tongue. The buds also occur in other parts of the digestive system.*

Skin receptors produce at least five different sensations: *light touch, pressure, pain, cold,* and *warmth.* Receptors with particular shapes appear to specialize somewhat in various sensations (see Fig. 4-21). However, the surface of the eye, which only has free nerve endings, produces all five sensations, so receptor shape is not critical (Carlson, 1981). Altogether, the skin has about 200,000 nerve endings for temperature, 500,000 for touch and pressure, and 3 million for pain.

Question: Does the number of receptors in an area of skin relate to its sensitivity?

Yes. Your skin could be "mapped" by applying heat, cold, touch, pressure, or pain to points all over your body. This procedure would show that the skin receptors are found in varying numbers and that sensitivity corresponds roughly to the number of receptors in a given area. As a rough-and-ready illustration, try this two-point touch test:

> The density of touch receptors on various body areas can be checked by having a friend apply two pencil points to your skin a number of times, varying the distance between the points each time. Without looking, you should respond "one" or "two" each time. Record the distance between the pencils whenever you experience the touch as two points rather than one.

You should find that two points are recognizable when they are 1⁄10 inch apart on the fingertips, 1⁄4 inch on the nose, and 3 inches at the middle of the back. Generally speaking, important areas such as the lips, tongue, face, hands, and genitals have higher concentrations of receptors.

Question: There are many more pain receptors than other kinds. Why is pain so heavily represented, and does the concentration of pain receptors also vary?

Like the other skin senses, pain receptors vary in their distribution. There is an average of about 232 pain points per square centimeter behind the knee, 184 per centimeter on the buttocks (an area preferred by many parents for spankings), 60 on the pad of the thumb, and 44 on the tip of the nose (Geldard, 1972). (Is it better, then, to be pinched on the nose than behind the knee? It depends on what you like!)

Actually, there are two kinds of pain. Pain carried by *large* nerve fibers is sharp, bright, fast, and associated with specific body areas. This is the body's **warning system**. Give yourself a small jab with a pin and you will feel this type of pain. As you do this, notice that warning pain quickly disappears. A second type of pain is carried by *small* nerve fibers. This type is slower, nagging, aching, widespread, and very unpleasant. It gets worse if the pain stimulus is repeated. This is the body's **reminding system** (Melzack & Dennis, 1978). A sad thing about the reminding system is that it often produces agony even when the re-

Fig. 4-21 *The skin senses include touch, pressure, pain, cold, and warmth. This drawing shows different forms the skin receptors can take. Other shapes were once recognized, but most turned out to be variations of the shapes shown. The only clearly specialized receptor is the Pacinian corpuscle, which is highly sensitive to pressure. Free nerve endings are receptors for pain and any of the other sensations. For reasons that are not clear, cold is sensed near the surface of the skin, and warmth is sensed deeper.* (Carlson, 1981)

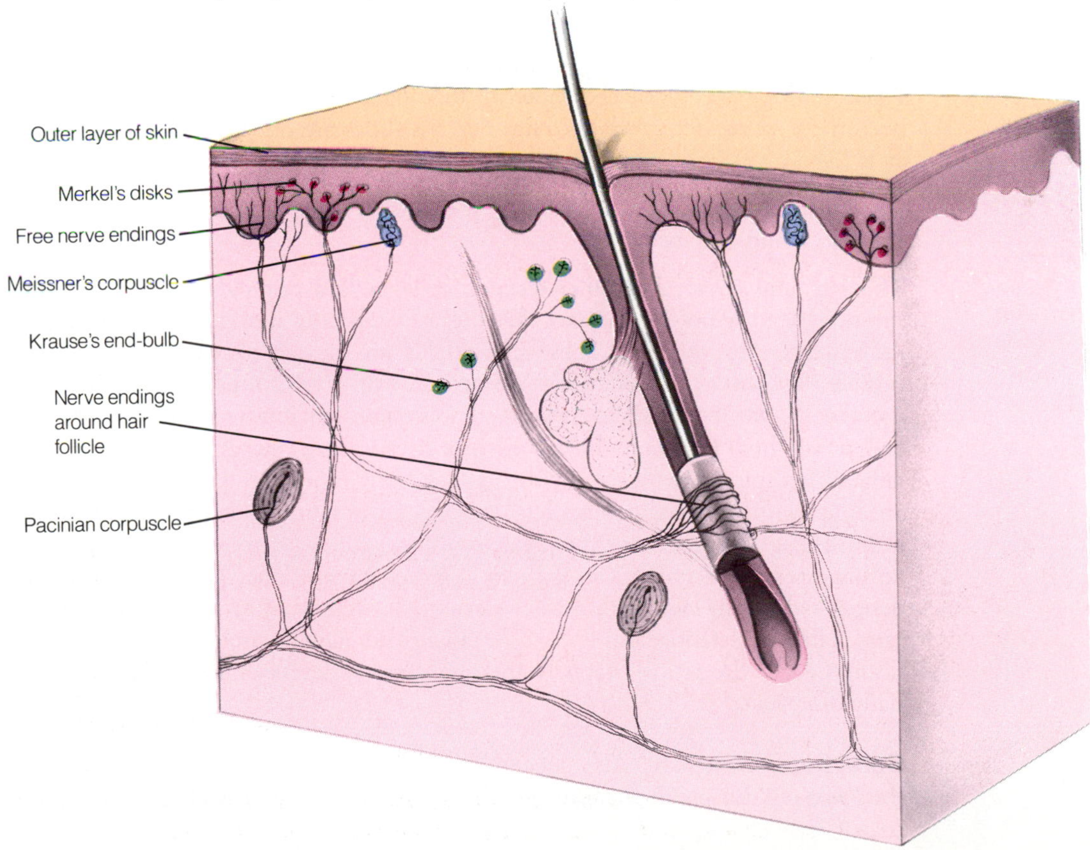

minder is useless, as in terminal cancer or when pain continues after an injury has healed. Later in the chapter we will return to pain to learn how it can be controlled. If you got carried away with the pin demonstration, maybe you should read ahead now....

Adaptation, Attention, and Gating—Tuning In and Tuning Out

Even though each of the senses we have described is continuously active, many sensory events never reach awareness. One reason for this is *sensory adaptation*, a second is *selective attention*, and a third is *sensory gating*. Let's see how information gets filtered by these processes.

Sensory Adaptation Think about walking into a house where fried fish, sauerkraut, and head cheese were prepared for dinner. (Some dinner!) You would probably pass out at the door, yet people who have been in the house for some time will be unaware of the food odors because of **sensory adaptation**. Sensory adaptation refers to a decrease in sensory response that accompanies a constant or unchanging stimulus.

Fortunately, the olfactory (smell) receptors are among the most quickly adapting. When exposed to a constant odor, they send fewer and fewer nerve impulses to the brain, until the odor is no longer noticed. Adaptation to sensations of pressure from a wristwatch, waistband, ring, or glasses is based on the same principle. Sensory receptors generally respond best to *changes* in stimulation. As David Hubel says, "We need above all to know about changes; no one wants or needs to be reminded 16 hours a day that his shoes are on" (Hubel, 1979).

Question: If change is necessary to prevent sensory adaptation, why doesn't vision undergo adaptation like the sense of smell does? If you stare at something, it certainly doesn't go away.

The rods and cones, like other receptor cells, would respond less to a constant stimulus were it not for the fact that the eye normally makes thousands of tiny movements every minute. These movements are caused by tremors in the eye muscles known as **physiological nystagmus** (nih-STAG-mus). Although these movements are too small to be seen, they shift visual images from one receptor cell to another. Constant shifting ensures that images always fall on fresh, unfatigued receptors. Evidence for this comes from experiments in which subjects are fitted with a special contact lens that has a miniature slide projector attached to it (see Fig. 4-22*a*). Since the projector follows the exact movements of the eye, an image can be stabilized on the retina. When this is done, projected geometric designs fade from view within a few seconds (Pritchard, 1961). You can get the same effect by staring at Fig. 4-22*b*. Since the lighter circle does not form a distinct edge, the retina adapts to the brightness difference, and the circle gradually disappears.

Selective Attention Also dependent on the functioning of sensory systems is the "seat-of-your-pants phenomenon." As you sit reading this chapter, receptors for touch and pressure in the seat of your pants are sending nerve impulses to your brain. Even though these sensations have been present all along, you were probably not aware of them until just now. The seat-of-your-pants phenomenon is an example of **selective attention.** Through selective attention, we are able to tune in on any of the many sensory messages bombarding us while excluding others. Another familiar example of this is the "cocktail party effect." When you are in a group of people, surrounded by voices, you can still select out and attend to the voice of the person with whom you are conversing. Or if that person gets dull, you can eavesdrop on conversations all over the room. (Be sure to smile and nod your head occasionally!)

Sensory adaptation A reduction in sensory response to unchanging stimuli.

Nystagmus Any involuntary vibration, oscillation, or movement of the eye.

Selective attention Voluntarily focusing on some stimulus or some portion of incoming sensory information.

Sensory gating Physiological control of the incoming flow of sensory messages.

Question: What makes this possible?

Selective attention appears to be based on the ability of various brain structures to select and divert incoming sensory messages (see Chapter 3). But what about messages on their way to the brain? Is it possible that some are blocked while others are allowed to pass? Recent evidence suggests there are **sensory gates** that control the flow of incoming nerve impulses in just this way.

Sensory Gating A fascinating example of sensory gating is provided by the work of Ronald Melzack and Patrick Wall, who are studying "pain gates" in the spinal cord (Melzack & Dennis, 1978; Wall, 1976). Melzack and Wall noticed, as you may have, that one type of pain will sometimes cancel another. This suggests that pain messages from different nerve fibers pass through the same neural "gate" in the spinal cord. If the gate is "closed" by one pain message, other messages may not be able to pass through.

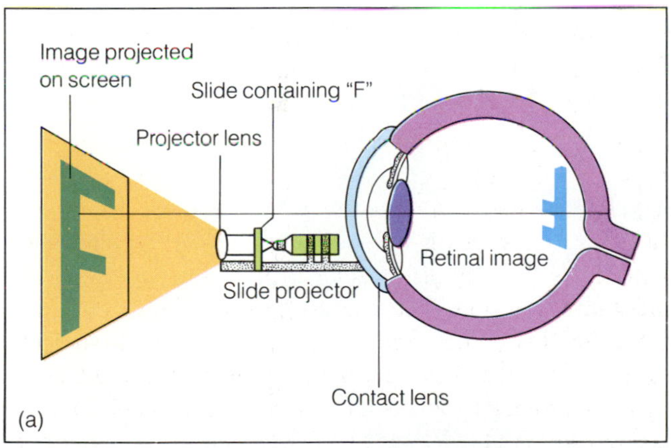

Fig. 4-22 *Stabilized images.* (a) *Miniature slide projector attached to a contact lens moves each time the eye moves. As a result the projected image disappears in a few seconds because it does not move on the retina.* (b) *A similar effect occurs when changes in brightness do not define a distinct edge. In this case eye movements cannot prevent adaptation: Therefore, if you stare at the dot, the lighter area will disappear. (After Cornsweet, 1970)*

Acupuncture The Chinese medical art of relieving pain and treating illness by inserting thin needles at various points on the body.

Beta endorphin A natural brain chemical similar in structure to morphine with powerful pain-killing properties.

Question: How is the gate closed?

Messages carried by large, fast nerve fibers seem to close the spinal pain gate directly. Doing so can prevent slower, "reminding system" pain from reaching the brain. Pain clinics use this effect by applying a mild electrical current to the skin. Such stimulation, felt only as a mild tingling, can greatly reduce more agonizing pain (Melzack & Dennis, 1978).

Messages from small, slow fibers seem to take a different route. After going through the pain gate, they pass on to a "central biasing system" in the brain. Under some circumstances the brain then sends a message back down the spinal cord, closing the pain gates (Melzack & Dennis, 1978) (see Fig. 4-23). Melzack and Wall believe this type of gating explains the pain-killing effects of **acupuncture.** As the acupuncturist's needles are twirled, heated, or electrified, they activate small pain fibers. These relay through the biasing system to close the gates to intense or chronic pain.

Acupuncture has an interesting side effect not predicted by sensory gating. People undergoing acupuncture often report feelings of light-headedness, relaxation, or euphoria. How are these feelings explained? The answer seems to lie in the body's newly discovered ability to produce opiatelike chemicals. To combat pain the brain releases a chemical called **beta-endorphin** (BAY-tah-en-DOR-fin), which is similar to morphine (Snyder & Childers, 1979). Both acupuncture and electrical stimulation cause a buildup of endorphins in the brain. In other words, the nervous system makes its own "drugs" to block pain. Actually, this ties in nicely with the idea of pain gates. The central biasing system, which closes pain

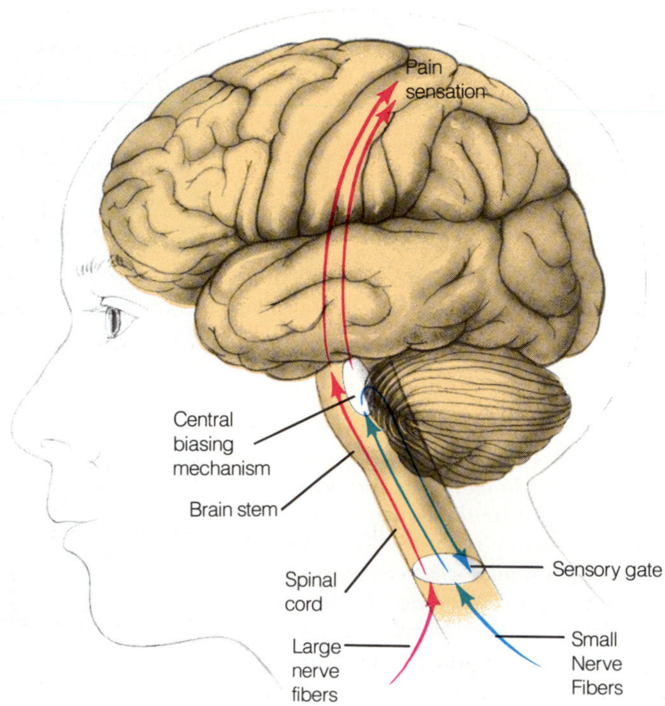

Fig. 4-23 *Diagram of a sensory gate for pain. A series of pain impulses going through the gate may prevent other pain messages from passing through. Or, pain messages may relay through a "central biasing mechanism" that exerts control over the gate, closing it to other impulses.*

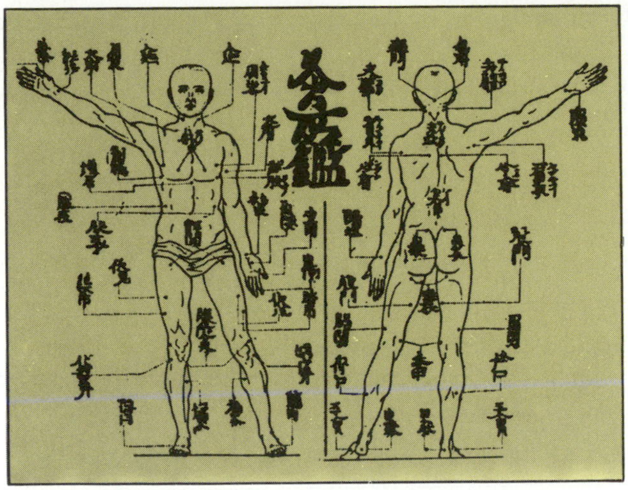

Fig. 4-24 *An acupuncturist's chart. Modern research has begun to explain the pain-killing effects of acupuncture. (See text.)*

gates in the spinal cord, is highly sensitive to morphine and other opiate painkillers (Melzack & Dennis, 1978).

The discovery of endorphins and their pain-killing effect has caused quite a stir in psychology. At long last it appears possible to explain a number of puzzling phenomena, including runner's "high," masochism, acupuncture, and the euphoria sometimes associated with childbirth and painful initiation rites in primitive cultures. In each instance there is reason to believe that pain and stress cause the brain to release endorphins (Kruger & Liebskind, 1984). These in turn induce feelings of pleasure or euphoria similar to morphine intoxication (Cannon et al., 1978). The "high" often felt by long-distance runners serves as a good example of this effect. In one experiment subjects were tested for pain tolerance. After running 1 mile, each was tested again. In the second test all could withstand pain about 70 percent longer than before. The runners were then given naloxone, a drug that blocks the effects of endorphins. Following another mile run, the subjects were tested again. This time they had lost their earlier protection from pain (Haier et al., 1981). People who say they are "addicted" to running may be closer to the truth than they realize. And more importantly, we may at last have an explanation for those hardy souls who take hot saunas followed by cold showers!

Since you may not want to try acupuncture or electrical stimulation to control everyday pain, the Applications section that follows describes some practical ways of reducing pain. Before we turn to this useful topic, here's a Learning Check.

Learning Check

1. Which of the following is *not* important for the transduction of sound? (circle)

pinna ossicles phosphenes oval window hair cells

2. Daily exposure to sounds with a loudness of ________ decibles may cause permanent hearing loss.

3. Cochlear implants have been used primarily to overcome
a. conduction deafness *b.* stimulation deafness *c.* nerve deafness *d.* tinnitus

4. Olfaction appears to be at least partially explained by the ______________________________ theory of molecule shapes and receptor sites.

5. From the standpoint of survival, we are fortunate that bitter tastes register primarily on the tip of the tongue. T or F?

6. Which of the following is a somesthetic sense? (circle)

   gustation olfaction rarefaction kinesthesis

7. Warning pain is carried by ______________ nerve fibers.

8. Sensory adaptation refers to an increase in sensory response that accompanies a constant or unchanging stimulus. T or F?

9. The brain-centered ability to influence what sensations we will receive is called (circle):

   sensory gating central adaptation selective attention sensory biasing

10. The pain-killing effects of acupuncture appear to result from ______________ ______________.

Answers: **1.** phosphenes **2.** 85 **3.** c **4.** lock and key **5.** F **6.** kinesthesis **7.** large **8.** F **9.** selective attention **10.** sensory gating

Applications

Controlling Pain—This Won't Hurt a Bit

Earlier sections of this chapter have dealt with useful information about each of the senses. Because so many applications have already been discussed, this will be a short discussion. Let's see how several ideas from this chapter can help you cope better with pain.

There are many indications that pain may be controlled psychologically. In India, fakirs pierce their cheeks with needles or sit on beds of spikes. In other cultures people endure tatooing, stretching, cutting, burning, and the like, with little apparent pain. How is such insensitivity achieved? There is no evidence that these people lack normal pain responses. Very likely the answer lies in four factors that can be used by anyone to alter the amount of pain felt in a particular situation. These are: (1) **anxiety,** (2) **control,** (3) **attention,** and (4) **interpretation.**

Anxiety The basic sensory message of pain can be separated from emotional reactions to it (Melzack, 1978). Studies have consistently shown that fear or high levels of anxiety increase pain (Barber, 1959). A dramatic reversal of this effect is the surprising *lack* of pain displayed by soldiers wounded in battle. Being excused from further combat apparently produces such relief that it leaves many soldiers insensitive to wounds that would agonize a civilian (Melzack, 1974).

Control A moment's reflection should convince you that pain over which you have no control is particularly upsetting. Loss of control seems to increase pain by increasing anxiety and emotional distress. People who are allowed to regulate, avoid, or control a painful stimulus suffer less (Craig, 1978). In general, the more control one *feels* over a painful stimulus, the less pain experienced (Kruger & Liebskind, 1984).

Attention Distraction can also radically reduce pain. Pain, even though it is highly persistent, can be selectively tuned out (at least partially) just like any other sensation. Subjects in one experiment who were exposed to intense pain experienced the greatest relief when they were distracted by the task of viewing color slides and describing them aloud (Kanfer & Goldfoot, 1968). In another experiment, pain was lessened when subjects concentrated on trying to name all their high school courses and teachers

Applications: Controlling Pain, continued

(Ahles et al., 1983). For the same reason, you may have temporarily forgotten about a toothache or similar pain while absorbed in a movie or book.

Interpretation The meaning or interpretation given a painful stimulus also affects pain (Keefe, 1982). For example, if you give a child a swat on the behind while playing, you'll probably get a burst of laughter. Yet the same swat given as punishment may bring tears. Childbirth provides a similar example. In some cultures birth is considered a relatively painless natural event, which it usually is for women reared in the culture. In our culture childbirth tends to be associated with fear and stress (Bresler & Trubo, 1979). It's not surprising, then, that painkillers are often required by women giving birth in the United States. The effects of interpretation have also been demonstrated in the lab. In one experiment it was found that thinking of pain as pleasurable (denying the pain) greatly increased pain tolerance (Neufeld, 1970).

Coping with Pain

Question: How can these facts be applied?

In a sense they have already been applied to childbirth. **Prepared childbirth training,** which emphasizes birth without drugs or painkillers, utilizes all four factors. To prepare for natural childbirth, the prospective mother learns in great detail what to expect at each stage of labor. This greatly relieves her fears and anxieties. During labor she pays attention to important sensations indicating the progress of labor and adjusts her breathing accordingly. Her attention is directed to sensations other than pain, and her positive attitude is maintained by use of the term *contractions* rather than *labor pains*. Finally, because of her months of preparation, and because of her active participation, she feels *in control* of the situation.

Reduced anxiety, redirected attention, and added control can be applied to other painful circumstances. In any situation where pain can be anticipated (a trip to the doctor, dentist, and so on), lowered anxiety may be achieved by making sure that you are *fully informed*. Be sure that everything that will happen or could happen to you is explained, and fully discuss any fears you have. If you are physically tense, the use of relaxation exercises can help lower your level of arousal. (Relaxation techniques are described in detail in the Chapter 22 Applications section. The desensitization procedure described there may also help reduce anxiety.)

Distraction and Reinterpretation Some dentists are now equipped to help you shift attention away from pain. Patients are actively distracted with video games and with headphones carrying music. Some dentists even put a clothespin on the patient's ear as a pain aid. In other situations you can shift attention away from pain by focusing on some external object. Pick a tree outside a window, a design on the wall, or some other stimulus and examine it in great detail. Prior practice in meditation can be a tremendous aid to such attention shifts. (Meditation techniques are described in Chapter 6.) Recent research suggests that distraction of this type works best for mild or brief pain. For chronic or strong pain, reinterpretation is more effective (McCaul & Malott, 1984).

Question: Is there any way to increase control over a painful stimulus?

Counterirritation Practically speaking, the possibilities may be limited. You may be able to arrange a signal with a doctor or dentist that will give you control over whether a painful procedure will continue. A second possibility is more unusual. Ronald Melzack's gate-control theory of pain suggests that sending *mild* pain messages to the spinal cord and brain may effectively close the neurological gates to more severe or unpredictable pain. Medical texts have long recognized this effect. Physicians have found that intense surface stimulation of the skin can control pain from other parts of the body, and that a brief, mildly painful stimulus can relieve more severe pain.

Applications: Controlling Pain, continued

Such procedures, known as **counterirritation**, are evident in some of the oldest techniques used to control pain: applying ice packs, hot-water bottles, or mustard packs to other parts of the body (Melzack, 1974).

This suggests a way to minimize pain that is based on increased control, counterirritation, and production of endorphins. If you pinch yourself, you can easily *create and endure* pain equal to that produced by many medical procedures (receiving an injection, having a tooth drilled, and so on). The pain doesn't seem too bad because you have control over it, and it is predictable. This fact might be used to *mask* one pain with a second painful stimulus that is under your control. For instance, if you are having a tooth filled, try pinching yourself or digging a fingernail into a knuckle while the dentist is working. Focus your attention on the pain you are creating, and increase its intensity any time the dentist's work becomes more painful. This suggestion may not work for you, but casual observation suggests that it can be a useful technique for controlling pain in some circumstances. Generations of children have used it to take the edge off of a spanking.

Learning Check

1. Like heightened anxiety, increased control tends to increase subjective pain. T or F?
2. In one experiment, subjects given the task of viewing color slides and describing them aloud experienced relief from pain. T or F?
3. Imagining a pleasant experience can be an effective way of reducing pain in some situations. T or F?
4. The concept of counterirritation holds that relaxation and desensitization are key elements of pain control. T or F?

Answers **1.** F **2.** T **3.** T **4.** F

Chapter Summary

- Sensory organs *transduce* physical energies into nerve impulses. Due to limited responsiveness, selectivity, *feature detection*, and *coding* patterns, the senses act as *data reduction systems*. Sensory response can be partially understood in terms of *localization of function* in the brain.
- The minimum amount of physical energy necessary to produce a sensation defines the *absolute threshold*. The study of thresholds and related topics is called *psychophysics*.
- Threatening or anxiety-provoking stimuli may raise the threshold for recognition, an effect called *perceptual defense*. Any stimulus below the level of conscious awareness is said to be *subliminal*. There is some evidence that *subliminal perception* occurs, but subliminal advertising is largely ineffective.
- The *visible spectrum* consists of electromagnetic radiation in a narrow range. The eye is in some ways like a camera, but ultimately it is a visual system, not a photographic one.

- Four common visual defects, correctable with glasses, are *myopia* (nearsightedness), *hyperopia* (farsightedness), *presbyopia* (loss of accommodation), and *astigmatism*.
- The *rods* and *cones* are *photoreceptors* making up the *retina* of the eye. The rods specialize in night vision, black and white reception, and motion detection. The cones, found exclusively in the *fovea* and otherwise toward the middle of the eye, specialize in color vision, *acuity* or perception of fine detail, and daylight vision. Much *peripheral vision* is supplied by the rods.
- The rods and cones differ in color sensitivity. Yellowish green is brightest for cones, blue-green for the rods (although they will see it as colorless). Color vision in the retina is explained by the *trichromatic theory*, and in the visual system beyond the eyes, by the *opponent-process theory*.
- Total color blindness is rare, but 8 percent of males and 1 percent of females are red-green color blind or color weak. Color blindness is a sex-linked trait carried on the X chromosome. Color blindness is revealed by the *Ishihara test*.
- *Dark adaptation*, an increase in sensitivity to light, is caused by increased concentration of visual pigments in both the rods and the cones, but mainly by recombination of *rhodopsin* in the rods. Vitamin A deficiencies may cause *night blindness*.
- *Sound waves* are the stimulus for hearing. They are transduced by the *eardrum*, *auditory ossicles*, *oval window*, *cochlea*, and, ultimately, the *hair cells*. Three basic types of deafness are: *nerve deafness*, *conduction deafness*, and *stimulation deafness*.
- *Olfaction* (smell) and *gustation* (taste) are *chemical* senses responsive to airborne or liquified molecules. The *lock and key* theory partially explains smell. Specific areas on the tongue are more responsive to sweet, salty, sour, and bitter tastes.
- The *somesthetic* senses include the *skin senses, vestibular senses*, and *kinesthetic senses*. The skin senses include touch, pressure, pain, cold, and warmth. Sensitivity to each is related to the number of receptors present.
- Incoming sensations are affected by *sensory adaptation* (a reduction in the number of nerve impulses sent), by *selective attention* (selection and diversion of messages in the brain), and by *sensory gating* (blocking or alteration of messages flowing toward the brain). Selective gating of pain messages apparently takes place in the spinal cord.
- Pain is greatly affected by *anxiety*, *attention*, *control* over the stimulus, the *interpretation* placed on an experience, and by *counterirritation*. Pain can therefore be reduced by controlling these factors.

Chapter 5

Perception

Chapter Preview

Murder!

The following is a true account. Only the degree of exaggeration has been changed for educational purposes.

I was in a supermarket when a girl suddenly came running around a corner. She looked back and screamed, "Stop! Stop! You're killing him! You're killing my father!" Naturally I was interested! As I hurriedly retraced her path, I was greeted by a grisly scene. There was a man stretched out on the floor with another on top of him. The guy on top was huge; at 6 feet 6 inches tall and 300 pounds, he looked only half human. He had his victim by the throat and was beating his head against the floor. There was blood everywhere. I decided to do the right thing. I ran. . . .

By the time the store manager and I returned to the "scene of the crime," the police were just arriving. It took quite a while to straighten things out, but here are the facts that emerged: The "guy on the bottom" had passed out and hit his head. This caused the cut (actually quite minor) that accounted for the "blood everywhere." The "guy on top" had seen the first man fall and was trying to prevent him from further injuring himself while unconscious. He was also loosening the man's collar.

If I had never returned, I would have sworn in court that I had seen a murder. The girl's description completely determined my own perceptions. This perhaps is understandable. But what I will never forget is the shock I felt when I met the "murderer"—the man I had seen a few moments before, in broad daylight, as a huge, vicious, horrible-looking creature. The man was not a stranger. He was a neighbor of mine. I had seen him dozens of times before. I know him by name. He is a rather small man.

The last chapter discussed sensation, the process of bringing information into the nervous system. This chapter is about **perception,** *or how we assemble sensations into a usable "picture" of the world. As we perceive events, the brain actively selects, organizes, and integrates sensory information. These mental processes are done so automatically that we are rarely aware of them. It may, in fact, take misperceptions as drastic as the one just described to call attention to this marvelous process. Perception creates faces, melodies, works of art, illusions, and, on occasion, "murders" out of the raw material of sensation. Let us see how this is accomplished.*

Survey Questions What are perceptual constancies and what is their role in perception? What basic principles do we use to group sensations into meaningful patterns? How is it possible to see depth and to judge distance? What effect does learning have on perception? How is perception altered by motives, values, and expectations? Is extrasensory perception possible? How reliable are eyewitness reports?

Perceptual Constancies—Taming an Unruly World

What would it be like to have your vision restored after a lifetime of blindness? In reality a first look at the world can be disappointing. A newly sighted person must *learn* to identify objects, read clocks, numbers, and letters, and judge sizes and distances (Senden, 1960). Indeed, learning to "see" can be quite frustrating. Richard Gregory (1977) has described the experiences of Mr. S. B., a 52-year-old cataract patient who had been blind since birth.

After an operation restored his sight, Mr. S. B. struggled to use his vision. At first, for instance, he could only judge distance in situations already familiar to him. One day, he was found crawling out of his hospital room window to get a closer look at the automobile traffic on the street. His curiosity is understandable, but he had to be restrained. His room was on the fourth floor!

Question: How could Mr. S. B. try to crawl out of a fourth-story window? Couldn't he at least tell distance from the size of the cars?

No, because using size to judge distance requires familiarity with the appearance of objects. Try holding your left hand a few inches in front of your eyes and your right hand at arm's length. The image of your right hand should be about half the size of your left hand. Still, because of the countless times you have viewed your hands from different distances, you know your right hand has not shrunk. This is called **size constancy.** The perceived size of an object remains the same even though the size of its retinal image changes.

In order to perceive your hand accurately, you had to draw on past experience. Some perceptions—like seeing a line on a piece of paper—are so basic they seem to be **native** (inborn). But much perception is **empirical,** or based on prior experience (Julesz, 1975). For example, Turnbull (1961) tells of the time he brought a Pygmy from the dense rain forests of Africa to the vast African plains. The Pygmy had no past experience with seeing objects at great distance. Hence, the first time he saw a herd of buffalo in the distance, he thought they were a swarm of insects. Imagine his confusion when he was then driven toward the animals. He concluded that witchcraft was being used to fool him because the "insects" seemed to grow into buffalo before his eyes.

Perhaps you have also experienced the failure of size constancy in unfamiliar situations. When viewed from an airplane, cars, houses, and people no longer seem normal in size; instead, they begin to look like toys.

A second important constancy is **shape constancy.** Shape constancy can be demonstrated by looking at this page from directly overhead and then from an angle. Obviously, the page is rectangular, but most of the time the image that

Resources

Perception The mental process of organizing sensations into meaningful patterns.

Size constancy The perceived size of objects remains unchanged despite changes in the size of the images they cast on the retina.

Shape constancy The perceived shape of objects is unaltered by changes in the shape of their images on the retina.

reaches your eye is distorted. In spite of this, there is no tendency for you to assume the book changes shape when the image does. (For additional examples see Fig. 5-1.)

Let's say that you are outside in bright sunlight with a friend who is wearing a white blouse. Suddenly a cloud shades the sun. It might seem that the blouse would grow dimmer, but it still appears bright white. This happens because the blouse continues to reflect a larger *proportion* of light than surrounding objects. The principle of **brightness constancy** states that the apparent brightness of an object stays the same under changing lighting conditions.

To summarize, the energy patterns reaching our senses are constantly changing, even when they come from the same object. Size, shape, and brightness constancy rescue us from a potentially confusing world in which objects would seem to shrink and grow, change shape as if made of rubber, and light up or fade like neon lamps. Establishing these constancies was only one of the hurdles Mr. S. B. faced in learning to "see." In the next section we will consider some others.

Perceptual Grouping—Getting It All Together

William James said that "to the infant the world is just a big, booming, buzzing confusion." Like an infant, Mr. S. B. had to find meaning in his visual sensations. He was soon able to tell time from a large wall clock and to recognize block letters he had previously known only from touch. At a zoo he recognized an

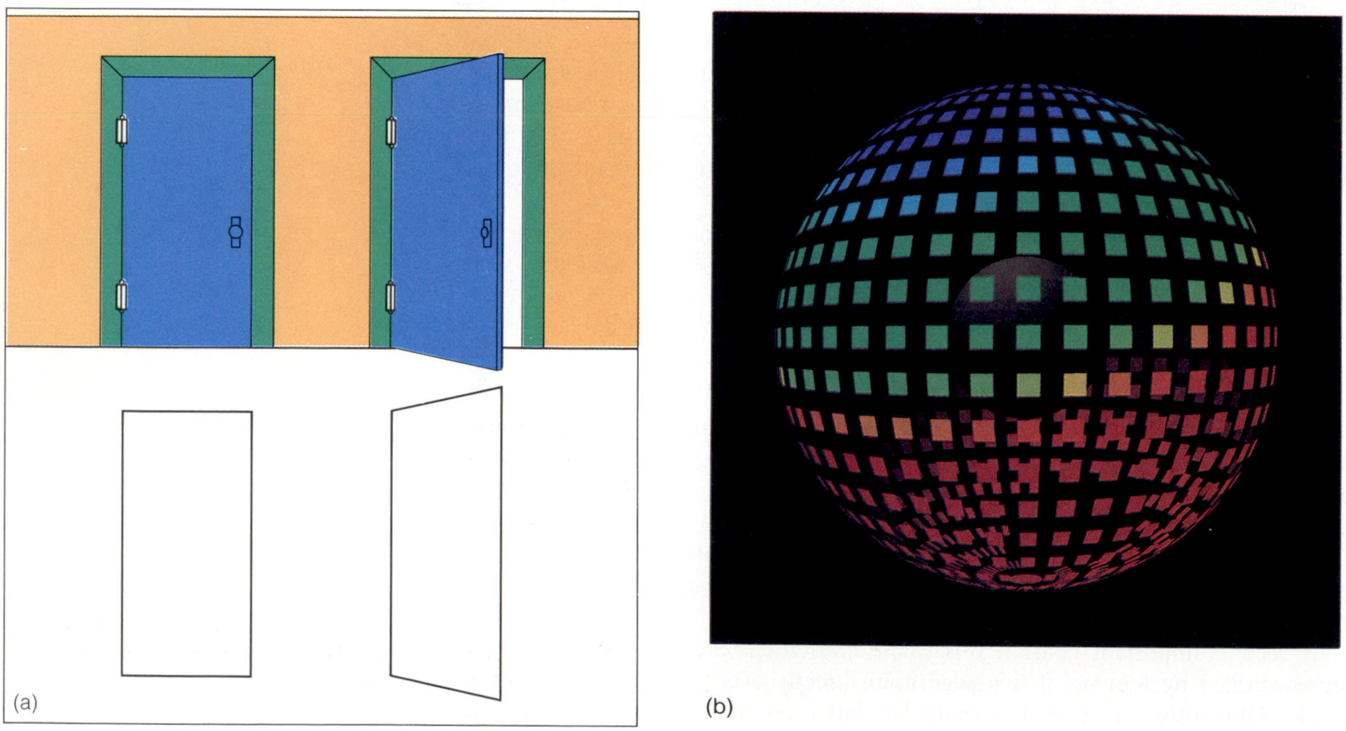

Fig. 5-1 *Shape constancy.* (a) *When a door is open, its image actually forms a trapezoid. Shape constancy is indicated by the fact that it is still perceived as a rectangle.* (b) *With great effort you may be able to see this design as a collection of flat shapes. However, if you maintain shape constancy, the distorted squares strongly suggest the surface of a sphere. (From "Spherescapes 1," by Scott Walter & Kevin McMahon, 1983)*

elephant from descriptions he had heard. However, handwriting meant nothing to him for more than a year after he regained his sight, and many objects remained meaningless until he touched them. Thus, while Mr. S. B. had visual *sensations*, his ability to *perceive* remained limited.

Question: How are sensations organized into meaningful perceptions?

The simplest organization is to group some sensations into an object, or "figure," that stands out on a plainer background. **Figure-ground organization** is probably inborn since it is the first perceptual ability to appear when a cataract patient regains sight (Hebb, 1949). In normal figure-ground perception only one figure is seen. However, in **reversible figures** figure and ground can be switched. In Fig. 5-2 it is equally possible to see either a wineglass figure on a dark background or two face profiles on a light background. As you shift from one possibility to the other, you should get a clear sense of what figure-ground organization means.

Question: What causes the formation of a "figure"?

The Gestalt psychologists (discussed in Chapter 1) studied this question in detail. Even if you were seeing for the first time, they concluded, the following factors would bring some order to your perceptions (refer to Fig. 5-3).

1. **Nearness.** Stimuli that are near each other tend to be grouped together (see Fig. 5-3*a*). Thus, for example, if three people stand near one another and one stands 10 feet away, the adjacent three will be seen as a group, and the distant person as an outsider.
2. **Similarity.** "Birds of a feather flock together," and stimuli that are similar in size, shape, color, or form tend to be grouped together (see Fig. 5-3*b*). For instance, picture two bands marching side by side. If their uniforms differ, the bands will probably be seen as two separate groups, not as a single large group.
3. **Continuation, or continuity.** Perceptions tend toward simplicity and continuity. In Fig. 5-3*c* it is easier to visualize a wavy line on a squared-off line than it is to see a complex row of shapes.
4. **Closure.** Closure refers to the tendency to *complete* a figure, so that it has a consistent overall form. Each of the drawings in Fig. 5-3*d* has one or more "gaps," yet each is perceived as a recognizable figure. The white "shapes" that appear in the middle of the right two drawings in Fig. 5-3*d* are called **illusory figures** (Parks, 1984). Even young children see these implied shapes, despite knowing that they are "not really there." Illusory figures reveal that our tendency to form shapes—even with minimal cues—is powerful.

In addition to these principles, learning and past experience greatly affect perceptual organization. Contrast Mr. S. B.'s immediate recognition of letters with his inability to read handwriting. Also, take a moment and look for the camouflaged insect in Fig. 5-4. **Camouflage** patterns are those that break up figure-ground organization. If you had never seen an insect before, could you have located the one pictured? Mr. S. B. would have been at a total loss to find meaning in such a picture.

In a way we are all detectives, seeking patterns in what we see. In this sense a meaningful pattern represents a **perceptual hypothesis,** or "guess," held until the

Brightness constancy The apparent, relative brightness of objects remains the same under differing conditions of illumination.

Figure-ground organization A basic perceptual organization wherein part of a stimulus appears to stand out as an object (figure) against a less prominent background (ground).

Reversible figure A stimulus pattern that allows perceivers to reverse figure-ground organization.

Illusory figure An implied shape that is not actually bounded by an outline.

Camouflage Designs that break up figure-ground organization, making objects more difficult to see.

Perceptual hypothesis An initial guess regarding the correct way to organize (perceive) a stimulus pattern.

Fig. 5-2 *A reversible figure-ground design. Do you see two faces in profile or a wineglass?*

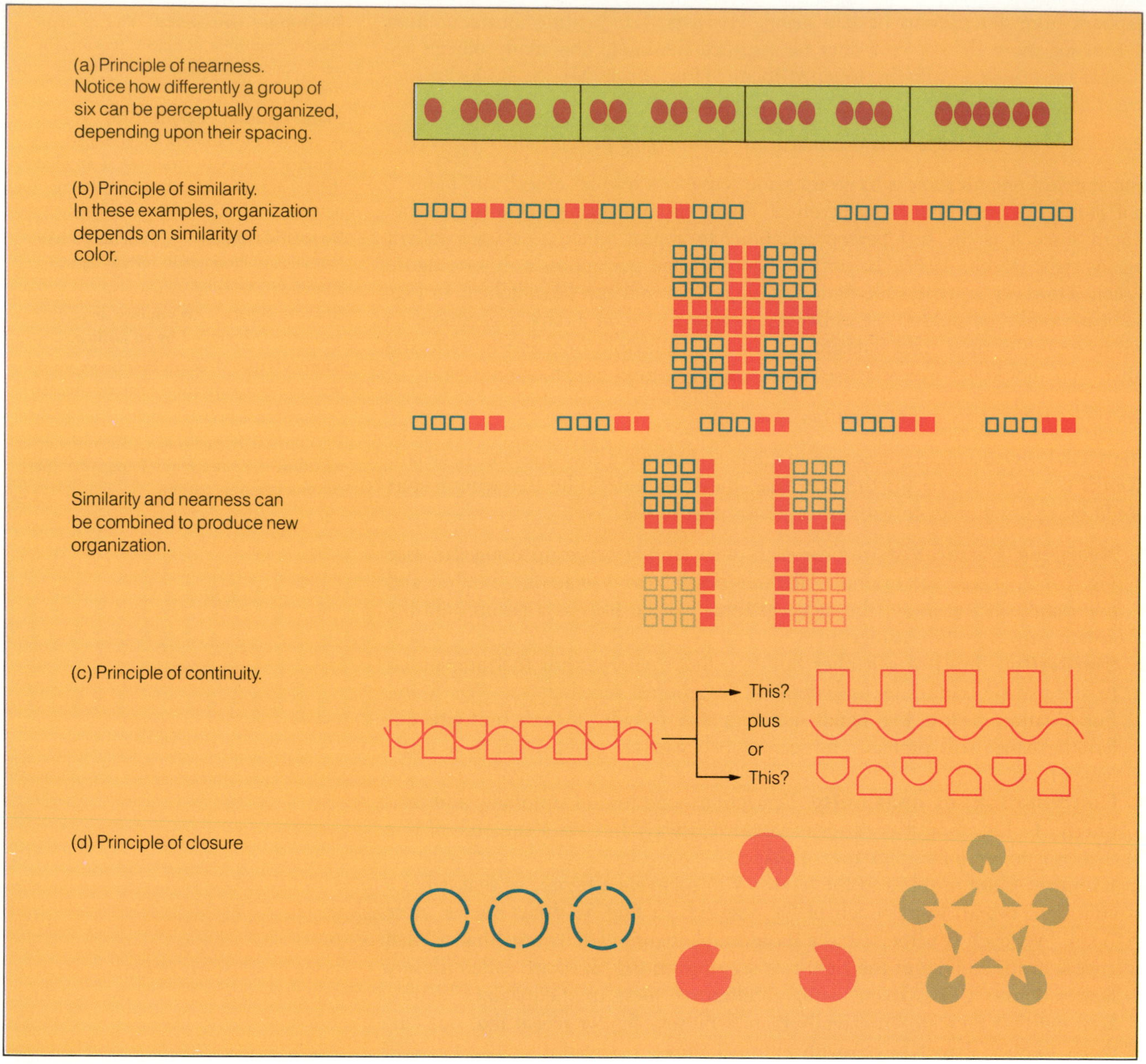

Fig. 5-3 *Perceptual grouping illustrations.*

Ambiguous stimuli Patterns that allow more than one perceptual organization

Impossible figure A stimulus pattern that cannot be organized into a stable, consistent, or meaningful perception.

evidence contradicts it. Have you ever seen a "friend" in the distance, only to have the friend turn into a stranger as you drew closer? Pre-existing ideas and expectations *actively* guide our interpretation of sensations (McBurney & Collings, 1984).

The active nature of perceptual organization is perhaps most apparent in the case of **ambiguous stimuli** (patterns allowing more than one interpretation). If you look at a cloud, you may discover dozens of ways to organize its contours into fanciful shapes and scenes. Even clearly defined stimuli may permit more than

Fig. 5-4 *An example of perceptual organization. Once the camouflaged insect (known as a giant walkingstick) becomes visible, it is almost impossible to view the picture again without seeing it.*

one interpretation. Stare at the designs in Fig. 5-5 and Fig. 5-6 if you doubt the active and fluctuating nature of perception.

Question: Is the ability to understand drawings learned?

Humans almost always appear to understand lines that represent the *edges of surfaces*. We also have no problem with a single line used to depict the *parallel edges* of a narrow object, such as a rope or telephone wire. One thing that we *do not* easily recognize is lines that show color boundaries on the surface of an object (Kennedy, 1983). Understanding this aspect of drawings seems to be learned.

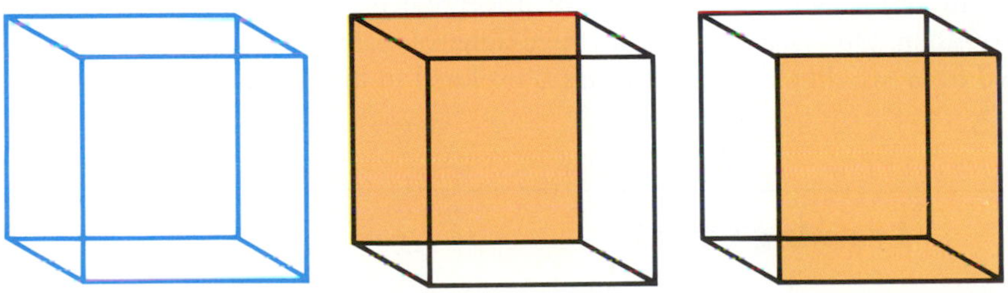

Fig. 5-5 *Necker's cube. Visualize the* left *cube as a wire box. If you stare at the cube, its organization will change. Sometimes it will seem to project upward, like the* center *cube; other times it will project downward. The difference lies in how the brain interprets the same information.*

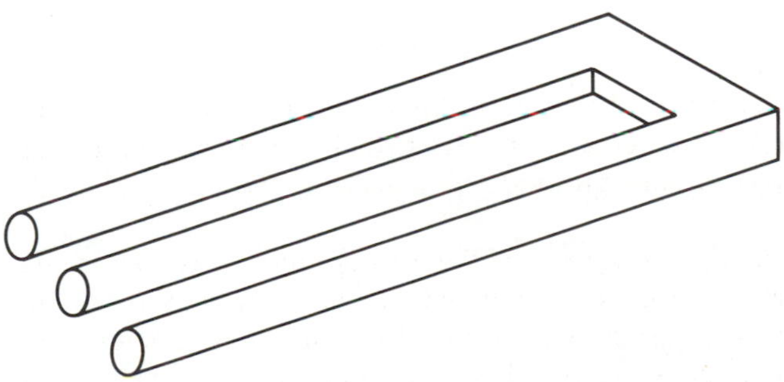

Fig. 5-6 *Some stimuli present such conflicts that a single perceptual organization becomes impossible. Here, for instance, the tendency to visualize drawings as three-dimensional objects is frustrated by the "three-pronged widget," an* impossible figure. *Impossible figures are patterns that cannot be organized as stable objects.*

Fig. 5-7 *A stimulus similar to one used by Kennedy (1983) to study the kinds of information universally recognized in drawings. (See text for explanation.)*

The last point is illustrated by the Songe, a small tribe in Papua New Guinea that does not make or use line drawings. As a test, the Songe were shown drawings like that in Fig. 5-7. They easily recognized the parrot from its outlines. But lines showing color boundaries confused them. Most thought that the parrot must have been cut repeatedly, even though the lines matched the colors of parrots they saw in daily life (Kennedy, 1983).

One of the most amazing feats of perceptual organization deserves a separate discussion. Our capacity to create three-dimensional space from flat retinal images and from two-dimensional drawings is explored in the next section.

Learning Check

Try these questions before reading more.

1. Which of the following are subject to basic perceptual constancy? (circle)

figure-ground size ambiguity brightness continuity closure shape nearness

2. The first and most basic perceptual organization to emerge when sight is restored to a blind person is:
a. continuity *b.* nearness constancy *c.* recognition of numbers and letters *d.* figure-ground

3. At times, meaningful perceptual organization represents a ________________, or "guess," held until the evidence contradicts it.

4. Ambiguous figures have more than one meaningful organization. T or F?

5. The design known as Necker's cube is a good example of an impossible figure. T or F?

6. There is evidence that humans universally recognize line drawings depicting the edges of ________________ and narrow parallel lines.

Answers: **1.** size, brightness, shape **2.** *d* **3.** hypothesis **4.** T **5.** F **6.** surfaces

Depth Perception—What if the World Were Flat?

Depth perception is the ability to see three-dimensional space and to accurately judge distances. Without depth perception you would be unable to successfully drive a car or ride a bicycle, play catch, shoot baskets, thread a needle, or simply navigate around a room. The world would look like a flat surface.

Question: Mr. S. B. had trouble with depth perception after his sight was restored. Does this mean that depth perception is learned?

Some psychologists (nativists) hold that depth perception is inborn. Others (the empiricists) view it as learned. Most likely, depth perception is partly learned and partly innate. Evidence of innate depth perception comes from work with the **visual cliff** (see Fig. 5-8). The visual cliff is basically a table covered with glass. On one side there is a checkered surface directly beneath the glass. On the other side, the checkered surface is 4 feet below. This makes the glass look like a table-top on one side and a cliff or drop-off on the other.

In a test for depth perception, 6- to 14-month-old infants were placed in the middle of the visual cliff. This gave them the choice of crawling to the "shallow" side or the "deep" side. (The glass prevented them from doing any "skydiving" if they chose the deep side.) Most infants chose the shallow side. In fact, most refused the deep side even when their mothers tried to call them toward it (Gibson & Walk, 1960). Psychologist Jane Gwiazada has recently tested babies in another interesting way. Gwiazada fits infants with goggles that make some designs stand out three-dimensionally, while others remain flat. By monitoring the babies' head movements, Gwiazada can tell when the infants first become aware of the 3-D designs. For most infants this occurs at age 4 months, give or take about 2 weeks. Together with evidence from the visual cliff, this work suggests that a basic level of depth perception is innate.

Depth perception The ability to see three-dimensional space and to accurately estimate distances.

Visual cliff An apparatus that looks like the edge of an elevated platform or cliff; used to test for depth perception in infants and baby animals.

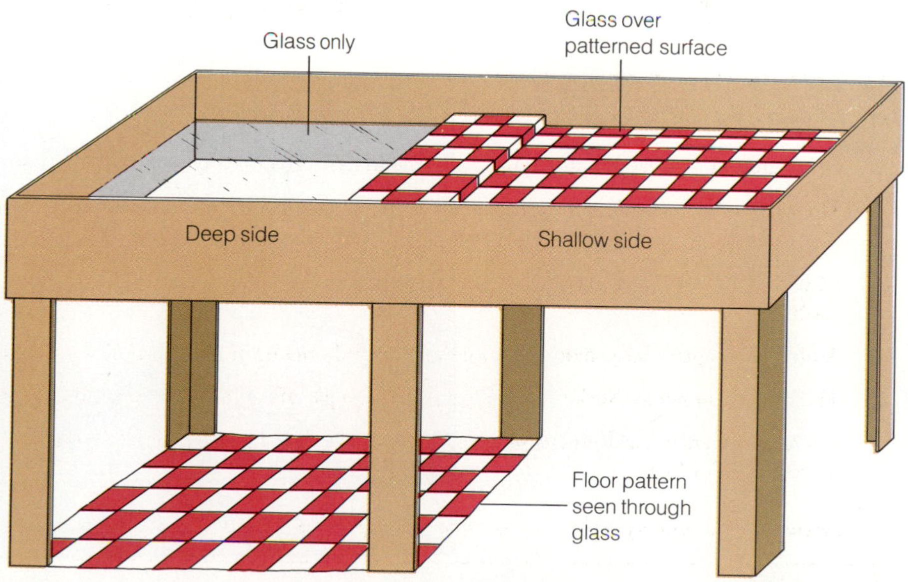

Fig. 5-8 *Human infants and newborn animals generally refuse to go over the edge of the visual cliff.*

Question: Then why do some babies crawl off of tables or beds?

As soon as infants become active crawlers, they refuse to cross the deep side of the visual cliff (Campos et al., 1978). But even babies who perceive depth may not be able to catch themselves if they slip. A lack of coordination—not an inability to see depth—probably explains most "crash landings" after about 4 months of age.

Question: How do adults perceive depth?

A number of **depth cues** combine to produce our experience of three-dimensional space. Depth cues are features of the environment, or messages from the body, which supply information about distance and space. Some cues will work with just one eye (**monocular cues**), while others require two eyes (**binocular cues**).

Muscular Cues As their name implies, muscular cues come from within the body. One is **accommodation,** a monocular cue for depth perception. You may recall from Chapter 4 that the lens in each eye must bend or bulge to focus nearby objects. Sensations coming from the muscles that support the lens are channeled back to the brain. Differences in these sensations help us judge distances that fall within about 4 feet of the eyes. Beyond 4 feet, accommodation contributes little to depth perception. Obviously, accommodation is more important to a watchmaker or a person trying to thread a needle than it is to a basketball player or an airline pilot.

A second bodily source of depth is **convergence,** a binocular cue. When you look at a distant object, the lines of vision from your eyes are parallel. However, when you look at something 50 feet or less in distance, your eyes must converge (turn in) to focus the object (see Fig. 5-9).

You are probably not aware of it, but whenever you estimate a distance under 50 feet (as when you approach a stop sign, play catch, or zap flies with your personal laser), you are using convergence. How? Again there is a relationship between muscle sensations and distance. Convergence is controlled by a group of muscles attached to the eyeball. These feed information on eye position to the

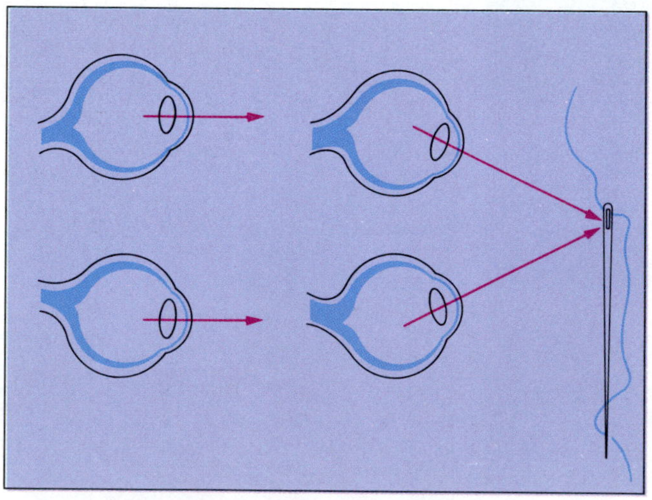

Fig. 5-9 *The eyes must converge or turn in toward the nose to focus close objects.*

brain to aid it in judging distance. You can feel convergence by exaggerating it: Focus on your fingertip and bring it toward your eyes until they almost cross. At this point you can feel sensations from the muscles that control eye movement.

Stereoscopic Vision The most important source of depth perception is **retinal disparity,** also a binocular cue. Retinal disparity is based on the simple fact that the eyes are about 2½ inches apart. Because of this, each eye receives a slightly different view of the world. When the resulting two images are *fused* into one overall image, **stereoscopic vision** occurs. This produces a powerful sensation of depth (see Fig. 5-10). Retinal disparity can be used to produce 3-D movies by filming with two cameras, separated by several inches. Later, both images are simultaneously projected on a screen. The audience then wears glasses that filter out one of the images to each eye. Since each eye gets a separate image, normal stereoscopic vision is duplicated. Try this demonstration of retinal disparity and fusion:

> Roll a piece of paper into a tube. Close your left eye. Hold the tube to your right eye like a telescope. Look through the tube at some object in the distance. Place your left hand against the tube halfway down its length and in front of your left eye. Now open your left eye. You should see a "hole" in your hand. You couldn't expect a professional photographer to do a better job of blending the two images than your visual system does automatically.

Question: If disparity is so important, can a person with one eye perceive depth?

A one-eyed person lacks convergence and retinal disparity, and accommodation is helpful only for judging small distances. This means that a person with only one eye will have restricted depth perception. Try driving a car or riding a bicycle some time with one eye closed. You will find yourself braking too soon or too late, and you will have difficulty estimating your speed. ("But officer, my psy-

Depth cues Features of the environment, or bodily sensations, that impart information about distance and three-dimensional space.

Monocular depth cues Depth cues that can be sensed with one eye.

Binocular depth cues Depth cues that function only when both eyes are used.

Accommodation Changes in the shape of the lens of the eye that serve to focus objects at varying distances.

Convergence The simultaneous turning inward of the two eyes as they focus on nearby objects.

Retinal disparity Small discrepancies in the images falling on each retina caused by separation of the eyes.

Stereoscopic vision The seeing of objects as three-dimensional and the perception of space caused chiefly by the separation of the eyes.

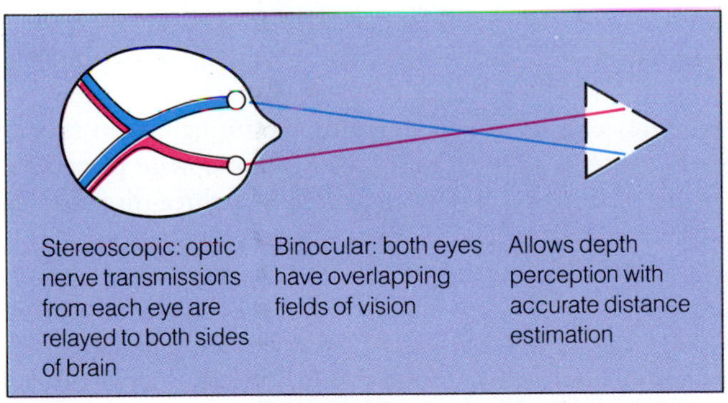

(a)

(b)

Fig. 5-10 (a) *Stereoscopic vision.* (b) *The photographs show what the right and left eye would see when viewing a vase. Hold a file card or small piece of paper (4 or 5 inches tall) vertically between the two photos. Place the bridge of your nose on the card so that each eye sees only one photo. Relax your eyes until the vase fuses into one image. The third dimension appears like magic.*

Pictorial depth cues Features found in paintings, drawings, and photographs that impart information about space, depth, and distance.

Moon illusion The apparent change in size that occurs as the moon moves from the horizon (large moon) to overhead (small moon).

chology text said to . . .") In spite of this, you will be able to drive, although with greater difficulty than usual. A person with one eye can even successfully land an airplane—a task strongly dependent on depth perception.

Pictorial Cues for Depth—A Deep Topic

A good movie, painting, or photograph can give a convincing sensation of depth where none exists, and as noted, a one-eyed person can learn to accurately gauge depth.

Question: How is the illusion of depth created on a two-dimensional surface, and how is it possible to judge depth with one eye?

The answers lie in the **pictorial depth cues,** all of which are monocular (they will work with just one eye). These cues contain much of the information present when a person looks at a real three-dimensional scene (Haber, 1980). To understand how the pictorial cues work, imagine that you are looking outdoors through a window. If you traced everything you saw onto the glass, you would have an excellent drawing, with convincing depth. If we then analyzed what was on the glass, we would find the following features.

Pictorial Depth Cues

1. **Linear perspective.** This refers to the apparent convergence of parallel lines in the environment. If you stand between two railroad tracks, they appear to come together near the horizon. Since you know they are parallel, this seeming convergence implies great distance (see Fig. 5-11).
2. **Relative size.** If an artist wishes to depict two objects of the same size at different distances, the artist makes the more distant object smaller (see Fig. 5-12). The films *Star Wars* and *Return of the Jedi* created sensational illusions of depth through rapid changes in the image size of planets, space stations, and starships.
3. **Light and shadow.** Most objects in the environment are lighted in such a way as to create definite patterns of light and shadow. Appropriate placement of light and shadow can give a two-dimensional design a three-dimensional feeling (see Fig. 5-13).
4. **Overlap.** Overlap (also known as *interposition*) is a depth cue that occurs when one object partially blocks the view of another. Hold your hands up and have a friend try to tell from across the room which is nearer. Relative size will give the answer if the difference between the two hands is large. But if one hand is only slightly closer than the other, your friend may have difficulty—until you slide one hand in front of the other. Overlap then removes any doubt (see Fig. 5-14).
5. **Texture gradients.** Changes in texture also contribute to depth perception. If you are standing in the middle of a cobblestone street, the street looks coarse near your feet, but the texture of the stones gets smaller and finer as you look off into the distance (see Fig. 5-15).
6. **Aerial perspective.** Smog, fog, dust, and haze add to the apparent distance of an object. Objects seen at great distance tend to be hazy, a washed-

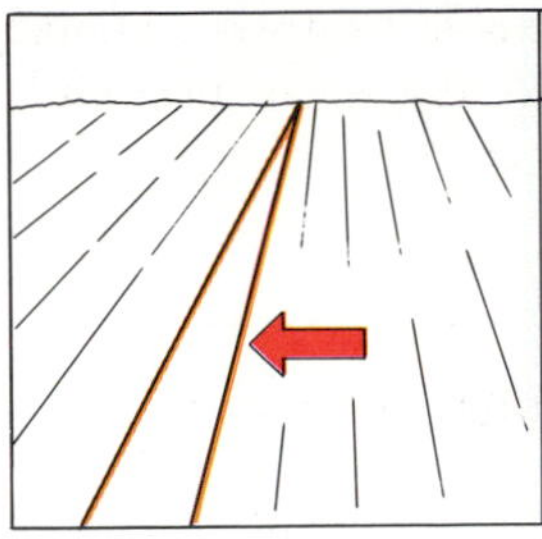

Fig. 5-11
Linear perspective.

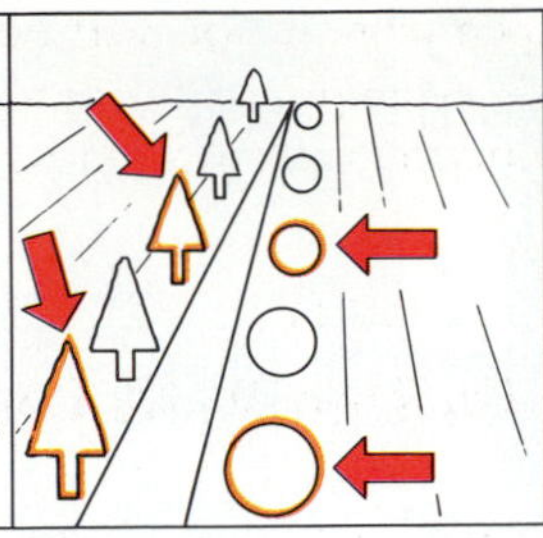

Fig. 5-12
Relative size.

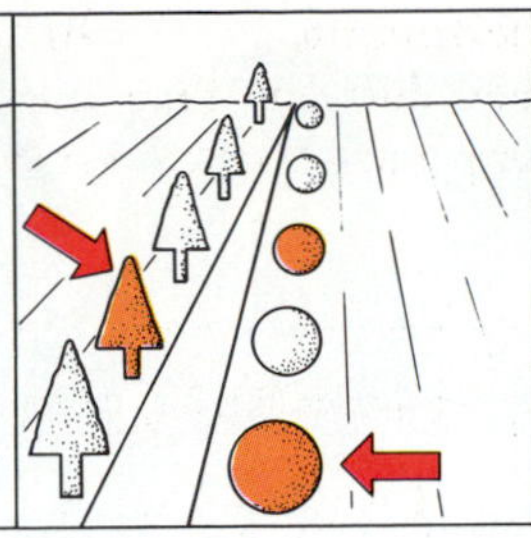

Fig. 5-13
Light and shadow.

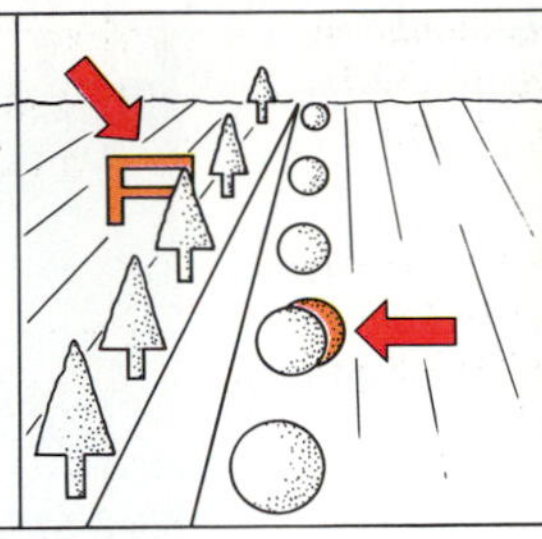

Fig. 5-14
Overlap

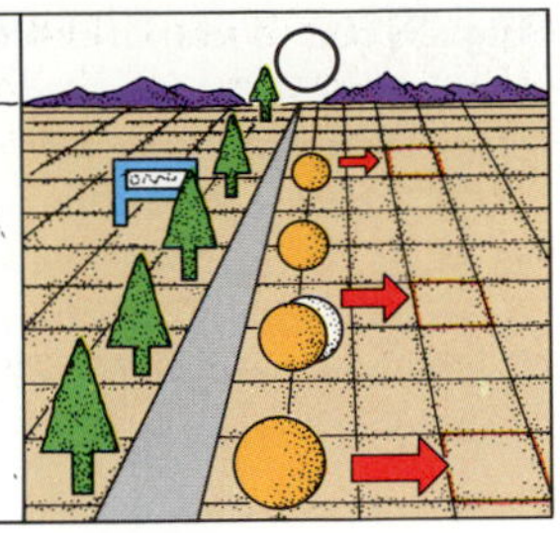

Fig. 5-15
Texture gradients.

out color, and lacking in detail due to aerial perspective. This is true even in clear air but is increasingly the case in our industrial society. As a matter of fact, aerial haze is often most noticeable when it is missing. If you have traveled the wide open spaces of states such as Colorado or Wyoming, you may have seen mountain ranges that looked only a few miles away, and then were shocked to find that you were actually viewing them through 50 miles of crystal-clear air.

7. **Relative motion.** Relative motion, also known as *motion parallax* (PAIR-ah-lax), can be seen by looking out a window and moving your head from side to side. You will notice that objects near you appear to move a sizable distance as your head moves. Trees, houses, and telephone poles at a greater distance appear to move slightly in relation to the background, and distant objects like hills, mountains, or clouds don't seem to move at all.

When combined, pictorial cues can create a powerful illusion of depth (see Fig. 5-16).

Question: Are pictorial depth cues universal, like the understanding of basic drawings noted earlier?

Not entirely. Some cultures use only selected pictorial cues to represent depth. People in these cultures may not easily recognize other cues (Deregowski, 1972). For example, researcher William Hudson has tested members of remote tribes who do not use relative size to show depth. These people see simplified drawings as two-dimensional designs (see Fig. 5-17).

Question: How do the depth perception cues relate to daily experience?

The Moon Illusion Like the bodily depth cues, you constantly use the pictorial cues to gauge depth and judge distances. This can be seen through an intriguing illusion. When the moon is on the horizon, it tends to look as large as a silver dollar. When it is directly overhead, it looks like a dime, very much smaller than it did earlier the same evening. Contrary to what some people believe, the moon's image is not magnified. If you take a photograph of the moon and measure its image, you will find that it is not larger on the horizon. But the moon *looks* larger when it's low in the sky. This is because the **apparent distance** of the moon is greater when it is on the horizon than when it is overhead.

Question: But if it seems farther away, shouldn't it appear smaller?

Fig. 5-16. *Pictorial depth. Look closely! The artist has used many of the pictorial depth cues to fool the eye. (M. C. Escher,* Still Life and Street. *© M. C. Escher Heirs c/o Cordon Art, Baarn, Holland. Collection Haags, Gemeentemuseum—The Hague. Reproduced by permission)*

No. When the moon is overhead, there is an absence of depth cues. In contrast, when the moon is on the horizon, it is seen behind houses, trees, telephone poles, and mountains. These objects add numerous depth cues, which cause the horizon to seem more distant than the sky overhead (Dember & Warm, 1980).

To better understand the moon illusion, picture two balloons, one 10 feet away and the other 20 feet away. Suppose the more distant balloon is inflated until its image matches that of the nearer balloon. We know the more distant balloon is larger because its image is the same size as a balloon that is closer. Similarly, the moon makes the same size image on the horizon as it does overhead. However, the horizon seems more distant because of the depth cues present. As a result, the horizon moon must be perceived as larger (Rock, 1962).

This explanation is known as the **apparent distance hypothesis.** You can test it by removing the normal depth cues present when you look at a full moon. Try looking at the moon through a rolled-up paper tube, or make your hands into a "telescope" and look at the next large moon you see. It will immediately "shrink" when viewed without depth cues.

Fig. 5-17 *A Hudson test picture. Two-dimensional perceivers assume the hunter is trying to spear the distant elephant rather than the nearby antelope. Some acquaintance with conventions for representing depth in pictures and photographs seems necessary. (From "Pictorial Perception and Culture" by J. B. Deregowski. © 1972 by Scientific American, Inc. All rights reserved)*

Learning Check

If you have difficulty with any of these questions, skim back over the previous material.

1. The visual cliff is used to test for depth perception. T or F?

2. Write an "M" or a "B" after each of the following to indicate if it is a monocular or binocular depth cue.

accommodation ____ retinal disparity ____ motion parallax ____ convergence ____ linear perspective ____

3. List one muscular cue for depth perception: ______________________

4. Interpretation of pictorial depth cues requires no prior experience. T or F?

5. The moon's image is greatly magnified by the atmosphere near the horizon. T or F?

Answers: **1.** T **2.** accommodation (M), convergence (B), retinal disparity (B), linear perspective (M), motion parallax (M) **3.** accommodation or convergence **4.** F **5.** F

Perceptual Learning—What If the World Were Upside Down?

There is a story, perhaps fictional, about a visit to the London symphony made by a diplomat from India. According to the story, the diplomat, to his great embarrassment, began clapping loudly after the orchestra finished tuning up. The point of this anecdote is that learning has a powerful impact on perception, something we have already seen in several ways.

Question: How does learning affect perception?

Perceptual Habits One way that learning affects perception is through established patterns of organization and attention, referred to as **perceptual habits.** Stop for a moment and look at Fig. 5-18. The left face looks somewhat unusual,

Apparent distance hypothesis An explanation of the moon illusion stating that the horizon seems more distant than the night sky because there are more depth cues near the horizon.

Perceptual habits Established patterns of perceptual organization and attention.

Fig. 5-18 *The effects of prior experience on perception. The doctored face looks far worse when viewed right-side up, because it can be related to past experience.*

to be sure. But the distortion appears mild—until the page is turned upside down. Viewed normally, the face looks quite grotesque. Why is there a difference? Apparently, most people have little experience with upside-down faces. Perceptual learning, therefore, has less impact on our perceptions of an upside-down face. With a face in normal position, you know what to expect and where to look.

Before we continue, read aloud the short phrase in Fig. 5-19. Did you read "Paris in the spring"? If so, look again. The word *the* appears twice in the phrase. Because of past experience with the English language, the repeated word is frequently overlooked. Again, the effects of perceptual learning are apparent.

Fig. 5-19

Magicians make use of perceptual habits when they use sleight of hand to distract observers while performing their tricks. Another kind of "magic" is related to consistency in the environment. It is usually safe to assume that the overall shape of a room is approximately that of a simple box. This need not be true, however. A decidedly lopsided room can be made to appear square by carefully distorting the proportions of the walls, floor, ceiling, and windows. One such room, called an **Ames room,** after the man who designed it, presents a unique problem for the perceptual habits and organization of an observer.

Since the left corner of the Ames room is farther from a viewer than the right, a person standing in that corner looks very small, whereas one standing in the right corner looks very large (see Fig. 5-20). If a person walks from the left corner of the room to the right, an observer is faced with maintaining shape constancy by perceiving the room as square, or maintaining size constancy by refusing to see the person "grow." Most people choose shape constancy and see people "shrink" and "grow" before their eyes.

As mentioned in the previous chapter, the brain is especially sensitive to important **perceptual features** of the environment. At least some of this sensitivity appears to be learned. Colin Blakemore and Graham Cooper of Cambridge University raised kittens in rooms with only vertical stripes or horizontal stripes on the

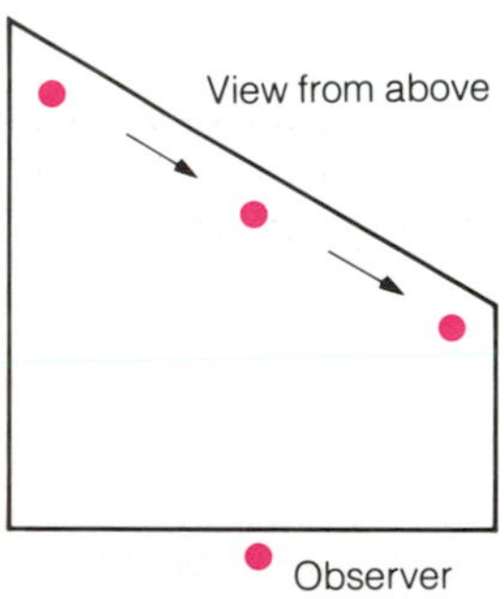

Fig. 5-20 *The Ames room. From the front the room looks normal; actually, the right-hand corner is very short, and the left-hand corner is very tall. In addition, the left side of the room slants away from viewers. The diagram shows the shape of the room and reveals why people appear to get bigger as they cross the room toward the nearer, shorter right corner.*

walls. When returned to normal environments, the "horizontal" cats could easily jump onto a chair, but when walking on the floor they bumped into chair legs. "Vertical" cats, on the other hand, had no difficulty avoiding chair legs, but they missed when trying to jump to horizontal surfaces. The cats reared with vertical stripes were "blind" to horizontal lines, and the "horizontal" cats acted as if vertical lines were invisible (Lewin, 1974). Other experiments show that there is an actual decrease in brain cells tuned to the missing features (Grobstein & Chow, 1975).

Ames room An intentionally distorted room that interrupts perceptual constancies.

Perceptual features Important elements of a stimulus pattern, such as lines, shapes, edges, spots, colors.

Question: Would it be possible, then, for an adult to adapt to a completely new perceptual world?

Inverted Vision An answer is offered by experiments in which people have worn lenses that invert visual images. In one such experiment a subject wore goggles that turned the world upside down and reversed objects from right to left. At first even the simplest tasks—walking, eating, and so forth—were extremely difficult. Imagine trying to reach for a door handle and watching your hand shoot off in the wrong direction.

Subjects also reported that head movements made the world swing violently through space, causing severe headaches and nausea. Yet, incredible as it may seem, after several days they began adapting to inverted vision. Their success was not complete, but it was impressive. Such a high degree of adaptation apparently is related to superior human learning abilities. If the eyes of goldfish are surgically turned upside down, the fish swim in circles and rarely adapt (Sperry, 1956).

Fig. 5-21 *Inverted vision. Adaptation to complete inversion of the visual world is possible but challenging.*

Context Surrounding information that gives meaning to an individual stimulus.

Frame of reference An internal psychological perspective relative to which events are perceived and evaluated.

Adaptation level An internal or mental "average" or "medium" point that is used to judge amounts.

Illusion An unreal or misleading impression presented to the senses; a perception that fails to accurately represent the stimulus.

Hallucination An imaginary sensation—such as seeing, hearing, or smelling something that does not exist in the external world.

Question: Did everything turn upright again for the humans?

No. While they wore the goggles, their visual images remained inverted. But, subjects regained ability to perform most routine activities, and their upside-down world began to seem relatively normal. In other experiments, subjects wearing inverting lenses have successfully driven cars, and one subject even flew an airplane after a few weeks of adaptation (Kohler, 1962). These feats are the equivalent of driving or flying upside down—with right and left reversed.

Active movement in a new visual world seems to be the key to rapid adaptation. In one experiment people wore glasses that grossly distorted vision. Those who walked on their own adapted more quickly than subjects pushed around in a wheeled cart (Held, 1971). Why does movement help? Probably because commands sent to the muscles can be related to sensory feedback (McBurney & Collings, 1984). Remaining immobile would be like watching a weird movie, over which you have no control. There would be little basis for any perceptual learning to occur.

Adaptation Level An important factor affecting perception is the external **context** in which a stimulus is judged. For example, a man 6 feet in height will look "tall" when surrounded by others of average height and "short" among a group of professional basketball players. In Fig. 5-22 the center circle is the same size in both designs. But, like the man in different company, the circle takes on a different apparent size depending on context. The importance of context is also shown by Fig. 5-23. What do you see in the middle? If you read across, context causes it to be organized as a 13. Reading down makes it a B.

Fig. 5-22 *Are the center dots in both figures the same?*

In addition to external contexts we all have *internal* **frames of reference,** or standards by which stimuli are judged. If you were asked to lift a 10-pound weight, would you label it "light," "medium," or "heavy"? The answer to this question depends on your **adaptation level** (Helson, 1964). This is your own personal "medium point," or frame of reference. Each person's adaptation level is constantly modified by experience. If most of the weights you lift in day-to-day life *average* around 10 pounds, you will call a 10-pound weight "medium." If you are a watchmaker and spend your days lifting tiny watch parts, you will probably call a 10-pound weight "heavy." If you work as a furniture mover, your adaptation level will exceed 10 pounds, and you will call a 10-pound weight "light." If you are an aging rock star, you will no doubt call everything "heavy," man.

Illusions Perceptual learning is responsible for a number of **illusions.** In an illusion, length, position, motion, curvature, or direction is consistently misjudged (Gillam, 1980). Illusions differ from **hallucinations** in that illusions distort stimuli that actually exist. People who are hallucinating perceive objects or events that have no external reality (for example, they hear "voices" that are not there). If you think you see a 3-foot-tall butterfly, you can confirm you are hallucinating by trying to touch its wings. To detect an illusion, it is often necessary to measure a drawing or apply a straight-edge to it.

Fig. 5-23 *Context alters the meaning of the middle figure.*

Generally speaking, size and shape constancy, habitual eye movements, continuity, and perceptual habits combine in various ways to produce the illusions in Fig. 5-24. Rather than attempt to explain all of the pictured illusions, let's focus on one "simple" example.

Consider drawing *a*, the familiar **Müller-Lyer illusion** (MUE-ler-LIE-er). In this illusion the horizontal line with arrowheads appears shorter than the line with V's on each end. A quick measurement will show that they are the same length. How can we explain this illusion? Evidence suggests it is based on a lifetime of experience with the edges and corners of rooms and buildings. Richard Gregory (1977) believes you see the horizontal line with the V's as if it were the corner of a room viewed from inside (see illustration). The line with arrowheads, on the other hand, suggests the corner of a room or building seen from outside (see Fig. 5-25).

Earlier, to explain the moon illusion, we said that if two objects make the same size image but one is more distant, the more distant object must be larger. This is known formally as **size-distance invariance.** Gregory believes the same concept explains the Müller-Lyer illusion. Thus, if the V-tipped line looks farther away than the arrowhead-tipped line, you must compensate by seeing the V-tipped line as larger. This explanation of the Müller-Lyer illusion presumes that you have had years of experience with straight lines, sharp edges, and corners—a pretty safe assumption in our culture.

Question: Is there any way to show that past experience causes this illusion?

If we could test someone who as a child had seen only curves and wavy lines, we would know if experience with a "square" culture is important. Fortunately, in South Africa there is a tribe of people, the Zulus, who live in a "round" culture.

Müller-Lyer illusion A stimulus consisting of two parallel lines tipped with inward or outward pointing Vs. Although they are of equal length, one of the lines appears longer than the other.

Size-distance invariance The strict relationship that exists between the distance an object lies from the eyes and the size of its image.

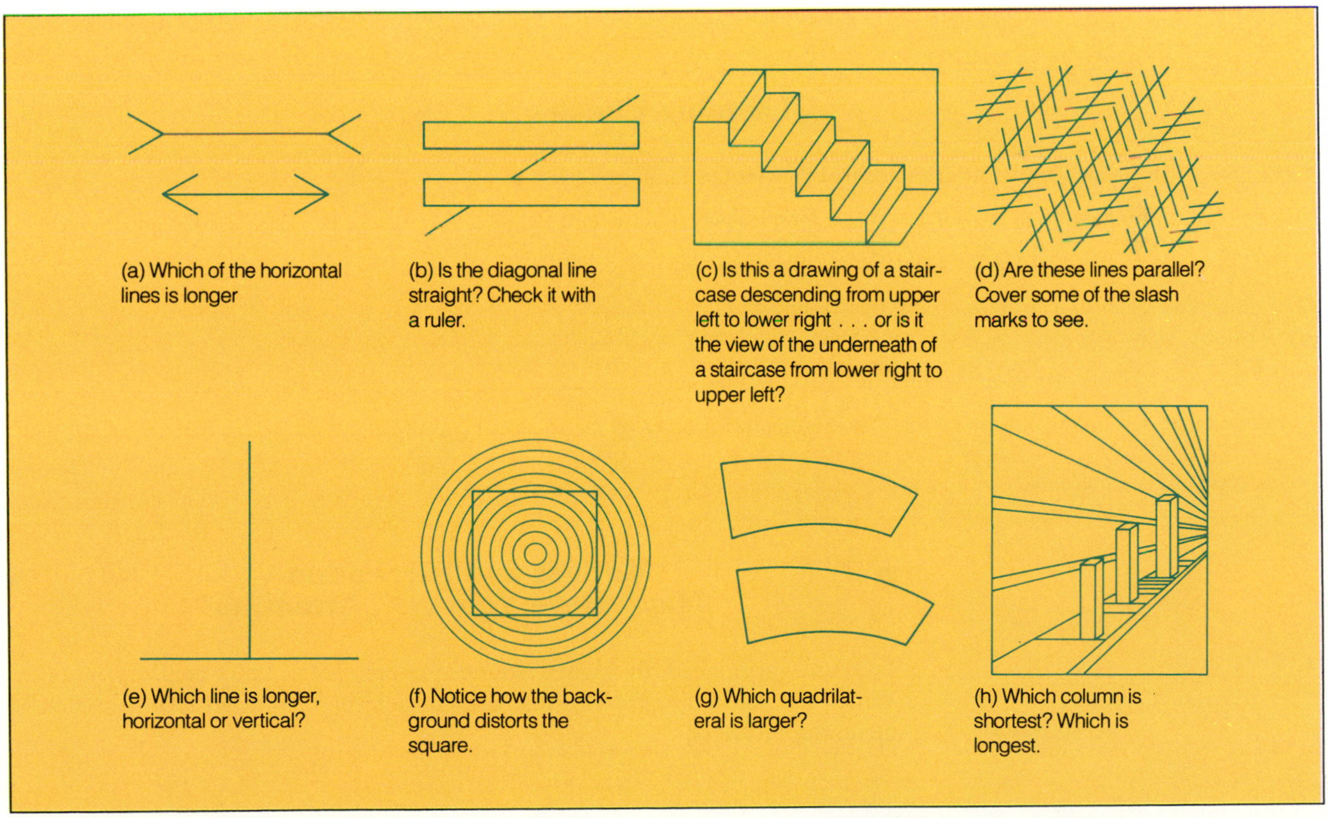

Fig. 5-24 *Some interesting perceptual illusions.*

(a) Which of the horizontal lines is longer

(b) Is the diagonal line straight? Check it with a ruler.

(c) Is this a drawing of a staircase descending from upper left to lower right . . . or is it the view of the underneath of a staircase from lower right to upper left?

(d) Are these lines parallel? Cover some of the slash marks to see.

(e) Which line is longer, horizontal or vertical?

(f) Notice how the background distorts the square.

(g) Which quadrilateral is larger?

(h) Which column is shortest? Which is longest.

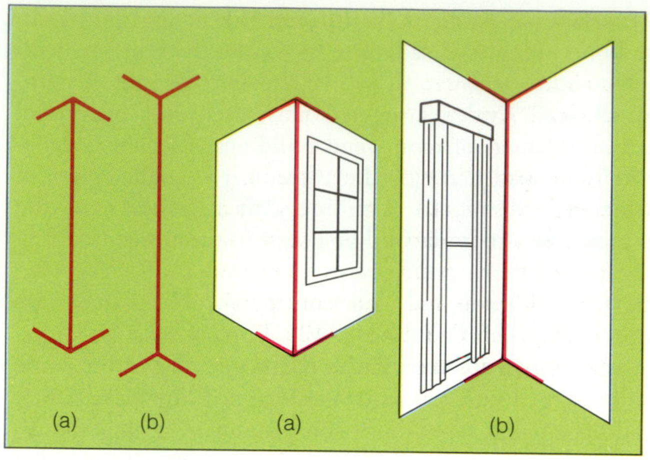

Fig. 5-25 *Why does line* (b) *in the Müller-Lyer illusion look longer than line* (a)*? Probably because it looks more like a distant corner than a nearer one. Since the vertical lines form images of the same length, the more "distant" line must be perceived as larger.*

In their daily lives Zulus rarely encounter a straight line: Huts are shaped like rounded mounds and are arranged in a circle; tools and toys are curved; and there are no straight roads or square buildings.

Question: What happens if a Zulu looks at the Müller-Lyer design?

The typical Zulu does not experience the illusion. At most he or she sees the V-shaped line as *slightly* longer than the other (Gregory, 1977). This seems to confirm the importance of past experience and perceptual habits in determining our view of the world.

Learning Check

1. Perceptual habits may become so ingrained that they lead us to misperceive a stimulus. T or F?

2. Perceptual learning seems to program the brain for sensitivity to important ______________ of the environment.

3. The Ames room is used to test for adaptation to inverted vision. T or F?

4. An important factor in adaptation to inverted vision is:
a. learning new categories *b.* active movement *c.* overcoming illusions *d.* the movement illusion

5. Size-distance relationships appear to underlie which two illusions? ______________ and ______________.

6. An adaptation level represents a personal "medium point" or internal ______________.

Answers: **1.** T **2.** features **3.** F **4.** *b* **5.** moon illusion and Müller-Lyer illusion **6.** frame of reference

Motives and Perception—May I Have Your . . . Attention!

You are surrounded by sights, sounds, odors, tastes, and tactile sensations. Which are you aware of? The first stage of perception is **attention**—selection of incoming messages.

Attention Very *intense* stimuli are attention getting. Stimuli that are brighter, louder, or larger tend to capture attention: A gunshot in a library would be hard to ignore. Big, bright cars probably get more tickets than small, dull ones. Loud, irritating comedian Don Rickles has made a career out of the first principle of attention.

Repetitious stimuli, repetitious stimuli, repetitious stimuli, repetitious stimuli, repetitious stimuli, repetitious stimuli are also attention getting. A dripping faucet at night makes little noise by normal standards, but because of repetition it may become as attention getting as a single sound many times louder. This effect is used repeatedly, so to speak, in television and radio commercials.

ATTENTION IS ALSO FREQUENTLY RELATED TO *contrast* OR *change* IN STIMULATION. Change is perhaps the most basic source of attention. We quickly **habituate** (respond less) to an unchanging stimulus.

Attention Focusing on a particular stimulus or some portion of sensory input.

Habituation A decrease in perceptual response to a repeated stimulus.

Orientation response The pattern of changes occurring throughout the body that prepares an organism to receive information from a particular stimulus.

Question: How does habituation differ from sensory adaptation?

Habituation As described in Chapter 4, *adaptation* decreases the actual number of sensory messages sent to the brain. When messages do reach the brain, the body makes a sort of "What is it?" reaction known as the **orientation response** (OR). An OR is characterized by enlarged pupils, brain wave changes, a short pause in breathing, increased blood flow to the head, and turning toward the stimulus (Dember & Warm, 1979). If you have ever seen someone do a double take, you have observed an orientation response.

Now, think about what happens when you buy a new record album. At first the album holds your attention all the way through. But when the album becomes "old," a whole side may play without your really attending to it. When a stimulus is repeated *without change*, the OR habituates, or decreases.

Motives Motives also play a role in attention. If you are riding in a car and are hungry, you will notice restaurants and billboards picturing food. If you are running low on gas, your attention will shift to gas stations. Advertisers, of course, know that their pitch will be more effective if it gets your attention. Ads are therefore loud, repetitious, and intentionally irritating. They are also designed to take advantage of two motives that are widespread in our society: *anxiety* and *sex*.

Everything from mouthwash to automobile tires is merchandised using sex as a source of attention. For instance, an ad for Triple Sec liqueur ran in national magazines under the heading "Sec's Appeal." Another liquor ad showed a woman in a seductive velvet dress as she says, "Feel the velvet." And what could be more obvious than ads for designer jeans that feature a shapely posterior pointed at the camera? Other ads combine sex with anxiety. Mouthwash, deodorant, soap, toothpaste, and countless other articles are pushed in ads that play on desires to be attractive or have sex appeal, and to avoid embarrassment.

In addition to directing attention, motives may alter what is perceived:

> As part of a supposed study of "the dating practices of college students," male volunteers were shown a picture of a female student and asked to give a first impression of how attractive she was. Before making these ratings, each subject read one of two short written passages: one was sexually arousing and the other was not. The important finding was that subjects who read the more arousing passage rated the female as more attractive. (Stephan, Bersheid, & Walster, 1971)

Fig. 5-26 *Emotionally significant stimuli influence attention. (Erdelyi & Appelbaum, 1973, p. 50. Reprinted by permission)*

This result may come as no surprise to you if you have ever been infatuated with someone and then "fallen out of love." A person who once seemed highly attractive may look quite different when your feelings change.

Another interesting experiment demonstrates that an emotional stimulus can shift attention away from other information. In this experiment members of a Jewish organization watched as pictures like Fig. 5-26 were flashed on a screen for a split second. Their recognition for symbols at the edge of the figure was impaired when the central item was an emotional symbol like the pictured swastika (Erdelyi & Appelbaum, 1973). This effect probably explains why fans of opposing sports teams often act as if they have seen two completely different games.

Perceptual Expectancies—On Your Mark, Get Set

Question: What is a perceptual expectancy?

A runner in the starting blocks at a track meet is **set** to respond in a certain way. In perception, past experience, motives, context, or suggestion may create a **perceptual expectancy** that sets you to perceive in a certain way. If a car backfires, runners at a track meet may jump the gun. As a matter of fact, we all frequently jump the gun when perceiving. To relate this idea to an earlier one: An expectancy is a perceptual hypothesis we are *very likely* to apply to a stimulus—even if it is inappropriate.

We respond according to a perceptual set by seeing what we expect to see. For example, let's say you are driving across the desert. You are very low on gas. Finally you see a distant sign. On it are the words FUEL AHEAD. You relax, knowing you will not be stranded. But as you draw nearer, the words on the sign become FOOD AHEAD. Most people have had similar experiences in which expectations altered their perceptions. To observe perceptual expectancies firsthand, perform the experiment described in Fig. 5-27.

Many perceptual expectancies are created by *suggestion*. This is especially true when one is perceiving other people. For example, a psychology professor once arranged an experiment in which a guest lecturer taught his class. Half the students in the class were given a page of notes that described the lecturer as a "rather *cold* person, industrious, critical, practical, and determined." The other students received notes describing him as a "rather *warm* person, industrious, critical, practical, and determined." (Kelley, 1950; italics added). Students who received the "cold" description perceived the lecturer as unhappy and irritable and didn't volunteer in class discussion. Those who got the "warm" description saw the lecturer as happy and good-natured, and they actively took part in discussion with him.

Expectancies may even explain why celebrities and persons of high status can seem "larger than life." In one experiment an individual was introduced to students as either a student, an assistant, a lecturer, or a professor at a prestigious university. When asked to estimate his height, students judged him to be progressively taller as his status increased (Wilson, 1968). Short people take note! Forget the high heels and get an education!

The concepts we have reviewed are basic to an understanding of perception. In the next section we will move beyond accepted perceptual principles to explore an interesting question: "Is there any evidence for the existence of extrasensory perception?"

Perceptual expectancy (or set) A readiness to perceive in a particular manner, induced by strong expectations.

Extrasensory perception The purported ability to perceive events in ways that cannot be explained by known capacities of the sensory organs.

Parapsychology The study of extranormal psychological events, such as extrasensory perception.

Psi phenomena Events that seem to lie outside the realm of accepted scientific laws.

Clairvoyance The purported ability to perceive events at a distance or through physical barriers.

Extrasensory Perception—Do You Believe in Magic?

In a quiet laboratory Uri Geller, a self-proclaimed "psychic," has agreed to demonstrate his claimed abilities. In the course of testing, Geller was supposedly able to: select from a row of 10 film canisters the one that contained an object, correctly guess 8 out of 8 times the number that would come up on a die shaken in a closed box, and reproduce drawings sealed in opaque envelopes.

Question: Was Geller cheating, or was he using some ability beyond normal perception?

There is now little doubt that Geller was cheating (Randi, 1980). But how? The answer lies in a discussion of **extrasensory perception** (ESP)—the purported ability to perceive events in ways that cannot be explained by accepted perceptual principles.

Parapsychology

Parapsychology is the study of ESP and other **psi** (sie) **phenomena**—events that seem to defy accepted scientific laws. Parapsychologists seek answers to the questions raised by three basic forms that ESP could take. These are:

1. **Clairvoyance:** the ability to perceive events or gain information in ways that appear unaffected by distance or normal physical barriers.

Fig. 5-27 *"Young woman/old woman" illustrations. As an interesting demonstration of perceptual expectancy, show some of your friends View I and some View II (cover all other views). Next show your friends View III and ask them what they see. Those who saw View I should see the old woman in View III; those who saw View II should see the young woman in View III. Can you see both? (After Leeper, 1935)*

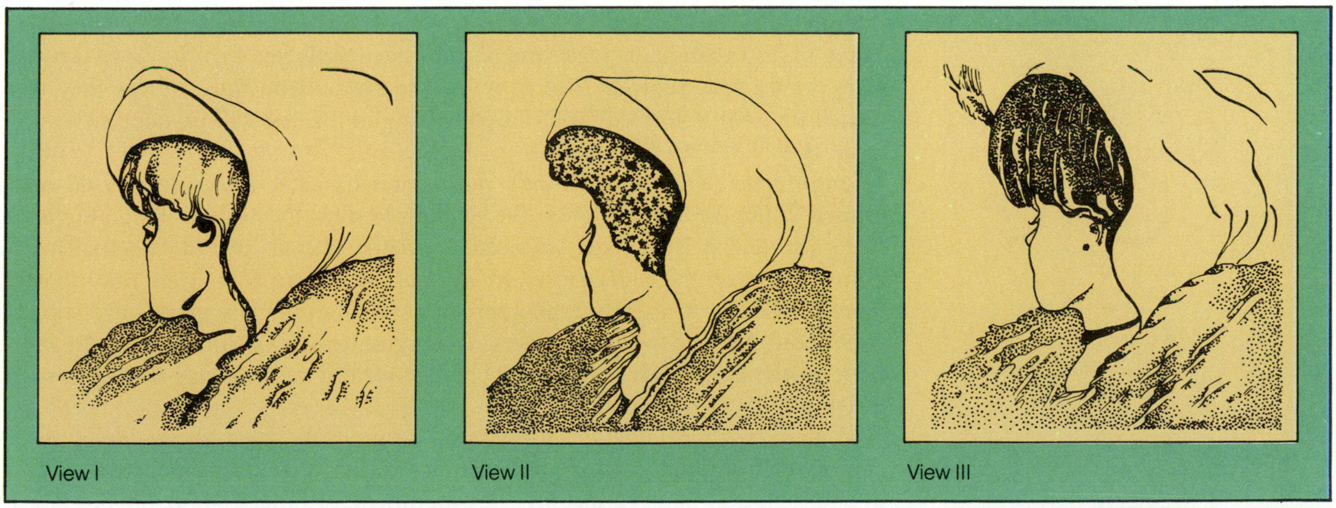

2. **Telepathy:** extrasensory perception of another person's thoughts, or, more simply, an ability to read someone else's mind.

3. **Precognition:** the ability to perceive or accurately predict future events. Precognition may take the form of *prophetic dreams* that foretell the future.

While we are at it, we might as well toss in another purported psi ability:

4. **Psychokinesis:** the ability to exert influence over inanimate objects by willpower ("mind over matter"). (Psychokinesis cannot be classed as a type of perception, extrasensory or otherwise, but it is frequently studied by parapsychologists.)

Question: Have parapsychologists confirmed the existence of ESP and other psi abilities?

American psychologists as a group remain skeptical about psi abilities. If you doubt ESP, then you should know that some experiments seem to support its existence. If you are among those who believe in ESP, then you should know why the scientific community doubts many of these experiments!

Coincidence Anyone who has ever had an apparent clairvoyant or telepathic experience may find it hard to question the existence of ESP. Yet, the difficulty of excluding *coincidence* makes natural ESP occurrences less conclusive than they might seem. For example, consider this typical psychic experience: During the middle of the night, a woman away for a weekend visit suddenly had a strong impulse to return home. When she arrived, she found the house on fire, with her husband asleep inside (Rhine, 1953). An experience like this is striking, but it does not confirm the existence of ESP. If, by coincidence, a "hunch" turns out to be correct, it may be *reinterpreted* as a premonition or case of clairvoyance (Marks & Kammann, 1979). If it is not confirmed, it will simply be forgotten.

Fig. 5-28 *ESP cards used by J. B. Rhine, an early experimenter in parapsychology.*

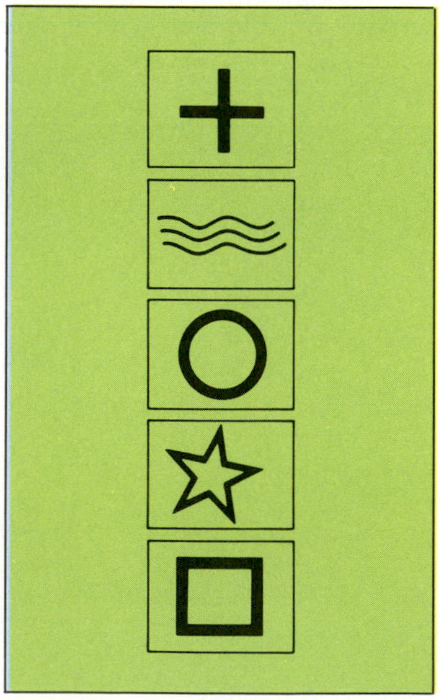

The formal study of psi events owes much to J. B. Rhine. Rhine established the first parapsychological laboratory at Duke University and spent the rest of his life trying to document ESP. To avoid problems of coincidence and after-the-fact interpretation of "natural" ESP events, Rhine tried to study ESP objectively. Many of his experiments made use of the **Zener cards** (see Fig. 5-28). In a typical clairvoyance test, subjects tried to guess the symbols on the cards as they were turned up from a shuffled deck. Pure guessing in this test will produce an average score of 5 "hits" out of 25 cards.

Unfortunately, some of Rhine's most dramatic early experiments used badly printed Zener cards that allowed the symbols to show through faintly on the back. Note also that it is very easy to cheat by marking cards with a fingernail or by noting marks on the cards caused by normal use. Even if this were not the case, there is evidence that early experimenters sometimes unconsciously gave subjects cues about the cards with their eyes, facial gestures, or lip movements. In short, none of the early studies in parapsychology were done in a way that eliminated the possibility of fraud (Alcock, 1981).

Modern parapsychologists are now well aware of the need for double-blind experiments, maximum security and accuracy in record keeping, meticulous experimental control, and repeatability of experiments (Rhine, 1974a). In the last 10 years hundreds of experiments have been reported in parapsychology journals, many of them supporting the existence of psi abilities (Hyman, 1979).

Question: Then why do most psychologists remain skeptical about psi abilities?

For one thing, fraud continues to plague the field. Walter J. Levy, former director of Rhine's laboratory, was caught faking records, as have some others who got positive results. Even honest scientists have been fooled by various frauds and cheats, so there is reason to remain skeptical and on guard.

Statistics and Chance A major criticism of psi research has to do with inconsistency. For every study with positive results, there are others that fail (Hansel, 1980). It is rare—in fact, almost unheard of—for a subject to maintain psi ability over any sustained period of time (Jahn, 1982; Schmeidler, 1977). ESP researchers consider this "decline effect" an indication that parapsychological skills are fragile and unpredictable (Rhine, 1977). But critics argue that subjects who only temporarily score above chance have just received credit for a **run of luck.** When the run is over, it is not fair to assume that ESP is temporarily gone, these critics say. We must count *all* attempts.

Research Methods Unfortunately, many of the most spectacular findings in parapsychology simply cannot be **replicated** (repeated) (Gardner, 1977; Hyman, 1977). More importantly, improvements in research methods usually result in fewer positive results. Proponents of parapsychology feel that they can point to experiments that meet all possible criticisms. But in virtually every case, the results cannot be repeated by doubters. Believers in ESP, such as ex-astronaut Edgar Mitchell, assume that other factors explain such negative results: "The scientist has to recognize that his own mental processes may influence the phenomenon he's observing. If he's really a total skeptic, the scientist may well turn off the psychic subject." This may sound convincing, but skeptics consider it unfair. With Mitchell's argument in effect, anyone attempting an objective experiment can only get two results: He or she may find evidence of ESP or be accused of having suppressed it. This makes it impossible to disprove ESP to believers, even if it truly does not exist.

Reinterpretation is also a problem in psi experiments. For example, Mitchell claimed he conducted a successful telepathy experiment from space. Yet news accounts never mentioned that on some trials Mitchell's "receivers" scored above chance, while on others they scored *below* chance. The second outcome, Mitchell decided, was also a "success" because it represented intentional "psi missing." But, as skeptics have noted, if both high scores and low scores count as "successes," how can you lose?

Stage ESP Skeptics and serious researchers in ESP both agree on one point. If psychic phenomena do occur, they cannot be controlled well enough to be used by entertainers. Stage ESP (like stage magic) is based on a combination of sleight of hand, deception, and patented gadgets (see Fig. 5-29). A case in point is Uri Geller, a former nightclub magician who "astounded" audiences—and some scientists—from coast to coast with apparent telepathy, psychokinesis, and precognition.

Geller's performance on tests was described earlier. Not mentioned is what Uni-

Telepathy The purported ability to directly know another person's thoughts.

Precognition The purported ability to accurately predict future events.

Psychokinesis The purported ability to mentally alter or influence objects or events.

Zener cards A deck of 25 cards bearing various symbols and used in early parapsychological research.

Run of luck A statistically unusual outcome (as in getting 5 heads in a row when flipping a coin) that could still occur by chance alone.

Replicate To reproduce or repeat.

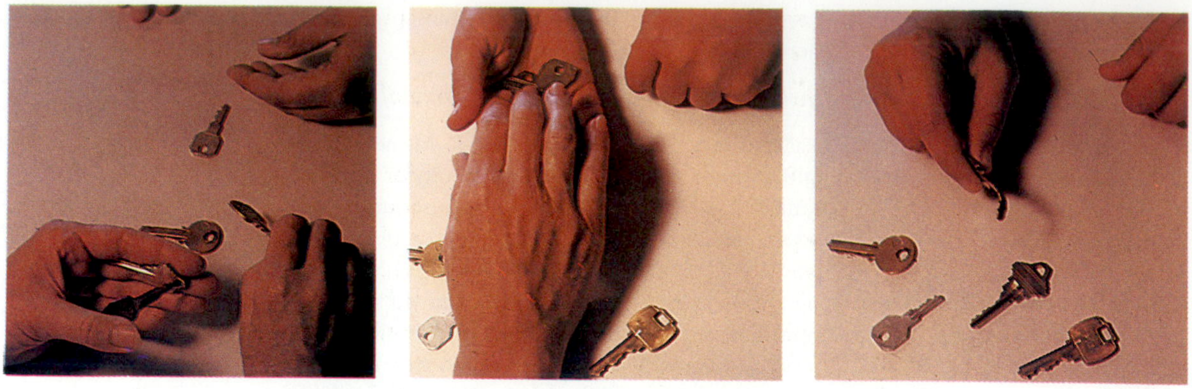

Fig. 5-29 *Fake psychokinesis.* (left) *The performer shows an observer several straight keys. While doing so, he bends one of the keys by placing its tip in the slot of another key. Normally, this is done out of sight, behind the "psychic's" hand. It is clearly shown here so you can see how the deception occurs.* (middle) *Next, the "psychic" places the two keys in the observer's hand and closes it. By skillful manipulation, the observer has been kept from seeing the bent key. The performer then "concentrates" on the keys to "bend them with psychic energy."* (right) *The bent key is revealed to the observer. "Miracle" accomplished! (Adapted from Randi, 1983)*

versity of Oregon professor Ray Hyman calls the "incredible sloppiness" of these tests. One example is Geller's reproductions of sealed drawings. These, it turns out, were done in a room next to the one where the drawings were made. Original reports of Geller's alleged "ability" failed to mention that there was a hole in the wall between the two rooms, through which Geller could easily hear discussions of the pictures being drawn. Also unreported was the fact that Geller's friend Shipi Stang was present at every test. Geller's manager has since testified that Stang frequently acted as Geller's accomplice in trickery (Alcock, 1981). Is it a coincidence that when a picture of a rocket ship was drawn, Stang hummed the theme music from the motion picture *2001: A Space Odyssey*? A similar lack of control pervaded every other test. In the "die in the box" tests, for instance, Geller was allowed to hold the box, shake it, and have the honor of opening it (Randi, 1980; Wilhelm, 1976). Why weren't such pertinent details reported?

Sensational and uncritical reporting of apparent paranormal events is widespread. Hundreds of books, articles, and television programs are produced each year by people who have become wealthy promoting unsupported claims. If a person did have psychic powers, he or she would not have to make a living by entertaining, giving demonstrations, or making personal appearances. A quick trip to the gaming tables of Las Vegas would allow the person to retire for life.

Conclusion After close to 100 years of investigation, it is still impossible to say conclusively that psi events occur, or that they don't. As we have seen, a close look at psi experiments often reveals serious problems of evidence, procedure, and scientific rigor (Alcock, 1981; Hansel, 1980; Marks & Kammann, 1979; Randi, 1980). Yet, being a skeptic does not mean a person is against something. It means that he or she is unconvinced. The purpose of this discussion, then, has been to balance the *uncritical* acceptance of psi events that is rampant in the media.

Question: What would it take to scientifically demonstrate the existence of ESP?

Quite simply, a set of instructions that would allow any competent, unbiased observer to produce a psi event under standardized conditions (Moss & Butler, 1978). Undoubtedly, some intrepid researchers will continue their attempts to supply just that. Others remain skeptics, and some consider 100 years of inconclusive efforts reason enough to abandon the concept of ESP. At the least it seems essential to be carefully skeptical of evidence reported in the popular press or by researchers who are uncritical "true believers." But then, you already knew I was going to say that, didn't you!

In the upcoming Applications section, we will return to "everyday" perception, with a look at objectivity and eyewitness testimony. Before we continue, here's a Learning Check.

Learning Check

1. Attention is elicited by all but one of the following. Which does not fit?
a. habituation *b.* repetition *c.* change *d.* intensity

2. The presence of an orientation response shows that habituation is complete. T or F?

3. Changes in brain waves and increased blood flow to the head are part of an OR. T or F?

4. Research shows that heightened sexual arousal can cause a person to perceive someone of the opposite sex as more physically attractive. T or F?

5. When a person is prepared to perceive events in a particular way, it is said that a perceptual expectancy or ______________ has been created.

6. Perceptual expectancies are greatly influenced by the existence of mental categories and labels. T or F?

7. Four purported psi events investigated by parapsychologists are clairvoyance, telepathy, precognition, and ______________.

8. Natural or "real life" occurrences are regarded as the best evidence for the existence of ESP. T or F?

9. Skeptics attribute positive results in psi experiments to statistical runs of luck. T or F?

10. Replication rates are high for ESP experiments. T or F?

Answers: **1.** *a* **2.** F **3.** T **4.** T **5.** set **6.** T **7.** psychokinesis **8.** F **9.** T **10.** F

Applications

Perception and Objectivity—Believing Is Seeing

Have you ever seen the sun set? An odd question perhaps, since we see the sun "go down" every day. Yet, in reality we know that the sun does not "set." Instead, our viewing angle changes as the earth turns, until finally the sun is blocked by the horizon. Want to try the alternative? Tonight stand facing the west. With practice you can learn to feel yourself being swept backward on the rotating surface of the earth—as you watch an unmoving sun recede in the distance (Fuller, 1969).

This radical shift in perspective illustrates the limitations of "objective" observation. As with most other perceptions, seeing a "sunset" is an active and creative **reconstruction** of events. As we have seen, perception reflects the needs, expectations, attitudes, values, and beliefs of the perceiver. In this light the phrase "seeing is believing" must be modified. Clearly, we see what we believe as well as believe what we see.

In some cases the highly subjective quality of perception contributes to the uniquely personal vision valued in art, music, poetry, and the creative parts of scientific research. Too often, though, it is a real liability.

Eyewitness In the courtroom eyewitness testimony can be a key element in establishing guilt or innocence. The claim "I saw it with my own eyes" carries a lot of weight with a jury. But, to put it bluntly, eyewitness testimony is frequently wrong. In fact, recent experiments show that a person's confidence in his or her testimony has almost no bearing on its accuracy (Wells & Murray, 1983)!

Psychologists interested in perception are gradually convincing lawyers, judges, and police officers of the fallibility of eyewitness testimony (Loftus & Monahan, 1980). In one court case a police officer testified that he saw the defendant, a black man, shoot the victim as both stood in a doorway 120 feet away. Measurements made by a psychologist showed that, at that distance, light from the dimly lit doorway was extremely weak—less than a fifth of that from a candle. To further show that identification was improbable, a black juror stood in the doorway under identical lighting conditions. None of the other jurors could identify him. The defendant was acquitted (Buckhout, 1974).

Unfortunately, perception rarely provides an instant replay of events. Even in broad daylight eyewitness testimony is untrustworthy. After a disastrous DC-10 airliner crash in Chicago in 1979, 84 pilots who saw the accident were interviewed. Forty-two said the DC-10's landing gear was up, and 42 said it was down! As one investigator commented, the best witness may be a "kid under 12 years old who doesn't have his parents around" (McKean, 1982). Adults, it seems, are easily swayed by their expectations.

Perceptions formed when a person is surprised, threatened, or under stress are especially prone to distortion. This is why witnesses to crimes so often disagree. As a dramatic demonstration of this problem, an assault was staged on a college campus in which a professor was attacked by an actor. Immediately after the event, 141 witnesses were questioned in detail. Their descriptions were then compared with a videotape made of the staged "crime." The total accuracy score for the group (on features such as appearance, age, weight, and height of the assailant) was only 25 *percent* of the maximum possible (Buckhout, 1974).

Question: Wouldn't the victim of a crime remember more than a mere witness?

A recent experiment found that eyewitness accuracy was virtually the same for witnessing a crime (seeing a pocket calculator stolen) as it was for being a victim (seeing one's own watch stolen) (Hosch & Cooper, 1982). Jurors who place more weight on the testimony of victims may be making a serious mistake.

Applications: Perception and Objectivity, continued

Also, it is worth repeating that witnesses who are confident in their testimony are no more likely to be accurate than those who have doubts.

In many crimes, victims also fall prey to the phenomenon of **weapon focus.** Understandably, victims often fix their entire attention on the knife, gun, or other weapon used by an attacker. In doing so, they fail to perceive details of appearance, dress, or other clues to identity (Loftus, 1979).

Implications How often are our everyday perceptions as inaccurate or distorted as those of an emotionally distraught eyewitness? The answer we have been moving toward is "very frequently." Bearing this in mind may help you develop tolerance for the views of others and be more cautious about the "objectivity" of your own perceptions. It may also encourage more frequent **reality testing** on your part.

Question: What do you mean by reality testing?

Reality Testing In any situation having an element of doubt or uncertainty, reality testing involves obtaining additional information as a check on perceptions. Even simple designs like those in Fig. 5-30 are easily misperceived. One of the designs in the drawing is a continuous line; the other is not. Most people cannot perceive this difference spontaneously. Instead, they must carefully trace and compare the two designs as a check on pure perception (Julesz, 1975).

Psychologist Sidney Jourard provided a more pertinent example of reality testing. One of Jourard's students believed her roommate was stealing from her. The student gradually became convinced of her roommate's guilt but said nothing. As her distrust and anger grew, their relationship turned cold and distant. Finally, at Jourard's urging, she confronted her roommate. The roommate cleared herself immediately and expressed relief when the puzzling change in their relationship was explained (Jourard, 1974). With their friendship reestablished, the true culprit was soon caught. (The cleaning woman did it!)

If you have ever concluded that someone was angry, upset, or unfriendly without checking the accuracy of your perceptions, you have fallen into a subtle trap. Personal objectivity is an elusive quality, requiring frequent reality testing to maintain. At the very least it pays to ask a person what he or she is feeling when you are in doubt. Undoubtedly, most of us could learn to be better "eyewitnesses" to daily events.

Question: Do some people perceive things more accurately than others?

Perceptual Awareness Humanistic psychologist Abraham Maslow (1969) believed that some people are unusually accurate in perceptions of themselves and of others. Maslow characterized these people as especially alive, open, aware, and mentally healthy. He found their perceptual styles were marked by: immersion in the present; a lack of self-consciousness; freedom from selecting, criticizing, or evaluating; and a general "surrender" to experience. The kind of perception Maslow described is like that of a mother with her newborn infant, a child at Christmas, or two people in love.

Other researchers have tested Zen masters for habituation to repeated stimuli. The results indicate that Zen masters fail to show the expected habituation (Kasamatsu & Hirai, 1966). This finding lends

Fig. 5-30 *Limits of pure perception. (Adapted from patterns devised by Marvin L. Minsky and Seymour A. Papert)*

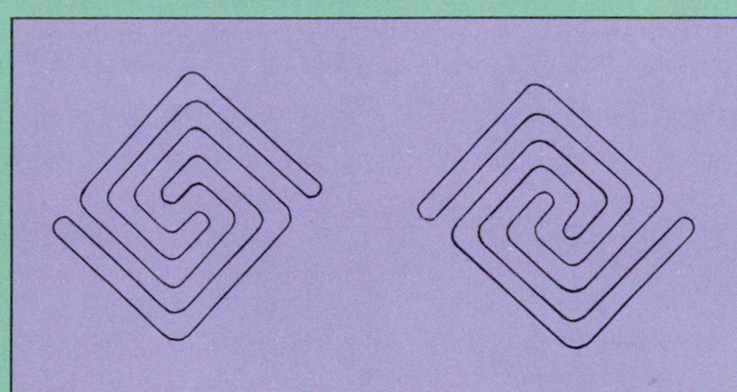

Applications: Perception and Objectivity, continued

some credibility to claims that Zen masters perceive a tree as vividly after seeing it 500 times as they did the first time.

Attention Whereas the average person has not reached perceptual restriction of the "if you've seen one tree, you've seen them all" variety, the fact remains that most of us tend to look at a tree and classify it into the perceptual category of "trees in general" without really appreciating the miracle standing before us. How then can we bring about a **dishabituation** of perception (without going through years of meditative discipline as a Zen master does)? The deceptively simple answer is: *Pay attention.*

The following quote summarizes the importance of attention:

> One day a man of the people said to Zen Master Ikkyu: "Master, will you please write for me some maxims of the highest wisdom?"
>
> Ikkyu immediately took his brush and wrote the word "Attention."
>
> "Is that all?" asked the man. "Will you not add something more?"
>
> Ikkyu then wrote twice running: "Attention. Attention."
>
> "Well," remarked the man rather irritably, "I really don't see much depth or subtlety in what you have just written."
>
> Then Ikkyu wrote the same word three times running: "Attention. Attention. Attention."
>
> Half angered, the man demanded, "What does that word 'Attention' mean anyway?"
>
> And Ikkyu answered gently: "Attention means attention." (Kapleau, 1966)

To this we can add only one thought, provided by the words of poet William Blake: "If the doors of perception were cleansed, man would see everything as it is, infinite."

Learning Check

1. Most perceptions can be described as active reconstructions of external reality. T or F?
2. Inaccuracies in eyewitness perceptions obviously occur in real life, but they cannot be reproduced in psychology experiments. T or F?
3. Accuracy scores for facts provided by witnesses to staged crimes may be as low as 25 percent correct. T or F?
4. Victims of crimes are more accurate eyewitnesses than are impartial observers. T or F?
5. *Reality testing* is another term for dishabituation. T or F?

Answers: **1.** T **2.** F **3.** T **4.** F **5.** F

Chapter Summary

- *Perception* is the process of assembling sensations into a usable mental representation of the world.
- In vision the image projected on the retina is constantly changing, but the external world appears stable and undistorted because of *size*, *shape*, and *brightness constancy*.
- The most basic organization of sensations is a division into *figure* and *ground* (object and background). A number of factors contribute to the organization of sensations. These include: *nearness*, *similarity*, *continuity*, *closure*, and *combinations* of the preceding. Basic elements of line drawings appear to be universally recognized.

- A perceptual organization may be thought of as a *hypothesis* held until evidence contradicts it. Perceptual organization shifts for *ambiguous stimuli*. *Impossible figures* resist stable organization altogether.
- *Depth perception* (the ability to perceive three-dimensional space and judge distances) is present in rudimentary form soon after birth, as shown by testing on the *visual cliff*.
- Depth perception depends on the *muscular cues* of accommodation (bending of the lens) and *convergence* (inward movement of the eyes). *Stereoscopic vision* is created mainly by *retinal disparity* and the resulting overlap of visual images.
- A number of *pictorial cues* also contribute to depth perception. These are: *linear perspective*, *relative size*, *light and shadow*, *overlap*, *texture gradients*, *aerial haze*, and *relative motion* (motion parallax). All are monocular depth cues (only one eye is needed to make use of them).
- The *moon illusion* is at least partially explained by the *apparent distance hypothesis*, which emphasizes the greater number of depth cues present when the moon is on the horizon. Another way of saying this is that a *size-distance invariance* underlies the moon illusion.
- The organization and interpretation of sensations are greatly influenced by the development of *perceptual habits*. Studies of *inverted vision* show that even the most basic organization is subject to a degree of change. *Active movement* speeds adaptation to a new perceptual environment.
- Perceptual judgments are almost always related to *context*, or to an internal frame of reference called the *adaptation level*.
- One of the most familiar of all perceptual illusions, the *Müller-Lyer illusion*, seems to be related to perceptual learning, linear perspective, and size-distance invariance relationships.
- Attention is closely related to *stimulus intensity*, *repetition*, *contrast*, and *change*. Attention is accompanied by an *orientation response*. When a stimulus is repeated without change, the orientation response undergoes *habituation*.
- Personal *motives* and *values* often alter perceptions by changing the evaluation of what is seen or by altering attention to specific details.
- Attention, prior experience, suggestion, and motives combine in various ways to create perceptual *sets*, or *expectancies*. These prepare a person to perceive, or misperceive, in a particular way.
- *Parapsychology* is the study of *extrasensory perception* (ESP) and other *psi* (psychic) events. Three purported forms of ESP are *clairvoyance*, *telepathy*, and *precognition*. A fourth purported psi ability is *psychokinesis* (mind affecting matter).
- The existence of psi phenomena is still debated because coincidence, inconsistency, statistical problems, deception, and sloppy research have invalidated many "proofs." At the same time, experiments have been performed that do appear to some to support the existence of psi events.
- Perception is an active *reconstruction* of events. This is one reason why *eyewitness testimony* is surprisingly unreliable and unrelated to the *confidence* of the witness. Eyewitness accuracy is further damaged by *weapon focus*. Perceptual accuracy is enhanced by *reality testing*, *dishabituation*, and conscious efforts to pay *attention*.

Chapter 6

States of Consciousness

Chapter Preview

Living Nightmares

January, 1959, in New York's Times Square: To raise money for charity, disc jockey Peter Tripp has agreed to go without sleep for 200 hours. All too soon Tripp's fight to stay awake turns brutal. After 100 hours, he begins to have visual hallucinations: He sees cobwebs in his shoes and watches in terror as a tweed coat becomes a suit of furry worms. When Tripp crosses the street to a hotel to change clothes, a dresser drawer seems to burst into flames.

After 170 hours, Tripp's agony becomes almost unbearable. He struggles with the simplest thought, memory, and reasoning problems. His brain wave patterns look like those of sleep, and he is no longer sure who he is. By the end of 200 hours, Tripp is unable to distinguish between his waking nightmares, hallucination, and reality (Luce, 1965).

The Womb Tank *We shift now to a scene far removed from Peter Tripp's ordeal: Some years ago, John Lilly, M.D., pioneered the use of an unusual* **sensory deprivation** *environment. Subjects in Lilly's (1972) experiments floated naked in a tank of body-temperature water. As they drifted weightlessly in this "womblike" environment, subjects were cut off from smell, touch, vision, hearing, and taste sensations.*

Question: What effect does sensory deprivation have?

Under such conditions, subjects often lose track of time, have difficulty concentrating, and experience strange alterations in consciousness. For example, one subject in an earlier experiment screamed in panic, "There is an animal having a long slender body with many legs. It's on the screen, crawling in back of me!" (Heron, 1957). Experiences of this sort are called **hypnogogic images** *(hip-no-GAH-jik). They are similar to images that occur just before falling asleep. That is, hypnogogic images are dreamlike, very vivid, and often surprising. Quite often, sensory deprivation increases their occurrence (Taylor, 1983).*

As you can see, both sleep loss and sensory deprivation have a major impact on consciousness. *In the discussion of consciousness that follows, we will begin with the familiar realms of sleep and dreaming and then move to points beyond.*

Survey Questions What are "states of consciousness"? How much sleep do we need? Can sleep patterns be changed? Are there different types of sleep? What are the most common sleep disorders? Do dreams have meaning? What happens during hypnosis? How do drugs affect consciousness? How is meditation done, and what are its benefits? How can dreams be used to promote personal understanding?

States of Consciousness—Beyond Normal Awareness?

William James described consciousness as a "stream"—an everchanging flow of awareness. Ordinary **waking consciousness** includes a mixture of external and internal sensations, memories of the past, images, daydreams, and expectations for the future. But, as James also noted, states of consciousness related to fatigue, delirium, dreaming, hypnosis, meditation, drugs, and ecstasy differ significantly from what might be considered "normal" awareness.

Question: There must be many altered states of consciousness—how are they distinguished from normal consciousness?

An **altered state of consciousness** (ASC) represents a distinct change in the *quality* and *pattern* of mental functioning, especially regarding sense impressions, emotion, memory, time sense, thinking, feelings of self-control and suggestibility (Tart, 1975). Definitions aside, most people have little difficulty recognizing that they have experienced an ASC.

Question: Aside from drugs, what causes ASCs?

The list of causes is practically endless. In addition to drugs, sleep, dreaming, and meditation, we could add: sensory overload (for example, a light show or a Mardi Gras crowd), monotonous stimulation ("highway hypnotism" on long drives is a good example), unusual physical conditions (high fever, hyperventilation, dehydration, sleep loss), sensory deprivation, long-distance running, music, and too many other possibilities to mention.

To get right to questions raised by the Chapter Preview, let's begin with the most familiar of all altered states of consciousness—sleep and dreaming.

Resources

Waking consciousness A state of normal, alert awareness.

Altered state of consciousness A condition of awareness distinctly different in quality or pattern from waking consciousness.

Sleep—A Nice Place to Visit

Each of us will spend some 25 years of life in a strange state of semiconsciousness called sleep. Contrary to common belief, we are not totally unresponsive during sleep. Experiments show that you are more likely to awaken if your own name is spoken, instead of another (Webb, 1978). Some people can even do simple tasks while asleep. In one experiment, subjects learned to avoid an electric shock by touching a switch each time a tone sounded—eventually they could do it without waking. Of course, sleep does impose limitations. There is no evidence, for in-

Microsleep A momentary shift in brain wave patterns to those of sleep.

Sleep deprivation Being deprived of wanted or needed amounts of sleep.

Sleep-deprivation psychosis A pronounced disruption of mental and emotional functioning brought about by lack of sleep.

Sleep patterns The ordering and duration of daily sleep and waking periods.

Sleep stages Various levels of sleep depth identified by brain wave patterns and behavioral changes.

Electroencephalograph (EEG) A device designed to detect, amplify, and record electrical activity in the brain.

stance, that a person can learn math, a foreign language, or other complex skills while asleep—especially when the snooze takes place in class (Aarons, 1976).

Because of its many contradictions, sleep has always aroused curiosity. What do we know about this daily retreat from the world?

Question: How strong is the need for sleep?

Sleep expert Wilse Webb (1975) describes sleep as a "gentle tyrant." Webb considers sleep an *innate biological rhythm* that can never be entirely side-stepped. But, if flexibility is needed, sleep will give way temporarily, especially at times of great danger. As comedian Woody Allen put it, "The lion and the lamb shall lie down together, but the lamb will not be very sleepy." You could choose, then, to stay awake for an extended period. But there *are* limits. Animals that are prevented from sleeping fall into a coma and die after several days (Kleitman, 1963; Rechtschaffen, 1983).

In one set of experiments, animals were placed on treadmills over a tank of water to minimize sleep. Even so, sleep won out. The animals soon began to engage in repeated microsleeps (Goleman, 1982). A **microsleep** is a brief shift in brain activity to patterns normally found in sleep. Microsleeps also occur in humans: When you drive, it's well worth remembering that a microsleep can lead to a macro-accident.

Question: How long could a person go without sleep?

Sleep Deprivation With few exceptions, 4 days or more without sleep becomes hell for anyone, but longer sleepless periods are possible. The world record for continuous wakefulness is held by Randy Gardner, who at age 17 went 268 hours (11 days) without sleep. Surprisingly, Randy needed only 14 hours of sleep to recover (Dement, 1972). It is usually not necessary to completely replace lost sleep. In fact, most symptoms of sleep deprivation are removed by a single night's rest.

What are the costs of sleep loss? Age and personality make a big difference. Randy Gardner remained coherent to the end of his vigil, whereas Peter Tripp's behavior became quite bizarre. In general, most persons show no impairment on complex mental tasks after 2 days without sleep. But most do decline in their ability to pay attention, remain vigilant, and follow simple routine (Webb, 1978). As Wilse Webb says, "It's not your thinking or memory that goes, it's your will to continue; you would prefer to be asleep" (Goleman, 1982).

Longer periods without sleep occasionally produce a temporary **sleep-deprivation psychosis** like that experienced by Peter Tripp. Common elements of this reaction are confusion and disorientation, delusions (false or distorted beliefs), and hallucinations. Fortunately, such "crazy" behavior is less common than once thought. Hallucinations and delusions are never evident before 60 hours of sleep loss (Webb, 1978).

Question: What is the normal range of sleep needs?

Sleep Needs and Patterns According to medical records, there is a man in England who gets by on only 15 minutes to an hour of sleep each night—and feels perfectly fine. However, this is quite a rarity. Only 8 percent of the population averages 5 hours of sleep or less per night. The majority sleep on a familiar 7- to 8-hour per night schedule. It is quite normal, however, to sleep as little as

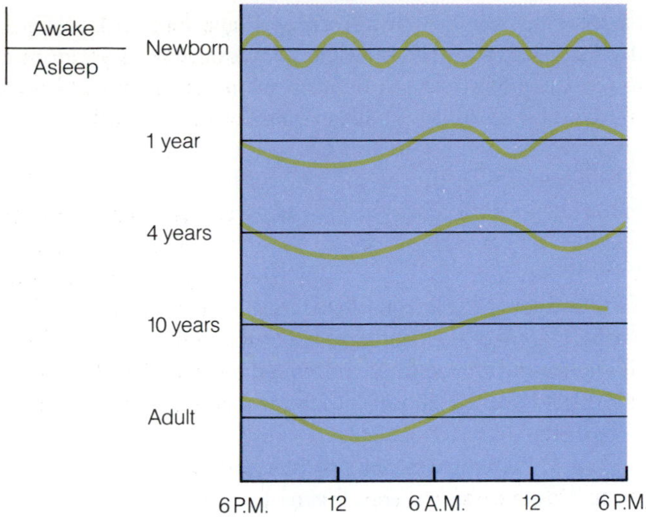

Fig. 6-1 *Development of sleep patterns. Short cycles of sleep and waking gradually become the night-day cycle of an adult. (After Williams, 1964)*

5 hours per night, or as much as 11. Urging everyone to sleep 8 hours a night would be like advising everyone to wear medium-size shoes.

Question: Do elderly people need more sleep?

They may need it, but they seldom get it! Increasing age usually brings a *reduction* in sleep time. People over the age of 50 average only 6 hours of sleep a night. In contrast, infants spend up to 20 hours a day sleeping, usually in 2- to 4-hour cycles. With increasing age, most children go through a "nap" stage and eventually settle into a steady cycle of sleeping once a day (see Fig. 6-1). Some people, of course, maintain the afternoon "siesta" as an adult pattern.

There is a great temptation to try to reduce sleep time. However, people on *shortened* cycles—for example, 3 hours of sleep followed by 6 hours awake—often can't get to sleep when the cycle calls for it (Webb, 1978). A more promising possibility is to adopt *longer*-than-normal "days." Such days can be tailored to match natural **sleep patterns,** which show a ratio of 2 to 1 between time awake and time asleep. One experiment indicated that 28-hour "days" are possible. Evidently, younger subjects find it easier to adapt to these longer "days"—presumably because their sleep habits are less firmly established (Kleitman & Kleitman, 1953).

Stages of Sleep—The Nightly Roller-Coaster Ride

Question: What causes sleep?

Early sleep experts thought that some substance related to fatigue must accumulate in the bloodstream and cause sleep. But studies of Siamese twins (individuals whose bodies are joined from birth) show this is false. One twin can frequently be observed sleeping while the second is awake (see Fig. 6-2). During wakefulness, a sleep-promoting chemical collects in the brain and spinal cord, *not* in the blood. If this substance is extracted from one animal and injected into another,

Beta waves Low-amplitude, high frequency brain waves observed when a subject is awake and alert.

Alpha waves High-amplitude brain waves in the 8- to 12-cycles-per-second range; observed when a subject is awake but relaxed.

Sleep spindles Short bursts of activity observed in brain wave recordings made during sleep.

Myoclonus Reflex contraction of a muscle that causes a jerking motion.

Delta waves Very high amplitude brain waves in the 0- to 4-cycles-per second range; observed in deep sleep.

REM sleep Rapid-eye-movement sleep; typically observed in Stage 1 sleep and associated with dreaming.

Non-REM sleep Sleep that is free of rapid eye movements, typically Stages 2, 3, and 4.

the second animal will fall asleep (Pappenheimer, 1976). Notice, however, that this explanation is incomplete. For example, how do we account for the well-rested student who must fight to stay awake during a boring lecture?

All that can be said with certainty is that sleep is *actively* generated by several important structures in the brain: the hypothalamus, reticular formation, and a "sleep center" in the brainstem. Rather than "shutting down" during sleep, the brain changes the *pattern* of its electrical and chemical activity, not the amount.

Question: What happens when you fall asleep?

The Stages of Sleep The changes that come with sleep can be measured with an **EEG (electroencephalograph,** or brain-wave machine). The brain gives off tiny electrical signals that can be amplified and recorded. When a person is awake and alert, the EEG shows a pattern of small, fast waves called **beta** (see Fig. 6-3). Immediately before sleep, the EEG shifts to a different pattern of larger and slower waves called **alpha.** (Alpha waves also occur at other times when one is relaxed and thoughts are allowed to drift.) As the eyes close, breathing becomes slow and regular, the pulse rate slows, and body temperature drops.

Stage 1 As the person loses consciousness and enters **light sleep,** the heart rate slows even more. Breathing becomes more irregular; the muscles of the body relax. This sometimes triggers a reflex muscle contraction called **myoclonus** (MY-oh-KLOE-nus), which is quite normal. In Stage 1 sleep the EEG is made up mainly of small, irregular waves with some alpha. Persons awakened at this time may or may not say they were asleep.

Stage 2 As sleep deepens, the EEG begins to show short bursts of activity called **sleep spindles,** and body temperature drops even more noticeably (see Fig. 6-3). Sleep spindles seem to mark the true boundary of sleep. Within 4 minutes after they appear, the majority of subjects who are awakened report that they were asleep (Bonnet & Moore, 1982).

Stage 3 In Stage 3 a new brain wave called **delta** begins to appear. Delta waves are very large and slow. Delta waves signal deeper sleep and a further loss of consciousness.

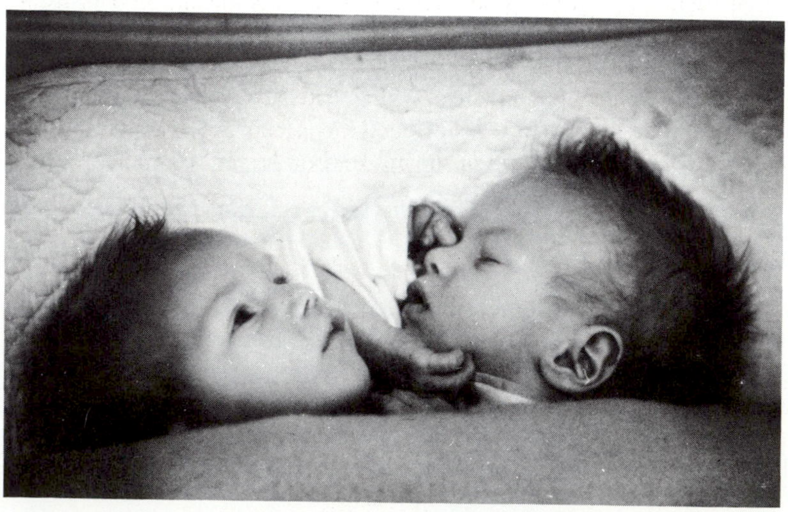

Fig. 6-2 *These Siamese twins share the same blood supply, yet one head sleeps while the other is awake. (Photo by Yale Joel,* Life Magazine. © 1954 *Time, Inc.)*

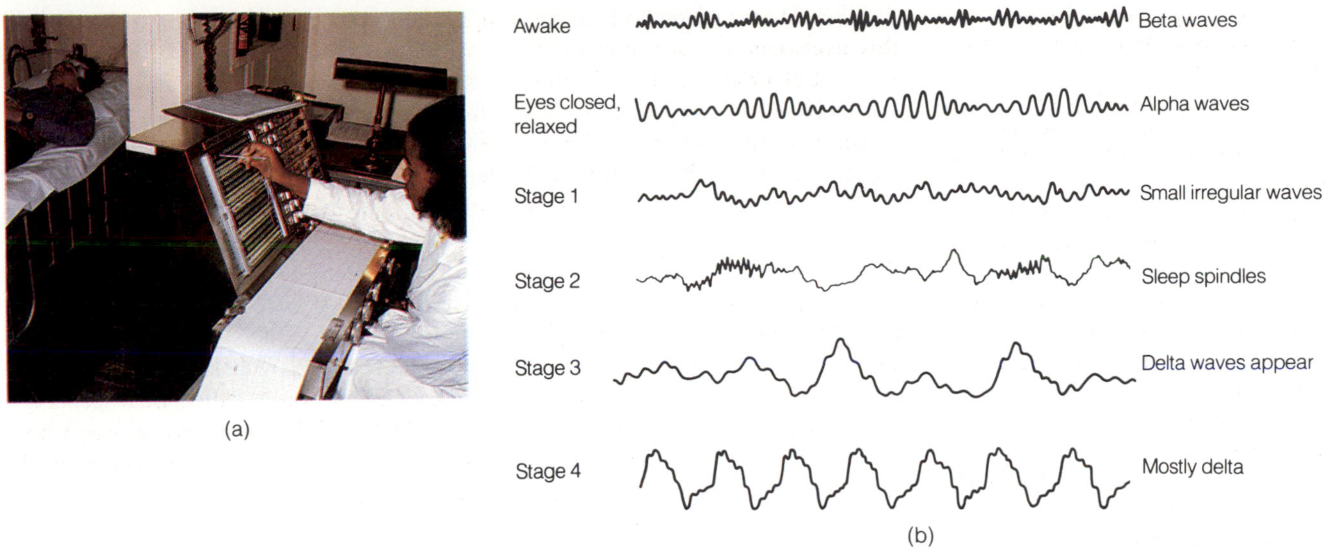

Fig. 6-3 (a) *Photograph of an EEG tracing.* (b) *Changes in brain wave patterns associated with various stages of sleep. Actually, most wave types are present at all times, but they occur more or less frequently in various sleep stages.*

Stage 4 About an hour after sleep begins, **deep sleep** is reached. In Stage 4 the brain wave pattern becomes almost pure delta waves, and the sleeper is in a state of nearly complete oblivion. If a loud noise is sounded during Stage 4, the sleeper will awaken in confusion and may not remember the noise.

After spending some time in Stage 4, the sleeper returns (through Stages 3 and 2) to Stage 1. Further shifts between deeper and lighter sleep occur throughout the night (see Fig. 6-4).

Two States of Sleep Along with the discovery of sleep stages, it was noticed that at various times the eyes of a sleeper make rapid movements. These rapid eye movements (or **REMs**) are strongly associated with dreaming. Roughly 85 percent of awakenings made during ongoing REMs produce reports of dreams (Cartwright, 1978). REMs usually occur in Stage 1 sleep. An exception is the very first Stage 1 period, which is usually free of REMs and dreams.

The two most basic states of sleep now appear to be REM sleep, with its associated dreaming, and **non-REM (NREM) sleep,** which occurs during Stages 2, 3, and 4 (Cartwright, 1978). NREM sleep is dream free about 90 percent of the time. While it's true that people awakened during NREM sleep occasionally say they were dreaming, dreams reported during REM sleep are usually longer, clearer, more detailed, and more vivid or dreamlike (Foulkes & Schmidt, 1983).

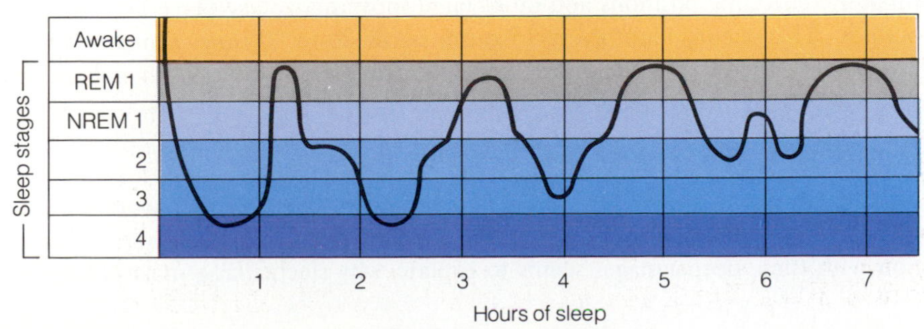

Fig. 6-4 *Typical changes in stages of sleep during the night. (After Van de Castle, 1971)*

NREM sleep seems to help us recover from fatigue built up during the day. It increases with exercise or physical exertion (Horne & Staff, 1983). In comparison, REM sleep increases when a person is subjected to added daytime stress. Although REM sleep totals only about 1½ hours per night (about the same as a feature movie), its connection with dreaming makes it as important as NREM sleep. REM sleep may become pronounced when there is a death in the family, a major occupational change, marital conflict, or other emotionally charged events (Hartmann, 1973).

REM Sleep—In the Theater of Dreams

When researchers Nathaniel Kleitman and Eugene Aserinsky discovered REM sleep in 1952, they ushered in a "golden era" of dream inquiry that has allowed us to answer some age-old questions. Let us consider some of the most interesting.

Question: Does everyone dream? Do dreams occur in an instant?

Most people dream 4 or 5 times a night, but not all people remember their dreams. "Nondreamers" are often shocked by the vividness of their dreams when first awakened during REM sleep. Dreams are usually spaced about 90 minutes apart, with each succeeding dream lasting a little longer. The first dream lasts only about 10 minutes; the last averages 30 minutes and may run as long as 50. Dreams, therefore, occur in real time, not as a "flash" (Cartwright, 1978; Dement, 1960).

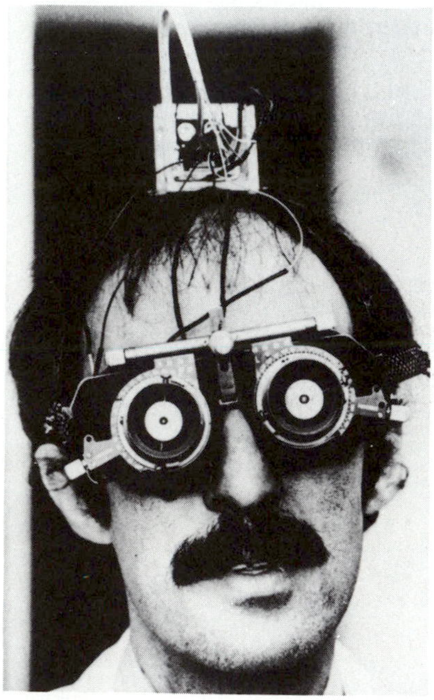

Fig. 6-5 *Dr. John Herman of the University of Texas may look like he just stepped out of the movie* Star Wars, *but he is actually involved in dream research. Dr. Herman is wearing goggles that electronically monitor eye movements during sleep. Use of such devices has greatly extended our understanding of dreaming.*

Question: What happens to the body when a person dreams?

REM Sleep As discussed before, the brain returns to light sleep and rapid eye movements begin. Some eye movements correspond to dream activity: Dream that you are watching a tennis match, and you will probably move your eyes from side to side (Dement & Kleitman, 1957).

REM sleep is a time of high emotion. The heart beats irregularly, and blood pressure and breathing waver. Both males and females appear to be sexually aroused. This occurs for all REM sleep, so it is not strictly related to erotic dreams. When an erotic dream does occur, evidence of sexual arousal becomes more pronounced (Cartwright, 1978). With all this emotional activity, it might be expected that muscles would be tense during dreaming. The reverse is true, however. During REM sleep, the body becomes quite still, as if the person were paralyzed. If we imagine the results that could come from acting out dreams, it seems that REM-sleep paralysis prevents some hilarious nighttime escapades. Fortunately, changing positions and other large movements take place *between* REM periods. This occurs about every 15 minutes, or 20 to 40 times a night. Interestingly, poor sleepers tend to move less and spend more time on their backs (De Koninck, Gagnon, & Lallier, 1983).

Question: Does sleepwalking occur during dreaming?

NREM Sleep Surprisingly, no. EEG studies have shown that **somnambulism** (sleepwalking) and **sleeptalking** occur in NREM sleep, Stages 3 and 4. Association with these deeper stages seems to explain why sleeptalking makes little sense and why a sleepwalker who is awakened is confused and remembers little (Jacobson et al., 1965; Luce, 1974). **Night terrors** also occur during NREM sleep. These are violent episodes of panic that may last 15 or 20 minutes. Affected individuals often scream and thrash about violently during the terror, but remember little afterward. In contrast, **nightmares** are merely "bad" dreams that occur during REM sleep.

Question: How important are dreams? Are they essential for normal functioning?

Dreams To answer these questions, dream researcher William Dement awakened subjects each time they entered REM sleep. People thus prevented from dreaming several nights in a row showed an increased tendency to dream. By the fifth night, 20 or 30 awakenings were often necessary to prevent dreaming. When uninterrupted sleep was finally allowed, subjects dreamed extra amounts. This effect, called a **REM rebound,** explains why alcoholics often have horrible nightmares after they quit drinking (Dement, 1960). Alcohol suppresses REM sleep and sets up a powerful rebound when it is withdrawn. It's worth remembering that while alcohol may help a person get to sleep, it often greatly reduces sleep quality.

While they were deprived of dream sleep, Dement's subjects complained of memory lapses, difficulty in concentrating, and feelings of anxiety during the day. For a time, this result led to widespread belief that a person would go crazy if kept from dreaming. But sleep researchers now refer to this as the "REM myth." Recent experiments indicate that missing *any* sleep stage can cause a rebound for that stage. More importantly, daytime disturbances are generally related to the total *amount* of sleep lost, not the type of sleep lost (Cartwright, 1978; Johnston et al., 1972).

What, then, is the purpose of REM sleep? For one thing, REM sleep increases after learning, so it may help restore brain chemicals needed for learning and memory (Hartmann, 1981; Stern, 1981). There is further evidence that dreams help integrate information learned during the day, prevent sensory deprivation during sleep, and aid the processing of emotional events. Although we have much to learn, it seems clear that REM sleep and dreaming are valuable for keeping the brain in good working order.

Somnambulism Walking or performing other actions while asleep.

Sleeptalking Speaking aloud while asleep.

Night terror Violent periods of emotional upheaval or panic that occur during deep sleep.

Nightmare Frightful or upsetting dreams occurring mainly during REM sleep.

REM rebound A significant increase in REM sleep observed on nights that follow a period during which REM sleep was reduced or prevented.

Dreams and Beyond—A Separate Reality?

Question: What do people usually dream about?

Calvin Hall, a noted authority on dreams, has collected and analyzed over 10,000 dreams. Hall (1966) found that most dreams reflect everyday experiences. The favorite dream setting is familiar rooms in a house. Action usually takes place between the dreamer and two or three other emotionally significant people—friends, enemies, parents, employers. Actions in dreams are also predominantly familiar: running, jumping, riding, sitting, talking, and watching. About half of the recorded dreams had sexual elements. Dreams of flying, floating, and falling occur less frequently. Hall also found that if you're dreaming more now, you may be enjoying it less. Unpleasant emotions such as fear, anger, and sadness are more frequent in dreams than pleasant emotions.

Wish fulfillment Freudian belief that the content of many dreams reflects unfulfilled desires that cannot be consciously expressed.

Psychodynamic theory Any theory of personality that emphasizes internal conflicts, motives, and unconscious forces.

Dream symbols Images in dreams that serve as visible signs of hidden ideas, desires, impulses, emotions, relationships, and so forth.

Activation-synthesis hypothesis Physiological theory that relates dream content to motor commands made, but not carried out, during sleep.

Hypnosis An altered state of consciousness characterized by narrowed attention and increased suggestibility.

Mesmerize To hypnotize.

Hypnotic susceptibility scale Any test designed to assess an individual's capacity for becoming hypnotized.

Question: How meaningful are dreams?

Dream Theories Sigmund Freud's book *The Interpretation of Dreams* (1900) opened a whole new world of psychological investigation. On analyzing his own dreams, Freud felt that many represented **wish fulfillment.** Thus, a student who is angry at a teacher may dream of successfully embarrassing the teacher in class; a lonely person may dream of romance, or a hungry child may dream of food.

Although Freud's **psychodynamic theory** of dreaming is attractive, there is evidence against it. For example, volunteers in a study of the effects of prolonged starvation showed no particular increase in dreams about food and eating (Keys, 1950). Freud's response, no doubt, would have been that dreams rarely express needs so directly. Freud believed that the conscience relaxes during sleep, allowing dreams to express unconscious impulses, desires, and conflicts in disguised **dream symbols.** Thus, a woman sexually attracted to her best friend's husband might dream of stealing her friend's wedding ring and placing it on her own hand, an indirect symbol of her true desires.

A radically different view of dreaming is offered by scientists Allan Hobson and Robert McCarley (1977). After studying REM sleep in cats, Hobson and McCarley believe that dreams are made in this way: During REM sleep, certain brain cells are activated that normally control eye movements, balance, and actions. However, messages from the cells are blocked from actually reaching the body, so no movement occurs. But the cells continue to tell higher brain areas of their activities. Struggling to come up with a reasonable interpretation of this information, the brain searches through stored memories and manufactures a dream. Hobson and McCarley call this explanation of dreaming the **activation-synthesis hypothesis.**

Question: How does this help explain dream content?

Let's use the classic chase dream as an example. In such dreams we feel we are running but not going anywhere as a pursuer bears down on us. Hobson and McCarley suggest that in such dreams the brain is being told the body is running, but it gets no feedback from the motionless body to confirm it. As it tries to make sense of this information, the brain creates a chase drama.

The activation-synthesis hypothesis certainly seems to explain some dreams. Most psychologists, however, continue to believe that dreams have deeper meaning (Cartwright, 1978; Winget & Kramer, 1979). As a result, many psychologists now urge people to collect and interpret their own dreams. The Applications section at the end of this chapter will offer some practical suggestions for doing just that.

Learning Check

See if you can answer these questions before reading on.

1. A momentary shift in brain activity to a pattern characteristic of sleep is referred to as:
a. delta sleep *b.* light sleep *c.* microsleep *d.* deprivation sleep

2. Delusions and hallucinations may continue for several days after a sleep-deprived individual returns to normal sleep. T or F?

3. Older adults, and particularly the elderly, sleep more than children because the elderly are more easily fatigued. T or F?

4. Most studies of sleep patterns show a consistent ratio of 2 to 1 between time awake and time asleep. T or F?

5. Rapid eye movement (REMs) indicate a person is in deep sleep. T or F?

6. Sleep spindles typically first appear in which stage of sleep? (circle)

Stage 1 Stage 2 Stage 3 Stage 4

7. Unpleasant emotions are more frequent in dreams than are pleasant emotions. T or F?

8. According to the activation-synthesis model, dreams reflect wish fulfillment and the symbolization of unconscious conflict. T or F?

Answers: **1.** c **2.** F **3.** F **4.** T **5.** F **6.** Stage 2 **7.** T **8.** F

Hypnosis—Look into My Eyes

"Your body is becoming heavy. Your eyes are so tired you can barely keep them open. You feel warm and relaxed and very heavy. You are so tired you can't move. Relax. Sleep, sleep, sleep." These are the last words a book should ever say to you, and the first a professional hypnotist might say.

Hypnosis, like dreaming, has an aura of mystery surrounding it. In reality, hypnosis is not nearly so mysterious as it might seem. Most psychologists regard **hypnosis** as an *altered state of consciousness, characterized by narrowed attention and an increased openness to suggestion.*

Interest in hypnosis began in the 1700s with Franz Mesmer (whose name is the basis for the term **mesmerize**). Mesmer, an Austrian physician, believed that he could cure diseases by passing magnets over the body. For a time, mesmerism enjoyed quite a following. In the end, however, Mesmer's theories of "animal magnetism" were rejected by the medical profession, and he was branded a quack and a fraud. The term *hypnosis* was coined later by an English surgeon named James Braid. The Greek word *hypnos* means "sleep," and Braid used it to describe the hypnotic trance. However, we now recognize that hypnosis is *not* sleep, since EEG (brain wave) recordings made during hypnosis are similar to those obtained when a person is awake.

Question: Can anyone be hypnotized?

Approximately 8 people out of 10 can be hypnotized, but only 4 out of 10 will be good hypnotic subjects. If you are willing to be hypnotized, chances are good that you could be. Hypnotic susceptibility can be measured by making a series of suggestions to a person and recording the number of suggestions to which he or she responds. A typical hypnotic test is the **Stanford Hypnotic Susceptibility Scale** shown in Table 6-1 (also see Fig. 6-6).

Question: How is hypnosis done? Could anyone be hypnotized against his or her will?

There are as many different hypnotic routines as there are hypnotists. The actual method of hypnotic induction doesn't seem to be too important. Common factors in all techniques are that they encourage a person: (1) to focus attention on what

Table 6-1 Stanford Hypnotic Susceptibility Scale

Suggested Behavior	Criterion of Passing (yielding score of +)
1. Postural sway	Falls without forcing.
2. Eye closure	Closes eyes without forcing.
3. Hand lowering (left)	Lowers at least 6 in. by end of 10 sec.
4. Immobilization (right arm)	Arm rises less than 1 in. in 10 sec.
5. Finger lock	Incomplete separation of fingers at end of 10 sec.
6. Arm rigidity (left arm)	Less than 2 in. of arm bending in 10 sec.
7. Hands moving together	Hands at least as close as 6 in. after 10 sec.
8. Verbal inhibition (name)	Name unspoken in 10 sec.
9. Hallucination (fly)	Any movement, grimacing, acknowledgment of effect.
10. Eye catalepsy	Eyes remain closed at end of 10 sec.
11. Posthypnotic (changes chairs)	Any partial movement response.
12. Amnesia test	Three or fewer items recalled.

(Adapted from Weitzenhoffer & Hilgard, 1959)

Fig. 6-6 *In one test of hypnotizability, subjects attempt to pull their hands apart after hearing suggestions that their fingers are "locked" together.*

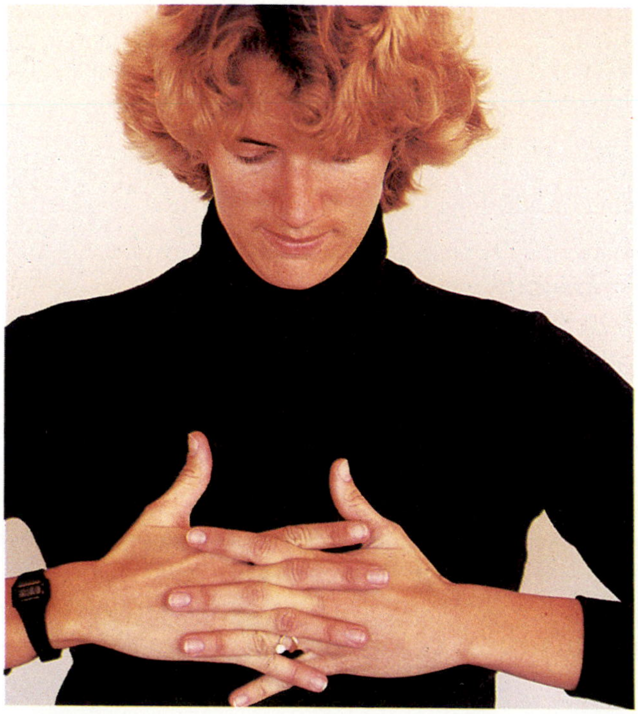

is being said, (2) to relax and feel tired, (3) to "let go" and accept suggestions easily, and (4) to use vivid imagination (Tart, 1975).

In deeper stages of hypnosis, "reality testing" may be relaxed so that a partial suspension of normal "will power" is achieved. But at first one must cooperate willingly in order to become hypnotized. Many theorists believe that all hypnosis is really **self-hypnosis** and that the hypnotist simply serves as a guide to help the subject achieve an altered state of awareness that could be achieved alone.

Self-hypnosis A state of hypnosis attained without the aid of a hypnotist; autosuggestion.

Basic suggestion effect The tendency of hypnotized persons to carry out suggested actions as if they were involuntary.

Disinhibition A reduction or removal of inhibitions.

Question: What does it feel like to be hypnotized?

You might be surprised at some of the actions you performed during hypnosis, and you might experience mild feelings of floating, sinking, anesthesia, or separation from your body. Personal experiences vary widely. However, in all but the deepest stages of hypnosis, people remain aware of what is going on. A key element in hypnosis is the **basic suggestion effect.** Hypnotized persons feel that suggested actions or experiences are involuntary—they seem to just "happen" without effort (Kihlstrom, 1985).

Question: Could someone be made to perform an immoral act while hypnotized?

Generally speaking, a person will not do something when hypnotized that he or she would not normally do. However, a person who would not undress in public *might* undress if given the suggestion that he or she is at home alone and that it is bedtime (Eysenck, 1957). Also, hypnosis may **disinhibit** a person by providing an excuse to engage in forbidden behavior. If you were hypnotized and told to throw a cream pie in your teacher's face, you would probably comply because you couldn't be held responsible. After all, you were hypnotized, weren't you?

Question: What can be achieved with hypnosis?

A vast array of abilities has been tested for responsiveness to hypnotic suggestion. In some cases the evidence is incomplete or contradictory, but the following conclusions seem reasonably justified (Kihlstrom, 1985):

1. **Superhuman acts of strength.** Hypnosis has no more effect on physical strength than instructions that encourage a subject to make his or her best effort (Barber, 1970).
2. **Memory.** There is some evidence that hypnosis can enhance memory. However, it also frequently increases the number of false memories as well (Dywan & Bowers, 1983). For this reason many states now bar persons who have been hypnotized from testifying in court cases. (See Chapter 9 for more information.)
3. **Pain relief.** Hypnosis can relieve pain (Hilgard & Hilgard, 1983). Therefore, it can be especially useful in situations where chemical painkillers cannot be used or are ineffective. One such situation is control of *phantom limb pain.* (Phantom limb pains are recurring pains that amputees sometimes feel coming from the missing limb.)
4. **Age regression.** Through hynposis, subjects have been "regressed" to childhood. Some theorists believe that regressed subjects are only acting childlike. Doubt is also cast by the fact that age-regressed persons continue to use knowledge they could only have learned as adults. The validity of age regression, therefore, remains doubtful (Kihlstrom, 1985).

Stage hypnosis Use of hypnosis to entertain; more often, merely a simulation of hypnosis for that purpose.

Psychoactive drug A mood- or consciousness-altering substance.

Stimulant A substance that produces a temporary increase of activity in the body and nervous system.

Depressant A substance that produces a temporary decrease of activity in the body and nervous system.

5. **Sensory changes.** Hypnotic suggestions concerning sensations seem to be among the most effective. Given the proper instructions, a person can be made to smell a bottle of ammonia and respond as if it were a wonderful perfume. It is also possible to alter color vision, hearing sensitivity, time sense, perception of illusions, and many other sensory responses (Kihlstrom, 1985).

Generally, hypnosis seems to have greatest value as a tool for inducing relaxation, as a means of controlling pain (in dentistry and childbirth, for example), as an aid to maintaining motivation (to study, diet, quit smoking, and so forth), and as an adjunct to other forms of psychological therapy and counseling. The effects that can be obtained with hypnosis are useful but seldom amazing (Hilgard, 1974; Rieger, 1976; Williams, 1974).

Stage Hypnotism

Question: How do entertainers use hypnosis on stage to get people to do strange things?

They don't. Little or no hypnosis is necessary to do a good stage hypnosis act. T. X. Barber, an authority on hypnosis, says that stage hypnotists make use of several characteristics of the stage setting to perform their act (Barber, 1970).

1. **Waking suggestibility.** We are all more or less open to suggestion, but on stage people are usually cooperative because they don't want to ruin the act. As a result they will readily follow almost any instruction given by the entertainer.
2. **Selection of responsive subjects.** Participants in stage hypnotism (all *volunteers*) are first "hypnotized" as a group. Thus, anyone who doesn't succumb (respond to instructions) is eliminated.
3. **The hypnosis label disinhibits.** As we noted before, once a person has been labeled "hypnotized," he or she can sing, dance, act silly, or whatever, without fear of embarrassment. Being "hypnotized" takes away all personal responsibility for one's actions.
4. **The hypnotist as a director.** After participants loosen up and respond to a few suggestions, they find that they are suddenly the star of the show. Audience response to the antics on stage brings out the "ham" in many participants so that all the "hypnotist" need do is direct the action.
5. **The stage hypnotist uses tricks.** Stage hypnosis is about 50 percent taking advantage of the situation and 50 percent deception. Here is a common deception:

   One of the more impressive stage tricks is to suspend a person horizontally between two chairs and then to stand on the person's chest. This is astounding only because the audience does not question it. Anyone can do it, as is demonstrated in the photographs and instructions in Fig. 6-7. Try it!

To summarize, hypnosis is real and is capable of causing a significant change in conscious experience. It is a useful tool that has been effectively applied in a variety of settings. The TV or nightclub stage, however, is not one of these settings. Stage "hypnotists" entertain; they rarely hypnotize.

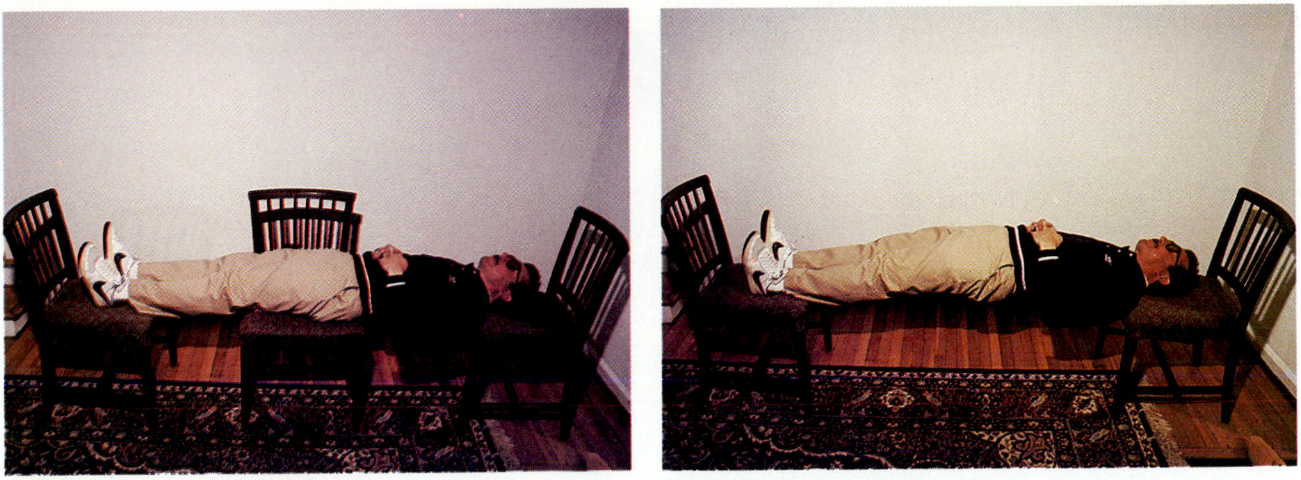

Fig. 6-7 *Arrange three chairs as shown. Have someone recline as shown. Ask him to lift slightly while you remove the middle chair. Accept the applause gracefully!*

Learning Check

Here are a few questions to test your memory of our discussion of hypnosis.

1. The term *hypnosis* was coined by a British surgeon named:
a. Franz Mesmer *b.* James Stanford *c.* T. A. Kreskin *d.* James Braid

2. Only 4 out of 10 people can be hypnotized. T or F?

3. Which of the following can most definitely be achieved with hypnosis?
a. superhuman acts of strength *b.* pain relief *c.* enhanced memory *d.* sleeplike brain waves

4. Could someone be made to perform an immoral act while hypnotized? Yes/No

Answers: **1.** *d* **2.** F **3.** *b* **4.** Generally no; however, hypnosis may provide an excuse to engage in prohibited behavior.

Drug-Altered Consciousness—The High and Low of It

Alcohol, heroin, amphetamines, barbiturates, marijuana, cocaine, LSD, caffeine, nicotine. . . . The list of consciousness-altering drugs—legal and illegal—is extensive. The surest way to alter human consciousness is to administer a **psychoactive drug.** A psychoactive drug is a substance capable of altering attention, memory, judgment, time sense, self-control, emotion, or perception (Ludwig, 1966).

Facts about Drugs Most psychoactive drugs can be placed on a scale ranging from **stimulation** to **depression.** Figure 6-8 shows the approximate relationships among various drugs and their effects on the central nervous system. A more complete summary of the most frequently abused psychoactive drugs is given in Table 6-2 (pp. 154-155).

Table 6-2 Comparison of Psychoactive Drugs

Name	Classification	Medical Use	Usual Dose	Duration of Effect
Alcohol	Sedative-hypnotic	Solvent, antiseptic	Varies	1–4 hr.
Amphetamines	Stimulant	Relief of mild depression, control of appetite and narcolepsy	2.5–5 milligrams	4 hr.
Barbiturates	Sedative-hypnotic	Sedation, relief of high blood pressure, hyperthyroidism	50–100 milligrams	4 hr.
Caffeine	Stimulant	Counteract depressant drugs, treatment of migraine headaches	Varies	Varies
Cocaine	Stimulant, local anesthesia	Local anesthesia	Varies	Varied, brief periods
Codeine	Narcotic	Ease pain and coughing	30 milligrams	4 hr.
Heroin	Narcotic	Pain relief	Varies	4 hr.
LSD	Hallucinogen	Experimental study of mental function, alcoholism	100–500 milligrams	10 hr.
Marijuana (THC)	Relaxant, euphoriant; in high doses, hallucinogen	Treatment of glaucoma	1–2 cigarettes	4 hr.
Mescaline	Hallucinogen	None	350 micrograms	12 hr.
Methadone	Narcotic	Pain relief	10 milligrams	4–6 hr.
Morphine	Narcotic	Pain relief	15 milligrams	6 hr.
Psilocybin	Hallucinogen	None	25 milligrams	6–8 hr.
Tobacco (nicotine)	Stimulant	Emetic (nicotine)	Varies	Varies

(Question marks indicate conflict of opinion. It should be noted that illicit drugs are frequently adulterated and thus pose unknown hazards to the user.)
*Persons who inject drugs under nonsterile conditions run a high risk of contracting AIDS, hepatitis, abscesses, or circulatory disorders.

Table 6-2 Comparison of Psychoactive Drugs (continued)

Effects Sought	Long-Term Symptoms	Physical Dependence Potential	Psychological Dependence Potential	Organic Damage Potential
Sense alteration, anxiety reduction, sociability	Cirrhosis, toxic psychosis, neurologic damage, addiction	Yes	Yes	Yes
Alertness, activeness	Loss of appetite, delusions, hallucinations, toxic psychosis	Yes	Yes	Yes
Anxiety reduction, euphoria	Addiction with severe withdrawal symptoms, possible convulsions, toxic psychosis, addiction	Yes	Yes	No
Wakefulness, alertness	Insomnia, heart arrhythmias, high blood pressure	No	Yes	Yes
Excitation, talkativeness	Depression, convulsions	Debated	Yes	Yes
Euphoria, prevent withdrawal discomfort	Addiction, constipation, loss of appetite	Yes	Yes	No
Euphoria, prevent withdrawal discomfort	Addiction, constipation, loss of appetite	Yes	Yes	No*
Insightful experiences, exhilaration, distortion of senses	May intensify existing psychosis, panic reactions	No	No?	No?
Relaxation; increased euphoria, perceptions, sociability	Possible lung cancer, other health risks	No	Yes	Yes
Insightful experiences, exhilaration, distortion of senses	May intensify existing psychosis, panic reactions	No	No?	No?
Prevent withdrawal discomfort	Addiction, constipation, loss of appetite	Yes	Yes	No
Euphoria, prevent withdrawal discomfort	Addiction, constipation, loss of appetite	Yes	Yes	No*
Insightful experiences, exhilaration, distortion of senses	May intensify existing psychosis, panic reactions	No	No?	No?
Alertness, calmness, sociability	Emphysema, lung cancer, mouth and throat cancer, cardiovascular damage, loss of appetite	Yes	Yes	Yes

Adapted and updated from *Resource Book for Drug Abuse Education*. NEA, 1969.

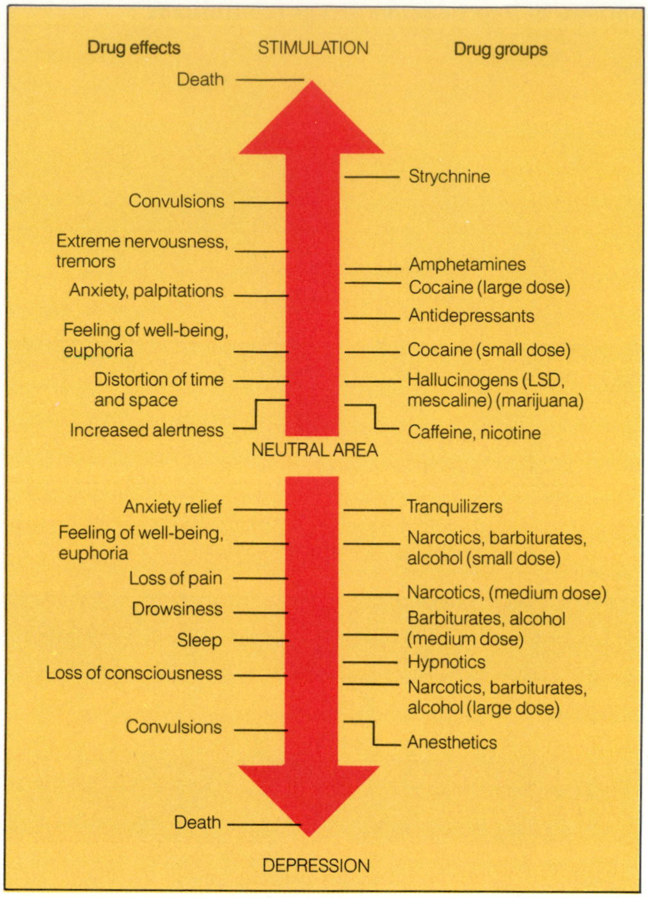

Fig. 6-8 *Spectrum and continuum of drug action. Drugs can be placed on a continuum of stimulation-depression according to their effect on the central nervous system.*

Drug dependence falls into two broad categories. When a person compulsively uses a drug to maintain bodily comfort, a **physical dependence** exists. Physical dependence, commonly referred to as **addiction,** occurs most often with drugs that cause **withdrawal symptoms** (painful or even agonizing reactions that take place when the drug is withheld). Addiction is often accompanied by a **drug tolerance,** in which the user must take larger and larger doses to achieve the desired effect. When a person develops a **psychological dependence,** he or she feels a drug is necessary to maintain emotional or psychological well-being. No withdrawal symptoms or physical cravings are involved, and yet psychological dependence may affect a drug user as powerfully as physical dependence does.

Note in Table 6-2 that the drugs most clearly associated with physical dependence are: alcohol, amphetamines, barbiturates, codeine, heroin, methadone, morphine, and tobacco. *All* of the drugs listed can lead to psychological dependence. The discussion that follows focuses on the drugs most frequently abused by college students.

Uppers—Amphetamines, Cocaine, Caffeine, Nicotine

Amphetamines form a large group of synthetic stimulants. Drugs commonly available in this group are *Dexedrine*, *Methedrine*, and *Benzedrine*. Amphetamines were once widely prescribed by doctors to aid weight loss or to combat mild depression. Both practices are now discouraged because patients frequently become dependent on their "legal" amphetamines. The only fully legitimate medical uses of amphetamines are to treat narcolepsy (sleep attacks) and to counteract overdoses of depressant drugs. Illicit use of amphetamines is widespread among individuals seeking an easy way to stay awake or who think drugs can improve mental or physical performance.

Amphetamines rapidly produce a drug tolerance. Most abusers begin with 1 or 2 pills a day and soon progress to dozens a day to get the same effect. Eventually, many users take amphetamines in large doses, or switch to injecting Methedrine ("speed") directly into the bloodstream. The true speed freak typically goes on binges lasting several days, after which he or she "crashes" from lack of sleep and food.

Question: How dangerous are amphetamines?

The dangers of amphetamine usage are multiple. To stay "high," the speed freak must take more and more of the drug as the body's tolerance increases. Higher doses can cause nausea, vomiting, high blood pressure, life-threatening heart arrhythmias, and crippling strokes. Also, it is important to realize that amphetamines speed the expenditure of bodily resources; they do not magically supply energy (AMA, 1968). Hence, the after-effects of an amphetamine high can be quite dangerous and uncomfortable. Possible effects include fatigue, depression, terrifying nightmares, confusion, and uncontrolled irritability and aggression. Repeatedly overextending one's body by speeding may lead to:

> considerable weight loss, sores and nonhealing ulcers, brittle fingernails, tooth grinding, chronic chest infections, liver disease, a variety of hypertensive disorders, and in some cases cerebral hemorrhage. (Canadian Government's Commission of Inquiry, 1971)

Amphetamines can also cause a loss of contact with reality known as **amphetamine psychosis.** Affected individuals feel threatened and suffer from paranoid delusions that someone is out to get them. Acting on these delusions, the speed freak may become violent, resulting in self-injury or injury to others (Snyder, 1972).

Cocaine Cocaine is a powerful central nervous system stimulant derived from the leaves of the coca plant. Its subjective effects are sensations of alertness, euphoria, well-being, power, boundless energy, or exhilaration (Spotts & Shontz, 1980). Cocaine has a long history of use and misuse in the United States. At the turn of the century, dozens of non-prescription potions and cure-alls containing cocaine were sold. It was during this time that Coca-Cola was indeed the "real thing." From 1886 until 1906, Coca-Cola contained cocaine (which has since been replaced with caffeine) (Grinspoon & Bakalar, 1977). Today, cocaine is

Physical dependence Physical addiction, as indicated by the presence of drug tolerance and withdrawal symptoms.

Withdrawal symptoms Physical illness and discomfort that accompany the withdrawal of an addictive drug.

Drug tolerance A reduction in the body's response to a drug.

Psychological dependence Drug dependence that is based primarily on emotional or psychological needs.

Amphetamines A class of synthetic drugs having stimulant effects on the nervous system.

Amphetamine psychosis A severe disruption of psychological functioning caused by abuse of amphetamines.

Cocaine A crystalline drug derived from coca leaves; used as a central nervous system stimulant and local anesthetic.

Caffeine A natural drug with stimulant properties; found in coffee and tea and added to artificial beverages and medicines.

Caffeinism Excessive consumption of caffeine, leading to dependence and a variety of physical and psychological complaints.

becoming one of the most widely abused drugs. An estimated 4 to 5 million Americans use it at least once a month (Hammer & Hazleton, 1984).

Question: How does cocaine differ from amphetamines?

The two are very much alike in their effect on the central nervous system, so much so that when experienced users are given both they can't tell the difference (Resnick et al., 1977). At high dosages the main difference is that amphetamine effects may last several hours; cocaine is quickly metabolized, so its effects last only about 15 to 30 minutes.

Question: How dangerous is cocaine?

Many scientists are beginning to think it is physically addicting, especially as the number of dependent abusers has continued to grow. On one hand, there is little evidence that withdrawal symptoms occur when a person stops taking cocaine. Yet, on the other hand, many users report powerful cravings for cocaine when they try to stop using it (Wilbur, 1986). Thus, while it remains debatable if cocaine is physically addicting in the classic sense, there is little doubt about its tremendous potential for abuse.

Cocaine is one of the most rewarding of all known chemicals. When rats and monkeys are given free access to cocaine, they find it irresistible. Many, in fact, end up dying of convulsions from self-administered overdoses of the drug (Hammer & Hazelton, 1984). In short, those who use cocaine run a high risk of becoming dependent and compulsive abusers. Many authorities estimate that if cocaine were cheaper, 9 out of 10 users would progress to compulsive abuse. In fact, rock cocaine (or "crack"), which is cheaper, appears to be producing very high abuse rates among those who try it.

The following is a list of increasingly serious signs of cocaine abuse (Pursch, 1983):

Compulsive use. If cocaine is available, say at a party, you will undoubtedly use it. You can't say no to it.

Loss of control. Once you have had some cocaine, you will keep using it until you are exhausted or the cocaine is gone.

Disregarding consequences. You don't care if the rent gets paid, your job is endangered, your lover disapproves, or your health is affected—you'll use cocaine anyway.

Cocaine has quite a reputation as a "glamour" drug. It is becoming increasingly clear, however, that it's capacity for abuse and social damage rivals that of the decidedly unglamorous drug, heroin. Anyone who thinks he or she may be developing a cocaine problem should seek advice at a drug clinic or a Cocaine Anonymous meeting.

Caffeine Caffeine is the most frequently used psychoactive drug in the United States. Caffeine stimulates the brain by blocking chemicals that normally inhibit or slow nerve activity. Its effects become apparent with doses as small as 100 to 200 milligrams (the amount found in about 2 cups of brewed coffee) (Julien, 1985). Psychologically, caffeine suppresses fatigue or drowsiness and increases feelings of alertness; some people have a hard time starting a day without it.

How much caffeine did you consume today? It is common to think of coffee as the major source of caffeine, but there are many others. Caffeine is found in tea, many soft drinks (especially colas), chocolate, and cocoa. Over 2,000 nonprescription drugs also contain caffeine, including stay-awake pills, cold remedies, and many name-brand aspirin products.

Question: Are there any serious drawbacks to using caffeine?

Serious abuse of caffeine may result in an unhealthy drug dependence known as **caffeinism** (Levitt, 1977) (Fig. 6-9). People with caffeinism suffer from insomnia, irritability, loss of appetite, chills, racing heart, and elevated body temperature. It is not uncommon to find that such individuals are consuming 15 or 20 cups of coffee a day. Even in the absence of caffeinism, there are some caffeine-related health risks. Caffeine encourages the development of breast cysts in women, and it may contribute to insomnia, stomach problems, heart problems, and high blood pressure in both men and women. Since 1980, health authorities have urged pregnant women to give up caffeine entirely because of a suspected link between caffeine and birth defects. More recently, a possible link between caffeine and miscarriages has also been detected (Grady, 1986). It is customary in our culture to think of caffeine as a nondrug. But, as this discussion shows, it is wise to remember that it *is* a drug and therefore should be used in moderation.

Nicotine Nicotine is a naturally occurring stimulant found mainly in tobacco. Next to caffeine, it is the most widely used psychoactive drug (Julien, 1985).

Fig. 6-9 *Like other drugs, caffeine is subject to abuse by some users.*

THE FAR SIDE By GARY LARSON

The real reason dinosaurs became extinct

Question: How does nicotine compare with other stimulants?

Nicotine is a potent drug. In large doses it causes stomach pain, vomiting and diarrhea, cold sweats, dizziness, confusion, and tremors. In very large doses, nicotine may cause convulsions, respiratory failure, and death (Levitt, 1977). Nicotine is so toxic that it is sometimes used as an insecticide!

Most beginning smokers get sick on 1 or 2 cigarettes. In contrast, a heavy smoker may consume 40 cigarettes a day without feeling ill. This difference indicates that regular smokers build a tolerance for nicotine (Levitt, 1977).

Question: Is it true that nicotine can be addicting?

There is growing evidence that, for some smokers, nicotine is addicting. For many, withdrawal from nicotine causes headache, sweating, cramps, insomnia, digestive upset, irritability, and a sharp craving for cigarettes (Shiffman, 1980). Indeed, relapse patterns are nearly identical for alcoholics, heroin addicts, and smokers who try to quit (Brownell et al., 1986).

Question: How serious are the health risks of smoking?

A burning cigarette releases more than 6,800 different chemicals. Many of these are potent *carcinogens* (cancer-causing substances). In addition, nicotine itself may be cancer-causing (Bock, 1980). Lung cancer and other cancers caused by smoking are now considered the single most preventable cause of death in the United States. Among men, 97 percent of lung cancer deaths are caused by smoking. For women, 74 percent of all lung cancers are due to smoking. If you think smoking is harmless, you're kidding yourself. As one expert says, "The scientific link between tobacco smoking and cancer is now as firmly established as any link between cause and effect in a human disease is likely to be" (Reif, 1981).

Question: Is it better for a person to quit smoking abruptly, or taper down gradually?

Many authorities recommend cutting down gradually, or at least switching to a low-tar cigarette. But researcher Stanley Schachter and others believe it is better to quit cold turkey rather than merely to cut down or smoke lighter cigarettes. Schachter's work shows that smokers who cut down are in a constant state of withdrawal. This causes irritability and discomfort without really ending smoking. Smokers who switch to low-tar cigarettes often end up smoking more to get the same total nicotine input. In doing so, they may expose themselves to more cancer-causing substances than before (Schachter, 1978; Shiffman, 1980). Whichever approach is taken, quitting smoking is not easy. Yet tens of millions of people have quit.

Downers—Barbiturates and Alcohol

Question: How do downers differ from the stimulant drugs?

The two most widely used downers, or depressant drugs, are **alcohol** and **barbiturates.** These drugs are so much alike in their effects that barbiturates are sometimes referred to as "solid alcohol." Let's examine the properties of each.

Barbiturates

Barbiturates are **sedative** drugs that depress activity in the brain. Medically, they are used to calm patients or to induce sleep. In mild doses barbiturates have an effect similar to alcohol intoxication, but an overdose can cause coma or death. Barbiturates combined with alcohol are particularly dangerous, as the combined effects of the two drugs are multiplied by a **drug interaction** (one drug enhances the effect of another). Barbiturates are often taken in excessive amounts because a first dose may be followed by a second or third as the user becomes uninhibited or forgetful. Marilyn Monroe, Judy Garland, and a number of other well-known personalities have died of barbiturate overdoses. An overdose of barbiturates first causes unconsciousness, and then so severely depresses activity in brain centers controlling heartbeat and respiration that death results.

Sedative A substance that calms, tranquilizes, or induces sleep by depressing activity in the nervous system.

Drug interaction A combined effect of two drugs that exceeds what would be expected from the mere addition of one drug to the other.

Barbiturate One of a large group of drugs used as sedatives because of their ability to suppress activity in the central nervous system.

Alcohol Common name for ethyl alcohol, the intoxicating element in fermented and distilled liquors.

Abuse The most frequently abused downers are newer, short-acting barbiturates, such as *Seconal* and *Tuinal*. Closely related to these (and to alcohol) is the nonbarbiturate drug *Methaqualone* (*Quaalude*, *Sopor*, and *Parest* are its trade names). These drugs seem to be preferred because they take effect quickly, and the "rush" of intoxication only lasts from 2 to 4 hours. Like the other depressants, repeated use can cause a physical dependence and emotional depression. Freddie Prinze, a popular television comedian, was on Quaaludes before he committed suicide.

All too often, the short-acting depressants are gulped down with alcohol, or added in uncounted quantities to a "spiked" punch bowl. This is the combination that left a young woman named Karen Ann Quinlan in a coma that lasted over 10 years, ending with her death in 1985. It is no exaggeration to restate that mixing barbiturates with alcohol can be fatal.

Alcohol

Contrary to popular belief, alcohol is not a stimulant. The apparent gaiety at drinking parties is due to alcohol's effect as a central nervous system **depressant.** As Fig. 6-10 shows, small amounts of alcohol reduce inhibition and produce feelings of relaxation and euphoria. Greater amounts of alcohol cause progressively more dangerous impairment of brain function until the drinker loses consciousness. Alcohol is also not an aphrodisiac. It usually impairs sexual performance, particularly in males. As William Shakespeare observed long ago, drink "provokes the desire, but it takes away the performance."

Abuse Alcohol, America's favorite depressant, generates this country's biggest drug problem. Over 100 million Americans use alcohol, and an estimated 10 to 13 million of these have a serious drinking problem. A particularly alarming trend is a dramatic increase in alcohol abuse among adolescents and young adults. A recent national survey of college students found that 17 percent (more than 1 out of 6) are heavy drinkers. For college males the figure was 25 percent, or 1 out of 4 (Olmstead, 1983).

Question: What are the signs of alcohol abuse?

Detoxification To remove poison or the effects of poison; in the treatment of alcoholism, the withdrawal of the patient from alcohol.

Recognizing Problem Drinking Because alcohol abuse is such a common problem, it is important to recognize the danger signals of alcoholism. Progression from a social drinker to a problem drinker to an alcoholic is often subtle. Coleman and Hammen (1974) and Jellinek (1960) have detailed steps in the development of a drinking problem:

1. **Initial phase.** Initially, the social drinker begins to turn more frequently to alcohol to relieve tension or to feel good. Four danger signals in this period that signal excessive dependence on alcohol are:

Fig. 6-10 *The behavioral effects of alcohol are related to blood alcohol content and the resulting suppression of higher mental function. (From Jozef Cohen,* Eyewitness Series in Psychology, *p. 44. Copyright © by Rand McNally and Company. Reprinted by permission)*

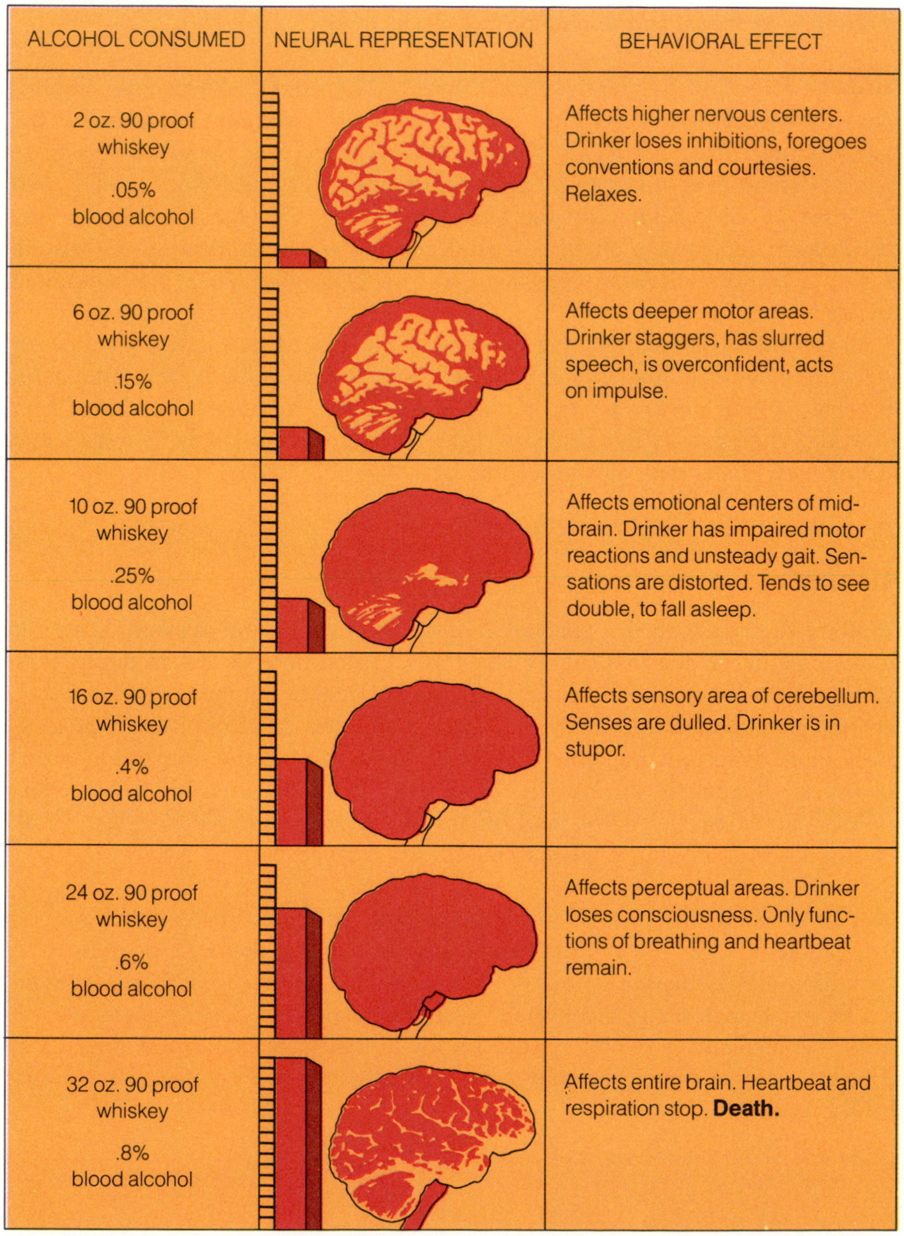

Box 6-1

The Development of a Drinking Problem

Early Warnings

You are beginning to feel guilty about your drinking.

You drink more than you used to and tend to gulp your drinks.

You try to have a few extra drinks before or after drinking with others.

You have begun to drink at certain times or to get through certain situations.

You drink to relieve feelings of boredom, depression, anxiety, or inadequacy.

You are sensitive when others mention your drinking.

You have had memory blackouts or have passed out while drinking.

Signals Not to Be Ignored

There are times when you need a drink.

You drink in the morning to overcome a hangover from previous drinking.

You promise to drink less and are lying about your drinking.

You often regret what you have said or done while drinking.

You have begun to drink alone.

You have weekend drinking bouts and Monday hangovers.

You have lost time at work or school because of drinking.

You are noticeably drunk on important occasions.

Your relationship to family and friends has changed because of your drinking.

Increasing consumption. The individual drinks more and more and may begin to worry about his or her drinking.

Morning drinking. Morning drinking is a dangerous sign, particularly when it is used to combat a hangover or to "get through the day."

Regretted behavior. While drunk, the individual engages in extreme behavior that later causes feelings of guilt or embarrassment.

Blackouts. Excessive drinking may be accompanied by an inability to remember what happened during intoxication.

2. **Crucial phase.** A crucial turning point comes as the person begins to lose control over drinking. At this stage there is usually control over when and where a first drink is taken, but one drink starts a chain reaction leading to a second and a third and so on.
3. **Chronic phase.** At this point alcoholics drink compulsively and continuously. They eat infrequently, become intoxicated from far less alcohol than before, and feel a powerful need for alcohol when deprived of it. Work, family ties, and social life all deteriorate. Their self-drugging is usually so compulsive that when given the choice, the bottle comes before friends, relatives, employment, and self-esteem. The alcoholic is an addict.

To add to this summary, Box 6-1 may help you form a clearer picture of how alcoholism begins.

Treatment Treatment for alcoholism begins by sobering up the person and cutting off the supply. This procedure is referred to as **detoxification.** It frequently

Cannabis sativa The hemp plant, from whose leaves and flowers marijuana and hashish are derived.

Hallucinogen Any substance that alters or distorts sensory impressions.

produces all the symptoms of drug withdrawal and can be excruciatingly unpleasant for the alcoholic. The next step is to try to restore the alcoholic's health. Continued heavy use of alcohol usually causes severe damage to the body and nervous system. Food, vitamins, and medical care cannot fully reverse this damage, but a reasonable state of health can be obtained. When alcoholics have "dried out" and health has been restored, they may be treated with tranquilizers, antidepressants, or psychotherapy. Unfortunately, the success of these procedures has been limited.

One lay group approach that has been fairly successful is Alcoholics Anonymous (AA), which functions on the premise that it takes a former alcoholic to understand and help a current alcoholic. Of those who remain in AA over 1 year, 81 percent get through the following year without a drink (Sexias, 1981). AA's success rate may simply reflect the fact that members participate voluntarily, meaning they have admitted to themselves that they have a serious problem. Sadly, it seems that problem drinkers often will not admit their problems until they have really "hit bottom." If they are willing, though, AA presents a practical approach to the problem.

Marijuana—What's in the Pot?

Marijuana and **hashish** are derived from the hemp plant **Cannabis sativa.** The main active chemical in cannabis is tetrahydrocannabinol, or **THC** for short. THC is a mild **hallucinogen**—a substance that alters sensory impressions. There have been no overdose deaths from marijuana use reported in the United States (Carr & Meyers, 1980). However, enough is now known about the effects of marijuana to make it clear that it cannot be considered harmless. Particularly worrisome is the fact that THC accumulates in the body's fatty tissues, especially in the brain and reproductive organs. Even if a person smokes marijuana just once a week, the body is never entirely free of THC (Nahas, 1979a).

Question: Does marijuana produce physical dependence?

Studies of long-term heavy users of marijuana in Jamaica, Greece, and Costa Rica failed to find any physical dependence (Carter, 1980; Rubin & Comitas, 1975; Stefanis et al., 1977). Marijuana's potential for abuse lies primarily in the realm of psychological dependence, not addiction.

Immediate Effects of Marijuana Marijuana's typical psychological effects are a sense of euphoria or well-being, relaxation, altered time sense, and perceptual distortions (Carr & Meyers, 1980). Being stoned on marijuana impairs short-term memory and slows learning—effects that can be a serious problem for frequent users (Nahas, 1979b). All considered, marijuana intoxication is relatively subtle by comparison to a drug such as alcohol (Carter, 1980). Despite this, it is now well established that driving a car or operating machinery while high on marijuana can be extremely hazardous (Carr & Meyers, 1980). As a matter of fact, driving under the influence of any intoxicating drug is dangerous.

Question: There have been many alarming reports in the press about the dangers of marijuana. Are they accurate?

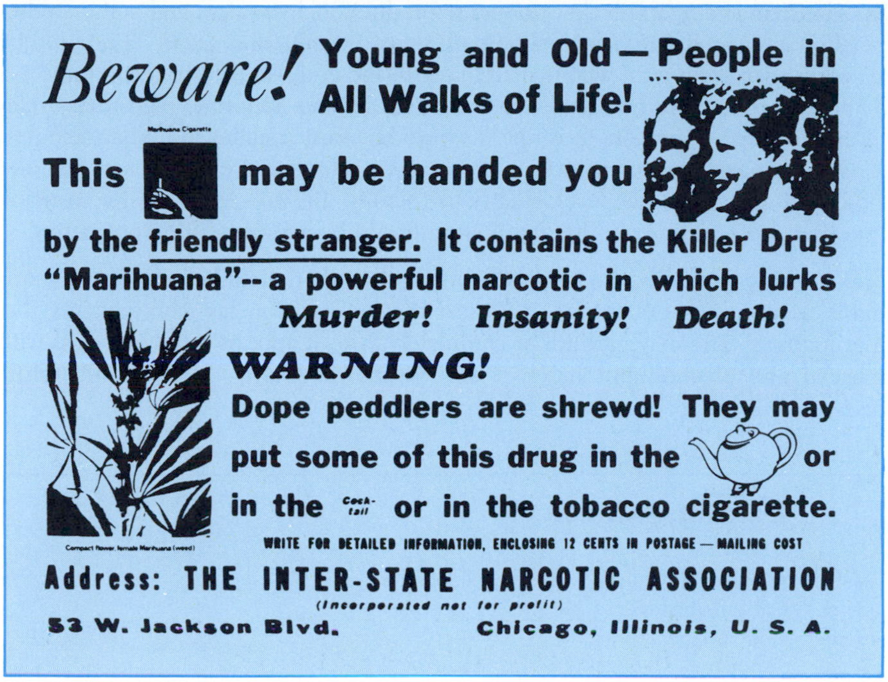

Fig. 6-11 *An outdated antimarijuana poster demonstrates the kind of misinformation that has long been attached to this drug. Research is beginning to sort out what risks are associated with continued use of marijuana.*

Dangers of Marijuana Use As one pharmacologist put it, "Those reading only *Good Housekeeping* would have to believe that marijuana is considerably more dangerous than the black plague." Unfortunately, an evaluation of marijuana's risks has been clouded by emotional debate. Let's see if we can make a realistic appraisal.

In the early 1970s it was widely reported that marijuana causes brain damage, genetic damage, loss of motivation, and a reduction in the body's natural immunity to diseases. These are serious charges, but each has been criticized for being based on poorly done or inconclusive research (Brecher, 1975a; Julien, 1985; NIDA, 1976; Zinberg, 1976). In addition, recent studies in Jamaica, Greece, and Costa Rica failed to find any serious health problems or mental impairment in long-term marijuana smokers (Carter, 1980; Rubin & Comitas, 1975; Stefanis et al., 1977). Does this mean that marijuana gets a clean bill of health? Not really. As is true of alcohol, some adults become highly dependent on marijuana. The use of any drug, including marijuana, can seriously impair mental, physical, and emotional development (Nahas, 1979b; Zinberg, 1976).

Health Risks After many years of conflicting and inadequate information, some of marijuana's potential health hazards have been clarified. After an extensive review of research, the National Academy of Sciences concluded in 1982 that marijuana's long-term effects include several health risks:

1. In regular users, marijuana causes chronic bronchitis and pre-cancerous changes in lung cells. At present no direct link between marijuana and lung cancer has been established, but it is suspected. Some doctors estimate that smoking several joints a week is the equivalent of smoking a dozen cigarettes a day (Nahas, 1979a).

2. Marijuana temporarily lowers sperm production in males, and some studies show increased numbers of abnormal sperm in men who use it. This could be a problem for a man who is marginally fertile and wants to have a family.
3. In experiments with female monkeys, THC causes abnormal menstrual cycles and disrupts ovulation. It is not known if the same applies to human females. Other animal studies show that THC causes a higher rate of miscarriages, and that it can reach the developing fetus (Nahas, 1979a). As is true for so many other drugs, it appears that marijuana should be avoided during pregnancy.

When the preceding findings are compared with the studies of veteran marijuana users in other countries, it is clear that no one can say with certainty that marijuana is extremely harmful or completely safe. It appears to be in a class with tobacco and alcohol, but much is still unknown (Carter, 1980). Only future research will tell for sure "what's in the pot."

Learning Check

1. Circle the letter of all the drugs listed below that are capable of causing a physical dependence:
   a. heroin *b.* morphine *c.* codeine *d.* methadone
   e. barbiturates *f.* alcohol *g.* caffeine *h.* amphetamines
2. Amphetamine psychosis is similar to extreme ____________, in which the individual feels threatened and suffers from delusions.
3. Cocaine is very similar to ____________ in its effects on the central nervous system.
   a. Quaaludes *b.* codeine *c.* cannabis *d.* amphetamine
4. The combination of ____________ and alcohol can be fatal.
5. One drink starts a chain reaction leading to a second and a third in the crucial phase of problem drinking. T or F?
6. This country's biggest drug problem centers on abuse of:
   a. marijuana *b.* alcohol *c.* tobacco *d.* cocaine
7. Most experts now acknowledge that marijuana is physically addicting. T or F?

Answers: **1.** All but *g* **2.** paranoia **3.** *d* **4.** barbiturates **5.** T **6.** *b* **7.** F

Meditation—The 20-Minute Vacation

People seek drug experiences for a variety of reasons, ranging from curiosity and a desire to belong to a group, to a search for meaning, or an escape from feelings of inadequacy (Lipinski & Lipinski, 1970). Perhaps there is an alternative. Many psychologists now regard **meditation** as a practical way to lower stress and enhance well-being. Meditation refers to any mental exercise designed to produce relaxation and heighten awareness.

Question: How is meditation done?

Concentrative meditation, which is the simplest of several related techniques, is easily learned. In one experiment (Maupin, 1965), college students were instructed to concentrate on breathing:

> While you are sitting let your breath become relaxed and natural. Then focus your attention on your own breathing: the movements of your belly, not your nose and throat. Do not allow extraneous thoughts or stimuli to pull your attention away from your breathing. This may be hard to do at first, but keep directing your attention back to it. Turn everything else aside if it comes up. (Maupin, 1965)

Meditation A contemplative mental exercise for the production of relaxation or heightened awareness.

Mantra A flowing word or sound repeated silently to oneself as the focus of attention in meditation.

Relaxation response The pattern of internal physiological changes that occurs in the body at times of relaxation.

Not all subjects responded to this exercise, but at the end of a 2-week period those who did reported satisfying changes in consciousness. Their experiences included deep concentration, pleasant bodily sensations, and extreme detachment from outside worries and distractions.

An alternative approach you may want to try involves the use of a **mantra.** Mantras are smooth, flowing words that are easily repeated. Instead of focusing on breathing, you can silently chant a mantra. Two widely used mantras are "om" and "om mani padme hum." Like breathing, a mantra is basically used as a focus for attention. If other thoughts arise during meditation, one should return attention to the mantra as often as necessary to maintain meditation.

The Relaxation Response A principal claim of many commerical meditation courses is that they offer a mantra tailored to the needs of each individual. But medical researcher Herbert Benson of Harvard Medical School has demonstrated that the physical benefits of meditation are the same no matter what word is used. These include lowered heart rate, blood pressure, muscle tension, and other signs of lowered stress.

Benson believes that the core of meditation is the **relaxation response.** By this he means an innate physiological pattern that opposes activation of the body's fight-or-flight mechanisms. Benson feels, quite simply, that most of us have forgotten how to relax deeply. Subjects in his experiments have had considerable success in producing the relaxation response by following these instructions:

> Sit quietly in a comfortable position. Close your eyes. Deeply relax all your muscles, beginning at your feet and progressing up to your face. Keep them deeply relaxed.
>
> Breathe through your nose. Become aware of your breathing. As you breathe out, say the word "one" silently to yourself.
>
> Do not worry about whether you are successful in achieving a deep level of relaxation. Maintain a passive attitude and permit relaxation to occur at its own pace. Expect distracting thoughts. When these distracting thoughts occur, ignore them and continue repeating "one. (Adapted from Benson, 1977)

Question: What effects does meditation have, other than producing relaxation?

Effects of Meditation Many extravagant claims have been made about meditation. For example, members of the Transcendental Meditation (TM) movement have stated that 20 minutes of meditation is as restful as a night's sleep. This, however, is simply not true. One recent study, for instance, found that merely resting for 20 minutes produces the same bodily effects as meditation (Holmes et al., 1983). Long-term meditators have also claimed improvements in memory, alertness, creativity, and intuition. Again, such claims must be judged cautiously. Most are based on personal testimonials or poorly controlled studies. Contrary to such claims, a study by Warrenburg and Pagano (1983) found no improvements in verbal, musical, or spatial skills that could be linked to TM.

Before you dismiss meditation, however, let's explore a little further. A thorough review of studies on meditation leads to a number of interesting conclusions (Pagano & Warrenburg, 1983).

As already stated, meditation does reliably elicit the relaxation response. The fact that other activities will do the same does not cancel the value of meditation as a way to achieve relaxation. Meditation may be the best choice for people who find it difficult to "turn off" upsetting thoughts when they need to relax.

Early reports that meditators produce more alpha waves (a brain wave pattern associated with lowered stress) have proved false. Meditation most often produces a *decrease* in alpha waves. Instead, meditators fall into hypnogogic drowsiness like that associated with sensory deprivation. In other words, they tend to remain in a twilight state between sleep and wakefulness (Pagano & Warrenburg, 1983; Schuman, 1980).

Regular meditators consistently report lower levels of day-to-day stress and a greater sense of well-being. This effect appears to be genuine. It is interesting to note, however, that similar stress reduction occurs when people set aside time daily to engage in other restful activities. Muscle relaxation, positive daydreaming, and even leisure reading can bring similar benefits.

Summary To summarize, recent research suggests that meditation is only one of several ways to elicit the relaxation response. For many people sitting quietly and resting can be as effective. However, if you are the type of person who finds it difficult to ignore upsetting thoughts, then concentrative meditation might be a better way to promote relaxation. More important than the method you choose, however, is a willingness to set aside time each day to intentionally relax. Meditation and similar techniques provide a valuable, stress-lowering time-out from the normal clamour of thoughts and worries—something almost everyone could use in our fast-paced society.

Learning Check

1. During meditation, there is an increase in hypnogogic drowsiness. T or F?

2. Mantras are words said silently to oneself to end a session of meditation. T or F?

3. Research conducted by Herbert Benson indicates that careful selection of a mantra is necessary to obtain the physical benefits of meditation. T or F?

4. The most immediate benefit of meditation appears to be its capacity for producing the relaxation response. T or F?

Answers: **1.** T **2.** F **3.** F **4.** T

Applications

Getting to Sleep/Exploring Your Dreams

Given that sleep and dreaming are the most familiar of all altered states of consciousness, it seems appropriate to return to these topics for this chapter's Applications. First, we will discuss ways of combating insomnia, then we will investigate collecting and interpreting dreams.

Insomnia

An estimated 40 million Americans suffer from chronic insomnia (Kripke & Simons, 1976). **Insomnia** includes difficulty in going to sleep, frequent nighttime awakenings, waking too early, or a combination of these. Almost everyone has had an occasional bout of insomnia.

Americans spend more than one-half billion dollars each year on drugs to help them sleep. There is real irony in this figure. Nonprescription sleeping pills such as *Sominex*, *Nytol*, and *Sleep-eze* have little or no sleep-inducing effect (Kales & Kales, 1973). Even worse are prescription *sedatives*. These drugs (usually barbiturates) decrease both Stage 4 and REM sleep and thereby drastically reduce sleep quality. In addition, a drug tolerance rapidly builds, so that the initial dosage becomes ineffective. Many users become "sleeping-pill junkies," as an ever greater number of pills is required to produce sleep. The resulting **drug-dependency insomnia** is a serious problem. Victims must be painstakingly withdrawn from all sleeping medications. Otherwise, terrible nightmares and sleep disturbances drive them back to drug use.

Question: If sleeping pills are a poor way to treat insomnia, what can be done?

Temporary insomnia caused by worry, stress, or excitement usually sets up a cycle in which heightened physical arousal interferes with sleep, then frustration and anger resulting from inability to sleep cause more arousal, which further interferes with sleep, which causes more frustration, and so on. This cycle suggests that one of the best ways to beat temporary insomnia is to avoid fighting it. It is usually best to get up and do something useful or satisfying when you have difficulty sleeping (reading a textbook might not be a bad choice of useful activities).

Some insomniacs have been found to have a drop in blood sugar during the night. The restlessness and hunger this causes can be avoided by having a small snack before sleeping. Also, it has been discovered that the amino acid **tryptophan** (TRIP-toe-fan) helps put people to sleep. Interestingly, tryptophan can be found in a glass of milk (Arehart-Treichel, 1977). So grandma was right after all! But she apparently didn't know that an egg-tuna-cottage cheese-soy bean-cashew-chicken-turkey sandwich would be even better for inducing sleep. All of the listed foods are also high in tryptophan (Hartmann, 1978).

Question: What about more serious cases of insomnia?

Treatment for **chronic insomnia** usually begins with training in relaxation techniques to lower arousal before sleep. (See Chapter 22 Applications for more about relaxation.) "Stimulus control" procedures are also helpful. For example, patients are told to strictly avoid doing anything in bed but sleeping. They are not to study, eat, watch TV, read, or even think in bed. In this way, only sleeping becomes associated with retiring (Bootzin, 1973).

One of the most helpful techniques for combating insomnia is also the simplest. Many insomniacs have scattered sleeping habits. For these people, adopting a regular schedule (getting up and going to sleep at exactly the same time each day) helps establish a firm body rhythm and greatly improves sleep. These and other ways of combating insomnia are summarized in Box 6-2.

Applications: Getting to Sleep/Exploring Your Dreams, continued

Box 6-2
Behavioral Remedies for Insomnia

All of the approaches listed here have been shown effective for treating insomnia (Borkovec, 1982; Hopson, 1986). With a little experimenting you should be able to find a combination that works for you.

Stimulants Avoid stimulants such as coffee or cigarettes. Remember too that alcohol, though not a stimulant, impairs sleep quality.

Worries Schedule time in the early evening to write down worries or concerns and what you will do about them the next day.

Relaxation Learn a physical or mental strategy for relaxing, such as progressive muscle relaxation (Chapter 22), meditation, or blotting out worries with calming images. Strenuous exercise during the day promotes sleep, but vigorous evening exercise is usually too stimulating. Very light evening exercise may be helpful, however.

Stimulus control Link only sleep with your bedroom so that it does not trigger worrying: (1) Go to bed only when you are feeling sleepy. (2) Avoid naps. (3) Awaken at the same time each morning. (4) Avoid nonsleep activities in bed. (5) Always leave the bedroom if sleep has not occurred within 10 minutes. (6) Do something else when you are upset about not being able to sleep.

Paradoxical intention To remove the pressures of trying to get to sleep, try instead to keep your eyes open (in the dark) and stay awake as long as possible. This lowers performance anxiety and allows sleep to overtake you unexpectedly.

An uninterpreted dream is like an unopened letter.
The Talmud

Exploring Dreams

As we have seen, Freud considered the meaning of dreams to be deeply hidden. But there are other points of view. Dream theorist Calvin Hall (1966, 1974) prefers to think of dreams as plays and the dreamer as a playwright. Hall does admit that the images and ideas in dreams tend to be more *primitive* than those experienced when one is awake. Nevertheless, much can be learned by simply considering the **setting, cast** of characters, **plot**, and **emotions** portrayed in a dream.

Another dream researcher, Rosalind Cartwright (1969, 1978) suggests that dreams be considered primarily as feeling statements. The overall **emotional tone** of a dream is a major clue to its meaning. Is the dream comical, threatening, joyous, or depressing? Were you lonely, jealous, frightened, in love, or angry? Cartwright encourages use of everyday dream life as a source of varied experience and personal enrichment, and considers dream explorations an avenue for personal growth.

Dream theorist Ann Faraday (1972) also believes in the value of studying one's own dreams. Faraday considers dreams a message *from* yourself *to* yourself. Thus, the way to understand dreams is to remember them, write them down, look for the message they contain, and become deeply acquainted with *your own* symbol system. Here's how:

How to Catch a Dream

1. Before retiring, plan to remember your dreams. Keep a pen and paper or a tape recorder beside your bed.
2. If possible, arrange to awaken gradually without an alarm. Natural awakening is almost always from a REM period.
3. If you rarely remember your dreams, you may want to set an alarm clock to go off 2 hours after you go to sleep, or for an hour before you usually awaken. Although less desirable than awakening naturally, this method may let you catch a dream.
4. On awakening, lie still and review the dream images with your eyes closed. Try to recall as many details as possible.

Applications: Getting to Sleep/Exploring Your Dreams, continued

5. If you can, make your first dream record (whether by writing or by tape) with your eyes closed. Opening your eyes will disrupt dream recall.
6. Review the dream again and record as many additional details as you can remember. Dream memories disappear quickly. Be sure to describe feelings as well as plot, characters, and actions.
7. Put your dreams into a permanent "dream diary." Keep dreams in chronological order and review them periodically. This procedure will reveal recurrent themes, conflicts, and emotions. It almost always produces valuable insights.
8. Remember, a number of drugs suppress dreaming (see Table 6-3).

Because each dream has several possible meanings or levels of meaning, there is no fixed way to work with it. Telling the dream to others and discussing its meaning can be a good start. Describing it may help you relive some of the feelings in the dream, and family or friends may be able to offer interpretations you would be blind to yourself. Watch for verbal or visual puns and other playful elements in dreams. If, for example, you dream that you are in a wrestling match and your arm is pinned behind your back, it may mean that you feel someone is "twisting your arm" in real life. Some people find it revealing to enact the dream as a play, or to draw, paint, or dance a dream.

The meaning of most dreams will yield to careful scrutiny and a little detective work. If you still have trouble seeing the meaning of a dream, you may find it helpful to use a technique developed by Fritz Perls. Perls, the originator of Gestalt therapy, considered most dreams a special message about what's missing in our lives, what we avoid doing, or feelings that need to be "reowned." Perls believed that dreams are a way of filling in gaps in personal experience (Perls, 1969).

An approach Perls found helpful in understanding a dream is to "take the part of" or "speak for" each of the characters and objects in the dream. In other words, if you dream about a strange man standing behind a doorway, you would speak aloud to the man, then answer for him. To use Perls' methods, you would even speak for the door, perhaps saying something like, "I am a barrier. I keep you safe, but I also keep you locked inside. The stranger has something to tell you. You must risk opening me to learn it."

Table 6-3 Effects of Selected Drugs on Dreaming

Drug	Effect on REM Sleep
Alcohol	Decrease
Amphetamines	Decrease
Barbiturates	Decrease
Caffeine	None
Cocaine	Unknown
LSD	Slight increase
Marijuana	Slight decrease or no effect

A particularly interesting dream exercise is to continue a dream as a waking fantasy so that it may be concluded or carried on to a more meaningful ending. It is also revealing to set up dialogues between people or objects in the dream, especially those that stand in opposition to one another. Speak for them both and you will perhaps discover conflicting aspects of yourself. As the world of dreams and your personal dream language become more familiar, you will doubtless find many answers, paradoxes, intuitions, and insights into your own behavior.

Using Your Dreams

History is full of cases where dreams have been a pathway to creativity and discovery. A striking example of a dream breakthrough is provided by Otto Loewi, a pharmacologist and winner of a Nobel Prize. Loewi had spent years on research relating to the chemical transmission of nerve impulses. A tremendous breakthrough in his research came when he dreamed of an experiment 3 nights in a row. The first 2 nights he woke up and scribbled the experiment on a pad, but the next morning he was unable to tell what the notes meant. On the third night, he got up after having the dream and, instead of making notes, went straight to his laboratory and performed the crucial experiment. Loewi later commented that if the experiment had occurred to him while awake, he would have rejected it.

Loewi's experience gives some insight into the po-

Applications: Getting to Sleep/Exploring Your Dreams, continued

tential value of dreams for the production of creative solutions. The dream state is one of reduced inhibition, and it may be especially useful in solving problems that require a fresh point of view. The likelihood of being able to take advantage of dreams for problem solving is improved if you "set" yourself before retiring by thinking intently about a problem you wish to solve. Try to steep yourself in the problem by stating it clearly and reviewing all relevant information. Then use the suggestions listed in the previous section to catch your dreams. While this cannot be guaranteed to produce a novel problem solution or a new insight, it is certain to be an adventure.

Learning Check

1. An excess of tryptophan in the body is now thought to cause most cases of chronic insomnia. T or F?

2. Remedies for insomnia that emphasize stimulus-control techniques attempt to strongly link sleep (and no other activities) with one's bed and bedroom. T or F?

3. Calvin Hall's approach to dream interpretation emphasizes the setting, cast, plot, and emotions portrayed in a dream. T or F?

4. Rosalind Cartwright stresses that dreaming is a relatively mechanical process having little personal meaning. T or F?

5. Both alcohol and LSD cause a slight increase in dreaming. T or F?

6. "Taking the part of" or "speaking for" dream elements is a dream interpretation technique originated by Fritz Perls. T or F?

7. Research shows that dreams have little value as an avenue for creative problem solving. T or F?

Answers: **1.** F **2.** T **3.** T **4.** F **5.** F **6.** T **7.** F

Chapter Summary

- States of awareness that differ significantly from normal, alert, *waking consciousness* are called *altered states of consciousness* (ASCs). Altered states are particularly associated with sleep and dreaming, hypnosis, psychoactive drugs, and meditation.
- Sleep is an innate *biological rhythm* essential for survival. Higher animals and people deprived of sleep experience involuntary *microsleeps*. Moderate sleep loss mainly affects vigilance and performance on routine or boring tasks. Extended sleep loss can (somewhat rarely) produce a temporary *sleep deprivation psychosis*.
- *Sleep patterns* show some flexibility, but 7 to 8 hours per night remains average. The amount of daily sleep decreases steadily from birth to old age. Once-a-day sleep schedules, with a 2-to-1 ratio of waking and sleep, are most efficient for most people.
- There are two basic sleep states, *rapid eye movement* (REM) sleep, and *non-REM* (NREM) sleep. REM sleep is much more strongly associated with dreaming than is non-REM sleep.
- Dreaming and REMs occur mainly during Stage 1 sleep. Dreaming is accompanied by emotional arousal, but relaxation of the skeletal muscles. *Somnam-*

bulism (sleepwalking) and *sleeptalking* occur during NREM sleep. *Night terrors* also take place in NREM sleep, whereas nightmares occur in REM sleep. People deprived of dream sleep show a *REM rebound* when allowed to sleep without interruption.

- Most dreams are about familiar settings, people, and actions. Dreams more often involve negative emotions than positive emotions. The Freudian, or *psychodynamic*, view is that dreams express unconscious wishes, frequently hidden by *dream symbols*. Many theorists have questioned Freud's view of dreams. For example, the *activation-synthesis model* portrays dreaming as a physiological process.
- *Hypnosis* is an altered state characterized by narrowed attention and increased suggestibility. Hypnosis seems capable of producing relaxation, controlling pain, maintaining motivation, and altering perceptions. *Stage hypnotism* makes use of deception and several characteristics of the stage setting to simulate hypnosis.
- A *psychoactive* drug is a substance capable of altering functioning of the brain and nervous system in ways that alter consciousness. Most psychoactive drugs can be placed on a scale ranging from *stimulation* to *depression*.
- Drugs may cause a *physical dependence* (addiction) or a *psychological dependence*, or both. The physically addicting drugs are: heroin, morphine, codeine, methadone, barbiturates, alcohol, amphetamines, tobacco, and possibly cocaine. All psychoactive drugs can lead to psychological dependence.
- *Stimulant drugs* are readily abused due to the period of depression that often follows stimulation. The greatest risks are associated wtih *amphetamines*, *cocaine*, and *nicotine*, but even *caffeine* can be a problem. Nicotine includes an added risk because smoking causes lung cancer and other health problems.
- *Barbiturates* are depressant drugs whose action is similar to alcohol intoxication. The overdose level for barbiturates is low, making them dangerous drugs. Mixing barbiturates and alcohol may be fatal, due to a *drug interaction*.
- *Alcohol* is the most heavily abused drug in common use today. The development of a drinking problem is usually marked by an *initial phase* of increasing consumption, a *crucial phase*, in which a single drink can set off a chain reaction, and a *chronic phase*, in which a person lives to drink and drinks to live.
- *Marijuana* is subject to an abuse pattern similar to alcoholism. Studies of long-term users have failed to find any drastic health changes due to marijuana. However, laboratory studies have implicated marijuana as a likely source of lung cancer and other health problems.
- *Concentrative meditation* is a deceptively simple technique for altering consciousness. A major physical benefit of meditation is its capacity to combat stress by producing the *relaxation response*.
- *Insomnia* may be temporary or chronic. When it is treated through use of drugs, sleep quality is often lowered and *drug-dependency insomnia* may develop. *Behavioral approaches* to managing insomnia have been shown to be effective.
- Dreams may be used to promote self-understanding. Hall's emphasis on the *setting*, *cast*, *plot*, and *emotions* of a dream can be helpful in this regard. Cartwright's view of dreams as *feeling statements* and Perls' technique of speaking for dream elements are also helpful.

Part Three

Learning, Memory, and Thinking

Chapter 7

Conditioning and Learning I

Chapter Preview

What Did You Learn in School Today?

When your aging author was in college, students discovered an interesting "game" that could be played with the plumbing in the dorms. If a toilet was flushed while someone was taking a shower, the cold-water pressure dropped suddenly, causing the shower to become scalding hot. Naturally, the shower victim screamed in terror as his reflexes caused him to leap back in pain. Soon it was further discovered that if several students flushed all *the toilets at once, the effects were multiplied many times over!*

A flushing toilet has to be one of the world's most uninspiring stimuli. But for a time there was a whole crop of University of California, Riverside, students who jumped involuntarily whenever they heard a toilet flush. Their reaction to this previously neutral stimulus was the result of a special form of learning called classical conditioning. *Details of how and why classical conditioning occurs are explored in this chapter.*

Now consider another learning situation: Let's say that you are at school and that you are "starving to death." Locating a vending machine, you deposit your last quarter to buy a candy bar. Your stomach growls in anticipation as you press the button, and . . . nothing happens. Being civilized and in complete control, you press the other buttons, try the coin return, and look for an attendant. Still nothing. Your stomach growls again. Being no longer either civilized or self-controlled, you give the machine a little kick (just to let it know how you feel). Then, as you turn away, the machine begins to whirr and out pops a candy bar plus 15 cents change. Once this happens, chances are you will repeat the "kicking process" in the future. If it pays off several times more, kicking vending machines may become a regular feature of your behavior. In this case, learning is based on operant conditioning.

Classical and operant conditioning underlie much human learning. In fact, conditioning reaches into every corner of our lives. You should certainly find it useful to learn more about it. Are you ready to learn more about learning? If so, read on! This chapter and the next explore conditioning and other forms of learning.

Survey Questions How is learning defined? What is classical conditioning, and what is its role in human learning? What factors affect classical conditioning? What is operant conditioning? What kinds of factors affect it? In what ways do classical and operant conditioning differ? How are conditioning principles applied to practical problems?

What Is Learning—Does Practice Make Perfect?

The weaver bird is a curious creature that ties a special knot with grass to hold its nest together. How does it learn to make the knot? It doesn't! Weaver birds raised in total isolation for several generations still tie the knot at their first opportunity to build a nest.

Knot tying in the weaver bird is a **fixed action pattern (FAP).** A fixed action pattern is an instinctual chain of movements found in all members of a species. Like other **innate** (inborn) **behaviors,** fixed action patterns help animals meet basic needs in their lives (picture a cat's face-washing routine, for instance). A simpler innate behavior is a **reflex,** such as blinking when a puff of air hits the eye. More complex patterns, such as the maternal instinct in lower animals, combine both fixed action patterns and reflexes.

Question: Do humans have instincts?

Humans have reflexes. But most psychologists reject the idea that people have instincts. To qualify as instinctual, a behavior must be both complex and "species specific." **Species-specific behaviors** occur uniformly in all members of a species, and, other than reflexes, no human behaviors seem to qualify. However, what humans lack in instinctual "programming" is more than made up for by learning capacity.

Our ability to learn is so advanced that the majority of our daily activities are either wholly learned, or at least greatly affected by learning. Imagine what you would be like if you suddenly lost everything you have ever learned. What could you do? You would be unable to read, write, or speak. You couldn't walk, feed yourself, find your way home, drive a car, or party. Needless to say, you would be totally incapacitated. (Dull too!)

Question: Learning is obviously important. What's a formal definition of learning?

Learning is a *relatively permanent change in behavior due to past experience*. Notice that this definition *excludes* temporary changes caused by motivation, fatigue, maturation, disease, injury, or drugs. Each of these can change behavior, but none constitutes learning.

Question: Isn't learning the result of practice?

It depends on what you mean by practice. Merely repeating a response will not necessarily produce learning. For conditioning to occur, some type of *reinforcement* must be present. **Reinforcement** refers to any event that increases the

Resources

Fixed action pattern (FAP) A genetically programmed sequence of actions that occurs mechanically and almost universally in a species.

Innate behavior A genetically programmed or inborn behavior pattern.

Reflex An innate, automatic response to a stimulus; for example, an eyeblink, knee jerk, or dilation of the pupil.

Species-specific behavior Patterned behavior that is exhibited by all normal members of a particular species.

Learning Any relatively permanent change in behavior that can be attributed to experience but not to fatigue, maturation, injury, and so forth.

Reinforcement Any event that brings about learning or increases the probability that a particular response will occur.

Antecedents Events that precede a response.

Consequences Effects that follow a response.

Classical conditioning A basic form of learning in which existing reflex responses come to be elicited by new stimuli (also known as respondent conditioning).

Neutral stimulus A stimulus that fails to elicit a response.

chances that a response will occur again. If I want to teach a dog a trick, I could reinforce correct responses by giving the dog food each time it sits up. Similarly, a child who consistently gets praise or a hug for picking up toys will learn to be neat. These, of course, are only examples. As we will see later, there are many ways in which learning can be reinforced.

Antecedents and Consequences Unlocking the secrets of learning begins with noting what happens just before, and just after, a response. Events before a response are called **antecedents.** Those that follow a response are called **consequences.** Paying careful attention to the "before and after" of learning is a key to understanding it.

In classical conditioning all the "action" occurs before a response. We begin with a stimulus that already triggers a response. For example, a puff of air to the eye (the stimulus) will make you blink (the response). This occurs without any prior learning. Now, assume that we sound a horn (another stimulus) just before each puff of air hits your eye. If the horn and the air puff occur together many times, what happens? Soon, the horn alone will make you blink. Since you didn't respond to the horn before, learning has occurred. Similarly, if your mouth waters each time you eat a sweet roll, you may learn to salivate when you merely *see* a sweet roll.

Classical conditioning, then, involves learning to *associate* antecedent events with one another. A stimulus that does not produce a response is associated with one that does. Learning is evident when the new stimulus also begins to elicit (bring forth) the response.

Operant conditioning involves learning affected by *consequences*. Each time a response is made, it may be followed by reinforcement, punishment, or nothing. These results determine whether a response is likely to be made again. For example, if you wear a particular shirt or blouse and get lots of compliments (reinforcement), you are likely to wear it more often. If people snicker, insult you, call the police, or scream (punishment), you will probably wear it less often.

Now that you have an idea of what happens in the two basic kinds of learning, let's look at classical conditioning in more detail.

Classical Conditioning— Does the Name Pavlov Ring a Bell?

Question: How was classical conditioning discovered?

At the beginning of the twentieth century, something happened in the lab of the Russian physiologist **Ivan Pavlov** that brought him international recognition. The event was so unastounding that a lesser man might have ignored it: Pavlov's experimental subjects drooled at him.

Actually, Pavlov was studying digestion. In order to observe salivation, he placed meat powder or some tidbit on a dog's tongue. After a time, Pavlov noticed that his animals were salivating *before* the food was placed in their mouths. Later, the dogs even began to salivate at the mere sight of Pavlov entering the room. Pavlov recognized this as something more than misplaced affection. Salivation is normally a reflex (automatic, nonlearned) response. Some form of learning had

Fig. 7-1 *Pavlov's conditioning apparatus. In Pavlov's early experiments a tube carried saliva from the dog's mouth to a lever that activated a recording device* (far left). *The placing of a dish of food in front of the dog was paired with various other stimuli for conditioning.*

to be taking place for the animals to salivate at the sight of food. Pavlov called this form of learning **conditioning.** Because of its importance in psychology's history, it is now called **classical conditioning** (also known as **respondent conditioning**).

Question: How did Pavlov study conditioning?

Pavlov's Experiment After Pavlov observed that meat powder caused reflex salivation, he began his classic experiments. To begin, he rang a bell. Then immediately afterward, he placed meat powder on the dog's tongue. Each time Pavlov rang the bell, he followed it with meat powder, which always caused salivation. This sequence was repeated many times: bell/meat powder/salivation, bell/meat powder/salivation. Eventually (as conditioning took place), the bell alone would cause salivation (see Fig. 7-2). By association, the bell, which was previously a **neutral stimulus,** began to have the same effect as food. This effect was shown by sometimes ringing the bell alone and observing that the dog salivated.

Fig. 7-2 *The conditioning procedure.*

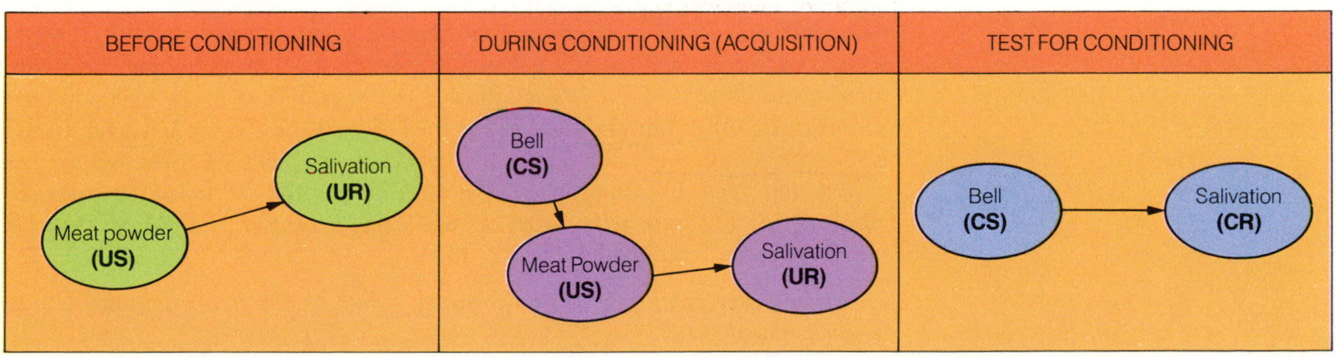

Conditioned stimulus A previously neutral stimulus that acquires the capacity to evoke a response by being paired with an unconditioned stimulus.

Unconditioned stimulus A stimulus innately capable of eliciting a response.

Unconditioned response An innate reflex response elicited by an unconditioned stimulus.

Conditioned response A learned response that becomes associated with a conditioned stimulus in classical conditioning.

Acquisition That period in conditioning during which a response is acquired through pairing of a conditioned stimulus and an unconditioned stimulus.

Respondent reinforcement In classical conditioning, reinforcement that occurs when the unconditioned stimulus closely follows the conditioned stimulus.

Extinction In classical conditioning, the weakening of a response that occurs when the conditioned stimulus is presented without the unconditioned stimulus.

Spontaneous recovery The reappearance of a learned response after apparent extinction.

Stimulus generalization The tendency to respond to stimuli similar to, but not identical to, a conditioned stimulus.

Psychologists use several special terms to describe these events. The bell in Pavlov's experiment is a **conditioned** (learned) **stimulus (CS).** The meat powder is an **unconditioned stimulus** (US) (because the dog does not have to learn to respond to it). Unconditioned stimuli typically produce reflex responses. Since a reflex is "built in," it is called an **unconditioned** (nonlearned) **response (UR).** In Pavlov's experiment, salivation was the UR. When the bell alone causes salivation, the response can no longer be called a simple reflex. Instead it is a **conditioned** (learned) **response (CR)** (Fig. 7-2).

Question: Are all these terms and code letters really necessary?

In a word, yes, because they help us recognize similarities in various instances of classical conditioning. As an example, see if you can apply the terms to explain the effects of the shower and flushing toilet described in the chapter Preview.

1. What is the unconditioned (nonlearned) response?

Hot water hurts jump back

2. What is the unconditioned stimulus that causes the response?

Hot water ~~burns; jump back.~~

3. What is the conditioned stimulus?

Toilet flushing

Now let's see if you understand the terms. The unconditioned, or nonlearned, response was a reflex jump from the hot water. The unconditioned stimulus was the hot water. The conditioned stimulus was the sound of a flushing toilet. That is, the flushing sound was at first neutral. But, due to conditioning, it began to elicit a reflex.

Elements of Classical Conditioning—Teach Your Little Brother to Salivate

A number of interesting events occur during classical conditioning. To observe them, you could ring a bell, squirt lemon juice into a child's mouth, and condition salivation to the bell. The child's reactions might then be used to demonstrate additional features of conditioning.

Acquisition During **acquisition,** or training, a conditioned response must be **reinforced,** or strengthened (see Fig. 7-3). In classical conditioning, reinforcement occurs whenever the CS is followed by, or paired with, an unconditioned stimulus (US). For our child the bell is the CS; salivating is the UR; and the US is the sour lemon juice. To reinforce salivation to the bell, we must pair the bell with lemon juice. Conditioning will be most rapid if the US follows *immediately* after the CS. For most reflexes the optimal delay between CS and US is from ½ second to about 5 seconds (Schwartz, 1984).

Question: After conditioning has occurred, what would happen if the US no longer followed the CS?

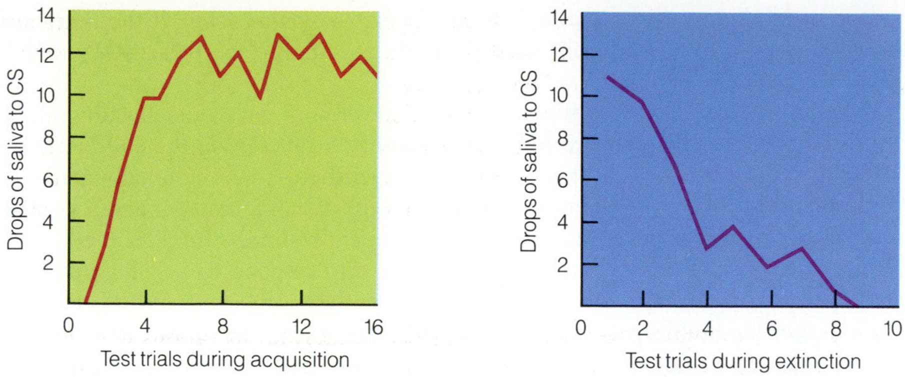

Fig. 7-3 *Acquisition and extinction of a conditioned response. (After Pavlov, 1927)*

Extinction and Spontaneous Recovery If the US never again follows the CS, conditioning will **extinguish.** If the bell (in our example) is rung repeatedly and not followed by lemon juice, the child's tendency to salivate to the ringing of the bell will be *inhibited* (or suppressed). Thus, we see that classical conditioning can be reversed by consistently omitting reinforcement (Fig 7-3). This process is called **extinction.**

Question: If conditioning takes a while to build up, shouldn't it take time to reverse?

Yes. After one session in which the bell is rung until the child quits responding, we might assume that extinction is complete. However, the next day, if the bell is rung, it would initially elicit a response. This reaction is called **spontaneous recovery.** Because of it, several extinction sessions may be necessary to completely reverse conditioning. Spontaneous recovery explains why a person who has been in a terrifying car accident may need many slow, calm rides before his or her fear is completely extinguished.

Generalization Once a person or an animal has learned to respond to a conditioned stimulus, other stimuli *similar* to the CS may also trigger a response. For example, we might expect the child in our conditioning experiment to salivate to sounds like the ringing of a telephone or doorbell. **Stimulus generalization,** as it is called, has been demonstrated many times in experiments involving humans and animals (Kimble, 1961).

It is easy to see the importance of stimulus generalization. Consider, for instance, the child who accidentally burns a finger while playing with matches. Conditioning principles predict that the sight of a lighted match will become a conditioned stimulus for fear. But will the child's fear be limited only to matches? Because of stimulus generalization, the child should also show a healthy fear of flames produced by cigarette lighters, fireplaces, stoves, and so forth. Fortunately, generalization tends to extend learning to new situations and similar circumstances. Were it not for this, we would be far less adaptable.

An important point to keep in mind about stimulus generalization is that it does have limits. Experiments show that there is a gradual decrease in generalization as test stimuli become less like the original CS (Siegel et al., 1968). In other words, if you condition a person to blink each time you play a particular note on

Stimulus discrimination The learned ability to detect differences in stimuli, often produced by reinforcing responses to one stimulus but not another.

Phobia An intense and unrealistic fear of some specific object or situation.

Conditioned emotional response The conditioning of autonomic nervous system responses and/or visceral responses to a previously nonemotional stimulus.

Desensitization A reduction in fear or anxiety brought about by repeated exposure to emotional stimuli, especially when they are coupled with relaxation.

a piano, blinking will decline as you play higher or lower notes. If the notes are *much* higher or lower, the person will not respond at all (Fig. 7-4).

Discrimination Let's consider one more possibility with our salivating child (who by now must be ready to hide in the closet). Suppose that the child is again conditioned with a bell as the CS. As an experiment we occasionally sound a buzzer instead of the bell but never follow it with the US (lemon juice). At first the buzzer would produce salivation (due to generalization). But after the buzzer is presented several times more, the child ceases to respond to it. The child has now learned to *discriminate*, or respond differently to, the bell and the buzzer. In essence, the child's generalized response to the buzzer has extinguished.

Stimulus discrimination is an important element of learning. As an example, you might remember the feelings of anxiety or fear you experienced as a child when your mother's or father's voice changed to its you're-about-to-get-swatted tone. Most children quickly learn to discriminate voice qualities associated with pain from voice qualities associated with praise or affection.

Classical Conditioning in Humans—An Emotional Topic

Question: How much human learning is based on classical conditioning?

In its simplest form classical conditioning depends on reflex responses. To expand a little on what we have said, a *reflex* is a dependable, inborn stimulus-response connection. For example, pain causes reflex withdrawal of various parts of the body. The pupil of the eye reflexively narrows to bright lights. Various foods cause

Fig. 7-4 (a) *Stimulus generalization. Stimuli similar to the CS also elicit a response.* (b) *This cat has learned to salivate when it sees a catfood box. Because of stimulus generalization, it also salivates when shown a similar-looking detergent box.*

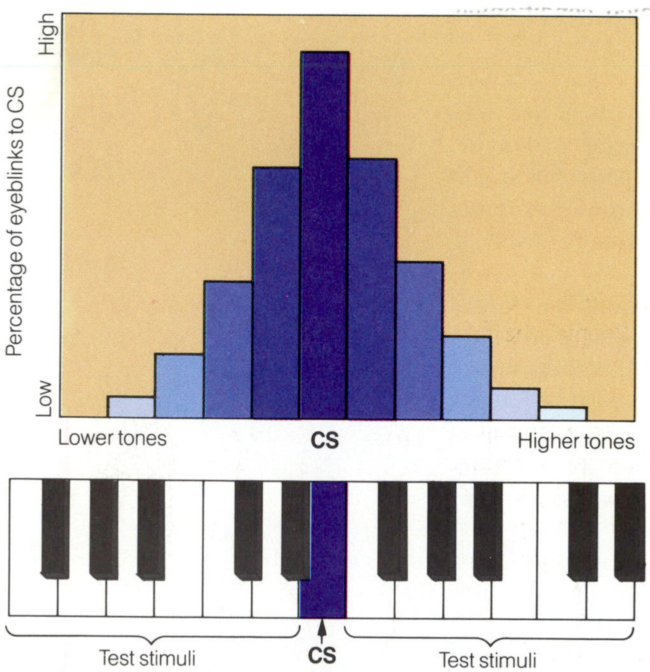

(a)

(b)

Fig. 7-5 *Hypothetical example of a CER becoming a phobia. Child approaches dog* (a) *and is frightened by it* (b). *Fear generalizes to other household pets* (c) *and later to virtually all furry animals* (d).

salivation. It is entirely possible for humans to associate any of these—or other—reflex responses with a new stimulus. At the very least you have probably noticed how your mouth waters when you see or smell a bakery. You may even have salivated to pictures of food (a picture of a lemon is great for this).

Of greater importance, perhaps, are more subtle ways in which conditioning affects human behavior. In addition to simple reflexes, more complex *emotional* or "gut" responses may be conditioned to new stimuli. For instance, if your face reddened as part of your emotional reaction to being punished as a child, you may blush now as an adult when you are embarrassed or ashamed. Or, think of the times you have experienced pain at a dentist's office. On your next visit did your heart pound and your palms sweat *before* the dentist began? Many *involuntary*, autonomic nervous system responses are linked to new stimuli and situations by classical conditioning.

Another common example of such conditioning is a **phobia** (FOE-bee-ah). Phobias are fears that persist even when no realistic danger exists. People who fear animals, water, heights, thunder, automobiles, or bugs can often trace their fear to a few unfortunate experiences in which they were frightened, injured, upset emotionally, or subjected to pain in the presence of the feared object or stimulus. Reactions of this type, called **conditioned emotional responses (CERs)**, are often broadened into phobias by stimulus generalization (see Fig. 7-5). In fact, a therapy technique called **desensitization** is now widely used to extinguish or counter-condition fears, anxieties, and phobias. (Desensitization is described in detail in Chapter 22.)

Vicarious, or Secondhand, Conditioning The importance of conditioned emotional responses is extended by the fact that they can be learned indirectly.

Vicarious classical conditioning Classical conditioning (especially of emotions) brought about by observing the reactions of another person to a particular stimulus.

Operant conditioning Learning that occurs when an organism "operates" on the environment and is affected by the consequences of its actions.

Operant reinforcer Any event that reliably increases the probability or frequency of responses it follows.

Conditioning chamber An apparatus designed for the study of operant conditioning in animals; a Skinner box.

One experiment, for example, showed that people could be conditioned to give an emotional response to a light, merely by watching another person get an electric shock each time the light came on. Even though subjects never directly received a shock, they developed a conditioned emotional response to seeing the light come on (Bandura & Rosenthal, 1966). Children who learn to fear thunder by watching their parents have undergone similar conditioning.

Vicarious classical conditioning, as it is called, probably affects emotional reactions in many situations. For example, the film *Jaws* made ocean swimming a conditioned fear stimulus for many viewers. If movies can affect us, we might expect the emotional reactions of parents, friends, and relatives to have even more impact. How, for instance, does a city child learn to fear snakes and to respond emotionally to mere pictures of them? Perhaps the child has been told that "snakes are dangerous," but the child's *emotional* response has probably been learned by observing the negative reactions of others.

The emotional attitudes we develop toward certain foods, political parties, minority groups, escalators—whatever—are probably not only conditioned by direct experience but vicariously as well. Parents may do well to look in a mirror if they wonder how or where a child has "picked up" a particular fear or emotional attitude.

Learning Check

Make certain you can answer these questions before continuing.

1. Complex responses known as ________ help many animals adapt to their environment.
   a. generalizations *b.* unconditioned discriminations *c.* fixed action patterns *d.* releasers
2. Classical conditioning, studied by the Russian physiologist ___Pavlov___, is also referred to as ___respondant___ conditioning.
3. Classical conditioning is strengthened or reinforced when the ___US___ follows the ___CS___.
   a. CS, US *b.* US, CS *c.* UR, CR *d.* CS, CR
4. Training that inhibits (or causes the loss of) a conditioned response is called ___extinction___.
5. Many phobias very likely begin with a CER that generalizes to similar situations. T or F?
6. Conditioning brought about by observing pain, joy, or fear of others is called ___vicarious___ conditioning.
7. A dependable, inborn stimulus-response connection is called a/an:
   a. unconditioned stimulus *b.* CER *c.* reflex *d.* reinforcer

Answers: **1.** *c* **2.** Ivan Pavlov, respondent **3.** *b* **4.** extinction **5.** T **6.** vicarious **7.** *c*

Operant Conditioning—Can Pigeons Play Ping-Pong?

As stated earlier, **operant conditioning** concerns how we learn to associate responses with their consequences. The basic principle of operant conditioning is quite simple: Acts followed by reinforcement tend to be repeated. Think of the

Table 7-1 Comparison of Classical Conditioning and Operant Conditioning

	Classical Conditioning	Operant Conditioning
Nature of response	Involuntary, reflex	Spontaneous, voluntary
Reinforcement	Occurs *before* response (conditioned stimulus paired with reinforcing stimulus)	Occurs *after* response (response is followed by reinforcing stimulus or event)
Role of subject	Passive (response is *elicited*)	Active (response is *emitted*)
Nature of learning	Association between antecedent stimuli	Probability of response altered by consequences

earlier example of the vending machine. Because kicking the machine was followed by reward, the odds of repeating the "kicking response" were increased.

As we have seen, classical conditioning is passive and involuntary. It simply "happens to" the learner when a CS and US are associated. In operant conditioning the learner actively "operates on" the environment. Thus, operant conditioning refers mainly to learning *voluntary* responses. For example, waving your hand in class to get a teacher's attention is a learned operant response. (See Table 7-1 for a further comparison of classical and operant conditioning.)

The idea that reward affects learning is certainly nothing new to parents (and other trainers of small animals). However, parents, as well as teachers, politicians, businesspeople, supervisors, and even you, may use reward in ways that are haphazard, inexact, or misguided. A case in point is the very term *reward*. To be correct, it is better to say *reinforcer*. Why? Because rewards do not always increase responding. If you try to give licorice candy to a child as a reward for good behavior, the reward will work only if the child likes licorice. As a practical rule of thumb, psychologists therefore define an **operant reinforcer** as any event that follows a response and increases its probability.

Acquisition of an Operant Response Most laboratory research on operant learning takes place in some form of **conditioning chamber**, also called a Skinner box (after B. F. Skinner, who invented it for experiments in operant conditioning) (see Fig. 7-6). A look into a typical Skinner box will clarify the process of operant conditioning.

The Adventures of Mickey Rat

A hungry rat is placed in a small cagelike chamber. The walls are bare except for a metal lever and a tray from which food pellets may be dispensed (see Fig. 7-6).

Frankly, there's not much to do in a Skinner box. This situation increases the chances that our subject will make the response that we want to reinforce, which is pressing the bar. Hunger also ensures that the animal will actively *emit*, or freely give off, a variety of responses. Now let's take another look at our subject.

Further Adventures of Mickey Rat

For a while our subject walks around, grooms, sniffs at the corners, or stands on his hind legs—all typical rat behaviors. Then it happens. He places his paw on the lever to get a better view of the top of the cage. *Click!* The lever depresses, and a food pellet

Fig. 7-6 *The Skinner box. This simple device, invented by B. F. Skinner, allows careful study of operant conditioning. When the rat presses the bar, a pellet of food or a drop of water is automatically released.*

drops into the tray. The rat walks to the tray, eats the pellet, and then grooms himself. Up and exploring the cage again, he leans on the lever. *Click!* After a trip to the food tray, he returns to the bar and sniffs it, then puts his foot on it. *Click!* Soon the rat's behavior settles into a smooth pattern of frequent bar pressing.

Notice that the rat did not acquire a new skill in this situation. He already had the responses necessary to depress the bar. Reward only alters how *frequently* he presses the bar. In operant conditioning, reinforcement is used to alter the frequency of responses or to assemble them into new patterns.

A good example of using operant reinforcement to change behavior patterns is shown in Fig 7-7. The results are from an effort to reduce the number of deviant behaviors performed by children in a special classroom. (Deviant behavior was defined as fighting, crying, and having temper tantrums.) As you can see, chaos reigned during the initial, baseline period. However, when good behavior (such as paying attention or remaining seated) was reinforced, disruptive actions declined rapidly (O'Leary & Becker, 1967).

To be effective, operant reinforcement like that used in the special classroom must be **response contingent.** That is, reinforcement is given only when a desired response is made. Contingent reinforcement also affects the *performance* of responses already learned. This is evident in situations ranging from childrearing to job performance and pay (see Fig. 7-8).

Shaping Even in a Skinner box, it might be a long time before a rat accidentally pressed the bar and received a food pellet. We might wait forever for more complicated responses to occur. For example, you would have to wait a long time for a duck to accidentally walk out of its cage, turn on a light, play a toy piano, turn off the light, and walk back to its cage. If this is what you wanted to reward, you would never get the chance.

Question: Then how are the animals on TV and at amusement parks taught to perform complicated tricks?

Response-contingent reinforcement Reinforcement given only when a particular response is made.

Shaping Gradual molding of responses to a final desired pattern.

Successive approximations A gradual series of steps that change behavior to a desired response pattern.

The answer lies in **shaping.** Let's look again at our subject, Mickey Rat.

Mickey Rat Shapes Up

Assume that the rat has not yet learned to press the bar. He also shows no signs of interest in the bar. Instead of waiting for the first accidental bar press, we can shape his behavior patterns. At first, we settle for just getting him to face the bar. Any time he turns toward the bar, he is reinforced with a bit of food. Soon Mickey spends much of his time facing the bar. Next, we reinforce him every time he takes a step toward the bar. When he turns toward the bar, then walks away, nothing happens. But when he faces the bar and takes a step forward, *click!* His responses are being shaped.

By changing the rules regarding what makes a successful response, the rat can gradually be trained to approach the bar and to press it. We can reward responses that come closer and closer to the final desired pattern until it occurs. The basic principle of shaping, then, is that **successive approximations** to the desired re-

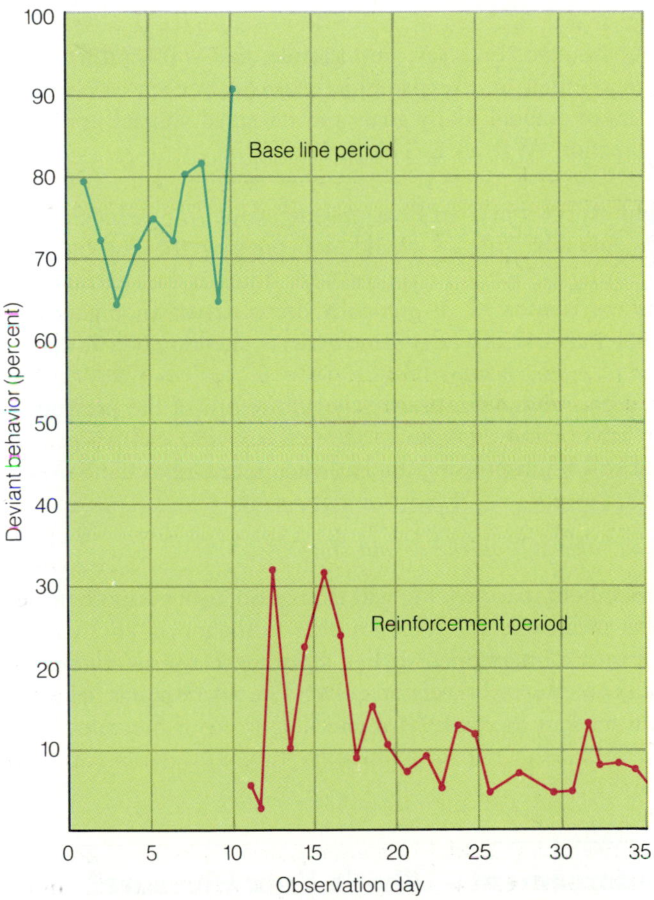

Fig. 7-7 *Reinforcement and human behavior. The amount of deviant behavior engaged in each day by children in a classroom setting is shown. Before reinforcement of good behavior began, disruptive actions were the rule. The effectiveness of reinforcement is indicated by the rapid drop in crying, fighting, and tantrums that occurred. (Adapted from O'Leary & Becker, 1967)*

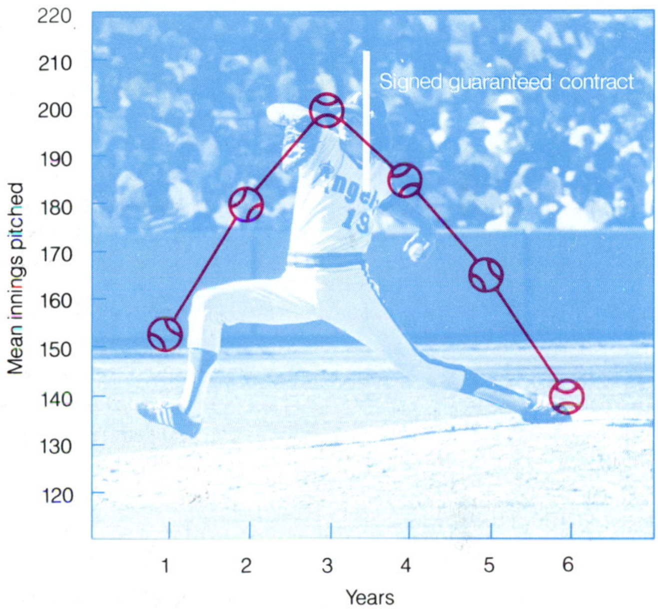

Fig. 7-8 *Mean number of innings pitched by major league baseball players before and after signing long-term guaranteed contracts. The performance of 38 pitchers who signed multiyear contracts for over $100,000 per season is shown. When salary was no longer contingent on good performance, there was a rapid decline in innings pitched and in the number of wins. During the same 6-year period, the performance of pitchers on 1-year contracts remained fairly steady. (Data from O'Brian et al., 1981)*

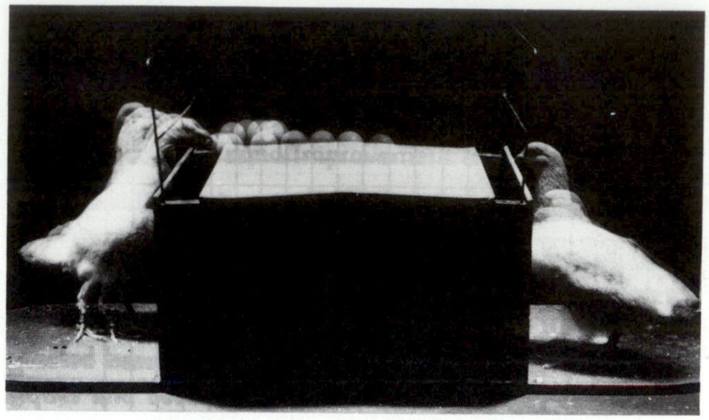

Fig. 7-9 *Operant conditioning principles were used to train these pigeons to play Ping-Pong.*

sponse are reinforced. B. F. Skinner once taught two pigeons to play Ping-Pong in this way. (See Fig. 7-9.)

Shaping applies to humans, too. Let's say, for example, that you want to study more, clean the house more often, or exercise more. Success in each case would be aided if you set a series of gradual, daily goals and rewarded yourself for each small step in the right direction (Watson & Tharp, 1981).

Extinction You might expect that a rat's bar pressing would immediately stop if food delivery ceased. Actually, the rat would stop pressing the bar but not immediately. Just as acquiring an operant response takes time, so does **extinction.** If a learned response is not reinforced, it gradually drops out of an organism's behavior. Extinction, therefore, refers to the same general phenomenon it did in classical conditioning.

Even after extinction seems complete, there may be a return of the previously rewarded response. If a rat is removed from a Skinner box after extinction and given a short rest, the rat will begin pressing the bar when returned to the Skinner box.

Question: Does extinction take as long the second time?

If reinforcement is still withheld, bar pressing will extinguish again, usually more quickly. The brief return of an operant response after extinction is another example of *spontaneous recovery* (mentioned earlier regarding classical conditioning). Spontaneous recovery seems to be very adaptive. The rat responds again in a situation that produced food in the past: "Just checking to see if the rules have changed!"

Operant Reinforcement—What's Your Pleasure?

As we have seen, reinforcement is a key element in learning. Reinforcers clearly have a large impact on our daily lives. Let's examine the reinforcement of operant behavior in more detail.

When dealing with humans, an effective reinforcer may be anything from an M&M candy to a pat on the back. In categorizing reinforcers, useful distinctions can be made between *primary reinforcers* and *secondary reinforcers.*

Primary Reinforcement

Primary reinforcers are natural, or unlearned. Hence, they apply almost universally to a species. They are usually biological in nature and produce comfort, end discomfort, or fill an immediate physical need. Food, water, and sex are obvious primary reinforcers. Every time you open the refrigerator, walk to a drinking fountain, turn up the heat, or make a trip to an ice cream parlor, your actions reflect the effect of primary reinforcement.

In addition to the most obvious examples, there are other, less natural primary reinforcers. One of the most unusual (and powerful) is **intra-cranial stimulation** (ICS). ICS involves direct stimulation of "pleasure centers" in the brain (Olds & Fobes, 1981) (see Fig. 7-10).

Wiring a Rat for Pleasure

Use of brain stimulation for reward requires the permanent implantation of tiny electrodes in specific areas of the brain. A rat "wired for pleasure" can be trained to press the bar in a Skinner box to deliver electrical stimulation to its own brain. Some rats will press the bar thousands of times per hour to obtain brain stimulation. After 15 or 20 hours of constant pressing, animals sometimes collapse from exhaustion. When they revive, they begin pressing again. If the reward circuit is not turned off, an animal will ignore food, water, and sex in favor of bar pressing.

One shudders to think what might happen if brain implants were easy and practical to do. (They are not.) Every company from *Playboy* to General Motors would have a device on the market, and we would have to keep a closer watch on politicians than usual!

Secondary Reinforcement

In some primitive societies learning is still strongly tied to primary reinforcement. Most of us, however, respond to a much broader range of rewards and reinfor-

Operant extinction Weakening or disappearance of an operant response that occurs when reinforcement is withheld.

Primary reinforcers Unlearned reinforcers; usually those that satisfy physiological needs.

Intracranial stimulation Direct electrical stimulation and activation of brain tissue.

Secondary reinforcer A learned reinforcer; often one that gains reinforcing properties by association with a primary reinforcer.

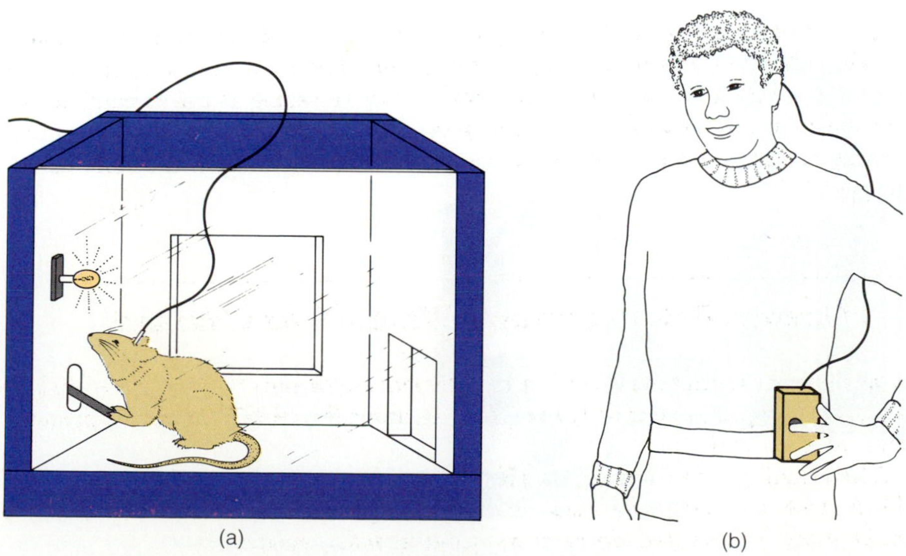

Fig. 7-10 *In the apparatus shown in* (a), *the rat can press a bar to deliver mild electric stimulation to a "pleasure center" in the brain. Humans also have been "wired" for brain stimulation, as shown in* (b).

Token reinforcer A tangible secondary reinforcer such as money, gold stars, poker chips, and the like.

cers. Money, praise, attention, approval, success, affection, and grades all serve as *learned*, or **secondary reinforcers.**

Question: How does a secondary reinforcer gain its ability to reward responding?

A secondary reinforcer may simply be associated with a primary reinforcer. This can be demonstrated experimentally in this way:

The Button-Down Rat

A rat caged in a Skinner box has learned through operant conditioning to press the bar for food pellets. Each rewarded bar press is also followed by a brief auditory tone. After a period of training in which bar pressing, food, and the tone are associated, the rat is moved to a new cage. This cage has no bar, but it does have a button mounted on the wall. If the rat pushes the button, the tone sounds, but no food is delivered. Even though no primary reinforcement (food) is given, the rat learns to press the button to turn on the tone. Because of its prior association with food, the tone has become a secondary reinforcer.

Tokens Secondary reinforcers may also gain their value more directly when they can be *exchanged* for primary reinforcers. Printed money obviously has little or no value on its own. You can't eat it, drink it, or sleep with it. However, it can be exchanged for water, lodging, and other . . . necessities.

In a series of classic experiments, chimpanzees were taught to work for **tokens.**

Chimps were first trained to put poker chips into a "Chimp-O-Mat" vending machine that dispensed a few grapes or raisins for each chip. Once the animals had learned to exchange tokens for food, they would learn new tasks to earn the chips. They also learned to lift a heavy weight to obtain them. Value of the tokens was maintained by occasionally allowing the chimps to use the "Chimp-O-Mat" to exchange chips for food. (Cowles, 1937; Wolfe, 1936) (See Fig 7-11.)

Fig. 7-11 *Poker chips normally have little or no value for chimpanzees, but this chimp will work hard to earn them once he learns that the "Chimp-O-Mat" will dispense food in exchange for the chips.*

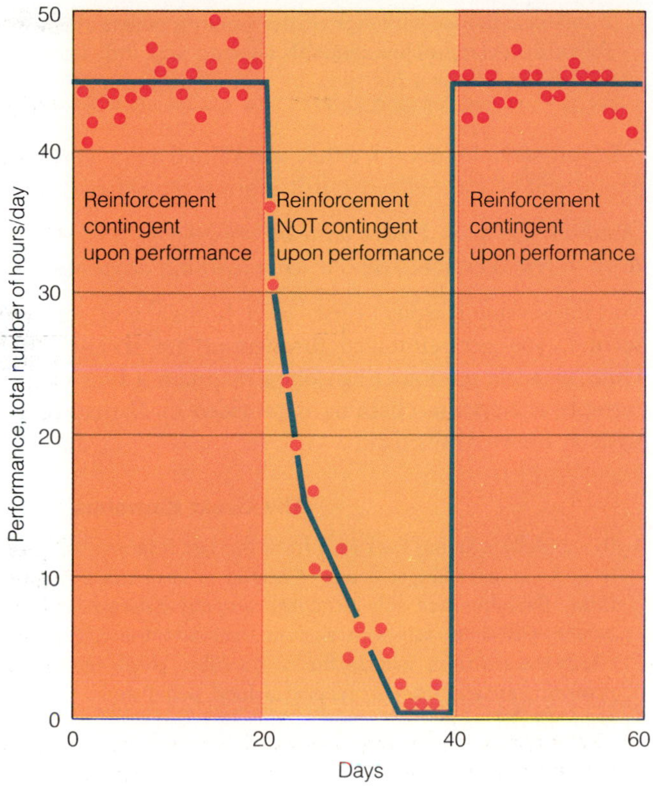

Fig. 7-12 *Reinforcement in a token economy. This graph shows the effects of using tokens to reward socially desirable behavior on a mental hospital ward. Desirable behavior was defined as cleaning the ward, bed making, attending therapy sessions, and so forth. Tokens earned by constructive behavior could be exchanged for basic amenities such as meals, snacks, coffee, game-room privileges, or weekend passes. (Adapted from Ayllon & Azrin, 1965)*

One problem with primary reinforcers is that people and animals receiving them may *satiate* quickly. (To be satiated means to be fully satisfied or to have reduced desire.) If, for example, you wanted to use candy to reinforce a retarded child for correctly naming things, the child might only show interest while still hungry. A major advantage of tokens is that they do not lose their reinforcing value as quickly as primary reinforcers do. This is why tokens (plastic chips, gold stars, and the like) have been quite useful in work with troubled children, adolescents, adults in special programs, and in education of the mentally retarded (see Fig. 7-12). Tokens are even used at times in ordinary elementary school classrooms. In each case the goal is to provide an immediate, tangible reward as an incentive for learning. Typically, tokens may be exchanged for food, desired goods, special privileges, or trips to movies, amusement parks, and so forth. (See Chapter 22 for more information on the use of tokens in therapy.)

Delay of Reinforcement

Reinforcement has its greatest effect on operant learning when the time lapse between a response and its consequences is short. This point can be demonstrated in a simple experiment.

Mickey Rat and Friends Get Delayed

Several groups of rats are trained to press the bar in a Skinner box for a food reward. For some of the animals, a bar press is followed immediately by a food pellet. Other

Response chaining The assembly of a series of responses into a chain of actions leading to reinforcement.

Superstitious behavior In conditioning, a behavior repeated because it seems to produce reinforcement, even though it is actually unnecessary.

animals are trained with ever greater amounts of delay between a bar press and a reward. When the delay reaches about 50 seconds, very little learning occurs. If delivery of the food pellet follows a bar press by more than about 1½ minutes, no learning occurs. (Perin, 1943) (See Fig. 7-13.)

If you wish to reward either an animal or a person for a correct response, reward will be most effective if it is given *immediately* after the response.

Question: Let's say I work hard all semester in a class to get an A. Wouldn't the delay in reinforcement keep me from learning anything?

No, for several reasons. First, as a human you can anticipate future reward. Second, you get reinforced throughout the semester by quiz and test grades. Third, a single reinforcer can often maintain a long *chain* of responses. A simple example of **response chaining** is provided by Barnabus, a rat trained by psychologists at Brown Univeristy.

The Great Barnabus

By carefully working backward from the last response to the first, Barnabus was trained to make an ever longer chain of responses to obtain a single food pellet. When in top form, Barnabus was able to: climb a spiral staircase, cross a narrow bridge, climb a ladder, pull a toy car with a chain, get into the car, pedal it to a second staircase, climb the staircase, wriggle through a tube, climb onto an elevator and descend to a platform, press a lever to receive a food pellet and . . . start over! (Pierrel & Sherman, 1963)

Many of the things we do every day involve similar response chains. The long sequence of events necessary to prepare a meal, for instance, is rewarded by the final eating. A violin maker may spend 3 months carrying out thousands of operations for the final reward of hearing the first note from an instrument. Tying a shoelace is a short but familiar response chain.

Superstitious Behavior Reinforcement affects not only the last response that precedes it but also other responses occurring shortly beforehand. This helps account for the learning of many human superstitions. If a golfer taps her club on the ground three times and then hits an unusually fine shot, the success of the shot rewards not only the swing but also the three taps. During operant training, animals often develop similar unnecessary responses. If a rat scratches its ear just before its first bar press, it may continue to scratch its ear before each subsequent bar press. Pressing the bar is all the animal actually has to do to receive food, but it may continue "superstitiously" scratching its ear each time, as if this were necessary.

Question: But if the superstitious behavior is unnecessary, why does it continue?

Superstitious acts probably *appear* to pay off to the person or animal. For example:

Why Pigeons Shouldn't Gamble

A pigeon has been placed in a Skinner box, where it is allowed to peck at the key 3 times to obtain food. Then the key is turned off. At random intervals food falls into the tray as the pigeon continues pecking. *There is no connection between pecking and food,* but there *appears* to be. During 20 testing periods, 20 minutes in length, the pigeon made an average of 2700 "superstitious" pecks. (Neuringer, 1970)

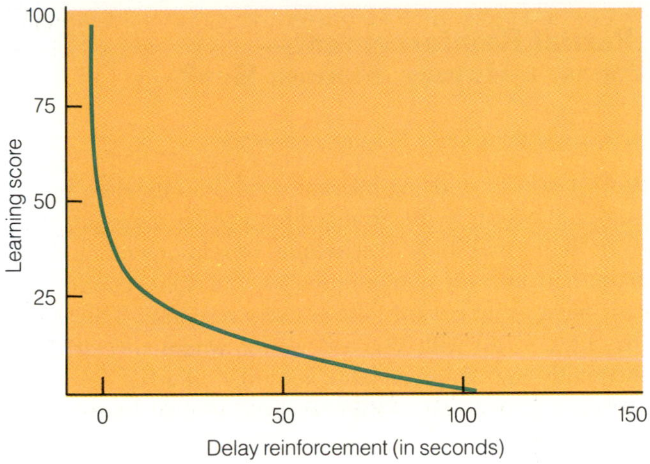

Fig. 7-13 *The effect of delay of reinforcement. Notice how rapidly the learning score drops when reward is delayed. Animals learning to press a bar in a Skinner box showed no signs of learning if food reward was given more than 100 seconds after a bar press. (Perin, 1943)*

Fig. 7-14 *Many gamblers rely on charms for good luck. Such superstitious behavior occurs because the charm is occasionally associated with reinforcement (winning).*

Many human superstitions seem to be based on the same phenomenon. If you get the large half of a wishbone and have good fortune soon thereafter, you may credit the wishbone for your luck (see Fig. 7-14). If you walk under a ladder and then break a leg, you may avoid ladders in the future. Each time you avoid a ladder and nothing unusually bad occurs, your superstitious response is reinforced. Belief in magic can also be interpreted along these lines. Primitive rituals to produce rain, ward off illness, or produce abundant crops very likely earned the faith of participants by occasionally appearing to succeed. Besides, better safe than sorry!

Learning Check

1. Responses in operant conditioning are ____________, whereas those in classical conditioning are passive, ____________ responses.
2. Changing the rules so that an animal (or person) is gradually trained to respond as desired is called ____________.
3. Extinction in operant conditioning is also subject to ______ of a response.
   a. successive approximations *b.* shaping *c.* automation *d.* spontaneous recovery
4. Reinforcement in operant conditioning depends on the consequences of a response, or what happens after it is made. T or F?
5. Primary reinforcers are those learned through classical conditioning. T or F?
6. Tokens basically are ____________ reinforcers.
7. Superstitious responses are those that are:
   a. shaped by secondary reinforcement *b.* extinguished *c.* prepotent *d.* unnecessary to obtain reinforcement

Answers: **1.** voluntary or emitted, involuntary or elicited **2.** shaping **3.** *d* **4.** T **5.** F **6.** secondary **7.** *d*

Partial Reinforcement—Las Vegas, a Human Skinner Box?

SERENDIPITY *(n)*: to discover one thing while looking for another

B. F. Skinner, so the story goes, was studying operant conditioning when he ran short of food pellets. In order to continue, he arranged for a pellet to reward every other response. Thus began the formal study of **schedules of reinforcement.** Until now we have treated reward in operant conditioning as if it were continuous. **Continuous reinforcement** means that reward follows every response. This is fine for the laboratory but has little to do with the real world, where successful responses are more inconsistently and unpredictably rewarded. **Partial reinforcement,** which does not follow every response, may be given in a number of patterns. Each has an effect on the rate at which a response is performed. In addition to these specific effects (to be explored in a moment), there is a general effect: *Responses acquired under conditions of partial reinforcement are highly resistant to extinction*. For some obscure reason, forever lost in the lore of psychology, this is called the **partial reinforcement effect.** It applies to both classical and operant conditioning.

Question: How does getting reinforced part of the time make a habit stronger?

If you have ever visited Las Vegas or a similar gambling mecca, you have probably been amused by the sight of row after row of people pulling slot machine handles. To get the flavor of what's happening here and to gain insight into partial reinforcement effects, imagine that you are making your first visit to Las Vegas.

Fig. 7-15 *The one-armed bandit (slot machine) is a dispenser of partial reinforcement.*

You put a nickel in a slot machine and pull the handle. Twenty-five cents in nickles spills into the tray. Taking one of your newly won nickels, you pull the handle again. Again there is a small payoff. Let's say this continues for 15 minutes. Every pull is followed by a payoff. Then, without your knowing it, someone turns off the payoff mechanism. Suddenly each pull is followed by nothing. Obviously, you would respond several times more before giving up. However, when continuous reinforcement is followed by extinction, the message soon becomes clear: No more payoffs.

Contrast this with partial reinforcement. You begin by placing five nickels in the machine, without a payoff. You are just about to quit, but decide to play one more. Bingo! The machine returns $2 in change. After this, payoffs continue on a partial schedule; some are large and some are small. All are unpredictable. Sometimes you hit two in a row, and sometimes 20 or 30 pulls go unrewarded. Now let's say the payoff mechanism is turned off again. How many times do you think you would respond this time before your handle-pulling response extinguished? Since you have developed the expectation that any play may be "the one," it will be hard to resist just one more play . . . and one more . . . and one more. Also, since acquisition on a schedule of partial reward includes long periods of nonreward, it will be harder to discriminate between conditions of reinforcement and extinction. It is no exaggeration to say that the partial reinforcement effect has left many people penniless. Even psychologists visiting Las Vegas often get cleaned out—and they should know better!

Schedule of reinforcement A rule or program for determining which responses will be reinforced.

Continuous reinforcement A pattern in which every response is followed by a reinforcer.

Partial reinforcement A pattern in which only a portion of responses are reinforced (also called intermittent reinforcement).

Partial reinforcement effect Greater resistance to extinction found in responses acquired on a schedule of partial reinforcement.

Fixed ratio schedule A schedule of reinforcement in which a predetermined number of responses must be made to obtain a reinforcer.

Variable ratio schedule A schedule in which the number of responses required to obtain a reinforcer varies.

Schedules of Partial Reinforcement

The patterns in which partial reinforcement could be given are limitless. We will consider only the four most basic possibilities.

Fixed Ratio (FR) During continuous reinforcement every response is followed by a reinforcer. A simple variation would be to follow every other response with reinforcement. Likewise, we could follow every third, fourth, fifth, or *n*th response with reinforcement. Each of these possibilities is a **fixed ratio (FR) schedule.** The ratio of reinforcers to responses is fixed: FR-2 means every other response is rewarded; FR-3 means every third response is reinforced; and so forth.

Question: What effect does an FR schedule have?

The most prominent characteristic of fixed ratio schedules is that they produce *very high rates of response* (Fig 7-16). A hungry rat on an FR-10 schedule will quickly run off 10 responses, pause to eat, and will then run off 10 more. A similar situation occurs when factory or farm workers are paid on a piecework basis. When a fixed number of items must be produced for a set amount of pay, work output is high.

Variable Ratio (VR) A **variable ratio (VR) schedule** is a slight variation on fixed ratio. Instead of reinforcing, for example, every fourth response (FR-4), a person or animal on a VR-4 schedule gets rewarded *on the average* every fourth response. Sometimes a response must be made two times to obtain a reinforcer, sometimes five times, sometimes four, and so on. The actual number of responses required varies, but it averages out to four (in this example).

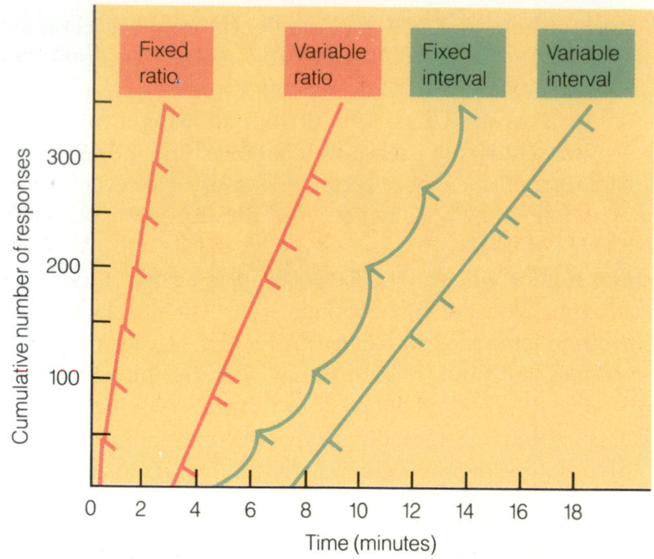

Fig. 7-16 *Typical response patterns for reinforcement schedules. Results such as these are obtained when a cumulative recorder is connected to a Skinner box. The device consists of a moving strip of paper and a mechanical pen that jumps upward each time a response is made. Rapid responding causes the pen to draw a steep line; a horizontal line indicates no response. Small tick marks on the lines show when a reinforcer was given.*

Variable ratio schedules also produce high response rates, although not quite as high as FR. Since reinforcement is less predictable. VR schedules tend to produce slightly greater resistance to extinction than fixed ratio schedules. Playing a slot machine is an example of behavior maintained by a variable ratio schedule of reward. Another would be a child asking for a treat at the supermarket. The number of times the child must ask varies, so the child becomes quite persistent. Golf, tennis, and many other sports are also reinforced on a variable ratio basis: An average of 1 good shot in 5 or 10 may be all that's needed to make a person into a sports fanatic.

Fixed Interval (FI) Another pattern involves reinforcing only the first response that occurs after a fixed amount of time has passed. In other words a rat on a FI 30-second schedule must wait 30 seconds after the last reinforced response before a bar press will pay off again. The rat can press the bar as often as it wants during the interval, but it will not be rewarded. **FI schedules** produce *moderate response rates*. These are punctuated by spurts of activity mixed with periods of inactivity. Animals working on an FI schedule seem to develop a keen sense of the passage of time. For example:

Mickey Rat Gets Put on Hold

Mickey Rat, trained on a FI 60-second schedule, has just been reinforced for a bar press. What does he do? He saunters around the cage, grooms himself, hums, whistles, reads magazines, and polishes his nails. After 50 seconds, he walks to the bar and gives it a press—just testing. After 55 seconds have passed, he gives it two or three presses. Fifty-eight seconds, and he settles down to rapid pressing; 59 seconds, 60 seconds, and he hits the reinforced press. After one or two more presses (unrewarded), he wanders off again for the next interval.

Question: Are there human examples of FI schedules?

Pure examples of fixed interval schedules are somewhat rare, but some situations come close. A parallel would be having a paper due in a class every 2 weeks. Immediately after turning in a paper, your work would probably drop to zero for a week or more, until the next due date draws near. Another example is checking a Thanksgiving turkey in the oven. Usually, the frequency of checking increases as the time for the turkey to be done draws near (Schwartz, 1984).

Variable Interval (VI) **VI schedules** are a logical variation on fixed intervals. Here, reinforcement is given for the first response made after a varied amount of time has passed. A VI 30-second schedule means that reinforcement follows an interval that *averages* 30 seconds duration. VI schedules produce *slow, steady rates* of response and tremendous resistance to extinction. When you dial a phone number and get a busy signal, reward (getting through) is on a VI schedule. You may have to wait 30 seconds or 30 minutes. If you are like most people, you will doggedly dial over and over again until you get a connection. Success in fishing is also on a VI schedule—which may explain the bull dog tenacity of many anglers (Schwartz, 1984).

Fixed interval schedule A schedule in which reinforcement is given following a fixed period of time after the previous reinforcement.

Variable interval schedule A schedule that varies the time period between reinforcements.

Stimulus control The tendency of operant responses acquired in the presence of certain stimuli to later be elicited by those stimuli.

Discriminative stimuli Stimuli that precede rewarded and unrewarded responses in operant conditioning and that come to exert some control over whether the response is made.

Stimulus Control—Putting Habits on a Leash

Thus far, we have focused on the consequences of making a response. The time has come to consider behavior in combination with the situation in which it occurs. Antecedent stimuli, or events that come before a response, also affect operant conditioning. If a response is reinforced in a particular situation, it tends to come under the control of stimuli present in that situation. This is called **stimulus control.** Notice how this works with our friend Mickey Rat.

Lights Out for Mickey Rat

While learning the bar-pressing response, Mickey has been in a Skinner box illuminated by a bright light. During several training sessions the light is alternately turned on and off. When the light is on, a bar press will produce food. When the light is off, bar pressing goes unrewarded. We soon observe that the rat presses vigorously when the light is on and ignores the bar when the light is off.

In this example the light signals what consequences will follow if a response is made. A similar situation would be a child learning to ask for candy when her mother is in a good mood but not asking at other times. In operant conditioning, stimuli that precede a rewarded response tend to influence *when* and *where* the response will occur. Evidence for stimulus control could be shown in the example above by turning the food delivery *on* when the light is *off*. A well-trained rat would never discover that the rules had changed.

Generalization Two important aspects of stimulus control are **generalization** and **discrimination.** Let's return to the example of the vending machine (from the chapter Preview) to illustrate these concepts. First, generalization.

Question: Is generalization the same in operant conditioning as it is in classical conditioning?

Basically, yes. Responses followed by reinforcement tend to be made again when similar antecedents are present. Assume, for instance, that you have been consistently rewarded for kicking one particular vending machine. Your kicking response tends to occur in the presence of that machine. It has come under stimulus

Box 7-1

Stimulus Control

The role of discriminative stimuli may be clarified by an interesting feat achieved by Jack, a psychologist friend of the author's. Jack decided to teach his cat to say its name. Here is how he proceeded. First he gave the cat a pat on the back. If the cat meowed in a way that sounded anything like its name, Jack immediately gave the cat a small amount of food. If the cat made this unusual meow at other times, it received nothing. This process was repeated many times each day. By gradual shaping, the cat's meow was made to sound very much like its name. Also, this peculiar meow came under stimulus control: When it received a pat on the back the cat said its name; without the pat it remained silent or meowed normally. Psychologists symbolize a stimulus that precedes reinforced responses as an S+. Discriminative stimuli that precede unrewarded responses are symbolized as S− (Schwartz, 1984). Thus, the accompanying diagram summarizes the cat's training.

I should add at this point that I was unaware that Jack had a new cat or that he had trained it. I went to visit him one night and met the cat on the front steps. I gave the cat a pat on the back and said, "Hi, kitty, what's your name?" Imagine my surprise when the cat clearly replied, "Ralph!"

ANTECEDENT	RESPONSE	CONSEQUENCE
S+ →	"Ralph" →	Food
S− →	"Ralph" →	Nothing
S+ →	"Meow" →	Nothing

control. Now let's say that there are three other machines on campus identical to the one that pays off. Because they are similar, your kicking response will very likely transfer to them. If each of these machines also pays off in response to a kick, your kicking response may *generalize* to other machines bearing only mild similarity to the original. Similar generalization explains why children may temporarily call all men *daddy*—much to the embarrassment of their parents.

Discrimination Meanwhile, back at the vending machine. . . . As stated earlier, to **discriminate** means to respond differently to different stimuli. Because

Fig. 7-17 *Stimulus control. Operant shaping was used to teach Flo, the pictured walrus, first to cover her face* (left) *and then to douse her trainer. A fish is her reward. Notice the trainer's hand signal, which serves as a discriminative stimulus to control Flo's performance. (Photographs* © *1984,* Los Angeles Times*)*

Fig. 7-18 *Operant discrimination training is used to sharpen the skills of "detective" dogs.*

one vending machine reinforced your kicking response, you began kicking other identical machines (generalization). Because these also paid off, you began kicking similar machines (more generalization). If kicking these new machines has no effect, the kicking response that generalized to them will extinguish due to nonreinforcement. Thus, your response to machines of a particular size and color is consistently rewarded, whereas the same response to different machines is extinguished. You have learned to discriminate between antecedent stimuli that signal reward and nonreward. As a result your response pattern will shift appropriately in the presence of these **discriminative stimuli.** (See Fig 7-17 and Box 7-1).

Stimulus discrimination is aptly illustrated by the "sniffer" dogs used at airports and border stations to locate drugs and explosives. Operant discrimination training is used to teach these dogs to recognize contraband. During training the dogs are reinforced only for approaching containers baited with drugs or explosives (Fig 7-18). Stimulus discrimination also has a tremendous impact on human behavior. Learning to recognize different automobile brands, birds, animals, wines, types of music, or even the answers on psychology tests all depend, in part, on operant discrimination learning.

Learning Check

1. Two aspects of stimulus control are ______________ and ______________.
2. Responding tends to occur in the presence of discriminative stimuli associated with reinforcement and tends not to occur in the presence of discriminative stimuli associated with nonreinforcement. T or F?
3. When stimuli similar to those that preceded reward also bring forth a response, this is called stimulus generalization. T or F?
4. When a reward follows every response, it is called:
   a. continuous reinforcement *b.* fixed reinforcement *c.* ratio reinforcement *d.* controlled reinforcement
5. Partial reinforcement tends to produce slower responding and reduced resistance to extinction. T or F?
6. The schedule of reward associated with playing slot machines and other types of gambling is:
   a. fixed ratio *b.* variable ratio *c.* fixed interval *d.* variable interval

Answers: **1.** generalization, discrimination **2.** T **3.** T **4.** *a* **5.** F **6.** *b*

Managing Behavior— Conditioning in Everyday Situations

To complete our discussion, let's briefly look at some examples of human and animal learning that are more realistic. As you will see, conditioning principles have found their way into business, education, industry, and the home. If you understand these principles, you will find frequent uses for them. It is impossible to detail all the possibilities, but some examples should extend your understanding. (For more information, also see Chapter 22.)

Conditioning Pets

One of the most common mistakes people make with pets (especially dogs) is hitting them if they do not come immediately when called. Calling the animal then becomes a conditioned stimulus for fear and withdrawal. No wonder the pet disobeys when summoned on future occasions.

Question: *How can conditioning be used to correct this?*

An excellent way to train an animal to come when you call is to give a distinctive call or whistle daily during feeding. This makes the signal a discriminative stimulus for reward (food). Effectiveness of the signal is greatly enhanced if it is also used at other times and in other settings and is followed first always, then frequently, then occasionally with a little food. Ultimately, very few "bribes" will be necessary to maintain the effectiveness of the signal if it is conditioned on a partial schedule of reward. Later, petting and praise can be substituted for food.

Question: *What can be done about an animal that begs at the table?*

Pets beg at the table for only one reason: They have been rewarded occasionally for doing so. The problem is usually that the owner finds begging bothersome most of the time and seeks to discourage it by not rewarding it with food. But there is always the time when Fido is just too cute to resist. If the owner gives in then, begging has been reinforced on a partial schedule, which makes it very resistant to extinction. Also, persistence has been reinforced. If you don't want your pets to beg, never give in and reward them. If you want them to beg quietly, reward them after a period of silence, not after a particularly sorrowful plea. Then, gradually extend the length of the silent period.

Conditioning in Business

Most business and industrial applications of reinforcement principles focus on the effects of various bonuses, payment schedules, incentives, commissions, and profit-sharing plans. Before this trend, most people worked for either a straight salary or for an hourly wage. A straight salary can be thought of as a fixed interval schedule of reward. There is little relationship between the amount of effort expended from one paycheck to the next and the amount of pay. This is also partially true of an hourly wage. While it is true that more hours worked means a larger paycheck, an employee gets paid the same amount for an hour of productive work as he or she does for an hour of goofing off. It can be demoralizing to see others do less work and receive the same pay.

Negative attention seeking Gaining attention from another person by engaging in irritating or disruptive behavior.

With these facts in mind, industrial psychologists have sought to make pay relate more directly to work output. The simplest alternative to hourly wages or salary is payment on a piecework (fixed ratio) basis. If an individual is paid a small amount for each item handled, pound picked, shirt sewed, or whatever, work output tends to be high because more items mean more pay. Piecework pay has something of a bad reputation because some employers pay so little on a per-item basis that tremendous amounts of work are necessary to earn a reasonable wage. But this need not be the case. For example, employees of a small leather factory in Los Angeles are paid for making a prearranged number of items per week (billfold backs, handbag handles, and so on). Employees are allowed to work as many or as few hours per day as they choose, and they can work at any rate. This allows great flexibility for the workers, and the company pays only for the work it gets.

The most widely used business adaptation of schedules of reinforcement is a combination of hourly wages and incentives for extra effort. Fixed interval rewards (hourly wage or salary) guarantee a good overall level of productivity and give workers a secure base pay, whereas fixed ratio reinforcement (incentives, bonuses, commissions, or profit sharing) ties extra effort to increased pay or other rewards. For example, in one recent study, clerks in a department store were given a chance to earn paid time off by meeting minimum standards for selling and stockwork. This strategy brought about a significant improvement in their performance. In comparison, a control group's behavior remained the same (Luthans, Paul, & Baker, 1981).

Conditioning and Children

Children seem to have an almost endless craving for attention. This makes attention and approval from parents very powerful reinforcers.

Question: How does this affect a child?

Parents often unknowingly reinforce **negative attention seeking** in children. Generally, children are *ignored* when they are quiet or are playing constructively. They get attention as they get louder and louder, when they yell "Hey Mom!" at the top of their lungs, when they throw a tantrum or show off, or when they break something. Granted, the attention they get is often a scolding, but it is still attention, and it still reinforces negative attention seeking. To avoid this, parents could ignore children when they seek attention this way. However, if attention seeking declines because it is not reinforced, some other behavior must be rewarded to take its place. Parents report dramatic changes in their children's behavior when they make a special effort to actively praise, attend to, or spend time with their children when the children are quiet or playing constructively.

Question: What can be done about a child who throws tantrums in a store if he or she isn't allowed to buy candy?

Children are realists. If you say, "No, you may not buy candy" and stick to it, the child will get the message. Children can discriminate between what is said in a situation and the *actual* possibility of a reward. Children learn to throw tantrums with one parent but not the other; they learn to discriminate between parents' and grandparents' susceptibility to their requests; and they discriminate between a casual no and an angry no. The problem is that no occasionally becomes, "OK, but shut up!" If so, whining or crying has been rewarded on a partial schedule, and it will occur even more frequently in the future. Consistency is the key. If tantrums *never* pay off, they will be abandoned.

Question: But what if the tantrum is really embarrassing? Sometimes parents are willing to do anything to quiet a child.

Beginning a program of nonreward for tantrums may require considerable courage, but it does work. If you don't mind the idea of buying a treat, but dislike the tantrum, try requiring the child to "help" you in some (quiet) way as a condition for receiving the treat. If necessary, walk away from the child and return only when the child has quieted down, or leave the store with the child when a tantrum starts and allow a return to the store only when the child has quieted down.

Conditioning Other Adults

Students seldom realize how much power they have over their teachers. Even tough-skinned veteran teachers are (believe it or not) still human and therefore sensitive to whether they are succeeding in class and being accepted by students. This fact can be used in a demonstration of the effects of reward on human behavior.

Shaping a Teacher

For this demonstration, approximately one-half (or more) of the students in a classroom must participate. First, a target behavior should be selected. This should be something like "lecturing from the right side of the room." (Keep it simple; teachers aren't too clever.) Begin training in this way: Each time the instructor turns toward the right side of the room or takes a step in that direction, participating students should look *really* interested. Also, smile, ask questions, lean forward, and make eye contact. If the teacher turns to the left or takes a step in that direction, participating students should lean back, yawn, check out their split ends, close their eyes, or generally look bored. Soon, without being aware of why, the instructor should be spending most of his or her time each class period lecturing from the right side of the classroom.

This trick has been a favorite of psychology graduate students for decades. For a time one of my professors delivered all of his lectures from the right side of the room while toying with the venetian blind cords. (We added the cords the second week!)

As we pointed out in the discussion of reinforcement with children, attention and approval are powerful rewards for human behavior. This is something to keep in mind when interacting with others.

Question: But how can this be applied?

An excellent example is provided by the work of two educators, Paul S. Graubard and Harry Rosenberg, who taught "incorrigible," "deviant," and "socially outcast" students to use reinforcement on classmates. They cite the example of Peggy, an attractive, intelligent student who was unable to make friends. Peggy encountered so much hostility that she was miserable and unhappy and because of this did poorly in school.

When asked to name three other students she would like to have as friends, Peggy named three students who frequently insulted her. Here is how Peggy began to put into effect the reinforcement principles she had learned: She began by ignoring Doris if Doris said anything bad to her. When Doris said anything nice, Peggy complimented her or sat down and asked Doris to join her. Doris soon began to say nice things about Peggy, to sit by her in class, and for the first time ever, they were able to ride on the bus together without fighting.

Peggy dealt with another student's hostility in the same way. Whenever Elwyn said something bad to her, she turned her back on him. But the first time he walked past her without saying something bad, she gave him a big smile and said, "Hi, Elwyn, how are you today?" The authors add that after Elwyn recovered from his initial shock, he grew to be Peggy's best friend (Graubard & Rosenberg, 1974).

Experimental Living In 1948, B. F. Skinner published *Walden Two*, a utopian novel about a model community based on behavioral engineering. Would such a community work? On a small scale, the answer appears to be yes. One such operant community organized at the University of Kansas was quite successful. College students took part in an Experimental Living Project in which 30 men and women shared a large house (Miller, 1976). In this "community," work, leadership, and self-government were tied directly to behavioral principles.

Worksharing provides a good example of the Project's operant approach. Basic jobs such as preparing food and cleaning were divided into approximately 100 tasks. Each task was described in terms of its expected end result. Residents performed all of these tasks themselves, and one community member checked daily to see that each job had been completed. (This role was rotated periodically.) To maintain job performance, credits were assigned for each of the tasks. At the end of the month, residents who had collected 400 credits got a sizable rent reduction.

This system was very effective in maintaining day-to-day work habits. As anyone who has shared living quarters knows, good intentions are no guarantee that the chores will get done. More importantly, residents rated the Project as superior to dormitory living and similar alternatives. Most were highly satisfied with the system (Miller 1976). The Experimental Living Project is a good example of the possibilities of applying conditioning principles to human behavior.

The examples cited here should give you an idea of the value of applying conditioning principles to everyday situations. If you would like to try these principles yourself, a good place to start is in managing your own behavior—the topic of this chapter's Applications section.

Learning Check

1. Pets who beg for food are often persistent because they have been rewarded on a schedule of partial reinforcement. T or F?

2. A straight salary can be though of as fixed interval reinforcement, whereas piecework pay is a fixed ratio schedule. T or F?

3. Negative attention seeking refers to the idea that parents tend to reward negative attention from their children. T or F?

4. Compliments, attention, and approval can serve as powerful reinforcers of human behavior. T or F?

Answers: **1.** T **2.** T **3.** F **4.** T

Applications

Behavioral Self-Management

This discussion could be the start of one of the most personal "Applications" in this book. There is now little doubt that self-administered reward affects behavior (Watson & Tharp, 1981). Many people have learned to successfully use self-administered reinforcement to alter or manage their own behavior. At the very least, trying self-management can make you more aware of your behavior and what controls it. This Application, then, is an invitation to carry out a self-management project of your own. Would you like to increase the number of hours you spend studying each week? Would you like to exercise more, attend more classes, concentrate longer, or read more books? All these activities and many others can be improved by following the rules described here.

1. Choose a target behavior. Identify the activity you want to change.
2. Record a baseline. Record how much time you currently spend performing the target activity or count the number of desired or undesired responses you make each day.
3. Establish goals. Remember the principle of shaping, and set realistic goals for gradual improvement on each successive week. Also, set daily goals that add up to the weekly goal.
4. Choose reinforcers. If you meet your daily goal, what reward will you allow yourself? Daily rewards might be watching television, eating a candy bar, socializing with friends, playing a musical instrument, or whatever you enjoy. Also establish a weekly reward. If you reach your weekly goal, what reward will you allow yourself? A movie? A dinner out? A weekend hike?
5. Record your progress. Keep accurate records of the amount of time spent each day on the desired activity.
6. Reward successes. If you meet your daily goal, collect your reward. If you fall short, be honest with yourself and skip the reward. Do the same for your weekly goal.
7. Adjust your plan as you learn more about your behavior. Overall progress will reinforce your attempts at self-management.

If you have trouble finding rewards or if you don't want to use the entire system, remember that anything *done often* can serve as reinforcement. For example, if you watch television every night and want to study more, make it a rule not to turn on the set until you have studied for an hour (or whatever length of time you choose). Then lengthen the requirement each week.

Here is a sample of one student's plan:

1. *Target behavior:* number of hours spent studying for school
2. *Recorded baseline:* an average of 15 minutes per day for a weekly total of 1¼ hours
3. *Goal for first week:* an increase in study time to 20 minutes per day; weekly goal of 2 hours total study time. Goal for second week: 25 minutes per day and 2½ hours per week. Goal for third week: 30 minutes per day and 3 hours per week. Ultimate goal: to reach and maintain 8 hours per week study time.
4. *Daily reward for reaching goal:* 1 hour of guitar playing in the evening; no playing if the goal is not met. Weekly reward for reaching goal: go to a movie or buy a record album.

Self-Recording Even if you find it difficult to give and withhold the rewards in your program, you are likely to succeed. Simply knowing that you are reaching a desired goal can be reward enough. The key to any self-management program therefore becomes accurate record keeping. This concept is demonstrated by a study in which some students in an introductory psychology course recorded study time and graphed daily and weekly study behavior. Even though no extra rewards were offered, students who

Applications: Behavioral Self-Management, continued

recorded their study time earned better grades than those who did not (Johnson & White, 1971).

Contracting If you try the techniques discussed and have difficulty sticking with them, you may want to try **behavioral contracting.** In a behavioral contract you state a *specific* problem behavior you want to control or a goal you want to achieve. Also state the rewards you will receive, privileges you will forfeit, or punishments you must accept. The contract should be typed and signed by you and a person you are close to.

A behavioral contract can be quite motivating, especially when mild punishment is part of the agreement. Here's an example reported by Nurnberger and Zimmerman (1970): A student working on his Ph.D. had completed all requirements except for his dissertation, yet for 2 years he had not written a single page. A contract was drawn up for him in which he agreed to meet weekly deadlines on the number of pages he would complete. To make sure he would meet the deadlines, he wrote postdated checks. These were to be forfeited if he failed to reach his goal for the week. The checks were made out to organizations he despised (the Ku Klux Klan and American Nazi Party). From the time he signed the contract until he finished his degree, the student's work output was greatly improved.

Getting Help Attempting to manage or alter your own behavior may be more difficult than it sounds. If you feel you need more information, consult either of the books listed below. You will also find helpful advice in the Applications for Chapters 8 and 22. If you do try a self-modification project but find it impossible to reach your goal, be aware that professional advice is available.

For more information, consult:

Watson, D. L., & Tharp, R. G. *Self-Directed Behavior.* Brooks/Cole, 1981.

Williams, R. L., & Long, J. D. *Toward a Self-Managed Life Style.* Houghton Mifflin, 1979.

Learning Check

1. After a target behavior has been selected for reinforcement, it's a good idea to record a baseline so you can set realistic goals for change. T or F?
2. Self-recording, even without the use of extra rewards, can bring about desired changes in target behavior. T or F?
3. Recording a baseline for target responses is the final step in behavioral contracting. T or F?
4. A self-management plan should make use of the principle of shaping by setting a graduated series of goals. T or F?

Answers: **1.** T **2.** T **3.** F **4.** T

Chapter Summary

- *Classical* (or *respondent*) conditioning and *operant* conditioning are two basic types of learning. In classical conditioning a previously neutral stimulus begins to elicit a response through *association* with another stimulus. In operant conditioning the frequency and pattern of voluntary responses are altered by their *consequences*.
- Many animals are born with *innate* behavior patterns far more complex than *reflexes*. These are organized into *fixed action patterns* (FAPs), which are stereotyped, *species-specific* behaviors.
- *Learning* is a relatively permanent change in behavior due to experience. Learning due to basic conditioning depends on *reinforcement*. Reinforcement increases the probability that a particular response will occur.
- Classical conditioning, studied by Pavlov, occurs when a *conditioned stimulus* (CS) is associated with an *unconditioned stimulus* (US). The US causes a reflex called the *unconditioned response* (UR). If the CS is consistently paired with the US, then the CS begins to produce a response by itself. This is called a *conditioned* (learned) *response* (CR).
- When the conditioned stimulus is followed by the unconditioned stimulus, conditioning is *reinforced* (strengthened). When the CS is repeatedly presented alone, conditioning is *extinguished* (weakened or inhibited). Temporary reappearance of a conditioned response after extinction seems to be complete is called *spontaneous recovery*.
- Through *stimulus generalization*, stimuli similar to the conditioned stimulus will also produce a response. Generalization gives way to *stimulus discrimination* when an organism learns to respond to one stimulus but not to similar stimuli.
- Conditioning applies to visceral or emotional responses as well as to simple reflexes. As a result, *conditioned emotional responses* (CERs) also occur. Irrational fears called *phobias* may be learned CERs. Conditioning of emotional responses can occur *vicariously* (secondhand) as well as directly.
- Operant conditioning occurs when a voluntary action is followed by a *reinforcer*. Reinforcement in operant conditioning increases the frequency or probability of a response.
- Complicated operant responses can be taught by reinforcing *successive approximations* to a final desired response. This is called *shaping*. It is particularly useful in training animals.
- If an operant response is not reinforced, it may *extinguish* (disappear). But after extinction seems complete, it may temporarily reappear (*spontaneous recovery*).
- *Primary reinforcers* are natural, physiologically based rewards. *Intra-cranial stimulation* of "pleasure centers" in the brain can also serve as a primary reinforcer.
- *Secondary reinforcers* are learned. They typically gain their reinforcing value by direct association with primary reinforcers or by being subject to exchange for primary reinforcers. *Tokens* and money gain their reinforcing value in this way.
- *Delay* of reinforcement greatly reduces its effectiveness, but long *chains* of responses may be built up in which a single reinforcer rewards many responses. *Superstitious behaviors* often become part of response chains because they appear to be associated with reinforcement.

- Reward or reinforcement may be given *continuously* (after every response) or on a *schedule of partial reinforcement*. Partial reinforcement produces greater resistance to extinction. Four of the most basic schedules of reinforcement are: *fixed ratio, variable ratio, fixed inverval*, and *variable interval*.
- Stimuli that precede a reinforced response tend to control the response on future occasions *(stimulus control)*. Two aspects of simulus control are *generalization* and *discrimination*. In generalization, an operant response tends to occur when stimuli similar to those preceding reinforcement are present. In discrimination, responses are given in the presence of *discriminative stimuli* associated with reinforcement (S+) and withheld for stimuli (S−) associated with nonreinforcement.
- Conditioning principles are applied in a wide variety of natural settings. In business and industry this typically involves such reinforcers as wages, bonuses, and time off. In other settings, attention and approval act as powerful reinforcers. Parents often unintentionally reinforce children's *negative attention seeking*.
- Operant conditioning can be used in self-management by choosing a *target behavior* and reinforcing desired changes. *Self-recording* of target behaviors and *behavioral contracting* can also help bring about beneficial changes in personal behavior.

Chapter 8

Conditioning and Learning II

Chapter Preview

Human history becomes more and more a race between education and catastrophe.

H. G. Wells

Any subject can be taught effectively in some intellectually honest form to any child at any stage of development.

Jerome Bruner

Dr. Moore's "Learning Machine"

Teaching 2- to 5-year-olds to read, write, type, and compose stories may sound impossible. However, under the proper conditions it can become a reality. In the early 1960s Omar Khayyam Moore of Yale University designed a "responsive learning environment" to take advantage of children's intellectual curiosity. In Moore's lab, children were allowed to "play" with a "talking typewriter." When a child pressed a key, the corresponding letter appeared on the paper and a voice named it through a loudspeaker. Surprised by this response, the children tried other keys. Soon the connection between keys and letters began to form.

After several sessions in which typing was fairly random, a new game began. Whenever a child's attention wandered, a letter appeared on a screen and was named aloud. Children who returned to random key pressing suddenly found that the keys no longer worked—until they pressed the key matching the letter on the screen. Then, the correct letter printed and the voice named it. Soon, a new letter appeared on the screen. Later, words began to appear. If a child pressed the key for the first letter, a pointer moved to the second letter. When the child had correctly typed all the letters of a word such as dog, *the machine pronounced the word. Then a new word appeared. By working with the talking typewriter, children rapidly went from random typing to reading and writing. Then they composed their own sentences and stories—all before age 5 (Pines, 1963)!*

Today, pocket-size electronic games duplicate many of the educational feats of Moore's bulky apparatus. And, by comparison to popular video games like "Space Invaders" or "Pac Man," Moore's talking typewriter looks pretty tame. Just the same, children in Moore's lab became lost in the joy of discovery, simply because the environment was responsive to their actions. As these children show, an ability to learn is every human's birthright. This chapter extends the discussion begun in Chapter 7. An important theme to watch for as you read is that learning is based on information.

Survey Questions What do classical conditioning and operant conditioning have in common? What is feedback and how does it affect learning? What impact does punishment have on learning? What is cognitive learning? Does learning occur by imitation? How are motor skills best learned? What can be done to break a bad habit?

Conditioning in Perspective—Great Expectations

An ice cream truck approaches with its bell ringing. A boy runs to the truck, buys an ice cream, and eats it, salivating as he does. What kind of learning is this? If it seems to you that both classical and operant conditioning are present in this example, you are right.

Resources

Two-factor learning Learning that involves both classical conditioning and operant conditioning.

Two-Factor Learning

In the real world, classical and operant conditioning are often intertwined. As you can see in Figure 8-1, the boy's behavior reflects both kinds of learning. Due to classical conditioning, the boy will salivate each time he hears the truck's bell. Also, the bell is a discriminative stimulus (S+) signaling that reward is available if certain responses are made. When he hears the bell, the boy will run to the truck, buy, and eat an ice cream (operant conditioning). The boy's involuntary responses are altered by classical conditioning, while his voluntary behavior is shaped by operant conditioning.

Question: Other than the fact that they often occur together, do operant and classical conditioning have anything in common?

Fig. 8-1 *Two-factor learning.*

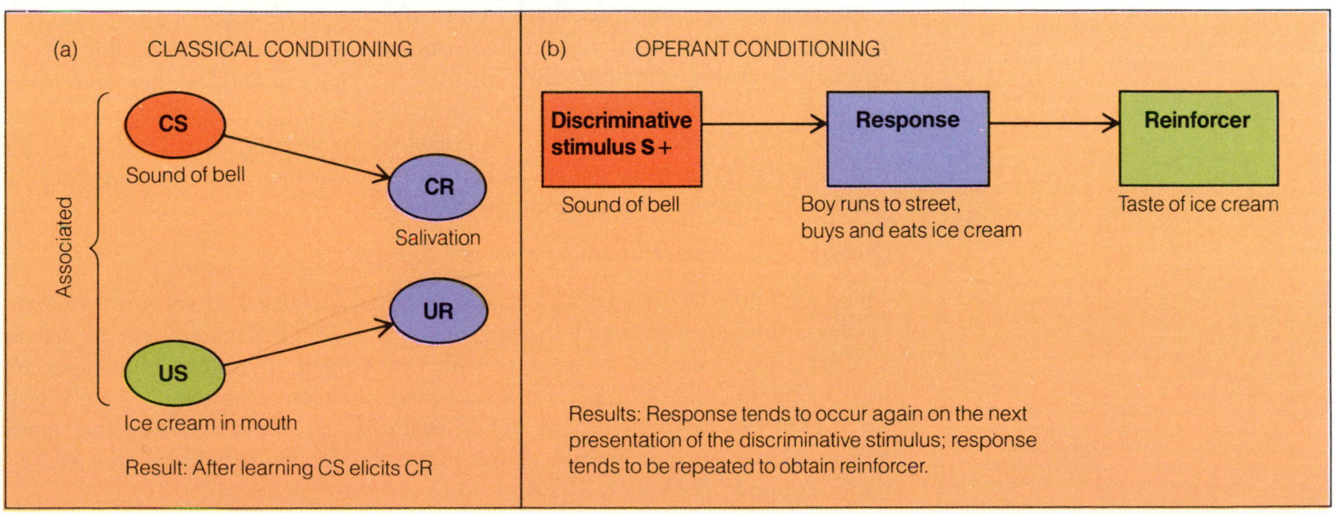

Expectancy An anticipation concerning future events or relationships.

Feedback Information on the effects a response has had that is returned to the person performing the response (also known as knowledge of results).

Programmed instruction Any learning format that presents information in small amounts, gives immediate practice, and provides continuous feedback to learners.

Computer-assisted instruction (CAI) Learning aided by computer-presented information and exercises.

Branching program A computer program that provides corrective information and exercises for learners depending on the nature of their errors.

Drill and practice A basic CAI format, typically consisting of questions and answers.

Instructional games Educational computer programs designed to resemble games in order to motivate learning.

Educational simulations Computer programs that simulate real-world settings or situations to promote learning.

Information Psychologists used to picture conditioning as a mechanical "stamping in" of responses. Now, many think of learning in terms of *information processing*. According to this **informational view,** learning creates mental **expectancies** (or expectations) about events. Once acquired, these expectancies alter behavior. For example, researcher Robert Rescorla (1980, 1987) explains classical conditioning this way: Because the conditioned stimulus reliably precedes the unconditioned stimulus, the CS *predicts* the US. When the CS is present, the brain *expects* the US to follow. Therefore, the brain prepares the body to respond to the US. In our example, whenever the boy hears the bell or sees the truck, his mouth waters to prepare for eating ice cream. Similarly, when you are about to get a shot with a hypodermic needle, your muscles tighten and there is a catch in your breathing as your body prepares for discomfort.

If you think about it, operant reinforcers also supply information. In operant conditioning we learn to *expect* that a certain response will have a certain effect at certain times (Bolles, 1979). From this point of view, reward tells a person or an animal that a response was "right" and worth repeating. Likewise, stimuli or events preceding actions tell what response to make to get a reinforcer. Thus, when the boy hears the bell, he *expects* that running to the truck and paying for an ice cream will lead to eating it. If his expectation changes, his behavior will too. Picture what would happen if the ice cream truck changed its route, and the boy repeatedly ran out to find, instead, a garbage truck with its safety bell ringing. Rapid extinction would follow as the boy's expectancy changed from "bell means ice cream" to "bell means garbage."

The adaptive value of information helps explain why much human learning occurs without obvious reinforcement by food, water, and the like. Humans readily learn responses that merely have a desired effect or that bring them closer to a goal. Let's explore this idea further.

Feedback

Imagine that you are asked to throw darts at a target. Each dart must pass over a screen, which prevents you from telling if you hit the target. If you threw 1000 darts this way, we would expect little improvement in your performance, because no **feedback** is provided. Feedback (information about what effect a response had) is particularly important in human learning. Recall, for instance, that O. K. Moore's "learning machine" did not explicitly reward children for correct responses. Yet, because it provided feedback, rapid learning took place.

The value of feedback (also called **knowledge of results,** or **KR**) is one of the most useful lessons to be gained from studies of learning. Increased feedback almost always improves learning and performance.

Question: How can feedback be applied?

There are numerous possibilities, many already widely used. If you want to learn to play a musical instrument, to sing, to speak a second language, or to deliver a speech, tape-recorded feedback can be very helpful. In sports, videotapes are used to improve everything from tennis serves to pick-off moves in baseball. If you would like to make similar use of feedback, it's worth knowing that taped replays are most helpful when a skilled coach directs attention to key details (Salmoni, Schmidt, & Walter, 1984).

Learning Aids Feedback is valuable in education too. In recent years operant learning and feedback have been combined in two interesting ways. These are *programmed instruction* and *computer-assisted instruction.*

Question: How do such techniques make use of feedback?

For feedback to be most effective, it should be *frequent, immediate,* and *detailed.* **Programmed instruction** teaches students in a format that requires precise answers about information as it is presented. This arrangement supplies frequent feedback to keep learners from practicing errors. It also has the advantage of letting students work at their own pace. (The Learning Check that follows this discussion is done in a programmed format so that you can see what one looks like.)

In **computer-assisted instruction (CAI),** students work at individual computer terminals. The computer displays lessons on a screen, and students respond by typing answers. In addition to giving immediate feedback, the computer can *analyze each answer.* This allows use of a **branching program** that supplies extra information and asks questions when errors are made.

Elementary school children seem to do especially well with a "computer tutor" due to the rapid feedback and individualized pacing. Adults, too, benefit from computer-assisted instruction. Although the final level of skill or knowledge is no higher than that gained with conventional methods, CAI can save much time and effort (Wexley, 1984).

The simplest computerized instruction consists of self-paced **drill and practice.** In this format students answer questions similar to those found in printed workbooks. This has the advantage of instantly providing correct answers. In addition, the computer can supply extra KR, such as how fast you worked, your percentage of correct answers, or how your work compared with previous scores (Lepper, 1985).

Higher level CAI programs include **instructional games** and **educational simulations.** Instructional games use stories, competition with a partner, sound effects, and gamelike graphics to increase interest and motivation (see Fig. 8-2). In educational simulations students face problems in an imaginary situation or "microworld." By observing the effects of their choices, students discover basic principles of physics, biology, psychology, or other subjects (Lepper, 1985).

Psychologists are only now beginning to fully explore the value and limits of computer-assisted instruction. Nevertheless, it seems likely that their efforts will improve not only education but our understanding of human learning as well.

Fig. 8-2 *Computer-assisted instruction. Screen on the left shows a typical drill-and-practice math problem, in which students must find the hypotenuse of a triangle. Center screen presents the same problem as an instructional game to increase interest and motivation. In the game a child is asked to set the proper distance on a ray gun in the hovering space ship to "vaporize" an attacker. The right screen depicts an educational simulation. Here students place a "probe" at various spots in a human brain. They then "stimulate," "destroy," or "restore" areas. As each area is altered, it is named on the screen, and the effects on behavior are described. This allows students to explore basic brain function on their own.*

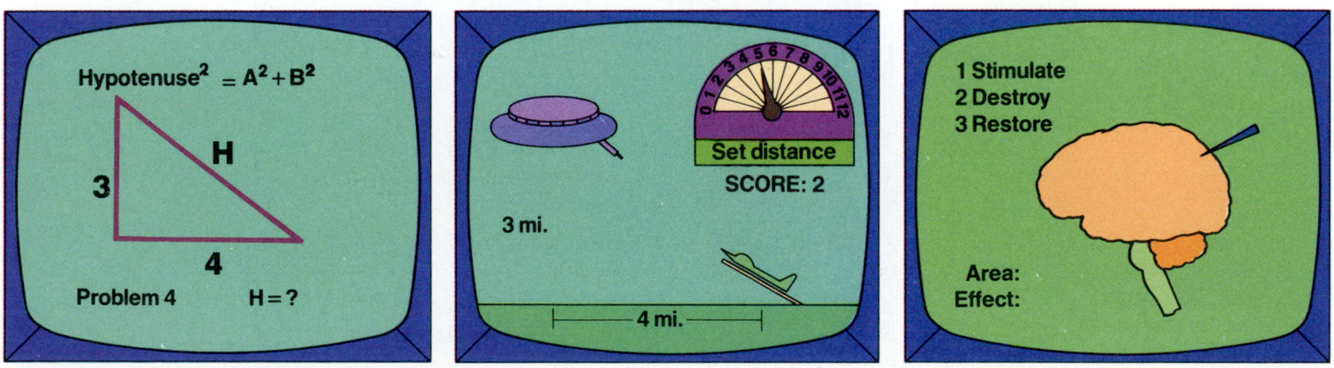

Learning Check

To give you an idea of what programmed instruction is like, this Learning Check is presented in a programmed format. To use it, cover the words on the left, and then uncover each answer after you have filled in a blank.

classical	In many learning situations ______ and operant conditioning occur simulta-
two-	neously. This circumstance is referred to as ______ factor learning. Often, a rein-
classical	forcer that strengthens an operant response also serves as an unconditioned stimulus for ______
	conditioning. The informational view of learning states that both classical and operant conditioning create
expectancies	mental ______ that alter behavior. Much human learning is based on informa-
knowledge	tional feedback about the effects a response has had. Feedback is also known as KR or ______
results	of ______. Programmed instruction is self-paced and gives immediate
feedback	______ to the learner. The simplest form of computer-assisted instruction is
drill	______ and practice.

Punishment—Putting the Brakes on Behavior

For better or worse, punishment is one of the most popular ways to control behavior in our society. Spankings, reprimands, loss of privileges, fines, jail sentences, firings, failing grades, and the like all reflect a widespread reliance on punishment (Fig. 8-3). Clearly, no account of learning can be complete without discussing punishment. Before we begin, however, let's return briefly to reinforcement.

Fig. 8-3 *Punishment has long been used to suppress undesirable behavior.*

> **Edict of Louis XI, King of France**
> **A.D. 1481**
>
> "Anyone who sells butter containing stones or other things (to add to the weight) will be put into our pillory, then said butter will be placed on his head until entirely melted by the sun. Dogs may lick him and people offend him with whatever defamatory epithets they please without offense to God or King. If the sun is not warm enough, the accused will be exposed in the great hall of the gaol in front of a roaring fire, where everyone will see him."

Negative Reinforcement versus Punishment Until now we have concentrated on **positive reinforcement,** which occurs when pleasant or desirable consequences follow a response. The time has come to also consider the "dark side" of conditioning: **Negative reinforcement,** as it is called, occurs when a response causes the *removal* of an *unpleasant* event. Like positive reinforcement, negative reinforcement also increases responding. However, it does so by *ending discomfort*. For example, if you have a headache and take an aspirin, your aspirin taking will be reinforced if the headache stops. Likewise, a rat could be taught to press a bar to get a food pellet (positive reinforcement); or, the rat could be shocked mildly until it pressed a bar that turned off the shock (negative reinforcement). Either way, bar pressing would increase. Often, positive and negative reinforcement combine. If you are uncomfortably hungry, eating a meal is reinforced by the good-tasting food (positive reinforcement) and by an end to nagging hunger (negative reinforcement).

Positive reinforcement Following a response with a reward or other positive event.

Negative reinforcement Following a response with an end to discomfort or the removal of a negative state of affairs.

Punishment Following a response with pain or an otherwise negative event; or, following a response with the removal of a positive stimulus.

Many people mistake negative reinforcement for punishment. However, **punishment** is "any event that follows a response and *decreases* its likelihood of occurring again" (Adams, 1980). As noted, negative reinforcement *increases* responding. The difference can be seen in a hypothetical example. Let's say you live in an apartment and your neighbor's stereo is blasting so loudly that your ears hurt. If you pound on the wall and the volume drops (negative reinforcement), future wall pounding will be more likely. If you pound on the wall and the volume increases (punishment), or the neighbor comes over and pounds on you (more punishment), pounding on the wall becomes less likely. For a more realistic example, consider the case of a drug addict undergoing withdrawal. Taking the drug ends painful withdrawal symptoms temporarily. Drug taking, therefore, is negatively reinforced. If, on the other hand, the drug intensified pain (punishment), the addict would quickly stop taking it.

Question: Isn't it also punishing to have privileges, money, or other positive things taken away?

Yes. Punishment is either the addition of an aversive (painful or disliked) event or the removal of a positive event. Parents who "ground" their teenage children for misbehavior are using the second kind of punishment. For your convenience, Figure 8-4 summarizes what we have covered so far.

Variables Affecting Punishment

Question: Reinforcement strengthens a response. Does punishment weaken a response?

Many people assume that punishment abolishes undesired behavior. Is this always true? Psychologists have learned that the effectiveness of punishment depends greatly on its *timing, consistency*, and *intensity*. Punishment suppresses behavior best when it occurs while a response is being made, or *immediately* afterward (timing), and when it is given *each time* a response occurs (consistency). Thus, a dog that has developed a habit of constantly barking can be effectively (and humanely) punished by spraying water on its nose each time it barks. Ten to fifteen such treatments are usually enough to greatly reduce barking. This would not be the case if punishment were applied occasionally or much later. If you discover

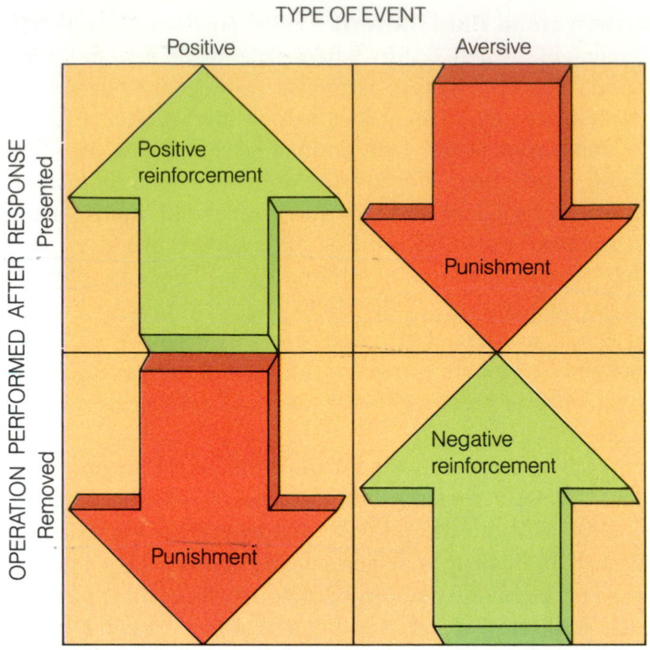

Fig. 8-4 *Types of reinforcement and punishment. The impact of an event depends on whether it is presented or removed after a response is made. Each square defines one possibility: Arrows pointing upward indicate that responding is increased; downward-pointing arrows indicate that responding is decreased. (Adapted from Kazdin, 1975)*

that your dog dug up and ate a tree while you were gone, it will do little good to punish him hours later. Likewise, the commonly heard childhood threat of, "Wait 'til your father comes home, then you'll be sorry," does more to make father an ogre than it does to effectively punish an undesirable response.

Severe punishment can be extremely effective in stopping behavior. If a child sticks a finger in a light socket and gets shocked, that may be the last time the child *ever* tries it. More often, however, punishment only temporarily *suppresses* a response. If the response is still reinforced, punishment may be particularly ineffective. Responses suppressed by **mild punishment** usually reappear later. If a child sneaks a snack from the refrigerator before dinner and is punished for it, the child may pass up snacks for a short time. But since snack sneaking was also rewarded by the sneaked snack, the child will probably try sneaky snacking again, sometime later.

This fact was demonstrated experimentally by arranging for rats to be slapped on the paw when bar pressing in a Skinner box. Two groups of well-trained rats were placed on extinction. One group was punished with a slap for each bar press, while the other was not. It might be expected that the slap would cause bar pressing to extinguish more quickly. Yet this was not the case, as can be seen in Fig. 8-5. Punishment temporarily slowed responding, but it did not cause more rapid extinction. Slapping the paws of rats or children has little permanent effect on a reinforced response. It is worth stating again, however, that intense punishment may permanently suppress a response. Experiments show that actions even as basic as eating can be suppressed. Animals severely punished while eating may never eat again (Bertsch, 1976).

Question: Then should punishment be used in the learning process?

Using Punishment Wisely Parents, educators, animal trainers, and the like have three basic tools available to control simple learning: (1) *reinforcement* (or reward) strengthens a response; (2) *nonreinforcement* causes a response to extinguish; (3) *punishment* suppresses a response. These tools work best in combination. When punishment is mild, as it should be, its effect may be limited if reinforcers are still available in the situation. If you choose to use punishment, it is best to also reward an alternate, desirable response. Used alone, punishment tells a person or animal that a response was "wrong," but it *does not teach new behaviors*. If reinforcement is missing from the formula, punishment becomes less effective.

Question: Are there drawbacks to the use of punishment?

Yes, several. Let's consider the case against punishment.

Severe punishment Intense punishment; by definition, punishment capable of suppressing a response for long periods.

Mild punishment Punishment that has a relatively weak effect, especially that which only temporarily suppresses responses.

Nonreinforcement Withholding reinforcement after selected responses (in other words, extinction training).

Escape learning Learning to make a response in order to end an aversive (painful or uncomfortable) stimulus.

Avoidance learning Learning to make a response in order to postpone or prevent discomfort.

Side Effects of Punishment

The basic problem with punishment is that it is usually *aversive* (painful or uncomfortable). As a result people and situations associated with punishment tend, through classical conditioning, to also become aversive (feared, resented, or disliked). This association, perhaps, is why children so often choose school windows to break when others are available. The aversive qualities of punishment make it especially inappropriate to use when teaching children to eat politely or when toilet training them.

Escape and Avoidance A second major problem is that aversive stimuli usually encourage **escape learning** and **avoidance learning.** Escape learning simply reflects the operation of negative reinforcement. For instance, if you work with a loud and obnoxious person, you may at first escape from conversations with him to obtain relief. Later you may learn to avoid him altogether. Each time you sidestep him, your avoidance is again reinforced by a sense of relief. In many

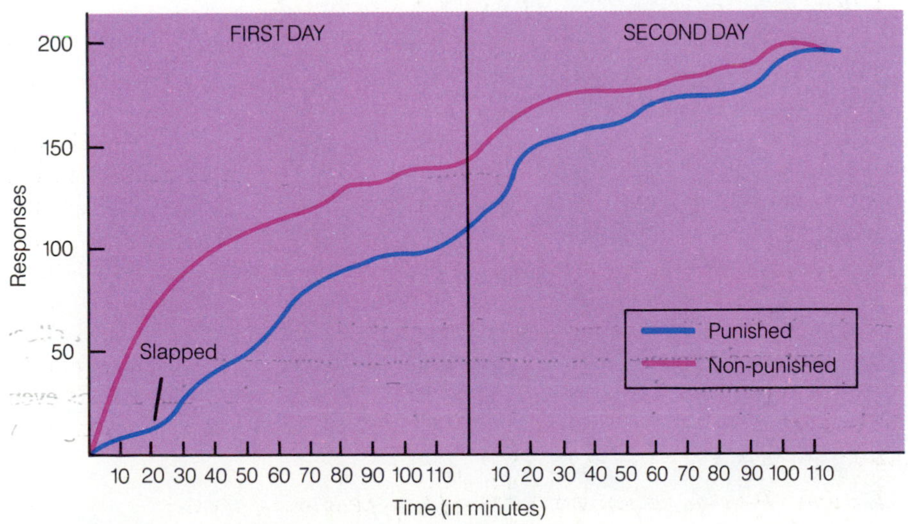

Fig. 8-5 *The effect of punishment on extinction. Immediately after punishment, the rate of bar pressing is suppressed, but by the end of the second day, the effects of punishment had disappeared. (After B. F. Skinner,* The Behavior of Organisms. *© 1938. D. Appleton-Century Co., Inc. Reprinted by permission of Prentice-Hall, Inc.)*

situations involving frequent punishment, similar desires to escape and avoid are activated. For example, children who run away from punishing parents (escape) may soon learn to lie about their behavior (avoidance) or to spend as much time away from home as possible (also an avoidance response).

Aggression A third problem with punishment is that it can greatly increase *aggression*. Researchers have shown that animals consistently react to pain by attacking whomever or whatever is around (Azrin et al., 1965). A common example of this effect is the faithful dog that nips its owner while undergoing a painful procedure at the veterinarian's office.

We also know that one of the most common responses to frustration is aggression (Fig. 8-6). Generally speaking, punishment is painful, frustrating, or both. Punishment therefore sets up a powerful learning environment for the promotion of aggression. When a child is spanked, the child may feel angry, frustrated, and hostile. What if the child then goes outside and hits a brother, sister, or a neighbor? The danger is that the child may feel good because anger and frustration have been released. If so, aggression has been rewarded and will tend to occur again in other frustrating situations. One study found that overly aggressive adolescent boys had been severely punished for aggression at home. Since aggression was suppressed at home, parents were frequently surprised to learn that their "good boys" were in trouble at school for fighting and other forms of aggression (Bandura & Walters, 1959).

To summarize, the most common error in the use of punishment is to rely on it exclusively as a means of training or discipline. The overall emotional adjustment of a child or pet disciplined mainly by reward is usually superior to one disciplined mainly by punishment. Frequent punishment makes a person or an animal unhappy, confused, anxious, aggressive, and fearful of the source of punishment. Children who receive a lot of punishment from parents or teachers

Fig. 8-6 *Frustration and aggression are frequent side effects of punishment.*

learn not only to dislike parents and teachers but also to dislike and avoid the activities associated with punishment (schoolwork or household chores, for instance) (Munn, 1969). It is not entirely unreasonable with 3- to 5-year-old children to occasionally use mild physical punishment (see the Chapter 15 Applications section). Otherwise, it would seem that the adage "Spare the rod and spoil the child" should at least be changed to "Use the rod sparingly or spoil the child" and perhaps simply to "Spare the rod."

Cognitive learning Higher-level learning involving thinking, knowing, understanding, and anticipation.

Cognitive map An internal image or other mental representation of an area (maze, city, campus, and so forth) that underlies an ability to choose alternate paths to the same goal.

Latent learning Learning that occurs without obvious reinforcement and that remains unexpressed until reinforcement is provided.

Cognitive Learning—Beyond Conditioning

Question: Is all learning just a connection between stimuli and responses?

Some learning can be thought of this way. But, as we have seen, even basic conditioning has "mental" elements. There is no doubt that human learning includes a large *cognitive*, or mental, dimension. As humans, we are greatly affected by information, expectations, perceptions, mental images, and the like. Loosely speaking, **cognitive learning** refers to understanding, knowing, anticipating, or otherwise making use of higher mental processes. Cognitive learning extends beyond basic conditioning into the realms of memory, thinking, problem solving, and language. Since these topics are covered in later chapters, our discussion here is limited to an initial look at learning beyond conditioning.

Cognitive Maps How do you navigate around the town you live in? Is it fair to assume that you have simply learned to make a series of right and left turns to get from one point to another? It is far more likely that you have developed an overall mental picture of how the town is laid out. This **cognitive map** (internal representation of relationships) acts as a guide even when you must detour or take a new route.

* cognitive maps

Question: Are animals capable of cognitive learning?

A little psychological "monkey business" shows that they are. In one experiment chimpanzees watched as a psychologist hid pieces of fruit in a field at various places. Later, the chimps were released into the field. Chimps who watched the hiding found about 12 pieces of fruit each. Control group chimps averaged only 1 find each—mostly by following the informed monkeys and sharing the "fruits of their labors" (Menzel, 1978). Actually, it's not surprising that higher animals are capable of cognitive learning. Even the lowly rat—not exactly a mental giant—learns *where* food is found in a maze, not just which turns to make to reach the food (Tolman, 1946).

Latent Learning Cognitive learning is also revealed by **latent** (or hidden) **learning.** That is, learning sometimes occurs without obvious reinforcement and remains hidden until reinforcement is provided:

Mickey Rat II Learns Where the Action Is

Two groups of rats are allowed to explore a maze. Rats in one group find food at the far end of the maze and soon learn to make their way rapidly through the maze when released. Rats in the second group are unrewarded and show no signs of learning. But

later, when the same rats are given food, they run the maze as well as the rewarded group. (Tolman & Honzik, 1930)

Although there was no outward sign of it, the unrewarded rats had learned their way around the maze. Their learning, therefore, remained latent at first (see Fig. 8-7).

Question: How did they learn if there was no reinforcement?

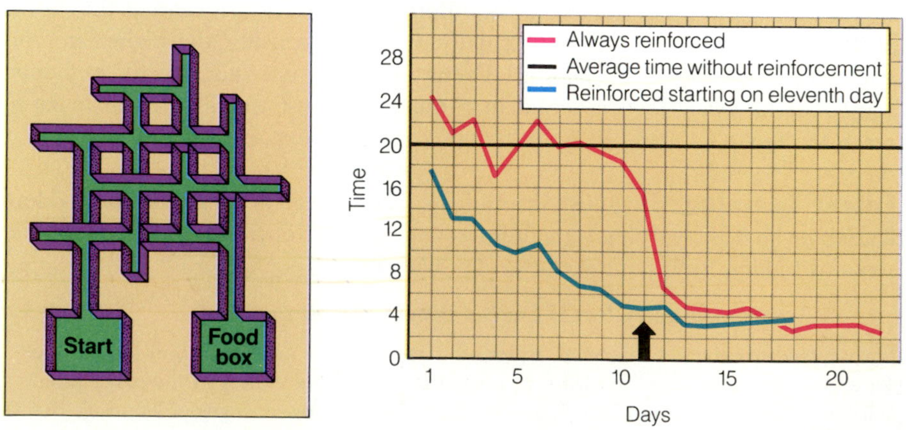

Fig. 8-7 *Latent learning. The maze used by Tolman and Honzik to demonstrate latent learning by rats (left). Results of the experiment are on the right. Notice the rapid improvement in performance that occurred when food was made available to the previously unreinforced animals. (Adapted from Tolman & Honzik, 1930)*

Apparently, satisfying curiosity can be enough to reward learning (Harlow & Harlow, 1962). In humans, latent learning is probably related to higher level abilities, such as anticipation of future reward. For example, if you give an attractive classmate a ride home, you may make mental notes about how to get to his or her house, even if a date only seems to be a remote future possibility.

Discovery learning Learning based on insight or understanding rather than on mechanical application of rules.

Discovery Learning Much of what is meant by cognitive learning is summarized by the word *understanding*. Each of us has, at times, learned ideas by *rote* (repetition and memorization). Although rote learning is efficient, many psychologists believe that learning is more lasting when people *discover* facts and principles on their own (Lepper, 1985). In **discovery learning,** skills are gained by insight and understanding instead of by rote (Bruner, 1968).

Question: As long as learning occurs, what difference does it make?

Figure 8-8 illustrates the difference. Two groups of students were taught to calculate the area of a parallelogram. Some were encouraged to see that a "piece" of a parallelogram could be "moved" to create a rectangle. Later, they were better able to solve unusual problems than were students who simply memorized a rule (Wertheimer, 1959). As this suggests, discovery learning tends to produce better understanding of new problems and situations (Lepper, 1985). In sum, it seems worthwhile to take extra steps to foster insight and deeper understanding, even if learning by discovery takes longer.

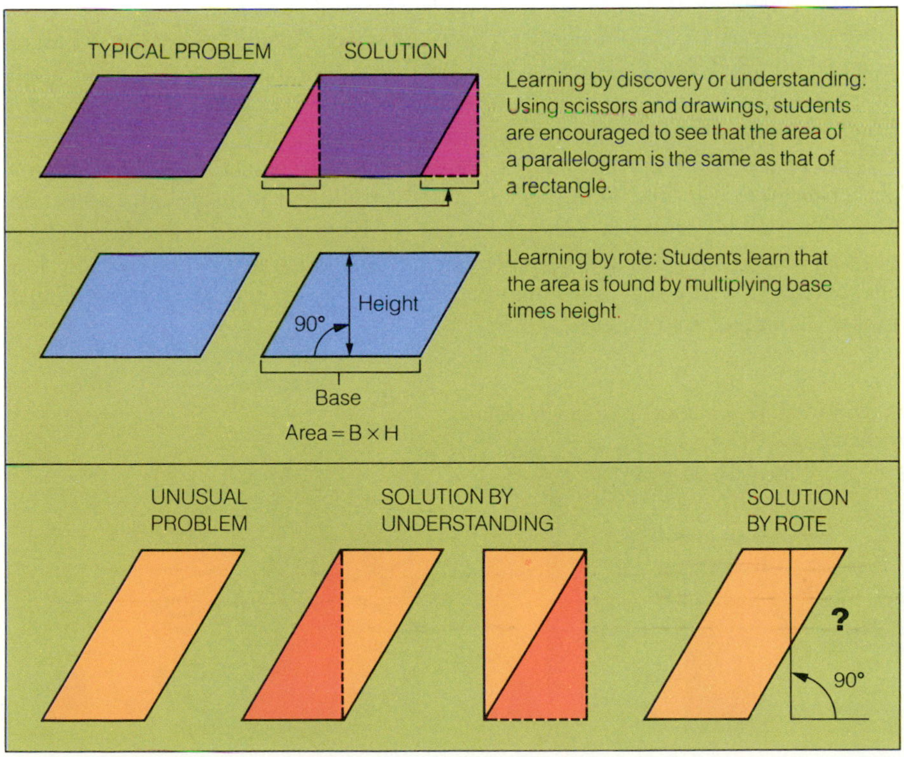

Fig. 8-8 *Learning by understanding and by rote. For some types of learning, understanding may be superior, although both types of learning are useful. (After Wertheimer, 1959)*

Modeling—Do as I Do, Not as I Say

The class watches intently as a skilled potter pulls a spinning ball of clay into the form of a vase. There is little doubt that many skills are learned by what Albert Bandura (1971) calls **observational learning, modeling,** or, simply, imitation. The value of learning by observation is obvious: Imagine trying to *tell* someone how to tie a shoelace, do a dance step, crochet, or play a guitar.

Question: It seems obvious that we learn by observation, but how does it occur?

By observing a **model** (someone who serves as an example), a person may: (1) learn new responses, (2) learn to carry out or avoid previously learned responses (depending on what happens to the model for doing the same thing), or (3) learn a general rule that can be applied to various situations (Rosenthal & Zimmerman, 1978).

For observational learning to occur, several things must take place. First, the learner must pay *attention* to the model and *remember* what was done. (A beginning auto mechanic might be interested enough to watch an entire tune-up but be unable to remember all the steps.) Next, the learner must be able to *reproduce* the modeled behavior. (Sometimes this is a matter of practice, but it may be that the learner will never be able to perform the behavior. I may admire the feats of world-class gymnasts, but with no amount of practice could I ever reproduce them.) If a model is *successful* or *rewarded*, the learner is more likely to imitate the behavior. This is also the case for models who are attractive, admired, or high in status (Bandura & Walters, 1963). Finally, once a new response is tried, normal *reinforcement determines if it will be repeated thereafter*.

Modeling has a powerful effect on behavior. In a classic experiment, children watched an adult attack a large blowup Bo-Bo doll. Some children saw an adult sit on the doll, punch it, hit it with a hammer, and kick it around the room (Fig. 8-9). Others saw a color movie of these actions. A third group saw a cartoon version of the aggression. Later, the children were frustrated (by having some attractive toys taken away from them) and then allowed to play with the Bo-Bo doll. Most imitated the attack they had seen the adult perform. Some even added new aggressive acts of their own! Interestingly, the cartoon was only slightly less effective in encouraging aggression than the live adult model and the filmed model (Bandura, Ross, & Ross, 1963).

Fig. 8-9 *A nursery school child imitates the aggressive behavior of an adult model he has just seen in a movie. (Photos courtesy of Albert Bandura)*

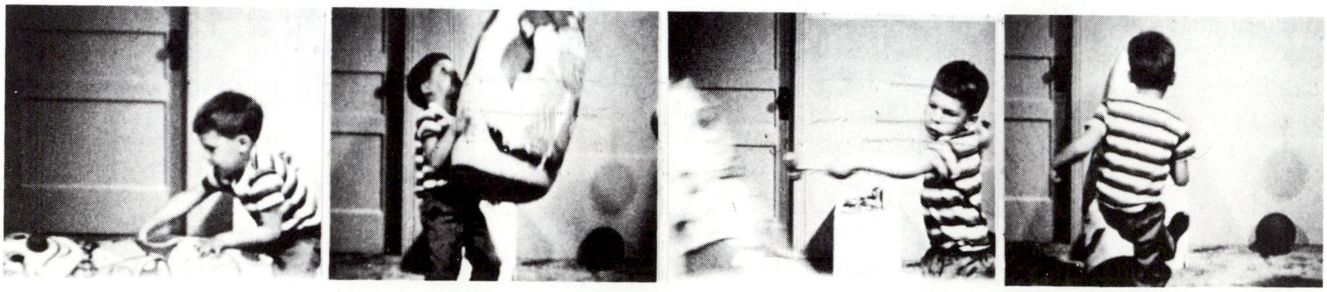

Question: Then do children blindly imitate adults?

No. Remember that observational learning equips a person to duplicate a response, but whether it is actually imitated depends on whether the model was rewarded or punished for what was done. Nevertheless, research shows that when parents tell a child to do one thing, but model a completely different response, children tend to imitate what the parents *do*, and *not* what they *say* (Bryan & Walbek, 1970). Thus, through modeling, children learn not only attitudes, gestures, emotions, and personality traits, but fears, anxieties, and bad habits as well.

Observational learning Learning achieved by watching and imitating the actions of another or noting the consequences of those actions.

Model A person who serves as an example in observational learning.

Consider a typical situation. Little Shawn-Erin-Ringo-Jeremy Jones has just been interrupted at play by his little brother. Angry and frustrated, he hits his little brother. This behavior interrupts his father's TV program. Father promptly spanks little Shawn-Erin-Ringo-Jeremy, saying "This will teach you to hit your little brother." And it will. Because of modeling effects, it is unrealistic to expect a child to "Do as I say, not as I do." The message the father has given the child is clear: "You have frustrated me; therefore, I will hit you." Is it any wonder that the child does the same when frustrated?

Question: Can television serve as a model for observational learning?

An indication of the potential impact of TV can be found in these figures: By the time the average person has graduated from high school, he or she will have viewed some 15,000 hours of TV, compared with only 11,000 hours spent in the classroom. In that time such viewers will have seen some 18,000 murders and countless acts of robbery, arson, bombing, torture, and beatings. Prime-time TV dramas average 8 acts of violence per hour and children's cartoons average 22 an hour (Oskamp, 1984). Many psychologists believe this flood of aggression adversely affects children.

"He said his first words today—'Bang you're dead.'"

Box 8-1

Television: An Unflattering Portrait

Did you know that the world is populated primarily by males, professionals, whites, and members of the middle class? Did you know that women make up only 28 percent of the population; that one-half of all women are teenagers or in their early 20s; that more than one-third are unemployed or have no identifiable purpose beyond offering emotional support to men or serving as objects of sexual desire? That minorities are generally service workers, criminals, victims, or students? That over one-half of all villains have accents (usually German or Russian)? If you watch much TV, these are the impressions you get daily on the tube (U.S. Commission on Civil Rights, 1977).

Televised violence is even more disturbing. Some 80 percent of all TV dramas, and 95 percent of televised cartoons, contain violence. Foreigners and nonwhites are more likely to die on TV than are whites. TV lawmen more often than not contribute to violence, rather than prevent it (Oskamp, 1984; U.S. National Commission on the Causes and Prevention of Violence, 1970).

Are the distortions and stereotypes of "TV land" cause for concern? It would seem so. In over 99 percent of all United States households, TV is practically a member of the family. By 1984 average daily TV viewing in America had exceeded 7 hours. If forced to choose between having indoor plumbing or television, many families would find it difficult to decide! Clearly, television is a major influence in the lives of most children and many adults (Oskamp, 1984).

At this point, hundreds of studies, involving well over 10,000 children, have been completed. The vast majority point to the same conclusion: "If large groups of children watch a great deal of televised violence they will be more prone to behave aggressively" (Comstock et al., 1978; Liebert et al., 1973; Rubinstein, 1978). In addition to encouraging imitation of aggression, TV violence tends to lower sensitivity to violent acts. When Victor Cline and his associates showed a bloody fight film to a group of boys, they found that heavy TV viewers showed much less emotion than those who watched little or no TV (Cline et al., 1972).

Question: Is it fair to say, then, that televised violence causes aggression in children?

No. That would be an exaggeration. Televised violence can make aggression more likely, but it does not cause it to occur (Freedman, 1984). Many other factors affect the chances that hostile thoughts will be translated into actions (Berkowitz, 1984). Among children one such factor is the extent to which a child *identifies* with aggressive characters (Huesmann et al., 1983). That's why it is so sad to find TV *heroes* behaving aggressively, as well as villains. (See Box 8-1.)

Even if television does not *cause* viewers to become violent, it clearly does often serve as a powerful teacher of aggression. Beyond this, televised models may **disinhibit** hostile or aggressive impulses that viewers already have. When a TV program gives viewers the message that violence is normal acceptable behavior, it can lower inhibitions against acting violently (Berkowitz, 1984). Disinhibition may even extend to self-destructive impulses. There is evidence that after a television soap opera character commits suicide, real suicides increase among viewers

(Phillips, 1982). In view of TV's tremendous power to inform and entertain, it is unfortunate it so often serves as a very poor model—especially for growing children.

Learning Check

1. Negative reinforcement increases responding; punishment suppresses responding. T or F?

2. Three factors that greatly influence the effects of punishment are timing, consistency, and ____________.

3. Mild punishment tends to only temporarily ________ a response that is also reinforced. (circle)

enhance aggravate replace suppress

4. Three undesired side effects of punishment are: (1) conditioning of fear and resentment, (2) encouragement of aggression, and (3) the learning of escape or ____________ responses.

5. An internal representation of relationships is referred to as a ____________ ____________.

6. Learning that suddenly appears when a reward or incentive for performance is given is called:
a. discovery learning *b.* latent learning *c.* rote learning *d.* reminiscence

7. Psychologists use the term ____________ to describe observational learning.

8. If a model is successful, rewarded, attractive, or high in status, his or her behavior is:
a. difficult to reproduce *b.* less likely to be attended to *c.* more likely to be imitated *d.* subject to positive transfer

9. Children who observed a live adult behaving aggressively became more aggressive; those who observed movie and cartoon aggression did not. T or F?

Answers: **1.** T **2.** intensity **3.** suppress **4.** avoidance **5.** cognitive map **6.** *b* **7.** modeling **8.** *c* **9.** F

Learning Principles in Action—Biofeedback

Psychologists have discovered that humans can learn to control bodily activities formerly believed to be involuntary. For years Yoga and Zen masters have demonstrated extraordinary control over "involuntary" functions like heart rate, blood pressure, oxygen consumption, and temperature of parts of the body. Now, Western technology is showing that under the proper conditions anyone can learn to duplicate these "impossible" effects.

Question: How is this possible?

Biofeedback A technique allowing individuals to monitor and control their own bodily functions.

Electronic Yoga? By applying the general principle of feedback to the control of bodily responses, we arrive at **biofeedback.** If I were to say to you, "Raise the temperature of your right hand," you probably couldn't because you wouldn't know when you were succeeding. However, your task could be made easier by attaching a sensitive thermometer to your hand. With the thermometer wired so that an increase in temperature would activate a signal light, all you would have to do is try to keep the light on as much as possible. With practice you could then learn to raise your hand temperature at will.

Question: If you succeed at raising hand temperatures, what are you actually doing?

If asked to describe what you did, you might say, "I thought warm thoughts," or, "I just had a feeling when the light was on and I kept trying to recapture that feeling." The point is that when you are given feedback, you can repeat successful responses, even if they are subtle mental states. In this sense biofeedback involves cognitive learning: Bodily processes are monitored (usually electronically) and converted into a clear signal that provides *information* about bodily activity.

Neal Miller and his research associates have found that almost any bodily function can be voluntarily controlled if feedback or reward follows a change in the function. In a typical experiment Miller taught rats to change the speed of their heart rate. Their reward was electrical stimulation of "pleasure centers" in the brain (Miller & DiCara, 1967). Miller initially thought the animals were directly speeding and slowing their hearts. But later experiments suggest the animals altered heart rate by moving their voluntary muscles (Miller & Dworkin, 1974). In any case Miller and others have shown that rats can also learn to change their blood pressure, the blood flow to their stomach or kidneys, and the frequency of stomach contractions. They can even increase blood flow in one ear without affecting the other (Miller, 1969). Can you blush in your left ear?

Question: Of what value is this?

Applications of Biofeedback

Biofeedback holds promise as a means of treating psychosomatic problems (illnesses caused mainly by stress or psychological factors) (see Fig. 8-10). For example, Elmer and Alyce Green have successfully trained people to prevent migraine headaches. With sensors taped to their hands and foreheads, patients are taught to redirect blood flow away from the head to their extremities. Since migraine headaches are caused by excessive blood flow to the head, biofeedback training equips patients to short-circuit headaches before they develop (Luce & Peper, 1971).

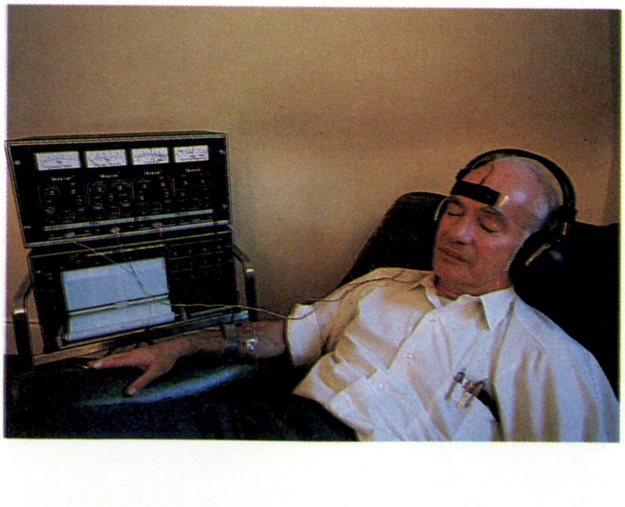

Fig. 8-10 *Biofeedback training involving muscle tension and blood flow has been used to relieve headaches and promote relaxation. Here, a biofeedback signal is routed back to the patient through headphones, allowing him to alter bodily activities.*

Early successes led many to predict that biofeedback would offer a cure for psychosomatic illnesses, anxiety, phobias, drug abuse, and a long list of other problems. In reality, biofeedback has proved helpful but not an instant cure. Biofeedback can definitely relieve muscle-tension headaches and migraine headaches (Adler & Adler, 1976; Blanchard et al., 1982; Budzynski, 1977). It shows promise for lowering blood pressure and alleviating irregular heart rhythms (Blanchard et al., 1984; Kristt & Engel, 1975). Biofeedback has special promise for the rehabilitation of people suffering from muscular disorders and stroke (Orne, 1982). The technique has even been used with some success to control epileptic seizures (Sterman, 1977). How does biofeedback help? Some researchers believe many of its benefits may simply reflect *general relaxation* (Blanchard & Epstein, 1978). Others stress that there is no magic in biofeedback itself. The procedure simply acts as a "mirror" that helps a person accomplish tasks involving *self-regulation* (Green & Shellenberger, 1986; Norris, 1986). Just as a mirror does not comb your hair, biofeedback does not do anything by itself. It can, however, help people make desired changes in their behavior.

Alpha control The ability to voluntarily increase the proportion of brain waves in the alpha frequencies, usually through biofeedback.

Motor skill Learned skills having an element of physical dexterity or requiring the coordination of muscular movements.

Motor program A mental representation or model of a skilled movement, similar in some ways to a computer program.

Question: Does biofeedback apply to brain waves?

Alpha Control Alpha waves are one of several distinctive patterns of brain activity that can be recorded with the EEG (electroencephalograph, or brain wave machine). Several years ago psychologist Joseph Kamiya developed a technique whereby subjects are signaled by a tone or light whenever they produce alpha waves (Kamiya, 1968). Subjects in early alpha-control experiments reported that high levels of alpha were linked with sensations of pleasure, relaxation, "passive alertness," or peaceful images. Some people looked on these findings as a potential avenue to "instant bliss." But more recently, serious questions have been raised about the use of alpha training to promote deep relaxation. Research has shown that for some people increased alpha output is the product of relaxation; but for others it occurs at times of *heightened* arousal (Orne & Wilson, 1978). For the moment it seems that the age of "electronic yoga" is not yet quite with us. This is especially true of inexpensive commercial "alpha-feedback" machines. These devices are so inaccurate that "blissed out" users frequently end up hearing electrical "noise" from their house wiring, rather than their own brain waves (Beyerstein, 1985).

Learning Principles in Action—Learning Skills Skillfully

A **motor skill** is a series of actions molded into a smooth and efficient performance. Typing, walking, pole vaulting, shooting baskets, playing golf, driving a car, writing, and skiing are examples of motor skills.

Question: How are motor skills learned?

Many begin as simple response chains. However, as skills improve, we typically develop **motor programs** for them (Blumenthal, 1976). Motor programs are mental plans or models of what a skilled movement should be like. A good example of this kind of learning is provided by a guitarist friend of the author's. The gui-

Fig. 8-11 *Strobe-light photograph of a motor skill. Multiple exposures reveal the complexity of skilled movement. Motor skills are guided by mental plans or programs.*

tarist once cut the first finger of his right hand before a performance. Normally he did his finger-picking with his thumb and first two fingers. How could he perform with an injured finger? No problem! He used the second and third fingers instead. His musical skills were in his head (as a motor program), not in his fingers.

New skills usually require conscious guidance. Think of when you learned to drive a car. Initially, almost all of your attention was focused on steering, signaling, accelerating, and braking; holding a conversation or tuning the radio was probably out of the question. However, as motor programs develop, we can pay less attention to specific movements. Eventually, skills become *automated*, or nearly automatic. This frees higher brain centers to make decisions and attend to other information (Singer, 1978). Thus, a skilled skier can enjoy the scenery on a downhill run, a knitter can watch television, or a driver can think about things other than driving.

Skillful Skill Learning

Throughout life you will repeatedly face the challenge of learning new motor skills. How can psychology help make your learning more effective? Research findings suggest that you should keep in mind the following points for optimal skill learning (sources: Drowatzky, 1975; Gagne & Fleishman, 1959; Klausmeir, 1975; Meichenbaum, 1977; Singer, 1978):

1. Begin by observing and imitating a *skilled model*. Modeling provides a good mental picture of the skill. At this point try simply to grasp a visual image of the skilled movement.
2. Learn *verbal rules* to back up motor learning. Such rules are usually most helpful in the early phases of skill learning. When first learning cross-country skiing, for example, it is helpful to say "left arm, right foot, right arm, left foot." Later, as a skill becomes more automated, internal speech may actually get in the way.
3. Practice should be as *lifelike* as possible so that artificial cues and responses do not become a part of the skill. A competitive diver should practice on the board, not on a trampoline. If you want to learn to ski, try to practice on snow, not straw.
4. Get *feedback* from a mirror, videotape, coach, or observer. Whenever possible, get someone experienced in the skill to direct attention to *correct responses* when they occur.
5. When possible, it is better to practice *natural units* rather than break the task into artificial parts. When learning to type, it is better to start with real words rather than exercises or nonsense syllables.
6. Learn to *evaluate* and *analyze* your own performance. Remember you are trying to learn a motor program, not just train your muscles. Motor skills are actually very mental.

The last point leads to one more suggestion. Research has shown that merely thinking about or imagining a skilled performance can aid learning (Annett, 1979; Kemeny & Maltzman, 1987). This technique, called **mental practice,** seems to help by refining motor programs. The more familiar you are with a skill, the more mental rehearsal helps (Drowatzky, 1975; Meichenbaum, 1977). When you begin to get really good at a skill you are interested in, give mental practice a try. You may be surprised at how effective it can be.

Practice Effects It is also helpful to know that improvement in performance of a motor skill is most rapid when short practice sessions are alternated with rest periods (Fig. 8-12). This pattern, called **spaced practice,** helps keep fatigue and boredom to a minimum. It can also prevent the learner from practicing errors while tired. (Perfect practice makes perfect.) The opposite of spaced practice is **massed practice,** in which little or no rest is given between learning sessions. Notice in Figure 8-12 that massed practice lowers performance during training. As you can also see, both massed and spaced practice produce similar amounts of learning after a short break in training. However, in the long run, skills learned with spaced practice are retained better than those learned by massed practice (Drowatzky, 1975). This suggests that you should keep practice sessions short and well spaced if you are learning to type, play a musical instrument, juggle, or master some other motor skill.

Question: Why is there a jump in the motor skill curves after the rest period?

Improved performance of a motor skill *after* practice is called **reminiscence.** Reminiscence is explained in this way: Learning increases during practice, but so does fatigue, boredom, and loss of motivation. These negative factors lower *performance* toward the end of a practice session even though *learning* continues. Later, when a rest period removes fatigue, performance rises sharply (Drowatzky, 1975).

Throughout this chapter we have emphasized various ways of enhancing learning. To turn things around a bit, the upcoming Applications section describes several techniques for breaking bad habits. While you probably have absolutely no bad habits of any kind, you may at least find some hints you can pass on to friends and relatives who are curiously blind to their own faults.

Mental practice Mentally rehearsing and refining a skilled performance.

Spaced practice Learning trials or practice sessions spread over a period of time and including a number of rest periods.

Massed practice Continuous practice without rest periods or interruptions.

Reminiscence Improvement in the performance of a motor skill that occurs sometime after practice has ended.

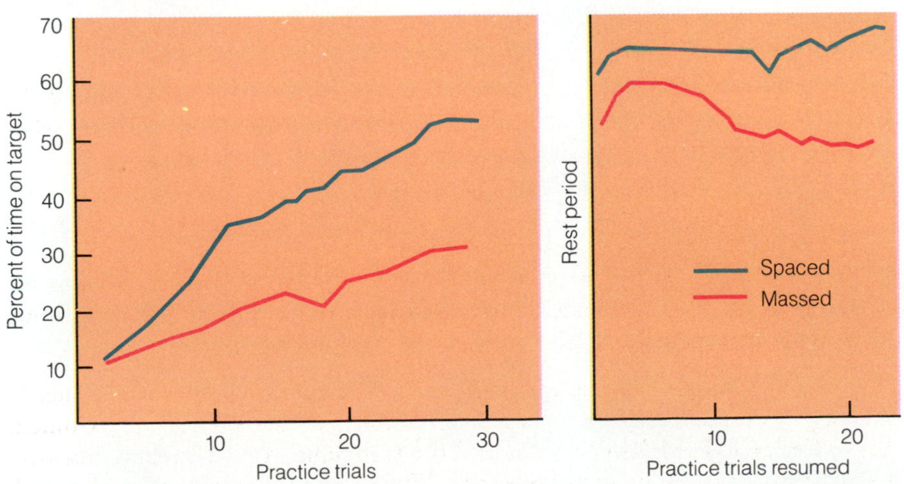

Fig. 8-12 *Performance curves for massed and spaced practice. Subjects learned to keep a pointer on a moving target. During the first learning session the spaced-practice group performed better. After a rest period, performance was similar for both groups, but further trials again lowered performance in the massed-practice group. (From Jones & Ellis, 1962)*

Learning Check

1. Biofeedback is a type of meditation in which the body is made very quiet so that bodily functioning can be detected. T or F?
2. Rats given electrical brain stimulation as a reward can be made to alter such bodily functions as heart rate, blood pressure, and stomach contractions. T or F?
3. Biofeedback can definitely relieve:
   a. depression *b.* diabetes *c.* stomach ulcers *d.* muscle-tension headaches
4. Joseph Kamiya developed a technique whereby subjects can gain control over the brain's production of ________.
5. An important step in the mastery of many motor skills is achieved when the skill becomes
   a. reversible *b.* automated *c.* graduated *d.* fixed
6. Mental models, called ________ ________, appear to underlie well-learned motor skills.
7. In motor skill learning, massed practice generally produces performance that is superior to spaced practice. T or F?
8. Learning verbal rules to back up motor learning is usually most helpful in the early stages of acquiring a skill. T or F?

Answers: **1.** F **2.** T **3.** *d* **4.** alpha waves **5.** *b* **6.** motor programs **7.** F **8.** T

Applications

Good Ways to Break Bad Habits

Question: How can I use learning principles to break a bad habit?

The following techniques offer some helpful possibilities. They combine ideas drawn both from this chapter and the last.

1. Try to discover what is reinforcing a habit and *remove, avoid,* or *delay* the reinforcement.

Example: A student who developed a habit of taking longer and longer breaks when studying realized that the breaks usually were lengthened by TV watching. A chance to watch TV was also reinforcing more frequent break taking.

Comment: To improve study habits, the student should either resolve to stay out of the room where the TV is located until work is done, or else require 2 hours of study for ½ hour of TV watching.

Example: Pam has a slightly different problem. When she reads in the evening, her periods of concentration last only about 15 minutes. They are usually followed by a trip to the kitchen for a snack. In addition to falling behind in her reading, she is gaining weight.

Comment: Snacking is rewarding her impulse to avoid reading. She should do her reading at school or at a library, so that there is a delay between the impulse to eat and the reward of snacking. At home she should keep only staples on hand or foods that require preparation, so that a separate trip to a store is required for "goodies." Requiring a walk around the block before eating a snack would also help (Ferster et al., 1962).

2. Try to get the *same reinforcement with new responses.*

Example: A young mother realized she was yelling at her children more often than she would like. This habit seemed to be reinforced by the periods of relative quiet that followed when she raised her voice.

Comment: To avoid this habit (which is negatively reinforced), she should (as much as possible) ignore her

Applications: Good Ways to Break Bad Habits, continued

children when they are noisy and should make a special effort to praise them, show approval, and pay attention to them when they are playing quietly and constructively.

Example: Frank has been drinking increasing amounts of beer after getting home from work in the evening. He usually feels more relaxed but often drinks too much and gets into arguments with other family members.

Comment: Frank's need to unwind and dissipate the frustrations of the workday might be better achieved by participation in an athletic activity, such as jogging, swimming, bowling, handball, and so forth. An organized team sport might ensure that he will actually stick with his substitute activity.

3. *Avoid* or *narrow down cues* that elicit the bad habit.

Example: A student has begun to notice how much impulse buying he does at the grocery store. As a first step in avoiding this habit, he has begun to shop after he has had a meal because he has observed that hunger is a cue for his food buying.

Comment: He should also make a shopping list and stick to it so that he only looks at items he intends to buy.

Example: A father has noticed that he nags and criticizes his 4-year-old son almost nightly because the boy pours ketchup all over his dinner. He is upset about this and other daily instances of criticizing the boy.

Comment: The father has identified one cue for his excessive criticizing. It could be avoided by giving the boy a small bowl of ketchup to prevent the regular dinner battle. Other cues for nagging can be avoided in similar ways as they are identified (Schmidt, 1976).

Example: Raul is not ready to give up smoking, but would like to cut down. He has taken many smoking cues out of his daily routine by removing ashtrays, matches, and extra cigarettes from his house, car, and office. He also has been making an effort to avoid situations in which most of his smoking occurs by staying away from other smokers, taking a walk after meals (leaving his cigarettes at home), and putting a piece of gum in his mouth when he feels nervous.

Comment: To improve his control of smoking, Raul should try narrowing cues. He could begin by smoking only inside buildings, never outside or in his car. He could then limit his smoking to home. Then to only one room at home. Then to one chair at home. If he succeeds in getting this far, he may want to limit his smoking to only one uninteresting place: a bathroom, basement, or garage, for example (Goldiamond, 1971).

4. Make an *incompatible response* in the presence of stimuli that usually precede the bad habit.

Example: A sprinter has developed a habit of jumping the gun at track meets and is frequently disqualified.

Comment: The sprinter should prepare for meets by remaining in the blocks while his coach fires the starter's pistol several times.

Example: A child has developed the habit of throwing her coat on the floor after coming in the front door. After being scolded, she would hang it up.

Comment: The parents should recognize that scolding has become the cue for hanging the coat up. The girl should not just be scolded, but should put her coat on again, go outside, come in the door, and hang her coat up. Soon, coming in the door will become the cue for hanging the coat up.

Example: June bites her nails so much they are painful and unsightly. She has identified several situations in which she is most likely to bite her nails and would like to break the connection between these and her habit.

Comment: June should make a list of incompatible behaviors she can engage in when she has the urge to bite her nails. These might include: putting her hands in her pockets, taking notes in class, sketching pictures, crossing her arms, leaning against something with her hands, chewing gum, playing a musical instrument, or combing her hair (Perkins & Perkins, 1976).

5. Use *negative practice* to associate a bad habit with discomfort.

Example: Rick has a facial tic that appears when he is nervous or tired. The tic looks like a wink made with his right eye.

Applications: Good Ways to Break Bad Habits, continued

Comment: In negative practice a response is repeated until it becomes boring, painful, or produces fatigue. This increases awareness of the habit and tends to discourage its recurrence. Rick should stand in front of a mirror and repeat the tic until the muscles used become quite uncomfortable. Similarly, if you have a habit of saying "you know" or "uh" too often when speaking, set aside 15 minutes a day and repeat the error over and over while thinking, "I hate the way this sounds when someone else says it."

6. Utilizing *feedback* is one of the most direct of all approaches to changing bad habits.

Example: Four college students who are renting a house together are concerned about their high utility bills. Also, they would like to make an effort to conserve energy. To date, however, their good intentions have not lowered their electric bill.

Comment: The roommates should keep a daily record of their energy consumption by writing down and posting the numbers shown on their electric meter. A study of families given this kind of daily feedback showed that their energy use was greatly reduced (Palmer et al., 1977).

The last technique described is worth emphasizing. As noted in the Applications for Chapter 7, almost any habit will benefit simply from keeping score. Keep track of the number of times daily that you arrive late to class, smoke a cigarette, watch an hour of TV, drink a cup of coffee, bite your fingernails, swear, or whatever other response you are interested in changing. A simple tally on a piece of paper will do, or you can get a small mechanical counter like those used to keep golf scores or count calories.

In this chapter and the last, we have tried to emphasize the practical applications of learning theories to everyday problems. Many simple difficulties can be handled effectively without special training. If you have a really troublesome habit, such as overeating or excessive use of alcohol, cigarettes, or marijuana, you may find it most expedient to consult a professional counselor. Additional learning techniques for overcoming mild difficulties can be found in Chapter 22, Chapter 11, and Chapter 7.

Learning Check

1. Removing or avoiding reinforcement of a bad habit can help eliminate it, but delaying reinforcement has no effect. T or F?

2. A mother who praises her children when they are quiet instead of yelling at them when they are noisy has received the same reinforcement for an alternate response. T or F?

3. Restricting smoking to only one room in a house is an example of using feedback to alter a bad habit. T or F?

4. To break the link between an undesired response and various situations in which it occurs, it can be helpful to practice making an incompatible response in the same situations. T or F?

5. In negative practice we learn to avoid or narrow down cues that elicit a bad habit. T or F?

Answers: **1.** F **2.** T **3.** F **4.** T **5.** F

Chapter Summary

- Many real-world situations involve *two-factor learning*—a combination of classical conditioning and operant conditioning.
- From an *informational viewpoint*, conditioning creates *expectancies*, which alter response patterns. In classical conditioning, the CS creates an expectancy that the US will follow. In operant conditioning, learning is based on the expectation that a response will have a specific effect.
- *Feedback* or *knowledge of results* aids learning and improves performance. It is most effective when it is *immediate*, *detailed*, and *frequent*.
- *Programmed instruction* breaks learning into a series of small steps and provides immediate feedback. *Computer-assisted instruction* (CAI) does the same but has the added advantage of being able to provide alternate exercises and information when needed. Three variations of CAI are *drill and practice*, *instructional games*, and *educational simulations*.
- In *positive reinforcement* a reward or a pleasant event follows a response. In *negative reinforcement* a response ends discomfort and is therefore repeated. Punishment decreases responding. *Punishment* is either the presentation of an aversive event or the removal of a positive event after a response is made.
- *Punishment* is most effective when it is *immediate*, *consistent*, and *intense*. Mild punishment tends only to temporarily suppress responses that are reinforced or were acquired by reinforcement.
- The undesirable side effects of punishment include: conditioning of *fear* to punishing agents and situations associated with punishment, the learning of *escape* and *avoidance* responses, and the encouragement of *aggression*.
- *Cognitive learning* involves higher mental processes, such as understanding, knowing, or anticipating. Even in relatively simple learning situations, animals and people seem to form *cognitive maps* (internal representations of relationships). In *latent learning*, learning remains hidden or unseen until a reward or incentive for performance is offered. *Discovery learning* emphasizes insight and understanding, in contrast to *rote learning*.
- Much human learning is achieved through observation or *modeling*. Modeling (or *observational learning*) is influenced by many factors, especially the personal characteristics of the model and the success or failure of the model's behavior. Studies have shown that aggression is readily learned and released by modeling.
- During *biofeedback*, bodily processes are monitored and converted to a signal that indicates what the body is doing. With practice, biofeedback allows alteration of many bodily activities. It shows promise for the alleviation of some stress-related illnesses. Its long-term effectiveness is still being evaluated. The usefulness of *alpha control* (voluntary control of brain waves) is debatable.
- *Motor skills* are nonverbal response chains assembled into a smooth performance. Motor skills are guided by internal mental models called *motor programs*. Motor skills often show improvement *after* practice *(reminiscence)*. Motor skill learning is usually best when practice is *spaced*, rather than *massed*.
- Bad habits may be altered by each of the following techniques: remove, avoid, or delay reinforcement of undesirable responses; try to get the same reinforcement with different responses; avoid or restrict cues that elicit undesirable responses. Use of negative practice and obtaining feedback about responses can also help alter troublesome behavior.

Chapter 9

Memory

Chapter Preview

"What the Hell's Going on Here?"

February, 1978: Steven Kubacki is cross-country skiing on the ice of Lake Michigan. He stops for a moment, pausing to enjoy the winter solitude. It's cold, colder in fact than he had realized. Steven decides to turn back. In a few minutes comes a new realization: He is lost. Wandering on the ice, he grows numb and very, very tired.

Put yourself in Steven Kubacki's shoes, and you will appreciate the shock of what happened next. Steven clearly recalls wandering lost and alone on the ice. Immediately after that, he remembers waking up in a field. But as he looked around, Steven knew something was wrong. It was spring! The backpack beside him contained running shoes, swimming goggles, and a pair of glasses—all unfamiliar. As he looked at his clothing—also unfamiliar—Steven thought to himself, "What the hell's going on here?" Fourteen months had passed since he left to go skiing (Loftus, 1980). How did he get to the field? Where did the strange gear come from? Steven couldn't say. He had lost over a year of his life to total amnesia.

As Steven Kubacki's amnesia vividly shows, life without memory would be meaningless. Imagine the terror and confusion of having all of your memories wiped out, from birth to present. You would have no identity, no knowledge, no life history, no recognition of friends or family. Your past would be a total blank. In a very real sense we are our memories.

This chapter discusses memory and forgetting. As an inquiring person you should find the information interesting. Also included is a large section on improving memory skills. As a student you should find this discussion particularly helpful. Almost anyone (including you) can learn to use memory more effectively.

Survey Questions How do we store information in memory? Is there more than one type of memory? How is memory measured? What are "photographic" memories? What causes forgetting? How accurate are everyday memories? How can memory be improved?

Stages of Memory—Do you Have a Mind Like a Steel Trap? Or a Sieve?

"A dusty storehouse of facts." That's how many people think of memory. In reality, **memory** is an *active system* that receives, stores, organizes, alters, and recovers information. In some ways memory acts like a computer (Fig. 9-1). Information to be recorded is first **encoded,** or changed into a usable form. This step is like punching data onto cards before feeding it into a computer. Next, information is **stored,** or held in the system. (As we will see in a moment, human memory actually has three separate storage systems.) Finally, memories must be **retrieved,** or taken out of storage, to be useful. In order to "remember" something, encoding, storage, and retrieval all must take place.

Question: What are the three separate memory systems just mentioned?

Psychologists have identified three stages of memory. To be stored for a long time, information must pass through all three (please refer to Fig 9-2).

Sensory Memory Let's say a friend asks you to pick up several things at a market. How do you remember them? Incoming information first enters **sensory memory.** Sensory memory holds an exact copy of what is seen or heard for a few seconds or less. For instance, if you see an object, an **icon** (EYE-kon: image)

Resources

Memory The mental capacity of storing, organizing, and recovering information.

Encoding Converting information into a form in which it will be retained in memory.

Storage Holding information in memory for later use.

Retrieval Recovering information from memory.

Sensory memory The first stage of memory, which holds an explicit and literal record of incoming information for one-half second or less.

Icon A mental image or representation.

Fig. 9-1 *In some ways a computer acts like an electronic memory system. Both systems process information, and both allow encoding, storage, and retrieval of data.*

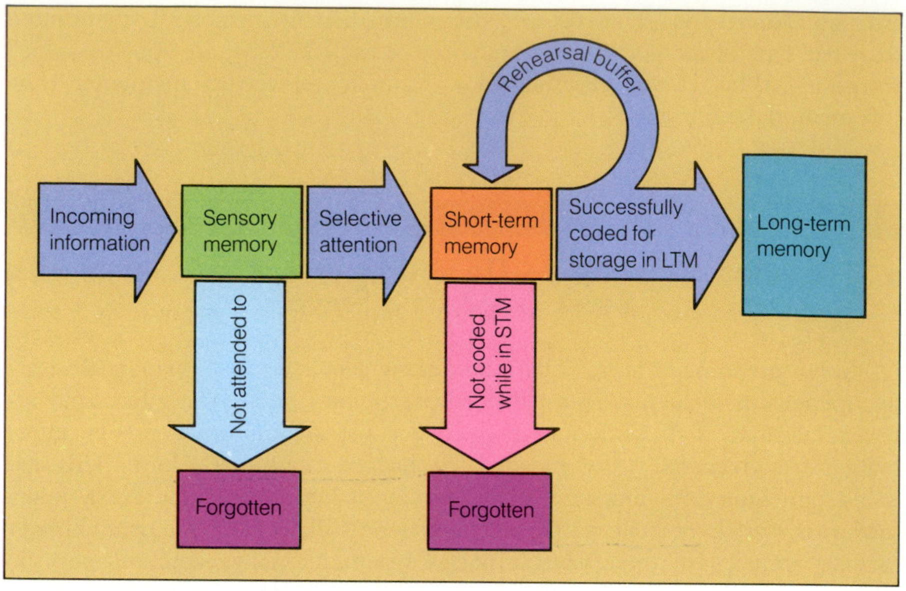

Fig. 9-2 *Memory is thought to involve at least three steps. Incoming information is first held for a second or two by sensory memory. Information selected by attention is then transferred to temporary storage in short-term memory. If new information is not rapidly encoded, or rehearsed, it is forgotten. If it is transferred to long-term memory, it becomes relatively permanent, although retrieving it may be a problem. The preceding is a useful* model *of memory; it may not be literally true of what happens in the brain.*

persists for about one-half second afterward (Klatzky, 1980). In general, sensory memory holds information just long enough to transfer it to the second memory system.

Short-Term Memory Not everything seen or heard is kept in memory. Let's say a radio is playing in the background as your friend reads you her shopping list. Do you remember what the announcer says too? Probably not, because *selective attention* (discussed in Chapter 4) determines what information moves on to **short-term memory (STM).** Short-term memories are also brief, but longer than sensory memories. Attending to your friend's words will place the shopping list in short-term memory (while allowing you to ignore the voice on the radio saying, "Buy Burpo Butter").

Short-term memory acts as a *temporary* storehouse for *small amounts* of information. Unless the information is important, it is quickly "dumped" from STM and forever lost. Short-term memory prevents our minds from collecting useless names, dates, telephone numbers, and other trivia (Miller, 1964). At the same time, it provides a **working memory** where we do much of our thinking. Dialing a phone number, doing mental arithmetic, remembering a shopping list, and the like all rely on STM (Atkinson & Shiffrin, 1971).

As you may have noticed when dialing a telephone, STM is very sensitive to *interruption* or *interference* (Adams, 1967). You've probably had the following experience with STM. You look up a number and walk to the phone, repeating it to yourself. You dial the number and get a busy signal. Returning a few minutes later, you find that you must look up the number again. This time as you are about to dial, someone asks you a question. You answer, turn to the phone, and find that you have forgotten the number.

Question: If short-term memory is brief, easily interrupted, and limited in "size," how do we remember for greater lengths of time?

Long-Term Memory Information that is important or *meaningful* is transferred to the third memory system, called long-term memory. In contrast to STM, **long-term memory (LTM)** acts as a permanent storehouse for information. LTM contains everything you know about the world—from aardvark to zucchini, math to Monopoly, facts to fantasy. And yet, there appears to be no danger of running out of room in LTM. LTM has a nearly limitless storage capacity (Klatzky, 1980).

Short-term memory (STM) The memory system used to hold small amounts of information for relatively brief time periods.

Working memory Another name for short-term memory, especially as it is used for thinking and problem solving.

Long-term memory (LTM) The memory system used for relatively permanent storage of meaningful information.

Dual Memory Most of our daily memory chores are handled by STM and LTM. To summarize their connection, picture short-term memory as a small desk at the front of an immense warehouse full of filing cabinets (LTM). As information is brought into the warehouse, it is first placed on the desk. Since the desk is small, it must be quickly cleared off to make room for new information. Some items are simply tossed away because they are unimportant. Meaningful or important information is placed in the permanent files (long-term memory). When we want to use knowledge from LTM to answer a question, the information is returned to STM. Or, in the analogy, a copy is taken out of the files (LTM) and moved to the desk, (STM) where it can be used.

Now that you have a general picture of STM and LTM, it is time to explore both in more detail. The discussions that follow should add to your understanding.

Learning Check

Match:

A. Sensory memory **B.** STM **C.** LTM

1. ____ Working memory

2. ____ Holds information for a few seconds or less

3. ____ Stores an exact image of information seen

4. ____ Permanent, unlimited capacity

5. ____ Temporarily holds small amounts of information

6. ____ Selective attention determines its contents

7. STM is improved by interruption or interference because attention is more focused at such times. T or F?

Answers: **1.** B **2.** A **3.** A **4.** C **5.** B **6.** B **7.** F

Short-Term Memory—Do You Know the Magic Number?

Question: How much information can be held in short-term memory?

For an answer read the following numbers once. Then close the book and write as many as you can in the correct order.

8 5 1 7 4 9 3

This is called a **digit-span test.** If you were able to correctly repeat this series of 7 digits, you have an average short-term memory. Now try to memorize the following list of digits, reading them only once.

7 1 8 3 5 4 2 9 1 6 3

This series was probably beyond your short-term memory capacity. Psychologist George Miller has shown that short-term memory is limited to what he calls the magic number **seven** (plus or minus two) **bits** of information (Miller, 1956). It is as if short-term memory has 7 "slots" or "bins" into which separate items can be placed.

When all of the "slots" in STM are filled, there is no room for new information (Klatzky, 1980). Picture how this works at a party: Let's say your hostess begins introducing everyone who is there, "Ted, Barbara, Donna, Roseanna, Wayne, Shawn, Linda. . . ." "Stop," you think to yourself. But the hostess continues, ". . . Eddie, Jay, Gordon, Frank, Marietta, Dan, Patty, Glen, Ricky." The hostess leaves, satisfied that you have met everyone. And you spend the evening talking with Ted, Barbara, and Ricky, the only people whose names you remember!

Recoding Before we continue, try your short-term memory again, this time on letters. Read the following letters once, then close the book and try to write them in the proper order.

TVF BIJF KY MCA

Notice that there are 12 letters, or "bits" of information. This should be beyond the 7-item limit of STM. However, since the letters are presented as 4 groups, or **chunks** of information, many students are able to memorize them.

Question: How does chunking help?

Chunking **recodes** information into larger units. Most often it does so by taking advantage of units already in LTM. For example, in the letter list above, you may have noticed that KY is the abbreviation for Kentucky. If so, the 2 bits "K" and "Y" become one chunk. In a memory experiment involving the list you have just memorized, subjects remembered best when the letters were read as: TV . . . FBI . . . JFK . . . YMCA (Bower & Springston, 1970). If you recoded the letters this way, you undoubtedly remembered the entire list.

Chunking suggests that STM holds about 7 of whatever units we are using, be they numbers, letters, words, phrases, or familiar sentences (Klatzky, 1980). Picture STM as a small desk again. Through chunking we combine several individual items into one "stack" of information. This allows us to place 7 stacks on the desk where before there was only room for 7 separate items.

Question: How long do short-term memories last?

Rehearsal Short-term memories appear to weaken and disappear very rapidly. However, a short-term memory can be prolonged quite easily by silently repeating it until it is needed. Remembering a telephone number you intend to use only once is often done this way.

Keeping a short-term memory alive by silently repeating it is called **rehearsal.** The longer a short-term memory is rehearsed, the greater is its chance of being stored in LTM. What if rehearsal is prevented, so that a memory cannot be recycled or moved to LTM? Without rehearsal STM is incredibly short.

> In one experiment subjects heard meaningless syllables like XAR followed by a number like 67. As soon as subjects heard the number, they began counting backwards by threes (to prevent them from repeating the syllable). After only 18 seconds of delay, memory scores fell to zero. (Peterson & Peterson, 1959)

After *18 seconds* without rehearsal, the short-term memories were gone forever! Keep this in mind when you get only one chance to hear information you want to remember. For example, if you are introduced to someone, and his or her name slips out of STM, there is no way to retrieve it. To escape this awkward situation, you might try saying something like, "I'm curious, how do you spell your name?" But unfortunately, the response is often an icy reply like, "B-O-B S-M-I-T-H, it's really not too difficult," To avoid embarrassment, pay careful attention to the name, repeat it to yourself several times, and try to use it in the next sentence or two—before you lose it.

Long-Term Memory—Where the Past Lives

An electrode was placed at location number 11 on the patient's brain. She immediately said, "Yes, sir, I think I heard a mother calling her little boy somewhere. It seemed to be something happening years ago. . . . It was somebody in the neighborhood where I live." A short time later the electrode was applied to the same spot. Again the patient said, "Yes, I hear the same familiar sounds, it seems to be a woman calling, the same lady" (Penfield, 1958). These statements were made by a woman undergoing brain surgery for epilepsy. Only local anesthetics were used (there are no pain receptors in the brain), so the patient was awake as her brain was electrically stimulated (Fig. 9-3). When activated, some brain areas seemed to produce vivid memories of long-forgotten events.

Question: Does this mean that every experience a person has ever had is recorded in memory?

Permanence Results like those described led neurosurgeon Wilder Penfield to claim that the brain records the past like a "continuous strip of movie film, complete with sound track" (Penfield, 1957). But as you now know, this is an exaggeration. Many events never get past short-term memory. More importantly, there is reason to doubt Penfield's conclusion. In only about 3 percent of cases does brain stimulation produce memorylike experiences. Most reports resemble dreams more than memories, and many are clearly fictional. Memory experts Elizabeth and Geoffrey Loftus have carefully examined Penfield's work as well as research on "truth serums" and hypnosis. They conclude there is little evidence that long-term memories are absolutely permanent (Loftus & Loftus, 1980). It is probably most accurate to say that long-term memories are *relatively* permanent, or long lasting.

Digit-span test A test of attention and short-term memory in which a number of digits are read to subjects who then must immediately try to recall them.

Information bits Meaningful units of information, such as numbers, letters, words, or phrases.

Information chunks Information bits grouped into larger units.

Recoding Reorganizing or otherwise transforming information to facilitate storage in memory.

Rehearsal Silently repeating or mentally reviewing information to hold it in short-term memory or aid its long-term storage.

TVF / BIJF / KY / MCA
TVFBI JFK YMCA

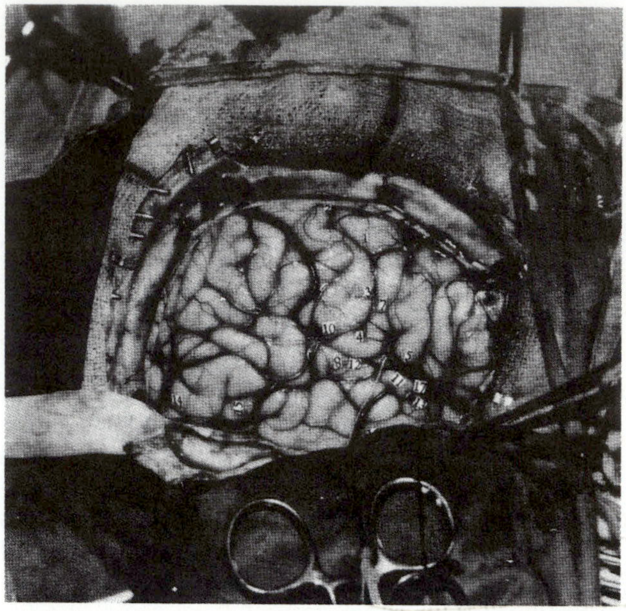

Fig. 9-3 *Exposed cerebral cortex of a patient undergoing brain surgery. Numbers represent points that reportedly produced "memories" when electrically stimulated. A critical evaluation of such reports suggests that they are more like dreams than memories. This fact raises questions about claims that long-term memories are permanent. (From Wilder Penfield,* The Excitable Cortex in Conscious Man, *1958. Courtesy of the author and Charles C Thomas, Publisher, Springfield, Illinois)*

Constructing Memories There is another reason to doubt Penfield's claim. As new long-term memories are formed, older memories are often updated, changed, lost, or *revised* (Cofer, 1975). Consider this illustration: Loftus and Palmer (1974) showed subjects a filmed automobile accident. Afterward, some subjects were asked to estimate how fast the cars were going when they "smashed" into each other. For others the words "bumped," "contacted," or "hit" replaced "smashed." One week later subjects were asked, "Did you see any broken glass?" Those asked earlier about the cars that "smashed" into each other were more likely to say yes. (No broken glass was shown in the film.) The new information ("smashed") was included in subjects' memories and altered them.

Updating memories is called **constructive processing.** Research shows that gaps in memory, which are common, may be filled in by logic, guesses, or new information (Loftus, 1977, 1980). Indeed, it is possible to have "memories" for things that never happened (such as remembering broken glass at an accident when there was none). People in Elizabeth Loftus' experiments who had **pseudo-memories** (false memories) were often quite upset to learn they had given false "testimony" (Loftus, 1980).

The updating of long-term memory is a common problem in police work. For example, a witness may select a photo of a suspect from police files or see a photo in the news. Later, the witness identifies the suspect in person (in a lineup or in court). Did the witness really remember the criminal? Or the more recently seen photograph? Even if the suspect is innocent, he or she may be "remembered" as the criminal. It is quite possible for a photo to update or *blend* with the original memory. Many tragic cases of mistaken identity have occurred in this way.

Question: Couldn't hypnosis be used to avoid such problems?

News stories often give the impression that it can. Is this true? For an answer see Box 9-1.

Box 9-1

Hypnosis, Imagination, and Memory

News reports often imply that hypnosis can improve memory. But does it? Read on and judge for yourself.

Recent research has shown that a hypnotized person is more likely than normal to use imagination to fill in gaps in memory. Also, when hypnotized subjects are given false information, they tend to weave it into their memories (Sheehan, Grigg, & McCann, 1984). It has been shown that "leading" questions asked during hypnosis can alter memories (Sanders & Simmons, 1983). And, even when a memory is completely false, the hypnotized person's confidence in it can be unshakable (Laurence & Perry, 1983). Most telling of all is the fact that hypnosis increases false memories more than it does true ones. Subjects in one experiment, for instance, were able to slightly improve their memory scores under hypnosis. But they did so at great cost: Eighty percent of their new memories were *incorrect* (Dywan & Bowers, 1983).

Overall, it can be concluded that hypnosis does not greatly improve memory (Kihlstrom, 1985). Even when hypnosis uncovers more information, there is no way to tell which memories are true and which are false. Clearly, hypnosis is not the magic bullet against forgetting that some police investigators hoped it would be.

Organization Long-term memory may record 1 quadrillion separate bits of information in a lifetime (Asimov, 1967). How is it possible, then, to quickly find specific memories? The answer is that each person's "memory index" is highly organized.

Question: Do you mean that information is arranged alphabetically, as in a dictionary?

Not a chance! If I ask you to name a black and white animal that lives on ice, is related to a chicken, and cannot fly, you don't have to go from aardvark to zebra to find the answer. Probably you will only think of black and white birds living in the Arctic. Which of these cannot fly? Voilà, the answer is penguin.

The arrangement of information in LTM may be based on rules, images, categories, symbols, similarity, formal meaning, or personal meaning (Atkinson & Shiffrin, 1971). In the last 15 years psychologists have begun to develop a picture of the **structure,** or arrangement, of memories. One example will serve to illustrate this research.

You are given the following two statements, to which you must answer yes or no: *A canary is an animal*. *A canary is a bird*. Which do you answer more quickly? Collins and Quillan (1969) found that *A canary is a bird* produced a faster yes than *A canary is an animal*. Why should this be so? Collins and Quillan believe a **network model** of memory explains why. According to them, LTM is organized as a network of linked ideas (see Fig. 9-4). When ideas are "farther" apart, it takes a longer chain of associations to connect them. The more two items are separated, the longer it takes to answer. In other words, *canary* is probably close to *bird* in your "mental dictionary." *Animal* and *canary* are farther apart.

Constructive processing Reorganizing memories on the basis of logic, inference, or the addition of new information.

Pseudo-memories False memories that a person believes are real or accurate.

Memory structure Patterns of associations among bits of information stored in memory.

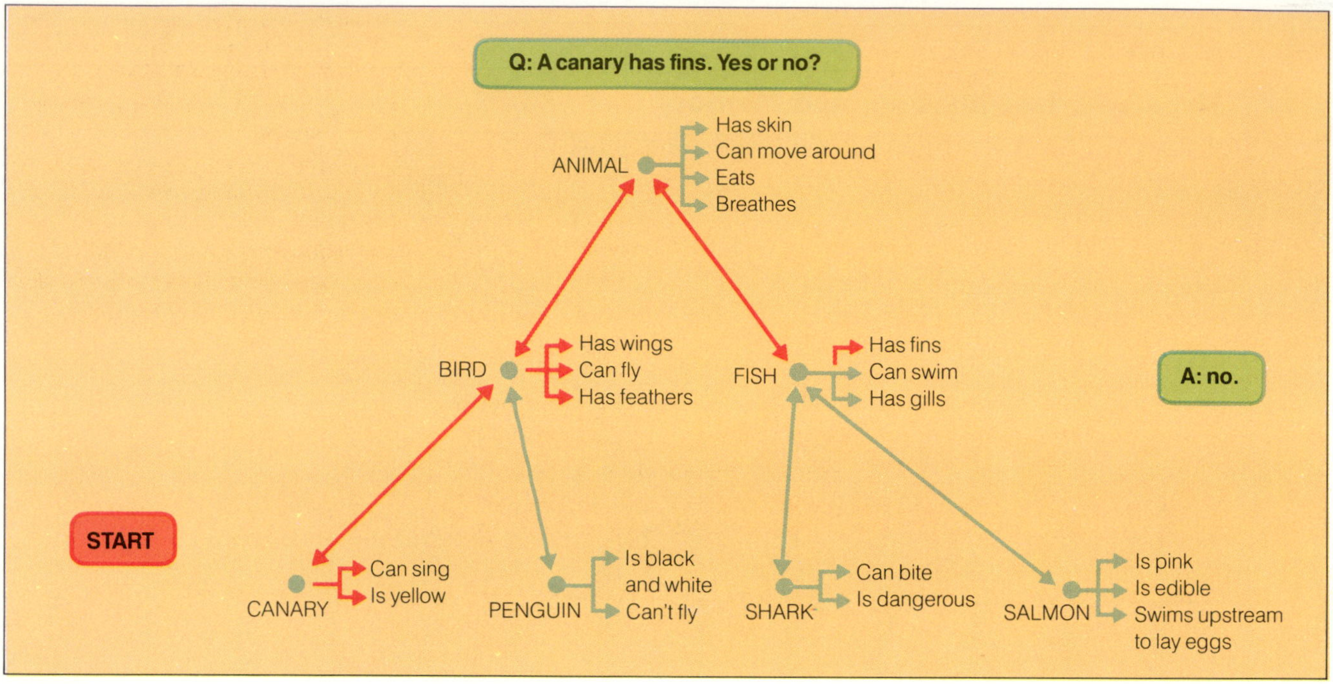

Fig. 9-4 *Hypothetical network of facts about animals shows what is meant by the structure of memory. Small networks of ideas such as this are probably organized into larger and larger units and higher levels of meaning. (Adapted from Collins & Quillian, 1969)*

Remember, though, this has nothing to do with alphabetical order. We are talking about organization based on meaning.

Psychologists still have much to learn about the nature of long-term memory. For now, one thing stands out clearly: People who have good memories excel at organizing information and making it meaningful (Mandler, 1968). With this in mind, the Applications for this chapter tells how you can use organization and meaning to improve your memory.

Learning Check

1. The digit-span test is commonly used to measure LTM. T or F?

2. There is evidence that STM lasts about 18 seconds, without rehearsal. T or F?

3. Information can be held indefinitely in STM by (circle):

chunking recoding networking rehearsal

4. Constructive processing is often responsible for creating pseudo-memories. T or F?

5. Electrical stimulation of the brain has shown conclusively that all memories are stored permanently, but not all memories can be retrieved. T or F?

6. Memories elicited under hypnosis are more vivid, complete, and reliable than normal. T or F?

7. ________________ of related information are an example of the structure or organization found in LTM.

Answers: **1.** F **2.** T **3.** rehearsal **4.** T **5.** F **6.** F **7.** Networks

Measuring Memory—The Answer Is on the Tip of My Tongue

Initially, it might seem that you either remember something or you don't. But a moment of thought should convince you that this is not always true. For instance, have you ever recognized someone you only saw once before and thought you had completely forgotten? If so you have used a form of partial memory called *recognition*. Partial memory is also demonstrated by the **tip-of-the-tongue phenomenon.** This is the experience of having an answer or a memory just out of reach—on the "tip of your tongue."

In one study of the tip-of-the-tongue effect, university students read the definitions of words such as *sextant*, *sampan*, and *ambergris*. Students who "drew a blank" and couldn't name a defined word were asked to give whatever other information they could about it. Often, they could accurately guess the first and last letter and even the number of syllables of the word they were seeking. They were also able to give words that sounded like or meant the same as the defined word (Brown & McNeill, 1966).

Because memory is not an all-or-nothing event, there are several ways of measuring it. Three commonly used **memory tasks** are *recall*, *recognition*, and *relearning*. Let's see how they differ.

Tip-of-the-tongue phenomenon The experience of feeling that a memory is available, while being unable to retrieve it.

Memory task Any task designed to test or assess memory.

Recall To supply or reproduce memorized information with a minimum of external cues.

Recognition Memory in which previously learned material is correctly identified as that which was seen before.

Recall What is the name of the first song on your favorite record album? Who won the World Series last year? Who wrote the *Gettysburg Address?* If you can answer these questions, you have demonstrated recall. To **recall** means to supply or reproduce facts or information. Tests of recall often require *verbatim* (word-for-word) memory. If you study a poem or a speech until you can recite it without looking, you will have recalled it. Recall is also used when you take an *essay* exam and provide facts and ideas without prompting. Essay tests tend to be difficult because they offer few cues to aid memory.

Recognition If you tried to write down all the facts you could remember from a class taken last year, you might conclude that you had learned very little. However, a more sensitive testing procedure based on **recognition** could be used. For instance, you could be given a *multiple-choice* test covering the facts and ideas from the course. Since multiple-choice tests only require you to recognize the correct answer, you would probably find evidence of considerable learning.

Recognition memory can be amazingly accurate for pictures, photographs, or other visual input. One investigator showed subjects 2560 photographs at a rate of one every 10 seconds. Subjects were then shown 280 pairs of photographs. One in each pair was from the first set of photos and the other was similar but new. Subjects could tell with 85 to 95 percent accuracy which photograph they had seen before (Haber, 1970). This finding may explain why people so often say, "I may forget a name, but I never forget a face."

Recognition is usually superior to recall. This is why police departments use photographs or a lineup to identify criminal suspects (Fig. 9-5). Witnesses who disagree in their recall of a suspect's height, weight, age, or eye color often agree completely when recognition is all that is required.

Fig. 9-5 *Police lineups make use of the sensitivity of recognition memory.*

Relearning In a classic experiment on memory, a psychologist read a short passage in Greek to his son. This was done daily when the boy was between 15 months and 3 years of age. At age 8 the boy was asked if he remembered the Greek passage. He showed no evidence of recall. He was then given selections from the passage he had heard and selections from other Greek passages. Could he recognize the one he had heard as an infant? "It's all Greek to me!" he said, indicating no recognition (and drawing a frown from everyone in the room).

Had the psychologist stopped, he might have concluded that no memory of the Greek remained. However, the child was then asked to memorize the original quotation and others of equal difficulty. This time his earlier learning became evident. The boy memorized the passage he had heard in childhood 25 percent faster than the others (Burtt, 1941). As this experiment suggests, relearning is typically the most sensitive measure of memory.

When a person is tested by **relearning,** how do we know a memory still exists? As with the boy described, relearning is measured by a **savings score.** Let's say it takes you 1 hour to memorize all the names in a telephone book. (It's a small town.) Two years later you relearn them in 45 minutes. Because you "saved" 15 minutes, your savings score would be 25 percent (15 divided by 60 times 100). Savings of this type are a good reason for studying a wide range of subjects. It may seem that time spent learning algebra, history, or a foreign language is wasted because little is remembered a year or two later. But if you ever need such information, you will find you can relearn it in far less time.

Redintegration There is a fourth way in which memories may be revealed. Imagine finding a picture taken on your sixth birthday or tenth Christmas. As you look at the photo, one memory leads to another, which leads to another, and another. (Picture this as following some of the "branches" of your memory network.) Soon you have unleashed a flood of seemingly forgotten details. This process is called **redintegration** (ruh-DIN-tuh-GRAY-shun). Many people find that such memories are also touched off by distinctive odors out of the past—from a farm visited in childhood, Grandma's kitchen, the seashore, a doctor's office, the perfume or after-shave of a former lover, and so on. The key idea in redintegration is that one memory serves as a cue to trigger another. As a result, an entire past experience may be reconstructed from one small recollection. Such memories usually involve personal experience rather than formal learning.

Relearning Learning again something that was previously learned. Used as a measure of memory for prior learning.

Savings score In testing memory by relearning, a savings score is the percentage of reduction in time needed to remaster previously learned information.

Redintegration The process of reconstructing an entire complex memory after observing or remembering only a part of it.

Eidetic imagery The ability to retain a "projected" image long enough to use it as a source of information. Sometimes referred to as photographic memory.

Internal images Mental images or representations used in memory and thinking.

Eidetic Imagery—Picture This!

Question: What is a photographic memory? How is it different from the types of memory already described?

Eidetic (eye-DET-ik) **imagery,** known informally as photographic memory, occurs when a person has visual images clear enough to be "scanned" or retained for at least 30 seconds. Eidetic imagery occurs most often in childhood, with about 8 children out of 100 having eidetic images (Haber, 1969).

In one series of tests, children were shown a picture from *Alice in Wonderland* (Fig. 9-6). To test your eidetic imagery, look at the picture and read the instructions there. Now, let's see how much you remember. Can you say (without looking again) which of Alice's apron strings is longer? Are the cat's front paws crossed? How many stripes are on the cat's tail? After the picture was removed from view, one 10-year-old boy was asked what he saw. He replied, "I see the tree, gray tree with three limbs. I see the cat with stripes around its tail." Asked to count the stripes, the boy replied, "There are about 16" (a correct count!). The boy then went on to describe the remainder of the picture in striking detail (Haber, 1969).

Don't be disappointed if you didn't do too well when you tried your eidetic skills. Most eidetic imagery disappears during adolescence and becomes quite rare by adulthood (Haber, 1974). Actually, this change may not be too much of a loss. The majority of eidetic memorizers have no better long-term memory than average.

Fig. 9-6 *Test picture used to identify children with eidetic imagery. To test your eidetic imagery, look at the picture for 30 seconds. Then look at a blank surface and try to "project" the picture on it. If you have good eidetic imagery, you will be able to see the picture in detail. Return now to the text and try to answer the questions there. (Redrawn from an illustration in Lewis Carroll's* Alice in Wonderland)

Internal Images Eidetic images are "projected" out in front of a person. Many psychologists believe that a second type of imagery is also used in memory. Can you remember how many doors there are in your house or apartment? To answer a question like this, many people form **internal images** of each room and count the doorways they "see."

Kosslyn, Ball, and Reisler (1978) found an interesting way to show that memories do exist as images. Subjects first memorized a sort of treasure map similar to the one shown in Figure 9-7*a*. They were then asked to picture a black dot moving from one object, such as the tree, to another, such as the hut at the top of the island. Did subjects really form an image to do this task? It seems they did.

Box 9-2

Can Exceptional Memory Be Learned?

In the beginning SF, a college student, could remember 7 digits—a typical score. Could he improve with practice? For 20 months psychologist William Chase guided SF as he practiced memorizing ever longer lists of digits. Ultimately, SF was able to memorize around 80 digits, like this sample:

9284204805084226895399019025291280799970
6606574717310601080585269726026357332135

How did SF reach such lofty heights of memory? He worked by chunking digits into meaningful groups containing 3 or 4 digits each. SF's avid interest in long-distance running helped greatly. For instance, to him the first 3 digits from the preceding sample represent 9 minutes and 28 seconds, a good time for a 2-mile run. When running times wouldn't work, SF used other associations, such as ages or dates, to chunk digits (Ericsson & Chase, 1982).

Chase and psychologist Anders Ericsson believe SF's performance shows that exceptional memory—even like that displayed by Mr. S—is merely a learned extension of normal memory. As further evidence, they note that SF's short-term memory did not improve during his months of practice. For example, he could still memorize only 7 consonants. SF's phenomenal memory for numbers grew as he figured out ways to encode digits so he could rapidly store them in LTM.

In sum, there is evidence that exceptional memory can be learned. It's an open question, however, about whether some exceptional memories, like Mr. S's, are based on unusually vivid images or other rare abilities.

As shown in Figure 9-7*b*, the time it took to "move" the dot was directly related to actual distances on the map.

Some people may have internal images so vivid that they too have "photographic" memory. A notable example was reported by A. R. Luria (1968) in his book, *The Mind of a Mnemonist*. Luria studied a man (Mr. S) who had practically unlimited memory for visual images. Mr. S could remember almost everything that ever happened to him with incredible accuracy. When Luria tried to test Mr. S's memory by using longer and longer lists of words or numbers, he discovered that no matter how long the list, Mr. S was able to reproduce it without error. Psychologists used to think that such exceptional memory was a biological gift and could not be learned. However, recent research has raised questions about this conclusion (see Box 9-2).

As fantastic as it might sound to a struggling student, Mr. S's memory caused great difficulty. He remembered so much that he could not separate important facts from trivia. For instance, if he were tested on the contents of this chapter after reading it, he might remember not only every word, but all the images each word made him think of and all the sights, sounds, and feelings that occurred as he was reading. Finding the answer for a specific question, writing a logical essay, or even understanding a single sentence therefore was very difficult for him.

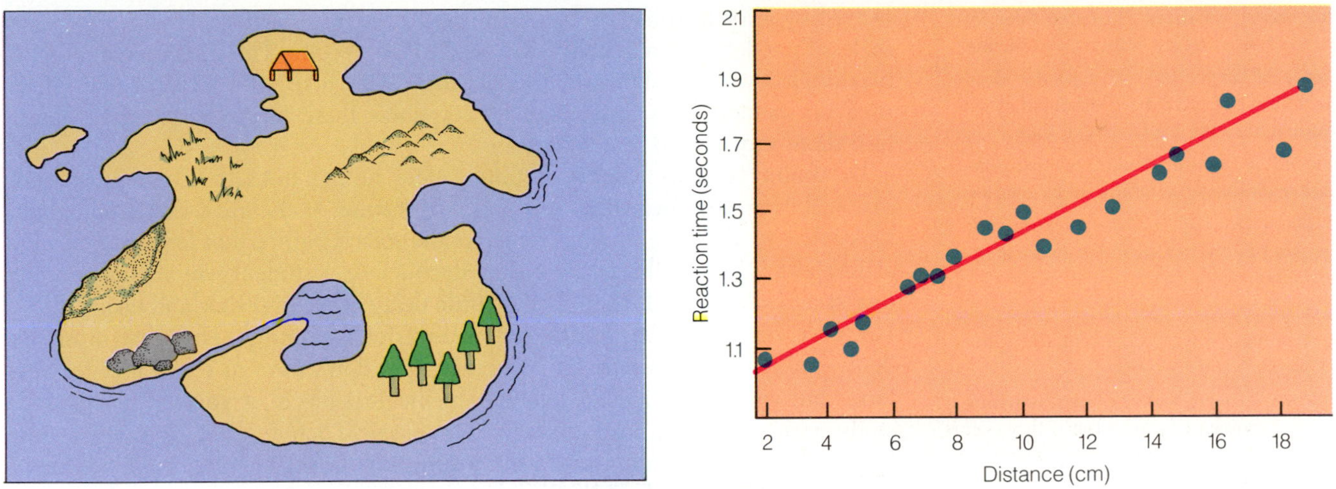

(a) (b)

Fig. 9-7 *"Treasure map" similar to the one used by Kosslyn, Ball, and Reisler (1978) to study images in memory. (See text for explanation.)*

Learning Check

Unless you have a memory like Mr. S's, it might be a good idea to see if you can answer these questions before reading on.

1. Four common techniques for measuring or demonstrating memory are: ________, ________, ________, and ________.

2. Multiple-choice tests primarily require ________ memory.

3. Essay tests require ________ of facts or ideas.

4. As a measure of memory, a "savings" score is associated with: (circle)

recognition eidetic images relearning reconstruction

5. Children with eidetic imagery typically have no better than average long-term memory. T or F?

Answers: **1.** recall, recognition, relearning, redintegration **2.** recognition **3.** recall **4.** relearning **5.** T

Why We, Uh, Let's See; Why, We, Uh . . . Forget!

Question: Why are some memories lost so quickly? For example, why is it hard to remember information a week or two after taking a test in class?

Generally speaking, most forgetting occurs immediately after memorization. In a famous set of experiments, **Hermann Ebbinghaus** (1885) tested his own memory at various times after learning. Ebbinghaus wanted to be sure he would not be

Nonsense syllables Invented three-letter words used to test learning and memory.

Curve of forgetting A graph that shows the amount of memorized information still retained after varying lengths of time.

Encoding failure Failure to store sufficient information to form a useful memory.

Memory traces Hypothesized physical changes that take place in the brain as it stores information.

Memory decay The fading or weakening of memories presumed to occur when memory traces become weaker.

Disuse Theory that attributes forgetting to a weakening of memory traces that occurs when the memories are not periodically used or retrieved.

swayed by prior learning, so he memorized **nonsense syllables.** These are meaningless three-letter words such as GEX, CEF, or WOL. The importance of using meaningless words is shown by the fact that VEL, FAB, and DUZ are no longer used on memory tests. Subjects who recognize these words as detergent names find them very easy to remember.

By waiting various lengths of time before testing himself, Ebbinghaus constructed a **curve of forgetting** (see Fig. 9-8). Owing to the great care Ebbinghaus took in his work, these findings remain valid today. Notice that forgetting is rapid at first and is then followed by a slow decline. As a student you should see that forgetting is minimized when there is little delay between review and taking a test. However, don't misinterpret this as a reason for cramming. The error most students make is to cram *only*. If you cram, you don't have to remember for very long, but you may not learn enough in the first place. If you use short, daily study sessions, and, in addition, review intensively before a test, you will get the benefit of good preparation and a minimum time lapse.

"I'll never forget old, old . . . oh, what's his name?" Forgetting is both frustrating and embarrassing. Why *do* we forget? The Ebbinghaus curve gives a general picture of forgetting, but it doesn't explain it. For explanations we must search further.

Encoding Failure

Whose head is on a United States penny? Which way is it facing? What is written on the top side of a penny? Can you accurately draw and label a penny? In an interesting experiment, Nickerson and Adams (1979) asked a large group of students to draw a penny. Few could. Well, then, could the students at least recognize a drawing of a real penny among fakes? (See Figure 9-9.) Again, few could.

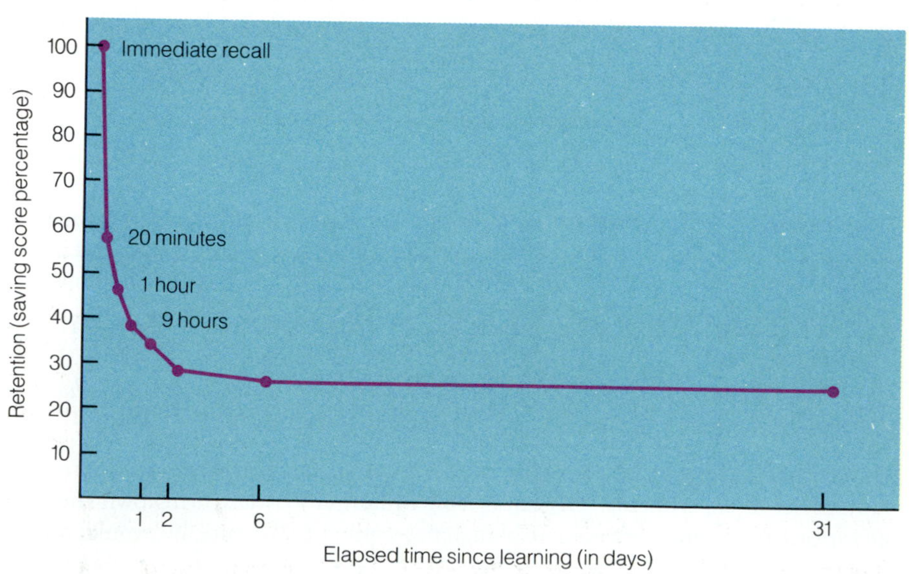

Fig. 9-8 *The curve of forgetting. This graph shows the amount remembered (measured by relearning) after varying lengths of time. Notice how rapidly forgetting occurs. Material learned was nonsense syllables. Meaningful information is not forgotten so quickly. (After Ebbinghaus, 1885)*

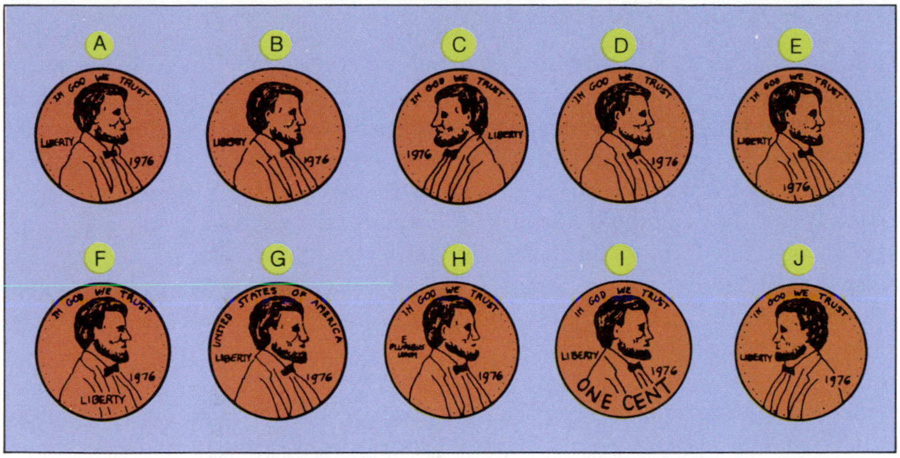

Fig. 9-9 *Some of the distractor items used in a study of recognition memory and encoding failure. Penny A is correct but was seldom recognized. Pennies G and J were popular wrong answers. (Adapted from Nickerson & Adams, 1979)*

The most obvious reason for forgetting is also the most commonly overlooked. In many cases we "forget" because a memory was never formed in the first place. Obviously, few of us ever encode the details of a penny. If you are bothered by frequent forgetting, it is wise to ask yourself, "Have I been storing the information in the first place?"

Decay

One view of forgetting says that **memory traces** (changes in nerve cells or brain activity) fade, or **decay,** over time. Decay appears definitely to be a factor in the loss of sensory memories. Such fading also applies to short-term memory. Information stored in STM seems to initiate a brief flurry of activity in the brain that quickly dies out (Shiffrin & Cook, 1978). Short-term memory therefore operates like a "leaky bucket": New information constantly pours in, but it rapidly fades away and is replaced by still newer information (Miller, 1956).

Disuse Is it possible that the decay of memory traces also explains long-term forgetting? That is, could long-term memory traces fade from **disuse** and eventually become so weak they cannot be retrieved? As tempting as this possibility may seem, there are reasons to doubt it. One already mentioned is the recovery of seemingly forgotten memories through redintegration. Another is that disuse fails to explain why some unused memories fade, while others are carried for life. A third contradiction will be recognized by anyone who has spent time with the elderly. People growing older may become so forgetful that they can't remember what happened a week ago. Yet at the same time your Uncle Oscar's recent memories are fading, he may have vivid memories of trivial and long-forgotten events from the past. "Why I remember it as clearly as if it were yesterday," he will say, forgetting that the story he is about to tell is one he told earlier the same day. In short, disuse alone does not adequately explain long-term forgetting.

Question: If decay and disuse don't fully explain forgetting, what does?

There are several additional possibilities. Let's briefly consider each.

Memory cue Any stimulus associated with a particular memory. The presence of such cues usually enhances memory retrieval.

State-dependent learning Improved memory that occurs when one's bodily state at the time of retrieval matches the state that existed at the time of learning.

Interference The capacity of old memories to inhibit retrieval of newer memories, and the reverse.

Retroactive inhibition The tendency for new memories to interfere with the retrieval of old memories.

Cue-Dependent Forgetting

Often memories appear to be *available* but not accessible. An example is having an answer on the tip of your tongue. You know the answer is there, but it remains just "out of reach." This situation indicates that many memories are "forgotten" because **cues** present at the time of learning are absent when the time comes to retrieve information. For example, if you were asked, "What were you doing on Monday afternoon of the third week in September 2 years ago?" your reply might be, "Come on. How should I know?" However, if you were reminded, "That was the day the courthouse burned," or "That was the day Mary had her automobile accident," you might remember immediately. The presence of such cues almost always enhances memory (Fig. 9-10).

State-Dependent Learning Nearly everyone has heard the story about the drunk who misplaced his wallet and had to get drunk again to find it. Although this tale is often told as a joke, it is not too farfetched. The *bodily state* that exists during learning can be a strong cue for later memory (Overton, 1985). For this reason information learned under the influence of a drug is best remembered when the drugged state occurs again—an effect known as **state-dependent learning.**

A similar effect applies to emotional states. For instance, Gordon Bower (1981) found that people who learned a list of words while in a happy mood recalled them better when they were happy again. People who learned a list while they felt sad remembered best when they were sad (see Fig. 9-11). The link between emotional cues and memory may explain why couples who quarrel often end up remembering—and rehashing—old arguments.

Interference

Further understanding of forgetting comes from an experiment in which college students learned lists of nonsense syllables. After studying, students in one group

Fig. 9-10 *Because of the many cues they provide, photographs often bring back numerous memories.*

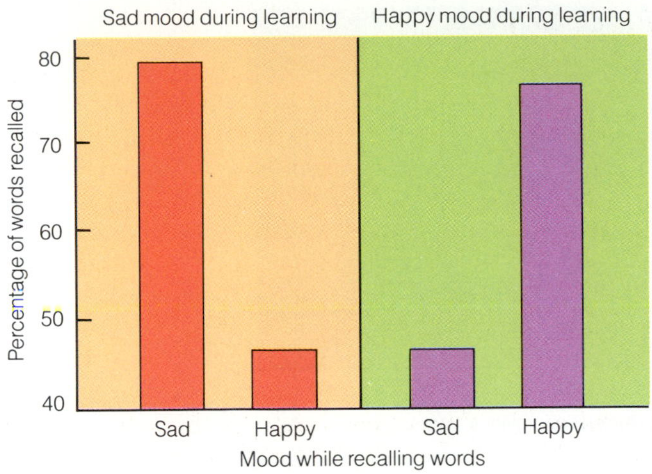

Fig. 9-11 *The effect of mood on memory. Subjects best remembered a list of words when their mood during testing was the same as their mood when they learned the list. (Adapted from Bower, 1981)*

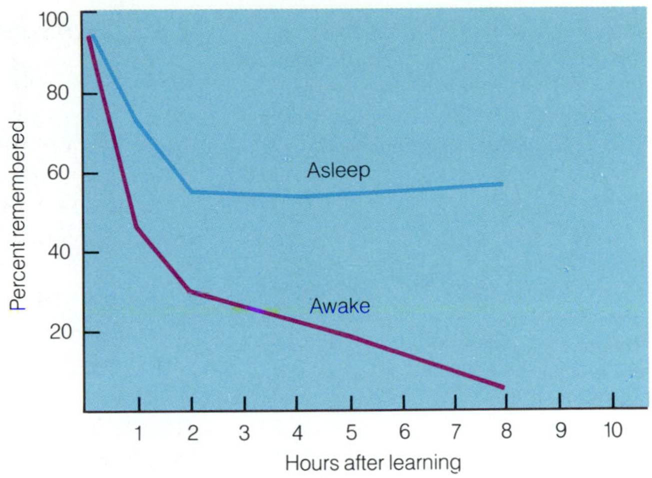

Fig. 9-12 *The amount of forgetting after sleep or waking activity. Notice that sleep causes less memory loss than waking. (After Jenkins & Dallenbach, 1924)*

slept for 8 hours and were then tested for memory of the lists. A second group remained awake for 8 hours and went about business as usual. When members of the second group were tested, they remembered *less* than the group that slept (see Fig. 9-12). This difference is based on the fact that new learning can **interfere** with previous learning (Shiffrin, 1970). Such interference seems to apply to both short-term and long-term memories (Klatzky, 1980).

It is not completely clear if new memories alter existing memory traces or if they make it harder to "locate" (retrieve) earlier memories. In either case there is no doubt that interference is a major cause of forgetting. College students who memorized 20 lists of words (1 list each day) were only able to recall 15 percent of the last list. Students who learned only 1 list remembered 80 percent (Underwood, 1957) (see Fig. 9-13).

Inhibition The sleeping college students remembered more because **retroactive** (RET-ro-AK-tiv) **inhibition** was held to a minimum. Retroactive inhibition refers to the tendency for new learning to interfere with the retrieval of old learning. Avoiding new learning prevents retroactive inhibition from occurring. This fact doesn't exactly mean you should hide in your closet after you study for an exam. However, you should avoid studying other subjects until the exam. Sleeping after study can help you retain memories, whereas reading, writing, or even watching TV may cause interference.

Retroactive inhibition is easily demonstrated in the laboratory by this arrangement:

Experimental group:	Learn A	Learn B	Test A
Control group:	Learn A	Rest	Test A

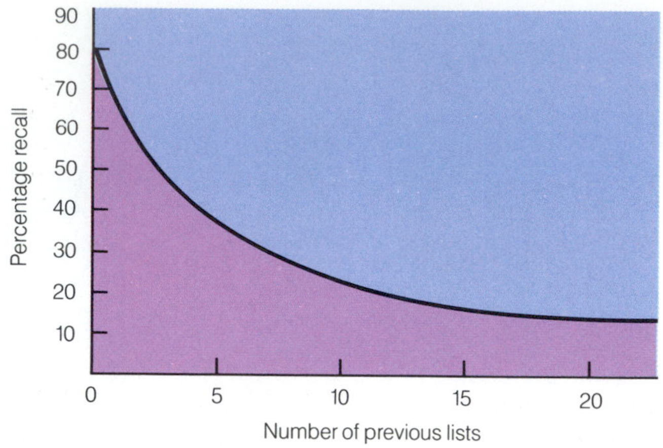

Fig. 9-13 *Effects of interference on memory. A graph of the approximate relationship between percentage recalled and number of different word lists memorized. (Adapted from Underwood, 1957)*

Imagine yourself as a member of the experimental group. In Task A you learn a list of telephone numbers. In Task B you learn a list of Social Security numbers. How do you do on a test of Task A (the telephone numbers)? If you do not remember as much as the control group that *only* learns Task A, retroactive inhibition has occurred. The second thing learned interfered with memory of the first thing learned; the interference went "backward," or was "retroactive" (see Fig. 9-14).

A second basic type of interference is **proactive** (pro-AK-tiv) **inhibition.** Proactive inhibition occurs when prior learning interferes with later learning. A test for proactive inhibition would take this form:

Experimental group:	Learn A	Learn B	Test B
Control group:	Rest	Learn B	Test B

If the experimental group remembers less than the control group on a test of Task B, then learning Task A interfered with memory of Task B.

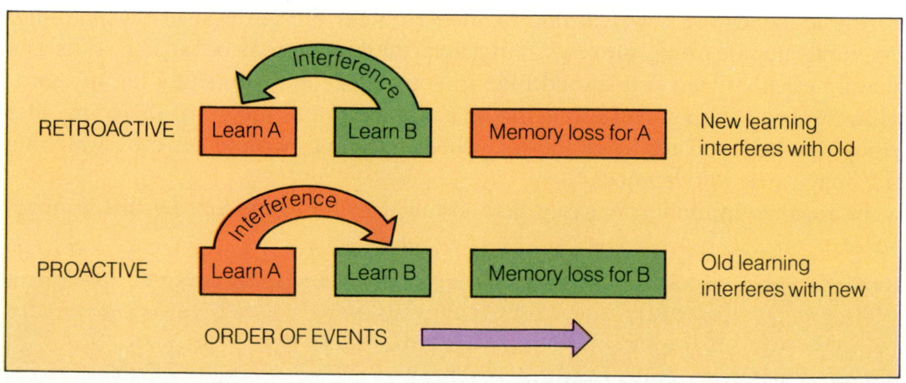

Fig. 9-14 *Retroactive and proactive inhibition. The order of learning and testing shows whether interference is retroactive (backward) or proactive (forward).*

Question: Then proactive interference goes "forward"?

Yes. For instance, if you cram for a psychology exam and then later the same night cram for a history exam, your memory for the second subject studied (history) will be less accurate than if you had studied only history. (Due to retroactive inhibition, your memory for psychology would probably also suffer.) The greater the similarity in the two subjects studied, the more interference takes place. The moral, of course, is don't procrastinate in preparing for exams.

Repression

Take a moment from reading and scan over the events of the last few years of your life. What kinds of things most easily come to mind? Many people find that they tend to remember happy, positive events better than disappointments and irritations. A clinical psychologist would call this tendency **repression,** or motivated forgetting (Linton, 1979).

Through repression, painful, threatening, or embarrassing memories are held out of consciousness by forces within one's personality. The forgetting of past failures, upsetting childhood events, the names of persons you dislike, or appointments you don't want to keep may indicate repression.

Question: If I try to forget a test I have failed, am I repressing it?

No. Repression can be distinguished from **suppression,** an active attempt to put something out of mind. By not thinking about the test, you have merely suppressed a memory. If you choose to, you can remember the test. Clinicians consider true repression an *unconscious* event. When a memory is repressed, we are unaware that forgetting has even occurred. (See Chapter 13 for more information on repression.)

An interesting, unanswered question is why some traumatic events are vividly remembered, whereas others are repressed. Psychologists Roger Brown and James Kulik (1977) use the term **flashbulb memories** to describe lasting images that are frozen in memory at times of personal tragedy, accident, or loss. One reason such memories can be so vivid is that the hormones adrenaline and ACTH are secreted at times of stress. Both substances have been shown to enhance memory formation, possibly by altering brain chemistry (McGaugh, 1983).

Proactive inhibition The tendency for old memories to interfere with the retrieval of newer memories.

Repression Unconsciously pushing out or barring from awareness unwanted memories.

Suppression A conscious effort to not think of something or to keep it from awareness.

Flashbulb memories Vivid and lasting memories created at times of high emotion.

Retrograde amnesia Loss of memory for some events that preceded a head injury or other amnesia-causing event.

Consolidation Theoretical process by which information is solidified as a relatively permanent memory in the brain.

Memory Formation—Some "Shocking" Findings

One possibility overlooked in our discussion of forgetting is that memories may be lost as they are being formed. For example, a head injury may cause a "gap" in memories preceding the accident. **Retrograde amnesia,** as it is called, can be understood by assuming that transferring memories from short-term storage to long-term memory takes a certain amount of time. The forming of a long-term memory is called **consolidation** (John, 1967). You can think of consolidation as being somewhat like writing your name in wet concrete. Once the concrete is set, the information (your name) is fairly lasting, but while it is setting it can be wiped out (amnesia) or scribbled over (interference).

Electroconvulsive shock An electric current passed directly through the brain, producing a convulsion.

Hippocampus A structure in the brain associated with the regulation of emotions and the transfer of information from short-term memory to long-term memory.

Consider a classic experiment on consolidation, in which a rat is placed on a small platform. The rat steps down to the floor and receives a painful electric shock. After one shock, the rat can be returned to the platform repeatedly, but it will not step down. Obviously, the rat remembers the shock. Would it remember if consolidation were disrupted?

Interestingly, one way to prevent consolidation is to give a different kind of shock called **electroconvulsive shock (ECS)** (Jarvik, 1964). ECS is an electric shock to the brain. It does not harm the animal, but it does destroy any memory that is being formed. If each painful shock (the one the animal remembers) is followed by ECS (which wipes out memories during consolidation), the rat will step down over and over. Each time, ECS will erase the memory of the painful shock. (ECS has been employed as a psychiatric treatment for severe depression in humans. Used in this way, electroshock therapy also causes memory loss. See Chapter 20 for details.)

Question: What would happen if ECS were given several hours after the learning?

If enough time is allowed to pass between learning and ECS, the memory is unaffected, apparently because consolidation is already complete. This is why people with head injuries usually only lose memories from immediately before the accident, while older memories remain intact (Baddeley, 1976). Likewise, you would forget more if you studied, stayed awake 8 hours, and then slept 8 hours than you would if you studied, slept 8 hours, and were then awake for 8 hours. Both cases involve the passage of 16 hours. However, in the second instance forgetting is reduced, because more consolidation takes place before interference begins.

Question: What part of the brain causes consolidation?

From STM to LTM Actually, many areas of the brain are responsible for memory, but the **hippocampus** is of particular importance. This structure, buried deep within the brain, seems to act as a sort of "switching station" between short-term and long-term memory.

Humans who have had the hippocampus damaged show a striking inability to store memories. HM, a patient described by Brenda Milner, is typical. Two years after an operation that affected the hippocampus, HM continued to give his age as 27 (it was actually 29) and reported that it seemed that the operation had just taken place (Milner, 1965). His memory of events before the operation remained clear, but HM found forming new long-term memories almost impossible. When his parents moved to a new house a few blocks away on the same street, HM could not remember the new address, and he was observed to read the same magazines over and over again without finding their contents familiar. If you were to meet HM, he would seem fairly normal since he still has short-term memory. But if you were to leave the room and return 15 minutes later, HM would act as if he had never seen you before (Milner, 1965). Years ago HM's favorite uncle died, but HM suffers the same grief anew each time he is told of the death. Lacking the ability to form lasting memories, HM lives eternally in the present.

Question: How are memories recorded in the brain?

The Brain and Memory Scientists studying simple animals are beginning to identify the exact mechanisms by which individual nerve cells record information. There is now extensive evidence that learning alters the electrical activity, struc-

Fig. 9-15 An Aplysia. *The relatively simple nervous system of this sea animal allows scientists to study memory as it occurs in single nerve cells.*

ture, and chemistry of the brain (McGaugh, 1983). For example, Eric Kandel and his colleagues have studied learning in the marine snail *Aplysia*. Kandel has found that learning in *Aplysia* occurs when certain nerve cells in a circuit alter the amount of transmitter chemicals they release (Kandel, 1976) (see Fig. 9-15). Such changes essentially determine which circuits get strengthened and which become weaker.

On the basis of such breakthroughs, scientists are now studying a bewildering array of chemicals and brain processes that affect memory (McGaugh, 1983). Should this research succeed, it may be possible to help the millions of persons who suffer from memory impairment. Will researchers ever produce a "memory pill" for those with normal memory? Some neuroscientists are confident that memory can be and will be artificially enhanced. At present, however, the possibility of something like a "physics pill" or a "math pill" seems especially remote.

Learning Check

1. According to the Ebbinghaus curve of forgetting, we forget slowly at first and then a rapid decline occurs. T or F?

2. Which explanation seems to account for loss of short-term memories? (circle)

decay disuse repression interference

3. When memories are available but not accessible, forgetting may be cue dependent. T or F?

4. When learning one thing makes it more difficult to recall another, forgetting may be caused by ______________.

5. You are asked to memorize long lists of telephone numbers. You learn a new list each day for 10 days. When tested on list 3, you remember less than a person who only learned the first three lists. Your larger memory loss is probably due to: (circle)

disuse retroactive inhibition regression proactive inhibition

6. Repression is thought of as a type of motivated forgetting. T or F?

7. Retrograde amnesia results when consolidation is speeded up. T or F?

Answers: **1.** F **2.** both decay and interference **3.** T **4.** interference or inhibition **5.** retroactive inhibition **6.** T **7.** F

How to Improve Your Memory—Keys to the Memory Bank

While you're waiting around for the development of a memory pill, let's focus on some ways of improving your memory right now.

Knowledge of Results Learning proceeds most effectively when feedback or knowledge of results allows you to check to see if you are learning. Feedback also helps you identify material that needs extra practice. In addition, knowing that you have remembered or answered correctly can be rewarding. A prime means of providing feedback for yourself when studying is *recitation*.

Recitation Recitation means repeating to yourself what you have learned. If you are going to remember something, eventually you will have to retrieve it. Recitation forces you to practice retrieving information as you are learning. When you are reading a text, you should stop frequently and try to remember what you have just read by summarizing it aloud. In one experiment the best memory score of all was earned by a group of students who spent 80 percent of their time reciting and only 20 percent reading (Gates, 1958). Maybe students who talk to themselves aren't crazy after all.

Overlearning Numerous studies have shown that memory is greatly improved when study is continued beyond bare mastery. In other words, after you have learned material well enough to remember it once without error, you should continue to study the material. Overlearning is your best insurance against going blank on a test because of nervousness or anxiety.

Selection The Dutch scholar Erasmus said that a good memory should be like a fisherman's net: It should keep all the big fish and let the little ones escape. If you boil down the paragraphs in most textbooks to one or two important terms or ideas, you will find your memorization chores more manageable and you will probably remember more than you would if you tried to retain everything. Practice careful and selective marking in your texts and use marginal notes to further summarize ideas. Most students mark their texts too much instead of too little. If everything is underlined, you haven't been selective.

Spaced Practice Spaced practice generally is superior to massed practice. By improving concentration, and consolidation, three 20-minute study sessions can produce more learning than 1 hour of continuous study. Perhaps the best way to make use of this principle is to *schedule* your time. If most students were to keep a totally honest record of their weekly activities, they would probably find that very few hours were spent really studying. To make an effective schedule, designate times during the week before, after, and between classes when you will study particular subjects. Then treat these times just as if they were classes you had to attend.

Organize Assume that you must memorize the following list of words: *north, man, red, spring, woman, east, autumn, yellow, summer, boy, blue, west, winter, girl, green, south.* This rather difficult list could be reorganized into *chunks* as follows: *north-east-south-west, spring-summer-autumn-winter, red-yellow-green-blue, man-woman-boy-girl.* This simple reordering made the second list much easier to learn when college students were tested on both lists (Deese & Hulse, 1967). In another experiment, students who made up stories using long lists of words to be memorized learned the lists better than those who didn't (Bower & Clark, 1969). Organizing class notes and outlining chapters can be helpful when studying. It may even be helpful to outline your outlines, so that the overall organization of ideas becomes clearer and simpler.

Whole versus Part Learning If you had to memorize a speech, would it be better to try to learn it from beginning to end or in smaller parts like paragraphs? Generally, it is better to practice whole packages of information rather than smaller parts. This is especially true for fairly short, organized information. An exception is that learning parts may be better for extremely long, complicated information. Try to study the largest *meaningful* amount of information possible at one time.

For very long or complex material, try the *progressive part method.* In this approach you break a learning task into short sections. At first, you study part A until it is mastered. Next, you study parts A and B; then A, B, and C; and so forth. This is a good way to learn the lines of a play, a long piece of music, or a poem. After the material is learned, you should also practice it by starting at points other than A (at C, D, or B, for example). This helps prevent getting "lost," or going blank in the middle of a performance.

Serial Position Whenever you must learn something in *order,* be aware of the *serial position effect.* This is the tendency to make the most errors in remembering the middle of a list. If you are introduced to a long line of people, the names you are likely to forget will be those in the middle, so you should make an extra effort to attend to them. The middle of a list, poem, or speech should also be given special attention and extra practice.

Sleep Remember that sleeping after study produces the least interference. Since you obviously can't sleep after every study session, or can't study everything just before you sleep, your study schedule (see the "Spaced Practice" section) should include ample breaks between subjects. Using your breaks and free time in a schedule is as important as living up to your study periods.

Review If you have spaced your practice and have overlearned, review will be like icing on your study cake. Reviewing shortly before an exam cuts down the time during which you must remember details that may be important for the test but not otherwise meaningful to you. When reviewing, hold the amount of new information you try to memorize to a minimum. It may be realistic to take what

Knowledge of results During learning, feedback or information provided about the correctness of responses or other aspects of performance.

Recitation As a memory aid, repeating aloud information one wishes to retain.

Overlearning Study or learning that continues after initial mastery of skills or information.

Spaced practice A practice schedule that alternates study periods with brief rests. (Massed practice, in comparison, continues for long periods, without interruption.)

Whole learning Studying an entire package of information (such as a complete poem) at once.

Part learning Separately studying subparts of a larger body of information (such as sections of a textbook chapter).

Serial position effect The tendency for the greatest number of memory errors to occur in the middle portion of an ordered list.

you have actually learned and add a little more to it at the last minute by cramming, but remember that more than a little new learning will confuse you and will interfere with what you already know.

If you consistently use the principles reviewed here, you should get grades at least one step higher without increasing your study time, or you should get the same grades after spending less time. Give this an honest try—the results are almost guaranteed. Besides, if you haven't adopted the SQ3R and LISAN techniques described in the first chapter, it might be time to give them a try.

Learning Check

1. To improve memory, it is reasonable to spend as much or more time reciting as reading. T or F?

2. Organizing information while studying has little effect on memory because memory is already highly organized. T or F?

3. The progressive part method of study is best suited for long and complex learning tasks. T or F?

4. Sleeping immediately after studying is highly disruptive to the consolidation of memories. T or F?

Answers: **1.** T **2.** F **3.** T **4.** F

Applications

Mnemonics—Memory Magic

Question: Some stage performers use memory as part of their acts. Do they have eidetic imagery?

Various "memory experts" entertain by giving demonstrations in which they memorize the names of everyone at a banquet, the order of all the cards in a deck, long lists of disconnected words, or other seemingly impossible amounts of information. Such feats may seem like magic, but if they are, you can have a magic memory too. These tricks are performed through the use of **mnemonics** (nee-MON-iks). A mnemonic is any kind of memory system or aid.

Some mnemonic systems have become so common that almost everyone knows them. If you are trying to remember how many days there are in a month, you may find the answer by reciting, "Thirty days hath September. . . ". Physics teachers often help their students remember the colors of the spectrum by giving them the mnemonic "Roy G. Biv": red, orange, yellow, green, blue, indigo, violet. The budding sailor who has trouble telling port from starboard may remember that port and left both have four letters or may remind herself, "I *left* port." And what beginning musician hasn't remembered the notes represented by the lines and spaces of the musical staff by learning "face" and "every good boy does fine."

Mnemonic techniques are ways of avoiding *rote* learning (learning by simple repetition). The superiority of mnemonic learning as opposed to rote learning has been demonstrated many times. For example, Bower (1973) asked college students to study five different lists of 20 unrelated words. At the end of a short study session, subjects were asked to recall all 100 items. Subjects using mnemonics remembered an average of 72 items, whereas a control group using simple, or rote, learning remembered an average of 28.

Stage performers rarely have a naturally superior

Applications: Mnemonics—Memory Magic, continued

memory. Instead, they make extensive use of memory systems to perform their feats. Few of these systems are of practical value to the student, but the principles underlying mnemonics are. By practicing mnemonics you should be able to greatly improve your memory with little effort.

The basic principles of mnemonics are:

1. Use mental pictures. There are at least two kinds of memory, *visual* and *verbal*. Visual pictures or images are generally easier to remember than words. Turning information into mental pictures is therefore very helpful (Paivio, 1969).

2. Make things meaningful. Transfer of information from short-term to long-term memory is aided by making the information meaningful. If you encounter technical terms that have little or no immediate meaning for you, *give* them meaning, even if you have to stretch the term to do so. (This point is clarified by the examples following this list.)

3. Make information familiar. Connect it to what you already know. Another way to get information into long-term memory is to connect it to information already stored there. If some facts or ideas in a chapter seem to stay in your memory easily, associate other more difficult facts with them.

4. Form bizarre, unusual, or exaggerated mental associations. When associating two ideas, terms, or mental images, you will find that the more outrageous and exaggerated the association, the more likely you are to remember it later.

A sampling of typical applications of mnemonics should make these four points clear to you.

Example 1 Let's say you have 30 new vocabulary words to memorize in Spanish. You can proceed by rote memorization (repeat them over and over until you begin to get them), or you can learn them with little effort by using the **key word method** (Pressley et al., 1980). To remember that the word *pajaro* (pronounced PA-ha-ro) means bird, you can link it to a "key" word in English: *Pajaro* (to me) sounds like "parked car-o." Therefore, to remember that *pajaro* means bird, I will visualize a parked car jam-packed full of birds. I will try to make this image as vivid and exaggerated as possible, with birds flapping and chirping and feathers flying everywhere. Similarly, for the word *carta* (which means letter), I will imagine a shopping *cart* filled with postal letters. If you link similar key words and images for the rest of the list, you may not remember them all, but you will get most without any further practice. As a matter of fact, if you have formed the *pajaro* and *carta* images just now, it is going to be almost impossible for you to ever see these words again without remembering what they mean.

Question: What if I think pajaro means "parked car" when I take my Spanish test?

This is why you should form one or two extra images so that the important feature (bird, in this case) is repeated.

Example 2 Let's say you have to learn the names of all the bones and muscles in the human body. You are trying to remember that the jawbone is the *mandible*. This one is easy because you can associate it with a *man nibbling*, or maybe you can picture a *man dribbling* a basketball with his jaw (make this image as ridiculous as possible). If the muscle name *latissimus dorsi* gives you trouble, familiarize it by turning it into "*the ladder misses the door, sigh.*" Then picture a ladder glued to your back where the muscle is found. Picture the ladder leading up to a small door at your shoulder. Picture the ladder missing the door. Picture the ladder sighing like an animated character in a cartoon.

Question: This seems like more to remember, not less; and it seems like it would cause you to misspell things.

Mnemonics are not a complete substitute for normal memory; they are an aid to normal memory. Mnemonics are not likely to be helpful unless you make extensive use of *images*. Your mental pictures will come back to you easily. As for misspellings, mnemonics can be thought of as a built-in hint in your memory. Often, when taking a test, you will find that the slightest hint is all you need in order to remember correctly. A mnemonic image is like having someone leaning over your shoulder who says, "Psst, the name of that muscle sounds like 'ladder misses the door, sigh.'" If misspelling continues to be a problem, try to create memory aids for spelling, too.

Here are two more examples to help you appreci-

Applications: Mnemonics—Memory Magic, continued

ate the flexibility of a mnemonic approach to studying.

Example 3 Your art history teacher expects you to be able to name the artist when you are shown slides as part of an exam. Many of the slides you have only seen once before in class. How will you remember them? As the slides are shown in class, make each artist's name into an object or image. Then picture the object *in* paintings done by the artist. For example, you can picture van Gogh as a *van* (automobile) *going* through the middle of each van Gogh painting. Picture the van running over things and knocking them down. Or, if you remember that van Gogh cut off his ear, picture a giant bloody ear in each of his paintings.

Example 4 If you have trouble remembering history, try to avoid thinking of it as something from the dim past. Picture each historical personality as a person you know right now (a friend, teacher, parent, and so on). Then picture these people doing whatever the historical figures did. Also try visualizing battles or other events as if they were happening in your town or make parks and schools in your town into foreign countries. Use your imagination.

Question: How can mnemonics be used to remember things in order?

Here are three techniques that are helpful.

1. Form a chain. To remember lists of ideas, objects, or words in order, try forming an exaggerated association (mental image) connecting the first item to the second, then the second to the third, and so on. To remember the following short list in order: *elephant, doorknob, string, watch, rifle, oranges,* picture a full-sized *elephant* balanced on a *doorknob* playing with a *string* tied to him. Picture a *watch* tied to the string, and a *rifle* shooting *oranges* at the watch. This technique can be used quite successfully for lists of 20 or more items. Try it next time you go shopping and leave your list at home.

2. Take a mental walk. Mnemonics were well known to ancient Greek orators, who would take a mental walk along a familiar path to associate ideas they wanted to cover in a speech with the images of statues found along the walk. You can do the same thing by "placing" objects or ideas along the way as you mentally take a familiar walk.

3. Use a system. Many times the first letter or syllables of words or ideas can be formed into another word that will serve as a reminder of order. "Roy G. Biv," just cited, is an example. As an alternative, learn the following: 1 is a bun, 2 is a shoe, 3 is a tree, 4 is a door, 5 is a hive, 6 is sticks, 7 is heaven, 8 is a gate, 9 is a line, 10 is a hen. To remember in order, form an image associating bun with a mental picture of the first item on your list. For example, if the first item is "frog," picture a "frog-burger" on a bun to remember it. Then, associate shoe with the second item, and so on.

If you have never used mnemonics, you may still be skeptical, but give this approach a fair trial. Most people find they can greatly extend their memory through the use of mnemonics. But remember, mnemonics only supplement the memory tips given earlier; they do not replace them. Like most things worthwhile, remembering takes effort.

Learning Check

1. Memory systems and aids are referred to as ____________________.

2. Which of the following is least likely to improve memory?
a. using exaggerated mental images
b. forming a chain of associations
c. turning visual information into verbal information
d. associating new information with information that is already known or familiar

3. Picturing your knee moaning as it tries to remember something could serve as a mnemonic for the term *mnemonic.* T or F?

4. Bower's 1973 study showed that, in general, mnemonics only improve memory for related words or ideas. T or F?

Answers: **1.** mnemonics **2.** c **3.** T **4.** F

Chapter Summary

- *Memory* is an active, computerlike system that *encodes, stores,* and *retrieves* information.
- Humans appear to have three interrelated memory systems: *sensory memory, short-term memory* (also called *working memory*), and *long-term memory.*
- Sensory memory is *exact* but very brief. Through *selective attention* some information is transferred to STM.
- STM has a capacity of about *seven bits* of information, but this can be extended by *chunking* or *recoding* the information. Short-term memories are brief and very sensitive to *interruption* or *interference;* however, they can be prolonged by *rehearsal.*
- LTM functions as a general storehouse of information, especially *meaningful* information. Long-term memories are *relatively* permanent, or lasting. LTM seems to have an almost unlimited storage capacity.
- LTM is subject to *constructive processing,* or ongoing revision and updating. LTM is highly *organized* to allow retrieval of needed information. The pattern, or *structure,* of memory *networks* is the subject of current memory research.
- *Hypnosis* may improve memory to a small degree, but it also increases the number of *false memories* reported.
- The *tip-of-the-tongue phenomenon* shows memory is not an all-or-nothing event. So, memories may be revealed by *recall, recognition, relearning,* or *redintegration.*
- In recall, memory proceeds *without explicit cues,* as in an *essay exam.* A common test of recognition is the *multiple-choice* question, which requires selection of a correct answer. In relearning, "forgotten" material is learned again and memory is indicated by a *savings score.* In redintegration, memories are *reconstructed* as each memory serves as a cue for the next memory.
- *Eidetic imagery* (photographic memory) occurs when a person is able to project an image onto a blank surface. Such images allow brief, nearly complete recall in some children. Eidetic imagery is rarely found in adults. However, many adults have *internal memory images,* which can be very vivid.
- *Exceptional* memory can be learned by finding ways to directly store information in LTM. Learning has no effect on the limits of STM. Some people may have exceptional memories that exceed what can be achieved through learning.
- Forgetting and memory were extensively studied by *Herman Ebbinghaus,* whose *curve of forgetting* shows that forgetting is most rapid immediately after learning. This is one reason why *periodic review* can be helpful in studying.
- *Failure to encode* information is a common cause of "forgetting." Forgetting in sensory memory and STM probably reflects *decay of memory traces* in the nervous system. Decay or *disuse* of memories may also account for some LTM loss, but much forgetting cannot be explained in this way.
- Often forgetting is *cue dependent.* That is, information is stored and *available* but is not *accessible* because the cues necessary to retrieve it are missing. The power of cues to trigger memories is revealed by *state-dependent learning* and the link between moods and memory.
- Much forgetting in both STM and LTM can be attributed to *interference* of memories with one another. When recent learning interferes with retrieval of prior learning, *retroactive inhibition* has occurred. If old learning interferes with new learning, *proactive inhibition* has occurred.

- *Repression* is the forgetting of painful, embarrassing, or traumatic memories. Repression is thought to be unconscious, in contrast to *suppression*, in which one consciously tries to avoid thinking about something.
- *Retrograde amnesia* and the effects of electroconvulsive shock (ECS) may be explained by the concept of *consolidation*. Consolidation theory holds that permanent memory traces are formed during a critical period after learning. Until they are consolidated, long-term memories are easily destroyed. The *hippocampus* is a brain area that has been connected to consolidation of memories.
- Memory can be improved by using *feedback* and *recitation*, by *overlearning*, by *selecting* and *organizing* information, and by using *spaced practice* and the *progressive part method*. Effects of *serial position*, *sleep*, and *review* should also be kept in mind when studying or memorizing.
- *Mnemonic systems* use mental images and unusual associations to link new information with familiar memories already stored in LTM. Such strategies organize information and give it personal meaning to make recall easier.

Chapter 10

Thinking, Problem Solving, and Creativity

Chapter Preview

Chess Anyone?

David Levy was in trouble. It was the fourth game of a six-game chess match and Levy was trying a new strategy. If he lost the match, Levy would forfeit $2500 of his own money. Game one was a tie. Levy won games two and three. Now in game four, he was locked in a sharp tactical battle, and he was losing. What was wrong? In the earlier games Levy relied on the kind of wide open maneuvering that had made him an International Master. In contrast, his opponent's strength was a powerful short-term, or tactical, style of play. Maybe "powerful" isn't the right word. Unbeatable is closer to the truth, as Levy soon learned. For the moment, David Levy had met his match. He watched silently as the robot arm of Chess 4.7 made its final move, winning game four.

Chess 4.7 is a computer program. In 1977 it won the Minnesota Open Chess Tournament—against humans. However, David Levy, the reigning Scottish champion, proved to be a tougher opponent. After losing game four, Levy quickly returned to his original style of play—and won the match (Ehara, 1980). For all their raw power computers are only able to plan five or six chess moves in advance (by considering over 1 billion possibilities). They don't make mistakes in the short run, but they can be beaten by strategy and foresight.

David Levy's victory symbolizes one of the most unique of all human capabilities: the ability to think intelligently and creatively. We know how computers "think" because we created them. But how do we explain David Levy's creativity and problem-solving ability? Or yours? Thinking, problem solving, and creativity are the challenging topics of this chapter.

Survey Questions What is the nature of thought? What basic units are used in thinking, and how do they differ? How do concepts and language influence thought? Can animals think? Can they be taught to use language? What do we know about effective problem solving and creativity? Can creativity be learned? How accurate is intuition?

What Is Thinking? It's All in Your Head!

Thinking refers to many things: daydreaming, fantasy, problem solving, and reasoning—to name but a few. Stated more formally, **thinking,** or **cognition,** refers to the mental manipulation and combination of images, concepts, words, rules, symbols, and precepts. Although an ability to think is not limited to humans, imagine trying to teach an animal to match the feats of Hans Eberstark, a "lightning calculator." Eberstark can multiply two 12-digit numbers in his head, supplying the correct answer in about 2 minutes!

Question: To what extent are animals capable of thought?

Most pet owners can readily supply stories about apparent thinking in animals. A friend might say, "Wow, you should have seen Studebaker figure out how to get into the closet where I hid the dog food." Are animals actually thinking in such situations? In a rudimentary sense they are. At its most basic, thinking is the **internal representation** of a problem or situation. (Picture a chess player who mentally tries out several possible moves before actually touching a chesspiece.)

Animals demonstrate internal representation in **delayed response problems.** For example, a hungry animal could be allowed to watch as food is hidden under one of three goal boxes. After a delay the animal is released. Can it select the correct box? If the delay is brief, the answer is yes (Hunter, 1913). Animals also show apparent problem-solving ability far exceeding that just described. In fact, German psychologist Wolfgang Köhler (VOOLF-gong KEAR-ler) believed that higher animals such as chimpanzees are capable of insight.

Insight is a sudden reorganization of the elements of a problem whereby the solution becomes evident. To test for insight, Köhler challenged Sultan, his brightest chimp, with a **multiple-stick problem.** In this problem several sticks of increasing length were arranged between the cage and a banana (see Fig. 10-1). To reach the banana, Sultan had to use the first stick to retrieve the second stick (which was longer than the first). The second stick could then be used to retrieve an even longer stick, which could then be used to reach the banana (Köhler, 1925).

When confronted with this problem, Sultan looked at the banana, then at the sticks . . . then at the banana. Picking up the first stick, Sultan smoothly and without further hesitation solved the problem and raked in the banana.

Psychologists have long debated whether Köhler's chimps actually displayed insight. More recently, however, David Premack (1983) has provided additional evidence of insightful problem solving by a chimp. In one fascinating experiment Premack showed a chimpanzee a videotape of an actor jumping up and down

Resources

Cognition The process of thinking, knowing, or mentally processing information.

Internal representation Any image, concept, precept, symbol, or process used to mentally represent information during thought.

Delayed response problem A problem in which an organism is required to make a correct choice some time after receiving information on which the choice is based.

Insight A sudden mental reorganization of a problem causing the solution to seem self-evident.

Multiple-stick problem A problem-solving test for primates in which sticks of increasing length must be used to successively retrieve each next-longer stick, and then some desired object, such as food.

below a bunch of bananas. The chimp was then shown several still photographs of the actor in various positions. From these, the chimp chose a photograph of the actor stepping up onto a chair. Note that this choice makes sense only if the chimp understood that the actor was trying to reach the bananas.

In recent years evidence for animal intelligence and thinking ability has continued to grow—but not without controversy (see Box 10-1).

Basic Units of Thought In the Chapter Preview we used chess playing as an example of human thought. Let's briefly consider another chess example. Chess Grand Master Miguel Najdorf once simultaneously played 45 chess games while *blindfolded*. It is estimated that over 3600 different positions arose during the evening of the exhibition (Hearst, 1969).

How did Najdorf perform his feat? Like most people he used several types of internal representation. The *basic units of thought* include (1) **images,** (2) **muscular responses,** (3) **concepts,** and (4) **language,** or **symbols.** All four units are usually combined in situations requiring complex thought and internal representation. Indeed, in some situations people need all the help they can get. To accomplish their mental feats, blindfolded chess players report that they use a combination of visual images, muscular sensations involving "lines of force," concepts ("Game 2 is an English opening"), and the special notational system or "language" used by chess players (Hearst, 1969). Because of their importance, each of the units of thought is discussed in greater detail in the following pages.

Image Most often, a mental representation that has picture-like qualities; an icon.

Muscular responses Visible movement of the muscles or unseen changes in their tension, which create kinesthetic sensations.

Concept A generalized idea representing a class of objects or events grouped together on some basis.

Language A body of words, or symbols, and rules for combining them that is used for communication and thought and is understood by a sizable community.

Fig. 10-1 *Psychologist Wolfgang Köhler believed that solution of a multiple-stick problem revealed a capacity for insight.*

Box 10-1
How Intelligent Are Animals?

Evidence for the idea that animals are capable of intelligent thought is varied and, to many researchers, convincing:

- Monkeys can learn to select, from among three objects, the one that differs from the other two.
- When a container of sugar water is moved a set distance farther from a beehive each day, the bees begin to go to the new location *before* the water is moved.
- Pigeons can learn to select photographs of humans from a group of photos that includes various objects.
- A chimpanzee is allowed to see itself in a mirror. It is then anesthetized and a red spot is placed on its forehead. When it awakens and looks in the mirror, it tries to rub away the colored spot.

Do such examples really demonstrate thinking by animals? Some psychologists say yes; some say no. What would it take, then, to verify animal thinking? Psychologist Donald Griffin suggests that we must observe behavior that is *versatile* and *appropriate* to changing circumstances. He also believes that thinking is implied by actions that appear to be planned with an awareness of likely results. As an example, sea otters select suitably sized rocks and use them to hammer shellfish loose for eating. They then use the rock to open the shell (Fig. 10-2).

As convincing as such examples may seem, they have not gone unchallenged. For example, Epstein, Lanza, and Skinner have conditioned pigeons to duplicate seemingly insightful behavior like that claimed for higher animals. David Premack, however, replies that the pigeons only achieved the *appearance* of thinking, because their behavior was strongly guided by reinforcement.

As stated before, it seems reasonable to assume that animals do think. However, debate is sure to continue about the limits of their intelligence and about whether specific examples demonstrate thinking, instinct, or conditioning. (Sources: Epstein et al., 1981; Griffin, 1984; Herrnstein, 1979; Premack, 1983; Rose, 1984.)

Fig. 10-2 *Does the seemingly intelligent behavior of sea otters and other animals reflect thinking ability, instinct, or conditioning? The evidence remains inconclusive, so psychologists disagree.*

Mental Imagery—Does a Frog Have Lips?

A survey of 500 people found that 97 percent have visual images and 92 percent have auditory images. Over 50 percent had imagery that included movement, touch, taste, smell, and pain (McKellar, 1965). When we speak of images, we usually think of mental "pictures." But, as you can see, "images" may involve the other senses as well. For example, your image of a bakery may include its delicious odor, as well as its appearance. Some people even have a rare form of imagery called **synesthesia** (sin-es-THEE-zyah). For these individuals, images cross normal sensory barriers (Marks, 1978). To the synesthetic individual, for instance, hearing music may include a burst of colors or tastes as well as sound sensations. Despite such variations, it is generally accepted that most people use images to think and to solve problems.

In recent years Stephen Kosslyn of Harvard University and other researchers have added greatly to our understanding of mental imagery. For instance, Kosslyn (1983) discovered that mental images are not flat, like photographs.

Synesthesia Experiencing one sense in terms of another; for example, "seeing" sounds as colors.

Stored image A mental image retained in memory.

Created image A mental image that has been assembled or invented rather than simply remembered.

Question: How could he determine that?

To sample Kosslyn's work, think about the following question: "Does a frog have lips and a stubby tail?" Unless you often kiss frogs, you will probably tackle this question by using mental images. To answer, most people report that they picture a frog, "look" at its mouth, and then mentally *rotate* the frog to check its tail (Kosslyn, 1983). Mental images, then, are not necessarily flat, and they can be moved about as needed (also see Fig. 10-3).

Question: How are images used to solve problems?

Stored images can be used to bring prior experience to bear on problem solving. If you were given the question "How many uses can you think of for an old automobile tire?" you might begin by picturing all the uses you have already seen. To generate more original solutions, you might use **created images.** Recent research indicates that people who have good imaging ability tend to score higher on tests of creativity (Shaw & Belmore, 1983). Thus, an artist may completely picture a proposed sculpture before beginning work.

Does the "size" of a mental image make any difference in thinking? To find out, first picture a cat sitting beside a housefly. Now try to "zoom in" on the cat's ears so you see them clearly. Next, picture a rabbit sitting beside an elephant. How quickly can you "see" the rabbit's front feet? Did it take longer than picturing the cat's ears?

Fig. 10-3 *Imagery in thinking. Subjects were shown a drawing similar to* (a) *and drawings of how* (a) *would look in other positions, such as* (b) *and* (c). *Subjects could recognize* (a) *after it had been "rotated" from its original position. However, the more* (a) *was rotated in space, the longer it took to recognize it. This result suggests that subjects actually formed a three-dimensional image of* (a) *and rotated the image to see if it matched. (Shepard, 1975)*

When a rabbit is pictured with an elephant, the rabbit's image must be small because the elephant is large. Using such tasks, Kosslyn (1975) found that the smaller an image is, the harder it is to "see" its details. To put this finding to use, try forming oversized images of things you want to think about. For example, to understand electricity, picture the wires as large pipes with electrons the size of golf balls moving through them; to understand the human ear, explore it (in your mind's eye) like a large cave; and so forth.

Muscular Imagery

Question: How do muscular responses relate to thinking?

It is somewhat surprising to recognize that we think with our bodies as well as our heads. Jerome Bruner (1966) believes that we often represent things in a kind of **muscular imagery** created by actions or *implicit* actions. For example, people who "talk" with their hands are using gestures to help themselves think as well as to communicate. A great deal of information is contained in *kinesthetic sensations* (feelings from the muscles and joints). As one talks, these sensations help structure the flow of ideas (Horowitz, 1970). If you try to tell a friend how to knead bread dough, you may find it impossible to resist moving your hands as you describe the proper motion.

Most thinking is accompanied by an undercurrent of muscular tension and **micromovements** throughout the body. In one classic study a subject was asked to imagine that he was hitting a nail with a hammer. As he did, there was a clearly recorded burst of activity in the muscles of his unmoving arm (Jacobson, 1932). If you would like to demonstrate the link between muscular activity and thinking, ask a friend who was in a sporting event to describe what occurred. Along with a description, you will probably get an "instant replay" of the high points!

Learning Check

1. A ____________ ____________ problem can be used to show that animals are capable of simple representative thought.

2. There is evidence that chimpanzees are capable of insightful solutions to problems, but some psychologists remain unconvinced that true thinking is involved. T or F?

3. List four basic units of thought:

____________, ____________

____________, ____________

4. Synesthesia is the use of kinesthetic sensations as a vehicle for thought. T or F?

5. Our reliance on imagery in thinking means that problem solving is impaired by micromovements. T or F?

6. Humans appear capable of forming three-dimensional images that can be moved or rotated in space. T or F?

Answers: **1.** delayed response **2.** T **3.** images, muscular responses, concepts, and language or symbols **4.** F **5.** F **6.** T

Concepts—I'm Positive, It's a Whatchamacallit

A **concept** is an idea that represents a class of objects or events. Concepts provide a powerful tool for thought because they allow us to think more *abstractly*, free from distracting details. Imagine, for instance, that you have shown a 5-year-old child two big toy frogs and four little frogs. You then ask the child, "Are there more frogs or more baby frogs?" When Markman and Seibert (1976) asked kindergarten children the same question, most children erred and said, "More baby frogs." The researchers then introduced the concept of *family* to the problem ("This is a family of frogs. Are there more frogs or more baby frogs?"). Adding the concept dramatically reduced the children's thinking errors.

Question: How are concepts learned?

Concept formation is the process of classifying information into meaningful categories. In early childhood much concept formation simply involves experience with **positive** and **negative instances** of the concept. This is not as simple as it might seem: Imagine a child learning the concept of *dog.*

Dog Daze

A child and her father go for a walk. At a neighbor's house, they see a medium-sized dog. The father says, "See the dog." As they pass the next yard, the child sees a cat and says "Dog!" Her father corrects her, "No, that's a *cat*." The child now thinks, "Aha, dogs are large and cats are small." In the next yard she sees a Pekingese and says, "Cat!" "No, that's a dog," replies her father.

The child's confusion is understandable. At first she might even mistake a Pekingese for a dust mop. However, with more positive and negative instances the child will eventually recognize everything from Great Danes to Chihuahuas as examples of the same category—dogs. As adults we more often acquire concepts by learning or forming **rules.** For example, a *triangle* must be a closed shape with three sides made of straight lines. Rule learning is generally more efficient than examples, but examples remain important (Rosenthal & Zimmerman, 1978). It is unlikely that memorizing a series of rules would allow an uninitiated listener to accurately categorize *punk, new wave, fusion, salsa,* and *techno-pop* music.

Question: Are there different kinds of concepts?

Several general types of concepts have been identified. A **conjunctive concept** refers to a class of objects having one or more features in common. Conjunctive concepts are sometimes referred to as *and concepts:* To belong to the concept class, an item must have "this feature, *and* this feature, *and* this feature." For example, a *motorcycle* must have two wheels, *and* an engine, *and* a seat, *and* handlebars. **Relational concepts** classify objects on the basis of their relationship to something else, or by the relationship between features of an object. *Large, above, left, north,* and *upside down* are all relational concepts. **Disjunctive concepts** refer to objects that have at least one of several possible features. These are *either-or concepts.* To belong, an item must have "this feature, *or* that feature, *or* another feature." For example, in the game of baseball, a *strike* is *either* a swing, *or* a miss, *or* a pitch down the middle, *or* a foul ball. The either-or quality of disjunctive concepts makes them difficult to learn.

Muscular imagery Internal representations of events in terms of generated, remembered, or imagined muscular sensations.

Micromovements Tiny, nearly imperceptible movements associated with changes in muscular tension and activity.

Concept formation The process of formulating or acquiring concepts by direct experience, rule learning, or exposure to prototypes.

Positive instance In concept learning, an object or event that exemplifies the concept class.

Negative instance In concept learning, an object or event that does not belong to the concept class.

Conceptual rule A formal rule by which one may decide if an object or event belongs to a particular conceptual class.

Conjunctive concept A concept defined by the joint presence of specific features. (For example, to belong an object must be both red *and* triangular.)

Relational concept A concept defined by the relationship between features of an object or between an object and its surroundings (for example, "greater than," "lopsided").

Disjunctive concept A concept defined by the presence of at least one of several possible features. (For example, to belong an object must be either blue *or* circular.)

Prototype An ideal, or model, used as a prime example of a particular concept.

Denotative meaning The objective dictionary meaning of a word or concept.

Connotative meaning The subjective, personal, or emotional meaning of a word or concept.

Semantic differential A psychological measure of connotative meaning obtained when words or concepts are rated on a number of dimensions.

Encoding Changing information into a form that allows it to be stored in memory and manipulated in thought.

Semantics The study of meanings in language.

Phonemes The basic sounds of a language that can be distinguished from one another.

Morphemes The smallest meaningful units in a language.

When you think of the concept *bird*, do you make a mental list of features that birds have? Probably not. In addition to rules and features, most people also use **prototypes,** or ideal models, to identify concepts (Rosch, 1977). A robin, for instance, is a model bird, whereas an ostrich is not. What this tells us is that not all examples of a concept are equally representative. The upshot is that identifying concepts is difficult when we cannot come up with a prototype relevant to what we see. What, for example, are the objects shown in Fig. 10-4?

Generally speaking, concepts have two types of meaning. The **denotative meaning** of a word or concept is its explicit definition. The **connotative meaning** is its emotional or personal meaning. For example, the denotative meaning of the word *naked* (having no clothes) is the same for a nudist as it is for a movie censor, but we could expect their connotations to differ.

Question: Can you give a clearer statement of what a connotative meaning is?

Researcher Charles Osgood (1952) used a method called the **semantic differential** to measure connotative meaning (see Fig. 10-5). Osgood found that when words or concepts are rated on a series of scales, most of their connotative meaning boils down to the dimensions: *good-bad*, *strong-weak*, and *active-passive*. (Sounds like a good movie title doesn't it: *The Good the Bad, the Strong the Weak, the Active and the Passive.*) Because concepts vary on these dimensions, words or phrases having roughly the same denotative meaning may have very different connotations. For example, I am *conscientious*; you are *careful*; he is *nit-picking!*

Language—Give Us a Sign, Washoe

As we have seen, thinking sometimes takes place without language. Everyone has had the experience of searching for a word to express an idea that exists as a vague image or feeling. Nevertheless, most thought leans heavily on language, because it allows the world to be **encoded** into symbols that are easy to manipulate.

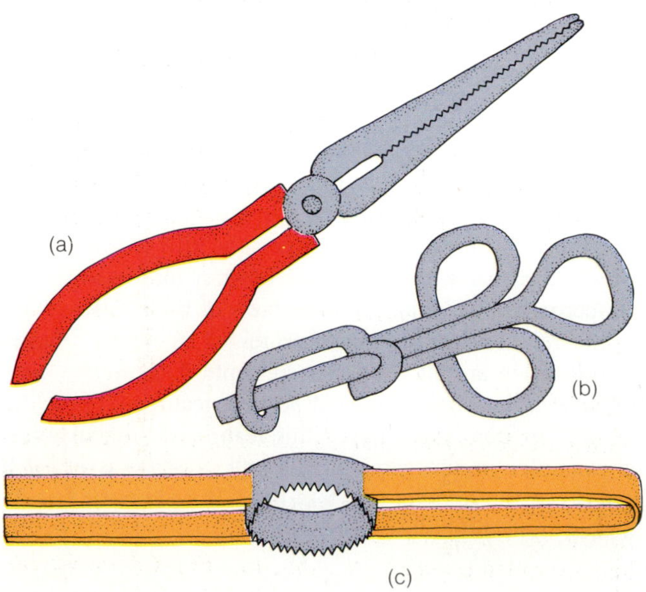

Fig. 10-4 *Use of prototypes in concept identification. Even though its shape is unusual, item* (a) *can be related to a model (an ordinary pair of pliers) and thus recognized. But what are items* (b) *and* (c)*? If you don't recognize them, look ahead to Fig. 10-6. (After Bransford & McCarrell, 1977)*

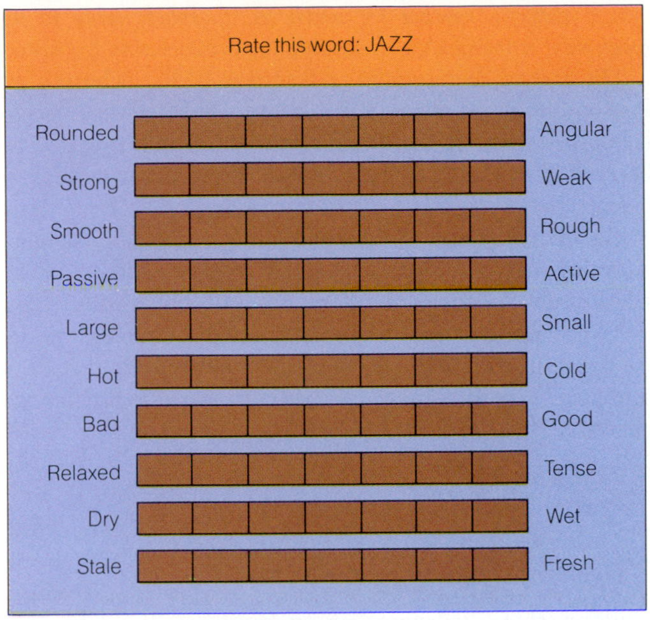

Fig. 10-5 *This is an example of Osgood's semantic differential. Connotative meaning of the word* jazz *can be established by rating it on the scales. Mark your own rating by placing dots or X's in the spaces. Connect the marks with a line; then have a friend rate the word and compare your responses. It might be interesting to do the same for* rock and roll, disco, *and* classical. *You also might want to try the word* psychology. *(From C. E. Osgood. Copyright © 1952 American Psychological Association. Reprinted by permission)*

Study of the meaning of words and language is called **semantics.** It is here that the connection between language and thought becomes most evident. Suppose, on an intelligence test, you were asked to circle the word that does not belong in this series:

SKYSCRAPER CATHEDRAL TEMPLE PRAYER

If you circled PRAYER, you answered as most people do. Now try another problem, again circling the odd item:

CATHEDRAL PRAYER TEMPLE SKYSCRAPER

Had you seen only this question, you probably would have circled SKYSCRAPER. There is a subtle change in meaning caused by re-ordering the words (Judson & Cofer, 1956; cited by Mayer, 1977).

Semantic problems often arise when a word has dual, or unclear, meaning: Does the sentence, "Tom was seated by the waiter," mean the waiter gave Tom a seat or that Tom was seated beside the waiter? Choice of words may directly influence thinking about important events by shifting meaning: Has one country's army "invaded" another? Or "effected a protective incursion"? Is the city reservoir "half full" or "half empty"? Would you rather eat "prime beef" or "dead cow"?! (See Fig. 10-7.)

Question: What does it take to make a language?

The Structure of Language

First of all, a language must provide *symbols* that can stand for objects and ideas. The symbols we call words are built out of **phonemes** (FOE-neems: basic speech sounds) and **morphemes** (MORE-feems: speech sounds collected into meaningful units). The units of speech can be arranged into countless combinations. Consider the possibilities in just four morphemes: *reach, to, able, un.* From these we can make: *able to, unable to, reach to, to reach, able to reach, unable to reach, reachable, unreachable, reachable to, unreachable to, unto, unto Able.*

The second requirement of language is that it have a **grammar,** or set of rules for combining sounds into words and words into sentences. One part of grammar is known as **syntax,** or rules for word order in sentences. Syntax is very important because rearranging words almost always changes the meaning of a sentence: "Dog bites man" versus "Man bites dog."

Traditional grammar has been concerned with "surface" language—the actual sentences spoken. More recently, American linguist Noam Chomsky has drawn attention to the rules used to change core ideas into various sentences. Chomsky (1968) argues that we do not learn all the sentences we might ever say. Rather, we actively *create* them by applying **transformation rules.** For example, the core sentence "Dog bites man" can be transformed to the following patterns (and others as well):

Past: The dog bit the man.
Passive: The man was bitten by the dog.
Negative: The dog did not bite the man.
Question: Did the dog bite the man?

Children show evidence of using transformation rules when they form sentences such as "I runned home." The child has applied the past tense rule to the irregular verb *to run.*

The third, and perhaps most essential, characteristic of language is that it is **productive.** The great strength of any true language is that it can produce new thoughts or ideas. Because words do not resemble the things they represent, they can be arranged to produce an infinite variety of meaningful sentences (Bruner, 1966). Some are silly: "Please don't feed me to the goldfish." Some are profound: "We hold these truths to be self-evident, that all men are created equal." In either case it is the productive quality of language that makes it such a powerful tool for thought.

Question: Do animals use language?

Animals do communicate. The cries, gestures, and mating calls of animals have broad meanings immediately understood by other animals of the same species

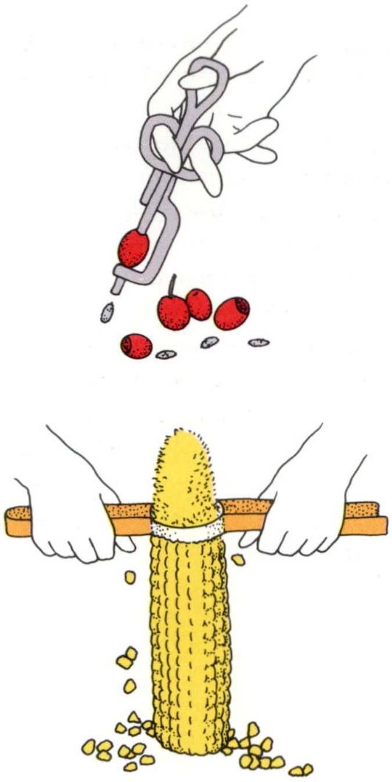

Fig. 10-6 *Context can substitute for a lack of appropriate prototypes in concept identification.*

Fig. 10-7 *The Stroop interference task. Test yourself by naming the colors in the top two rows as quickly as you can. Then name the colors of the ink used to print the words in the bottom two rows (do not read the words themselves). The greater difficulty of naming colors in the bottom rows shows how intimately thought is linked to language. The meaning of words has a powerful impact on our response to them. (After Tzeng & Wang, 1983)*

(Premack, 1983). For the most part, however, natural animal communication is quite limited. Even apes and monkeys make only a few dozen distinct cries, which carry messages such as "attack," "flee," or "food here." More importantly, animal communication seems to lack the productive quality of human language. For example, when a monkey gives an "eagle distress" call, it means something like, "I see an eagle." The monkey has no way of saying, "I don't see an eagle," or "Thank heavens that wasn't an eagle," or "That sucker I saw yesterday was some huge eagle" (Glass, Holyoak, & Santa, 1979).

Question: Could an animal be taught to use language?

Psychologists have made several intriguing attempts to teach animals to use language. Let's consider some of their successes and failures.

Talking Chimps Early attempts to teach chimps to talk were a dismal failure. The world record for talking was held by Viki, a chimp who could say only four words (*mama, papa, cup,* and *up*) after 6 years of intensive training (Fleming, 1974; Hayes, 1951). (Actually, all four words sounded something like a belch.) Then there was a breakthrough. Beatrice Gardner and Allen Gardner of the University of Reno, Nevada, used a combination of operant conditioning and imitation to teach a female chimp named Washoe to use **American Sign Language (ASL).** ASL is a set of hand gestures used by the hearing impaired (each gesture stands for a word).

Washoe's communication skills blossomed rapidly as her "vocabulary" grew. Soon she began to put together primitive sentence strings like: "Come-gimme sweet," "Out please," "Gimme tickle," and "Open food drink." She now has a vocabulary of about 240 signs and can construct six-word sentences. She even communicates with other chimpanzees using sign language, and she is "teaching" her adopted son Loulis to use signs (Gardner & Gardner, 1969; Rose, 1984).

Some critics are skeptical about Washoe's achievements since her arrangement of "words" is somewhat haphazard. Children quickly learn the difference between word orders like "Give me candy" and "me give candy." An answer to this criticism has come from the work of David Premack (1970), who taught a female chimp named Sarah to use 130 "words" consisting of plastic chips arranged on a magnetized board (see Fig. 10-8).

From the beginning of her training, Sarah was required to use proper word order. She has learned to answer questions, to label things "same" or "different," to classify objects by color, shape, and size, and to construct compound sentences (Premack & Premack, 1983). One of her most outstanding achievements is use of sentences involving **conditional relationships:** "If Sarah take apple, then Mary give Sarah chocolate"; "If Sarah take banana, then Mary no give Sarah chocolate."

Question: Can it be said with certainty that the chimps understand such interchanges?

Most researchers working with chimps believe that they have indeed communicated with them. Especially convincing are the chimp's spontaneous responses. Washoe once "wet" on psychologist Roger Fouts' back while riding on his shoulders. When Fouts asked, with some annoyance, why she had done it, Washoe signed, "It's funny!"

Grammar A set of rules for combining language units into meaningful speech or writing.

Syntax The study of word orderings in the formation of sentences.

Transformation rules Rules by which a simple declarative sentence may be converted to other voices or forms (past tense, passive voice, and so forth).

Productivity The capacity of language for generating new ideas and possibilities.

American Sign Language A standardized system of hand gestures used by hearing-impaired persons for communication.

Conditional statement A statement that contains a qualification, often of the *if-then* form.

Fig. 10-8 *After reading the message, "Sarah insert apple pail banana dish" on the magnetic board, Sarah performed the actions as directed. (From "Teaching Language to an Ape" by Ann J. Premack and David Premack. Copyright © 1972 by Scientific American, Inc. All rights reserved)*

Some of the most convincing evidence on language comprehension by an animal has come from recent work by Penny Patterson. Patterson has trained a young gorilla named Koko to use over 300 signs. Patterson considers conversations held about *past events* and *feelings* a strong indication of Koko's comprehension. For example, 3 days after Koko bit Patterson, the following conversation took place:

Me: "What did you do to Penny?"
Koko: "Bite."
Me: "You admit it?"
Koko: "Sorry bite scratch. Wrong bite."
Me: "Why bite?"
Koko: "Because mad."
Me: "Why mad?"
Koko: "Don't know."
(Adapted from Patterson, 1978, p. 459.)

Such interchanges are impressive. But communication and actual language use are two different things. Several psychologists have recently expressed doubt that apes can really use language. For one thing, the chimps rarely "speak" without prompting. Many of their seemingly original sentences turn out to be responses to questions or imitations of signs made by the teacher. Also, it appears that the apes may be simply performing chains of *operant responses* to get food or other goodies (Savage-Rumbaugh et al., 1979; Terrace, 1985). By using such responses, the apes then manipulate their trainers to get what they want.

You might say that the critics believe the apes have made monkeys out of their trainers. However, psychologists Roger and Debbi Fouts have recently countered such criticism. An analysis they performed of some 6000 conversations between chimps showed that only 5 percent had anything to do with food. The Fouts have also videotaped conversations between chimps that took place when no humans were present to cue them (Fouts, Fouts, & Schoenfield, 1984). So, maybe the chimps will make monkeys out of the critics. Although the issue is far from resolved, such research promises to unravel some of the mysteries of language learning. In fact, it has already proved helpful for teaching language to aphasic children (children with serious language impairment) (Huges, 1974).

Learning Check

Before you read more, it might be a good idea to see if you can answer these questions.

1. A *mup* is defined as anything that is small, blue, and hairy. *Mup* is a ________________ concept.
2. The connotative meaning of the work *naked* is "having no clothes." T or F?
3. True languages are ________________ because they can be used to generate new possibilities.
4. The basic speech sounds are called ________________; the smallest meaningful units of speech are called ________________.
5. One of the chimpanzee Sarah's most oustanding achievements has been the construction of sentences involving: (circle)

   negation   adult grammar   unprompted questions   conditional relationships
6. Critics consider "sentences" constructed by apes to be simple ________________ responses having little meaning to the animal.

Answers: **1.** conjunctive **2.** F **3.** productive **4.** phonemes, morphemes **5.** conditional relationships **6.** operant

Problem Solving—Getting an Answer in Sight

A good way to start off a discussion of problem solving is to solve a problem. Give this one a try.

> A famous ocean liner (the *Queen Ralph*) is steaming toward port at 20 miles per hour. It is 50 miles from shore when a seagull takes off from its deck and flies toward port. At the same instant, a speedboat leaves port at 30 miles per hour. The bird flies back and forth between the speedboat and the *Queen Ralph* at a speed of 40 miles per hour. How far will the bird have flown when the two boats pass?

If you don't immediately see the answer to this problem, read it again. (The answer is revealed in the "Solution by Insight" section that follows.)

We all do a tremendous amount of problem solving every day. Problem solving can be as commonplace as figuring out how to make a nonpoisonous meal out of the leftovers in the refrigerator or as significant as developing a cure for cancer. In either case we begin with an awareness that an answer probably exists and that by proper manipulation of the elements of thought a solution can be found. A number of different approaches to problem solving can be identified.

Mechanical solution A problem solution achieved by trial and error or by a fixed procedure specified by learned rules.

General solution A solution that correctly states the requirements for success but not in sufficient detail for further action.

Functional solution A detailed, practical, and workable solution.

Selective encoding The mental ability to select relevant information while ignoring useless or distracting information.

Selective combination In problem solving, the ability to connect seemingly unrelated items of information.

Selective comparison The ability to relate a present problem to similar problems solved in the past or to prior experience.

Fixation The tendency to repeat wrong solutions or faulty responses, especially in response to frustration.

Functional fixedness Rigidity in problem solving caused by an inability to see new uses for familiar objects.

Mechanical Solutions Mechanical solutions may be achieved by *trial and error* or by *rote*. If I have forgotten the combination to my bike lock, I may be able to discover it by trial and error. In an era of high-speed computers, many trial-and-error solutions are best left to machines. A computer could generate all possible combinations of the five numbers on my lock in a split second.

When a solution is achieved by rote, we mean that thinking advanced according to a learned set of rules. If you have a good background in mathematics, you may have solved the problem of the bird and the boats by rote. (I hope you didn't. There is an easier solution.)

Solutions by Understanding Many problems are unsolvable by mechanical means or by the use of habitual modes of thought. In this case a higher level of thinking based on *understanding* is necessary. A classic series of studies on this type of thinking has been performed by German psychologist Karl Duncker (1945). Duncker gave college students this problem:

> Given an inoperable stomach tumor and rays which at high intensity will destroy tissue (both healthy and diseased), how can the tumor be destroyed without damaging surrounding tissue? (Students were also shown the sketch in Fig. 10-9.)

Question: What did this problem show about problem solving?

Duncker asked the students to think aloud as they worked. By "eavesdropping" on their thoughts, he found that there were two phases to successful problem solving. First, students had to discover the **general properties** of a correct solution. Once they realized that the intensity of the rays had to be lowered on their way to the tumor, a number of **functional** (workable) **solutions** could be proposed. This marked the second stage of problem solving, during which a specific solution was selected. (The correct solution is to focus weak rays from several sources on the tumor, or to rotate the person's body so that the exposure of healthy tissue is minimized.)

Solution by Insight Recall that Köhler's apes sometimes seemed to show *insight* in their problem solving. With humans we say that insight has occurred when an answer suddenly appears after a period of unsuccessful thought. An insight is usually so rapid and clear that we often wonder how such an "obvious" solution could have been missed.

Perhaps you experienced insight when trying to solve the problem of the boats and the bird. Because the boats will cover the 50-mile distance in exactly 1 hour, and the bird flies 40 miles per hour, the bird will have flown 40 miles when the boats meet. No math is necessary if you have insight into this problem.

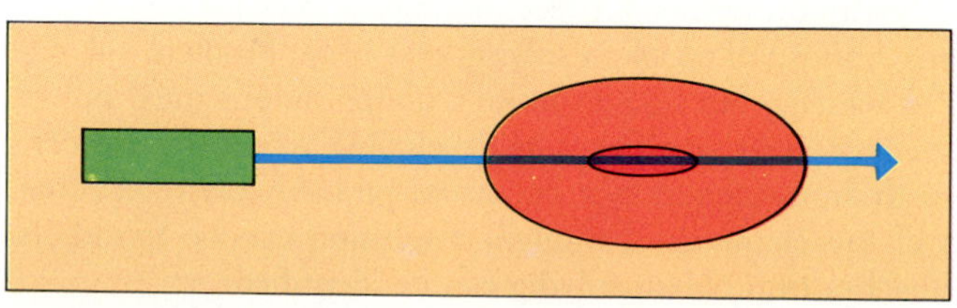

Fig. 10-9 *A schematic representation of Duncker's tumor problem. The dark spot represents a tumor surrounded by healthy tissue. How can the tumor be destroyed without injuring surrounding tissue? (After Duncker, 1945)*

Question: What, really, does it mean to have an insight?

Psychologists Robert Sternberg and Janet Davidson (1982) have studied people as they solve problems that require insight or "leaps of logic" for solution. According to their work, insight involves three abilities. The first is **selective encoding,** which refers to the ability to select information that is relevant to a problem, while ignoring that which is not. For example, consider the following problem:

> If you have white socks and black socks in your drawer, mixed in the ratio of 4 to 5, how many socks will you have to take out to make sure you have a pair of the same color?

A person who fails to recognize that "mixed in a ratio of 4 to 5" is irrelevant information will be less likely to come up with the correct answer of three socks.

According to Sternberg and Davidson, a second source of insights is **selective combination,** which involves bringing together seemingly unrelated bits of useful information.

A third source of insight is **selective comparison,** which is the ability to compare new problems with old information or with problems already solved. A good example is the hatrack problem. This problem calls on subjects to build a structure in the middle of a room that will support an overcoat. Subjects are given only two long sticks and a C-clamp to work with. The solution, shown in Fig. 10-10, is to clamp the two sticks together, so they are wedged between floor and ceiling. If you were given this problem, you would be more likely to solve it if you first thought of the way pole lamps are wedged between floor and ceiling.

Fixations The ease with which problems are solved is related to a variety of factors. One of the most important barriers to problem solving is called **fixation.** Fixation is the tendency to get "hung up" on wrong solutions or to become blind to other alternatives. A prime example of fixation is **functional fixedness.** Func-

Fig. 10-10 *Solution to the hatrack problem.*

Inductive thought A type of thinking in which a general rule or principle is inferred from a series of specific examples; for example, inferring the laws of gravity by observing many falling bodies.

Deductive thought Thought that applies a general set of rules to specific situations; for example, using the laws of gravity to predict the behavior of a single falling body.

tional fixedness is the inability to see new uses (functions) for familiar objects or for objects that have been used in a particular way. If you have ever used a dime as a screwdriver, you've overcome functional fixedness.

Question: How does functional fixedness affect problem solving?

Karl Duncker, who originated the concept of functional fixedness, performed a clever study to demonstrate its operation. Duncker challenged students to mount a candle on a vertical board so that it could burn in the normal way. Duncker gave each student three candles, some matches, some cardboard boxes, some thumbtacks, and other items. Half of Duncker's subjects received these items *inside* the cardboard boxes. The others received all the items, including the boxes, laid out on a tabletop. Duncker found that when the items were in the boxes, solution of the problem was very difficult. This is because the boxes were seen as *containers*, not as items that might be part of the solution. (If you haven't guessed the solution, check Fig. 10-11.)

Functional fixedness is just one example of the mental blocks that prevent insight. Here's another: How would you remove a $5 bill placed below a stack of precariously balanced objects (without touching or moving the objects)? A good answer is to split the bill at the edge and tear it in half, gently pulling from opposite ends. Many people fail to see this solution because they have learned not to destroy things of value. In a book entitled *Conceptual Blockbusting*, James Adams (1980) lists other sources of fixations (see Box 10-2).

Creative Thinking— Fluency, Flexibility, and Originality

Question: What distinguishes creative thinking from more routine problem solving?

As we have noted, problem solving may be the result of thinking that is mechanical, insightful, or based on understanding. To this we can add that thought may be **inductive** (going from specific facts or observations to general principles) or

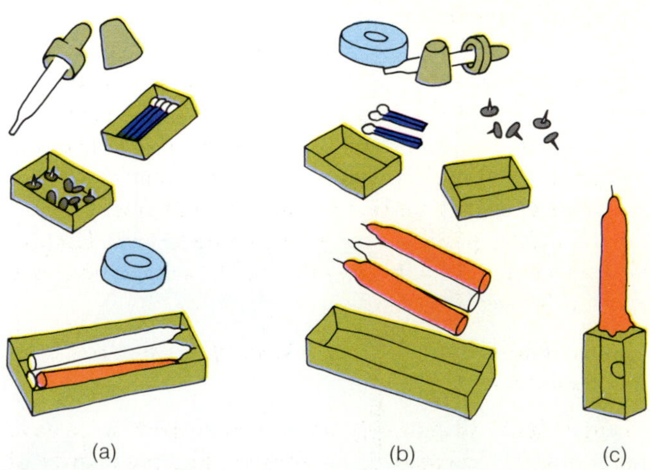

Fig. 10-11 *Materials for solving the candle problem were given to subjects in boxes* (a) *or separately* (b). *Functional fixedness caused by condition* (a) *interfered with solving the problem. The solution to the problem is shown in* (c).

Box 10-2

Common Barriers to Creative Thinking

1. Emotional barriers: Inhibition and fear of making a fool of oneself, fear of making a mistake, inability to tolerate ambiguity, excessive self-criticism.
2. Cultural barriers: Values that hold that fantasy is a waste of time, playfulness is for children only; reason, logic, and numbers are good; feelings, intuitions, pleasure, and humor are bad or have no place in the serious business of problem solving.
3. Learned barriers: Conventions about uses (functional fixedness), meanings, possibilities, taboos.
4. Perceptual barriers: Habits leading to a failure to identify important elements of a problem.

deductive (going from general principles to specific situations). Thinking may also be **logical** (proceeding from given information to new conclusions on the basis of explicit rules) or **illogical** (intuitive, associative, or personal).

Creative thinking involves all these styles of thought (in varying combinations) *plus* fluency, flexibility, and originality (Guilford, 1950). The meaning of these terms can be illustrated by returning to an earlier example. Let's say that you would like to find a creative use (or uses) for the millions of automobile tires discarded each year. The creativity of your suggestions could be rated in this way: **Fluency** is defined as the total number of suggestions you are able to make. **Flexibility** is defined as the number of times you shift from one class of possible uses to another. **Originality** refers to how novel or unusual your suggestions are. By totaling the number of times you showed fluency, flexibility, and originality, we could rate the creativity of your thinking on this problem. Speaking more generally, we would be rating your capacity for **divergent thinking.**

Divergent thinking is the most widely used measure of creative problem solving. In routine problem solving or thinking, there is one correct answer, and the problem is to find it. This leads to **convergent thought** (lines of thought that converge on the correct answer). Divergent thinking is the reverse, in which many possibilities are developed from one starting place.

There are several tests of divergent thinking. In the **Unusual Uses Test** a person is asked to think of as many uses for an object (such as the tires just mentioned) as possible. In the **Consequences Test** the object is to answer a question such as, "What would be the results if everyone suddenly lost the sense of balance and were unable to stay in an upright position?" Subjects are to list as many reactions as possible. In the **Anagrams Test** subjects are given a word such as *creativity* and asked to make as many new words as possible by rearranging the letters. Each of these tests can be scored for fluency, flexibility, and originality. (For an example of other tests of divergent thought, see Fig. 10-12.)

Question: Isn't creativity more than divergent thought? What if a person comes up with a large number of useless answers to a problem?

A good question. Divergent thought is definitely an important part of creative thinking, but there is more to it. To be creative, the solution to a problem must

Logical thought Drawing conclusions on the basis of formal principles of reasoning.

Illogical thought Thought that is intuitive, invalid, or haphazard.

Fluency In tests of creativity, fluency refers to the total number of solutions produced.

Flexibility In tests of creativity, flexibility is indicated by the number of different types of solutions produced.

Originality In tests of creativity, originality refers to the degree of novelty or unusualness of the solutions produced.

Divergent thought Thinking that produces many ideas or alternatives; a major element in original or creative thought.

Convergent thought Thinking directed toward discovery of a single established correct answer; conventional thinking.

Unusual Uses Test A test of creativity in which subjects try to think of new uses for a common object.

Consequences Test A test of creativity in which subjects try to list as many consequences as possible that would follow if some change were made.

Anagrams Test A test of creativity in which subjects try to make as many new words as possible from the letters in a given word.

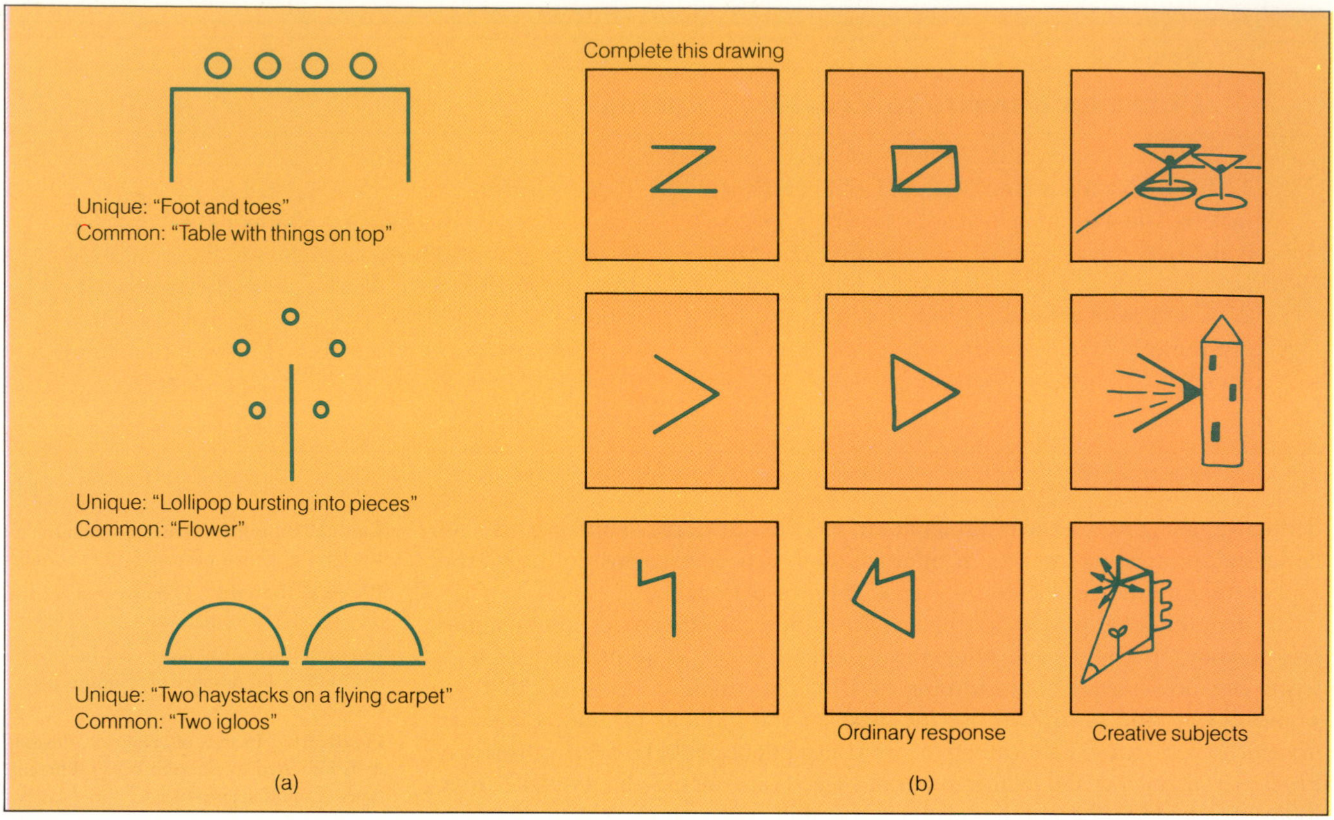

Fig. 10-12 *Some tests of divergent thinking. Creative responses are more original and more complex.* [(a) *After Wallach & Kogan, 1965;* (b) *after Barron, 1958*]

be more than novel, unusual, or original. It must also be potentially useful or meaningful, and it must meet the demands of the problem (MacKinnon, 1962). This is the dividing line between a "harebrained scheme" and a "stroke of genius." (See Fig. 10-13 and Fig. 10-14.) In other words, the creative person brings reasoning and critical thinking to bear on novel ideas once they are produced (Snow, 1986).

Question: Is there any pattern to creative thinking?

Stages of Creative Thought A good summary of the sequence of events in creative thinking proposes five stages that usually occur:

1. **Orientation.** As a first step, the problem must be defined and important dimensions identified.
2. **Preparation.** In the second stage, creative thinkers saturate themselves with as much information pertaining to the problem as possible.
3. **Incubation.** Most major problems produce a period during which all attempted solutions will have proved futile. At this point problem solving may proceed on a subconscious level: While the problem seems to have been set aside, it is still "cooking" in the background.
4. **Illumination.** The stage of incubation is often ended by a rapid insight or series of insights. These produce the "Aha!" experience, often depicted in cartoons as a light bulb appearing over the thinker's head.

5. Verification. The final step is to test and critically evaluate the solution obtained during the stage of illumination. If the solution proves faulty, the thinker reverts to the stage of incubation.

Of course, creative thought is not always so neat. Nevertheless, the stages listed are a good summary of the most typical sequence of events.

You may find it helpful to attach the stages to the following more or less true story. Legend has it that the king of Syracuse (a city in ancient Greece) once suspected that his goldsmith had substituted cheaper metals for some of the gold in a crown and had pocketed the difference. Archimedes, a famous mathematician and thinker, was presented with the problem of discovering whether the king had been cheated.

Archimedes began by defining the problem (orientation): "How can I determine what metals have been used in the crown without damaging it?" He then investigated all known methods of analyzing metals (preparation). All involved cutting or melting the crown, so he was forced to temporarily set the problem aside (incubation). Then one day as he stepped into his bath, Archimedes suddenly knew he had the solution (illumination). He was so excited he is said to have run naked through the streets shouting, "Eureka, eureka!" (I have found it, I have found it!)

On observing his own body floating in the bath, Archimedes realized that different metals of equal weight would displace different amounts of water. A pound of brass, for example, occupies more space than a pound of gold, which is denser. All that remained was to test the solution (verification). Archimedes placed an amount of gold (equal in weight to that given the goldsmith) in a tub of water. He marked the water level and removed the gold. He then placed the crown in the water. Was the crown pure gold? If it was, it would raise the water to exactly the same level. Unfortunately, the purity of the crown and the fate of the goldsmith are to this day unknown!

Question: What makes a person creative?

The Creative Personality According to the popular stereotype, highly creative people are eccentric, introverted, neurotic, socially inept, unbalanced in their interests, and, frequently, on the edge of madness. Although some well-known artists and musicians cultivate a public image to fit the stereotype, there is

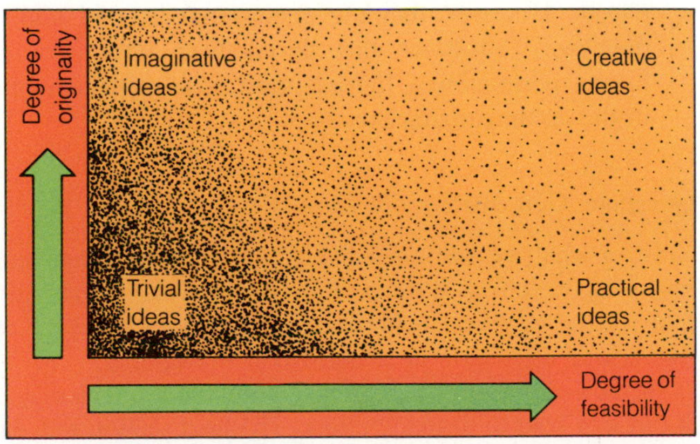

Fig. 10-13 *Creative ideas combine originality with feasibility. (Adapted from McMullan & Stocking, 1978)*

Box 10-3

Creativity Profile

The following qualities have repeatedly been found to characterize creative individuals:

1. An unusual awareness of people, events, and problems.
2. A high degree of verbal fluency.
3. Flexibility with numbers, concepts, media; flexibility in social situations.
4. Originality of ideas and expressions, a sense of humor.
5. An ability to abstract, organize, and synthesize.
6. A high energy/activity level.
7. Persistence at tasks of interest.
8. Impatience with routine or repetitive tasks.
9. A willingness to take risks.
10. A vivid and spontaneous imagination; in childhood this may take the form of "fibbing" or imaginary companions.

(Source: Meeker, 1978.)

little truth in it (see Box 10-3). Studies by psychologist Donald MacKinnon paint a very different picture of the creative person. After extensive interviews and testing of creative writers, architects, mathematicians, and scientists, MacKinnon (1968) and others have drawn these conclusions:

1. At any given level of IQ, some people are creative and some are not. There is little correlation between creativity and IQ (Nelson & Crutchfield, 1970; Taylor, 1978).
2. Creative people usually have a greater than average range of knowledge and interests, and they are more fluent in combining ideas from various sources.
3. Creative people have an openness to experience. They accept irrational thought and are uninhibited about their feelings and fantasies.
4. MacKinnon's subjects enjoyed symbolic thought, ideas, concepts, and possibilities. They tended to be interested in truth, form, and beauty, rather than in recognition or success. Their creative work was an end in itself.
5. Highly creative people value independence and have a preference for complexity. However, they are unconventional and nonconforming primarily in their work; otherwise, they do not have particularly unusual, outlandish, or bizarre personalities. Indeed, most creative personalities resemble the profile in the accompanying Box 10-3.

Fig. 10-14 *Hat-tipping device. According to the patent, it is for "automatically effecting polite salutations by the elevation and rotation of the hat on the head of the saluting party when said person bows to the person or persons saluted." In addition to being original or novel, a creative solution must fit the demands of the problem. Is this a creative solution to the "problem" of hat tipping?*

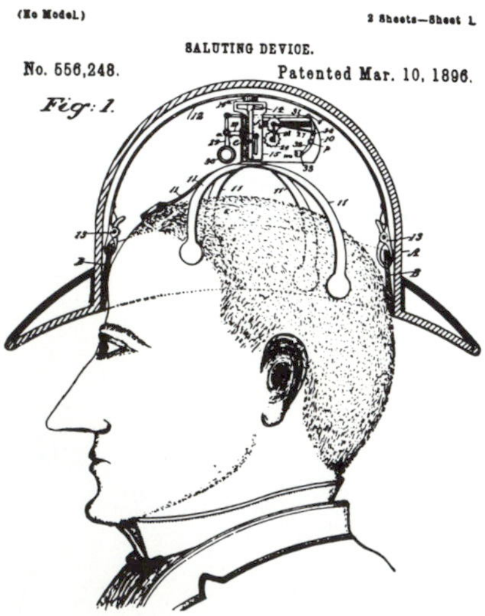

Question: Can creativity be learned?

Most of what we know about creativity remains preliminary. Nevertheless, it is beginning to look as if some of the thinking skills that contribute to creative problem solving can be taught. In the Applications section of this chapter you will find a brief discussion of some helpful strategies.

At the same time that irrational, intuitive thought may contribute to creativity, it can also lead to thinking errors. The next section tells how this can happen.

Intuition— Mental Shortcut? Or Dangerous Detour?

Decision 1: An epidemic breaks out and 600 people are about to die. Doctors have two choices. If they give drug A, 200 lives will be saved. If they give drug B, there is a one-third chance that 600 people will be saved and a two-thirds chance that none will be saved. Which drug should they choose?

Decision 2: Again, 600 people are about to die, and doctors must make a choice. If they give drug A, 400 people will die. If they give drug B, there is a one-third chance that no one will die and a two-thirds chance that 600 will die. Which drug should they choose?

Intuition Quick, instinctive thought that does not make use of formal logic or clear reasoning.

Representativeness error A tendency to select wrong answers because they seem to match pre-existing mental categories.

Base rate The basic rate at which an event occurs over time; the basic probability of an event.

Most people choose drug A for the first problem and drug B for the second. This is fascinating because the two problems are identical. The only difference is that the first is stated in terms of lives saved, the second in lives lost. Yet, even people who realize their answers are contradictory find it difficult to change them (Kahneman & Tversky, 1972, 1973).

Intuition As the example shows, we often make decisions on the basis of intuition, rather than by logic. Doing so may provide quick answers, but it can also be misleading and sometimes disastrous. Two noted psychologists, Daniel Kahneman and Amos Tversky, have spent nearly 20 years studying how people make decisions and predictions in situations involving uncertainty. They have found, to put it bluntly, that human judgment is often seriously flawed (Kahneman et al., 1982). Understanding the thinking errors they have identified may help you avoid them. Let's explore some common errors.

Representativeness One very common pitfall is illustrated by the following question:
Which is more probable?

A. Bjorn Borg will lose the first set of a tennis match but win the match.
B. Bjorn Borg will lose the first set.

Tversky and Kahneman (1982) found that most people regard A as more probable than B. However, this intuitive answer overlooks an important fact: The likelihood of two events occurring together is lower than the probability of either alone. (For example, the probability of getting one head when flipping a coin is one-half, or .5. The probability of getting two heads when flipping two coins is .25, or one-fourth.) Therefore, A is less likely to be true than B.

Tversky and Kahneman believe that such faulty conclusions are based on an intuitive error called **representativeness.** That is, a choice that seems to be representative of what we already know is given greater weight. Thus, the information given in the question about Borg is compared with a mental model of what a tennis pro's behavior should be like. The first choice seems to better represent this model and therefore seems more likely, even though it isn't.

Underlying Odds A second common error in judgment involves ignoring the **base rate,** or underlying probability of an event. In one experiment, for instance,

Framing In thought, the terms in which a problem is stated or the way in which it is structured.

subjects were told that they would be given descriptions of 100 people—70 lawyers and 30 engineers. Subjects were then asked to guess, without knowing anything about a person, whether he or she was an engineer or a lawyer. All correctly stated the probabilities as 70 percent for lawyer and 30 percent for engineer. Subjects were then given this description:

> Dick is a 30-year-old man. He is married with no children. A man of high ability and high motivation, he promises to be quite successful in his field. He is well liked by his colleagues.

Notice that the description gives no new information about Dick. He could still be either an engineer or a lawyer. Therefore, the odds should again be estimated as 70-30. However, most people changed the odds to 50-50. Intuitively, it seems that Dick has a 50 percent chance of being either an engineer or a lawyer. But this guess completely ignores the underlying odds.

Perhaps it is fortunate that we do at times ignore underlying odds. Were this not the case, how many people would get married in the face of a 50 percent divorce rate? Or how many would start high-risk businesses? On the other hand, people who smoke, drink, and then drive, or skip wearing auto seat belts ignore rather high odds of injury or illness. In many high-risk situations ignoring base rates is the same as thinking you are an exception to the rule.

Framing Perhaps the most general conclusion from Kahneman and Tversky's work is that the way a problem is stated, or **framed**, affects decisions (Tversky & Kahneman, 1981). This is especially true if the problem is stated in terms of either losses or gains—like the epidemic problem described earlier.

Usually, the broadest way of framing or stating a problem produces the most rational decision. However, people often state problems in increasingly narrow terms until a single, seemingly "obvious" answer emerges. For example, to select a career, it would be wise to consider pay, working conditions, job satisfaction, needed skills, future employment outlook, and many other factors. Instead, such decisions are often narrowed to thoughts such as, "I like to write, so I'll be a journalist," "I want to make good money and law pays well," or "I can be creative in photography." Framing decisions so narrowly greatly increases the risk of making a poor choice.

Conclusion We have discussed only some of the intuitive errors made in the face of uncertainty. The study of intuitive decision making is rapidly finding application to medical diagnosis, business decisions, military strategy, investing and finance, international relations, and more. In each area people are learning to think twice before they decide. With practice you too can learn to spot errors like those described: Remember, shortcuts to answers often short-circuit clear thinking—a point we will explore further in the upcoming Applications section.

Learning Check

1. Insight refers to rote, or deductive, problem solving. T or F?
2. The first phase in problem solving by understanding is to discover the general properties of a correct solution. T or F?
3. The term *fixation* refers to the point at which a helpful insight becomes fixed in one's thinking. T or F?

4. Functional fixedness is usually an aid to problem solving. T or F?

5. Fluency, flexibility, and originality are characteristics of:
a. convergent thought *b.* deductive thinking *c.* creative thought *d.* trial-and-error solutions

6. List the stages of creative thinking in the correct order:

________________, ________________,

________________, ________________,

________________.

7. An ability to organize, abstract, and synthesize ideas blocks creativity; these are noncreative qualities. T or F?

8. To be creative, an original idea must also be practical or feasible. T or F?

9. According to Sternberg and Davidson, insights are the result of selective encoding, selective combination, and selective ________________ of information.

10. Kate is single, outspoken, and very bright. As a college student she was deeply concerned with discrimination and other social issues and participated in several protests. Which statement is more likely:
a. Kate is a bank teller. *b.* Kate is a bank teller and a feminist

11. The probability of two events occurring together is lower than the probability of either one occurring alone. T or F?

12. Usually, the broadest way of ________________ a problem yields the most rational decision.

Answers: **1.** F **2.** T **3.** F **4.** F **5.** c **6.** orientation, preparation, incubation, illumination, verification **7.** F **8.** T **9.** comparison **10.** *a* **11.** T **12.** framing

Applications

Steps to Better Thinking and Problem Solving

We all at one time or another experience difficulties in thinking and problem solving. The following should alert you to some of the more common problems.

Rigid Mental Set Try the problems pictured in Fig. 10-15. If you have difficulty, try asking yourself what *assumptions* you are making. The problems are designed to demonstrate the limiting effects of a mental set. (The answers to these problems, along with an explanation of the mental sets that prevent their solution, are found on p. 284.) In addition to the assumptions and mental sets we bring to a problem, problems themselves may produce a disruptive set. A simple example is the following: The name *Polk* is pronounced "poke," the word *folk* is pronounced "foke," and the white of an egg is pro-

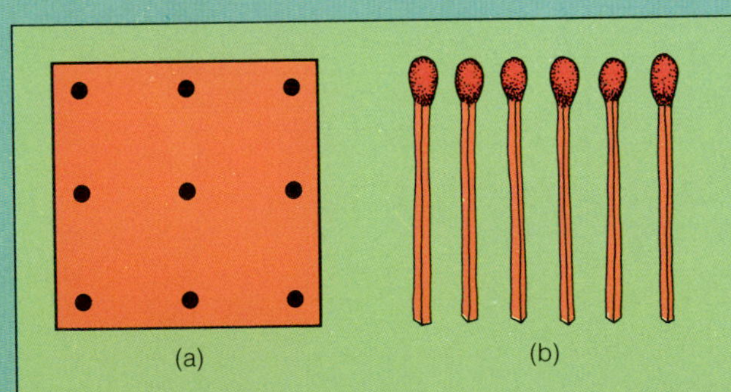

Fig. 10-15 (a) *Nine dots are arranged in a square. Can you connect them by drawing four continuous straight lines (without lifting your pencil from the paper)?* (b) *Six matches must be arranged to make four triangles. The triangles must be the same size, with each side equal to the length of one match. (The solutions to these problems appear on page 284.)*

Applications: Steps to Better Thinking and Problem Solving, continued

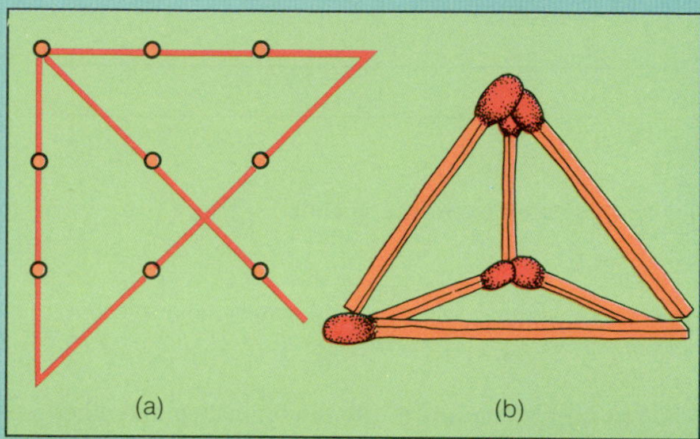

Fig. 10-16 *Problem solutions.* (a) *The dot problem can be solved by extending the lines beyond the square formed by the dots. Most people assume incorrectly that they may not do this.* (b) *The match problem can be solved by building a three-dimensional pyramid. Most people assume that the matches must be arranged on a flat surface.*

nounced ____________________? Here is another example. See if you can unscramble each set of letters to make a word that uses all the letters:

MEST ____________________

LFAE ____________________

DUB ____________________

STAKL ____________________

OTOR ____________________

LTEPA ____________________

Now try a new list:

FINEK ____________________

OPONS ____________________

KROF ____________________

PUC ____________________

SDIH ____________________

LTEPA ____________________

Did you notice that the last set of letters was the same in each list? Many people don't and end up solving the problem twice. To complete the first list *(stem, leaf, bud, stalk, root)*, the item LTEPA is usually unscrambled as PETAL. In the second list *(knife, spoon, fork, cup, dish)* LTEPA becomes PLATE for many people.

Now that you have been forewarned about the danger of faulty assumptions, see if you can correctly answer the following questions.

1. Argentineans do not have a fourth of July. T or F?
2. How many birthdays does the average person have?
3. A farmer had 19 sheep. All but 9 died. How many sheep did he have left?
4. It is not unlawful for a man living in Winston-Salem, North Carolina, to be buried west of the Mississippi River. T or F?
5. Some months have 30 days, some have 31. How many months have 28 days?
6. I have two coins that together total 55 cents. One of the coins is not a nickel. What are the two coins?
7. It would be far better to have an elephant eat you than a gorilla. T or F?

These questions are designed to cause thinking errors. Here are the answers:

1. F. Of course they have a fourth of July. What would they do, go from the third to the fifth? **2.** One, celebrated each year. **3.** 19—9 alive and 10 dead. **4.** F. It is against the law to bury a living man anywhere. **5.** All of them. **6.** A half-dollar and a nickel. One of the coins is not a nickel, but the other one is! **7.** F. It would be better to have the elephant eat the gorilla. (Read it again.)

If you got caught on any of the questions, consider it an additional reminder of the value of actively challenging the assumptions you are making in any instance of problem solving.

Problems with Logic A major thinking difficulty centers on the process of *logical reasoning.* Simple

Applications: Steps to Better Thinking and Problem Solving, continued

sequences of logical thought can be arranged as a set of *premises* (assumptions) and a *conclusion*. This format is called a **syllogism.** A syllogism can be evaluated for the *validity* of its *reasoning* and for the *truth* of its *conclusion*. It is entirely possible to draw true conclusions using faulty logic, or to draw false conclusions using valid logic. The examples below show how this is possible.

Syllogism I

All humans are mortal. (Major premise)
All women are human. (Minor premise)
Therefore, all women are mortal. (Conclusion)

Comment: As you can see from the diagram in Fig. 10-17, the logic of the syllogism is valid. Since our premises are true, this means the conclusion is true. The diagram shows all women included within the boundaries of mortals.

Syllogism II

All women are humans.
All humans are mortal.
Therefore, all mortals are women.

Comment: In this example the conclusion drawn is false because the reasoning is invalid. The diagram for Syllogism I shows that all mortals are not women. Notice how little the syllogism has to be changed to produce a false conclusion. Now consider Syllogism III.

Syllogism III

All psychologists are weird.
Mary is a psychologist.
Therefore, Mary is weird.

Comment: In this case the reasoning is valid, but the conclusion is false, because the first premise is false. All psychologists are *not* weird. (Honest!) Now, let's consider one more syllogism.

Syllogism IV

All ducks have wings.
All birds have wings.
Therefore, all ducks are birds.

Comment: This syllogism shows the importance of paying close attention to logic. The reasoning appears to be valid since the conclusion is true, but substitute *bats* or *airplanes* for *ducks* and see how the conclusion reads. It is a good idea to get in the habit of questioning the logic used by politicans and advertisers—-psychologists, too, for that matter.

Oversimplification It may be an oversimplification to say so, but oversimplification is another basic source of thinking errors. There are two types of oversimplification that are particularly troublesome. The first is **all-or-nothing thinking.** Classifying things as absolutely right or wrong, good or bad, acceptable or unacceptable, or honest or dishonest prevents appreciation of the complexity of most life problems. The second problem is thinking in terms of **stereotypes.** Stereotypes are particularly troublesome when human relationships are involved. An overly simplified, inaccurate, or rigid picture of men, blacks, women, Republicans, liberals, police officers, or any other group of people leads to muddled thinking about individual members of the group. Look for this and the other errors in your own thinking habits.

Enhancing Creativity—Brainstorms

Thomas Edison once explained his creativity by saying, "Genius is 1 percent inspiration and 99 percent perspiration." Many studies of creativity show that

Fig. 10-17

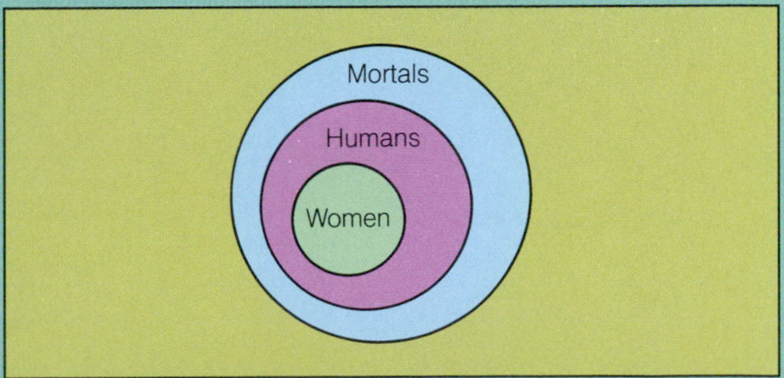

Applications: Steps to Better Thinking and Problem Solving, continued

"genius" owes as much to persistence and dedication as it does to inspiration (Hunt, 1982). Once it is recognized that creativity can be hard work, then something can be done to enhance it. Here are some suggestions on how to begin (from Hayes, 1978, and indicated sources).

1. Define the problem broadly. Whenever possible enlarge the definition of a problem. For instance, assume your problem is, "Design a better doorway." This is likely to lead to ordinary solutions. Why not change the problem to, "Design a better way to get through a wall"? Now your solutions will be more original. Best of all might be to state the problem as, "Find a better way to define separate areas for living and working." This could lead to truly creative solutions (Adams, 1980).

Let's say that you are the leader of a group interested in designing a new can opener. Wisely, you ask the group to think about *opening* in general, rather than about can openers. This was just the approach used in developing the pop-top can. As the design group discussed the concept of opening, one member suggested that nature has its own openers, like the soft seam on a pea pod. Instead of a new can-opening tool, the group invented the self-opening can (Fig. 10-18) (Stein, 1974).

2. Create the right atmosphere. A variety of experiments show that people make more original, spontaneous, and imaginative responses when exposed to others (models) doing the same (Amabile, 1983). If you want to become more creative, spend time around creative people. This is the premise underlying much education in art, theater, dance, and music.

Fig. 10-18

3. Allow time for incubation. Trying to hurry, or to force a problem's solution, may simply encourage fixation on a dead end. In one experiment subjects were asked to list as many consequences as possible that would follow if people no longer needed to eat. Most subjects rapidly produced several ideas and then ran dry. After working for a time, some subjects were interrupted and required to do another task for 20 minutes. Then they returned to the original question. The interruption improved their scores, even though they worked no longer than the control group (Fulgosi & Guilford, 1968).

4. Seek varied input. Remember, creativity requires divergent thinking. Rather than digging deeper with logic, you are attempting to shift your mental "prospecting" to new areas. As an example of this strategy, Edward de Bono (1970) recommends that you randomly look up words in the dictionary and relate each to the problem. Often this activity will trigger a fresh perspective or open a new avenue. For instance, let's say you are asked to come up with new ways to clean oil off a beach, and you draw a blank. Following de Bono's suggestion, you would read the following randomly selected words, relate each to the problem, and see what thoughts are triggered: *weed, rust, poor, magnify, foam, gold, frame, hole, diagonal, vacuum, tribe, puppet, nose, link, drift, portrait, cheese, coal.*

5. Look for analogies. As the principle of selective comparison (described earlier) suggests, many "new" problems are really old problems in new clothing. Representing a problem in a variety of ways is often the key to solution. Most problems become easier to solve when they are effectively represented. For example, consider this problem:

> Two backpackers start up a steep trail at 6 a.m. They hike all day, resting occasionally, and arrive at the top

Applications: Steps to Better Thinking and Problem Solving, continued

at 6 p.m. The next day they start back down the trail at 6 a.m. On the way down they stop several times and vary their pace. They arrive back at 6 p.m. On the way down one of the hikers, who is a mathematician, tells the other that she has realized that they will pass a point on the trail at exactly the same time as they did the day before. Her nonmathematical friend finds this hard to believe, since on both days they have stopped and started many times and have changed their pace. The problem: Is the mathematician right?

Perhaps you will see the answer to this problem immediately. If not, think of it this way: What if there are *two* pairs of backpackers, one going up the trail, the second coming down, and both hiking on the *same day?* It becomes obvious that the two pairs of hikers will pass each other at some point on the trail. Therefore, they will be at the same place at the same time. The mathematician was right (adapted from Hayes, 1978).

6. Delay evaluation. Various studies suggest that people are most likely to be creative when they are given the freedom to play with ideas and solutions without having to worry about being evaluated. In the first stages of creative thinking, it is important to avoid criticizing your efforts. Worrying about the correctness of solutions tends to inhibit creativity (Amabile, 1983). This idea is expanded in the discussion that follows.

An alternative approach to enhancing creativity is called *brainstorming*. Although brainstorming is a group technique, it can be applied to individual problem solving as well.

Brainstorming The essence of brainstorming is that *production* and *criticism* of ideas are kept separate. To encourage divergent thinking in group problem solving, participants are encouraged to produce as many ideas as possible without fear of criticism or evaluation. Only *after* a brainstorming session is complete are ideas reconsidered and evaluated (Haefele, 1962). As ideas are freely generated, an interesting **cross-stimulation effect** takes place in which one participant's ideas trigger ideas for others. The four basic rules for successful brainstorming are:

1. Criticism of an idea is absolutely barred. All evaluation is deferred until after the session.
2. Modification or combination with other ideas is encouraged. Don't worry about giving credit for ideas or keeping them neat. Mix them up!
3. Quantity of ideas is sought. In the early stages of brainstorming, quantity is more important than quality. Try to generate lots of ideas.
4. Unusual, remote, or wild ideas are sought. Let your imagination run amok!

Question: How is brainstorming applied to individual problem solving?

The essential point to remember is to *suspend judgment*. Ideas should first be produced without regard for logic, organization, accuracy, practicality, or any other evaluation. In writing an essay, for instance, you would begin by writing ideas in any order, the more the better, just as they occur to you. Later you would go back and reorganize, rewrite, and criticize your efforts.

As an aid to achieving steps 2, 3, and 4 of the brainstorming method, you might find the following checklist helpful for encouraging original thought. It can be used to see if you have overlooked a possible solution (adapted from Parnes, 1967).

Creativity Checklist

1. Redefine. Consider other uses for all elements of the problem. (This is designed to alert you to fixations that may be blocking creativity.)
2. Adapt. How could other objects, ideas, procedures, or solutions be adapted to this particular problem?
3. Modify. Imagine changing anything and everything that could be changed.
4. Magnify. Exaggerate everything you can think of. Think on a grand scale.
5. Minify. What if everything were scaled down? What if there were no differences between elements of the problem? "Shrink" the problem down to size.

Applications: Steps to Better Thinking and Problem Solving, continued

6. Substitute. How could one object, idea, or procedure be substituted for another?
7. Rearrange. Break the problem into pieces and shuffle them.
8. Reverse. Consider reverse orders, opposites, and turn things inside out.
9. Combine. This one speaks for itself.

By making a habit of subjecting a problem to each of these procedures, you should be able to greatly reduce the chances that you will overlook a useful, original, or "creative" solution.

Learning Check

1. In evaluating a syllogism, it is possible to draw a true conclusion with faulty logic, or a false conclusion with valid logic. T or F?
2. Stereotyping is an example of oversimplification in thinking. T or F?
3. Exposure to creative models has been shown to enhance creativity. T or F?
4. In brainstorming, each idea is critically evaluated as it is generated. T or F?
5. Defining a problem broadly produces a cross-simulation effect that can inhibit creative thinking. T or F?

Answers: **1.** T **2.** T **3.** T **4.** F **5.** F

Chapter Summary

- Thinking is the manipulation and combination of *internal representations* of external stimuli or situations.
- Animals reveal a capacity for thought when they solve *delayed response problems* and, in some cases, problems that appear to require understanding or *insight*. Some psychologists remain unconvinced about such abilities, however.
- Four basic units of thought are *images*, *concepts*, *muscular responses*, and *language*.
- Most people have internal images of one kind or another. Images may be *stored or created*. Sometimes they cross normal sense boundaries in a type of imagery called *synesthesia*. Images used in problem solving may be three-dimensional, and their size may change.
- Muscular images are created by memory of actions or by *implicit actions*. *Kinesthetic sensations* and *micromovements* seem to help structure the flow of thought for many people.
- A *concept* is a generalized idea of a class of objects or events. *Concept formation* is often based on *positive* and *negative instances* and on *rule learning*. In practice, concept identification frequently makes use of *prototypes*, or general models of the concept class. Concepts may be classified as *conjunctive* (*and* concepts), *disjunctive* (*either-or* concepts), or *relational*.

- The *denotative* meaning of a word or concept is its dictionary definition. *Connotative* meaning is personal or emotional. Connotative meaning can be measured with the *semantic differential*.
- Language allows events to be *encoded* into *symbols* for easy mental manipulation. Thinking in language is influenced by meaning. The study of meaning is called *semantics*.
- Language carries meaning by combining a set of symbols according to a set of rules *(grammar)*, which includes rules about word order *(syntax)*. A true language is *productive* and can be used to generate new ideas or possibilities.
- Animal communication is relatively limited because it lacks *symbols* that can be rearranged easily. Attempts to teach chimpanzees systems such as American Sign Language suggest to some that primates are capable of language use. Others question this conclusion.
- The solution to a problem may be arrived at *mechanically* (by trial and error or by rote application of rules), but mechanical solutions are frequently inefficient or ineffective except where aided by computer.
- Solutions by *understanding* usually begin with discovery of the *general properties* of an answer. Next comes proposal of a number of *functional solutions*.
- When understanding leads to a rapid reorganization of a problem whereby the solution becomes obvious, it is said that *insight* has occurred. Three elements of insight are *selective encoding*, *selective combination*, and *selective comparison*.
- Insight and other problem solving can be blocked by *fixation*. *Functional fixedness* is a common fixation, but *emotional blocks*, *cultural values*, *learned conventions*, and *perceptual habits* are also problems.
- Creative thinking requires *divergent* thought, characterized by *fluency*, *flexibility*, and *originality*. To be creative, a solution must be useful or meaningful as well as original.
- Five stages often seen in creative problem solving are *orientation*, *preparation*, *incubation*, *illumination*, and *verification*. Not all creative thinking fits this pattern.
- Studies suggest the *creative personality* has a number of identifiable characteristics, most of which contradict popular stereotypes. There appears to be little or no correlation between IQ and creativity.
- Intuitive thinking often leads to errors. Wrong conclusions may be drawn when an answer seems highly *representative* of what we already believe to be true. Another problem occurs when people ignore the *underlying probability* (or *base rate*) of an event. Clear thinking is usually aided by stating or *framing* a problem in broad terms.
- *Rigid mental set*, *faulty logic*, and *oversimplification* are major sources of thinking errors. Various strategies, including *brainstorming*, tend to enhance creative problem solving.

Part Four

Actions and Reactions

Chapter 11

Motivation

Chapter Preview

Flight of the *Gossamer Albatross*

What would it feel like to pedal *an airplane over the English Channel? In 1979 cyclist Bryan Allen found out the hard way by serving as pilot and "engine" for the first human-powered flight from England to France. Allen pedaled a delicate aircraft, the* Gossamer Albatross, *in a grueling 3-hour flight. The flight took Allen to the limits of endurance, as he fought head winds, thirst, leg cramps, and exhaustion. The following excerpts are from Allen's (1979) account:*

> 6:59 A.M. At last, word comes over the radio . . . "We have France in sight—four miles to go. . . ."
>
> Four miles or four hundred. I'm fading now and know it. Gradually the head winds have been building up . . . I talk to myself . . . Don't give up now, you *can* do it! As I waver between hope and despair, the radio crackles again:
>
> "Altitude six inches, six inches; get it up, you've got to get it up!"
>
> 7:29 A.M. One mile. Less distance than I had flown *Gossamer Condor* two years before for the original Kremer prize. Then, however, there were no head winds or turbulence, no thirst, no cramps. . . . Despite the cramps, I struggle back up to five feet. "Against all hope," I repeat to myself, "against all hope."
>
> 7:36 A.M. Four hundred yards to shore. . . . One hundred yards now. I am running on reserves I never knew I had. . . .

Motivation *This chapter is about the goals, needs, and motives that underlie Bryan Allen's behavior—and your own. Allen's final burst of effort ("I am running on reserves I never knew I had") is but one example of highly motivated behavior—behavior ranging from eating and drinking to feats like Allen's historic flight. How do we explain such diversity? The answer is by considering a broad sweep of ideas—from "feeding systems" in the brain to Abraham Maslow's concept of self-actualization. The pages that follow are an introduction to some of the most interesting and useful of these ideas.*

Survey Questions Are there different types of motives? What causes hunger? Thirst? Overeating? In what ways are pain avoidance and the sex drive unusual? How does arousal relate to motivation? How are motives learned? Are some motives more basic than others? What is intrinsic motivation? Can psychology be applied to dieting?

Motivation—Forces That Push and Pull

We move. We seek different goals, some more vigorously than others. The same goal may be pursued for different reasons, or different goals may be pursued for the same reasons. We use the concept of motivation to explain each of these basic aspects of behavior. To be more specific, **motivation** refers to the "dynamics of behavior, the process of initiating, sustaining, and directing activities of the organism" (Goldenson, 1970).

Question: Can you clarify that?

Yes. Let's relate the concept of motivation to a simple sequence of activity:

> Liz is studying (psychology, of course) in the library. She begins to feel hungry and has difficulty concentrating. Her stomach growls. She grows restless and decides to buy an apple from a vending machine. The machine is empty, so she goes to the cafeteria. Closed. She returns to the library, packs up her books, and drives home, where she prepares a meal and eats. At last her hunger is satisfied, and she again resumes studying.

Liz's food seeking was *initiated* by her bodily need for food; it was *sustained* because her need was not immediately met; and her activities were *directed* by possible sources of food. Notice too that her food seeking was *terminated* by achieving her goal.

A Model of Motivation Many motivated activities can be thought of as beginning with a **need.** The need that initiated Liz's search was a depletion of necessary substances within the cells of her body. Needs cause a psychological state or feeling called a **drive** to develop. (In Liz's case the drive was hunger.) Drives activate a **response** (or a series of actions) designed to attain a **goal** that will satisfy the need. Meeting the need temporarily ends the motivational sequence. Thus, a simple model of motivation can be shown in this way:

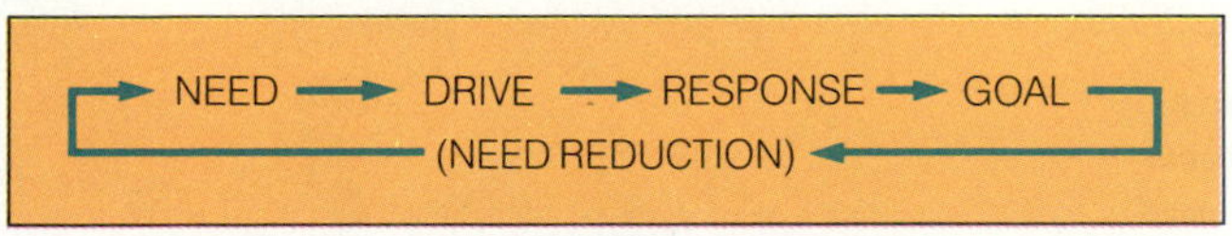

Question: Why use the terms "need" and "drive"? Aren't they the same thing?

Both terms are necessary because the strength of needs and drives can differ. If you were to begin fasting, your bodily need for food would increase daily, but you would probably be less "hungry" on the seventh day than you were on the first. Your need steadily increases, but the hunger drive comes and goes.

Resources

Motive (or motivation) A force within an organism that activates behavior or directs behavior toward some goal.

Need A specific state within the organism that may energize behavior that satisfies the need. Needs are often related to the depletion of essential body substances.

Drive The psychological expression of an internal need state; for example, hunger or thirst.

Response Any muscular action, glandular activity, or other identifiable behavior.

Goal The object of a motivated and directed sequence of behavior.

Before we assume that we have a complete model of motivation, let us observe Liz's eating behavior on another occasion:

> For dinner, Liz has just eaten soup, salad, a large steak, a large baked potato, one-half of a loaf of bread, two pieces of cheesecake, and four cups of coffee. After the meal she remarks about her discomfort from overeating. Soon after, Liz's roommate arrives with a strawberry pie. Liz exclaims that strawberry pie is her favorite dessert and proceeds to eat three good-sized pieces and has a cup of coffee to wash them down.

Is this hunger? Certainly we can believe that Liz's extra large meal was enough to satisfy her biological needs for food.

Question: How does that change the model of motivation?

The story illustrates that motivated behavior can be energized by the "pull" of external stimuli as well as by the "push" of internal needs. The pull exerted by a goal is called its **incentive value.** Some goals are so desirable (strawberry pie, for example) that they motivate behavior in the absence of internal need. Other goals are so low in incentive value that they will be rejected even though they might meet the internal need. Fresh, live grubworms, for instance, are considered a delicacy in some parts of the world, but it is doubtful that the average American could eat one no matter how hungry he or she might be.

In most instances it is helpful to recognize that actions are energized by a combination of internal needs *and* external incentives, and that a strong state of need may make a less attractive incentive into a desirable goal. You may never have eaten a grubworm, but chances are good that you have eaten some pretty horrible leftovers when the refrigerator was bare. Incentives also help account for motives that do not seem to have any identifiable internal need, such as drives for success, status, or approval (see Fig. 11-1).

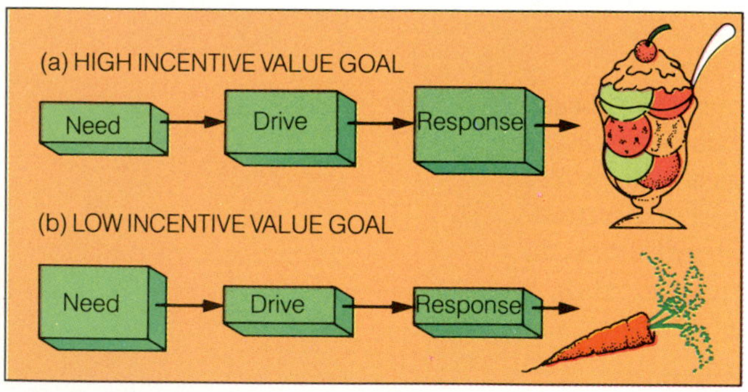

Fig. 11-1 *Needs and incentives interact to determine drive strength* (top). (a) *Moderate need, combined with a high-incentive goal, produces a strong drive.* (b) *Even when a strong need exists, drive strength may be moderate if a goal's incentive value is low. It is important to remember, however, that incentive value lies "in the eye of the beholder"* (photo). *No matter how hungry, few people would be able to eat the pictured grubworms.*

Types of Motives For the purpose of study, motives can be divided into three major categories:

1. **Primary motives** are based on biological needs that must be met for survival. The most important primary motives are hunger, thirst, pain avoidance, and needs for air, sleep, elimination of wastes, and regulation of body temperature. Primary motives are innate.
2. **Stimulus motives** also appear to be innate, but they are not necessary for mere survival of the organism. Their purpose seems to be to provide the nervous system with useful information and stimulation. The stimulus motives include activity, curiosity, exploration, manipulation, and physical contact.
3. **Learned,** or **secondary, motives** account for the great diversity of human activities suggested by the Chapter Preview. Behavior like Bryan Allen's flight over the English Channel is probably best understood in terms of learned motives or goals. Many secondary motives are related to acquired needs for power, affiliation (the need to be with others), approval, status, security, and achievement. The important motives of fear and aggression also appear to be subject to learning.

Incentive value The value a goal holds for a person or animal above and beyond its ability to fill a need.

Primary motives Innate motives based on biological needs.

Stimulus motives Innate needs for stimulation and information.

Secondary motives Motives based on learned psychological needs.

Homeostasis A steady state of bodily equilibrium normally maintained automatically by various physiological mechanisms.

primary motives – innate, surviv

stimulus motives – innate, provide nervous system w/ curiosity, exploration ect.

Learned, secondary – power, status, approval, security.

Primary Motives and Homeostasis—Keeping the Home Fires Burning

How important is food in your life? Water? Sleep? Air? Temperature regulation? For most of us, satisfying these biological needs is so habitual we tend to overlook how much of our behavior they actually direct. But exaggerate any of these needs through famine, shipwreck, poverty, near-drowning, or exposure, and their powerful grip on behavior becomes evident. We are, after all, still animals in many ways.

Biological drives are essential because they maintain **homeostasis** (HOE-me-oh-STAY-sis), or bodily equilibrium (Cannon, 1932).

Question: What is homeostasis?

The term *homeostasis* means standing steady, or steady state. Within the body there are "ideal" levels for body temperature, for concentration of various chemicals in the blood, for blood pressure, and so forth. When the body deviates from these ideal levels, automatic reactions restore equilibrium. You might find it helpful to think of the homeostatic mechanisms as being similar in operation to a *thermostat* set at a particular temperature.

A (Very) Short Course on Thermostats

If room temperature falls below the level set on a thermostat, the heat is automatically turned on to warm the room. When the heat equals or slightly exceeds the ideal temperature, it is automatically turned off. In this way room temperature is maintained in a state of equilibrium hovering around the ideal level.

In the human body the first reactions to disequilibrium are also automatic. For example, if you become too hot, blood flow to body surfaces is increased and perspiring begins, thus lowering body temperature. We become aware of the need to maintain homeostasis only when driven by continued disequilibrium to seek shade, warmth, food, or water.

Since hunger is one of the most interesting and better understood of the primary drives, we will examine it in detail before we discuss biological drives in general. Before reading more, you may find it helpful to complete the Learning Check that follows.

Learning Check

1. Motives __initiate__, sustain, and __direct__ activities.

2. Needs provide the __push__ of motivation, whereas incentives provide the __pull__.

Classify the following needs or motives by placing the correct letter in the blank.

A. Primary motive **B.** Stimulus motive **C.** Secondary motive

3. _B_ curiosity **6.** _A_ thirst

4. _C_ status **7.** _C_ achievement

5. _A_ sleep **8.** _B_ physical contact

9. The maintenance of bodily equilibrium is called thermostasis. T or F?

10. A goal high in incentive value may create a drive in the absence of any internal need. T or F?

Answers: **1.** initiate, direct **2.** push, pull **3.** B **4.** C **5.** A **6.** A **7.** C **8.** B **9.** F **10.** T

Hunger— Pardon Me, That's Just My Hypothalamus Growling

Question: What causes hunger?

When you feel hungry, you probably associate a desire for food with sensations from your stomach. This, sensibly enough, is where the search for hunger began. In an early study Cannon and Washburn (1912) decided to see if the contractions of an empty stomach cause hunger. To do this, Washburn trained himself to swallow a balloon. Once it was in his stomach, the balloon was inflated through an attached tube so that stomach contractions could be recorded (see Fig. 11-2). Cannon and Washburn observed that when Washburn's stomach contracted, he felt "hunger pangs." They concluded that hunger is nothing more than stomach contractions.

Later research contradicted this conclusion. Perhaps you already guessed that something more than the stomach is involved in hunger. Many people experience hunger as an overall feeling of weakness or shakiness that does not seem to be associated with the stomach. And, while eating *is* limited when the stomach is distended (full), it can be shown that the stomach is not essential for experiencing hunger.

Question: How has that been demonstrated?

For one thing, cutting the sensory nerves from the stomach (so that stomach sensations can no longer be felt) does not abolish hunger. Even more convincing is the fact that many people have had their stomachs removed surgically. These people continue to feel hungry and to eat regularly. It would seem that some *central* factor must be the cause of hunger. One important element now appears to be the level of sugar in the blood. If insulin is injected in a human, it produces **hypoglycemia** (HI-po-gli-SEE-me-ah: low blood sugar) and stimulates feelings of hunger and stomach contractions (Hoyenga & Hoyenga, 1984). Strange as it may seem, the liver may also affect hunger.

Question: The liver?

Yes, the liver. Evidence suggests that the liver responds to a lack of bodily "fuel" by sending nerve impulses to the brain, thus triggering the desire to eat (Friedman & Stricker, 1976).

Question: What part of the brain controls hunger?

When you are hungry, many brain areas are affected, so no single "hunger center" exists. However, one of the most important areas for the control of hunger is the **hypothalamus** (HI-po-THAL-ah-mus), a small structure near the base of the brain (see Fig. 11-3).

Cells in the hypothalamus are sensitive to levels of sugar (and perhaps other substances) in the blood. The hypothalamus also receives messages from the liver and the stomach (Hoyenga & Hoyenga, 1984). These messages combine to produce hunger. One area of the hypothalamus acts somewhat like a **feeding system.** If the *lateral hypothalamus* is activated electrically, even a well-fed animal will immediately begin eating. (The term *lateral* simply means side—in this case the sides of the hypothalamus.) If the same area is destroyed, the animal will refuse to eat and will die if not force-fed (Anand & Brobeck, 1951).

A second area within the hypothalamus seems to serve as a **satiety system** (or "stop system") for eating. If the *ventromedial hypothalamus* is destroyed, dramatic

Hypoglycemia Below-normal blood sugar level.

Hypothalamus A small area at the base of the brain that regulates many aspects of motivation and emotion, especially hunger, thirst, and sexual behavior.

Feeding system Areas on each side of the hypothalamus that initiate eating when stimulated.

Satiety system Areas on the bottom middle of the hypothalamus that terminate eating.

Fig. 11-2 *In Cannon's early study of hunger, a simple apparatus was used to simultaneously record hunger pangs and stomach contractions. (After Cannon, 1934)*

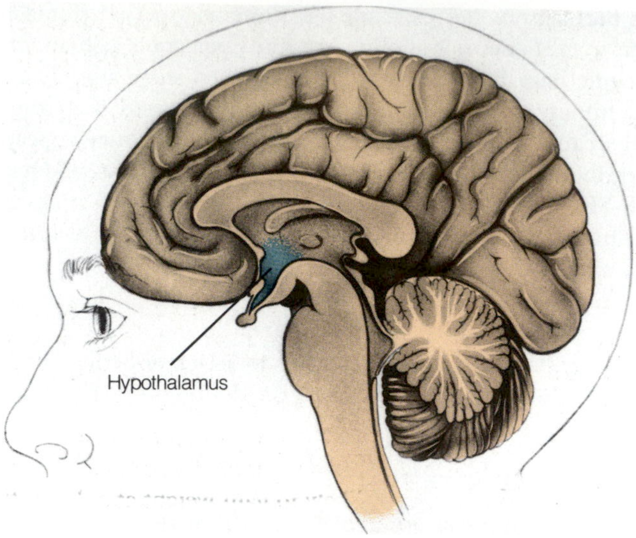

Fig. 11-3 *Location of the hypothalamus in the human brain.*

overeating results. (*Ventromedial* refers to the bottom middle of the hypothalamus.) Rats with such damage overeat to the point of total obesity. Some balloon up to weights of 1000 grams or more and get so large that they can barely move (see Fig. 11-4). A normal rat weighs about 180 grams. To picture this weight change in human terms, envision someone you know who weighs 180 pounds growing to a weight of 1000 pounds!

Fig. 11-4 *Damage to the hunger-satiety system in the hypothalamus can produce a very fat rat, a condition called hypothalamic* hyperphagia *(overeating). This rat weighs 1080 grams. (The pointer has gone completely around the dial and beyond.) (Photo courtesy of Neal Miller)*

It should come as no surprise that there is more to hunger than simple "start" and "stop" systems in the brain. Recent evidence suggests that fat stored in the body also influences hunger. The body acts as if there is a **set point** for the *proportion* of body fat that is maintained (Le Magnen, 1980). That is, the set point acts like a "thermostat" for body fat. Your personal set point is the weight you maintain when you are making no effort to gain or lose weight. When your body goes below its set point, you are likely to feel hungry most of the time (Friedman & Stricker, 1976).

Question: Do people have different set points?

Yes. The set point appears to be partly inherited and partly determined by early feeding patterns. Persons with overweight parents are much more likely to be overweight themselves. Also, the set point may be lastingly altered when a child is overfed. If a weight problem begins in childhood, the person will, as an adult, have *more* fat cells and *larger* fat cells in the body. If the person does not become overweight until adulthood, his or her fat cells will be larger, but their number usually does not increase. Thus, when a weight problem begins in childhood, it is much more difficult to control.

Question: Why do people overeat?

Obesity Set points are only one piece in a complex puzzle that scientists are still trying to solve. Their search is fueled by the fact that obesity is a major health risk and, for many, a source of social stigma and low self-esteem (Brownell, 1982).

Perhaps if eating were controlled only by internal needs, fewer people would overeat. As noted earlier, however, the sight or aroma of food often makes people want to eat, even when they do not feel hungry. It seems that many people are sensitive to **external eating cues** (signs and signals linked with food) (Rodin, 1978). If you are sensitive to external cues, you are most likely to eat when food is attractive, highly visible, and easy to obtain (Schachter & Rodin, 1974).

Question: Does that mean that people who are overweight are more sensitive to external eating cues?

Until recently, the obese were thought to be "externally cued eaters." Lean people, in contrast, were assumed to be better attuned to internal hunger signals. Unfortunately, this idea is now recognized as too simple. People of all weights can be found who are unusually sensitive to external eating cues, so this is not strictly a problem of the obese (Rodin, 1981). Just the same, eating cues do appear to be a factor in some overeating. For example, psychologist Judith Rodin found that externally responsive girls were most likely to gain weight at a 2-month summer camp (Rodin, 1978).

It is highly likely that **diet** also contributes to overeating. Placing animals on a "supermarket" diet, for instance, can lead to gross obesity. In one experiment rats were given meals of chocolate chip cookies, salami, cheese, bananas, marshmallows, milk chocolate, peanut butter, and fat. Rats on this diet gained almost three times as much weight as controls who ate only standard laboratory rat chow (Sclafani & Springer, 1976). (Rat chow is a dry mixture of several bland foods. If you were a rat, you'd probably eat more cookies than rat chow too!) We humans also appear to be sensitive to dietary content. In general, *sweetness*, high *fat content*, and *variety* tend to encourage overeating (Ball & Grinker, 1981). It seems that our culture may provide the worst possible kinds of foods for those with a tendency toward obesity.

It is tempting to assume that fatness comes from constant overeating, but this is a myth. Studies by Albert Stunkard (1980) and Judith Rodin (1978) show that overeating occurs mainly when a person is gaining weight. Once excess weight is gained, it can be maintained with a normal diet. An added problem is that as people gain weight, many reduce their activity level and burn fewer calories. As a result, some overweight persons may continue to gain weight while consuming fewer calories than their slimmer neighbors (Ball & Grinker, 1981).

Question: Is it true that people also overeat when they are emotionally upset?

Yes. People with weight problems are just as likely to eat when they are anxious, angry, bored, or distressed as when hungry (Bruch, 1973; Hoyenga & Hoyenga, 1984). Furthermore, unhappiness often accompanies obesity in our fat-conscious culture (Rodin, 1978). The result is a pattern of overeating that leads to emotional distress and still more overeating, making weight control extremely difficult.

To summarize, overeating is the result of a complex interplay of internal and external influences, diet, emotions, genetics, exercise, and many other factors (Rodin, 1978). To answer the question we began with, people become obese in different ways and for different reasons. Clearly, scientists are still a long way from winning the "battle of the bulge." (For another perspective on overeating, see Box 11-1.)

Set point A theoretical proportion of body fat that tends to be maintained by changes in hunger and eating.

External eating cue Any external stimulus that tends to encourage hunger or to elicit eating.

Diet The types and amounts of food and drink regularly consumed over a period of time.

Box 11-1

The Dieter's Dilemma

If dieting works, why are hundreds of "new" diets published each year? The answer is that while dieters do lose weight, most regain it soon after the diet ends. Indeed, many people experience a rebound that can push weight higher than before the diet began. Why should this be so? Many theorists now believe that dieting (starving) alters the physiology of the body. In effect, dieting causes the body to become highly efficient at *conserving* calories and storing them as fat (Bennet & Gurin, 1982; Hoyenga & Hoyenga, 1984).

Apparently, evolution has prepared us to save energy when food is scarce and to stock up on fat when food is plentiful. Briefly starving yourself, therefore, may have little lasting effect on weight. To avoid ineffectively bounding between feast and famine requires a change in basic eating habits—a topic covered in this chapter's Applications.

Other Factors in Hunger

As research on overeating suggests, "hunger" is affected by more than bodily needs for food. Let us consider some additional factors of interest.

Cultural Factors Learning to think of some foods as desirable and others as revolting obviously has much to do with eating habits. In America we would never consider eating the eyes out of the steamed head of a monkey, but in some parts of the world this dish is considered a real delicacy. By the same token, our willingness to consume large quantities of meat, to eat cows, and to cook fish would be considered barbaric in many cultures. Thus, **cultural values** greatly affect the incentive value of various foods.

Taste Even tastes for "normal" foods may vary considerably. One experiment demonstrated that the hungrier a person is, the more pleasant a sweet food tastes (Cabanac & Duclaux, 1970). It is also interesting to note that a **taste aversion** can be easily learned if a food causes sickness, or if it is eaten just before nausea is caused by something else (Nachman, 1970). Not only will such foods be avoided, they too can become nauseating. A friend of the author's, who once became ill after eating a cheese Danish (well, actually, *several*), has never again been able to come face to face with this delightful pastry. Such learning usually helps protect both animals and people (Garcia et al., 1984).

If you like animals, you will be interested in an imaginative approach to an age-old problem. In many parts of the country, predators are poisoned, trapped, or shot on sight by livestock owners. These practices have virtually extinguished the timber wolf, and in some areas the coyote faces a similar end. How might the coyote be saved, without an unacceptable loss of livestock?

In a now classic experiment, coyotes were given lamb tainted with lithium chloride. Coyotes who took the bait rapidly became nauseated and vomited. After one or two such treatments, they developed **bait shyness**—a lasting distaste for the tainted food (Gustavson & Garcia, 1974). If applied consistently, taste aversion conditioning might solve many predator-livestock problems at less expense than traditional methods (Fig. 11-5). Perhaps this technique could even be used to protect roadrunners from the Wiley Coyote!

Specific Hungers Evidence exists that animals and people are able to develop **specific hungers** for nutritional substances lacking in their diet. For example, if animals are made ill by being deprived of vitamin B, they develop a marked preference for foods containing this essential vitamin (Scott & Verrey, 1947).

Question: Then do humans have specific hungers?

There is some direct evidence of specific hungers occurring in humans, particularly in children. In one classic experiment on **self-selection feeding,** human infants were given a daily "cafeteria" choice of foods. Over a period of several months they selected a balanced diet, and their health and growth were normal (Davis, 1928). In fact, one child who began the study suffering from rickets voluntarily drank large amounts of foul-tasting cod-liver oil and apparently cured himself of his nutritional disease.

It should be noted, however, that the "wisdom of the body" is actually fairly limited. In the experiment described, the babies could only select from nutritious foods. If candy had been a choice, they might not have done so well. Even by early childhood, learned food preferences tend to override specific hungers, so that poor diets of sweets and junk food are not uncommon in our society.

Eating Disorders

Under the sheets of her hospital bed Krystal looks like a starved skeleton. If her self-destructive course cannot be changed, Krystal may die of malnutrition. How could things go so desperately wrong with a motive as basic as hunger?

Serious cases of undereating like Krystal's are called **anorexia nervosa** (AN-uh-REK-see-yah ner-VOH-sah). Victims of anorexia, who are mostly adolescent females (5 to 10 percent are male), suffer devastating weight loss from self-inflicted starvation.

Question: Do anorexics lose their appetite?

Anorexia nervosa is not a simple loss of desire for food. Many anorexics continue to feel hunger, and yet they struggle to starve themselves. The problem can best be described as a *relentless pursuit of excessive thinness*. Persons who suffer from anorexia nervosa have an obsessive fear of gaining weight. Often, the problem starts with normal dieting that gradually begins to dominate the person's life. In time, anorexics suffer physical weakness, absence of menstrual cycles, and a dangerous risk of infection. Five to eight percent (that's more than 1 in 20) die of malnutrition or related health problems.

Bulimia (bue-LIHM-ee-yah), also known as the binge-purge syndrome, is a second major eating disorder. Bulimics gorge on food, then induce vomiting or take laxatives to avoid gaining weight. Like anorexia, bulimia is far more prevalent in women than in men. A recent study of college women found that 5 percent (1 out of 20) are bulimic (Ollendick & Hart, 1985).

In a culture that values slimness, bulimia may seem relatively harmless. However, like anorexia nervosa, binging and purging can cause serious health prob-

Cultural values The values attached to various objects and activities by the majority of people in a given culture.

Taste aversion An active dislike for a particular food; frequently created when the food is associated with illness or discomfort.

Bait shyness An unwillingness or hesitation on the part of animals to eat a particular food; often caused by the presence of a taste aversion.

Specific hunger A heightened desire for, or consumption of, a particular food item, especially one that remedies a nutritional deficiency.

Self-selection feeding Allowing persons or animals to feed themselves by choosing freely from a large variety of foods.

Anorexia nervosa A sustained loss of appetite that has psychological origins; self-starvation.

Bulimia Excessive eating (gorging) usually followed by self-induced vomiting and/or taking laxatives.

Fig. 11-5 *Like humans and other animals, coyotes develop taste aversions when food is associated with nausea.*

lems. Typical risks include sore throat, hair loss, muscle spasms, kidney damage, dehydration, erosion of tooth enamel, swelling of the salivary glands, menstrual irregularity, loss of sex drive, and even heart attack.

Question: What causes anorexia and bulimia?

Causes Both anorexics and bulimics have exaggerated fears of becoming fat and unrealistic views of what constitutes normal size. Anorexics, especially, have distorted body images. Most overestimate their body size by 25 percent or more and continue to see themselves as "fat" when in fact they are wasting away.

Anorexics are usually described as "perfect" daughters—helpful, considerate, conforming, and obedient. Many are would-be-high achievers who frantically try to be "perfect" in one area—to have complete control over their weight and to be perfectly slim. The thought of gaining weight fills them with terror—they literally feel that they are losing control. Bulimics also seem to be concerned with control. For them, however, maintaining control is an ongoing struggle. Bulimics are obsessed with thoughts of weight, food, eating, and ridding themselves of food. As a result, most feel guilt, shame, self-contempt, and anxiety after a binge. For many, vomiting reduces the anxiety triggered by a binge. This makes purging highly reinforcing.

Treatment In almost all cases, a person with anorexia or bulimia will need professional help to restore normal eating. Treatment for anorexia usually begins with admitting the person to a hospital. There, a carefully controlled diet is used to restore weight and health. As a second step the client enters counseling to work on the personal conflicts and family issues that led to weight loss. For bulimia, psychologists have had some success with behavioral counseling that includes careful self-monitoring of food intake and work on extinguishing the urge to vomit after eating.

Although much progress is being made in treating eating disorders, most anorexics and bulimics do not seek help, and many actively resist it. With this in mind, it is worth emphasizing again that eating disorders are serious, health-threatening problems that rarely disappear on their own. (Sources: DSM Ill, 1980; Moore, 1981; Polivy & Herman, 1985; Rosen & Leitenburg, 1982; Schlessier-Stroop, 1984.)

Primary Motives Revisited—The Strange Case of Sex and Pain

The pattern we observed in the control of hunger is similar to that found for most other primary motives. For example, thirst is only partially related to dryness of the mouth and throat. When drugs are used to keep the mouth constantly wet or dry, thirst and water intake remain normal. Like hunger, thirst appears to be controlled through the hypothalamus, where separate *thirst* and *thirst-satiety* systems are found. Also like hunger, thirst is strongly affected by individual learning and by cultural values.

Question: Is there such a thing as a "specific thirst"?

In a sense there is. Before the body can retain water, minerals lost through perspiration (mainly salt) must be replaced. Therefore, animals develop a marked preference for salt water when their salt levels are lowered experimentally (Carlson, 1981).

You may not have noticed, but there are actually two kinds of thirst. **Extracellular thirst** occurs when there is a loss of water from the fluids surrounding the cells of your body. Bleeding, vomiting, diarrhea, sweating, and drinking alcohol cause this type of thirst (Houston, 1985). When a person loses both water and minerals in any of these ways—especially by perspiring—a slightly salty liquid may be more satisfying than plain water. Among some nomadic peoples of the Sahara Desert, blood is a highly prized beverage, perhaps because of its saltiness. (Maybe they should try Gatorade?)

A second type of thirst occurs when you eat a salty meal. In this instance your body does not lose fluid. Instead, an increase in salt causes fluid to be drawn out of cells. As the cells "shrink," **intracellular thirst** is triggered. Thirst of this type is best quenched with plain water.

The drives for food, water, air, sleep, and elimination are all fairly similar in that they are generated by a combination of activities in the body and the brain, are modified by learning and culture, and are influenced by external factors. Two of the primary drives are unlike the others. These are the sex drive and the drive to avoid pain. Each differs from the other primary drives in some interesting ways.

Question: How is the drive to avoid pain different?

Pain Drives such as hunger, thirst, and sleepiness come and go in a fairly regular cycle each day. Pain, by contrast, is an **episodic drive** (ep-ih-SOD-ik). That is, it occurs in distinct episodes, since it is aroused only when damage to the tissues of the body is threatened. Most of the primary drives cause a person to actively seek a desired goal (food, drink, sleep, and so forth). The pain drive has as its goal the avoidance or elimination of pain.

The desire to end pain seems so basic that it may come as a surprise that avoiding pain appears to be partially learned. This fact was demonstrated by a study in which dogs were totally isolated (in special cages) from the normal bumps, bites, and other pains of puppyhood. As adults, the dogs reacted strangely to pain. For example, when a lighted match was held near their noses, many pushed toward it as if they felt no pain (Melzack & Scott, 1957). Apparently, the dogs had not learned the meaning of pain or how to avoid it.

Human pain avoidance is also affected by learning. Some people, for instance, feel they must be "tough" and not show any discomfort; others complain loudly at the smallest ache or pain. As you might expect, the first attitude raises pain tolerance, and the second lowers it (Klienke, 1978). Such attitudes explain why members of some societies endure cutting, burning, whipping, tatooing, and piercing of the skin that would agonize the typical American.

The Sex Drive Sexual motivation is quite unusual compared with other biological motives. In fact, many psychologists do not think of sex as a primary motive because sex (contrary to anything your personal experience might suggest) is not necessary for *individual* survival. It is necessary, of course, for *group* survival among humans and other creatures.

In lower animals the sex drive is directly related to the action of bodily hormones. Females of the lower species are only interested in mating when their fertility cycle is in the stage of **estrus,** or "heat" (caused by secretion of the hormone **estrogen** into the bloodstream). Hormones are important in the male animal as well. In most lower animals castration will abolish the sex drive. But in

Extracellular thirst Thirst caused by a reduction in the volume of fluids found between body cells.

Intracellular thirst Thirst triggered when fluid is drawn out of cells due to an increased concentration of salts and minerals outside the cell.

Episodic drive A non-cyclical drive that occurs in distinct episodes associated with particular conditions (for example, pain avoidance, sexual motivation).

Estrus Changes in the reproductive organs and sexual drives of animals associated with a desire for mating, particularly used to refer to females in heat.

Estrogen Any of a number of female sex hormones.

Nonhomeostatic drive A drive that is relatively independent of physiological deprivation cycles or bodily need states.

contrast to the female, the normal male animal is always ready to mate. His sex drive is primarily aroused by the behavior of a receptive female. In animals, mating is therefore closely tied to the fertility cycle of the female.

Question: How much do hormones affect the sex drive in humans?

The link between hormones and the sex drive grows weaker as we ascend the biological scale. Hormones do affect the human sex drive but only to a limited degree. For example, one careful study found no connection between female sexual activity and the monthly menstrual cycle (Udry & Morris, 1977). In humans, mental, cultural, and emotional factors determine sexual expression. However, our liberation from hormones is not total. Human males show a loss of sex drive after castration, and some women lose sexual desire when using birth control pills (McCauley & Ehrhardt, 1976).

Human sexual behavior and attitudes are discussed in detail in Chapter 23. For now it is enough to note that the sex drive is largely **nonhomeostatic.** In humans the sex drive can be aroused at virtually any time by almost anything. It therefore shows no clear relationship to deprivation (the amount of time since the drive was last satisfied). True, an increase in desire may occur as time passes. But, on the other hand, recent sexual activity does not prevent sexual desire from occurring again. The sex drive is also unusual in that its arousal is as actively sought as its reduction. This quality of the sex drive makes it capable of motivating an unusually wide range of behaviors. It also accounts for its use to sell almost everything imaginable.

Learning Check

1. Systems for the control of hunger and thirst are found in the ______________ of the brain.

2. The satiety system in the hypothalamus signals the body to start eating when it receives signals from the liver or detects changes in blood sugar. T or F?

3. Varied diets containing high levels of sweets and fats encourage overeating only for people who tend to eat when they are anxious. T or F?

4. Bait shyness occurs when:
a. a specific hunger develops
b. the set point for body fat is altered
c. the hypothalamus is activated electrically
d. a taste aversion is formed

5. If an animal is deprived of a necessary food substance, the animal may develop a/an: (circle)

taste aversion estrus drive specific hunger

6. Anorexia nervosa is also known as the binge-purge syndrome. T or F?

7. Five to eight percent of anorexics die of malnutrition or related problems. T or F?

8. Thirst may be either intracellular or ______________.

9. Pain avoidance is an ______________ drive.

10. Sexual behavior in animals is largely controlled by estrogen levels in the female and the occurrence of estrus in the male. T or F?

Answers: **1.** hypothalamus **2.** F **3.** F **4.** *d* **5.** specific hunger **6.** F **7.** T **8.** extracellular **9.** episodic **10.** F

Stimulus Needs— Skydiving, Horror Movies, and the Fun Zone

"Curiosity killed the cat" is sometimes said, but nothing could be further from the truth. Drives for **exploration, manipulation,** or simply for **curiosity** seem to exist in most animals. As mentioned earlier, such drives might be explained by the life-and-death necessity of keeping track of sources of food, danger, and other important details of the environment. However, the curiosity drives seem to go beyond such needs.

Exploration drive A hypothesized drive assumed to underlie an organism's tendency to investigate unfamiliar areas of its environment.

Manipulation drive A hypothesized drive assumed to explain the tendency of organisms to investigate objects by touching and handling them.

Curiosity drive A hypothesized drive assumed to underlie a wide range of investigative and stimulus-seeking behaviors.

Sensory deprivation A condition in which there is a marked reduction in the amount of sensory stimulation to which one is exposed.

Monkey Business

In an experiment, monkeys confined to a dimly lit box learned to perform a simple task to open a window that allowed them to view the outside world (Butler & Harlow, 1954). In a similar experiment, monkeys quickly learned to solve a mechanical puzzle made up of interlocking metal pins, hooks, and hasps (Butler, 1954) (see Fig. 11-6). In both situations no external reward was offered for exploration or manipulation.

The monkeys seemed to work for the sheer fun of it. An interest in video games, chess, puzzles, Rubick's cube, and the like offers a human parallel. Curiosity, the drive to *know*, also seems to be powerful in humans. Scientific investigation, intellectual curiosity, and other advanced activities may be an extension of this basic drive.

Closely related to curiosity is the need for sensory stimulation. It is now well established that humans and animals demand and actively seek stimulation (Reykowski, 1982). As discussed in Chapter 6, people who have undergone prolonged or severe **sensory deprivation**—for example, prisoners, arctic explorers, radar operators, and truck drivers—often report sensory distortions and disturbed thinking. The nervous system seems to require varied, patterned stimulation in order to respond normally (Suedfeld, 1975).

The drive for stimulation can even be observed in infants. When babies are shown patterns of varying complexity (Fig. 11-7), they spend more time looking at complex patterns than at simpler ones (Berlyne, 1966). Indeed, human infants

Fig. 11-6 *Monkeys happily open locks that are placed in their cage. Since no reward is given for this activity, it provides evidence of the existence of stimulus needs. (Photo courtesy of Harry F. Harlow)*

Fig. 11-7 *Berlyne studied curiosity in infants by showing them these designs. Babies looked first at the more complex patterns on the right. (From* Science *153:25–33. Copyright © 1966 by the American Association for the Advancement of Science)*

seem to have an almost limitless appetite for stimulation. By the time a child can walk, there are few things in the home that have not been tasted, touched, viewed, handled, or, in the case of toys, destroyed!

Question: Are stimulus needs homeostatic?

Arousal Theory Some psychologists would argue that they are not. However, by relating drives for stimulation to the concept of homeostasis, we get a useful model for understanding many human activities. This position, called the **arousal theory** of motivation, assumes that there is an ideal level of arousal for various activities and that individuals behave in ways that keep arousal near this ideal level (Hebb, 1966).

Question: What do you mean by "arousal"?

Arousal refers to variations in activation of the body and the nervous system. Arousal is zero at death; it is low during sleep; it is moderate during daily activities; and it is high at times of excitement, emotion, or panic. Arousal theory assumes that an individual becomes uncomfortable when arousal is too low (as when a person is bored) or when it is too high (as might be the case during intense fear, anxiety, or panic). Curiosity and the drive to seek stimulation can be interpreted as an attempt to raise the level of arousal when it is too low. Most adults seem to vary their activities to maintain a comfortable level of activation. Music, parties, athletics, conversation, sleep, and many other activities may be mixed to keep arousal at moderate levels, thus preventing both boredom and overstimulation.

Question: Do people vary in their needs for stimulation?

Sensation Seekers The city dweller who visits the country complains that it is "too quiet," and seeks some "action." The country dweller finds the city "hectic," "overwhelming," or "too much," and seeks peace and quiet. The arousal theory of motivation also assumes that the ideal level of arousal varies from one person to the next and that individuals learn to seek a particular arousal level.

Marvin Zuckerman has devised a test to measure such differences. The *Sensation-Seeking Scale* (SSS), as he calls it, includes statements like the samples shown here (from Zuckerman et al., 1978).

Arousal theory A theory of motivation that assumes people prefer to maintain "ideal," or comfortable, levels of arousal.

Arousal The overall level of excitation or activation present at any given time in a person or animal.

Sensation seeking A personality characteristic of persons who prefer high levels of stimulation.

Thrill and Adventure Seeking

I would like to try parachute jumping.
I think I would enjoy the sensations of skiing very fast down a high mountain slope.

Experience Seeking

I like to explore a strange city or section of town myself, even if it means getting lost.
I like to try new foods that I have never tasted before.

Disinhibition

I like wild, "uninhibited" parties.
I often like to get high (drinking liquor or smoking marijuana).

Boredom Susceptibility

I can't stand watching a movie that I've seen before.
I like people who are sharp and witty, even if they do sometimes insult others.

People who score high on the full-length version of this test tend to be extroverted, independent individuals who value change and stimulation (Fig. 11-8). In addition, high scorers are more likely to smoke and to prefer spicy, sour, and crunchy foods over blander foods. Low sensation seekers are orderly, nurturant, giving, and enjoy the company of others (Zuckerman, 1978). Which are you? (Most people fall somewhere in between.)

Question: Is there an ideal level of arousal?

Levels of Arousal Discounting individual differences, performance of a task is usually best when arousal is moderate. Let's say that you have to take an essay exam in one of your classes. If you are sleepy or feeling lazy (arousal level too low), your performance will suffer. If you are in a state of anxiety or panic about

Fig. 11-8 *Thrill seeking is an element of the sensation-seeking personality.*

Inverted U function A curve, roughly in the shape of an upside-down U, that relates the quality of performance to levels of arousal.

Yerkes-Dodson law A qualification of the inverted U function that states the relationships among arousal, task complexity, and performance.

Test anxiety High levels of arousal and worry that can seriously impair test performance.

Circadian rhythms Cyclical changes in bodily function and arousal that vary on a schedule approximating one 24-hour day.

the test (arousal level too high), you will also perform below par. This relationship between arousal and efficiency of behavior can be expressed as an **inverted U function** (see Fig. 11-9). At very low levels of arousal, the body is not sufficiently energized to perform effectively. With increased arousal, performance continues to improve up to the middle regions of the curve; then it begins to drop off as an individual becomes emotional, frenzied, or disorganized. Such disorganization might occur if you were trying to start a car stalled on a railroad track, with a speeding train bearing down on you.

Question: Is performance always best at moderate levels of arousal?

No, the optimal level of arousal depends on the complexity of the task to be performed. For simple tasks, greater activation runs little risk of disorganizing performance. If a task is relatively *simple*, the optimal level of arousal will be *high*. When a task is more *complex*, the best performance occurs at *low* levels of arousal. This relationship is called the **Yerkes-Dodson law** (see Fig. 11-9). It applies to a wide variety of tasks and to measures of motivation other than arousal.

Some examples of the Yerkes-Dodson law in operation might be helpful. At a track meet it is almost impossible for a sprinter to get too aroused for a race. The task is direct and uncomplicated: Run as fast as you can for a short distance. On the other hand, a golfer making the last putt in an important tournament faces a more sensitive and complex task, as does a basketball player making a game-deciding free throw. Excessive arousal is almost certain to hurt such performances. In school, most students have had experience with "test anxiety" as a familiar example of the effects of excessive arousal on performance.

Question: Then is it true that by learning to calm down, a person would do better on tests?

Usually, but not always. Studies of anxious students show that they typically are most anxious when they don't know the material. If this is the case, calming down simply means you will remain calm while failing. One of the best ways to overcome test anxiety is to be overprepared (Spielberger et al., 1976). (See Box 11-2.)

Fig. 11-9 (a) *The general relationship between arousal and efficiency can be described by an inverted U curve. The optimal level of arousal or motivation is higher for a simple task* (b) *than for a complex task* (c).

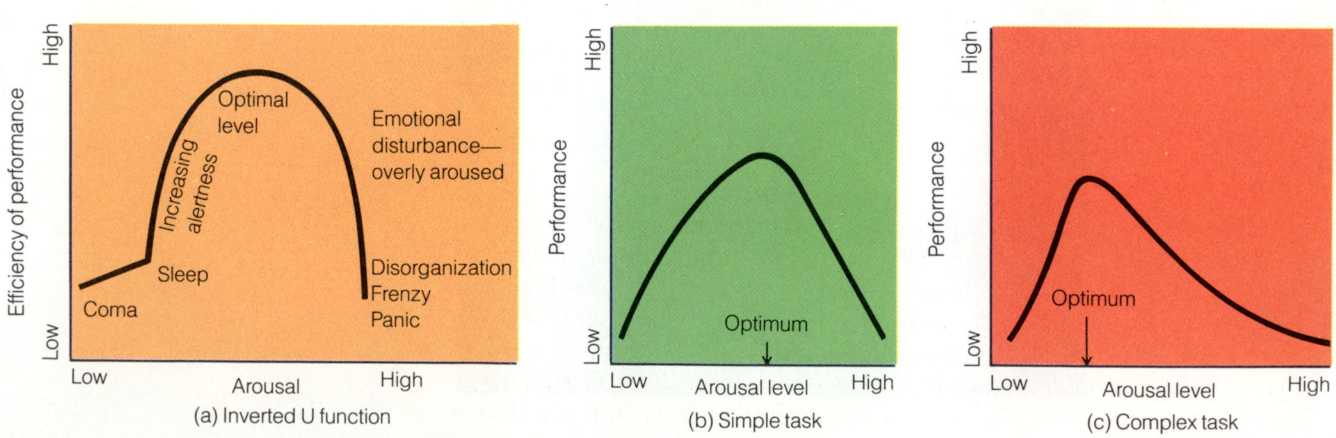

Box 11-2

Coping with Test Anxiety

Test anxiety refers to a combination of heightened *physiological arousal* (uneasiness, tension, sweating, pounding heart, nervousness) plus excessive *worry* during test taking. This potent combination—worry plus arousal—tends to distract students with a rush of upsetting thoughts and feelings (Mueller & Thompson, 1984).

Treating Test Anxiety

In recent years psychologists have become relatively successful in treating test anxiety. Let's see what can be learned from their efforts.

Preparation The most direct antidote for test anxiety is *hard work.* Many test-anxious students simply study too little and too late (Becker, 1982). Thus, one solution for test anxiety is to *overprepare* by studying well in advance of the "big day." Students who are well prepared score higher, worry less, and they are less likely to become overly aroused (Lazarus & Folkman, 1984).

Relaxation Learning to relax can also help lower test anxiety (Ricketts & Galloway, 1984). Students interested in learning self-relaxation skills should look ahead to Chapter 22, where a relaxation technique is described. Test anxiety is also lowered by support from others (Sarason, 1981). If you tend to be overly anxious during tests, you may find it helpful to discuss the problem with your professor. Preparing for the test with a supportive friend or classmate can also help.

Rehearsal Some students find that nervousness during tests can be lessened by carefully *rehearsing* how they will cope with upsetting events. Before taking a test, imagine yourself going blank, running out of time, or feeling panicked. Then calmly plan how you will handle each situation—by keeping your attention on the task, by focusing on one question at a time, and so forth (Watson & Tharp, 1981).

Restructuring Thoughts Because worries are a major part of test anxiety, changing self-defeating thinking can be the best solution of all (Wise & Haynes, 1983). Test-anxious students often benefit from listing the kinds of distracting and self-defeating thoughts they have during exams. They then work on learning to counter their worries with calming, rational replies. (See Chapter 13 Applications for more information.)

Let's say, for example, that a student thinks, "I'm going to fail this test, and all my friends will think I'm stupid." To counter this upsetting thought, he or she might say, "If I prepare well and control my worries, I will probably pass the test. Even if I don't, it won't be the end of the world. My friends will still like me, and I can try to improve on the next test."

Students who cope well with testing typically take a practical attitude and try to do the best they can, even under trying circumstances. With practice, most students can learn to be less testy at test-taking time.

Circadian Rhythms

We have seen that moment-to-moment changes in arousal can have a large impact on performance in many situations. What about larger cycles of arousal? Do they also affect energy levels, motivation, and performance? Scientists have long known that the body operates like a finely tuned instrument, guided by internal "biological clocks." Every 24 hours your body undergoes a complex cycle of changes called **circadian** (SUR-kay-dee-AN) **rhythms** (*circa:* about; *diem:* a day).

Throughout the day, large changes take place in body temperature, blood pres-

Social motives Learned motives acquired as part of growing up in a particular society or culture.

sure, urine volume, and amino acid level. Also affected are the liver, kidneys, and endocrine glands. These bodily activities, and many others, peak sometime each day (Moore-Ede et al., 1982). Especially important is the output of the hormone adrenaline, which causes general arousal. Adrenaline is often 3 to 5 times greater during the day (Luce, 1971).

Most people are more energetic and alert during the high point of their circadian rhythm (Horne et al., 1980). Differences in such peaks are so basic that even personal compatibility may be affected. When a "day person" rooms with a "night person," for example, both are more likely to give their relationship a negative rating (Watts, 1982). This is easy to understand: What could be worse than having someone bounding around cheerily when you're half asleep, or the reverse?

Shift Work and Jet Lag The effects of circadian rhythms become especially noticeable whenever there is a major shift in time schedules. It is well documented, for example, that businesspersons, diplomats, athletes, and other time zone travelers often make errors or perform poorly when their body rhythms are disturbed by jet lag (Rader & Hicks, 1987). If you travel great distances east or west, the peaks and valleys of your circadian rhythms will be out of phase with the sun and clocks. For example, you might find that your period of peak arousal occurs at 4 A.M., while your low point falls during the middle of the day. Shift work has the same effect, causing lower efficiency, as well as fatigue, irritability, upset stomach, nervousness, depression, and a decline in mental agility (Akerstedt, Torsvall, & Gillberg, 1982).

Question: How fast do people adapt to such time shifts?

For major time zone shifts (5 hours or more), it can take from several days to 2 weeks to resynchronize. Adaptation to jet lag is slowest when you stay indoors (in a hotel room, for instance), where you can continue to sleep and eat on "home time." Getting outdoors, where you must sleep, eat, and socialize on the new schedule, tends to speed adaptation (Moore-Ede et al., 1982).

The *direction* of travel also affects adaptation. If you fly west, adapting is relatively easy, taking an average of 4 to 5 days. If you fly east, adapting takes 50 percent longer or more. (See Fig. 11-10.) Why is there a difference? The answer is that when you fly east the sun comes up earlier (relative to your "home" time). As you fly west it comes up later. Most people find that it is easier to "advance" (stay up later and sleep in) than it is to shift backwards. When you travel east, you must go to sleep during your former afternoon and get up when your body thinks it is the middle of the night. Likewise, work shifts that "rotate" backward (night, evening, day) are more disruptive than those that advance (day, evening, night). Best of all are work shifts that do not change: Even continuous night work is less disruptive than shifts that change.

Question: What does all of this have to do with those of us who are not shift workers or world travelers?

There are few college students who have not at one time or another "burned the midnight oil," especially for final exams. During this or any other strenuous period, it is wise to remember the effects of disturbed bodily rhythms. Any major deviation from your regular schedule is likely to cost more than it's worth. Often, you can accomplish as much during 1 hour in the morning as you could have in

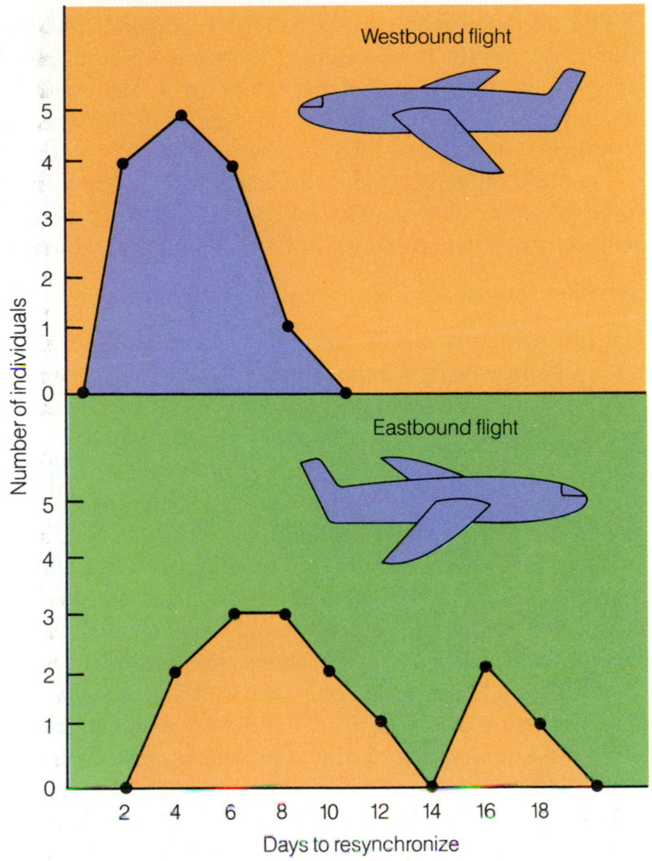

Fig. 11-10 *Time required to adjust to air travel across six time zones. The average time to resynchronize was faster for westbound travel than for eastbound flights. (Data from Beljan et al., 1972; cited by Moore-Ede et al., 1982)*

3 hours of work after midnight. The 2-hour difference in efficiency might as well be spent sleeping. If you feel you must depart from your normal schedule, do it gradually over a period of days.

In general, if you can anticipate an upcoming body rhythm change (when traveling, before finals week, or when doing shift work), it is best to *preadapt* yourself to your new schedule beforehand. Before traveling, for instance, you should go to sleep 1 hour later (or earlier) each day until your sleep cycle matches the time at your destination.

Learned Motives—The Pursuit of Excellence

Competition and achievement are highly valued in American culture. In less industrialized nations, the desire to achieve may be minimal. Some of your friends are more interested than others in success, money, possessions, status, love, approval, grades, dominance, power, or belonging to groups. In each case we are referring to differences in **social motives** or goals. Social motives are acquired in complex ways through socialization and cultural conditioning. The behavior of outstanding artists, scientists, athletes, educators, and leaders is best understood in terms of such learned needs, particularly the need for achievement.

Need for achievement (nAch) The desire to excel or meet some internalized standard of excellence.

Need for power The desire to have social impact and control over others.

Fear of success An aversion to success; anxiety triggered by success.

The **need for achievement (nAch)** is certainly not the only social motive of importance, but it is a prominent motive in American culture. To many people, being "motivated" means being interested in achievement. In other chapters we will investigate the motives behind aggression, love, affiliation, and seeking approval. For now, let us focus on the need for achievement.

The need for achievement can be defined as a desire to meet some *internalized standard of excellence* (McClelland, 1961). The person with high needs for achievement strives to do well in any situation in which evaluation takes place.

Question: Is that like the aggressive businessperson who strives for success?

Not necessarily. Needs for achievement may lead to material wealth and prestige, but a person who is a high achiever in art, music, science, or amateur athletics may be striving for excellence without concern for material reward. The need for achievement differs from a **need for power,** which is a desire to have *impact* or control over others (McClelland, 1975). People with strong needs for power want their importance to be visible: They buy expensive possessions, read flashy magazines, and try to exploit relationships.

David McClelland (1958, 1961) and a number of other psychologists have been interested in the effects of high or low needs for achievement. Using a simple measure of nAch, McClelland found that he could predict the behavior of high and low achievers in many situations. In one study, for example, the occupations of college graduates were compared with scores on a need for achievement test given in their sophomore year. Fourteen years after graduation, those who scored high in nAch were found more often in careers involving an element of risk and responsibility than were those with low nAch scores (McClelland, 1965). Interestingly, scores for achievement motivation have declined for students in recent years (Lueptow, 1980). Some psychologists believe this may help account for the dramatic decline in *Scholastic Aptitude Test* scores observed in the last decade (Hoyenga & Hoyenga, 1984).

Fig. 11-11 *The person with high needs for achievement strives to do well in any situation in which evaluation takes place.*

Characteristics of Achievers In front of you are five targets placed at various distances from where you are standing. You are given a beanbag to toss at the target of your choice. Target A, anyone can hit; target B, most people can hit; target C, some people can hit; target D, very few people can hit; target E is rarely if ever hit. If you hit A, you will receive $2; B, $4; C, $8; D, $16; and E, $32. You get only one toss. Which one would you choose? McClelland's research suggests that if you have a high need for achievement, you will select C or perhaps D.

Those high in nAch are *moderate* risk takers. When faced with a problem or challenge, persons high in nAch avoid goals that are too easy because such goals offer no sense of satisfaction. They also avoid long shots because there is no hope of success or because if success occurs, it will be due to luck rather than skill. Persons low in nAch select either sure things or impossible goals. Either way, there is no risk of personal responsibility for failure.

Desires for achievement and calculated risk taking are converted into successful performances of tasks in many situations. People high in nAch do better on various tasks in the laboratory. They are more likely to complete difficult tasks. They earn better grades in high school and college, and they tend to excel in their chosen occupations. College students high in nAch tend to attribute success to their own ability and failure to insufficient effort (Kleinke, 1978). Thus, high

Box 11-3

Who's Afraid of a Little Success?

Which of the following statements do you agree with?

1. I am happy only when I am doing better than others.
2. Achievement commands respect.
3. It is extremely important for me to do well in all things that I undertake.
4. Often the cost of success is greater than the reward.
5. I believe that successful people are often sad and lonely.
6. I think "success" has been emphasized too much in our culture.

(Source: Zuckerman & Allison, 1976.)

Agreement with the first three statements shows a positive attitude toward success. People who agree with the last three statements tend to avoid success. It might seem that avoiding success is always undesirable. In reality, an overemphasis on achievement can be as big a handicap as avoidance of success. Our society is notorious for its successful but unhappy workaholics. In the final analysis, a truly successful life strikes a balance between achievement and other needs.

nAch students are more likely to renew their efforts when faced with a poor performance. When the going gets tough, high achievers get going.

Fear of Success Have you ever hidden your talents in favor of blending into a group? Have you ever backed off from "winning" in sports or school? Have you ever "played dumb" with friends? Everyone has probably done so at times. Each of these actions involves an avoidance, or fear, of success (see Box 11-3). Obviously, fearing success can stifle efforts to achieve.

Why would anyone avoid success? Most often because: (1) Success can require a stressful shift in self-concept; (2) many people fear rejection when they stand out in a group; and (3) some people fear the extra demands of being a "successful person" (Tresemer, 1977). All three reasons are illustrated by a secretary who quit when she was offered a job as a supervisor. When asked why she quit, she said it was because she didn't want to be a "career woman," because she feared her former friends in the office would reject her, and because she disliked telling others what to do.

Question: Do fears of success occur more in women or men?

Both men and women appear to be equally subject to **fear of success** (Kearney, 1984). But in our culture there is often an extra conflict for women. By adulthood many men and women have learned to consider it "unfeminine" for a woman to excel (de Charms & Muir, 1978). Understandably, then, successful women are most often those who define achievement as an acceptable feminine quality (Kleinke, 1978). Perhaps the women's movement and changing attitudes will help remove this unnecessary stumbling block for future generations of talented and aspiring women.

Hierarchy of needs A rank ordering of needs based on their presumed potency.

Basic needs In Maslow's need hierarchy, the first two levels of needs, which are considered powerful but not personally enriching.

Growth needs In Maslow's need hierarchy, the higher-level needs associated with personal growth and development of personal potential.

Meta-needs In Maslow's hierarchy, those needs above and beyond the ordinary; needs associated with impulses for self-actualization.

The Key to Success? What does it take to achieve extraordinary success? Educational psychologist Benjamin Bloom conducted a study of America's top performers in six fields: concert pianists, Olympic swimmers, sculptors, tennis players, mathematicians, and research neurologists. Bloom (1985) found that drive and determination, not great natural talent, led to success in the lives of the high achievers studied.

The development of Bloom's subjects began when parents exposed the child to music, swimming, scientific ideas, and so forth, "just for fun." Many of the children were initially quite ordinary in their skills. One Olympic swimmer, for instance, remembers repeatedly losing races as a 10-year-old. At some point, however, the children began to get recognition for their abilities and pursued them more actively. Before long, parents became aware of the child's rapid progress and sought out a more expert instructor or coach. After more successes and encouragement, the youngsters began "living" for their talent. Most spent many hours each day practicing their skills. This continued for many years before they reached truly extraordinary heights of achievement.

The upshot of Bloom's work is that talent is nurtured through dedication and hard work. It appears that this is most likely to happen when parents give their wholehearted support to a child's special interest and when they place emphasis on doing one's best at all times. The old belief that "talent will out" of its own accord is largely a myth.

Motives in Perspective—A View from the Pyramid

As you may recall from Chapter 1, humanistic psychologist Abraham Maslow defined self-actualization as the full development of personal potential. As a sidelight to his work on self-actualization, Maslow proposed that there is a **hierarchy** (or ordering) of human needs. By this he meant that some needs are more basic or powerful than others. Think for a moment about the needs that influence your behavior. Which seems strongest? Which do you spend the most time and energy satisfying? Now look at Maslow's hierarchy (Fig. 11-12).

Note that physiological needs are at the bottom. Since these are necessary for

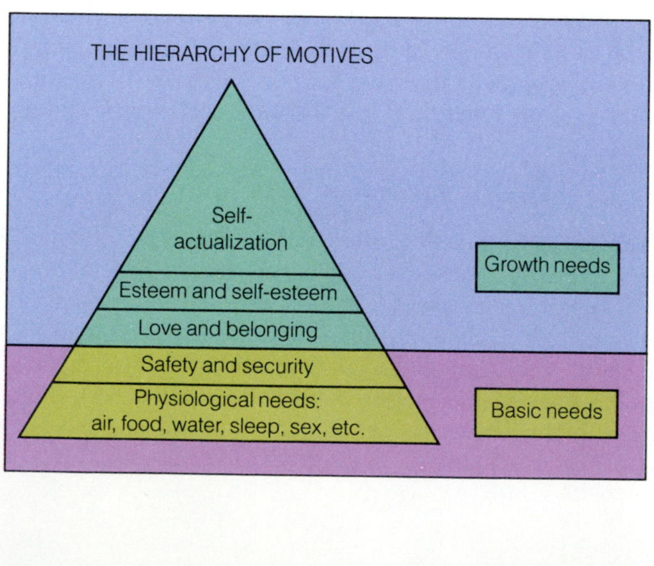

Fig. 11-12 *Maslow believed that lower needs in the hierarchy are dominant. Basic needs must be satisfied before growth motives are fully expressed. Desires for self-actualization are reflected in various meta-needs (see text).*

Fig. 11-13 *Wheelchair athletes engage in vigorous competition. Maslow considered such behavior an expression of needs for self-actualization.*

survival, they tend to be ***prepotent***, or dominant over the higher needs. It could be said, for example, that "to a starving person, food is god."

Maslow believed that higher needs are expressed only when the prepotent physiological needs are satisfied. This is also true of needs for safety and security. Until there is a basic amount of order and stability in meeting the lower needs, a person may have little interest in higher pursuits. For this reason Maslow described the first two levels of the hierarchy as **basic needs.** Higher, or **growth needs,** include love and belonging (family, friendship, caring), needs for esteem and self-esteem (recognition and self-respect), and self-actualization needs (Fig. 11-13). Although Maslow believed that a desire for self-actualization is universal, he placed it at the top of the hierarchy. This placement indicates that he viewed it as fragile and easily interrupted by lower needs.

Question: How are needs for self-actualization expressed?

Maslow called the less powerful but humanly important actualization motives **meta-needs** (Maslow, 1970). These are listed in Table 11-1. According to Maslow, there is a tendency to move up the hierarchy to the meta-needs.

Table 11-1 Maslow's List of Meta-Needs

Meta-needs are seen as an expression of tendencies for self-actualization, the full development of personal potential.	
1. Wholeness (unity)	**8.** Beauty (rightness of form)
2. Perfection (balance and harmony)	**9.** Goodness (benevolence)
3. Completion (ending)	**10.** Uniqueness (individuality)
4. Justice (fairness)	**11.** Playfulness (ease)
5. Richness (complexity)	**12.** Truth (reality)
6. Simplicity (essence)	**13.** Autonomy (self-sufficiency)
7. Aliveness (spontaneity)	**14.** Meaningfulness (values)

Intrinsic motivation Motivation that comes from within, rather than from the presence of external rewards; motivation that derives from personal enjoyment of a task or activity.

Extrinsic motivation Motivation based on obvious external rewards, obligations, or similar factors, not on the inherent satisfactions of a task or activity.

Maslow's hierarchy is not well documented by research, and questions can be raised about it. How, for instance, do we explain the use of fasting as a means of social protest? How has the meta-need for justice overcome the more basic need for food? (Perhaps the answer is that fasting is temporary.) Despite such objections Maslow's views have been widely influential as a way of understanding and appreciating the rich interplay of human motives.

Intrinsic and Extrinsic Motivation

Some people cook for a living and consider it hard work. Others cook for pleasure and dream of opening a restaurant. For some people carpentry, gardening, writing, photography, or jewelry making is fun. For others the same activities are drudgery they must be paid to do. How can the same activity be "work" for one person and "play" for another?

When you undertake an activity for enjoyment, to demonstrate competence, or to gain skill, your motivation is usually *intrinsic*. **Intrinsic motivation** occurs when there is no obvious external reward or ulterior purpose behind your actions. The activity is an end in itself. Intrinsic motivation is closely related to the higher levels of Maslow's hierarchy.

In contrast, **extrinsic motivation** stems from obvious external factors, such as pay, grades, rewards, obligations, or approval. Most of the activities we think of as "work" are extrinsically rewarded.

Turning Play into Work It might seem that increasing extrinsic incentives would strengthen motivation, but this is not always the case. Research with children shows that excessive rewards can undermine spontaneous interest (Ross et al., 1976). For instance, children lavishly rewarded for drawing with Magic Markers (felt-tip pens) later showed little interest in playing with them (Greene & Lepper, 1974). Apparently, "play" can be turned into "work" by *requiring* a person to do something he or she would otherwise enjoy. A similar effect occurred when adult college students were rewarded for working on puzzles (Daniel & Esser, 1980). Also important is the finding that intrinsic motivation encourages creativity, whereas extrinsic motivation blocks creativity (Amabile, 1985).

Question: How can the concept of intrinsic motivation be applied?

Motivation can't always be intrinsic. Nor should it be. Not every worthwhile activity is intrinsically satisfying. In addition, extrinsic motivation is often needed if we are to develop enough skill or knowledge for an activity to become intrinsically rewarding. This effect can be observed in learning to read, to play a musical instrument, or to enjoy a sport. At first, external encouragement or incentives may be needed to get a person to the level of ability needed for intrinsic motivation to occur.

So, both extrinsic and intrinsic motivation are necessary. But extrinsic motivation should not be overused. Greene and Lepper (1974) summarize: (1) If there is no intrinsic interest in an activity to begin with, there is nothing to lose by using extrinsic rewards; (2) if needed skills are lacking, extrinsic rewards may be necessary to begin; (3) extrinsic rewards may focus attention on an activity so that real interest can develop—this is especially true for motivating learning in children; (4) if extrinsic rewards or incentives are to be used, they should be as small as possible, used only when absolutely necessary, and faded out as soon as possible. By following these rules, you can avoid taking spontaneous interest and satisfaction out of motivation for others, especially children.

Learning Check

1. Drives for exploration, manipulation, and curiosity provide evidence for the existence of ______________ needs.
2. People who score high on the SSS tend to be extroverted and independent and to value change. T or F?
3. When a task is complex, the ideal level of arousal is ______________; when a task is simple, the optimal level of arousal is ______________.
4. The overall relationship between arousal and efficiency can be described as:
   a. nonhomeostatic *b.* a negative correlation *c.* an inverted U function *d.* an SSS score
5. The need for achievement can be described as a desire to meet an internalized ______________ of ______________.
6. People with high nAch are attracted to "long shots" and "sure things." T or F?
7. Fears of success are common in men but occur less often in women. T or F?
8. According to Maslow, meta-needs are the most basic and prepotent sources of human motivation. T or F?
9. Intrinsic motivation is often undermined in situations in which obvious external rewards are applied to a naturally enjoyable activity. T or F?
10. Mentally rehearsing ways to calmly deal with anticipated test-taking problems can help lower test anxiety. T or F?

Answers: **1.** stimulus **2.** T **3.** low, high **4.** c **5.** standard, excellence **6.** F **7.** F **8.** F **9.** T **10.** T

Applications

Behavioral Dieting—Kicking the Food Habit

The goal of the previous discussion was to help you better understand a number of basic motives. In this section we will consider an application of motivational research by looking at psychological techniques for weight control.

Most people today are aware that obesity can be hazardous to health, yet all around us are people who suffer from being overweight. The overweight run a high risk of developing heart and kidney diseases, of encountering dangerous complications in surgery, and of simply living fewer years than slimmer people (Lappe, 1971).

Question: What can be done to control weight?

For years the basic approach has been to "diet"; that is, to restrict food intake drastically for a brief period. This, of course, is perfectly sensible in theory: You must eat less to lose weight. As noted earlier, however, most people who lose weight by dieting regain it rapidly.

What is really needed if one wishes to lose weight is to overhaul *eating habits* and to control *cues* for eating. The person who succeeds in changing eating habits can expect a permanent weight reduction. This approach, called **behavioral dieting,** is greatly superior to simple dieting for weight control. The following list summarizes several behavioral techniques that have proved helpful (compiled from Kiell, 1973; Lake, 1973; Mayer, 1968; Trotter, 1974).

1. **Begin any weight control program with a physical checkup.** About 5 percent of all weight problems are physical.
2. **Learn your eating habits by observing yourself and keeping a diet diary.** Begin by keeping a complete record of your eating habits for 2 weeks. Record when and where you eat, what you eat, and the feelings and events that occur just before and after eating. How do others around you respond to your eating? Is someone encouraging you to overeat?
3. **Count calories, but don't starve yourself.** To lose, you must eat less, and calories allow you to keep an accurate record of your food intake.
4. **Develop techniques to control the act of eating.** Begin by taking smaller portions. Carry only what you plan to eat to the table. Put all other food away before leaving the kitchen. Eat slowly, finish one mouthful before taking another, count your mouthfuls, leave food on your plate, avoid eating alone (you're less likely to overeat in front of others).
5. **Learn to weaken your personal eating cues.** When you have learned when and where you do most of your eating, avoid these situations. Try to restrict your eating to one room, and do not read, watch TV, study, or talk on the phone while eating. Require yourself to interrupt what you are doing in order to eat. Be especially aware of the "night-eating syndrome." Most calories are consumed late in the day or at night. Keep food out of sight and find things to do to keep yourself busy during this dangerous period.
6. **Avoid snacks.** Buy low-calorie foods that require preparation, and fix only a single portion at a time. If you have an impulse to snack, set a timer for 20 minutes and see if you are still hungry then. Delay the impulse to snack several times if possible. Dull your appetite by filling up on raw carrots, bouillon, water, coffee, or tea.
7. **Exercise.** Physical activity burns calories. Stop saving steps and riding elevators. Add activity to your routine in every way you can think of. Contrary to popular opinion, regular exercise does not increase appetite. For reasons that are not well understood, exercise lowers the body's set point for fat storage (Bennet & Gurin, 1982). Some psychologists are convinced that no diet can succeed for long *without* an increase in exercise (Katahn, 1984).

Applications: Behavioral Dieting, continued

8. Get yourself committed to weight loss. Involve as many people in your program as you can.

9. Make a list of rewards you will receive if you change your eating habits and punishments that will occur if you don't. You may find it helpful to set up specific rewards (see Chapter 22 for more details). Don't reward yourself with food!

10. Chart your progress daily. Record your weight, the number of calories eaten, whether you met your daily goal. (Set realistic goals by cutting down calories gradually. About a pound per week weight loss is realistic, but remember, you are changing habits, not just losing weight.) Take pride in your successes. Post your chart in a prominent place. This feedback on your progress is possibly the most important of all the techniques.

Be patient with this program. It takes years to develop eating habits. You can expect it to take at least several months to change them. If you are unsuccessful at losing weight with these techniques, you might find it helpful to seek the aid of a psychologist familiar with behavioral weight-loss techniques.

Learning Check

1. According to behavioral dieting specialists, about 45 percent of all weight problems are physical. T or F?
2. In addition to burning calories, physical exercise can lower the body's set point. T or F?
3. For behavioral dieting you should maintain a diet diary and chart your progress, but you should avoid the trap of counting calories. T or F?

Answers: **1.** F **2.** T **3.** F

Chapter Summary

- Motives *initiate*, *sustain*, and *direct* activities. Motivation typically involves the sequence: *need*, *drive*, *goal*, and *goal attainment* (need reduction).
- Behavior can be activated either by *needs* (push) or by *goals* (pull). The attractiveness of a goal and its ability to initiate action are related to its *incentive value*.
- Three principal types of motives are: *primary motives* (based on biological survival needs), *stimulus motives* (which serve needs for activity, exploration, manipulation, and so forth), and *secondary motives* (activated by learned needs and valued goals). Most primary motives operate to maintain *homeostasis*.
- Hunger is influenced by a complex interplay of factors. These include fullness of the stomach, blood sugar levels, metabolism in the liver, and fat stores in the body. The most direct control of eating is effected by the *hypothalamus*, which has areas that act like *feeding* and *satiety* systems.
- Other factors influencing hunger are: the body's *set point*, *external eating cues*, the attractiveness and variety of *diet*, *emotions*, learned *taste preferences* or *taste aversions*, and *cultural values*.
- Lack of nutritional substances in the diet can sometimes produce *specific hungers*, as demonstrated by *self-selection* feeding experiments with animals and infants.

- *Anorexia nervosa* (self-inflicted starvation) and *bulimia* (gorging and purging) are two prominent eating disorders. Both problems tend to involve conflicts about self-image, self-control, and anxiety.
- Like hunger, thirst and other basic motives are affected by a number of bodily factors but are primarily under the central control of the hypothalamus. Thirst may be either *intracellular* or *extracellular*.
- Pain avoidance is an unusual primary drive because it is *episodic* as opposed to *cyclic*. Pain avoidance and pain tolerance are partially learned. The sex drive is also unusual in that it is *nonhomeostatic* (both increases and decreases in drive level are actively sought).
- The stimulus motives include needs for *exploration*, *manipulation*, *change*, and *sensory stimulation*. Stimulus motives appear to be innate because they operate independent of other rewards.
- Drives for stimulation are partially explained by *arousal theory*, which states that an ideal level of bodily arousal will be maintained if possible. The desired level of arousal or stimulation varies from person to person. Stimulus needs have been measured with the *Sensation Seeking Scale (SSS)*.
- Optimal performance on a task usually occurs at moderate levels of arousal. This relationship is described by an *inverted U function*. An added qualification, known as the *Yerkes-Dodson law*, states that for simple tasks the ideal arousal level is higher, and for complex tasks it is lower.
- *Test anxiety* is a combination of heightened arousal and excessive worry that impairs performance. Students can lower test anxiety by learning to overprepare, through relaxation training, by mentally rehearsing calm test taking, and by replacing upsetting thoughts with calm rational statements.
- *Circadian rhythms* of bodily activity are closely tied to sleep cycles. Time zone travel or shift work can seriously disrupt sleep and bodily rhythms. Traveling east intensifies jet lag; backward work shift rotations are more stressful than forward rotations. *Preadapting* to new time schedules can minimize these effects.
- *Social motives* are learned through socialization and cultural conditioning. Such motives account for much of the diversity of human motivation.
- One of the most prominent and intensely studied social motives is the *need for achievement (nAch)*. Achievement striving differs from the *need for power*. Higher nAch is correlated with success in many situations, with occupational choice, and with moderate risk taking. There is evidence that at times both men and women experience a *fear of success*.
- Maslow's *hierarchy of motives* categorizes needs as: *basic* and *growth oriented*. Lower needs in the hierarchy are assumed to be *prepotent* (dominant) over higher needs. Self-actualization, the highest and most fragile need, is reflected in *meta-needs*.
- Higher needs in Maslow's hierarchy are closely related to the concept of *intrinsic motivation*. In many situations *extrinsic motivation* (that which is induced by obvious external rewards) can reduce intrinsic motivation.
- Because of the limitations of traditional dieting, changing basic eating patterns and habits is usually more effective. *Behavioral dieting* brings about such changes by use of self-control techniques.

Chapter 12

Emotion

Chapter Preview

Voodoo Death

Few events are more bizarre than sudden death caused by voodoo or "magic." Yet, many explorers and anthropologists have witnessed this strange phenomenon. Here is an account of what happens in one tribe when a man discovers that he has been cursed by an enemy:

> He stands aghast, with his eyes staring at the treacherous pointers, with his hands lifted as though to ward off the lethal medium. . . . His cheeks blanch and his eyes become glassy and the expression of his face becomes horribly distorted. . . . His body begins to tremble and the muscles twist involuntarily. He sways backwards and falls to the ground. . . . From this time onwards he sickens and frets, refusing to eat and keeping aloof from the daily affairs of the tribe. Unless help is forthcoming in the shape of a counter-charm, death is only a matter of a comparatively short time. (Basedow, 1925; cited in Cannon, 1942)

At first glance voodoo deaths seem to require belief in the power of magic. Actually, all they require is belief in the power of emotion. Walter Cannon (1942), a well-known physiologist, studied a large number of voodoo deaths and concluded that they really do occur.

Question: How could a voodoo curse cause death?

Cannon believed that these deaths are explained by changes in the body that accompany strong emotion. Specifically, he believed that cursed victims experience fear so intense and lasting that it causes a heart attack or other bodily disaster.

More recent research suggests that Cannon's explanation was only partly correct. It now appears that such deaths are caused not by fear itself but by the body's reaction to fear. After a period of strong emotion, the parasympathetic nervous system normally restores balance by reversing the bodily changes caused by emotion. For example, during intense fear, heart rate is dramatically increased; to counteract this increase, the parasympathetic system later slows the heart. It is now believed that the cursed person's emotional response is so intense that the parasympathetic nervous system overreacts and slows the heart to a stop (Seligman, 1974).

There is more to this story, as we will see in a later section of this chapter. For now, it is enough to say that emotions are not only the spice of life; for some they may be the spice of death as well.

Survey Questions What causes emotion? How do psychologists explain emotions? What happens to the body during emotion? Can "lie detectors" really detect lies? How do emotions develop? How accurately are they expressed by "body language" and the face? What do we know about coping with threatening situations, helplessness, death, and depression?

Resources

Adaptive behaviors Actions that aid humans and animals in their attempts to survive and adapt to changing conditions.

Physiological changes in emotion Changes in bodily activities (especially involuntary responses) that accompany emotional states.

Adrenaline A hormone produced by the adrenal glands that tends, in general, to arouse the body.

Emotional expression Any behavior that gives an outward sign that an emotion is occurring, especially those signs that communicate the presence of an emotional state to others.

Primary emotions According to Plutchik, the most basic emotions are fear, surprise, sadness, disgust, anger, anticipation, joy, and acceptance.

Commonsense theory of emotion A simple, but naive and unlikely account of the events that occur during an emotional episode.

James-Lange theory According to this theory, emotional feelings follow bodily arousal and come from awareness of such arousal.

Dissecting an Emotion—How Do You Feel?

Have you ever waited until someone was in a good mood to ask for a favor? If so, you are aware that emotions have a powerful influence on everyday behavior. The root of the word **emotion** means "to move," and emotions do, indeed, move us. First, the body is physically aroused during emotion. Such bodily stirrings are what cause people to say they were "moved" by a play, a funeral, or an act of kindness. Second, we are often motivated, or moved to take action, by emotions such as fear, anger, or joy. Underlying all this, perhaps, is the fact that emotions are linked to such basic **adaptive behaviors** as attack, retreat, seeking comfort, helping others, reproduction, and the like (Plutchik, 1980). Of course, human emotions can be disruptive—as in having stage fright or "blowing" an athletic performance. But more often, emotions aid survival. This seems to be why emotional reactions were retained in evolution.

Most people closely identify a pounding heart, sweating palms, and "butterflies" in the stomach with emotion. This observation is valid since **physiological changes** within the body are a major element of fear, anger, joy, and other emotions. These changes include alterations in heart rate, blood pressure, perspiration, and other bodily stirrings. (More on this later.) Most such reactions are caused by release of **adrenaline** into the bloodstream. Adrenaline is a hormone that stimulates the sympathetic nervous system, which in turn activates the body.

Emotional expressions, or outward signs of what a person is feeling, are a second major element of emotion. For example, when you are intensely afraid, your hands tremble, your face contorts, and your posture becomes tense and defensive. Emotion is also revealed by marked shifts in voice tone or modulation. Such emotional expressions are particularly important because they communicate emotion from one person to another (Fig. 12-1).

Question: Are some emotions more basic than others?

Based on his research, Robert Plutchik (1980) believes there are eight **primary emotions: fear, surprise, sadness, disgust, anger, anticipation, joy,** and **acceptance** (receptivity). If the list seems too short, it's because each listed emotion can vary in *intensity*. Anger, for instance, may vary from rage to simple annoyance.

One of Plutchik's most interesting ideas concerns the mixing of primary emotions. As shown in Fig. 12-2, each pair of emotions can be mixed to yield a third, more complex emotion. Other mixtures are also possible. For example, a child about to eat a stolen cookie may feel both joy and fear. The result? Guilt—as you may recall from your own childhood. Likewise, jealousy could be considered a mixture of love, anger, and fear.

Fig. 12-1 *How accurately do facial expressions reveal emotion? After you have guessed what emotion these people are feeling,* *turn to page 335.*

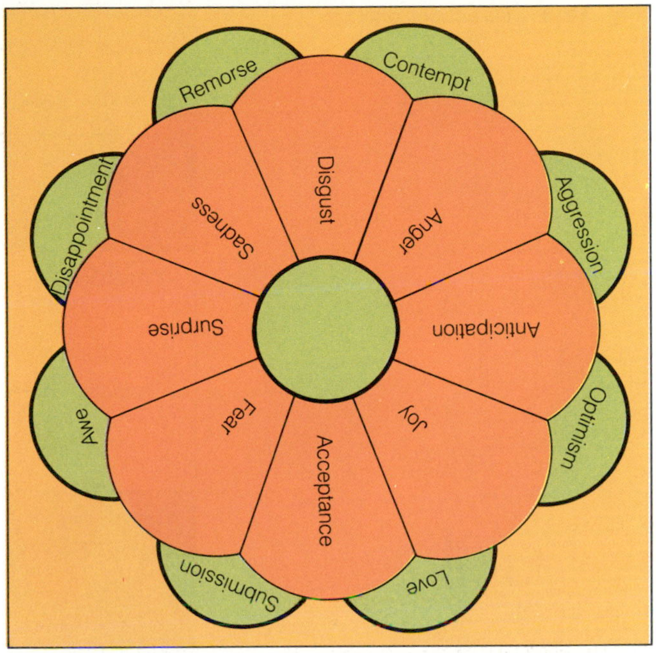

Fig. 12-2 *Primary and mixed emotions. In Robert Plutchik's model there are eight primary emotions, as listed in the inner areas. Adjacent emotions may combine to give the emotions listed around the perimeter. Mixtures involving more widely separated emotions are also possible. (Adapted from Plutchik, 1980)*

Theories of Emotion—Four Ways to Fear a Bear

Question: What is the typical sequence of events in experiencing an emotion?

There are many theories about what takes place during emotion. Let's take a brief look at four of the most popular views.

The Commonsense Theory of Emotion Common sense tells us that when we see a bear, we feel fear, become aroused, and run (and sweat and yell). For various reasons, psychologists have questioned this ordering of events. The theories of emotion that follow tell why. (Refer to Fig. 12-3.)

The James-Lange Theory (1884–1885) In the 1880s American psychologist William James (the functionalist) and Danish psychologist Carl Lange proposed a different relationship between emotional feelings and the body. James and Lange suggested that "We are afraid of a bear because we run, or are angry because we strike." In doing so, they turned the tables on our usual view of emotion. According to James and Lange, bodily arousal (such as increased heart rate) does not follow a feeling such as fear. Instead, they argued, *emotional feelings follow bodily arousal.* Thus, we see a bear, run, are aroused, and *then* feel fear as we become aware of our bodily reactions.

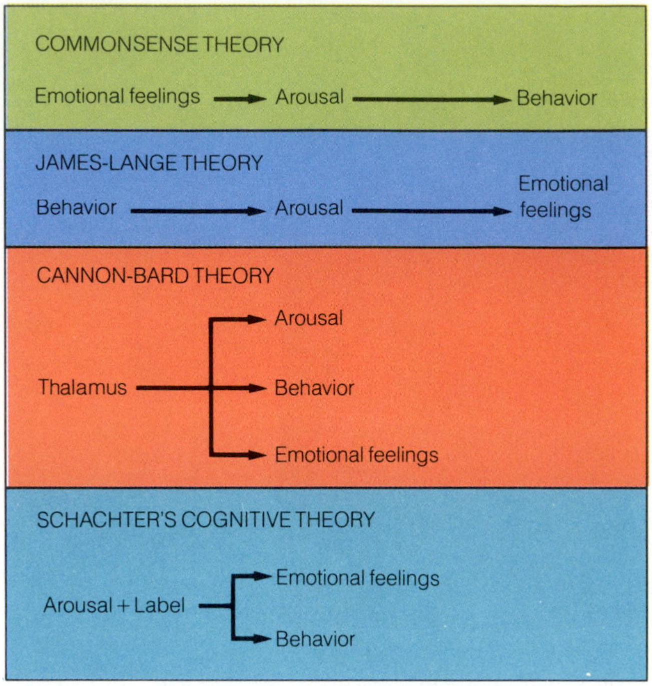

Fig. 12-3 *Theories of emotion.*

To support this line of thought, James pointed out that we often do not experience an emotion until after reacting. For example, imagine that you are driving and that a car suddenly pulls out in front of you. You swerve and skid to an abrupt halt. Only after you have stopped do you notice your pounding heart, rapid breathing, and tense muscles—and recognize your fear.

The Cannon-Bard Theory (1927) American physiologist Walter Cannon and his student Phillip Bard found a number of reasons to question the James-Lange theory. While agreeing that the body becomes stirred up during emotion, Cannon and Bard noted that the physical changes accompanying various emotions are almost identical. This fact casts doubt on the idea that emotional feelings come primarily from the body.

Question: What does account for the variety of emotions, the body or the brain?

For the reason just stated, and a number of others, Walter Cannon (1932) proposed that emotional feelings and bodily arousal are both organized in the brain. In this version, seeing a bear activates the thalamus, which in turn alerts both the cortex and the hypothalamus for action. The cortex is responsible for emotional feelings and emotional behavior. The hypothalamus is responsible for arousing the body. Thus, if the bear is seen as dangerous, bodily arousal, running, and feelings of fear will all be generated at the same time by brain activity.

Schachter's Cognitive Theory of Emotion (1971) The previous theories are mostly concerned with emotion as a physical response. In Stanley Schachter's view, cognitive (mental) factors also enter into emotion. According to Schachter, emotion occurs when a particular *label* is applied to general physical *arousal*. Schachter assumes that when we are aroused, we have a need to interpret our feelings. Assume, for instance, that someone sneaks up behind you on a dark street and says "Boo!" No matter who the person is, your body will be aroused (pounding heart, sweating palms, and so on). If the person is a total stranger, you may interpret this arousal as fear; if the person is a close friend, the arousal may be labeled as surprise or delight. The label (such as anger, fear, or happiness) applied to bodily arousal is influenced by past experience, the situation, and the reactions of others.

Support for the cognitive theory of emotion comes from an experiment in which subjects watched a slapstick movie (Schachter & Wheeler, 1962). Before viewing the movie, one-third of the subjects received an injection of adrenaline, one-third got a placebo injection, and the remaining subjects were given a tranquilizer. Subjects who received the adrenaline rated the movie the funniest and showed the most amusement while watching it. In contrast, those given the tranquilizer were least amused, and the placebo group fell in between.

According to the cognitive theory of emotion, subjects who received adrenaline had a stirred-up body but no explanation for the way they were feeling. Consequently, subjects became happy when the movie implied that their arousal was due to amusement. This and similar experiments make it clear that emotion is much more than just an agitated body. Perception, experience, attitudes, judgment, and many other more clearly "mental" factors also affect emotion. Schachter would predict, then, that if you met a bear, you would be aroused. If the bear seemed unfriendly, you would interpret your arousal as fear; and if the bear offered to shake your paw, you would be happy, amazed, and relieved!

Cannon-Bard theory According to this theory, emotional feelings and bodily arousal occur simultaneously and both begin with activity in the thalamus.

Cognitive theory Schachter's "mental" theory of emotion states that emotions occur when physical arousal is labeled or interpreted on the basis of experience and situational cues.

Attribution We now move from slapstick movies and fear of bear bodies to appreciation of bare bodies. Stuart Valins (1967) has added an interesting refinement to Schachter's theory of emotion. According to Valins, arousal can be attributed to various sources—a process that alters perceptions of emotion. To dem-

Fig. 12-4 *Which theory of emotion best describes the reaction of these people? Given the complexity of emotion, each theory appears to possess an element of truth.*

Attribution The mental process of assigning causes to events. In emotion, the process of attributing perceived arousal to a particular source.

Autonomic nervous system The system of nerves that carries information to and from the brain and the internal organs and glands of the body.

Sympathetic branch A part of the autonomic nervous system responsible for activating the body at times of stress.

Parasympathetic branch A part of the autonomic system responsible for quieting the body and conserving energy.

onstrate such **attribution**, Valins (1966) showed undergraduate male students a series of slides of nude females. While watching the slides, subjects heard an amplified heartbeat that they believed was their own. In reality they were listening to a recorded heartbeat carefully designed to beat *louder* and *stronger* when some, but not all, of the slides were shown.

After viewing the slides, subjects were asked to say which they found most attractive. Students exposed to the false heartbeat consistently rated slides paired with a "pounding heart" as the most attractive. In other words, when a subject saw a slide and heard his heartbeat become more pronounced, he attributed his "emotion" to the slide. His interpretation then seems to have been, "Now that one I like!" His next reaction, perhaps, was "But why?" Recent research suggests that subjects persuade themselves that the slide really is more attractive in order to explain their apparent arousal (Truax, 1983).

Question: That seems somewhat artificial. Does it really make any difference what arousal is attributed to?

Yes. To illustrate how attribution works in the real world, consider what happens when parents interfere with the budding romance of a son or daughter. Often, trying to break up a young couple's relationship *intensifies* their feelings for one another. Parental interference adds frustration, anger, and fear or excitement (as in seeing each other on the sly) to the couple's feelings. Since they already care for one another, they are likely to attribute all this added emotion to "true love" (Walster, 1971).

Attribution theory predicts that you are most likely to "love" someone who gets you stirred up emotionally, even when fear, anger, frustration, or rejection is part of the formula. Thus, if you want to successfully propose marriage, take your intended to the middle of a narrow, windswept suspension bridge over a deep chasm and look deeply into his or her eyes. As your beloved's heart pounds wildly (from being on the bridge, not from your irresistible charms), say "I love you." Attribution theory predicts your companion will conclude, "Oh wow, I must love you too."

The preceding is not as farfetched as it may seem. In an ingenious study, a female experimenter interviewed men in a park, some on a swaying suspension bridge 230 feet above a river and others on a solid wooden bridge just 10 feet above the ground. After the interview each subject was given the experimenter's telephone number, so he could "find out about the results" of the study if he wanted. Men interviewed on the suspension bridge were much more likely to give the "lady from the park" a call (Dutton & Aron, 1974). Apparently, these men experienced heightened arousal, which they interpreted as attraction to the experimenter—a clear case of love at first fright! (Love is discussed further in Chapter 24.)

Learning Check

Check your comprehension by answering these questions.

1. Many of the physiological changes associated with emotions are caused by secretion of the hormone
a. atropine *b.* adrenaline *c.* attributine *d.* amoduline

2. Emotional ________________ often serves to communicate one's emotional state to others.

3. Awe, remorse, and disappointment are among the primary emotions listed by Robert Plutchik. T or F?

4. According to the James-Lange theory of emotion, we see a bear, are frightened, and run. T or F?

5. The Cannon-Bard theory of emotion says that bodily arousal and emotional experience occur ________________.

6. According to Schachter's cognitive theory, bodily arousal must be labeled or interpreted for an emotional experience to occur. T or F?

7. Subjects in Valin's false heart-rate study attributed increases in their heart rate to the action of a placebo. T or F?

Answers: **1.** b **2.** expression **3.** F **4.** F **5.** simultaneously **6.** T **7.** F

Physiology and Emotion—Arousal, Sudden Death, and Lying

To a large degree, the physical aspects of emotion are innate, or built into the body. The physical reactions of an African Bushman frightened by a wild animal and an urbane city dweller frightened by a prowler are quite similar. Unpleasant emotions produce especially consistent reactions. Among the most frequent are: pounding heart, muscular tenseness, irritability, dryness of the throat and mouth, sweating, butterflies in the stomach, frequent urination, trembling, restlessness, sensitivity to loud noises, and a large number of internal reactions (Shaffer, 1947). The consistency of these reactions is tied to the fact that they are caused by the **autonomic nervous system (ANS)**. As you may recall from the discussion in Chapter 3, the reactions of the ANS are *automatic* and not normally under voluntary control. There are two divisions of the ANS, one called the **sympathetic branch** and the other the **parasympathetic branch**.

Question: What do these do during emotion?

Fight or Flight The sympathetic branch prepares the body for emergency action—"fight or flight"—by arousing a number of bodily systems and inhibiting others. (Sympathetic nervous system effects are listed in Table 12-1.) These changes have a purpose. Sugar is released into the bloodstream for quick energy, the heart beats faster to distribute blood to the muscles, the process of digestion is temporarily inhibited, blood flow in the skin is restricted to reduce bleeding, and so forth. Most of the sympathetic reactions increase the chances that a person or an animal will survive an emergency. (To learn about an interesting sidelight of sympathetic arousal, see Box 12-1.)

The actions of the parasympathetic branch generally reverse emotional arousal and calm and relax the body. After a period of high emotion, the heart is slowed, the pupils return to normal size, blood flow shifts away from the muscles and back to the internal organs, and so forth. In addition to restoring balance, the parasympathetic system helps build up and conserve bodily energy.

The parasympathetic system responds much more slowly than the sympathetic. This is why increased heart rate, muscular tension, and similar signs of arousal do not subside for 20 or 30 minutes after you experience an intense emotion, such as fear.

Table 12-1 Autonomic Nervous System Effects

Organ	Parasympathetic System	Sympathetic System
Pupil of eyes	Constricts to diminish light	Dilates to increase light
Tear glands Mucous membrane of nose and throat Salivary glands	Stimulate secretion	Inhibit secretion, cause dryness
Heart	Slowing, constriction of blood vessels	Acceleration, dilation of blood vessels to increase blood flow
Lungs, windpipe	Constrict bronchi of lungs to relax breathing	Dilate bronchi to increase breathing
Esophagus Stomach Abdominal blood vessels	Stimulate secretion and movement	Inhibit secretion and movement, divert blood flow
Liver	Liberates bile	Retains bile
Pancreas	—	Releases blood sugar
Intestines	Stimulate secretion	Inhibit secretion
Rectum Kidney Bladder	Excitation, expulsion of feces and urine	Inhibition, retention of feces and urine
Skin blood vessels	Dilate, increase blood flow	Constrict; skin becomes cold and clammy
Sweat glands	Inhibited	Stimulated to increase perspiration
Hair follicles	Relaxed	Tensed to make hair stand on end

Sudden Death As we noted in the Chapter Preview, the parasympathetic system may overreact during intense fear, sometimes causing death. Voodoo curses are not the only cause of such deaths. There is evidence that in times of war the pressures of combat can be so intense that some soldiers literally die of fear (Moritz & Zamchech, 1946). Even in civilian life such deaths apparently are possible. In one case a terrified woman was admitted to a hospital because she felt she was going to die. A backwoods midwife had predicted that the woman's two sisters would die before their sixteenth and twenty-first birthdays. Both died as predicted. The midwife also predicted that this woman would die before her twenty-third birthday. She was found dead in her hospital bed the day after she was admitted. It was 2 days before her twenty-third birthday (Zimbardo, 1975). The woman was an apparent victim of her own terror.

Box 12–1

Emotion—The Eyes Have It

Question: Is there any truth to the idea that the eyes can reveal emotion?

The eyes have long been considered "windows on the soul" and indicators of emotion. For instance, if you doubt someone's word, you may ask them to "look you in the eye." Many seasoned poker players claim to have detected a bluff by watching the eyes of their opponents. Psychologist Eckhard Hess (1975) believes that in such instances we are mainly interested in the size of a person's *pupils*. As shown in Table 12-1, emotion affects the pupils. Specifically, *arousal*, *interest*, or *attention* can activate the sympathetic nervous system and cause the pupils to dilate (enlarge).

Dilation of the pupils can occur during both pleasant and unpleasant emotions (Woodmansee, 1970). Despite this fact, most people tend to interpret *large* pupils as a sign of pleasant feelings and *small* pupils as a sign of negative feelings. To illustrate, Hess (1975) showed two photos of an attractive young woman to a group of men. In one photograph the woman's pupils were large. In the other they were small. The men consistently described the woman with large pupils as "soft," "feminine," or "pretty."

Fig. 12-5 *Select the face you think looks more attractive, warm, or friendly. Research by Eckhard Hess (1975) suggests you will choose the face on the left because the pupils of the eyes are larger.*

The same woman, with small pupils, was described as "hard," "selfish," and "cold" (Fig. 12-5).

This effect, of course, does not apply only to women. In another experiment subjects were introduced to two individuals of the opposite sex and asked to choose one as a partner for the experiment. Subjects of both sexes tended to select the person with the larger pupils as a partner. Perhaps at long last we know why the bad guys in movies always have beady eyes!

Question: Is the parasympathetic nervous system always responsible for such deaths?

Probably not. In the case of older individuals or people with heart problems, the direct effects of sympathetic activation may be enough to bring about heart attack and collapse. For example, at a memorial concert honoring the late Louis Armstrong, his widow was stricken with a heart attack as she played the final chord of "St. Louis Blues." Psychiatrist George Engel (1977) has studied hundreds of similar occurrences and concludes that many lead to death. He found that almost half of all sudden deaths are associated with the extremely traumatic disruption of a close relationship or the anniversary of the loss of a loved one. Clearly, relationships are one of the most potent sources of human emotional response.

Lie Detectors Because bodily changes caused by the autonomic nervous system are good indicators of emotion, several ways of measuring them have been developed. One use of such measures is the "lie detector." If you have not yet done so, chances are good that sooner or later you will take a lie detector test. Of course this doesn't mean you are likely to become a criminal. It simply reflects the fact that a growing number of businesses use lie detectors to screen job applicants and to check the honesty of current employees. These practices must be questioned for two reasons: First, the lie detector's accuracy is doubtful; and second, such testing is often a serious invasion of privacy (Lykken, 1981).

Question: What is a lie detector? Do lie detectors really detect lies?

The lie detector is more accurately referred to as a **polygraph** (Fig. 12-6). A polygraph (the word means "many writings") is a portable device capable of drawing a record of changes in **heart rate, blood pressure, breathing rate,** and the **galvanic skin response (GSR).** (The GSR is recorded from the surface of the hand by electrodes that measure skin conductance, or, more simply, sweating.) The polygraph has become popularly known as a lie detector because of its frequent use in criminology and job interviewing. In reality the polygraph is not a lie detector at all. As critic David Lykken (1981) points out, there is no unique "lie response" that everyone gives when not telling the truth. The machine only records *general emotional arousal*—it can't tell the difference between fear, anxiety, lying, or excitement.

When attempting to detect a lie, the polygraph operator begins by asking a number of **irrelevant** (nonemotional) **questions.** ("What is your name?" "What did you have for lunch?" and so forth.) This procedure establishes a "baseline," or normal emotional responsiveness. Then **relevant questions** can be asked: "Did

Fig. 12-6 *A typical polygraph* (left) *includes devices for measuring heart rate, blood pressure, respiration, and galvanic skin response. Pens mounted on the top of the machine make a record of bodily responses on a moving strip of paper. Changes in the area* (right) *marked by the arrow indicate emotional arousal. If such responses appear when a person answers a question, he or she may be lying, but other causes of arousal are also possible.*

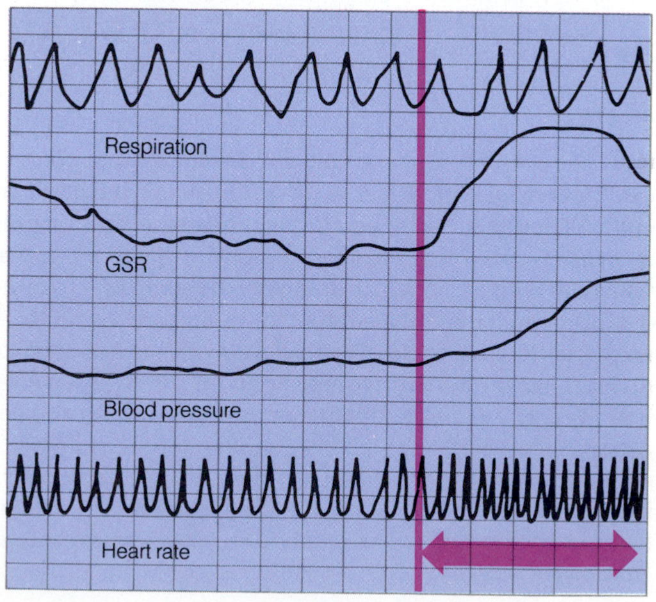

you murder Hensley?" A person who lies presumably will become anxious or emotional when answering relevant questions.

Question: Wouldn't a person be nervous just from being questioned?

Yes, and to minimize this problem, a skilled polygraph examiner asks a *series* of questions with critical items mixed among them. An innocent person may respond emotionally to the whole procedure, but supposedly only a guilty person will show increased response to key questions. For example, a suspected bank robber might be shown a picture and asked, "Was the teller who was robbed this person? Was it this person?" (Lykken 1974). As an alternative, subjects may be asked **control questions** for comparison to critical questions (Saxe, Dougherty, & Cross, 1985). Control questions are designed to make almost anyone anxious: "Have you every stolen anything from a place you worked?" Typically, control questions are extremely difficult to answer truthfully with an unqualified "No." In theory, they allow the examiner to see how a person reacts to doubt or misgivings. The person's reaction to critical questions can then be compared with his or her response to control questions.

Even when questioning is done properly, "lie detection" may be inaccurate. For example, in August 1978 Floyd Fay was convicted of murdering his friend Fred Ery. To prove his innocence, Fay volunteered to take a lie detector test, which he failed. Fay spent 2 years in prison before the real killer confessed to the crime. Psychologist David Lykken (1981) has documented three such cases in which innocent people spent from 1 to 5 years behind bars after being convicted on the basis of polygraph evidence.

Question: If Floyd Fay was innocent, why did he fail the test?

Put yourself in his place, and it's easy to see why. Imagine the examiner asking, "Did you kill Fred?" Since you knew Fred, and you are a suspect, it's no secret that this is a critical question. What would happen to *your* heart rate, blood pressure, breathing, and perspiration under such circumstances?

Proponents of lie detection claim 90 to 95 percent accuracy. But in one laboratory experiment accuracy was lowered to 25 percent by subjects who intentionally thought exciting or upsetting thoughts during questioning (Smith, 1971). Similarly, the polygraph may be thrown off by self-inflicted pain or by people who can lie without anxiety. One recent experiment showed that tranquilizing drugs interfere with the detection of lies (Waid & Orne, 1982). Worst of all, the test's most common error is to label an innocent person guilty, rather than a guilty person innocent (Lykken, 1981). In field studies involving real crimes and criminal suspects, an average of approximately 1 innocent person in 5 was rated as guilty by the "lie detector" (Saxe, Dougherty, & Cross, 1985). In some instances these false positives reached 75 percent, or 3 persons out of 4.

Each year hundreds of thousands of ordinary workers are forced to take polygraph exams. In some cases unsatisfactory results or failure to submit to an exam may lead to demotion, transfer, or outright firing. In view of what we have said here, it is ironic that only a few states have passed laws requiring operators of lie detection devices to be licensed. True, some states have adopted laws forbidding employers to require job applicants to take polygraph tests. The fact remains, however, that there is a good chance you will at some time be given a "lie detector" test. Should this occur, the best advice is to remain calm; then actively challenge the outcome if your honesty is wrongly questioned.

Polygraph A device for recording several physiological activities, typically including heart rate, blood pressure, respiration, and galvanic skin response; commonly called a "lie detector."

Galvanic skin response (GSR) A change in the electrical resistance (or inversely, the conductance) of the skin, due to activity in the sweat glands and associated with arousal or anxiety.

Irrelevant questions In a polygraph exam, neutral, nonthreatening, or nonemotional questions.

Relevant questions In a polygraph exam, questions to which only a guilty person should react.

Control questions In a polygraph exam, questions that almost always provoke anxiety, thus providing a baseline of emotional responsiveness.

Learning Check

See if you can correctly answer these questions.

1. Emotional arousal is closely related to activity of the ___[autonomic]___ nervous system.

2. The sympathetic system prepares the body for "fight or flight." T or F?

3. The parasympathetic system inhibits digestion and raises blood pressure and heart rate. T or F?

4. What bodily changes are measured by a polygraph? ___[heart rate, blood ~~rate~~ pressure, breathing rate galvanic skin response]___

5. The polygraph is really an ___[arousal and emotion]___ detector.

6. The pupils of the eyes dilate during pleasant emotions and constrict during unpleasant emotions. T or F?

Answers: **1.** autonomic **2.** T **3.** F **4.** heart rate, blood pressure, breathing rate, galvanic skin response **5.** arousal or emotion **6.** F

Development and Expression of Emotions—Feeling Babies and Talking Bodies

Question: How soon do emotions develop?

Even the basic reactions of **anger, fear,** and **joy**—which appear to be unlearned—take time to develop. General **excitement** is the only emotional response newborn infants clearly express. However, as any parent can tell you, the emotional life of a baby blossoms rapidly. One researcher (Bridges, 1932) observed a large number of babies and found that all the basic human emotions appear before age 2. Bridges found that there is a consistent order in which emotions appear and that the first basic split is between pleasant and unpleasant emotions (see Fig. 12-7).

More recent research suggests that even by the end of the first year, babies can express happiness, surprise, fear, anger, disgust, and interest (Saarni, 1982). This is an important development because it contributes to a fascinating interplay of emotions between infants and adults. For example, when new parents see and hear a crying baby, they feel annoyed, irritated, disturbed, or unhappy. In addition, their blood pressure and perspiration increase (Frodi et al., 1978). Such reactions encourage parents to tend to a baby's needs, thus increasing its chances for survival.

Question: Does the ordering Bridges observed apply to children of all cultures?

Development of the ability to express emotion is probably related to maturation of the brain, since children of all cultures show a similar pattern (Greenberg, 1977). Babies the world over, it seems, rapidly become capable of letting others know what they like and dislike. (Prove this to yourself sometime by driving a baby buggy.)

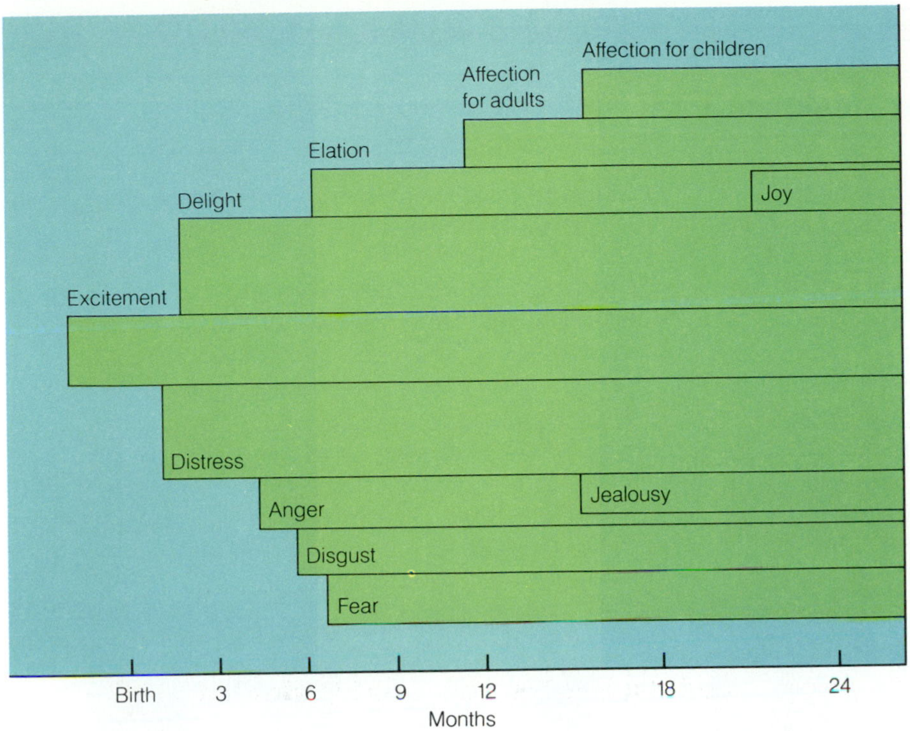

Fig. 12-7 *In the human infant, emotions are rapidly differentiated from an initial capacity for excitement.* (After K. M. B. Bridges, 1932. Reprinted by permission of The Society for Research in Child Development, Inc.)

Emotional Expression

Are human emotional expressions a carryover from more primitive and animal-like stages of human evolution? Charles Darwin thought so. Darwin (1872) observed that tigers, monkeys, dogs, and human beings all bare their teeth in the same way during rage. Darwin believed that emotional expressions were retained during the course of human evolution because communicating feelings to others is an aid to survival (Fig. 12-8). (For more information on the link between facial expressions and emotion, see Box 12-2.)

Fig. 12-8 *The "yawn" of this baboon is actually a threat. Emotional expressions allow dominance relationships among animals to be maintained with little actual fighting.*

Question: Are emotional expressions the same for all people?

The most basic expressions appear to be fairly universal. Children who are born deaf and blind and who therefore have little opportunity to learn emotional expressions from others use the same facial gestures as others to display joy, sadness, disgust, and so on (Knapp, 1978). In fact, the gestures of such children may be one of the few examples of "pure" emotional expression. By adulthood most people have learned to carefully control facial expression so that many gestures become unique to various cultures. Among the Chinese, for example, sticking out the tongue is a gesture of surprise, not of disrespect or teasing. Despite such differences, facial expressions of *fear*, *surprise*, *sadness*, *disgust*, *anger*, and *happiness* are recognized by people of all cultures (Ekman, 1980). Notice that this covers most of the primary emotions listed earlier in the chapter. It's also nice to note that a smile is the most universal and easily recognized facial expression of emotion.

Box 12-2

Emotional Expression—Making Faces

It may seem like a case of the tail wagging the dog, but scientists have recently found that "making faces" alters activity in the rest of the body. Paul Ekman and his colleagues carefully guided subjects as they arranged their faces, muscle by muscle, into expressions of surprise, disgust, sadness, anger, fear, and happiness (Fig 12-9). At the same time, subjects' bodily reactions were monitored. Contrary to what might be expected, making faces brought about changes in the autonomic nervous system, as reflected by heart rate and skin temperature. In addition, each facial expression produced a different pattern of activity. An angry face, for instance, raised heart rate and skin temperature, whereas disgust lowered heart rate and skin temperature (Ekman, Levenson, & Friesen, 1983).

It appears, then, that not only do emotions determine expressions, but expressions may determine emotions (Laird, 1984). Such findings also emphasize the central role played by the face in emotion—as first suggested by Charles Darwin. They may also help explain an interesting effect you have probably observed. When you are feeling "down" or sad, forcing yourself to smile will sometimes be followed by an actual improvement in your mood (Laird, 1974).

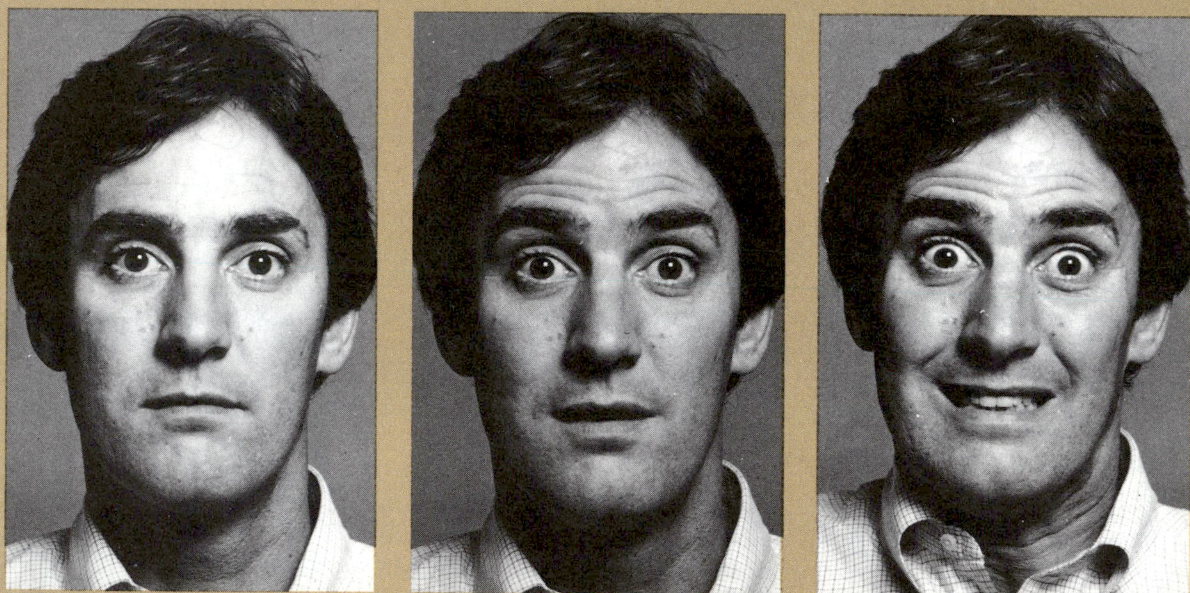

Fig. 12-9

Body Language If a friend approached you and said, "Hey, ugly, what are you doing?" would you be offended? Probably not, because such expressions are usually accompanied with a big grin. The facial and bodily gestures of emotion speak a language all their own and add an additional message to what is said verbally. The study of communication through body movement, posture, gestures, and facial expressions is called **kinesics** (ki-NEE-ziks) and is informally referred to as body language.

Question: What kinds of messages are sent with body language?

Most of the popular books on body language (for example, Fast, 1970) tend to list particular meanings for gestures. For instance, a woman who stands rigidly, crosses her arms over her chest, or sits with her legs tightly crossed supposedly is sending a "hands off" message. But researchers in the field of kinesics emphasize that gestures are rarely this fixed in meaning (Swensen, 1973). The message might simply be, "This room is cold." Being more realistic, we would say that an overall **emotional tone** is usually communicated by body language.

The most expressive and frequently noticed part of the body is the face. Physiologists estimate that the face is capable of producing some 20,000 different expressions. Most of these are **facial blends**, involving a mixture of two or more basic expressions. Imagine, for example, that you just received an F on an unfair test. Quite likely, your eyes, eyebrows, and forehead would show anger, while your mouth would express sadness (Knapp, 1978).

Most of us believe we can fairly accurately tell what others are feeling by observing facial expressions. If thousands of facial blends occur, how do we make such judgments? The answer seems to lie in the fact that facial expressions can be boiled down to basic dimensions of **pleasantness-unpleasantness, attention-rejection,** and **activation** (or arousal) (Schlosberg, 1954). By smiling when giving a friend a hard time, you add the emotional message of pleasantness and acceptance to the verbal insult and change its meaning. As they say in movie Westerns, it makes a big difference to "smile when you say that, pardner."

Other emotional feelings are telegraphed by the body. The most general seem to be **relaxation** or **tension**, and **liking** or **disliking.** Relaxation is expressed by casual positioning of the arms and legs, leaning back (if sitting), and spreading the arms and legs. Liking is expressed mainly by leaning toward a person or object (Mehrabian, 1969) (Fig. 12-11). Thus, body positioning can reveal feelings that would normally be concealed. Who do you "lean toward"?

Kinesics Study of the meaning of body movements, posture, hand gestures, and facial expressions, commonly called body language.

Emotional tone The underlying emotional state an individual is experiencing at any given moment.

Facial blend An arrangement of facial features that mixes parts of two or more basic facial expressions.

Pleasantness-unpleasantness As reflected in facial expressions, the degree to which a person is experiencing pleasure or displeasure.

Attention-rejection As reflected in facial expressions, the degree to which a person is directing attention at the perceiver or some other stimulus.

Activation As reflected in facial expressions, the degree of arousal experienced by the person making the expression.

Fig. 12-10 *Facial and bodily gestures do not always allow an observer to accurately "read" emotion. The agonized expression on the face of Frank De Vito is deceptive. Mr. De Vito and his wife have just learned that he has won $1 million in the New Jersey state lottery.*

Fig. 12-11 *Emotions are often unconsciously revealed by gestures and body positioning.*

Imagine that you are standing 30 yards from a classroom in which test grades are being announced. As students file out, do you think you could tell—without the aid of facial expressions—who got A's and who got F's? Actually, your task might not be too difficult. Recent research suggests that overall *posture* can also indicate one's emotional state. Specifically, when a person is successful, his or her posture is likely to be more erect (Weisfeld & Beresford, 1982) (see Fig. 12-12). It remains debatable whether this tendency is a product of evolution or is simply learned. In any case, standing tall with pride and slumping with dejection do seem to be consistent patterns.

Question: Does body positioning or movement ever reveal lying or deception?

If you know a person well, you may be able to detect deception from expressive changes (Ekman & Friesen, 1975). But don't count on it. Most people learn to maintain careful control over their facial expressions. A good example is smiling to avoid hurting someone's feelings when you have received a disappointing gift. Often, because of such control, deception is best revealed by the lower body. Tense leg positions and restless or repetitive foot and leg movements are associated with fibbing in most people (Ekman & Friesen, 1975). Even a good con artist may be too busy attending to his or her voice and face to control bodily cues.

Coping with Emotion—"Am I Okay or in Trouble?"

Situation: You have been selected to give a speech to 300 people. Or, a physician has informed you that you must undergo a dangerous and painful operation. Or, the one true love of your life walks out the door. What would your emotional response to these events be? How do you cope with an emotional threat? According to Richard Lazarus (1975, 1981), there are two important steps in the process of coping with a threatening situation. The first is **primary appraisal,** in which

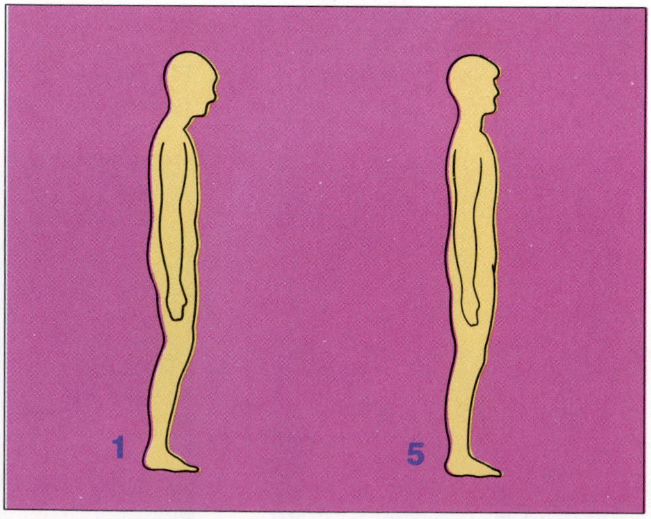

Fig. 12-12 *Posture and success. These drawings show the endpoints of a five-point rating scale used to measure erectness of posture. Success by human subjects in various situations was found to be reflected by erect posture. (Adapted from Weisfeld & Beresford, 1982)*

Primary appraisal The first step in coping with a threatening situation, consisting of deciding if the situation is indeed a threat.

Secondary appraisal After a situation is deemed a threat, the secondary appraisal is made in order to find a way to counter the threat.

Problem-focused coping Coping with a stressful or threatening situation by attempting to manage or remedy the situation itself.

Emotion-focused coping Coping with a stressful or threatening situation by attempting to manage or control one's emotional reaction to the situation.

you decide if a situation is relevant or irrelevant, positive or threatening. In essence, this appraisal answers the question, "Am I okay or in trouble?" (Lazarus & Folkman, 1984). Then you make a **secondary appraisal,** during which you choose a means of meeting the threat or challenge. ("What can I do about this situation?")

The emotional effects of appraising a threatening situation were demonstrated in a fascinating experiment by Joseph Spiesman and his associates (1964). These researchers used a graphic film called *Subincision* to stimulate emotional responses in volunteer subjects. Subincision is a ritual used to initiate adolescent boys into manhood in a primitive Australian tribe. The filmed procedure begins with three or four adults holding a boy down to prevent escape. Then a crude and obviously painful operation is performed in which the adolescent's penis is slit on the underside for its entire length. To add insult to injury, the operation is performed with a sharpened flintstone. Needless to say, American viewers respond emotionally to the gory details of this film.

The film was shown in four different versions to test the emotional effects of different appraisals. The first had no sound track. The second emphasized the painful and traumatic aspects of the operation. The third treated the operation in an intellectual and distant way. The fourth glossed over the threatening aspects of the operation and denied that it was painful.

Question: Did the sound tracks affect emotional reactions?

Recordings of heart rate and GSR showed quite clearly that appraisal of a situation affects emotional response. The film emphasizing traumatic aspects of the operation produced an increase in emotion over that caused by the silent film. On the other hand, the intellectual and denial sound tracks reduced emotion. The way a situation is "sized up" therefore becomes important to coping with it. Public speaking, for instance, can be appraised as an intense threat or as a challenge and a chance to perform. Emphasizing the threat by imagining failure, rejection, or embarrassment obviously invites disaster.

Coping with Threat After a person makes a secondary appraisal, his or her coping attempts can be either problem-focused or emotion-focused (Lazarus & Folkman, 1984). **Problem-focused coping** is aimed at managing or altering the distressing situation itself. In **emotion-focused coping** the person tries instead to control his or her emotional reaction.

Question: Couldn't both types of coping occur together?

Yes. Sometimes problem- and emotion-focused coping aid one another. Say, for example, that a woman experiences anxiety as she steps to the podium to give a speech. If she does some deep breathing to reduce her anxiety (emotion-focused coping), she will be better able to glance over her notes to improve her delivery (problem-focused coping). It is also possible, however, for the two types of coping to clash or impede one another. If you have to make a difficult decision, for instance, you may suffer unbearable emotional stress. In such circumstances there is a temptation to make a premature and ill-advised choice, just to end the emotional suffering. Doing so may allow you to cope with your emotions, but it shortchanges problem-focused coping (Lazarus & Folkman, 1984).

Coping effectively with emotional reactions is a major topic in its own right. In the following chapter we will further discuss reactions to stressful, threatening, and emotional situations. To conclude our discussion here, let's see what happens when coping attempts fail.

Learned Helplessness—Is There Hope?

Question: What would happen if a person appraised a threatening situation as hopeless?

Bruno Bettelheim (1960), who survived imprisonment in Nazi concentration camps, has described a reaction he calls "give-up-itis." Many of the prisoners felt so helpless that they developed a "zombie-like" detachment that made them into "walking corpses." Martin Seligman (1974) has described a similar reaction in Vietnam prisoner of war camps. Seligman reports the case of a young marine who had adapted unusually well to the stress of being a POW. His health was apparently related to a promise made by his captors that if he would cooperate he would be released on a certain date. As the date approached, his spirits soared. Then came a devastating blow. He had been deceived. His captors had never intended to release him. Immediately, he lapsed into a deep depression, refused to eat or drink, and died shortly thereafter.

Examples such as these are extreme, but they demonstrate once again the power of emotions. Recent attempts to understand such events have focused on the concept of **learned helplessness.**

Learned helplessness has been demonstrated in the laboratory with animals tested in a shuttle box (Fig. 12-13). If placed in one side of a divided box, dogs

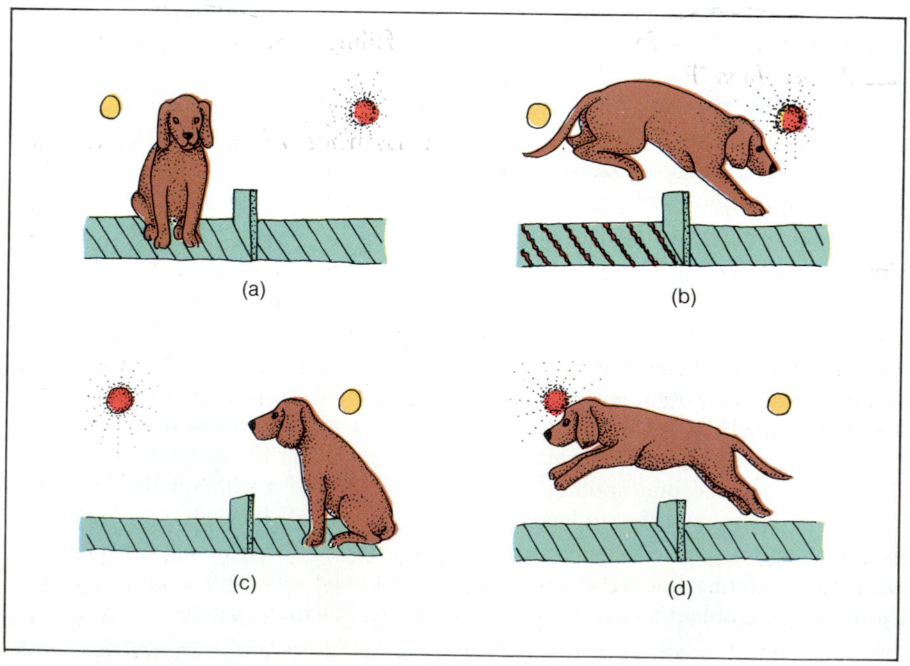

Fig. 12-13 *In the normal course of escape and avoidance learning, a light dims shortly before the floor is electrified* (a). *Since the light does not yet have meaning for the dog, the dog receives a shock (noninjurious, by the way) and leaps the barrier* (b). *Dogs soon learn to watch for the dimming of the light* (c) *and to jump before receiving a shock* (d). *Dogs made to feel "helpless" rarely even learn to escape shock, much less to avoid it.*

will quickly learn to leap to the other side to escape an electric shock. If they are given a warning before the shock occurs (for example, a light dims), most dogs will learn to avoid the shock by leaping the barrier before the shock arrives. This is true of most dogs but not those who have learned to feel helpless.

Question: How is a dog made to feel helpless?

Before being tested in the shuttle box, some dogs were placed in a harness (from which they could not escape) and were given several painful shocks. The animals were helpless to prevent these shocks (Overmier & Seligman, 1967). When placed in the shuttle box, these dogs reacted to the first shock by crouching, howling, and whining. None tried to escape. They helplessly resigned themselves to their fate—after all, they had already learned that there was nothing they could do about shock.

Similar effects occur when humans are made to fail or when they receive punishment they cannot predict or prevent (Fox & Oakes, 1984). However, where humans are concerned, attributions (remember attribution?) have a large effect on helplessness. Persons who are made to feel helpless in one situation are more likely to act helpless in other situations if they blame their failure on *lasting, general* factors. An example would be concluding "I must be stupid" after failing to solve a series of puzzles. In contrast, attributing failure to specific factors in the situation ("I'm not too good at puzzles," or "I wasn't really interested") tends to prevent learned helplessness from spreading (Alloy, Peterson, Abramson, & Seligman, 1984; Anderson, Anderson, Fleming, & Kinghorn, 1984).

Question: What does learned helplessness have to do with emotion?

Depression Seligman and his associates have drawn attention to the similarities between learned helplessness and depression. Symptoms that occur in both **depression** and learned helplessness include: feelings of powerlessness and hopelessness, decreased activity, lowered aggression, loss of sexual drive and appetite, and, in humans, a tendency to see oneself as failing, even when this is not the case (Miller, Rossellini, & Seligman, 1977).

Depression is one of the most widespread emotional problems, and it undoubtedly has many causes. However, Seligman has made a good case for learned helplessness as a major factor in many cases of depression and hopelessness. For example, Seligman (1972) describes the fate of Archie, a 15-year-old boy. For Archie school is an unending series of shocks and failures. Other students treat him as if he's stupid; in class he rarely answers questions because he doesn't know some of the words. He feels knocked down every direction he turns. These may not be electric shocks, but they are certainly psychological "shocks," and Archie has learned to feel helpless to prevent them. When he leaves school, his chances of success will be poor. He has learned to passively endure whatever shocks life has in store for him.

Question: Does Seligman's research give any clues about how to "unlearn" helplessness?

Hope With dogs one effective technique has been to forcibly drag them away from the shock into the "safe" compartment. After this is done several times, the animals regain "hope" and feelings of control over the environment. Just how this can be accomplished with humans is a question for further research. It seems

Learned helplessness A learned inability to overcome environmental obstacles or to avoid punishment. A learned state of passivity and inaction in the face of aversive stimuli.

Depression A state of deep despondency and emotional negativity.

Mastery training Learning that reinforces responses leading to mastery of a threat or control over one's environment.

obvious, however, that someone like Archie would benefit from an educational program that would allow him to "succeed" repeatedly. This prediction is backed up by animal experiments. When animals are given **mastery training,** they become more resistant to learned helplessness (Volpicelli, Ulm, Altenor, & Seligman, 1983). For example, animals that first learned to successfully escape shock were more persistent later in trying to escape inescapable shock. In effect, they wouldn't give up, even when the situation was hopeless.

Such findings suggest that we might even be able to "immunize" people against helplessness and depression by giving them experience at mastering seemingly impossible challenges. The Outward Bound schools, in which people pit themselves against the rigors of mountaineering, white-water canoeing, and wilderness survival, might serve as a model for such a program.

As a final note, the value of hope should not be overlooked. As fragile as this emotion seems to be, it is a powerful antidote to depression and helplessness. As an individual, you may find hope in religion, nature, human companionship, or even technology. Wherever you find it, remember its value: Hope is among the most important of all human emotions.

Learning Check

1. The first recognizable emotional response in a newborn baby is fear. T or F?

2. The pattern of emotional development in human infants varies greatly from one culture to another. T or F?

3. Charles Darwin held that emotional expressions aid survival for animals. T or F?

4. A formal term for "body language" is ____________.

5. Circle the three dimensions of emotion communicated by facial expressions:

pleasantness-unpleasantness complexity attention-rejection anger curiosity-disinterest activation

6. According to Richard Lazarus, coping with threatening situations can be both problem-focused and ____________ focused.

7. Depression in humans is similar to ____________ ____________ observed in animal experiments.

Answers:

1. F **2.** F **3.** T **4.** kinesics **5.** pleasantness-unpleasantness, attention-rejection, activation **6.** emotion- **7.** learned helplessness

Applications

Coping with Death and Depression—Problems for Everyone

DEAR ABBY: Do you think about dying much?

CURIOUS

DEAR CURIOUS: No, it's the last thing I want to do.

There are a number of situations in each person's life that are heavily charged with emotion. The second most difficult to handle is probably the death of a close friend or relative; the first is one's own impending death.

Death is a topic of importance to us all. The statistics on death are very convincing: One out of one dies. In spite of this, there tends to be a conspiracy of silence surrounding the topic of death. Perhaps this is because most of us would rather not be reminded of our ultimate demise. Modern medical practice and the funeral industry have also served to insulate most people from contact with death. As a result, most of us are poorly informed about a process that is as basic as birth.

We have seen in this chapter that it is valuable to understand one's own emotions and those of others. With this in mind, this section begins with an investigation of emotional responses before, during, and after death.

Fears of Death

Fears of death are not so extensive as might be supposed. In a public opinion poll of 1500 adults, only about 4 percent showed evidence of directly fearing their own death (Kastenbaum & Aisenberg, 1972). It might seem that as people grow older they would become more fearful of death. However, a study of individuals ranging in age from 30 to 82 found no overall differences in death anxiety associated with age (Conte, Weiner, & Plutchik, 1982). Those fears that do exist apparently change with age. Hall (1922) found that younger individuals fear the *occurrence* of death, whereas older people fear the *circumstances* of death.

These findings seem to indicate a general lack of fear about death, but there is another possible interpretation. It may be more accurate to say that they reflect a deeply ingrained tendency to deny death. The mere fact that death has been something of a taboo subject suggests that underlying fears do exist. When *Psychology Today* surveyed its readers on the subject of death, it found that less than one-third of those who replied grew up in families in which death was openly discussed (Schneidman, 1971). The average person's exposure to death unfortunately consists of the unrealistic portrayals of death on TV. It has been estimated that by the time a person is 14 years old, he or she will have witnessed 18,000 TV deaths. With few exceptions these will have been *homicides*, not deaths due to illness or aging (Tobin, 1972).

Reactions to Impending Death

A more direct account of emotional responses to death comes from the work of Elizabeth Kübler-Ross (1975). Kübler-Ross, a **thanatologist** (THAN-ah-TOL-oh-jist: one who studies death), has spent hundreds of hours at the bedsides of the terminally ill. She has found that dying persons tend to display several emotional reactions as they prepare for death. The five basic reactions are:

1. Denial and isolation. A typical first reaction to impending death is an attempt to deny its reality and to isolate oneself from information confirming that death is really going to occur. Initially, the person may be sure that "It's all a mistake," that lab reports or X rays have been mixed up, or that a physician is in error. This initial response may proceed to attempts to ignore or avoid any reminder of the situation.

2. Anger. Many dying individuals feel anger that often takes the form of asking, "Why me?" As they face the ultimate frustration of having everything

Applications: Coping with Death and Depression, continued

they value stripped away, their anger can spill over into rage or envy toward those who will continue living. Even good friends may temporarily evoke anger because their health is envied.

3. Bargaining. In another common reaction, the dying bargain with themselves or with God. The dying person says, "Just let me live a little longer and I'll do anything to earn it." Individuals may bargain for time by trying to be "good" ("I'll never smoke again"), by righting past wrongs, or by praying that if they are granted more time they will dedicate themselves to their religion.

4. Depression. As death draws near and the person begins to recognize that it cannot be prevented, feelings of futility, exhaustion, and deep depression may set in. The person recognizes that he or she will be separated from friends, loved ones, and the familiar routines of life, and this causes a profound sadness.

5. Acceptance. Assuming that death is not sudden, many people manage to come to terms with death and accept it calmly. The person who accepts death is neither happy nor sad, but at peace with the inevitable. Acceptance usually signals that the struggle with death has been resolved. The need to talk about death is ended, and silent companionship from others frequently is all that is desired.

Not all terminally ill individuals display all these reactions, nor do the reactions always occur in this order. Personal styles of dying vary greatly, according to emotional maturity, religious belief, age, education, the attitudes of relatives, and so forth. Generally, there does tend to be movement from initial shock, denial, and anger toward eventual acceptance. However, some people who seem to have accepted death may die angry and raging against the inevitable. Conversely, the angry fighter may let go of the struggle and die peacefully. In general, one's approach to dying will mirror his or her style of living (DeSpelder & Strickland, 1983). Thus, it is best not to think of Kübler-Ross' list as a fixed series of stages to go through. Rather, the list describes typical and appropriate reactions to impending death. It is also interesting to note that many of the same reactions accompany any major loss, be it divorce, loss of a home due to fire, death of a pet, or loss of a job.

Question: How can I make use of this information?

This information can be put to use in a number of ways. First of all, it can help both the dying individual and survivors recognize periods of depression, anger, denial, or bargaining and cope with them. Secondly, it is helpful to realize that close friends or relatives of the dying person may feel many of the same emotions before or after the person's death because they, too, are facing a loss.

Perhaps the most important thing to recognize is that the dying person may have a need to share feelings with others and to discuss death openly. Too often, the dying person feels isolated and separated from others by the wall of silence erected by doctors, nurses, and family members. Adults tend to "freeze up" with a dying person, saying things such as, "I don't know how to deal with this."

Understanding what the dying person is going through may make it easier for you to offer support at this important time. A simple willingness to be with the person and to honestly share his or her feelings can help bring dignity, acceptance, and meaning to death.

Bereavement After a friend or relative has died, a period of grief typically follows. Grief is a natural and normal reaction to loss, and most psychologists regard it as an essential part of adjusting to death. In our culture funeral services frequently serve as useful outlets for grief by encouraging the release of emotions.

Grief usually follows a predictable pattern (Parkes, 1979; Schulz, 1978). Grief normally begins with a period of **shock** or numbness. For a brief time the bereaved remain in a dazed state in which they may show little emotion. Most find it extremely difficult to accept the reality of their loss. This phase usually ends by the time of the funeral, which unleashes tears and bottled-up feelings of despair.

Applications: Coping with Death and Depression, continued

Initial shock is followed by sharp **pangs of grief.** These are episodes of painful yearning for the dead person and, sometimes, anguished outbursts of anger. During this period the wish to have the dead person back is intense. Often, mourners continue to think of the dead person as alive; they may hear his or her voice or may encounter the deceased in vivid dreams. During this period agitated distress alternates with silent despair, and suffering is acute.

The first powerful reactions of grief gradually give way to weeks or months of **apathy, dejection,** and **depression.** The person faces a new emotional landscape with a large gap that cannot be filled. Life seems to lose much of its meaning, and a sense of futility dominates the person's outlook. The mourner is usually able to resume work or other activities after 2 or 3 weeks, but insomnia, loss of energy and appetite, and similar signs of depression may continue.

Little by little the bereaved person accepts that which cannot be changed and makes a new beginning. Pangs of grief may still occur, but they are less severe and less frequent. Memories of the dead person, though still painful, now include positive images and nostalgic pleasure. At this stage the bereaved person can be said to be moving toward **resolution.** As was true of approaching death, individual reactions to grief vary considerably. In general, however, a month or two typically passes before the more intense stages of grief have run their course.

Table 12-2 Coping with Grief

- Face the loss directly and do not isolate yourself.
- Discuss your feelings with relatives and friends.
- Do not block out your feelings with drugs or alcohol.
- Allow grief to progress naturally; neither hurry nor suppress it.

(From Coni, Davison, & Webster, 1984)

As you can see, grief allows survivors to discharge their anguish and to prepare to go on living. A person who avoids this "grief work" by suppressing feelings may later experience a much more severe and lasting depression. Therefore, it is important for people who suffer a loss to accept the need to grieve and for those around them to encourage this necessary expression of emotion (Schulz, 1978). Some additional suggestions for coping with grief are given in Table 12-2.

Coping with Depression

Recent studies show that during the school year up to 78 percent of students at American colleges suffer some of the symptoms of depression. At any given time roughly one-quarter of the student population is involved (Beck & Young, 1978). Why should so many students be "blue"? A variety of problems typically contributes to such depressive feelings. Among the most common are:

1. Stresses from the increased difficulty of college work and pressures to make a career choice often leave students feeling that they are missing out on fun or that all their hard work is meaningless.
2. Isolation and loneliness are common when a student leaves his or her support group behind. Formerly, family, a circle of high school friends, and

Applications: Coping with Death and Depression, continued

often an intimate boyfriend or girlfriend could be counted on for support or encouragement.

3. Problems with studying and grades frequently trigger depression. Many students enter college with high aspirations and little former experience with failure. At the same time, many lack basic skills necessary for academic success.

4. Another common cause of college depression is the breakup of an intimate relationship, either with a former boyfriend or girlfriend or with a newly formed college romance (Beck & Young, 1978).

Recognizing Depression Most people know, obviously enough, when they are "down." Aaron Beck, a nationally recognized authority on depression, suggests you should assume that more than a minor fluctuation in mood is involved when five conditions exist:

1. You have a consistently negative opinion of yourself.

2. You engage in frequent self-criticism and self-blame.

3. You place negative interpretations on events that usually wouldn't bother you.

4. The future looks bleak and negative.

5. You feel that your responsibilities are overwhelming.

Question: What can be done to combat depression?

Combating Depression Beck and Greenberg (1974) suggest that you begin by making a *daily schedule* for yourself. Try to schedule activities to fill up every hour during the day. It is best to start with easy activities and progress to more difficult tasks. Check off each activity as it is completed. In this way you will begin to break the self-defeating cycle of feeling helpless and falling further behind (depressed students spend much of their time sleeping). A series of small accomplishments, successes, or pleasures may be all you need to get going again. However, if you are lacking skills needed for success in college, ask for help in getting them. Don't remain "helpless."

Beck and Greenberg also believe that feelings of worthlessness and hopelessness are supported by thoughts such as those listed in the five preceding conditions. They recommend writing down self-critical or negative thoughts as they occur, especially those that immediately precede feelings of sadness. After you have collected these thoughts, write a rational answer to each. For example, the thought, "No one loves me," should be answered with a list of people who do care. (See Chapter 22 for more information on this point.)

Attacks of the "college blues" are common and should be distinguished from more serious cases of depression. Severe depression is a serious problem that can lead to suicide or a major impairment of emotional functioning.

Question: How can mild depression be distinguished from more serious problems?

This is a rather difficult judgment to make because it is related to many psychological dimensions. Practically speaking, a useful answer can be found in a list of 10 danger signals compiled by the National Association for Mental Health to help people distinguish normal depression from reactions that require professional help. Here is the list:

1. A general and lasting feeling of hopelessness and despair.

2. Inability to concentrate, making reading, writing, and conversation difficult. Thinking and activity are slowed because the mind is absorbed by inner anguish.

3. Changes in physical activities such as eating, sleeping, and sex. Frequent physical complaints with no evidence of physical illness.

4. Loss of self-esteem, which brings on continual questioning of personal worth.

5. Withdrawal from others due to immense fear of rejection.

6. Threats or attempts to commit suicide, viewed as a way out of a hostile environment and a belief that life is worthless.

Applications: Coping with Death and Depression, continued

7. Hypersensitivity to words and actions of others and general irritability.
8. Misdirected anger and difficulty in handling most feelings. Self-directed anger because of perceived worthlessness may produce general anger directed at others.
9. Feelings of guilt in many situations. A depressed person assumes he or she is wrong or responsible for the unhappiness of others.
10. Extreme dependency on others. Feelings of helplessness and then anger at the helplessness.

No single item (except number 6) necessarily indicates dangerous depression, but if several are observed, it should be assumed that seeking professional help would be wise.

Learning Check

1. The majority of deaths portrayed on TV involve elderly people who die of some fatal disease. T or F?
2. In the reaction that Küber-Ross describes as bargaining, the dying individual asks, "Why me?" T or F?
3. A dazed state of shock or numbness is typical of the first phase of grief. T or F?
4. Many authorities stress that suppression of grief often leads to later problems, such as severe depression. T or F?
5. At any given time, close to one-half of the college student population suffers some of the symptoms of depression. T or F?
6. To break a cycle of depression and helplessness, Beck and Greenberg suggest it is best to start with easy activities and progress to more difficult tasks. T or F?

Answers: **1.** F **2.** F **3.** T **4.** T **5.** F **6.** T

Chapter Summary

- There is evidence that voodoo deaths actually occur. They are probably caused by intense and prolonged emotion. Despite this, emotions were probably retained in evolution because they are linked to many basic *adaptive behaviors*.
- Two major parts of an emotion are *physiological changes* in the body and *emotional expressions* (outward signs of emotion).
- The following are considered to be *primary emotions: fear, surprise, sadness, disgust, anger, anticipation, joy,* and *acceptance*. Other emotions seem to represent mixtures of the primaries.
- The *James-Lange theory* of emotion says that emotional *experience* follows the bodily reactions of emotion. In contrast, the *Cannon-Bard theory* says that bodily reactions and emotional experience occur at the same time and that emotions are organized in the brain.
- Schachter's *cognitive theory* of emotion emphasizes the importance of labels or interpretations applied to feelings of bodily arousal. Also important is the process of *attribution*. Attribution refers to the effects of associating bodily arousal with a particular person, object, or situation.
- Physical changes associated with emotion are caused by the action of *adrenaline*, a hormone released into the bloodstream, and by activity in the *autonomic nervous system* (ANS).
- The *sympathetic branch* of the ANS is primarily responsible for arousing the body, the *parasympathetic branch* for quieting it. Sudden death due to prolonged and intense emotion is probably a parasympathetic effect. Heart attacks caused by sudden intense emotion are more likely due to sympathetic arousal.
- The *polygraph*, or "lie detector," measures emotional arousal by monitoring *heart rate, blood pressure, breathing rate,* and the *galvanic skin response* (GSR). The lie detector's accuracy has been challenged by many researchers.
- Emotions develop from the *generalized excitement* observed in newborn babies. Three of the basic emotions—*fear, rage,* and *joy*—may be unlearned. Basic emotional expressions, such as smiling, frowning, or baring one's teeth when angry, also appear to be unlearned. *Facial expressions* appear to be central to emotion. As a result, some psychologists consider them a carryover from earlier stages of evolution.
- Body gestures and movements (body language) also express feelings, mainly by communicating *emotional tone* rather than specific messages. Three dimensions of facial expressions are *pleasantness-unpleasantness, attention-rejection,* and *activation*. The formal study of body language is known as *kinesics*.
- The *primary appraisal* of a situation greatly affects emotional response to it. Fear reactions in particular are related to the appraisal of threat. During a *secondary appraisal*, some means of coping with a situation is selected. Coping may be either *problem-focused* or *emotion-focused*.
- The concept of *learned helplessness* has been used to explain failure to cope with threatening situations and as a model for understanding *depression*. *Mastery training* acts as one major antidote to helplessness.
- Typical emotional reactions to impending death are *denial, anger, bargaining, depression,* and *acceptance*. Bereavement also brings forth a typical series of reactions ranging from shock to final acceptance.
- *Depression* is a major, and surprisingly common, emotional problem. Actions and thoughts that counter feelings of helplessness tend to reduce depression.

Chapter 13

Frustration, Conflict, Stress, and Defense

Chapter Preview

How to Build a Human Time Bomb

When he was arrested, John was sitting atop a 3-ton bulldozer staring into space. Behind him lay a mile-long path of destruction—John had cut a broad, straight path through yards, roads, and fields. The path led back to his house where the dozer was usually kept. Why did he do it? John explained that his father had denied him use of the family car that morning. Hours later, his anger reached the exploding point.

Question: What would cause someone to react so drastically to a family disagreement?

In John's case, the answer is that he was frustrated*—very frustrated! Perhaps you have been as frustrated as John must have been when he climbed into the driver's seat. For example, picture yourself looking for a parking place in a crowded lot. Imagine that you are late for a test and have already been delayed by an irritating traffic jam. After 15 minutes of frantic searching, you finally spy an empty space, but as you start toward it, a Volkswagen darts around the corner and into the space. A car behind you begins to honk impatiently. Your car's radiator boils over. In such a situation you might be seized by an overwhelming desire to run over anything in sight—cars, pedestrians, lampposts, trees, and flower beds. Few people actually carry out such impulses, but the feeling is common. Aggressive urges frequently accompany frustration.*

Question: Is frustration the same as anger?

No. **Frustration** *can be defined as a negative emotional state that occurs when one is prevented from reaching a goal. John's desire to use the family car was blocked by his father. Similarly, in the imaginary parking lot the goal of finding a parking space was blocked by the presence of other cars.*

This chapter will discuss frustration and some of the ways people deal with it. We will also discuss some common forms of **conflict.** *Conflicts develop when a person has two or more competing or contradictory motives or goals. Choosing between college and work, marriage and single life, or study and failure are conflicts many students face.*

Frustration and conflicts are major causes of stress. **Stress** *occurs when demands are placed on an organism to adjust or adapt. Stress is a normal part of life, but when it is severe or prolonged, it can do much damage. Therefore, the Applications section of this chapter focuses on ways for you to cope with frustration, conflict, and stress.*

Survey Questions What causes frustration and what are typical reactions to it? When and why do people use psychological defense mechanisms? Are there different types of conflict? How is stress related to health and disease? What can be done to manage stress?

Resources

External frustration - delay, failure, rejection, loss.

Personal frustrations - individual's characteristics

Sources of Frustration—Blind Alleys and Lead Balloons

Question: What causes frustration?

Obstacles of many kinds cause frustration. A useful distinction can be made between *external* and *personal* sources of frustration. **External frustration** is based on conditions outside the individual that impede progress toward a goal. All of the following are external frustrations: getting stuck with a flat tire, having a marriage proposal rejected, finding the cupboard bare when you go to get your poor dog a bone, finding the refrigerator bare when you go to get your poor tummy a T-bone, finding the refrigerator gone when you return home, being chased out of the house by your starving dog. In other words, external frustrations are based on *delay*, *failure*, *rejection*, *loss*, and other direct blocking of motives.

Frustration usually increases as the **strength, urgency,** or **importance** of a blocked motive increases. An escape artist submerged in a tank of water and bound with 200 pounds of chain could be expected to become *quite* frustrated by the jamming of a trick lock. Remember too that motivation becomes stronger as we near a goal. As a result, frustration is more intense when a person encounters an obstacle very close to a goal. If you've ever missed an A grade by two points, you were probably very frustrated. If you've missed an A by *one* point—well, frustration builds character, right?

A final factor affecting frustration is summarized by the old phrase "the straw that broke the camel's back." *Repeated* frustrations can accumulate in their effect until a small irritation unleashes an unexpectedly violent response. The boy who bulldozed the countryside probably had been frustrated by his father many times before.

Personal frustrations are based on an individual's personal characteristics. If you are 4 feet tall and aspire to be a professional basketball player, you very likely will be frustrated. If you want to go to medical school but can only earn D grades, you will likewise be frustrated. In both examples, frustration is ultimately based on personal limitations, although the resulting failures may be *experienced* as externally caused. We will return to this point in the Applications section of this chapter. In the meantime, let's look at some typical reactions to frustration.

Reactions to Frustration—Irresistible Force Meets Immovable Object

Question: Does frustration always cause aggression? Aren't there other reactions?

Although the connection is strong, frustration does not always provoke aggression. Later, in Chapter 25, we will explore factors that influence when and where aggression is likely to occur. For now, it is enough to note that **aggression** is one of the most persistent and frequent responses to frustration (Miller, 1941). The frustration-aggression link is so common, in fact, that experiments are hardly necessary to show it. A glance at almost any newspaper will provide examples such as the one that follows.

Justifiable Autocide

Burien, Washington (AP)—Barbara Smith committed the assault, but police aren't likely to press charges. Her victim was a 1964 Oldsmobile which failed once too often to start.

When Officer Jim Fuda arrived at the scene, he found one beat-up car, a broken baseball bat, and a satisfied 23-year-old Seattle woman.

"I feel good," Ms. Smith reportedly told the officer. "That car's been giving me misery for years and I killed it."

Aggression is not usually the first reaction to frustration. More often, frustration is met with **persistence,** characterized by more **vigorous efforts** and more **variable responses.** For example, if you put your last quarter in a vending machine and find that pressing the button has no effect, you will probably press harder and faster (vigorous effort), and then you will press all the other buttons (varied response). Persistence may help you get *around* a barrier and achieve your goal. However, if the machine *still* refuses to deliver or to return your quarter, you may then become aggressive and kick the machine (or at least tell it what you think of it). (See Fig. 13-1 for a summary of common reactions to frustration.)

Persistence can be very adaptive. Overcoming a barrier ends the frustration and

External frustration A negative emotional state caused by conditions outside an individual that impede satisfaction of a motive or block progress toward a goal.

Personal frustration A negative emotional state caused by personal characteristics that impede satisfaction of a motive or block progress toward a goal.

Aggression Any response made with the intention of bringing harm to some person or object.

Persistence As a response to frustration, persistence refers to repeated, more vigorous efforts and more variable responding.

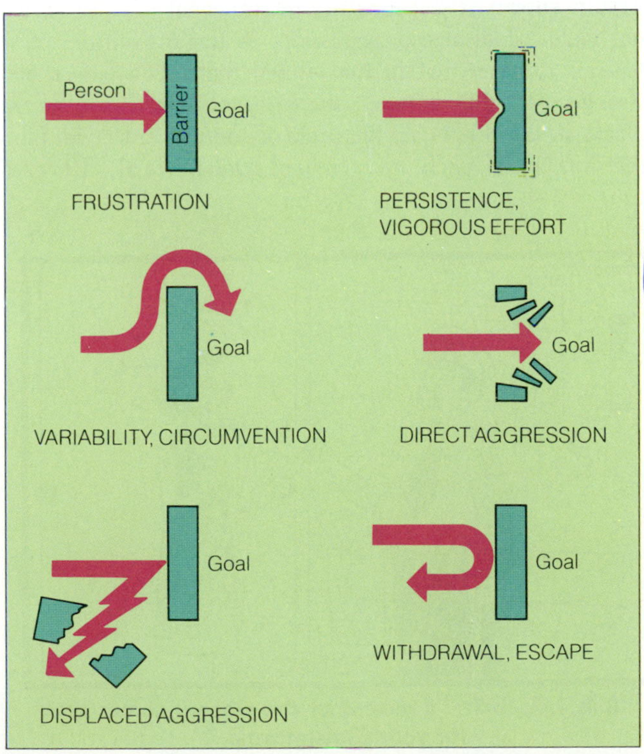

Fig. 13-1 *Frustration, and reactions to it.*

Displaced aggression Redirecting aggression to a target other than the actual source of one's frustration.

Scapegoating The tendency to select a person or group of people to take the blame for conditions not of their making; habitual redirection of aggression toward some person or group.

Escapism Reducing discomfort by leaving frustrating situations or by psychologically withdrawing from them.

displaced aggression - redirecting aggression at something else.

Scapegoat - person who has become a target of displaced aggression,

satisfies the need or motive directed toward the goal. The same is true of aggression that removes or destroys a barrier. Picture a small band of primitive humans, parched with thirst but separated from a water hole by a menacing animal. It is easy to see that attacking the animal may ensure their survival. In modern society such direct aggression is seldom acceptable. If you encounter a long line at the drinking fountain, aggression is hardly an appropriate response. Since direct aggression is disruptive and generally discouraged, it is frequently *displaced*.

Question: How is aggression displaced? Does displaced aggression occur often?

Directing aggression toward a source of frustration may be impossible or it may be too dangerous. If you are frustrated by your boss at work or by a teacher at school, the cost of direct aggression may be too high (loss of a job or failure of a needed class). Instead, the aggression may be displaced or *redirected* toward whomever or whatever is available (see cartoon).

Targets of **displaced aggression** tend to be "safer," or less likely to retaliate, than the original source of frustration. Attacking the helpless countryside when the real source of frustration is one's father is a clear case of displaced aggression. Sometimes long *chains* of displacement can be observed, in which one person displaces aggression to the next. For instance, a businessman who is frustrated by high taxes reprimands an employee, who swallows his anger until he reaches home and then yells at his wife, who in turn yells at the children, who then tease the dog; the dog chases the cat, who later knocks over the canary cage.

Psychologists attribute much hostility and destructiveness in our society to displaced aggression. A disturbing example is the finding that when unemployment increases, so does child abuse (Steinberg et al., 1981). Particularly damaging is a pattern known as **scapegoating.** A scapegoat is a person who has become a habitual target of displaced aggression. A tragic example of scapegoating on a large scale is the fact that in the United States between 1880 and 1930 there was a strong correlation between the price of cotton and the number of lynchings of blacks in the South. As the price of cotton went down (and frustration increased), the number of lynchings increased (Dollard et al., 1939). Despite recent progress,

"Bills, bills, bills! I'll remember this when it comes time for your Christmas tip."

many minority groups continue to suffer from hostility based on scapegoating. Think, for example, about the hostility that was expressed toward Arabic persons in the United States at the time when Americans were being held hostage in Iran.

Question: I have a friend who dropped out of school to hitchhike around the country. He seemed very frustrated before he quit. What type of response to frustration is this?

Another major reaction to frustration is **escape,** or **withdrawal.** Being frustrated is unpleasant. If other reactions do not reduce feelings of frustration, a person may try to escape. Escape may mean actually leaving a source of frustration (dropping out of school, quitting a job, leaving an unhappy marriage), or it may mean *psychologically* escaping. Two common forms of psychological escape are *apathy* (pretending not to care) and the *use of drugs* such as alcohol, marijuana, or narcotics.

Thus far we have examined only the most obvious responses to frustration. A whole class of *defensive* reactions also exists. Let's see how they operate.

Learning Check

Be sure you can answer these questions before continuing.

1. When progress toward a goal is blocked, the resulting psychological state is called ______.

2. Delays, rejections, and losses may be thought of as what kind of frustration? ______.

3. Which of the following is not considered a common reaction to frustration?
a. ambivalence *c.* displaced aggression
b. aggression *d.* persistence

4. Scapegoating can be thought of as a type of displaced aggression. T or F?

5. Sampson Goliath is 7 feet tall and weighs 300 pounds. He has failed miserably in his aspiration to become a jockey. The source of his frustration is mainly ______.

6. As a reaction to frustration, apathy may be viewed as a form of ______.

7. Being very close to a goal and then encountering a barrier typically increases the intensity of frustration. T or F?

Answers: 1. frustration **2.** external **3.** *a* **4.** T **5.** personal **6.** escape or withdrawal **7.** T

Psychological Defense—Mental Karate?

Situations causing frustration, conflict, or stress are often accompanied by an unpleasant emotion known as **anxiety.** A person who is anxious becomes tense, uneasy, apprehensive, worried, and feels vaguely threatened. Since anxiety is unpleasant and uncomfortable, we are usually motivated to avoid it. Anxiety caused by stressful situations, or by our own shortcomings and limitations, frequently leads to use of **psychological defense mechanisms.**

Question: What are psychological defense mechanisms, and how do they lessen anxiety?

A defense mechanism is any technique used to avoid, deny, or distort sources of anxiety. Defense mechanisms are also used to maintain an idealized self-image, so that we can comfortably live with ourselves. Many of the defenses were first identified by Sigmund Freud, who assumed they operated *unconsciously*. Often, unconscious defensiveness creates large blind spots in awareness, as when an extremely stingy person fails to recognize that he or she is a tightwad. Everyone has at one time or another used such defenses. Let's consider a few of the most common. (A more complete listing is given in Table 13-1.)

Denial One of the most basic defense mechanisms is **denial.** Denial means to protect oneself from an unpleasant reality by refusing to accept it or believe it. Denial is closely linked with experiences such as death, illness, and similar painful and threatening situations. For instance, if you were told that you had only 3 months to live, how would you react? Your first thoughts might be: "Aw, come on, someone must have mixed up the X rays," or "The doctor must be mistaken," or, simply, "It can't be true!" Similar denial and disbelief are common reactions to the unexpected death of a friend or relative: "It's just not real. I don't believe it. I just don't believe it!"

Repression Freud noticed that his patients had tremendous difficulty recalling shocking or traumatic events from childhood. It seemed that powerful forces were holding these painful memories from awareness. Freud called this **repression.** Apparently, we protect ourselves by repressing thoughts or impulses that are painful or threatening. Feelings of hostility toward a loved one, the names of disliked people, and past failures and embarrassments are common targets of repression.

Reaction Formation **Reaction formation** is a defense in which impulses are not only repressed, they are also held in check by exaggerated opposite behavior.

Table 13-1 Psychological Defense Mechanisms

Compensation	Counteracting a real or imagined weakness by emphasizing desirable traits or by seeking to excel in other areas.
Denial	Protecting oneself from an unpleasant reality by refusing to perceive it.
Fantasy	Fulfilling frustrated desires in imaginary achievements or activities.
Intellectualization	Separating emotion from a hurtful, threatening, or anxiety-provoking situation by talking and thinking about it in formal or intellectual terms.
Isolation	Separating contradictory thoughts or feelings into "logic-tight compartments" so that no conflict is created.
Projection	Attributing one's own feelings, shortcomings, or unacceptable impulses to others.
Rationalization	Justifying one's own behavior by giving reasonable and rational but false reasons for it.
Reaction formation	Preventing dangerous impulses from being expressed by exaggerating opposite behavior.
Regression	Retreating to an earlier level of development or to earlier, less demanding habits or situations.
Repression	Preventing painful or dangerous thoughts from entering consciousness.
Sublimation	Working off frustrated desires, or unacceptable impulses, in activities that are constructive.

For example, a mother who unconsciously resents her children may, through reaction formation, become absurdly overprotective and overindulgent. Her real thoughts of "I hate them" and "I wish they were gone" are replaced by "I love them" and "I don't know what I would do without them." The mother's hostile impulses are traded for "smother" love, so that she will not have to admit her dislike of her children. The basic idea in reaction formation is that the individual acts out an opposite behavior in order to block threatening impulses or feelings.

Regression In its broadest meaning, **regression** refers to any return to earlier, less demanding situations or habits. Most parents who have a second child have to put up with at least some regression by the older child. Frustrated by a new rival for attention, an older child may regress to childish speech, bed-wetting, or infantile play after the new baby arrives. However, regression is usually not this severe. The child at summer camp who gets homesick and longs for the security of familiar surroundings is undergoing mild regression. An adult who throws a temper tantrum or a married adult who "goes home to mother" is also regressing.

Projection Projection is an unconscious process that protects us from the anxiety that would occur from recognizing our own faults or unacceptable traits.

Question: How does projection work?

A person who is **projecting** tends to see his or her own shortcomings or unacceptable impulses in others. By exaggerating the unacceptable traits of *others*, the individual lessens his or her own failings.

The author once worked for a greedy shop owner who cheated many of his customers. This same man considered himself a pillar of the community and a good Christian. How did he justify to himself his greed and dishonesty? He believed that everyone who entered his store was bent on cheating *him* any way they could. In reality, few, if any, of his customers shared his motives, but he projected his own greed and dishonesty onto them.

Rationalization Every teacher is familiar with a strange phenomenon that occurs when a test is scheduled. On the day of the exam, an incredible wave of disasters sweeps through the city. An amazing number of mothers, fathers, sisters, brothers, aunts, uncles, grandparents, friends, relatives, and pets become ill or die. Motors suddenly fall out of automobiles. Books are lost or stolen. Alarm clocks go belly-up and ring no more.

The making of excuses comes from a natural tendency to explain one's behavior. When the explanation offered is reasonable, rational, and convincing—but not the real reason—we say a person is *rationalizing*. **Rationalization** unconsciously provides us with reasons for behavior we ourselves find somewhat questionable. Here is a typical example of rationalization. A student who fails to turn in an assignment he has known about since the beginning of the semester explains:

> My car broke down 2 days ago and I couldn't get to the library until yesterday. Then I couldn't get all the books I needed because some were checked out, but I wrote what I could. Then last night, as the last straw, the ribbon in my typewriter broke, and since all the stores were closed I couldn't finish the paper on time.

Anxiety Apprehension, dread, or uneasiness similar to fear but based on an unclear threat.

Psychological defense mechanisms Habitual and often unconscious psychological strategies used to avoid or reduce anxiety.

Denial Protecting oneself from an unpleasant reality by refusing to perceive it or believe it.

Repression Preventing painful or dangerous thoughts from entering consciousness.

Reaction formation Preventing dangerous or threatening impulses from being expressed by exaggerating opposite behavior.

Regression Retreating to an earlier stage of development or to earlier, less demanding habits or situations.

Projection Attributing one's own feelings, shortcomings, or unacceptable impulses to others.

Rationalization Justifying one's own behavior by giving reasonable and "rational" but false reasons for it.

Regression - retreating to earlier situations.
Projection - see your own unacceptable impulses on others.

Rationalization - an acceptable excuse that is not true.

If asked why he left the assignment until the last minute (the real reason for its being late), the student would probably launch into another set of rationalizations. If these are questioned, the student will probably become emotional as he is forced to see himself without the protection of his rationalizations.

Question: All of the defense mechanisms described seem pretty undesirable. Do they have a positive side?

People who overuse defense mechanisms become less adaptable, because they consume greater amounts of emotional energy to control anxiety and to maintain an unrealistic self-image. Defense mechanisms do have value, however. Often, they help keep us from being overwhelmed by immediate threats. This can provide time for learning to cope with continuing threats and frustrations. If you recognize some of your own behavior in the descriptions here, it is hardly a sign that you are hopelessly defensive. As noted earlier, most people make occasional use of defense mechanisms.

Two defense mechanisms that have a decidedly more positive quality are *compensation* and *sublimation*.

Compensation Compensation is a form of behavior in which a person tries to make up for some personal defect or fault. **Compensatory reactions** are defenses against feelings of inferiority. A person who has a deficiency or weakness (real or imagined) may go to unusual lengths to overcome the weakness or to compensate for it by excelling in other areas.

Two of the better known muscle men in America are Jack LaLanne and Charles Atlas. Both made successful careers out of body building, in spite of the fact that as young men they were thin and sickly. Perhaps it would be more accurate to say *because* they were thin and sickly. There are dozens of examples of compensation. A childhood stutterer may excel in debate at college. Franklin D. Roosevelt's outstanding achievements in politics came after he was stricken with polio. Although she was unable to see or hear, Helen Keller became an outstanding thinker and writer. Doc Watson, Ray Charles, Stevie Wonder, Ronnie Milsap, and a number of other well-known musicians are blind.

Sublimation **Sublimation** (sub-lih-MAY-shun) is defined as working off frustrated desires (especially sexual desires) in substitute activities that are constructive and accepted by society (Fig. 13-2). Freud believed that art, music, dance, poetry, scientific investigation, and most other creative activities can serve to rechannel sexual energies into productive and acceptable behavior. Freud also believed that almost any strong desire can be sublimated. For example, a very aggressive person might find social acceptance as a professional soldier, boxer, or football player. Greed may be refined into a successful business career. Lying may be sublimated into storytelling, creative writing, or politics.

Sexual motives appear to be the most easily and widely sublimated. Freud would have had a field day with such modern pastimes as surfing, motorcycle riding, drag racing, and dancing to or playing rock music, to name but a few. People enjoy each of these activities for a multitude of reasons, but it is hard to overlook the rich, sexual symbolism possible in each.

Compensation Counteracting a real or imagined weakness by emphasizing desirable traits or by seeking to excel in other areas.

Sublimation Working off frustrated desires or unacceptable impulses in substitute activities that are constructive or accepted by society.

Approach-approach conflict A condition in which a person or animal must choose between two positive, or desirable, alternatives.

Avoidance-avoidance conflict An unpleasant condition requiring a choice between two negative, or undesirable, alternatives.

Approach-avoidance conflicts An unpleasant condition in which a person or animal is simultaneously attracted to and repelled by the same goal.

2 Defense mechanisms more positive quality

1) Compensation · person tries to make up for some personal defect or default

2) Sublimation - working off frustrated behaviors.

Fig. 13-2 *For some players—and fans—football probably allows sublimation of aggressive urges.*

Conflict— Yes-No-Yes-No-Yes-No-Yes-No-Yes-No . . . Well, Maybe

Conflict creates a special kind of frustration. When an individual must make a decision between *incompatible* or *contradictory* needs, desires, motives, wishes, or external demands, he or she experiences conflict. There are four basic forms of conflict, each with its own characteristics (Lewin, 1935) (see Fig. 13-3 and Fig. 13-4).

4 Basic Forms of Conflict
1) Approach - Approach
2) Avoidance - Avoidance
3) Approach - Avoidance
4) Double Approach Avoidance

Approach-Approach Conflicts The simplest conflict comes from having to choose between two *positive*, or desirable, alternatives. Choosing between tutti-frutti-coconut-mocha-champagne-ice and orange-marmalade-peanut-butter-coffee-swirl at the ice cream parlor may throw you into a temporary conflict, but if you really like both choices, your decision will be quickly made. Even when more important decisions are involved, **approach-approach conflicts** tend to be the easiest kind of conflict to resolve. The old fable about the mule who died of thirst and starvation while standing between a bucket of water and a bucket of oats is clearly unrealistic. When both alternatives are positive, the scales of decision are easily tipped one direction or the other.

Approach-Approach - between 2 positive choices.
Avoidance - Avoidance - between 2 negative choices

Avoidance-Avoidance Conflicts Avoidance **conflicts** are based on being forced to choose between two *negative*, or undesirable, alternatives. A person in an avoidance conflict is "caught between the devil and the deep blue sea" or "caught between the frying pan and the fire." In real life, avoidance conflicts involve choosing between things like studying and failure, unwanted pregnancy and abortion, the dentist and tooth decay, a monotonous job and poverty.

Fig. 13-3 *Three basic forms of conflict.*

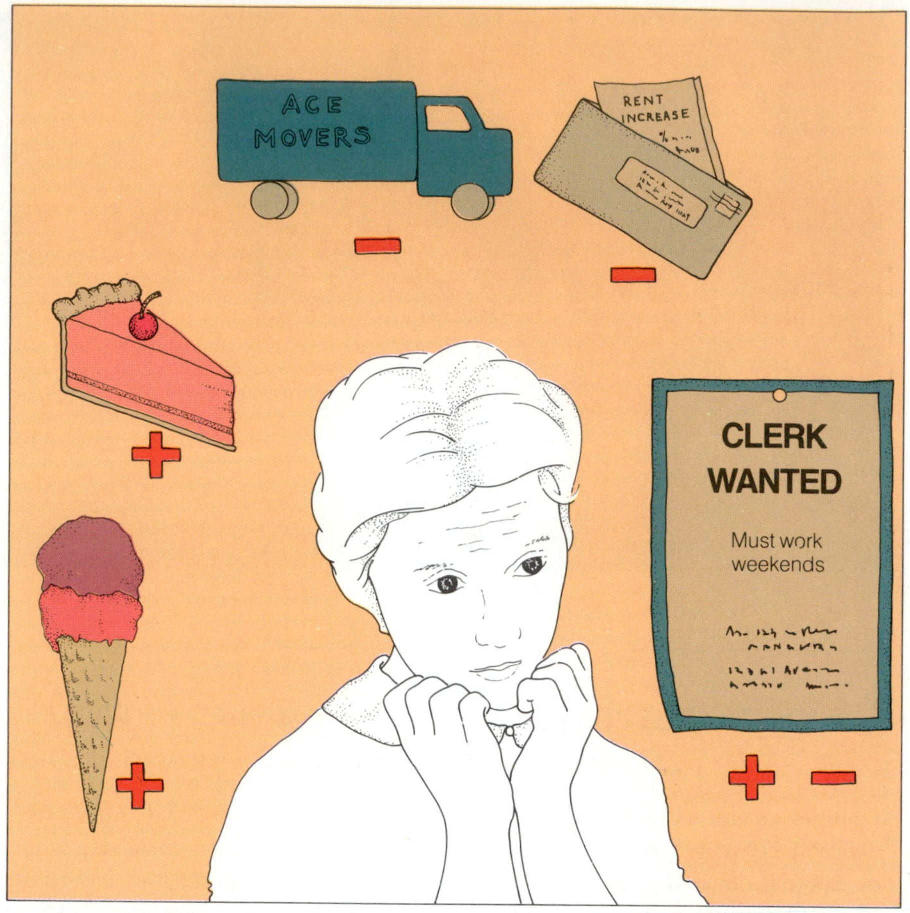

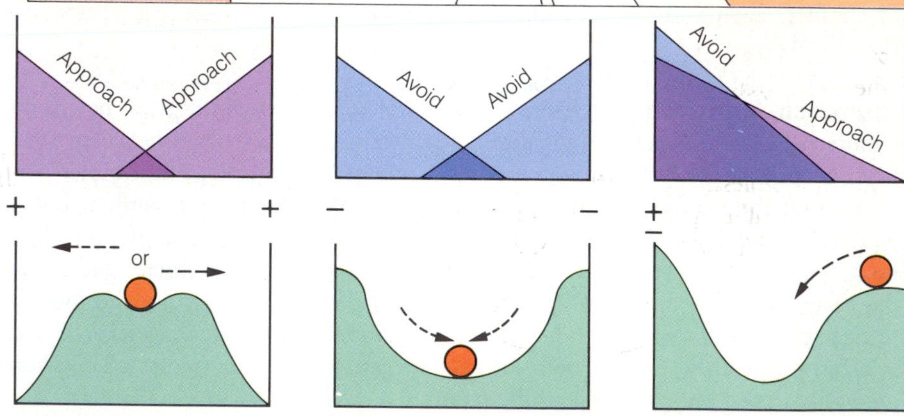

Fig. 13-4 *Conflict diagrams. As shown by the colored areas in the graphs, desires to approach, and to avoid, increase near a goal. The effects of these tendencies are depicted below each graph. The "behavior" of the ball in each example illustrates the nature of the conflict above it. An approach conflict (left) is easily decided. Moving toward one goal will increase its attraction (graph) and will lead to a rapid resolution. (If the ball moves in either direction, it will go all the way to one of the goals.) In an avoidance conflict (center), tendencies to avoid are deadlocked, resulting in inaction. In an approach-avoidance conflict (right), approach proceeds to the point where desires to approach and avoid cancel each other. Again, these tendencies are depicted (below) by the action of the ball. (Graphs after Miller, 1944)*

Question: Suppose I don't object to abortion. Or suppose that I consider any pregnancy sacred and not to be tampered with?

Ambivalence Mixed positive and negative feelings or simultaneous attraction and repulsion.

Approach-Avoidance - being simultaneously attracted to and repelled by same goal.

Notice that these examples can only be defined as conflicts on the basis of an individual's own needs and values. If a woman wants to terminate a pregnancy and has no personal objection to abortion, she experiences no conflict. Or, if she would not consider abortion under any circumstances, there is no conflict.

Avoidance conflicts often have a "damned if you do, damned if you don't" quality. In other words, both choices are negative, but *not choosing* is impossible or equally undesirable. To illustrate, imagine the plight of a person trapped in a hotel fire 20 stories from the ground. Should the person jump from the window and almost surely die on the pavement? Or should he or she try to dash through the flames and almost surely die of smoke inhalation and burns? When people are faced with choices such as these, it is easy to see why they often *freeze*, finding it impossible to decide or take action. A trapped individual may first think about the window, approach it, and then back away after looking down 20 stories. Next the person may try the door and again back away as heat and smoke billow in. In actual disasters of this sort, people are often found dead in their rooms, victims of an inability to take action.

Indecision, inaction, and freezing are not the only reactions to avoidance conflicts. Since avoidance conflicts are stressful and rarely solved, people sometimes pull out of avoidance situations entirely. This reaction, called *leaving the field*, is a form of escape. It may explain the behavior of a student the author knows who could not afford to attend school unless he worked. However, if he worked, he could not earn passing grades. His solution after much conflict and indecision? He joined the navy.

Approach-Avoidance Conflicts Approach-avoidance conflicts are also difficult to resolve. Since people seldom escape them, such conflicts are in some ways more troublesome than avoidance conflicts. A person in an **approach-avoidance conflict** is "caught"—being simultaneously attracted to, and repelled by, the same goal or activity. Attraction keeps the person in the situation, but its negative aspects cause turmoil and distress. For example, a high school student arrives to pick up his date for the first time. He is met at the door by her father, who is a professional wrestler—7 feet tall, 300 pounds, and entirely covered with hair. The father gives the boy a crushing handshake and growls that he will break him in half if the girl is not home on time. The student considers the girl attractive and has a good time. But does he ask her out again? It depends on the relative strength of his attraction and his fear. Almost certainly he will feel *ambivalent* about asking her out again, knowing that another encounter with her father is involved.

Ambivalence (mixed positive and negative feelings) is a central characteristic of approach-avoidance conflicts. Ambivalence is usually translated into *partial approach* (Miller, 1944). Since our student is still attracted to the girl, he may spend time with her at school and elsewhere but may not actually date her again. Some more realistic examples of approach-avoidance conflicts are: planning marriage to someone your parents strongly disapprove of, wanting to be an actor but suffering stage fright, wanting to buy a car but not wanting to be tied to monthly payments, wanting to eat when overweight, and wanting to go to school but hating to study. Many of life's important decisions have approach-avoidance dimensions.

Double approach-avoidance conflict An unpleasant state in which one is simultaneously attracted to and repelled by each of two separate alternatives.

Vacillation Wavering in intention or feelings.

Stress Condition that occurs when an organism must adjust or adapt to external circumstances.

Pressure A stressful condition that occurs when a person must respond at, or near, maximum capacity for long time periods.

Control With regard to stress, the ability to exert some influence over one's circumstances.

Double-Approach-Avoidance- ~~a good~~ a pos but neg, or a neg but pos.

Question: Aren't real-life conflicts more complex than the ones described here?

In reality, conflicts are rarely as clear-cut as those described. People in conflict are usually faced with several dilemmas at once, so several types of conflict are intermingled. The fourth type of conflict moves us closer to this realistic state of affairs.

Double Approach-Avoidance Conflicts You are offered two jobs, one with good pay but poor hours and dull work, the second with interesting work and excellent hours, but low pay. Which do you select? This situation is more typical of the choices we must usually make. It offers neither completely positive, nor completely negative, alternatives. It is, in other words, a **double approach-avoidance conflict,** since each alternative has both positive and negative qualities.

When faced with double approach-avoidance conflicts, people tend to **vacillate,** or waver, between the alternatives. Just as you are about to choose one alternative, its undesirable aspects tend to loom large, so you swing back toward the other. If you have ever been romantically attracted to two people at once, each having qualities you like and dislike, then you have probably experienced vacillation.

On a day-to-day basis, most double approach-avoidance conflicts are little more than an annoyance. When they involve major life decisions, such as choice of a career, school, mate, job, whether to have children, and so forth, they add significantly to the amount of stress experienced.

Learning Check

1. The psychological defense known as denial refers to the natural tendency to explain or justify one's actions. T or F? [F circled]
2. Fulfilling frustrated desires in imaginary achievements or activities defines the defense mechanism of:
   a. compensation *b.* isolation *c.* fantasy [c circled] *d.* sublimation
3. In compensation, one's own undesirable characteristics or motives are attributed to others. T or F? [T circled]
4. Of the defense mechanisms, two that are considered relatively constructive are: (circle)
   compensation [circled] denial isolation projection regression rationalization sublimation [circled]
5. Conflict is related to the presence of contradictory motives or an attempt to reach contradictory goal.
6. The easiest type of conflict to resolve is typically an Approach, Approach conflict.
7. Inaction and freezing are most characteristic of avoidance conflicts. T or F? [T circled]
8. Approach-avoidance conflicts produce mixed feelings called ambivalence.

Answers: **1.** F **2.** c **3.** F **4.** compensation and sublimation **5.** motives, goals **6.** approach-approach **7.** T **8.** ambivalence

Stress—Invisible Killer on the Loose

It is common to assume that stress is always bad or that a complete lack of stress is ideal. However, as stress researcher Hans Selye (1976) observed, "To be totally without stress is to be dead." **Stress** occurs any time we must adjust or adapt to the environment. Naturally, unpleasant situations such as work pressures, marital problems, or financial troubles produce stress. But so do travel, sports, a new job, ski jumping, dating, and other pleasant activities. Even if you aren't a thrill seeker, a healthy lifestyle may include a fair amount of stress.

Question: Why is stress sometimes damaging and sometimes not?

Psychologists are learning that stress reactions in humans are more complex than once thought. Let's examine some of the chief factors that determine whether stress is harmful.

When Is Stress a Strain? It goes almost without saying that some situations are inherently more stressful than others. Police officers, for instance, suffer from an unusually high rate of stress-related diseases. The threat of injury or death, coupled with periodic confrontations with drunk or belligerent citizens, takes a toll. A major factor here is the *unpredictable* nature of police work. An officer who stops to issue a traffic ticket never knows if he or she will encounter a cooperative citizen or an armed fugitive.

The effect of unpredictability in creating stress is shown by an interesting experiment involving three groups of rats. In the experiment one group was given shocks preceded by a warning tone; a second group got shocks without warning; the third group received no shocks but heard the tone. Later, autopsies were performed on the rats. It was found that animals that received no shocks had no stomach ulcers; those receiving unpredictable shocks had severe ulcers; and those given predictable shocks showed little or no ulceration (Weiss, 1972).

Pressure is another element in stress, especially job stress. **Pressure** occurs when activities must be speeded up, when deadlines must be met, when extra work is added unexpectedly, or when a person must work at, or near, maximum capacity for long periods. Most students who have survived final exams are familiar with the effects of pressure.

Question: What if I set deadlines for myself? Does it make a difference where the pressure comes from?

Yes. People generally experience more stress in situations over which they have little **control.** For example, DeGood (1975) subjected male college students to an unpleasant shock-avoidance task. Some subjects were allowed to select their own rest periods, while others rested at times selected by the experimenter. Subjects allowed to control their own rest periods showed lower stress levels (as measured by blood pressure) than those given no choice (Fig. 13-5). Notice that being unable to control stressors is similar to conditions that cause learned helplessness, as described in Chapter 12.

Another experiment shows that lack of control even carries over to the aftereffects of stress. Subjects jolted by uncontrollable blasts of noise did more poorly later on tests of concentration than people given control over the noise (Glass &

Fig. 13-5 *Assembly-line work can be quite stressful due to the lack of control employees have over the pace of work.*

Singer, 1972). If you have ever worked in a noisy office, factory, child-care center, restaurant, or similar setting, you will recognize this effect.

The evidence we have reviewed indicates that when emotional "shocks" are *intense* or *repeated*, *unpredictable*, *uncontrollable*, and linked to *pressure*, stress will be magnified and damage is likely to result. At work such damage sometimes takes the form of **burnout**, a pattern of emotional exhaustion described in Box 13-1.

As important as *external* conditions may be, they are not the whole story where stress is concerned. You have probably noted, for instance, that some people are stressed by events that others view as a thrill or a stimulating challenge. Ultimately, stress depends on how a situation is perceived. As you may recall from Chapter 12, whenever a stressor is appraised as a *threat*, a powerful stress reaction follows (Lazarus et al., 1985; Roskies & Lazarus, 1980). Further, stress is increased when a person believes he or she lacks *competence* to meet a particular demand (Bandura, 1977; Woolfolk & Richardson, 1978). Thus, the intensity of the body's stress response often depends on what we think and tell ourselves about stressors.

Psychosomatic Disorders

Chronic or repeated stress can damage physical health, as well as upset emotional well-being (Selye, 1976). Prolonged stress reactions are related to a large number of psychosomatic (SI-koh-so-MAT-ik) illnesses. Most people recognize that stomach ulcers are stress related, but so are many other illnesses. In **psychosomatic disorders** (*psyche:* mind; *soma:* body), psychological and emotional factors are associated with actual damage to tissues of the body. Psychosomatic problems, therefore, are *not* the same as *hypochondria*. **Hypochondriacs** (HI-po-KON-dree-aks) suffer from imaginary diseases. There is nothing imaginary about a bleeding

Box 13-1

Burnout—The High Cost of Caring

Job burnout is a condition in which an employee is physically, mentally, and emotionally drained (Farber, 1983). What does it mean to be "burned out"? Psychologist Christina Maslach (1982) has identified three aspects of the problem.

First of all, burnout involves *emotional exhaustion*. Affected persons are fatigued, tense, apathetic, and suffer various physical complaints. They feel "used up" and have an "I don't give a damn anymore" attitude toward work. A second aspect of burnout is *depersonalization*, or detachment from others. Burned-out workers coldly treat clients as if they were objects and find it difficult to care about them. The third aspect of burnout is a feeling of *reduced personal accomplishment*. Workers who have burned out do poor work and feel helpless, hopeless, and angry. Their self-esteem suffers and they yearn to change jobs or careers.

Burnout may occur in any job, but it is a marked problem in emotionally demanding helping professions, such as nursing, teaching, social work, counseling, or police work (Farber, 1983).

The irony of burnout is that the same work that tends to produce it can also be highly rewarding. If our society wishes to keep caring, committed people in the helping professions, several changes may be needed. A good start might include redesigning jobs to create a better balance between demands and satisfactions. Building stronger social support systems at work could also help. A good example is the increased use of support groups by nurses and other caregivers. Such groups allow workers to give and receive emotional support as they talk about feelings, problems, and stresses (Sully, 1983). Ultimately, however, the best solution may be for each of us to show greater understanding of the stresses felt by those whose work requires caring about the needs of others.

ulcer. A severe case could be fatal. The person who says, "Oh, it's *just* psychosomatic," misunderstands the seriousness of stress-related diseases.

Question: What diseases are psychosomatic? Who gets them?

The most common problems are gastrointestinal and respiratory (ulcers and asthma, for example), but there are many others. Included are problems such as eczema (skin rash), hives, migraine headaches, rheumatoid arthritis, hypertension (high blood pressure), colitis (ulceration of the colon), and heart disease. Actually, these represent only the major problems. Lesser health complaints are also frequently stress related. Typical examples include muscle tension, headaches, neckaches, backaches, indigestion, constipation, fatigue, insomnia, and sexual dysfunction (Brown, 1980; Hurst, Jenkins, & Rose, 1979). It is estimated that one-half or more of all patients who see a doctor have a psychosomatic disorder or have an illness complicated by psychosomatic symptoms.

It would be a mistake to assume that stress is the sole cause of psychosomatic disease. Usually several factors combine to produce damage. These include hereditary differences, specific organ weaknesses, and learned reactions to stress. Personality also enters the picture. To a degree, there are "ulcer personalities," "asthma personalities," and so on. The best documented of such patterns is the "cardiac personality"—an individual prone to heart disease.

Burnout A job-related condition of mental, physical, and emotional exhaustion.

Psychosomatic disorders Illnesses in which actual physical damage results from emotional reactions to stress.

Hypochondriac A person who is excessively preoccupied with minor bodily problems or who complains about illnesses that appear to be imaginary.

Type A Two noted cardiologists, Meyer Friedman and Ray Rosenman, offer a glimpse at how some people create unnecessary stress. On the basis of a long-term study of heart problems, Friedman and Rosenman (1974) classified people into two categories: **Type A personalities** (those who run a high risk of heart attack) and **Type B personalities** (those who are unlikely to have a heart attack). Friedman and Rosenman then did an 8-year follow-up, finding more than twice the rate of heart disease in Type A's than in Type B's (Rosenman et al., 1975).

Question: What is the Type A personality like?

Type A people are hard driving, ambitious, highly competitive, achievement oriented, and striving (Fig. 13-6). Type A people believe that with enough effort they can overcome any obstacle, and they "push" themselves accordingly. In tests of physical capacity (on a treadmill), Type A's work closer to their actual limits of endurance but say they are less fatigued than do Type B people (Glass, 1977). Type A's don't know when to quit!

Perhaps the most telltale of all Type A characteristics are *time urgency* and chronic *anger* or *hostility*. Type A's seem unsatisfied with the normal pace of events. They hurry from one activity to another, racing the clock in self-imposed urgency. As they do, they feel a constant sense of frustration, anger, and hostility. Feelings of anger and hostility, in particular, are strongly related to increased risk of heart attack (Lenfant & Schweizer, 1985).

Question: Some news reports have stated that Type A behavior is not a factor in heart attacks. Why is that?

It's true some studies have failed to show a link between Type A behavior and heart attacks (Case et al., 1985). However, many researchers believe it is possible that these studies did not accurately classify people as Type A's and Type B's in

Fig. 13-6 *Individuals with Type A personalities feel a continuous sense of time pressure, irritation, and hostility.*

the first place. Beyond that, hundreds of studies *have* supported the validity of the Type A concept. At this point it still seems that Type A's would be wise to take their increased health risks seriously.

Question: How are Type A people identified?

Many of the destructive habits of Type A people are summarized in the short self-identification test presented in Table 13-2. If all or most of the list applies to you, you may be a Type A. Your future plans may also provide a clue. When asked what they would do after college, 60 percent of Type A's said "go to graduate or professional school." In contrast, 70 percent of Type B's said, "go to work, get a job" (Glass, 1977).

Since our society places a premium on achievement, competition, and mastery, it is not surprising that many people develop Type A personalities. The best way to avoid the destructive stress this produces is to adopt behavior that is the opposite to that listed in Table 13-2 (Suinn, 1982). It is entirely possible to succeed without sacrificing your health in the process. (For additional suggestions on combating Type A behavior, consult Friedman and Rosenman, *Type A Behavior and Your Heart*.)

A very basic question remains unanswered in our discussion of stress. How does stress, and our response to it, translate into bodily damage? The answer seems to lie in the body's defenses against stress, a pattern of reactions known as the **general adaptation syndrome.**

Type A personality A personality type associated with elevated risk of heart disease; characterized by a chronic sense of time urgency and a hard-driving personal style.

Type B personality All personality types other than Type A; a low cardiac-risk personality.

General adaptation syndrome (G.A.S.) A consistent series of bodily reactions to prolonged stress, occurring in three stages: alarm, resistance, and exhaustion.

Table 13-2 Characteristics of the Type A Person*

Check the items that apply to you.

Do you:

____ Have a habit of explosively accentuating various key words in ordinary speech even when there is no need for such accentuation?

____ Finish other persons' sentences for them?

____ *Always* move, walk, and eat rapidly?

____ Quickly skim reading material and prefer summaries or condensations of books?

____ Become easily angered by slow moving lines or traffic?

____ Feel an impatience with the rate at which most events take place?

____ Tend to be unaware of the details or beauty of your surroundings?

____ Frequently strive to think of or do two or more things simultaneously?

____ Almost always feel vaguely guilty when you relax, vacation, or do absolutely nothing for several days?

____ Tend to evaluate your worth in quantitative terms (number of A's earned, amount of income, number of games won, and so forth)?

____ Have nervous gestures or muscle twitches such as grinding your teeth, clenching your fists, or drumming your fingers?

____ Attempt to schedule more and more activities into less time and in so doing make fewer allowances for unforeseen problems?

____ Frequently think about other things while talking to someone?

____ Repeatedly take on more responsibilities than you can comfortably handle?

*Shortened and adapted from Meyer Friedman and Ray H. Rosenman, *Type A Behavior and Your Heart*. New York: Alfred A. Knopf, 1974.

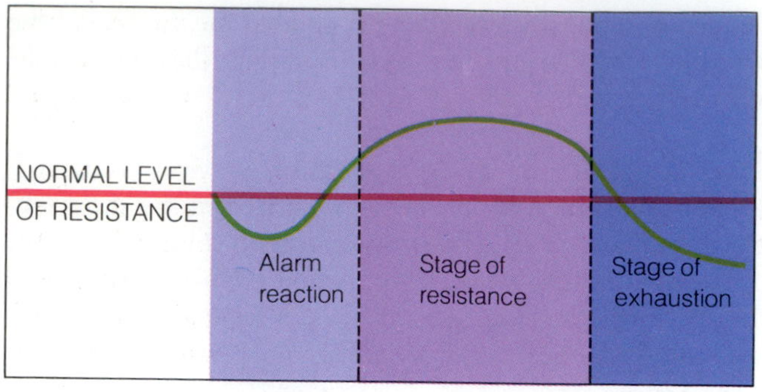

Fig. 13-7 *The general adaptation syndrome. During the initial alarm reaction to stress, resistance falls below normal. It rises again as bodily resources are mobilized, and it remains high during the stage of resistance. Eventually, resistance falls again as the stage of exhaustion is reached. (From* The Stress of Life *by Hans Selye. Copyright© 1956, 1976 by Hans Selye. Used by permission of McGraw-Hill Book Company)*

The General Adaptation Syndrome Study of the general adaptation syndrome (G.A.S.) began when Canadian physiologist Hans Selye (1976) noticed that the initial symptoms of almost any disease or trauma (poisoning, infection, injury, or stress) are almost identical. After more research Selye concluded that the body responds in the same way to any stress, be it infection, failure, embarrassment, adjustment to a new job, school difficulties, or a stormy romance.

Question: What pattern does the body's response to stress take?

The G.A.S. consists of three stages: an *alarm reaction*, a *stage of resistance*, and a *stage of exhaustion* (Selye, 1976).

In the **alarm reaction** the body mobilizes its resources to cope with added stress. The pituitary gland secretes a hormone that causes the adrenal glands to step up their output of adrenaline and noradrenaline. As these hormones are added to the bloodstream, some bodily processes are speeded and others are slowed, to concentrate bodily resources where they are needed.

In the first phase of the alarm reaction, people have such symptoms as headache, fever, fatigue, sore muscles, shortness of breath, diarrhea, upset stomach, loss of appetite, and lack of energy. Notice that these are also the symptoms of being sick, of stressful travel, of high-altitude sickness, final exams week, and (possibly) of falling in love!

Soon the body's defenses are stabilized, and symptoms of the alarm reaction disappear. Physically the body has made adjustments to resist stress. However, the outward appearance of normality is maintained at a high cost. During the **stage of resistance,** the body is better able to cope with the original source of stress (see Fig. 13-7), but resistance to other stresses is lowered. For example, animals placed in an extremely cold environment become more resistant to the cold, but more susceptible to infection. It is during the stage of resistance that the first signs of psychosomatic disorders begin to appear.

If stress continues, the **stage of exhaustion** may be reached. In this stage the body's resources are exhausted and the stress hormones are depleted. Unless a way of alleviating stress is found, the result will be a psychosomatic disease, organ failure, serious loss of health, or complete collapse.

The stages of the G.A.S. may sound melodramatic if you are young and healthy or if you have never had a personal encounter with prolonged stress. However, stress is not to be taken lightly. When Selye examined animals in the later stages of the G.A.S., he found enlargement and discoloration of their adrenal glands; intense shrinkage of the thymus, spleen, and lymph nodes; and deep bleeding stomach ulcers (Cox, 1978). In addition to such direct effects, there is growing evidence that stress can disrupt the body's **immune system,** making people more susceptible to illness (Jemmott & Locke, 1984). There is even evidence that severe life stresses, such as the death of a spouse, frequently precede the appearance of some forms of cancer (Eysenck, 1983).

Question: How do I know if I am subjecting myself to too much stress?

Although much has been learned about stress, this question remains difficult to answer. We can get some help, however, from research that links stressful events to changes in health, as described in the next section.

Alarm reaction First stage of the G.A.S., during which bodily resources are mobilized to cope with a stressor.

Stage of resistance Second stage of the G.A.S., during which bodily adjustments to stress stabilize but at a high physical cost.

Stage of exhaustion Third stage of the G.A.S., at which time the body's resources are exhaused and serious health consequences occur.

Immune system System that mobilizes bodily defenses (such as white blood cells) against invading microbes and other disease agents.

Social Readjustment Rating Scale (SRRS) A scale that rates the impact of various life events on the likelihood of illness.

Life change units (LCU's) Numerical values assigned to each life event on the Social Readjustment Rating Scale and used to predict the likelihood of illness.

Stress and Health—The Hazards of Hassles

At the University of Washington, Dr. Thomas Holmes and his associates have confirmed something long suspected: Stressful events reduce the body's natural defenses against disease and increase the likelihood of illness (Holmes & Masuda, 1972). Holmes found that disaster and sorrow often precede illness. More surprising is the finding that almost any major *change* in one's life requires adjustment and increases susceptibility to accident and illness.

Life Change Units Holmes and his associates have developed a rating scale to estimate the potential health hazards faced when stresses accumulate. Their **Social Readjustment Rating Scale (SRRS)** is reprinted in Table 13-3. Notice that the effect of life events is expressed in **life change units (LCU's).**

As you read the scale, notice too that a positive life event may be as costly as a disaster. Marriage rates 50 life change units, even though it is usually considered a happy event. Notice also that many items read "Change in . . . ". This means that an improvement in life conditions is as costly as a decline.

To use the scale, add up the LCU's for all life events you have experienced during the last year and compare the total with these standards:

0 to 150—No significant problems
150 to 199—Mild life crisis (33 percent chance of illness)
200 to 299—Moderate life crisis (50 percent chance of illness)
300 or over—Major life crisis (80 percent chance of illness)

When the LCU total exceeds 300 points, there is an 80 percent chance of illness or accident in the near future.

Table 13-3 Social Readjustment Rating Scale (SRRS).
The SRRS Lists Significant Life Events and Offers a Rating of Their Contribution to Susceptibility to Illness.

Rank	Life Event	Life Change Units	Rank	Life Event	Life Change Units
1	Death of spouse	100	22	Change in responsibilities at work	29
2	Divorce	73	23	Son or daughter leaving home	29
3	Marital separation	65	24	Trouble with in-laws	29
4	Jail term	63	25	Outstanding personal achievement	28
5	Death of a close family member	63	26	Wife begins or stops work	26
6	Personal injury or illness	53	27	Begin or end school	26
7	Marriage	50	28	Change in living conditions	25
8	Fired at work	47	29	Revision of personal habits	24
9	Marital reconciliation	45	30	Trouble with boss	23
10	Retirement	45	31	Change in work hours or conditions	20
11	Change in health of family member	44	32	Change in residence	20
12	Pregnancy	40	33	Change in school	20
13	Sex difficulties	39	34	Change in recreation	19
14	Gain of new family member	39	35	Change in church activities	19
15	Business readjustment	39	36	Change in social activities	18
16	Change in financial state	38	37	Take out loan less than $20,000	17
17	Death of close friend	37	38	Change in sleeping habits	16
18	Change to different line of work	36	39	Change in number of family get-togethers	15
19	Change in number of arguments with spouse	35	40	Change in eating habits	15
20	Take out mortgage or loan for major purchase	31	41	Vacation	13
			42	Christmas	12
21	Foreclosure of mortgage or loan	30	43	Minor violations of the law	11

Adapted with permission from "Social Readjustment Rating Scale," by T. H. Holmes and R. H. Rahe, *Journal of Psychosomatic Research*, 1967. Reprinted with permission from Pergamon Press, Ltd.

A more conservative rating of stress can be obtained by totaling LCU points for events occurring only during the previous 6 months. Studies of U.S. Navy personnel produced these figures for 6-month totals (Rahe, 1972):

LCU's	Average Number of Illnesses Reported for 6-Month Period
0 to 100	1.4
300 to 400	1.9
500 to 600	2.1

Question: Many of the listed life changes don't seem relevant to young adults or college students. Does the SRRS apply to these people?

The SRRS tends to be more appropriate for older, more established adults. However, research has shown that the health of college students is also affected by stressful events such as entering college, changing majors, or the breakup of a steady relationship (Martin et al., 1975).

The SRRS is not a foolproof way to rate stress, and some studies have failed to confirm the LCU-illness link (Schless, 1977). Nevertheless, a high LCU score should be taken seriously. It would be a good idea to total your LCU's once or twice a year as a rough index of stress levels. If your score goes much over 300, an adjustment in your activities or lifestyle may be called for. Remember, "to be forewarned is to be forearmed."

Hassle Lazarus' term for any distressing, day-to-day annoyance.

Stress management The application of behavioral strategies to reduce stress and improve coping skills.

Question: There must be more to stress than major life changes. Isn't there a link between ongoing stresses and health?

Hassles In addition to their immediate impact, major life changes often create a kind of ripple effect—that is, countless daily frustrations and irritations spring from the original event. In addition many of us face ongoing stresses at work or at home that do not involve major life changes. In recognition of these facts, psychologist Richard Lazarus and his associates recently studied the impact of minor, but frequent stresses. Lazarus (1981) aptly refers to such stresses as **hassles,** which he defines as distressing daily annoyances. Hassles range from traffic jams to losing classroom notes; from an argument with a roommate to an employer's unrealistic demands.

In a year-long study Lazarus had 100 men and women keep track of the frequency and severity of the hassles they encountered. Subjects in the study also filled out questionnaires concerning their physical and mental health. As Lazarus and his associates had suspected, frequent and severe hassles turned out to be better predictors of day-to-day psychological and physical health than were major life events. However, major life events did predict changes in health a year or two after the events took place. So, it appears that daily hassles are closely linked to immediate health, whereas major life changes have more of a long-term impact.

In follow-up work, Lazarus and others have found that the personal importance of hassles affects the amount of stress they produce (Lazarus et al., 1985). Hassles that are viewed as central to one's self-worth are most likely to cause trouble. For many people, central hassles are linked to work, family, and relationships. But as psychologist Rand Gruen notes, "Taking care of paperwork or being organized can be central for some people" (Fisher, 1984). This observation again emphasizes that stress occurs in people, not in the environment. Stress is always related to personality, values, perceptions, and personal resources.

Question: What can be done about a high LCU score or feeling excessively hassled?

A good response is to use **stress management** skills. For serious problems, stress management should be learned directly from a therapist or at a stress clinic. When ordinary stresses are involved, there is much you can do on your own. This chapter's Applications section will give you a start. In the meantime, take it easy!

Learning Check

1. Ulcers developed by persons in high-stress occupations and by animals in stress experiments are an example of a psychosomatic disorder.
2. Greater control over a source of stress is usually associated with a reduction in the amount of stress experienced. T or F?
3. People suffering from hypochondria have serious tissue damage caused by stress or prolonged emotion. T or F?

4. Which of the following is *not* classified as a psychosomatic disorder?
a. hypertension *b.* colitis *c.* eczema *d.* thymus

5. The first stage of the G.A.S. is called the ______________ reaction.

6. Most outward symptoms of stress disappear during the stage of ______________.

7. According to Friedman and Rosenman, Type A persons tend to be angry or hostile but they rarely suffer from a sense of time urgency. T or F?

8. Holmes' SRRS appears to predict long-range changes in health, whereas the frequency and severity of daily hassles is closely related to immediate ratings of health. T or F?

Answers: **1.** psychosomatic **2.** T **3.** F **4.** *d* **5.** alarm **6.** resistance **7.** F **8.** T

Applications

Stress Management

The simplest way of coping with stress is to modify or remove its source—by leaving a stressful job, for example. Obviously this is often impossible, which is why learning to manage stress is so important.

As shown in Figure 13-8, stress triggers *bodily effects, upsetting thoughts*, and *ineffective behavior.* Also shown is the fact that each element worsens the others, creating a vicious cycle. Indeed, the basic idea of the "Stress Game" is that once it begins, *you lose*—unless you take action to break the cycle. The information that follows tells how. (Stress management techniques are derived from Davis, McKay, & Eshelman, 1980; Meichenbaum, 1977; Woolfolk & Richardson, 1978, and other sources as indicated.)

Bodily Reactions

Much of the immediate discomfort of stress is caused by the body's fight/flight emotional response. The body is ready to act, with tight muscles and a pounding heart. When action is prevented, we merely remain "uptight." A sensible remedy is to learn a reliable, drug-free way of relaxing.

Exercise Because stress prepares the body for action, its effects can be dissipated by using the body. Any full-body exercise can be effective. Swimming, dancing, jumping rope, yoga, most sports, and especially walking are valuable outlets. Be sure to choose activities that are vigorous enough to relieve tension, yet enjoyable enough to be done repeatedly. Exercising for stress management is most effective when it is done daily.

Meditation Many stress counselors recommend meditation for quieting the body and promoting relaxation. The meditation technique described in Chapter 6 is a good starting place. Remember that meditation is easy to learn—taking an expensive commercial course is unnecessary. Remember too that listening to or playing music, taking nature walks, doing hobbies, and the like can be meditations of sorts.

Progressive Relaxation Progressive relaxation refers to a method in which people learn to relax systematically, completely, and by choice. To learn the full technique, consult Chapter 22 of this book. The basic idea is to tighten all the muscles in a given area of the body (the arms, for instance) and then voluntarily relax them. By tensing and relaxing each area of the body, you can learn to greatly reduce tension.

Ineffective Behavior

Stress is often made worse by our response to it. The following suggestions may help you deal with stress more effectively.

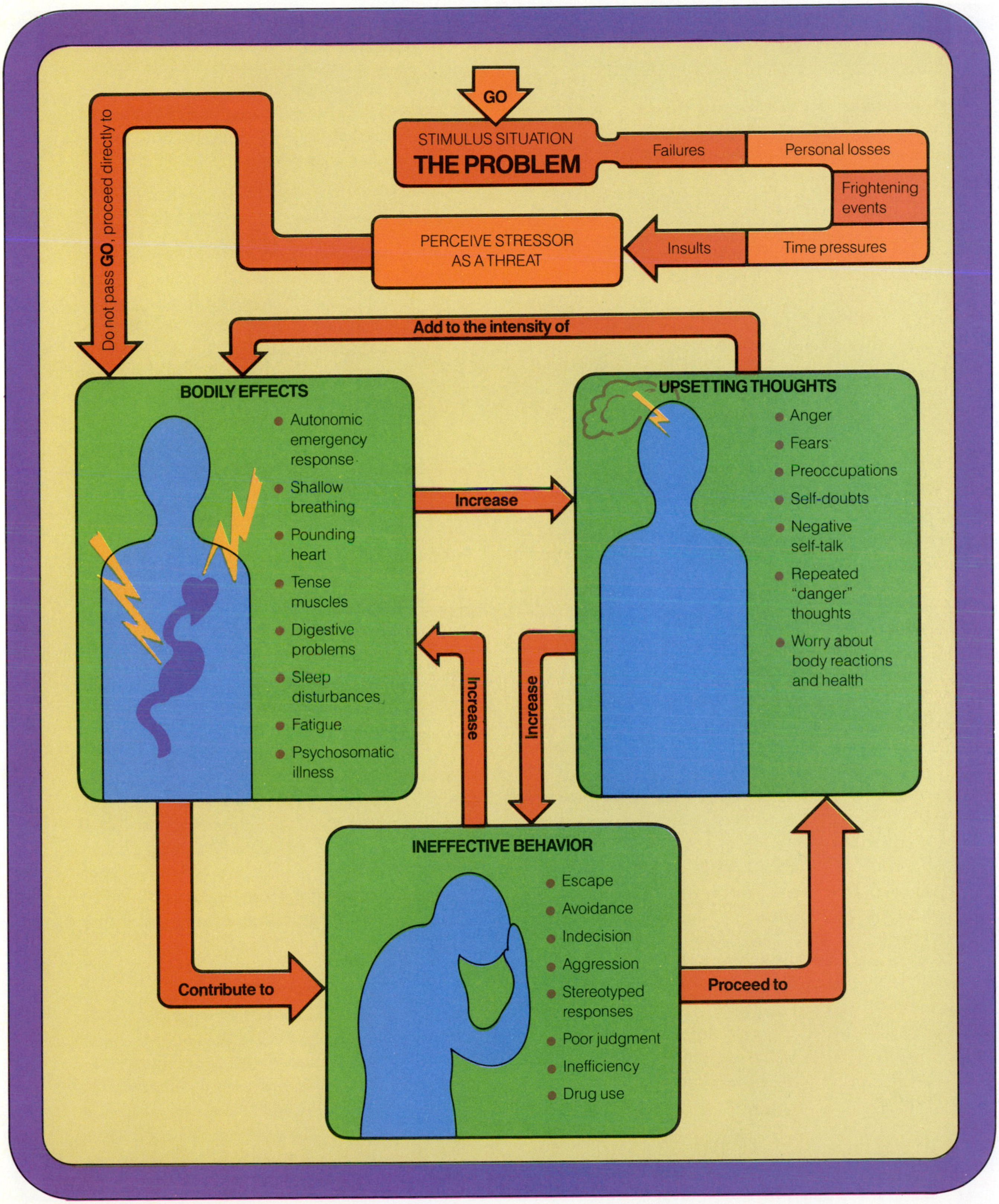

Fig. 13-8 *The stress game. (Adapted from Rosenthal & Rosenthal, 1980)*

Applications: Stress Management, continued

Slow Down Remember that stress can be self-generated. Try to deliberately do things at a slower pace—especially if your pace has speeded up over the years. Tell yourself, "What counts most is not if I get there first, but if I get there at all." Or, "My goal is distance, not speed."

Organize Disorganization creates stress. Try to take a fresh look at your situation and get organized. Setting priorities can be a real stress fighter. Ask yourself what's really important and concentrate on the things that count. Learn to let go of trivial but upsetting irritations. And above all, when you are feeling stressed, remember to K.I.S.: *Keep It Simple*.

Strike a Balance Work, school, family, friends, interests, hobbies, recreation, community, church—there are many important elements in a satisfying life. Damaging stress often comes from letting one element get blown out of proportion, especially work or school. Your goal should be *quality* in life, not quantity. Try to strike a balance between "good stress" and relaxation. Remember, when you are "doing nothing," you are actually doing something very important: Set aside time for "me acts" such as loafing, browsing, puttering, playing, napping.

Recognize and Accept Your Limits Many of us set unrealistic and perfectionistic goals. Given that no one can ever be perfect, this attitude leaves many people feeling inadequate, no matter how well they have performed. Set gradual, achievable goals for yourself. Also, set realistic limits on what you try to do on any given day. Learn to say no to added demands or responsibilities.

Seek Social Support Studies have shown that close, positive relationships with others facilitate good health and morale (Cobb, 1976). One reason for this is that support from family and friends serves as a buffer to cushion the impact of stressful events (Pardine et al., 1981). Talking out problems and expressing tensions can be incredibly helpful. If things really get bad, seek help from a therapist, counselor, or clergyman (please note that bartender is not on the list).

Upsetting Thoughts

Assume you are taking a test. Suddenly you realize you are running short of time. If you say to yourself, "Oh no, this is terrible, I've blown it now," your body's reponse will probably be sweating, tenseness, and a knot in your stomach. On the other hand, if you say, "I should have watched the time, but getting upset won't help now, so I'll just take one question at a time," your stress level will be much lower. (More information on test taking and anxiety appears in Chapter 11.)

As stated earlier, stress is greatly affected by the views we take of events. Physical symptoms and a tendency to make poor decisions are increased by negative thoughts or "self-talk." In many cases what you say to yourself can be the difference between coping and collapsing.

Coping Statements Donald Meichenbaum of the University of Waterloo, Canada, has popularized a technique called **stress inoculation.** In it, clients learn to fight fear and anxiety with an internal monologue of positive **coping statements.** First, clients learn to identify and monitor **negative self-statements.** Negative, self-critical thoughts are a problem because they tend to directly elevate physical arousal (Schuele & Wiesenfeld, 1983). To counter this effect, clients learn to replace negative statements with coping statements from a supplied list. Eventually, they are encouraged to make their own lists.

Question: How are coping statements applied?

Coping statements are used to block out, or counteract, negative self-talk in stressful situations. In giving a short speech, for instance, you would replace "I'm scared," "I can't do this," "My mind will go blank and I'll panic," or "I'll sound stupid and boring"

Applications: Stress Management, continued

with "I'll give my speech on something I like," or "I'll breathe deeply before I start my speech," or "My pounding heart just means I'm psyched up to do my best." Additional examples of coping statements follow.

Preparing for a Stressful Situation

I'll just take things one step at a time.
If I get nervous, I'll just pause a moment.
Tomorrow I'll be through it.
I've managed to do this before.
What exactly do I have to do?

Confronting the Stressful Situation

Relax now, this can't really hurt me.
Stay organized, focus on the task.
There's no hurry, take it step-by-step.
Nobody's perfect, I'll just do my best.
It will be over soon, just be calm.

Meichenbaum cautions that saying the "right" things to yourself may not be sufficient to bring about real improvement in stress tolerance. You must practice this approach in actual stress situations. Also, it is important to develop your own personal list of coping statements by finding what works for you. Ultimately, the value of learning this, and other stress management skills, ties back into the idea that much stress is self-generated. Knowing that you can manage a demanding situation is, in itself, a major antidote for stress.

Coping with Frustration and Conflict

A psychologist studying frustration placed rats on a small platform at the top of a tall pole. Then he forced them to jump off the platform toward two elevated doors, one locked and the other unlocked. If the rat chose the correct door, it swung open and he landed safely on another platform. If he chose the locked door, he bounced off it and fell into a net far below.

The problem of choosing the open door was made unsolvable and very frustrating by randomly alternating which door was locked. After a time most rats adopted a **stereotyped response.** That is, they chose the same door every time. This door was then *permanently* locked. All the rat had to do was to jump to the other door to avoid a fall, but time after time the rat bounced off the locked door (Maier, 1949).

Question: Isn't this an example of persistence?

No. Persistence that is not *flexible* can become "stupid," stereotyped behavior like that of a rat on a jumping stand. When dealing with frustration, it is important to know when to quit and establish a new direction. Here are some suggestions to help you avoid needless frustration.

1. Try to identify the source of your frustration. Is it internal, external, or personal?
2. Is the source of frustration something that can be changed? How hard would you have to work to change it? Is it under your control at all?
3. If the source of your frustration can be changed or removed, are the necessary efforts worth it?

The answers to these questions help determine if persistence will be futile. There is value in learning to accept gracefully those things that cannot be changed.

It is also important to distinguish between *real* barriers and *imagined* barriers. All too often we create our own imaginary barriers. For example:

> Anita wants a part-time job to earn extra money. At the first place she applied, she was told that she didn't have enough "experience." Now she complains of being frustrated because she wants to work but cannot. She needs "experience" to work but can't get experience without working. She has quit looking for a job.

Is Anita's need for experience a real barrier? Unless she applies for *many* jobs, it is impossible to tell if she has overestimated its importance. For her the barrier is real enough to prevent further efforts, but with persistent looking she might locate an "unlocked door." If a reasonable amount of persistence does show that "experience" is essential, it might be ob-

Applications: Stress Management, continued

tained in other ways—through temporary volunteer work, for instance.

Question: How can I handle conflicts more effectively?

Most of the suggestions just made also apply to conflict. However, here are some additional things to remember when you are in conflict or must make a difficult decision.

1. Don't be hasty when making important decisions. Take time to collect information and to weigh pros and cons. Hasty decisions are often regretted. Even if you do make a faulty decision, it will trouble you less if you know that you did everything possible to avoid a mistake.

2. Try out important decisions *partially* when possible. If you are thinking about moving to a new town, try to spend a few days there first. If you are choosing between colleges, do the same. If classes are in progress, sit in on some. If you want to learn to skin-dive, rent equipment for a reasonable length of time before buying.

3. Look for workable compromises. Again, it is important to get all available information. If you think that you only have one or two alternatives and they are undesirable or unbearable, seek the aid of a teacher, counselor, minister, or social service agency. You may be overlooking possible alternatives these people will know about.

4. When all else fails, make a decision and live with it. Indecision and conflict exact a high cost. Sometimes it is best to select a course of action and stick with it unless it is *very obviously* wrong *after* you have taken it.

Learning Check

1. Exercise, meditation, and progressive relaxation are considered effective ways of countering negative self-statements. T or F?

2. Research shows that social support from family and friends has little effect on the health consequences of stress. T or F?

3. One element of stress inoculation is training in the use of positive coping statements. T or F?

4. Stereotyped responding can be particularly troublesome in coping with frustration. T or F?

Answers: **1.** F **2.** F **3.** T **4.** T

Chapter Summary

- *Frustration* is the negative emotional state that occurs when progress toward a goal is blocked. Sources of frustration may be usefully classified as *external* or *personal*.
- External frustrations are based on *delay*, *failure*, *rejection*, *loss*, and other direct blocking of motives. Personal frustration is related to *personal characteristics* over which one has little control. Frustrations of all types become more intense as the *strength*, *urgency*, or *importance* of the blocked motive increases.
- Major behavioral reactions to frustration include *persistence*, *more vigorous responding*, *circumvention*, *direct aggression*, *displaced aggression* (including *scapegoating*), and *escape* or *withdrawal*.

- Frustration and attendant feelings of anxiety or inadequacy frequently lead to use of *psychological defense mechanisms*. A large number of defense mechanisms have been identified, including *compensation*, *denial*, *fantasy*, *intellectualization*, *isolation*, *projection*, *rationalization*, *reaction formation*, *regression*, *repression*, and *sublimation*. Each helps people deny, avoid, or distort sources of anxiety.
- *Conflict* occurs when one must choose between contradictory alternatives. Four major types of conflict are: *approach-approach* (choice between two desirable alternatives); *avoidance-avoidance* (both alternatives are negative); *approach-avoidance* (a goal or activity has both positive and negative aspects); and *double approach-avoidance* (both alternatives have advantages and disadvantages).
- Approach-approach conflicts are usually the easiest to resolve. Avoidance conflicts are difficult to resolve and are characterized by *inaction*, *indecision*, *freezing*, and a *desire to escape* (called *leaving the field*). People usually remain in approach-avoidance conflicts but fail to fully resolve them. Approach-avoidance conflicts are associated with *ambivalence* and *partial approach*. *Vacillation* (a wavering between alternatives) is probably the most common reaction to double approach-avoidance conflicts.
- *Stress* occurs when demands are placed on an organism to adjust or adapt. When stress is intense or prolonged (especially when associated with negative emotional response), it may cause damage in the form of ulcers and other *psychosomatic* problems. Psychosomatic (mind-body) disorders have no connection to *hypochondria*, the tendency to imagine that one has a disease.
- Stress is more damaging in situations involving *pressure*, a lack of *control*, *unpredictability* of the stressor, and *intense* or *repeated* emotional shocks. Stress is intensified when a situation is perceived as a *threat* and when a person does not feel *competent* to cope with it. In work settings prolonged stress, especially when associated with caregiving, can lead to *burnout*.
- People with *Type A personalities* are competitive, striving, frequently angry or hostile, and they have a chronic sense of time urgency. These characteristics combine to double the chances of heart attack.
- The body reacts to stress in a series of stages called the *general adaptation syndrome (G.A.S.)*. The stages of the G.A.S. are *alarm*, *resistance*, and *exhaustion*. The pattern of bodily reactions and changes in resistance observed in the G.A.S. follow closely the pattern observed in the development of psychosomatic disorders. In addition, stress may lower the body's *immunity* to disease.
- Work with the *Social Readjustment Rating Scale* indicates that an accumulation of life changes can increase susceptibility to accident or illness. However, immediate psychological and mental health is more closely related to the intensity and severity of daily annoyances, or *hassles*.
- A sizable number of coping skills can be applied to manage stress: Most of these focus on one of three areas: *bodily effects*, *ineffective behavior*, and *upsetting thoughts*.

Part Five

Human Development and Personality

Chapter 14

Human Development

Chapter Preview

Alien Minds

You may not have noticed. Not everyone has. There are alien creatures among us. More arrive daily. They look a lot like you and me, but they're smaller, and they think differently. Their speech is strange. They ask many questions. It's obvious they are trying to understand how we live. Their goal is to inhabit the planet Earth in our place. Who are these creatures? Where are they from? You need not be alarmed; they come not from outer space, but from inner space. They are the product of a biological union—of life perpetuating life. They are children.

Studying children helps answer the question, "How did I become the person I am today?" To understand ourselves as adults, we must get to know the child in our past. This fact makes the study of children rewarding, but there is another reason for interest: A child's understanding of the world is qualitatively *different from yours and mine. Entry into a child's circle of awareness has much of the intrigue of meeting a person from another culture. It might even be compared to an encounter with an alien mind. In short, children are extremely interesting creatures, and a tremendous amount of psychological research has focused on them.*

Question: What branch of psychology studies children?

The study of children is the heart of **developmental psychology.** *However, you should recognize that developmental psychologists are interested in every stage of life from "the womb to the tomb." Developmental psychology can therefore be described as the* study of progressive changes in behavior and abilities from conception to death. *With a definition like this, it's clear that developmental psychology includes many topics—so many, in fact, that some appear in other chapters.*

In this chapter you will find a number of general principles of development, including an account of the far-reaching events in the first years of life. Perhaps learning about development will contribute to your own development. Find out by reading more!

Survey Questions What can newborn babies do? How aware are infants of their surroundings? How do heredity and environment affect development? How important are parenting styles? Of what significance is a child's emotional attachment to parents? How do children acquire language and thinking abilities? What are the effects of a poor early environment? What can be done to enhance early development?

The Newborn Baby— The Basic Model Comes with Options

At birth the human **neonate** (NEE-oh-NATE, *neo:* new *nate:* born) is completely helpless and will die if not cared for. Newborn babies cannot lift their heads, turn over, or feed themselves. Does this mean they are inert and unfeeling? Definitely not! Neonates can see, hear, smell, taste, and respond to pain and touch. Although their senses are less acute at birth, babies are immediately responsive to their surroundings. Babies will, in fact, follow a moving object with their eyes and will turn in the direction of sounds.

A number of adaptive *reflexes* can also be observed in the newborn. An object pressed into the neonate's palm will be grasped with surprising strength. The **grasping reflex** is so strong that many infants can hang from a raised bar, like little trapeze artists. Very likely, the grasping reflex improves an infant's chances of survival by helping prevent falling. Another adaptive reflex can be demonstrated by touching a baby's cheek. Immediately the baby will turn toward your finger, as if searching for something.

Question: How is such turning adaptive?

The **rooting reflex,** as this is called, helps the infant find a bottle or breast. Then, when a nipple touches the infant's mouth, the **sucking reflex** helps the baby obtain needed food. At the same time, food rewards nursing which rapidly increases in vigor during the first days after birth. Thus, we see that learning begins immediately in the newborn.

Also of interest is the **Moro reflex.** If a baby's head is allowed to drop, or if the baby is startled by a loud noise, the infant will make movements similar to an embrace. These movements have been compared with those used by baby monkeys to cling to their mothers. (It is left to the reader's imagination to decide if there is any connection.)

We are tempted to think of newborn babies as mere bundles of reflexes. But a number of observations show that infants respond in ways that are more subtle than was once imagined. For example, Andrew Meltzoff and Keith Moore (1977) found that babies are born mimics. Figure 14-1 shows Meltzoff as he sticks out his tongue, opens his mouth, and purses his lips at a 20-day-old girl. Will the baby imitate him? Videotapes made of the babies tested in this way confirm that they consistently imitate adult facial gestures. Such mimicry is obviously an aid to rapid learning in infancy.

Question: How much intelligence does a newborn have?

Resources

Neonate A term used for newborn infants during the first weeks following birth.

Grasping reflex A neonatal reflex consisting of grasping objects placed in the palms.

Rooting reflex Neonatal reflex elicited by a light touch to the cheek, causing the infant to turn toward the object and attempt to nurse.

Sucking reflex Neonatal reflex elicited by touching the mouth, whereupon the infant makes rhythmic sucking movements.

Moro reflex Neonatal reflex elicited by sudden loss of support or the sounding of a loud noise; in response, the arms are extended and then brought toward each other.

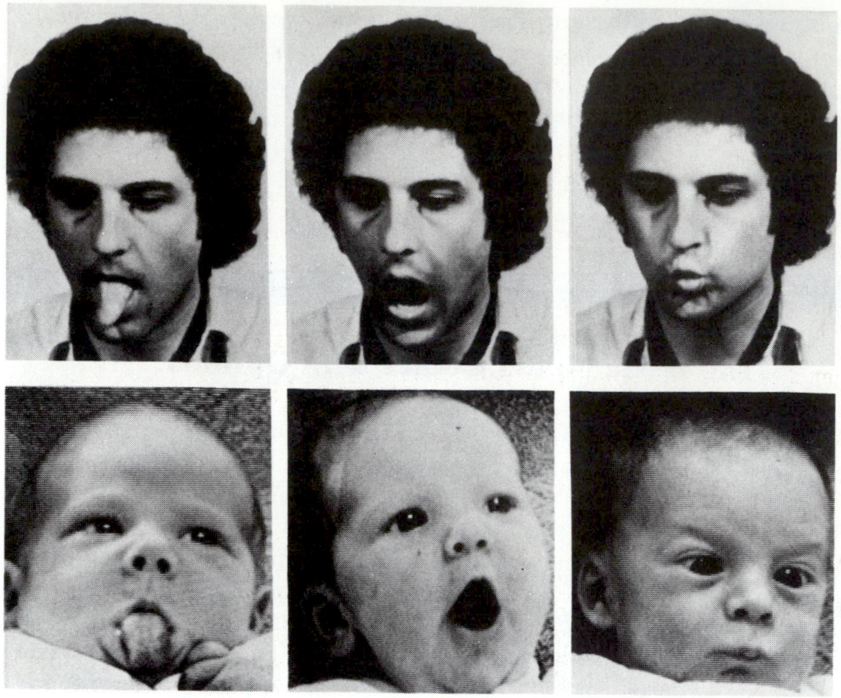

Fig. 14-1 *Infant imitation. In the top row of photos, Andrew Meltzoff makes facial gestures at an infant. The bottom row records the infant's responses. Videotapes of Meltzoff and of tested infants helped ensure objectivity. (Photos courtesy of Andrew N. Meltzoff)*

Child psychologist Jerome Bruner believes babies are smarter than most people think. Bruner cites an experiment in which 3- to 8-week-old babies showed signs of understanding that a person's voice and body are connected. If babies heard their mother's voice coming from where she was standing, they remained calm. If her voice came from a loudspeaker several feet away, the babies became agitated and began to cry. Bruner considers this and similar experiments a sign that the human mind is quite active from birth onward (Pines, 1970).

Another look into the private world of infants can be drawn from tests of their vision.

Question: How is it possible to test a baby's vision?

Working with infants always requires imagination because they cannot talk. To test infant vision, Robert Fantz (1963) invented a device called a **looking chamber** (Fig. 14-2*a*). A child is placed on his or her back inside the chamber, facing a lighted area above. Next, two objects are placed in the chamber. By observing the movements of the infant's eyes and the images they reflect, it is possible to tell what the infant is looking at.

Fantz found that 3-day-old babies prefer complex patterns such as checkerboards and bull's-eyes to simpler colored rectangles. Other researchers have determined that infants are more excited by circles and curves and that they will look longer at red and blue than at other colors (see Fig. 14-2*b*; Bornstein, 1975; Ruff & Birch, 1974). Findings such as these demonstrate (as a friend of the author's once put it) that, "There really is a person inside that little body."

Of possibly greater interest is the finding that infants will spend more time looking at a human face pattern than at a scrambled face or a colored oval (see

Fig. 14-2*c*). When real human faces were used, Fantz found that familiar faces were preferred to unfamiliar faces. However, preference for the familiar reverses at about age 2, when unusual objects begin to hold greater interest for the child. For instance, Jerome Kagan (1971) showed three-dimensional face masks to 2-year-olds and found they were fascinated by a face with eyes on the chin and a nose in the middle of the forehead. Kagan believes their interest came from a need to understand why the scrambled face differed from what they had come to expect.

Looking chamber An experimental apparatus used to test infant perception by presenting visual stimuli and observing infant responses.

Perhaps the most striking aspect of the human infant is the dazzling speed with which he or she is transformed from a helpless baby to an independent person. During this period there is a fascinating interplay of forces shaping the child's development—most importantly, heredity and environment.

Fig. 14-2 (a) *Eye movements and fixation points of infants are observed in Fantz's "looking chamber."* (b) *Thirteen-week-old infants preferred concentric and curved patterns like those on the left to nonconcentric and straight-line patterns like those on the right.* (c) *Infants tested in a looking chamber look at the normal face longer than at the scrambled face and at both faces longer than at the design on the right. (Photo courtesy of David Linton. Drawing from "The Origin of Form Perception" by Robert L. Fantz. Copyright © 1961 by Scientific American, Inc. All rights reserved)*

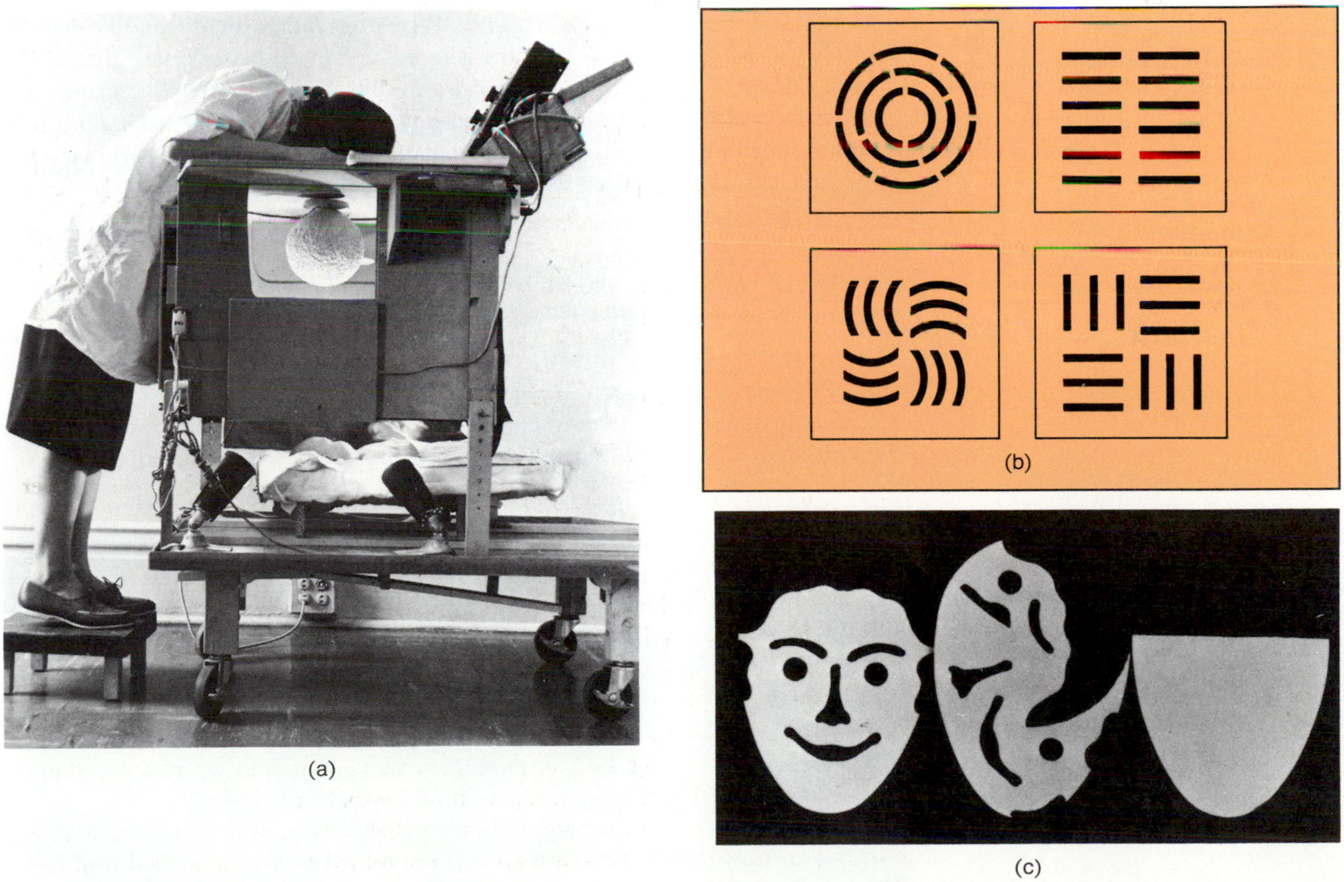

Heredity ("nature") The transmission of physical and psychological characteristics from parents to offspring through genes.

Chromosomes Threadlike structures ("colored bodies") in the nucleus of each cell that carry the genes. Normal human cells have 23 pairs of chromosomes.

Genes Areas on the chromosomes that carry hereditary information affecting various personal characteristics.

Polygenetic characteristics Personal traits or physical properties that are influenced by many genes.

Dominant gene A gene whose influence will be expressed on every occasion in which it is present.

Recessive gene A gene whose influence will only be expressed when it is paired with a second recessive gene (that is, it cannot be expressed when paired with a dominant gene).

Human growth sequence The general pattern of physical development from conception to death.

Environment ("nurture") The sum total of all external conditions and influences affecting the life and development of a person or animal.

Heredity and Environment— The Nature of Nurture and the Nurture of Nature

Question: Which has a greater effect on development, heredity or environment?

For many years psychologists debated—sometimes heatedly—the relative importance of nature versus nurture in determining behavior. The potent effects of **heredity** (nature) certainly cannot be denied. At the moment of conception, when a sperm and egg unite, an incredible number of personal features and growth patterns are determined. It is estimated that the genetic information carried in each human cell would fill thousands of 1000-page books—and that's in fine print!

Question: How does heredity operate?

Nature The nucleus of every cell in the body contains 46 threadlike structures called **chromosomes** that transmit the coded instructions of heredity. **Genes** are small areas on chromosomes. Each gene carries instructions that affect a particular process or personal characteristic. There are at least 100,000 genes in every human cell, and perhaps more. In some cases a single gene is responsible for a particular feature, such as eye color. Most characteristics, however, are **polygenetic,** or determined by many genes working in combination.

Genes may be *dominant* or *recessive*. When a gene is **dominant,** the trait it controls will be present every time the gene is present. When a gene is **recessive,** it must be paired with a second recessive gene before its effect will be expressed. Some examples should make the relationship clearer. We receive one-half of our chromosomes (and genes) from each parent. If you were to get a brown-eye gene from your father and a blue-green gene from your mother, you would be brown-eyed, because brown-eye genes are dominant.

Question: If brown-eye genes are dominant, how is it that two brown-eyed parents sometimes have a blue-eyed child?

If each parent has two brown-eye genes, the couple's children can only be brown-eyed. But what if each parent has one brown-eye gene and one blue-eye gene? In this case the parents would have brown eyes, but there is one chance in four that their children will get two blue-eye genes and have blue eyes (see Fig. 14-3).

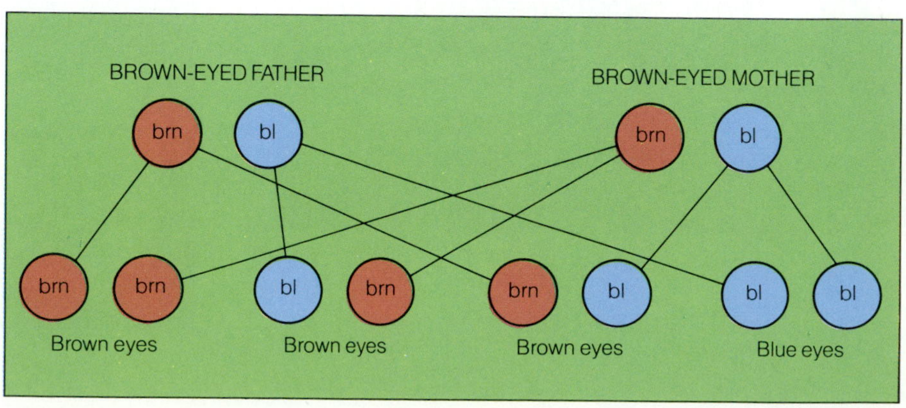

Fig. 14-3 *Gene patterns for children of brown-eyed parents, each with one brown-eye and one blue-eye gene. Since the brown-eye gene is dominant, only one child in four will be blue-eyed.*

Hereditary instructions carried by the chromosomes influence development throughout life by affecting the sequence of growth, the timing of puberty, and the course of aging. The broad outlines of the **human growth sequence** are therefore universal. They extend from conception to old age and death, as Table 14-1 shows. In addition, heredity determines eye and skin color, the order of motor development, and susceptibility to some diseases. Heredity also exerts considerable influence over body size and shape, height, intelligence, athletic potential, and a host of other details (Fig. 14-4). Score "1" for those who favor heredity as more important than environment in human development!

Nurture Does the preceding mean that nurture takes a back seat in development? Consider Aldous Huxley's (1965) summary of the influence of **environment:**

> Anatomically and physiologically man has changed very little during the last 20 or 30 thousand years. The native or genetic capacities of today's bright city child are no better

Table 14-1 Human Growth Sequence

Period*	Duration (Approximate)	Descriptive Name
Germinal	First two weeks after conception.	Zygote
Embryonic	Two to eight weeks after conception.	Embryo
Fetal	From eight weeks after conception to birth.	Fetus
Neonatal	From birth to a few weeks after birth.	Neonate
Infancy	From a few weeks after birth until child is walking securely. Some children walk securely at less than a year while others may not be able to until age 17-18 months.	Infant
No designated name for this period	From about 15-18 months until about 2-2½ years	Toddler
No specific name. Sometimes called "run-about years"	From age 2-3 to about age 6.	Preschool child
Middle years of childhood	From about age 6 to about age 12.	No specific name
Pubescence	Period of about 2 years before puberty.	No specific name
Puberty	Point of development at which biological changes of pubescence reach a climax marked by sexual maturity.	No specific name
Adolescence	From the beginning of pubescence until full social maturity is reached (difficult to fix duration of this period).	Adolescent
Adulthood Young adulthood (19-25) Adulthood (26-40) Maturity (41 plus)	From adolescence to death. Sometimes subdivided into other periods as shown at left.	Adult
Senescence	No defined limit that would apply to all people. Extremely variable. Characterized by marked physiological and psychological deterioration.	Adult (senile), "old age"

(Table courtesy of Tom Bond)

*Note: There is no exact beginning or ending point for the various growth periods. The ages are approximate, and each period may be thought of as blending into the next.

Fig. 14-4 *Twins who share identical genes—identical twins—demonstrate the powerful influence of heredity. Even when they are reared apart, identical twins are strikingly alike in motor skills, physical development, and appearance. (Horn, Plomin, & Rosenman, 1976)*

> than the native capacities of a bright child born into a family of Upper Paleolithic cave-dwellers. But whereas the contemporary bright baby may grow up to become almost anything—a Presbyterian engineer, for example, a piano-playing Marxist, a professor of biochemistry who is a mystical agnostic and likes to paint in water-colors—the Paleolithic baby could not possibly have grown into anything except a hunter or food-gatherer. (From "Human Potentialities" by A. Huxley. In R. E. Farson, ed., *Science and Human Affairs*. Palo Alto, CA: Science and Behavior Books, 1965)

Score "1" for the environmentalists!

Nature-Nurture Interactions The outcome of this debate (we have only viewed an opening round) is recognition that *both* heredity and environment are important. In fact, the two are inseparable. As a person grows, there is a constant interplay, or *interaction*, between the forces of nature and nurture. Heredity shapes development by providing a framework of personal potentials and limitations that are altered by learning, nutrition, disease, culture, and other environmental factors.

Question: How soon after birth do hereditary differences appear?

They appear immediately. From birth onward, infants are unique individuals. Jerome Kagan (1969) found that newborn babies differ noticeably in activity, irritability, attention, and other aspects of **temperament.** (Temperament refers to the physical foundations of personality, such as prevailing mood, sensitivity, and energy levels.) Another study found that babies can be separated into three major categories: *Easy children* (about 40 percent of those observed) are relaxed and agreeable. *Difficult children* (about 10 percent) are moody, intense, and easily angered. *Slow-to-warm-up children* (about 15 percent) are restrained and unexpressive, or shy. The remaining children do not fit neatly into any single category (Thomas & Chess, 1977). (Perhaps we should call them "generic" children?)

Because of inborn differences in readiness to smile, cry, vocalize, reach out, or pay attention, babies rapidly become *active participants* in their own development. Growing infants alter parents' behavior at the same time they are changed by it. For example, Amy is an easy baby who smiles frequently and is easily fed. This encourages touching, feeding, and affection from her mother. The mother's responses, in turn, reward Amy and cause more smiling and other positive reactions. A dynamic *relationship* has been established between mother and child.

Consistent differences in temperament can be detected for at least the first 2 years of life (Matheny, Wilson, & Nuss, 1984). Yet by age 10 children's personalities show little connection to the irritability, activity, or attentiveness observed in infancy (Kagan, 1976). Such findings emphasize again that environmental forces continue to modify inborn potentials with each passing year.

To summarize, we might say that three factors combine to determine a person's **developmental level** at any stage of life. These are *heredity*, *environment*, and the individual's *own behavior*, each tightly interwoven with the others.

Temperament The physical foundation of personality, including emotional and perceptual sensitivity, energy levels, typical mood, and so forth.

Developmental level An individual's current state of physical, emotional, and intellectual development.

Maturation The orderly emergence of personal characteristics and abilities as a result of progressive physical growth.

Maturation—Heredity at the Helm

Question: What, specifically, is maturation?

Maturation refers to growth and development of the body—or more specifically, of muscle, bone, and the nervous system. Maturation underlies the *orderly sequence* observed in the unfolding of many abilities, such as learning to crawl or walk.

While the *rate* of maturation varies from child to child, the *order* is virtually universal. For instance, the strength and coordination needed for sitting appear before that needed for crawling. Therefore, infants the world over typically sit before they crawl (and crawl before they stand, stand before they walk, and so on) (see Fig. 14-5).

Fig. 14-5 *Motor development. Most infants follow an orderly pattern of motor development. Although the order in which children progress is similar, there are large individual differences in the ages at which each ability appears. The ages listed are averages for American children. It is not unusual for many of the skills to appear 1 or 2 months earlier than average or several months later. (Frankenberg & Dodds, 1967)*

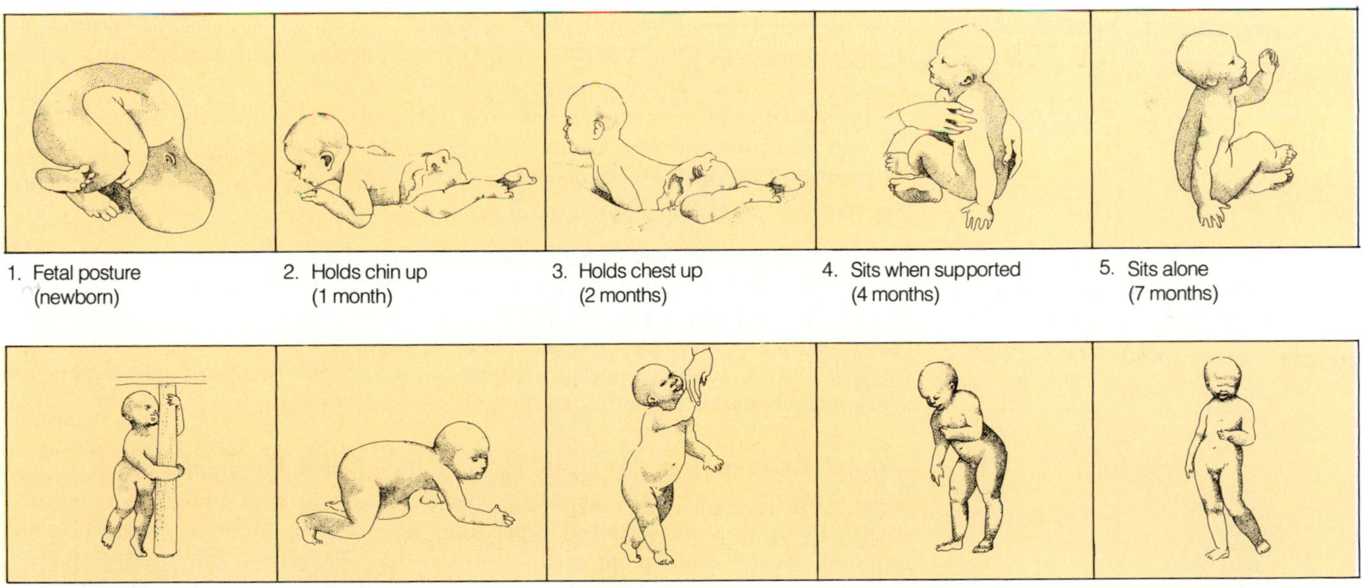

1. Fetal posture (newborn)
2. Holds chin up (1 month)
3. Holds chest up (2 months)
4. Sits when supported (4 months)
5. Sits alone (7 months)
6. Stands holding furniture (9 months)
7. Crawls (10 months)
8. Walks if led (11 months)
9. Stands alone (14 months)
10. Walks alone (15 months)

Readiness A condition that exists when maturation is sufficiently advanced to allow the rapid acquisition of a particular skill.

Principle of motor primacy Principle stating that minimum levels of motor, muscular, and physical development must precede the learning of certain skills.

Self-awareness Consciousness of oneself as a person.

Social referencing Observing others in social situations to obtain information or guidance.

Intrauterine environment The physical and chemical environment within the uterus during prenatal development.

Congenital problems Problems or defects that originate during prenatal development in the womb.

Genetic problems Problems caused by defects in the genes or by inherited characteristics.

readiness · maturation creates a condition of readiness for learning.

Principle of motor primacy - until necessary physical structures are mature, no amount of practice will be sufficient to establish skill.

Social Referencing - See who people are reference them.

Question: What about my weird cousin Emo who never crawled?

Like cousin Emo, a few children substitute rolling, creeping, or shuffling for crawling. A very small percentage move directly from sitting to standing and walking (Robson, 1984). Even so, an orderly sequence of motor development remains evident. In general, increased muscular control in infants proceeds from *head to toe*, and from the *center* of the body *to the extremities*.

Readiness Maturation often creates a condition of **readiness** for learning. The principle of readiness (also known as the **principle of motor primacy**) states: Until the necessary physical structures are mature, no amount of practice will be sufficient to establish a skill. It is impossible, for instance, to teach children to walk or to use a toilet before they have matured enough to control the necessary muscles. Parents who try to force children to learn skills for which they are not yet ready invite failure and run the risk of needlessly frustrating the child.

Question: Then are there definite ages at which children become ready to learn particular skills?

No. Readiness is not an all-or-nothing effect. Training that comes too early will be unsuccessful; training that is only a little early may succeed but will be inefficient; and training when a child is maturationally ready produces rapid learning.

Many parents are anxious to see their children move through the developmental stages, and there is always a temptation to try to hurry a child along. However, it is valuable to recognize that much needless grief can be avoided by respecting a child's personal rate of growth. For instance, eager parents who toilet trained an 18-month-old child in 10 trying weeks of false alarms and accidents might have done it in 3 weeks by waiting until the child was 24 months old. A recent study found that parents may control when toilet training starts, but maturation tends to determine when it will be completed (Martin et al., 1984). Around 30 months is average for completion. So why fight nature? (The wet look is in.)

Self-Awareness When you look in a mirror, you recognize the image looking back as your own—except, perhaps, early on Monday mornings. At what age did this sense of recognition develop? Like many other events in development, **self-awareness** depends on maturation of the nervous system.

Question: How is self-awareness demonstrated in a baby?

In one test of self-recognition, infants were shown their own videotaped images on a TV screen. Most infants had to be 15 months old before they could recognize their own images (Lewis & Brooks-Gunn, 1979). Increased self-awareness, then, closely parallels the human growth sequence (Kagan, 1976).

Social Referencing At about the same time that self-awareness develops, infants become increasingly aware of others. Have you ever noticed how adults sometimes glance at the facial expressions of others in order to decide how to respond? **Social referencing** of this sort can also be observed in babies. By 12 months of age, most babies *reference* (glance at) their mothers when placed in an unfamiliar situation.

In one study of social referencing, babies were placed on a visual cliff. (A visual cliff is pictured in Chapter 5.) The deep side of the cliff was just high enough so that the babies were tempted to cross it, but did not. Most babies placed on the edge of the cliff repeatedly looked at their mothers. As they did, the mothers made faces at them. (All for science, of course.) When the mothers posed faces of joy or interest, most babies crossed the deep side of the cliff. When they posed fear or anger, few babies crossed (Sorce et al., 1985). Thus, by the end of their first year, infants are aware of the facial expressions of others and seek guidance from them (Klinnert, 1984).

Learning Check

1. If an infant is startled, it will make movements similar to an embrace, known as the:
a. grasping reflex *b.* rooting reflex *c.* Moro reflex *d.* adaptive reflex

2. After age 2, infants tested in a looking chamber show a marked preference for familiar faces and simpler designs. T or F?

3. As a child develops, there is a continuous ______________ between the forces of heredity and environment.

4. Which of the following shows the correct sequence?
a. zygote, fetus, embryo, neonate, infant *b.* zygote, embryo, neonate, fetus, infant
c. embryo, zygote, fetus, neonate, infant *d.* zygote, embryo, fetus, neonate, infant

5. Slow-to-warm-up children can be described as restrained, unexpressive, or shy. T of F?

6. The orderly sequence observed in the unfolding of many basic responses can be attributed to ______________.

7. Clear signs of self-awareness or self-recognition are evident in most infants by the time they reach 8 months of age. T or F?

8. The principle of motor primacy is also known as ______________.

9. Social ______________ of parents' facial expressions is evident in infants by the time they are 1 year old.

Answers: **1.** c **2.** F **3.** interaction **4.** *d* **5.** T **6.** maturation **7.** F **8.** readiness **9.** referencing

---

Early Environment—As the Twig Is Bent

Environment obviously begins to affect development immediately after birth, but it may come as a surprise that the prenatal environment is also important. Normally we think of the **intrauterine environment** of the womb as highly protected and stable. In general it is, but a number of conditions can affect development before birth.

Prenatal Development

During embryonic and fetal development, it is quite possible for the effects of environment to reach the interior of the womb. If a mother's health or nutrition is poor, if she contracts certain diseases such as German measles or syphilis, if she uses drugs, or if she is exposed to X rays or atomic radiation, the fetus may be harmed. The resultant damage is referred to as a **congenital problem** (Fig. 14-6). Congenital problems (or *birth defects* as they are sometimes called) are distinct from **genetic problems,** which are inherited.

Question: How is it possible for the embryo or the fetus to be harmed?

Effects of Drugs As you may know, there is no direct intermixing of blood between the mother and the unborn child. Nevertheless, some substances, especially drugs, reach the fetus. If the mother is addicted to morphine, heroin, or methadone, the infant may be born with a drug addiction. Most common prescription drugs—many of them capable of producing fetal malformations—also reach the fetus.

Fetal alcohol syndrome - repeatedly heavy drinking by mother

Even a partial listing of troublesome drugs underscores the need for caution in drug use during pregnancy. Potentially damaging substances include: general anesthetics; cortisone; tetracycline; excessive amounts of vitamins A, D, B_6, and K; some barbiturates; opiates; tranquilizers; synthetic sex hormones; and possibly even caffeine and aspirin (Cox, 1984; Jacobson et al., 1984).

Question: What about alcohol and tobacco?

Repeated heavy drinking by a pregnant woman can produce a pattern known as **fetal alcohol syndrome.** It includes miscarriage or premature birth, infants with low birth weight, and infants with a variety of bodily defects and deformations (Jones & Smith, 1973). With such risks the safest course during pregnancy is to avoid drinking entirely. There is increasing evidence that even modest use of alcohol during pregnancy can be damaging (Streissguth et al., 1984). The *maximum* amount a pregnant woman should drink on any day is 1 ounce of hard liquor, or one glass of wine, or two glasses of beer (Furey, 1982). During the first 3 months of pregnancy, frequent drinking of even such small amounts of alcohol may cause damage.

Smoking also has an adverse effect on prenatal development. Smoking can elevate or lower the heart rate of the unborn child, and a mother who smokes heavily is more likely to miscarry. Heavy smokers run a higher risk of premature birth and tend to give birth to underweight babies. Both premature birth and low birth weight increase the chances of infant sickness and death (Cox, 1984).

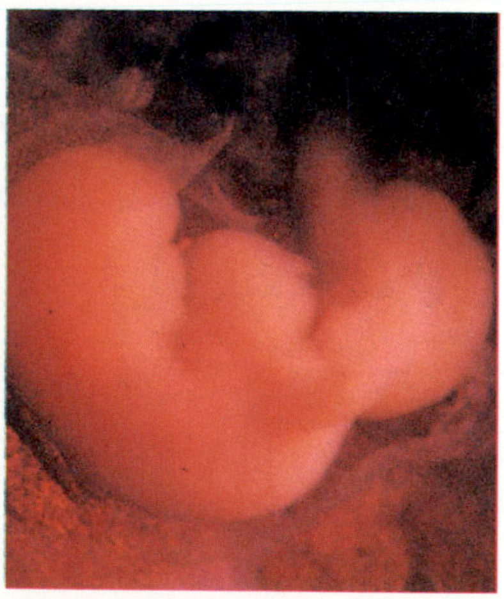

Fig. 14-6 *Due to the rapid growth of basic structures, the developing fetus is sensitive to a variety of diseases, drugs, and sources of radiation. This is especially true during the first trimester (3 months) of gestation.*

Birth

More than ever before, parents can choose how their child will be born. Should they choose a conventional hospital birth? Or should they try natural childbirth? Should the father be present for the birth? In recent years researchers have carefully probed the effects of such choices. Let's briefly explore what they have learned.

Conventional Delivery Until recently, **medicated births** in hospital delivery rooms were the rule in Western societies. In such births the mother is assisted by a physician and is given drugs to relieve pain. The drugs used range from local analgesics (painkillers) to general anesthetics that cause a loss of consciousness. Increasingly, doctors and parents have come to realize that general anesthesia during birth has major drawbacks. For one thing, drugs dull or block the mother's awareness of birth. They also reduce oxygen flow to the fetus and can cause the infant to be born partially anesthetized. For such reasons, babies whose mothers were given heavy doses of anesthetic tend to lag in muscular and neural development (Brackbill, 1979).

In the last 5 years there has been a marked move away from use of general anesthesia during birth. Nevertheless, some form of painkiller is used in 95 percent of all deliveries in the United States. Certainly, mothers should not feel guilty if they need a painkiller during birth. However, it appears wise to use as few drugs as possible.

Fetal alcohol syndrome A pattern of birth complications and bodily defects in infants caused by excessive consumption of alcohol by the mother during pregnancy.

Medicated birth The common practice in Western medicine of giving painkilling drugs during labor and birth.

Prepared childbirth A collection of techniques designed to manage discomfort and facilitate birth so that the use of painkilling drugs can be avoided or minimized. Also called natural childbirth.

Prepared Childbirth What can parents do to minimize the discomfort of birth—while giving their babies the best possible start in life? Many psychologists are convinced that **natural,** or **prepared, childbirth** is the answer. The most widely used approach to natural childbirth is the *Lamaze method* (la-MAHZ), developed by French physician Ferdinand Lamaze.

Couples begin learning the Lamaze method during pregnancy. Part of the training explains what will happen physically during birth. Women who thoroughly understand what is happening in their bodies tend to have fewer fears and less anxiety. Couples are also taught methods of breathing and muscular control to minimize pain during birth. Another important element is training the father or a friend to give support to the mother during birth. By coaching the mother in breathing and by assisting her in other ways, the father is made an active participant in the birth.

Natural childbirth typically shortens labor and minimizes pain. In addition, it treats birth as a celebration of life, rather than a medical problem or a disease. Accordingly, parents are more likely to experience birth as a time of great happiness when natural childbirth is used *and* the father is present (Tanzer & Block, 1976).

Question: How important is it for fathers to participate in birth?

Researchers have found that fathers generally make a better transition to parenthood when they participate in preparing for childbirth (Fig. 14-7) (Grossman et al., 1980). But, while participation in the birth itself is valuable for fathers, it is apparently not essential. The father's *attitude* toward the birth of his child is probably more important. A recent study found that fathers who *wanted* to be present during delivery showed greater interest in their infants during the first year and were more likely to help care for the baby (Grossman & Volkmer, 1984). This was true whether or not the father was actually able to attend the birth.

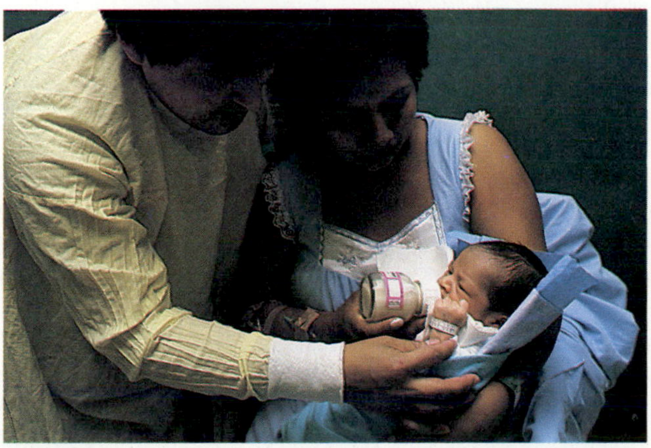

Fig. 14-7 *Changing attitudes toward childbirth have encouraged mothers and fathers to actively prepare for birth and to participate more fully in caring for the newborn.*

Maternal and Paternal Influences

Maternal influences The aggregate of all psychological effects mothers have on their children.

Caretaking styles Identifiable patterns of parental caretaking and interaction with children.

Paternal influences The aggregate of all psychological effects fathers have on their children.

Cooing Spontaneous repetition of vowel sounds by infants.

Babbling The repetition by infants of meaningless language sounds (including both vowel and consonant sounds).

maternal influence - all phychological effects mothers have on child

paternal - all phychological effects father has on child

In later years a child's environment expands to include the effects of culture, subculture, family, school, television, and peers. Immediately after birth and for the first few years, the most important influences come from an infant's caretakers. The quality of "mothering" and "fathering" is therefore of prime importance.

One revealing study of **maternal influences** began with selection of children who were unusually competent ("A" children) or who had a low degree of competence ("C" children). As increasingly younger children were observed, it became apparent that A and C patterns were already set by age 3.

To learn how this was possible, researchers visited homes and observed children under 3 and their mothers (White & Watts, 1973). Observed **caretaking styles** ranged from the "super mother" to the "zoo-keeper mother." Super mothers went out of their way to provide educational experiences for their children and allowed the child to initiate some activities. This caretaking style produced an A child, competent in most areas of development. At the other end of the spectrum, zoo-keeper mothers gave their children good physical care but interacted with them very little. Their child-care routines were rigid and highly structured. The result was C children who tended to approach problems inflexibly (Pines, 1969).

Another study found that children's intellectual abilities at age 6 can be predicted, to some extent, by their mothers' *responsiveness* to them during infancy (Coates & Lewis, 1984). Effective mothers, it seems, are those who are sensitive to their children's needs. Put another way, effective mothers alter their own behavior to meet their children's changing needs at each stage of development.

Taken together, such findings support two beliefs long held by developmental psychologists: First, that mothering *does* make a difference; and second, that early development has lasting effects on a person.

Fig. 14-8 *"Fathering" typically makes a contribution to early development differing in emphasis from "mothering."*

Question: Aren't you overlooking the effects of fathering?

Yes. Fathers also contribute significantly to an infant's social and intellectual growth. In fact, fathers make a unique contribution to development by interacting with the infant in ways that differ from those typical of mothers.

Recent studies of **paternal influences** have shown that even in nontraditional families, the father's main role tends to be that of a *playmate* for the infant. Fathers typically spend four to five times as much time playing with their infants as they do in caretaking (Parke & Sawin, 1977).

It might seem that the father's role as a playmate makes him less important in the child's development. Not so. From birth of the child onward, fathers are more visually attentive to the child than are mothers. They are much more tactile (lifting, tickling, and handling the baby), more physically arousing (engaging in rough-and-tumble play), and more likely to engage in unusual play (imitating baby, for example) (Crawley & Sherrod, 1984; Parke & Sawin, 1977). Mothers speak to the infant more, play more conventional games (such as peekaboo), and, as previously noted, spend more time in caretaking activities (see Fig. 14-9).

Thus, from the first days of life, infants get very different views of males and females. Females, who offer comfort, nurturance, and verbal stimulation, also tend to be close at hand. Males come and go, and when they are present, action,

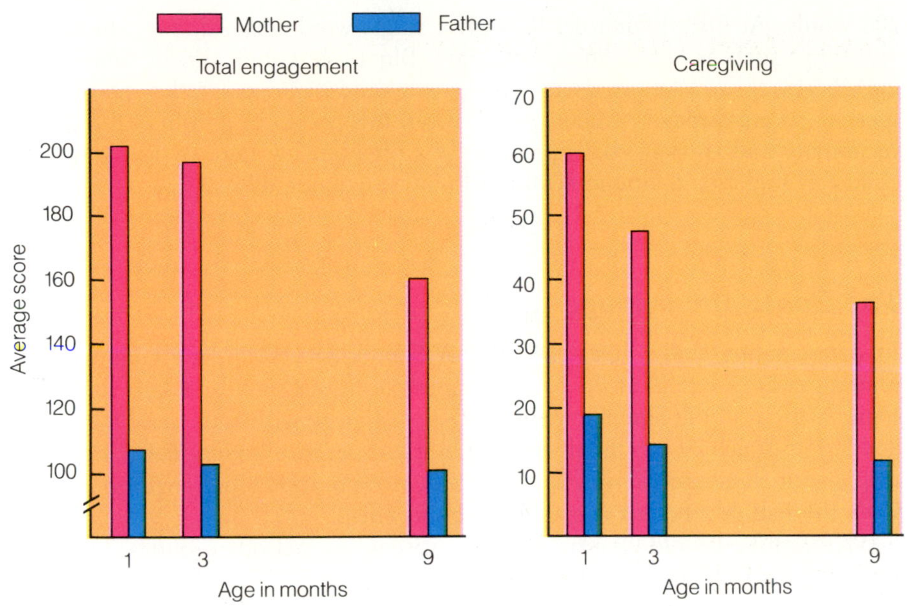

Fig. 14-9 *Mother-infant and father-infant interactions. These graphs show what occurred on routine days in a sample of 72 American homes. The graph on the left records the total amount of contact parents had with their babies, including such actions as talking to, touching, hugging, or smiling at the infant. The graph on the left shows the amount of caregiving (diapering, washing, feeding, and so forth) done by each parent. Note that in both cases mother-infant interactions greatly exceed father-infant interactions. (Adapted from Belsky, Gilstrap, & Rovine, 1984)*

exploration, and risk taking prevail (Herbert & Greenberg, 1983). It's no wonder, then, that maternal and paternal styles appear to have a major impact on children's sex-role development (Biller, 1982).

Cooing - (6-8 weeks) babies begin "oo" "ah"
babble- consonant and vowels continuous outpouring of sounds.

Language Development—Fast-Talking Babies

There's something almost miraculous about hearing a baby's first words. As infants, how did we manage to leap into the world of language? To gain an understanding, let's begin with a survey of language development.

Language Acquisition The development of language is closely tied to maturation. As any parent can tell you, babies can cry from birth on. By 4 weeks of age, the infant can control crying enough to use it as an attention-getting device, and parents can tell the nature of the infant's needs from the tone of the crying. Around 6 to 8 weeks of age, babies begin **cooing** (repeating vowel sounds like "oo" and "ah").

By age 6 months, the nervous system has matured enough to allow the child to grasp objects, to smile, laugh, sit up, and to **babble.** In the babbling stage, consonant sounds are added to produce a continuous outpouring of repeated language sounds. The influence of environment at this stage is indicated by the fact that babbling increases when parents talk to the child (Mussen et al., 1979).

At about 1 year of age, the child can stand alone for a short time and can respond to words such as "no" or "hi." Soon afterward, the first connection between words and objects is formed, and children may address their parents as "Mama" or "Dada." Between the ages of 1½ and 2 years, children become able to stand and walk alone. By this time their vocabulary may include from 24 to

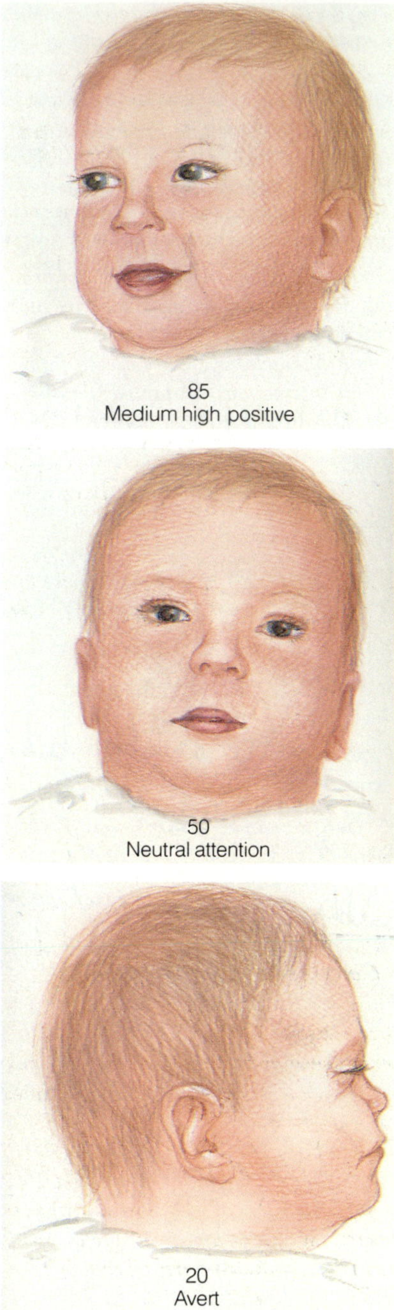

Fig. 14-10 *Infant engagement scale. These samples from a 90-point scale show various levels of infant engagement, or attention. Babies participate in prelanguage "conversations" with parents by giving and withholding attention, and by smiling, gazing, or vocalizing. (Source: Beebe et al., 1982)*

200 words. At first children go through a **single-word stage,** during which they say things such as "go," "juice," or "up" (Bloom & Lahey, 1978). Soon after, they begin to arrange words in simple two-word sentences called **telegraphic speech:** "Want Teddy," "Mama gone." From this point on, growth of the child's vocabulary and language skills proceeds at a phenomenal rate. By first grade the child can understand around 8000 words and use about 4000.

The Roots of Language

In a fascinating study, researchers Louis Sander and William Condon (1974) filmed newborn infants as the babies listened to various sounds. A later frame-by-frame analysis of the films showed something astonishing: Infants move their arms and legs in synchrony to the rhythms of human speech. Random noise, rhythmic tapping, or disconnected vowel sounds will not produce this "language dance." Only the natural rhythms of speech have this effect.

Why would day-old infants "dance" to speech but not other sounds? One possibility is that language recognition is innate. Linguist Noam Chomsky (1968, 1975) has long claimed that humans have a **biological predisposition** to develop language. According to Chomsky, language organization is inborn, much like a child's ability to coordinate walking. If such inborn language recognition does exist, it may explain why children around the world use a limited number of patterns in their first sentences. Typical patterns include (Mussen et al., 1979):

Identification:	See kitty.	Agent-action:	Mama give
Nonexistence:	Allgone milk.	Negation:	Not ball.
Possession:	My doll.	Question:	Where doggie?

Question: Does Chomsky's theory explain why language develops so rapidly?

Perhaps. But many psychologists believe that Chomsky underestimates the importance of learning (Bruner, 1983). **Psycholinguists** (specialists in the psychology of language) have shown that language is not magically "switched on" by adult speech. Imitation of adults and rewards for correctly using words (as when a child asks for a cookie) are also a part of language learning. More importantly, parents and children begin to communicate long before the child can speak. Months of shared effort precede the child's first word (Miller, 1977). From this point of view, the filmed infants' behavior reflects a readiness to interact *socially* with parents, not innate language recognition.

Question: How do parents communicate with infants before they can talk?

Early Communication Parents go to a great deal of trouble to get babies to smile and vocalize (Fig. 14-10). In doing so, they quickly learn to change their actions to keep the infant's attention, arousal, and activity at optimal levels (Brazelton et al., 1974). A familiar example is the "I'm-Going-to-Get-You Game." In it the adult says, "I'm gonna getcha . . . I'm gonna getcha . . . I'm gonna getcha . . . Gotcha!" Through such games, adults and babies come to share similar rhythms and expectations (Stern, 1982). Soon a system of shared **signals** is created. Touching, vocalizing, gazing, and smiling help lay a foundation for later language use. Specificially, these signals establish a pattern of "conversational" **turn taking** (Bruner, 1983; Snow, 1977):

Mother	Ann	Mother	Ann
	(smiles)		
Oh, what a nice little smile!		*Well pardon you!*	
Yes, isn't that nice?		*Yes, that's better, isn't it?*	
There.		*Yes.*	(vocalizes)
There's a nice little smile.	(burps)	*Yes.*	
		What's so funny?	(smiles)

From the outside such exchanges may look meaningless. In reality they represent real communication. A baby's vocalizations and attention provide a way of interacting emotionally with parents (Stern et al., 1975). (For another perspective on turn taking, see Fig. 14-11.)

In summary, some elements of language may be innate, but a full flowering of speech requires careful cultivation. Now that we have our subjects (babies) walking and talking, let's move on to some other facets of development.

Single-word stage In language development, the period during which a child first begins to use single words.

Telegraphic speech In language development, the formation of simple two-word sentences that "telegraph" (communicate) a simple idea.

Biological predisposition In language development, the presumed hereditary readiness of humans to learn and use language.

Psycholinguist A specialist in the psychology of language and language development.

Signal In early language development, any behavior, such as touching, vocalizing, gazing, or smiling, which allows nonverbal interaction and turn taking between parent and child.

Turn taking In early language development, the tendency of parent and child to alternate in the sending and receiving of signals or messages.

Critical Periods in Development—Imprinting, Attachment, and Motherless Monkeys

Question: Why do experiences early in life often have such lasting effects?

Part of the answer lies in the existence of critical periods for acquiring particular behaviors. A **critical period** is a time of increased sensitivity to environmental influences (both positive and negative). Critical periods usually correspond to times of rapid development. For example, the infamous drug thalidomide interferes with limb formation in the developing fetus. Before its use was banned, many pregnant women in the United States and Europe took thalidomide during the period of fetal limb formation (the sixth to eighth weeks of pregnancy). The result was severe birth defects.

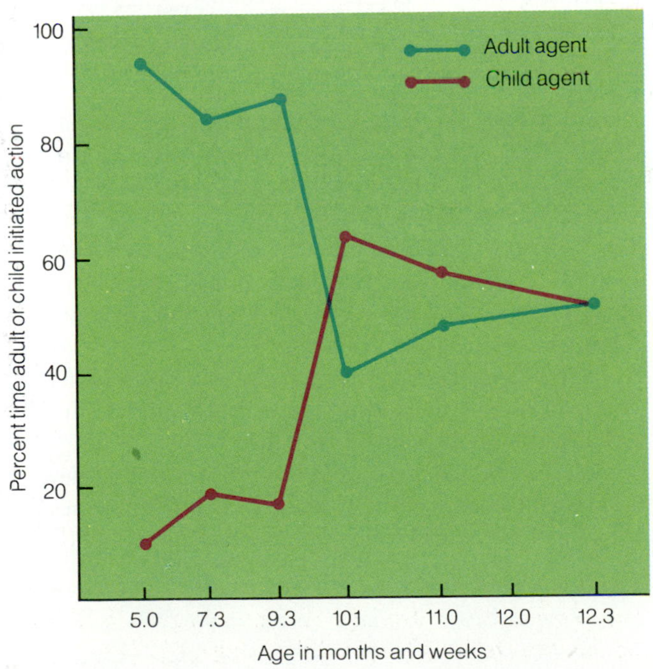

Fig. 14-11 *This graph shows the development of turn taking in games played by an infant and his mother. For several months Richard responded to games such as peekaboo and "hand-the-toy-back" only when his mother initiated action. At about 9 months, however, he rapidly began to initiate action in the games. Soon he was the one to take the lead about half of the time. Learning to take turns and to direct actions at another person underlie basic language skills. (From Bruner, 1983)*

Critical period A period in development during which susceptibility to environmental influences is heightened. Also, a time during which certain events must take place for normal development to occur.

Imprinting A rapid and relatively permanent type of learning occurring during a limited time period early in life.

Emotional attachment An especially close emotional bond that infants form with their parents, caretakers, or others.

Separation anxiety Distress displayed by infants when they are separated from their parents or principal caretakers.

Affectional needs One's emotional needs in general but, especially, needs for love, attention, and affection.

Imprinting Often, certain events must occur during a critical period in order for a person or an animal to develop normally. For example, Konrad Lorenz, an ethologist who studies animal behavior, was curious about why baby geese follow their mother. The obvious explanation seemed to be, "It's instinctive," but Lorenz showed otherwise.

Mother Lorenz

Normally the first large moving object a baby goose sees is its mother. Lorenz hatched geese in an incubator, so the first moving object they saw was Lorenz. From then on, these baby geese followed Lorenz. They even reacted to his call as if he were their mother (Lorenz, 1937) (Fig. 14-12).

It can be seen that the response pattern of "mother-goose following" is not automatic. Rather, it is established during a critical period by the essential experience of seeing a large moving object. The rapid and early learning of a permanent behavior pattern of this type has been called **imprinting.**

In most birds the critical period for imprinting is very brief. For instance, Hess (1959) found that if ducklings are not allowed to imprint on their mother or some other object within 30 hours after hatching, they never will. (Ducklings have been imprinted on decoys, rubber balls, wooden blocks, and other unlikely objects.) In many animals, imprinting and other events taking place during critical periods have lifelong consequences (Lorenz, 1962):

Revenge of the Jackdaw

Imprinting normally serves to attach a young animal to its mother. It also guides the selection of a mate of the same species at sexual maturity. In another of Lorenz's experiments, a jackdaw (European blackbird) imprinted on him. When the bird reached sexual maturity, Lorenz became the object of its mating ritual. Part of this ritual involves stuffing worms into the mouth of the intended mate—as a surprised Lorenz learned while asleep on the lawn one day. When Lorenz refused its gift, the jackdaw stuffed a worm in Lorenz's ear (showing, perhaps, that it's not nice to fool Mother Nature)!

Fig. 14-12 *"Mother" Lorenz leads his charges. The goslings have imprinted on Lorenz because he was the first moving object they saw after they hatched.*

Question: Does imprinting occur in humans?

Attachment True cases of imprinting are limited to birds and other animals (Hess, 1959). However, human infants form an **emotional attachment** to their *primary caretakers* (usually parents), and there is a critical period (roughly the first year of life) during which this must occur for healthy development (Bowlby, 1969, 1973). A direct sign that an emotional bond has been formed appears when infants are around 8 to 12 months of age. At that time babies display **separation anxiety** (crying and signs of fear) when their parents leave them alone or leave them with a stranger (Kagan, 1976).

In recent years a major controversy has raged over whether attachment is influenced by events that occur immediately after birth. Please see Box 14-1 for a discussion of mother-infant bonding.

Attachment can have quite an effect on early development. Infants who are securely attached to their parents later show more resiliency, curiosity, problem-solving ability, and social competence in preschool (Parke & Asher, 1983).

Question: Does day-care for young children interfere with normal attachment?

Box 14-1

Mother-Infant Bonding—A Touching Debate

In one hospital ward new mothers are given traditional contact with their infants: a glimpse after birth and 30-minute visits every 4 hours for feeding. In a second hospital ward, "extended contact group" mothers are given their babies for 1 hour during the first 3 hours after birth and for an extra 5 hours each afternoon for the first 3 days after delivery. Does the extra contact make a difference?

An initial series of studies reported by Marshall Klaus and John Kennel (1982) seemed to suggest that there are lasting benefits to close, early contact between a mother and her infant. According to Klaus and Kennel, there is a sensitive period in the first hours after birth. Therefore, mother-child pairs who spend extra time together form a stronger **emotional bond.** This is especially true, they believe, if skin-to-skin touching is part of early contact. However, the majority of later, more carefully conducted studies have failed to support the idea that extended, early contact is crucial to the mother-infant bond (Myers, 1984).

Even Klaus and Kennel now acknowledge that it is unlikely that something as important as emotional attachment would depend *solely* on the first few hours of life (Klaus & Kennel, 1984). Humans are highly adaptable, and there are many opportunities for attachment during the first year of life.

Advocates of bonding continue to believe that early contact between mothers and infants can have beneficial effects. Even those researchers who doubt that early contact makes a difference agree that allowing mother, father, and infant to be together during the first few hours is humane and natural. So, while most evidence suggests that early contact is not necessary, it is undoubtedly a positive, emotionally satisfying experience.

Fortunately, it seems that it does not. A major survey of day-care effects concluded that *high-quality* nonmaternal care does not appear to have harmful effects on preschool children (Etaugh, 1980). A second, more recent, study also concluded that mother-infant attachment is not threatened by quality day care (Tephy & Elardo, 1984). Attachment also appears not be harmed when the mother works (Owen et al., 1984). The key ingredient for secure attachment is a mother who is accepting and sensitive to her baby's signals and rhythms (Belsky, Rovine, & Taylor, 1984).

Motherless Monkeys Research with rhesus monkeys suggests that, like imprinting, infant attachments can have lasting effects. Harry Harlow (1966, 1967) has shown that baby monkeys separated from their mothers and raised in isolation become troubled adult animals. Among other things, these motherless monkeys never develop normal sexual behaviors, and they make poor mothers if mated. They are coldly rejecting or indifferent to their babies and may brutalize or injure them. It has been suggested that human parents who abuse, reject, or physically injure their children may be displaying a similar pattern. Most abusive parents were themselves rejected or mistreated as children.

Meeting a baby's **affectional needs** is every bit as important as meeting more obvious needs for food, water, and physical care. All things considered, one of the most important developments of the first year of life appears to be creation of

Deprivation In development, the loss or withholding of normal stimulation, nutrition, comfort, love, and so forth; a condition of lacking.

Deprivation dwarfism A stunting of early growth associated with isolation, rejection, or general deprivation.

Hospitalism A pattern of deep depression observed in institutionalized infants, marked by weeping and sadness and a lack of normal responsiveness to other humans.

Perceptual stimulation Varied, patterned, and meaningful sensory input.

Surrogate mother A substitute mother (often an inanimate dummy in animal research).

Contact comfort A pleasant and reassuring feeling human and animal infants get from touching or clinging to something soft and warm, usually the mother.

a bond of trust and affection between the infant and at least one other person. Parents are sometimes afraid of "spoiling" a baby with too much attention, but for the first year or two this is nearly impossible. As a matter of fact, a later capacity to experience warm and loving relationships may depend on it.

Deprivation and Enrichment— A Practical Definition of Tender Loving Care

NEWS ITEM: "Wild Child Raised by Apes Found in Africa." Over the years there have been several reported discoveries of feral (wild) children. These are children who supposedly have grown up in the care of animals and who act like animals when found. Actually, there is little documented evidence that such children have existed, but we needn't go this far afield for proof of the destructive effects of early **deprivation.**

There are numerous confirmed cases of children who have spent the first 5 or 6 years of life in closets, attics, and other restricted environments. When discovered, these children are usually mute, severely retarded, and emotionally damaged. Some suffer from **deprivation dwarfism**—stunted growth associated with isolation, rejection, or general deprivation in the home environment. (See inset news excerpt.) Special efforts to teach such children to speak and function normally often meet with limited success.

Question: What aspects of such experiences are responsible for the damage done?

One of the earliest hints came when psychoanalyst René Spitz (1945) compared two groups of infants. One group was made up of healthy and lively babies in an institution Spitz called the "nursery." In the "foundling home" was a second group of babies who suffered from a condition called **hospitalism.** This is a pattern of deep depression marked by weeping and sadness, long periods of immobility or mechanical rocking, and a lack of normal response to other humans. The foundling home also had an unusually high rate of infant deaths, and development of the living babies was severely retarded.

By comparing conditions at the two institutions, Spitz found some striking differences. At the nursery each baby had a separate attendant; at the foundling home there were eight babies to a nurse. Spitz considered the "wasting away" of the foundling home babies a result of their lack of dependable mother figures.

Question: In other words, the babies failed to form an attachment to an adult, right?

Yes. Recent work shows that lack of attachment is a major element in early deprivation. For example, making living conditions better for a group of children in a Canadian institution failed to reverse their declining mental health. The children improved only when they were placed with caring foster parents or adoptive parents (Flint, 1978).

A second major factor in many cases of deprivation is a lack of **perceptual stimulation.** All of the "wasted" babies studied by Spitz were well cared for physically. However, they were kept in bare rooms in cribs with white sheets hung on the sides. The infants could see only the blank ceiling, and their only contact

"Closet Child" Now with Loving Parents

LONG BEACH (AP)—Becky's story began to unfold when the Sheriff's Department responded to a tip like hundreds of others. They found Becky in urine-soaked clothes, asleep on a hard cot in her parents' bedroom.

"She was almost like an animal," one of the deputies reported.

Her world then was the bedroom and its closet, in which she was kept for untold hours. Now Becky lives in a spacious foster home.

Since Becky's rescue, she has gained 12 pounds and grown 6 inches. But she is still a mite, for she weighed only 24 pounds and stood only 32 inches tall last April.

When she was found, Becky couldn't even crawl; now she walks. Then, she knew only a few words—now she speaks in sentences. She is, except for the hurt in her eyes, like almost any toddler.

But Rebecca is no toddler. She is 9 years old, and her pediatrician says she may never catch up.

with others came during a few brief periods each day when they were quickly fed or changed. To put it mildly, there was *nothing happening* for these children—no change, no input, no cuddling, no attention, and most of all, no stimulation. This was deprivation in the fullest sense of the word.

Early Stimulation

Experiments with animals have confirmed the destructive effects of a lack of stimulation in infancy. For example, Harry Harlow separated infant rhesus monkeys from their mothers at birth. The real mothers were replaced with **surrogate** (artificial) **mothers**—essentially, dummies of approximately the same size and shape as real monkeys. Some of the surrogates were made of cold, unyielding wire, and others were covered with soft terry cloth (Fig. 14-13). When the infants were given a choice between the two mothers, they consistently chose to spend most of their time clinging to the cuddly terry cloth mother. This was true even when a bottle was mounted in the wire mother, making it the source of food.

The "love" and attachment displayed toward the cloth mothers was identical to that shown toward natural mothers. When frightened by rubber snakes, wind-up toys, and other "fear stimuli," the infant monkeys ran to their cloth mothers and clung to them for security (Harlow & Zimmerman, 1958). Harlow concluded that one of the most important dimensions of early stimulation is **contact comfort,** supplied by touching, holding, and stroking an infant. Harlow's findings may be inconclusive where humans are concerned, but other findings back them up. For example, one researcher found that just 20 minutes of extra touching a day could accelerate the developmental rate of infants in an institution (Casler, 1965).

Fig. 14-13 *An infant monkey clings to a cloth-covered surrogate mother. Baby monkeys become attached to the cloth "contact-comfort" mother but not to a similar wire mother. This is true even when the wire mother provides food. (Photo courtesy of Harry Harlow, University of Wisconsin Primate Laboratory)*

For many psychologists the concept of contact comfort has become part of the rationale for advocating breast feeding of infants. Breast feeding almost guarantees a baby will receive an adequate amount of touching and handling, and it appears to aid attachment (Jensen et al., 1981). In addition, the breast-feeding mother

Colostrum The first milk secreted by a woman for a few days after giving birth. Colostrum is rich in antibodies to disease.

Enriched environment An environment deliberately made more novel, complex, and perceptually stimulating.

Visually directed reaching Coordinated, visually guided reaching for a particular object.

produces **colostrum** (ko-LOSS-trum) rather than milk for the first few days after birth. Colostrum is a fluid rich in proteins that carries antibodies from the mother to the newborn and helps prevent certain infectious diseases.

Question: What about the mother who can't breast-feed or who prefers not to?

The advantages of breast feeding are not overriding. If a mother is aware of the importance of touching and cuddling, bottle feeding is in no way psychologically inferior to breast feeding. In fact, a mother's warmth or coldness, relaxation or tension, and acceptance or rejection are more important than the choice of breast or bottle (Heinstein, 1963). Being sensitive to a baby's feeding rhythms and needs seems to be a key element in promoting healthy infant attachment (Ainsworth, 1979).

Enrichment If too little stimulation limits development, can an abundance of stimulation enhance it? A number of attempts to answer this question have made use of **enriched environments.** An enriched environment is one that has been deliberately made more novel, complex, and richly stimulating. Enriched environments for infants may be the "soil" from which brighter children grow. To illustrate, let us begin with an experiment in which rats were raised in an enriched environment (Kretch et al., 1962):

Building Bigger and Better Brains

To begin with, infant rats were divided into two groups. One group was raised in *stimulus-poor* conditions. These animals were housed in adequate but unstimulating cages that had gray walls and contained nothing to explore or investigate. The second group was housed in a sort of rat wonderland. The walls of the *stimulus-enriched* environment were decorated with colored patterns, and the cage was filled with platforms, ladders, and cubbyholes to be explored. When both groups of rats reached adulthood, they were tested for ability to learn mazes. The stimulated rats dramatically out-performed their deprived relatives. In addition, later tests showed that the stimulated rats had brains that were larger and heavier, with a thicker cortex.

It is a long leap from rats to people, yet it is hard to overlook the significance of an increase in brain size caused by sensory stimulation. If stimulation can enhance the "intelligence" of a lowly rat, it is reasonable to assume that human infants also benefit from stimulation.

Question: Is there any evidence that this is actually the case?

As might be expected, it is much harder to prove that such things occur in humans. In Chapter 16 you will find a full discussion of the effects of environment on intelligence. For now, let us examine one case of enrichment applied to humans.

Infants like to reach out and touch things, but normally it takes about 5 months after birth for this skill to develop. In an experiment conducted at a state hospital, newborn infants were given several kinds of extra stimulation each day for several months (White & Held, 1966):

Each child in the stimulus enrichment condition was handled an extra 15 minutes daily; each was placed in a position that allowed visual exploration outside the crib; white crib sheets were replaced by patterned sheets with colorful animal designs; and a collection of bright and colorful objects was hung over each child's crib.

As limited as these changes may seem, they caused **visually directed reaching** to occur an average of a 1½ months early. This may not sound like an earthshaking improvement in adult terms, but for an infant it is a substantial acceleration of development.

This is only one of many experiments showing a positive relationship between stimulation and improvements in various abilities, particularly those that might be labeled "intellectual." Most people recognize that babies need lots of "tender loving care" where physical needs are concerned. But as the previous discussion shows, a complete definition of tender loving care should include a baby's psychological needs as well. It would be a good idea to place stimulation, affectionate touching, and personal warmth high on any list of infant needs.

Learning Check

The preceding sections of this chapter contain a large amount of information. Check your comprehension by answering the questions below. Skim back over the material if you miss any.

1. A duckling can be imprinted after the critical period has passed if the environment is enriched. T or F?

2. The development of separation anxiety in an infant corresponds to formation of an attachment to parents. T or F?

3. A baby's affectional needs can be met by supplying adequate food, water, and physical care. T or F?

4. Harlow's "motherless monkeys" became attached to the surrogate mother that fed them. T or F?

5. René Spitz attributed hospitalism to an absence of perceptual stimulation. T or F?

6. Bottle feeding prevents a mother from providing an adequate amount of contact comfort for an infant. T or F?

7. The intrauterine environment has little effect on a person's development. T or F?

8. The "super mother" goes out of her way to provide educational experiences yet accepts the child as he or she is. T or F?

9. The development of speech and language usually occurs in which order:
a. crying, cooing, babbling, telegraphic speech
b. cooing, crying, babbling, telegraphic speech
c. babbling, crying, cooing, telegraphic speech
d. crying, babbling, cooing, identification

10. Research has shown conclusively that mother-infant contact immediately after birth is essential for optimal development. T or F?

Answers: **1.** F **2.** T **3.** F **4.** F **5.** F **6.** F **7.** F **8.** T **9.** *a* **10.** F

Cognitive Growth—How Do Children Learn to Think? How Do Children Think to Learn?

Question: How different is a child's understanding of the world from that of an adult?

Generally speaking, a child's thinking is *less abstract* than that of an adult. Children use fewer generalizations, categories, or principles and tend to base their understanding of the world on particular examples, tangible sensations, and concrete objects.

An indication of the concrete nature of thinking in very young children is their failure to recognize the permanence of objects. Older children and adults realize

Assimilation In Piaget's theory, the application of existing mental patterns to new situations (that is, the new situation is *assimilated* to existing mental schemes).

Accommodation In Piaget's theory, the modification of existing mental patterns to fit new demands (that is, mental schemes are changed to *accommodate* new information or experiences).

Sensorimotor stage Stage of intellectual development during which sensory input and motor responses become coordinated.

Object permanence Concept, gained in infancy, that objects continue to exist even when they are hidden from view.

Preoperational stage Period of intellectual development during which children begin to use language and think symbolically, yet remain intuitive and egocentric in their thought.

Intuitive thought Thinking that makes little or no use of reasoning and logic.

Egocentric thought Thought that is self-centered and fails to consider the viewpoints of others.

Fig. 14-14 *Jean Piaget—philosopher, psychologist, and keen observer of children.*

that an object that is out of sight still exists. With a very young child, "out of sight" can literally mean "out of mind." If a ball rolls behind something while a 4- or 5-month-old child is playing with it, the child behaves as if the ball has ceased to exist and stops looking for it.

Question: Is there any pattern to the growth of intellect in childhood?

Piaget's Theory of Cognitive Development

According to the Swiss psychologist and philosopher Jean Piaget (1951, 1952), there is. Piaget (pronounced pea-ah-JAY) believed all children pass through a series of distinct stages in intellectual development (Fig. 14-14). Many of his ideas came from observing his own children as they solved various thought problems. (It is tempting to imagine that Piaget's illustrious career may have been launched one day when his wife said to him, "Watch the children for a while, will you, Jean?") Piaget's many observations convinced him that intellect grows through what he called "assimilation" and "accommodation."

Assimilation refers to using existing patterns in new situations. Let's say a plastic hammer is Ben's favorite toy. Ben uses the hammer properly and pounds on the blocks that came with it. For his birthday Ben gets an oversize toy wrench. If he uses the wrench for pounding, it has been assimilated to an existing mental structure.

In **accommodation,** existing ideas are modified to fit new requirements. For instance, a young child might think that a dime is worth less than a (larger) nickel. As the child begins to spend money, he or she will be forced to alter ideas about what "more" and "less" mean. Thus, new situations are assimilated to existing ideas, and new ideas are created to accommodate new experiences.

Piaget's theories have had a profound effect on our thinking about children. The following is a brief summary of what he found.

The Sensorimotor Stage (0–2 Years) In the first 2 years of life, a child's intellectual development is largely *nonverbal.* The child is mainly concerned with learning to coordinate *purposeful* movements with information from the senses. Also important at this time is gradual emergence of the concept of **object permanence.** At about age 1½ the child begins to pursue disappearing objects. By age 2 the child can anticipate the movement of an object behind a screen. When watching an electric train, for example, the child looks ahead to the end of a tunnel rather than staring at the spot where the train disappeared.

In general, developments in this stage indicate that the child's conceptions are becoming more *stable.* Objects cease to appear and disappear magically, and a more orderly and predictable world takes shape.

The Preoperational Stage (2–7 Years) During the preoperational period the child is developing an ability to think *symbolically* and to use language. But the child's thinking is still very **intuitive.** (Do you remember thinking as a child that the sun and the moon followed you when you took a walk?) In addition, the child's use of language is not as sophisticated as it might seem. Children have a tendency to confuse words with the objects they represent. If the child calls a toy block a "car" and you use it to make a "train," the child may be upset. To children the name of an object is as much a part of the object as its size, shape, and color. This seems to underlie a preoccupation with name calling. To the preoperational child an insulting name may hurt as much as "sticks and stones." Consider, for instance, one rather protected youngster who was angered by her older brother. Searching for a way to retaliate against her larger and stronger foe, she settled on, "You panty girdle!" It was the worst thing she could think of.

During the preoperational stage the child is also quite **egocentric,** or unable to take the viewpoint of other people. The ego seems to stand at the center of his or her world. The concept of egocentrism helps us understand why children can seem exasperatingly selfish or uncooperative at times. A child who blocks your view by standing in front of a television set assumes that you can see if he can. If you ask him to move so you can see, he may move so that he can see better!

The Concrete Operational Stage (7–11 Years) An important development during this stage is mastery of the concept of **conservation.** Children have learned the concept of conservation when they understand that rolling a ball of clay into a "snake" does not increase the amount of clay and that pouring liquid from a tall, narrow glass into a shallow dish does not reduce the amount of liquid. In each case the volume remains the same despite a change in shape or appearance. The original amount is "conserved" (Fig. 14-15).

During the concrete operational stage a child's thought begins to include the concepts of time, space, and number. Categories and principles are used, and the child can think logically about concrete objects or situations. These abilities explain why children stop believing in Santa Claus when they reach the stage of

Concrete operational stage Period of intellectual development during which children become able to use the concepts of time, space, volume, and number, but in ways that remain simplified and concrete, rather than abstract.

Conservation In Piaget's theory, mastery of the concept that the volume of matter remains unchanged (is conserved) even when the shape or appearance of objects changes.

Fig. 14-15 *Children under age 7 intuitively assume that a volume of liquid is increased when it is poured from a short, wide container into a tall, thin one.*

Box 14-2

Monopoly à la Piaget

Piaget's stages of cognitive development may be easier to remember if we relate them to a single example. What would happen at each stage if we played a game of *Monopoly* with the child?

Sensorimotor stage: The child puts houses, hotels, and dice in mouth, plays with "Chance" cards.

Preoperational stage: The child plays *Monopoly* but makes up own rules and cannot understand instructions.

Concrete operational stage: The child understands basic instructions and will play by the rules but is not capable of hypothetical transactions dealing with mortgages, loans, and special pacts and bargains with other players.

Formal operations stage: The child no longer plays game mechanically; complex and hypothetical transactions unique to each game are now possible.

Reversibility of thought Recognition that relationships involving equality or identity can be reversed (for example, if A = B, then B = A).

Formal operations stage Period of intellectual development characterized by thinking that includes abstract, theoretical, and hypothetical ideas.

Abstract principles Concepts and ideas removed from specific examples and concrete situations.

Hypothetical possibilities Suppositions, guesses, or projections.

concrete operations. Because of their ability to conserve, they come to realize such things as: Santa couldn't possibly visit everyone's house in one evening, or Santa's sack couldn't hold that many toys (Fehr, 1976).

Another important development at this time is the ability to reverse thoughts or operations. Lack of *reversibility* is illustrated by this conversation with a 4-year-old boy still in the *preoperational* stage (Phillips, 1969):

"Do you have a brother?"
"Yes."
"What's his name?"
"Jim."
"Does Jim have a brother?"
"No."

Reversibility of thought allows children in the concrete operational stage to recognize that if 4 × 2 = 8, then 2 × 4 does, too. Younger children must memorize each relationship separately. Thus, preoperational a child may know that 4 × 9 = 36 but not remember that 9 × 4 also equals 36.

The Formal Operations Stage (11 Years and Up) Sometime after about the age of 11, the child begins to break away from concrete objects and specific examples. Thinking is based more on **abstract principles.** Children can think about their thoughts, and they become less egocentric. The older child or adolescent also gradually becomes able to consider **hypothetical possibilities** (see Box 14-2). For example, if you ask a younger child: "What do you think would happen if people were able to fly?" the child might respond, "But people can't fly." Older children are able to consider the possibilites and to discuss their implications.

The stage of formal operations represents attainment of full adult intellectual ability. The older adolescent is capable of inductive and deductive reasoning and can conceptualize mathematics, physics, philosophy, psychology, and other theoretical and abstract systems. From this point on, improvements in intellectual ability are based on the accumulation of knowledge, experience, and wisdom, rather than on an enlargement of basic thinking capacity.

Learning Check

Match each item with one of these stages:

A. Sensorimotor **B.** Preoperational **C.** Concrete operational **D.** Formal operations

1. ____ egocentric thought

2. ____ abstract or hypothetical thought

3. ____ purposeful movement

4. ____ intuitive thought

5. ____ conservation

6. ____ reversibility

7. ____ object permanence

8. ____ nonverbal development

9. Assimilation refers to applying existing patterns or knowledge to new situations. T or F?

Answers: **1.** B **2.** D **3.** A **4.** B **5.** C **6.** C **7.** A **8.** A **9.** T

Applications

Making the Most of a Magic Time of Life

Many applications of the ideas presented in this chapter are self-evident. A few bear additional emphasis or extension.

Maturation It is valuable to remember that individual differences in maturation rates are the rule in human development. Aware parents recognize the difference between the **statistical child** and the **particular child**.

Developmental norms specifying ages at which particular abilities appear are based on *averages*. There is always a wide range of normal variation around each average. Thus, it is reasonable to expect plateaus, reversals, and periods of rapid advancement in the development of a particular child. This applies not only to the appearance of motor skills such as crawling and walking but also to language development and the stages of cognitive development described by Piaget. In all areas of development, the uniqueness of a child should be respected. This means resisting the temptation to compare the child with others, particularly in the child's presence. Each child is an individual and should be viewed as such.

Enrichment

As we have already noted, babies need stimulation. By keeping this need in mind, parents can do much to provide opportunities for varied sensory experience during infancy. A baby should be surrounded by colors, music, people, and things to see, taste, smell, and touch. Babies are not vegetables. It makes perfect sense to talk to infants, to take them outside, to hang mobiles over their cribs, or to rearrange their rooms. Also, the more time babies spend interacting with parents, the faster they develop language and thinking abilities (Clarke-Stewart & Koch, 1983).

Applications: Making the Most of a Magic Time of Life, continued

Most parents could put far more imagination into attempts to enrich an infant's surroundings than they typically do.

Question: Can enrichment be overdone?

The answer depends more on the *quality* of enrichment than on its quantity. Remember that the goal in enrichment is to create a world that *responds* to the infant—not one that bombards the infant with stimuli.

Responsiveness The concept of **responsiveness,** mentioned earlier, applies to toys and objects, as well as to parents' behavior. Toys that respond to a child's actions, such as balls, rattles, mirrors—even a spoon and a pie tin—help speed infant learning. Particularly effective are experiences that allow children to see cause-effect results from their own behavior. As psychologist Paul Chance points out, the most responsive toys tend to be the least expensive. The least responsive toy available is probably a $500 color television, while one of the most responsive is a $1 rubber ball (Chance, 1982).

Many authorities are concerned about parents who try to *push* their children's intellectual development in a misguided attempt to produce "super babies." It's worth stating again that forcing a barrage of stimuli, flash cards, exercises, and the like on infants is not enriching. Parents who approach play and learning as if their preschooler were on the fast track for Harvard are filling their own needs at the expense of the child's (Alvino et al., 1985). True enrichment is responsive to the child's curiosity and interests. It does not make the child feel pressured to perform.

Question: Is enrichment useful only during infancy?

Definitely not. An enriched, responsive environment is beneficial at any stage of childhood. As a matter of fact, Jerome Kagan has reported that stimulation in later childhood can have a greater effect on intellect than previously believed.

Kagan studied babies who were raised in darkened huts in an isolated Guatemalan village. Without the benefit of even a moderate amount of stimulation, these children were severely retarded by age 2. Yet by age 11 they had become beautiful children—gay, alert, and active (Kagan & Klein, 1973). The rich stimulation of village life during later childhood was enough to reverse the effects of early deprivation.

Question: In general, what kinds of experiences are most likely to encourage intellectual development?

Piaget Revisited

Piaget's theory suggests that the ideal is to provide experiences that are only slightly novel, unusual, or challenging. Remember, a child's intellect develops mainly through accommodation. As old concepts and thinking habits become obsolete, they are discarded or adapted to fit new demands.

To stretch a child's intellect, demands must be made, but experiences that are too far beyond the familiar may cause frustration and withdrawal. Therefore, gradually expanding beyond a child's current level of understanding is usually most productive.

Parents can contribute greatly to intellectual growth through their attitudes toward a child's *investigation* or exploration of the world. The child who repeatedly hears, "Don't touch that" (chair, handle, trash, radio, pencil, flower, and so forth) or "I told you not to" (go up there, play with that, leave this spot, get dirty, and so forth) may become passive and intellectually dulled (Carew, Chan, & Halfor, 1976). Placing virtually all common objects off limits for a child is a serious mistake.

In addition, Piaget's work shows the importance of relating to a child on the appropriate level. If you give a physical explanation to a very young child who asks, "Why does the sun come up in the morning?" you may have missed the point. Answering in terms of the child's egocentric viewpoint is more likely to be meaningful. An answer such as, "So that you will know it's time to get up" is completely satisfactory for a young child. Later, explanations can be made increasingly abstract and accurate.

It is also valuable to remember that children are newcomers to language. Many of the "silly" things

Applications: Making the Most of a Magic Time of Life, continued

children say have meanings that become apparent only to the adult patient enough to look for them. For example, language expert S. I. Hayakawa (1965) relates this incident:

> Once when our little girl was three years old, she found the bath too hot and said, "Make it warmer." It took me a moment to figure out that she meant, "Bring the water more nearly to the condition we call warm." It makes perfectly good sense if you look at it that way. (From "The Use and Misuse of Language" by S. I. Hayakawa. In R. E. Farson, Ed., *Science and Human Affairs*. Palo Alto, CA: Science and Behavior Books, 1965)

Intellectual growth is encouraged when children feel free to express ideas and when they feel understood when they do.

Question: Are there any guidelines for relating to children at their level:

In a delightful book entitled *Using Psychology*, psychologist Morris Holland offers some suggestions about how best to relate to children at different stages of intellectual development. The following points are drawn from this discussion (Holland, 1975).

1. Sensorimotor stage (0-2). Active play with a child is most effective at this stage. Encourage explorations in touching, smelling, and manipulating objects. Playing peekaboo is a good way to establish the permanence of objects.

2. Preoperational stage (2-7). Although children are beginning to talk to themselves and to act out solutions to problems, touching and seeing things will continue to be more useful than verbal explanations. Concrete examples will also have more meaning than generalizations. The child should be encouraged to classify things in different ways. Learning the concept of conservation may be aided by demonstrations involving liquids, beads, clay, and other substances.

3. Concrete operational stage (7-11). Children in this stage are beginning to us eneralizations, but they still require specific examples to grasp many ideas. Expect a degree of inconsistency in the child's ability to apply concepts of time, space, quantity, and volume to new situations.

4. Formal operations stage (11-adult). At this point it becomes more realistic to explain things verbally or symbolically to a child. Helping the child master general rules and principles now becomes productive. Encourage the child to create hypotheses and to imagine how things "could be."

Keeping this general outline in mind should help you adjust to the changing patterns of intellect displayed by developing children.

Learning Check

1. The idea that the particular child is different from the "statistical child" applies to language development and cognitive skills but not to motor development. T or F?
2. In his study of a Guatemalan village, Kagan found that a stimulating environment can sometimes reverse severe early deprivation. T or F?
3. To promote accommodation, it is best to provide information or experiences only moderately beyond a child's current level of comprehension. T or F?
4. Playing peekaboo is a good way to help the sensorimotor child master the concept of conservation. T or F?

Answers: 1. F 2. T 3. T 4. F

Chapter Summary

- The human *neonate* has a number of *adaptive reflexes*, including the *grasping*, *rooting*, *sucking*, and *Moro reflexes*. Neonates show immediate evidence of learning and of appreciating the consequences of their actions.
- Tests in a *looking chamber* reveal a number of visual preferences in the newborn. The neonate is drawn to complex, circular, curved, red or blue designs; human face patterns are also preferred, especially familiar faces. In later infancy, interest in the unfamiliar emerges.
- The *nature-nurture controversy* concerns the relative contributions of *heredity* (nature) and *environment* (nurture) to development. Hereditary instructions are carried by the *chromosomes* and *genes* in each cell of the body. Most characteristics are *polygenetic* and reflect the combined effects of *dominant* and *recessive* genes. Heredity influences a large number of personal characteristics as well as programming the general *human growth sequence*.
- Heredity is also involved in differences in *temperament* present at birth. Most infants reliably fall into one of three temperament categories: *easy* children, *difficult* children, and *slow-to-warm-up* children.
- Most psychologists accept that heredity and environment are inseparable and *interacting* forces. A child's *developmental level* therefore reflects *heredity*, *environment*, and the effects of the child's *own behavior*.
- *Maturation* of the body and nervous system underlies the orderly *sequence* of motor, cognitive, and language development. The *rate* of maturation, however, varies from individual to individual.
- The development of self-awareness, walking, bowel and bladder control, and many other basic capacities closely parallels maturation. Many early skills are subject to the principle of *readiness* (or *motor primacy*).
- *Prenatal development* is subject to environmental influences in the form of diseases, drugs, radiation, and the mother's diet, health, or emotions. Prenatal damage to the fetus may cause *congenital problems*, or birth defects.
- Healthy children are produced both by *conventional birth* and by *natural* (or *prepared*) *childbirth*. Prepared births, however, have the advantage of minimizing the use of anesthetics. The father's presence at birth appears to be desirable, although his attitude toward the birth may be of more basic importance.
- Studies of parents and their children suggest that *caretaking styles* have a substantial impact on emotional and intellectual development. Whereas mothers typically emphasize caretaking, fathers tend to function as playmates for their children.
- *Language development* proceeds from *control of crying*, to *cooing*, to *babbling*, to use of *single words*, then to *telegraphic speech*.
- The underlying patterns of telegraphic speech suggest a *biological predisposition* to acquire language. This innate predisposition is augmented by learning. *Prelanguage communication* between parent and child involves *shared rhythms*, nonverbal *signals*, and *turn taking*.
- A variety of *critical periods* exists throughout development, including periods before birth. Many animals display critical periods in *imprinting*.
- *Emotional attachment* of human infants to their caretakers is a critical early event. Infant attachment is reflected by *separation anxiety*. Although the issue

is controversial, it is doubtful that immediate *mother-infant contact* is crucial for forming lasting emotional bonds.

- Early *preceptual* and *emotional deprivation* seriously retard development. Even physical growth may be affected, as is the case in *deprivation dwarfism*.
- Research on deprivation suggests that perceptual stimulation is essential for normal development. Work with subhuman primates (monkeys) has also pointed to *contact comfort* as an important source of infant stimulation and attachment.
- Deliberate *enrichment* of the environment in infancy has a beneficial effect on the development of animals. Research with human infants has also demonstrated the value of enrichment.
- The intellect of a child is *less abstract* than that of an adult. Jean Piaget theorized that intellectual growth occurs through a combination of *assimilation* and *accommodation*. He also held that children go through a fixed series of *cognitive stages*. The stages and their approximate age ranges are: *sensorimotor* (0-2), *preoperational* (2–7), *concrete operational* (7–11), and *formal operations* (11–adult).
- Wise parents recognize the difference between the *statistical child* and a *particular child*. Effective *enrichment* is *responsive* to the child's interests and needs, and it takes into account the child's level of cognitive development.

Chapter 15

Challenges of Development: The Cycle of Life

Chapter Preview

Life with Billy

By the time he was 5, Billy's "record" read like the script of a parent's worst nightmare. Billy threw uncontrollable temper tantrums and never seemed to sleep. He had not learned to talk. He got into closets and tore up his mother's dresses and urinated on her clothes. He smashed furniture and spread soap powder and breakfast food all over the floors. He attacked his mother at every opportunity, once going for her throat with his teeth. He tried to stuff his baby brother in a toy box. When Billy's parents bought him a doll they called by the baby's name, they began finding the doll pushed head down in the toilet bowl.

Billy refused to eat anything but cold, greasy hamburgers from a certain drive-in. To get through a week, his parents were forced to buy hamburgers by the sack and hide them around the house so Billy wouldn't eat them all at once. When his parents went out driving, they had to detour around drive-ins to prevent Billy from frothing at the mouth and trying to jump out the window (Moser, 1965). Billy, you may note, was not an average 5-year-old.

Question: What was his problem?

Billy was an autistic child. His problem is rare. Few children get off to as bad a start in life as Billy. Nevertheless, every individual faces certain challenges and problems on the path to healthy development. Some obstacles, such as toilet training or establishing an identity, can be considered universal. Others are specialized problems. In either case, the challenges of development extend far beyond childhood and on into old age.

In this chapter we will examine some of the special challenges and problems presented by each stage of life. Be alert for information pertinent to your own life. Be alert for Billy, too. You'll meet him again later in the chapter.

Survey Questions What are the typical tasks and dilemmas of childhood, adolescence, adulthood, and old age? What are some of the more serious childhood problems? In what ways is adolescent development especially challenging? What happens psychologically during adulthood and aging? How do effective parents rear their children?

The Cycle of Life—Rocky Road or Garden Path?

If you pride yourself on being one of a kind, you have good reason. There is no such thing as a "typical person" or a "typical life." Nevertheless, there are certain broad similarities in the universal **life stages** of infancy, childhood, adolescence, young adulthood, middle adulthood, and old age. Each period confronts a person with a new set of **developmental tasks** to be mastered. These are skills that must be acquired or personal changes that must take place for optimal development. Examples are learning to read in childhood, adjusting to sexual maturity in adolescence, and establishing a vocation as an adult (Havighurst, 1979).

In an influential book entitled *Childhood and Society* (1963), personality theorist Erik Erikson suggests that we also face a specific **psychosocial dilemma**, or "crisis," at each stage of life. According to Erikson, resolving each dilemma creates a new balance between a person and the social world. An unfavorable outcome throws us off balance and makes it harder to deal with later crises. A string of "successes" produces healthy development and a satisfying life. Those who are plagued with unfavorable outcomes may experience life as a "rocky road."

Question: What are the major developmental tasks and life crises?

This is a broad question requiring an extended answer. Read on!

Stage One, First Year of Life: Trust versus Mistrust During the first year of life, children are completely dependent on others. Erikson believes that a basic attitude of **trust** or **mistrust** is formed at this time. Trust is established when babies are given adequate warmth, touching, love, and physical care. Mistrust is caused by inadequate or unpredictable care and by parents who are cold, indifferent, or rejecting. Basic mistrust may later cause insecurity, suspiciousness, or inability to relate to others. Notice that basic trust is encouraged by the same conditions that help babies become securely attached to their parents (Chapter 14).

Stage Two, 1–3 Years: Autonomy versus Shame and Doubt In stage two, children's growing self-control is expressed by climbing, touching, exploring, and a general desire to do things for themselves. Parents help foster a sense of **autonomy** by encouraging children to try new skills. However, the child's crude efforts often result in spilling, falling, wetting, and other "accidents." Thus, parents who *ridicule* their children, or *overprotect* them, may cause them to feel **shame** and to **doubt** their abilities.

Stage Three, 3–5 Years: Initiative versus Guilt In stage three, the child moves from simple self-control to an ability to take initiative. Through play the

Resources

Life stages Widely recognized periods of life corresponding to various ages and broad phases of development.

Developmental task Any skill that must be mastered, or personal change that must take place, for optimal development at a particular life stage.

Psychosocial dilemma A conflict between personal impulses and the social world that affects personality development.

Trust versus mistrust A conflict early in life centered on learning to trust others and the world.

Autonomy versus shame and doubt A conflict created when growing self-control (autonomy) is pitted against feelings of shame or doubt.

Initiative versus guilt A conflict centered around learning to take initiative while at the same time overcoming feelings of guilt about doing so.

child learns to plan, undertake, and carry out a task. Parents reinforce **initiative** by giving freedom to play, to ask questions, to use imagination, and to choose activities (Fig. 15-1). Children may be emotionally handicapped by parents who criticize severely, prevent play, or discourage questions. In this case, children learn to feel **guilty** about the activities they initiate.

Stage Four, 6–12 Years: Industry versus Inferiority Many of the events of middle childhood are symbolized by that fateful day when you first entered school. With dizzying speed your world expanded beyond your family, and you faced a whole series of new challenges.

Erikson describes the elementary school years as the child's "entrance into life." In school, children begin to learn skills valued by society, and success or failure can have lasting effects on their feelings of adequacy. Children learn a sense of **industry** if they win praise for building, painting, cooking, reading, studying, and other productive activities. If a child's efforts are regarded as messy, childish, or inadequate, feelings of **inferiority** result. For the first time, teachers, classmates, and adults outside the home become as important as parents in shaping attitudes toward oneself.

Stage Five, Adolescence: Identity versus Role Confusion Adolescence is a turbulent time for many persons in our culture. Caught between childhood and adulthood, the adolescent faces some unique problems. Erikson considers a need to answer the question, "Who am I?" the primary task during this stage of life. Mental and physical maturation bring to the individual new feelings, a new

Fig. 15-1 *According to Erikson, children aged 3 to 5 learn to plan and initiate activities through play.*

body, and new attitudes (Fig. 15-2). The adolescent must build a consistent **identity** out of self-perceptions and relationships with others. Conflicting experiences as a student, friend, athlete, worker, son or daughter, lover, and so forth must be integrated into a unified sense of self (more on this later). According to Erikson, persons who fail to develop a sense of identity suffer from **role confusion,** an uncertainty about who they are and where they are going.

Question: What does Erikson consider the major conflict in early adulthood?

Stage Six, Young Adulthood: Intimacy versus Isolation In stage six, Erikson emphasizes the need to achieve an essential quality of **intimacy** in one's life. After establishing a stable identity, a person is prepared to share meaningful love or deep friendship with others. By "intimacy" Erikson means an ability to care about others and to share experiences with them. In line with Erikson's view, 75 percent of college-age men and women rank a good marriage and family life as their primary adult goal (Bachman & Johnson, 1979). And yet, marriage or sexual involvement is no guarantee that intimacy will prevail: Many adult relationships remain superficial and unfulfilling. Failure to establish intimacy with others leads to a deep sense of **isolation.** The person feels alone and uncared for in life. This circumstance often sets the stage for later difficulties.

Stage Seven, Middle Adulthood: Generativity versus Stagnation According to Erikson, an interest in guiding the next generation is the main source of balance in mature adulthood. This quality, called **generativity,** is expressed by caring about oneself, one's children, and the future (Fig. 15-3). Gen-

Industry versus inferiority A conflict in middle childhood centered around lack of support for industrious behavior, which can result in feelings of inferiority.

Identity versus role confusion A major conflict of adolescence, involving the need to establish a consistent personality identity.

Intimacy versus isolation The challenge in early adulthood of establishing intimacy with friends, family, a lover, or a spouse versus experiencing a sense of isolation.

Generativity versus stagnation A conflict of middle adulthood in which stagnant concern for oneself is countered by interest in guiding the next generation.

Fig. 15-2 *Dramatic differences in physical size and maturity are found in adolescents of the same age. The girls pictured are all 13, the boys 16. Maturation that occurs earlier or later than average can affect the "search for identity." (From "Growing Up" by J. M. Tanner. Copyright © September 1973 by Scientific American, Inc. All rights reserved)*

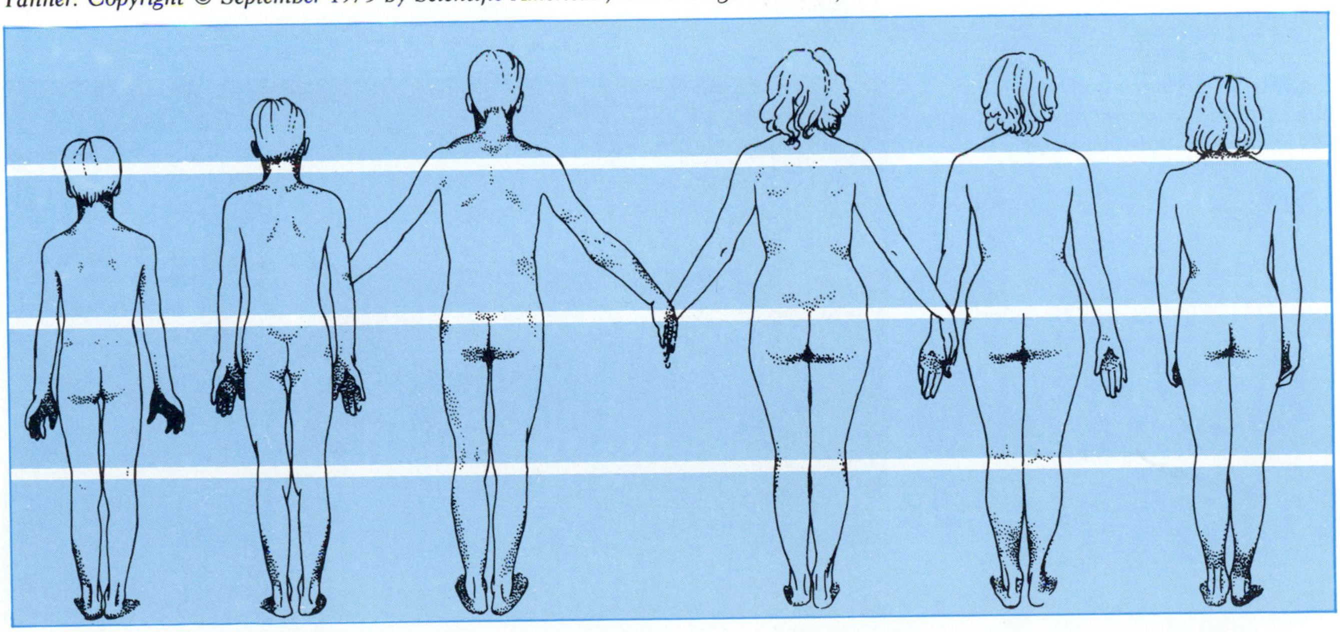

Integrity versus despair A major challenge in late adulthood consisting of maintaining a sense of integrity rather than falling into a pattern of despair.

erativity may be achieved by guiding one's own children or by helping other children (as a teacher, clergyman, or coach might do). It may also be achieved through productive or creative work. In any case a person's concern and energies must be broadened to include the welfare of others and society as a whole. Failure in this is marked by a **stagnant** concern with one's own needs and comforts. Life loses meaning, and the person feels bitter, dreary, and trapped.

Question: What does Erikson see as the conflicts of old age?

Stage Eight, Late Adulthood: Integrity versus Despair Because old age is a time of reflection, a person must be able to look over the events of a lifetime with a sense of acceptance and satisfaction. According to Erikson, the previous seven stages of life become the basis for successful aging. The person who has lived richly and responsibly develops a sense of **integrity.** This sense allows the person to face aging and death with dignity. If previous life events are viewed with regret, the elderly person falls into **despair.** In this case there is a feeling that life has been a series of missed opportunities, that one has failed, and that it is too late to reverse what has been done. Aging and the threat of death then become a source of fear and depression.

In squeezing the events of a lifetime into a few pages, we must ignore countless details. Although much is lost, the net effect is a clearer picture of an entire life cycle. Is Erikson's description, then, an exact map of your future? Probably not. Still, the dilemmas we have discussed reflect major psychological events in the lives of many people. Knowing about such events may allow you to anticipate typical trouble spots in life. You may also be better prepared to understand the problems and feelings of friends and relatives at various stages in the life cycle.

Having completed our whirlwind birth-to-death tour, we will revisit several life stages for a closer look at some of the challenges, landmarks, tasks, and problems of each. Before we begin, it might be a good idea to complete the Learning Check that follows.

Fig. 15-3 *According to Erikson, an interest in future generations characterizes optimal adult development.*

Learning Check

Since Erikson's eight life stages are scattered through the previous pages, you might find it helpful to summarize them. Complete the following do-it-yourself summary to check your recall of the stages. Compare your answers with those listed below to make sure you have a correct summary.

Stage	**Crisis**	**Favorable outcome**
First year of life	**1.** ______________ vs. **2.** ______________	Faith in the environment and in others
Ages 1–3	Autonomy vs. **3.** ______________	Feelings of self-control and adequacy
Ages 3–5	**4.** ______________ vs. guilt	Ability to begin one's own activities
Ages 6–12	Industry vs. **5.** ______________	Confidence in productive skills, learning how to work
Adolescence	**6.** ______________ vs. role confusion	An integrated image of oneself as a unique person
Early adulthood	Intimacy vs. **7.** ______________	Ability to form bonds of love and friendship with others
Middle adulthood	Generativity vs. **8.** ______________	Concern for family, society, and future generations
Late adulthood	**9.** ______________ vs. **10.** ______________	Sense of dignity and fulfillment, willingness to face death

Answers: **1.** trust **2.** mistrust **3.** shame or doubt **4.** initiative **5.** inferiority **6.** identity **7.** isolation **8.** stagnation **9.** integrity **10.** despair

Problems of Childhood— Why Parents Get Gray Hair

Can you remember a time in your childhood when your actions led to a disaster or a near disaster? It shouldn't be hard. It's a wonder that many of us survive childhood at all. Where I grew up, digging underground tunnels, wriggling down chimneys, hopping on trains, jumping off houses, crawling through storm drains, making bombs—and worse—were common childhood adventures.

Question: If initiative and industry are important in childhood, what limits should parents place on a child's freedom to explore the world?

An answer is provided by psychologist Diana Baumrind (1980), who has studied the effects of three major styles of parenting. According to Baumrind, each style tends to have a different effect on children's behavior. See if you recognize the styles she describes.

Authoritarian parents view children as having few rights but adultlike responsibilities. The authoritarian parent tends to demand strict adherence to rigid standards of behavior. The child is expected to stay out of trouble and to accept without question parents' word on right or wrong behavior. The children of such parents typically are obedient and self-controlled, but they also tend to be emotionally stiff, withdrawn, apprehensive, and lacking in curiosity.

In contrast, **overly permissive parents** view children as having few responsibilities but rights similar to adults. Such parents require little in the way of responsible behavior from their children. Rules are not enforced and the child usually gets his or her own way. This tends to produce dependent, immature children who misbehave frequently. Such children tend to "run amok" and to be aimless in their approach to life.

Baumrind describes **effective parents** as those who balance their own rights with those of their children. Such parents are *authoritative* but not authoritarian. That is, they control their children's behavior, but they are also loving and caring. Effective parents approach discipline in a way that is firm and consistent, not harsh or rigid. In general they encourage the child to act responsibly. This parenting style produces children who tend to be competent, self-controlled, independent, assertive, and inquiring. Thus, by balancing freedom and restraint, effective parents help children become responsible adults.

As an added guide to parenting, it may help to remember that stress is a normal part of life—even in childhood. Certainly this does not mean that parents should go out of their way to stress a child. However, it does suggest that there is no point in trying to shield children completely from stressful stimulation. **Overprotection** (sometimes called "smother love") can be as damaging as overstressing a child or being excessively strict or permissive.

Most children do a good job of keeping stress at comfortable levels when *they* initiate an activity (Murphy & Moriarty, 1976) (Fig. 15-4). At a public swimming pool, for instance, some children can be observed making death-defying leaps from the high dive, while others stick close to the wading area. If no immediate danger is present, it is reasonable to let children get stuck in trees, make them-

Fig. 15-4 *Most children do a good job of keeping stress at comfortable levels when they initiate an activity.*

selves dizzy, squabble with neighbor children, and so forth. Getting into a few scrapes can help prepare a child to cope with later stresses. Just think, if your author hadn't crawled through a few storm pipes, his adult interest in plumbing the depths of the psyche might have gone down the drain.

Question: How can you tell if a child is being subjected to too much stress?

Normal Childhood Problems Child specialists Chess, Thomas, and Birch (1965) have listed a number of difficulties experienced at times by almost every child. These can be considered normal reactions to the unavoidable stress of growing up.

1. All children experience occasional **sleep disturbances,** including wakefulness, frightening dreams, or a desire to get into their parents' bed.
2. **Specific fears** of the dark, dogs, school, or of a particular room or person are also common.
3. Most children will be **overly timid** at times, allowing themselves to be bullied by other children into giving up toys, a place in line, and the like.
4. Temporary periods of **general dissatisfaction** may occur during which nothing pleases the child.
5. Children also normally display periods of **general negativism** marked by tantrums, refusal to do anything requested, or a tendency to say no on principle.
6. Another normal problem is **clinging,** in which children refuse to leave the side of their mothers or to do anything on their own.
7. Development does not always advance smoothly. Every child will show occasional **reversals** or **regressions** to more infantile behavior.

An additional problem common to the elementary school years is **sibling rivalry**. Where there is more than one child in a family, it is normal for a certain amount of jealousy, rivalry, and even hostility to develop between brothers and sisters. Some sibling conflict may even be constructive. A limited amount of aggressive give-and-take between siblings provides an opportunity to learn emotional control, self-assertion, and being a good sport (Bank & Kahn, 1982). Parents can help keep such conflicts within bounds by not "playing favorites" and by resisting the temptation to compare one child to another.

Parents should also expect some **rebellion** from their children. Most schoolchildren rebel at times against rules and limitations of the adult world. For many children the company of peers offers a chance to "let off steam" by doing some of the things adults forbid. Being messy, noisy, hostile, or destructive is normal when engaged in to a moderate degree.

It is important to keep in mind that "normal problems" can signal a more serious disturbance if they are displayed for prolonged periods or if they become exaggerated. Problems of a more serious nature are identified in the next section.

Authoritarian parents Parents who demand strict obedience to authority and rigid rules.

Overly permissive parents Parents who give their children little guidance, allow them an excessive amount of freedom, or who do not require the child to take responsibility for his or her actions.

Effective parents Parents who supply firm and consistent guidance combined with love and affection.

Overprotection Excessively guarding and shielding a child from possible stresses.

General negativism A tendency to respond negatively to almost all situations or social interactions.

Clinging A problem in which a child literally clings to a parent or refuses to leave the parent's side.

Regression Any return to an earlier, less demanding and more infantile behavior pattern.

Sibling rivalry Competition among brothers and sisters for attention, dominance, status within the family, and so forth.

Childhood rebellion Open resistance to, or defiance of, adult authority.

Significant Childhood Problems—Off to a Bad Start

Although severe emotional disturbances affect only a minority of children, the number involved is larger than most people realize.

Question: What is the nature of these problems?

Enuresis An inability to control urination, particularly with regard to bed-wetting.

Encopresis A lack of bowel control; "soiling."

Overeating Eating in excess of one's daily caloric needs.

Anorexia nervosa A serious loss of appetite apparently of psychological origin.

Pica A craving for unnatural foods or substances such as chalk, ashes, and the like.

Delayed speech Speech that is developmentally delayed; that is, speech that begins well after the normal age for language development has passed.

Stuttering Chronic hesitation or stumbling in speech.

Learning disability Any problem with thinking, perception, language, attention, or activity levels that tends to impair learning ability.

Dyslexia An inability to read with understanding, often caused by a tendency to misread letters (by seeing their mirror images, for instance).

Hyperactivity A behavioral state characterized by short attention span, restless movement, and impaired learning capacity.

Minimal brain dysfunction (MBD) A hypothesized explanation for hyperactivity, involving a lag in brain development or low-level damage to the brain.

Toilet-Training Disturbances Difficulty sometimes centers on toilet training or bowel and bladder habits. The two most common problems are **enuresis** (EN-you-REE-sis: lack of bladder control) and **encopresis** (EN-coh-PREE-sis: lack of bowel control). Enuresis is more common than encopresis and many times more common among males than females. Both wetting and soiling can be a means of expressing frustration or pent-up hostility.

Parents should not be overly alarmed by some delays in toilet training or by a few "accidents." As mentioned in the last chapter, 30 months is the average age for completing toilet training. It is not unusual, however, for some children to take 6 months longer. Even when problems persist, they may be purely physical. Many bed wetters, for instance, have difficulty because they become extremely relaxed when asleep. These children can be helped by limiting the amount they drink during the evening. They should also use the toilet just before going to bed, and they can be rewarded for "dry" nights. Understanding, tact, and sympathy can do much to alleviate mild disturbances. Where more serious problems exist, parents should seek professional help.

Feeding Disturbances Feeding disturbances take a variety of forms. The disturbed child may vomit or refuse food for no reason or may drastically overeat or undereat. **Overeating** is sometimes encouraged by a parent who feels unloved and compensates by showering the child with "love" in the form of food. Some parents overfeed simply because they consider a fat baby healthy or desirable. Whatever the case, overfed children develop eating habits and conflicts that have lifelong consequences.

As described in Chapter 11, serious cases of *undereating* are called **anorexia nervosa** (AN-uh-REX-yah ner-VOH-sah: nervous loss of appetite). The victims of anorexia nervosa are mostly adolescent females. In addition to the causes decribed in Chapter 11, anorexia may reflect conflicts about maturing sexually. In other words, by starving themselves, adolescent girls can limit figure development and prevent menstruation (Palazolli, 1978). This delays the time when they must face adult responsibilities.

Another childhood eating difficulty is a condition called **pica** (PIE-ka). Some children go through a period of intense appetite during which they eat or chew on all sorts of inedible substances. Most commonly these are plaster or chalk, but some children displaying pica try to eat things like buttons, rubber bands, mud, or paint flakes. The latter can be quite dangerous because some paint contains lead, which is highly poisonous.

Speech Disturbances The two most common speech problems are **delayed speech** and **stuttering.** A serious delay in learning to talk is sometimes caused by too little stimulation in early childhood. Other possible causes are parents who discourage the child's attempts to grow up, and stresses such as separation from the mother, hospitalization, or birth of a sibling.

Stuttering was once held to be primarily a psychological disturbance. Now, researchers believe that stuttering is usually of physical origin. For example, stuttering is four times more common in males than in females, and there seem to be hereditary factors underlying its occurrence (Sheehan & Costley, 1977). Nevertheless, in some instances stuttering seems to reflect learned speech patterns or tension or frustration in the child. Because of such factors, parental reactions can add considerably to the child's anxiety, thus perpetuating the problem.

Learning Disorders Soon after Gary entered school, he became shy and difficult. Gary's teacher suspected a learning disability, and a specialist confirmed this. **Learning disabilities** include problems with thinking, perception, language, attention, or activity levels. Gary's specific problem was **dyslexia** (dis-LEX-yah), an inability to read with understanding. Because of it, he often felt confused and "stupid" in class, although his intelligence was normal.

The causes of dyslexia are not known at present. However, researchers suspect that it is related to brain dominance. As you may recall from Chapter 3, the left side of the brain is usually dominant over the right in language ability. In a minority of people the right brain is language dominant or it shares language ability with the left brain. People with shared or reversed dominance of this sort seem to be more prone to language disorders, including dyslexia (Durden-Smith & DeSimone, 1984; Marx, 1983).

One of the most significant learning disorders is **hyperactivity**. The hyperactive child is constantly in motion and cannot concentrate (Fig. 15-5). The child talks rapidly, cannot sit still, rarely finishes work, acts on impulse, and cannot pay attention. Hyperactivity occurs in 3 to 5 percent of American children, with five times as many boys as girls being affected (Varley, 1984). Unless it is carefully managed, hyperactivity can severely limit a child's ability to learn.

Question: What causes hyperactivity?

The most widely held theory is that hyperactivity is the result of **minimal brain dysfunction (MBD)**. Experts who support this theory link hyperactivity to a lag in brain maturation or to undetected damage to the brain. Medical authorities typically advocate the use of stimulant drugs to control hyperactivity. On one hand, such drugs do appear to lessen activity and increase the child's ability to focus attention (Solanto, 1984). On the other hand, however, a number of psychologists have objected to this blanket use of powerful drugs, which they regard as dangerous and unnecessary (Havighurst, 1976).

Fig. 15-5 *The hyperactive child's inability to hold still and pay attention can seriously disrupt learning.*

Behavior modification Application of principles of learning to change or to eliminate maladaptive or abnormal behavior.

Autism A severe disorder of childhood involving mutism, sensory spin-outs, sensory blocking, tantrums, unresponsiveness to others, and additional difficulties.

Echolalia A compulsion, sometimes observed in autistic children, to repeat everything that is said.

Operant shaping Gradual molding of responses through reinforcement of successive approximations to a final desired pattern.

Adolescence The socially defined period between childhood and adulthood.

Puberty The biologically defined period during which a person matures sexually and becomes capable of reproduction.

Question: What kind of treatment do they suggest?

Some researchers have found **behavior modification** as effective as drug treatment (Pelham, 1977; Wulbert & Dries, 1977). Behavior modification essentially is the application of learning principles to human problems (see Chapter 22 for more information). The basic idea is to find times when the hyperactive child is calm and attentive and to reward the child for such behavior.

Childhood Autism Childhood **autism** (AH-tism) is a problem that affects 1 in 2500 children, boys four times more often than girls. Autism is one of the most severe childhood problems. The autistic child is locked into a private world and appears to have no need for affection or contact with others. Autistic children do not even seem to know or care who their parents are.

In addition to being extremely isolated, the autistic child may throw gigantic temper tantrums—sometimes including self-destructive behavior such as head banging. Sadly, many well-meaning parents unintentionally reward such behavior with attention and concern (Edelson, 1984). Language learning in the autistic is usually so retarded that the child is mute. If they speak at all, autistic children often infuriatingly parrot back everything said, a response known as **echolalia** (EK-oh-LAY-lee-ah). These children also engage in frequent repetitive actions such as rocking, flapping their arms, or waving their fingers in front of their eyes. Additionally, they may show no response to an extremely loud noise (sensory blocking) or may spend hours watching a water faucet drip (sensory "spinout") (Ferster, 1968; Rimland, 1978).

Question: Do parents cause autism?

At one time experts blamed parents for autism. It is now recognized that autism is caused by congenital defects in the nervous system (Schopler, 1978). This is why, even as babies, autistic children are aloof and do not cuddle or mold to their parents' arms.

Question: Can anything be done for an autistic child?

Even with help, only one autistic child in four approaches normalcy. Nevertheless, almost all autistic children can make progress with proper care (Schopler, 1978). When treatment is begun early, behavior modification can be particularly successful.

Do you remember the child described in the Chapter Preview? Billy was one of the first patients in a pioneering program designed by psychologist Ivar Lovaas. Billy was selected for the program because of his unusual appetite for hamburgers. Teaching Billy to talk illustrates one aspect of his treatment. It began with his learning to blow out a match—making a sound like "who." Each time he made the "who" sound, Billy was rewarded with a bite of his beloved hamburgers. Next he was rewarded for babbling meaningless sounds. If he accidentally said a word, he was rewarded. After several weeks, he was able to say words such as "ball," "milk," "mama," and "me." By a painstaking continuation of this process, Billy was eventually taught to talk. Notice that this process is basically an example of **operant shaping,** discussed in Chapter 7.

In a behavior modification program, each of an autistic child's maladaptive behaviors is altered using combinations of reward and punishment. In addition to food, therapists are finding that sensory stimulation, such as tickling or music, is often very reinforcing for the autistic child (Rincover et al., 1977). And, strangely enough, researchers have found that following actions such as head banging and hand biting by punishment can bring a swift end to self-destructive behavior (Haywood et al., 1982). When such efforts are combined with parental involvement in treatment at home, considerable progress can be made (Short, 1984).

Autism and other severe childhood problems represent a monumental challenge to the ingenuity of psychologists, educators, and parents. However, great strides have been made in the last few years, and there is reason to believe that in the future even more help will be available to children who get a bad start in life.

Learning Check

See if you can answer these questions before you continue reading.

1. Occasional reversals and regressions to more infantile behavior are sure signs that a significant childhood problem exists. T or F?

2. Sleep disturbances and specific fears can be a sign of significant childhood problems when they are prolonged or exaggerated. T or F?

3. A moderate amount of sibling rivalry is considered normal. T or F?

4. Encopresis is the formal term for lack of bladder control. T or F?

5. The hyperactive child is lost in his or her own private world. T or F?

6. According to Diana Baumrind's research, effective parents are authoritarian in their approach to their children's behavior. T or F?

Answers: **1.** F **2.** T **3.** T **4.** F **5.** F **6.** F

Adolescence—The Best of Times, the Worst of Times

Adolescence is a time of change, exploration, exuberance, and youthful searching. It is also a time of worry and problems, especially in today's world. It might even be fair to describe adolescence as "the best of times, the worst of times." Just in case you weren't taking notes in junior high, let's survey problems and challenges of this colorful chapter of life.

Adolescence and Puberty

Adolescence refers to the period during which we move from childhood to acceptance as an adult. This change is recognized in almost all cultures. However, the length of adolescence varies greatly from culture to culture (Siegel, 1982). For example, most 14-year-old girls in America live at home and go to school. In contrast, many 14-year-old females in rural villages of the Near East are married and have children (Santrock, 1984). In our culture, 14-year-olds are adolescents. In others, they may be adults.

Many people confuse adolescence with puberty. But as you can see, the culturally defined period of adolescence differs from puberty, which is a *biological*

Growth spurt An often dramatic acceleration in physical growth that coincides with puberty.

Social markers Visible or tangible signs that indicate a person's social status or role.

event. **Puberty** refers to rapid physical growth, coupled with hormonal changes that bring sexual maturity. Interestingly, the peak **growth spurt** during puberty occurs earlier for girls than for boys (Fig. 15-6). This difference accounts for the 1- to 2-year period when girls tend to be taller than boys. (Remember going to dances where the girls towered over the boys?) For girls the onset of puberty typically occurs between 11 and 14 years of age. For most boys the age range is 13 to 16 years (Kaluger & Kaluger, 1984).

When you were going through puberty, did you ever spend *hours* preparing to attend a party, dance, or other social event? If you did, you weren't alone. Puberty tends to dramatically increase body awareness and concerns about physical appearance (Siegel, 1982). Beyond this, about one-half of all boys and one-third of all girls report being dissatisfied with their appearance during early adolescence (Rosenbaum, 1979). In many instances, such feelings are related to the *timing* of puberty. Girls who are temporarily "too tall," boys who are "too small," and both boys and girls who lag in sexual development are likely to be upset about their bodies.

Question: How much difference does the timing of puberty make?

Early and Late Maturation Because puberty involves so many rapid changes, it can be stressful for just about anyone. When puberty comes unusually early or late, its impact may be magnified—for both good and bad.

For boys, early maturation is generally beneficial. Typically, it enhances their self-image and gives them an advantage athletically and socially. For such reasons

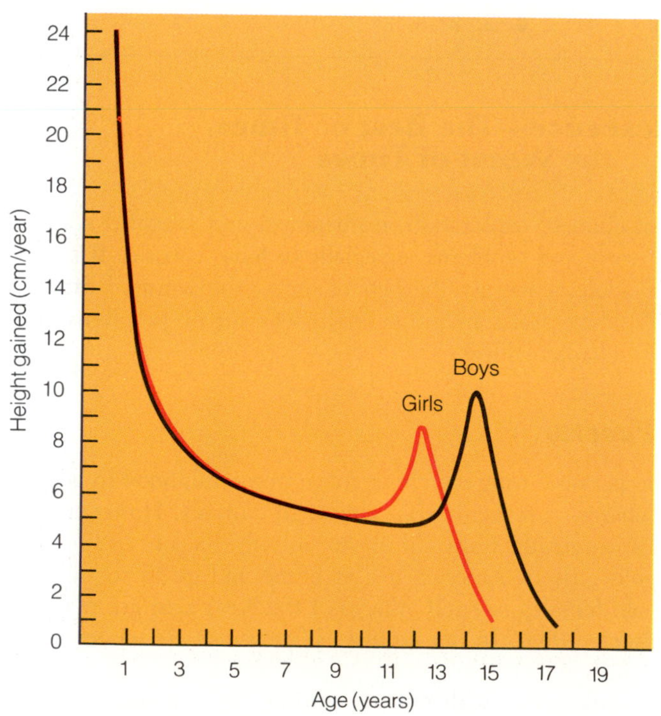

Fig. 15-6 *The typical rate of growth for boys and girls. Notice that the rate of growth in early adolescence equals that for ages 1 to 3. Note too the earlier growth spurt for girls.*

Box 15-1

Hurried into Adulthood

Psychologist David Elkind (1981) believes that a large number of American parents are hurrying their children's development. Elkind is concerned about parents who try to raise their babies' IQs or who have them reading, swimming, and doing gymnastics before they are 3 months old. Such pushing, he believes, partly explains why more children than ever show serious stress symptoms. Moreover, hurried children are becoming hurried teenagers—urged by parents and media alike to grow up fast. Elkind believes that too many teenagers are left without sufficient guidance, direction, and support to make a healthy transition to adulthood (Elkind, 1984).

Elkind's main thesis is that today teenagers have adulthood thrust on them prematurely. Violence, drug abuse, X-rated movies, teenage crime, teenage pregnancy, divorce and single parent households, date rape, aimless schools—all this, and more, strikes Elkind as evidence that there is no place for teenagers in today's society.

According to Elkind, the traditional **social markers** of adolescence have all but disappeared. (Markers are signs that tell where a person stands socially—such as a driver's license or a wedding ring.) As an example, Elkind notes that clothing for children and teenagers is increasingly adultlike. Girls especially are encouraged to wear revealing and seductive clothing and swimsuits.

Clearly, Elkind is stating a clinical opinion, not a demonstrated fact. It's possible that his view will prove exaggerated—indeed, much of what he says is debatable. Nevertheless, his portrayal of hurried adolescents as "all grown up with no place to go" is highly thought provoking.

early-maturing boys tend to be more poised, relaxed, dominant, self-assured, and popular with their peers (Santrock, 1984; Siegel, 1982). Many late-maturing boys are anxious about being behind in development. However, after they catch up, they tend to be more eager, talkative, self-assertive, and tolerant of themselves.

For girls, the advantages of early maturation are less clear-cut. In elementary school, developmentally advanced girls tend to have *less* prestige among peers. Presumably, this is because they are larger and heavier than their classmates. By junior high, however, early development leads to *greater* peer prestige and adult approval. In contrast, later-maturing girls have the possible advantage of usually growing taller and thinner than early-maturing girls. Other relevant findings are that early-maturing girls date sooner and are more independent and more active in school; they are also more often in trouble at school (Siegel, 1982).

As you can see, there are costs and benefits associated with both early and late puberty. One added cost of early maturation is that it may force premature identity formation (Siegel, 1982). When a teenager begins to look like an adult, he or she may be treated like an adult. Ideally, this change can encourage greater maturity and independence. But what happens when a person is treated as an adult before he or she is emotionally ready? Then the search for identity may end too soon, leaving the person with a distorted, poorly formed sense of self (see Box 15-1).

Imaginary audience The group of people a person imagines is watching (or will watch) his or her actions.

Menopause The female "change of life" signaled by the end of regular monthly menstrual periods.

Climacteric A point during late middle age when males experience a significant change in health, vigor, or appearance; roughly analogous to menopause in women.

Search for Identity

As discussed earlier, many psychologists regard identity formation as a key task of adolescence. To be sure, problems of identity occur at other times too. But in a very real sense, puberty signals that the time has arrived to begin forming a new, more mature image of oneself. Answering the question "Who am I?" is also spurred by cognitive development. After adolescents have attained the stage of formal operations, they are better able to ask questions about their place in the world and about morals, values, politics, social relationships, and private thoughts. Then too, being able to think about hypothetical possibilities allows the adolescent to contemplate the future and ask more realistically, "Who will I be?" (Coleman, Hersberg, & Morris, 1977).

David Elkind has noted another interesting pattern in adolescent thought. According to Elkind (1984), many teenagers are preoccupied with **imaginary audiences.** That is, they act like others are as aware of their thoughts and feelings as they are themselves. Sometimes this leads to painful self-consciousness—as in thinking *everyone* is staring at a bad haircut you just received. The imaginary audience also seems to underlie attention-seeking "performances" involving outlandish dress or behavior. In any case, adolescents become very concerned with controlling the impressions thay make on others (Santrock, 1984). For many, being "on stage" in this way helps define the shape of an emerging identity.

Question: What effects do parents have on identity formation?

Parents and Peers The adolescent search for identity often results in increased conflict with parents. However, this is not necessarily a problem. Some conflict with parents is probably necessary for growth of a separate identity. A complete lack of conflict may mean that the adolescent is afraid to seek independence (Siegel, 1982). Actually, there is usually a good deal of agreement between adolescents and their parents on basic topics such as religion, marriage, morals, and so forth. The largest conflicts tend to be over more superficial differences in styles of dress, manners, social behavior, and the like. In general, adolescents tend to overestimate differences between themselves and their parents (Lerner & Shea, 1982).

In high school were you a jock, preppy, brain, hacker, surfer, cowboy, punk, mod, warthog, dervish, gargoyle, or aardvark? (Well, okay, I made up the last four—the rest are real.) Increased identification with peer groups is quite common during adolescence. To an extent, membership in such groups gives a measure of security and a sense of identity apart from the family. Beyond this, group membership provides practice in belonging to a social network. Children tend to see themselves more as members of families and small friendship groups, not as members of society as a whole. Therefore, gaining a broader, member-of-society perspective can be a major step toward adulthood (Kohlberg, 1976) (Fig. 15-7).

Question: But aren't groups also limiting?

Yes, they are. Conformity to peer values peaks in early adolescence, but it remains strong at least through high school (Newman, 1982). Throughout this period there is always a danger of allowing group pressure to foreclose personal growth. By the end of high school, many adolescents have not yet sufficiently explored various interests, values, vocations, skills, or ideologies on their own.

Fig. 15-7 *Membership in friendship groups and cliques helps adolescents build an identity apart from their relationship to parents. However, overidentification with a clannish group that rejects anyone who looks or acts different can limit personal growth.*

Perhaps this is why many students view moving on to work or college as a chance to break out of earlier roles—to expand or reshape personal identity. For many who choose college, the effect may be more a matter of placing further changes in identity on hold. By doing so, college students keep open the possibility of changing majors, career plans, personal style, and so on. Typically, commitment to an emerging adult identity grows stronger in later college years (Santrock, 1984).

The search for identity we have discussed here may be intensified during adolescence, but it does not end there. In the next section we will move on into early adulthood for a look at further developments. Before you read more, here's a chance to check your memory.

Learning Check

1. In most societies, adolescence begins with the onset of puberty and ends with its completion. T or F?

2. Early-maturing boys tend to experience more clear-cut advantages than do early-maturing girls. T or F?

3. According to David Elkind, the traditional markers of adolescence and adulthood have been blurred. T or F?

4. The imaginary audience refers to conformity pressures that adolescents believe adults apply to them. T or F?

Answers: **1.** F **2.** T **3.** T **4.** F

Challenges of Adulthood—Charting Life's Ups and Downs

After a "settling down" period somewhere in the twenties, adult development is uniform and uninteresting, right? Wrong! A fairly predictable series of challenges is associated with development from adolescence to old age.

Question: What personality changes and psychological developments can a person look forward to in adulthood?

Recent research has added several important substages to the events discussed by Erikson. One of the most informative accounts is based on clinical work by Roger Gould, a psychiatrist interested in adult personality. Gould's research (1975) reveals that the most common patterns for American adults are as follows.

Ages 16–18: Escape from Dominance Ages 16 to 18 are marked by a struggle to escape from parental dominance. Efforts to do so cause considerable anxiety about the future and conflicts about continuing dependence on parents.

Ages 18–22: Leaving the Family The majority of people break away from their families in their early twenties. Leaving home is usually associated with building new friendships with other adults. These friends serve as substitutes for the family and as allies in the process of breaking ties.

Ages 22–28: Building a Workable Life The trend in the mid-twenties is to seek mastery of the real world. Two dominant activities are: striving for accomplishment (seeking competence) and reaching out to others. Note that the second activity corresponds to Erikson's emphasis on seeking intimacy at this time. Married couples in this age group tend to place a high value on "togetherness."

Ages 29–34: Crisis of Questions Around the age of 30 many people experience a minor life "crisis." The heart of this crisis is a serious questioning of what life is all about. Assurance about previous choices and values tends to waver. Unsettled by these developments, the person actively searches for a style of living that will bring meaning to the second half of life. Marriages are particularly vulnerable during this time of dissatisfaction. Extramarital affairs and divorces are common symptoms of the "crisis of questions."

Ages 35–43: Crisis of Urgency People of ages 35 to 43 are typically beginning to become more aware of the reality of death. Having a limited number of years to live begins to exert pressure on the individual. Intensified attempts are made to succeed at a career or to achieve one's life goals. Generativity, in the form of nurturing, teaching, or serving others, helps alleviate many of the anxieties of this stage.

Ages 43–50: Attaining Stability The urgency of the previous stage gives way to a calmer acceptance of one's fate in the late forties. The predominant feeling is that the die is cast and that former decisions can be lived with. Those who have families begin to appreciate their children as individuals and to ease up on their tendency to extend their own goals to their children's behavior.

Ages 50 and Up: Mellowing After age 50 a noticeable mellowing occurs. Emphasis is placed on sharing day-to-day joys and sorrows. There is less concern with glamor, wealth, accomplishment, and abstract goals. Many of the tensions of earlier years give way to a desire to savor life and its small pleasures.

Question: Don't many people undergo a midlife crisis?

A Midlife Crisis? Obviously, not everyone has difficulty at the midpoint of life. However, psychologist Daniel J. Levinson at Yale University has carried out an in-depth study of lives from early adulthood to later maturity. Levinson (1978) found that most of his subjects (all males) went through a period of instability, anxiety, and change between the ages of 37 and 41 (Gould's "crisis of urgency" period).

Roughly one-half of the people studied by Levinson defined the midlife period as a sort of "last chance" to achieve their goals. Such goals were often stated as a key event; for example, attaining a supervisory position, achieving a certain income, becoming a full professor, becoming shop steward, and so forth. For these individuals the midlife period is stressful yet manageable. A second pattern involved a serious midlife decline, often related to choice of a dead-end job or lifestyle. In other cases it meant that subjects had experienced external success but felt that what they were doing was pointless. And in a third pattern a few hearty individuals appeared to be "breaking out" of a seriously flawed life structure. For them, a decision to "start over" was typically followed by 8 to 10 years of rebuilding.

Thus, it can be seen that the midlife crisis, if it takes place at all, can be both a danger and an opportunity. Ideally it is a time of reworking old identities, of achieving long-sought goals, of finding one's own truths, and of preparation for later maturity and aging (Barrow & Smith, 1979).

Middle Age When individuals reach their forties and fifties, declining vigor, strength, and youthfulness make it clear that more than half of their time is gone. At the same time, greater stability comes from letting go of the "impossible dream" (Sheehy, 1976). That is, there is an increased attempt to be satisfied with the direction one's life has taken and to accept that hoped-for life goals may no longer be possible.

For most women during this era, **menopause** represents the first real encounter with aging. At menopause monthly menstruation ends, and a woman is no longer able to bear children. In menopause the level of the hormone estrogen drops—sometimes causing drastic changes in mood or appearance and the occurrence of physical symptoms such as hot flashes (a sudden uncomfortable sensation of heat).

Some women find menopause as difficult to adjust to as adolescence, and many experience anxiety, irritability, or depression at this time. Most postmenopausal women, however, report that menopause was not as bad as they expected and that much of their anxiety came from not knowing what to expect (Mussen et al., 1979).

Question: Do men go through similar changes?

Males do not undergo any physical change that is directly comparable to menopause. Just the same, some authorities now believe that 40- to 60-year-old males often pass through a **climacteric** (kly-MAK-ter-ik), or significant physiological change (Zaludek, 1976). During the climacteric, decreases in male hormone

Biological aging Physiological changes that accompany increasing age and alter a variety of physical and psychological functions.

Maximum life span The biologically determined maximum number of years humans could live under optimal conditions.

Life expectancy The average number of years a person of a given sex, race, and nationality can expect to live.

Gerontologist One who scientifically studies aging and its effects.

Fluid abilities Innate abilities based on perceptual, motor, or intellectual speed and flexibility; abilities that are not based on prior intentional learning.

Crystalized abilities Abilities that a person has intentionally acquired in the past and has practiced to a high level of mastery; accumulated knowledge and skills.

Disengagement theory of aging Theory stating that as people age it is normal and desirable for them to withdraw from society and from roles they held earlier.

output may cause psychological symptoms similar to those experienced by women in menopause. However, men remain fertile at this time, and many of their symptoms (depression, anxiety, irritability) are more likely related to self-doubts caused by declining vigor and changing physical appearance.

After the late fifties, problems an individual faces in maintaining a healthy and meaningful life are complicated by the inevitable process of aging. How unique are the problems of older people, and how severely do they challenge the need to maintain integrity and personal comfort? We will look at some answers in the next section.

Aging—Will You Still Need Me When I'm 64?

In 1978 students at Long Beach City College in California elected Pearl Taylor their spring festival queen. Ms. Taylor had everything necessary to win: looks, intelligence, personality, and campuswide popularity. At about the same time, citizens of Raleigh, North Carolina, elected Isabella Cannon as their mayor.

Question: What's so remarkable about these events?

Not too much really, except that Pearl was 90 years old when elected, and Isabella was 73 (Barrow & Smith, 1979). Both were part of the graying of America. Currently, some 21 million Americans are over the age of 65. By the year 2020, some 40 million persons, or *1 out of every 5*, will be 65 years of age or older. These figures make the aged the fastest growing segment of society. Understandably, psychologists have become increasingly interested in aging.

Question: What is life like for the aged?

There are large variations in aging. Most of us have known elderly individuals at both extremes: those who are active, healthy, satisfied, and whose minds are clear and alert and those who are confused, childlike, dependent, or senile. Despite such variations, some generalizations can be made.

Aging **Biological aging** is a gradual process that begins quite early in life. Peak functioning in most physical capacities reaches a maximum by about 25 to 30 years of age. Thereafter, gradual declines can be observed in muscular strength, flexibility, circulatory efficiency, speed of response, sensory acuity, and other functions.

Question: So people are "over the hill" by 30?

Hardly! Prime abilities come at different ages for different activities. Peak performances for professional football and baseball players usually occur in the mid-twenties; for professional bowlers, the mid-thirties; for artists and musicians, the fifties; and for politicians, philosophers, business or industrial leaders and others, the early sixties.

For those who are still young, the prospect of physical aging may be the greatest threat of old age (see Box 15-2). However, it is a misconception to believe that most elderly people are sickly, infirm, or senile. Only about 5 percent of the elderly are in nursing homes. As for the possibility of mental deterioration, phy-

Box 15-2

Biological Aging—How Long Is a Lifetime?

Whatever the biological causes of aging, humans seem to grow, mature, age, and die within a set time. The length of our lives is limited by a boundary called the **maximum life span.** Humans, like other animals, appear to live a limited number of years, even under the best of circumstances. Estimates of the average human life span place it around 95 to 110 years (Botwinick, 1984).

For most people, **life expectancy** (the actual number of years the average person lives) is shorter than a life span. In the 1800s the average life expectancy was 36 years. Now, average life expectancy for American males is 72 years and for females it is 79 years. With improved health care, life expectancy should move even closer to the maximum life span.

At present there is no known way to extend the human life span. On the other hand, there is every reason to believe that life expectancy can be increased. If you would personally like to add to a new, higher average, here are some deceptively simple rules for living a long life (Coni, Davison, & Webster, 1984):

1. Do not smoke.
2. Use alcohol in moderation or not at all.
3. Avoid becoming overweight.
4. If you suffer from high blood pressure, have it treated.
5. Remain socially and economically active in retirement.
6. Exercise regularly throughout life.

To this we can add: Get married (married persons live longer), learn to manage stress, and choose long-lived parents!

sician Alex Comfort (1976) comments, "The human brain does not shrink, wilt, perish, or deteriorate with age. It normally continues to function well through as many as nine decades." As a **gerontologist** (JER-on-TOL-o-jist: one who studies aging), Comfort estimates that only 25 percent of the disability of old people is medically based. The remaining 75 percent is social, political, and cultural (Fig. 15-8).

Comfort's view is backed up by studies of the intellectual capacities of aging individuals. Little overall decline occurs in intelligence test scores with aging. Although it is true that **fluid abilities** (those requiring speed or rapid learning) may decline, **crystallized abilities** such as vocabulary and accumulated knowledge actually improve at least into the seventies (Baltes & Schaie, 1974). The general intellectual decline attributed to old age is largely a myth.

Question: What kind of person adjusts most successfully to aging?

Activity and Disengagement Two principal theories have been proposed to explain successful adjustment to the physical and social changes of aging. **Disengagement theory** assumes that it is normal and desirable that people will withdraw from society as they age (Cumming & Henry, 1961). According to this theory, elderly persons welcome disengagement since it relieves them of roles and responsibilities they have become less able to fulfill. Likewise, society benefits from disengagement as younger persons with new energy and skills fill positions vacated by aging individuals.

Activity theory Theory of aging stating that the best adjustment to aging occurs for individuals who remain active mentally, socially, and physically.

Ageism Discrimination or prejudice based on a person's age.

Certainly we have all known people who disengaged from society as they grew older. Nevertheless, the disengagement theory can be criticized for describing successful aging as an orderly retreat.

Question: What does the second theory say?

A second view of optimal aging is provided by **activity theory,** which assumes that activity is the essence of life for people of all ages. Activity theory predicts that people who remain active physically, mentally, and socially will adjust better to aging (Havighurst, 1961).

Proponents of activity theory believe that aging persons should maintain the activities of their earlier years for as long as possible. If a person is forced to give up particular roles or activities, it is recommended that these activities or roles be replaced with others. In so doing, the aging person is able to maintain a better self-image, greater satisfaction, and more social support—resulting in more successful aging.

Question: Which theory is correct?

The majority of studies conducted on aging support the *activity theory*, although there have been exceptions (Barrow & Smith, 1979). At the same time, some people do seek disengagement, so neither theory is absolutely "correct." Actually, successful aging probably requires a combination of activity and disengagement. For example, one researcher has shown that the elderly tend to disengage from activities that are no longer satisfying while maintaining those that are (Brown, 1974).

Ageism In one way or another you have encountered ageism. **Ageism** refers to discrimination or prejudice on the basis of age. It applies to people of all ages and can oppress the young as well as the old. For instance, a person applying for a job may just as likely be told, "You're too young," as "You're too old." Ageism, however, probably has more negative impact on older individuals because it is usually expressed as an aversion, hatred, or rejection of the elderly. As Alex Comfort (1976) points out, the concept of "oldness" is often used to expel people from useful work. According to Comfort, retirement is frequently just another name for dismissal and unemployment.

Fig. 15-8 *Aging is a fact. But is "oldness" a social convention? Do the needs of "old people" differ from those of the young?*

Another facet of ageism is stereotyping of the aged. Popular stereotypes of the "dirty old man," "meddling old woman," "senile old fool," and the like, especially as seen in films and on TV, help perpetuate the myths underlying ageism. Contrast such images to those associated with youthfulness: The young are perceived as fresh, whole, attractive, energetic, active, emerging, appealing, and so forth.

Question: What can be done about ageism?

One of the best ways to combat ageism as it applies to older persons is to counter stereotypes with facts. As one example, studies show that in many occupations older workers perform better at jobs requiring *both* speed and skill (Giniger et al., 1983). Taking a broader view, Bernice Neugarten (1971) examined the lives of 200 people between the ages of 70 and 79. Neugarten found that 75 percent of these people were satisfied with their lives after retirement. Other myths about aging identified by Neugarten are:

1. Old persons generally do not become isolated and neglected by their families. Most *prefer* to live apart from their children.
2. Old persons are rarely placed in mental hospitals by uncaring children.
3. Old persons who live alone are not neccessarily lonely or desolate.
4. Few elderly persons ever show signs of senility or mental decay, and few ever become mentally ill.

In short, most of the elderly studied by Neugarten were integrated, active, and psychologically healthy. Findings such as these call for an end to the forced obsolescence of the elderly. As a group, older people represent a valuable source of skills, knowledge, and energy that we can no longer afford to cast aside. As we face the challenges of this planet's uncertain future, we need all the help we can get!

Learning Check

Check your comprehension with these questions.

1. Building a workable life tends to be the dominant activity during which age range?
   a. 18–22 *b.* 22–28 *c.* 29–34 *d.* 35–43
2. Levinson's description of the "midlife crisis" corresponds roughly to Gould's
   a. escape from dominance *b.* crisis of questions *c.* crisis of urgency *d.* settling-down period
3. The average male experiences the menopause between the ages of 45 and 50. T or F?
4. Many indications of biological aging start to become evident as early as the mid-twenties. T or F?
5. An expert on the problems of aging is called a ______________________.
6. The activity theory of optimal aging holds that aging individuals should restrict their activities and withdraw from former community activities. T or F?
7. After age 65 a large proportion of older people show significant signs of senility and most require special care. T or F?

Answers: **1.** b **2.** c **3.** F **4.** T **5.** gerontologist **6.** F **7.** F

Applications

Parenting—The World's Most Important Job

Raising children draws many of the problems of development into a single arena. When parenting is effective, both adult and child benefit. When parents fail to give their children a good start in life, everybody suffers—the child, the parents, and society as a whole. Healthy development requires emotional and social competence as well as intellectual ability. In addition to the skills needed for achievement, effective parents give their children a capacity for love, joy, and fulfillment.

Question: What can parents do to promote healthy development in their children?

Much of the answer can be found in two key areas of parent-child relationships. These are *communication* and *discipline*. In each area parents can set an exam-

Applications: Parenting, continued

ple of tolerance, understanding, and acceptance that goes beyond their traditional role as mere dispensers of "dos" and "don'ts."

Rearing Children

No psychologist would deny that love is essential for healthy development, but *discipline* can be of equal importance. Parents with unmanageable, delinquent, or unhappy children often can honestly claim that they have given them lots of love. Yet when parents fail to provide a framework of guidelines for behavior, children become antisocial, aggressive, and insecure. As noted earlier in this chapter, overly permissive parents—those who allow themselves to be dominated or manipulated—create lifelong patterns of self-serving behavior in their children.

Question: Does that mean discipline should be strict and unbending?

No. Recall too that authoritarian parents also have undesirable effects on their children. Families do not need to be run like military boot camps. Effective discipline is authoritative yet sensitive. The goal is to socialize the child without undue frustration and without destroying the bond of love and trust between parent and child.

Question: How can a balance be maintained?

Many experts are advocating a style of childrearing that recognizes a child's psychological needs. Discipline should give children freedom to express their deepest feelings through speech and actions. This does not mean freedom to do entirely as one pleases. It means the child has room to move about freely *within* well-defined limits. Of course, individual parents may choose limits that are more "strict" or less "strict." But this choice is less important than the consistency of parental standards. *Consistent* discipline gives a child a sense of security and stability; inconsistency makes the child's world seem unreliable and unpredictable.

Question: How can limits best be maintained?

Parents tend to base discipline on one or more of the following techniques: **power assertion, withdrawal of love,** or **child management** (Coopersmith, 1968; Hoffman, 1977).

Power assertion refers to physical punishment or to a show of force in which parents take away toys or privileges. As an alternative, some parents may temporarily withdraw love by refusing to speak to a child, by threatening to leave, by rejecting the child, or by otherwise acting as if the child is temporarily unlovable. Management techniques combine praise, recognition, approval, rules, reasoning, and the like to encourage desirable behavior. Each of these approaches can effectively control a child's behavior, but their side effects differ considerably.

Question: What are the side effects?

Power-oriented techniques—particularly harsh or severe physical punishment—are associated with fear, hatred of parents, and a lack of spontaneity and warmth. Severely punished children also tend to be defiant, rebellious, and aggressive (Patterson, 1982).

Withdrawal of love, which is a major middle-class mode of discipline, produces children who tend to be self-disciplined. We might say that such children have developed a good conscience. They are often described as "model" children or as unusually "good." But as a side effect, they are also frequently anxious, insecure, and dependent on adults for approval.

Management techniques also have their limitations. Most important is the need to carefully adjust them to a child's level of understanding. Younger children may not always see the connection between rules, explanations, and their own behavior. In spite of this limitation, management techniques receive a big plus in an important area of child development. Psychologist Stanley Coopersmith (1968) has found a direct connection between parental styles of discipline and a child's **self-esteem.**

Question: What is self-esteem?

Self-esteem refers to a quiet confidence that comes from regarding oneself as a worthwhile person. Many

Applications: Parenting, continued

theorists consider high self-esteem essential for emotional health. Individuals with low self-esteem have a low estimation of their value as people.

In direct studies of children, Coopersmith found that low self-esteem is related to the use of physical punishment or withholding of love. High self-esteem, in contrast, was related to management techniques that emphasized clear and consistent discipline coupled with high parental interest and concern for the child. Thus, it seems best for parents to minimize physical punishment and to avoid unnecessary withdrawal of love.

Question: Are you saying that physical punishment and withdrawal of love should not be used?

Effective parents use each of the three major types of discipline at one time or another, and each has its place. Coopersmith's findings simply suggest that physical punishment and withdrawal of love should be used with caution. In using these two forms of punishment, parents should observe the following guidelines.

1. Parents should separate disapproval of the act from disapproval of the child. Instead of saying, "I'm going to punish you because *you are bad*," say, "I'm upset about *what you did*."
2. Punishment should never be harsh or injurious to a child. Don't physically punish a child while you are angry. Also remember that giving a child the message "I don't love you right now" can be more painful than any spanking.
3. Punishment is most effective when it is administered immediately. This statement is especially true for younger children.
4. Spanking and other forms of physical punishment are not particularly effective for children under age 2. The child will only be confused and frightened. Spankings also become less effective after age 5 because they tend to humiliate the child and breed resentment.
5. Reserve physical punishment for situations that pose an immediate danger to the younger child, for example, when a child runs into the street.
6. Remember too that it is usually more effective to reinforce children when they are being good than it is to punish them for misbehavior.

After age 5, management techniques are the most effective form of discipline, especially techniques that emphasize communication.

Communication between Parent and Child

When clear communication is maintained between parent and child, many discipline problems can be avoided before they develop. Haim Ginott (1965) has suggested that it is essential to make a distinction between a child's feelings and a child's behavior. Since children (and parents, too) do not choose how they will feel, it is important to allow the free expression of feelings.

The child who learns to regard some feelings as "bad," or unacceptable, is being asked to deny a very real part of his or her experience. Ginott encourages parents to teach their children that all feelings are appropriate; it is only actions that are subject to disapproval. Many parents are unaware of just how often they block communication and the expression of feelings in their children. Consider this typical conversion taken from Ginott's book (1965):

Son:	I am stupid, and I know it. Look at my grades in school.
Father:	You just have to work harder.
Son:	I already work harder and it doesn't help. I have no brains.
Father:	You are smart, I know.
Son:	I am stupid, I know.
Father:	(loudly) You are not stupid!
Son:	Yes, I am!
Father:	You are not stupid. Stupid!

By debating with the child, the father misses the point that his son *feels* stupid. It would be far more helpful for the father to encourage the boy to talk about his feelings.

Question: How could he do that?

He might say, "You really feel that you are not as smart as others, don't you? Do you feel that way of-

Applications: Parenting, continued

ten? Are you feeling bad at school?" In this way the child is given a chance to express his emotions and to feel understood. The father might conclude the conversation by saying, "Look, son, in my eyes you are a fine person. But I understand how you feel. Everyone feels stupid at times."

Communication with a child can also be the basis of effective discipline. Thomas Gordon (1970), a child psychologist who has developed a program called Parent Effectiveness Training (PET), offers a useful suggestion. Gordon believes that parents should send "I" messages to their children, rather than "you" messages.

Question: What's the difference?

"You" messages take the form of threats, name calling, accusing, bossing, lecturing, or analyzing. Generally, "you" messages tell children what's "wrong" with them.

An "I" message is a form of communication that tells children what effect their behavior has had on you. To illustrate the difference, consider this example. After a hard day's work, Susan wants to sit down and rest a while. She begins to relax with a newspaper when her 5-year-old daughter starts banging loudly on a toy drum. Most parents would respond with a "you" message:

"You go play outside this instant." (bossing)

"Don't ever make such a racket when someone is reading." (lecturing)

"You're really pushing it today, aren't you?" (accusing)

"You're a spoiled brat." (name calling)

"Do you want me to swat you?" (threatening)

Gordon suggests sending an "I" message such as, "I am very tired, and I would like to read. I feel upset and can't read when you make so much noise." This forces the child to accept responsibility for the effects of her actions. If this doesn't curb misbehavior, the consequences can also be stated as an "I" message: "I would like for you to stop banging on that drum; otherwise, please take it outside." If the child continues to bang on the drum inside the house, then she has caused the toy to be put away. If she takes it outside, she has made a decision to play with the drum in a way that respects her mother's wishes. In this way both parent and child are allowed to maintain a sense of self-respect, and a needless clash is averted.

Only two additional points on communicating with children need be noted. They are: "Listen more than you talk"; and "Live the message you wish to communicate."

Child Abuse

Sadly, no account of parenting would be complete without a brief discussion of child abuse. Much as we might like to believe otherwise, child abuse is widespread—from 200,000 to 400,000 cases of physical abuse are reported each year in this country alone. Undoubtedly, many more go unreported (President's Commission on Mental Health, 1978). In about one-third of all cases of physical abuse, the child is seriously injured (Giovannoni & Becerra, 1979). Every year hundreds of children are killed by their own parents.

Question: What are abusive parents like?

Characteristics of Abusive Parents Abusive parents are usually young (under 30) and from lower income levels. However, professionals who treat child abuse see parents of all ages and income levels.

Abusive parents often have a high level of stress and frustration in their lives. Typical problems include loneliness, marital discord, unemployment, drug abuse, divorce, family violence, heavy drinking, and work anxieties (Giovannoni & Becerra, 1979). Some parents are aware that they are mistreating a child, but they are unable to stop. Other abusive parents literally hate their children or are disgusted by them. The child's sloppiness, diapers, crying, or needs are unbearable to the parent. Often these parents expect the child to love them and make them happy. When the child (who is usually under 3 years old) cannot meet their unrealistic demands, they react with lethal anger.

As mentioned previously, the core of much child abuse is a cycle of violence that flows from one gen-

Applications: Parenting, continued

eration to the next. That is, most abusive parents were themselves mistreated as children (Williams & Money, 1980). Such parents simply never learned to love, communicate with, or discipline a child.

When does the cycle of violence begin? Sad to say, it shows up almost immediately:

Abusive Toddlers

> In a recent study, abused 1- to 3-year olds were observed as they interacted with playmates. The question of interest was, "How do abused children react when another child is crying or distressed?" In almost every instance abused children responded to distress with fear, threats, or physical assault. (Main & George, 1985)

In short, abused children rapidly become abusive children and, later, abusive adults.

Question: What can be done about child abuse?

Preventing Child Abuse Many public agencies now have teams to identify battered or neglected children. However, legal "cures" for child abuse are not very satisfying. The courts can take custody of a child, or the parents may voluntarily agree to place the child in a foster home. Foster care can be an improvement, but it may also further traumatize the child. In some cases the child is allowed to remain with the parents but under court supervision. Even then, there is a chance of further injury unless the parents get help.

Self-help groups staffed by former child abusers and concerned volunteers are a major aid to parents. One such group is Parents Anonymous, a national organization of parents determined to help each other stop abusing children. Local groups set up networks of members that parents can call in an abuse crisis or when they feel one coming on. Parents also learn how to curb violent impulses and how to cope with their children. Such training may be especially effective when carried out at home, where abuse usually occurs (Nomellini & Katz, 1983).

Another way of preventing child abuse is by changing attitudes. Despite newspaper and TV coverage of the problem, many parents believe it is their "right" to slap or hit their children. A survey found that physical punishment is widely accepted in this country. Even hitting a child with a leather strap or a wooden stick was rated as only "moderately serious" (Giovannoni & Becerra, 1979). A child had to be "banged against a wall" or "hit in the face with a fist" before the parents considered the act abusive. As the authors of the survey put it, the public attitude appears to be, "It's all right to hit your child, but not too hard; in fact it's all right to hurt your child—but not too badly."

To face the problem squarely, we must realize that the line between acceptable discipline and child abuse is blurred. As a society we seem to say, "Violence is okay if the child isn't injured; if the child is injured, then it's child abuse." Of course, when the child is injured, it's too late to take back the violence. By condoning punishment that borders on being abusive, we greatly raise the chances of injury. The best solution to physical abuse, then, may lie in rethinking our attitudes toward physical punishment and toward the rights of children.

Learning Check

1. According to the text, effective discipline gives children freedom within a structure of consistent and well-defined limits. T or F?
2. Coopersmith found that high self-esteem in childhood is related to discipline based on either management techniques or withdrawal of love. T or F?
3. Spankings and other physical punishment are most effective for children under the age of 2. T or F?
4. Authoritarian parents view children as having few rights but many responsibilities. T or F?
5. Most parents who abuse children were themselves mistreated as children. T or F?

Answers: **1.** T **2.** F **3.** F **4.** T **5.** T

Chapter Summary

- According to Erikson, each life stage provokes a specific *psychosocial crisis*. In order of occurrence, these are: *trust versus mistrust*, *autonomy versus shame and doubt*, *initiative versus guilt*, *industry versus inferiority*, *identity versus role confusion*, *intimacy versus isolation*, *generativity versus stagnation*, and *integrity versus despair*.
- Three major parental styles are *authoritarian*, *permissive*, and *effective (authoritative) parenting*. When judged by its effects on children, authoritative parenting appears to be most effective.
- Few children grow up without experiencing some of the normal problems of childhood: *negativism*, *clinging*, *specific fears*, *sleep disturbances*, *general dissatisfaction*, *regression*, *sibling rivalry*, and *rebellion*.
- Significant problems affect about 1 child in 10. Major areas of difficulty are: *toilet training* (including *enuresis* and *encopresis*); *feeding disturbances*, such as *overeating*, *anorexia nervosa* (self-starvation), and *pica* (eating nonfood substances); speech *(delayed speech*, *stuttering)*; and *learning disorders* (*dyslexia*, *hyperactivity*, and other problems). *Childhood autism* is representative of some of the more severe problems that can occur. Some cases of hyperactivity and autism are being treated successfully with *behavior modification*.
- *Adolescence* is a culturally defined social status; *puberty* is a biological event. *Early maturation* is beneficial mostly for boys; its effects are mixed for girls. One danger of early maturation is *premature identity formation*. Adolescent identity formation is accelerated by cognitive development and is influenced by parents and peers.
- Certain relatively consistent events mark adult development in our society. These range from escaping parental dominance in the late teens to a noticeable acceptance of one's lot in life during the fifties. Some research indicates that a *midlife crisis* affects many people in the 37-to-41 age range. Adjustment to later middle age may be complicated for women by *menopause* and for men by a *climacteric*.
- Both the *number* and *proportion* of older people in the population have grown. *Biological aging* begins between 25 and 30; however, peak performance in a particular pursuit may come at various points throughout life. Maximum *life span* can be distinguished from *life expectancy*. Intellectual decline is quite limited, at least through one's seventies.
- *Gerontologists* have proposed two major theories of successful aging: The *disengagement theory* holds that withdrawal from society is necessary and desirable in old age. The *activity theory* counters that optimal adjustment to aging is tied to continuing activity and involvement. There is an element of truth to each; however, the activity theory has received more support.
- *Ageism* refers to prejudice, discrimination, and stereotyping on the basis of age. It affects people of all ages but is especially damaging to older people. Most ageism is based on myths and misinformation.
- Effective parental discipline tends to emphasize *child management* techniques (especially communication) rather than *power assertion* or *withdrawal of love*. *Child abuse* is a major problem for which few solutions exist at present. Abused children tend to become abusive adults.

Chapter 16

Intelligence

Chapter Preview

What Day Is It?

Ask George in which recent years April 21 fell on a Sunday. Without hesitation he will answer: "1985, 1974, 1968, 1963, 1957, 1946." Surprisingly, this gives only the slightest hint of his ability. If encouraged, George will go back as far as 1700—with complete accuracy! His calendar calculations cover a range of at least 6000 years, extending centuries beyond present perpetual calendars. With equal ease he can identify February 15, 2002, as a Friday or August 28, 1591, as a Wednesday.

Question: Is he a genius?

George's abilities are all the more amazing in view of the fact that he is mentally retarded and cannot add, subtract, multiply, or divide even simple numbers (Horwitz et al., 1965). George's strange talent is an example of the savant syndrome, *in which "an island of brilliance is found in a sea of retardation." The savant syndrome occurs when a person of subnormal intelligence shows highly developed mental ability in one or more very limited areas.*

Question: How could he be retarded and have this ability both at the same time?

The striking contrast between George's general retardation and unusual mental ability is a fitting introduction to the challenge psychologists face in trying to define and measure intelligence. Quite frankly, we are still searching for answers to such questions as: Is intelligence a general trait or a collection of specific skills? Is intelligence determined by the genetic "wheel of fortune" or is it nurtured by environment? Is it possible to construct an intelligence test that is fair to all people? How important is intelligence for "success"? Because our understanding of intelligence is rapidly changing, we cannot hope to give final answers.

For the sake of clarity, this chapter is divided into two parts. In the Resources section we will assume that intelligence can be measured, and we will use measurements as a way of answering questions about intelligence. In the Applications section we will consider questions that have been raised about intelligence tests and the meaning of their results.

Survey Questions How do psychologists define intelligence? What are the qualities of a good psychological test? What are typical IQ tests like? How do IQ scores relate to gender, age, and occupation? What does IQ tell us about genius? What causes mental retardation? Does heredity or environment determine intelligence? Are IQ tests fair to all racial and cultural groups?

Resources

Defining Intelligence—Intelligence Is . . . It's . . . You Know, It's . . .

Like so many important concepts in psychology, intelligence cannot be observed directly: It has no mass, occupies no space, and is invisible. Nevertheless, we feel certain it exists. Consider the following two individuals:

> When she was 14 months old, Anne H. wrote her own name. She taught herself to read at age 2. At age 5, she astounded her kindergarten teacher by walking into class with a stack of encyclopedias—which she proceeded to read. At 10 she breezed through an entire high school algebra course in 12 hours.

> At age 10 Billy A. can write his name and can count, but he has trouble with simple addition and subtraction problems and finds multiplication impossible. He has been held back in school twice and is still incapable of doing the work his 8-year-old classmates find easy. His teachers have suggested placing him in a special educational program for slow learners.

Anne is considered a genius; Billy, a slow learner. There seems little doubt that they differ in intelligence.

Question: Wait! Anne's ability is obvious, but how do we know that Billy isn't just lazy?

This dilemma is one that **Alfred Binet** faced in 1904. The minister of education in Paris had given Binet the task of devising a way to distinguish slower students from the more capable (or the capable but lazy). In a flash of brilliance, Binet and an associate created a test made up of "intellectual" questions and problems. Next, they determined which questions an average child could answer at each age. Children low in intellectual ability were identified by below-par performance on the test.

Binet's approach gave rise to modern intelligence tests. At the same time, it launched 80 years of debate that has often been heated and at times bitter. Part of the debate is related to the basic difficulty of defining intelligence.

Question: Is there an accepted definition of intelligence?

Most psychologists would probably agree with David Wechsler's general description of **intelligence** as the: *global capacity of the individual to act purposefully, to think rationally, and to deal effectively with the environment*. Beyond this, there is so much disagreement that many psychologists simply accept an **operational definition** of intelligence. (A concept is defined "operationally" by specifying what procedures will be used to measure it.) In other words, by selecting test items, a psychologist is saying in a very direct way: "This is what I mean by intelligence." A test that measures memory, reasoning, and verbal fluency offers a very different definition of intelligence than one that measures strength of grip, shoe size, length of the nose, or the person's best Pac Man score.

Reliability and Validity Suppose that a famous educator and psychologist, Ike Q. Tester, is dissatisfied with existing intelligence tests and decides to develop his own (the *I. Q. Tester IQ Test*). As a concerned citizen, there are two questions you should ask about Professor Tester's test: "Is it *reliable*?" and, "Is it *valid*?"

Question: What does reliability refer to?

A reliable bathroom scale gives the same weight on several successive weighings. For a test to be **reliable**, it must yield the same score, or close to the same score, each time it is administered to the same individual. It is quite easy to see that a test has little value if it is unreliable. Imagine a medical test for pregnancy, for instance, which gives positive and negative responses for the same woman on different occasions.

Question: How is the validity of a test established?

A test has **validity** when it measures what it claims to measure. One way to determine validity is to compare test scores with actual performance. A test of legal aptitude, for example, might be validated by comparing test scores with grades in law school. Even when they are reliable, many of the psychological tests you will encounter have little or no validity. This is especially true of "personality" tests found in magazines or offered by commercial "self-improvement" courses.

Later in this chapter we will address the question of whether intelligence tests are valid. For now, let's take a practical approach, by examining some widely used intelligence tests and the meaning of scores on them.

Intelligence An individual's overall capacity to think rationally, act purposefully, and deal effectively with the environment.

Operational definition Definition that specifies the operations (actions or procedures) used to measure a concept or variable.

Reliability The ability of a test to yield the same score, or nearly the same score, each time it is given to the same person.

Validity The ability of a test to measure what it purports to measure.

Stanford-Binet Intelligence Scale A widely used individual test of intelligence directly descended from Alfred Binet's first intelligence test.

Mental age A measure of mental ability defined in terms of the average capabilities of individuals at each age; that is, mental ability apart from age in years.

Testing Intelligence—The IQ and You

American psychologists quickly recognized the usefulness of Binet's test. In 1916 **Lewis Terman** and others at Stanford University revised it for use in this country. After several more revisions, the **Stanford-Binet Intelligence Scale** is still widely used. The Stanford-Binet assumes that mental ability in childhood improves with increasing age. As a result, the Stanford-Binet is really a set of increasingly more difficult tests, one for each age group.

The age-ranked questions of the Stanford-Binet allow a person's **mental age** to be determined. For example, at ages 8 or 9, few children can define the word *connection*. At age 10, 10 percent can. At age 13, 60 percent can. In other words, the ability to define *connection* indicates mental ability comparable to that of the average 13-year-old and gives a mental age of 13 (on this single item). Table 16-1 is a sample of items that persons of average intelligence can answer at various ages.

Mental age gives a good indication of actual abilities, but it says nothing about whether overall intelligence is high or low. To know the meaning of mental age,

Fig. 16-1 *Modern intelligence tests are widely used to measure intellectual abilities. When properly administered, such tests provide an operational definition of intelligence.*

Table 16-1 Sample Items from the Stanford-Binet Intelligence Scale

Two years old	On a large paper doll, points out the hair, mouth, feet, ears, nose, hands, and eyes. When shown a tower built of four blocks, builds one like it.
Three years old	When shown a bridge built of three blocks, builds one like it. When shown a drawing of a circle, copies it with a pencil.
Four years old	Fills in the missing word when asked, "Brother is a boy; sister is a ________." "In daytime it is light; at night it is ________." Answers correctly when asked, "Why do we have houses?" "Why do we have books?"
Five years old	Defines *ball*, *hat*, and *stove*. When shown a drawing of a square, copies it with a pencil.
Nine years old	Answers correctly when examiner says, "In an old graveyard in Spain they have discovered a small skull which they believe to be that of Christopher Columbus when he was about ten years old. What is foolish about that?" Answers correctly when asked, "Tell me the name of a color that rhymes with head." "Tell me a number that rhymes with tree."
Adult	Can describe the difference between laziness and idleness, poverty and misery, character and reputation. Answers correctly when asked, "Which direction would you have to face so your right hand would be toward the north?"

(Terman & Merrill, 1960)

chronological age (age in years) must also be considered. Mental age can then be related to chronological age to yield an **IQ,** or **intelligence quotient.** When the Stanford-Binet was first used in the United States, IQ was defined as mental age (MA) divided by chronological age (CA) and multiplied by 100:

$$\frac{\textbf{MA}}{\textbf{CA}} \times 100 = \textbf{IQ}$$

An advantage of the IQ is that intelligence can be compared in children with different chronological and mental ages. For instance a 10-year-old child with a mental age of 12 has an IQ of 120:

$$\frac{\text{(MA) } 12}{\text{(CA) } 10} \times 100 = 120 \text{ (IQ)}$$

A second child having a mental age of 12, but with a chronological age of 12 would have an IQ of 100:

$$\frac{(\text{MA})\ 12}{(\text{CA})\ 12} \times 100 = 100\ (\text{IQ})$$

The IQ shows that the younger child is brighter than his 12-year-old friend, even though their intellectual skills are actually the same. Notice that IQ equals 100 when MA = CA. An IQ score of 100 is therefore defined as average intelligence.

Question: Then does a person with an IQ score below 100 have below average intelligence?

Not unless the IQ is significantly below 100. An IQ of 100 is the *mathematical* average (or mean) for such scores. "Average intelligence" is usually defined as any score from 90 to 109. The important point to note is that IQ scores will be over 100 when mental age is higher than age in years, and IQ scores will be below 100 when mental age is lower than age in years. An example of the second possibility would be a 15-year-old with a MA of 12:

$$\frac{12}{15} \times 100 = 80\ (\text{IQ})$$

The preceding calculations were presented to give you insight into the meaning of IQ scores. However, with tests currently in use, there is no longer any need to calculate IQs. Instead, a **deviation IQ** score is used. To find a deviation IQ, we determine how far above or below average a person's score is, relative to others taking the test. Tables supplied with the test are then used to convert a person's *relative standing* in the group to an IQ score. This approach removes certain troublesome errors that occur when IQ is calculated directly.

Question: How old do children have to be before their IQ scores become stable?

Stability of IQ IQ scores are not very dependable until about age 6 (Honzik, 1983). The correlation between IQ scores obtained at age 2 and those obtained at age 18 is only .31. (Recall that a perfect correlation is 1.00 and a correlation of 0.00 occurs when scores are unrelated.) With increasing age, IQs become more reliable. The average change (median change) in IQ on retesting is roughly 5 points in either direction. However, children may show small ups and downs in tested intelligence as they develop. No typical pattern exists, and in some cases changes in IQ of 15 points or more may take place. Overall, though, changes are usually quite small after middle childhood.

Question: Is the Stanford-Binet the only intelligence test?

The Wechsler Test A widely used alternative to the Stanford-Binet is the **Wechsler Adult Intelligence Scale–Revised**, or **WAIS–R**. This test also has a form adapted for use with children, called the **Wechsler Intelligence Scale for Children–Revised (WISC–R)**.

The Wechsler tests bear an overall similarity to the Stanford-Binet but differ in some important respects. The WAIS–R is specifically designed to test adult intelligence, and both the WISC–R and the WAIS–R rate **performance** (nonverbal) intelligence in addition to **verbal** intelligence. The Stanford-Binet only gives one overall IQ, whereas the Wechsler tests can be broken down to reveal strengths

Chronological age One's age in years.

Intelligence quotient (IQ) An index of intelligence defined as a person's mental age divided by his or her chronological age and multiplied by 100.

Deviation IQ An IQ obtained statistically from a person's relative standing in his or her age group (that is, how far above or below average the person's score was relative to other scores).

Wechsler Adult Intelligence Scale–Revised (WAIS–R) The most recent version of a widely used adult intelligence test that rates both verbal and performance intelligence.

Wechsler Intelligence Scale for Children–Revised (WISC–R) The most recent version of a widely used intelligence test for children that rates both verbal and performance intelligence.

Performance intelligence Intelligence as demonstrated in solving puzzles, assembling objects, completing pictures, and other nonverbal tasks.

Verbal intelligence Intelligence as revealed by answering questions involving vocabulary, general information, arithmetic, and other language- or symbol-oriented tasks.

Individual intelligence test A test of intelligence designed for administration to a single individual by a trained specialist.

Group intelligence test Any intelligence test that can be administered to a group of people with minimal supervision.

Normal curve A bell-shaped curve having known mathematical properties, characterized by a large number of scores in a middle area, tapering to very few extremely high and low scores.

and weaknesses in various areas. The intellectual skills revealed by the Wechsler tests and some sample items are listed in Table 16-2.

Group Tests Both the Stanford-Binet and the Wechsler tests are **individual intelligence tests** that must be given on a one-to-one basis by a specially trained tester. Other tests of intelligence have been designed for use with large groups of people. **Group intelligence tests** are usually paper-and-pencil tests that require test-takers to read, to follow instructions, and to solve problems of logic, mathematics, or the visual arrangement of geometric designs. The first group intelligence test was the Army Alpha, developed for use in classifying World War I military inductees.

Table 16-2 Sample Items Similar to Those Used on the WAIS–R

Verbal Subtests	**Sample Items**
Information	How many wings does a bird have? Who wrote *Paradise Lost?*
Digit Span	Repeat from memory a series of digits, such as 3 1 0 6 7 4 2 5, after hearing them once.
General	What is the advantage of keeping money in a bank?
Comprehension	Why is copper often used in electrical wires?
Arithmetic	Three men divided 18 golf balls equally among themselves. How many golf balls did each man receive? If two apples cost 15¢, what will be the cost of a dozen apples?
Similarities	In what way are a lion and a tiger alike? In what way are a saw and a hammer alike?
Vocabulary	This test consists simply of asking, "What is a ________?" or "What does ________ mean?" The words cover a wide range of difficulty or familiarity.
Performance Subtests	**Description of Item**
Picture Arrangement	Arrange a series of cartoon panels to make a meaningful story.
Picture Completion	What is missing from these pictures?
Block Design	Copy designs with blocks (as shown at right).
Object Assembly	Put together a jigsaw puzzle
Digit Symbol	

1	2	3	4
X	III	I	0

Fill in the symbols:

3	4	1	3	4	2	1	2

(Courtesy of The Psychological Corporation)

If you're wondering if you have ever taken an intelligence test, the answer is probably yes. The Scholastic Aptitude Test (SAT), the American College Test (ACT), and the College Qualification Test (CQT) all are group tests that can be used to estimate a person's intelligence as well as his or her chances for college success.

Learning Check

Check your comprehension before you continue reading.

1. The first successful intelligence test was developed by ________.

2. If we define intelligence by writing a test, we are using:
a. a circular definition *b.* an abstract definition
c. an operational definition *d.* chronological age as the definition of intelligence

3. If a psychologist compares scores on a test with grades, performance ratings, or other measures, the psychologist is probably interested in the ________ of the test.

4. IQ is defined as $\frac{(\ \ )}{(\ \ )} \times 100$.

5. Scores on modern intelligence tests are based on one's deviation IQ (relative standing among test-takers) rather than on the ratio between mental age and chronological age. T or F?

6. The WAIS–R is a group intelligence test? T or F?

Answers: **1.** Alfred Binet **2.** c **3.** validity **4.** $\frac{MA}{CA}$ **5.** T **6.** F

Variations in Intelligence—The Numbers Game

Based on scores from a large number of randomly selected people, the classifications shown in Table 16-3 have been set for various IQ ranges. A look at the percentages reveals a definite pattern. The distribution of IQs approximates a **normal** (bell-shaped) **curve,** in which the majority of scores fall close to the average, with far fewer at the extremes. Figure 16-2 shows this characteristic of measured intelligence.

Question: On the average, do males and females differ in intelligence?

Sex IQ does not give a definite answer to this question since intelligence test items are selected to be equally difficult for both sexes. It seems safe to assume that men and women do not differ in overall intelligence, and no significant IQ difference has been found. However, tests like the WAIS–R allow a comparison of the intellectual strengths and weaknesses of men and women. Here a difference does emerge: Women perform better on test items that require verbal ability, vocabulary, and rote learning; men are better at items that require visualization of spatial relationships and arithmetic reasoning (Wechsler, 1958). However, such differences are small and are based on *averages*. It is important to recognize

Table 16-3 Distribution of Adult IQ Scores on WAIS–R

IQ	Verbal Description	Percent of Adults
Above 130	Very superior	2.2
120-129	Superior	6.7
110-119	Bright normal	16.1
90-109	Average	50.0
80-89	Dull normal	16.1
70-79	Borderline	6.7
Below 70	Mentally retarded	2.2

(Wechsler, 1958)

that many women are better than men at math, that many men are better than women at verbal skills, and so forth.

Question: How do IQ scores relate to success in school, jobs, and other undertakings?

School and Occupation IQ differences of a few points tell little about intellectual potential. But when a broader range of scores is considered, meaningful differences emerge. The correlation between IQ and school grades is .50—a sizable association.

As you might expect, there is also a relationship between IQ and job classification. Persons holding "high-status" positions average higher IQ than those in "lower status" occupational settings. (The term *high status* refers to traditionally higher paid business and professional occupations.) For example, accountants average about 120 in IQ and miners about 90 (Anastasi & Foley, 1958). It is important to note, however, that there is a range of IQ scores in all occupations. Many people of high intelligence, because of choice or circumstance, can be found in "low-ranking" occupations (Fig. 16-3).

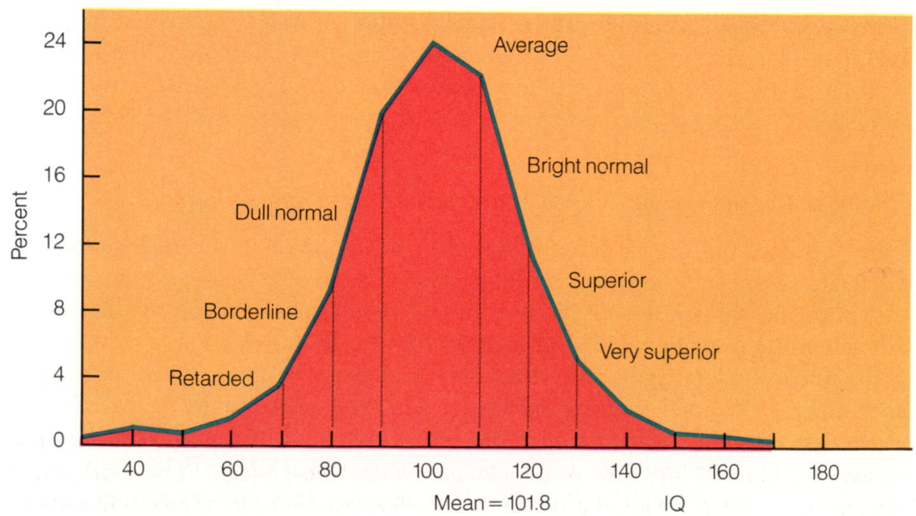

Fig. 16-2 *Distribution of Stanford-Binet Intelligence Test scores for 3184 children. (After Terman & Merrill, 1960)*

It is tempting to interpret the link between IQ and occupation as evidence that professional jobs require more intelligence. This interpretation is dangerous because IQ tests require the same types of mental gymnastics needed for success in school. Since higher status jobs often require an academic degree, the apparent link between IQ and job status may be misleading. Selection procedures for professional jobs appear to be biased in favor of a particular type of intelligence; namely, the kind measured by intelligence tests.

When variations in IQ are extreme—below 70 or above 130—influences on adjustment and one's potential for success become unmistakable. Only 4.5 percent of the population falls in these ranges, but this means that about 10 million people in the United States are exceptional by way of having very high or very low IQs. Discussions of the mentally gifted and the mentally retarded follow.

The Mentally Gifted—Is Genius Next to Insanity?

Question: How high is the IQ of a genius?

Only about 1 percent of the population scores above 140 on IQ tests. A person scoring this high is at least "gifted" and, depending on the standards used, he or she may be considered a genius. However, some psychologists reserve the term *genius* for even higher IQs or for other qualities, such as exceptional creativity.

Are high IQ scores in childhood associated with later ability? To directly answer this question, Lewis Terman selected 1500 children with IQs of 140 or more. By following the development of this gifted group into adulthood, Terman countered a number of popular misconceptions about genius.

Misconception: The gifted tend to be peculiar, socially backward people.
Fact: On the contrary, Terman's gifted subjects were socially well adjusted and showed above-average leadership capacity.

Misconception: "Early ripe means later rot": The gifted tend to fizzle out as adults.
Fact: This is false. When retested as adults, Terman's subjects again scored in the upper IQ ranges.

Misconception: The very bright are usually physically inferior "eggheads" or weaklings.
Fact: This is also a misconception. As a group the gifted were above average in height, weight, and physical appearance.

Misconception: The highly intelligent person is more susceptible to mental illness ("Genius is next to insanity").
Fact: Terman demonstrated conclusively that the gifted have better than average mental health records, indicating a greater *resistance* to mental illness.

Misconception: Intelligence has nothing to do with success, especially in practical matters.
Fact: The later success of Terman's subjects was the most striking finding of the study. Far more of them than average had completed college, earned advanced degrees, or held professional positions. Many had been recognized for outstanding

Fig. 16-3 *John Kirtley has an IQ score of 174, yet he prefers to do custodial work, feeling that his unusual intellect would be "used" by his employers if he pursued a technical occupation.*

Mental retardation The presence of a developmental disability, a formal IQ score below 70, or a significant impairment of adaptive behavior.

Adaptive behaviors Basic skills and actions considered necessary for self-care and dealing successfully with the environment.

Profound retardation Traditionally defined as an IQ score below 20.

Severe retardation Traditionally defined as an IQ score from 20 to 35.

Moderate retardation Traditionally defined as an IQ score between 36 and 51.

Mild retardation Traditionally defined as an IQ score in the 52–67 range.

achievments. As a group the gifted had produced dozens of books, thousands of scientific articles, and hundreds of short stories and other publications (Terman & Oden, 1959).

Question: Were all of the gifted children superior as adults?

No. Remember that high IQ reveals *potential,* not capacity. A high IQ is no guarantee of success. Some of the gifted had committed crimes, were unemployable, or were poorly adjusted.

Question: How did the more successful subjects differ from the less successful?

A recent follow-up found that the highly successful subjects differed mainly in their greater *persistence* and motivation to succeed (Feldman, 1982). The meaning of this finding is clear: As one educator put it, "No one is paid to sit around being capable of achievement—what you do is always more important than what you should be able to do" (Whimbey, 1980).

Question: How might a parent spot an unusually bright child?

Early signs frequently observed in gifted children include: a tendency to seek out and identify with older children and adults; an early fascination with explanations and problem solving; talking in complete sentences as early as 2 or 3 years of age; an unusually good memory; precocious talent in art, music, or number skills; an early interest in books, early reading (often by age 3); showing of kindness, understanding, and cooperation toward others (Alvino et al., 1985).

Notice that this list includes behavior other than straight "academic" intelligence. Children may be gifted in ways other than that reflected by a high IQ score. In fact, if such things as artistic talent, mechanical aptitude, musical aptitude, athletic potential, and so on, are considered, 19 out of 20 children could be labeled "gifted" in some respect (Fig. 16-4) (Feldman & Bratton, 1972). It

Fig. 16-4 *It is wise to remember that there are many ways in which a child may be "gifted." Many schools now offer gifted and talented education programs for students with a variety of special abilities—not just for those who score well on IQ tests.*

Box 16-1

Frames of Mind—Seven Intelligences?

At an elementary school a student who is two grades behind in reading shows his teacher how to solve a difficult computer programming problem. In a nearby room one of his classmates, who is poor in math, plays an intricate piece of music on a piano. Both of these children show clear signs of intelligence. And yet, each might score below average on a traditional IQ test. Such observations have convinced many psychologists that it is time to forge new, broader definitions of intelligence. Their basic goal is to better predict "real world" success—not just the likelihood of success in school (Sternberg, 1985).

One such psychologist is Howard Gardner of Harvard University. Gardner (1985) theorizes that there are actually seven different kinds of intelligence. These include abilities in language, logic and math, visual and spatial thinking, music, bodily-kinesthetic skills (such as dance or athletics), intrapersonal skills (self-knowledge), and interpersonal skills (leadership, social abilities).

If Gardner's theory is correct, traditional IQ tests measure only a part of real-world intelligence—namely, linguistic, logical-mathematical, and spatial abilities. A further implication is that our schools may be wasting a lot of human potential.

Not all psychologists agree with Gardner's broader definition of intelligence. But whether or not he is right, it seems likely that in the future intelligence will not be so strongly equated with IQ.

may therefore be a mistake to identify giftedness primarily with intelligence tests (Alvino et al., 1985). Such limited definitions of giftedness may shortchange many children who have special talents or potentials. (See Box 16-1.)

Mental Retardation—A Difference that Makes a Difference

A person with mental abilities far below average is termed **mentally retarded** or **developmentally disabled.** An IQ of 70 or below traditionally has been the dividing line between normal intelligence and retardation. However, a person's ability to perform **adaptive behaviors**—such as dressing, eating, communicating, shopping, and working—also figures into such classifications (Haywood et al., 1982). Below an IQ of 70, additional distinctions may be made, as shown in Table 16-4.

Question: Are the retarded usually placed in institutions?

No. Total care is only necessary for the **profoundly** retarded. The **severely** and **moderately** retarded are capable of mastering basic language skills and routine self-help skills. Many become financially self-supporting by working in *sheltered workshops* (special simplified work environments). The **mildly** retarded benefit from carefully structured and supervised education. As adults they are capable of living alone and may marry (although they tend to have difficulties with many of the demands of adult life) (Suinn, 1975).

Table 16-4 Levels of Mental Retardation

IQ Range	Degree of Retardation	Educational Classification
68-83	Borderline	Slow learner
52-67	Mild	Educable retarded
36-51	Moderate	Trainable retarded
20-35	Severe	Dependent retarded
Below 20	Profound	Life-support retarded

(Robinson & Robinson, 1976)

It is important to realize that retarded persons have no handicap where feelings are concerned. They are sensitive to rejection and are easily hurt by teasing or ridicule. Likewise, they respond warmly to love and acceptance. Professionals working with them emphasize their rights to self-respect and to a place in the community. This is especially important during childhood, when the support of others adds greatly to the person's chances of becoming a well-adjusted member of society (Fig. 16-5).

Question: What causes mental retardation?

Causes of Retardation

About 25 percent of all cases of mental retardation are *organic*, or related to known physical disorders, including **birth injuries** (such as lack of oxygen), **fetal damage** (from maternal drug abuse, disease, or infection), **metabolic disorders,** such as cretinism and phenylketonuria (discussed in the next section), and **genetic abnormalities.**

Fig. 16-5 *This youngster is a participant in the Special Olympics—an athletic event for the mentally retarded. It is often said of the Special Olympics that "everyone is a winner—participants, coaches, and spectators."*

Family Environment In the majority of instances, no known biological problem can be identified. In such cases the degree of retardation is usually mild, in the 50-to-70 IQ range, and quite often other family members are also mildly retarded (DSM-III, 1980). **Familial retardation,** as this is called, occurs most often in very low income or impoverished households. In some such homes, nutrition, early stimulation, medical care, intellectual stimulation, and emotional support are inadequate. The positive side of this picture is that most cases of familial retardation could be prevented by better nutrition, education, and early childhood enrichment programs.

To conclude our discussion, let's briefly return to organic retardation for a look at several distinctive problems.

Phenylketonuria (PKU) Phenylketonuria (FEN-ul-KEET-uh-NURE-ee-ah) is a genetically induced lack of an important enzyme. Lack of the enzyme causes the buildup of phenylpyruvic acid (a destructive chemical) within the body. If PKU goes untreated, severe retardation typically occurs by age 3 (Kopp & Parmelee, 1979). PKU is now easily detected in babies by medical testing during the first month of life. It can usually be controlled by a special diet low in foods containing substances the child's body can't handle.

Microcephaly Microcephaly (MY-kro-SEF-ah-lee) means small-headedness. The microcephalic suffers a rare abnormality in which the skull is extremely small or fails to grow. The brain is forced to develop in a limited space, causing severe retardation that usually requires the individual to be placed in an institution.

Hydrocephaly Hydrocephaly (HI-dro-SEF-ah-lee: water on the brain) is caused by a buildup of cerebrospinal fluid within brain cavities. Pressure from this fluid can damage the brain and greatly enlarge the head. Hydrocephaly is not uncommon—about 8000 babies are born with the problem each year in the United States. Thanks to new medical procedures, most of these infants now will lead normal lives. Treatment involves surgically implanting a tube that drains fluid from the brain into the abdomen. If this is done within the first 3 months of life, retardation can usually be avoided.

Cretinism Cretinism (KREET-un-iz-um) is a form of retardation that develops in infancy due to an insufficient supply of thyroid hormone. In some parts of the world, cretinism is caused by too little iodine in the diet (iodine is necessary for normal thyroid function). Widespread use of iodized salt makes this cause of the condition rare in the United States. Cretinism causes stunted physical and intellectual growth that cannot be corrected unless detected early. Fortunately, it is easily and routinely detected in infancy and may be treated by thyroid hormone replacement.

Down Syndrome The disorder known as Down syndrome causes moderate to severe retardation and a shortened life expectancy (usually around 40 years) in 1 out of 800 babies. Distinctive physical features of this problem, once referred to as mongolism, are almond-shaped eyes, a slightly protruding tongue, stubby hands, a stocky build, and sometimes a deep crease on the palm of the hand. It is now known that Down children have an extra chromosome. That is, cells in the child's body have 47 chromosomes, instead of the usual 46. This condition

Birth injury Any injury or damage that occurs to an infant during delivery.

Fetal damage A congenital problem; that is, damage or injury that occurs in the uterus during prenatal development.

Metabolic disorder Any disorder in metabolism (the rate of energy production and use in the body).

Genetic abnormality Any abnormality in the genes, including missing genes, extra genes, or defective genes.

Familial retardation Mild retardation associated with intellectually, nutritionally, and emotionally impoverished home life.

Phenylketonuria (PKU) An inherited lack of an enzyme that causes a destructive chemical to build up within the nervous system and leads to mental retardation.

Microcephaly Extreme small-headness, which limits brain growth and is often accompanied by mental retardation.

Hydrocephaly The destructive accumulation of fluid within the brain, which, if not controlled, can lead to brain damage and retardation.

Cretinism Stunted physical and mental growth and a lowered metabolic rate caused by insufficient secretion of thyroid hormone.

Down syndrome A pattern of physical malformation and mental retardation caused by the presence of an extra chromosome.

results from flaws in the parents' egg or sperm cells. Thus, while Down syndrome is *genetic*, it is usually not *hereditary* and does not "run in the family."

A very significant factor in Down syndrome appears to be the age of parents at the time of conception. The reproductive cells of older men and women are more prone to errors during cell division, which raises the odds that an extra chromosome will be present. Mothers in their early twenties have about 1 chance in 2000 of giving birth to a Down syndrome baby. At age 40 the odds increase to about 1 in 105. By age 48 the risk reaches 1 in 12. Recent research has determined that the age of the father is also linked to increased risk. In about 25 percent of cases the father is the source of the extra chromosome (de la Cruz & Muller, 1983).

These rather significant changes in risk should be considered in family planning. There is no "cure" for Down syndrome. However, these children are usually loving and responsive, and they can make progress in a caring environment. Experts working with Down syndrome children emphasize that they can do most of the things that other children can do, only more slowly (Pueschel et al., 1978). There is evidence that Down children continue to learn and to make slow mental progress well into adulthood (Berry et al., 1984). The best hope for Down syndrome victims therefore lies in specially tailored educational programs that enable them to lead fuller lives.

Learning Check

1. The distribution of IQs approximates a ______________________ (bell-shaped) curve.
2. The association between IQ and "high-status" jobs shows that "high-status" jobs require more intelligence. T or F?
3. Women tend to excel on test items that require verbal ability, vocabulary, and rote learning. T or F?
4. Only about 6 percent of the population scores above 140 on IQ tests. T or F?
5. An IQ score below 90 indicates mental retardation. T or F?
6. Many cases of mental retardation without known organic causes appear to be ______________________ .
7. According to Howard Gardner's theory, the three basic human intelligences are: linguistic skills, logic, and spatial skills. T or F?

Match:

8. ____ PKU
9. ____ Microcephaly
10. ____ Hydrocephaly
11. ____ Cretinism
12. ____ Down syndrome

A. Too little thyroid hormone
B. Very small brain
C. 47 chromosomes
D. Lack of an important enzyme
E. Excess of cerebrospinal fluid
F. Caused by a lack of oxygen at birth

Answers: **1.** normal **2.** F **3.** T **4.** F **5.** F **6.** familial **7.** F **8.** D **9.** B **10.** E **11.** A **12.** C

Eugenics The improvement of a species or race through selective breeding for desirable characteristics.

Heredity and Environment—Super Rats and Family Trees

Question: Is intelligence inherited?

This seemingly simple question is loaded with controversy. Some psychologists believe intelligence is strongly affected by heredity. Many others think that environment is dominant. Let's examine some of the evidence for each view.

In a classic study of genetic factors in learning, Tryon (1929) managed to breed separate strains of "maze-bright" and "maze-dull" rats (animals that were extremely "bright" or "stupid" at learning mazes). After several generations of breeding, the slowest "super rat" outperformed the best "dull" rat. This and other studies of **eugenics** (selective breeding for desirable characteristics) suggest that some traits are highly influenced by heredity.

Question: That may be true, but is maze learning really a measure of intelligence?

No, it isn't. Tryon's study seemed to show that intelligence is inherited, but later researchers found the "bright" rats were simply more motivated by food and less easily distracted during testing (Whimbey, 1980). When they weren't chasing after rat chow, the "bright" rats were no more intelligent than the supposedly dull rats. Because of such problems, animal studies cannot tell us with certainty how heredity and environment affect intelligence. Let's see what human studies reveal.

Most people are aware that there is a moderate similarity in the intelligence of parents and their children, or between brothers and sisters. As Figure 16-6 shows, the similarity in IQ scores among relatives grows in proportion to their closeness on the family tree.

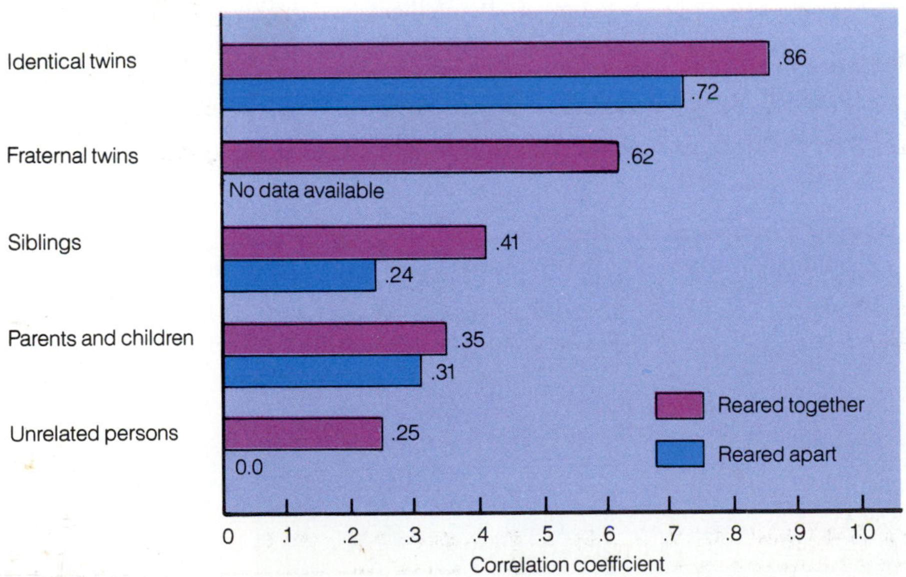

Fig. 16-6 *Approximate correlations between IQ scores for persons with varying degrees of genetic and environmental similarity. Notice that the correlations grow smaller as the degree of genetic similarity declines. Also note that a shared environment increases the correlation in all cases. (Estimates from Bouchard, 1983; Henderson, 1982)*

Fraternal twins Twins conceived from two separate eggs. Fraternal twins are no more alike genetically than other siblings.

Identical twins Twins who develop from the same egg and who, therefore, have identical genes.

Question: Does that indicate that intelligence is hereditary?

Not necessarily, because brothers, sisters, and parents share similar environments as well as similar heredity. To separate heredity and environment, we need to make some selected comparisons.

Twin Studies Notice in Fig. 16-6 that the IQ scores of fraternal twins are more alike than those of ordinary siblings. **Fraternal twins** come from two separate eggs fertilized at the same time. Thus, they are no more genetically alike than ordinary siblings. Why, then, should the twins' IQ scores be more similar? The reason is environmental: Parents treat twins more alike than ordinary siblings, resulting in a closer match in IQs.

More striking similarities are observed with **identical twins,** who develop from a single egg and have *identical* genes. At the top of Fig. 16-6 you can see that identical twins who grow up in the same family have highly correlated IQs. This is what we would expect with identical heredity and highly similar environments. Now, let's consider what happens when identical twins are reared apart. As you can see, the correlation drops, but only from .86 to .72. Psychologists who emphasize genetics believe these figures show that intelligence is 70 to 80 percent hereditary (Eysenck, 1981).

Question: How do environmentalists interpret the figures?

Environmentalists point out that some separated twins differ by as much as 20 IQ points. In every case where this occurs there are large educational and environmental differences between the twins (Whimbey, 1980). Also, separated twins are almost always placed in homes socially and educationally similar to their biological parents. This fact would tend to inflate apparent genetic effects by making the separated twins' IQs more alike (Kamin, 1981).

Strong evidence for an environmental view of intelligence comes from families having one adopted child and one biological child. As Figure 16-7 shows, parents contribute genes *and* environment to their biological child. With an adopted child they contribute only environment. If intelligence is highly genetic, the IQs of biological children should be more like their parents' IQs than are the IQs of adopted children. However, studies show that children reared by the same mother resemble her in IQ to the same degree; it does not matter whether they share her genes (Horn et al., 1979; Kamin, 1981; Weinberg, 1977).

Question: How much can environment alter intelligence?

IQ and Environment In one study, striking increases in IQ were observed in 25 children who were moved from an orphanage to more stimulating environ-

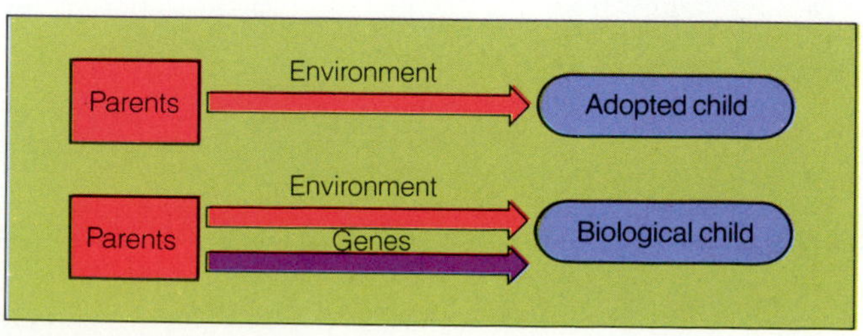

Fig. 16-7 *Comparison of an adopted child and a biological child reared in the same family. (After Kamin, 1981)*

Box 16-2

Can Intelligence Be Taught?

The traditional answer to the question, "Can intelligence be taught?" is "No." Coaching, for instance, has little positive effect on aptitude and intelligence test scores (Kulik, Bangert-Drowns, & Kulik, 1984). But is a brief period of coaching a fair test of the modifiability of intelligence? Apparently not. There is increasing evidence that extended, in-depth training in thinking skills can increase tested intelligence (Whimbey, 1980).

At the forefront of such efforts is Israeli psychologist Reuven Feuerstein (FOY-er-shtine). Feuerstein and his colleagues have developed a program they call Instrumental Enrichment. The program involves hundreds of hours of guided problem solving. The emphasis throughout is on remedying the kinds of gaps and flaws in thinking that cause lower IQ scores (Feuerstein et al., 1980). Feuerstein and other researchers have shown that such training can, in fact, raise IQ scores (Haywood, Meyers, & Switsky, 1982; Messerer et al., 1984).

A difficulty with such training is that it is very time consuming. In recognition of this problem, other psychologists are now developing computer programs to teach problem solving, effective thinking, and other elements of intelligence (Pellegrino, 1985). With our growing understanding of how people think, and with the tireless aid of computers, it may indeed become common in schools to "teach intelligence."

ments. The children, all considered mentally retarded and unadoptable, were moved to an institution where they received personal attention from adults. Later, these supposedly retarded children were adopted by parents who gave them love, a family, and a stimulating environment. The IQs of the children showed an average gain of 29 points. For one child the increase was an amazing 58 points. A second group of initially less "retarded" children who remained in the orphanage *lost* an average of 26 IQ points (Skeels, 1966)!

The educational level of parents creates another interesting environmental effect. In a study done in France, IQ scores for 32 adopted children were compared with the scores of brothers and sisters who stayed with the biological parents. In most cases the biological parents were poorly educated and worked in nonprofessional jobs. The adopted children had mostly gone to families of higher educational and economic status. It was found that average IQ scores matched almost perfectly those of children from similar family backgrounds. That is, children who stayed with their biological parents had lower IQs than their adopted brothers and sisters. Basically, the adoptees performed the same as nonadopted upper-middle-class children (Schiff et al., 1978). This and the preceding study are an encouraging indication that intelligence can be raised by an improved environment. (Also, see Box 16-2.)

Summary In summary, few psychologists seriously believe that heredity is not a factor in intelligence, and all accept that environment affects it. Estimates of the contributions of each factor continue to vary. But ultimately, both camps agree that improving social conditions or education can raise intelligence. There is probably no limit to how far *down* intelligence can go in a poor environment, but heredity may impose some limits on how far up IQ can go, even under ideal conditions (Scarr-Salapatek, 1971). It might help, then, to think of inherited intellectual potential as a rubber band that is stretched by outside forces. A long rubber band may be stretched more easily, but a shorter one can be stretched to the same length if enough force is applied (Stern, 1956). Of course a superior genetic "gift" may allow for a higher maximum IQ. However, in the final analysis intelligence reflects development as well as potential, nurture as well as nature.

Learning Check

1. Selective breeding for desirable characteristics is called ______________ .

2. The closest similarity in IQs would be observed for:
a. parents and their children
b. identical twins reared apart
c. fraternal twins reared together
d. siblings reared together

3. Most psychologists believe that intelligence is 90 percent hereditary. T or F?

4. Except for slight variations during testing, IQ cannot be changed. T or F?

5. Environmental effects are probably more capable of lowering IQ than of raising it. T or F?

Answers: **1.** eugenics **2.** *b* **3.** F **4.** F **5.** T

Applications

Intelligence in Perspective—Are Intelligence Tests Intelligent?

Almost everyone has some curiosity about how they would score on an intelligence test. If you would like to get a rough estimate of your IQ, take the following self-administered test.

Dove Counterbalance Intelligence Test

Time limit: 5 minutes
Circle the correct answer.

1. T-bone Walker got famous for playing what?
a. trombone *c.* T-flute *e.* "hambone"
b. piano *d.* guitar

2. A "gas head" is a person who has a _____.
a. fast-moving car *d.* habit of stealing cars
b. stable of "lace" *e.* long jail record for arson
c. "process"

3. If you throw the dice and 7 is showing on the top, what is facing down?
a. 7 *c.* boxcars *e.* 11
b. snake eyes *d.* little joes

4. Cheap chitlings (not the kind you purchase at a frozen-food counter) will taste rubbery unless they are cooked long enough. How soon can you quit cooking them to eat and enjoy them?
a. 45 minutes *d.* one week (on a low flame)
b. two hours *e.* one hour
c. 24 hours

5. Bird or Yardbird was the jacket jazz lovers from coast to coast hung on _____?
a. Lester Young *d.* Charlie Parker
b. Peggy Lee *e.* Birdman of Alcatraz
c. Benny Goodman

6. A "hankerchief head" is:
a. a cool cat *d.* a hoddi
b. a porter *e.* a preacher
c. an Uncle Tom

7. Jet is _____.
a. an East Oakland motorcyle club
b. one of the gangs in West Side Story
c. a news and gossip magazine
d. a way of life for the very rich

8. "Bo Diddly" is a _____.
a. game for children *d.* new dance
b. down-home cheap wine *e.* Moejoe call
c. down-home singer

9. Which word is most out of place here?
a. splib *c.* gray *e.* black
b. blood *d.* spook

10. If a pimp is uptight with a woman who gets state aid, what does he mean when he talks about "Mother's Day"?
a. second Sunday in May
b. third Sunday in June
c. first of every month
d. none of these
e. first and fifteenth of every month

11. How much does a "short dog" cost?
a. 15¢ *c.* 35¢ *e.* 86¢ plus tax
b. $2 *d.* 5¢

12. Many people say that "Juneteenth" (June 10th) should be made a legal holiday because this was the day when:
a. the slaves were freed in the United States
b. the slaves were freed in Texas
c. the slaves were freed in Jamaica
d. the slaves were freed in California
e. Martin Luther King was born
f. Booker T. Washington died

13. If a man is called a "blood," then he is a _____.
a. fighter *d.* hungry hemophile
b. Mexican-American *e.* red man or Indian
c. Negro

14. What are the Dixie Hummingbirds?
a. a part of the KKK
b. a swamp disease
c. a modern gospel group
d. a Mississippi Negro paramilitary strike force
e. deacons

15. The opposite of square is _____.
a. round *c.* down *e.* lame
b. up *d.* hip

Answers: **1.** *d* **2.** *c* **3.** *a* **4.** *c* **5.** *d* **6.** *c* **7.** *c* **8.** *c* **8.** *c* **9.** *c* **10.** *c* **11.** *c* **12.** *b* **13.** *c* **14.** *c* **15.** *d*

Applications: Intelligence in Perspective, continued

If you scored 14 on this exam, your IQ is approximately 100, indicating average intelligence. If you scored 11 or less, you are mentally retarded. With luck and the help of a special educational program, we may be able to teach you a few simple skills!

Race and IQ

Question: Isn't this test a little unfair?

No. it is *very* unfair. It was constructed by black sociologist Adrian Dove as "a half serious attempt to show that we're just not talking the same language." Dove tried to slant his test as much in favor of urban black culture as he believes the typical intelligence test is biased toward a white middle-class background. (Due to its age, the test is probably now also unfair for anyone under 30.)

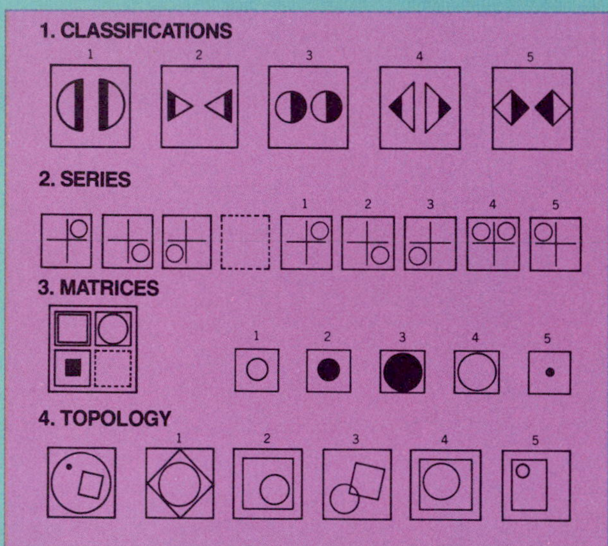

Fig. 16-8 *Sample items from a culture-fair test. 1. Which pattern is different from the remaining four? (Number 3.) 2. Which of the five figures on the right would properly continue the three on the left—that is, fill the blank? (Number 5.) 3. Which of the figures on the right should go in the square on the left to make it look right? (Number 2.) 4. At left the dot is outside the square and inside the circle. In which of the figures on the right could you put a dot outside the square and inside the circle? (Number 3.) (Courtesy of R. B. Cattell)*

Dove's test is a thought-provoking reply to the fact that black children in the United States score an average of about 15 points lower on standardized IQ tests than do white children. By reversing the bias, Dove has shown that intelligence tests are not equally valid for all groups. As Kagan (1973) has commented, "If the Wechsler and Binet scales were translated into Spanish, Swahili, and Chinese and given to every 10-year-old in Latin America, East Africa, or China, the majority would obtain IQ scores in the mentally retarded range."

Certainly we cannot believe that children of different cultures are all retarded. The fault must lie in the test. To avoid this problem, some psychologists have tried to develop **culture-fair tests** that do not disadvantage certain groups. (For a sample of culture-fair test items, see Fig. 16-8.)

Biased tests are not the only IQ issue blacks have confronted. Arthur Jensen, writing in the *Harvard Educational Review*, claimed in 1969 that the lower IQ scores of blacks can be primarily attributed to "genetic heritage."

Before we go any further, it is important to note that few psychologists support Jensen. Soon after Jensen made his claim, psychologists responded with a number of counterarguments.

First, it is no secret that as a group blacks in the United States are more likely than whites to live in environments that are physically, educationally, and intellectually impoverished. As one critic notes, test scores are meaningless if they result from unequal educational opportunity. Further, it is tragic if these scores are then used to deny further educational opportunities (Grover, 1983).

Second, the gap in IQ between blacks and whites is small enough to be closed by environment. Jensen's reply to this claim is that special educational programs such as Head Start have proved incapable of narrowing the IQ gap. But it is essentially ridiculous to expect that a brief summer program or a few hours a day are enough to counteract the differences in educational and environmental advantages of blacks and whites.

Third, Jensen ignores the point made by the Dove Test. The assumptions, biases, and content of stan-

Applications: Intelligence in Perspective, continued

dard IQ tests do not allow meaningful comparisons between ethnic, cultural, or racial groups (Garcia, 1977). As Leon Kamin (1981) says, "The important fact is that we cannot say which sex (or race) might be more intelligent, because we have no way of measuring 'intelligence.' We have only IQ tests." Kamin's point is that the makers of IQ tests designed test items that would give men and women equal IQ scores. They could just as easily put together an IQ test that would give blacks and whites in this country equal scores. Differences in IQ scores are not a fact of nature, but a decision by the test makers.

Perhaps the most devastating criticism of Jensen is that his logic is faulty. Consider this example: Corn comes in different varieties bred to grow to a certain height. If we plant tall and short varieties side by side in the same field, we will observe a genetically determined difference in their height at maturity. But what if we take corn (all the same variety) and plant half in a fertile field and half in poor soil? Again we observe a difference in maximum height, but this time it is clearly a mistake to assume the difference is genetically caused.

Only when black children are raised in exactly the same surroundings as white children can hereditary factors be clearly assessed. Along this line, one revealing study looked at black children adopted by white families. These children had IQ scores averaging 106, which is comparable to the national average for white children (Scarr-Salapatek & Weinberg, 1975). It is not clear if the black children were actually "brighter" as a result of being raised by white families or if they were just better prepared to take a "white" test. The fact remains, that when an equal opportunity for intellectual development can close the IQ gap, we must abandon narrow genetic views of IQ differences.

Questioning the Concept of IQ—Beyond the Numbers Game

Blacks are not the only segment of the population with reason to question the validity of intelligence testing and the role of heredity in determining intelligence. The clarifications won by blacks extend to others as well.

Consider the 9-year-old child facing this question on an intelligence test: "Which of the following does not belong with the others? Roller skates, airplane, train, bicycle." If the child fails to answer "airplane" does this reveal a lack of intelligence? It can be argued that an intelligent choice could be based on any of the following: Roller skates are not typically used for transportation; an airplane is the only nonland item; a train can't be steered; a bicycle is the only item with just two wheels (Sheils & Monroe, 1976). The parents of a child who misses this question may have reason to be angry since educational systems tend to classify children and then make the label stick.

Recent court decisions have led some states to outlaw use of intelligence tests in public schools. Criticism of intelligence testing has also come from the academic community. Harvard University psychologist David McClelland (1973) believes IQ is of little value in predicting real competence in dealing effectively with the world. McClelland concedes that IQ predicts school performance, but when he compared a group of straight-A college students with another group having poor grades, he found no differences in later career success.

Standardized Testing In addition to IQ tests, 400 to 500 million standardized multiple-choice tests are given in schools and workplaces around the nation each year. Many, like the Scholastic Aptitude Test, may determine whether a person is admitted to college. Other tests—for employment, licensing, and certification—directly affect the lives of thousands by qualifying or disqualifying them for jobs.

Widespread reliance on standardized intelligence tests and aptitude tests raises questions about the relative good and harm they do. On the positive side, tests can open opportunities as well as close them. A high test score may allow a disadvantaged youth to enter college, or it may identify a child who is bright but emotionally disturbed. Test scores may also be fairer and more objective than judgments made by admissions officers or employment interviewers. Also, tests *do* accurately predict academic performance. The fact that academic performance *does not*

Applications: Intelligence in Perspective, continued

predict later success may call for an overhaul of college course work, not an end to testing.

On the negative side, mass testing can occasionally exclude people of obvious ability. In one case a student who was seventh in his class at Columbia University, and a member of Phi Beta Kappa, was denied entrance to law school because he had low scores on the Law School Admissions Test (*U.S. News and World Report*, 1979). Other complaints relate to the frequent appearance of bad or ambiguous questions on standardized tests, overuse of class time to prepare students for the tests (instead of teaching general skills), and in the case of intelligence tests the charge that tests are often biased.

What should we make of the positive and negative aspects of standardized testing? Robert Glaser (1977) says we should remember that tests are "limited tools for limited purposes." Glaser also says that tests are now used primarily to *select people*. In schools they could instead be used to *adapt instruction* to the strengths, weaknesses, and needs of each student—thereby increasing the chances of success.

Conclusion

An application of the preceding discussion to your personal understanding of intelligence can be summarized in this way. Intelligence tests are a two-edged sword; we have learned much from their use, yet they have the potential to do great harm. In the final analysis, it is important to remember—as Howard Gardner has pointed out—that creativity, motivation, physical health, mechanical aptitude, artistic ability, and numerous other qualities not measured by intelligence tests contribute to achievement of life goals. Also remember that IQ is *not intelligence*. IQ is an *index* of intelligence—as defined by a particular test. Change the test and you change the score. An IQ is not some permanent number stamped on the forehead of a child that forever determines potential.

Let us end on an optimistic note. As discussed earlier in Box 16-2, some psychologists and educators are seeking ways to teach necessary intellectual skills to all children. In some cases their success has been striking. One experiment divided 40 children from extremely disadvantaged (slum) families into two groups. Children in the control group received no extra attention or training. Beginning shortly after birth, the experimental group was given a wide variety of stimulation to develop perceptual, motor, and language abilities. At age 2 the children were placed in small classes with other children and several teachers. Each child received lots of teacher attention and exposure to a broad range of topics and thinking exercises. When tested at age 5½, the control group had an average IQ of about 95; the average for the experimental group was 124 (reported by Whimbey, 1980). These results should be encouraging to everyone interested in the fulfillment of human potentials.

Learning Check

1. The WAIS–R, Stanford-Binet, and Dove Test are all culture-fair intelligence scales. T or F?
2. Jensen's claim that genetics accounts for racial differences in average IQ ignores environmental differences and the cultural bias inherent in standard IQ tests. T or F?
3. IQ scores predict school performance. T or F?
4. IQ is not intelligence; it is an index of intelligence. T or F?

Answers: **1.** F **2.** T **3.** T **4.** T

Chapter Summary

- *Intelligence* refers to one's general capacity to act purposefully, think rationally, and deal effectively with the environment. In practice, intelligence is *operationally defined* by the creation of intelligence tests.
- To be of any value, a psychological test must be *reliable* (give consistent results). A worthwhile test must also have *validity*, meaning that it measures what it claims to measure.
- The first practical intelligence test was assembled by Alfred Binet. A modern version of Binet's test is the *Stanford-Binet Intelligence Scale*. A second major intelligence test is the *Wechsler Adult Intelligence Scale–Revised* (WAIS–R). The WAIS–R measures both *verbal* and *performance* intelligence. Intelligence tests have also been produced for use with groups. *Group tests* include the *Army Alpha*, the *SAT*, the ACT, and the CQT.
- Intelligence is expressed in terms of an *intelligence quotient* (IQ). IQ is defined as *mental age* (MA) divided by *chronological age* (CA) and then multiplied by 100. An "average" IQ of 100 occurs when mental age equals chronological age. In practice, intelligence tests now report *deviation IQs*, rather than IQ scores calculated with mental age and chronological age.
- IQ scores become fairly stable at about age 6 and they become increasingly reliable thereafter. On the average, IQ scores continue to gradually increase until middle age. Later intellectual declines are slight for most people until their seventies.
- The distribution of IQ scores approximates a *normal curve*. There are no overall differences between males and females in tested intelligence, but intellectual strengths exist for each. IQ is strongly related to school grades and job status. The second association may be somewhat artificial.
- People with IQs in the *gifted* or "genius" range of above 140 tend to be superior in many respects. By criteria other than IQ, a large proportion of children might be considered as gifted in one way or another.
- The term *mentally retarded* is traditionally applied to those whose IQ falls below 70, or who lack various *adaptive behaviors*. Further classifications of retardation are: *mild* (52–67), *moderate* (36–51), *severe* (20–35), and *profound* (below 20). Chances for educational success are related to the degree of retardation.
- About 25 percent of the cases of mental retardation are *organic*, being caused by *birth injuries*, *fetal damage*, *metabolic disorders*, or *genetic abnormalities*. The remaining 75 percent are of undetermined cause. Many of these are thought to be the result of *familial retardation*, a generally low level of educational and intellectual stimulation in the home, coupled with poverty and poor nutrition.
- Five specific forms of organic retardation are: *phenylketonuria* (PKU), *microcephaly*, *hydrocephaly*, *cretinism*, and *Down Syndrome*.
- Studies of *eugenics* in animals and familial relationships in humans demonstrate that intelligence is partially determined by heredity. However, environment is also important, as revealed by changes in tested intelligence induced by stimulating environments. There is increasing evidence that some elements of intelligence can be taught. Intelligence therefore reflects the combined effects of heredity and environment in the development of intellectual abilities.

Chapter 17

Personality: Traits, Types, and Testing

Chapter Preview

The Hidden Essence

Rural Colorado. The car lurched over the last few yards of brain-jarring ruts. There before us stood an ancient farmhouse, a hulking monument to neglect.

Annette was out of the house—hooting and whooping—before we had stopped. If anyone was suited for a move to the "wilds" of Colorado, it was Annette, the "terror of Tenth Street." Still, it was hard to imagine a more radical change. After separating from her husband, she had traded housewifery in the city for survival in the hinterlands. Survival, by the way, is no exaggeration. Annette was working as a ranch hand and as a lumberjack (lumberjill?), trying to make it alone through some hard winters.

So radical were the changes in Annette's life, I must confess I expected just as radical a change in her. She was, on the contrary, more her "old self" than ever.

Perhaps you have had a similar experience. After several years of separation, it is always intriguing to see an old friend. Often you will be struck at first by ways in which the person has changed. Soon, however, you will probably be pleased to discover how superficial such changes really are. Under it all there is a core that ties the semistranger before you to the person you once knew. It is exactly this core of consistency that psychologists have in mind when they use the term personality.

The Extra Dimension *Despite our advanced technology, the human dimension still determines success or failure in many situations. Errors in human judgment contributed significantly to the* Challenger *spacecraft accident. Similarly, it is often said that the most dangerous part of an automobile is "the nut at the wheel." Without doubt, personality touches many aspects of our daily lives. Selecting a mate, choosing friends, getting along with co-workers, voting for a president, and numerous other activities raise questions about personality. But what is personality? How does it differ from temperament, character, or attitudes? How stable are personality characteristics? These and related questions are the concerns of this chapter.*

Survey Questions How do psychologists use the term *personality*? Are some personality traits more basic or important than others? Does heredity influence personality? What is psychological androgyny (and is it contagious)? How do psychologists measure personality? What causes shyness? What can be done about it?

Do You Have Personality?

"Jim's not handsome, but he has a great personality." "My father's business friends think he's a nice guy, but they should see him at home where his real personality comes out." "It's hard to believe they're sisters. They have such opposite personalities."

It's obvious from such statements that we all frequently use the term *personality*. But when questioned, many people seem hard-pressed to define personality. Most simply end up saying something about "charm," "charisma," or "style." If you have used *personality* in such ways, you have given it a different meaning than psychologists do. To a psychologist it makes little sense to ask, "Do I have personality?" or to proclaim, "She has lots of personality." In psychological terms, everyone has personality.

Question: Then how do psychologists use the term?

Since personality is a *hypothetical construct*,* psychologists give it different meanings. Most, however, regard **personality** as a person's *unique and enduring behavior patterns*. In other words, personality refers to the consistency in who you are, have been, and will become. It also refers to the special combination of talents, aptitudes, values, hopes, loves, hates, and habits that makes each of us a unique person.

Question: How is psychologists' use of the term different from the way most people use it?

Many people confuse personality with what is technically known as **character.** The term *character* implies that a person has been *judged* or *evaluated*, not just described. If, by saying someone has "personality," you mean the person is friendly, outgoing, and attractive, you are really referring to what is considered good character in our culture. But in some cultures it is deemed good for a person to be fierce, warlike, and cruel. So, while everyone in a particular culture has personality, not everyone has character—or at least not good character. (Do you know any good characters?)

Personality can also be distinguished from **temperament.** As mentioned in Chapter 14, temperament is the "raw material" from which personality is formed. Temperament refers to the hereditary aspects of one's emotional nature: sensitivity, strength and speed of response, prevailing mood, and fluctuations in mood (Allport, 1961). As you may recall, differences in temperament are apparent from birth onward.

*An explanatory concept that is not directly observable.

Resources

Personality An individual's unique and relatively unchanging traits, psychological characteristics, and behavior patterns.

Character A subjective evaluation of personality, particularly with regard to a person's desirable or undesirable attributes.

Temperament The physical foundation of personality, including prevailing mood, sensitivity, energy levels, and so forth.

Fig. 17-1 *Does this man have personality? Do you?*

Psychology Looks at Personality

The psychology of personality employs a large number of concepts. It might be wise, therefore, to start with a few key terms. These ideas should help you keep your bearings as you read this chapter and the next.

Traits We use the idea of traits every day in talking about the personalities of friends and acquaintances. For instance, my friend Dan is *sociable, orderly,* and *intelligent;* his sister Andrea is *shy, sensitive,* and *creative.* In general, psychologists think of **traits** as *lasting qualities* within a person that are inferred from behavior. If you observe Dan talking to strangers—first at a supermarket and later at a party—you might infer that he is "sociable." You might then predict from this trait that he will also be sociable at school or at work. As you can see, we often use traits to predict future behavior from previous behavior (Rowe, 1987). Traits also imply consistency in behavior. As an example, think about how little your friends' personality traits have changed in the last 5 years.

Types Have you ever asked the question, "What type of person is she (or he)?" before meeting someone new? An interest in personality *types* is quite natural. A **personality type** represents a category of individuals who have a number of traits or characteristics in common (Potkay & Allen, 1986). Informally, it is quite common to speak of personality types. Your own thinking might include the executive type, the athletic type, the motherly type, the Yuppie type, the strong silent type, and so forth.

Question: How valid is it to speak of personality "types"?

Over the years, psychologists have proposed various ways to categorize personalities. Consider the idea, first advanced by Swiss psychiatrist Carl Jung (yung), that a person is either an **introvert** (shy, self-centered person) or an **extrovert** (bold, outgoing person). These terms are so widely used that you may think of yourself and your friends as being one or the other. However, the wildest, wittiest, most party-loving "extrovert" you know is introverted at times, and extremely introverted persons are assertive and sociable in some situations. In short, two categories (or even several) are often insufficient to fully capture individual personalities.

Even though types tend to oversimplify personality, they do have value. Most often, types are used by psychologists as a shorthand way of labeling people who share similar personality traits. You might recall from Chapter 13, for instance, that classifying people as Type A or Type B personalities helps predict their chances of suffering a heart attack. Similarly, you will read in Chapter 19 about unhealthy personality types such as the paranoid personality, the dependent personality, and the antisocial personality.

Self-Concept Another way of understanding personality is to focus on a person's self-concept. The rough outlines of your own self-concept would be revealed by this request: "Please tell us about yourself." In other words, a **self-concept** represents a person's *perception* of his or her own personality traits. It consists of all your ideas and feelings about who you are (Potkay & Allen, 1986).

Many psychologists believe that one's self-concept has a major influence on behavior. We creatively build our self-concepts out of daily experience. Then we slowly revise them on the basis of new experience. Once a stable self-concept exists, it tends to shape further experience by determining what we pay attention to, what we remember, and how we interpret events (Markus & Nurius, 1986). In this way, an individual's self-concept can greatly affect personal adjustment—especially when the self-concept is *inaccurate* or *inadequate* (Potkay & Allen, 1986). As an example, imagine a student who thinks she is stupid, worthless, and a failure, despite having completed three years of college with good grades. With such a negative self-concept, the student will probably be depressed or anxious no matter how well she does. Problems of this type are explored further in the next chapter.

Personality Theories Personality is so complex that we might easily become lost without a guiding framework for understanding it. How do the observations we make about personality fit together? Can we explain and predict behavior from our knowledge of personality? How does personality develop? Why do people become emotionally unhealthy? How can they be helped? To answer such questions, psychologists have created a fascinating array of theories. A **personality theory** is a system of assumptions, ideas, and principles proposed to explain personality. In this chapter you will find two examples of trait theories of personality. The next chapter is devoted entirely to more elaborate personality theories proposed by thinkers such as Sigmund Freud, B. F. Skinner, and Carl Rogers.

Now that you are oriented, let's take a deeper look at personality.

Traits (personality) Relatively permanent and enduring qualities that a person displays in most situations.

Personality types System of personality description employing only a few categories, with each category representing a collection of related traits.

Introvert An individual whose attention is focused inward; thus, a person who prefers to be alone or withdraws from social contact.

Extrovert An individual whose energy and interests are directed outward; thus, a person who seeks social contact or is outgoing.

Self-concept Knowledge of one's own personality traits; a collection of beliefs, ideas, and feelings about one's own identity.

Personality theory An interrelated system of concepts and principles used to understand and explain personality.

Trait theorist A psychologist who is interested in classifying, analyzing, and interrelating traits, and in discovering their origins, to understand and explain personality.

The Trait Approach—Describe Yourself in 18,000 Words or Less

How many words can you think of to describe the personality of a close friend? You should have little trouble making a long list: Over 18,000 English words refer to personality traits (Allport & Odbert, 1936). As stated earlier, **traits** are *relatively permanent and enduring qualities* that a person shows in most situations. (See Box 17-1.) For example, if you are usually optimistic, reserved, or friendly, these qualities might be considered stable traits of your personality.

Question: What if I am sometimes pessimistic, uninhibited, or shy?

The first three qualities are still traits as long as they are most *typical* of your behavior. Let's say Ima Student approaches most situations with optimism, but has a habit of expecting the worst each time she takes a test. If her pessimism is limited to this situation or to a few others, it is still accurate and useful to describe her as an optimistic person.

In general, the trait approach attempts to identify traits that best describe a particular individual. Take a moment to check traits in Table 17-1 that you feel describe your personality. Are the traits you checked of equal importance? Are some stronger or more basic than others? Do any overlap? For example, if you checked "dominant," did you also check "confident" and "bold"? Answers to these questions would interest a **trait theorist.** To understand personality, trait theorists attempt to classify traits and to discover which are most basic.

Box 17-1

Extroverted Study Habits

Where do you prefer to study in the library? The answer may reveal a basic trait of your personality.

As we noted, splitting people into introverted and extroverted *types* is an oversimplification. On the other hand, many psychologists regard one's *degree* of introversion/extroversion as one of several important personality *traits*. Viewed in this way, a person's level of introversion/extroversion can have interesting links to behavior.

One study found that students scoring high in extroversion chose study locations that provided more chances for socializing and that had higher noise levels (Campbell & Hawley, 1982). In the campus library at Colgate University (where the study was done), you can find extroverted students in the second-floor lounge. Or, if you prefer, more introverted students can be found studying in the carrels on the first and third floors!

Question: Are there different kinds of traits?

Classifying Traits Psychologist Gordon Allport (1961), who was deeply interested in personality, identified several kinds of traits. **Common traits** are those shared by most members of a culture. Common traits show how people from a particular nation or culture are similar, or which traits the culture emphasizes. In American culture, for example, competitiveness is a fairly common trait. Among the Hopi of northern Arizona, it is a relatively rare trait. Of course, common traits tell us little about individuals. While many people are competitive

Table 17-1 Adjective Checklist

Check the traits you feel are characteristic of your personality. Are some more basic than others?

aggressive	organized	ambitious
confident	loyal	generous
warm	bold	cautious
sensitive	mature	talented
sociable	busy	funny
dominant	dull	accurate
humble	uninhibited	future-oriented
thoughtful	serious	helpful
orderly	anxious	conforming
liberal	curious	optimistic
meek	neighborly	passionate
kind	compulsive	honest
cheerful	emotional	good-natured
clever	calm	reliable
jealous	religious	nervous

in American culture, each person may rate high or low in this trait. Even if we study only highly competitive personalities, we know that no two are exactly alike. Allport therefore believed that we must also consider each person's unique qualities, or **individual traits.**

If the difference between common traits and individual traits is unclear, consider this analogy: If you were going to buy a pet dog, you would want to know the general characteristics of a particular breed (its common traits). In addition, you would want to know about the "personality" of a specific dog before selecting it (its individual traits).

Allport also made distinctions among **cardinal traits, central traits,** and **secondary traits.** A cardinal trait is so basic that all of a person's activities can be traced to existence of the trait. It is said, for instance, that an overriding factor in the life of Albert Schweitzer was "reverence for every living thing." Likewise, Abraham Lincoln's personality was dominated by the cardinal trait of honesty. According to Allport, few people have cardinal traits.

Question: How do central and secondary traits differ from cardinal traits?

Central traits are the basic building blocks of personality. Allport found that a surprisingly small number of central traits are enough to capture the essence of a person. College students asked to write a short description of someone they knew well mentioned an average of only 7.2 central traits (Allport, 1961).

In contrast, secondary traits are less consistent and less important aspects of a person. For this reason, any number of secondary traits could be listed in a personality description. Your own secondary traits include such things as food preferences, attitudes, political opinions, musical tastes, and so forth. In Allport's terms, a personality description might therefore include:

Name: Jane Doe
Age: 22
Cardinal traits: None
Central traits: Possessive, autonomous, artistic, dramatic, self-centered, trusting
Secondary traits: Prefers colorful clothes, likes to work alone, politically liberal, always late, and so forth

Source Traits A second major approach to the study of traits is illustrated by the work of Raymond B. Cattell (1965). Cattell was dissatisfied with merely classifying traits. Instead, he wanted to reach deeper into personality to learn how traits are organized and interlinked.

Cattell began by studying features that make up the visible portions of personality. He called these **surface traits.** Through use of questionnaires, direct observation, and life records, Cattell gathered data on the surface traits of a large number of people. He then noted that surface traits often appear in *clusters*, or groups. In fact, some traits appeared together so often they seemed to represent a single more basic trait. Cattell called such underlying personality characteristics **source traits.**

Question: How do source traits differ from Allport's central traits?

The main difference is that Allport classified traits subjectively, whereas Cattell used a statistical technique called **factor analysis** to reduce surface traits to source traits. Factor analysis uses correlations to identify traits that are interrelated. Using

Common traits Personality traits that are shared by most members of a particular culture.

Individual traits Personality traits that comprise a person's unique individual qualities.

Cardinal trait A personality trait so basic or powerful that all or most of a person's activities spring from existence of the trait.

Central traits The core traits that characterize an individual personality.

Secondary traits Personality traits of secondary importance; traits that are less consistent or relatively superficial.

Surface traits The visible or observable traits of one's personality.

Source traits Basic underlying traits of personality; each source trait is reflected in a larger number of surface traits.

Factor analysis A statistical technique whereby multiple measures are intercorrelated. Measures that form "clusters" of correlations are assumed to reflect some general underlying factor.

Trait profile A graphic representation of the ratings obtained by an individual (or sometimes a group) on each of several personality traits.

Trait-situation interaction Variations in behavior that occur when the expression of a trait is influenced by settings or circumstances.

Psychological androgyny The presence of both "masculine" and "feminine" personality traits (as masculinity and femininity are traditionally defined within one's culture).

this approach, Cattell developed a list of 16 underlying source traits. He considers this the basic number necessary to describe an individual personality.

Cattell's source traits are measured by a test called the *Sixteen Personality Factor Questionnaire* (often referred to as the 16 PF). Like many tests of its type, the 16 PF can be used to produce a **trait profile.** A trait profile presents a graph of a person's scores for each trait. Trait profiles can be very helpful for obtaining a "picture" of an individual personality or for making comparisons between two or more persons (see Fig. 17-2).

Question: Does heredity affect personality traits?

The clearest answer to this question comes from studying identical twins—especially those who were separated at birth.

Twins and Traits Over the past several years, psychologists at the University of Minnesota have been studying identical twins who grew up in separate homes. At the university, reunited twins take a wide range of medical and psychological tests (Fig. 17-3). The results of these tests, and earlier work by other psychologists, indicate that identical twins are much alike, even when they are reared apart (Bouchard et al., 1981). Like all identical twins, the reunited twins are astonishingly similar in appearance and voice quality. Observers are also struck by how often the twins display identical facial gestures, hand movements, and nervous tics, such as nail biting or finger tapping.

On many of the physical tests, results for reunited twins are so similar that they might have been produced by the same person on different days. Separated twins also tend to share similar talents. If one twin excels at art, music, dance, drama,

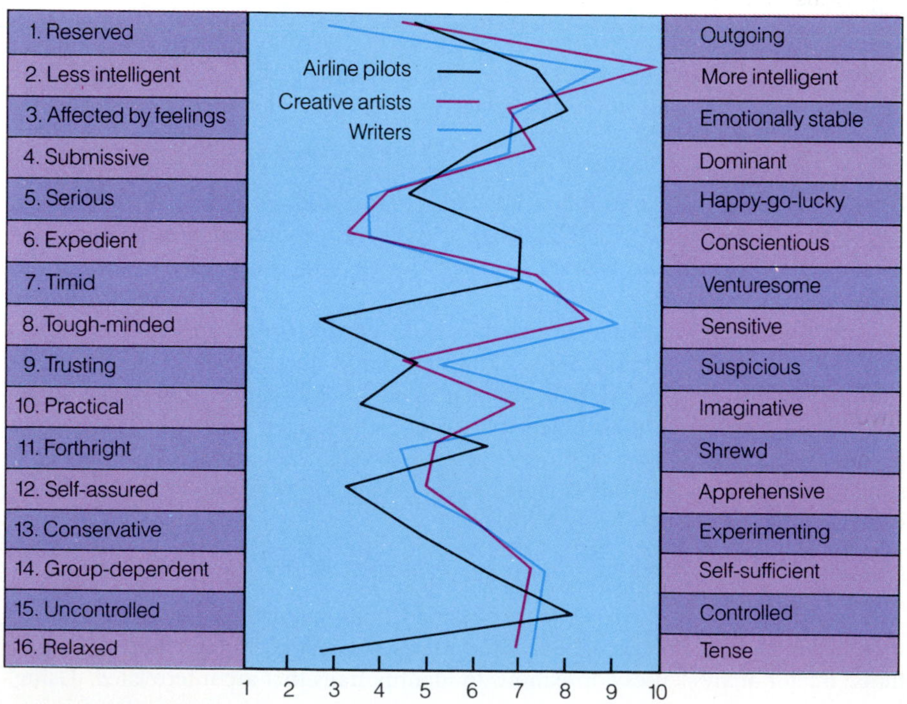

Fig. 17-2 *The 16 source traits measured by Cattell's 16 PF are listed on the left. Scores can be graphed as a profile for an individual or a group. Profiles shown are group averages for airline pilots, creative artists, and writers. Notice the similarity between artists and writers and the difference between these two and pilots. (After Cattell, 1973)*

or athletics, the other is likely to also—despite wide differences in childhood environment (Farber, 1981).

Such observations make it clear that heredity has a sizable effect on each of us. Where personality is concerned, similarities also exist, but they are not as strong. For instance, identical twins frequently differ in dominance and extroversion. That is, one twin is usually more extroverted or dominant than the other (Farber, 1981). Due to such differences, personality profiles for separated twins may have much in common, but they are usually far from identical.

All told, it seems reasonable to conclude that there is a genetic factor in personality (Farber, 1981). However, it is relatively small in comparison to the great physical similarity of identical twins (Scarr et al., 1981).

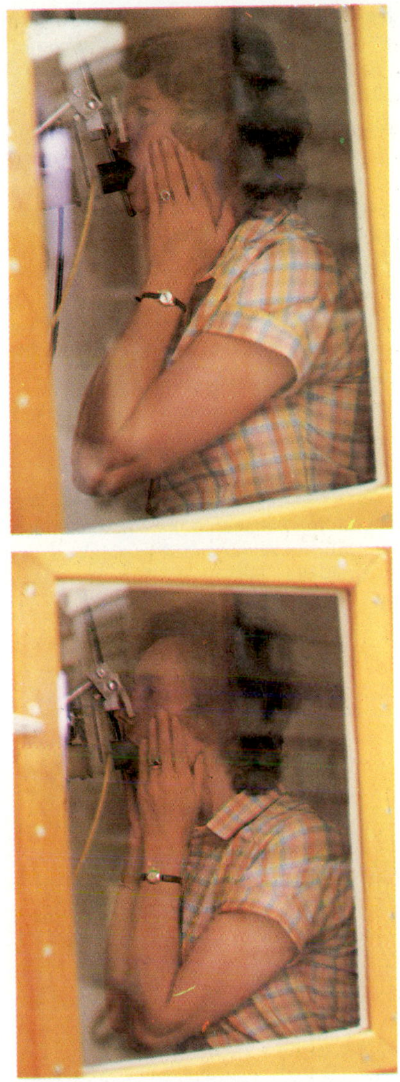

Fig. 17-3 *Reunited identical twins Terry and Margaret undergo lung function tests at the University of Minnesota. Researchers collected a wide range of medical and psychological data for each set of reunited twins.*

Traits, Consistency, and Situations

There is now little doubt that personality traits show a degree of consistency over long periods of time (Conley, 1984; Moss & Susman, 1980). And yet, *situations* also exert a powerful influence on our behavior. For instance, it would be unusual to find someone reading a book at a football game or dancing at a movie. Likewise, few people sleep in roller coasters or laugh at funerals. On the other hand, your personality traits may help predict whether you choose to read a book, go to a movie, or attend a football game in the first place.

In view of such observations, most psychologists now agree that traits *interact* with situations to determine behavior (Loevinger & Knoll, 1983). (This point is discussed further in Chapter 18.)

To illustrate what is meant by **trait-situation interactions,** imagine what would happen if you moved from a church to a classroom to a party to a football game. As the setting changed, your behavior would probably become more loud and boisterous. This change would demonstrate situational effects on behavior. Yet, at the same time, your personality traits would also be apparent: If you were quieter than average in class, you would probably be quieter than average in the other settings too (Rorer & Widiger, 1983).

The concept of traits allows us to address some interesting questions about personality. Let's take a moment to explore an intriguing example of trait research.

Psychological Androgyny—Are You Masculine, Feminine, or Androgynous?

Are you a leader, aggressive, ambitious, analytical, assertive, athletic, competitive, decisive, dominant, forceful, independent, individualistic, self-reliant, and willing to take risks? If so, you are quite "masculine." Are you affectionate, cheerful, childlike, compassionate, flatterable, gentle, gullible, a lover of children, loyal, sensitive, shy, soft-spoken, sympathetic, tender, understanding, warm, and yielding? If so, then you are quite "feminine."

Question: What if I have traits from both lists?

Then you may be **androgynous** (an-DROJ-ih-nus). The two lists just given are from the work of psychologist Sandra Bem. Using lists of various traits, Bem

Bem Sex Role Inventory (BSRI) A list of 60 personal traits including "masculine," "feminine," and "neutral" traits; used to rate one's degree of androgyny.

Interview (personality) A face-to-face meeting held for the purpose of gaining information about an individual's personal history, personality traits, current psychological state, and so forth.

Direct observation (personality) Any observation of a person's behavior in a natural or prearranged situation undertaken to form an impression of his or her personality.

Personality questionnaire A paper-and-pencil test consisting of questions designed to reveal various aspects of the respondent's personality.

Projective tests Psychological tests making use of ambiguous or unstructured stimuli. Subjects are presumed to project their own thoughts and impulses onto these stimuli.

constructed the **Bem Sex Role Inventory (BSRI),** a list of 20 "masculine" traits (self-reliant, assertive, and so forth), 20 "feminine" traits (affectionate, gentle), and 20 neutral traits (truthful, friendly). Next, Bem and her associates gave the BSRI to thousands of people, asking them to say whether each trait applied to them. Of those surveyed, 50 percent fell into traditional masculine or feminine categories; 15 percent scored higher on traits of the opposite gender; and 35 percent were androgynous, getting high scores on both the masculine and feminine items.

Question: You haven't said yet what it means to be androgynous. Is it having both male and female traits?

Psychological Androgyny The word **androgyny** (an-DROJ-ih-nee) literally means "man-woman." Androgyny sounds as if it might have something to do with androids, asexuality, or sex-change operations, but it actually refers to persons who have both masculine and feminine traits.

Bem's interest in androgyny stems from her belief that our complex society requires flexibility with respect to sex roles. She believes that it is right, and more than ever necessary, for men to be gentle, compassionate, sensitive, and yielding, and for women to be forceful, self-reliant, independent, and ambitious—*as the situation requires*. In short, Bem feels that more people should be androgynous (Fig. 17-4).

Fig. 17-4 *Androgynous individuals adapt easily to both traditional "masculine" and "feminine" situations.*

Adaptability In an interesting series of experiments, Bem and her associates sought to show that androgynous individuals are more adaptable, that they are less hindered by sex roles or images of what is appropriate "masculine" or "feminine" behavior. For example, in one experiment Bem gave people the choice of performing either a "masculine" activity (oil a hinge, nail boards together, and so forth) or a "feminine" activity (prepare a baby bottle, wind yarn into a ball, and so on). Masculine men and feminine women consistently chose sex-appropriate activities, even when the opposite choice paid more!

Bem's conclusion from a number of studies is that rigid sex roles can seriously restrict behavior, especially for men (Bem, 1974, 1975a, 1975b, 1981). She believes masculine males have great difficulty expressing warmth, playfulness, and concern—even when these are appropriate—because they view such actions as "feminine." Likewise, feminine women have trouble being independent and assertive, even when these qualities are called for.

In the years since Bem's first studies, androgyny has been variously supported, attacked, and debated. Now, as the dust begins to settle, the picture looks like this:

- Having "masculine" traits primarily means a person is independent and assertive. Scoring high in "masculinity," therefore, is related to high self-esteem and to success in many situations.
- Having "feminine" traits primarily means a person is nurturant and interpersonally oriented. People who score high in "femininity," therefore, tend to experience greater social closeness with others and more happiness in marriage.

In sum, there are advantages to possessing both "masculine" and "feminine" traits, whatever one's gender may be (Spence, 1984).

Many people, of course, remain comfortable with traditional views of masculinity and femininity. Nevertheless, personality researchers have done much to show that "masculine" traits and "feminine" traits can exist in the same person, and that androgyny can be a highly adaptive balance.

Learning Check

1. ____________________ refers to the hereditary aspects of a person's emotional nature.

2. The term ________ refers to the presence or absence of desirable personal qualities.
a. personality *b.* character *c.* source trait *d.* temperament

3. A system that classifies all people as either introverts or extroverts constitutes a ____________________ approach to personality.

4. An individual's perception of his or her own personality constitutes that person's ____________________.

5. According to Allport, few people have ____________________ traits.

6. Central traits are those shared by most members of a particular culture. T or F?

7. Cattell believes that clusters of ____________________ traits reveal the presence of underlying ____________________ traits.

8. Cattell's personality questionnaire provides ratings on 16 surface traits. T or F?

9. Research with identical twins has shown that heredity is the single most powerful influence on adult personality traits. T or F?

10. Trait-situation interactions suggest that expressing one's personality traits is influenced by settings and circumstances. T or F?

11. The Bem Sex Role Inventory is used to identify source traits in androgynous individuals. T or F?

Answers: **1.** Temperament **2.** *b* **3.** type **4.** self-concept **5.** cardinal **6.** F **7.** surface, source **8.** F **9.** F **10.** T **11.** F

Personality Assessment—Psychological Yardsticks

One of the greatest values of the trait approach is the refinement it has brought to personality measurement and testing. To study traits, psychologists have found it helpful to create ways of assessing personality. The results have been of tremendous value in research, industry, education, and clinical work.

Question: How is personality assessed?

Psychologists use **interviews, observation, questionnaires,** and **projective tests** to measure personality. Each method is a refinement of more informal ways of evaluating people.

At one time or another, you have probably "sized up" a potential date, friend, or employer by engaging in conversation (interview). Perhaps you have asked a friend, "When I am delayed, I get angry. Do you?" (questionnaire). Maybe you watch your professors when they are angry or embarrassed to learn what they are "really" like (observation). Or possibly you have noticed that when you say, "I think people feel . . .," you may be expressing your own feelings (projection).

Let's see how psychologists apply each approach to probe personality more formally.

The Interview

A very direct way to learn about a person's personality is to engage in conversation. An interview is described as **unstructured** if the conversation is informal and the interviewee determines what subjects are discussed. In a **structured** interview, information is obtained by asking a series of planned questions.

Question: How are interviews used?

Interviews are used to identify personality disturbances; to select persons for employment, college, or special programs; and for research on personality dynamics. Interviews also provide information for counseling or therapy. For instance, a counselor might ask a depressed person, "Have you ever contemplated suicide? What were the circumstances?" The counselor might then follow by asking, "How did you feel about it?" or, "How is what you are now feeling different from what you felt then?"

In addition to providing information, interviews make it possible to observe a person's tone of voice, hand gestures, posture, and facial expressions. Such "body language" cues are important because they may radically alter what is said, as when a person claims to be "completely calm" yet trembles uncontrollably.

Limitations Interviews give rapid insight into personality, but they are subject to certain limitations. For one thing, interviews can be swayed by preconceptions. A person identified as a "housewife," "college student," "high school athlete," "punk," or "ski bum" may be misjudged because of an interviewer's attitude toward a particular lifestyle. Second, an interviewer's own personality may cause an accentuation or distortion of the interviewee's traits.

A third problem is the **halo effect.** The halo effect is a tendency to generalize a favorable or unfavorable impression to unrelated details of personality (Fig. 17-5). A person who is likable or physically attractive may be rated more mature,

Fig. 17-5 *What is your impression of this person? Interviewers are often influenced by the halo effect (see text).*

intelligent, or adjusted than he or she actually is. The halo effect is something to keep in mind when you are interviewed for employment. First impressions do make a difference.

Even with their limitations, interviews are a respected method of personality assessment. In many cases, interviews are an essential step to additional personality testing and to counseling or therapy.

Unstructured interview An interview in which conversation is informal and topics are taken up freely as they arise.

Structured interview An interview that follows a prearranged plan, usually defined by asking a series of planned questions.

Halo effect The tendency to generalize a favorable or unfavorable first impression to unrelated details of personality.

Rating scale A list of various personality traits or aspects of behavior on which a person is rated, during or after observation of the person's behavior.

Direct Observation and Rating Scales

Are you fascinated by bus depots, airports, subway stations, or other public places? Many people relish a chance to observe the behavior of others. When used for assessment, direct observation is an extension of this natural interest in "people watching." For instance, a psychologist might arrange to observe a disturbed child playing with other children. Does the child remain withdrawn from others? Does she become hostile or aggressive without warning? By careful observation, the psychologist will form an impression of the child's personality and clarify the nature of her problems.

Question: Wouldn't observation be subject to the same problems of misperception as an interview?

Yes. Misperceiving can be a difficulty. Because of it, **rating scales** are sometimes used (see Table 17-2). Rating scales limit the chance that some traits will be

Table 17-2 Sample Rating Scale Items

How would you rate the subject's emotional self-control?				
In control at all times, shows no emotion	Remains calm and controlled in most situations	Expresses moderate emotion at times	Is easily aroused to emotional display	Has little control over emotions
Place a check at the point that describes the person's degree of introversion/extroversion.				
Very introverted, withdrawn	Moderately introverted, shy	Balanced mixture of introversion and extroversion	Moderately extroverted, outgoing	Very extroverted, friendly, active, and assertive
How would you rate the subject's potential for leadership?				
Very low	Below average	Average	Above average	Very high
How would you describe the subject's prevailing mood?				
Depressed, despondent	Sad, subdued	Neutral	Happy, relaxed	Euphoric

overlooked while others are exaggerated. Perhaps such scales should be standard procedures for choosing a roommate, spouse, or lover!

An alternative to rating scales is to do a **behavioral assessment.** In this case, observers record how often various *actions* occur, not what traits they think a person has. For example, psychologists working with hospitalized mental patients may find it helpful to record the frequency of patients' aggression, self-care, speech, and unusual behaviors (Alevizos & Callahan, 1977).

Situational Testing A specialized form of direct observation is called **situational testing.** Situational tests are based on the premise that the best way to learn how a person reacts is to simulate "real-life" situations. Situational tests expose a person to frustration, temptation, pressure, boredom, or other conditions capable of revealing personality characteristics.

Question: How are situational tests done?

An interesting example of situational testing is the "Shoot–Don't Shoot" training done by many police departments (Fig. 17-6). At times, police officers must make split-second decisions about using their guns. A mistake may be fatal. In the Shoot–Don't Shoot Test, actors play the part of armed juveniles or criminals. As various high-risk scenes are acted out live, or on videotape, officers must decide to shoot or hold fire: A newspaper reporter who took the test (and failed it) gives this account (Gersh, 1982):

> I judged wrong. I was killed by a man in a closet, a man with a hostage, a woman interrupted when kissing her lover, and a man I thought was cleaning a shotgun. . . . I shot a drunk who reached for a comb, and a teenager who pulled out a black water pistol. Looked real to me.

In addition to the training it provides, the Shoot–Don't Shoot Test uncovers police cadets who lack the good judgment needed to carry a gun on the street.

Fig. 17-6 *A police officer undergoes a Shoot–Don't Shoot Test. Variations on this situational test are used by a growing number of police departments. All officers must score a passing grade.*

Personality Questionnaires

Most **personality questionnaires** are paper-and-pencil tests requiring people to answer questions about themselves. As measures of personality, questionnaires are more **objective** than interviews or observation. Questions, administration, and scoring are all standardized so that scores are unaffected by the opinions or prejudices of the examiner.

Many personality tests have been created, including tests such as the *Guilford-Zimmerman Temperament Survey*, the *California Psychological Inventory*, the *Allport-Vernon Study of Values*, the *16 PF*, and many more. One of the best known and most widely used is the *Minnesota Multiphasic Personality Inventory (MMPI)*. The MMPI is composed of 550 items to which a subject must respond "true," "false," or "cannot say." Items include statements such as:

Everything tastes the same.
There is something wrong with my mind.
I enjoy animals.
Whenever possible I avoid being in a crowd.
I have never indulged in any unusual sex practices.
Someone has been trying to poison me.
I daydream often.*

Question: How can these items show anything about personality? For instance what if a person has a cold so that "everything tastes the same?"

The answer to a single item tells nothing about personality. A person who agrees that "everything tastes the same" might indeed have a cold. It is only through *patterns* of response that personality is revealed. Items on the MMPI were selected for their ability to correctly identify persons with particular psychological problems. If items are consistently answered in a particular way by depressed persons, it is assumed that others who answer the same way are also prone to depression.

The MMPI measures 10 major aspects of personality (listed in Table 17-3). After the MMPI is scored, results are charted as an **MMPI profile** (see Fig. 17-7). By comparing a person's profile with scores produced by normal adults, various disorders can be identified.

Question: How accurate is the MMPI?

For the MMPI or any other personality questionnaire to be accurate, people must be willing to tell the truth about themselves.

Because truthful answers are important, the MMPI has an additional "Lie Scale" to detect attempts of subjects to make themselves look better (or worse) than they really are. However, the Lie Scale alone is not enough to ensure accuracy. If MMPI scores were used as the only basis for classifying a person as overly anxious, severely depressed, or schizophrenic, a large number of people would be incorrectly labeled (Cronbach, 1970). Fortunately, such judgments usually take into account information from interviews or other sources.

Most psychologists are well aware of the limitations of psychological tests (see Box 17-2). If psychologists were the only persons giving these tests, there would

Behavioral assessment A technique in which the frequency of various behaviors is recorded to gain a picture of a person's behavior patterns.

Situational test A form of testing in which persons are placed in a situation that simulates real-life conditions of interest so that their reactions may be directly observed.

Personality questionnaire A paper-and-pencil test consisting of questions designed to reveal various aspects of the respondent's personality.

Objective test A test that gives the same score when different people correct it.

Minnesota Multiphasic Personality Inventory (MMPI) One of the best known and most widely used objective personality questionnaires.

MMPI profile A graphic representation of an individual's scores on each of the subscales of the MMPI.

*Reproduced by permission. Copyright 1943, renewed 1970 by the University of Minnesota. Published by The Psychological Corporation, New York, NY. All rights reserved.

Table 17-3 MMPI Subscales

1. Hypochondriasis. (HI-po-kon-DRY-uh-sis). Reflects exaggerated concern about one's physical health.

2. Depression. High scorers are marked by feelings of worthlessness, hopelessness, and pessimism.

3. Hysteria. Reflects somatic complaints related to psychological disturbances (psychosomatic problems).

4. Psychopathic deviancy. Shows a disregard for social and moral standards and emotional shallowness in relationships.

5. Masculinity/femininity. Indicates degree of traditional "masculine" aggressiveness or "feminine" sensitivity.

6. Paranoia. Indicates extreme suspiciousness and feelings of persecution.

7. Psychasthenia. (psych-as-THEE-nee-ah). Suggests presence of irrational fears (phobias) and compulsive (ritualistic) actions.

8. Schizophrenia. Reflects withdrawal, unusual and bizarre thinking or actions.

9. Hypomania. Suggests emotional excitability, manic moods or behavior, and excessive activity.

10. Social introversion. High score indicates a tendency to be socially withdrawn.

be few problems. However, many organizations, including businesses, routinely use personality tests; and errors or abuses sometimes occur. With this in mind, you should be aware that the United States Supreme Court handed down a decision in 1971 limiting the use of tests as conditions of employment or promotion. If you think a test was unfair, you may have a case.

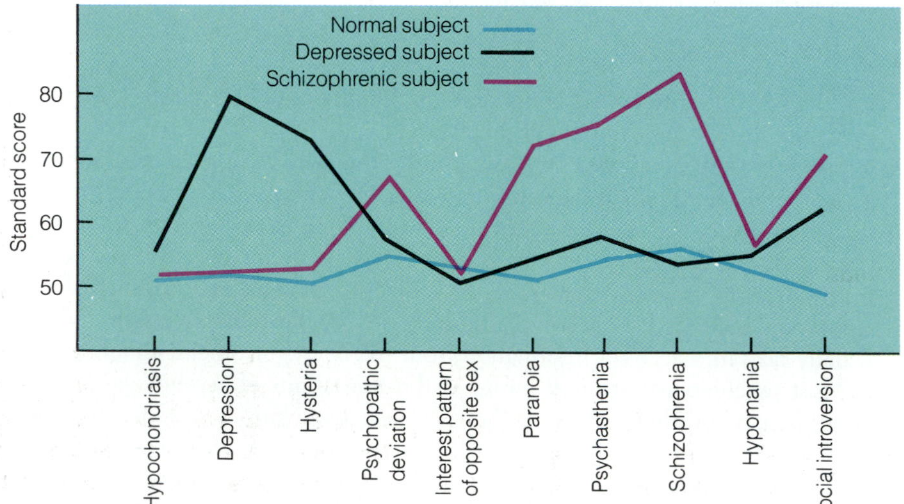

Fig. 17-7 *An MMPI profile showing hypothetical scores indicating normality, depression, and psychosis.*

Box 17-2

"Roasting" Personality Tests

Humorist Art Buchwald (1965) once lampooned personality questionnaires by writing his own test. Here is a sample of his items:

Answer, "Yes," "No," or "Don't bother me, I can't cope!"

I would enjoy the work of a chicken flicker.
My eyes are always cold.
Frantic screams make me nervous.
I believe I smell as good as most people.
Most of the time I go to sleep without saying good-bye.
I use shoe polish to excess.
The sight of blood no longer excites me.

Buchwald's questions may seem ridiculous, but they are not very different from the real thing. To avoid the problems of traditional tests, psychologist Frank McMahon (1964) once constructed an "above-board" test with clearly stated questions. For example, the true-false question: "Some people have it in for me" is followed by: "If True, I can't seem to get them off my mind." Although McMahon's test has not been widely used, his approach clearly takes much of the mystery out of personality testing.

Projective Tests of Personality—Inkblots and Hidden Plots

Projective tests take a very different approach to personality than the techniques already discussed. Interviews, observation, rating scales, and inventories typically identify overt, observable traits. By contrast, projective tests attempt to uncover deep-seated or *unconscious* wishes, thoughts, and needs.

Projective tests Psychological tests making use of ambiguous or unstructured stimuli. Subjects are presumed to project their own thoughts and impulses onto these stimuli.

Question: How is a test able to do that?

As a child you may have delighted in finding faces and objects in cloud formations. Or perhaps you have learned something about your friends' personalities from their reactions to movies or paintings. If so, you will have some insight into the rationale for projective tests. A **projective test** provides an *ambiguous stimulus* that a person must describe or make up a story about. Describing an unambiguous stimulus (a picture of an automobile, for example) tells little about your personality. But when you are faced with an unstructured stimulus or situation, you must organize and interpret what you see in terms of your own life experiences. Everyone sees something different in a projective stimulus, and what is perceived can reveal inner workings of the personality.

Since projective tests have no right or wrong answers, the ability of subjects to fake or "see through" the tests is greatly reduced. Moreover, projective tests can be an unusually rich source of information, since responses are not restricted to simple true-false or yes-no answers.

Question: Is the inkblot test a projective technique?

Rorschach Inkblot Test A projective test comprised of 10 standardized inkblots that are described by the person taking the test.

Thematic Apperception Test (TAT) A projective test consisting of 20 different scenes and life situations about which respondents make up stories.

The Rorschach Inkblot Test The inkblot test, or Rorschach (ROR-shock), is one of the oldest and most widely used projective tests. Developed by Swiss psychologist Hermann Rorschach in the 1920s, it consists of a set of 10 standardized inkblots. These vary in color, shading, form, and complexity.

Question: How does testing take place?

First, subjects are shown each blot and asked to describe what they see in it (Fig. 17-8). Later, the psychologist may return to a blot, asking a subject to identify specific sections, to elaborate on previous descriptions, or to suggest a completely new story. Obvious differences in content—such as "blood dripping from a dagger" versus "flowers blooming in a field"—are important for identifying conflicts and fantasies. But surprisingly, content is considered less important than what parts of the inkblot are used to form an image and how the image is organized. These factors allow a psychologist to view the ways in which a subject perceives the world and to detect disorders in personality function.

The Thematic Apperception Test Another popular projective test is the Thematic Apperception Test (TAT) developed by Harvard psychologist and personality theorist Henry Murray.

Question: How does the TAT differ from the Rorschach?

The TAT consists of 20 sketches depicting various scenes and life situations (see Fig. 17-9). The subject is shown each sketch and is asked to make up a story about the people in it. Later the subject is shown each sketch a second or perhaps third time. The subject is then asked to elaborate on previous stories or to construct new stories for each sketch.

Question: How is the TAT scored?

Scoring of the TAT is restricted to analyzing the content of the stories. In particular, the psychologist is concerned with what the basic issues are in each story: Interpretation focuses on how people in the stories feel, how they interact, what

Fig. 17-8 *Inkblots similar to those used on the Rorschach. What do you see?*

Fig. 17-9 *This is a picture like those used for the Thematic Apperception Test. If you wish to simulate the test, tell a story that explains what led up to the pictured situation, what is happening now, and how the action will end.*

events led to the incidents depicted in the sketch, and how the story will end. The psychologist might also count the number of times the central figure in each story is angry, overlooked, apathetic, jealous, or threatened. For example, here is a story written by a student to describe Fig. 17-9.

> The girl has been seeing this guy her mother doesn't like. The mother is telling her that she better not see him again. The mother says, "He's just like your father." The mother and father are divorced. The mother is smiling because she thinks she is right. But she doesn't really know what the girl wants. The girl is going to see the guy again, anyway.

Question: How accurate are projective tests?

Limitations of Projective Testing Although projective tests have been popular with clinical psychologists, their *validity* is considered lowest among tests of personality. (Recall that a test is valid when it measures what it claims to measure.) Because of the subjectivity involved in scoring, *objectivity* (consistency) of judgments among different users of the TAT and Rorschach is also low. Note that after the subject interprets an ambiguous stimulus, the scorer must interpret the subject's (sometimes) ambiguous responses. In a sense, the interpretation of a projective test may be a projective test for the scorer!

Test battery A group of tests and interviews given to the same individual.

Despite the drawbacks of projective tests, many psychologists attest to their value, especially as part of a **battery** of tests and interviews. It is said that in the hands of a skillful clinician, projective tests help detect major conflicts and define the goals of therapy. Moreover, since projective tests are unstructured, they may be more effective for getting clients to talk about anxiety-provoking topics than are the direct questions found in inventories and interviews.

Sudden Murderers—A Research Example

Personality studies provide us with clues to some of the most perplexing human events. Consider Fred Cowan, a model student in school and described by those who knew him as quiet, gentle, and a man who loved children. Despite his size (6 feet tall, 250 pounds), Fred was described by a co-worker as "someone you could easily push around."

Fred Cowan is representative of a puzzling phenomenon: the sudden murderer—a gentle, quiet, shy, good-natured person who explodes without warning into violence (Lee et al., 1977). Two weeks after being suspended from his job, Fred returned to work determined to get even with his supervisor. Unable to find the man, he killed four co-workers and a policeman before taking his own life.

Question: Isn't such behavior contrary to the idea of personality traits?

It might seem that sudden murderers are newsworthy simply because they seem such unlikely candidates for violence. On the contrary, research conducted by Melvin Lee, Philip Zimbardo, and Minerva Bertholf suggests that sudden murderers explode into violence *because* they are shy, restrained, and inexpressive, not in spite of it. These researchers studied prisoners at a California prison: 10 were inmates whose homicide was an unexpected first offense; 9 were criminals with a record of habitual violence prior to murder; and 16 were inmates convicted of nonviolent crimes.

Question: Did the inmates differ in personality makeup?

Lee and his associates administered a battery of tests to the inmates. Included were the MMPI, a test measuring shyness, an adjective checklist, and personal interviews. As expected, the sudden murderers were passive, shy, and overcontrolled (restrained) individuals. The habitually violent inmates were "masculine" (aggressive), undercontrolled (impulsive), and less likely to view themselves as shy than the average person (Lee et al., 1977).

Interviews and other observations have revealed that quiet, overcontrolled individuals are likely to be especially violent if they ever lose control. Their attacks are usually triggered by a minor irritation or frustration, but the attack reflects years of unexpressed anger and feelings of belittlement. When sudden murderers finally release the strict controls they have maintained on their behavior, a furious and frenzied attack ensues. Usually it is totally out of proportion to the offense against them, and often they have amnesia for some or all of their violent actions.

In comparison, the previously violent murderers showed very different reactions. Although they killed, their violence was moderate—usually only enough to do the necessary damage. Typically, they felt they had been cheated or betrayed and that they were doing what was necessary to remedy the situation or to maintain their manhood (Lee et al., 1977).

This brief example illustrates how some of the concepts and techniques discussed in this chapter can be applied to further our understanding. The Applications section that follows should add balance to your view of personality. Don't be shy: Read on!

Learning Check

1. Planned questions are used in a ____________________ interview.

2. The halo effect is the tendency of an interviewer to influence what is said by the interviewee. T or F?

3. Which of the following is considered the most objective measure of personality? (circle):

rating scales   personality questionnaires   projective tests   the TAT

4. Situational testing allows direct ____________________ of personality characteristics.

5. A psychotic person would probably score highest on which MMPI scale? (circle):

depression   hysteria   schizophrenia   hypomania

6. The use of ambiguous stimuli is most characteristic of (circle):

interviews   projective tests   personality inventories   direct observation

7. The content of one's responses to the MMPI is considered an indication of unconscious wishes, thoughts, and needs. T or F?

8. Doing a behavioral assessment requires direct observation of the person's actions. T or F?

9. A surprising finding is that sudden murderers are usually overcontrolled, very masculine, and more impulsive than average. T or F?

Answers: **1.** structured **2.** F **3.** personality questionnaires **4.** observation **5.** schizophrenia **6.** projective tests **7.** F **8.** T **9.** F

Applications

Shrinking Violets and Bashful Beaux—Understanding Shyness

Do you:

Find it hard to talk to strangers?
Lack confidence with people?
Find it difficult to make friends?
Feel awkward in social situations?
Feel nervous with people who are not close friends?

If so you may be one of the *40 percent* of American college students who consider themselves shy. If you are shy and wish you weren't, it may help to know that many others are shy too. However, three-fourths of those who are shy say they don't like it (Zimbardo et al., 1978).

Touch a snail and it retreats into its shell. Speak to a shy person, and he or she may shrink back as if threatened. As a personality trait, **shyness** refers to an avoidance of others, coupled with social inhibition (restraint and signs of strain when socializing) (Buss, 1980). Shy persons fail to make eye contact, retreat when spoken to, speak too quietly, pause too long in conversations, and display little interest or animation.

Question: What causes shyness?

Elements of Shyness To begin with, shy persons often lack **social skills.** Many simply have not learned how to meet others, how to start a conversation and keep it going, or how to end social encounters. A second factor in shyness is **social anxiety.** Most people are nervous in some social situations (such as meeting an attractive stranger). Such anxiety is typically a reaction to *evaluation fears* (fears of being embarrassed, ridiculed, rejected, or of seeming inadequate). Such fears occur for both the shy and the nonshy. However, social anxieties are more frequent or intense for shy persons. A third problem for shy persons is a **self-defeating bias** in their thinking. Specifically, shy persons almost always blame themselves when a social encounter doesn't go well (Girodo, 1978).

Immediate Causes of Shyness Have you ever had to deliver a speech to a group of strangers? If you have, you are probably aware that shyness is most often triggered by *novel* or *unfamiliar* social situations. A person who does fine with family or close friends may become shy and awkward when meeting a stranger. Shyness is also magnified by formality, meeting someone of higher status, being noticeably different from others, or being the focus of attention (as in giving a speech) (Buss, 1980; Pilkonis, 1977).

Question: Don't most people become cautious and inhibited in such circumstances?

Yes. That's why we need to see how the personalities of shy and nonshy persons differ.

Dynamics of the Shy Personality There is a tendency to think that shy persons are wrapped up in their own feelings and thoughts. In some cases this may be true. But surprisingly, researchers Jonathan Cheek and Arnold Buss (1979) found no connection between shyness and *private* self-consciousness (attention to inner feelings, thoughts, and fantasies). Instead, they discovered that shyness is linked to *public* self-consciousness.

Persons who rate high in **public self-consciousness** are intensely aware of themselves as social objects (Buss, 1980). They are concerned about what others think of them, and they feel others are evaluating them. They worry about saying the wrong thing or appearing foolish. With such concerns, many shy persons feel they are being rejected even when they are not. In public they may feel "naked" or as if others can "see through them." Such feelings trigger anxiety or outright fear during social encounters, leading to awkwardness and inhibition.

As mentioned, almost everyone feels anxious in at least some social situations. But there is a key difference in the way shy and nonshy persons *label* this anxiety. Shy persons tend to consider their social anxiety a *lasting personality trait*. Shyness, in other words, becomes part of their self-concept. In contrast, nonshy persons believe that *external situations* cause their occasional feelings of shyness. Particular

Applications: Shrinking Violets and Bashful Beaux, continued

people or situations may trigger anxiety or "stage fright" for the nonshy, but this group assumes that almost anyone would feel as they do under the same circumstances (Zimbardo et al., 1978).

Why should labeling make such a difference? The answer seems to lie in its effect on *self-esteem*. Nonshy persons tend to have higher self-esteem than shy persons. The greater confidence of the nonshy comes from an ability to benefit more from successful social encounters. Nonshy persons give themselves credit for successes, and they recognize that failures are often due to circumstances. Shy people, in contrast, blame themselves for social failures and never give themselves credit for successes. It's no wonder they often have lower self-esteem (Buss, 1980; Girodo, 1978).

Consequences of Shyness Even when it is mild, shyness can cause problems. Among the most common are:

1. Difficulties in making new friends or meeting people.
2. Feelings of isolation and loneliness.
3. Misperception by others: a shy person may strike others as vain, bored, unfriendly, or uninterested.
4. A general lack of self-projection and confidence in social settings.

Unless shyness is intense and quite painful, it is a mistake to think of it as a major problem. Yet, as the preceding list shows, shyness does have its costs. As one author notes, people who were once shy look back on the shyness of their youth "with about the same tenderness that they recall adolescent pimples."

Question: What can be done to reduce shyness?

Overcoming Shyness

Visitors to China frequently marvel at the almost total lack of shyness among the Chinese. In America many children seem to "outgrow" shyness as they gain social skills and wider social experience. Some adults overcome shyness with the aid of a "shyness clinic" or similar program. (Shyness clinics are sometimes offered on college campuses or by private psychologists.) Many previously shy people simply made an effort to learn new social skills and break out of old routines. Each of these observations suggests that shyness is to a large extent learned and open to change. If you are shy and would like to change, the information that follows may offer a starting point. Even if you are not shy, you may find some of the ideas useful.

Shy Beliefs While directing a shyness clinic, Michel Girodo (1978) observed that shyness is often maintained by a number of unrealistic or unproductive beliefs. Here's a sample:

1. *If you wait around long enough at a social gathering, something will happen.*
Comment: This is really a cover-up for fear of initiating conversation. For two people to meet, at least one has to make an effort—it might as well be you.
2. *Other people who are popular are just lucky when it comes to being invited to social events or asked out.*
Comment: Except for times when a person is formally introduced to new acquaintances, this is false. People who are more active socially typically make an effort to meet and spend time with others: They join clubs, invite others to do things, strike up conversations, and generally leave little to "luck."
3. *The odds of meeting someone interested in socializing are always the same, no matter where I am.*
Comment: This is another rationalization for inaction. It pays to seek out settings and events that have a higher probability of leading to social contact. Drama clubs, hiking clubs, sports teams, school events, and so forth often serve as a convenient way to bring together people interested in socializing.
4. *If someone doesn't seem to like you right away, they really don't like you and never will.*
Comment: This belief leads to much unnecessary withdrawal and isolation. Even when a person doesn't show immediate interest, it doesn't mean the person dislikes you. Liking takes time and opportunity to develop.

Unproductive beliefs like the preceding can be replaced with statements such as these:

Applications: Shrinking Violets and Bashful Beaux, continued

1. I've got to be active in social situations.
2. I can't wait until I'm completely relaxed or comfortable before taking a social risk.
3. I don't need to pretend to be someone I'm not; it just makes me more anxious.
4. I may think other people are harshly evaluating me, but actually I'm being too hard on myself.
5. I can set reasonable goals for expanding my social experience and skills.
6. Even people who are very socially skillful are never successful 100 percent of the time. I shouldn't get so upset when an encounter goes badly. (Adapted from Girodo, 1978)

Social Skills Learning to play a musical instrument, ski, or speak a foreign language takes practice. So does the learning of social skills. There is nothing "innate" about knowing how to meet people or enjoy a conversation. There are many ways in which social skills can be directly practiced. It can be helpful, for instance, to get a tape recorder and listen to several of your conversations. You may be surprised by the way you pause, interrupt, miss cues, or seem disinterested. Similarly, it can be useful to look at yourself in a mirror and exaggerate facial expressions of surprise, interest, dislike, pleasure, and so forth. By such methods most people can learn to put more animation and skill into their self-presentation.

One of the simplest ways to make better conversation is by learning to ask questions. A good series of questions shifts attention to the other person and shows you are interested in her or him. Nothing elaborate is needed. You can do fine with questions such as, "Where do you (work, study, live)?" "Do you like (dancing, travel, music)?" "How long have you (been at this school, worked here, lived here)?" The best questions are often *open-ended* (Girodo, 1978):

> "Do you get a chance to travel much?" (as opposed to: "Have you ever been to Florida?").
>
> "What's it like living on the west side?" (as opposed to: "Do you like living on the west side?").
>
> "What kinds of food do you like?" (as opposed to "Do you like Chinese cooking?").

It's easy to see why open-ended questions are helpful. Because a number of words are needed to answer them, it takes only a few questions to keep a conversation alive. Also, in replying to open-ended questions, people often give "free information" about themselves. This extra information can then be used to ask other questions or to lead into other topics of conversation.

This brief sampling of ideas is no substitute for actual practice. Overcoming shyness requires a real effort to learn new skills and test old beliefs and attitudes. It may even require the help of a counselor or therapist. At the very least, it requires a willingness to take social risks. Breaking down the barriers of shyness will always include some awkward or unsuccessful encounters. Nevertheless, the rewards are powerful: human companionship and personal freedom.

Learning Check

1. Surveys show that 14 percent of American college students consider themselves shy. T or F?
2. Social anxiety and evaluation fears are seen almost exclusively in shy individuals; the nonshy rarely have such experiences. T or F?
3. Unfamiliar people and situations most often trigger shyness. T or F?
4. Public self-consciousness plus a tendency to label oneself as shy are major characteristics of the shy personality. T or F?
5. Misperception by others is a common problem associated with shyness. T or F?
6. Changing personal beliefs and practicing social skills can be helpful in overcoming shyness. T or F?

Answers: **1.** F **2.** F **3.** T **4.** T **5.** T **6.** T

Chapter Summary

- *Personality* is made up of one's unique and enduring behavior patterns. *Character* is personality evaluated, or the possession of culturally desirable qualities. *Temperament* refers to the hereditary and physiological aspects of one's emotional nature.
- Personality *traits* are lasting personal qualities that are inferred from behavior. Traits imply a degree of personal consistency and help predict future behavior. Personality *types* group people into categories on the basis of shared traits or similar characteristics. Although type systems tend to oversimplify personality, they remain useful at times. Behavior is influenced by *self-concept*, which is one's perception of one's own personality traits. *Personality theories* combine interrelated assumptions, ideas, and principles to explain personality.
- *Trait theories* attempt to specify qualities of personality that are most lasting or characteristic of a person. Allport makes useful distinctions between *common traits* and *individual traits* and among *cardinal*, *central*, and *secondary traits*.
- A second trait approach, developed by Cattell, attributes visible or *surface traits* to the existence of underlying *source traits*. Cattell identified 16 source traits by use of a statistical method called *factor analysis*.
- Cattell's source traits are measured by the *Sixteen Personality Factor Questionnaire* (16 PF). Like other trait measures, the outcome of the 16 PF may be graphically displayed as a *trait profile*.
- Research with identical twins suggests that personality traits are influenced by heredity. However, heredity does not appear to be a dominant or overriding factor in personality differences.
- Traits appear to *interact* with *situations* to determine behavior. Neither factor alone fully explains our actions.
- Research done by Bem and others indicates that roughly one-third of all persons are *androgynous*. Psychological androgyny (possessing both masculine and feminine traits) appears related to greater adaptability or flexibility in behavior.
- Accurate *assessment* of personality is of great importance to psychologists. Techniques typically used to measure personality are: *interviews*, *observation*, *questionnaires*, and *projective tests*.
- *Structured* and *unstructured* interviews provide much information, but they are subject to interviewer bias and misperceptions. The *halo effect* (a tendency to generalize first impressions) may also lower the accuracy of an interview.
- *Direct observation*, sometimes involving *situational tests*, *behavioral assessment*, or use of *rating scales*, allows evaluation of a person's actual behavior.
- *Personality questionnaires*, such as the *Minnesota Multiphasic Personality Inventory (MMPI)*, are objective, but their accuracy and validity are open to question.
- *Projective tests* ask a subject to project thoughts or feelings to an ambiguous stimulus or unstructured situation. The *Rorschach*, or *inkblot test*, is a well-known projective technique. A second is the *Thematic Apperception Test (TAT)*. The validity and objectivity of projective tests are quite low. Nevertheless, projective techniques are considered useful by many clinicians, particularly as part of a *battery* of tests.
- *Shyness* is a combination of *social inhibition* and *social anxiety*. It is marked by heightened *public self-consciousness* and a tendency to regard one's shyness as a lasting *trait*. Shyness can be lessened by changing *self-defeating beliefs* and by improving *social skills*.

Chapter 18

Theories of Personality

Chapter Preview

Eels, Cocaine, Hypnosis, and Dreams

One of his earliest scientific discoveries was the location of the testes in an eel. Later he obtained some cocaine and began to study its value as a medicine. He was soon convinced it was a wonder drug. He proclaimed, "I took coca again and a small dose lifted me to heights in a wonderful fashion. I am just now busy collecting the literature for a song of praise to this magical substance" (Jones, 1953, p. 84). But his praise came to a rapid end when he prescribed cocaine to aid a friend addicted to morphine. Instead of improving, the friend became dependent on both drugs. His next interest was hypnosis, but he abandoned it when it did not meet his needs. At age 44, criticized by friends and virtually unknown in intellectual circles, he published his first book. It was a masterwork entitled The Interpretation of Dreams *(1900). Less than 1000 copies were sold.*

Question: Who are you talking about?

The hero of this little essay is no less than the best known of all personality theorists—Sigmund Freud. Volume after volume followed Freud's initial work until he had built a theory of personality that deeply influenced modern thought. Other theorists owe a debt to his pioneering efforts.

As there are dozens of personality theories, it is possible to introduce only a few of the most influential. For clarity, we will confine ourselves to three broad perspectives: (1) psychodynamic theories, *(2)* behavioristic theories, *and (3)* humanistic theories. *Psychodynamic theories focus on the inner workings of personality, especially internal conflicts and struggles. Behavioristic theories place greater importance on the external environment and on the effects of conditioning and learning. Humanists stress subjective experience and personal growth.*

Survey Questions How do psychodynamic theories explain personality? What do behaviorists emphasize in their approach to personality? How do humanistic theories differ from other perspectives? According to each of these major viewpoints, what childhood events shape adult personality? What can be done to promote self-actualization?

My life has been aimed at one goal only; to infer or to guess how the mental apparatus is constructed and what forces interplay and counteract in it.

Sigmund Freud

Psychoanalytic Theory— Id Came to Me in a Dream

Psychoanalytic theory, the best-known psychodynamic approach, grew out of the clinical study of disturbed individuals. Sigmund Freud, a Viennese physician, became interested in personality when he realized that many of his patients' problems seemed not to have physical causes. Starting about 1890 and continuing until he died in 1939, Freud evolved a theory of personality that is more complex than a short description can show. We will consider only its main features.

Question: How did Freud view personality?

The Structure of Personality

Freud conceived of personality as a dynamic system directed by three structures: the **id,** the **ego,** and the **superego.** Each is a complex system in its own right, and behavior in most situations involves the activity of all three.

The Id The id is made up of innate biological instincts and urges present at birth. It is self-serving, irrational, impulsive, and totally **unconscious.** The id operates on the **pleasure principle,** meaning that pleasure-seeking impulses of all kinds are freely expressed. If everyone's personality were solely under control of the id, the world would be chaotic beyond belief.

Freud thought of the id as a wellspring of energy for the entire **psyche** (sie-KEY), or personality. This energy, called **libido** (lih-BEED-oh), derives from the **life instincts** (called **Eros**). According to Freud, libido promotes survival, underlies sexual desires, and is expressed whenever we seek pleasure. Freud also described a **death instinct (Thanatos),** which he deemed responsible for aggressive and destructive urges (Fig. 18-1). Freud offered humanity's long history of wars and violence as evidence of such urges. Most id energies, then, are directed toward discharging tensions associated with sex and aggression.

The Ego The ego is sometimes described as the "executive," because it draws energy from the id. The id is like a blind king or queen whose power is awesome

Resources

Psychoanalytic theory Freudian theory of personality that emphasizes unconscious forces and internal conflicts in its explanations of behavior.

Id According to Freud, the most primitive part of personality, which remains unconscious, supplies energy to other parts of the psyche, and demands immediate gratification.

Unconscious Contents of the mind that are beyond awareness, especially impulses and desires not directly known to a person.

Pleasure principle Principle under which the id operates, consisting of a desire for immediate satisfaction of wishes, desires, or needs.

Psyche The mind, mental life, and personality as a whole.

Libido In Freudian theory, the force, primarily pleasure-oriented, that energizes the subparts of personality.

Eros Freud's name for the "life instincts" postulated by his theory.

Thanatos The death instinct postulated by Freud.

Ego The executive portion of personality in Freudian theory charged with directing rational, realistic behavior.

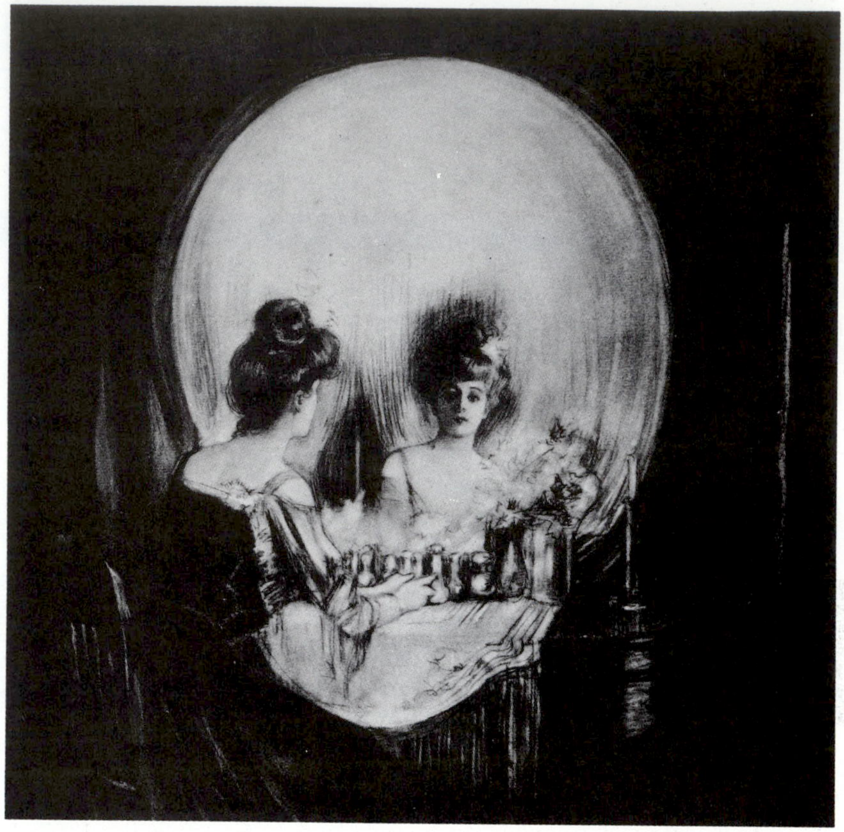

Fig. 18-1 *Freud considered personality an expression of two conflicting forces: life instincts and the death instinct. Both are symbolized in this drawing by Allan Gilbert. (If you don't immediately see the death symbolism, stand farther from the drawing.)*

but who must rely on others to carry out orders. The id can only produce mental images of things it desires. (This is called "primary process thinking.") The ego wins power to direct behavior by matching the desires of the id with external reality.

Question: Are there other differences between the ego and the id?

Yes. In contrast to the id, which operates on the pleasure principle, the ego is directed by the **reality principle.** That is, the ego delays action until it is appropriate. The reality principle results in "secondary process thinking," which basically is realistic problem solving. The ego is the system of thinking, planning, and deciding. It is in conscious control of the personality.

Question: What is the role of the superego?

The Superego The superego acts as a judge or censor for the thoughts and actions of the ego. One part of the superego, called the **conscience,** represents all actions for which a person has been punished. When standards of the conscience are not met, you are punished internally by *guilt* feelings. The **ego ideal** represents all behavior one's parents approved or rewarded. The ego ideal is a source of goals and aspirations. When its standards are met, *pride* is felt. By these processes the superego acts as an "internalized parent" to bring behavior under control. In Freudian terms, a person with a poorly developed superego will be a delinquent, a criminal, or an antisocial personality. In contrast, an overly strict or harsh superego will cause inhibition, rigidity, or intolerable guilt.

Reality principle The principle by which the ego functions, involving delaying action (or need satisfaction) until it is appropriate.

Superego In Freudian theory, an internalization of parental values and societal standards.

Conscience In Freudian theory, the part of the superego that causes guilt when its standards are not met.

Ego ideal In Freudian theory, the part of the superego representing ideal behavior; a source of pride when its standards are met.

Neurotic anxiety Apprehension felt when the ego must struggle to maintain control over id impulses.

Moral anxiety Apprehension felt when one's thoughts, impulses, or actions conflict with standards enforced by the superego.

Unconscious In Freudian theory, contents of the mind that are beyond awareness, especially impulses and desires not directly known to a person.

The Dynamics of Personality

Question: How do the id, ego, and superego interact?

It is important to recognize that Freud did not envision the id, ego, and superego as parts of the brain, or as "little people" running the human psyche. In reality they are distinct and conflicting psychological processes. Freud theorized a delicate balance of power among the three. For example, the demands of the id for immediate gratification often clash with the superego's moral restrictions. Perhaps the role of each division of the personality can be clarified by an example.

Freud in a Nutshell

Let's say you are sexually attracted to someone. The id clamors for immediate satisfaction of its sexual desires but is opposed by the superego (which finds the very thought of sexual behavior appalling). The id says, "Now, now, now!" The superego icily responds, "Never!" And what does the ego say? The ego says, "I have a plan!"

To be sure, the oversimplification is drastic, but it captures the core of Freudian personality dynamics. To reduce tension, the ego could initiate actions leading to friendship or romance. If the id is unusually powerful, the ego may direct an attempted seduction. If the superego is dominant, the ego may be forced to *displace* or *sublimate* sexual energies to other activities (sports, music, dancing, push-ups, cold showers). According to Freud, similar internal struggles and rechanneling of energies typify most personality functioning.

Question: Is the ego always caught in the middle?

Basically, yes, and the pressures on it can be quite strong. In addition to meeting the conflicting demands of the id and the superego, the overworked ego must deal with external reality. When the ego is threatened or overwhelmed, the person feels anxiety. Impulses from the id that threaten a loss of control cause **neurotic anxiety.** Threats of punishment from the superego cause **moral anxiety.** Each person develops habitual ways of reducing these anxieties, and many resort to use of *ego-defense mechanisms* to lessen internal conflicts (see Chapter 13).

Levels of Awareness A major principle of psychoanalytic theory, and other psychodynamic theories, is that behavior often expresses unconscious forces within the personality. The **unconscious** includes repressed memories and emotions as well as the instinctual drives of the id. Interestingly, modern scientists are beginning to identify brain areas that seem to have the kinds of unconscious effects Freud described. Especially important are areas linked with emotion and memory—such as the hippocampus in the limbic system (Reiser, 1985; Wilson, 1985).

Even though they are beyond awareness, unconscious thoughts, feelings, or impulses may slip into behavior in disguised or symbolized form. For example, if you meet someone you would like to know better, you may unconsciously leave a book or a jacket at his or her house to ensure another meeting.

Conscious Region of the mind that includes all mental contents (thoughts, images, feelings, memories, and so forth) a person is aware of at any given moment.

Preconscious A part of the mind that contains information not currently in consciousness, but that can be voluntarily brought to awareness.

Socialization The process of learning to live in a particular culture by adopting socially acceptable values and behavior.

Psychosexual stages In Freud's theory of personality development, the oral, anal, phallic, and genital stages, during which various personality traits are formed.

Erogenous zone Any body area that produces pleasurable sensations.

Fixation In Freudian theory, lasting conflicts developed during a particular psychosexual stage as a result of frustration or overindulgence.

Oral stage In Freud's theory, the period early in life when infants are preoccupied with the mouth as a source of pleasure and means of expression.

Oral-dependent personality According to Freud, a person who wants to passively receive attention, gifts, love, and so forth.

Oral-aggressive personality In Freudian terms, a person who uses the mouth to express hostility by shouting, cursing, biting, and so forth. Also, one who actively exploits others.

Anal stage In Freud's theory, the psychosexual stage corresponding roughly to the period of toilet training (age 1 to 3) and characterized by a preoccupation with the process of elimination.

Question: Earlier you said the id is completely unconscious. Are the actions of the ego and superego unconscious?

At times, yes, but they also operate on two other levels of awareness (Fig. 18-2). The **conscious** level includes everything we are aware of at a given moment: thoughts, perceptions, feelings, and memories. The **preconscious** contains material that can be readily brought to awareness. If you stop to think about a time when you have felt angry or rejected, you will be moving this memory from the preconscious to the conscious level of awareness.

Another illustration of the levels of awareness is found in the operation of the superego. At times we consciously attempt to live up to moral codes or standards; at other times we may feel guilty without knowing why. Psychoanalytic theory attributes the latter instances to unconscious workings of the superego. In Freudian psychology, events that are truly unconscious cannot be readily brought to awareness or directly known by the individual.

Personality Development

Every society must bring about the **socialization** of its children by teaching them language, customs, rules, roles, and morals. The job of preparing children to participate in society is typically placed in the hands of parents. This arrangement is convenient and fateful. While carrying out socialization, parents impart something of their own personality to children.

Question: How does this occur? What factors are most influential in the development of adult personality?

Each theory offers a different version of the important events in personality formation. Let's continue with a look at Freud's psychodynamic viewpoint.

A Freudian Fable? Freud theorized that the core of personality is formed before age 6 in a series of **psychosexual stages.** His account holds that childhood urges for erotic pleasure have lasting effects on development. Freud's emphasis on infantile sexuality is one of the most controversial aspects of his thinking. However, Freud used the term *sex* very broadly to mean any pleasurable activity.

Freud identified four psychosexual stages: the **oral, anal, phallic,** and **genital.** At each stage a different part of the body becomes an **erogenous zone** (an area

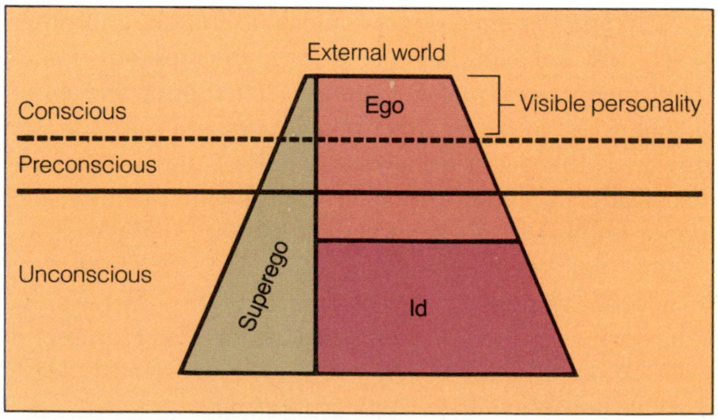

Fig. 18-2 *The approximate relationship among the id, ego, superego, and levels of awareness.*

capable of producing pleasure). Each then serves as the main source of pleasure, frustration, and self-expression. Freud believed that many adult personality traits can be traced to **fixations** in one or more of the stages.

Question: What is a fixation?

A fixation is an unresolved conflict or emotional hang-up caused by overindulgence or by frustration. A description of the psychosexual stages shows why Freud considered fixations important.

The Oral Stage During the first year of life, most of the infant's pleasure comes from stimulation of the mouth. If a child is overfed or frustrated, oral traits may be created. Adult expressions of oral needs include gum chewing, nail biting, smoking, kissing, overeating, and alcoholism (Fig. 18-3).

Question: What if there is an oral fixation?

Fixation early in the oral stage produces an **oral-dependent** personality. Oral-dependent persons are gullible (they swallow things easily!), passive, and need lots of attention (they want to be mothered). Frustrations later in the oral stage cause aggression, often in the form of biting. Fixation here causes **oral-aggressive** adults to be argumentative ("biting sarcasm" is their forte!), cynical, and exploitive of others.

The Anal Stage Between the ages of 1 and 3, the child's attention shifts to the process of elimination. When parents attempt toilet training, the child can gain approval or express rebellion or aggression by "holding on" or "letting go." Therefore, harsh or indulgent toilet training may lock such responses into personality. Freud described the **anal-retentive** (holding-on) personality as obstinate, stingy, orderly, and compulsively clean. The **anal-expulsive** (letting-go) personality is disorderly, destructive, cruel, and messy.

The Phallic Stage Adult traits of the **phallic personality** are: vanity, exhibitionism, sensitive pride, and narcissism (self-love). Freud theorized that such traits develop between the ages of 3 and 6. At this time, increased sexual interest causes the child to become physically attracted to the parent of the opposite sex. In males this attraction leads to an **Oedipus conflict.** The core of the conflict is that the boy feels rivalry with his father for the affection of the mother. Freud believed the male child feels threatened by the father (specifically, the boy fears castration). To lower his anxieties, the boy must **identify** with the father. Identification causes him to take on the father's values and to form a conscience.

Question: What about the female child?

The female counterpart to the Oedipus conflict is called the **Electra conflict.** In it the girl loves her father and competes with her mother. However, according to Freud, the girl's identification with the mother is more gradual and less effective in creating a conscience. Freud believed that females already feel castrated and so are less driven to identify with their mothers than boys are with their fathers. This particular aspect of Freudian thought has been thoroughly (and rightfully) denounced by modern feminists. It is probably best understood as a reflection of the male-dominated times in which Freud lived.

Anal-retentive personality Freud's term for a person who is obstinate, stingy, or compulsive, and who generally has difficulty "letting go."

Anal-expulsive personality In Freudian terms, a disorderly, destructive, cruel, or messy person.

Phallic stage In Freud's theory, the psychosexual stage (roughly age 3 to 6) when a person is preoccupied with the genitals as a source of pleasure.

Phallic personality According to Freud, a person who is vain, exhibitionistic, sensitive, and narcissistic.

Oedipus conflict Freudian concept referring to a boy's sexual attachment to his mother, and feelings of rivalry with his father.

Electra conflict Freudian concept referring to a girl's sexual attraction to her father and resultant feelings of rivalry with her mother.

Fig. 18-3 *Was Freud's ever-present cigar a sign of an oral fixation?*

Latency According to Freud, a period in childhood when psychosexual development is more or less interrupted.

Genital stage In Freud's theory, the culmination of personality development, marked, among other things, by the attainment of mature adult sexuality.

Behavioral personality theory Any model of personality that emphasizes observable behavior, stimuli and responses, and the impact of learning.

Learning theorist With regard to personality, a psychologist interested in the ways that learning principles shape and explain personality.

Latency According to Freud there is a period of **latency** from age 6 to puberty. Latency is not actually a stage. Rather, it is a time during which psychosexual development is interrupted. Freud's belief that psychosexual development is "on hold" at this time is difficult to accept. Nevertheless, Freud saw latency as a relatively quiet time compared with the stormy first 6 years of life.

The Genital Stage At puberty a resurgence of sexual energies activates all the unresolved conflicts of earlier years. This resurgence, according to Freud, is the reason why adolescence can be such a trying time, filled with emotion and turmoil. The genital stage begins at puberty and is marked, through adolescence, by a growing capacity for mature and responsible social-sexual relationships. The genital stage ends with heterosexual love and the attainment of full adult sexuality.

Critical Comments As bizarre as Freud's developmental theory might seem, it has been influential for several reasons. First, it pioneered the idea that the first years of life help shape adult personality. Second, it identified feeding, toilet training, and early sexual experiences as critical events in personality formation. Third, Freud was among the first to propose that development proceeds through a series of stages. (Erik Erikson's psycho*social* stages, described in Chapter 15, are a modern extension of Freudian thinking.)

Question: Is the Freudian view of development widely accepted?

Despite its contributions, Freud's theory remains controversial, and few psychologists embrace it without reservation. In some cases Freud was clearly wrong. His portrayal of the elementary school years (latency) as free from sexuality and unimportant for personality development defies belief. His idea that a stern or threatening father helps develop a strong conscience in males has also been challenged. Studies show that an affectionate and accepting father is more likely than a stern one to create a strong conscience in a son (Mussen et al., 1969; Sears et al., 1957). Freud also overemphasized sexuality in personality development; other motives and cognitive factors are of equal importance. Many more criticisms could be listed, but the fact remains that there is an element of truth to much of what Freud said.

Learning Check

1. List the three divisions of personality postulated by Freud: ______________________.

2. Which division is totally unconscious? ______________.

3. Which division is responsible for moral anxiety? ______________.

4. Freud proposed the existence of a death instinct known as Eros. T or F?

5. Freud's version of personality development is based on the concept of ______________ stages.

6. Arrange these stages in the proper order: phallic, anal, genital, oral. ______________________

7. Freud considered the anal-retentive personality obstinate and stingy. T or F?

Answers: **1.** id, ego, superego **2.** id **3.** superego **4.** F **5.** psychosexual **6.** oral, anal, phallic, genital **7.** T

Learning Theories of Personality—Habit I Seen You Somewhere Before?

Question: How do behaviorists approach personality?

According to some critics, as if people are robots like R2D2 of *Star Wars* fame. Actually, the behaviorist position is not nearly as mechanistic as some critics would have us believe, and its value is now well established. For one thing, the behaviorists have shown repeatedly that children can *learn* things like kindness or hostility, generosity or destructiveness (Bandura & Walters, 1963; Hoffman, 1975). But what does this have to do with personality? Everything, according to the behavioral viewpoint.

The behaviorist position is that personality is no more (or less) than a collection of learned behavior patterns. Personality, like other learned behavior, is acquired through classical and operant conditioning, observational learning, reinforcement, extinction, generalization, and discrimination (Fig. 18-4). When Mother says, "It's not nice to make mud pies with Mommy's blender. If we want to grow up to be a big girl, we won't do it again, will we?" she serves as a model and in other ways shapes her daughter's personality.

Strict learning theorists reject the idea that personality is made up of consistent traits. They would contend, for instance, that there is no such thing as a trait of "honesty" (Bandura, 1973; Mischel, 1968).

Question: Certainly some people are honest while others are not. How can honesty not be a trait?

A **learning theorist** would agree that some people are *more often* honest than others. But knowing this does not allow us to predict whether a person will be honest in a specific situation. It would not be unusual, for example, to find that a person honored for returning a lost wallet had cheated on a test. If you were to ask a learning theorist, "Are you an honest person?" the reply might be, "In what situation?"

Fig. 18-4 *Freud believed that aggressive urges are "instinctual." In contrast, behavioral theories assume that personal characteristics such as aggressiveness are learned. Is this boy's aggression the result of observational learning, harsh punishment, or prior reinforcement?*

Situational determinants Immediate conditions (for example, rewards and punishments) that determine what behavior is likely to occur in a given situation, regardless of the actor's personality traits.

Habit A deeply ingrained, learned pattern of behavior.

Drive Any stimulus (especially an internal stimulus such as hunger) strong enough to goad a person to action.

Cue External stimuli or signs that guide responses, especially those that signal the likely presence or absence of reinforcement.

Response Any behavior, either observable or internal.

Social learning theory An approach that combines behavioral principles with cognitive variables (perception, thinking, anticipation), plus the effects of social relationships and observational learning, to explain personality.

Psychological situation A situation as it is perceived and interpreted by an individual, not as it exists objectively.

Expectancy One's anticipation or expectation concerning the effect some response will have, especially regarding reinforcement.

Reinforcement value The subjective value a person attaches to a particular activity or reinforcer.

Self-reinforcement Praising oneself or allowing oneself a special treat or reward for having made a particular response (such as completing a school assignment).

Radical behaviorism An approach that avoids any reference to thoughts or other internal processes. Radical behaviorists are interested strictly in the functional relationships between stimuli and responses.

In drawing our attention to **situational determinants** of behavior, learning theorists have not entirely removed the "person" from personality. Walter Mischel (1973) acknowledges that some situations strongly determine behavior (for instance, an escaped lion walks into the supermarket; you accidentally sit on a lighted cigarette; you find your lover in bed with your best friend). Other situations are trivial and have little impact. Thus, external events *interact* with each person's unique learning history to produce behavior in any given situation. As discussed in Chapter 17, trait theorists also believe that situations affect behavior, but by interacting with traits. So, in essence, learning theorists favor substituting the concept of past learning for "traits" in order to explain behavior.

Question: How do learning theorists view the structure of personality?

Behavior = Personality The behavioral view of personality can be illustrated with a theory proposed by John Dollard and Neal Miller (1950). In their view, **habits** form the structure of personality. As for the dynamics of personality, Dollard and Miller believe habits are governed by four elements of learning: **drive, cue, response,** and **reward.** A drive is any stimulus strong enough to goad a person to action (hunger, pain, lust, frustration, fear, and so on). Cues are signals from the environment that guide responses so they are most likely to bring about reward or reinforcement.

Question: How does that relate to personality?

An example may clarify this viewpoint. Let's say a child is frustrated by an older brother who takes a toy from her. A number of responses are open to the child. She can throw a temper tantrum, hit her brother, tell Mother, and so forth. The response she chooses is guided by available cues and the previous effects of each response. If telling Mother has paid off in the past, and Mother is present, telling may be the immediate response. If a different set of cues exists (if Mother is absent or if the older brother looks particularly menacing), some other response may be selected. To an outside observer, the child's actions seem to reflect her personality. To the learning theorist, they are a direct reaction to the combined effects of drive, cue, response, and reward.

Question: Doesn't this analysis leave out a lot?

Yes. Learning theorists originally set out to provide a simple, clear model of personality. But in recent years they have had to face a fact they originally tended to overlook. The fact is: People think. The new breed of behavioral psychologists—who include perception, thinking, and other mental events in their views—are called **social learning theorists.** (The label *social* is used because they also stress social relationships and modeling.)

Social Learning Theory The "cognitive behaviorism" of social learning theory can be illustrated by three concepts proposed by Julian Rotter (1975). They are: the psychological situation, expectancy, and reinforcement value. Let's examine each.

Someone trips you. How do you respond? Your response probably depends on whether you think it was an accident or intentional. It is not enough to know the setting in which a person responds. We also need to know the person's **psycholog-**

ical situation—that is, how the person *interprets* or *defines* the situation. Here's another example. Let's say you do poorly on an exam. Do you consider this a challenge to work harder, an indication that it's time to drop the class, or an excuse to get drunk? Again, your interpretation is important.

An **expectancy** refers to your anticipation that a response will lead to reinforcement. To continue the example, if working harder has paid off in the past, it is a likely reaction to a low test score. But according to Rotter, behavior is not automatic. To predict your response, we would also have to know if you *expect* your efforts to pay off in the present situation. In fact, expected reinforcement may be more important than actual past reinforcement. And what about the *value* you attach to grades, school success, or personal ability? Rotter's third concept, **reinforcement value,** states that humans attach different values to various activities or rewards. This too must be taken into account to understand personality.

One additional idea deserves mention here. We all at times evaluate our actions and may reward ourselves with special privileges or treats when the evaluation is positive (Fig. 18-5). With this in mind, social learning theory adds the concept of **self-reinforcement** to the behavioristic view. Thus, habits of self-praise or self-reproach become important dimensions of personality. In fact, self-reinforcement might be considered the behaviorist's equivalent of the Freudian superego. (See Box 18-1.)

Radical Behaviorism As you have probably noted, social learning theory is only moderately behavioristic. The most extreme view of personality is held by radical behaviorist B. F. Skinner, who has said, "Intelligent people no longer believe that men are possessed by demons . . . but human behavior is still commonly attributed to indwelling agents" (Skinner, 1971). For Skinner, "personality" is a convenient fiction we invent to pretend we have explained behavior that

Fig. 18-5 *Through self-reinforcement we reward ourselves for personal achievements and other "good" behavior.*

Box 18-1

Self-Reinforcement

The following statements, adapted from a scale developed by Elaine Heiby (1983), will add to your understanding of self-reinforcement.

I often think positive thoughts about myself.
I frequently meet standards that I set for myself.
I try not to blame myself when things go wrong.
I usually don't get upset when I make mistakes because I learn from them.
I can get satisfaction out of what I do even if it's not perfect.
When I make mistakes, I take time to reassure myself.
I don't think talking about what you've done is too boastful.
Praising yourself is healthy and normal.
I don't think I have to be upset every time I make a mistake.
My feelings of self-confidence and self-esteem stay pretty steady.

People who agree with all or most of the preceding statements tend to have high rates of self-reinforcement. And, as the last item suggests, high rates of self-reinforcement are related to high self-esteem. The reverse is also true: Numerous studies have shown that mildly depressed college students tend to have low rates of self-reinforcement (Heiby, 1983).

It is not known if low self-reinforcement leads to depression, or if the reverse is true. But, in any case, learning to be more self-reinforcing appears to lessen depression (Fuchs & Rehm, 1977). From a behavioral viewpoint, there is value in learning to be "good to yourself."

is actually controlled by the environment. Skinner believes that everything a person does is ultimately based on past and present rewards and punishments. Perhaps Skinner's point of view has been shaped by his environment.

Question: How do learning theorists account for personality development?

Behavioristic View of Development

Many of the major points Freud made about development can be restated in terms of modern learning theory. Miller and Dollard (1950) agree with Freud that the first 6 years are crucial for personality development, but for different reasons. Rather than thinking in terms of psychosexual urges and fixations, they ask, "What makes early learning experiences so lasting in their effects?" Their answer is that childhood is a time of urgent and tearing drives, powerful rewards and punishments, and crushing frustration. Also important is **social reinforcement** based on the effects of attention and approval from others. These forces combine to shape the core of personality.

Critical Situations Miller and Dollard consider four developmental situations to be of critical importance. These are: (1) **feeding,** (2) **toilet** or **cleanliness training,** (3) **sex training,** and (4) learning to express **anger** or **aggression.**

Question: Why are these of special importance?

Feeding serves as an illustration. If children are fed when they cry, they are encouraged to actively manipulate the environment. The child allowed to cry without being fed learns to be passive. Thus, a basic active or passive orientation toward the world may be formed by early feeding experiences. Feeding can also affect later social relationships because the child learns to associate satisfaction and pleasure, or frustration and discomfort, with the presence of others.

Toilet and cleanliness training can be a particularly strong source of emotion for both parents and children. Parents are usually aghast the first time they find a child smearing feces about with gay abandon. Their reaction is often sharp punishment. For the child the result is frustration and confusion. Many attitudes toward cleanliness, conformity, and bodily functions are formed at such times. Studies also show that severe, punishing, or frustrating toilet training can have undesirable effects on personality development (Sears et al., 1957). Toilet and cleanliness training therefore require patience and a sense of humor.

Question: What about sex and anger?

When, where, and how a child learns to express anger and aggression are of obvious importance. So too is expression of sexual behavior. Both types of experiences can leave an imprint on personality. Specifically, permissiveness for sexual and aggressive behavior in childhood is linked to adult needs for power (McCelland & Pilon, 1983). This link probably occurs because permitting such behaviors allows children to get pleasure from asserting themselves.

Sex training also involves learning "male" and "female" behaviors—which creates an even broader basis for shaping personality.

Becoming Male or Female From birth onward children are identified as boys or girls and encouraged to learn sex-appropriate behavior. According to social learning theory, two processes that contribute greatly to personality development in general, and to sex training, are *identification* and *imitation*. **Identification** refers to the child's emotional attachment to admired adults, especially to those the child depends on for love and care. Identification typically encourages **imitation,** a desire to be like the valued or admired adult (Fig. 18-6). Many of a child's "male" or "female" traits come from conscious or unconscious attempts to pattern behavior after that of the same-sex parent with which the child identifies.

Question: When children are around parents of both sexes, why don't they imitate behavior typical of the opposite sex as well as the same sex?

You may recall from Chapter 8 that Albert Bandura and others have shown that learning takes place vicariously as well as directly (Bandura, 1965). This means we can learn without direct reward by observing and remembering the actions of others. But imitation of actions depends on their outcome. For example, boys and girls have equal opportunities to observe adults and other children acting aggressively. However, girls are less likely than boys to imitate aggressive behavior because they rarely see female aggression rewarded or approved. Thus, many arbitrary dimensions of "maleness" or "femaleness" are perpetuated at the same time sexual identity is established.

Social reinforcement Praise, attention, approval, and/or affection from others.

Critical situations Situations in development regarded by behaviorists as capable of leaving a lasting imprint on personality, including: feeding, toilet training, sex (or gender) training, and anger or aggression training.

Identification Incorporating the goals and values of another person into one's own behavior; feeling emotionally connected to a person and wanting to be like him or her.

Imitation An attempt to match one's own behavior to another person's behavior.

Fig. 18-6 *Adult personality is influenced by identification with parents.*

A study of preschool children by Lisa Serbin and Daniel O'Leary (1975) found that boys are three times more likely to get teacher attention for aggressive or disruptive behavior than girls are. Boys who hit other students or who broke things typically got a loud scolding that drew the attention of the whole class. When teachers responded to disruptive girls, they gave brief, soft rebukes that others couldn't hear. Since we know that attention of almost any kind reinforces children's behavior, it is clear that the boys were being encouraged to be active and aggressive. Serbin and O'Leary found that girls got the most attention when they were within arm's reach, literally or figuratively clinging to the teacher.

It's easy to see that the teachers were unwittingly encouraging the girls to be submissive, dependent, and passive. Similar differences in reinforcement probably explain why males are responsible for much more aggression in society than females are. Murder and assault rates, for example, are consistently higher for men (Deaux, 1985).

Learning Check

1. Learning theorists believe personality "traits" really are ____________________ acquired through prior learning. They also emphasize ____________________ determinants of behavior.

2. Dollard and Miller consider cues the basic structure of personality. T or F?

3. To explain behavior, social learning theorists include mental elements, such as ____________________ (the anticipation that a response will lead to reinforcement).

4. Self-reinforcement is to behavioristic theory as superego is to psychoanalytic theory. T or F?

5. The radical behaviorist view of personality is represented by:
a. Neal Miller *b.* John Dollard *c.* Julian Rotter *d.* B. F. Skinner

6. Which of the following is *not* a "critical situation" in the behaviorist theory of personality development? (circle)

feeding sex training language training anger training

7. Social learning theories of personality development emphasize identification and ____________________.

Answers: **1.** habits, situational **2.** F **3.** expectancies **4.** T **5.** *d* **6.** language training **7.** imitation

---

Humanistic Theory—A Peek at Peak Experiences

Humanism is a reaction to the pessimism of psychoanalytic theory and the mechanism of learning theory. At its core is an optimistic image of what it means to be human. Humanists reject the Freudian view of personality as a battleground for biological instincts and unconscious forces. Instead, they view **human nature** as inherently *good* and seek ways to allow our positive potentials to emerge. Humanists also oppose the mechanical, "thing-like" overtones of the behaviorist viewpoint. We are not, they say, merely a bundle of moldable responses; rather, we are creative beings capable of **free choice.** To a humanist the person you are today is largely the product of all of your previous choices. The humanistic viewpoint also places emphasis on immediate **subjective experience** rather than on prior learning. Humanists believe that, "There are as many 'real worlds' as there are people." To understand behavior we must learn how a person subjectively views the world, what is "real" for her or him.

Humanism An approach to psychology that focuses on human experience, problems, potentials, and ideals.

Human nature Those traits, qualities, potentials, behavior patterns most characteristic of the human species.

Free choice An expression of one's free will; the ability to make choices or decisions that are not controlled by heredity, prior conditioning, or other such determinants.

Subjective experience Reality as it is perceived and interpreted, not as it exists objectively; personal, private, nonobjective experience.

Self-actualization The full development of personal potential.

Question: Who are the major humanistic theorists?

There are many psychologists whose theories fall within the humanistic tradition. Of these, the best known are Carl Rogers (1902–1987) and Abraham Maslow (1908–1970). Since Maslow's idea of self-actualization was briefly introduced earlier in the text, let's begin with a more detailed look at this facet of his thinking.

Maslow and Self-Actualization

Psychologists have had a tendency to study human problems more than human strengths. A notable exception to this can be found in Abraham Maslow's studies of people living unusually effective lives. Maslow became interested in people who seemed to be using almost all of their talents and potentials. How were they different from the average person? To find an answer, Maslow began by studying the lives of great men and women: Albert Einstein, William James, Jane Adams, Eleanor Roosevelt, Abraham Lincoln, John Muir, Walt Whitman, and others. From there he moved on to direct studies of artists, writers, poets, and other creative individuals.

Along the way Maslow's thinking changed radically. At first he studied only people of obvious creativity or high achievement. Eventually, however, it be-

Box 18-2

Characteristics of Self-Actualizers

As he continued his studies, Maslow found that **self-actualizers** shared a great number of similarities. Whether famous or unknown, academically distinguished or uneducated, rich or poor, self-actualizers tended to fit this profile:

1. Efficient perceptions of reality. Subjects were able to judge situations correctly and honestly and were very sensitive to the fake and dishonest.

2. Comfortable acceptance of self, others, nature. Subjects were able to accept their own human nature with all its shortcomings. The shortcomings of others and the contradictions of the human condition were also accepted with humor and tolerance.

3. Spontaneity. Maslow's subjects extended their creativity into everyday activities. They tended to be unusually alive, engaged, and spontaneous.

4. Task-centering. Most subjects had a mission to fulfill in life or some task or problem outside of themselves to pursue. Humanitarians such as Albert Schweitzer or Mother Teresa represent this quality.

5. Autonomy. Subjects were free from dependence on external authority or other people. They tended to be resourceful and independent.

6. Continued freshness of appreciation. The self-actualizer seems to constantly renew appreciation of life's basic goods. A sunset or a flower will be experienced as intensely the one-thousandth time as it was the first. There is an "innocence of vision," like that of an artist or a child.

7. Fellowship with humanity. Maslow's subjects felt a deep identification with others and the human situation in general.

8. Profound interpersonal relationships. The interpersonal relationships of self-actualizers are marked by deep, loving bonds.

9. Unhostile sense of humor. This refers to the wonderful capacity to laugh at oneself. It also refers to the kind of humor a man like Abraham Lincoln had. Lincoln probably never made a joke that hurt anybody. His wry comments were a gentle prodding at human shortcomings.

10. Peak experiences. All of Maslow's subjects reported the frequent occurrence of "peak" experiences. These were marked by feelings of ecstasy, harmony, and deep meaning. Subjects reported feeling at one with the universe, stronger and calmer than ever before, filled with light, beautiful and good, and so forth. In short, self-actualizers feel safe and unanxious, accepted, loved, loving, and alive.

Self-actualizer One who is living creatively and making full use of his or her potentials.

Task-centering Focusing on the task at hand, rather than on one's own feelings or needs.

Autonomy Freedom from dependence on external authority or the opinions of others.

Peak experiences Temporary moments of self-actualization, marked by feelings of ecstasy, harmony, and deep meaning.

came clear that a housewife, carpenter, clerk, or student could live creatively and make full use of his or her potentials. Maslow referred to this tendency as **self-actualization** (Maslow, 1954). (See Box 18-2.)

Question: Maslow's list of self-actualizing people seems pretty subjective. Is it really a fair representation of self-actualization?

You have noticed that Maslow tried to investigate self-actualization empirically, but his choice of people for study was subjective. Undoubtedly there are many ways to reach full development of personal potential. Maslow's primary contribution was to draw attention to the *possibility* of continued personal growth. Maslow considered self-actualization an ongoing process, not a simple end point to be attained only once.

Carl Rogers' Self Theory

Like Freud, Carl Rogers based his theory on clinical experience. Unlike Freud, who portrayed the normal personality as "adjusted" to internal conflict, Rogers saw greater possibility for inner harmony. The **fully functioning person,** he said, is one who has achieved an openness to feelings and experiences and has learned to trust inner urges and intuitions (Rogers, 1961). Rogers believed this attitude is most likely to occur when a person receives ample amounts of love and acceptance from others.

Personality Structure and Dynamics Rogers' theory of personality centers on the concept of the **self,** a flexible and changing perception of personal identity that emerges from the **phenomenal field.**

Question: What is the "phenomenal field"?

The phenomenal field is the person's total *subjective* experience of reality. The self is made up of those experiences identified as "I" or "me" that are separated from "not me" experiences. As stated in the previous chapter, much human behavior can be understood as an attempt to maintain consistency between one's **self-image** and one's actions. For example, individuals who think of themselves as kind and considerate will act accordingly in most situations.

Question: Let's say I know a person who thinks she is kind and considerate, but she really isn't. How does this fit with Rogers' theory?

According to Rogers, experiences that match the self-image are **symbolized** (admitted to consciousness) and contribute to gradual changes in the self. Information or feelings inconsistent with the self-image are said to be **incongruent.** It is incongruent, for example, to think of yourself as a considerate person if others frequently mention your rudeness. It is also incongruent to pretend you are kind when you are feeling callous or to say you are not angry when you are seething inside.

Experiences seriously incongruent with the self-image can be threatening, and they are often distorted or denied conscious recognition. Blocking, denying, or distorting experiences prevents the self from changing and creates a gulf between the self-image and reality. As the self-image grows more unrealistic, the **incongruent person** becomes confused, vulnerable, dissatisfied, or seriously maladjusted (see Chapter 19).

When your self-image is consistent with what you really think, feel, do, and experience, you are best able to actualize your potentials. Rogers also considered it essential to have a degree of congruence between the self-image and the **ideal self.** The ideal self is similar to Freud's ego ideal. It is an image of the person you would most like to be. (For another perspective, see Box 18-3.)

Question: Is it really incongruent not to live up to one's ideal self?

Rogers was aware that we never fully attain our ideals, but the greater the gap between the way you see yourself and the way you would like to be, the greater the tension and anxiety experienced. The Rogerian view of personality can therefore be summarized as a process of maximizing potentials by accepting information about oneself as realistically and honestly as possible. In accord with Rogers' thinking, researchers have found that people with a close match between their

Fully functioning person Rogers' term for persons living in harmony with their deepest feelings, impulses, and intuitions.

Self A continuously evolving conception of one's personal identity.

Phenomenal field A person's total subjective experience of reality; his or her private psychological world.

Self-image Total subjective perception of oneself, including an image of one's body and impressions of one's personality, capabilities, and so on (another term for one's self-concept).

Symbolization In Rogers' theory, the process of admitting an experience to awareness.

Incongruence A mismatch or inconsistency. In Rogers' theory, experiences that are inconsistent with one's self-image are said to be incongruent.

Incongruent person A person who has a distorted or inaccurate self-image.

Ideal self An idealized image of oneself (the person one would like to be) that, optimally, closely matches one's overall self-image.

Fig. 18-7 *Humanists consider self-image a central determinant of behavior and personal adjustment.*

Box 18-3

Possible Selves

Your ideal self may be only one of many personal identities you have thought about. Psychologists Hazel Markus and Paula Nurius (1986) believe that each of us holds images of many **possible selves.** These selves include the person we would most like to become (the ideal self), as well as other selves we could become, or are afraid of becoming. In other words, possible selves translate our hopes, fears, fantasies, and goals into personal images of who we *could* be. Thus, a beginning law student might picture herself as a successful attorney; the husband in a troubled marriage might picture himself as a divorcé; a person on a diet might imagine both slim and grossly obese possible selves. Such self-images tend to direct future behavior. They also give meaning to current behavior and help us evaluate it. For example, the unhappy spouse might be moved by negative images of his "divorcé self" to try saving the marriage.

Even day-to-day decisions may be guided by possible selves. Purchasing new clothes, a car, cologne, membership in a health club, and the like may be influenced by images of a valued future self. Of course, identities are not all equally possible. As Markus and Nurius point out, almost everyone over age 30 has probably felt the anguish of realizing that some cherished possible selves will never be realized.

Possible self A collection of thoughts, beliefs, feelings, and images concerning a self one could become.

Conditions of worth Internalized standards of evaluation used to judge the worth of one's thoughts, actions, feelings, or experiences.

Positive self-regard Thinking of oneself as a good, lovable, worthwhile person.

Organismic valuing Placing value on an experience on the basis of how one responds to it as an entire organism; judgment made directly on the basis of one's perceptions and feelings.

Unconditional positive regard Unshakable love and approval given without qualification.

self-image and ideal self tend to be socially poised, confident, and resourceful. Those with a poor match tend to be anxious, insecure, and lacking in social skills (Gough, Fioravanti, & Lazzari, 1983).

A Humanistic View of Development

Why do mirrors, photographs, tape recorders, and the reactions of others hold such fascination and threat for most people? Carl Rogers would say it is because they provide information about one's self. The development of a self-image is highly dependent on information from the environment. It begins with a sorting of perceptions and feelings—my body, my toes, my nose, I want, I like, I am, and so on—and soon expands to include self-evaluation: I am a good person, I did something bad just now, and so forth.

Question: How does development of the self contribute to later personality functioning?

Rogers held that positive and negative evaluations by others cause a child to develop internal standards of evaluation called **conditions of worth.** In other words, we learn that some actions win our parents' love and approval whereas others are rejected.

Learning to evaluate some experiences or feelings as "good" and others as "bad" is directly related to a later capacity for self-esteem, positive self-evaluation, or

positive self-regard, to use Rogers' term. To think of yourself as a good, lovable, worthwhile person, your behavior and experiences must match your internal conditions of worth. The problem is that this can cause incongruence by leading to the denial of many legitimate feelings and experiences.

To put it simply, Rogers saw many adult adjustment problems as an attempt to live by the standards of others. He believed congruence and self-actualization are encouraged by substituting **organismic valuing** for conditions of worth. Organismic valuing is a direct, gut-level response to life experiences that avoids the filtering and distortion of incongruence. It is the ability to trust one's own feelings and perceptions—to become one's own "locus of evaluation." Organismic valuing is most likely to develop, Rogers felt, when children (or adults) receive "unconditional positive regard" from others. That is, when they are "prized" just for being themselves, without any conditions or strings attached.

Learning Check

1. Humanists view human nature as basically good and they emphasize the effects of subjective learning and unconscious choice. T or F?
2. Maslow used the term ______________________ to describe individuals who seem to be fully using their talents and potentials.
3. According to Rogers, a close match between the self-image and the ideal self creates a condition called incongruence. T or F?
4. Markus and Nurius describe alternative self-concepts that a person may have as "possible selves." T or F?
5. Rogers' theory regards conditions of ______________ as a troublesome aspect in development of the self.

Answers: **1.** F **2.** self-actualizers **3.** F **4.** T **5.** worth

---

Personality Theories—Overview and Comparison

Question: Which personality theory is right?

Each theory has made significant contributions to our understanding of personality by meaningfully organizing observations of human behavior. Nevertheless, none of the major theories can be fully proved or disproved. (If a theory could be proved true, it would no longer be a theory. It would be a law.) At the same time that theories are neither true nor false, their implications or predictions may be. The best way to judge a theory, then, is in terms of its *usefulness* for explaining behavior, for stimulating research, and for suggesting ways of treating psychological disorders. Each theory has fared differently in these areas.

In the final analysis, we need the concepts of all three perspectives (and those discussed in the previous chapter) to account adequately for the complexities of personality. There is an element of truth to each view, and a balanced picture emerges only when all are considered. Table 18-1 provides a final overview of the three principal theories we have discussed.

Table 18-1 Comparison of Three Views of Personality

	Psychoanalytic Theory	Behavioristic Theory	Humanistic Theory
View of human nature	negative	neutral	positive
Is behavior free or determined?	determined	determined	free choice
Principal motives	sex and aggression	drives of all kinds	self-actualization
Personality structure	id, ego, superego	habits	self
Role of unconscious	maximized	practically nonexistent	minimized
Conception of conscience	superego	self-reinforcement	ideal self, valuing process
Developmental emphasis	psychosexual stages	critical learning situations: identification and imitation	development of self-image
Barriers to personal growth	unconscious conflicts; fixations	maladaptive habits; pathological environment	conditions of worth; incongruence

Applications

The Search for Self-Actualization

> Some people fear finding themselves alone—and so they don't find themselves at all.
>
> André Gide

> What a man can be, he must be. This need we may call self-actualization.
>
> Abraham Maslow

Self-actualization is a concept that has appeared several times in this book. Perhaps you have been attracted to the promise it holds for personal growth. Self-actualizers lead rich, creative, and fulfilling lives.

Question: What steps can be taken to promote self-actualization?

Promoting self-actualization is more difficult than might be imagined. Many people are caught in a struggle for survival or security and never get a chance to develop their potentials fully. Others show little interest in personal growth or in the qualities Maslow described. Moreover, Maslow made few specific recommendations about how to proceed. Nevertheless, a number of helpful suggestions can be gleaned from his writings (Maslow, 1954, 1967, 1971).

Steps toward Self-Actualization

There is no magic formula for leading a more creative life. Knowing or even imitating the traits of unusually effective people cannot be counted on to promote self-actualization. Self-actualization is primarily a *process*, not a goal or an end point. As such, it requires hard work, patience, and commitment. Here are some ways to begin.

Be Willing to Change Begin by asking yourself, "Am I living in a way that is deeply satisfying to me and that truly expresses me?" If not, be prepared to make changes in your life. Indeed, ask yourself this question often and accept the need for continual change.

Take Responsibility You can become an architect of self by acting as if you are *personally* responsible for every aspect of your life. Shouldering respon-

Applications: The Search for Self-Actualization, continued

sibility in this way is not totally realistic, but it helps end the habit of blaming others for your own shortcomings. This attitude is illustrated by a young woman who realized in a counseling session, "I can't depend on someone else to give me an education. I'll have to get it myself" (Rogers, 1962).

Examine Your Motives Self-discovery involves an element of risk. To learn your strengths, limitations, and true feelings, you must be willing to go out on a limb, speak your mind, and take some chances. Fears of failure, rejection, loneliness, or disagreement with others are a tremendous barrier to personal change. If most of your behavior seems to be directed by a desire for "safety" or "security," it may be time to test the limits of those needs. Try to make each life decision a choice for growth, not a response to fear or anxiety.

Experience Honestly and Directly Wishful thinking is another barrier to personal growth. Self-actualizers trust themselves enough to accept all kinds of information without distorting it to fit their fears and desires. Try to see yourself as others do. Be willing to admit, "I was wrong" or, "I failed because I was irresponsible." This basic honesty can be extended to perception in general. Try to experience the world as you did when you were a child: fully, vividly, and directly. Try to see things as they are, not as you would like them to be.

Make Use of Positive Experiences As a rule of thumb, growth-promoting activities usually feel good. Perhaps you have felt unusually alert and alive when expressing yourself through art, music, dance, writing, or athletics. Or perhaps life seems especially rich when you are alone in nature, surrounded by friends, or when you are helping others. Whatever their source, Maslow considered peak experiences temporary moments of self-actualization. Therefore, you might actively repeat activities that have caused feelings of awe, amazement, exaltation, renewal, reverence, humility, fulfillment, or joy.

Be Prepared to Be Different Maslow believed that everyone has a potential for "greatness," but most fear becoming what they might. Much of this fear is related to the fact that actualizing potentials may place you at odds with cultural expectations or with others who are important in your life. As part of personal growth, be prepared to be unpopular when your views don't agree with others. Trust your own impulses and feelings; don't automatically judge yourself by the standards of others. Accept your uniqueness: As one young woman put it, "I've always tried to be what others thought I should be, but now I'm wondering whether I shouldn't just see that I am what I am" (Rogers, 1962).

Get Involved Maslow found with few exceptions that self-actualizers tend to have a mission or "calling" in life. For these people "work" is not done just to fill deficiency needs, but to satisfy higher yearnings for truth, beauty, brotherhood, and meaning. Many of the things you do may be motivated by more commonplace needs, but you can add meaning to these activities by endeavoring to work hard at whatever you do. Get personally involved and committed. Turn your attention to problems outside yourself.

Slow Down Try to avoid hurrying or overscheduling your time. Self-awareness takes time to develop, and a certain amount of leisure is essential for contemplation and self-exploration. Time pressures tend to force a person to rely compulsively on old habits.

Start a Journal Although this suggestion does not come from Maslow's writings, it is a valuable way of promoting self-awareness. Many people find a journal provides the kind of information necessary to make growth-oriented life changes. A journal should include a description of significant events in your daily life. In addition thoughts, feelings, fears, wishes, frustrations, and dreams should be recorded. Some find it useful to write dialogues in their journal in which they speak to parents, teachers, lovers, ob-

Applications: The Search for Self-Actualization, continued

jects, and so forth. Review and reread your journal periodically. You will find it is easier to learn from an event after it has "cooled off" and you can view it objectively.

Assess Your Progress Since there is no final point at which one becomes self-actualized, it is important frequently to gauge your progress and to renew your efforts. Boredom is a good sign you are in need of change. If you feel bored at school, at a job, or in a relationship, consider it a challenge or an indication that you have not taken responsibility for personal growth. A situation is only as "boring" as you allow it to be. Almost any activity can be used as a chance for self-exploration if it is approached creatively.

What to Expect As we have already noted, growth-promoting activities are usually personally satisfying.

Question: Are there other signs that one is moving in the right direction?

Yes. There should be a noticeable improvement in the quality of your daily life and a greater acceptance of yourself and of others. You should feel more confident and should carry out daily routines with less strain or conflict. These changes do not happen overnight, and your first steps toward self-actualization may be threatening at the same time they are exhilarating. Positive changes can be quite subtle. An idea of what to expect is provided by the words of Henry David Thoreau. After he had spent 2 years in the wilderness at Walden Pond, Thoreau had this to say about his experience:

> I learned this, at least, by my experiment: that as one advances confidently in the direction of his dreams, and endeavors to live the life which he has imagined, he will meet with a success unexpected in common hours. He will put some things behind, will pass an invisible boundary; new universal and more liberal laws will begin to establish themselves around and within him. . . . The laws of the universe will appear less complex, and solitude will not be solitude, nor poverty, poverty, nor weakness, weakness.

Learning Check

1. In his writings, Maslow emphasized that self-actualization is a process, not a goal or end point. T or F?
2. Making fuller use of personal potentials requires learning to live up to the expectations of others. T or F?
3. Maslow described peak experiences as temporary moments of self-actualization. T or F?
4. A major characteristic of self-actualizers is their interest in status and personal recognition. T or F?
5. According to Maslow, wishful thinking and distorted self-perceptions are barriers to self-actualization. T or F?

Answers: 1. T 2. F 3. T 4. F 5. T

Chapter Summary

- Like other *psychodynamic* approaches, Freud's psychoanalytic theory emphasizes unconscious forces and conflicts within the personality. In his theory, personality is made up of the *id*, *ego*, and *superego*. *Libido*, derived from the life instincts, is the primary energy running the personality. Conflicts within the personality may cause *neurotic anxiety* or *moral anxiety* and motivate use of *ego-defense mechanisms*. The personality operates on three levels: the *conscious*, *preconscious*, and *unconscious*.
- The Freudian view of personality development is based on a series of *psychosexual stages*: the *oral*, *anal*, *phallic*, and *genital* stages. *Fixation* at any stage can leave a lasting imprint on personality.
- Behavioral theories of personality emphasize learning, conditioning, and immediate effects of the environment. Learning theorists generally reject the idea of stable personality "traits," preferring instead to stress the effects of *prior learning* and *situational determinants* of behavior.
- Learning theorists John Dollard and Neal Miller consider *habits* the basic core of personality. Habits express the combined effects of *drive*, *cue*, *response*, and *reward*.
- *Social learning theory* adds cognitive elements, such as perception, thinking, and understanding to the behavioral view of personality. Such elements are exemplified by Julian Rotter's concepts of the *psychological situation*, *expectancies*, and *reinforcement value*. Some social learning theorists treat "conscience" as a case of *self-reinforcement*.
- The behavioristic view of personality development holds that social *reinforcement* in four situations is critical. The situations are: *feeding*; *toilet* or *cleanliness training*; *sex training*; and *anger* or *aggression training*. *Identification* and *imitation* are of particular importance in gender training.
- Humanistic theory emphasizes *freedom of choice*, *subjective experience*, a *positive* view of human nature, and needs for *self-actualization*. Abraham Maslow's study of *self-actualizers* showed that they have a variety of characteristics in common, ranging from efficient perceptions of reality to frequent peak experiences.
- Carl Rogers' theory views the *self* as an entity that emerges from the *phenomenal field*. Experiences that match the *self-image* are *symbolized* (admitted to consciousness), whereas those that are *incongruent* are excluded. The *incongruent person* has a highly unrealistic self-image. *Congruent* or *fully functioning persons* are flexible and open to experiences and feelings. They also have a self-image that corresponds closely to their *ideal selves*. According to recent thought, a person's ideal self is only one of many alternate self-concepts or *possible selves* that can influence behavior.
- In the development of personality, humanists are primarily interested in the emergence of a *self-image* and *self-evaluations*. As parents apply *conditions of worth* to children's behavior, thoughts, and feelings, children begin to do the same. Internalized conditions of worth then contribute to incongruence and interrupt the *organismic valuing process*.
- Self-actualization can be viewed as an ongoing process of personal growth, rather than a destination. In this sense, self-actualization may be actively pursued at any point in life.

Part Six

Abnormal Behavior and Psychotherapy

Chapter 19

Deviance and Disorder: The Unhealthy Personality

Chapter Preview

Catch-22: A Practical Definition of "Crazy"

"Can't you ground someone who's crazy?"

"Oh, sure, I have to. There's a rule saying I have to ground anyone who's crazy."

"Then why don't you ground me? I'm crazy. Ask Clevinger."

"Clevinger? Where is Clevinger? You find Clevinger and I'll ask him."

"Then ask any of the others. They'll tell you how crazy I am."

"They're crazy."

"Then why don't you ground them?"

"Why don't they ask me to ground them?"

"Because they're crazy, that's why."

"Of course they're crazy," Doc Daneeka replied. "I just told you they're crazy, didn't I? And you can't let crazy people decide whether you're crazy or not, can you?"

Yossarian looked at him soberly and tried another approach. "Is Orr crazy?"

"He sure is," Doc Daneeka said.

"Can you ground him?"

"I sure can. But first he has to ask me to. That's part of the rule."

"Then why doesn't he ask you to?"

"Because he's crazy," Doc Daneeka said. "He has to be crazy to keep flying combat missions after all the close calls he's had. Sure, I can ground Orr. But first he has to ask me to."

"That's all he has to do to be grounded?"

"That's all. Let him ask me."

"And then you can ground him?" Yossarian asked.

"No. Then I can't ground him."

"You mean there's a catch?"

"Sure there's a catch." Doc Daneeka replied. "Catch-22. Anyone who wants to get out of combat duty isn't really crazy."

There was only one catch and that was Catch-22, which specified that a concern for one's own safety in the face of dangers that were real and immediate was the process of a rational mind. Orr was crazy and could be grounded. All he had to do was ask; and as soon as he did, he would no longer be crazy and would have to fly more missions. Orr would be crazy to fly more missions and sane if he didn't, but if he was sane he had to fly them. If he flew them he was crazy and didn't have to; but if he didn't want to he was sane and had to. Yossarian was moved very deeply by the absolute simplicity of this clause of Catch-22 and let out a respectful whistle.

"That's some catch, that Catch-22," he observed.

*"It's the best there is," Doc Daneeka agreed.**

This excerpt from Joseph Heller's novel Catch 22 *captures the ambiguities presented by the classic question, "What is normal?" In the 1800s, doctors, and laymen alike used such terms as "crazy," "insane," "cracked," and "lunatic" quite freely. The "insane" were considered bizarre and definitely different from you or me.*

Today our understanding of "mental illness" or emotional disturbance is becoming increasingly sophisticated. Drawing lines between normal and abnormal can be done only by considering some complex issues. In this chapter and the next, we will summarize major psychological disturbances and their characteristics.

Survey Questions How is normality defined, and what are the major psychological disorders? What is a personality disorder? Is the term *neurosis* still used? What problems result when a person suffers high levels of anxiety? What are affective disorders? What can be done about them? What causes suicide, and how can it be prevented?

Psychopathology—Defining Major Psychological Problems

Resources

In 1978 William Milligan was accused of being the "university rapist" who attacked four women near Ohio State University. At his trial, psychiatrists testified that Milligan had nine separate personalities. The rapist was assumed to have been a personality identified as an "18-year-old lesbian" named Adelena.

Unlike the *Catch* 22 excerpt, William Milligan's problem is "nonfiction." It is but one hint of the magnitude of mental health problems in this country. Here are the facts on psychopathology:

Psychopathology An inability to behave in ways that foster personal well-being; abnormal or maladaptive behavior.

Organic mental disorder A mental or emotional problem caused by malfunction of the brain.

Substance use disorder Psychological dependence on a mood- or behavior-altering drug.

Psychotic disorder A severe psychological disorder characterized by a retreat from reality, by hallucinations and delusions, and by social withdrawal.

Mood disorder A psychological problem involving major disturbances in mood or emotion, such as depression or mania.

Anxiety disorder A disorder characterized by disruptive feelings of fear, apprehension, or anxiety.

Somatoform disorder The presence of physical symptoms that mimic disease or injury for which there is no identifiable physical cause.

Dissociative disorder A problem marked by a separation of thoughts and actions, as in temporary amnesia or multiple personality.

Personality disorder A deeply ingrained, unhealthy, maladaptive personality pattern.

Psychosexual disorder Any of a wide range of difficulties with sexual identity, sexual behavior, or sexual adjustment.

Neurosis An outdated term once used to refer, as a group, to anxiety disorders, somatoform disorders, dissociative disorders, and some affective disorders.

- Nearly half of all hospital beds in all types of hospitals are occupied by the mentally ill.
- 1 out of every 10 children born will experience either a major or a minor mental disorder.
- 1 out of every 100 persons will become so severely disturbed as to required hospitalization at some point in his or her lifetime.
- Each year over 2 million persons are admitted or readmitted to outpatient services or psychiatric treatment in general hospitals.

A tremendous variety of problems falls under the general heading of *psychopathology*. **Psychopathology** may be defined as the *inability to behave in ways that foster the well-being of the individual and ultimately of society*. This definition covers not only obviously maladaptive behavior such as drug addiction, compulsive gambling, or loss of contact with reality, but also any behavior that interferes with personal growth and self-fulfillment (Carson, Butcher, & Coleman, 1988).

Psychological problems are grouped into broad categories of maladaptive behavior. The most widely used system of classification is found in the *Diagnostic and Statistical Manual of Mental Disorders* (DSM-III-R, 1987). If you were to glance through this manual, you would find a wide range of disorders described, including those that follow.

Organic mental disorders are problems caused by brain pathology; that is, by senility, drug damage, diseases of the brain, injuries, the toxic effects of poisons, and so on. Organic disorders are often accompanied by such symptoms as severe emotional disturbances, impairment of thinking, memory loss, personality changes, and delirium.

Psychoactive Substance use disorders are defined as psychological dependence on mood- or behavior-altering drugs: alcohol, barbiturates, opiates, cocaine, amphetamines, hallucinogens, marijuana, tobacco, and others. Problems in this category center on damaged social or occupational functioning and an inability to stop using the drug (Fig. 19-1).

Psychotic disorders are the most severe type of psychopathology, often requiring hospitalization. In psychosis there is a retreat from reality: The person can no longer tell what is fantasy or hallucination, and what is real. In addition, there is usually a major loss of ability to control thoughts and actions.

Mood disorders primarily involve disturbances in mood or emotion (affect = emotion). In an affective disorder, individuals may be *manic*, meaning agitated, euphoric, and hyperactive, or they may be *depressed*. In either case, extremes of mood are intense or long lasting. Depressed individuals run a high risk of suicide.

Anxiety disorders may take the form of *phobias* (irrational fears of objects, activities, or situations), *panic* (in which the person suffers sudden unexplainable feelings of terror), or *generalized anxiety* (chronic and persistent anxiety). Also associated with anxiety disorders is a pattern known as *obsessive-compulsive* behavior (more on this later).

Somatoform disorders are indicated when a person has physical symptoms that mimic physical disease or injury (paralysis, blindness, or chronic pain, for example) but for which there is no identifiable cause. The assumption in such cases is that psychological factors underlie the symptoms.

Fig. 19-1 *The self-portraits shown here were painted by Andy Wilf between 1978 and 1981. During that time Wilf is said to have increasingly abused drugs and alcohol. This dramatic series of images is a record of his self-destructive descent into a private hell. The third painting shows a shrouded skull—and foretells the artist's fate. Wilf died of a drug overdose early in 1982. Drug abuse is but one of the many psychopathologies, or "problems in living," psychologists seek to alleviate. (Courtesy of Ulrike Kantor, Ulrike Kantor Gallery)*

Dissociative disorders include cases of sudden temporary *amnesia* and instances of *multiple personality*, like that displayed by William Milligan.

Personality disorders are deeply ingrained, unhealthy personality patterns. Such patterns are usually apparent by adolescence and continue throughout most of adult life. They include paranoid (overly suspicious), narcissistic (self-loving), dependent, compulsive, antisocial, and other personality types.

Psychosexual disorders include *gender identity disorders* (where a person's sexual identity does not match his or her physical gender), *transsexualism* (a persistent discomfort about one's sex and a desire to change to the opposite sex), and a wide range of deviations in sexual behavior (fetishism, voyeurism, and so on). Also related to this category are a variety of *sexual dysfunctions* (problems in sexual desire or sexual response; see Chapter 23).

Question: Shouldn't neurosis *be included on the list?*

The former *Diagnostic and Statistical Manual* (DSM-II) listed **neurosis** as a disorder, but the new version (DSM-III-R) discourages use of the term. Why? Because the label "neurosis" tends to lump together too many separate problems. Behavior once considered "neurotic" is now found under anxiety, somatoform, and dissociative disorders (as well as milder mood disorders). Of course, it still

Insanity Legally, a mental disability shown by an inability to manage one's affairs or to be aware of the consequences of one's actions.

Expert witness A person recognized by a court of law as being qualified to give expert testimony on a specific topic.

Subjective discomfort Personal, private feelings of discomfort or unhappiness.

Statistical abnormality Abnormality defined on the basis of an extreme score on some measure or dimension, such as IQ or anxiety.

Normal curve A bell-shaped curve having known mathematical properties; characterized by a large number of scores in a middle area, tapering to very few extremely high and low scores.

Social nonconformity Failure to match one's behavior to widely accepted norms or to the usual minimum rules for social conduct in a particular society.

Context With regard to behavior, the social situation, behavioral setting, or other surrounding circumstances in which an action takes place.

makes sense to distinguish these milder problems from psychosis, because they do not involve a major loss of contact with reality.

Question: Is psychosis the same as insanity?

No. Psychosis is a *psychiatric* term that describes a particular type of psychopathology. **Insanity** is a *legal* term. Persons who are declared "insane" are not legally responsible for their actions, and they can be involuntarily committed to a mental institution. Insanity is usually established through the testimony of psychologists and psychiatrists who serve as **expert witnesses** in a court of law (Carelli, 1982).

Normality—What Is Normal?

Setting aside certain behaviors or certain people as psychologically unhealthy raises the age-old issue of what is normal. Defining normality can be a tricky business. We might begin by saying that **subjective discomfort** is characteristic of psychopathology; that is, the unhealthy personality will be marked by unhappiness, anxiety, depression, or other signs of emotional upset.

Question: But couldn't a person be psychotic without feeling subjective discomfort?

Yes. A problem with this definition is that a person's behavior might be quite maladaptive without causing personal discomfort. A psychotic person displaying obviously bizarre and maladjusted behavior might feel on top of the world. It could be said, also, that a *lack* of discomfort may reveal a problem. If you were to show no signs of grief or depression in response to the death of a friend or loved one, we might suspect psychopathology. In practice, subjective discomfort accounts for most instances in which a person voluntarily seeks professional help.

Some psychologists have tried to pin down normality more objectively by using **statistical definitions.** For example, since we know that anxiety is a characteristic of several milder disorders, we could devise a test to learn how many people show low, medium, or high levels of anxiety. Usually the results of such a test will fall into a **normal** (bell-shaped) **curve** (see Fig. 19-2). (*Normal* in this case is a statistical concept referring only to the shape of the curve.) Notice that most people score in the center region of such a curve. Those people who deviate from the average by being anxious all the time (high anxiety) might be considered abnormal. Incidentally, a person who never feels anxiety might also be considered abnormal.

Question: Then a statistical definition of abnormality tells us nothing about the meaning of a deviation from the norm?

Right. It is as statistically "abnormal" (unusual) for a person to score above 145 on an IQ test as it is to score below 55, but only in the second case would we consider the score "abnormal" or undesirable.

Another major problem with statistical definitions is the question of *where to draw the line* between normality and abnormality. To take a new example, we

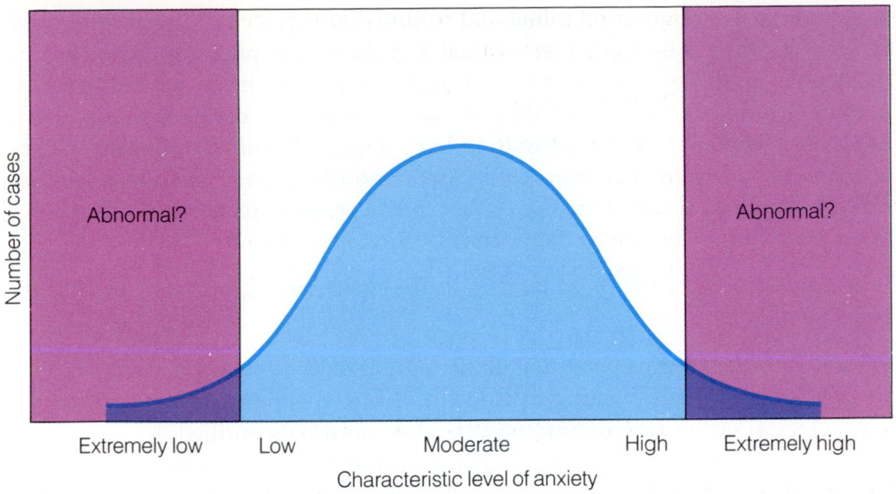

Fig. 19-2 *The number of people displaying a personal characteristic may help define what is statistically abnormal.*

could obtain the average frequency of sexual intercourse for persons of a particular age, sex, and marital status. Obviously, a person who feels driven to seek sexual release dozens of times a day has a problem. But as we move back toward the norm, we face the statistical problem of drawing lines. How often must an otherwise normal behavior occur before it becomes abnormal?

Social nonconformity may also serve as a basis for judging normality. Abnormal behavior can sometimes be viewed as a failure in *socialization*. Here we refer to the person who has not adopted the usual minimum rules for social conduct, or who has learned to engage in socially destructive or self-destructive behavior. This type of nonconformity must be carefully distinguished from that shown by highly creative individuals or those who have a unique lifestyle. It should be noted also that strict adherence to social norms is no guarantee of mental health (Fig. 19-3). In some cases psychopathology takes the form of rigid conformity.

Before any behavior can be defined as normal or abnormal, we must consider the **context** in which it occurs. Is it normal to stand outside and water a lawn? It depends on whether it is raining. Is it abnormal for a grown man to remove his pants and expose himself to another man or woman in a place of business? It depends on whether the other person is a bank clerk or a doctor! Almost any imaginable behavior can be considered normal in some context, as the following example indicates:

> In mid-October, 1973, an airplane carrying a rugby team called the Old Christians crashed in the snowcapped Andes of South America. Incredibly, 16 of the 45 people who had been aboard at the time of the crash survived 73 days in deep snow and subfreezing temperatures. They were forced to use extremely grim measures to do so—they ate the bodies of those who had died in the crash. (Adapted from *Time*, Jan. 8, 1973)

Cultural relativity Concept referring to the fact that a variety of perceptions and judgments are made relative to the values of one's culture.

Culture is one of the most influential contexts in which any behavior is judged. In some cultures it is considered normal to believe that plants and trees are inhabited by spirits, or to defecate or urinate in public, or to appear naked in public. In our culture each of these behaviors would be considered unusual or abnormal. There is, in other words, a high degree of **cultural relativity** in perceptions of normality and abnormality (see Box 19-1). Still, all known cultures classify people as abnormal if they either fail to communicate with others or are consistently unpredictable in their actions.

Question: If abnormality is so hard to define, how are judgments of psychopathology made?

It should be clear at this point that all definitions of abnormality are **relative.** Yet, in spite of the great difficulty of formally defining abnormality, we know that psychological disturbances occur and that they must be identified.

In practice, the judgment that a person needs help usually occurs when the person *does something* (hits a person, hallucinates, stares into space, collects rolls of toilet paper, and so forth) that *annoys* or *gains the attention* of a person in a *position of power* (an employer, teacher, parent, spouse, or the person himself or herself), who then *does something* about it. A police officer may be called, the person may be urged to see a psychologist, a relative may start commitment proceedings, or the person may voluntarily seek help.

The sections that follow continue our discussion by describing in greater detail some of the problems already mentioned. A full discussion of schizophrenia and other more severe problems is reserved for the next chapter. Before you read further, see if you can answer these questions.

Fig. 19-3 *Social nonconformity does not automatically indicate psychopathology.*

Box 19-1
Women, Culture, and "Madness"

Many more women than men are treated for psychological problems. Why?

- Due to cultural training, women may be more willing than men to reveal distress and to seek help for their problems.
- Because women are often denied power, responsibility, and independence in our society, they may more often feel depressed, anxious, or hopeless—for good reason.
- There may be a damaging male bias to traditional conceptions of normality.

The third possibility is perhaps the most controversial. According to psychologist Marcie Kaplan (1983), DSM-III-R has a distinct male bias. Kaplan believes that women are penalized both for conforming to female stereotypes and for ignoring them. If a woman is independent, aggressive, and unemotional, she may be considered "unhealthy." Yet, at the same time, a woman who is vain, emotional, irrational, and dependent on others (all are "feminine" traits in our culture) may be classified as a histrionic, or dependent, personality.

For the most part, DSM-III-R is a highly useful system. Nevertheless, Kaplan's critique helps illustrate the subtle influence that culture may have on perceptions of normality.

Learning Check

1. Approximately what percentage of hospital beds are occupied by the mentally ill? (circle)

10 percent   25 percent   50 percent   75 percent   90 percent

2. Which among the following are *not* major psychological problems listed in DSM-III-R? (circle)

psychotic disorders   mood disorders   neurosis   personality disorders   insanity   anxiety disorders

3. A major difference between psychotic disorders and anxiety disorders (or other milder problems) is that in psychosis the individual has ______________________.

4. Statistical definitions of abnormality successfully avoid the limitations of other approaches. T or F?

5. One of the most powerful contexts in which judgments of normality and abnormality are made is:

a. the family
b. religious systems
c. occupational settings
d. culture

Answers: **1.** 50 percent **2.** neurosis, insanity **3.** retreated from reality **4.** F **5.** *d.*

The Antisocial Personality—Rebel without a Cause

As stated earlier, personality disorders are deeply ingrained maladaptive personality patterns. For example, the *paranoid personality* is overly suspicious, mistrusting, or hypersensitive, guarded, and distrustful of the honesty of others. Persons having a *narcissistic personality* are preoccupied with their own self-importance; they need constant admiration, and they are absorbed in fantasies of power, wealth, brilliance, beauty, and love. The *dependent personality* involves an extreme lack of self-confidence, in which others are allowed to run the person's life, and the person places his or her own needs second to others. The list of such maladaptive patterns is long, so let us focus on a single frequently misunderstood personality disorder: the antisocial personality

Question: What are the characteristics of an antisocial personality?

The individual with an **antisocial personality** (sometimes referred to as a *sociopath* or *psychopath*) typically has a long history of conflict with society. Antisocial persons are irresponsible, impulsive, selfish, lacking in judgment, unable to feel guilt, emotionally shallow, unable to learn from experience, and lacking in moral values. In short, the sociopath is poorly socialized, has a general disregard for the truth, and seems to lack a conscience (Cleckley, 1964; DSM-III-R, 1987).

Question: Are sociopaths dangerous?

Sociopaths are rarely the crazed murderers that have been portrayed on TV and in movies. It is true that many sociopaths are delinquents or criminals who may pose a threat to the general public. However, most sociopaths create a good first impression and are frequently described as "charming." Their lying, self-serving manipulation, and lack of dependability only gradually become evident to their "friends."

Many successful businesspeople, entertainers, politicians, and other "normal" individuals reveal sociopathic leanings in their willingness to coldly use other people for their own ends. Some psychologists believe that the "manipulative personality" may be a better description of the problem as it occurs in noncriminal individuals (Bursten, 1973).

Question: What causes sociopathy?

People with antisocial personalities usually have a childhood history of emotional deprivation and neglect. This, perhaps, is chiefly responsible for their failure to develop concern for the feelings of others. In addition, adult sociopaths tend to be *emotionally cold.* They simply do not feel normal pangs of conscience, guilt, or anxiety. This coldness seems to account for an unusual ability to calmly lie, cheat, steal, or manipulate others. This condition may explain why many sociopaths are thrill seekers. Quite likely, they are searching for stimulation strong enough to overcome their chronic underarousal and "boredom" (Carson, Butcher, & Coleman, 1988).

Question: Can sociopathy be treated?

Antisocial personality disorders are rarely treated with success. All too often, sociopaths manipulate therapy like any other situation. If it is to their advantage to act "cured" they will do so, but they return to former patterns of behavior at the first opportunity. There is, however, some evidence that antisocial behavior declines somewhat after age 30.

Sexual Deviance— Trench Coats, Whips, Leathers, and Lace

Sexual deviance implies a departure from accepted standards of proper behavior. By the most strict standards (including the law in some states), any sexual activity other than face-to-face heterosexual intercourse between married adults is "deviant." But public standards and behavior found privately acceptable by consenting adults are often at odds. By private standards, oral-genital contact, masturbation, and premarital sex cannot be considered sexual deviations.

From a psychological point of view, the mark of true sexual deviations is that they are compulsive and destructive. Typically, they cause guilt, anxiety, or discomfort for one or both participants. Deviations fitting this definition are related to a wide variety of behaviors, including **pedophilia** (sex with children), **incest** (sex with blood relatives), **fetishism** (sexual arousal associated with inanimate objects), **exhibitionism** (displaying the genitals), **voyeurism** (viewing the genitals of others), **transvestic fetishism** (achieving sexual arousal by wearing clothing of the opposite sex), **sexual sadism** (deriving sexual pleasure from inflicting pain), **sexual masochism** (receiving pain as part of the sex act), and **frotteurism** (sexually touching or rubbing against a nonconsenting person, usually in a public place such as a streetcar).

Misconceptions Sexual deviance is a highly emotional subject, and many misconceptions have developed. Two of the most misunderstood problems are exhibitionism and pedophilia. Check your understanding against the information that follows.

Exhibitionism is a common problem: Roughly 35 percent of all sexual arrests are for "flashing." Exhibitionists are typically male, married, and most come from strict and repressive backgrounds. Exhibitionists have the highest repeat rate among sexual offenders. Most of them feel a deep sense of inadequacy, which produces a compulsive need to prove their manhood by frightening women. While exhibitionists are usually harmless, those who approach closer than arm's reach may be dangerous (Sue et al., 1981). In general, a woman confronted by an exhibitionist can assume that his goal is to shock and alarm her. By becoming visibly upset, she actually encourages him (Hyde, 1984).

Child molesters, who are usually males, are often pictured as despicable perverts lurking in dark alleys. In fact, most are married and two-thirds are fathers. Many are rigid, passive, puritanical, or religious. In one-half to two-thirds of all cases of molestation, the offender is a friend, acquaintance, or relative of the child. Molesters are also often thought of as child rapists. But most molestations rarely exceed fondling (Sue et al., 1981).

Question: How serious are the effects of a molestation?

The impact varies widely. Many authorities feel that a single incident of fondling is unlikely to cause severe psychological harm to a child. For most children the event is frightening, but not a lasting trauma. This is why parents are urged not

Antisocial personality A person who seems to lack a conscience, is emotionally shallow, impulsive, selfish, and tends to manipulate others; also referred to as a sociopath or psychopath.

Pedophilia Sex with children, or child molesting.

Incest Sexual contact with a close relative or family member.

Fetishism Gaining sexual gratification from inanimate objects; especially, an inability to achieve sexual arousal without the object.

Exhibitionism Deriving sexual pleasure from displaying the genitals (usually), to an unwilling viewer.

Voyeurism Deriving sexual pleasure from viewing the genitals of others, usually without their knowledge or permission (peeping).

Transvestism Achieving sexual arousal by wearing clothing of the opposite sex.

Sadism Gaining sexual pleasure by inflicting pain during the sex act.

Masochism Deriving sexual arousal or pleasure from having pain inflicted during the sex act.

Box 19-2

Sex Role Stereotyping and Rape

A number of writers have suggested that rape is in some ways related to sex role socialization. That is, many people learn to believe that women should not show direct interest in sex. Men, on the other hand, are taught to take the initiative and to persist in attempts at sexual intimacy—even when the woman says no.

Psychologists James Check and Neil Malamuth believe that such attitudes create a "rape-supportive culture." They point out, for instance, that the single, most used cry of rapists to their victims is, "You know you want it." And afterward, "There now, you really enjoyed it, didn't you."

To test the hypothesis that *stereotyped* images contribute to rape, male college students were classified as either high or low in sex role stereotyping. Each student then read one of three stories. The first described voluntary intercourse; the second depicted stranger rape; and the third described acquaintance rape (forced intercourse on a date).

As predicted, college males high in sex role stereotyping were more aroused by the rape stories. Their arousal patterns, in fact, were similar to those found among actual rapists. Moreover, a chilling 44 percent of those tested indicated they would consider raping someone—especially if they could be sure of not being caught (Check & Malamuth, 1983).

In view of such attitudes—and the continuing widespread belief that when a woman says no she means yes—it is little wonder that rape occurs every 6 minutes in the United States. Perhaps the time has come for our culture to make it clear that no means no.

to overreact to such incidents or to become hysterical. Doing so only further frightens the child (Wilson et al., 1984). This does not mean, however, that parents should ignore hints from a child that a molestation may have occurred. Repeated molestations, those that involve force or threats, and incidents that exceed fondling can leave lasting emotional scars. This is especially true if the molester is someone the child deeply trusts. Molestations by parents, close relatives, teachers, youth leaders, and similar persons can be quite damaging. In such cases professional counseling is often needed.

As the preceding suggests, the picture of sexual deviance that most often emerges is one of sexual inhibition and immaturity. Quite often, some relatively infantile sexual expression (like exhibitionism or pedophilia) is selected because it is less threatening than normal sexuality.

Rape Forcible rapists are a notable exception to the preceding description. Rapists often inflict more violence on their victims than is necessary to achieve their goal. Most authorities no longer think of rape as a sexual act. Rather, it is an act of brutality or aggression based on the need to debase others. Many rapists are antisocial personalities who impulsively take what they want without concern for the feelings of the victim or guilt about their deed. Others harbor deep-seated resentment or outright hatred toward women. However, the problem may reach far deeper (see Box 19-2).

Quite often, the rapist's goal is not strictly sexual intercourse; it is to attack, subordinate, humiliate, and degrade the victim. Typical after-effects for the victim include rage, guilt, depression, loss of self-esteem, shame, and, in many cases, a lasting mistrust of male-female relationships. The male who doubts the seriousness of rape should imagine himself mistakenly placed in jail, where he is violently raped (sodomized) by other inmates. There is no pleasure in rape for victims of either sex. It is truly a despicable crime.

Learning Check

1. Which of the following personality disorders is associated with an inflated sense of self-importance and a constant need for attention and admiration?
a. narcissistic *b.* paranoid *c.* antisocial *d.* manipulative

2. Almost all persons with antisocial personalities are criminals or delinquents. T or F?

3. Antisocial personality disorders are difficult to treat, but there is typically a decline in antisocial behavior after adolescence. T or F?

4. The formal term for child molesting is:
a. sadism *b.* bestiality *c.* pedophilia *d.* fetishism

5. What percentage of arrests for sexual offenses involve exhibitionism? ______________.

6. Rape is primarily an act of brutality or aggression, rather than an exclusively sexual act. T or F?

Answers: **1.** *a* **2.** F **3.** F **4.** *c* **5.** 35 percent **6.** T

Nonpsychotic Disorders—When Anxiety Rules

Imagine for a moment the feeling of waiting to take an important test for which you are unprepared; or waiting to give a speech to a large audience of strangers; or waiting for a dentist to start work. You have almost certainly felt **anxiety** in one of these situations. Anxiety is similar to fear except that it is a response to a *nonspecific threat* or an *anticipation of harm*. When people get stage fright, we say that they are anxious, because it is unclear what they fear.

Question: Is it abnormal to feel anxiety?

We all occasionally feel anxiety, and at times of great stress, anxiety may be intense, but anxiety that is out of proportion to a given situation may reveal a problem:

> A college student appeared at a counseling center with a complaint that he was deathly afraid of examinations. . . . He had previously been involved in a confrontation with an instructor whom he accused of having administered an unfair test in that there was not enough time to answer all the questions. . . . He soon realized that the time limit had not been long enough because he had wasted most of his time in attempting to control his anxieties. He had already skipped two other examinations by remaining in bed petrified with his fears of failure. (Adapted from Suinn, 1975)*

Forcible rape Sexual intercourse carried out against the victim's will, under the threat of force.

Anxiety Apprehension, dread, or uneasiness similar to fear, but based on an unclear threat.

*From *Fundamentals of Behavior Pathology* by R. M. Suinn. Copyright © 1975. Reprinted by permission of John Wiley & Sons, Inc. Additional Suinn quotes in this chapter and the next are from the same source.

Adjustment disorder A combination of emotional, psychological, and physical disturbances caused by identifiable life stresses.

Generalized anxiety disorder Defined as at least 6 months of persistent anxiety.

Panic disorder Persistently high levels of anxiety coupled with sudden episodes of intense, but unfocused, panic (anxiety attacks).

Phobic disorder A type of anxiety disorder in which irrational fears (phobias) are focused on specific objects, activities, or situations.

Agoraphobia An intense fear of leaving familiar surroundings, such as one's home.

Life-Disruptive, Nonpsychotic Disorders The student just described shows signs of having a disruptive emotional problem, but one that does not involve a loss of contact with reality. As mentioned earlier, such problems were once called neuroses. Now they are classified separately as anxiety disorders, dissociative disorders, and somatoform disorders. In general, these problems involve:

High levels of anxiety and/or restrictive, self-defeating behavior patterns.

A tendency to use elaborate defense mechanisms or avoidance responses to maintain minimal functioning.

Pervasive feelings of stress, insecurity, inferiority, unhappiness, and dissatisfaction with life.

Persons with such disorders struggle to preserve control but remain ineffective and accomplish little.

Question: Do such problems constitute a "nervous breakdown"?

Adjustment Disorders The problems mentioned seriously disrupt people's lives and almost always cause considerable misery. However, they rarely bring about a total "breakdown." Actually, the term *nervous breakdown* has no formal meaning. There is nothing wrong with the nerves of an anxious or emotionally troubled individual. What many people have in mind when they use the term is properly called an **adjustment disorder.**

Adjustment disorders occur when life stresses push people beyond their ability to cope effectively. Examples of such stresses are prolonged unemployment, extreme marital strife, and chronic physical illness. The presence of an adjustment disorder is signaled by extreme irritability, sleep disturbances, loss of appetite, physical complaints, and apathy, anxiety, or depression. Often these problems are successfully treated with rest, sedation, supportive counseling, and a chance to "talk through" fears and anxieties.

Question: How is an adjustment disorder different from an anxiety disorder?

The outward symptoms can be similar. However, adjustment disorders typically disappear when life circumstances improve. This demonstrates their link to stressful events.

Anxiety Disorders

In most anxiety disorders the person's distress seems greatly out of proportion to the situation. Consider, for example, the following description of Ethel B:

> She was never completely relaxed, and complained of vague feelings of restlessness, and a fear that something was "just around the corner." Although she felt that she had to go to work to help pay the family bills, she could not bring herself to start anything new for fear that something terrible would happen on the job. She had experienced a few extreme anxiety attacks during which she felt "like I couldn't breathe, like I was sealed up in a transparent envelope. I thought I was going to have a heart attack. I couldn't stop shaking." (Suinn, 1975)

Distress such as Ethel B's is a key element in anxiety disorders. Many psychologists believe it also underlies dissociative and somatoform disorders—where maladaptive behavior serves to reduce anxiety and personal discomfort. To deepen your understanding, let's examine several related nonpsychotic disorders.

Generalized Anxiety Disorder The essential feature of the simplest anxiety disorder—known as a **generalized anxiety disorder**—is at least 6 months of persistent anxiety. Affected individuals typically complain of sweating, racing heart, dizziness, upset stomach, rapid breathing, and other symptoms of autonomic nervous system activity. They also continually worry, anticipating disasters such as fainting, losing control, dying, injury, or death of close relatives, and so forth.

Question: Was Ethel B's problem a generalized anxiety disorder?

No. The added presence of *anxiety attacks* indicates she suffered from a **panic disorder.**

Panic Disorder In this relatively simple but very disturbing pattern, continuous tension, worry, and anxiety occasionally explode into sudden episodes of intense panic. During a panic, or anxiety, attack, affected individuals experience heart palpitations or chest pain, choking or smothering sensations, vertigo, feelings of unreality, trembling, and fear of dying, going crazy, or doing something uncontrollable during the attack (DSM-III-R, 1987). Many believe that they are having a heart attack, are going insane, or are about to die. Needless to say, individuals showing this pattern are unhappy and uncomfortable much of the time.

Phobic Disorders Phobias are irrational fears that persist even when there is no real danger. In **phobic disorders,** irrational fears, anxiety, and avoidance are focused on specific objects, activities, or situations (Fig. 19-4).

Acrophobia—fear of heights
Agoraphobia—fear of public places
Claustrophobia—fear of closed spaces
Nyctophobia—fear of darkness
Pathophobia—fear of disease
Zoophobia—fear of animals

Fig. 19-4 *For a person with a strong fear of snakes (ophidiophobia), merely looking at this picture may be unsettling.*

This list of possibilities is only partial: Phobias may be attached to almost any object or situation.* Almost everyone has a few mild phobias: Fears of heights, closed spaces, or bugs and crawly things are common. A phobic disorder differs from such garden-variety fears in that it produces overwhelming anxiety that may cause vomiting, wild climbing and running, or fainting. Phobic persons are so threatened that they will go to almost any length to avoid the feared object or situation.

Question: Are some phobias more common than others?

The most common problem is **agoraphobia** (ah-go-rah-FOBE-ee-ah). One expert estimates that 1 out of every 100 people has agoraphobia severe enough to restrict his or her life to a serious degree (Hardy, 1976).

Agoraphobia often starts after a stressful life event, such as interpersonal conflict (Last, Barlow, & O'Brien, 1984). Soon after the event, the agoraphobic person develops an intense fear of leaving the familiar setting of the home. Typically, he or she creates elaborate alibis to avoid areas of insecurity—such as crowds, open roads, supermarkets, automobiles, and so on (Zane & Milt, 1984). As a result, agoraphobics depend heavily on others to maintain a semblance of a normal life. Some are literally housebound and never leave the security of their homes (DSM-III-R, 1987).

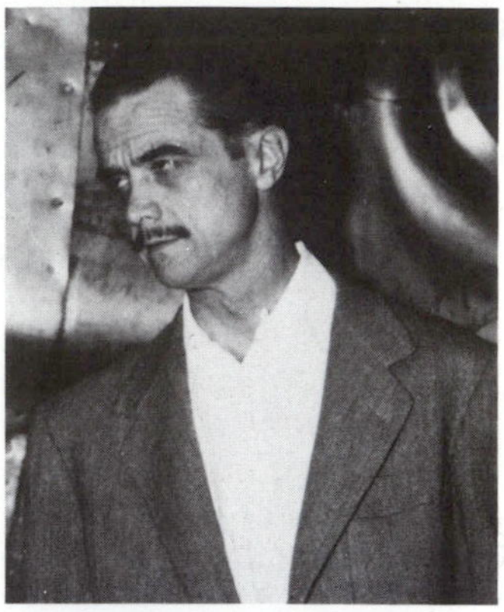

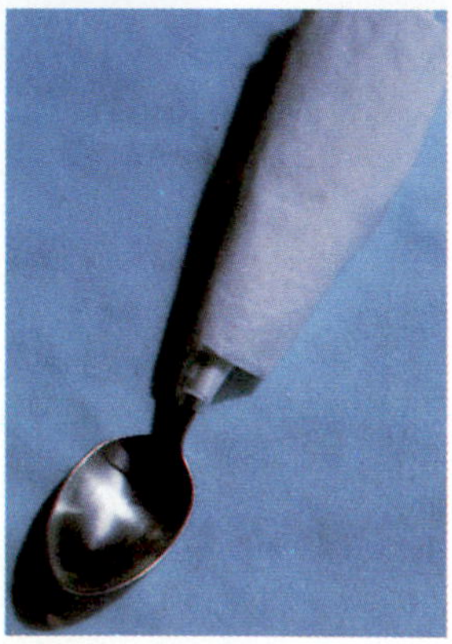

Fig. 19-5 *The severe obsessions and compulsions of billionaire Howard Hughes led him to live as a recluse for over 20 years. Hughes had an intense fear of contamination. To avoid infection, he constructed sterile, isolated environments in which his contact with people and objects was strictly limited by complicated rituals. Before handling a spoon, for instance, Hughes had his attendants wrap the handle in tissue paper and seal it with tape. A second piece of tissue was then wrapped around the first before he would touch it (Hodgson & Miller, 1982). A spoon prepared as Hughes required is shown at bottom.*

Obsessive-Compulsive Disorder **Obsessions** are images or thoughts that intrude into consciousness against a person's will. You have probably experienced a mild obsessional thought in the form of some song or stupid commercial jingle that is repeated over and over in your mind. This may be irritating, but it is certainly not disturbing in any major sense. True obsessions are so disturbing that they cause anxiety or extreme discomfort. Such obsessions may center on images of one's own violent death, feelings of being "dirty" or "unclean," feelings that one is about to lose control, or similar threatening preoccupations.

Obsessions usually give rise to **compulsions.** These are irrational acts a person feels driven to repeat (Fig. 19-5). Often, the compulsive act helps control or block out anxiety caused by the obsession. A person who feels guilty or unclean because of a conflict about masturbation might be driven to wash his hands hundreds of times a day. A minister who finds profanities popping into his mind might take up compulsively counting his heartbeats to prevent himself from thinking "dirty" words. A young mother who repeatedly has an image of a knife plunging into her infant might count all the knives in the house several times a day and insist that they always be locked up.

Of course, not all obsessive-compulsive disorders are so dramatic; many simply involve extreme orderliness and rigid routine. Compulsive attention to detail and rigid adherence to procedures and rules make the highly anxious person feel more secure by keeping activities totally predictable and under control.

Post-Traumatic Disorders Most anxiety disorders are relatively lasting patterns. As such, they have little connection to the actual degree of threat present.

*Obviously, by combining the appropriate root word with the word *phobia*, any number of unlikely fears can be named. Some are: *acarophobia*, fear of itching; *zemmiphobia*, fear of the great mole rat; *nictophobia*, fear of backing into doorknobs; *phobiaphobia*, fear of fear; and *hippopotomonstrosesquipedaliophobia*, fear of long words!

A notable exception is found in **post-traumatic stress disorders.** These problems occur when stresses *outside the range of normal human experience* cause a significant psychological and emotional disturbance. Such reactions frequently follow sudden disasters, such as floods, tornadoes, earthquakes, or serious accidents (Fig. 19-6).

Military combat is also a major source of post-traumatic stress disorders. For instance, many soldiers suffer **combat exhaustion** after extended periods of severe stress. Like other anxiety disorders, combat exhaustion is characterized by insomnia or repeated nightmares, loss of appetite, extreme sensitivity, unexplained crying, body tremor, hand wringing, and attacks of uncontrollable anxiety. Reactions of this sort may also surface long after the stress has passed—as is sometimes observed in former political hostages, prisoners of war, and combat veterans.

Obsessive-compulsive disorder An extreme, unavoidable preoccupation with certain thoughts and compulsive performance of certain behaviors.

Obsession Recurring irrational or disturbing thoughts a person cannot prevent.

Compulsion An act an individual feels driven to repeat, often against his or her will.

Post-traumatic stress disorder Psychological and emotional disturbance following exposure to stresses outside the range of normal human experience, such as natural disasters or military combat.

Combat exhaustion Psychological and emotional disturbance caused by the severe stresses of military combat.

Dissociative Disorders

A dissociative reaction is marked by striking episodes of *amnesia*, *fugue*, or *multiple personality*. **Amnesia** is the inability to recall one's name, address, or past. **Fugue** (sounds like fewg) is physical flight to escape extreme conflict or threat. Fugue and amnesia are sometimes coupled. A person may wander away from

Amnesia Loss of memory (partial or complete) for past events and, especially, loss of memory for one's identity.

Fugue Taking flight to escape extreme emotional conflict, anxiety, or threat.

Fig. 19-6 *In the aftermath of natural disasters, some survivors suffer from post-traumatic stress reactions. For some, the flare-up of anxiety and distress may occur months or years after the stressful event is over.*

Multiple personality A form of dissociative disorder in which an individual develops two or more distinct personalities.

Dual personality A case of multiple personality in which there are two personalities.

Schizophrenia A type of psychosis characterized by withdrawal from reality, delusions, hallucinations, and a "split" between thought and emotion.

Hypochondriasis A preoccupation with minor bodily problems and the presence of illnesses that appear to be imaginary.

Somatoform pain Pain that has no identifiable physical cause and appears to be of psychological origin.

Conversion reaction A symptom or disability that appears to be physical but that actually results from anxiety, stress, or emotional conflict.

work or school only to later arrive in a strange place with no knowledge of the journey. It's easy to see that forgetting one's identity or fleeing unpleasant situations can serve as a defense against intolerable anxiety.

Multiple personality is a relatively rare condition in which two or more separate personalities exist in an individual. The fictional story of *Dr. Jekyll and Mr. Hyde* is a well-known example of **dual personality.** (Note that dual personality is *not* schizophrenia; **schizophrenia** is a form of psychosis, as discussed in the next chapter.) One of the most dramatic examples of multiple personality ever recorded is described in the book *Sybil* (Schreiber, 1973). Sybil is a woman who had 16 different personalities. Each personality had a distinct voice, vocabulary, and posture. One personality could play the piano (not Sybil), but the others could not.

When a personality other than Sybil was in control, Sybil experienced a "time lapse," or memory blackout. For example, as a child she once "awoke" as a fifth grader and couldn't understand why she was not in her third-grade classroom. When she was asked to do a multiplication problem she couldn't begin. Two years of her life were missing, and the personality that had inhabited her body had learned multiplication, but Sybil had not.

Sybil's amnesia and alternate personalities developed during childhood when she was regularly beaten, locked in closets, perversely tortured, and almost killed. Sybil's first dissociations allowed her to escape by creating another person who would suffer torture in her place. Multiple personality often begins with similar unbearable childhood experiences. In later years Sybil continued the pattern by developing additional personalities to defend against new stresses. Fortunately, multiple personality is far rarer in real life than it is in TV dramas!

Somatoform Disorders

Perhaps you have known someone, particularly someone prone to anxiety, who seems to suffer from an unending series of physical complaints. Usually such individuals believe they have been "sickly" for much of their lives. Often, they have a complicated medical history, and they have, over the years, consulted numerous doctors, sometimes two or more at once. Life for these people is marked by endless preoccupation with bodily sensations and various "diseases"—despite the fact that there is no physical basis for their complaints.

Question: Are you describing hypochondria?

Basically, yes. In **hypochondriasis** (HI-po-kon-DRY-uh-sis) the person has multiple physical complaints for which medical attention is sought, but for which no clear physical cause can be found. **Somatoform pain** is a related problem in which the person is disabled by pain that has no identifiable physical basis. A rarer form of somatoform disorder (or "body-form" disorder) is called a *conversion reaction*.

Question: How does a conversion reaction differ from hypochondriasis?

Conversion reactions occur when anxiety or severe emotional conflicts are "converted" into symptoms that actually disturb bodily functioning or closely resemble physical disability. Conversion disorders are usually quite dramatic. For instance, a soldier might go deaf or lame or might develop "glove anesthesia" just before a battle.

Question: What is glove anesthesia?

Glove anesthesia is a loss of sensitivity in the areas of skin that would normally be covered by a glove. Glove anesthesia demonstrates that conversion symptoms often contradict known medical facts. The system of nerves in the hands does not form a glovelike pattern and therefore could not cause the observed symptoms. Conversion reactions are also revealed by a disappearance of symptoms when the "victim" is asleep, hypnotized, or anesthetized (Fig. 19-7).

The physical symptoms of a conversion disorder usually serve to excuse the person from a threatening situation. In one case a college student who had a minor traffic accident awakened the following morning with a numbness in his legs and found himself unable to move them. A conversion reaction was suspected when it was noted that he did not seem at all upset by his inability to walk. Investigation revealed that his parents were pressuring him to stay in school (although he wanted to quit) and that he was not prepared for his final exams. If he failed his exams, he expected to be drafted (Suinn, 1975).

A final note of interest: Conversion disorders probably account for many of the so-called miracle cures attributed to faith healers or medical quacks. Persons with conversion symptoms who firmly believe they are being helped may undergo a miraculous cure, but they usually develop new symptoms later.

Fig. 19-7 (left) *"Glove" anesthesia is a conversion reaction involving loss of feeling in areas of the hand that would be covered by a glove* (a). *If the anesthesia were physically caused, it would follow the pattern shown in* (b). (right) *To test for organic paralysis of the arm, an examiner can suddenly extend the arm, stretching the muscles. A conversion reaction is indicated if the arm pulls back involuntarily. (Adapted from* Weintraub, 1983)

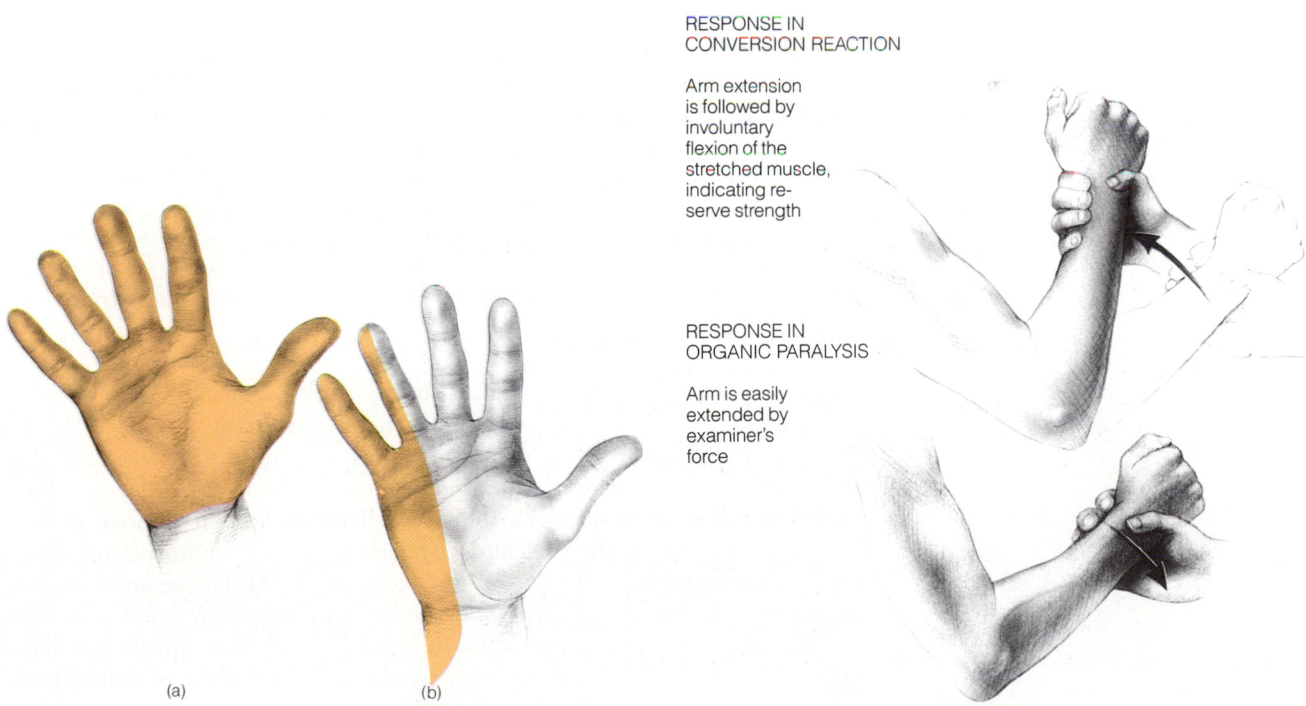

Learning Check

We have discussed problems from four major categories of DSM-III-R, as listed below. See if you can correctly match specific disorders with items on the right, by placing letters in the parentheses.

1. Adjustment disorders ( )

2. Anxiety disorders:
generalized anxiety disorder ( )
panic disorder ( )
phobic disorders ( )
obsessive-compulsive disorders ( )
post-traumatic stress disorders ( )

3. Dissociative disorders ( )

4. Somatoform disorders ( )

A. Disturbing thoughts, rigid routine, mechanical behavior
B. Hypochondriasis, psychogenic pain, and conversion reactions
C. Free-floating anxiety and anxiety attacks
D. Persistent, specific, irrational fears
E. Emotional distress linked to ongoing life stresses
F. Amnesia, fugue, multiple personality
G. Chronic worry, anxiety, nervousness without apparent external source
H. Triggered by events outside the range of normal human experience

Answers: **1.** E **2.** G, C, D, A, H **3.** F **4.** B

Three Theories—Pathways to Anxiety and Disorder

Question: What causes the problems described in the preceding section?

At least three major perspectives on the causes of dissociative, anxiety, and somatoform disorders can be identified. These are: (1) the psychodynamic approach, (2) the humanistic approach, and (3) the behavioristic approach.

Psychodynamic Approach Freud was the first to propose an explanation for what was then called neurosis. According to Freud, disturbances like those we have described represent a raging conflict between subparts of the personality—the id, ego, and superego.

Freud emphasized that intense anxiety can be caused by forbidden id impulses for sex or aggression that threaten to break through into behavior. Also important is guilt generated by the superego's response to these impulses. The ego is caught in the middle and overwhelmed. This forces the person to adopt rigid defense mechanisms and misguided, inflexible behavior to prevent a disastrous loss of control.

Humanistic Approaches Humanistic psychologist Carl Rogers interpreted emotional disorders as the end product of a faulty self-image (Rogers, 1959). Rogers believed that anxious individuals have built up unrealistic pictures of themselves, leaving them vulnerable to contradictory information. Let's say, for example, that an essential part of a student's self-image is seeing himself or herself as highly intelligent. If the student does poorly in school, he or she may deny or distort self-perceptions and views of the situation. Rigid defense mechanisms, a conversion reaction, anxiety attacks, or similar symptoms may result from threats to one's self-image. These symptoms in turn become new threats and require further distortions. We have, in other words, a vicious cycle of maladjustment and anxiety that feeds on itself once started.

Behavioristic Approach Behaviorists generally assume that the "symptoms" we have discussed are learned, just as other behaviors are. You might recall from Chapter 7, for instance, that phobias can be learned through classical conditioning. Similarly, anxiety attacks may reflect a generalization of conditioned emotional responses to new situations. As another example, the hypochondriac's "sickness behavior" may be reinforced by the sympathy and attention he or she gets.

One aspect of disordered behavior all theorists agree on is that it is self-defeating and *paradoxical.* A paradox is a contradiction. The contradiction in self-defeating behavior is that in the long run it makes the person more miserable, but its immediate effect is to temporarily lower anxiety.

Question: But if the person becomes more miserable in the long run, how does the pattern get started?

The behavioristic explanation is that self-defeating behavior begins with **avoidance learning** (described earlier, in Chapter 8). Here's a quick review of avoidance learning to refresh your memory:

> An animal is placed in a special cage. After a few minutes a light comes on, followed a moment later by a painful shock. Quickly, the animal escapes into a second chamber. After a few minutes a light comes on in this chamber, and the shock is repeated. Soon the animal learns to *avoid* pain by moving *before* the shock occurs. Once an animal learns to avoid, the shock can be turned off altogether. A well-trained animal may avoid the nonexistent shock indefinitely.

The same analysis can be applied to disordered human behavior. A behaviorist would say that the powerful reward of *immediate relief* from anxiety keeps self-defeating avoidance behavior alive. This view, known as the **anxiety reduction hypothesis** seems to explain why the behavior patterns we have discussed often look very "stupid" to outside observers.

There is probably a core of truth to each of the three explanations. For this reason, understanding a particular example of anxiety disorders, dissociation, or somatoform disorders may be aided by combining parts of all three perspectives. Each viewpoint also suggests a different approach to treatment. Since there are many possibilities, a full discussion of therapy is found later, in Chapters 21 and 22.

Psychodynamic Pertaining to internal motives, conflicts, unconscious forces, and other dynamics of mental life.

Humanistic Any system of thought focused on subjective experience and human problems and potentials.

Self-image Total subjective perception of oneself; another term for self-concept.

Behavioristic Any approach that emphasizes overt, observable behavior and the effects of learning and conditioning.

Avoidance learning A learning procedure in which making a particular response delays or prevents the onset of an unpleasant stimulus.

Anxiety reduction hypothesis An explanation of the self-defeating nature of many avoidance responses that emphasizes the immediate reinforcing effects of relief from anxiety.

Depressive Disorders— On the Dark Side of the Mood

Nobody loves you when you're down and out—or so it seems. Psychologists have gradually come to realize that disturbances in mood—the **affective disorders**—are among the most serious of all. In terms of sheer numbers, studies show that in Europe and the United States between 10 and 20 percent of the adult population has had a major depressive episode at some time (DSM-III-R, 1987). Roughly 25 percent of all cases treated by private psychiatrists and psychologists are for depression (Marmon, 1975).

Question: Don't mood disorders include manic behavior?

Dysthymia A chronic emotional disturbance marked by a predominately depressed mood, but not involving severe depression.

Cyclothymia A chronic emotional disturbance involving periods of depression mixed with periods of manic behavior, but not involving extreme depression or mania.

Reactive depression A serious depression that appears to be a reaction to some identifiable event.

Lithium carbonate A drug used to lessen mood swings in persons suffering from some types of affective disorders.

Maternity blues A brief and relatively mild state of depression often experienced by mothers 2 or 3 days after giving birth.

Postpartum depression A mild to moderately severe depression that begins within 3 months following childbirth.

Although manic behavior is included, depression is by far the most common problem. In depressive disorders, sadness and despondency are exaggerated, prolonged, or unreasonable. Indications of a depressive disorder are: sadness, hopelessness, inability to feel pleasure or to take interest in anything, fatigue, sleep and eating disturbances, feelings of worthlessness, an extremely negative self-image, and, often, recurrent thoughts of suicide. If a person is depressed more days than not, for at least two years, the problem is termed **dysthymia.** If depression alternates with periods when the person's mood is elevated, expansive, or irritable, the problem is called **cyclothymia** (DSM-III-R, 1987).

In serious cases of depression, it becomes impossible for a person to function at work or at school. Sometimes, depressed individuals cannot even feed or clothe themselves. When depression and/or mania is even more severe, the person may become psychotic and lose touch with reality. (Affective psychosis is discussed in the next chapter.)

Question: How are depressive disorders different from milder, more normal feelings of depression?

If a loved one dies or a person suffers a major failure, loss, or setback, a period of mourning or depression is to be expected. Depression at such times represents an emotional adjustment that is completed within a reasonable time. When someone is continuously or intensely depressed, we must look for causes that go beyond the apparent triggering incident. In many **reactive depressions** we find that the person was unprepared to cope with a major loss because of an earlier series of disappointments. In other instances the person is simply emotionally dependent or immature. In any case, the triggering incident in a reactive depression is often merely the "last straw" that reveals an underlying emotional disturbance.

Question: Is there an explanation for severe depression?

Depression and other affective disorders have resisted explanation and treatment. Some scientists are focusing on the biology of mood changes. These researchers are interested in brain chemicals and transmitter substances, electrolytes, serotonin and noradrenaline levels, and so forth. Their findings are complex and inconclusive, but progress has been made. For example, the chemical **lithium carbonate** can be effective in treatment of some cases of depression, particularly those also showing manic behavior (Depue & Monroe, 1978). Others have looked for psychological explanations. Psychoanalytic theory, for instance, holds that depression is caused by repressed anger that is turned inward as self-blame and self-hate (Isenberg & Schatzberg, 1976). As discussed earlier, in Chapter 12, behavioral theories of depression emphasize *learned helplessness*.

Adequate understanding and treatment of depression is a challenge to the ingenuity of psychologists, psychiatrists, and other investigators. It is to their credit that this major source of human misery has recently become the target of intensified research (see Box 19-3). While we await the outcome of their efforts, a problem remains: Thousands of depressed people commit suicide each year. What can be done about it? This chapter's Applications section provides some answers.

Box 19-3

Postpartum Depression

Two weeks after the birth of her child, Cheryl realized something was wrong. She could no longer ignore that she was extremely irritable, fatigued, tearful, and depressed. "Shouldn't I be happy?" she wondered. "What's wrong with me?"

Many women are surprised to learn that they run an increased risk of depression after giving birth. The two most common forms of the problem are **maternity blues** and **postpartum depression.** (The term *postpartum* refers to the time period following childbirth.)

An estimated 50 to 80 percent of all women undergo a temporary disturbance in mood, usually lasting from 24 to 48 hours after childbirth. These "third day" maternity blues are marked by crying, fitful sleep, tension, anger, and irritability. For most women this reaction is a normal part of adjusting to childbirth. Their depression is brief and relatively mild. For some women, however, the maternity blues can be the beginning of a more lasting depression.

As many as 20 percent (1 in 5) of all women who give birth may develop a mild to moderate depressive disorder. Typical signs of postpartum depression are mood swings, despondency, feeling inadequate, and feeling unable to cope with the new baby. Depression of this kind may last anywhere from 2 months to about a year.

Predicting postpartum depression is difficult. However, the risk is increased by high levels of anxiety during pregnancy and by negative attitudes toward childrearing. The occurrence of stressful life events before birth is also a major concern. Mothers who have temperamentally "difficult" infants are especially prone to depression (Cutrona & Troutman, 1987). Because birth and adjusting to parenthood can both be stressful, it may be that any extra problems push women toward depression.

Psychologists are still studying the best ways to prevent and treat postpartum depression. Presently, the amount of social support a woman receives seems to be an important part of the problem. That is, women who become depressed are also likely to view their husbands as unsupportive. Efforts to educate prospective parents about postpartum depression and the value of mutual support may therefore prove helpful. (Source: Hopkins, Marcus, & Campbell, 1984)

A Final Note—You're Okay, Really!

It is the author's hope that you will not fall prey to a psychological version of "medical student's disease" after reading this chapter. Medical students, it seems, have a tendency to notice in themselves the symptoms of each disease they study. As a psychology student you may have noticed what seem to be abnormal tendencies in your own behavior. If so, don't panic: This only shows that pathological behavior is an *exaggeration* of normal defenses and reactions, not that your behavior is pathological.

Learning Check

1. The humanistic explanation of anxiety and related disorders emphasizes the importance of faulty self-image. T or F?
2. According to the behavioristic view, anxious, self-defeating behavior is explaind by________________learning.
3. Freud's original psychodynamic explanation of "neurosis" was based on the anxiety reduction hypothesis. T or F?
4. Learned helplessness is emphasized by________________theories of depression.
   a. humanistic *b.* behavioristic *c.* biological *d.* psychoanalytic
5. The drug lithium carbonate has been shown to be an effective treatment for anxiety disorders. T or F?

Answers: **1.** T **2.** avoidance **3.** F **4.** *b* **5.** F

Applications

Suicide: Life in Balance

"Suicide: A permanent solution to a temporary problem."

By the time you finish reading this page, someone in the United States will have attempted suicide. Suicide is a very disturbing and widely misunderstood problem. It ranks as the seventh cause of death in the United States, and approximately 1 person out of 100 attempts suicide at some time in his or her life. Given these figures, it seems likely that you will sooner or later be affected by the suicide attempt of a friend, relative, neighbor, or co-worker. Check your knowledge of suicide against the following information.

Question: What factors affect suicide rates?

Season Suicide rates vary from city to city and time to time, but some general patterns emerge. Contrary to popular belief, there is little connection between major holidays, such as Christmas, and the suicide rate. For reasons not clearly understood, the peak actually comes in May (Zung & Green, 1974).

Sex Men have the questionable honor of being better at suicide than women. Three times as many men as women *complete* suicide, but women make more attempts. More men than women succeed at suicide because they typically use a gun or an equally fatal technique. Women most often attempt a drug overdose, a method that leaves greater chance of help arriving before death occurs (Lester, 1972).

Age Age is also a factor in suicide. More than half of all suicides are committed by individuals over 45 years old. This may be changing, however. There has been a recent increase in suicide rates for adolescents and young adults.

Part of this increase comes from the ranks of college students, where suicide is the leading cause of death. Contrary to popular belief, the most dangerous time for student suicide is the beginning (first 6 weeks) of a semester, not during final exams.

School is a factor in some suicides, but only in the sense that suicidal students were not living up to their own extremely high standards. Many were good students. Other important factors in student suicide are chronic health problems (real or imagined) and interpersonal difficulties (some suicides are rejected lovers, but others are simply withdrawn and friendless people) (Seiden, 1966).

Of special concern to psychologists is the recent dramatic increase in adolescent suicides. At present, about 5000 teenagers and young adults commit sui-

Applications: Suicide: Life in Balance, continued

cide each year in the United States. This rate—about 13 deaths per day—is double the number reported 10 years ago. In some cities, authorities have reported **suicide clusters**—virtual "epidemics" of adolescent suicide that occur in rapid succession. Also distressing is the fact that an increasing number of youths employ such highly lethal methods as shooting themselves.

Income Some professions, such as medicine and psychiatry, show higher than average suicide rates. Overall, however, suicide is quite democratic. It is equally a problem of the rich and the poor (Labovity & Hagedorn, 1971).

Marital Status An additional factor in suicide is martial status. Marriage (when successful) may be the best natural deterrent to suicidal impulses. The highest suicide rates are found among the divorced; the next highest rates occur among the widowed; lower rates are recorded for single persons; and married individuals have the lowest rate of all.

Question: Why do people try to kill themselves?

Immediate Causes The best explanation for suicide may simply come from a look at the conditions that precede it. Usually there is a history of interpersonal troubles with family, in-laws, or a lover or spouse. Often there may be drinking problems, sexual adjustment problems, or job difficulties (Humphrey et al., 1972).

A combination of factors such as these lead to severe depression and a preoccupation with death as the "answer" to the person's suffering. There is usually a break in communication with others that causes the person to feel isolated and misunderstood. Self-image becomes very negative. The person feels worthless and helpless and wants to die (Lester, 1972).

A long history of such conditions is not always necessary to produce a desire for suicide. People who attempt suicide are not necessarily "mentally ill." Anyone may temporarily reach a state of depression severe enough to attempt suicide. Most dangerous for the average person are times of divorce, separation, failure, and bereavement. Each can create what seems like an intolerable situation and can motivate an intense desire for escape.

The causes of increased adolescent suicide remain unclear. As with adults, there is often a backdrop of problems with drugs, depression, school, peers, family, divorced parents, or the breakup of a romance. However, many victims come from stable and affluent homes. Some experts suggest that many cases of adolescent suicide result from *unrealistic expectations*. For example, parents may create feelings of despair by pressuring their children to meet impossibly high standards.

Even without parental pressure, teenagers may expect the impossible of themselves in school, sports, romance, or progress toward a future career. Extremely high expectations can bring self-esteem to rock bottom over even the smallest "failure" (Serban, 1982). Again, the outcome is feelings of helplessness, hopelessness, and a desire to escape.

Preventing Suicide—You Can Help

Question: Is it true that people who talk about or threaten suicide are rarely the ones who try it?

No. This is one of the major fallacies about suicide. Of every 10 potential suicides, 8 give warning beforehand (Rudestam, 1971; Schneidman et al., 1965). A person who threatens suicide should be taken seriously. A potential suicide may say nothing more than, "I feel sometimes like I'd be better off dead." Warnings may also come indirectly. If a friend gives you a favorite ring and says, "Here, I won't be needing this any more," or comments, "I guess I won't get my watch fixed—it doesn't matter anyway," it may be a plea for help.

Question: Is it true that suicide can't be prevented, that the person will find a way to do it anyway?

No. The decision to attempt suicide usually comes when a person is alone, depressed, and unable to view matters objectively. You *should* intervene if someone seems to be threatening suicide.

Applications: Suicide: Life in Balance, continued

It is estimated that about two-thirds of all suicide attempts fall in the "to be" category. That is, they are made by people who do not really want to die. Almost a third more are characterized by a "to be or not to be" attitude. These people are *ambivalent* or undecided about dying. Only about 3 to 5 percent of cases represent individuals who definitely want to die. Most people, therefore, are relieved when someone comes to their aid (Schneidman et al., 1965). Remember that suicide is almost always a cry for help and that you *can* help.

Question: What is the best thing to do if someone hints they are thinking about suicide?

It helps to know some of the common characteristics of suicidal thoughts and feelings. Suicide expert Edwin Schneidman (1987) has identified several.

1. Escape. Everyone at times feels like running away from an upsetting situation. Running away from home, quitting school, or abandoning a marriage are all departures. Suicide, of course, is the ultimate, irreversible escape. It helps when suicidal persons see that the natural wish for escape doesn't have to be expressed by ending it all.

2. Unbearable psychological pain. Emotional pain is what the suicidal person is seeking to escape. A goal of anyone hoping to prevent suicide should be to reduce the pain in any way possible. Ask the person, "Where does it hurt?"

3. Frustrated psychological needs. Often, suicide can be prevented if a distraught person's frustrated needs can be identified and eased. Is the person deeply frustrated in his or her search for love, achievement, trust, security, or friendship?

4. Constriction of options. The suicidal person feels helpless and decides that death is the *only* solution. The person has narrowed all his or her options solely to death. The rescuer's goal, then, is to help broaden the suicidal person's perspective. Even when all the choices are unpleasant, suicidal persons can usually be made to see that their *least unpleasant option* is better than death.

Knowing these patterns will give some guidance in talking to a suicidal person. In addition, suicide expert David Lester (1971b) suggests that your most important task may be to establish *rapport* with the person. You should offer support, acceptance, and legitimate caring.

Remember that a suicidal person feels misunderstood. You should therefore try to accept and understand the feelings the person is expressing. Acceptance should extend to the idea of suicide itself. One of the worst things you can do is to say something like, "You're not thinking of doing something drastic, are you?" Hiding from suicide or trying to avoid talking about it makes the person feel wrong, unaccepted, and alone. Don't be afraid to talk about suicide directly. It is completely acceptable to ask, "Are you thinking of suicide?"

Establishing communication with suicidal persons may be enough to carry them through a difficult time. You may also find it helpful to get day-by-day commitments from them to meet for lunch, to share a ride, and the like. Let the person know you *expect* her or him to be there. Such commitments, even though small, can be enough to tip the scales when a person is alone and thinking about suicide.

Don't end your efforts too soon. One of the most dangerous times for suicide is when a person suddenly seems to get better after a severe depression. Many experts agree that this often means the person has finally made the decision to end it all. The improvement in mood is deceptive because it comes from an anticipation that suffering is at an end (Lester & Lester, 1971).

Crisis Intervention There are over 200 centers for suicide prevention in the United States, and most sizable cities have mental health crisis intervention teams. Both services have staff trained to talk to potential suicides over the phone. Give a person who seems to be suicidal the number of one of these services to place near a phone. Urge the person to call you or the other number if he or she becomes frightened or impulsive.

Applications: Suicide: Life in Balance, continued

The preceding applies mainly to persons who are having mild suicidal thoughts. If a person actually threatens suicide, you must act more quickly. Ask how the person plans to carry out the suicide. A person who has a *concrete, workable plan* should be asked to accompany you to the emergency ward of a hospital.

If a person seems on the verge of attempting suicide, don't worry about over-reacting; call the police, crisis intervention, or a rescue unit. Needless to say, you should call immediately if a person is in the act of attempting suicide or if a drug has already been taken. The majority of suicide attempts come at temporary low points in a person's life and may never be repeated. Get involved—you may save a life!

Suicide—A Summary of Facts

The following is a list of useful facts to know about suicide.

1. More men than women commit suicide, but women make more attempts.

2. College students are most likely to attempt suicide during the first part of the school quarter or semester.

3. Many people temporarily become depressed enough to contemplate suicide. Those who would attempt suicide are not usually psychotic or suffering from lasting mental illness.

4. Suicide strikes both the rich and the poor.

5. A person who is suicidal once may never again become suicidal. Preventing suicide is well worth the effort.

6. Most potentially suicidal persons give warning.

7. People who talk about suicide *do* often attempt it.

8. The majority of people (two-thirds) who attempt suicide do not really want to die, and most of the remainder are ambivalent about dying.

9. A *sudden* improvement in mood after a suicidal depression can mean that the person has decided to carry out a suicide attempt.

10. Four major characteristics of the suicidal state are (1) psychological pain, (2) frustrated needs, (3) a desire to escape, and (4) constricted options.

11. Suicide can often be prevented by the efforts of family, friends, and mental health professionals.

Learning Check

1. More women use guns in their suicide attempts than do men. T or F?
2. While the overall suicide rate has remained about the same, there has been a decrease in adolescent suicides. T or F?
3. Suicide is equally a problem of the rich and the poor. T or F?
4. The highest suicide rates are found among the divorced. T or F?
5. The majority (two-thirds) of suicide attempts fall in the "to be" category. T or F?

Answers: 1. F 2. F 3. T 4. T 5. T

Chapter 20

Psychosis

Chapter Preview

Psychosis—"Losing It"

> I'm a man 36 years of age, that in 1956–57 they changed the flag of the United States of America once by adding Alaska as a State to the Union and thus paving the way for Hawaii to become a state in 1959. That of course, gives me the "*capacity of the flag itself*" and therefore like any Congressional Medal of Honor winner, gives me the "*capacity of the President of the United States of America. . . .*"
>
> . . . in 1955–56 civil authorities . . . some "small time" politicians got together on me and sand-bagged me brainwashed me and bugged me with a "*short-wave* Radio grid center, with an ultra-violet cross grid" called a "bug." Its sole purpose is to use a person's senses against himself so as to perjure and distort him to no end of humiliation . . . they vibrate your nerves physically with it and never ceases.
>
> . . . I'd been there several months before they gave me "ground privileges" and once on the grounds they started frequencing my time all the more, vibrating the back of my neck, first flicking it to the front of my face, like a "whip" or a cat of 9 tails. (Suinn, 1975)

The excerpts above are taken from a letter written by a man experiencing a psychosis. They reveal some of the severe disturbances in thinking, behavior, speech, and emotions that accompany psychosis.

Psychosis also represents a loss of contact with reality. Novelist Joanne Greenberg (1964) describes a split from reality this way:

> The walls dissolved and the world became a combination of shadows . . . all direction became a lie. The laws of physics and solid matter were repealed and the experience of a lifetime of tactile sensation, motion, form, gravity, and light were invalidated. She did not know whether she was standing or sitting down, which way was upright, and from where the light, which was a stab as it touched her, was coming. She lost track of the parts of her body; where her arms were and how to move them. As light went spinning erratically away and back she tried to clutch at thoughts only to find that she had lost all memory of the English language.*

What is psychosis really like? What causes it? What can be done about it? For answers to these and related questions, read on.

*From *I Never Promised You a Rose Garden* by Hannah Green (Joanne Greenberg). Copyright © 1964 by Hannah Green. Reprinted by permission of Holt, Rinehart and Winston, Publishers.

Survey Questions What are the general characteristics of psychosis? How do delusional disorders, schizophrenia, and psychotic mood disorders differ? What causes schizophrenia? How are psychotic disorders treated? Is psychiatric labeling damaging?

Resources

Psychosis—Life in the Shadow of Madness

Psychosis—a major loss of contact with shared views of reality—is among the most serious of all mental problems.

Question: What is psychosis like?

A person experiencing a psychotic break undergoes a number of important changes. Following are descriptions of some of the major characteristics of psychoses (psycho*sis:* singular; psycho*ses:* plural).

Presence of Delusions **Delusions** are false beliefs that are held even when the facts contradict them. Individuals with the psychotic delusion that they are Jesus Christ will not be disturbed by an inability to walk on water or to perform miracles. Some common types of delusion are: (1) *depressive* delusions, in which people feel that they have committed horrible crimes or sinful deeds; (2) *somatic* delusions, such as belief that one's body is "rotting away" or that it is ravaged by disease; (3) delusions of *grandeur,* in which individuals think they are extremely important persons; (4) delusions of *influence,* in which people feel they are being controlled or influenced by others or by unseen forces; (5) delusions of *persecution,* in which people feel others are "out to get them"; and (6) delusions of *reference,* in which unrelated events are given personal meaning (as when a person assumes that a newspaper article or a television program is giving a special message directly to her or him) (DSM-III-R, 1987). If you reread the opening quote of the Chapter Preview, you will find evidence of delusions of grandeur, influence, and persecution.

Hallucinations and Sensory Changes **Hallucinations** are sensory experiences that occur in the absence of a stimulus. The most common psychotic hallucination is hearing voices, which may be familiar, may be answered, and frequently are insulting. More rarely, psychotic individuals may also feel "insects crawling under the skin," taste "poisons" in their food, or smell "gas" their "enemies" are using to "get" them. Sensory changes may bring about extreme sensitivity to heat, cold, pain, or touch. Anesthesia, a loss of normal sensitivity, is also possible.

Disturbed Emotions Emotions may swing violently between extremes of elation and depression, or the psychotic person may be hyperemotional, depressed, emotionally "flat," or apathetic. In **flat affect** there are almost no signs of emotion. In such cases a person's face is frozen and his or her voice is monotonous.

Psychosis A severe psychological disturbance characterized by withdrawal from reality, by hallucinations and delusions, by disturbed emotions, and often by personality disorganization.

Delusions False beliefs held against all contradictory evidence.

Hallucinations Imaginary sensations, such as seeing, hearing, or smelling things that don't exist in the real world.

Flat affect An extreme lack of emotional responsiveness.

Personality disintegration A shattering of the coordination among thoughts, actions, and emotions normally found in personality.

Organic psychosis A psychosis caused by a known brain injury or disease.

Functional psychosis A psychosis of unknown origin or one presumed to be caused by psychological factors.

General paresis An organic psychosis that results when syphilis attacks the brain.

Personality Disorganization or Disintegration Major disturbances such as those just described, plus added problems in thought, speech, memory, actions, and attention, bring about *personality disintegration* and a break with reality. As a result, significant impairment almost always occurs in work, social relations, and self-care. When psychotic disturbances and a shattered personality are evident for weeks or months (often including a period of deterioration, an active phase, and a residual phase), then the individual is said to have suffered a psychosis (DSM-III-R, 1987).

Question: How could a person function with such problems?

Actually, the preceding description is somewhat exaggerated, since it is rare to find all these changes occurring at once. As a matter of fact, you would probably find a trip to a psychiatric ward disappointing if you expected to see flamboyant, dramatic, or bizarre behavior. Typically, extreme psychotic behavior occurs in brief *episodes*. The symptoms of psychosis come and go and may be quite subtle much of the time (Fig. 20-1).

Question: Does psychosis occur without warning?

No. Usually there are signs of impending trouble. A recent study of psychotic patients found that for most, symptoms such as insomnia, emotional changes, or feeling "high" signaled a coming crisis (Brier & Strauss, 1983). In fact, most of the patients were aware of their symptoms and tried to fight off the psychosis.

Even after a psychotic break, people are not totally unresponsive to their surroundings. In one interesting experiment psychotic patients were interviewed in two ways. Some were told that the purpose of the interview was to determine if they were "ready for discharge." In this group, patients who were known to like the hospital acted very bizarre and disturbed during the interviews. A second group was told that the interview was to determine if the patient should be allowed "open ward" privileges. In this case, disturbed patients suddenly became amazingly free of symptoms (Braginsky & Braginsky, 1967).

Fig. 20-1 *A scene in a state mental hospital.*

This experiment shows that some psychotic symptoms can be considered a primitive form of communication, the message being, "I need help" or, "I can't handle it anymore." This view becomes more evident in light of the fact that an almost universal symptom of psychosis is difficulty in talking to others. Psychotic speech tends to be garbled and chaotic, sometimes sounding like no more than a "word salad":

> The lion will have to change from dogs into cats until I can meet my father and mother and we dispart from rats. . . . It's all over for a squab true tray and there ain't no squabs, there ain't no men, there ain't no music, there ain't nothing besides my mother and my father who stand alone upon the Island of Capri where is no ice. Well it's my suitcase sir. (Rodgers, 1982)

Question: Are there different types of psychosis?

A psychosis based on known brain pathology related to disease, gunshot wound, accident, or other physical causes is termed an **organic psychosis.** A psychosis based on unknown or psychological factors is called a **functional psychosis.** The possible causes of functional psychoses are explored later in this chapter.

Organic Psychosis One example of organic psychosis is **general paresis** (pah-REE-sis), which occurs in some cases of untreated syphilis. In advanced stages, syphilis attacks brain cells and gradually brings about a deterioration in behavior. A common sign of general paresis is a loss of inhibition that leads to inappropriate comments, shocking profanity, and obscenity—the "dirty old man" syndrome.

A second source of organic psychosis that gives special cause for alarm is lead and mercury poisoning (see Fig. 20-2). Although such poisoning is relatively rare, it can damage the brain and cause hallucinations, delusions, or a loss of emotional control. A particularly dangerous situation is found in old buildings, since many are painted with old-style leaded paints. Children who eat this paint may become psychotic or retarded. Other more subtle sources of lead can also be a problem. For example, children who live near congested streets may absorb lead from breathing automobile exhaust. Testing shows that high levels of lead are related to difficulties in thinking and attention at school (Yule et al., 1984).

Fig. 20-2 *The Mad Hatter, from Lewis Carroll's book,* Alice in Wonderland. *History provides numerous examples of psychosis caused by toxic chemicals. Carroll's Mad Hatter character is modeled after an occupational disease of the 18th and 19th centuries. In that era hatmakers were heavily exposed to mercury used in the preparation of felt. Consequently, many suffered brain damage and became psychotic, or "mad" (Kety, 1979).*

Box 20-1

Alzheimer's Disease

Alzheimer's disease (ALLS-hi-merz) is one of the most fearsome and devastating problems of aging. In addition to being the most common form of organic brain damage, it is the major cause of senility. Alzheimer's disease afflicts about 5 to 10 percent of all people over age 65, or about 2 million Americans.

Alzheimer's victims at first have difficulty remembering recent events. Then they slowly become more disoriented, suspicious, and confused. In time they lose the ability to work, cook, drive, or use tools. As their condition worsens, victims can no longer read, write, and calculate. Eventually they are mute, bedridden, and unable to walk, sit up, or smile (Roach, 1985).

Researchers are urgently seeking the causes of Alzheimer's disease. It is now known that selective damage to nerve cells in the brain is probably to blame. Especially important is the presence of unusual webs and tangles of nerve cells leading to and from the hippocampus—an area important for learning and memory (Chapter 3) (Hyman et al., 1984). Important changes also take place in an area called the nucleus basalis and in chemicals necessary for carrying messages within the brain (Coyle, Price, & DeLong, 1983).

By the year 2000 it is estimated that 1 of every 10 adults over 65 will be a victim of Alzheimer's disease (Shodell, 1984). At present, increased efforts are being made to find a cure for Alzheimer's. For some of us such efforts may prove to be a race against time.

Senile dementia Serious mental impairment in old age caused by physical deterioration of the brain.

Alzheimer's disease An age-related disease characterized by memory loss, mental confusion, and in its later stages by a nearly total loss of mental abilities.

Delusional disorder A psychotic state characterized by the presence of powerful delusions of grandeur or persecution.

Paranoid psychosis A delusional disorder centered especially on delusions of grandeur, jealousy, or persecution.

Delusions of grandeur False beliefs that one is a very important person or that one's actions are of earth-shaking importance.

Delusions of persecution False beliefs that one is being persecuted or cheated, injured, harassed, or plotted against by others.

Major mood disorders Disorders marked by lasting extremes of mood or emotion and often accompanied by psychotic symptoms.

Senile dementia is probably the most common organic problem. In senile dementia (duh-MEN-sha), there are marked disturbances in memory, reasoning, judgment, impulse control, and personality—a combination that usually leaves victims confused, suspicious, apathetic, or withdrawn. Senile dementia is closely associated with physical deterioration of the brain. Common causes are circulatory problems, repeated strokes, or general shrinkage and atrophy of the brain (see Box 20-1).

Three major types of functional psychoses are *delusional disorders*, *major mood disorders*, and *schizophrenia*. Information on each follows.

Delusional Disorders— An Enemy Behind Every Tree

People with **delusional disorders** usually do not suffer from hallucinations, emotional excesses, or personality disintegration. Even so, their break with reality is unmistakable. The main feature of this problem is the presence of deeply held false beliefs. The affected person's delusions may involve feelings of grandeur, jealousy, persecution, bodily complaints, or romantic attraction.

When delusions of grandeur, jealousy, or persecution are especially prominent a **paranoid psychosis** may be said to exist. Many self-styled reformers, absurdly jealous husbands or wives, crank letter writers, "communist hunters," and the like, suffer paranoid delusions.

Paranoid individuals often believe they are being cheated, spied upon, followed, poisoned, harassed, or that someone is plotting against them. Usually they are intensely suspicious, believing they must be on guard at all times. The evidence such individuals find to support their beliefs is usually unconvincing to others. Every detail of the paranoid's existence is woven into a personal version of "what's really going on." Buzzing during a telephone conversation may be interpreted as "someone listening," a stranger who comes to the door asking for directions may be seen as "really trying to get information," and so forth.

Persons suffering paranoid delusions are rarely treated because it is almost impossible to suggest to them that they need help. Anyone who does so simply becomes part of the "conspiracy" to "persecute" them. Paranoids frequently lead lonely, isolated, and humorless lives marked by constant suspicion and hostility toward others. While they are not necessarily dangerous to others, they can be. A person who believes that "the Mafia" is slowly closing in on him may be moved to violence by his irrational fears. A person standing at the door with his hand in his coat pocket could become the target of a paranoid attempt at "self-defense."

Because our next topics involve several new terms and ideas, let's stop for a quick Learning Check before proceeding.

Bipolar disorders Emotional disorders in which a person is manic (excited), or depressed, or swings between mania and depression. If a person appears only to be depressed, he or she must have had a manic episode at some other time before a bipolar disorder is indicated.

Manic Extremely excited, hyperactive, or irritable.

Unipolar disorder An emotional disorder in which a person experiences extended periods of deep depression but has no history of ever having been manic.

Major depression A severe and lasting state of depression accompanied by psychotic symptoms such as delusions and hallucinations.

Learning Check

1. A person who wrongly believes that his or her body is "rotting away" is suffering from:
   a. depressive delusions *b.* delusions of grandeur *c.* somatic delusions *d.* delusions of persecution
2. Persons suffering from psychoses are totally unresponsive to their surroundings. T or F?
3. A psychosis caused by lead poisoning would be termed a *functional* disorder. T or F?
4. Hallucinations are the principal feature of paranoid psychosis. T or F?
5. In *flat affect,* a sensory experience—such as hearing voices—occurs in the absence of a stimulus. T or F?
6. Alzheimer's disease is thought to be caused by lead poisoning in the hippocampus. T or F?

Answers: **1.** c **2.** F **3.** F **4.** F **5.** F **6.** F

Major Mood Disorders—Peaks and Valleys

About 14 percent of patients admitted to mental hospitals suffer from psychosis associated with major mood disorders.

Question: How do such problems differ from other types of psychosis?

In addition to the usual symptoms of psychosis, **major mood disorders** are marked by lasting extremes of emotion. Typically, one of the following patterns predominates: In **bipolar disorders,** persons go up and down emotionally. The individual may be continuously loud, elated, hyperactive, and energetic *(manic type)* or may swing between mania and deep depression *(mixed type)*. Even when a person is sad and guilt-ridden, the problem is considered a bipolar disorder *(depressive type)* if the person has ever been manic in the past (DSM-III-R, 1987). The person who only goes down emotionally, suffers from a **unipolar disorder.** If the psychotic depression occurs without any history of mania, it is called a **major depression.**

Endogenous depression Depression that appears to be produced from within (perhaps by chemical imbalances in the brain), rather than as a reaction to life events.

Schizophrenia A form of psychosis characterized by withdrawal from reality, apathy or inappropriate emotion, and, in many cases, delusions and hallucinations.

Schizotypal personality A nonpsychotic personality disorder involving withdrawal, social isolation, and odd behavior. A schizotypal personality resembles true schizophrenia but lacks symptoms of psychosis such as hallucinations or delusional thoughts.

Disorganized schizophrenia A type of schizophrenia marked by severe disorganization of thought, emotion, and behavior; schizophrenia involving personality disintegration.

Manic individuals throw themselves into fits of activity marked by extreme distractibility, rapid shifts in thoughts ("flights of ideas"), constant talking, and restless movement. In advanced stages manic behavior becomes more and more incoherent, agitated, and out of control. Eating or sleeping may be ignored until individuals push themselves into states of total delirium. (Such behavior accounts for public images of the "raving maniac.") This brief excerpt from a case history illustrates manic behavior:

> Her husband had returned home to find her twirling around the living room bizarrely draped in her wedding gown tied with a bathtowel and wearing a lampshade. She gaily greeted him, laughed with an ear-piercing shrillness, and invited him to stay for the exciting "coming-out" party she was giving. Strewn on the table were a thousand handwritten invitations signed with a flourish and addressed to such dignitaries as the President of the United States, the justices of the Supreme Court, the Emperor of Japan. She made incessant noises: singing her own ballads, shouting mottoes, which she devised, reciting limericks, making rhyming sounds, and yelling obscenities. (Suinn, 1970)

Depressive reactions show a reverse pattern, in which feelings of failure, sinfulness, worthlessness, and total despair predominate. The person becomes extremely subdued or withdrawn and may be intensely suicidal. Depressive reactions pose a serious threat to the survival of a disturbed individual. Suicide attempted during a psychotic depression is rarely a plea for help. Usually, the person intends to succeed and may give no prior warning (Fig. 20-3).

Manic and depressive states often appear to be interrelated in bipolar disorders. That is, when manic behavior occurs, it may still be a reaction to depression. The manic individual seeks to escape feelings of worthlessness and depression in an unending rush of activity.

Question: How do major mood disorders differ from the mood disorders described in Chapter 19?

Major mood disorders usually involve more severe emotional changes. Also, of course, the person's emotional excesses are often accompanied by psychotic delusions and hallucinations. As a further distinction, major mood disorders more often appear to be **endogenous** (en-DODGE-eh-nus: produced from within), rather than a reaction to external events.

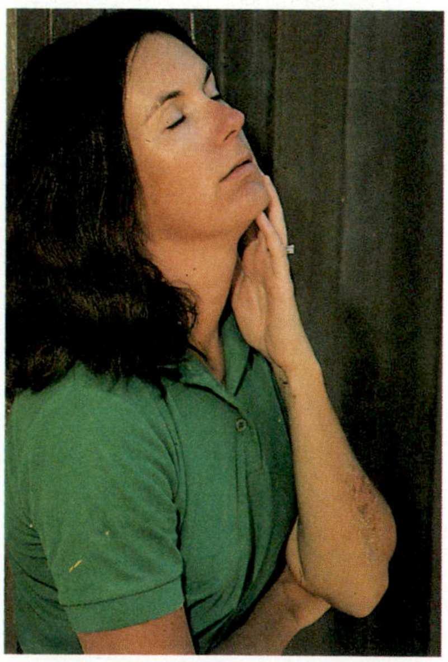

Fig. 20-3 *In a depressive psychosis, suicidal impulses can be intense and despair total.*

Schizophrenia—Shattered Reality

Approximately half of all admissions to mental hospitals are diagnosed as *schizophrenic*. **Schizophrenia** (SKIT-soh-FREE-nee-uh) is a major health problem: 1 person in 100 will become schizophrenic, and one-fourth of all hospital beds in the United States are occupied by schizophrenics. Most schizophrenics are young adults, but schizophrenia can occur at any age.

Question: Does a schizophrenic have two personalities?

Schizophrenia does not refer to having more than one personality. Recall from the previous chapter that multiple personality is a nonpsychotic, dissociative disorder. (Also, see Box 20-2.)

Box 20-2

"Schizophrenic" Confusion

"David was so warm and friendly yesterday but today he's as cold as ice. He's so schizophrenic sometimes I don't know how to react." Such statements illustrate how commonly the term *schizophrenic* is misused. As you know, even a person who displays two or more personalities (a dissociative disorder) is not "schizophrenic." Neither, of course, is a person like David, whose behavior is merely inconsistent.

On a more technical level, schizophrenia is often confused with a personality disorder that resembles it somewhat. Recall from Chapter 19 that personality disorders are maladaptive personality patterns. One such pattern is known as the **schizotypal personality.** Starting in adolescence, affected persons slowly become isolated and emotionally withdrawn. They are typically seen as listless and apathetic, and they are often considered "odd," "shiftless," or eccentric. Their behavior at times may be markedly peculiar (collecting garbage, eating cigarette butts, talking to themselves, and so forth).

Problems of this type do resemble some aspects of schizophrenia. But the schizotypal personality, like other personality disorders, does not involve a psychotic "break with reality." Many schizotypal personalities simply live colorless and isolated lives on the fringes of society as vagrants, eccentrics, derelicts, or prostitutes.

The word *schizophrenia* does mean "split mind," but this refers to a split between thought and emotion. In schizophrenia, emotions may become blunted or flat, or they may be very inappropriate. For example, a schizophrenic may smile or giggle when told his mother has died, or may describe her death with no visible emotion. In addition, schizophrenia is characterized by: withdrawal from contact with others and a loss of interest in external activities; a breakdown of personal habits and ability to deal with daily events; and the delusions, hallucinations, and thought abnormalities found in other types of psychosis. Schizophrenic delusions can be particularly bizarre. They often include the idea that the person's thoughts and actions are being controlled, that his or her thoughts are being broadcast so others can hear them, that thoughts have been "inserted" into the person's mind, or that thoughts have been removed.

Question: Is there more than one type of schizophrenia?

Schizophrenia may ultimately turn out to be a whole group of related disturbances. For now, we can identify four major types of schizophrenia.

Disorganized Schizophrenia **Disorganized schizophrenia** comes as close as any true psychiatric problem to matching the stereotyped images of "insanity" seen in movies and on television. In disorganized schizophrenia, personality disintegration is almost complete. The result is silliness, laughter, and bizarre or often obscene behavior (Fig. 20-4), as shown by this intake interview of a patient:

Dr. I am Dr. ______. I would like to know something more about you.
Patient You have a nasty mind. Lord!! Lord!! Cat's in a cradle.
Dr. Tell me, how do you feel?
Patient London's bell is a long, long dock. Hee! Hee! (Giggles uncontrollably)

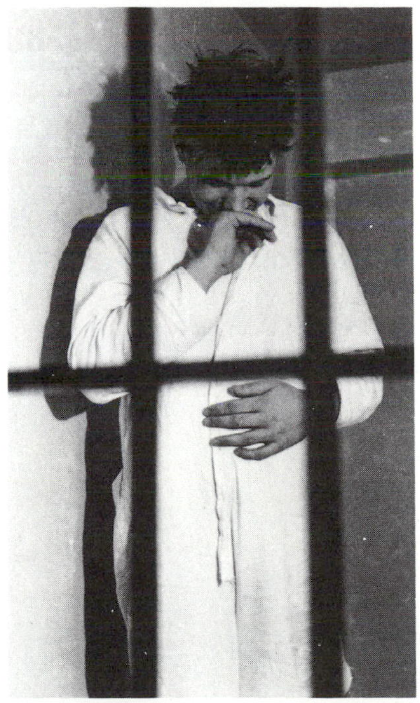

Fig. 20-4 *In disorganized schizophrenia, behavior is marked by silliness and laughter or bizarre and often obscene behavior.*

> *Dr.* Do you know where you are now?
> *Patient* D_____n! S_____t on you all who rip into my internals! The grudgerometer will take care of you all! (Shouting) I am the Queen, see my magic. I shall turn you all into smidgelings forever!
> *Dr.* Your husband is concerned about you. Do you know his name?
> *Patient* (Stands, walks to and faces the wall) Who am I, who are we, who are you, who are they (Turns) I . . . I . . . I . . . I! (Makes grotesque faces)
>
> Edna was placed in the women's ward where she proceeded to masturbate. She always sat in a chosen spot and in a chosen way, with her feet propped under her. Occasionally, she would scream or shout obscenities. At other times, she giggled to herself. She was known to attack other patients. She began to complain that her uterus was attached to a "pipeline to the Kremlin" and that she was being "infernally invaded" by Communism. (Suinn, 1975)

Disorganized schizophrenia typically develops in early adolescence or young adulthood and is often preceded by serious personality disorganization in earlier years. Chances of improvement are limited, and social impairment is usually extreme (DSM-III-R, 1987).

Catatonic Schizophrenia The catatonic seems to be in a state of total panic. This brings about a stuporous condition in which odd positions may be held for hours or even days. Sometimes, a condition called *waxy flexibility* occurs. At such times the catatonic can be arranged into any position like a mannequin. These periods of immobility may be similar to the tendency to "freeze" at times of great emergency or panic. There is evidence that catatonic individuals are struggling desperately to control their inner turmoil, because stupor may occasionally give way to outbursts of agitated and sometimes violent behavior. The following excerpt describes a **catatonic episode:**

> Manuel appeared to be physically healthy upon examination. Yet he did not regain his awareness of his surroundings. He remained motionless, speechless, and seemingly unconscious. One evening an aide turned him on his side to straighten out the sheet, was called away to tend another patient, and forgot to return. Manuel was found the next morning, still on his side, his arm tucked under his body, as he had been left the night before. His arm was turning blue from lack of circulation but he seemed to be experiencing no discomfort. Further examination confirmed that he was in a state of waxy flexibility. (Suinn, 1975)

Notice that, in addition to his other problems, Manuel was unable to talk. *Mutism* plus a marked decrease in responsiveness to the environment make the catatonic patient difficult to reach. Fortunately, this bizarre form of schizophrenia is rare in Europe and North America.

Paranoid Schizophrenia Paranoid schizophrenia is the most common schizophrenic disorder. **Paranoid schizophrenia,** like delusional disorders, centers around delusions of grandeur and persecution, but in paranoid schizophrenia there is personality disintegration that is not evident in paranoid psychosis. The paranoid schizophrenic also has hallucinations and delusions that are more fragmented and unconvincing than those seen in delusional disorders.

Thinking that their minds are being controlled by god, the government, or "cosmic rays from space," or that someone is trying to poison them, paranoid schizophrenics may feel forced into violence to "protect" themselves. Do you remember James Huberty, who brutally murdered 21 people at a fast-food restaurant in San Ysidro, California, in 1984? Some observers believe that Huberty was a paranoid schizophrenic who felt persecuted and cheated by life. Shortly before he announced to his wife that he was "Going hunting humans," Huberty had been hearing hallucinated voices.

Undifferentiated Schizophrenia The three "types" of schizophrenia just described occur most often in textbooks. In reality there is considerable overlap among the types, and a real patient may shift from one pattern of behavior to another at different times. Many patients, therefore, are simply classified as suffering from **undifferentiated schizophrenia.**

The diagnosis of schizophrenia is fairly subjective and open to considerable error (see this chapter's Applications) (McCabe, 1976). All things considered, however, there is no doubt that schizophrenia is real or that it is a major challenge to medical and psychological researchers.

Catatonic schizophrenia A type of schizophrenia involving occasional outbursts of agitated or violent behavior, but more often, a mute and stuporous condition of immobility and unresponsiveness.

Catatonic episode Period of extreme stupor, immobility, and unresponsiveness.

Paranoid schizophrenia A type of schizophrenia in which delusions of grandeur or persecution are prominent.

Undifferentiated schizophrenia Schizophrenia that does not fit any other distinct subtype.

Psychological trauma A psychological injury or shock, such as that caused by violence, abuse, neglect, separation, and so forth.

Disturbed family environment Stressful or unhealthy family relationships, communication patterns, and emotional atmosphere.

Double-bind communication A message that contradicts itself and places the person who receives it in an unsolvable conflict.

The Causes of Schizophrenia—An Unsolved Riddle

Former British Prime Minister Winston Churchill once described a question that perplexed him as "a riddle wrapped in a mystery inside an enigma." The same words might be used to describe the causes of schizophrenia, the most common and devastating psychosis.

Question: What do we know about the causes of schizophrenia?

Environment Some psychologists suspect that early **psychological trauma** may contribute to the later development of schizophrenia. Case studies of schizophrenia often show its victims were exposed to violence, sexual abuse, death, divorce, or separation in childhood. In general, there seems to be a greater than average degree of stress in the childhood of those who develop schizophrenia. A question that remains unanswered is why childhood trauma leaves some individuals emotionally crippled and others not.

Many psychologists theorize that a **disturbed family environment** is a causal factor in schizophrenia. For example, one intriguing theory is that the schizophrenic is *forced* to escape into psychosis by being placed in what British psychiatrist R. D. Laing (1967, 1970) calls a *position of checkmate.* This idea can be illustrated by imagining that someone is standing over you with a large stick. This person gives you these instructions:

> In a moment I'm going to ask you if this stick is real. If you say yes, I will hit you with it. If you say no, then I will hit you with it. If you refuse to answer, I will hit you with it.

Your reaction to this dilemma might very well be stammering, emotion, and a defensive crouch. To a person outside the situation your reactions might look "crazy" (Fig. 20-5). Similarly, Laing believes that the schizophrenic's strange thoughts and behavior are really an adaptation to an impossible environment. Laing and others also believe the families of schizophrenics constantly engage in **double-bind communication.**

Biochemical abnormality A disturbance of the body's chemical systems, especially in brain chemicals or neurotransmitters.

Dopamine An important transmitter substance found in the brain, especially in the limbic system, an area associated with emotional response.

A double-bind message is one that places the listener in an unsolvable conflict like that just posed. For example, the mother of a schizophrenic might issue this typical double-bind message, "You don't really love me; you're only pretending you do." This statement asks for a show of love but makes showing love impossible. Anything the person does becomes "wrong."

Although environmental explanations are attractive, they are not enough to account for schizophrenia. For example, when the children of schizophrenic parents are raised away from their chaotic home environments, they are still likely to become psychotic (Page, 1971).

Question: Does that mean that heredity is a factor in schizophrenia?

Heredity Evidence for heredity as a factor in schizophrenia has been growing ever stronger in recent years. It now appears that some individuals inherit a *potential* for developing schizophrenia.

Question: How can that be shown?

Here is a prime example: If one identical twin becomes schizophrenic (remember, identical twins have identical genes), then the other twin has a *46 percent* chance of also becoming schizophrenic (Nicol & Gottesman, 1983). There is even a case on record of *four* identical quadruplets *all* developing schizophrenia (Rosenthal & Quinn, 1977). (See Box 20-3.)

Question: What about other family relationships?

If *both* parents are schizophrenic, a child again has a 46 percent chance of developing the disorder; persons with a brother or sister and one parent who are schizophrenic run a 17 percent risk; persons with a schizophrenic brother or sister

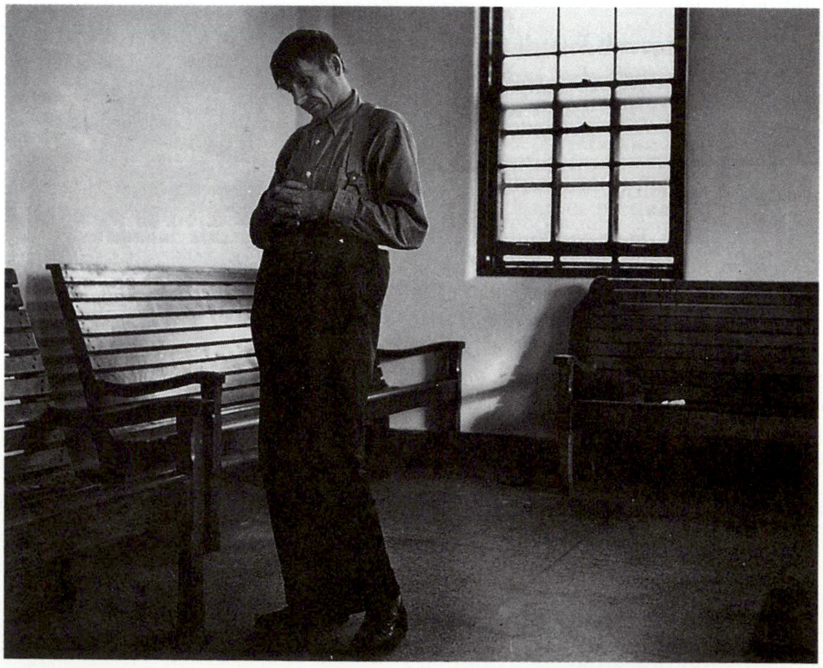

Fig. 20-5 *Can the catatonic's rigid postures and stupor be understood in terms of abnormal body chemistry? Environment? Heredity?*

Box 20-3

The Genain Sisters—Trouble Times Four

By the time the Genain quadruplets reached high school, they began to act strangely. Hester broke light bulbs and tore buttons off her clothes. By age 20 Nora moaned at meals and complained that the bones in her neck were slipping. At night she stood on her knees and elbows in bed until they bled. At age 22 Iris quit her job, and "went to pieces." She screamed, drooled at meals, and talked about hearing voices. Myra, who was the fourth identical quad, panicked easily and couldn't be reassured but did not actually break down until age 24 (Rosenthal, 1963).

In addition to sharing identical heredity, the Genain sisters—Nora, Iris, Myra, and Hester—have something else in common: All four became schizophrenic before age 25. The women, who are now in their fifties, have been in and out of mental hospitals all their lives.

You may be tempted immediately to assume that the Genain quads' psychoses were caused by heredity. However, it would be a mistake to overlook the nightmarish family life in which the girls grew up. Mr. Genain was an alcoholic who hounded, spied on, terrorized, and sexually molested the girls. Mrs. Genain added her own bizarre thinking and sexual preoccupations to the family's already warped relationships. To put it mildly, the girls' mother and father failed spectacularly as parents. In the final analysis, it seems that both heredity and an unhealthy environment led to the Genain sisters' problems (Carson, Butcher, & Coleman, 1988).

In sum, it appears that heredity may set higher or lower thresholds for psychosis. Whether a person "crosses the line" and becomes actively disturbed, however, may depend on the kind of stresses he or she is exposed to.

have a 10 percent chance; and for *fraternal* twins the chance of mutual schizophrenia is about 14 percent (Nicol & Gottesman, 1983).

These figures can be compared with the risk for the population in general, which is 1 percent (Fig. 20-6). Comparisons such as these, and a variety of other studies, have shown that schizophrenia is more common among close relatives than distant relatives and that it tends to run in families (Gottesman & Shields, 1982).

Question: How could someone inherit a susceptibility to schizophrenia?

Body Chemistry LSD, PCP (angel dust), and similar drugs produce effects that partially mimic the symptoms of psychosis. Also, the same drugs (phenothiazines) that are used to treat an LSD overdose are effective in treating schizophrenia (Mandell et al., 1972). Such similarities have suggested to many scientists that psychosis may be based on **biochemical abnormalities** that cause the body to produce some substance similar to a *psychedelic* (mind-altering) drug. At present the most likely candidate is **dopamine** (DOPE-ah-meen), an important chemical messenger in the brain (Fig. 20-7).

Question: How does dopamine fit into the picture?

By far the most exciting discovery in recent years is the close link between dopamine and schizophrenia. Many researchers now believe that schizophrenia is di-

Fig. 20-6 *Lifetime risk of developing schizophrenia is related to how closely a person is genetically related to a schizophrenic. A shared environment also increases the risk (Nicol & Gottesman, 1983). (Data from Gottesman & Shields, 1982)*

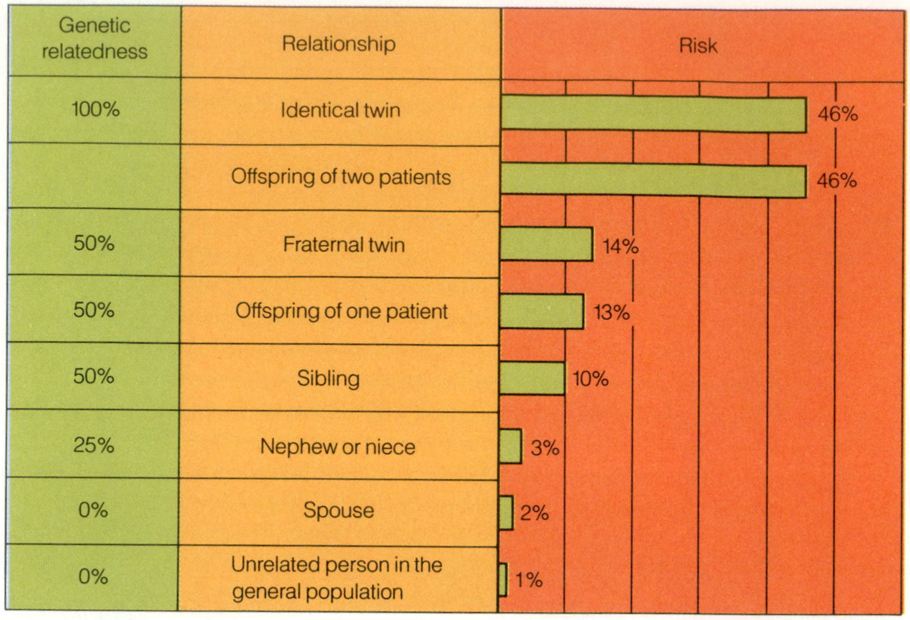

Antipsychotic drug Any drug that tends to eliminate various symptoms of psychosis.

Dopamine receptors Areas on certain nerve cells that are sensitive to dopamine and that activate the nerve cell when dopamine is present.

CT scan Computed tomography scan; a computer-enhanced X-ray image of the brain.

rectly related to overactivity in brain dopamine systems (Barchas et al., 1978; Nicol & Gottesman, 1983).

Early hints of a dopamine-psychosis link came when researchers noted that large doses of amphetamines (speed) produce symptoms that are almost identical to paranoid schizophrenia. Amphetamines, it turns out, also raise brain dopamine levels. Another piece of the puzzle fell into place when it was discovered that all major *antipsychotic* drugs *block* the action of dopamine at receptor areas in the brain (Iversen, 1979).

Question: Then is schizophrenia a "dopamine high"?

For a time it seemed so. But no extra or abnormal amounts of dopamine could be found in the brains of schizophrenics (Davis, 1978). So much for the dopamine theory!

But wait. Our story is not over. In a dramatic breakthrough a team of researchers at the University of Toronto found nearly *double* the normal number of dopamine receptors in the brains of schizophrenics. These extra receptors exist in especially large numbers in the limbic system (a major emotional system of the brain) (Lee & Seeman, 1980).

Many scientists now believe that dopamine activation triggers a flood of unrelated thoughts, feelings, and perceptions, and directly accounts for the voices, hallucinations, delusions, and other disturbances of schizophrenia (Iversen, 1979). Because of the extra receptors, schizophrenics may get psychedelic effects from normal levels of dopamine in the brain. The implication of this, and related research on other brain chemicals, is that schizophrenics may be on a sort of drug trip caused by their own bodies (Bushbaum & Haier, 1982; Hoffer, 1972).

Medical researchers have long hoped for a way to directly observe the schizophrenic brain. Two new medical techniques are now making this possible. One, called a **CT scan**, provides an X-ray picture of the brain. (CT stands for computed

Fig. 20-7 *This series of paintings by Louis Wain reflects a troubled personality. Wain was a British illustrator who became schizophrenic in middle age. As Wain's psychosis progressed, his cat paintings became highly abstract and fragmented. In many ways Wain's paintings resemble the perceptual changes caused by psychedelic drugs such as mescaline and LSD. Recent research suggests that psychosis may, in fact, be the result of mind-altering changes in brain chemistry. (Derik Bayes/Courtesy* Guttman-Maclay Life Picture *Service)*

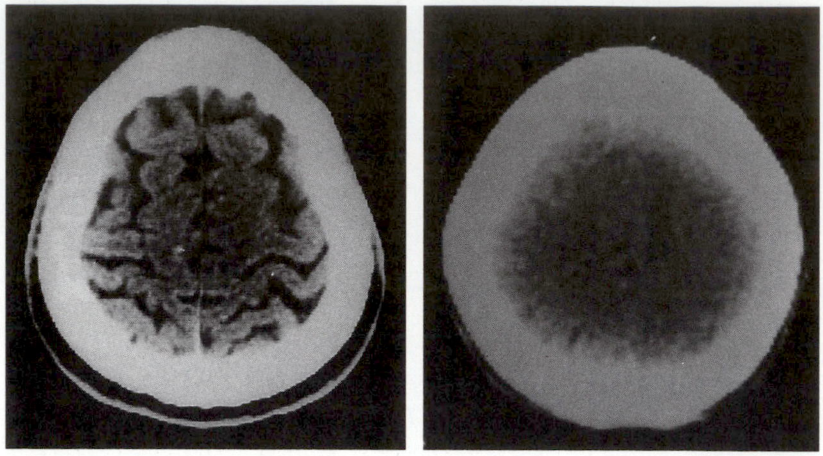

Fig. 20-8 (left) *CT scan of would-be presidential assassin John Hinkley, Jr., taken when he was 25. The X-ray image shows widened fissures in the wrinkled surface of Hinkley's brain.* (right) *CT scan of a normal 25-year-old's brain. In most young adults, the surface folds of the brain are pressed together too tightly to be seen. As a person ages, surface folds of the brain normally become more visible. Pronounced brain fissuring in young adults may be a sign of schizophrenia, chronic alcoholism, or other problems (McKean, 1982).*

tomography, or computer-enhanced X-ray images.) Figure 20-8 shows a CT scan of John Hinkley, Jr.,'s brain. Hinkley, you may recall, shot President Ronald Reagan and three other men in 1981. In the ensuing trial Hinkley was judged insane.

As you can see, Hinkley's brain differs from the norm. Specifically, it has wide surface fissuring and enlarged ventricles (fluid-filled spaces within the brain). Similar changes, which are normal in older people, are found in about 1 out of 10 young schizophrenics. Although the meaning of such changes is still in doubt, the CT scan promises to aid in diagnosing schizophrenia and to provide new information on its causes (McKean, 1982).

A second new technique, called a **PET scan,** provides an image of brain *activity*. (PET stands for positron emission tomography.) A PET scan is made by injecting a radioactive sugar solution into a vein. When the sugar reaches the brain, a device measures how much is used in each area. This information is then translated into a colored map, or scan, of brain activity (Fig. 20-9). Researchers are already finding patterns in such scans that are consistently linked with schizo-

Fig. 20-9 *Positron emission tomography produces PET scans of the human brain. In the scans shown here, red, pink, and orange indicate lower levels of brain activity; white and blue indicate higher activity levels. Notice that activity in the schizophrenic brain is quite low in the frontal lobes (top area of each scan). Activity in the manic-depressive brain is low in the left brain hemisphere and high in the right brain hemisphere. Researchers are trying to identify consistent patterns like these to aid diagnosis of mental disorder.*

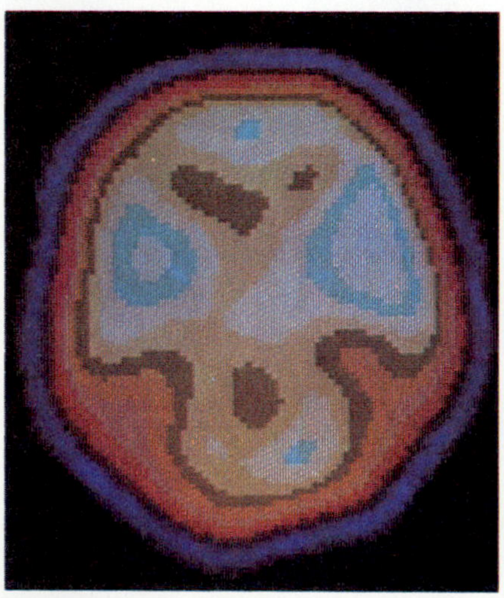
NORMAL

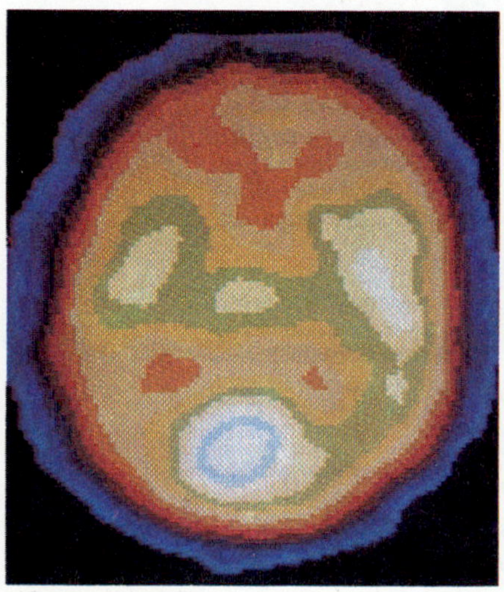
SCHIZOPHRENIC

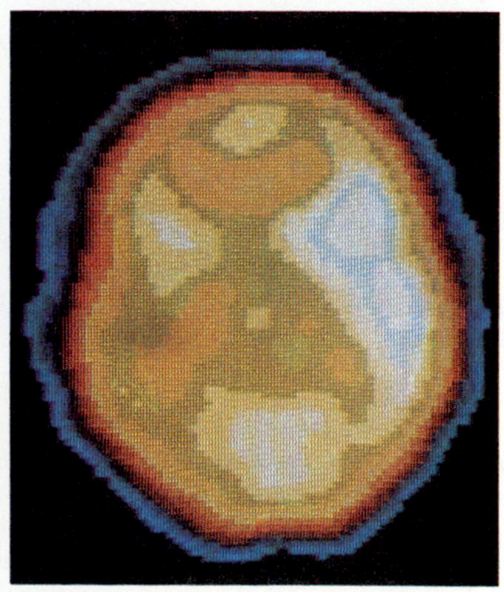
MANIC-DEPRESSIVE

phrenia, affective disorders, and other problems. Some researchers believe that in the future PET scans will be routinely used to diagnose schizophrenia (Landis, 1980). For now, PET scans show that there is a clear difference between normal and schizophrenic brain activity.

PET scan Positron emission tomography; a colored image of brain areas and their activity levels, as shown by concentrations of radioactive sugar in each area.

Summary In summary, the emerging picture of psychosis takes this form: *Anyone* subjected to enough stress may be pushed to a psychotic break, but some people inherit a difference in body chemistry or brain structure that makes them more susceptible. Thus, the right combination of inherited potential and environmental stress brings about changes in brain chemicals or generates mind-altering substances in the body (Gottesman & Shields, 1982).

Ultimately, distinctions between organic and functional psychoses may be dropped, and treatment of major disturbances may become more chemical than psychological. But for now psychosis remains "a riddle wrapped in a mystery inside an enigma." Let us hope the recent advances that we have so briefly explored are as promising as they appear to be.

Learning Check

Match the following:

_____ **1.** Schizotypal personality

_____ **2.** Disorganized schizophrenia

_____ **3.** Catatonic schizophrenia

_____ **4.** Paranoid schizophrenia

_____ **5.** Major mood disorders

A. Manic or depressive behavior
B. Mutism, odd postures, immobility
C. Nonpsychotic disorder
D. Silliness, disorganization, bizarre behavior
E. Delusions of grandeur or persecution

6. Schizophrenics have two or more personalities. T or F?

7. R. D. Laing attributes psychotic behavior to a "crazy" or impossible environment, often created in the home by:
a. manic parents *b.* schizoaffective interactions *c.* psychedelic interactions *d.* double-bind communication

8. The ____________ ____________ of a schizophrenic person runs a 46 percent chance of also becoming psychotic.

9. Abnormally high numbers of noradrenaline receptors have been found in the brains of schizophrenics. T or F?

10. Enlarged surface fissures and ventricles, as revealed by CT scans, are found only in the brains of chronic schizophrenics. T or F?

Answers: **1.** C **2.** D **3.** B **4.** E **5.** A **6.** F **7.** *d* **8.** identical twin **9.** F (dopamine receptors) **10.** F

Treatment—Medical Approaches

Question: Is psychosis incurable? If a person's symptoms temporarily disappear, can an unexpected relapse occur?

An organic psychosis cannot be "cured" in the usual sense, but it may be controlled with drugs and other techniques. With functional psychoses the outlook is

Psychotherapy Any form of psychological treatment for behavioral or emotional disorders. Most often refers to verbal interaction between trained mental health professionals and their clients.

Somatic therapy Any therapy directly involving bodily processes; for example, drug therapy, electroconvulsive therapy, or psychosurgery.

Chemotherapy Use of psychoactive drugs to treat mental or emotional disturbances.

Minor tranquilizers Drugs (such as Valium) that produce relaxation or reduce anxiety.

Energizers Mood-elevating drugs.

Major tranquilizers (antipsychotics) Drugs that, in addition to having tranquilizing properties, also serve as antipsychotics by reducing hallucinations and delusional thinking.

Tardive dyskinesia A neurological disorder associated with excessive use of major tranquilizers; characterized by rhythmic facial movements and unusual movements of the arms and legs.

Electroconvulsive therapy (ECT) A medical treatment for severe depression, consisting of an electric shock passed directly through the brain, which produces a convulsion.

still rather negative, but many people are *permanently* cured. It is wrong to fear "former mental patients" or to exclude them from work, friendships, or other social situations. A psychotic episode does not inevitably lead to a lifelong maladjustment, but too often it leads to rejection based on groundless fears.

Question: What can be done about psychosis?

Two basic forms of treatment can be distinguished. The first, called **psychotherapy,** can be described as two people talking about one person's problems. Psychotherapy is a special relationship between a therapist and a person in trouble. Psychotherapy is applied to everything from a brief crisis to a full-scale psychosis. Because approaches currently in use are so varied, a complete discussion of psychotherapy is found in the next two chapters.

A second major approach to treatment is **somatic** (bodily) **therapy.** The principal somatic treatments are *chemotherapy*, *electroconvulsive therapy*, and *psychosurgery*. Somatic therapy is often done in the context of psychiatric *hospitalization*. All of the somatic approaches have a distinct medical slant, and they are used primarily to treat psychoses. For these reasons, somatic therapy provides an appropriate conclusion to our discussion of psychosis.

Drugs The atmosphere in mental hospitals changed radically in the mid-1950s with the widespread adoption of chemotherapy (KEE-mo-therapy). **Chemotherapy** is the use of drugs or chemical substances to alleviate the symptoms of emotional disturbance. Drugs may relieve the anxiety attacks and other discomforts of nonpsychotic disorders, but they are more frequently used to combat psychosis. Drugs such as Thorazine are credited with emptying mental hospitals, reducing the hospital population from a peak of 560,000 to fewer than 200,000 patients in barely a generation.

Question: What types of drugs are used in chemotherapy?

The three major classes of drugs are: *minor tranquilizers*, *major tranquilizers (antipsychotics)*, and *energizers*. **Minor tranquilizers** calm anxious or agitated persons; **antipsychotics** control hallucinations and other symptoms of psychosis; and **energizers** improve the mood of those who are depressed.

Question: Are drugs a valid approach to treatment?

Drugs have greatly improved the chances for recovery from a psychiatric disorder. They have shortened the length of hospital stays and have made it possible for more individuals to be returned to the community where they may be treated on an outpatient basis.

Few experts would argue for a return to the conditions that existed before chemotherapy became available. But there are some drawbacks. First of all, drugs do not *cure* mental illness. In many instances, they only temporarily relieve symptoms. Such relief may allow patients to benefit more fully from psychotherapy and other attempts to help them, but drugs alone do not remove underlying problems. As a matter of fact, patients may separate temporary improvement caused by a drug from improvement they consider genuine. As one patient told the author, "The drugs made me talk more and seem happy, but I knew I really wasn't."

The use of drugs also raises the issue of balancing benefits against possible side effects. For example, as many as 10 percent of patients taking major tranquilizers for extended periods develop ***tardive dyskinesia*** (TARD-iv dis-cah-NEE-zyah). In this neurological condition patients develop rhythmical facial and mouth movements, as well as unusual movements of the limbs and other parts of the body.

Perhaps the most valid criticism of chemotherapy is the simple observation that it is often overused. Apparently the temptation to reach for the prescription pad is great. Most observers agree that too many drugs are being given to too many people. Researcher David Rosenhan (see the Applications section of this chapter) believes that drugs are often used to keep patients docile and easy to manage. Many critics believe that the locks that came off the doors of old-style asylums have simply been replaced by "chemical locks." In the long run, concern over side effects and the overuse of drugs may temper the popularity of chemotherapy. But where psychosis is concerned, drugs are usually helpful and will remain a major mode of treatment.

Shock **Electroconvulsive therapy (ECT)** is a rather drastic medical treatment for depression. In the usual ECT session a 150-volt electrical current is passed through the brain for slightly less than a second (Fig. 20-10). The current triggers a convulsion and causes the patient to lose consciousness for a short time. Muscle relaxants and sedative drugs are given before ECT to soften its impact. Treatments are administered in a series of 6 to 8 sessions spread over 3 to 4 weeks. There is some loss of memory for the period of treatments, but memory usually returns within 6 months.

Question: How does shock help?

Actually, it is the seizure activity that is considered helpful. Proponents of ECT claim that shock-induced seizures alter the biochemical balance in the brain, bringing an end to severe depression and suicidal or self-destructive behavior (Frankl, 1977).

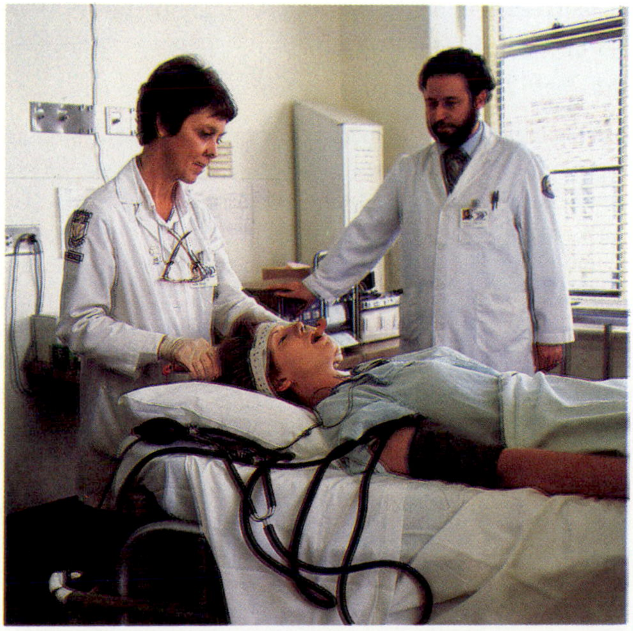

Fig. 20-10 *In electroconvulsive therapy, electrodes are attached to the head, and a brief electrical current is passed through the brain. ECT is used in the treatment of severe depression.*

Psychosurgery Any surgical alteration of the brain designed to bring about desirable behavioral or emotional changes.

Prefrontal lobotomy An antiquated form of psychosurgery in which portions of the frontal lobes of the brain were destroyed or in which major fiber tracts to the frontal lobes were cut.

Deep lesioning A type of psychosurgery in which small areas deep within the brain are destroyed with an electrical current passed from the tip of an electrode (needle) lowered into the target area.

Mental hospitalization Confinement to a protected environment that provides various forms of therapy for mental, emotional, and behavioral problems.

Half-way house A facility within the community that provides housing and supervision for individuals making the transition from living in an institution (mental hospital, prison, and so forth) to independent living in the community.

Community mental health center A facility offering a wide range of mental health services, such as counseling, consultation, and crisis intervention. Community mental health centers also emphasize the prevention of mental health problems.

Many people consider ECT a distasteful procedure, and not all professionals support its use. In fact, a heated debate has raged over the effectiveness of ECT and the seriousness of its side effects. Critics claim that memory losses caused by ECT are often permanent and that there is evidence of occasional brain damage (Friedberg, 1977). Others have charged that ECT is no more effective than drugs and that it is used for all types of problems, even though it is only effective for depression (Costello, 1976; Turek & Hanlon, 1977).

Defenders of ECT argue that evidence of damage comes mainly from studies done before sedation, muscle relaxants, and the use of oxygen reduced chances of injury. And recently there have been reports that if electrodes are applied to only one side of the head, memory loss is greatly reduced (Rosenberg & Pettinati, 1984). Those who support ECT view it as being like any other medical treatment: It involves calculated risks (Fink, 1977; Weiner, 1984).

As is the case with chemotherapy, the major problem with ECT seems to lie in overuse and misuse. Some patients have had literally hundreds of shock treatments and have suffered damage in the process. In spite of such abuses, ECT, when carefully used, is still considered a valid treatment for selected cases of depression—especially when it brings a rapid end to wildly self-destructive behavior.

Surgery The most extreme biological treatment is **psychosurgery,** a general term applied to any surgical alteration of the brain. The best known psychosurgery is the *lobotomy*. In the **prefrontal lobotomy** and related techniques, the frontal lobes are disconnected from other areas of the brain. The original goal of this procedure was to calm persons who had not responded to any other type of treatment.

When the lobotomy was first introduced in the early 1950s, there were enthusiastic claims for its success. But later studies suggest that some patients were calmed, some showed no change, and some became "vegetables." Lobotomies also caused a high rate of undesirable side effects, such as seizures, extreme lack of emotional response, and even stupor (Barahal, 1958; Valenstein, 1980). As such problems became apparent, the lobotomy was abandoned.

Question: To what extent is psychosurgery used now?

Psychosurgery is still considered a valid treatment by many neurosurgeons. However, most now use sophisticated **deep lesioning** techniques. In this approach small target areas in the brain's interior are destroyed. The appeal of deep lesioning is that it can have fairly specific effects. For instance, a patient with uncontrollable aggressive impulses may be calmed by psychosurgery (Valenstein, 1980).

It is worth remembering that all forms of psychosurgery are *irreversible*. A drug can be given or taken away. You can't take back psychosurgery. Many critics argue that psychosurgery should be banned altogether. Others continue to report success with psychosurgical procedures (Mitchell-Heggs et al., 1976). All things considered, it is perhaps most accurate, even after decades of use, to describe psychosurgery as an "experimental" technique (Perkoff, 1980).

Hospitalization Somatic therapy, psychotherapy, and other techniques may require a special setting or special control for a period of time. Traditionally, this has meant a trip to a psychiatric hospital or state institution. **Hospitalization** by itself may be considered a form of treatment since it removes a troubled individual from situations that may be provoking or maintaining the problem.

At its best the hospital is a sanctuary—a controlled environment in which diagnosis, support, refuge, and psychotherapy are provided (Bachrach, 1984). At worst an institution can be a brutalizing experience that leaves a person less prepared to face the world than before (Fig. 20-11).

Fig. 20-11 *Depending on the quality of the institution, hospitalization may be a refuge or a brutalizing experience. Many state "asylums" or mental hospitals are antiquated and in need of drastic improvement.*

In the last 20 years the resident population in large mental hospitals throughout the United States has been reduced by two-thirds. This reduction is largely due to policies designed to improve the odds that hospitalization will be constructive.

Ideally, hospitals are used as a last resort after other forms of treatment within the community have been exhausted. Recent research indicates that most psychiatric patients do as well with short-term hospitalization (3 to 4 weeks) as they do with longer periods (3 to 4 months) (Glick et al., 1979). In view of this, hospital stays are now held to a minimum through use of *revolving-door* policies, in which patients are released as soon as possible and readmitted only if necessary. Also, modern hospitals provide recreation and rehabilitation to help end an old problem—the tendency for many patients to become so "institutionalized" that they have difficulty returning to the community. Also helpful are halfway houses and voluntary support groups that ease the patient's return to the community.

Question: How successful have such policies been?

In truth their success has been limited. Many states have welcomed a reduction in mental hospital populations as a way to save money. The upsetting result is that many chronic patients are being discharged to a lonely existence in hostile communities without adequate care. A large percentage of homeless persons interviewed recently at an emergency shelter had psychiatric problems (Bassuk, Rubin, & Lauriat, 1984). In short, critics point out that the revolving door turns inward, too. Patients who move from hospitalization to unemployment and social isolation all too often must return for further treatment (Goering et al., 1984).

Large mental hospitals may no longer be warehouses for society's unwanted, but many former patients are no better off leading bleak lives in nursing homes, single-room hotels, or board and care homes (Bassuk & Gerson, 1978). Ironically, high-quality psychological and psychiatric care is available in almost every community. As much as anything, a simple lack of sufficient funding prevents large numbers of people from getting the care they need. It would be especially helpful if better rehabilitation programs were offered as a follow-up treatment (Goering et al., 1984).

Community Mental Health Programs—Hope and Help for Many

The creation of community mental health centers has been a bright spot in mental health care. **Community mental health centers** de-emphasize hospitalization and seek new answers to mental health problems through short-term treatment, outpatient care, and crisis or emergency services (Perlmutter & Silverman, 1972).

If it is like most, the primary aim of the mental health center in your community is to directly aid troubled citizens. The second goal of mental health

Paraprofessional An individual who works in a near-professional capacity under the supervision of a more highly trained person.

centers is *prevention*. Consultation, education, and crisis intervention are used to end or prevent problems before they become serious. Also, some centers attempt to raise the general level of mental health in target areas by combating problems such as unemployment, delinquency, and drug abuse.

Question: How have community mental health centers fared in meeting their goals?

In practice they have concentrated much more on providing clinical services than they have on prevention (Bloom & Parad, 1977). This situation appears to be primarily the result of wavering government support (translation: money).

Overall, community mental health centers have succeeded in making mental health services more accessible than ever before. Many of their programs are made possible by **paraprofessionals,** individuals who work under the supervision of more highly trained staff. Some paraprofessionals are ex-addicts, ex-alcoholics, or ex-patients who have "been there." Many more are persons (paid or volunteer) who have skills in tutoring, crafts, counseling, or simply are warm, empathetic, and skilled at communication. There is a severe shortage of people working in mental health care. The contributions of paraprofessionals will undoubtedly continue to grow. A career as a paraprofessional should not be overlooked by students planning to work in the field of mental health (see Appendix A).

Learning Check

1. The use of chemotherapy has required longer hospital stays because drugs can be given only under hospital supervision. T or F?
2. ECT is a modern form of chemotherapy. T or F?
3. Electroconvulsive therapy is mainly used as a treatment for depression. T or F?
4. Tardive dyskinesia is a possible complication in long-term use of:
   a. major tranquilizers *b.* minor tranquilizers *c.* energizers *d.* ECT
5. Currently, the frontal lobotomy is the most widely used form of psychosurgery. T or F?
6. Psychosurgery can be reversed if it is unsuccessful. T or F?
7. Whenever possible, the community mental health movement emphasizes prevention of mental health problems. T or F?
8. Research indicates that relatively short periods of psychiatric hospitalization are as beneficial as long-term hospital stays. T or F?

Answers: **1.** F **2.** F **3.** T **4.** *a* **5.** F **6.** F **7.** T **8.** T

Applications

On Being Sane in Insane Places

Question: Suppose someone were committed to a psychiatric hospital by accident. Would the staff notice? Would the person be able to get out?

David Rosenhan of Stanford University set out to answer these questions and another: "How accurately do psychiatric hospitals distinguish between people who are psychotic and those who are healthy?"

To find out, Rosenhan and several colleagues had themselves committed (Rosenhan, 1973). Entrance to mental hospitals was gained by faking only one symptom: Rosenhan and the others complained of hearing voices that said "empty," "hollow," and "thud." In 11 out of 12 tries, they were admitted with a diagnosis of schizophrenia.

Pseudo-patients After being admitted, these *pseudo-patients* dropped all pretense of mental illness. Yet, even though they acted completely normal, none of the researchers was ever recognized by hospital *staff* as a phony patient. Other patients were not so easily fooled. It was not unusual for a real patient to say to one of the researchers, "You're not crazy, you're checking up on the hospital!" or, "You're a journalist."

Rosenhan and the others spent from 1 to 7 weeks in hospitals before being discharged. The hospitals ranged from very modern and plush to ancient and shoddy. No matter how good the facilities or the hospital's reputation, Rosenhan found some disturbing conditions.

Contact between staff and patients was very limited and was sometimes marked by fear or hostility. It was found that attendants and staff only spent an average of 11.3 percent of their time out of the "cage," the glassed-in central compartment in the ward.

It was not unusual for the morning attendants to wake patients with a hostile call of: "Come on, you m_____ f_____s, out of bed!" When patients tried to talk with staff, they were often ignored or received strange replies. One pseudo-patient approached a psychiatrist and politely asked when he might get grounds privileges. The doctor's reply was "Good morning, Dave. How are you today?"

Rosenhan found that therapy other than drugs was very limited. Daily contact of patients with psychiatrists, psychologists, or physicians averaged about 7 *minutes*. On the other hand, the researchers were given a total of 2100 pills to swallow. (They took only 2 of these; the rest were pocketed or flushed down the toilet.)

Nonpersons Patients tended to be treated as nonpersons. A nurse unbuttoned her uniform to adjust her bra in front of a roomful of male patients. She was not being sexy; she just didn't consider the patients men. A patient would often be discussed by the staff while the patient was standing nearby. It was as if patients were invisible.

A situation that sums up Rosenhan's findings better than any other is his notetaking. Rosenhan began taking notes by carefully jotting things on a small piece of paper hidden in his hand. He learned quickly that hiding was totally unnecessary. He was soon walking around with a clipboard and notepads, recording observations and collecting data.

No one questioned this behavior. Notetaking was simply seen as a symptom of his "illness." As a matter of fact, Rosenhan found that anything he did was ignored. When a staff member manhandled a patient (as happened occasionally), Rosenhan would be right there—taking notes on the whole incident!

Labels These observations clarify the failure of staff members to detect the fake patients. Because the pseudo-patients were seen in the *context* of a mental ward and because they had been *labeled* schizophrenic, *anything* they did was seen as a symptom of their "illness."

To return to the original hypothetical question about talking your way out of an accidental commitment, it should be clear that it could be quite futile

On Being Sane in Insane Places, continued

to say, "Look, this is all a mistake, I'm not crazy. You've got to let me out." The response might very well be, "Have you had these paranoid delusions for long?"

Many mental health professionals found Rosenhan's findings hard to believe. This led to a follow-up study, in which researchers warned the staff of another hospital that one or more pseudo-patients were going to try to gain admission over the next 3 months. Thus alerted, the staff at this hospital tried to identify fake incoming patients. Among 193 candidates, 41 were labeled fakes by at least one staff member, and 19 more were labeled "suspicious." This only served to confirm Rosenhan's original findings, because he never sent *any* patients—fake or otherwise—to this hospital!

An important final note is that all of the normal people who served as pseudo-patients in the original studies were discharged as schizophrenics "in remission" (temporarily free of symptoms). In other words the label that prevented hospital staff from seeing the normality of the researchers stayed with them when they left. Psychiatrist Karl Menninger (1964) once commented on a similar situation:

> A label can blight the life of a person even after his recovery from mental illness. A young doctor I knew suffered for a time from some anxiety and indecision. He consulted a psychiatrist and soon recovered. Unfortunately, a "tentative" diagnosis of schizophrenia got abroad—I don't know how—and the young doctor's professional career was seriously impaired. He was injured, not by mental illness but by a word.

Observations such as these are not a total condemnation of psychiatric hospitals. Many of the conditions Rosenhan encountered will be found in *any* hospital or other large institution. But Rosenhan's findings do carry an important message for professionals and nonprofessionals alike: *labels can be dangerous.* As Stoller (1967) has said:

> When a person is labeled—neurotic, psychotic, executive, teacher, salesman, psychologist—either by himself or by others, he restricts his behavior to the role and even may rely upon the role for security. This diminishes the kind of experiences he is likely to have. Indeed, it is those groups whose members have shared labels—be it schizophrenic or executive—which are hardest to help move into intimate contact.

Implications The terms reviewed in this and the previous chapter can, and do, aid communication about human problems. But if used carelessly, they may do great damage. Everyone has felt or acted "crazy" during brief periods of stress or high emotion. The person whose adjustment problems extend over a longer period of time is different from you or me only in the severity of his or her difficulty.

It is therefore more productive to label problems than to label people. Think of the difference in impact between saying, "He is experiencing a serious emotional disturbance" and saying, "He is a *psychotic.*" Which statement would you choose to have said about yourself?

It is also important to realize that a severely disturbed person will appreciate being treated normally. Rosenhan's research makes it clear that the person is not helped by being thrust into the role of a "patient." One former patient's comments clarify this last point:

> After I got back from the hospital, my friends tried to *act* like nothing had changed. But I could tell they weren't being honest. For instance, a friend invited me to dinner and everything went fine until I dropped my fork. Both my friend and his wife jumped up and stared at me like they thought I might explode. I was quite embarrassed.

On Being Sane in Insane Places, continued

Learning Check

1. In the majority of their attempts, Rosenhan's pseudo-patients were admitted to mental hospitals after complaining only that they were hearing voices. T or F?
2. Although they were often detected by professional staff members, the normality of the pseudo-patients was never recognized by other patients. T or F?
3. During their hospital stay, pseudo-patients were denied psychiatric drugs even though they requested them. T or F?
4. Rosenhan found that almost anything pseudo-patients said or did was interpreted as a symptom of their "illness." T or F?
5. When they were alerted that a number of pseudo-patients might try to gain entry, hospital staff members were able to more accurately detect the fakes. T or F?

Answers: **1.** T **2.** F **3.** F **4.** T **5.** F

Chapter Summary

- Psychosis is a break in contact with reality that is marked by *delusions*, *hallucinations*, *sensory changes*, *emotional disturbances*, and, in some cases, *personality disintegration*.
- Psychotic symptoms, as well as lesser problems in thought, speech, memory, and attention, tend to be most prominent during short episodes of increased disturbance. There is evidence that some such symptoms are partially under voluntary control.
- An *organic psychosis* is based on known injuries or diseases of the brain. Problems of unknown origin are termed *functional psychoses*. Three common causes of organic psychosis are untreated syphilis *(general paresis)*, *poisoning*, and *senile dementia* (especially *Alzheimer's disease*).
- *Delusional disorders* are defined almost exclusively by the presence of persistent delusions. A diagnosis of *paranoid psychosis* is almost totally based on delusions of jealousy, grandeur or persecution and rarely involves personality disintegration. Because they often have intense and irrational delusions of persecution, paranoid persons may be violent if they believe they are threatened.
- *Major mood disorders* involve extremes of mood, plus psychotic symptoms, in many ways. *Bipolar disorders* combine mania and depression, and occur in *manic*, *depressive*, and *mixed* types. *Major depressions* involve extreme sadness and despondency but no evidence of mania.
- *Schizophrenia* is the most common psychosis. It is distinguished by a split between thought and emotion and by delusions, hallucinations, and communication difficulties. Several subtypes of schizophrenia have been identified. They should not be confused with *schizotypal personality disorder*, which involves gradual withdrawal into isolation from others and odd, apathetic behavior.

- *Disorganized schizophrenia* shows extreme personality disintegration and silly, bizarre, or obscene behavior. Social impairment is usually extreme.
- *Catatonic schizophrenia* is associated with stupor, mutism, and odd postures. Sometimes, violent agitated behavior also occurs.
- In *paranoid schizophrenia* (the most common subtype), delusions of grandeur and persecution are coupled with psychotic symptoms and personality breakdown.
- *Undifferentiated schizophrenia* is the term used to indicate a lack of clear-cut patterns of disturbance.
- Current explanations of schizophrenia emphasize a combination of *environmental stress*, *inherited susceptibility*, and *biochemical abnormalities* in the body or brain. One popular environmental theory is that schizophrenics have been subject to unsolvable dilemmas through *double-bind communication*. A better case can be made for the importance of early *traumatic experiences* and *disturbed family environments* as underlying factors in schizophrenia. In addition, studies of twins and other close relatives strongly support a *genetic* view of schizophrenia. Recent biochemical studies have focused on abnormalities in brain transmitter substances, especially *dopamine* and its receptor sites.
- Three somatic or medical approaches to treatment of psychosis are *chemotherapy* (use of drugs), *electroconvulsive therapy* (ECT—brain shock for the treatment of depression), and *psychosurgery* (surgical alteration of the brain). All three techniques are capable of producing serious side effects, and all are controversial to a degree (due to questions about effectiveness and the cost/benefit ratio).
- *Hospitalization* is often associated with somatic therapy, and it is also considered a form of treatment. Prolonged hospitalization is now discouraged by *revolving-door* admissions policies and by an emphasis on providing care within the community. As long as community care remains poor, however, repeated hospitalization is likely.
- A development in mental health care that seeks to avoid or minimize hospitalization is the creation of *community mental health centers*. Community mental health centers also have as their goal the *prevention* of mental health problems through education, consultation, and crisis intervention.
- David Rosenhan's use of *pseudo-patients* to study mental hospitals suggests that problems in diagnosis exist and that *psychiatric labeling* can affect our perceptions of others' behavior.

Chapter 21

Insight Therapy

Chapter Preview

Quiet Terror on a Spring Afternoon

The warm California sun shone brightly. A light breeze danced inland from the ocean. Outside my office window an assortment of small birds sang to a beautiful spring day. I could hear them between Susan's frightened sobs.

As a psychologist I see many students who have personal problems. Still, I was somewhat surprised to see Susan at my office door. Her excellent work in class and her healthy, casual appearance left me unprepared for her first words. "I feel like I'm losing my mind," she said. "Can I talk to you?"

In the next hour Susan sketched the features of her own personal hell. Her calm exterior hid a world of overwhelming fear, anxiety, and depression. She had lost several part-time jobs because at each one she began to fear her co-workers and the customers so much that she could barely bring herself to speak to them. Her absenteeism and embarrassing interchanges with customers would gradually lead to her dismissal.

At school Susan felt "different" and was sure that other students could tell she was "weird." Several disastrous romances had left her terrified of men. Lately she had become so depressed that she had begun to think frequently of suicide. At times she became so terrified for no apparent reason that her heart pounded wildly and she felt that she was about to lose control of herself completely.

Susan's visit to my office was an important turning point. Emotional conflicts had made her existence a living nightmare. At a time when she was becoming her own worst enemy, Susan had realized that she needed the help and support of another person. In Susan's case that person was a talented psychologist to whom I referred her. By combining various forms of psychotherapy, the psychologist was able to help Susan come to grips with her emotions and return a healthy balance to her personality.

This chapter and the next discuss psychological methods used to ease problems like Susan's. Here we will describe therapies that emphasize the value of gaining insight *into personal problems. In the next chapter we will focus on* behavior therapy *and* cognitive therapy, *which are used to directly change troublesome thoughts and behaviors.*

Survey Questions How did modern psychotherapies develop? Is Freudian psychoanalysis still used? What are the characteristics of humanistic therapies? Can psychotherapy be done with groups of people? What are group therapies like? What do various therapies have in common? How would a person go about finding professional help? What can be done to help a troubled friend?

Resources

Humpty-Dumpty sat on a wall.
Humpty-Dumpty had a great fall.
All the King's horses and all the King's men
Couldn't put Humpty together again.

Psychotherapy—Getting Better by the Hour

In our age of stress, conflict, and anxiety, who will put you together again, and how will they do it? Actually, the odds are that you will *not* experience a life-impairing emotional problem like Susan's, but if you did, what kind of help is available? In most cases the answer is some form of *psychotherapy*.

Question: What is psychotherapy?

Psychotherapy is any psychological technique that is used to facilitate positive changes in a person's personality, behavior, or adjustment. The psychotherapist has many approaches to choose from: psychoanalysis, desensitization, Gestalt therapy, logotherapy, client-centered therapy, reality therapy, transactional analysis, behavior modification—to name but a few.

Due to a recent explosive growth in the number of therapies, some confusion may exist about how they differ. To begin, it may help to recognize that psychological problems are complex, and that the best approach for a particular person or problem will not always be the same. Also, psychotherapies vary widely in emphasis, as described in Table 21-1.

Myths Popular accounts tend to depict psychotherapy as a complete personal transformation—a sort of "major overhaul" of the psyche. But this ignores the realities of solving human problems. As clinical psychologist Bernie Zilbergeld (1983) points out, therapy is *not* equally effective for all problems. Chances of improvement are fairly good for phobias, low self-esteem, some sexual problems, and marital conflicts. More complex problems, however, can be difficult to treat. Also, contrary to what many people think, therapy usually does not bring about dramatic changes in behavior or an end to personal problems. For many people, therapy's major benefit is that it provides comfort, support, and a way to make positive changes.

In short, it is often unrealistic to expect psychotherapy to undo a person's entire past history. Yet even when problems are severe, therapy may help a person gain a new perspective or learn ways to better cope with life (Coleman, Butcher, & Carson, 1984). Psychotherapy can be hard work for both client and therapist. But when it succeeds, there are few activities more rewarding.

Table 21-1 Dimensions of Therapy

The term *psychotherapy* most often refers to verbal interaction between trained mental health professionals and their patients. Many therapists also use learning principles to directly alter troublesome behaviors, as described in Chapter 22.

The terms listed here describe basic aspects of various therapies. Notice that more than one term may apply to the same therapy. For example, it would be possible to have a directive, action-oriented, group therapy or a nondirective, individual, insight-oriented therapy.

Individual therapy	A therapy session involving only one client and one therapist
Group therapy	A therapy session in which several clients participate at one time with one or more therapists
Insight therapy	Any psychotherapy whose goal is to lead clients to a deeper understanding of their thoughts, emotions, and behavior
Action therapy	Any therapy designed to bring about direct changes in troublesome thoughts, habits, feelings, or behavior
Directive therapy	Any approach in which the therapist provides strong guidance during therapy sessions
Nondirective therapy	A style of therapy in which clients assume responsibility for solving their own problems; the therapist assists but does not guide or give advice

As a final point, you also should realize that psychotherapy is not done only to solve psychological problems. Some therapies are designed to encourage personal growth and enrichment for people who are already functioning effectively.

Origins of Therapy—Bored Skulls and Hysteria on the Couch

History gives ample reason for appreciating the humanity of modern therapies. Archaeological findings dating to the Stone Age suggest that most primitive approaches were marked by fear and superstitious belief in demons, witchcraft, and magic. One of the more dramatic "cures" practiced by primitive "psychotherapists" was a process called **trepanning** (treh-PAN-ing). A hole was bored, chipped, or bashed into the skull of the patient, presumably to relieve pressure or release evil spirits. Actually, trepanning may have simply been an excuse to kill people who were unusual, since many of the "patients" didn't survive the "treatment."

During the Middle Ages, treatment for the mentally ill in Europe focused on **demonology.** Abnormal behavior was blamed on supernatural forces such as possession by the devil or the curses of witches and wizards. As treatment, **exorcism** was used to drive out the evil. For the fortunate, exorcism was a religious ritual. More often, though, it took the form of physical torture to make the body an inhospitable place for the devil to reside (Fig. 21-1).

One explanation for the rise of demonology may lie in a condition called **ergotism** (ER-got-ism). In the Middle Ages, rye fields were often infested with ergot fungus (Fig. 21-2). Ergot, we now know, is a natural source of LSD and other mind-altering chemicals. Eating bread made from tainted grain can cause symptoms that might easily be interpreted as possession, bewitchment, or madness. Pinching sensations, convulsions, muscle twitches, facial spasms, delirium, and visual hallucinations are all common reactions to ergot poisoning (Kety, 1979;

Psychotherapy Any form of psychological treatment for behavioral or emotional problems; most often refers to verbal interaction between trained mental health professionals and their clients.

Trepanning In modern usage, any surgical procedure in which a hole is bored in the skull; historically, the chipping or boring of holes in the skull to "treat" mental disturbance.

Demonology In Medieval Europe, that branch of knowledge dealing with the study of demons and the treatment of persons "possessed" by demons.

Exorcism In Medieval Europe, the practice of expelling or driving off an "evil spirit," especially one residing in the body of a person who is "possessed."

Ergotism A pattern of psychotic-like symptoms that accompany poisoning by ergot fungus.

Fig. 21-1 *Early approaches to the treatment of mental illness.* (a) *Primitive "treatment" for mental disorder sometimes took the form of boring a hole in the skull.* (b) *Many early asylums were no more than prisons with inmates held in chains.* (c) *One late nineteenth-century "treatment" was based on swinging the patient in a harness—presumably to calm the patient's nerves.*

Fig. 21-2 *Two ears of rye infested with ergot fungus (dark areas). The psychedelic effects of the fungus may explain some cases of "possession" in Medieval Europe and "bewitchment" in colonial New England.*

Matossian, 1982). Thus, many of the "patients" of demonology may have been doubly victimized.

The idea that the emotionally disturbed are "mentally ill" and that they should be treated compassionately emerged after 1793. This was the year **Philippe Pinel** changed the Bicêtre Asylum in Paris from a squalid "madhouse" into a mental hospital by personally unchaining the inmates. Although almost 200 years have passed since Pinel began humane treatment for the emotionally disturbed, the process of improving conditions in psychiatric hospitals and of changing public attitudes toward psychotherapy continues today. Increased acceptance of the value of psychotherapy is a positive sign, but public attitudes toward the disturbed still tend to be colored by suspicion and fear. Perhaps as more people take part in psychotherapy as a growth experience, it will become more widely understood.

Question: When was psychotherapy developed?

The first true psychotherapy was developed around the turn of the century by Sigmund Freud.

As a physician in Vienna, Freud was intrigued by the cases of **hysteria** (physical symptoms such as paralysis or numbness without known physical cause) he encountered. As you may recall, such problems are now called *somatoform disorders* (see Chapter 19). Slowly Freud became convinced that the symptoms of hysteria were only the tip of the iceberg, that deeply hidden unconscious conflicts (frequently sexual in nature) were to blame. Based on this insight, Freud went on to develop his own form of therapy. Because **psychoanalysis,** as Freud called his technique, is the "granddaddy" of most modern psychotherapies, let us examine it in some detail.

Hysteria Wild emotional excitability sometimes associated with the development of apparent physical disabilities (numbness, blindness, and the like) without known physical cause.

Psychoanalysis Freud's approach to therapy, emphasizing the use of free association, dream interpretation, and transference to uncover unconscious conflicts.

Free association In psychoanalysis, the technique of having the client say anything that comes to mind, regardless of how embarrassing or unimportant it may seem.

Psychoanalysis—Expedition into the Unconscious

Question: Isn't psychoanalysis the therapy where the patient lies on a couch?

Freud's patients usually reclined on a couch during therapy, while Freud sat out of sight taking notes and offering interpretations. This arrangement was selected to encourage relaxation and a free flow of thoughts and images from the patient's unconscious (Fig. 21-3). This aspect is the least important of several features of psychoanalysis and has been abandoned by many modern analysts.

Question: How did Freud treat emotional problems?

Freud's theory stressed that repressed memories, motives, and conflicts—particularly those stemming from instinctual drives for sex and aggression—were the cause of neurosis. Although unconscious and repressed, these factors remained active in the personality, forcing the person to develop rigid ego-defense mechanisms and to devote excessive amounts of time and energy to compulsive and self-defeating behavior. Freud relied on four basic techniques to uncover the unconscious roots of neurosis (Freud, 1949):

1. **Free association.** During psychoanalysis the patient must say whatever comes to mind without regard for whether it makes sense or is painful or embarrassing. Thoughts are allowed to move freely from one association to the next.

Fig. 21-3 *Pioneering psychotherapist Sigmund Freud in his office.*

2. **Dream analysis.** The purpose of free association is to lower defenses so that unconscious material may emerge. Freud considered dreams an unusually good additional way to tap the unconscious. Freud referred to dreams as "the royal road to the unconscious" because he believed that forbidden desires and unconscious feelings are more freely expressed in dreams. He distinguished between the **manifest** (obvious, visible) **content** and the **latent** (hidden) **content** of dreams.

   To appreciate fully the unconscious message of a dream, Freud sought to reveal its latent meaning by interpreting **dream symbols.** Let's say a young husband reports a dream in which he pulls a pistol from his waistband and aims at a target while his wife watches. The pistol repeatedly fails to discharge, and the man's wife laughs at him. Freud might see this as an indication of repressed feelings of sexual impotence, with the gun serving as a disguised image of the penis.
3. **Analysis of resistance.** When free associating or describing dreams, the patient may *resist* talking about or thinking about certain topics. Such resistances are said to reveal important unconscious conflicts. As the analyst becomes aware of resistances, he or she brings them to the patient's awareness so they can be explored.
4. **Analysis of transference.** The individual undergoing psychoanalysis may transfer feelings to the therapist that relate to important past relationships with others. At times the patient may act as if the analyst were a rejecting father, an unloving or overprotective mother, or a former lover. This is considered a prime opportunity to help the patient undergo an emotional reeducation. As the patient reexperiences repressed emotions, the therapist can help the patient recognize and understand them.

Question: Is psychoanalysis still used?

Traditional psychoanalysis called for 3 to 5 therapy sessions a week for up to 7 years. Because of the huge amounts of time and money this requires, psychoanalysts have become relatively rare. Today, most therapists who use psychoanalytic theory have switched to **short-term dynamic therapy.** In this approach, therapists rely on direct interviewing to uncover unconscious conflicts more rapidly. They also seek to actively lower defenses and provide insights. By such means, the length of therapy has been shortened considerably (Been & Sklar, 1985).

The development of newer, more streamlined dynamic therapies is in part due to questions about the effectiveness of traditional psychoanalysis. One critic, H. J. Eysenck (1967), went so far as to suggest that psychoanalysis simply takes so long that there is a **spontaneous remission** of symptoms (improvement due to the mere passage of time).

How seriously should this criticism be taken? It is true that problems ranging from hyperactivity to anxiety improve with the passage of time. However, more recent work affirms that psychoanalysis is usually better than no treatment at all (Bergin & Suinn, 1975). The main value of Eysenck's critique and others that followed is that they encouraged psychologists to try new ideas and techniques. Researchers began to ask, "When psychoanalysis works, why does it work? Which procedures are essential and which are unnecessary?" Based on intuition, personal philosophy, clinical experience, and the personality theory they find most acceptable, modern psychotherapists have posed surprisingly varied answers to these questions. The following sections will acquaint you with some of the therapies currently in use.

Manifest dream content The surface, "visible" content of a dream; dream images as they are remembered by the dreamer.

Latent dream content The hidden or symbolic meaning of a dream, as revealed by dream interpretation and analysis.

Dream symbols Images in dreams whose personal or emotional meanings differ from their literal meaning.

Resistance Blocks that occur in psychoanalysis during free association; topics the client resists thinking or talking about.

Transference In psychoanalysis, the tendency of a client to transfer to the therapist feelings that correspond to those the client had for important persons in his or her past.

Short-term dynamic therapy Modern psychodynamic therapy based on psychoanalytic theory but designed to produce insight within a briefer time period than required by traditional psychoanalysis.

Spontaneous remission In psychiatry and clinical psychology, the spontaneous disappearance of a psychological disturbance without therapy.

Learning Check

See if you can answer the following questions. If you miss any, review the previous sections.

Match

____ **1.** Directive therapies

____ **2.** Action therapies

____ **3.** Insight therapies

____ **4.** Nondirective therapies

A. Change behavior
B. Place responsibility on client
C. The client is strongly guided
D. Seek understanding

5. Pinel is famous for his use of exorcism. T or F?

6. Freud developed trepanning. T or F?

7. A spontaneous remission of symptoms means that psychotherapy has succeeded. T or F?

8. In psychoanalysis an emotional attachment to the therapist by the patient is called:
a. free association *b.* resistance *c.* manifest association *d.* transference

Answers: **1.** C **2.** A **3.** D **4.** B **5.** F **6.** F **7.** F **8.** d

Client-centered therapy Nondirective therapy created by Carl Rogers; based on insights discovered while exploring conscious thoughts and feelings with the aid of a supportive therapist.

Unconditional positive regard Unshakable personal acceptance given without qualification or evaluation.

Empathy A capacity for taking another's point of view; the ability to feel what another is feeling.

Authenticity In Carl Rogers' terms, the ability of a therapist to be genuine and honest regarding his or her feelings.

Reflection In client-centered therapy, the process of rephrasing or repeating thoughts and feelings so that clients become aware of what they are saying about themselves.

Fig. 21-4 *Carl Rogers, originator of client-centered therapy.*

Humanistic Therapies—Restoring Human Potential

The goal of traditional psychoanalysis is adjustment. Freud was actually quite conservative in his claims: Any of his patients, he said, could expect only to change their "hysterical misery into common unhappiness"! The humanistic therapies outlined in upcoming sections are generally more optimistic. Most assume that it is possible for people to live rich and rewarding lives and to make full use of their potential. Psychotherapy is seen as a means of giving natural tendencies toward mental health a chance to emerge.

Question: What is client-centered therapy? How is it different from psychoanalysis?

Client-Centered Therapy Psychoanalysts delve into childhood, dreams, and the unconscious. Psychologist Carl Rogers (1902–1987) found it more productive to explore *conscious* thoughts and feelings (Fig. 21-4). The psychoanalyst tends to take a position of authority from which he or she offers interpretations of what is "wrong" with the patient or of what dreams or childhood experiences "mean." Rogers believed that what is right or valuable for the therapist may not be right and valuable for the client. (Rogers preferred the term *client* to *patient*.) Accordingly, **client-centered therapy** (also called person-centered therapy) is *nondirective*. The client is the center of the process. He or she determines what will be discussed during each session.

Question: If the client runs things, what does the therapist do?

The therapist's job is to create an "atmosphere of growth" by maintaining four basic conditions.

First, the therapist offers the client **unconditional positive regard.** In other words, the client is accepted *totally*. The therapist refuses to react with shock, dismay, or disapproval to anything the client says or feels. Total acceptance by the therapist is the first step to self-acceptance by the client.

Second, the therapist attempts to achieve genuine **empathy** for the client by trying to see the world through the client's eyes and to feel some part of what he or she is feeling.

As a third essential condition, the therapist strives to be **authentic** in his or her relationship with clients. The therapist must not hide behind a professional role. Rogers believed that phony fronts and facades destroy the growth atmosphere sought in client-centered therapy (see Box 21-1).

Fourth, the therapist does not make interpretations, pose solutions, or offer advice. Instead, the therapist **reflects** the client's thoughts and feelings. By repeating or restating what the client has said or by telling the client what emotion he or she seems to be displaying, the therapist serves as a psychological "mirror" in which clients learn to see themselves more clearly and realistically. Rogers believed that a person armed with a realistic self-image and with a new level of self-acceptance will gradually discover solutions to life problems.

Box 21-1

Carl Rogers on Personal Growth

Like other humanistic psychologists, Carl Rogers (1980) believed deeply that there is a natural human urge to seek health and self-growth. Rogers' belief is vividly expressed by the following quotation:

> I remember that in my boyhood the bin in which we stored our winter's supply of potatoes was in the basement, several feet below a small window. The conditions were unfavorable, but pale white sprouts . . . would grow two or three feet in length as they reached toward the light of the distant window. The sprouts were, in their bizarre, futile growth, a sort of desperate expression of the directional tendency I have been describing. . . . In dealing with clients whose lives have been terribly warped, in working with men and women on the back wards of state hospitals, I often think of those potato sprouts. . . . The clue to understanding their behavior is that they are striving, in the only ways that they perceive as available to them, to move toward growth, toward becoming. To healthy persons, the results may seem bizarre and futile but they are life's desperate attempt to become itself. This potent constructive tendency is an underlying basis of the person-centered approach.

Existential Therapy According to existentialists, "being in the world" (existence) creates deep and unavoidable conflicts. Each of us, they say, must deal with the realities of death. We must face the fact that each person creates his or her private world by making choices. We must overcome the isolation of living on a vast and indifferent planet. We must confront feelings of meaninglessness.

Question: What do these concerns have to do with psychotherapy?

Like client-centered therapy, **existential therapy** tries to promote self-knowledge and self-actualization. However, there are important differences. Client-centered therapy seeks to uncover a "true self" hidden behind an artificial screen of defenses. In contrast, existential therapy emphasizes the idea of **free will.** That is, through *choices* one can *become* the person he or she wants to be.

Existential therapy attempts to restore meaning and vitality to life so that the individual has the *courage* to make rewarding and socially constructive choices. Typically, existential therapy focuses on the "ultimate concerns" of human existence. These include the inescapable givens of **death, freedom, isolation,** and **meaninglessness** (Yalom, 1980).

Question: What does an existential therapist do?

One example of existential therapy is Victor Frankl's **logotherapy.**

Frankl (1955) developed his approach on the basis of experiences in a Nazi concentration camp. In the camp Frankl observed the breakdown of countless prisoners as they were stripped of all hope and human dignity. Frankl believed that those who survived with their sanity did so because they had managed to hang on to a sense of *meaning* (logos). In some cases this was nothing more than the ultimate human freedom—the freedom to choose one's own attitude in any set of circumstances.

Existential therapy Insight therapy that focuses on the elemental problems of existence, such as death, meaning, choice, and responsibility.

Free will The presumed ability of humans to freely make choices not determined by heredity, past conditioning, or other dictates.

Death, freedom, isolation, meaninglessness The universal challenges of existence, including: an awareness of one's mortality; the responsibility that comes with freedom to choose; the fact that each person is ultimately isolated and alone in his or her private world; and the reality that meaning must be created in life.

Logotherapy A form of existential therapy that emphasizes the need to find and maintain meaning in one's life.

Confrontation In existential therapy, the process of confronting clients with their own values and with the need to take responsibility for the quality of their existence.

Gestalt A German word meaning form, pattern, or whole.

Gestalt therapy An approach that focuses on immediate experience and awareness to help clients rebuild thinking, feeling, and acting into connected wholes.

Like most existential therapists, Frankl uses a flexible approach centered around **confrontation.** The person is challenged to examine the quality of his or her existence and choices and to *encounter* the unique, intense, here-and-now interaction of two human beings. When existential therapy is successful, it brings about a reappraisal of what's important in life. Indeed, some clients experience an emotional rebirth not unlike that seen in people who have survived a close brush with death.

Gestalt Therapy Gestalt therapy, which is most often associated with Frederick (Fritz) Perls (1969), is built around the idea that perception, or *awareness*, becomes disjointed and incomplete in the maladjusted individual. The Gestalt approach is more directive than either client-centered therapy or existential therapy, and it places a special emphasis on immediate experience.

Question: What does Gestalt mean?

The German word **Gestalt** means *whole*, or complete. The Gestalt therapist seeks to help the individual rebuild thinking, feeling, and acting into connected wholes. This is achieved by expanding personal awareness, by accepting responsibility for one's thoughts, feelings, and actions, and by filling in gaps in experience.

Question: What do you mean by "gaps in experience"?

Gestalt therapists believe that we often shy away from expressing or "owning" upsetting feelings. This creates a gap in self-awareness that may become a barrier to personal growth. For example, a person who feels anger after the death of a parent might go for years without expressing it. This and similar threatening gaps may block emotional health.

Working either one-to-one or in a group setting, the Gestalt therapist encourages the individual to become more aware of his or her immediate experience. Rather than discussing "why" he or she feels guilt, anger, fear, or boredom, the client is encouraged to have these feelings in the "here and now" and to become fully aware of them. The therapist helps promote awareness by drawing attention to the client's posture, voice, and eye or hand movements. The client may also be asked to exaggerate a vague feeling until it becomes clear. Gestalt therapists believe that expressing such feelings allows people to "take care of unfinished business" and break through emotional impasses.

In all his writings, Perls' basic message comes through clearly: Emotional health comes from knowing what you *want* to do, not dwelling on what you *should* do, *ought* to do, or *should want* to do. Another way of stating this idea is that emotional health comes from taking full responsibility for one's feelings and actions. It means changing "I can't" to "I won't," for example, or "I must" to "I choose to."

Question: How does Gestalt therapy help people discover their real wants?

Above all else, Gestalt therapy emphasizes *present* experience. Clients are urged to stop intellectualizing and talking *about* feelings. Instead they learn to: live now; live here; stop imagining; experience the real; stop unnecessary thinking; taste and see; express rather than explain, justify, or judge; give in to unpleasantness and pain just as to pleasure; surrender to being as you are (adapted from Naranjo, 1970).

Learning Check

See if you can answer the following questions.

Match

____ **1.** Client-centered therapy	**A.** Meaning
____ **2.** Gestalt therapy	**B.** Unconditional positive regard
____ **3.** Existential therapy	**C.** Gaps in awareness
____ **4.** Logotherapy	**D.** Choice and becoming

5. A Gestalt therapist tries to *reflect* a client's thoughts and feelings. T or F?

6. Client-centered therapy is directive. T or F?

7. Confrontation and encounter are concepts of existential therapy. T or F?

Answers: **1.** B **2.** C **3.** D **4.** A **5.** F **6.** F **7.** T

Group Therapy—People Who Need People

Question: Is group therapy just individual therapy with more than one person?

Most psychotherapies can be adapted for use in groups. Psychologists first tried working with groups as a practical response to the need for more therapists than were available. To their surprise, group therapy not only worked, it also offered some special advantages (Fig. 21-5).

In group therapy a person can *act out* or directly experience problems. Doing so often produces insights that might not occur from merely talking about prob-

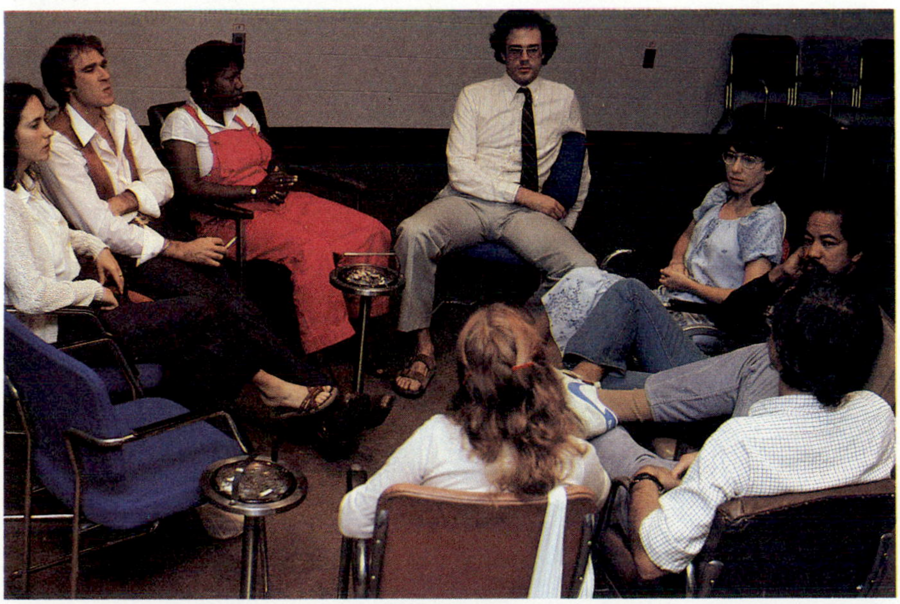

Fig. 21-5 *A group therapy session. Group members offer mutual support while sharing problems, insights.*

Box 21-2

"Psych Jockeys"

By now you have probably heard a phone-in radio psychologist. On a typical program callers describe problems arising from child abuse, loneliness, love affairs, phobias, sexual adjustment, or depression. The radio psychologist then offers reassurance, advice, or suggestions for getting help.

Talk-radio psychology may seem harmless, but it raises some important questions. For instance, is it reasonable to give advice without knowing anything about a person's background? Might the advice do harm? What good can a psychologist do in 3 minutes?

In defense of themselves, radio psychologists point out that listeners may learn solutions to their own problems by hearing others talk. Many also stress that their work is educational, not therapeutic. And certainly for some callers a radio psychologist may be the only person willing to listen to their problem.

The real issue seems to be the question of when advice becomes therapy. The American Psychological Association has taken the position that media psychologists should discuss only problems of a general nature, instead of actually counseling a person. For example, if a caller complains about insomnia, the radio psychologist should talk about insomnia in general, not probe the caller's personal life (Schommer, 1984).

By giving information and advice, radio psychologists probably do help some listeners. Even so, a good guide for anyone tempted to call a radio psychologist might be "let the consumer beware." Or, to use an analogy, how much confidence would you have in a physician who would make a diagnosis over the phone?

lems. In addition, other group members with similar problems can offer support and useful input. Groups also help form a bridge between therapy and real-life problems by providing a situation that is more realistic than the protected atmosphere of individual therapy. For reasons such as these, a number of specialized group techniques have emerged. Because they range from Alcoholics Anonymous to marriage encounter, we will sample only a few representative approaches. (The largest group therapy of all may be on your radio—see Box 21-2.)

Psychodrama. One of the first group approaches was developed by J. L. Moreno (1953), who called his technique **psychodrama.** In psychodrama an individual **role plays** (acts out) dramatic incidents resembling those that cause problems in real life. For example, a disturbed teenager might act out a typical family fight, with the therapist playing his father and other clients taking the roles of mother, brothers, and sisters. Moreno believed that insights and the emotional relearning from these enactments transfer to real-life situations. Therapists using psychodrama often find **role reversals** especially helpful (Leveton, 1977). For instance, the teenager just described would be asked to role play his father or mother in order to better understand their feelings.

Family Therapy Family relationships are the source of great pleasure and, all too often, of great pain for many people. In **family therapy,** husband, wife, and children work as a group to resolve the problems of each family member. Family therapy tends to be brief and focused on specific problems, such as frequent fights, a depressed teenager, and so forth (Berman, 1982).

Family therapists believe that problems are rarely limited to a single family member: A problem for one is considered a problem for all. Thus, family members work together to improve communication, to change destructive patterns, and to see themselves and each other in new ways.

Question: Does the therapist work with the whole family at once?

The family therapist treats the family as a unit but may not meet with the entire family at each session. If a family crisis is at hand, the therapist may first try to identify the most resourceful family members, who can help solve the immediate problem. The therapist and family members may then work on resolving more basic conflicts and on improving family relationships.

Group Awareness Training During the 1960s and 1970s, the human potential movement led many people to become interested in personal growth experiences. Often, their interest was expressed by participation in sensitivity training or encounter groups.

Question: What is the difference between sensitivity and encounter groups?

Sensitivity groups tend to be less confrontive than encounter groups. Participants in sensitivity groups take part in exercises that gently enlarge awareness of oneself and others. For example, in a "trust walk," participants expand their confidence in others by allowing themselves to be led while blindfolded.

In **encounter groups,** more intense emotion and communication may take place. Here, the emphasis is on tearing down defenses and false fronts through discussion that can be brutally honest (Stoller, 1972). Because there is a danger of hostile confrontation and psychological damage, encounter group participation is safest when members are carefully screened and a trained leader guides the group.

Sensitivity and encounter techniques are used by many businesses to improve employee morale and relationships. Specially designed encounter groups for married couples are also widely held. However, in the last decade there has been a shift away from public participation in sensitivity and encounter groups. Instead, hundreds of thousands of people have taken part in various forms of **large group awareness training** (Finkelstein et al., 1982). Lifespring, Actualizations, est, and similar commercial programs are well-known examples. Like the smaller groups that preceded them, large group trainings combine psychological exercises, confrontation, new viewpoints, and group dynamics to promote personal change.

Question: Are sensitivity, encounter, and awareness groups really psychotherapies?

Judging from the glowing testimonials given by many participants, such groups must fill some need not met by society or traditional psychotherapy. However, there is, at present, little evidence that these experiences are truly therapeutic (Finkelstein et al., 1982). Many of the claimed benefits may simply result from a kind of **therapy placebo effect** related to positive expectations, a break in daily routine, and an excuse to act differently. The importance of such factors is easily

Psychodrama A therapy technique in which clients act out personal conflicts and feelings in the presence of others who play supporting roles.

Role playing The dramatic enactment or re-enactment of significant life events.

Role reversal Taking the role of another person to learn how one's own behavior appears from the other person's perspective.

Family therapy Therapeutic technique in which all family members participate, both individually and as a group, to change destructive relationships and communication patterns.

Sensitivity group A group experience consisting of exercises designed to increase self-awareness and sensitivity to others.

Encounter group A group experience that emphasizes intensely honest interchanges among participants regarding feelings and reactions to one another.

Large group awareness training Any of a number of programs (many of them commercialized) that claim to increase self-awareness and facilitate constructive personal change.

Therapy placebo effect Improvement caused not by the actual process of therapy but by a client's expectation that therapy will help.

Transactional analysis (TA) A therapeutic technique designed to improve transactions (interchanges) with others through an awareness of ego-states and games.

Ego-states In transactional analysis, any of three distinct modes of self-expression: the Child, the Parent, and the Adult.

Child In TA, the impulsive, playful, childlike portion of one's personality.

Parent In TA, an internal representation of one's parents; the judging and nurturing portion of the personality.

Adult In TA, the mature, rational, decision-making portion of the personality.

Games In TA, habitual modes of interacting that are used to structure time and provide emotional "payoffs" at the expense of intimacy and honest communication.

illustrated: Participants in a weekend "retreat" that featured nothing more than volleyball, charades, and ballroom dancing also reported enhanced mental health (McCardel & Murray, 1974)! Kurt Back (1972) may have summarized it best when he said, "Encounter groups may comfort, but they do not cure anything." For some the experience is positive, for some negative, and for many it is merely a diversion.

Transactional Analysis—Different Strokes for Different Folks

Transactional analysis (TA) is a therapy that blends humanistic thought with some updated elements of psychoanalysis. TA teaches people a model of behavior to use in becoming more aware of themselves and their *interactions* with others—especially those involving various "games." Because TA emphasizes relationships, it is often conducted as a group therapy.

Question: How does TA enhance awareness?

TA is based on a relatively simple concept proposed by Eric Berne (1961, 1964). According to Berne, the personality has three basic parts or **ego-states,** known as the *Parent*, the *Adult*, and the *Child*. These can be distinguished from one another by distinct behaviors, words, tones, gestures, attitudes, and expressions.

Although Berne denied it, it is easy to see that the three ego-stages are an updated version of Freud's concepts of the id, ego, and superego: The Child corresponds to the id, the Adult to the ego, and the Parent to the superego.

Ego-States The **Child** is a carryover from youth. The Child can be primitive, impulsive, demanding, creative, playful, or manipulative. The Child tends to say things such as "I want"; "I need"; "I won't"; or, simply, "Wow."

In addition to this perpetual Child, Berne says we carry another product of our past, in the form of the Parent ego-state. The **Parent** is an internal record of all the messages received from one's parents or other authorities as our personality developed. The Parent can be evaluative and restrictive or nurturing and allowing. It is activated whenever you judge or nurture yourself or another person. The Parent makes such statements as: "You should"; "You ought to"; "Why didn't you?"; "That's good";"You can do it"; "That's bad"; and "Try harder."

According to TA, people get into trouble when they use an inappropriate ego-state. TA teaches people how to develop each ego-state and helps them decide when to use each one. The **Adult** is a mature and rational decision-making part of the personality. With the Adult in charge, an individual can explore alternatives and their consequences and decide which ego-state is needed. TA gives people a thinking strategy to use in exploring alternatives and deciding what changes they wish to make, especially in *relationships* with others.

Question: How does the ego-state analysis apply to relationships?

Transactions The Parent-Adult-Child analysis can be extended to interactions between two people. That is, a person can send a message from any of his or her ego-states to any of the ego-states in another person. TA holds that trouble comes in relationships when *crossed* or *ulterior transactions* (exchanges) occur. (See Fig. 21-6.) Diagram *a* represents an Adult-to-Adult transaction, such as, "What time

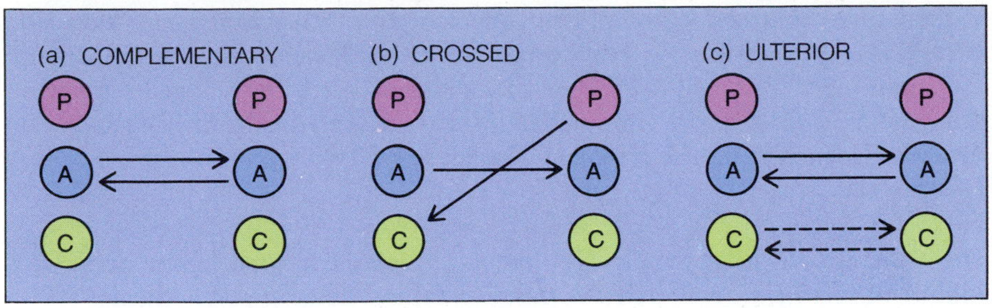

Fig. 21-6 *Basic TA transactions.*

is it?" "It's one o'clock." Communication continues because the expected response was received. But what if the reply is Parent-to-Child, such as, "Why don't you just forget about the time and see if you can get some work done for a change?" Now communication breaks down, or is "crossed" (diagram *b*).

Question: What happens in an ulterior transaction?

In an ulterior transaction the exchange *appears* to take place on one level, but actually takes place on another. For example, the apparent Adult-to-Adult question, "Isn't it getting late?" might carry with it an unspoken (ulterior) cue: "Hey, why don't we quit early tonight?" The reply, "Yeah, it's getting late," might have nothing to do with the time; it may instead be a Child-to-Child reply, "Yeah, let's go play, the supervisor won't know if we leave early."

Games Ulterior transactions may sound harmless enough, but they form the basis of **games,** which are indirect ways of communicating. For example, one spouse might ask another, "How much money is in the checking account?" in such a way that the real message is, "What are you trying to do, put us in the poorhouse?" Games keep people from being close and honest, and at worst they may be physically or emotionally destructive. By the way, the most common game in marriage is, "If it weren't for you" (I would be doing all the things I pretend I want to do but am afraid to try). A major goal of TA is to teach people more direct and creative ways of living, by exploring alternatives to games.

Psychotherapy—An Overview

Question: How effective is psychotherapy?

Judging the outcome of therapy is tricky. Nevertheless, there is evidence that therapy is beneficial. In surveys of hundreds of studies of psychotherapy, a modest but consistent positive effect for therapy was found to exist (Shapiro & Shapiro, 1982; Smith & Glass, 1977). These findings, of course, are based on averages: For some people therapy was tremendously helpful; for others it was unsuccessful; overall it was effective for more people than not. Speaking more subjectively, one real success—in which a person's life is lastingly changed for the better—can be worth the frustration of several cases in which little progress is made.

It is common to think of therapy as a long, slow process. But this need not be the case. Recent research reveals that most people can expect improvement in a reasonably brief time. An analysis of over 2400 persons found that about 50 percent felt better after only 8 therapy sessions. After 26 sessions roughly 75 percent had improved (Howard et al., 1986) (See Figure 21-7.) The typical "dose" of therapy is one hourly session per week. This means that the majority of patients had improved after 6 months of therapy and half felt better in just 2 months. Keep in mind that people often suffer for several years before seeking help. In view of this, such rapid improvement is impressive.

Question: What do psychotherapies have in common?

The therapies we have sampled are but a few of the approaches in use. One author, writing in 1959, counted at least 36 major systems of psychotherapy (Harper, 1959). The count could easily exceed 200 today. The examples cited were selected because they represent some of the basic variations in philosophy or techniques and because they offer ideas that may be of immediate use to you. For a summary of the major differences among psychotherapies, see Table 21-2. To add to your understanding, let us briefly summarize what all of the techniques have in common.

All the psychotherapies we have discussed include some combination of the following goals: insight, resolution of conflicts, an improved sense of self, a change in unacceptable patterns of behavior, better interpersonal relations, and an improved picture of oneself and the world. To accomplish these goals, psychotherapies offer:

1. A *caring relationship* between client and therapist. *Emotional rapport* based on warmth, understanding, acceptance, and empathy forms the basis for this relationship.
2. A *protected setting* in which emotional *catharsis* (release) can take place. Therapy provides a sanctuary in which the client is free to express fears, anxieties, and personal secrets without fear of rejection or loss of confidentiality.

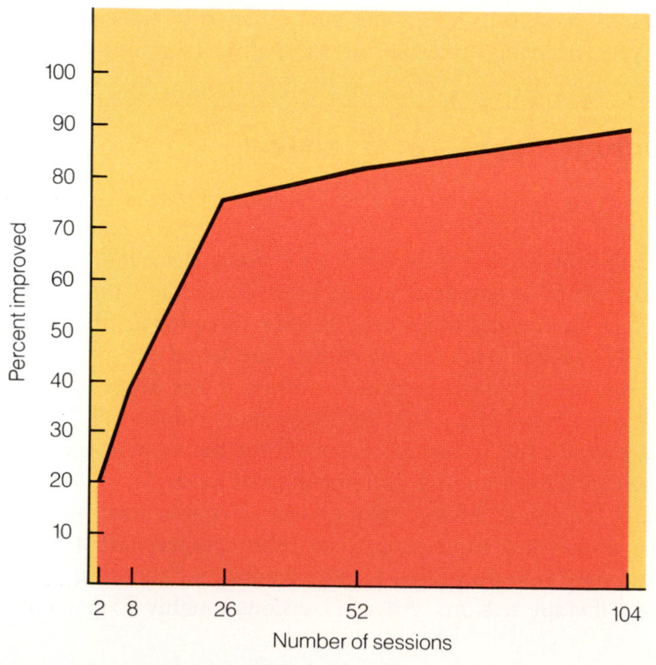

Fig. 21-7 *The dose-improvement relationship in psychotherapy. This graph shows the percentage of patients improved after varying numbers of therapy sessions. Notice that the most rapid improvement took place during the first 6 months of once-a-week sessions. (From Howard, Kopta, Krause, & Orlinsky, 1986, p. 160)*

Table 21-2 Comparison of Psychotherapies

	Insight or Action?	Directive or Nondirective?	Time Orientation	Individual or Group?
Psychoanalysis	insight	directive	past	individual
Short-term dynamic	insight	directive	past and present	individual
Client-centered	insight	nondirective	past and present	individual
Existential	insight	both	present and future	individual
Gestalt	insight	directive	present	both
Transactional analysis	both	directive	past and present	both
Psychodrama	insight	directive	present	group
Family	both	directive	present	group
Behavior modification*	action	directive	present	both
Cognitive*	action	directive	present	individual
Rational-emotive*	action	directive	present	individual

*Discussed in Chapter 22.

3. All therapies to some extent offer an *explanation* or *rationale* for the suffering the client has experienced, and they propose a line of action that if followed will end this suffering.
4. Therapy also provides clients with a *new perspective* about themselves and their situation (Stiles, Shapiro, & Elliott, 1986).

These basic foundations of psychotherapy represent one of the more valuable lessons to be learned from this chapter. Together, they offer a useful perspective for meeting the challenge of helping a troubled friend or relative. More specific suggestions on this point will be found in the discussion that concludes the Applications section of this chapter.

Learning Check

1. In psychodrama, people attempt to form meaningful wholes out of disjointed thoughts, feelings, and actions. T or F?
2. Most large group awareness trainings make use of Gestalt therapy. T or F?
3. There are no dangers in participating in an encounter group. T or F?
4. Which therapy places great emphasis on role playing?
   a. psychodrama *b.* family therapy *c.* TA *d.* encounter
5. The Adult is a mature and rational decision-making part of the personality. T or F?
6. According to TA, destructive psychological games are based on ________________ transactions.
7. Emotional ________________ (release) in a protected setting is an element of most psychotherapies.

Answers: **1.** F **2.** F **3.** F **4.** *a* **5.** T **6.** ulterior **7.** catharsis

Applications

Seeking Professional Help—When, Where, and How?

Question: How would I know if I should seek professional help at some point in my life?

Although there is no simple answer to this question, the following guidelines may be helpful.

1. If your level of psychological discomfort (unhappiness, anxiety, or depression, for example) becomes comparable to a level of physical discomfort that would cause you to see a doctor or dentist, you should consider seeing a psychologist or a psychiatrist.

2. Another sign that should influence your decision is the occurrence of significant changes in observable behavior, such as the quality of your work (or schoolwork), your rate of absenteeism, your use of drugs (including alcohol), or your relationships with others who are important to you.

3. Perhaps you have at some time urged a friend or relative to seek professional help and were then dismayed because they refused to recognize the extent of their problem. If *you* find friends or relatives making a similar suggestion, recognize that they may be seeing things more objectively than you.

4. If you have persistent or disturbing suicidal thoughts or impulses, you should seek help immediately.

Question: If I wanted to talk to a therapist, how would I find one?

1. *The yellow pages.* Psychologists are listed under "Psychologist" or in some cases under "Counseling Services." Psychiatrists are generally listed as a subheading under "Physicians." Counselors are usually found under the heading "Marriage and Family Counselors." These listings will usually put you in touch with individuals in private practice.

2. *Community or county mental health centers.* Most counties and many cities in the United States now offer public mental health services. (These are listed in the phone book.) Public mental health centers usually provide counseling and therapy services directly and can make referrals to private therapists.

3. *Mental health associations.* Many cities have mental health associations organized by concerned citizens. Groups such as these usually keep listings of qualified therapists and of other services and programs in the community.

4. *Colleges and universities.* If you are a student, don't overlook counseling services offered by a student health center or special student counseling facilities.

5. *Newspaper advertisements.* Professional ethics discourage advertisements. Occasionally there are exceptions to this rule as when low-cost outreach clinics try to make their presence known to the public, but in the case of an advertised service you should carefully inquire into the training and qualifications of its staff.

Question: How would I know what kind of a therapist to see? How would I pick one?

The choice between a psychiatrist and a psychologist is somewhat arbitrary. Both are trained to do psychotherapy, and whereas a psychiatrist can administer somatic therapy and prescribe drugs, a psychologist can work in conjunction with a physician if such services seem indicated. Fees for psychiatrists are usually higher, averaging about $90 an hour. Psychologists average from $40 to $60 an hour.

With fees in mind, your decision may be influenced by whether you have health insurance that will cover the expense. If fees are a problem, keep in mind that many individual therapists charge on a sliding scale, or ability-to-pay basis, and that community mental health centers almost always charge on a sliding scale.

Some communities now have counseling services staffed by sympathetic paraprofessional counselors, whose fees are much lower. There is a natural tendency, perhaps, to doubt the abilities of paraprofes-

Applications: Seeking Professional Help, continued

sionals. However, many studies have shown that paraprofessional counselors are often as effective as professionals (Hattie, Sharpley, & Rogers, 1984). Group therapy is also much less expensive because the therapist's fee is divided among several people.

The training and qualifications of a therapist usually can be learned simply by asking. A reputable therapist will be glad to reveal his or her background. If you have any doubts, you can check credentials or obtain other helpful information from local branches of any of the following organizations. You can also write to the addresses listed below.

The National Association for Mental Health
1800 North Kent Street
Rosslyn, VA 22209

The American Psychiatric Association
1700 18th Street N.W.
Washington, DC 20009

The American Psychological Association
1200 17th Street N.W.
Washington, DC 20036

The American Association of Humanistic Psychology
7 Hartwood Drive
Amherst, NY 14226

The question of how to pick a particular therapist remains. The best way is to start with a short consultation with a respected psychiatrist or psychologist or with a counselor at a mental health center. This will allow the person you visit to evaluate your problem and recommend an appropriate type of therapy or a therapist who is likely to be helpful. As an alternative you might ask the person teaching this course for a referral.

Question: How would I know whether to quit or ignore a therapist?

A balanced look at psychotherapies suggests that all *techniques* are about equally successful (Gomes-Schwartz et al., 1978; Stiles, Shapiro, & Elliot, 1986). However, all *therapists* are not equally successful.

Far more important than the approach used are the therapist's personal qualities. The most consistently successful psychotherapists are those who are willing to use whatever method seems most helpful for a client. They are also marked by personal characteristics of warmth, integrity, sincerity, and empathy (Frank, 1973; Katz, 1972).

It is perhaps most accurate to say that at this stage of development, psychotherapy is an art, not a science. Since the *relationship* between a client and therapist is the therapist's most basic tool, you must trust and easily relate to a therapist for therapy to be effective.

Becoming a Community Mental Health Resource—How to Help

Question: What can be done to help a friend or relative who has a temporary personal problem or emotional crisis?

Everyone is occasionally faced with the task of comforting a troubled friend. For the majority of such upsets any caring, emotionally stable, empathic person can aid effectively. For example, Carl Rogers (1980) cites hotline volunteers who with minimal training sometimes "use skill and judgment that would make a professional green with envy." But how can you best give support? Jerome Frank (1973), Carl Rogers (1957), and others agree about two essential conditions for aiding constructive change. These are:

1. An unconditional acceptance of the troubled person, an unshakable positive regard for him or her as a human.
2. A capacity to communicate to the person an understanding of the discomfort he or she is feeling.

We may call the second quality *empathy*, the ability to enter another person's private world, to understand feelings, and to share psychological pain. Because empathy and true caring cannot be faked, your support at times of crisis can be more valuable than anything the best-trained professional can offer. John O. Stevens (1971) has summarized:

Applications: Seeking Professional Help, continued

> The way to really help someone is not to help him do anything but become more aware of his own experience—his feelings, his actions, his fantasies—and insist that he explore his own experience more deeply and take responsibility for it, no matter what that experience is.

Question: I'm still not sure exactly what is best to do when a friend wants to talk about a problem.

Several points may be kept in mind when "counseling" a friend. (Also, see Table 21-3.)

Active Listening People frequently talk "at" each other without really listening. A person with problems needs to be heard. Make a sincere effort to listen to and understand the person. Try to accept the person's message without judging it or immediately leaping to conclusions (Kottler & Brown, 1985). Let the person know you are listening—through eye contact, posture, your tone of voice, and your replies (Ivey & Galvin, 1984).

Clarify the Problem People who have a clear idea of what is wrong in their lives are in a better position to discover solutions. Try to understand the problem from the person's point of view. As you do, check your understanding often. For example, you might ask, "Are you saying that you feel depressed just at school? Or in general?" Remember, a problem well defined is often half solved.

Focus on Feelings Feelings are neither right nor wrong. By focusing on feelings, you can avoid making the person defensive. Passing judgment on what is said prevents the free outpouring of emotion that is the basis for catharsis. For example, a friend confides that he has failed a test. Perhaps you know that he studies very little. If you say, "Maybe if you studied a little more, you would do better," he will probably become defensive or hostile. Much more can be accomplished by saying, "You must feel very frustrated" or, simply, "How do you feel about it?" Remember too that feelings are often revealed by facial gestures, tone of voice, and movements (Ivey & Galvin, 1984).

Avoid Giving Advice Many people mistakenly think that they must solve others' problems for them. Remember that your goal is to provide understanding and support, not solutions (Egan, 1984). Of course, it is reasonable to give advice when you are asked for it, but beware of the trap of the "Why don't you . . . ? Yes, but . . ." game. According to Berne (1964), this "game" follows a pattern: Someone says, "I have this problem." You say, "Why don't you do thus and so?" The person replies, "Yes, but . . ." and then gives several reasons why your suggestion won't work. If you make a new suggestion, the reply will once again be, "Yes, but . . ." because the person either knows more about his or her personal situation than you do or because he or she has reasons for avoiding your advice. The student described earlier knows he needs to study. His problem is to understand why he doesn't *want* to study.

Accept the Person's Frame of Reference W. I. Thomas said, "Things perceived as real are real in their effect." Try to resist the temptation to contradict the person with your point of view. Since we all live in different psychological worlds, there is no "correct" view of a life situation. A person who feels that his or her point of view is understood feels freer to examine it objectively and to question it.

Reflect Thoughts and Feelings One of the best things you can do when "counseling" a friend is to give feedback by simply restating what is said. This is also a good way to encourage a person to talk. If your friend seems to be at a loss for words, *restate* or *paraphrase* his or her last sentence: For example:

Friend: I'm really down about school. I can't get interested in any of my classes. I flunked my Spanish test, and somebody stole my notebook for psychology.
You: You're really upset about school, aren't you?
Friend: Yeah, and my parents are hassling me about my grades again.
You: You're feeling pressured by your parents?
Friend: Yeah, damn.
You: It must make you angry to be pressured by them.

As simple as this sounds, it is very helpful to someone trying to sort out feelings. Try it. If nothing

Applications: Seeking Professional Help, continued

else, you'll develop a reputation as a fantastic conversationalist!

Silence Studies of counselors show that they tend to wait longer before responding than do people in everyday conversations. Pauses of 5 seconds or more are not unusual, and interrupting is rare. Listening patiently lets the person feel unhurried and encourages her or him to speak freely (Goodman, 1984).

Questions Because your goal is to encourage free expression, *open questions* tend to be the most helpful (Goodman, 1984). A *closed* question is one that can be answered yes or no. Open questions call for an open-ended reply. Say, for example, that a friend tells you, "I feel like my boss has it in for me at work." A closed question response would be, "Oh yeah? So, are you going to quit?" Open questions, such as, "Do you want to tell me about it?" or "How do you feel about it?" are more likely to be helpful.

Maintain Confidentiality Your efforts to help will be wasted if you fail to respect the privacy of someone who has confided in you. Put yourself in the person's place. Don't gossip.

These guidelines are not an invitation to play "junior therapist." Professional therapists are trained to approach serious problems with skills far exceeding those described here. Also, formal therapy provides a protected and confidential arena for problem solving. The point of this discussion is that each of us can supply two of the greatest mental health resources available at any cost: friendship and honest communication.

Table 21-3 Helping Behaviors

To help another person gain insight into a personal problem, it is valuable to keep the following comparison in mind (adapted from Kottler & Brown, 1985, p. 45).

Behaviors that Help	Behaviors that Hinder
Active listening	Probing painful topics
Acceptance	Judging/moralizing
Reflecting feelings	Criticism
Open-ended questioning	Threats
Supportive statements	Rejection
Respect	Ridicule/sarcasm
Patience	Impatience
Genuineness	Placing blame
Paraphrasing	Opinionated statements

Chapter Summary

- *Psychotherapies* may be classified as *insight* therapies, *action* therapies, *directive* therapies, *nondirective* therapies, and combinations of these. *Behavior therapy* and *cognitive behavior therapy* are major action-oriented approaches. Therapies may be conducted either *individually* or in *groups*.
- Primitive approaches to mental illness were often superstitious and misguided. *Trepanning* involved boring a hole in the skull. *Demonology*, used in the Middle Ages, attributed mental disturbance to supernatural forces and prescribed *exorcism* as the cure. In some instances, the actual cause of bizarre behavior may have been *ergot poisoning*. More humane treatment began in 1793 with the work of *Philippe Pinel* in Paris.
- Freud's *psychoanalysis* was the first formal psychotherapy. Psychoanalysis seeks a release of repressed thoughts and emotions from the unconscious. The psy-

choanalyst uses the techniques of *free association*, *dream analysis*, and *analysis of resistance* and *transference* to reveal health-producing insights.

- Some critics have argued that traditional psychoanalysis takes so long that patients may simply experience a *spontaneous remission* of symptoms. However, psychoanalysis has been shown to be better than no treatment at all. Also, *short-term dynamic therapy* (which relies on psychoanalytic theory but is brief and focused) is as effective as other major therapies.
- *Client-centered* (or *person-centered*) therapy is nondirective and is dedicated to creation of an *atmosphere of growth*. *Unconditional positive regard*, *empathy*, *authenticity*, and *reflection* are combined to give clients a chance to solve their own problems.
- *Existential therapies*, such as Frankl's *logotherapy*, focus on the end result of the choices one makes in life. Clients are encouraged through *confrontation* and *encounter* to exercise *free will* and to take responsibility for their choices. The goal of existential therapy is to reestablish meaning in one's life.
- *Gestalt therapy* emphasizes immediate awareness of thoughts and feelings. Its goal is to rebuild thinking, feeling, and acting into connected wholes and to help clients break through emotional blocks.
- *Group therapy* may be a simple extension of individual methods or it may be based on techniques developed specifically for groups. In *psychodrama*, individuals enact roles and incidents resembling their real-life problems. In *family therapy*, the family group is treated as a unit.
- Although they are not literally psychotherapies, sensitivity and encounter groups attempt to encourage positive personality change. *Sensitivity groups* tend to be nonconfrontive, their emphasis being on self-awareness, trust, and communication. In *encounter groups*, participants actively tear down false fronts and defenses. In recent years, commercially offered *large group awareness trainings* have become popular. However, the therapeutic benefits of such programs are questionable.
- In *transactional analysis (TA)*, people learn to apply the P-A-C (Parent-Adult-Child) analysis to their own and others' behavior. By placing the Adult in control, people learn to draw on the strengths of each *ego-state*. They also learn to recognize *complementary*, *crossed*, and *ulterior transactions* and to avoid *games*.
- Outcome studies of psychotherapy show that it is generally effective. The majority of clients show improvement within 6 months of beginning therapy. However, there are large differences in how various individuals respond to therapy.
- All psychotherapies offer a *caring relationship*, *emotional rapport*, a *protected setting*, *catharsis*, *explanations* for clients' problems, and a *line of action* to follow in alleviating them.
- Sources of psychological help exist in most communities. A competent and reputable therapist can usually be located through a *referral*. Providing *empathy* is a major way to support a troubled friend. Other points to keep in mind are to *listen actively*, try to help the person *clarify the problem*, *focus on feelings*, avoid giving *unwanted advice*, accept the person's *perspective*, *reflect* thoughts and feelings, be *patient* during silences, use *open questions* when possible, and maintain *confidentiality*.

Chapter 22

Behavior Therapy

Chapter Preview

Behavior Therapy and the Twilight Zone

Five times a day, for several days, Brooks Workman stopped what she was doing and vividly imagined opening a soft drink can. She made a point of picturing herself bringing the can to her mouth and placing her lips on it. Just as she was about to drink, hordes of roaches poured out of the can and scurried into her mouth—writhing, twitching, and wiggling their feelers (Williams & Long, 1979).

Question: Why would anyone imagine such a thing?

Brooks Workman's behavior is not as strange as it sounds. Her goal was self-control: Brooks felt that she was drinking too many colas and she wanted to cut down. The method she chose (called covert sensitization*) is a form of* behavior therapy*. Behavioral approaches include* **behavior modification** *(the use of learning principles to change behavior) and* **cognitive behavior therapy** *(the use of learning principles to change upsetting thoughts and beliefs).*

Behavior Therapy *In the previous chapter we discussed therapies based on insight or self-awareness. Here we will consider* action-oriented *approaches. Behavior therapists believe that insight or deep understanding of one's problems is often unnecessary for improvement. Instead, behavior therapists try to directly alter troublesome thoughts and behaviors.*

Brooks Workman didn't need to probe into her past or her emotions and conflicts; she simply wanted to break a bothersome habit. Even when serious problems are at stake, techniques like the one she used have proved valuable. Behavior therapy has helped people stop drinking, smoking, hiccuping, stuttering, and molesting children. Behavior modification can be used to lose weight or to increase eating in the pathologically underweight. It has improved study habits, work output in factories, and speech in retarded and disturbed children, and it has increased the amount of time psychotic patients will go without hallucinating. Also, through behavior modification, people have conquered fears of heights, snakes, public speaking, sexual intimacy, and automobiles.

The list of possible applications for behavioral approaches is practically endless. It is almost certain that you will discover a useful technique for self-improvement in this chapter. But before we begin, here is something to think about.

The Twilight Zone? *Pretend for a moment that you work for the telephone company and that you have been sent to repair a phone. Picture a professional building similar to those in which your doctor and dentist are found. Inside the front door is an office bustling with quiet activity. As you look down the hall, you see the offices of several therapists. You ask where the broken phone is. A secretary tells you it is at the opposite end of the building and asks you to follow. The secretary opens a door on your left. As you step through it, your mind reels.*

In confusion you rapidly scan your surroundings. You are in a tavern! In the dim light you see a bar and heavily padded stools. Behind the counter, a bartender polishes glasses in front of a large mirror and a row of bottles. Lighted displays advertising beer glow softly from the wall, and music flows from an unseen speaker.

Catching sight of the secretary again, you wind your way through the tables and hurry to a door on the opposite side of the room. Once again you are in an ordinary office. But over your shoulder you see the bartender close the door behind you, and the strains of music die abruptly with the click of the latch.

What's happening here? Was it a hallucination? A movie set? A modern version of Alice in Wonderland? *A hideout for the CIA? For an answer, read further.*

Survey Questions How are learning principles applied in aversion therapy? Can behavior therapy be used to treat phobias, fears, and anxieties? What role does reinforcement play in behavior modification? Can behavior therapy change thoughts and emotions? How are behavioral principles applied to everyday problems?

Resources

Behavior Modification—Animal, Vegetable, or Mineral?

Question: In general, how does behavior therapy work?

Behavior therapy is based on one basic assumption: People have *learned* to be the way they are. Consequently, if they have learned responses that cause problems, then they can change them or *relearn* more appropriate responses. Broadly speaking, **behavior modification** refers to any attempt to use the learning principles of *classical* or *operant conditioning* to change human behavior.

Question: How does classical conditioning work? I'm not sure I remember.

Classical conditioning was described in Chapter 7. It is the process of learning originally studied by Russian physiologist Ivan Pavlov. Here is a brief review of Pavlov's principles:

> A previously neutral stimulus (the *conditioned stimulus*) is followed by a stimulus (the *unconditioned stimulus*) that always produces a response (the *unconditioned response*).

Eventually the conditioning stimulus begins to produce the response directly. The response is then called a *conditioned response*. Thus, for a child the sight of a hypodermic needle (CS) is followed by pain (US), which causes anxiety or emotional discomfort (UR). Eventually the sight of a hypodermic (the conditioned stimulus) may produce anxiety (a conditioned response) *before* the child feels any pain.

Question: What does classical conditioning have to do with behavior modification?

Classical conditioning can be used to associate discomfort with a bad habit. Psychologists call discomfort used in this way an *aversion*. An aversion may be used to combat an undesirable habit as it was in the case of the woman who wanted to drink fewer colas. When more powerful versions of this approach are used, it is called *aversion therapy*.

Behavior modification Application of learning principles to change or eliminate maladaptive or undesirable behavior.

Classical conditioning A basic form of learning discovered by Pavlov in which existing (reflex) responses become associated with new stimuli.

Conditioned aversion A learned dislike or conditioned negative emotional response to some stimulus.

Aversion therapy Suppression of an undesirable response by associating it with aversive (painful or uncomfortable) stimuli.

Response contingent Applying reinforcement, punishment, or other consequences only when a certain response is made.

Aversion Therapy—A Little Pain Goes a Long Way

Imagine that you are eating an apple. Suddenly you discover that you just bit a large green worm in half. You vomit. Months pass before you can eat an apple again without feeling ill. You have experienced a **conditioned aversion** to apples.

Question: Conditioning an aversion was mentioned as an application of classical conditioning in behavior modification. How is a conditioned aversion used in therapy?

In **aversion therapy** an individual learns to associate a strong aversion (or negative emotional response) with an undesirable habit such as drinking, overeating, or gambling. Aversion therapy has been used to cure hiccups, sneezing, stuttering (Goldiamond, 1965), vomiting (Lang & Melamed, 1969), bed-wetting (Wickes, 1958), and for treatment of fetishism, transvestism, and other "maladaptive" sexual behaviors (Fuastman, 1976). Aversion therapy can also be an aid to persons who want to quit smoking (see Box 22-1).

An excellent example of aversion therapy is provided by the work of Roger Vogler and his associates (1977). Vogler works with alcoholics who have been unable to stop drinking. For many clients aversion therapy is a last chance. They have often been threatened with desertion by relatives and friends, have lost their jobs, and have tried Alcoholics Anonymous, psychotherapy, detoxification, vitamin therapy, and even Antabuse therapy. (Antabuse is a drug that causes an alcoholic to become violently nauseated after he or she drinks.) Here is a typical aversion procedure:

> While drinking an alcoholic beverage, painful (although noninjurious) electric shocks are delivered to the client's hand. From the client's point of view, the shocks are unpredictable; he or she never knows for sure when one is due. Most of the time, however, the shocks come as the client is beginning to take a drink of alcohol (Fig. 22-1).

This *response-contingent* (or response-connected) shock obviously takes the immediate pleasure out of drinking. It also causes the alcohol abuser to develop a conditioned aversion to drinking. The sight and smell of alcohol and the motions of drinking begin to have a capacity to make the individual very uncomfortable.

Box 22-1

Puffing Up an Aversion

The fact that nicotine is toxic makes it easy to create an aversion to smoking. Behavior therapists have found that electric shock, nauseating drugs, and similar aversive stimuli are not required to make smokers uncomfortable. All that is needed is for the smoker to smoke—rapidly and for a long time.

Rapid smoking is the most widely used aversion therapy for smoking (Lichtenstein, 1982). In this method subjects are told to smoke continuously, taking a puff every 6 to 8 seconds. Rapid smoking continues until the smoker is miserable and can stand it no more. By then, most clients are thinking, "I never want to see another cigarette for the rest of my life."

A number of studies suggest that rapid smoking is the most effective behavior therapy for smoking. Research also indicates that the health risks of rapid smoking are small (Hall et al., 1984). Nevertheless, anyone tempted to try rapid smoking should realize that it is very unpleasant. Without the help of a therapist, most people quit too soon for the procedure to succeed. (An alternative method that is more practical is described in the Applications section of this chapter.)

The most basic problem with rapid smoking—like other stop-smoking methods—is that about one-half of those who quit smoking begin again (Hall et al., 1984). Because the "evil weed" calls so strongly to former smokers, support from a stop-smoking group or a close, caring person can make a big difference. Former smokers who get encouragement from others are much more likely to stay smoke-free (Lichtenstein, 1982).

Fig. 22-1 *Aversion therapy for drinking. The sights, smells, and tastes of drinking are associated with unpleasant electrical shocks applied to the hand.*

Question: But can't the person tell when it is "safe" to drink and when it is not?

Transfer, or *generalization*, of aversion conditioning to the "real world" is a problem. With this in mind, Vogler constructed in his office a vivid recreation of a "friendly neighborhood tavern," complete with a bar, tables, soft lights, music, and a bartender. Also provided are a "living room," a "bedroom," and a "kitchen." Clients undergo aversion therapy in a setting as much like the normal site of their drinking as possible, which helps assure that carryover of the aversion training will occur.

Actually, aversion therapy is used as a last resort, even for problems as serious as alcohol abuse. Vogler and his associates also train alcoholics to discriminate blood alcohol levels (so clients can tell how drunk they are). They teach alcoholics alternatives to drinking, and they offer education programs on alcohol abuse as well as general counseling (Vogler et al., 1977). They have also added an interesting twist to their aversion therapy: Alcohol abusers are videotaped as they go from sober to drunk. Later, they watch the videotaped drinking bout and see themselves with slurred speech, dropping cigarette ashes in their drinks, saying stupid and belligerent things. Most react with shame and embarrassment when they see the tapes. Apparently, few people have any idea of how unattractive they are when drunk.

To add to the videotape effect, the bartender is trained to provoke clients into becoming argumentative and obnoxious. Presumably, this is not too hard to do by the time the client is saying, "I am 'masshhhed'" (Vils, 1976). In the videotape self-confrontation held later, grossly drunken behaviors are replayed until the client says, "Okay, okay, I've seen enough." Seeing themselves as obnoxious drunks adds to the aversion people feel for drinking, and it increases their determination to quit.

Question: I'm not sure I'm comfortable with the idea of treating humans this way.

People are often disturbed (shocked?) by such methods. It must be emphasized that clients usually volunteer for aversion therapy because it helps them overcome a destructive habit. Indeed, commercial aversion programs for overeating, smoking, and alcohol abuse have attracted large numbers of willing customers.

When psychologists use aversion therapy, they often back it up with supportive counseling. Also, for mild problems, such as nail biting, a person may not have to undergo pain at all. Merely watching a trained actor (who *appears* to get electric shocks while biting his nails) can curb the problem (Rosenthal et al., 1978). Last, and most important, aversion therapy can be justified by its long-term benefits. As behaviorist Donald Baer puts it, "A small number of brief, painful experiences is a reasonable exchange for the interminable pain of a lifelong maladjustment" (Baer, 1971).

Generalization Transfer of a learned response from one stimulus situation to other similar situations.

Hierarchy A rank-ordered series of higher and lower amounts, levels, degrees, or steps.

Rapid smoking Prolonged smoking at a forced pace; used to produce discomfort in aversion therapy for smoking.

Learning Check

Before continuing, see if you can answer these questions. If not, review the preceding section.

1. What two types of conditioning are used in behavior modification? ____________ and ____________.

2. Aversion therapy is used to combat what? ____________.

3. Shock, pain, and discomfort play what role in conditioning an aversion?
a. conditioned stimulus *b.* unconditioned stimulus *c.* unconditioned response *d.* conditioned response

4. If shock is used to control drinking, it must be ____________ contingent.

5. A potential problem with aversion therapy is transfer of the aversion to settings outside the clinic or laboratory. T or F?

Answers: **1.** classical, operant **2.** undesirable responses or destructive habits **3.** *b* **4.** response **5.** T

Desensitization—Who's Afraid of a Big, Bad Hierarchy?

Assume you are a swimming instructor who wants to help a child overcome fear of the high diving board. How might you proceed? Directly forcing a terrified child off the high board could be a psychological disaster. Obviously, a better approach would be to begin by teaching the child to dive off the edge of the pool. Then the child could be taught to dive off the low board, followed by a platform 6 feet above the water, and then an 8-foot platform. As a last step the child could try the high board.

This *ordered set of steps* is called a **hierarchy.** The hierarchy allows the child to undergo *adaptation*. Gradually the child adapts to the high dive and overcomes fear, much as one adapts gradually to the cold water of a swimming pool on a

Desensitization A reduction in sensitivity to a stimulus; most often, a reduction in fear, anxiety, or aversion.

Reciprocal inhibition Principle stating that the presence of one emotional state can inhibit the occurrence of another, such as joy preventing fear or anxiety inhibiting pleasure.

Phobia An intense and unrealistic fear of some object or situation.

Vicarious desensitization A reduction in fear or anxiety that takes place vicariously ("second hand") when a client watches models perform the feared behavior.

Model A person (either live or filmed) who serves as an example for observational learning or vicarious conditioning.

hot day. When the child has overcome the fear, a psychologist would say that **desensitization** (dee-SEN-sih-tih-ZAY-shun) has occurred (Fig. 22-2).

Desensitization is also based on the principle of **reciprocal inhibition,** named by Joseph Wolpe (1974). Reciprocal inhibition means that one emotional state can prevent the occurrence of another. For instance, it is impossible to be anxious and relaxed at the same time. If we have managed to get our subject onto the high board in a relaxed state, anxiety and fear responses will be inhibited. Repeated times on the high board should cause fear in the situation to disappear. Again, we would say that the person has been *desensitized.* In general, desensitization (that is, a reduction in fears) is usually brought about by gradually approaching a feared stimulus while maintaining complete relaxation.

Question: What is desensitization used for?

Densensitization is primarily used to help people unlearn or countercondition phobias or strong anxieties. Almost everyone has a phobia or two. Many people fear heights, snakes, public speaking, spiders, and so forth. Usually these cause little difficulty because the individual carefully avoids fear-producing situations. However, consider the following: a teacher with stage fright, a student with test anxiety, a salesperson who fears people, an aspiring pole-vaulter who fears heights, or a newlywed with a fear of sexual intimacy. Each may be hampered enough by fears or anxieties to seek aid.

Question: How is desensitization done?

Desensitization usually involves three steps. First, the client and the therapist *construct a hierarchy.* This is a list of fear-provoking situations involving the phobia and ranging from the least disturbing situation to the most disturbing one. Second, the client is taught *exercises that produce total relaxation.* Once the client is relaxed, he or she proceeds to the third step by trying to *perform the least disturbing item* on the list. For a fear of heights (acrophobia), this might be: "(1)

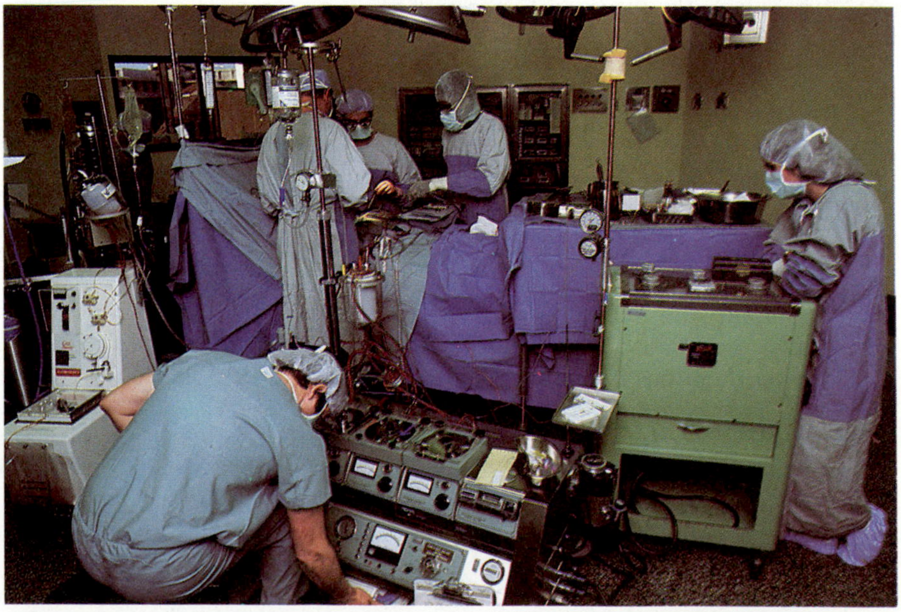

Fig. 22-2 *A case of natural desensitization: Doctors and nurses learn to remain calm at the sight of blood because of their frequent exposure to it.*

standing on a chair." The first item is repeated until no anxiety is felt. Any change from complete relaxation is a signal to clients that they must repeat the relaxation process before continuing. Slowly clients move up the hierarchy: "(2) climb to the top of a small stepladder"; "(3) look down a flight of stairs"; and so on, until the last item is performed without fear: "(20) fly in an airplane."

Question: I understand how some fears could be desensitized by gradual approach—like the child on the high dive. But how would a therapist use desensitization to combat fear of sexual intimacy?

For a person with a fear of heights, the steps of the hierarchy might be acted out. Often, however, acting out is totally impractical. In some cases this problem can be handled by having clients observe models (live or filmed) who are performing the feared behavior (Fig. 22-3). If such **vicarious desensitization** is not practical, there is yet another alternative. Fortunately, desensitization works almost as well when a person *vividly imagines* each step in the hierarchy. If the person can visualize the steps without anxiety, fear in the actual situation is reduced.

Here is a sample of the hierarchy imagined by a 24-year-old married woman to overcome the fear and disgust she felt for sexual intercourse. (Some steps are left out to shorten the list.)

1. Dancing with and embracing husband while fully clothed.
2. Being kissed on cheeks and forehead.
3. Being kissed on lips.
4. Sitting on husband's lap, both fully dressed.
5. Husband kisses neck and ears.
6. Husband caresses hair and face.

.
.
.

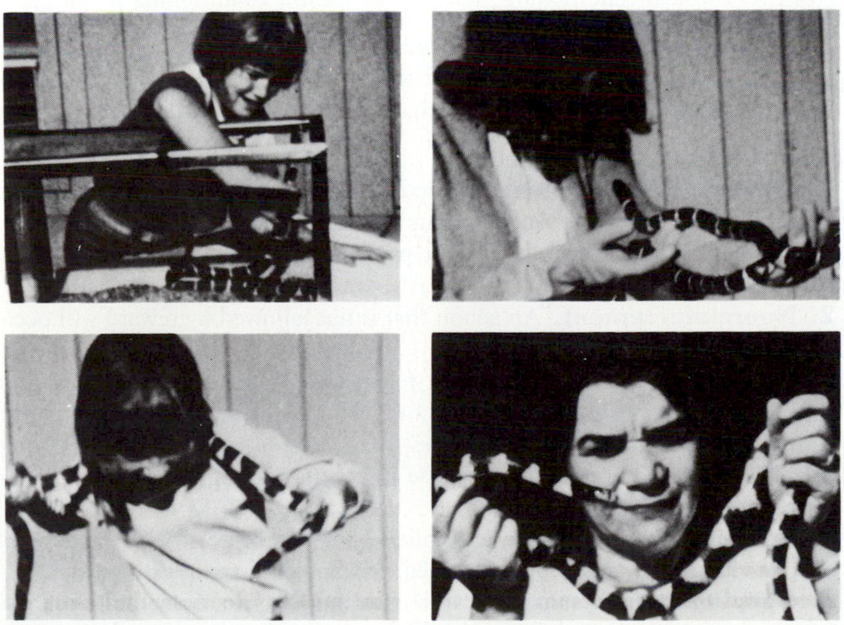

Fig. 22-3 *Treatment of a snake phobia by vicarious desensitization. The photographs show models interacting with snakes. To overcome their own fears, phobic subjects observed the models. (Bandura et al., 1969. Photos courtesy of Albert Bandura)*

17. Having intercourse in bed in the dark.
18. Having intercourse in the nude in the dining room or living room.
19. Changing positions during intercourse.
20. Having intercourse in the nude while sitting on husband's lap. (Adapted from Lazarus, 1964)

Mrs. A was able to imagine the last steps in this hierarchy without experiencing anxiety after a 3-month period of desensitization. Accordingly, she and her husband reported that their sexual and marital adjustments were greatly improved.

Learning Check

Answer these questions before reading on.

1. The ordered series of steps used in desensitization make up a ____________________ of feared situations.
2. What two principles underlie desensitization? ____________________ and ____________________.
3. When desensitization is carried out through the use of live or filmed models, it is called:
   a. cognitive therapy *b.* covert desensitization *c.* relaxation training *d.* vicarious desensitization
4. Three basic steps in desensitization are: construct a hierarchy, flood the person with anxiety, imagine relaxation. T or F?

Answers: **1.** hierarchy **2.** adaptation, reciprocal inhibition **3.** *d* **4.** F

Operant Principles—All the World Is a . . . Skinner Box?

Question: Aversion therapy and desensitization are forms of behavior modification based on classical conditioning. Where does operant conditioning fit in?

The principles of operant conditioning have been developed by B. F. Skinner and other psychologists mostly through laboratory research with animals. The operant principles most frequently used by behavior therapists to deal with *human* behavior are:

1. **Positive reinforcement.** An action that is followed by reward will occur more frequently. If children whine and get attention, they will whine more frequently. If you get A's in your psychology class, you may become a psychology major.
2. **Nonreinforcement.** An action that is not followed by reward will occur less frequently.
3. **Extinction.** If a response is not followed by a reward after it has been repeated many times, it will go away. After winning 3 times, you pull the handle on a slot machine 30 times more without a payoff. What do you do? You go away. So does the response of handle pulling (for that particular machine, at any rate).
4. **Punishment.** If a response is followed by discomfort or an undesirable effect, the response will be suppressed (but not necessarily extinguished).
5. **Shaping.** Shaping means rewarding actions that are closer and closer approximations to a desired response. If a response is complicated, it may never

occur and therefore cannot be rewarded. If I want to reward a retarded child for saying "ball," I may begin by rewarding the child for saying anything that starts with a *b* sound.

6. **Stimulus control.** Responses tend to come under the control of the situation in which they occur. If I set my clock 10 minutes fast, I can get to work on time in the morning. My departure is under the stimulus control of the clock even though I know it is fast.
7. **Time out.** A time-out procedure usually involves removing the individual from a situation in which reinforcement occurs. Time out prevents reward from following an undesirable response; it is a variation of nonreinforcement.

(For a more thorough review of operant principles, return to Chapter 7.) As simple as these principles may seem, they have been used very effectively by behavior modification specialists to overcome difficulties in work, home, school, and industrial settings. Let's see how.

Operant conditioning Type of learning that occurs when an organism actively "operates" on its environment and changes its behavior in response to the consequences of actions.

Extinction The result of consistently not reinforcing a response, which leads to a gradual decrease in the frequency with which the response occurs.

Time out Usually refers to removing a person from a situation in which rewards for maladaptive behavior are available, in order to produce extinction; also, the withholding of social reinforcers (attention, approval) when undesirable responses are made.

Nonreinforcement and Extinction—Time Out in the Attention Game

An extremely overweight mental patient had a persistent and disturbing habit: She stole food from other patients. No one could persuade her to stop stealing or to diet. For the sake of her health, a behavior therapist assigned her a special table in the ward dining room. If she approached any other table, she was immediately removed from the dining room. Since her attempts to steal food went unrewarded, they rapidly disappeared. Additionally, any attempt to steal from others usually resulted in the patient's missing her own meal (Ayllon, 1963).

Question: What operant principles did the therapist use?

The therapist used *nonreward* to produce *extinction*. Most frequently occurring human behaviors lead to some form of reward. An undesirable response can be eliminated by *identifying* and *removing* the rewards that maintain it. But people don't always do things for food, money, or other obvious rewards. Most of the rewards maintaining human behavior are more subtle. *Attention*, *approval*, and *concern* are common yet powerful reinforcers for humans (Fig. 22-4).

For instance, in a classroom we often find that misbehaving children are surrounded by others who giggle and pay attention to them. If seating is rearranged so that the disruptive children are surrounded by less responsive students, misbehavior decreases. Attention from a teacher (even scolding) can also be a reinforcer. An experiment showed that when teachers paid extra attention to classroom misbehavior, it increased. It increased even when the attention took the form of saying things such as "Sit down!" When misbehaving children were *ignored* and attention was given to children who were *not* misbehaving, misbehavior decreased (Madsen et al., 1968).

Question: How are nonreward and extinction applied in therapy?

Nonreward and extinction can eliminate many problem behaviors. Frequently, difficulties center around a limited number of particularly disturbing responses. A typical strategy used in institutions is called *time out*. Time out means refusing to

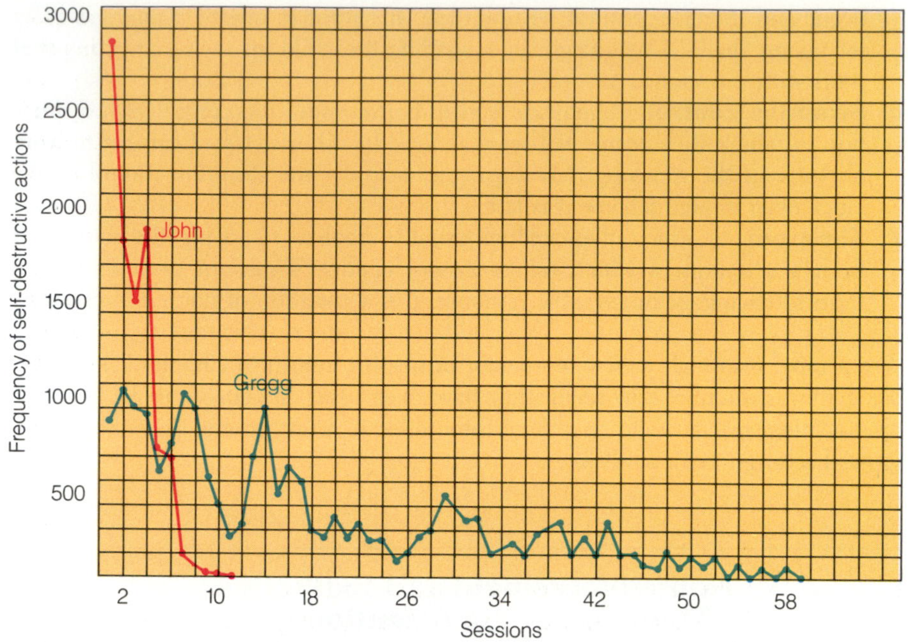

Fig. 22-4 *This graph shows extinction of self-destructive behavior in two autistic boys. Before extinction began, the boys received attention and concern from adults for injuring themselves. During extinction, self-damaging behavior was ignored. (Adapted from Lovaas & Simons, 1969)*

reward maladaptive responses, usually by refusing to play the *attention* game. Another form of time out is to remove an individual immediately from the setting in which an undesirable response occurs, so that the response will not be rewarded. For example:

> Fourteen-year-old Josh periodically appeared in the nude in the activity room of a training center for disturbed juveniles. This behavior always generated a great deal of attention from staff and other patients. Usually Josh was returned to his room and confined there. During this "confinement," he often missed doing his usual chores. As an experiment he was placed on time out. The next time he appeared nude, counselors and other staff members greeted him normally and then ignored him. Attention from other patients rapidly subsided. Sheepishly he returned to his room and dressed.

Reinforcement and Token Economies—The Target Is Health

This section might be called "Throwing a Lifeline to the Unreachable." A distressing problem faced when dealing with severe mental illness is how to "break through" to a patient who cannot, or will not, communicate. Mental patients sometimes spend years in hospitals without noticeable improvement. Even the patient who is willing to talk about his or her problem may make little visible progress toward mental health.

Question: What can be done in such circumstances?

An approach to therapy that is rapidly growing in popularity is based on the use of *tokens*. **Tokens** are *symbolic* rewards that can be exchanged for real rewards. (As you may recall from Chapter 7, tokens are secondary reinforcers.)

Tokens may be printed slips of paper, plastic "poker" chips, check marks, points, or "gold stars." Whatever form they take, tokens serve as rewards because they may be exchanged for candy, food, cigarettes, recreation, or other privileges, such as private time with a therapist, outings, using the record player, and so forth. Tokens are being used in mental hospitals, halfway houses for drug addicts, schools for the retarded, programs for delinquents, and ordinary classrooms. Their use is usually associated with dramatic improvements in behavior and overall adjustment.

Learning research and everyday experience point out the power of positive reinforcement to change behavior. If a response is followed by reward, it will occur more frequently. Using tokens, a therapist can *immediately* reward a positive response. This feature of tokens allows a therapist to use operant shaping to influence behavior instead of vaguely urging patients to "get themselves together."

So that incentives will have maximum impact, the therapist selects specific **target behaviors** that could or should be improved, then reinforces them with tokens. For example, an uncommunicative mental patient might initially be given a token each time he or she says a word. Next, tokens may be given for speaking a complete sentence. Later, the patient could gradually be required to speak more frequently, then to answer questions, and eventually to carry on a short conversation in order to receive tokens. In this way patients who have not spoken more than a few words for months or years have been returned to the world of normal communication.

Full-scale use of tokens in an institutional setting leads to the development of a **token economy.** In a token economy patients are rewarded with tokens for a wide range of socially desirable or productive activities. They must *pay* tokens for privileges and for engaging in problem behavior (Fig. 22-5). For example, tokens

Tokens Symbolic rewards, or secondary reinforcers (such as plastic chips, gold stars, or points) that can be exchanged for real reinforcers.

Target behaviors Actions or other behaviors (such as speech) selected by a therapist for reinforcement.

Token economy A therapeutic program in which a wide range of desirable behaviors is reinforced with tokens that can be exchanged for goods, services, activities, and privileges.

Fig. 22-5 *Pictured below are the tokens used in one token economy system; also pictured are credit values for various activities. Tokens may be exchanged for items or for privileges listed on the board. (Photographs courtesy of Dr. Robert P. Liberman)*

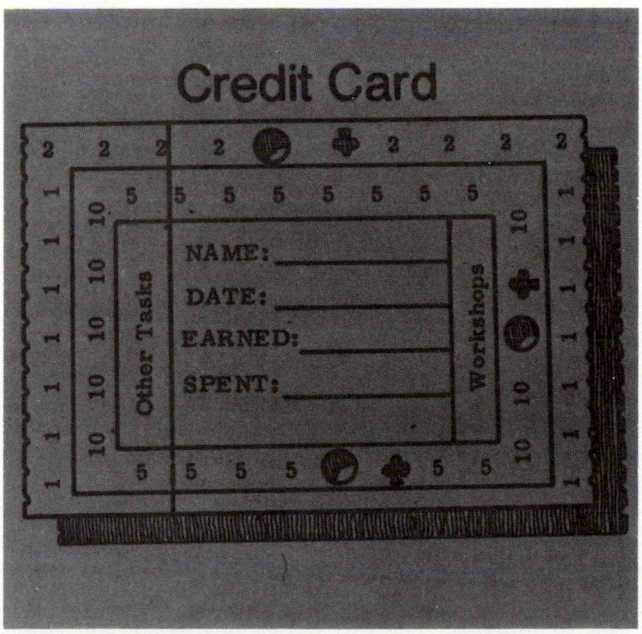

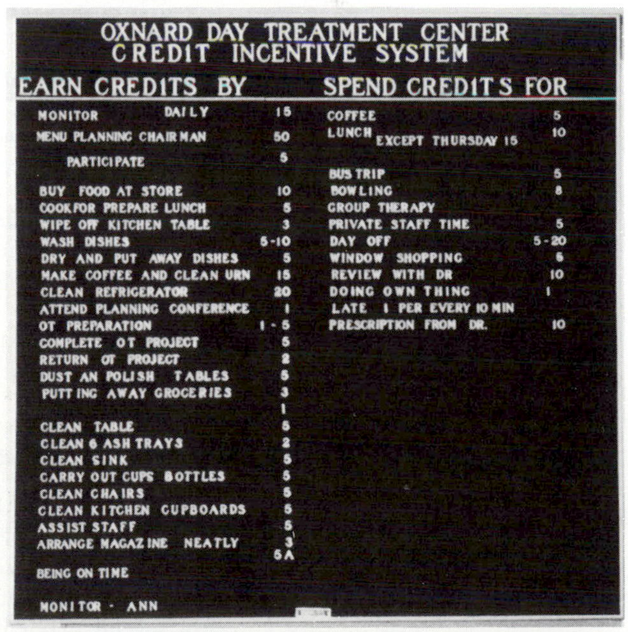

are given to patients who get out of bed, dress themselves, take required medication, arrive for meals in time, and the like. Work at constructive activity, such as gardening, cooking, or custodial duties, may also earn tokens. Patients *must exchange* tokens for meals and for private rooms, movies, passes, off-ward activities, and other privileges. Sometimes tokens can be exchanged for items at a commissary or ward store. Patients are *charged* tokens for staying in bed, disrobing in public, talking to themselves, fighting, crying, and similar target behaviors.

In a token economy program, staff members ensure that patients earn tokens easily for constructive behavior, but fine them heavily for destructive responses. This system provides the therapist with leverage. Patients are both pushed and enticed toward normality. The result can be a radical change in a patient's overall adjustment and morale. Patients have an incentive to change and are held responsible for their maladaptive habits and actions. Many "hopelessly" retarded, mentally ill, and delinquent people have been returned to a productive life by means of token economies.

Question: Wouldn't there be a problem with generalization of improvements brought about by a token economy?

Yes. As was the case with aversion therapy, lack of generalization can be a problem. To minimize this, patients are praised and given social recognition when they receive tokens. Each time a token is given, the therapist says something like "That was very good," or "You're doing so well."

By the time they are ready to leave the program, patients may be earning tokens on a weekly basis for maintaining sane, responsible, and productive behavior (Binder, 1976). The results of recent experiments suggest that the most effective token economies are those that ultimately depend on *social rewards* such as recognition and approval (Lieberman et al., 1976). Such rewards are what patients will receive when they return to family, friends, and community.

Cognitive Behavior Therapy—Think Positive!

Question: How would a behavior therapist treat a problem like depression? None of the techniques described seem to apply.

As we have discussed, behavior therapists usually try to change troublesome actions. However, in recent years a new breed of therapist has appeared. **Cognitive behavior therapists,** as they are called, are interested in thoughts as well as visible behavior. Rather than looking only at actions, cognitive therapists try to learn what people think, believe, and feel. They then help clients change *thinking patterns* that lead to trouble (Meichenbaum, 1977).

Cognitive Therapy for Depression

Cognitive therapy has been especially effective for treating depression. As you may recall from Chapter 12, Aron Beck believes that negative, self-defeating thoughts underlie depression. According to Beck, depressed persons see themselves, the world, and the future in negative terms. Beck (1985) believes this occurs because of several major distortions in thinking. The first is *selective perception:* If five good things happen during the day and three bad, the depressed person will focus only on the bad. *Overgeneralization* is a second thinking error underlying depression. An example would be considering yourself a total failure, or worthless, if you were to lose a job or fail a class. To complete the picture, Beck says that depressed persons tend to *magnify* the importance of undesirable events, and they engage in *all-or-nothing thinking* (seeing events, or themselves, as completely good or bad, right or wrong, successful or a failure) (Beck, 1985).

Question: What do cognitive behavior therapists do to alter such patterns?

Cognitive therapists make a step-by-step effort to correct negative thoughts that lead to depression or similar problems. At first, clients are taught to recognize and keep track of their own thoughts. The client and therapist then look for ideas and beliefs that cause depression, anger, avoidance, and so forth. For example, here's how a therapist might challenge all-or-nothing thinking (Burns & Persons, 1982):

Client: I'm feeling even more depressed. No one wants to hire me, and I can't even clean up my apartment. I feel completely incompetent!

Therapist: I see. The fact that you are unemployed and have a messy apartment proves that you are completely incompetent?

Client: Well . . . I can see that doesn't add up.

Next, clients are asked to gather information to test their beliefs. For instance, a depressed person might list his or her activities for a week. The list is then used to challenge all-or-nothing thoughts, such as "I had a terrible week" or "I'm a complete failure." With more coaching, clients learn to alter thoughts in ways that improve their moods, actions, and relationships.

In an alternate approach, the cognitive therapist looks for an *absence* of effective coping skills and thought patterns, not for the *presence* of self-defeating thinking (Meichenbaum, 1977). The aim is to teach clients how to cope with anger, depression, shyness, stress, and similar problems. Stress inoculation, which was described in Chapter 13, is a good example of this approach.

Cognitive behavior therapy is a promising and rapidly expanding specialty. Before we leave the topic, let's explore one more widely used form of cognitive therapy.

Rational-Emotive Therapy

According to Albert Ellis (1962, 1973), the basic idea of **rational-emotive therapy (RET)** is as easy as A-B-C. Ellis assumes that people become unhappy and develop self-defeating habits because of unrealistic or faulty *beliefs*.

Question: How are beliefs important?

Ellis analyzes problems in this way: The letter A stands for an **activating experience,** which the person assumes to be the cause of C, an emotional **consequence.** For instance, a person who is rejected (the activating experience) feels depressed, threatened, or hurt (the consequence). Rational-emotive therapy shows the client that the true cause of difficulty is what comes between A and C: In between is B, the client's irrational and unrealistic **beliefs.** In this example the

Cognitive behavior therapy The application of learning principles to change maladaptive thoughts, beliefs, and feelings that underlie emotional and behavioral problems.

Selective perception Perceiving only certain stimuli among a larger stimulus array.

Overgeneralization Extending the implications of a single event to a large number of unrelated situations.

All-or-nothing thinking Classifying objects or events as absolutely right or wrong, good or bad, acceptable or unacceptable, and so forth.

Rational-emotive therapy (RET) An approach stating that unrealistic and irrational beliefs cause many emotional problems and that such beliefs must be changed or abandoned.

Activating experience In rational-emotive therapy, any personal experience that appears to evoke a response, especially an emotional response.

Emotional consequence In RET, a person's emotional reaction to any given situation.

Belief In RET, a conviction or assumption that affects emotional reactions to various experiences.

Irrational assumption In RET, an unrealistic or self-defeating belief that causes emotional upsets and maladaptive behavior.

unrealistic belief leading to unnecessary suffering is: "I must be loved and approved of by almost everyone at all times" (see Table 22-1).

Ellis (1979) believes that most irrational beliefs come from three ideas, each of which is unrealistic:

1. I *must* perform well and be approved of by significant others. If I don't, then it is awful, I cannot stand it, and I am a rotten person.
2. You *must* treat me fairly. When you don't, it is horrible and I cannot bear it.
3. Conditions *must* be the way I want them to be. It is terrible when they are not, and I cannot stand living in such an awful world.

It's easy to see that such beliefs can lead to much grief and needless suffering in a less than perfect world.

Rational-emotive therapists are very directive in their attempts to change a client's irrational beliefs and self-talk. The therapist may directly attack clients' logic, challenge their thinking, confront them with evidence contrary to their beliefs, and may even assign homework.

RET has been criticized as superficial and argumentative by some, but Ellis' basic insight has considerable merit. For instance, one study found that having irrational beliefs, like those listed in Table 22-1, is related to feelings of anger and unhappiness (Rohsenow & Smith, 1982). Many of us would probably do well to surrender our irrational beliefs. Improved self-acceptance and a better tolerance of daily annoyances are the benefits of doing so (Ellis, 1976).

The value of cognitive approaches is further illustrated by three techniques (covert sensitization, thought stopping, and covert reinforcement) described in the Applications section that follows. See what you think of them.

Table 22-1 Ten Irrational Beliefs

1. I must be loved and approved of by almost every significant person in my life.
2. I should be completely competent and achieving in all ways to be a worthwhile person.
3. Certain people I must deal with are thoroughly bad and should be severely blamed and punished for it.
4. It is awful and upsetting when things are not the way I would very much like them to be.
5. My unhappiness is always caused by external events; I cannot control my emotional reactions.
6. If something unpleasant might happen, I should keep dwelling on it.
7. It is easier to avoid difficulties and responsibilities than to face them.
8. I should depend on others who are stronger than I am.
9. Because something once strongly affected my life, it will do so indefinitely.
10. There is always a perfect solution to human problems, and it is awful if this solution is not found.

(Adapted from Rohsenow & Smith, 1982.)

Learning Check

1. Behavior modification programs aimed at extinction of an undesirable behavior typically make use of what operant principles?
a. punishment and stimulus control
b. punishment and shaping
c. nonreinforcement and time out
d. stimulus control and time out

2. Attention can be a powerful ________________ for humans.

3. Token economies depend on use of the time-out procedure. T or F?

4. An advantage of tokens is that they can be used to ________________ ________________ a desired response.

5. Tokens are used at first to change specific actions called ________________ ________________.

6. Tokens basically allow the operant shaping of desired responses. T or F?

7. According to Beck, selective perception, overgeneralization, and ________________ thinking are cognitive habits that underlie depression.

8. RET teaches people to change the antecedents of irrational behavior. T or F?

Answers: **1.** c **2.** reinforcer **3.** F **4.** immediately reinforce **5.** target behaviors **6.** T **7.** all-or-nothing **8.** F

Applications

Self-Management—Applying Behavioral Principles to Yourself

"Throw out the snake oil, ladies and gentlemen, and throw away your troubles. Doctor B. Havior Modification is here to put an end to all human suffering."

True? Well, not quite. Behavior therapy is not a cure-all. Its use is often quite complicated and requires a great deal of experience and expertise. Also, there are times when therapists regard insight therapy as more appropriate than behavior therapy. Still, behavior therapy offers a straightforward solution to many problems.

It would be a serious mistake to presume that you could apply the principles of behavior therapy to major personal problems. As mentioned elsewhere in this book, professional help is available and should be sought when a significant problem exists. For lesser difficulties there is a good chance that you might succeed in modest attempts to apply the principles of behavior modification to yourself. Let us see how this might be done.

Covert Reward and Punishment—Boosting Your "Will Power"

"Have you ever decided to quit smoking cigarettes, watching television too much, eating too much, drinking too much, or driving too fast?"

"Well, one of those applies. I have decided several times to quit smoking."

"When have you decided?"

"Usually after I am reminded of how dangerous smoking is—like when I heard that my uncle had died of lung cancer. He smoked constantly."

"If you have decided to quit 'several times,' I assume you haven't succeeded?"

"No, the usual pattern is for me to become upset about smoking and then to cut down for a day or two."

"You forget the disturbing image of your uncle's death, or whatever, and start smoking again."

"Yes, I suppose if I had an uncle die every day or so, I might actually quit!"

The use of electric shock to condition an aversion seems remote for everyday problems. Even naturally

Applications: Self-Management, continued

aversive actions are difficult to apply to personal behavior. As mentioned earlier, for instance, rapid smoking is difficult for most smokers to carry out on their own. And, what about a problem like overeating? It would be difficult indeed to eat enough to create a lasting aversion to overeating.

In view of such limitations, psychologists have developed an alternative procedure that can be used to curb smoking, overeating, and other habits (Cautela & Bennett, 1981).

Covert Sensitization Obtain six 3-by-5 cards and on each write a brief description of a scene related to the habit you wish to control. The scene should be so *disturbing* or *disgusting* that thinking about it would temporarily make you very uncomfortable about indulging in the habit. For smoking, the cards might read:

1. I am in a doctor's office. The doctor looks at some X rays and tells me I have lung cancer. She says a lung will have to be removed and she sets a date for the operation.
2. I am in bed under an oxygen tent. My chest feels caved in. There is a tube in my throat. I can barely breathe.
3. I wake up in the morning and smoke a cigarette. I begin to cough up blood.
4. Other cards would continue along the same line.

For overeating the cards might read:

1. I am at the beach. I get up to go for a swim and I overhear people whispering to each other, "Isn't that fat disgusting?"
2. I am at a store buying clothes. I try on several things that are too small. The only things that fit look like rumpled sacks. Salespeople are staring at me.
3. And so forth.

The trick, of course, is to get yourself to imagine or picture vividly each of these disturbing scenes *several times* a day. Imagining the scenes can be accomplished by placing them under *stimulus control*. Simply choose something you do *frequently* each day (such as getting a cup of coffee or getting up from your chair). Next make a rule. Before you can get a cup of coffee, or get up from your chair, or whatever you have selected as a cue, you must take out your cards and *vividly picture* yourself engaging in the action you wish to curb (eating or smoking, for example). Then *vividly picture* the scene described on the top card. Imagine the scene for 30 seconds. After visualizing the top card, move it to the bottom so the cards are rotated. Make new cards each week. The scenes can be made much more upsetting than the samples given here. The samples are toned down to keep you from being "grossed out."

Covert sensitization may sound as if you are "playing games with yourself," but it can be a great help if you want to cut down on a bad habit (Cautela, 1973). Try it!

Thought Stopping As discussed earlier, behavior therapists have begun to realize that thoughts, like visible responses, can also cause trouble. Think of times when you have repeatedly "put yourself down" mentally or when you have been preoccupied by needless worries, fears, or other negative and upsetting thoughts. If you would like to gain control over such thoughts, recent experiments show how it can be done.

The simplest thought-stopping technique makes use of mild punishment to suppress upsetting mental images and internal "talk." Simply place a large, flat rubber band around your wrist. As you go through the day, apply this rule: Each time you catch yourself thinking the upsetting image or thought, pull the rubber band away from your wrist and snap it. You need not make this terribly painful. Its value lies in drawing your attention to how often you form negative thoughts and in interrupting the flow of thoughts. Strong punishment is not required.

Question: It seems like this procedure might be abandoned rapidly. Is there an alternative?

A second thought-stopping procedure requires only that you interrupt upsetting thoughts each time they occur. Begin by setting aside time each day during which you will deliberately think the unwanted thought. As you begin to form the thought, shout

Applications: Self-Management, continued

"Stop!" aloud, with conviction. (Obviously you should choose a private spot for this part of the procedure!)

Repeat the thought-stopping procedure 10 to 20 times for the first 2 or 3 days. Then switch to shouting "Stop!" covertly (to yourself) rather than aloud. Thereafter, thought stopping can be carried out throughout the day, whenever upsetting thoughts occur (adapted from Williams & Long, 1979). After several days of practice, you should be able to stop unwanted thoughts whenever they occur.

Covert Reinforcement Earlier we discussed how punishing images can be linked to undesirable responses, such as smoking or overeating, to decrease their occurrence. Many people also find it helpful to covertly *reinforce* desired actions. For example, suppose your target behavior is "not eating dessert." If this were the case, you could (Cautela & Bennett, 1981):

> Imagine that you are standing at the dessert table with your friends. As dessert is passed, you politely refuse, and you feel good about staying on your diet.

These images would then be followed by imagining a pleasant, reinforcing scene:

> Imagine that you are your ideal weight. You look really slim in your favorite color and style. Someone you like says to you, "Gee, you've lost weight. I've never seen you look so good."

For many people, of course, actual direct reinforcement (as described in the Chapter 7 Applications) is the most powerful way to alter behavior. Nevertheless, covert or "visualized" reinforcement can have similar effects. To make use of covert reinforcement, choose one or more target behaviors and rehearse them mentally. Then follow each rehearsal with a vivid rewarding image.

Applying Desensitization—Overcoming Common Fears

You have prepared for 2 weeks to give a speech in a large class. As your turn approaches, your hands begin to tremble and perspire. Your heart pounds and you find it difficult to breathe. You say to your body, "Relax!" What happens? Nothing!

Relaxation The key to desensitization is relaxation. To inhibit fear, one must *learn* to relax. Here is a method for achieving deep-muscle relaxation.

> Tense the muscles in your right arm until they tremble. Hold them tight for about 5 seconds and then let go. Allow your hand and arm to go limp and to relax completely. Repeat the procedure. Releasing tension two or three times will allow you to feel whether your arm muscles have relaxed. Repeat the tension-release procedure with your left arm. Compare it with your right arm. Repeat until the left arm is equally relaxed. Apply the tension-release technique to your right leg; to your left leg; to your abdomen; to your chest and shoulders. Clench and release your chin, neck, and throat. Wrinkle and release your forehead and scalp. Tighten and release your mouth and face muscles. As a last step, curl your toes and tense your feet. Then release. Practice relaxation with the tension-release method until you can achieve complete relaxation quickly (5 to 10 minutes).

After you have practiced relaxation once a day for a week or two, you will begin to be able to tell when your body (or a group of muscles) is tense. Also, you will begin to be able to relax on command. As an alternative you might want to try imagining a very safe, pleasant, and relaxing scene. Some people find such images as relaxing as the tension-release method (Crits-Christoph & Singer, 1984).

Once you have learned to relax, the next step is to identify the fear you would like to control and construct a *hierarchy*.

Procedure for Constructing a Hierarchy
Make a list of situations (related to the fear) that make you anxious. Try to list at least 10 situations. Some should be very frightening and others only mildly frightening. Write a short description of each situation on a separate 3-by-5 card. Place the cards in order from the least disturbing situation to the most disturbing. Here is a sample hierarchy for a student afraid of public speaking:

Applications: Self-Management, continued

1. Given an assignment to speak in class.
2. Thinking about the topic and the date the speech must be given.
3. Writing the speech; thinking about delivering the speech.
4. Watching other students speak in class the week before the speech date.
5. Rehearsing the speech alone; pretending to give it to the class.
6. Delivering the speech to my roommate; pretending my roommate is the teacher.
7. Reviewing the speech on the day it is to be presented.
8. Entering the classroom; waiting and thinking about the speech.
9. Being called; standing up; facing the audience.
10. Delivering the speech.

Using the Hierarchy When you have mastered the relaxation exercises and have the hierarchy constructed, set aside time each day to work on reducing your fear. Begin by performing the relaxation exercises. When you are completely relaxed, visualize the scene on the first card (the least frightening scene). If you can *vividly* picture and imagine yourself in the first situation twice *without a noticeable increase in muscle tension*, proceed to the next card. Also, as you progress through the cards, relax yourself between each card.

Each day, stop when you reach a card that you cannot visualize without tension after making three attempts. Each day, begin one or two cards before the one on which you stopped the previous day. Continue to work with the cards until you can visualize the last situation without experiencing tension (techniques are based on Wolpe, 1974).

By using this approach, you should be able to reduce the fear or anxiety associated with things such as public speaking, entering darkened rooms, asking questions in large classes, heights, talking to members of the opposite sex, taking tests, and so forth. Even if you are unable to reduce a fear, you will have learned to place relaxation under voluntary control. This alone is valuable because controlling unnecessary tension can increase energy and efficiency.

Learning Check

1. Covert sensitization and thought stopping combine aversion therapy and cognitive therapy. T or F?
2. Like covert aversion conditioning, covert reinforcement of desired responses is also possible. T or F?
3. Exercises that bring about deep-muscle relaxation are an essential element in covert sensitization. T or F?
4. Items in a desensitization hierarchy should be placed in order from least disturbing to most disturbing. T or F?
5. The first step in desensitization is to place the visualization of disturbing images under stimulus control. T or F?

Answers: **1.** T **2.** T **3.** F **4.** T **5.** F

Chapter Summary

- *Behavior therapists* use variations of *behavior modification*, therapeutic techniques that apply the learning principles of *operant* and *classical conditioning*, to bring about positive changes in human behavior.
- Classical conditioning, the pairing of a *conditioned stimulus* (CS) and an *unconditioned stimulus* (US), can be used to condition an *aversion* when the US causes pain or discomfort.
- In *aversion therapy*, the sights, sounds, odors, and motions of a maladaptive response or bad habit (such as smoking or drinking) are associated with pain or other aversive events. Thus, the undesirable response becomes linked with an aversion that inhibits occurrence of the response.
- Classical conditioning also underlies *desensitization*, a technique used to overcome fears and anxieties. In desensitization, gradual *adaptation* and *reciprocal inhibition* serve to break the link between fear and particular situations. Typical steps in desensitization are: *constructing a hierarchy* of feared situations, *learning to produce total relaxation*, and *performing items on the hierarchy* (from least to most disturbing).
- Desensitization may be carried out with real settings and situations in the environment or it may be carried out by *vivid imagination* of the fear hierarchy. Desensitization is also effective when it is administered *vicariously;* that is, when clients watch *models* perform the feared responses.
- Behavior modification also makes use of operant principles. The most commonly used principles are: *positive reinforcement*, *nonreinforcement*, *extinction*, *punishment*, *shaping*, *stimulus control*, and *time out*. Through the application of these principles, behavior modification is used to extinguish undesirable responses and to promote constructive behavior.
- Nonreward can be used to produce extinction of troublesome behaviors. Often this is done by simply *identifying* and *eliminating* reinforcers, particularly *attention* and *approval*.
- In the application of positive reinforcement and operant shaping, symbolic rewards known as *tokens* are often used. Tokens allow *immediate reinforcement* of selected *target behaviors* so that rapid shaping is possible.
- Full-scale use of tokens in an institutional setting produces a *token economy*. In a token economy, responsibilities, goods, services, and privileges are assigned values, and tokens are earned and exchanged. Toward the end of a token economy program, patients are shifted to *social rewards* such as recognition and approval.
- *Cognitive behavior therapy* is a new specialty that emphasizes changing thought patterns that underlie emotional or behavioral problems. Its goals are to correct distorted thinking and/or to teach improved coping skills.
- In a variation of cognitive therapy called *rational-emotive therapy* (RET), clients learn to recognize and challenge their own *irrational beliefs*. In the ABC *analysis* of RET, changing B (beliefs) alters the emotional consequences (C) of activating events (A).
- Cognitive-behavioral techniques can be an aid to managing one's own behavior. In *covert sensitization*, *aversive images* are used to discourage unwanted behavior. *Thought stopping* uses mild punishment to prevent upsetting thoughts. *Covert reinforcement* is a way to encourage desired responses by mental rehearsal. *Desensitization* pairs relaxation with a hierarchy of upsetting images in order to lessen fears.

Part Seven

Self and Others

Chapter 23
Human Sexuality

The Development of Sex Differences
Sex Roles and Sex Role Socialization
Sexual Behavior
Human Sexual Response
Male and Female Responses Compared
Attitudes and Sexual Behavior
Applications: Sexual Problems

Chapter 24
Social Psychology I

Humans in a Social Context—People, People Everywhere
Personal Space—Invisible Boundaries
Social Perception—Behind the Mask
The Need for Affiliation—Come Together
Interpersonal Attraction—Social Magnetism?
Social Influence—Follow the Leader
Social Power—Who Can Do What to Whom?
Obedience—Would You Electrocute a Stranger?
Compliance—A Foot in the Door
Applications: Assertiveness Training—Standing Up for Your Rights

Chapter 25
Social Psychology II

Attitudes—Belief + Emotion + Action
Attitude Change—Why the "Seekers" Went Public
Forced Attitude Change—Brainwashing and Cults
Prejudice—Attitudes That Injure
Intergroup Conflict—The Roots of Prejudice
Aggression—The World's Most Dangerous Animal
Applications: Helping—Prosocial Behavior

Chapter 26
Applied Psychology

Introduction to Applied Psychology
Industrial/Organizational Psychology—Psychology at Work
Environmental Psychology—Life in the Big City
A Panorama of Applied Psychology
Applications: Vocational Choice and Occupational Survival—Charting Your Course in the World of Work

Chapter 23

Human Sexuality

Chapter Preview

That Magic Word

Sex \seks n 1. one of the two divisions of organisms formed on the distinction of male and female.

"Sex" has many meanings: reproduction, gender, sexual identity, recreation, intimacy, and much more. Of the various meanings, the simplest would seem to be the reference to gender. What, really, could be simpler? Males are males and females are females, right? Wrong. Even something as basic as gender is complicated and many-sided.

Gender *The complexity of gender is illustrated by the attempt (1976) of Dr. Renée Richards to enter a women's tennis tournament. You may recall from news stories that Dr. Richards is a transsexual. Formerly she was Dr. Richard Raskin, a Newport Beach, California, opthalmologist. As a man Richard Raskin was a modestly successful tennis player. After a sex-change operation and hormone therapy to alter gender, Dr. Richards tried to launch a new tennis career as a woman. Understandably, other women players protested. Officials finally decided to use a genetic sex test to determine if Dr. Richards could compete. She, in turn, protested this test. Genetically she would still be considered male, but psychologically she is female—she has female genitals, and she functions socially as a female (Hyde, 1984). Is Dr. Richards, then, male or female?*

You might consider the case of Renée Richards an unfair example because the transsexual seeks an alteration of natural gender. For most people the various indicators of gender are in agreement. Nevertheless, it is not unusual to find occasional ambiguities among the various dimensions of a person's "sex." Contrary to common belief, gender is not a simple either-or classification. In the first part of this chapter we will consider some basic dimensions of "maleness" and "femaleness." An essential question we will address is, "How does one become male or female?"

Sexual Behavior *Each of us is by nature a sexual creature, an inescapable reality that springs from the basic biology of reproduction. With this reality in mind, later sections of this chapter discuss sexual behavior, sexual arousal and response, sexual problems, and attitudes toward sexuality. These are topics you may feel you already know a lot about. Therefore, before reading further you may find it interesting to see if you can correctly answer the* Human Sexuality Quiz. *Answers follow the quiz. The reasons for the answers can be found in this chapter.*

Human Sexuality Quiz *Indicate which of the statements are true and which are false.*

1. *Women are generally incapable of multiple orgasm.*
2. *Impotence in males is usually psychologically caused.*
3. *Frequent nocturnal emissions ("wet dreams") in males indicate the presence of a sexual disorder.*
4. *Male sexual potency and female pleasure in intercourse are closely related to penis size.*
5. *Of the various sexual dysfunctions, premature ejaculation is one of the easiest to treat.*
6. *In recent years medical advances have brought about a decline in the overall occurrence of sexually transmitted diseases.*
7. *For women, masturbation typically involves stimulation of the clitoris.*
8. *Sterilization in both men and women usually abolishes the sex drive.*
9. *Women have two kinds of orgasm, vaginal and clitoral.*
10. *Changes in sexual behavior brought about by the "sexual revolution" have had more impact on women than on men.*
11. *Men are more aroused by explicit erotic stimuli (such as pornographic films) than are women.*
12. *Maximum sexual responsiveness generally occurs at a later age for women than it does for men.*

Answers: 1. F 2. T 3. F 4. F 5. T 6. F 7. T 8. F 9. F 10. T 11. F 12. T

Survey Questions What are the basic dimensions of gender? How does one's sense of maleness or femaleness develop? How are sex roles acquired? What are the most typical patterns of human sexual behavior? To what extent do males and females differ in sexual response? Have recent changes in attitudes affected sexual behavior? What are the most common sexual adjustment problems? How are they treated?

The Development of Sex Differences

It has been said that the one thing you will never forget about a person is that person's sex. Considering the number of activities, relationships, conflicts, and choices influenced by gender, it is no wonder that we pay close attention to it. Let's begin with a few basic questions: What does it mean to be male or female? What are the dimensions of gender? How do gender and sex role differences develop?

Male or Female? Traditionally, the basic physical differences between males and females have been divided into *primary* and *secondary* sexual characteristics.

Primary sexual characteristics refer to the sexual and reproductive organs themselves: the penis, testes, and scrotum in males; and the ovaries, uterus, and vagina in females (Figs. 23-1 and 23-2). As described in Chapter 15, **secondary sexual characteristics** appear at puberty in response to hormonal signals from the

Resources

Primary sexual characteristics
Gender as defined by the genitals and internal reproductive organs.

Secondary sexual characteristics
Sexual features other than the genitals and reproductive organs—such as the breasts, body shape, facial hair, and so forth.

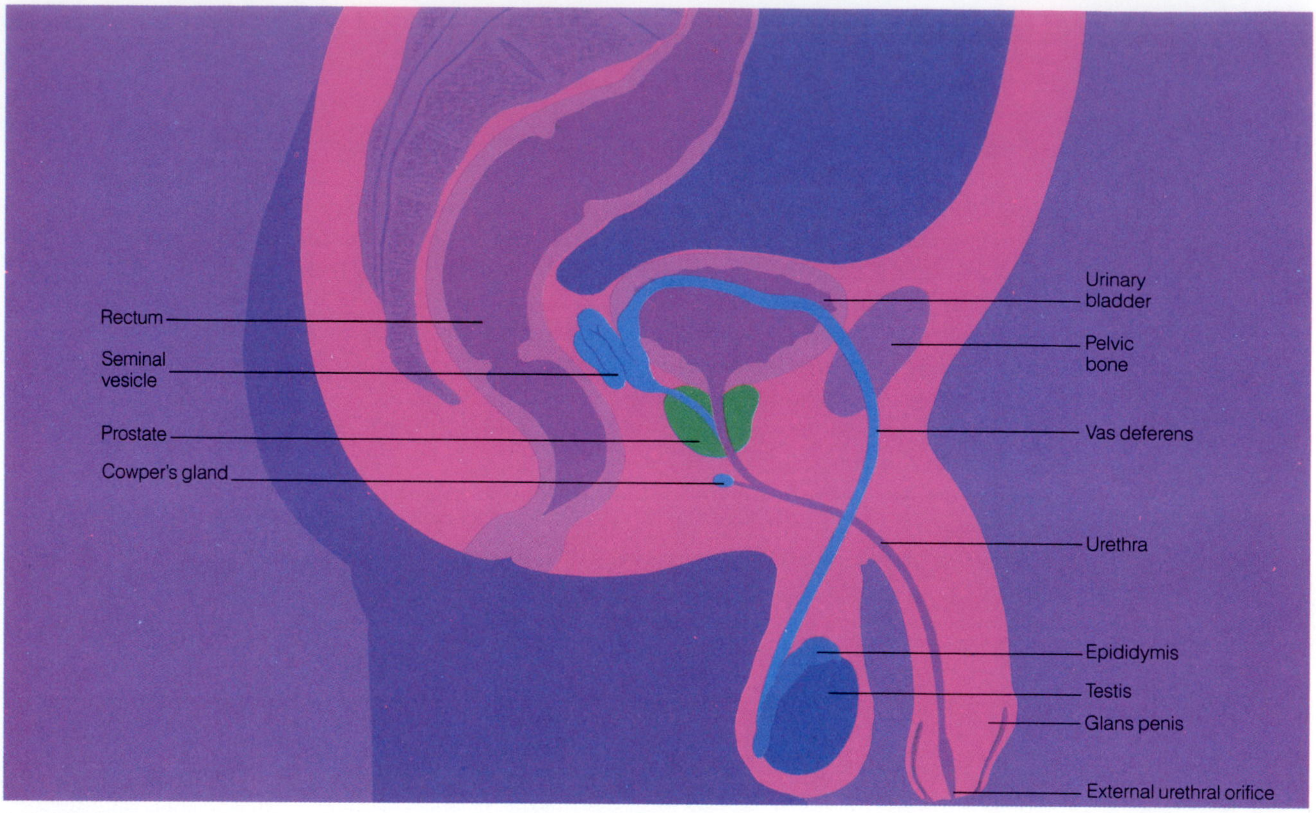

Fig. 23-1 *Cutaway view of internal and external male reproductive structures.*

Menarche The onset of menstruation; a woman's first menstrual period.

Menopause An end to regular monthly menstrual periods.

Gonads The primary sex glands—the testes in males and ovaries in females.

Estrogen Any of a number of female sex hormones.

Androgen Any of a number of male sex hormones, especially testosterone.

Testosterone Male sex hormone, secreted mainly by the testes and responsible for the development of male sexual characteristics.

pituitary gland. In females, secondary sexual characteristics involve development of the breasts, broadening of the hips, and other changes in body shape. Males develop facial and body hair, and the voice deepens. These changes signal readiness for reproduction. Reproductive maturity is especially evident in the female **menarche** (MEN-ar-kee: the onset of menstruation). From menarche until **menopause** (the end of regular monthly fertility cycles), women can bear children.

Question: What causes the development of sex differences?

In general terms, both primary and secondary sexual characteristics are related to the action of sex hormones in the body. (*Hormones* are chemical substances secreted by glands of the endocrine system.) The **gonads** (or sex glands) affect sexual development and behavior by secreting **estrogens** (female hormones) and **androgens** (male hormones). The gonads in the male are the testes, and in the female the ovaries. The adrenal glands (located above the kidneys) also supply sex hormones in both males and females. At puberty, adrenal secretions add to the development of secondary sexual characteristics.

Interestingly, all individuals normally produce both estrogens and androgens. It is the proportion of these substances that influences sex differences. In fact, the development of male or female anatomy is largely due to the presence or absence—before birth—of **testosterone** (one of the androgens).

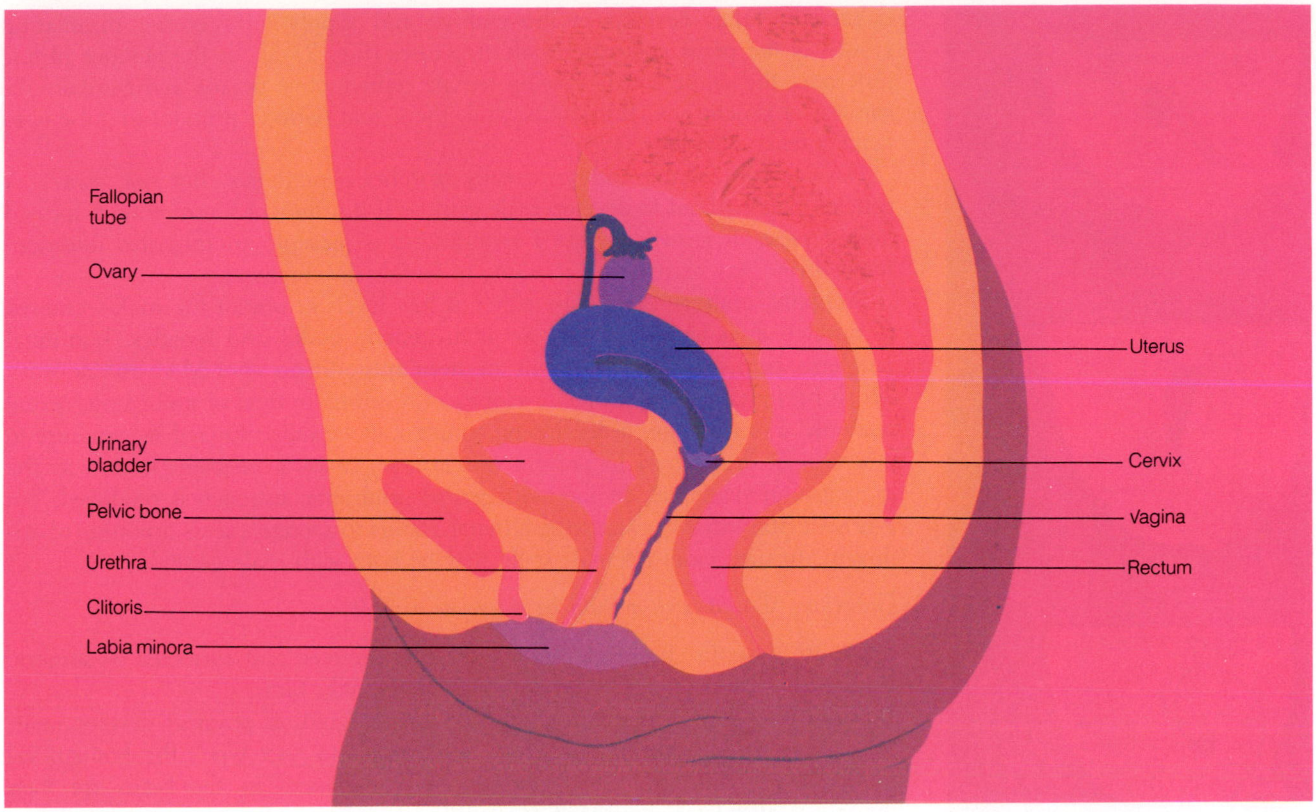

Fig. 23-2 *Cutaway view of internal and external female reproductive structures.*

Question: Then is biological sex determined by the sex hormones?

Not entirely. As suggested by our discussion in the Chapter Preview, gender cannot be reduced to a single dimension.

Dimensions of Gender At the very least, any designation of gender must include: (1) **genetic sex** (XX or XY chromosomes), (2) **gonadal sex** (ovaries or testes), (3) **hormonal sex** (predominance of androgens or estrogens), (4) **genital sex** (clitoris and vagina in females, penis and scrotum in males), and (5) **gender identity** (one's personal sense of maleness or femaleness) (Money & Ehrhardt, 1972).

To see why gender must be defined along several dimensions, let's follow the sequence of events involved in becoming male or female.

Gender Development Becoming male or female starts simply enough. Genetic sex is determined at the instant of conception: Two X chromosomes initiate development of a female; an X chromosome and a Y chromosome produce a male. Genetic sex remains the same throughout life, but it alone does not determine gender. We must also consider hormonal effects before birth.

For the first 6 weeks of prenatal development, there is no difference between a genetically male and a genetically female embryo. However, if a Y chromosome

Genetic sex Gender as indicated by the presence of XX (female) or XY (male) chromosomes.

Gonadal sex Gender as indicated by the presence of ovaries (female) or testes (male).

Hormonal sex Gender as indicated by a preponderance of estrogens (female) or androgens (male) in the body.

Genital sex Gender as indicated by the presence of male or female genitals.

Gender identity One's personal, private sense of maleness or femaleness.

is present, testes develop in the embryo and supply testosterone, stimulating growth of the penis and other male structures (Fig. 23-3). In the absence of testosterone, the embryo will develop female reproductive organs and genitals, regardless of genetic sex. It might be said, then, that nature's primary impulse is to make a female (Money, 1965).

Development of the embryo usually matches genetic sex, but not always. A genetic male will fail to develop male genitals if insufficient testosterone is formed during prenatal growth. Even if testosterone is present, an inherited *androgen insensitivity* may exist, again resulting in female development.

Similarly, androgens must be either at low levels or absent for an XX embryo to develop as a female. Thus, for both genetic males and females, hormonal problems before birth may result in **hermaphroditism** (her-MAF-ro-dite-ism), which means defects in sexual development resulting in dual or ambiguous sexual anatomy. For instance, a developing female may be masculinized by exposure to *progestin* (a drug given to prevent miscarriage) or by a problem known as the *androgenital syndrome*. In the androgenital syndrome, estrogen is produced, but a genetic abnormality causes the adrenal glands to secrete excess amounts of androgen. In such cases a female child may be born with male genitals.

Question: Would such a child be reared as a male?

Some are. Usually, however, the condition is detected and corrected by surgery. If necessary, extra estrogen may be administered after birth.

Some researchers believe that, in addition to guiding physical development, the balance of sex hormones before birth may also "sex type" the brain (Diamond, 1977; Kimura, 1985; Money, 1987). Changes in the brain are then thought to alter later chances of developing masculine or feminine characteristics.

Question: Does that mean there is a physical basis for male and female traits?

In animals, clear connections exist between prenatal hormones and later emergence of male or female behaviors. However, for humans evidence suggests that most sex-linked behavior is learned (Caplan et al., 1985, 1986; Weisstein, 1975). Be that as it may, some researchers believe that prenatal exposure to androgens or estrogens exerts a **biological biasing effect** on later psychosexual development in humans.

Question: Is there any evidence for this?

Consider females who have been exposed to androgens before birth. After birth, their hormone balance shifts to female and they are raised as girls. Does prenatal exposure to male hormones have any masculinizing effect on their psychological development? Medical psychologist John Money has observed that during childhood such girls are typically "tomboys" who prefer the company of males (Money, 1977). However, this masculinization does not persist into adulthood. After adolescence the girls' tomboyism usually gives way to traditional interests in marriage and motherhood (Money, 1987; Money & Mathews, 1982). Ultimately, cases like these seem to show that both prenatal hormones and later social factors contribute to adult sexual identity.

At the risk of getting entangled in the "battle of the sexes," let's consider one more idea. Some researchers believe that biology underlies male-female differences in thinking abilities. Women, they contend, are more often "left brained"

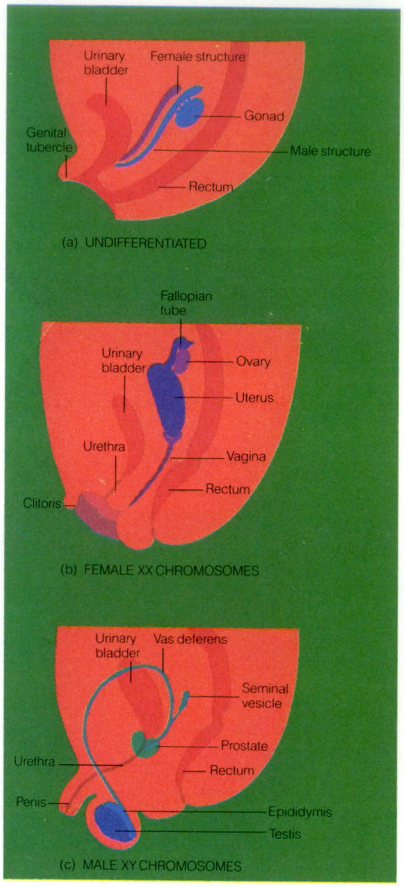

Fig. 23-3 *Prenatal development of the reproductive organs. Early development of ovaries or testes affects hormonal balance and alters sexual anatomy.* (a) *At first the sex organs are the same in the human male and female.* (b) *When androgens are absent, female structures develop.* (c) *Male sex organs are produced when androgens are present.*

and men "right brained." The left brain, you may recall, is largely responsible for language and rote learning. The right brain is superior at spatial reasoning. Thus, some psychologists believe biological differences explain why men (as a group) do better on spatial tasks and why women are better at language skills. Others, however, strongly reject this theory. To them, such claims are based on shakey evidence and sexist thinking (Caplan et al., 1985, 1986; Parlee, 1979; Unger, 1979). The one thing that is certain in this debate is that males and females are more alike than they are different (Maccoby & Jacklin, 1974). There is no biological basis for the unequal treatment women have often faced at work, school, and elsewhere.

Androgen insensitivity An inherited disorder in which male embryos fail to develop male genitals because of an unresponsiveness to testosterone.

Hermaphroditism The condition of having genitals suggestive of both sexes; ambiguous genital sexuality.

Androgenital syndrome An inherited disorder that causes the adrenal glands to produce excess androgens, sometimes masculinizing developing females before birth.

Biological biasing effect Hypothesized effect that prenatal exposure to male or female hormones has on development of the body, nervous system, and later behavior patterns.

Gender Identity One's personal, private sense of maleness or femaleness is referred to as *gender identity*, which can be distinguished from *sex roles*. Sex roles are observable traits, mannerisms, interests, and behaviors defined by one's culture as "male" or "female."

Gender identity appears to be a *learned* self-perception—a point emphasized by cases of hermaphroditism. If we compare two individuals having the same degree of hermaphroditism—one raised as a boy and the other as a girl—we will find that the person raised as a girl will act like and consider herself a girl, and the individual raised as a boy will act like and identify himself as a boy (Money, 1987).

Question: At what age is gender identity acquired?

Gender identity is essentially formed by 3 or 4 years of age (Money, 1977). Accordingly, children born with ambiguous gender have few problems as long as a final decision concerning their sex is made by the age of 18 months. If the parents consistently treat the child as a boy or a girl, the child should develop a clear sense of gender. Delaying the decision can create a situation in which the child develops a gender identity at odds with his or her biological sex, or a confused sense of sexual identity.

Question: How is gender identity acquired?

Obviously, it begins with *labeling* ("It's a boy"; "It's a girl"). Thereafter it is influenced by **sex role socialization**; that is, by the countless, subtle pressures exerted by parents, peers, and cultural forces that urge boys to "act like boys" and girls to "act like girls." In the next section we will investigate sex roles and sex role socialization in more detail.

Sex Roles and Sex Role Socialization

In determining adult sexual behavior and sex-linked personality traits, *sex roles* are probably as important as chromosomal, genital, or hormonal sex. **Sex role** refers to the pattern of behavior encouraged and expected of individuals on the basis of gender. In our culture boys are usually encouraged to be strong, fast, aggressive, dominant, achieving, and otherwise "male." Females have typically been expected to be sensitive, intuitive, passive, emotional, and "naturally" interested in household tasks and childrearing. The "naturalness" of such sex roles

Sex role socialization The process of learning behaviors considered appropriate for one's gender in a given culture.

Sex roles Separate patterns of traits, mannerisms, interests, and behaviors that are regarded as "male" and "female" by one's culture.

Instrumental behavior Behavior directed toward the achievement of some goal; behavior that is instrumental in producing some effect.

Expressive behavior Behavior that expresses or communicates emotion.

becomes questionable when they are compared with variations in different cultures. For example, Ethel Albert (1963) has identified numerous cultures in which women do the heavy work because men are considered too weak for it. In the Soviet Union approximately 75 percent of the medical doctors and a large proportion of the work force are women. Many more examples can be cited, but perhaps one of the most pertinent is anthropologist Margaret Mead's (1935) observations of the Tchambuli people of New Guinea.

Sex roles for the Tchambuli are a nearly perfect reversal of the American stereotypes. Tchambuli women handle the fishing and manufacturing and are expected to control the power and economic life of the community. Women also take the initiative in courting and sexual relations. Tchambuli men, on the other hand, are expected to be dependent, flirtatious, and concerned with their appearance. Art, games, and theatrics occupy most of the Tchambuli males' time, and males are particularly fond of adorning themselves with flowers and jewelry.

As the Tchambuli demonstrate, activities considered "appropriate" for males and females vary in different cultures. The arbitrary nature of sex roles is also apparent. A man is no less a man if he cooks, sews, or cares for children; a woman is no less a woman if she excels in sports, succeeds in business, or works as a mechanic. Still, adult personality and gender identity are closely tied to cultural definitions of "masculinity" and "femininity."

An interesting side effect of sex role socialization is the imprint left on activities having nothing to do with gender. On the average, for example, boys are superior to girls in math and visual-spatial skills. And, as previously mentioned, girls are superior to boys in language and verbal skills. There is also considerable evidence that boys are more aggressive than girls, that girls are more empathetic than boys, and so on (Block, 1979; Maccoby & Jacklin, 1974).

Question: How are such differences created?

Sex Role Socialization Learning sex roles begins immediately after birth. Infant girls are held more gently and treated more tenderly than boys are. Both parents play more roughly with their sons than with their daughters (who are presumed to be more "delicate"). Later, boys are allowed to roam over a wider area without special permission. They are also expected to run errands earlier than girls. Daughters are told that they are pretty and that "nice girls don't fight." Boys are told to be strong and that "boys don't cry." Sons are more often urged to control emotions than are daughters, and parents tolerate aggression toward other children more in boys than in girls.

The toys purchased for boys and girls are strongly sex typed: dolls for girls, trucks and guns for boys. Even bicycles come in "boys" and "girls" models (Hoffman, 1977; Wilson et al., 1984). By the time children reach kindergarten, they have learned to think that doctors, fire fighters, and pilots are men and that nurses, secretaries, and hairdressers are women (Blaske, 1984). And why not? The work force in America is still highly segregated by sex, and children learn from what they see.

Overall, parents tend to encourage their sons to engage in **instrumental** (goal-directed) **behaviors,** to control their emotions, and to prepare for the world of work. Daughters, on the other hand, are encouraged in **expressive** (emotion-oriented) **behaviors** and, to a lesser degree, are socialized for the maternal role.

When told that they respond differently to boys and girls, parents often explain that it is because there are "natural" differences between the sexes (Wilson et al., 1984). But what comes first, "natural differences" or the expectations that create them?

Question: Many people have become interested in the limitations imposed by stereotyped sex roles. Would such parental behavior apply to feminist mothers?

Sex roles are so pervasive that even feminists can be influenced by them. One study found that feminist women had little trouble treating their daughters in a nonstereotyped manner, but they seemed to want their sons to be "liberated but masculine." In other words, they had no anxieties when their daughters engaged in traditional "masculine" play, but they were upset if their sons played "dress up," preferred frilly clothes, imitated "female" mannerisms, or played with dolls (Van Gelder & Carmichael, 1975).

In our culture "male" seems—for many—to be defined as "not female." That is, many parents have a vague fear of expressive and emotional behavior in male children, because to them it seems to imply effeminacy (Wilson et al., 1984).

To summarize, sex role socialization in our society prepares children for an adult world in which men are expected to be instrumental, conquering, controlling, and unemotional, and in which women are expected to be expressive, emotional, passive, and dependent. Thus, sex role socialization prepares us to be highly competent in some respects and handicapped in others. Of course, many people find traditional sex roles comfortable and desirable. It seems evident, however, that just about everyone will benefit when the more stereotyped and burdensome aspects of sex roles are set aside.

Learning Check

To check your progress, answer the following questions:

1. ____________ sexual characteristics refer to the sexual and reproductive organs; ____________ sexual characteristics refer to other bodily changes that take place at puberty.

2. All individuals normally produce both androgens and estrogens, although the balance differs in males and females. T or F?

3. Five basic dimensions of gender are: ____________

4. In females, hermaphroditism may result from:
a. an androgen insensitivity *b.* excessive estrogen *c.* the androgenital syndrome *d.* all of the preceding

5. For humans, the biological biasing effect of prenatal hormones tends to override all other influences. T or F?

6. One's private sense of maleness or femaleness is referred to as ____________.

7. Traditional sex role socialization encourages ____________ behavior in males.
a. instrumental *b.* expressive *c.* emotional *d.* dependent

Answers: **1.** Primary, secondary **2.** T **3.** genetic sex, gonadal sex, hormonal sex, genital sex, gender identity **4.** c **5.** F **6.** gender identity **7.** *a*

Erogenous zones Areas of the body that produce pleasure and/or provoke erotic desire.

Sexual script An unspoken mental plan that defines a "plot," dialogue, and actions expected to take place in a sexual encounter.

Sex drive The strength of one's motivation to engage in sexual behavior.

Nocturnal orgasm An orgasm that occurs spontaneously during sleep or dreaming.

Sexual Behavior

Question: When does sexual behavior first appear in humans?

A capacity for sexual arousal is apparent at birth or soon after. Sexual researcher Alfred Kinsey verified instances of *orgasm* (sexual climax) in boys as young as 5 months old and girls as young as 4 months (Kinsey et al., 1948, 1953). Kinsey also found that children aged 2 to 5 years spontaneously manipulate and exhibit their genitals.

Various forms of sexual behavior continue through childhood and adolescence, but as the child matures, cultural norms place greater restrictions on sexual activities. Still, 50 percent of males and 25 percent of females report having engaged in preadolescent sex play. In adulthood, norms continue to shape sexual activity along socially approved lines. In our culture, sex between children, incest (sex between close relatives), prostitution, homosexuality, and extramarital sex all tend to be discouraged.

As was the case with sex role behavior, it can be seen that such restrictions are somewhat arbitrary. A comparison of many cultures shows that less restriction is usually matched by more sexual activity of all kinds. Apart from cultural restrictions, it can be said that any sexual act engaged in by consenting adults is "normal" if it does not hurt anyone.

Sexual Arousal Sexual arousal in humans is a complex phenomenon. It may, of course, be produced by direct stimulation of the body's **erogenous zones** (eh-ROJ-eh-nus: productive of pleasure or erotic desire). Human erogenous zones include the genitals, mouth, breasts, ears, anus, and to a lesser degree the surface of the entire body. It is clear, however, that more than physical contact is involved: A urological or gynecological examination rarely results in any sexual arousal. Human sexual arousal obviously includes a large cognitive element (see Box 23-1). Indeed, arousal may be triggered by mere thoughts or images.

Question: Are men more easily sexually aroused than women?

Apparently not. To answer the question, one study used medical recording devices to measure sexual arousal in males and females as they listened to erotic tape recordings. It was found that the erotic material was equally arousing for both sexes (Heiman, 1977). This and similar findings suggest that women are no less *physically* aroused by erotic stimuli than are men. However, compared with men, women more often have a negative *emotional* response to explicit pictures of sex. That is, women more often report feeling upset and disgusted by these stimuli (Hoyenga & Hoyenga, 1984).

If capacity for sexual arousal is measured by frequency of orgasm (brought about by masturbation or intercourse), the peak of male sexual activity is at age 18. Kinsey's studies (done in the early 1950s) placed the peak of female sexual activity at about 30 years of age. However, in recent years women have participated more fully in sexual activities, and at an earlier age (Hunt, 1974). The peak rate of female sexual activity still appears to occur later than that of males. However, male and female sexual behavior is gradually becoming more alike.

Question: What causes differences in sex drive?

Box 23-1

Sexual Scripts

In a restaurant, we commonly expect certain things to occur. It could even be said that each of us has a restaurant "script" that defines a plot, dialogue, and actions that should take place. Researcher John Gagnon (1977) believes that, similarly, we learn a variety of **sexual scripts** that guide our behavior.

Sexual scripts determine when and where we are likely to express sexual feelings, and with whom. They provide a "plot" for the order of events in lovemaking, and they outline "approved" actions, motives, and outcomes.

When two people follow markedly different scripts, misunderstandings are almost sure to occur. Consider, for instance, what happens when a woman acting out a "friendly first date" script is paired with a man following a "seduction" script: The result is often anger, hurt feelings, or worse. Even newlyweds may find that their sexual agendas differ. In such cases considerable "rewriting" of scripts is often needed for sexual compatibility.

However you may feel about the reality of sexual scripts, one implication seems inescapable: For humans the mind (or brain) is the ultimate erogenous zone (Knox, 1984).

Sex Drive Attitudes toward sex, sexual experience, and recency of sexual release are all obviously important, but physical factors may also play a role. In males the strength of the sex drive is related to the amount of androgens secreted by the testes. When the supply of androgens dramatically increases at puberty, sex drive increases too.

Surprisingly, the "male" hormones, or androgens, may also affect female sex drive. In addition to estrogen, a woman's body produces small amounts of androgens. Evidence suggests that these androgens may increase the sex drive in women just as they do in men. One study found that frequency of intercourse for married women was highest when their androgen levels were at a peak (Persky et al., 1978). Furthermore, when women are given androgens for medical reasons, some report increased sexual desire (Carlson, 1981). Some women also report variations in arousal at various times during their monthly cycle. If such a relationship does exist, its effects are probably small, since women may engage in sexual activity at any time during their monthly cycles (including during menstruation).

Question: Are nocturnal emissions ("wet dreams") an indication of an unusually strong sex drive? Do they ever indicate sexual disorders? Do both men and women experience nocturnal orgasms?

According to Kinsey's studies, about 85 percent of males and 35 percent of females have had sexual dreams that resulted in orgasm. These experiences typically begin during adolescence and may continue throughout adulthood. Kinsey found some reduction in the number of men experiencing noctural orgasms after marriage, but no change among women. Nocturnal orgasm may best be considered a completely normal (if relatively infrequent) form of sexual release.

Question: Does alcohol stimulate the sex drive?

In general, no. Alcohol is a *depressant*. As such, it may, in small doses, stimulate erotic desire by lowering inhibitions. This effect no doubt accounts for alcohol's reputation as an aid to seduction. (Humorist Ogden Nash once summarized this bit of folklore by saying, "Candy is dandy, but liquor is quicker.") However, in larger doses alcohol suppresses orgasm in women and erection in men. Increasing levels of drunkenness cause a progressive decrease in sexual desire, arousal, pleasure, and performance (Malatesta et al., 1979).

Question: Does removal of the testes or ovaries abolish the sex drive? Also, what happens to the sex drive in old age?

In lower animals, castration (surgical removal of the testicles) or removal of the ovaries usually completely abolishes sexual activity in *inexperienced* animals. Sexually experienced animals (particularly higher animals such as monkeys) may show little immediate change in sexual behavior after castration. In humans, the effects of male and female castration vary. Initially, some individuals show a decline in sex drive, while others experience no change. However, after several years have passed, almost all subjects report a decrease in sex drive.

The preceding observations have nothing to do with the effects of *sterilization*. Men and women who choose surgically based birth control (such as a vasectomy or a tubal ligation) experience no loss of sex drive. If anything, they may become more sexually active when pregnancy is no longer a concern.

There is typically a natural decline in sex drive that accompanies aging and reduction in sex hormone output. However, sexual activity does not come to an unavoidable end. In some cases men and women in their nineties have continued active sex lives. The crucial factor for an extended sex life appears to be regularity and opportunity. Individuals who fairly regularly engage in intercourse after ages 40 to 50 have little difficulty in later years (Masters & Johnson, 1970).

Masturbation One of the most basic human sexual behaviors is masturbation. **Masturbation** may be defined as deliberate self-stimulation that causes sexual pleasure or orgasm. Rhythmic self-stimulation has been observed in infants under 1 year of age. In adulthood, masturbation in the male usually takes the form of stroking or other manipulation of the penis. Female masturbation most often centers on stimulation of the clitoris or the areas immediately surrounding it.

The following are some questions commonly asked about masturbation.

Question: In adulthood do more men masturbate than women?

Yes. Of the women who took part in Kinsey's survey (1953), 60 percent reported that they had masturbated at some time. Of the males, 95 percent reported that they had masturbated (Kinsey et al., 1948). (Some cynics add, "And the other 5 percent lied!")

A survey conducted in the 1970s by Morton Hunt (1974) showed almost identical rates: 94 percent for males and 63 percent for females. Hunt believes, however, that a liberalization of attitudes toward masturbation has taken place. This change is reflected in the fact that adolescents now begin masturbation at a younger age.

Question: What purpose does masturbation serve?

Through masturbation people discover what is pleasing sexually and what their natural rhythms and preferences are. Masturbation is therefore an important part of the psychosexual development of most adolescents. Among other things, it provides a biologically healthy substitute for sexual intercourse during a period when sexual activity is discouraged and young people are maturing emotionally (Wilson et al., 1984).

Question: Is it immature for masturbation to continue after marriage?

If it is, there are a large number of "immature" people around! Morton Hunt found that approximately 70 percent of married men and women masturbate at least occasionally.

Generally speaking, masturbation is a valid sexual activity at any age, and it may continue after marriage without posing any threat to a relationship. There is nothing immature or infantile about masturbation. As a matter of fact, masturbation may be related to sexual response in other activities. For example, 85 percent of a group of women who had masturbated before marriage reported having an orgasm during the first year of marriage. In contrast, only about 65 percent of a group of women who did not masturbate experienced orgasm during the first year of marriage (Kinsey et al., 1953).

Question: Is there any way in which masturbation can cause harm?

In the past, frightening stories about possible physical and mental damage abounded in folklore about masturbation. Thirty years ago, a child might be told that masturbation would cause insanity, acne, sterility, or other such nonsense. "Self-abuse," as it was often called, has enjoyed a long and unfortunate history of religious and medical condemnation.

The contemporary view is that masturbation is a normal and acceptable sexual outlet. No knowledgeable psychologist would deny this, and enlightened parents are well aware of it. Still, many a child has been punished or made to feel guilty for touching his or her genitals. This situation is unfortunate since there is no harm caused by masturbation itself. Typically, the only negative effects of masturbation are the fear, guilt, or anxiety that occur when an individual has learned negative attitudes toward it.

Sexual Variations Male **homosexuality** and female **lesbianism** are two significant variations in sexuality. It is estimated that about 5 to 10 percent of all adult men in Western societies are predominantly homosexual. Adult women who are predominantly homosexual represent 3 to 5 percent of all women (Marmor, 1980). These percentages are small, but they indicate that there may be 6 to 12 million lesbians and gay men in the United States.

When evaluating homosexuality, one should remember that cultural standards for sexual behavior vary greatly. A major survey of 76 cultures found that almost two-thirds accept some form of homosexuality (Weinberg & Williams, 1974). Moreover, psychological testing consistently shows no differences in personality or adjustment between heterosexuals and homosexuals (Bell et al., 1981; Marmor, 1980). For these and other reasons, homosexuality cannot be considered a sexual disorder on psychological grounds (DSM-III-R, 1987).

Castration Surgical removal of the testicles. Castration differs from sterilization, a procedure (such as vasectomy or tubal ligation) that merely makes a man or woman infertile.

Masturbation Production of sexual pleasure or orgasm by manipulation or stimulation of the genitals other than by intercourse.

Homosexuality A capacity for erotic attraction to members of the same sex.

Lesbianism Female homosexuality.

Psychologically, homosexuality is regarded as a problem only if a person feels lasting guilt, self-hate, or similar negative emotions—a condition that has been referred to as *ego-dystonic homosexuality*. This condition is probably rare, however. The majority of adult homosexuals display adjustment patterns and occupational histories similar to those of heterosexuals (Marmor, 1980). The problems faced by homosexuals are more often related to rejection by family, discrimination in employment and housing, and to the undercurrent of homophobia in American society. (*Homophobia* refers to prejudice, fear, and dislike aimed at homosexuals.)

Homosexuals are found in all walks of life, at all social and economic levels, and in all cultural groups. As more gay and lesbian people make themselves known to friends, relatives, and co-workers, it may be reasonable to expect that the prejudices against them will wane.

Learning Check

1. A capacity for sexual arousal is apparent at birth or soon after. T or F?

2. Areas of the body that produce erotic pleasure are called ________________ zones.

3. When exposed to erotic stimuli, men and women vary in their most common emotional reactions, but there appears to be no difference in their levels of physical arousal. T or F?

4. There is some evidence to suggest that sexual activity and sex drives peak later for males than they do for females. T or F?

5. It is possible (and normal) for sexual activity to continue to ages 80 or 90. T or F?

6. More males than females report that they masturbate. T or F?

7. Masturbation can cause physical harm, according to the latest research reports. T or F?

8. The percentage of women who are homosexual is greater than the percentage of men who are homosexual. T or F?

Answers: **1.** T **2.** erogenous **3.** T **4.** F **5.** T **6.** T **7.** F **8.** F

Human Sexual Response

Objective information about human sexual response has been expanded by the work of gynecologist William Masters and psychologist Virginia Johnson (1966, 1970). In a series of experiments, interviews, and controlled observations, Masters and Johnson directly studied sexual intercourse and masturbation in nearly 700 males and females. The information they obtained has significantly improved our understanding of human sexuality.

According to Masters and Johnson, sexual response in both males and females can be divided into four phases: (1) **excitement,** (2) **plateau,** (3) **orgasm,** and (4) **resolution.** (See Fig. 23-4 and Fig. 23-5.)

Male Response Sexual arousal in the male is signaled by erection of the penis during the excitement phase. There is also a speedup in heart rate, increased blood flow to the genitals, enlargement of the testicles, erection of the nipples, and numerous other bodily changes. If sexual stimulation ends, the excitement

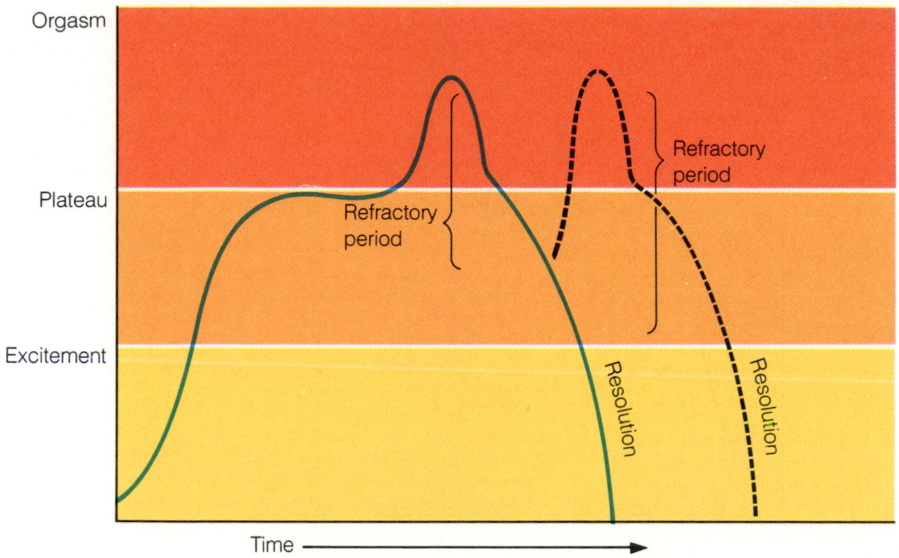

Fig. 23-4 *Male sexual response cycle. (Reproduced by permission from Frank A. Beach (ed.),* Sex and Behavior. *New York: John Wiley & Sons, Inc., 1965)*

phase will gradually subside. Continued stimulation moves the individual into the plateau phase, in which physical changes and subjective feelings of arousal become more intense. If stimulation ends during this phase, sexual arousal will subside more slowly and may produce considerable frustration.

Further stimulation during the plateau phase brings about a reflex release of accumulated tension resulting in sexual climax, or orgasm. Orgasm in the mature male is usually accompanied by **ejaculation** (release of seminal fluid) and is followed by a short **refractory period** during which continued stimulation will not produce a second orgasm. (Many men cannot even be stimulated to erection until the refractory phase has passed.) Only rarely is the male refractory period followed by a second orgasm. Orgasm is usually followed by *resolution*, a return to lower levels of sexual tension and arousal.

Female Response Although the timing and intensity of the phases vary considerably from person to person, the basic pattern of response for women is the same as that for men. During the excitement phase of arousal, a complex pattern of changes take place to prepare the vagina for intercourse. These changes correspond to erection in the male. Also (as in the male), the nipples become erect, pulse rate changes, and the skin may become flushed. Most women go through a plateau stage comparable to that in the male, although a few follow a pattern of response that essentially skips the plateau (Fig. 23-5).

During orgasm, from 3 to 10 muscular contractions of the vagina, uterus, and related structures serve to release accumulated sexual tension. Both orgasm and resolution in the female usually last longer than they do in the male. After orgasm, about 15 percent of all females return to the plateau phase and may have another orgasm before resolution.

Before the work of Masters and Johnson, there was considerable debate about whether a difference existed between female orgasm associated with the vagina and orgasm derived from stimulation of the clitoris. Sigmund Freud had contended in his writings that a clitoral orgasm was an "immature" form of female

Ego-dystonic homosexuality A hypothesized condition in which a homosexual person is painfully uncomfortable with his or her sexual orientation.

Homophobia A powerful fear of homosexuality.

Excitement phase The first phase of sexual response, indicated by initial signs of sexual arousal.

Plateau phase The second phase of sexual response during which physical arousal is further heightened.

Orgasm A climax and release of sexual excitement.

Resolution The fourth phase of sexual response, involving a return to lower levels of sexual tension and arousal.

Ejaculation The release of sperm and seminal fluid by the male at the time of orgasm.

Refractory period A short time period after orgasm during which males are unable to again reach orgasm.

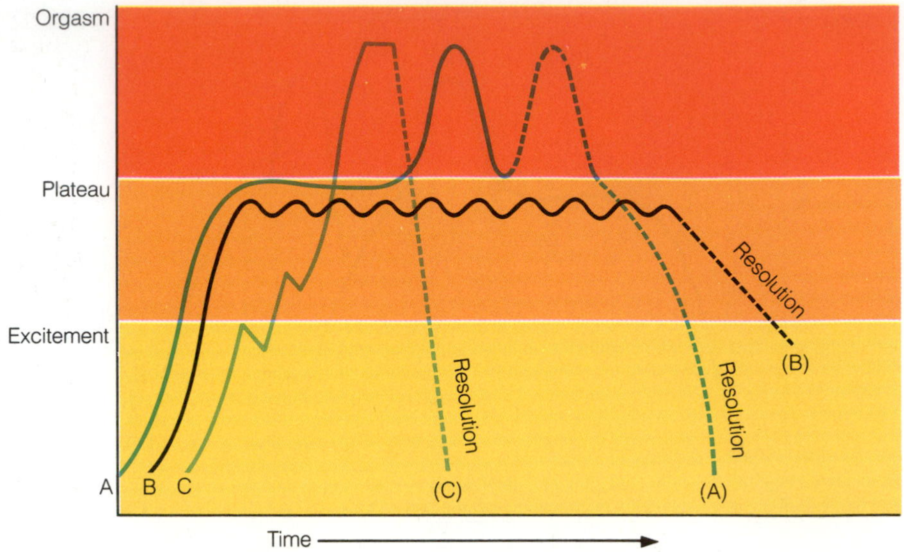

Fig. 23-5 *Female sexual response cycle. (Reproduced by permission from Frank A. Beach (ed.),* Sex and Behavior. *New York: John Wiley & Sons, Inc., 1965)*

response. Since the clitoris is the female structure comparable to the penis, Freud believed that women whose orgasmic experiences centered on the clitoris had not fully accepted their femininity.

Masters and Johnson exploded the Freudian myth by showing that there is no difference in physical response no matter what form of stimulation produces orgasm. As a matter of fact, the vagina is relatively insensitive to touch. Most sensations during intercourse, therefore, come from stimulation of the clitoris and other external structures. It now seems apparent that sensations from many sources are fused together into the total experience of orgasm and that, for the majority of women, one of the more important sources of these sensations is the clitoris.

When women in one study were asked to express a preference for vaginal or clitoral stimulation, most said they would rather not choose, but if forced to choose, two-thirds preferred clitoral sensations (Fisher, 1973). Similarly, researcher Shere Hite has reported the results of an unscientific, yet thought-provoking survey of 3000 women. Among these women only 26 percent reported regularly reaching orgasm during intercourse without separate massaging of the clitoris (Hite, 1976). To downgrade the "clitoral orgasm" ignores the basic physiology of female sexual response.

Male and Female Responses Compared

The research of Masters and Johnson indicates that similarities between male and female sexual responses outweigh the differences. However, differences that do exist may have a significant effect on sexual adjustment. For example, it was found that women typically go through the sexual phases more slowly than do men. During lovemaking, a woman may require from 10 to 20 minutes to go from excitement to orgasm,* whereas a man may experience all four stages in as little as 4 minutes. These differences should be kept in mind by couples seeking sexual compatibility.

Question: Does that mean a couple should try to time lovemaking to promote simultaneous orgasm?

At one time the concept of simultaneous orgasm (both partners reaching sexual climax at the same time) was considered the ideal "goal" of lovemaking. More recently, it has been rejected as an artificial concern that may reduce satisfaction instead of enhance it. To paraphrase one expert (Lowen, 1965):

> To govern the timing of orgasm can destroy the natural flow of feeling that guarantees mutual satisfaction. This point cannot be stressed too strongly. Inhibiting the buildup of excitation may limit pleasure, whereas spontaneity enhances it.

It is more advisable to aim for the satisfaction of both partners through some combination of intercourse and manual stimulation than it is to self-consciously inhibit spontaneity, communication, and pleasure.

Question: Does slower response mean that women are less sexual than men?

Definitely not. During masturbation 70 percent of females reach orgasm in 4 minutes or less. This finding casts serious doubts on the idea that female response is actually slower. Slower female response during intercourse probably occurs because stimulation to the clitoris is less direct. It might be said that the male anatomy simply provides too little stimulation during intercourse for more rapid female response, not that the female is in any way inferior.

Question: Does penis size affect female response?

Masters and Johnson found that the vagina adjusts to the size of the penis, and that subjective feelings of pleasure and intensity of orgasm are not related to penis size. They also found that while individual differences exist in flaccid penis size, there tends to be much less variation in erect penis size. (This is why erection has been referred to as the great equalizer.) Contrary to popular belief, there is no relationship between penis size and male sexual potency.

Question: Men almost always reach orgasm during intercourse, but many women do not. Does this indicate that women are less sexually responsive?

Again, the evidence argues against any lack of female sexual responsiveness. It is true that about 1 woman in 3 does not experience orgasm during the first year of marriage, and only about 30 percent regularly reach orgasm through intercourse alone. However, this does not imply lack of physical responsiveness since approximately 90 percent of all women reach orgasm when masturbating (Knox, 1984).

In another regard the female is clearly more responsive. Only about 5 percent of males are capable of multiple orgasm (and then only after an unavoidable refractory period). Most males are almost always limited to a second orgasm at

*There is much variation, however. A study of 1000 married women found that 50 percent of them reached orgasm if intercourse lasted 1 to 11 minutes; if intercourse lasted 15 minutes or more, the rate increased to 66 percent. Twenty-five percent of the wives said that orgasm occurred within 1 minute of the start of intercourse (Brewer, 1981). (Note that these times refer only to intercourse, not to an entire arousal sequence.)

best. In contrast, Masters and Johnson's findings suggest that most women who regularly experience orgasm are capable of multiple orgasm. Remember, though, that only about 15 percent of all women regularly experience multiple orgasm. A woman should not assume that something is wrong if she isn't multiorgasmic.

Attitudes and Sexual Behavior

Question: Has there been a "sexual revolution"?

Some observers have argued that liberalized attitudes toward sexual expression and the simultaneous development of effective contraceptives have brought about a "revolution" in sexual behavior. Others believe that sexual behavior has remained essentially unchanged for the past 20 years. From this point of view, the "sexual revolution" has been mostly verbal—people are simply talking more about sex now than they were in the past (Miller & Siegal, 1972).

Attitudes An accurate description of changing sexual attitudes and behavior seems to lie somewhere between the two views just expressed. Attitudes have changed significantly in the direction of greater tolerance. Behavior has also changed, but more moderately.

Changing attitudes are graphically illustrated by the result of national polls concerning the acceptability of premarital intercourse. In a 1959 Roper Poll, 88 percent of those interviewed agreed that premarital sex is "wrong." In 1969 only 68 percent of the respondents to a Gallup Poll rejected premarital sex. By 1973 only 48 percent felt likewise. And in 1979 only 5 percent of college-age men and 12 percent of women endorsed abstaining from sex before marriage (DeLamater & MacCorquodale, 1979; cited by Knox, 1984). Similar changes have been observed in attitudes toward extramarital sex, homosexuality, legalized prostitution, sex education, no-fault divorce, and a variety of related issues.

Question: Have changing attitudes been translated into behavior?

As we shall see in a moment, they have to some extent. Largely, however, there is greater *tolerance* for sexual behavior, especially that *engaged in by others*. For example, *Psychology Today* magazine found in polls of its readers that 80 percent considered extramarital sex acceptable under some circumstances (Athenasiou et al., 1970). But, in practice only one-third of all married men and women had actually had extramarital sexual experience (Rubenstein, 1983). Another survey of more conservative couples found that only 28 percent reported extramarital sexual experience (Johnson, 1970).

Question: How do such figures compare with earlier generations?

The figures cited do not allow a good comparison because they represent selected groups of people. A better indication is given by comparing Kinsey's findings from the early 1950s to Hunt's from the early 1970s. These researchers obtained similar figures: About 50 percent of males and 20 percent of females have at least one extramarital contact during their lifetime (Hunt, 1974; Kinsey, 1953). Thus, changing attitudes have not greatly altered behavior in this area.

Question: What kinds of changes have taken place?

Behavior Premarital intercourse rates have traditionally been considered a good indication of overall sexual activity. Kinsey found that 70 percent of males and 33 percent of females had engaged in premarital intercourse by age 25. Twenty years later, Hunt obtained premarital intercourse rates of 97 percent for males and about 70 percent for females by age 25. Another study found that 93 percent of women married after 1973 had engaged in premarital relations (Levin & Levin, 1975). A variety of additional studies support the idea that premarital intercourse rates have definitely increased.

A major element of the "sexual revolution" is earlier participation in sexual behavior by both sexes. A recent survey of American teenagers found that 43 percent of boys and 31 percent of girls have had intercourse by age 16 (Hass, 1983). There has also been a marked increase in sexual expression among females. Other studies show higher rates of intercourse in marriage for couples of all ages and a greater variety of sexual expression in marital relations (Hunt, 1974; Levin & Levin, 1975).

Question: Has a "sexual revolution" taken place then?

A Sexual Revolution? In all, there certainly seems to be adequate evidence that sexual behavior has increased in the last 20 to 25 years. However, this trend does not seem to represent a move toward sexual promiscuity. Although it is true that sexual intercourse by unmarried couples is more common, most couples emphasize mutual commitment and a loving relationship as a requirement for sexual involvement. In this regard, premarital sex can be said to parallel the behavior of engaged couples in past years (Simon & Gagnon, 1973).

Or, as one author has noted (Hyde, 1984), many young people today have just changed the sequence of events. For their parents the sequence was: fall in love, marry, begin a sexual relationship. For many the sequence now is: fall in love, begin a sexual relationship, marry. Most women have only 1 premarital sexual partner whom they eventually marry. Men typically have about 6 premarital partners (Hyde, 1984). Overall, an image of rampant sexual behavior is not supported.

We have noted that extramarital intercourse rates seem to have changed little in the past 30 years. Thus, liberalized sexual attitudes seem not to have jeopardized the basic concept of marriage. Even premarital intercourse does not appear to represent a major rejection of traditional values and responsible behavior. The association between sexuality and love or affection remains strong for the majority of the population. Likewise, other changes in attitudes and behavior appear to reflect a greater acceptance of sexuality, rather than a true "revolution."

A good summary of the changes that have occurred in sexual behavior is found in the phrase, "the slow death of the double standard." In the past decades distinctly different standards were often applied to male and female sexuality. Males, for instance, were largely forgiven for engaging in premarital sex. Young males who "sowed wild oats" not only were tolerated but in some cases tacitly encouraged to do so as a step toward manhood. On the other hand, women who were sexually active before marriage ran the risk of being labeled "easy," "bad," or "promiscuous" (Knox, 1984).

Similar differences pervaded sexual mores and placed women in a separate-but-

Box 23-2

AIDS, STD, and Sexual Responsibility

The incidence of **sexually transmitted disease** (STD) has risen steadily in the United States for the last 20 years. Today, sexually active individuals run an elevated risk of contracting chlamydia, gonorrhea, hepatitis B, herpes, syphilis, and other STDs. For many people the emergence of **acquired immune deficiency syndrome (AIDS)** has added a new fear. Whereas most other STDs are treatable, AIDS is almost always fatal once symptoms appear. You probably already know about AIDS. In case you don't, a short summary of facts may be valuable.

AIDS is caused by a virus. In time, the disease disables the body's immune system. This allows various other "opportunistic" diseases to invade the body without resistance. Most AIDS victims eventually die of multiple infections. The first symptoms of AIDS may show up as little as two months after infection, or they may not appear for up to 7 years. This long incubation period allows many infected persons to pass the disease on without knowing it.

AIDS is transmitted by direct contact with body fluids—especially blood, semen, and vaginal secretions. The AIDS virus cannot be transmitted by casual contact. People do not get AIDS from shaking hands, touching or using objects used by an AIDS patient, social kissing, sharing drinking glasses, sharing towels, and so forth.

AIDS has been called the "gay plague" because male homosexuals were its first victims. However, this label is in error. AIDS can be transmitted by all forms of sexual intercourse and has affected persons of all sexual orientations (Denning, 1987). Those who are at greatest risk include: men who have had sex with other men (homosexual and bisexual men), people who have shared needles (for tattoos or for intravenous drug use), blood transfusion recipients (between 1977 and spring 1985), hemophiliacs (who require frequent transfusions), sexual partners of people in the above groups, heterosexuals with a history of multiple partners.

Perhaps because it is fatal, AIDS is having a strong impact on sexual behavior in some populations. Among gay men there has been a sharp increase in monogamous relationships and in abstaining from sex. Gay men have also significantly reduced participation in high-risk sexual behaviors ("High risk," 1987). Evidence is growing that the risk of AIDS infection is lower for heterosexuals than once predicted (Scheer, 1987). Nevertheless, all sexually active persons are at risk. This has forced many people to face new issues of risk and responsibility.

The "sexual revolution" was fueled, in part, by the "pill" and other effective birth control methods. Will the threat of AIDS reverse the tide of changes that occurred in previous decades? Will STD come to mean Sudden Total Disinterest in sex? Will the "germs of endearment" change the terms of endearment? The answers may depend on how quickly AIDS spreads into the general population and how soon its prevention or its cure can be achieved.

Sexually transmitted diseases Any of a variety of diseases transmitted primarily by sexual intercourse or other sexual contact; venereal diseases.

Acquired immune deficiency syndrome (AIDS) A lethal breakdown of the body's immune system caused by a viral infection that is transmitted by contact with the body fluids of an infected person.

not-equal position with regard to sexual behavior. However, as the gap between male and female sexual patterns has continued to close, it is increasingly likely that an end to the double standard is in sight.

A more comfortable acceptance of a natural element of human relationships—sexuality—is the positive side of changing sexual attitudes and values. The negative side is represented by the plight of the individual who is not ready for, or interested in, greater sexual freedom. As one of the women who responded to Shere Hite's survey said:

> The Sexual Revolution tells me I am abnormal if I don't desire to make it with every Tom, Dick, or Jane that I see. I am only free to say yes. (Hite, 1976, cited by Hyde, 1984)

Apparently, some individuals feel pressured into sexual behavior because it is "expected." However, pressures such as these probably come as much from the individual as from others. If a greater acceptance of human sexuality is to be constructive, it must be perceived as a general increase in personal freedom—as the right to say no, as well as a right to choose when, where, how, and with whom one's sexuality will be expressed. As Box 23-2 suggests, there are compelling reasons for caution. As is true in other areas of human functioning, freedom must be combined with responsibility, commitment, and caring if it is to have meaning.

Learning Check

1. List the four phases of sexual response identified by Masters and Johnson: ______________________________

____

2. Males typically experience ______________________ after ejaculation.

a. an increased potential for orgasm
b. a short refractory period
c. the excitement phase
d. muscular contractions of the uterus

3. The research of Masters and Johnson suggests that the similarities between male and female sexual responses outweigh the differences. T or F?

4. During lovemaking, a female may require from 10 to 20 minutes to go from excitement to orgasm, whereas the male may experience all four stages of sexual response in as little as 4 minutes. T or F?

5. Simultaneous orgasm of the male and female should be the ultimate goal in lovemaking. T or F?

6. Recent research shows there is considerable evidence that open discussion and more liberal views regarding sexual behavior are causing loose or promiscuous sexuality. T or F?

7. Contrary to long-standing belief, it now appears that much female sexuality is focused on:
a. the uterus *b.* the urethra *c.* the clitoris *d.* the cervix

Answers: **1.** excitement, plateau, orgasm, resolution **2.** *b.* **3.** T **4.** T **5.** F **6.** F **7.** *c.*

Applications

Sexual Problems

Question: What are the most common sexual problems? How are they treated?

Most people who seek sexual counseling have one or more of the following six problems (Kaplan, 1974):

A. For the male:

1. Impotence: inability to produce or maintain an erection.
2. Premature ejaculation: inability to delay or control orgasm.
3. Retarded ejaculation: inability to reach orgasm.

B. For the female:

1. General sexual dysfunction: lack of erotic response to sexual stimulation (frigidity).
2. Orgasmic dysfunction: inability to reach orgasm.
3. Vaginismus: spasm of muscles at the entrance of the vagina, preventing intercourse.

There was a time when couples and individuals endured such dysfunctions in silence. However, in recent years effective treatments have been found for each problem. Let's briefly investigate the causes and treatments of the six barriers to sexual adjustment and fulfillment.

Male Impotence Impotence (also known as erectile dysfunction) is the inability to maintain an erection for sexual intercourse. Males suffering from *primary impotence* have never had an erection. Those who have previously performed successfully, but then have become impotent, are said to suffer from *secondary impotence*. In either case, when impotence becomes a repeated problem, it is usually very disturbing to the man and his sexual partner.

Question: How often must a man experience failure to be considered impotent?

Sex therapists Masters and Johnson (1970) believe that a problem exists when failure occurs on 25 percent or more of a man's lovemaking attempts. Repeated impotence should therefore be distinguished from *occasional* erectile problems. Fatigue, anger, anxiety, and excessive consumption of alcohol can cause temporary impotence in healthy males. True impotence typically persists for months or years.

It is important to recognize that occasional impotence is normal. In fact, overreaction to it may generate fears and doubts that can contribute to further impotence. At such times, it is particularly important for the man's partner to avoid expressing anger, disappointment, or embarrassment. Patient reassurance helps prevent the establishment of a vicious cycle.

Question: What causes impotence?

For years, experts held that impotence rarely was caused by physical illness, disease, or damage. Now it is recognized that roughly 40 percent of cases are *organic*, or physically caused. The origin of the remaining cases is *psychogenic* (resulting from emotional factors). Even when impotence is organic, however, it is almost always made worse by anxiety and other emotional reactions. If a man can have an erection during occasions other than lovemaking (during sleep, for instance), the problem probably is not physical (Knox, 1984).

Organic impotence has many causes. Typical problems include alcohol or drug abuse, diabetes, vascular disease, prostate and urological disorders, neurological problems, and reactions to medication for high blood pressure, heart disease, or stomach ulcers.

According to Masters and Johnson (1970), primary psychogenic impotence is often related to harsh religious training, early sexual experience with a seductive mother, or other experiences leading to guilt, fear, and sexual inhibition. In a few instances unrecognized homosexual feelings may also be a source of conflict.

Secondary psychogenic impotence may be related to anxiety about sex in general, guilt because of an extramarital affair, resentment or hostility toward a

Applications: Sexual Problems, continued

sexual partner, fear of ability to perform, and similar emotions and conflicts. Often the problem starts with repeated sexual failures caused by drinking too much alcohol or by the presence of premature ejaculation. In either case, initial doubts soon become severe fears of failure—which further inhibit sexual response.

Medical treatment for organic impotence may employ drugs or surgery. Treatment for both organic and psychogenic impotence also usually includes counseling to remove fears and psychological blocks. The man learns that he cannot consciously will an erection and that his disability is not a reflection on his manhood. To further free him of his fears (particularly fear of failure), the man and his partner are usually assigned a series of exercises to perform. This technique, called **sensate focus,** directs attention to natural sensations of pleasure and builds communication skills.

In sensate focus the couple is initially told to take turns stroking various parts of each other's bodies. They are instructed to carefully avoid any genital contact at first. Instead, they are to concentrate on giving pleasure and on signaling what is most gratifying to them. This takes the pressure to perform off the male and allows him to learn to give pleasure as a means of receiving it.

Over a period of days or weeks, the couple proceeds to more intense physical contact involving the breasts and genitals. As inhibitions are reduced and natural arousal begins to replace fear, the couple moves on to intercourse.

Premature Ejaculation Masters and Johnson (1970) consider ejaculation to be premature if a man cannot delay sexual climax long enough to satisfy his partner in at least one-half of their lovemaking attempts. However, Helen Kaplan, of Cornell University Medical School, finds this definition unsatisfactory because of large variations in the time different women take to reach orgasm. Kaplan (1974) says that prematurity exists when ejaculation occurs reflexively, or when there is an inability to tolerate high levels of excitement at the plateau stage of arousal.

Question: Do many men have difficulties with premature ejaculation?

Premature ejaculation is a common problem in male sexual adjustment. Theories advanced to explain it have ranged from the idea that it may represent hostility toward the female partner (since it deprives her of satisfaction) to the suggestion that most early male sexual experiences tend to encourage rapid climax (such as those taking place in the back seat of a car and masturbation). Kaplan (1974) adds that excessive arousal and anxiety over performance are usually present, and that some men simply engage in techniques that maximize sensation and make rapid orgasm inevitable. Whatever the causes, premature ejaculation can be a serious difficulty, especially in the context of long-term relationships.

Treatment for premature ejaculation is highly successful and relatively simple. The most common treatment procedure is the *squeeze technique* used by Masters and Johnson. The woman stimulates her partner manually until he signals that ejaculation is about to occur. She then firmly squeezes the tip of the penis to inhibit orgasm. When the man feels he has control, stimulation is repeated. Gradually, the man acquires the ability to delay orgasm sufficiently for satisfactory intercourse. During treatment, skills that improve communication between partners are developed, along with a better understanding of the male's sexual response cues.

Retarded Ejaculation Among males an inability to reach orgasm was once considered a rare problem. But milder forms of this dysfunction have recently accounted for increasing numbers of clients seeking therapy (Kaplan, 1974). Background factors often observed are: strict religious training, fear of impregnating, lack of interest in the sexual partner, symbolic inability to give of oneself, unacknowledged homosexuality, or the recent occurrence of traumatic life events. Power and commitment struggles within relationships may be important added factors.

Treatment for retarded ejaculation consists of sensate focus, manual stimulation by the female (which is designed to orient the male to the female as a

Applications: Sexual Problems, continued

source of pleasure), and stimulation to the point of orgasm followed by immediate intercourse and ejaculation. Therapy also focuses on resolving personal conflicts and marital difficulties underlying the problem.

Female General Sexual Dysfunction This difficulty, commonly referred to as *frigidity*, is usually defined as a persistent inability to derive pleasure from sexual stimulation. Women who show general sexual dysfunction respond with little or no physical arousal to sexual stimulation. The problem thus appears to correspond directly to male impotence (Kaplan, 1974). As in male impotence, general female sexual dysfunction may be primary or secondary.

The causes of female general sexual dysfunction bear some similarity to those seen in psychogenic impotence. Frigidity can often be traced to frightening childhood experiences such as molestations (often by older relatives), incestuous relations that produce lasting guilt, a harshly religious background in which sex is considered evil, or cold, unloving childhood relationships. Also common is the need to maintain control over emotions, deep-seated conflicts over being female, and extreme distrust of others, especially males (Masters & Johnson, 1970).

Question: How does treatment proceed?

Treatment at the Cornell clinic includes sensate focus, genital stimulation by the woman's partner, and "nondemanding" intercourse controlled by the woman. With success in these initial stages, full intercourse is gradually instituted. As sexual training proceeds, psychological conflicts and dynamics typically appear, and as they do, they are treated in separate counseling sessions (Kaplan, 1974).

Female Orgasmic Dysfunction The most prevalent sexual complaint among women is orgasmic dysfunction, an inability to reach orgasm during intercourse. Often it is clear in such cases that the woman is not completely unresponsive; rather, she is unresponsive in the context of a relationship—she may easily reach orgasm by masturbation but not in intercourse.

Question: Then couldn't the woman's partner be at fault?

Sex therapists try to avoid finding fault or placing blame. However, it is true that the male partner must be sexually adequate in terms of freedom from premature ejaculation, and that he must have a commitment to ensuring gratification of the woman. Some instances of "orgasmic dysfunction" can be traced to inadequate stimulation or faulty technique on the part of the male. Even when this is the case, sexual adjustment difficulties are best viewed as a problem the couple shares, not just as the "woman's problem" or the "man's problem."

If we focus only on the woman, the most common source of orgasmic difficulties is overcontrol of sexual response. Female orgasm requires a degree of abandonment to erotic feelings. It is therefore inhibited by ambivalence or hostility toward the relationship, by guilt, by fears of expressing sexual needs, and by tendencies to control and intellectualize erotic feelings. The woman is unable to let go and enjoy the flow of pleasurable sensations.

In Helen Kaplan's treatment program, nonorgasmic women are first trained to focus on their sexual responsiveness through masturbation or manual stimulation by a partner. As the woman becomes consistently orgasmic in these circumstances, her responsiveness is gradually transferred to intercourse. Couples also typically learn alternative positions and techniques of lovemaking designed to increase clitoral stimulation. At the same time, communication between partners is stressed, especially with reference to the woman's sexual value system (expectations, motivations, preferences).

Vaginismus In the condition known as *vaginismus*, muscle spasms make intercourse impossible. Vaginismus is often accompanied by obvious fears of intercourse, and where fear is absent, high levels of anxiety are present. Vaginismus therefore appears to be a phobic response to intercourse. Predictably, causative factors include experiences of painful intercourse, rape and/or brutal and frightening sexual encounters, fear of men, misinformation about sex

Applications: Sexual Problems, continued

(belief that it is injurious), and fear of the specific male partner (Kaplan, 1974).

Treatment of vaginismus is similar to what might be done for a nonsexual phobia. It includes extinction of conditioned muscle spasms by progressive relaxation of the vagina, desensitization of fears of intercourse, and masturbation or manual stimulation to associate pleasure with sexual approach by the male partner. Hypnosis has also been used in some cases with success (Kaplan, 1974).

Summary Solving sexual problems can be difficult. The problems described are rarely solved without professional help (a possible exception is premature ejaculation). If a serious sexual difficulty is not resolved in a reasonable amount of time, the aid of an appropriately trained psychologist, physician, or counselor should be sought. The longer the problem is ignored, the more difficult it is to solve.

Sexual Adjustment

Question: What can be done to improve sexual adjustment?

Often it is best to view sexual adjustment within the broader context of a relationship. Conflict and unresolved anger in other areas frequently take their toll in sexual adjustment; conversely, mutually satisfying relationships tend to carry over into sexual relations. Sex is not just a performance or a skill to be mastered like playing tennis. It is a form of communication and an extension of a relationship. Couples with strong and open relationships can probably survive most sexual problems. A couple with a satisfactory sex life but a poor relationship rarely lasts.

Sex researchers and therapists Masters and Johnson (1970) have discussed how sexual partners can best approach disagreements about each other's sexual needs and wishes. When disagreements arise over issues such as frequency of intercourse, who initiates lovemaking, or what behavior is appropriate, Masters and Johnson believe that the rule should be "each partner must accept the other as the final authority on his or her own feelings."

Partners are urged to give feedback about their feelings by following what therapists call the "touch and ask" rule: Touching and caressing should often be followed by questions such as, "Does that feel good?" "Do you like that?" and so forth (Knox, 1984). When problems do arise, partners are urged to be *responsive* to each other's needs at an *emotional* level and to recognize that all sexual problems are *mutual.* Failures should always be shared without placing blame. Masters and Johnson believe that it is particularly important to avoid the "numbers game." That is, couples should avoid being influenced by statistics on the "average" frequency of intercourse, by stereotypes about sexual potency, and by the superhuman sexual exploits portrayed in movies and magazines.

Question: Are there any other guidelines for maintaining a healthy emotional relationship?

In a study that compared happily married couples with unhappily married couples, Navran (1967) found that in almost every regard the happily married couples showed superior *communication* skills. Many theorists agree that communication is facilitated by observing the following guidelines (after Bach & Wyden, 1969).

Avoid "Gunnysacking" Persistent feelings, whether positive or negative, need to be expressed. Gunnysacking refers to saving up feelings and complaints. These are then "dumped" during an argument or used as ammunition in a fight. Gunnysacking is very destructive to a relationship.

Be Open about Feelings Happy couples not only talk more, they convey more personal feelings and show greater sensitivity to their partners' feelings.

> . . . in a healthy relationship, each partner feels free to express his likes, dislikes, wants, wishes, feelings, impulses, and the other person feels free to react with like honesty to these. In such a relationship, there will be tears, laughter, sensuality, irritation, anger, fear, baby-like behavior, and so on. (Jourard, 1963)

Don't Attack the Other Person's Character Whenever possible, expressions of negative feelings should be given as statements of one's own feelings,

Applications: Sexual Problems, continued

not as statements of blame. It is far more constructive to say, "It makes me angry when you leave things around the house" than it is to say, "You're a slob!"

Don't Try to "Win" a Fight Constructive fights are aimed at resolving shared differences, not at establishing who is right or wrong, superior or inferior.

Recognize that Anger Is Appropriate Constructive and destructive fights are not distinguished by whether anger is expressed. A fight is a fight, and anger is appropriate. As is the case with any other emotion in a relationship, anger should be expressed. However, constructive expression of anger requires that couples fight fair by sticking to the real issues and by not "hitting below the belt."

As a last point, it is worth restating that sexual adjustment and loving relationships are interdependent. As one observer put it, when sex goes well it's 15 percent of a relationship, and when it goes badly it's 85 percent (Knox, 1984). As a shared pleasure, a form of intimacy, a means of communication, and a haven from everyday tensions, a positive sexual relationship can do much to enhance a couple's mutual understanding and caring. Likewise, an honest, equitable, and affectionate out-of-bed relationship contributes greatly to sexual satisfaction (Hatfield et al., 1982).

Learning Check

1. Males suffering from primary impotence have never been able to produce or maintain an erection. T or F?
2. According to the latest figures, most cases of impotence are caused by physical problems. T or F?
3. Sensate focus is the most common treatment for premature ejaculation. T or F?
4. Premature ejaculation is considered the rarest of the male sexual adjustment problems. T or F?
5. As it is for psychogenic impotence, the sensate focus technique is a primary treatment for female general sexual dysfunction. T or F?
6. Vaginismus appears to be a phobic response to sexual intercourse. T or F?
7. Masters and Johnson urge sexual partners to recognize that all sexual problems are mutual, they are not just one partner's problem. T or F?

Answers: **1.** T **2.** F **3.** F **4.** F **5.** T **6.** T **7.** T

Chapter Summary

- Physical differences between males and females can be divided into *primary sexual characteristics* (genital and reproductive organs) and *secondary sexual characteristics* (other bodily features). Reproductive maturity in females is signaled by the *menarche* (the onset of menstruation). The development of both primary and secondary sexual characteristics is influenced by *androgens* (male sex hormones) and *estrogens* (female sex hormones).
- Gender can be broken down into *genetic sex*, *gonadal sex*, *hormonal sex*, *genital sex*, and *gender identity*.
- Gender development begins with genetic sex (XX or XY chromosomes). It is

then influenced by prenatal hormonal influences. *Androgen insensitivity*, exposure to *progestin*, the *androgenital syndrome*, and similar problems can cause problems in the formation of the genitals. Resulting gender ambiguities are called *hermaphroditism*.

- Many researchers believe that prenatal hormones exert a *biological biasing effect* that combines with *social factors* present after birth to influence psychosexual development. Social factors are especially apparent in learned *gender identity* and the effect of *sex roles* and *sex role socialization* on behavior. Sex role socialization in particular seems to account for most observed male/female differences.
- Sexual behavior is quite "natural," being apparent soon after birth and expressed in various ways throughout life. There appears to be little difference in sexual responsiveness between males and females.
- There is some evidence that the sex drive peaks at a later age for females than it does for males. Sex drive in both males and females may be related to bodily levels of androgen. *Nocturnal orgasms* are a normal, but relatively minor, form of sexual release. *Castration* may or may not influence sex drive in humans.
- *Masturbation* is a normal and completely acceptable behavior practiced by large portions of the population. For many, masturbation is an important part of sexual self-discovery. It is valid in marriage and normally has no harmful effects.
- A significant minority of adults are *homosexual*, being consistently attracted to sexual activity with members of the same sex. As a group homosexual men and women do not differ psychologically from heterosexuals.
- Human sexual response can be divided into four phases: (1) *excitement*, (2) *plateau*, (3) *orgasm*, and (4) *resolution*. Both males and females may go through all four stages in 4 or 5 minutes. But during intercourse, most females typically take longer than this—from 10 to 20 minutes. There do not appear to be any differences between "vaginal orgasms" and "clitoral orgasms" in the female. Mutual orgasm is no longer considered the ideal in lovemaking.
- Attitudes toward sex have become more liberalized, but actual changes in sexual behavior have been rather gradual. Generally speaking, the greatest change has been in the number of people willing to talk openly about sex. The next greatest change has been a greater acceptance of female sexuality and narrowing of differences in male and female patterns of sexual behavior.
- During the last 20 years there has been a steady increase in the incidence of *sexually transmitted diseases*. This increase, coupled with the emergence of AIDS, has had an impact on the sexual behavior of many persons.
- The principal male problems in sexual adjustment are: *impotence*, *premature ejaculation*, and *retarded ejaculation*; for women they are: *general sexual dysfunction*, *orgasmic dysfunction*, and *vaginismus*. Behavioral methods and counseling techniques have been developed to alleviate each problem. However, most sexual adjustment problems are closely linked to the general health of a couple's overall relationship.

Chapter 24

Social Psychology I

Chapter Preview

To live alone, one must be either an animal or a god.

ARISTOTLE

No man is an Iland, intire of itselfe.

JOHN DONNE

The Social Animal

Your assignment, should you accept it, is this: You have been given a written message and the name, address, and occupation of the person who should receive it. This "target person" lives over 1500 miles away in a city you have never visited. You are allowed to move the message through the mail, but you may send it only to a first-name acquaintance. That person, in turn, must mail the message only to one of his or her first-name acquaintances. The message is to be moved in this manner until it reaches the target person, whom the previous person must know by name.

Sound impossible? Social psychologist Stanley Milgram and his associates asked a number of people to try moving a message in this way. Amazingly, about one message in five made it. Even more amazing was the number of people needed to complete a chain between two strangers separated by half a continent. The average number of "links" required was about seven people (Korte & Milgram, 1970; Milgram, 1967)!

Question: How is that possible?

Actually, the seven-link average is not as astounding as it might seem. Each of us is enmeshed in a complex network of social relationships, and each person's network overlaps with many others. If you know hundreds of people, and each of them knows hundreds more, a chain of seven people can create millions of possible interconnections. Undeniably, humans are social animals.

***Social psychology** is the study of how people behave in the presence (real or implied) of others. Some groups are formal and organized; others are unorganized. All influence the behavior of their members. The fascinating interplay of individual and group behavior has been the target of an immense amount of psychological study; too much, in fact, for us to cover in any detail. Therefore, this chapter and the next are social psychology "samplers." It is hoped that you will find the topics selected interesting and thought provoking.*

Survey Questions How does group membership affect individual behavior? What unspoken rules govern the use of personal space? How do we perceive the motives of others and the causes of our own behavior? Why do people affiliate? What factors influence interpersonal attraction? What have social psychologists learned about conformity, social power, obedience, and compliance? How does self-assertion differ from aggression?

Humans in a Social Context—People, People Everywhere

We are born into an organized society. Established values, expectations, and behavior patterns are present when we arrive. So too is **culture**, an ongoing pattern of life that is passed from one generation to the next. Some readily visible aspects of culture are language, marriage customs, concepts of ownership, and sex roles.

Groups The groups to which a person belongs form his or her most immediate day-to-day social environment. Each person is a member of many groups: the family, teams, church groups, work groups, and so on. In each group we occupy a *position* in the structure of the group. **Roles** are different expected behavior patterns displayed in connection with various social positions. Different expectations are associated with playing each of the following roles: mother, teacher, employer, student. Some roles are **ascribed,** meaning they are not under the individual's control: male or female, adolescent, inmate. **Achieved** roles are those attained voluntarily, or by special effort: wife, teacher, scientist, bandleader (Fig. 24-1).

Resources

Culture An ongoing pattern of life characterizing a society at a particular stage in its development or historical period.

Social role Expected behavior patterns associated with particular social positions (such as daughter, worker, student).

Ascribed role A role that is assigned to a person; a role one has no choice about playing.

Achieved role A role that is assumed voluntarily.

Fig. 24-1 *Roles have a powerful impact on social behavior.*

Status An individual's position in a group or social structure, especially with respect to power, privilege, importance, and so forth.

Group structure The network of roles, communication pathways, and power in a group.

Group cohesiveness The degree of attraction among group members or their degree of commitment to remaining in the group.

Norms Accepted (but often unspoken) rules of behavior to which individual group members tend to conform.

Autokinetic effect The apparent movement of a stationary pinpoint of light displayed in a darkened room.

Personal space An area immediately surrounding the body that is regarded as private and subject to personal control.

Proxemics Systematic study of the human use of space, particularly interpersonal space in various social settings.

Intimate distance The most private space immediately surrounding the body (about 18 inches from the skin).

Question: What effect does role playing have on behavior?

Roles allow us to anticipate the behavior of others. When a person is acting as a physician, mother, clerk, or police officer, certain behaviors are expected. In general, roles are quite useful because they streamline many of our daily interactions with others. However, roles have a negative side too. It is not unusual for a person to ocupy two or more conflicting roles. Getting caught in a **role conflict** can be quite uncomfortable or frustrating. Consider, for example, the traffic court judge whose son is brought before her with a violation, or the teacher who must flunk a close friend's daughter.

The impact of roles is dramatically illustrated by an experiment conducted by psychologist Philip Zimbardo and his students at Stanford University. In this experiment normal, healthy, male college students were paid $15 a day to serve as "inmates" and "guards" in a simulated prison (Zimbardo et al., 1973).

On the second day of their "imprisonment," the prisoners staged a number of disturbances, but their rebellion was quickly suppressed by the guards. Over the next few days the guards behaved with increasing brutality and the prisoners became more traumatized, passive, and dehumanized. Four prisoners had to be released in the first 4 days because of reactions such as hysterical crying, confusion, and severe depression. Each day the guards tormented the prisoners with more frequent commands, insults, and demeaning tasks. After 6 days the experiment was halted.

What had happened? Zimbardo's interpretation is that the roles—prisoner and guard—assigned to participants were so powerful that in just a matter of days the experiment had become "reality" for those involved. Afterward, many of the guards found it hard to believe their own behavior. As one recalled, "I was surprised at myself. . . . I made them call each other names and clean toilets with their bare hands. I practically considered the prisoners cattle" (Zimbardo, 1973). It would seem that the source of many destructive human relationships can be found in destructive roles.

Position in a group also determines one's **status.** In most groups higher status is associated with special privileges and respect. Status can operate very subtly to influence behavior in many situations. For example, in one interesting experiment researchers left dimes in phone booths. When subjects entered the booths, they were approached by a researcher who said, "Excuse me, I think I left a dime in this phone booth a few minutes ago. Did you find it?" When the researcher was well dressed, 75 percent of the people returned the dime, but only 38 percent returned it to poorly dressed researchers (Bickman, 1974). Perhaps the better treatment given "higher status" individuals in this situation explains some of the American preoccupation with status symbols.

Question: Are there other dimensions of group membership?

Groups are made up of people who are in some way interrelated. Two important dimensions of any group are its *structure* and *cohesiveness.* **Group structure** is the organization of roles, communication pathways, and power in the group. Organized groups such as an army or an athletic team have a high degree of structure. Informal friendship groups may or may not be highly structured. **Group cohesiveness** is basically an indication of the degree of attraction among group members. Cohesiveness is the basis for much of the power that groups exert over their members.

A very important aspect of the functioning of any group is its norms. **Norms** are standards of conduct that prescribe appropriate behavior in a given situation. If you have the slightest doubt about the existence of powerful group norms, Stanley Milgram suggests this test: Board a crowded bus, find a seat, and begin singing loudly in your fullest voice. Milgram's guess is that no more than 1 person in 100 could actually carry out these instructions.

Question: How are norms formed?

One early investigation of the formation of group norms made use of a striking illusion called the **autokinetic effect.** In a completely darkened room, a stationary pinpoint of light will appear to drift or move about (it is therefore "autokinetic" or "self-moving"). Muzafer Sherif (1935) found that estimates of how far the light moves vary widely from person to person. However, when two or more people give estimates at the same time, their judgments rapidly converge. There is a similar convergence of attitudes, beliefs, and behavior among members of most groups. A good example of such convergence can be found in norms governing the use of *personal space.* Since personal space is an intriguing topic in its own right, let's take a moment to examine it.

Personal Space—Invisible Boundaries

An interesting aspect of social behavior is the effort people expend to regulate the space around their bodies. Each person has an invisible "spatial envelope" that defines his or her **personal space** and extends "I" or "me" boundaries past the skin.

Question: What effect does personal space have on behavior?

Maintaining and regulating personal space directly affects many social interactions. There are unspoken rules covering the interpersonal distance considered appropriate for formal business, casual conversation, waiting in line with strangers, and other situations. The study of rules for the personal use of space is called **proxemics** (Hall, 1974) (Fig. 24-2).

The existence of personal space and the nature of proxemics can be demonstrated by "invading" the space of another person. The next time you are talking with an acquaintance, move closer and watch the reaction. Most people show immediate signs of discomfort and step back to reestablish their original distance. Those who hold their ground will turn to the side, look away, or position an arm in front of themselves as a kind of barrier to intrusion. If you persistently edge toward your subjects, you should find it easy to move them several feet from their original positions.

Question: Would this technique work with a good friend?

Possibly not. Conventions governing comfortable or acceptable distances vary according to relationships as well as activities. Hall (1966) identifies four basic zones (listed distances apply to North American culture):

1. **Intimate distance.** For most American adults the most private personal space extends about 18 inches out from the skin. Entry within this space is reserved for special people or circumstances. Lovemaking, comforting others,

Fig. 24-2 *The use of space in public places is governed by unspoken norms, or "rules," about what is appropriate.*

cuddling children, and massage all take place within this space. So does wrestling!

2. **Personal distance.** This is the distance maintained in comfortable interaction with friends. It extends from about 1½ to 4 feet from the body. Personal distance basically keeps people within "arm's reach" of each other.
3. **Social distance.** Impersonal business and casual social gatherings take place in a range of about 4 to 12 feet. This distance eliminates most possibilities of touching and formalizes conversation by requiring greater voice projection. "Important people" in many offices use the width of their imposing desks to maintain social distance while conducting business.
4. **Public distance.** When people are separated by more than 12 feet, interactions take on a decidedly formal quality. People look "flat," and the voice must be raised. Formal speeches, lectures, business meetings, and the like are conducted at public distance.

Because of the consistencies of spatial behavior in our culture, you can learn much about your relationship to others by observing the distance you most comfortably hold between yourselves. Watch for this dimension in your daily social activities.

We have now explored some basic facts of social life as well as a striking example of group norms. In the next section we will consider another interesting aspect of social behavior: a kind of impromptu detective work that we engage in each day, in which we try to guess the motives of others and the causes of their actions. Let's see how this is done.

Social Perception—Behind the Mask

As much as we might like to think otherwise, it is probably impossible to completely know another person. In fact, in many instances we must form impressions of people from only the smallest shreds of evidence. How do we form such impressions? How do they affect our behavior? Many of the answers lie in **attribution,** the process of making inferences about behavior. (Attribution was also discussed briefly in Chapter 12.) To learn how we fill in the "person behind the mask," let's further explore the making of attributions.

Attribution Theory

Two people enter a restaurant and order different meals. One person tastes her food, then salts it. The second salts his food before tasting it. How would you explain their behavior? In the first instance you might assume that the *food* needed salt. If so, you have attributed the woman's actions to an **external** cause. In the second case you might be more inclined to conclude that the man must really *like* salt. If so, you would be saying that the cause of his behavior is **internal** (McGee & Snyder, 1975).

Question: What effects do such interpretations have?

It is difficult to fully understand social behavior without considering internal and external attributions. For instance, let's say that Jim, who is in one of your classes, seems to avoid you. You see Jim at a market. Do you say hello to him? It could depend on how you have explained Jim's actions to yourself (Wegner & Vallacher, 1977). Have you assumed his avoidance is caused by shyness? Coincidence? Dislike?

Question: How do people make such judgments?

Making Attributions Two factors that greatly influence attribution are the **consistency** and **distinctiveness** of a person's behavior (Kelly, 1967). If Jim has consistently avoided you, it is clear that he was not just in a bad mood on several occasions, so coincidence is ruled out. Still, Jim's avoidance could mean he is shy, not that he dislikes you. This is why distinctiveness is also important. If Jim seems to avoid others too, you may conclude that he is shy. If his avoidance is consistently and distinctively linked with you, you will probably assume that he dislikes you. You could be wrong, of course, but your behavior toward Jim will change just the same.

To infer causes, we typically take into account the behavior of the **actor,** the **object** of the action, and the **setting** in which the action occurs (Kelly, 1967). Imagine, for example, that someone compliments your taste in clothes. If you are at a picnic, you may attribute this compliment to what you are wearing (the "object"), unless, of course, you're wearing your worst "grubbies." If you are, you may simply assume the person (or "actor") is friendly, or tactful. However, if you are at a clothing store and a salesperson compliments you, you will probably attribute it to the setting—not to what you are wearing or to the salesperson's true feelings. In making attributions we are very sensitive to **situational demands.** When a person is quiet and polite in church or at a funeral, it tells us little about the individual's motives. The situation demands such behavior.

Consensus (or agreement) is another factor affecting attribution. A consensus in the behavior of a number of people implies that the behavior has an external cause. If millions of people go to see a particular movie, we tend to say *the movie* is good. If someone you know goes to see a movie six times when others are staying away in droves, the tendency is to assume *the person* likes "that type of movie."

Personal distance The distance maintained when interacting with close friends (about 18 inches to 4 feet from the body).

Social distance Distance at which impersonal interaction takes place (about 4 to 12 feet from the body).

Public distance Distance at which formal interactions, such as giving a speech, occur (about 12 feet or more from the body).

Attribution The process of mentally ascribing one's own behavior, and that of others, to various causes.

External cause A cause of behavior that is assumed to lie outside a person.

Internal cause A cause of behavior that is assumed to lie within a person—for instance, a need, preference, or personality trait.

Consistency As a basis for making causal attributions, consistency refers to a behavior that shows very little change from time to time in similar situations.

Distinctiveness As a basis for making causal attributions, distinctiveness means that a behavior occurs only under a specific (distinct) set of circumstances.

Actor In making attributions, the person whose behavior is being interpreted.

Object In making attributions, the aim, motive, or target of an action.

Setting In making attributions, the social and/or physical environment in which an action occurs.

Situational demands Unstated expectations that exist in various settings and social situations regarding appropriate behavior.

Consensus The degree to which people respond alike. In making attributions, a high degree of consensus among people with different personalities and preferences implies that their responses are externally caused.

Fundamental attributional error The tendency to attribute the behavior of others to internal causes (personality, likes, and so forth) while attributing one's own behavior to external causes (situations and circumstances).

Need to affiliate The desire to associate with other people.

Social comparison Making judgments about ourselves through comparison with others.

Actor and Observer Let's say that at the last five parties you have attended, you've seen a woman named Pam. Based on this, you assume Pam is outgoing and likes to socialize. You see Pam at yet another gathering and mention that she seems to like parties. She says, "Actually, I hate these parties, but I get invited to play my tuba at them. My music teacher says I need to practice in front of an audience, so I keep attending these dumb events. Want to hear a Sousa march?"

We seldom know the real reasons for others' actions. This is why we tend to infer causes from *circumstances*. However, in doing so, we often make mistakes like the one just described. The most common error is to attribute the actions of *others* to *internal causes* while attributing our *own* behavior to situations *(external causes)* (Jones & Nisbett, 1971; Kelly, 1971). This mistake is made so often that it is called the **fundamental attributional error** (Ross, 1977)

Psychologists have found that we consistently attribute the behavior of others to their wants, motives, and personality traits. In contrast, we tend to find external explanations for our own behavior. No doubt you chose *your* major in school because of what it has to offer; other students choose *their* majors because of the kind of people they are (Wegner & Vallacher, 1977). Or, other people who don't leave tips in restaurants are cheapskates; if you don't leave a tip, it's because the service was bad.

Implications As you can see, attribution theory attempts to summarize how we think about ourselves and others. It also tries to identify some of the consistent errors or biases in our interpretations. In addition to providing a better understanding of behavior, attribution theory has helped identify some practical problems. Let's conclude with a brief example.

Ye Old Double Standard Attribution research has uncovered an interesting double standard for men and women. In a study by Deaux and Emswiller (1974), men and women overheard a male or female perform extremely well on a perception task. Subjects where then asked to rate whether the test taker's success was due to his or her ability, to luck, or to some combination of the two. Both men and women attributed male success mainly to skill and women's performances mainly to luck! This was true, even though male and female performances were identical. No doubt, such attributions dog the heels of many talented and successful women.

Learning Check

1. *Male, female,* and *adolescent* are examples of ________________ roles.
2. Status refers to a set of expected behaviors associated with a social position. T or F?
3. Research has shown that the number of first-name acquaintances needed to interconnect two widely separated strangers averages about seven people. T or F?
4. The Stanford prison experiment demonstrated the powerful influence of the autokinetic effect on behavior. T or F?
5. Social psychology is the study of how people behave ________________________________.
6. If two people position themselves 5 feet apart while conversing, they are separated by a gap referred to as ________________ distance.

7. When situational demands are strong, we tend to attribute a person's actions to internal motives. T or F?

8. The fundamental attributional error is to attribute the actions of others to internal causes while attributing our own behavior to external causes. T or F?

Answers: **1.** ascribed **2.** F **3.** T **4.** F **5.** in the presence of others **6.** social **7.** F **8.** T

The Need for Affiliation—Come Together

Question: Why do people choose to associate with others?

We have already observed that the **need to affiliate** appears to be a basic human characteristic. Why? Probably because affiliation helps meet needs for approval, support, friendship, and information. We also seek company to alleviate fear or anxiety. An experiment in which college women were threatened with painful electric shock serves as an illustration.

Zilstein's Shock Shop

A man introduced as Dr. Gregor Zilstein ominously explained to arriving subjects, "We would like to give each of you a series of electric shocks. . . . These shocks will hurt, they will be painful." In the room was a frightening electrical device that seemed to verify Zilstein's intentions. While waiting to be shocked, each subject was given a choice of waiting alone or with other subjects. Women frightened in this way more often chose to wait with others than did subjects told that the shock would be a mild tickle or tingle. (Schachter, 1959).

Apparently the frightened women found it comforting or reassuring to be with others. The tempting conclusion is: "Misery loves company." But this is not completely accurate. In a later experiment, women expecting to be shocked were given the option of waiting with other shock subjects, with women waiting to see their advisers, or alone. Most subjects chose to wait with other future "victims." In short, misery seems to love miserable company! In general, we tend to seek the company of people in circumstances similar to our own.

Question: Is there a reason for this?

Yes. Other people provide information for evaluating one's own reactions. When a situation is threatening or unfamiliar, or when a person is in doubt, *social comparisons* serve as a guide for behavior.

Social Comparison Theory In some cases objective standards for self-evaluation exist. If I want to know how tall I am, I simply get out a yardstick. But how do I know if I am a good athlete, guitarist, worker, parent, or friend? How do I know if my views on politics, religion, or the latest rock album are correct? The only yardstick available for such evaluations is provided by comparing myself with others.

Eminent social psychologist Leon Festinger (1954) was among the first to point out that group membership fills needs for **social comparison.** When there are no objective standards, we must turn to others as a way of evaluating our actions, feelings, opinions, or abilities. When students congregate to compare notes after a classroom exam, they satisfy needs for social comparison.

Interpersonal attraction Social attraction to another person.

Physical proximity As a factor in interpersonal attraction, one's actual physical nearness to others in terms of housing, work, school, and so forth.

Physical attractiveness A person's degree of physical beauty, as defined by his or her culture.

Competence As a factor in interpersonal attraction, the degree of general ability or proficiency a person displays.

Festinger emphasizes that social comparisons are not made randomly or on some ultimate scale. To illustrate, let's say we ask a student if she is a good tennis player. If she were to compare herself with a professional, the answer would be no. But this tells little about her relative ability. In her group of tennis partners, she might be considered an excellent player. Useful personal evaluation requires comparison with people of similar backgrounds, abilities, and circumstances. On a fair scale of comparison, our tennis player knows she is good and takes pride in her skills.

In the same way, thinking of yourself as successful, talented, responsible, or fairly paid depends entirely on whom you compare yourself to. Social comparison theory holds that a desire for self-evaluation determines what groups one joins, and it provides a general motive for associating with others.

Question: Don't people also affiliate out of attraction for one another?

They do, of course. The next section tells why.

Interpersonal Attraction—Social Magnetism?

"Birds of a feather flock together." "Familiarity breeds contempt." "Opposites attract." "Absence makes the heart grow fonder." Interest in what attracts people to one another has spawned an extensive folklore about what factors are important. This is understandable since **interpersonal attraction** is the basis for most voluntary social relationships.

Question: What attracts people to each other?

Social psychologist Elliot Aronson (1969) lists several factors that determine with whom you are likely to become friends.

1. **Physical proximity.** It may be difficult to admit, but our friends (or even lovers) are selected more on the basis of opportunity than we might like to believe. Nearness plays a powerful role in determining friendships. In a study of friendship patterns in a married-student housing complex, it was found that the closer people lived to each other, the more likely they were to be friends (Festinger et al., 1950). People in love like to think they have found the "one and only" person in the universe for them. In reality they have probably found the one and only person in a 5-mile radius—or at least within driving distance (Buss, 1985)!

   A main reason for proximity's effect is that it increases the *frequency of contact* between people. A variety of laboratory studies show that we are generally attracted to people with whom we have had frequent contact (Saegert et al., 1973). In other words, there does seem to be a boy-next-door or girl-next-door effect in romantic attraction and a folks-next-door effect in friendship (Fig. 24-3).

2. **Physical attractiveness.** As might be expected, beautiful people are consistently rated more attractive than those of average appearance. This is another example of the *halo effect* (Chapter 17), in which it is assumed that attractive people are also intelligent, witty, honest, and so on.

Fig. 24-3 *What attracts people to each other? Proximity and frequency of contact have a surprisingly large impact.*

Being physically attractive seems to be an advantage for both males and females, but in our culture beauty has more influence on a woman's fate than on a man's. For instance, a study of dating patterns of college dormitory residents found a strong relationship between physical beauty in women and their frequency of dating. For men, looks were unrelated to dating frequency (Krebs & Adinolfi, 1975). After marriage there is a tendency for attractive women to be paired with highly educated men with high incomes. For men, however, there is little relationship between attractiveness and the achievement of status (Udry & Eckland, 1984).

If you view this state of affairs as rather shallow and sexist, it may be reassuring to know that beauty is a factor mainly in initial acquaintance. Later, more substantial personal qualities become important (Bersheid & Walster, 1974). It takes more than appearance to make a lasting relationship.

3. **Competence.** We are also attracted to the talented or competent, but there is an interesting twist to this.

Clever but Clumsy

In an experiment on attraction, college students listened to one of four tapes of a supposed candidate for the "College Quiz Bowl." On two of the tapes the person was represented as highly intelligent; on the other two he was depicted as average in ability. One of the "intelligent" and one of the "average" tapes included an incident in which the candidate clumsily spilled coffee on himself. Those listening to the tapes rated as *most* attractive the superior candidate who blundered, and as *least* attractive the student who was average and clumsy. The superior but clumsy student was more attractive than the student who was only superior. (Aronson, 1969)

Box 24-1

Selecting a Mate—Reflections in a Social Mirror

Ninety percent of all people in Western societies marry at some point. What, beyond attraction, determines how people pair up? The answer is that we tend to marry someone who is like us in almost every way.

A variety of studies show that people who marry are highly similar in age, education, race, religion, and ethnic background. In addition, the correlation of attitudes and opinions for married couples is .5. For mental abilities it is .4, and for socioeconomic status, height, weight, and eye color it is .3. In general, you are far more likely to choose someone similar to yourself as a mate than someone very different.

A second question of interest concerns what traits people look for in a mate. In the United States both men and women agree that the following six qualities are most important: kindness and understanding, intelligence, exciting personality, good health, adaptability, and physical attractiveness. Despite such agreement, men and women do differ on some rankings. Men, for instance, rank physical attractiveness as the third most important feature, whereas women rank it sixth. A second major difference concerns good earning capacity: men rank it eleventh; women rank it eighth. Apparently, for most people romance is leavened with a dash of practicality. Even so, kindness and understanding are ranked first by almost everyone. (Source: Buss, 1985)

Similarity In interpersonal attraction, the extent to which two people are alike in background, age, interests, attitudes, beliefs, and so forth.

Self-disclosure The process of revealing private thoughts, feelings, and personal history to others.

Reciprocity A reciprocal interchange or return in kind.

Overdisclosure Self-disclosure that exceeds what is appropriate for a particular relationship or social situation.

Social exchange theory Theory stating that rewards must exceed costs for relationships to endure.

Social exchange Any exchange between two people of attention, information, affection, favors, or the like.

Romantic love Love, apart from love of family or friends, that is associated with high levels of interpersonal attraction, heightened arousal, and mutual absorption.

The upshot of this experiment seems to be that we like people who are competent, but human.

4. **Similarity.** Take a moment to mentally list as many of your friends as you can. What do they have in common (other than the joys of knowing you)? It is highly likely that most are close to you in age and of the same sex and race as you are. There will be exceptions, of course. However, similarity on these three dimensions is the general rule for friendships in American culture (Huston & Levinger, 1978).

One of the most consistent findings about interpersonal attraction is that people with similar backgrounds, interests, attitudes, or beliefs are attracted to each other (Byrne, 1971). This is probably at least partially due to the reinforcing value of seeing our beliefs and attitudes affirmed by others. It shows we are "right" and reveals that they are clever people as well! Similarity also affects mate selection—see Box 24-1.

Question: How do people who are not yet friends learn if they are similar?

Self-Disclosure Getting to know others requires a willingness to talk about more than just the weather, sports, or nuclear physics. At some point you must begin to share private thoughts and feelings and reveal more of your true self. Engaging in such **self-disclosure** is a major step toward friendship. Experiments confirm that we more often reveal ourselves to persons we like than to those we find less attractive (Chaiken & Derlega, 1974).

Disclosing oneself to others requires a degree of trust. Many people play it safe, or "close to the vest," with people they do not know well. Indeed, there are definite norms about when self-disclosure is acceptable and when it is not. Moderate self-disclosure leads to **reciprocity** (a return in kind) (Huston & Levinger, 1978). **Overdisclosure,** however, gives rise to suspicion and reduced attraction (Rubin, 1975). (Imagine standing in line at a market and having the person in front of you say: "Lately I've been thinking about how I really feel about myself. I think that I'm pretty well adjusted, but I occasionally have some questions about my sexual adequacy.") When self-disclosure proceeds at a moderate pace, it is accompanied by growing trust and intimacy. When it is too rapid, or inappropriate, we are likely to back off and wonder about the person's motives.

Social Exchange Theory As relationships progress, quite often they can be understood in terms of maximizing rewards while minimizing "costs" in any **social exchange.** When a relationship ceases to be attractive, people often say, "I'm not getting anything out of it any more." Actually, they probably are, but their costs—in terms of effort, irritation, or lowered self-esteem—have exceeded their rewards. According to social exchange theory, we unconsciously weigh such rewards and costs. For a relationship to last, it must be *profitable* (its rewards must exceed its costs) for both parties.

Question: Does romantic attraction differ from interpersonal attraction?

Romantic Love One well-known newspaper columnist likes to ask of teenage romance, "Is it love or sex?" For those involved, this may be an academic question, since mutual attraction is strong either way. Just the same, it may be more accurate on occasion to say, "I'm in lust" than it is to say, "I'm in love." All of which raises the question, What is love? Can it be measured? Is love distinct from intense liking? An innovative research program carried out by Zick Rubin (1973) provides some answers.

In order to study love, Rubin chose to think of it as an attitude held by one person toward another. This allowed him to develop "liking" and "love" scales (see Box 24-2) for the measurement of each "attitude." Next, he asked dating couples to complete each scale twice: once with their date in mind and once for a close friend of the same sex.

Question: What were the results?

Scores for love of partner and love of friend differed more than those for liking (see Table 24-1). In other words, dating couples liked *and* loved their partners,

Box 24-2 *Sample love-scale and liking-scale items. Each scale consists of 13 items similar to those shown. Scores on these scales correspond to other indications of love and liking (reprinted by permission of Zick Rubin).*

Love Scale

1. If ______________ were feeling bad, my first duty would be to cheer him (her) up.
2. I feel that I can confide in ______________ about virtually everything.
3. I find it easy to ignore ______________'s faults.

Liking Scale

1. When I am with ______________, we are almost always in the same mood.
2. I think that ______________ is unusually well adjusted.
3. I would highly recommend ______________ for a responsible job.

Table 24-1 Love and Liking for Date and Same-Sex Close Friend

Condition	Mean Scores: Women	Mean Scores: Men
Love for partner	89.46	89.37
Liking for partner	88.48	84.65
Love for friend	65.27	55.07
Liking for friend	80.47	79.10

(Source: Rubin, 1970)

Mutual absorption With regard to romantic love, the almost exclusive attention lovers give to one another.

Heightened arousal An elevated level of general excitement and activation within the body and nervous system.

Passionate love A highly emotional state most often observed in the early stages of romantic love relationships.

Companionate love Deep affection and attachment based on mutual respect and shared interests.

Social influence Changes in a person's behavior induced by the presence or actions of others.

but mostly liked their friends. Women, however, were a little more "loving" of their friends than were men. Does this reflect real differences in the strength of male friendships and female friendships? Probably not, since it is more acceptable in our culture for women to express love for one another than it is for men.

Another way in which love and friendship differ is mutual absorption. Romantic love, in contrast to simple liking, usually involves deep **mutual absorption** of the lovers. In other words, lovers (unlike friends) attend almost exclusively to one another. It's not surprising, then, that couples scoring high on Rubin's love scale spend more time gazing into each other's eyes than do couples who score low on the scale (Rubin, 1970). As the song says, "Millions of people go by, but they all disappear from view—'cause I only have eyes for you."

Rubin's research helps clarify differences between love and liking, but something still seems missing. The chief feature that sets romantic love apart from other types is probably *heightened arousal*. **Passionate love** is a wildly emotional state—a mixture of tenderness and sexuality, elation and pain, anxiety and relief, altruism and jealousy (Walster & Walster, 1978). Passionate love is often associated with restlessness (in the absence of one's lover), appetite loss, agitation, emotional activation, and other signs of arousal. Also, passionate love frequently occurs against a backdrop of danger, adversity, stress, or frustration—especially in soap operas and romance novels! As discussed in Chapter 12, some psychologists believe that heightened arousal, no matter what its cause, may be interpreted as passionate love in a romantic relationship (Bersheid & Walster, 1974b). In any case a variety of experiments support the idea that passionate love is associated with heightened emotional arousal.

Companionate Love Do you believe that to be truly in love is to be in love forever? Do you believe that as long as two people love each other, they can overcome any obstacle? Do you believe that a person should marry whomever he or she loves, regardless of circumstances? If you agree with such statements, you probably believe strongly in the importance of passionate love. If so, you may be overlooking a second major kind of love. **Companionate love** refers to affection and deep attachment that is built on respect, shared interests, and firm friendship. Companionate love is lower key emotionally than passionate love. However, it is steady, long term, and tends to grow with time (Walster & Walster, 1978).

Question: Are you suggesting that one type of love is better than the other?

Passionate love is certainly responsible for launching many relationships. However, the passionate, breathless stage of love typically lasts only about 6 to 30 months (Walster & Walster, 1978). What happens when this period ends? Quite often, people separate. There is a degree of danger, then, in expecting to live forever on a romantic cloud. People who are primarily caught up in passionate love may neglect to build a more lasting relationship. In this sense companionate love—the "kind of affection we feel for those with whom our lives are deeply intertwined"—is as important as passionate love (Walster & Walster, 1978).

Rather than downplaying companionate love, it is helpful to realize that lovers must also be friends. It could even be said that passionate love merely brings people together long enough so that they can become friends as well as lovers. All considered, the best relationships probably involve a mixture of both types of love.

Learning Check

Before reading more, check your comprehension by answering the following questions.

1. Women threatened with electric shock in an experiment generally chose to wait alone or with other women not taking part in the experiment. T or F?

2. The need to affiliate is related to interest in social comparison. T or F?

3. Social comparisons are made pretty much at random. T or F?

4. Interpersonal attraction is increased by all but one of the following. (Which does not fit?)

physical proximity competence similarity social costs

5. High levels of self-disclosure are reciprocated in most social encounters. T or F?

6. Women rate their friends higher on the love scale than do men. T or F?

7. The most striking finding about marriage patterns in the United States is that most people choose mates whose personalities are quite unlike their own. T or F?

8. ______________________ love is the kind of affection we feel for those with whom our lives are deeply intertwined.

Answers: **1.** F **2.** T **3.** F **4.** social costs **5.** F **6.** T **7.** F **8.** Companionate

Social Influence—Follow the Leader

Question: What is social influence?

Imagine a traffic signal brightly flashing the word WAIT. As you and a number of other pedestrians wait for it to change, a well-dressed man in a suit crosses against the light. How many people follow him? Do you think the answer would be different if the man were dressed in a denim shirt, patched pants, and scuffed shoes?

One of the most heavily researched topics in social psychology concerns the effects of **social influence.** When people interact, they almost always affect one another's behavior. The street-corner setting just described was used in an early experiment on social influence. As you might have guessed, more people followed the well-dressed man than the one dressed in shabby clothes (Lefkowitz et al., 1955).

In another sidewalk experiment, various numbers of people were assembled on a busy New York City street. On cue they all looked at a sixth-floor window across the street. A camera recorded the number of passersby who also stopped to stare. The larger the initial group, the more people were influenced to join in staring at the window (Milgram et al., 1969).

Question: Are there different kinds of social influence?

Social influence ranges from simple suggestion to intensive indoctrination (brainwashing). Everyday behavior is probably most influenced by group pressures for conformity. Conformity situations develop when individuals become aware of differences between themselves and group actions, norms, or values (McGuire, 1969). Let us consider this important dimension of social life in more detail.

Conformity Bringing one's behavior into agreement or harmony with norms or the behavior of others in a group.

Group sanctions Rewards and punishments (such as approval or disapproval) administered by groups to enforce a degree of conformity among members.

Conformity

When John first started working at the Fleegle Flange Factory, he found it easy to process 300 flanges an hour, while those around him averaged only 200. Other workers told him to slow down and take it easy. "I get bored," he said and continued to do 300 flanges an hour. At first John had been welcomed, but now conversations broke up when he approached and other workers laughed at or ignored him when he spoke. Although he never made a conscious decision to conform, in another week John's output had slowed to 200 flanges an hour.

As mentioned earlier, all groups have shared rules of conduct called *norms.* The broadest norms, as defined by overall society, establish "normal" or acceptable behavior in most situations. Comparing hairstyles, habits of speech, dress, eating habits, and social customs in two or more cultures makes it clear that we all conform to social norms. In fact, a degree of uniformity is necessary if we are to interact comfortably. Imagine being totally unable to anticipate the actions of others. In stores, schools, and homes this would be frustrating and disturbing. On the highways it would be lethal.

Perhaps the most basic of all group norms is (as John discovered), "Thou shalt conform!" (Suedfeld, 1966). This is equally true for the Hell's Angels, the Daughters of the American Revolution, a street-corner gang, or the board of directors of a large corporation. Groups of all kinds exert considerable pressures toward uniformity on their members. Like it or not, everyday life is filled with instances of conformity (Fig. 24-4).

Question: How strong are group pressures for conformity?

Fig. 24-4 *Conformity is a subtle dimension of daily life. Notice the similarities of clothing and hairstyles among these couples.*

The Asch Experiment One of the better known experiments on conformity was staged by Solomon Asch in the early 1950s. You can best appreciate Asch's experiment by placing yourself in the position of a subject. Assume that you are seated at a table with six other students. Your task is actually quite simple. On each trial you are asked to select from among three lines the one that matches a standard line (see Fig. 24-5).

As the testing begins, each subject announces an answer for the first card. When your turn comes, you find yourself in complete agreement with the others. "This isn't hard at all," you say to yourself. For several more trials your answers correspond to those of the group. Then comes a shock. All six people announce that line one matches the standard, and you were about to say line three. Suddenly you feel alone and upset. You nervously look at the lines again as the room falls silent. Everyone seems to be staring at you as the experimenter awaits your answer. Do you yield to the group?

In this experiment the other "students" were all accomplices coached to give the wrong answer on about a third of the trials. Few real subjects suspected trickery; hence, the group pressure created was very realistic (Asch, 1956).

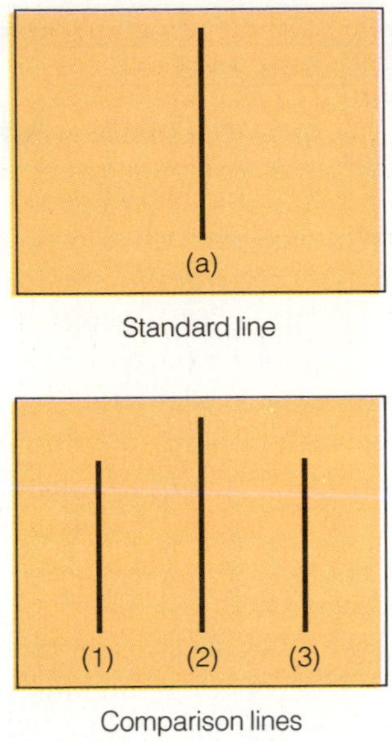

Fig. 24-5 *Stimuli used in Solomon Asch's conformity experiments.*

Question: How many people yielded to group pressure?

Subjects conformed to the group on about one-third of the critical trials. Of those tested, 75 percent yielded at least once. The significance of these results is underscored by the fact that subjects tested alone erred in less than 1 percent of their judgments. Those who yielded to group pressures were clearly denying what their eyes told them.

Question: Are some people more susceptible to group pressures than others?

A variety of experiments have shown that people with high needs for structure or certainty are more likely to be influenced. People who are anxious, low in self-confidence, or who are concerned with the opinions or approval of others are also more susceptible. Certain situations also encourage conformity, somtimes with disastrous results (see Box 24-3).

Question: How do groups enforce norms?

Group Factors in Conformity In most of our experiences with groups, we have been rewarded with acceptance and approval for conformity and threatened with rejection or ridicule for nonconformity. These reactions are called **group sanctions.** Negative sanctions (or punishments) for nonconformity range from laughter, staring, or social disapproval to complete rejection or formal ostracism. This is illustrated by later experiments in which Asch made up groups of six real subjects and one trained dissenter. When "Mr. Odd" announced his wrong answers, he was greeted with derisive laughter and sidelong glances.

Question: Wouldn't the effectiveness of group sanctions depend on the importance of the group?

Yes. And this is why the Asch experiments are impressive. Since these were only temporary groups, sanctions were informal and rejection had no lasting importance.

Question: What factors, besides importance of the group, affect the degree of conformity?

Box 24-3

Groupthink—Agreement at Any Cost

What happens when people in positions of power fall prey to pressures for conformity? To find out, Yale psychologist Irving Janis analyzed a collection of disastrous decisions made by government officials. His conclusion? Many such fiascoes are the result of **groupthink**—a compulsion by decision makers to maintain each other's approval, even at the cost of critical thinking. Groupthink has been blamed for many embarrassments, such as the Susan B. Anthony dollar and John F. Kennedy's backing of the Bay of Pigs invasion in Cuba.

The core of groupthink is misguided group loyalty, which prevents members from "rocking the boat" or questioning weak arguments and sloppy thinking. The resulting conformity pressures and self-censorship cause members to believe that there is greater agreement and unanimity than actually exist (Janis & Mann, 1977).

To prevent groupthink, Janis suggests that group leaders should: (1) define each group member's role as that of critical evaluator; (2) avoid stating any personal preferences in the beginning; (3) state the problem factually, without bias; (4) invite a group member or outside person to play devil's advocate. In addition, Janis suggests that there should be a "second-chance" meeting to reevaluate important decisions. That is, each decision should be reached twice. In an age clouded by the threat of nuclear war and similar disasters, even stronger solutions to the problem of groupthink would be welcome. Perhaps we should form a group to think about it?!

Groupthink A compulsion by members of decision-making groups to maintain agreement, even at the cost of critical thinking.

Earlier, we described an experiment in which passersby were influenced by a group of people staring at a building. We noted that the larger the group, the greater the number of passersby influenced. In Asch's face-to-face groups, the size of the majority also made a difference, but a surprisingly small one. The number of conforming subjects increased dramatically as the majority was increased from two to three people. However, a majority of three produced about as much yielding as a majority of eight. Next time you want to talk someone into (or out of) something, take two friends along and see what a difference it makes! (Sometimes it helps if the two are large and mean looking.)

Even more important than the size of the majority is its **unanimity.** Having at least one person in your corner can greatly reduce pressures to conform. When Asch provided subjects with an ally (who also opposed the majority by giving the correct answer), conformity was lessened. In terms of numbers, a unanimous majority of three is more powerful than eight with one dissenting. Perhaps this accounts for the rich diversity of human attitudes, beliefs, opinions, and lifestyles. If you can find at least one other person who sees things as you do (no matter how weird), you can be relatively secure in your opposition to other viewpoints.

Learning Check

1. The effect one person's behavior has on another is called ______________ ______________.

2. Conformity is a normal aspect of social life. T or F?

3. Subjects on Solomon Asch's conformity study yielded on about 75 percent of the critical trials. T or F?

4. Nonconformity is punished by negative group ______________________.

5. Janis uses the term ______________________ to describe a compulsion among decision-making groups to maintain an illusion of unanimity.

Answers: **1.** social influence **2.** T **3.** F **4.** sanctions **5.** groupthink

---

Social Power—Who Can Do What to Whom?

Here's something to think about: Whereas *strength* is a quality possessed by individuals, *power* is always social—it arises when people come together and disappears when they disperse. In trying to understand the ways people are able to influence each other, it is helpful to distinguish among five types of **social power** (Raven, 1974).

Reward power lies in the ability to reward a person for complying with desired behavior. Teachers try to exert reward power over their students through the use of grades. Employers command reward power by their control of wages and bonuses.

Coercive power is based on the ability to punish a person for failure to comply. Coercive power is the basis for most statute law, in that fines or imprisonment are used to control behavior.

Legitimate power comes from acceptance of a person as an agent of an established social order. For example, elected leaders and supervisors have legitimate power. So does a teacher in the classroom, but outside the classroom that power would have to come from another source.

Referent power is based on respect for or identification with a person or a group. The person "refers to" the source of referent power for direction. Referent power is responsible for much of the conformity observed in groups.

Expert power is based on recognition that another person has knowledge or expertise necessary for achieving a goal. An example is allowing teachers or experts to guide behavior because you believe in their ability to produce desirable results. Physicians, lawyers, psychologists, and plumbers have expert power.

A person who has power in one situation may have very little in another. In those situations where a person has power, he or she is described as an *authority*. In the next section we will investigate *obedience*. Obedience is a special type of conformity to the demands of an authority.

Unanimity Being unanimous or of one mind; agreement.

Social power The capacity to control, alter, or influence the behavior of another person.

Reward power Social power based on the capacity to reward a person for acting as desired.

Coercive power Social power based on the ability to punish others.

Legitimate power Social power based on a person's position as an agent of an accepted social order.

Referent power Social power gained when one is used as a point of reference by others.

Expert power Social power derived from possession of knowledge or expertise.

Obedience Conformity to the demands of an authority.

Obedience—Would You Electrocute a Stranger?

The question is this: If ordered to do so, would you administer an electric shock to a man with a known heart condition who is screaming and asking to be released? Certainly we can assume that few people would do so. Or can we? In Nazi Germany obedient soldiers (once average citizens) helped slaughter over 9 million people. Another example of the same phenomenon is an infamous incident during the Vietnam War when Lt. William Calley led a bloody massacre of helpless civilians at My Lai. Do such inhumane acts reflect deep character flaws?

Are they the acts of heartless psychopaths or crazed killers? Or are they simply the result of obedience to authority? What are the limits of such obedience? These are questions that puzzled social psychologist Stanley Milgram (1965) when he began a provocative series of studies on obedience.

Question: How did Milgram study obedience?

As was true of the Asch experiments, Milgram's research is best appreciated by imagining yourself as a subject. Place yourself in this situation.

Milgram's Study Imagine answering a newspaper ad to take part in a "learning" experiment at Yale University. When you arrive, a coin is flipped and a second subject, a pleasant-looking man in his fifties, is designated the "learner." By chance you have become the "teacher."

Your task is to read a list of word pairs to be memorized by the learner. You are to punish him with an electric shock each time he makes a mistake. The learner is taken to an adjacent room and you watch as he is seated in an "electric chair" apparatus and electrodes are attached to his wrists. You are then escorted to your position in front of a "shock generator." On this device is a row of 30 switches labeled from 15 to 450 volts and accompanied by descriptions ranging from "Slight Shock" to "Extreme Intensity Shock" and finally "Danger: Severe Shock." Your instructions are to administer a shock each time the learner makes a mistake. You are to begin with 15 volts and then move one switch (15 volts) higher for each additional mistake.

The experiment begins, and the learner soon makes his first error. You flip a switch. More mistakes. Rapidly you reach the 75-volt level. The learner moans after each shock. At 100 volts he complains he has a heart condition. At 150 volts he no longer wants to continue and demands release. At 300 volts he screams and says he can no longer give answers.

At some point during the experiment, you begin to protest to the experimenter. "That man has a heart condition," you say; "I'm not going to kill that man." The experimenter says, "Please continue." Another shock and another scream from the learner, and you say, "You mean I've got to keep going up the scale? No, sir. I'm not going to give him 450 volts!" The experimenter says, "The experiment requires that you continue." For the remainder of the experiment, the learner refuses to answer any more questions and screams with each shock (Milgram, 1965).

Question: I can't believe many people would do this. What happened?

Milgram also doubted that many people would obey such orders, and when he polled a group of psychiatrists before the experiment, they predicted that less than 1 percent of those tested would obey. The astounding fact is that 65 percent of those tested obeyed completely by going all the way to the 450-volt level. Virtually no one stopped short of 300 volts ("Severe Shock") (see Fig. 24-6).

Question: Was the "learner" injured?

The time has come to reveal that the "learner" was actually an actor who turned a tape recorder on and off in the "shock room." No shocks were ever administered, but the dilemma for the "teacher" was quite real. Subjects protested, sweated, trembled, stuttered, bit their lips, and laughed nervously. Clearly, they

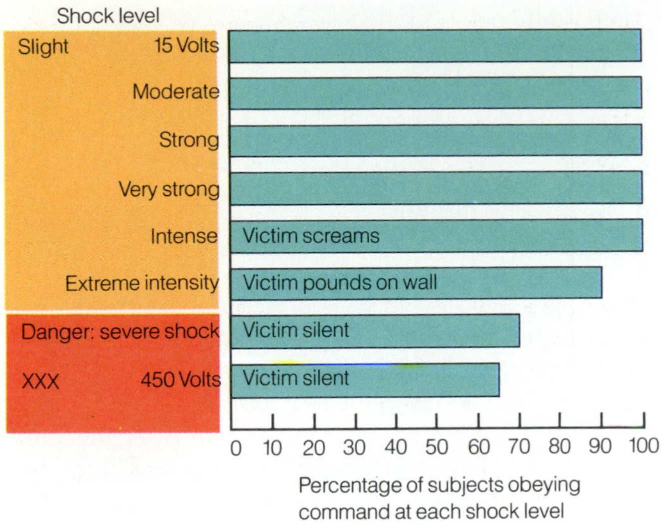

Fig. 24-6 *Results of Milgram's obedience experiment. Only a minority of subjects refused to provide shocks, even at the most extreme intensities. The first substantial drop in obedience occurred at the 300-volt level. (Milgram, 1963)*

were disturbed by what they were doing, but most obeyed the experimenter's orders.

Question: Why did so many people obey?

Milgram's Follow-up Some have suggested that the prestige of Yale University contributed to subjects' willingness to obey. Could subjects have assumed that the professor running the experiment would not really allow anyone to be hurt? To investigate this possibility, the experiment was rerun in a shabby office building in nearby Bridgeport, Connecticut. There was nothing in either the location or the experimenter's appearance to inspire confidence. Under these conditions fewer people obeyed (48 percent), but the reduction was minor.

Milgram was quite disturbed by the willingness of people to knuckle under to authority and to senselessly shock someone. In later experiments he tried in various ways to reduce obedience. He found that distance between the "teacher" and the "learner" was of importance. When subjects were in the *same room* as the learner, only 40 percent were fully obedient. When they were *face-to-face* with the learner and were required to force his hand down on a "shock plate," only 30 percent obeyed (Fig. 24-7). *Distance* from the authority also had an effect. When the experimenter delivered his orders over the phone, only 22 percent obeyed.

Milgram's research raises nagging questions about our willingness to commit antisocial or inhumane acts commanded by a "legitimate authority." The excuse so often given by war criminals—"I was only following orders"—takes on new meaning in this light. Milgram suggests that when directions come from an authority, people rationalize that they are not personally responsible for their actions (Fig. 24-8).

Question: Aren't you taking an overly dim view of obedience?

Obedience to authority is obviously necessary and desirable in many circumstances. Just the same, it is probably true, as C. P. Snow (1961) has observed, "When you think of the long and gloomy history of man, you will find more hideous crimes have been committed in the name of obedience than in the name

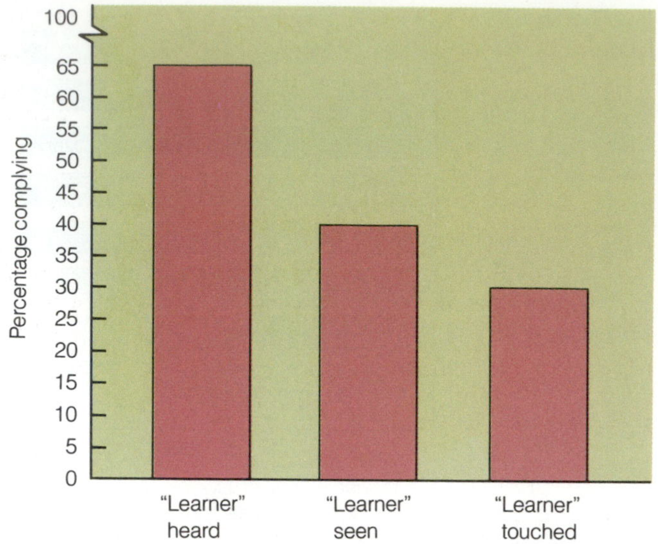

Fig. 24-7 *Physical distance from the "learner" had a significant effect on the percentage of subjects obeying orders.*

of rebellion." With this in mind, let us end this discussion on a more positive note. In one of his experiments, Milgram found that group support can greatly reduce destructive obedience. When real subjects saw two other "teachers" (both actors) resist orders and walk out of the experiment, only 10 percent continued to obey. Thus, a personal act of courage or moral fortitude by one or two members of a group may free others to disobey misguided or unjust authority.

Fig. 24-8 *Obedience to authority is often necessary and reasonable; however, it can also be destructive.*

Compliance—A Foot in the Door

In *conformity* situations the pressure to "get in line" is usually indirect. When an authority commands *obedience*, the pressure is direct and difficult to resist. There is a third possibility of interest. The term **compliance** has been used to describe situations in which a person with little or no authority makes a direct request to another person (Wrightsman & Deaux, 1981).

Pressures to comply are quite common. For example, a stranger might ask you to yield a phone booth so he can make a call, a saleswoman might suggest that you buy a more expensive watch than you had planned on, or a co-worker might ask you for some money to buy a cup of coffee.

Question: What determines whether a person will comply with a request?

Many factors could be listed, but three stand out as especially interesting. Let's briefly consider each.

The Foot-in-the-Door Effect People who sell door-to-door have long recognized that once they get a foot in the door, a sale is almost a sure thing. To state the **foot-in-the-door** principle more formally, a person who agrees to a small request is later more likely to comply with a larger demand. Evidence suggests, for instance, that if someone asked you to put a large, ugly sign in your front yard to promote safe driving, you would refuse. If, however, you had first agreed to put a small sign in your window, you would later be much more likely to allow the big sign to be placed in your yard (Freedman & Fraser, 1966).

The Door-in-the-Face Effect Let's say that a neighbor comes to your door and asks you to feed his dogs, water his plants, and mow his yard while he is out of town for a month. This is quite a major request—one that most people would probably turn down. Feeling only slightly guilty, you tell your neighbor that you're sorry but you can't help him out. Now, what if the same neighbor returns the next day and asks you if you would at least pick up his mail while he is gone. Chances are very good that you would honor this request, even if you might have resisted it otherwise.

Psychologist Robert Cialdini and his associates coined the term **door-in-the-face effect** to describe the reverse of the foot-in-the-door effect (Cialdini et al., 1975). On some occasions the best way to get a person to agree to a small request is to first make a major request. After the person has turned down the major request ("slammed the door in your face"), he or she may be more willing to agree to a lesser demand.

The Low-Ball Technique Anyone who has purchased an automobile will recognize a third way of inducing compliance. Automobile dealers are notorious for convincing customers to buy a car by offering "low-ball' prices that undercut the competition. The dealer first gets the customer to agree to buy at an attractively low price. Then, once the customer is committed, various techniques are used to bump the price up before the sale is concluded (see Box 24-4). The **low-ball technique,** then, consists of getting a person committed to act and then making the terms of acting less desirable. Another example would be asking some-

Compliance Bending to the requests of a person who has little or no authority or other basis for exercising social power.

Foot-in-the-door effect The tendency for a person who has first complied with a small request to be more likely later to fulfill a larger request.

Door-in-the-face effect The tendency for a person who has refused a major request to subsequently be more likely to comply with a minor request.

Low-ball technique A strategy in which commitment is gained first to reasonable or desirable terms, which are then made less reasonable or desirable.

Box 24-4

How to Drive a Hard Bargain

Your local car lot is a good place to see compliance take place. Automobile salespersons play the compliance game daily and get very good at it. If you understand what they are up to, you will have a far better chance of resisting their tactics.

Foot in the Door The salesperson offers you a test drive. If you accept, you will have made a small commitment of time to a particular car and to the salesperson. The salesperson will then ask you to go to an office and fill out some papers, "just to see what kind of a price" he or she can offer. If you go along, you will be further committed.

The Low-Ball Technique To get things underway, the salesperson will offer you a very good price for your trade-in or she/he will ask you to make an offer on the new car, "any offer, no matter how low." The salesperson will then ask if you will buy the car if she/he can sell it for the price you state. If you say yes, you have virtually bought the car. Most people find it very difficult to walk away once bargaining has reached this stage.

Once buyers are "hooked" by a low-ball offer, the salesperson goes to the manager to have the sale "approved." On returning, the salesperson will tell you with great disappointment that the dealership would lose money on the deal. "Couldn't you just take a little less for the trade-in or pay a little more for the car?" he or she will ask. At this point many people hesitate and grumble, but most give in and accept some "compromise" price or trade-in amount.

By the time you strike a deal, you can assume that the price you accept will give the dealership the minimum profit it requires on all sales—and probably much more. To add insult to injury, the salesperson will then try to increase the profit by convincing you to add various options to your car—extra mirrors, a stereo system, cruise control, and so forth. All of these items cost less from independent suppliers, so many people pay hundreds of dollars too much for them alone.

To combat all of the preceding, get a final "best offer" in writing. Then walk out. Go to another dealer and see if the salesperson will better the price, in writing. When she/he does, return to the first dealership and negotiate for an even better price—*then* decide where to buy.

one to loan you $5 and then upping it to $15. Or, you might ask someone if he or she would give you a ride to school in the morning. Only after the person has agreed would you tell her or him that you had to be there at 6 A.M.

Passive Compliance Complying with requests is a normal part of daily social life. At times, however, a willingness to comply can exceed what is reasonable. Researcher Thomas Moriarty (1975) has demonstrated excessive, passive compliance under realistic conditions. Moriarty became interested in the "little murders" of daily life: the personal insults, rebuffs, and sacrifices of dignity that are common. Moriarty observed that many people will put up with almost anything to avoid a confrontation. He decided to put this passive, "no-hassle" attitude to experimental test.

In one experiment, two subjects (one actually an accomplice) were given a difficult test in a very small room. The subjects were seated back-to-back and left alone to work. As soon as the experimenter left, the phoney subject turned on a portable cassette player at full volume. Real subjects who failed to complain were

Passive compliance Passively bending to unreasonable demands or circumstances.

treated to a 17-minute blast of nerve-wracking rock music. The accomplice was instructed to turn the music off only after a third request. In this particular experiment, 80 percent of the subjects said nothing, although they glared, cupped their ears, stopped work, and so forth. Interviews conducted later showed that most subjects were angry or annoyed but were afraid to tell the other "subject" to be quiet.

Question: Could it be that people failed to complain because they didn't want to disrupt the testing?

Yes, it is possible that the passivity observed in this study is unique to the experimental setting. However, when Moriarty and his students staged loud conversations behind theater patrons or people studying in a library, very few protested. In other naturalistic experiments, people were accosted in phone booths. The experimenter explained that he had left a ring in the booth and asked if the subject had found it. When the subject said "no," the experimenter demanded that the subject empty his pockets. Most did.

In these and similar situations, people passively accepted having their personal rights trampled, even when objecting presented no threat to their safety. Have we become, as Moriarty puts it, "a nation of willing victims"? Certainly we would hope not. Nevertheless, researchers such as Milgram and Moriarty have identified a significant social problem. We will address this problem again in the Applications section that follows.

Learning Check

1. An ability to punish others for failure to obey is the basis for:
a. referent power *b.* expert power *c.* legitimate power *d.* coercive power

2. Would you "electrocute" a stranger? ____________

3. Obedience in Milgram's experiments was related to:
a. distance between learner and teacher
b. distance between experimenter and teacher
c. obedience of other teachers
d. all of the above

4. Obedience is conformity to ____________.

5. By repeating his obedience experiment in a downtown office building, Milgram demonstrated that the prestige of Yale University was the main reason for subjects' willingness to obey in the original experiment. T or F?

6. The research of Thomas Moriarty and others has shifted to an interest in ____________ ____________ rather than obedience to authority.

Answers: **1.** *d.* **2.** answer will vary **3.** *d.* **4.** authority **5.** F **6.** passive compliance

Applications

Assertiveness Training—Standing Up for Your Rights

Have you ever:

Hesitated to question an error on a restaurant bill because you were afraid of making a scene?

Backed out of asking for a raise or a change in working conditions?

Said "yes" when you wanted to say "no"?

Been afraid to question a grade that seemed unfair?

Most of us have been rewarded, first as children, and later as adults, for compliant, obedient, or "good" behavior. Perhaps this is why so many people find it difficult to assert themselves. Or perhaps nonassertion is related to the anxiety that accompanies "making a scene" or feeling disliked by others. Whatever the causes, some people are so seriously inhibited that they suffer tremendous anguish in any situation requiring poise, self-confidence, or self-assertion. Fortunately for these people, behavior therapist Joseph Wolpe (and others) have pioneered a therapeutic technique called *assertiveness training*.

Question: What is done in assertiveness training?

Assertiveness training is a very direct procedure. By using group exercises, videotapes, mirrors, and staged conflicts, the behavior therapist teaches assertive behavior. People learn to practice honesty, disagreeing, questioning authority, and assertive postures and gestures. As their self-confidence improves, nonassertive clients are taken on "field trips" to shops and restaurants where they practice what they have learned.

Nonassertion severe enough to require therapy is unusual. Nevertheless, many people become tense or upset in at least some situations in which they must stand up for their rights. For this reason many people have found the techniques and exercises of assertiveness training helpful. If you have ever eaten a carbonized steak when you ordered rare, or stood in silent rage as a clerk ignored you, the following discussion will be of interest.

Self-Assertion The first step in assertiveness training is to convince yourself of three basic rights: You have the right to refuse, to request, and to right a wrong. Self-assertion involves standing up for these rights by speaking out in your own behalf.

Question: Is self-assertion just getting things your own way?

Not at all. A basic distinction can be made between *self-assertion* and *aggressive* behavior. Assertion is a direct, honest expression of feelings and desires. It is not exclusively self-serving, because pent-up anger can be very destructive to relationships. People who are nonassertive are usually patient to a fault. In contrast, aggression does not take into account the feelings or rights of others. Aggression is an attempt to get one's own way no matter what. Assertion techniques emphasize firmness, not attack (see Table 24-2).

The basic idea in assertiveness training is that each assertive action is practiced until it can be repeated even under stress. For example, let's say it really angers you when a store clerk waits on several people who arrived after you did. To improve your assertiveness in this situation, you would begin by *rehearsing* the dialogue, posture, and gestures you would use to confront the clerk or the other customer. Working in front of a mirror can be very helpful. If possible, you should *role play* the scene with a friend. Be sure to have your friend take the part of a really aggressive or irresponsible clerk, as well as a cooperative one. Rehearsal and role playing should also be used when you expect a possible confrontation with someone—for example, if you were going to ask for a raise, challenge a grade, or confront a landlord.

Question: Is that all there is to it?

No. Another important principle is *overlearning*. When you rehearse or role play assertive behavior, it is essential to continue practice until your responses become almost automatic. This helps prevent you from getting flustered in the actual situation.

Applications: Assertiveness Training, continued

Table 24-2 Comparison of Assertive, Aggressive, and Nonassertive Behavior

	Actor	Receiver of Behavior
Nonassertive behavior	Self-denying, inhibited, hurt, and anxious; lets others make choices; goals not achieved	Feels sympathy, guilt, or contempt for actor; achieves goals at actor's expense
Aggressive behavior	Achieves goals at others' expense; expresses feelings, but hurts others; chooses for others or puts them down	Feels hurt, defensive, humiliated, or taken advantage of; does not meet own needs
Assertive behavior	Self-enhancing; acts in own best interests; expresses feelings; respects rights of others; goals usually achieved, self-respect maintained	Needs respected and feelings expressed; may achieve goal; self-worth maintained

(After Alberti & Emmons, 1978)

One more technique you may find useful is the *broken record*. A good way to prevent assertion from becoming aggression is to simply restate your request as many times and as many ways as necessary. As an illustration, let's say you are returning a pair of shoes to a store. After two wearings the shoes fell apart, but you bought them 2 months ago and no longer have a receipt. The broken-record technique sounds something like this:

Customer: I would like to have these shoes replaced.
Clerk: Do you have a receipt?
Customer: No, but I bought them here and since they are defective, I would like to have you replace them.
Clerk: I can't do that without a receipt.
Customer: I understand that, but I want them replaced.
Clerk: Well, if you'll come back this afternoon and talk to the manager. . .
Customer: I've brought these shoes in because they are defective.
Clerk: Well, I'm not authorized to replace them.
Customer: Yes, well, if you'll replace these, I'll be on my way.

Notice that the customer has not attacked the clerk or created an angry confrontation. Simple persistence is often all that is necessary for successful self-assertion.

Question: How would I respond assertively to a put-down?

Responding assertively to verbal aggression (a put-down) is a real challenge. The tendency is to respond aggressively, which usually makes things worse. A good way to respond to a put-down is this: (1) If you are wrong, admit it; (2) acknowledge the person's feelings; (3) assert yourself about the other person's aggression; (4) briskly end the interchange.

Psychologists Robert Alberti and Michael Emmons (1978) offer an example of using the four steps: Let's say you accidently bump into someone. The person responds angrily, "Damn it! Why don't you watch where you're going! You fool, you could have hurt me!" A good response would be to say, "I'm sorry I bumped you. I didn't do it intentionally. It's obvious you're upset, but I don't like your calling me names or yelling. I can get your point without that."

Now, what if someone insults you indirectly ("I love your taste in clothing, it's so 'folksy.'")? Alberti

Applications: Assertiveness Training, continued

and Emmons suggest you ask for a clarification ("What are you trying to say?"). This will force the person to take responsibility for the aggression. It can also provide an opportunity to change the way the person interacts with you: "If you really don't like what I'm wearing, I'd like to know it. I'm not always sure I like the things I buy, and I value your opinion."

To summarize, self-assertion is not instant poise, confidence, or self-assurance. It is a way of combating anxieties associated with living in an impersonal and sometimes intimidating society. If you are interested in more information, see Alberti and Emmons' book, *Your Perfect Right* (Impact, 1978).

Learning Check

1. In assertiveness training, people learn techniques for getting their way in social situations and angry interchanges. T or F?

2. Nonassertive behavior causes hurt, anxiety, and self-denial in the actor, and sympathy, guilt, or contempt in the receiver. T or F?

3. Overlearning should be avoided when rehearsing assertive behaviors. T or F?

4. The "broken record" must be avoided, because it is a basic nonassertive behavior. T or F?

Answers: **1.** F **2.** T **3.** F **4.** F

Chapter Summary

- Humans are social animals enmeshed in a complex network of social relationships. *Social psychology* studies humans as members of groups. Its focus is how people behave in the presence (real or implied) of others.
- *Culture* provides a broad social context for our behavior. One's *position* in groups defines a variety of *roles* to be played. Roles, which may be *achieved* or *ascribed*, are particular behavior patterns associated with social positions. When a person holds two or more contradictory roles, *role conflict* may occur. The Stanford prison experiment showed that destructive roles may override individual determinants of behavior.
- Positions within groups typically carry higher or lower levels of *status*. High status is associated with special privileges and respect.
- *Group structure* refers to the organization of roles, communication pathways, and power within a group. *Group cohesiveness* is basically the degree of attraction among group members. *Norms* are standards of conduct enforced (formally or informally) by groups. The *autokinetic effect* has been used to demonstrate that norms rapidly form even in temporary groups.
- The study of personal space is called *proxemics*. Four basic spatial zones around each person's body are: *intimate distance* (0 to 18 inches), *personal distance* (1½ to 4 feet), *social distance* (4 to 12 feet), and *public distance* (12 feet or more).

- *Attribution theory* is concerned with how we make inferences about behavior. A variety of factors affect attribution, including *consistency, distinctiveness, situational demands,* and *consensus.* The *fundamental attributional error* is to ascribe the actions of others to internal causes, while attributing one's own behavior to external causes.
- The *need to affiliate* is tied to needs for approval, support, friendship, and information. Research indicates that affiliation is also related to reducing anxiety and uncertainty. *Social comparison theory* holds that we also affiliate to evaluate our actions, feelings, and abilities.
- *Interpersonal attraction* is increased by *physical proximity* (nearness), *frequent contact, physical attractiveness, competence,* and *similarity.* A large degree of similarity on many dimensions is characteristic of mate selection in most marriages.
- *Self-disclosure* occurs more when two people like one another. A *reciprocity norm* exists for self-disclosure: Low levels of self-disclosure are met with low levels in return, whereas moderate self-disclosure elicits more personal replies. However, *overdisclosure* tends to inhibit self-disclosure by others.
- According to *social exchange theory,* we tend to maintain relationships that are *profitable;* that is, those for which perceived rewards exceed perceived costs.
- *Romantic love* has been studied as a special kind of attitude. Love can be distinguished from liking by the use of attitude scales. Dating couples like *and* love their partners but only like their friends. *Passionate love* is associated with *heightened arousal* and *mutual absorption* between lovers. *Companionate love,* in contrast, is steady, long term, and lower key emotionally. Companionate love is an element of most lasting marriages.
- In general, *social influence* refers to alterations in behavior brought about by the behavior of others, especially situations in which *conformity* occurs.
- Virtually everyone conforms to a variety of broad social and cultural norms. *Conformity pressures* also exist within smaller groups. The Asch experiments demonstrated that various *group sanctions* encourage conformity.
- *Groupthink* refers to compulsive conformity in group decision making. Victims of groupthink seek to maintain each other's approval, even at the cost of critical thinking.
- Social influence is also related to five types of *social power.* The types are: *reward power, coercive power, legitimate power, referent power,* and *expert power.*
- *Obedience* to authority has been investigated in a variety of experiments, particularly those by Milgram. Obedience in Milgram's studies decreased when the victim was in the same room, when the victim and subject were face-to-face, when the authority figure was absent, and when others refused to obey.
- *Compliance* with direct requests is another means by which behavior is influenced. Three strategies for inducing compliance are the *foot-in-the-door technique,* the *door-in-the-face approach,* and the *low-ball technique.* Research suggests that in addition to excessive obedience to authority, many people show a surprising *passive compliance* to unreasonable requests.

Chapter 25

Social Psychology II

Chapter Preview

Doomsday for the Seekers

Hardly a year passes, it seems, without a doomsday group of one kind or another making the news. In one classic example of such groups, a woman named Mrs. Keech claimed she was receiving messages from beings on a planet called Clarion. The beings told Mrs. Keech that they had detected a fault in the Earth's crust that would submerge the North American continent in an unimaginable natural disaster. The date of this event was to be December 21. However, Mrs. Keech and her band of followers, who called themselves the Seekers, had no fear: On December 20 they expected to be met at midnight by a flying saucer and taken to safety in outer space.

The night of December 20 arrived, and the Seekers gathered at Mrs. Keech's house. Many had given up jobs and possessions to prepare for departure. Expectations were high and commitment was total, but as the night wore on, midnight passed and the world continued to exist. It was a bitter and embarrassing disappointment for all concerned.

Question: Did the group break up then?

The amazing twist to this story, and the aspect that intrigued social psychologists, was that the Seekers became more *convinced than ever before that they had been right. At about 5 A.M. Mrs. Keech announced that she had received a message explaining that the Seekers had saved the world. Before the night of December 20, the group had been uninterested in convincing other people that the world was coming to an end. Now they called newspapers, magazines, and radio stations to explain what had happened and to convince others of their accomplishment.*

How do we explain this strange turn in the behavior of Mrs. Keech's doomsday group? The answer seems to lie in the concept of cognitive dissonance. *Cognitive dissonance also helps explain many aspects of attitude change. Watch for a discussion of cognitive dissonance later in this chapter.*

Survey Questions What are attitudes? How are they acquired, measured, and changed? Under what conditions is persuasion most effective? What is cognitive dissonance? What does it have to do with attitudes and behavior? Is brainwashing actually possible? How are people converted to cult membership? What causes prejudice and intergroup conflict? What can be done about these problems? How do psychologists explain human aggression? Why are bystanders so often unwilling to help in an emergency?

Attitudes—Belief + Emotion + Action

What is your attitude toward birth control, marijuana, Republicans, higher education, Chevrolets, psychology? The answers have far-reaching effects on your behavior. The effects of attitudes are intimately woven into our actions and views of the world. Our tastes, friendships, votes, preferences, and goals are all touched by attitudes.

Question: What specifically is an attitude?

An **attitude** is a learned predisposition to respond to people, objects, or institutions in a positive or negative way. Attitudes are one of the most studied aspects of social functioning. This is because attitudes summarize past experience and *predict* or direct future actions. For example, an approach known as the **misdirected letter technique** demonstrates that actions are closely connected to attitudes:

The Luck of the Irish

During a period of civil violence in Ireland, researchers measured attitudes held toward the Irish in a sample of English households. Later, wrongly addressed letters were sent to the same households. Each letter had either an English name on it or an Irish name. The question was: Would the "Irish" letters be returned to the post office or thrown away? As predicted, the number of "Irish" letters returned corresponded directly to pro- or anti-Irish attitudes measured earlier. (Howitt et al., 1977)

"Your attitude is showing," is sometimes said. This statement seems simple, but actually there are three ways in which attitudes are expressed. Most attitudes have a **belief component,** an **emotional component,** and an **action component.** Consider, as an example, your attitude toward gun control. You will have beliefs about whether gun control would affect rates of crime or violence. You will have emotional responses to guns, find them either attractive and desirable or threatening and destructive. And you will have a tendency to seek out or avoid gun ownership. The action component of your attitude will probably also include support of organizations that urge or oppose gun control.

Question: How do people acquire attitudes?

Attitude Formation Attitudes are acquired in several basic ways. Sometimes we form them through **direct contact** with the object of the attitude—such as opposing pollution when a nearby factory ruins your favorite river. Attitudes are

Resources

Attitude A learned tendency to respond to people, objects, or institutions in a positive or negative way.

Misdirected letter technique A way of measuring attitudes toward a group that involves misdirecting letters addressed to the group to a large number of households and then noting how many letters are forwarded.

Belief component That part of an attitude consisting of what a person thinks or believes about the object of the attitude.

Emotional component That part of an attitude consisting of one's feelings toward the object of the attitude.

Action component That part of an attitude consisting of how one tends to act toward the object of the attitude.

Direct contact In forming attitudes, the effects of direct experience with the object of the attitude.

also learned through **interaction with others** holding the same attitude—if you live in a vegetarian household, chances are you will become a vegetarian. Attitudes are also acquired through the effects of **childrearing.** For example, if both parents belong to the same political party, chances are two out of three that as an adult the child will belong to the same party (Campbell et al., 1954).

In the previous chapter we discussed group forces that operate to bring about conformity. There is little doubt that many of the attitudes we hold are influenced by **group membership** (Fig. 25-1). In one classic study, for example, groups were formed to discuss the case of a juvenile delinquent. Most participants believed that what the boy needed was love, kindness, and friendship. To test group pressures on attitudes, a person who advocated severe punishment was added to each group.

Question: How did group members react to the "deviate"?

At first they directed almost all of their comments to him. But when the deviate stuck to his position, an interesting thing happened: Soon, he was almost completely excluded from conversation. And later, the deviate was strongly rejected in ratings made by other group members (Schachter, 1951). Group pressures for conformity and the difficulty of holding deviant attitudes can be clearly seen in this outcome.

Attitudes are also influenced by the **mass media.** As Marshall McLuhan put it, we are "massaged" by the media, meaning: threatened, urged, cajoled, persuaded, and otherwise influenced. Ninety-eight percent of American homes have

Fig. 25-1 *Attitudes are an important dimension of social behavior. They are often rooted in reference groups (see text).*

a television set, which is on an average of almost 7 hours a day (Comstock et al., 1978). The values and information thus channeled into homes exert a powerful influence on how people perceive, think about, and react to their world. For instance, the heavy dose of violence on television may lead viewers to develop a **"mean" world view.** That is, frequent viewers overestimate their chances of being involved in a violent incident (Roberts & Bachen, 1981). Heavy viewers are also less likely to feel that most people can be trusted (Gerbner & Gross, 1976). Of added concern are the stereotyped images of male and female roles and of racial or ethnic minorities found on the "tube."

Some attitudes are formed inadvertently through **chance conditioning.** Let's say, for instance, that you have had three encounters in your lifetime with psychologists. If by chance all three were negative, you might take an unduly dim view of psychology and psychologists. In the same way, people often develop strong attitudes toward cities, restaurants, or parts of the country on the basis of one or two unusually good or bad experiences.

Question: Why are some attitudes acted on while others are not?

To answer the question, let's consider an example. Assume that a person accepts that automobiles add to pollution, and strongly objects to smog, but continues to drive to work every day. How are such discrepancies explained? For one thing, the *immediate consequences* of our actions weigh heavily on the choices we make. A person who objects to air pollution but continues to drive is responding to the immediate convenience of driving.

A second factor is our expectation of how *others will evaluate* our actions (Fishbein & Ajzen, 1975). By taking this factor into account, researchers have been able to accurately predict family planning choices, alcohol use by adolescents, reenlistment in the National Guard, voting on a nuclear power plant initiative, and so forth (Cialdini et al., 1981).

Finally, we must not overlook the effect that long-standing *habits* have on action (Triandis, 1977). Say a "male chauvinist" boss vows to change his sexist attitudes toward female employees. Two months later it would not be unusual for his behavior to show the effects of habit rather than his intention to change. In short, there are often large differences between attitudes and behavior—particularly between privately held attitudes and public behavior.

Question: Can attitudes be measured?

Attitude Measurement There are a number of approaches to the measurement of attitudes. In some cases individuals are simply asked in a straightforward way to express attitudes toward a particular issue. For example, a person might be asked in an **open-ended interview,** "What are your thoughts about strip mining?" The second approach, which has been particularly useful as a measure of attitudes toward various groups, uses a **social distance scale.** Social distance indicates the degree to which one person would be willing to have contact with another person. The individual is asked to state his or her willingness to admit members of a particular group to various levels of social closeness, ranging from "would exclude from my country" to "would admit to marriage in my family."

Use of **attitude scales** is one of the most common methods of measurement. Attitude scales consist of statements expressing various possible views on a particular issue. For example, "socialized medicine would destroy the quality of health

Interaction with others In forming attitudes, the influence of discussions with others who hold particular attitudes.

Childrearing In forming attitudes, the effects of parental values, beliefs, and practices.

Group membership As a factor in forming attitudes, social influences associated with belonging to various groups.

Mass media Collectively, all media that reach very large audiences (magazines, for instance, are a medium of mass communication).

Chance conditioning Conditioning that takes place by chance or coincidence

Open-ended interview An interview in which respondents are allowed to freely expound their views.

Social distance scale An attitude measure that asks people to rate the degree to which they would be willing to have contact with a member of another group.

Attitude scale A collection of attitude statements with which respondents indicate agreement or disagreement.

care in this country" or, "this country desperately needs a national health care program." People are asked to agree or disagree with each item by ranking it on a five-point scale ranging from "strongly agree" to "strongly disagree." When scores on all items are computed, a person can be rated in terms of overall acceptance or rejection of a particular issue.

Attitude measures, particularly as they have been used in public polls, have provided much useful information about the feelings of large segments of the population. Again, though, it is important to remember that expressed attitudes and behavior may differ. Publicly expressed attitudes favoring racial or sexual equality often crumble in situations involving a conflict of interest. A "racially enlightened" individual, for instance, may act quite bigoted when equal employment opportunity laws threaten a chance for employment.

Attitude Change—Why the "Seekers" Went Public

Although attitudes are relatively stable, they are subject to change. Some attitude change can be understood in terms of the concept of **reference groups.** A reference group is one whose values and attitudes are seen by the individual as being relevant to his or her own. Reference group membership need not be physical. It depends instead on whom you identify with or care about.

In the 1930s Theodore Newcomb studied real-life attitude change among students at Bennington College. Most of the students came from conservative homes, but Bennington was a very liberal school. Newcomb found that most students shifted significantly toward more liberal attitudes during their 4 years at Bennington. Those who did not change maintained parents and hometown friends as their primary reference group (typified by one student's statement, "I decided I'd rather stick to my father's ideas"). Those who did change identified primarily with the campus community. Notice that all students could count both the college and their families as *membership* groups, but that one or the other tended to become their reference group.

Fig. 25-2 *Persuasion. Would you be likely to be swayed by this person's message? Successful persuasion is related to characteristics of the communicator, the message, and the audience.*

Question: What about advertising and other direct attempts to change attitudes? Are they effective?

Business corporations, politicians, and others who seek to persuade us obviously believe that attitude change can be engineered. Over $5 billion is spent yearly on television advertising in the United States alone.

Persuasion refers to any deliberate attempt to bring about attitude change by the transmission of information. Persuasion can range from the daily bombardment of media commercials to personal discussion among friends. In most cases the success or failure of attempted persuasion can be understood by considering characteristics of the **communicator,** the **message,** and the **audience** (Fig. 25-2). Let's say you have a chance to promote an issue important to you (pro or anti nuclear power, for instance) at a community gathering. Whom should you choose to make the presentation, and how should that person present it?

Research on persuasion suggests that attitude change is encouraged when: (1) the communicator is likeable, trustworthy, an expert on the topic, and similar to the audience in some respect; (2) the message appeals to emotions, particularly to fear or anxiety; (3) the message also provides a clear course of action that will, if followed, reduce fear or anxiety; (4) the message states clear-cut conclusions; (5) both sides of the argument are presented (for a well-informed audience); (6) only one side of the argument is presented (for a poorly informed audience); (7) the persuader appears to have nothing to gain if the audience accepts the message; and (8) the message is repeated as frequently as possible (Aronson, 1972; McGuire, 1969). You should have little difficulty seeing how these principles are applied in the selling of everything from underarm deodorants to presidents.

We all know from personal observation that emotional experiences also dramatically alter attitudes. Those individuals who give up drinking after nearly dying in an automobile accident caused by their own drunkenness serve as an example. To bring about such attitude change, psychologists have experimented with creating similar experiences through role playing.

Question: For example?

Janis and Mann (1965) asked women who were known smokers to play the role of a cancer patient. A physician told each of the women that he had some bad news: She had lung cancer and would have to undergo immediate surgery. The women played out the part by asking questions about the surgery, by asking if it might fail, and so on. Women in the role-playing group drastically reduced their smoking. Those who listened to a tape recording of similar information showed little change.

Question: Why should role playing have more effect than hearing the same information?

Cognitive Dissonance Theory Certainly, emotional impact and realism have some effect, but part of the explanation also lies in the concept of **cognitive dissonance.**

Question: What is cognitive dissonance?

Cognitions are thoughts. Dissonance means clashing. The influential theory of cognitive dissonance (Festinger, 1957) states that contradicting or clashing thoughts cause discomfort. We have a need for *consistency* in our thoughts and our perceptions.

If individuals can be made to act in ways that are inconsistent with their attitudes, they may change their thoughts to bring them into agreement with their actions. For example, smokers are told on every pack that cigarettes may endanger their lives. They light up and smoke. How do they resolve the tension between this information and their actions? They could quit smoking, but it may be easier to convince themselves that smoking is not really so dangerous. To do this, they will seek examples of people who have lived long lives as heavy smokers, and they will associate with other smokers who support this attitude. They will also avoid information concerning the link between smoking and cancer. Cognitive dissonance theory also suggests that people tend to reject new information that contradicts ideas they already hold, in a sort of "don't bother me with the facts my mind is made up" strategy.

Recall now Mrs. Keech and her doomsday group. Why did their belief in Mrs. Keech's messages *increase* after the world failed to end? Why did they suddenly become interested in convincing others of the correctness of their beliefs? Cogni-

Reference group Any group that an individual identifies with psychologically and uses as a standard for social comparison.

Persuasion A deliberate attempt to change attitudes or beliefs with information and arguments.

Communicator In persuasion, the person presenting arguments or information.

Message In persuasion, the content of a communicator's arguments or presentation.

Audience The person or group toward whom a persuasive message is directed.

Cognitive dissonance An uncomfortable clash between thoughts, beliefs, or attitudes, and one's behavior.

Justification In cognitive dissonance theory, the degree to which one's actions are justified by rewards or other circumstances. Low justification often causes high levels of dissonance.

tive dissonance explains that after publicly committing themselves to their beliefs, they had a strong need to maintain their stand. No matter what the evidence, convincing others was a way of adding additional proof that they were right.

Question: Acting contrary to one's attitudes does not always bring about change. How does cognitive dissonance account for this?

The amount of **reward,** or **justification,** for acting contrary to one's beliefs can influence the amount of dissonance created. In a now classic study, college students performed an extremely boring task consisting of turning wooden pegs on a board for an extended time. Afterward, they were asked to help lure others into the experiment by pretending it was interesting and enjoyable. Students paid $20 for lying to others did not change their own negative opinion of the task. Those who were paid only $1 later rated the experience as actually being pleasant and interesting. In other words, those paid $20 experienced no dissonance. These students could reassure themselves that anybody would lie for $20. Those paid $1 were faced with the conflicting thought, "I lied, but I had no good reason to." Rather than admit to themselves that they had lied, these students changed their attitude toward what they had done (Fig. 25-3) (Festinger & Carlsmith, 1959).

More recent experiments indicate that we are especially likely to experience dissonance when we cause an event to occur that we would rather hadn't occurred (Cooper & Fazio, 1984). Let's say, for example, that you agree to help a friend move. The big day arrives and you feel like staying in bed. Actually, you wish you hadn't promised to help. Thus, to reduce the dissonance you feel, you will probably convince yourself that the work will actually be "sort of fun" or that your friend really deserves the help. We make such adjustments in attitudes countless times in order to minimize cognitive dissonance (Fig. 25-4).

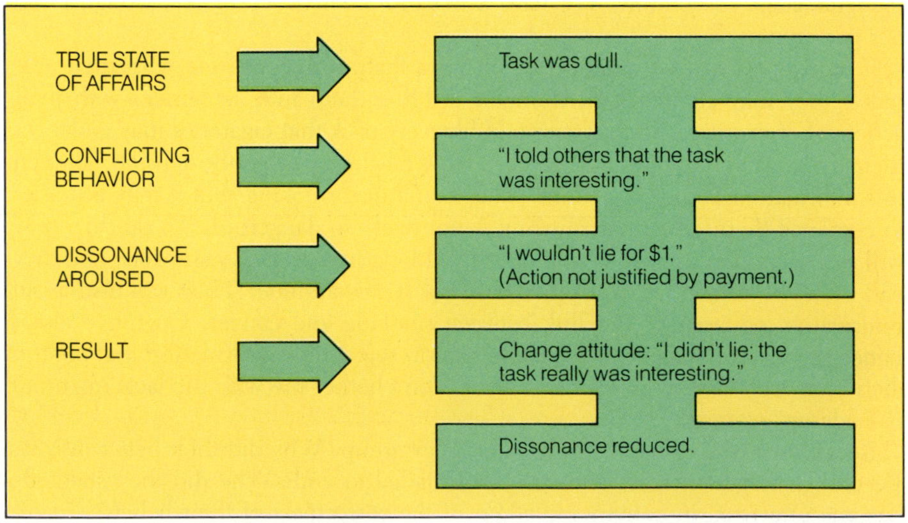

Fig. 25-3 *Summary of the Festinger and Carlsmith (1959) study from the viewpoint of a person experiencing cognitive dissonance.*

Fig. 25-4 *Making choices often causes dissonance. This is especially true if the rejected alternative is perceived as better than the one selected. To minimize such dissonance, we tend to emphasize positive aspects of what we choose, while downgrading other alternatives. Thus, college students are more likely to think their courses will be good* after *they have registered than they did* before *making a commitment. (Rosenfeld, Giacalone, & Tedeschi, 1983)*

Learning Check

1. Attitudes have three parts: a ________________ component, an ________________ component, and an ________________ component.

2. Which of the following is associated with attitude formation?
a. group membership *c.* childrearing *e.* all of the preceding
b. chance conditioning *d.* mass media *f.* *a* and *d* only

3. Because of the immediate consequences of actions, behavior contrary to one's attitudes is often enacted. T or F?

4. Items such as, "would exclude from my country" or "would admit to marriage in my family" would be found in which attitude measure?
a. a reference group scale *b.* an attitude scale *c.* a social distance scale *d.* an open-ended interview

5. In presenting a persuasive message, it is best to give both sides of the argument if the audience is already well informed on the topic. T or F?

6. Much attitude change is related to a desire to avoid clashing or contradictory thoughts, an idea summarized by ________________ ________________ theory.

Answers: **1.** belief, emotional, action **2.** *e* **3.** T **4.** *c* **5.** T **6.** cognitive dissonance

Forced Attitude Change—Brainwashing and Cults

Most people associate the term *brainwashing* with techniques used by the Chinese on American prisoners during the Korean War. Through various types of "thought reform," the Chinese were able to coerce approximately 16 percent of these prisoners to sign false confessions (Schein et al., 1957). More recently, the mass murder/suicide at Jonestown rekindled public interest in forced changes in attitudes, beliefs, or personal loyalties.

Brainwashing Engineered or forced attitude change involving a captive audience.

Unfreezing In brainwashing, a loosening of convictions about former values, attitudes, and beliefs.

Change In brainwashing, the point at which a person begins to repudiate former beliefs.

Refreezing In brainwashing, the process of rewarding and strengthening new attitudes and beliefs.

Cult A group that professes great devotion to some person, idea, or thing.

Prejudice A negative attitude or prejudgment held against members of a particular group of people.

Racism Racial prejudice that has become institutionalized (that is, it is reflected in government policy, schools, and so forth) and that is enforced by the existing social power structure.

Sexism Institutionalized prejudice against members of either sex, based solely on their gender.

Ageism An institutionalized tendency to discriminate on the basis of age; prejudice based on age.

Discrimination Treating members of various social groups differently in circumstances where their rights or treatment should be identical.

Question: What is brainwashing? How does it differ from other persuasive techniques?

As we have noted, advertisers, politicians, educators, religious organizations, and others actively seek to alter attitudes and opinions. To an extent their persuasive efforts resemble brainwashing, but there is an important difference: **Brainwashing** requires a *captive* audience. If you are offended by a television commercial, you can tune it out. Prisoners in the POW camps in Korea (and later in Vietnam) were completely at the mercy of their captors. James McConnell has noted that complete control over the environment allows a degree of psychological manipulation that would be impossible in a normal setting.

Question: How does captivity facilitate persuasion?

Brainwashing McConnell identifies three techniques used for brainwashing: (1) The target person is isolated from others who would support his or her original attitudes; (2) the target person is made completely dependent on his or her captors for satisfaction of needs; (3) the indoctrinating agent is in a position to reward the target person for changes in attitude or behavior.

Brainwashing typically begins with an attempt to make the target feel completely helpless. Physical and psychological abuse, lack of sleep, humiliation, and isolation serve to **unfreeze** former values and beliefs. **Change** comes about when exhaustion, pressure, and fear become unbearable. Prisoners reach the breaking point and sign a false confession or cooperate to gain relief. When they do, they are suddenly rewarded with praise, privileges, food, or rest. The continued coupling of hope and fear with additional pressures for conformity then serves to **refreeze** new attitudes (Schein et al., 1961).

Question: How permanent are changes caused by brainwashing?

In most cases, the dramatic alteration in attitudes brought about by brainwashing is temporary. Most "converted" prisoners who returned to the United States after the Korean War eventually reverted to their original beliefs and repudiated their indoctrinators.

Cults Exhorted by their leader, some 900 members of the Reverend Jim Jones' People's Temple picked up paper cups and drank purple Kool-Aid laced with the deadly poison cyanide. Psychologically, the mass suicide at Jonestown in 1978 is not so incredible as it might seem. Isolated in the jungles of Guyana, intimidated by guards, lulled with sedatives, cut off from friends and relatives, and totally accustomed to obeying rigid rules of conduct, the inhabitants of Jonestown were primed for Jones' final "loyalty test." Of greater psychological interest is the question of how people reach such a state of commitment and dependency.

Question: Why do people join groups such as the People's Temple?

Psychologist Margaret Singer (1979) has studied and aided hundreds of former cult members. Her interviews reveal that, in recruiting new members, cults make use of a powerful blend of guilt, manipulation, isolation, deception, fear, and escalating commitment. In this respect cults employ high-pressure indoctrination techniques not unlike those used in brainwashing.

Some of those interviewed by Singer were suffering from marked psychological distress when they joined a cult. Most, however, were simply undergoing a period of mild depression, indecision, or alienation from family and friends. Cult members try to catch potential converts at a time of need, especially when a sense of belonging will be attractive. For instance, many were approached just after a romance had broken up, or when they were struggling with exams or choice of a major, or when they were simply at loose ends and "on the street."

Question: How is conversion achieved?

Often it begins with intense displays of affection and understanding ("love bombing"). Next comes isolation from noncult members, together with drills, disciplines, and rituals (all-night meditation or continuous chanting, for instance) to wear down physical and emotional resistance, as well as to generate commitment.

At first, recruits make small commitments (to stay after a meeting, for example). Then, large commitments are encouraged (to stay an extra day, to call in sick at work, and so forth). Making a major commitment is usually the final step. The new devotee signs over a bank account or property to the group, takes up residence with the group, and so forth. Such major public commitments create a powerful cognitive dissonance effect in which it becomes virtually impossible for converts to admit they have made a mistake.

Once in the group, members are cut off from family and friends (former reference groups), and the cult can thus control the flow and the interpretation of information to them. Members are isolated physically (by continuous activity) and psychologically from their former value systems and social structure.

Question: Why do people stay in cults?

Most former members mention guilt and fear as the main reasons for not leaving even when they wished they could. Most had been reduced to childlike dependency on the group for meeting all their daily needs (Singer, 1979).

Behind the "throne" from which Jim Jones ruled Jonestown was a sign bearing these words: "Those who do not remember the past are condemned to repeat it" (Fig. 25-5). If we are to take the Reverend Jones at his word, then we should remember that cults are but one example of the danger of trading independence for security. Cults are merely a highly visible indication of the extent to which we all can be influenced by sophisticated psychological coercion and by our needs for approval from others.

Fig. 25-5 *Aftermath of the mass suicide at Jonestown. How do cult-like groups recruit new devotees? (See text.)*

Prejudice—Attitudes That Injure

Prejudice is a negative attitude or prejudgment tinged with unreasonable suspicion, fear, or hatred. Often prejudice is institutionalized and backed by social power structures. In such cases it is referred to as **racism, sexism,** or **ageism,** depending on the group discriminated against. Since sexism and ageism were discussed in earlier chapters, let's focus on racial prejudice and racism. Both racial prejudice and institutionalized racism may contribute to *discrimination.* **Discrimination** refers to behavior that prevents individuals from doing things they might reasonably expect to be able to do, such as buying a house, riding a bus, or attending a high-quality school.

An indication of just how pervasive discrimination can be comes from a rather remarkable study by F. K. Heussenstamm (1971). Subjects in the study were 15 college students, all of whom had received no traffic citations in the previous year. Each subject attached a bumper sticker for a well-known, militant black

Scapegoating The act of causing a person or a group to bear the blame for the actions of others or for conditions not of their making.

Personal prejudice Prejudicial attitudes held toward persons who are perceived as a direct threat to one's own interests.

Group prejudice Prejudice held out of conformity to group views.

Authoritarian personality A personality pattern characterized by rigidity, inhibition, prejudice, and an excessive concern with power, authority, and obedience.

Ethnocentrism Placing one's own group or race at the center—that is, tending to reject all other groups but one's own.

Dogmatism An unwarranted positiveness or certainty in matters of belief or opinion.

organization to his or her car. During the next 17 days the group received a total of 33 traffic citations! The power relationship between the white establishment and black militants (at least as interpreted by individual police officers) is clear.

Question: How do prejudices develop?

Becoming Prejudiced One theory suggests that prejudice represents a form of **scapegoating.** Scapegoating, you may recall, is a form of displaced aggression in which hostilities generated by frustration are redirected to other targets. One interesting test of this hypothesis was conducted at a summer camp for young men. Subjects were given a difficult test they were sure to fail. Additionally, completing the test caused them to miss a trip to the theater (normally the high point of their weekly entertainment). Attitudes toward Mexicans and Japanese were measured before the test and after the men had failed the test and missed the entertainment. Subjects in this study consistently rated members of these two groups lower after having been frustrated (Miller & Bugelski, 1970).

At times the development of prejudice (like other attitudes) can be traced to direct experiences with members of the rejected group. A child who is repeatedly bullied by members of a particular racial or ethnic group may develop resentment that forms the core of a lifelong dislike for members of the group. The tragedy in such cases is that once such an antipathy is established, it prevents accepting additional, more positive experiences that could reverse the damage.

Gordon Allport (1958) concluded that there are two important sources of prejudice. **Personal prejudice** occurs when members of another racial or ethnic group represent a threat to the individual's security or comfort. For example, members of another group may be viewed as competitors for jobs. **Group prejudice** occurs simply through the individual's adherence to *group norms*. In other words, you may have no personal reason for disliking out-group members, but you do so because you are expected to.

The Prejudiced Personality Other research suggests that prejudice at times is a general personality characteristic.

Question: Do you mean some people are more prone to prejudice than others?

Apparently some are. Theodore Adorno and his associates (1950) conducted extensive research on what they called the **authoritarian personality.** These researchers started out by studying anti-Semitism as a means of understanding the social climate that existed in Germany during World War II. In the process they found that people who are prejudiced against one group tend to be prejudiced against *all* out-groups.

Question: What are the characteristics of the prejudice-prone personality?

The authoritarian personality can be described as a collection of personal attitudes and values marked by rigidity, inhibition, and oversimplification. Authoritarians tend to be very **ethnocentric**—they consider only members of their own national, ethnic, or religious group acceptable. They are also overwhelmingly concerned with power, authority, and obedience. To measure these qualities, Adorno and his associates created the "F" scale. (The "F" stands for fascism.) This attitude scale is made up of statements such as the following—to which the authoritarian readily agrees (Adorno et al., 1950):

Authoritarian Beliefs

Obedience and respect for authority are the most important virtues children should learn.

People can be divided into two distinct classes: the weak and the strong.

If people would talk less and work more, everybody would be better off.

What this country needs most, more than laws and political programs, is a few courageous, tireless, devoted leaders, in whom the people can put their faith.

Nobody ever learns anything really important except through suffering.

Every person should have complete faith in some supernatural power whose decisions are obeyed without question.

Certain religious sects that refuse to salute the flag should be forced to conform to such patriotic action or else be abolished.

As children, authoritarians were usually severely punished and learned to fear authority (and to covet it) at an early age. Authoritarians are not happy people.

It should be readily apparent from the list of authoritarian beliefs that the "F" scale is slanted toward politically conservative authoritarians. Psychologist Milton Rokeach (1960) has noted that rigid and authoritarian personalities can be found at both ends of the political spectrum. Rokeach therefore prefers to describe rigid and intolerant thinking as **dogmatism.**

Even if we discount the obvious bigotry of the dogmatic or authoritarian personality, racial prejudice runs deeps in American society. To illustrate, an experiment showed that liberal, white, male college students were more willing to give shocks (under laboratory conditions) to a black victim than to a white victim (Shulman, 1974). We will probe deeper into the roots of such prejudiced behavior in an upcoming discussion, but first let's stop for a Learning Check.

Learning Check

1. Brainwashing differs from other persuasive attempts in that brainwashing requires a ______________________ ______________________.

2. Which statement about brainwashing is *false?*
a. The target person is isolated from others.
b. Attitude changes brought about by brainwashing are almost always permanent.
c. The first step is unfreezing former values and beliefs.
d. Cooperation with the indoctrinating agent is rewarded.

3. Margaret Singer found that most former cult members had experienced a major psychological disturbance just before joining the cult. T or F?

4. Which of the following is *not* a technique typically used by cults to recruit new members?
a. "love bombing" and isolation
b. drills and rituals to wear down resistance
c. physical intimidation and veiled threats
d. a succession of smaller to larger commitments

5. The authoritarian personality tends to be prejudiced against all out-groups, a quality referred to as ______________________.

Answers: **1.** captive audience **2.** *b* **3.** F **4.** *c* **5.** ethnocentrism

---

Social stereotypes Oversimplified images of the traits of individuals who belong to a particular social group.

Intergroup Conflict—The Roots of Prejudice

An unfortunate by-product of the human proclivity for forming groups is that group membership often limits contact with people in other groups. Additionally, groups themselves may come into conflict. Both events tend to foster unpleasant feelings and prejudices toward the out-group. The bloody clash of opposing forces in Ireland, in South Africa, and in hometown U.S.A. are reminders that intergroup conflict is a widespread problem of modern life. Daily we read of jarring clashes between nations, communities, races, and political, religious, or ethnic groups. In many cases, intergroup conflict is accompanied by *stereotyped* images of out-group members and by bitter prejudice.

Question: What exactly do you mean by a stereotype?

Social stereotypes are oversimplified images of people who fall into a particular category. As psychologist Gordon Allport (1958) put it: "Given a thimbleful of facts . . . [we] rush to make generalizations as large as a tub." Stereotypes tend to simplify people into "us" and "them" categories. Actually, aside from the fact that they always oversimplify, stereotypes may be either *positive* or *negative*. Table 25-1 shows stereotyped images of various national and ethnic groups and their changes over the years (Fig. 25-6). Notice that many of the qualities listed are desirable.

Stereotypes held by the prejudiced tend to be unusually irrational. When given a list of negative statements about other groups, prejudiced individuals agree with most of them. Particularly revealing is the fact that they often agree with conflicting statements. Thus, Jews are both "pushy" and "standoffish" or blacks are "ignorant" and "sly" to the prejudiced person. In one study, prejudiced subjects even expressed negative attitudes toward two nonexistent groups, the "Piraneans" and

Table 25-1 University Students' Characterization of Ethnic Groups, 1933 and 1967

Trait	Percent Checking Trait 1933	1967	Trait	Percent Checking Trait 1933	1967	Trait	Percent Checking Trait 1933	1967
Americans			**Italians**			**Jews**		
Industrious	48	23	Artistic	53	30	Shrewd	79	30
Intelligent	47	20	Impulsive	44	28	Mercenary	49	15
Materialistic	33	67	Musical	32	9	Grasping	34	17
Progressive	27	17	Imaginative	30	7	Intelligent	29	37
			Revengeful	17	0			
Germans			**Irish**			**Blacks**		
Scientific	78	47	Pugnacious	45	13	Superstitious	84	13
Stolid	44	9	Witty	38	7	Lazy	75	26
Methodical	31	21	Honest	32	17	Ignorant	38	11
Efficient	16	46	Nationalistic	21	41	Religious	24	8

Source: M. Karlins, T. L. Coffman, and G. Walters, "On the Fading of Social Stereotypes: Studies in Three Generations of College Students." *Journal of Personality and Social Psychology*, 1969, 13:1, 1-16.

Fig. 25-6 *Racial and ethnic pride are gradually replacing stereotypes and discrimination.*

the "Danirians." As further testimony to the irrationality of stereotypes, we may note that when a prejudiced person meets a pleasant or likeable member of a rejected group, the out-group member tends to be perceived as "an exception to the rule," not as a disconfirmation of the stereotype.

Question: How do stereotypes and intergroup tensions develop?

Two experiments, both in unlikely settings and both using children as subjects, offer some insight into these problems.

An Experiment in Prejudice What is it like to be discriminated against? Those who have never experienced discrimination probably can't imagine it. In a unique experiment, elementary school teacher Jane Elliot sought to give her pupils direct experience with prejudice.

On the first day of the experiment, Elliot announced that brown-eyed children were to sit in the back of the room and that they could not use the drinking fountain. Blue-eyed children were given extra recess time and got to leave first for lunch. At lunch brown-eyed children were prevented from taking second helpings, because they would "just waste it." Mixing of brown-eyed and blue-eyed children was prevented, and the blue-eyed children were told they were cleaner and smarter (Peters, 1971).

At first Elliot had to maintain these imposed conditions of prejudice. She also made an effort to constantly criticize and belittle the brown-eyed children. To her surprise, the blue-eyed children rapidly joined in and soon were outdoing her in the viciousness of their attacks. The blue-eyed children began to feel superior, and the brown-eyed children felt just plain awful. Fights broke out. Test scores of the brown-eyed children fell.

Question: How lasting were the effects of this experiment?

The effects were short-lived, because 2 days later the roles of the children were reversed. Before long the same destructive effects occurred again, but this time in reverse. The implications of this experiment are unmistakable. In less than one day it was possible to get children to hate each other because of their eye color and **status inequalities.** Certainly, the effects of a lifetime of real racial or ethnic prejudice are infinitely more powerful and destructive.

Question: What can be done to combat prejudice?

Equal-Status Contact Progress has been made through attempts to educate the general public about the lack of justification for prejudicial attitudes. Changing the belief component of an attitude has long been known to be one of the most direct means of changing the entire attitude. Thus, when people are made aware that minority group members share the same goals, ambitions, feelings, and frustrations as they do, intergroup relations may be improved.

However, this is not the whole answer. As we noted earlier, often there is a wide difference between attitudes and actual behavior. Until unprejudicial behavior is engineered, changes can be quite superficial. Several lines of thought (including cognitive dissonance theory) suggest that more frequent **equal-status contact** between groups in conflict should reduce prejudice and stereotypes.

Question: But does it?

Much evidence suggests it does. For example, in one early study white women who lived in integrated and segregated housing projects were compared for changes in attitude toward their black neighbors. Women in the integrated project showed a favorable shift in attitudes toward members of the other racial group. Those in the segregated project showed no change or actually became more prejudiced than before (Deutsch & Collins, 1951). In other studies, mixed-race groups have been formed at work, in the laboratory, and at schools. The conclusion from such research is that personal contact with a disliked group will induce friendly interracial behavior, respect, and liking. However, these benefits occur only when personal contact is on an equal footing (Cook, 1985).

To test the importance of equal-status contact directly, Gerald Clore and his associates set up a unique summer camp for children. The camp was administered by one white male, one white female, one black male, and one black female. Each campsite had three black and three white campers and one black and one white counselor. Thus, blacks and whites were equally divided in number, power, privileges, and duties. Did the experience make a difference? Apparently it did: Testing showed the children had significantly more positive attitudes toward opposite-race children after attending the camp than they did before (Clore, 1976).

Superordinate Goals Let us now consider a revealing study of intergroup conflict and its reduction. Muzafer Sherif and his associates conducted an ingenious experiment—also at a summer camp—with 11-year-old boys. When they arrived at camp, the boys were separated into two groups and housed in cabins that were physically separated. At first the groups were kept apart to build up in-group friendships. Development of pride and identification with the in-group was encouraged by participation in cooperative games and activities. Soon each group had a flag, a name (the "Rattlers" and the "Eagles"), and had staked out its own territory. At this point the two groups were placed in competition with each other.

After a number of clashes, disliking between the two groups bordered on hatred. Outright hostility erupted as the boys baited each other, started fights, and raided each other's cabins (Sherif et al., 1961).

Question: Were they allowed to go home hating each other?

As an experiment in the reduction of intergroup conflict, and to prevent the boys from remaining enemies, various strategies were tried to reduce tensions. Having leaders from each group meet did nothing. Just getting the groups together also did little. When the groups were invited to eat together, the event became a free-for-all.

Finally, emergencies were staged that required cooperation among members of the groups. For example, the water supply was damaged in a way that required all the boys to work together to repair it. Creation of this and other **superordinate goals** served to restore relations between the two groups. As members were forced to cooperate, hostilities subsided.

"Jigsaw" Classrooms Contrary to the hopes of many, integrating public schools often has little positive effect on racial prejudice. In fact, prejudice may be made worse, and the self-esteem of minority students frequently decreases (Aronson, 1980).

Question: If integrated schools provide equal-status contact, shouldn't prejudice be reduced?

Theoretically, yes. But in practice, minority-group children often enter newly integrated schools unprepared to compete on an equal footing. Elliot Aronson and his colleagues (1978) argue that the competitive nature of schools almost guarantees that children will *not* learn to like and understand each other. In the typical classroom, children compete fiercely for the approval of the teacher. Successful students learn to feel superior and often hold unsuccessful students in contempt. This is a high-stakes game in which only a few can win. It is clearly not a good way to reduce prejudice.

Based on the preceding ideas, Aronson has pioneered a way to apply the concept of superordinate goals to ordinary classrooms. According to Aronson, such goals are effective because they make people **mutually interdependent.** Each person's needs are linked to those of others in the group, and cooperation is encouraged.

Question: How has this idea been applied?

Aronson has successfully created **"jigsaw" classrooms** that emphasize cooperation rather than competition. The term *jigsaw* refers to the pieces of a jigsaw puzzle. In Aronson's method, each child is given a "piece" of the information needed to prepare for a test (Fig. 25-7).

In a typical session, children are divided into groups of five or six and given a topic to study for a later exam. Each child is given his or her "piece" of information and asked to learn it. For example, one child might have information on Thomas Edison's invention of the light bulb; another, facts about his invention of the telephone; and a third, information on Edison's childhood. After the children have learned their individual parts, they teach them to others in the group.

Status inequalities Differences in the power, prestige, or privileges of two or more persons or groups.

Equal-status interaction Communication that occurs on an equal footing, without obvious differences in power or status.

Superordinate goal A goal that exceeds or overrides all others; a goal that renders other goals relatively less important.

Mutual interdependence A condition in which two or more persons must depend on one another to meet each person's needs or goals.

Jigsaw classroom A method of reducing prejudice in which each student receives a different part of a body of information needed to complete a project or prepare for a test.

Fig. 25-7 *In a "jigsaw" classroom, children help each other prepare for tests. As they "teach" each other what they know, the children learn to cooperate and to respect the unique strengths of each individual.*

Even the most competitive children quickly realize that they cannot do well without the aid of everyone in the group. Each child makes a unique and essential contribution, so the children learn to listen to, and respect, each other.

Does the jigsaw method work? Compared with children in traditional classrooms, children in jigsaw groups were less prejudiced, they liked their classmates more, they had more positive attitudes toward school, their grades improved, and their self-esteem increased (Aronson et al., 1979). Such results are quite encouraging. As Kenneth Clark (1965) has said, "Racial prejudice . . . debases all human beings—those who are its victims, those who victimize, and in quite subtle ways, those who are merely accessories."

Aggression—The World's Most Dangerous Animal

For a time, the City Zoo of Los Angeles had on display two examples of the world's most dangerous animal—the only animal capable of destroying the earth and all other animal species. Perhaps you have already guessed which animal this was. In the cage were two college students, representing the species *Homo sapiens!*

The human capacity for aggression is staggering. It has been estimated that during the 125-year period ending with World War II, 58 million humans were killed by other humans (an average of nearly 1 person per minute). Murder now ranks as a major cause of death in the United States. One American kills another every 23 minutes—making the United States one of the world's most violent nations (Meredith, 1984). It is estimated that more than 1.4 million American children are subjected to physical abuse by parents each year. War, homicide, riots, family violence, assassination, rape, assault, forcible robbery, and other violent acts offer further testimony to the realities of human aggression (Fig. 25-8).

Question: What causes aggression?

The complexity of aggression has given rise to a number of potential explanations for its occurrence. Brief descriptions of some of the major possibilities follow.

Aggression Any response made with the intention of bringing harm to another person.

Ethologist A person who studies the natural behavior patterns of animals.

Instincts Some theorists argue that, as humans, we are naturally aggressive, having inherited a "killer instinct" from our animal ancestors. Ethologists such as Konrad Lorenz (1966, 1974) believe that aggression is a biologically rooted behavior observed in all animals, including humans. Lorenz also believes that humans lack certain innate patterns that inhibit aggression in other animal species. For example, in a dispute over territory or dominance, two wolves may growl, lunge, bare their teeth, and fiercely threaten each other. In most instances, though, neither is killed or even wounded. One wolf, recognizing the dominance of the other, will typically bare its throat in a gesture of submission. The dominant wolf could kill in an instant, but it is inhibited by the submissive gesture. In contrast, human confrontations of equal intensity almost always end in injury or homicide.

The idea that humans are "naturally" aggressive has an intuitive appeal, but many psychologists question it. Many of Lorenz's "explanations" of aggression are little more than loose comparisons between human and animal behavior. Just labeling a behavior as "instinctive" does little to explain it. More importantly, we are left with the question of why some individuals or human groups (the Arapesh, the Senoi, the Navajo, the Eskimo, and others) show little hostility or aggression.

Fig. 25-8 *Ritualized human aggression. Violent and aggressive behavior is so commonplace it may be viewed as entertainment. How "natural" is aggressive behavior?*

Frustration-aggression hypothesis Hypothesis stating that frustration tends to lead to aggression.

Aggression cues Stimuli or signals that are associated with aggression and tend to elicit it.

Social learning theory An approach that combines learning principles with cognitive processes (perception, thinking, anticipation), plus the effects of observational learning, to explain behavior.

Aggressive pornography Media depictions of sexual violence or of forced participation in sexual activity.

Biology Despite problems with the instinctive view, there is evidence that a biological basis for aggression may exist. Physiological studies have shown that there are brain areas capable of triggering or ending aggressive behavior (see Chapter 3). Also, researchers have found a relationship between aggression and such physical factors as hypoglycemia (low blood sugar), allergy, and specific brain injuries and disorders (Bandura, 1973; Bolton, 1976; Mark & Ervin, 1970). None of these conditions, however, can be considered a direct *cause* of aggression. Instead, they probably lower the threshold for aggression, making hostile behavior more likely to occur.

The effects of alcohol and other drugs provide another indication of the role of the brain and biology in violence and aggression. A variety of studies show that alcohol is involved in large percentages of murders and violent crimes (Collins, 1981; Lagerspetz, 1981). Intoxicating drugs lower inhibitions to act aggressively—often with tragic results.

Frustration Step on a dog's tail and you may get nipped. Frustrate a human and you may get insulted. The **frustration-aggression hypothesis** states that frustration is closely associated with aggression (Dollard et al., 1939). At several points in earlier chapters we have considered examples of the link between frustration and aggression.

Question: Does frustration always produce aggression?

Although the connection is strong, a moment's thought will show that frustration does not *always* lead to aggression, and that aggression can occur in the absence of frustration. Frustration, for instance, may lead to stereotyped responding, or perhaps to a state of "learned helplessness" (see Chapters 12 and 13). Aggression in the absence of frustration might be demonstrated by sports spectators who start fights, throw bottles, tear down goalposts, and the like after their team has *won.*

Frustration probably encourages aggression because it is aversive (uncomfortable). Many experiments have shown that unpleasant stimuli, such as pain, insults, sweltering rooms, and disgusting scenes or odors tend to increase aggression. Such stimuli probably raise overall arousal levels so that we become more sensitive to **cues for aggression** (Berkowitz, 1976, 1982).

Question: What do you mean by "cues" for aggression?

Some cues, or signals, for aggression are internal (angry thoughts, for instance). Many are external: Certain words, actions, and gestures of others are strongly associated with aggressive response (a raised middle finger, for instance, is an almost universal invitation to aggression).

Even inanimate objects may serve as cues for aggression. In one classic experiment, subjects administered shocks to another person in a laboratory. Before doing so, they were ridiculed and shocked by the other person. Just before subjects get a chance to "return the favor," they saw either a couple of badminton rackets, or a shotgun and a revolver on a table in the testing room. In either case, the experimenter explained that someone had left the objects there, and he casually moved them aside. Subjects who glimpsed the guns gave stronger shocks to the person who had angered them than did subjects who saw the sports equipment (Berkowitz, 1968). The implication of this **weapons effect** seems to be that the symbols and trappings of aggression encourage aggression.

Box 25-1

Aggression and Pornography—Is There a Link?

The debate on the effects of pornography is heating up again. Until recently, most evidence suggested that viewing pornography has no major adverse effects. This conclusion appears to remain valid for stimuli that can be described as merely erotic or sexual in content. However, in the last 10 years there has been a dramatic increase in the number of aggressive-pornographic stimuli appearing in the mass media. **Aggressive pornography** refers to depictions in which violence, threats, or obvious power differences are used to force someone (usually a woman) to engage in sex.

The principal finding of studies on aggressive-pornographic stimuli is that they do increase aggression by males against females. In a summary of various experiments, researchers Neil Malamuth and Ed Donnerstein (1982) conclude that "exposure to mass media stimuli that have violent and sexual content increases the audience's aggressive-sexual fantasies, beliefs in rape myths, and aggressive behavior." Donnerstein and Daniel Linz (1986) further conclude that it is media *violence* that is most damaging. As they put it, "violent images, rather than sexual ones, are most responsible for people's attitudes about women and rape." The problem, then, extends far beyond X-rated films and books. Mainstream movies, magazines, videos, and television programs are equally to blame for reinforcing the myth that women find force or aggression pleasurable.

Social Learning One of the most widely accepted explanations of aggression is also the simplest. **Social learning theory** holds that we learn to be aggressive by observing aggression in others (Bandura, 1973). According to this view, there is no instinctive human programming for fist-fighting, pipe bombing, knife wielding, gun loading, or other elements of violent or aggressive behavior. Hence, aggression must be learned.

Social learning theorists predict that individuals growing up in nonaggressive cultures will themselves be nonaggressive. Those raised in a culture with aggressive models and heroes will learn aggressive responses.

Considered in such terms, it is no wonder that America has become one of the most violent of all countries. It is estimated that a violent crime occurs every 54 seconds in the United States. Approximately 40 percent of the population own firearms. Nationally, 70 percent agree that "When a boy is growing up, it is very important for him to have a few fistfights." Eighteen percent of the population admit to having slapped or kicked another person (Stark & McEvoy, 1970). Children and adults are treated to an almost nonstop parade of aggressive models (in the media as well as in actual behavior—see Box 25-1). We are, without a doubt, an aggressive culture.

Question: What can be done about aggression?

Social learning theory implies that "aggression begets aggression." In other words, watching a prize fight, sporting event, or violent televison program may increase aggression, rather than drain off aggressive urges. A case in point is provided by psychologist Leonard Eron, who spent 22 years following over 600 children into

Prosocial behavior Behavior toward others that is helpful, constructive, or altruistic.

adulthood. Eron (1987) observes: "Among the most influential models for children were those observed on television. One of the best predictors of how aggressive a young man would be at age 19 was the violence of the television programs he preferred when he was 8 years old" (see Fig. 25-9). According to Eron, children learn aggressive strategies and actions from TV violence. Because of this, they are more prone to aggression when they face frustrating situations or cues. Thus, the spiral of aggression might be broken if we did not so often portray it, reward it, and glorify it.

Anger Control On a personal level, some psychologists have succeeded in teaching people to control their anger and aggressive impulses. The key to **anger control** is the fact that people who respond calmly to upsetting situations tend to see them as *problems to be solved*. Therefore, to limit anger, people are taught to:

1. Define the problem as precisely as possible.
2. Make a list of possible solutions.
3. Rank the likely success of each solution.
4. Choose a solution and try it.
5. Assess how successful the solution was and make adjustments if necessary.

Taking these steps has helped many people lessen tendencies toward child abuse, family violence, and other destructive outbursts (Meichenbaum, Henshaw, & Himel, 1982).

Beyond this, the question remains, "How shall we tame the world's most dangerous animal?" There is no easy answer—only a challenge of pressing importance. The solution will undoubtedly involve the best efforts of thinkers and researchers from many disciplines.

For the more immediate future it is clear that we need more people who are willing to engage in helpful, altruistic, *prosocial* behavior. In the following Applications section we will examine some of the forces that operate to prevent people from helping others. Also discussed are a few glimmerings about how to encourage prosocial behavior.

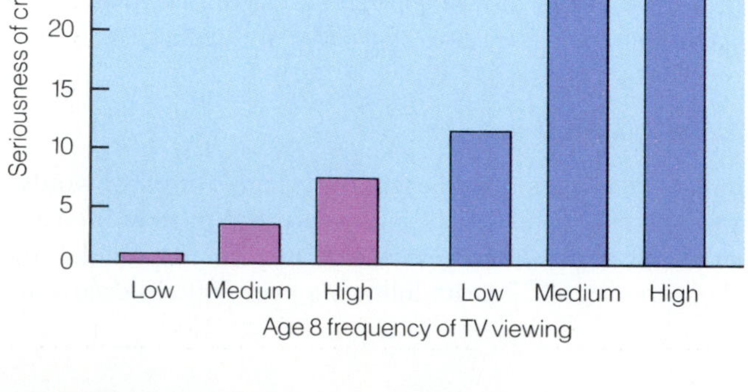

Fig. 25-9 *Although TV violence does not cause aggression, it can encourage it. The likelihood of committing criminal acts by age 30 is related to the amount of TV watching a person did when he or she was a child (Eron, 1987). (Graph copyright 1987 by the American Psychological Association, Inc. Reprinted by permission of the author.)*

Learning Check

1. Social stereotypes may be both positive and negative. T or F?
2. The stereotypes underlying racial and ethnic prejudice tend to be irrational. T or F?
3. Over the last 30 to 40 years there has been a marked increase in stereotyped images held by college students. T or F?
4. Jane Elliot's classroom experiment in prejudice showed that children could be made to dislike one another
   a. by setting up group competition *b.* by imposing status inequalities *c.* by role playing
   d. by frustrating all the students
5. Research suggests that prejudice and intergroup conflict may be reduced by ____________ ____________ interaction and ____________ goals.
6. Some researchers view aggression as related to such factors as hypoglycemia, allergy, and specific brain injuries and disorders. T or F?
7. Frustration is more likely to produce aggression when cues for aggressive behavior are present. T or F?
8. Social learning theory holds that exposure to aggressive models ____________ aggressive behavior.

Answers: **1.** T **2.** T **3.** F **4.** *b* **5.** equal status, superordinate **6.** T **7.** T **8.** increases

Applications

Helping—Prosocial Behavior

Late one night in March 1964, tenants of a Queens, New York, apartment building watched and listened in horror as a young woman named Kitty Genovese was murdered on the sidewalk outside. From the safety of their rooms, no fewer than 38 people heard the agonized screams as her assailant stabbed her, was frightened off, and returned to stab her again.

Kitty Genovese's murder took over 30 minutes, but none of her neighbors tried to help. None even called the police. Perhaps it is understandable that no one wanted to get involved. After all, it could have been a violent lovers' quarrel, or helping might have meant risking personal injury. But what prevented these people from at least calling the police?

Question: Isn't this an example of the alienation of city life?

News reports treated this incident as evidence of a breakdown in social ties caused by the impersonality of the city. While it is true that urban living can be dehumanizing, this does not fully explain such **bystander apathy.** According to psychologists Bibb Latane and John Darley (1968), failure to help is related to the number of people present. Over the years numerous studies have shown that the more potential helpers present, the *lower* the chances that help will be given (Latane, Nida, & Wilson, 1981).

Question: Why would people be less willing to help when others are present?

In Kitty Genovese's case the answer is that everyone thought *someone else* would help. The dynamics of this effect can be illustrated in this way: Suppose that two motorists have stalled at roadside, one on a sparsely traveled country road and the other on a busy freeway. Who gets help first?

On the freeway, where hundreds of cars pass every minute, each driver can assume that someone else

Applications: Helping—Prosocial Behavior, continued

will help. Personal responsibility for helping is spread so thin that no one takes action. On the country road, one of the first few people to arrive will probably stop, since the responsibility is clearly theirs. In general, Latane and Darley assume that bystanders are not apathetic or uncaring; they are inhibited by the presence of others.

Bystander Intervention There are four **decision points** individuals must pass through before giving help. First they must **notice** that something is happening. Next they must **define** the event as an emergency. Then they must **take responsibility.** Finally, they must **select** a course of action. Laboratory experiments have shown that each step can be influenced by the presence of other people.

Noticing What would happen if you fainted and collapsed on the sidewalk? Would someone stop to help? Would people think you were drunk? Would they even *notice* you? Latane and Darley suggest that if the sidewalk is crowded, few people will even see you. This has nothing to do with people blocking each other's vision. Instead, it is related to widely accepted norms against staring at others in public. People in crowds typically "keep their eyes to themselves."

Question: Is there any way to show this is a factor in bystander apathy?

To test this idea, students were asked to fill out a questionnaire either alone or in a room full of people. While the students worked, a thick cloud of smoke was blown into the room through a ventilator.

Most students alone in the room noticed the smoke immediately. Few of the people in groups noticed the smoke, even when it became difficult to see through it. Subjects working in groups politely kept their eyes on their papers and avoided looking at others (or the smoke). In contrast, those who were alone scanned the room from time to time.

Defining an Emergency The smoke-filled room also shows the influence others have on defining a situation as an emergency. After subjects in groups noticed the smoke, they cast sidelong glances at others in the room. Apparently they were searching for clues to help interpret what was happening. No one wanted to overreact or make a fool of himself or herself if there were no emergency. However, as subjects coolly surveyed the reactions of others, they were themselves being surveyed. In real emergencies, people sometimes underestimate the need for action because each person attempts to appear calm. In short, until someone acts, no one acts.

Taking Responsibility Perhaps the most crucial step in the helping sequence is assuming responsibility. In this case, groups limit helping by causing a **diffusion of responsibility.**

Question: Is that like the unwillingness of drivers to offer help on a crowded freeway?

Exactly. It is the feeling that no one is personally responsible for helping.

This problem was demonstrated in an experiment in which students took part in a group discussion over an intercom system. Actually, there was only one real subject in each group; the others were tape-recorded confederates of the experimenter. Each subject was placed in a separate room (supposedly to maintain confidentiality), and discussions of college life were begun.

During the discussion, one of the "students" simulated an epileptic-like seizure and called out for help. In some cases, subjects thought they were alone with the seizure victim. Others believed they were members of three- or six-person groups.

Subjects who thought they were alone with the "victim" of this staged emergency reported it immediately or tried to help. Some subjects on the three-person groups failed to respond and those who did were slower. In the six-person groups over a third of the subjects took no action at all.

People in this experiment were obviously faced with a conflict like that in many real emergencies: should they be helpful and responsible, or should they mind their own business? Many were influenced toward inaction by the presence of others.

Question: People do help in some emergencies. How are these different?

Applications: Helping—Prosocial Behavior, continued

It is not always clear what makes the difference. Helping behavior is a complex event, influenced by many variables.

One naturalistic experiment staged in a New York City subway gives a hint of the kind of things that may be important. When a "victim" (actor) "passed out" in a subway car, he received more help when carrying a cane than when carrying a liquor bottle. More importantly, however, was the fact that most people were willing to help in either case (Piliavin et al., 1969).

To better answer the question, we need to consider some factors not included in Latane and Darley's account of helping.

Who Will Help Whom? Psychologist John Dovido (1984) has summarized some of the major factors that affect helping behavior. Many studies suggest that when we see a person in trouble, this tends to cause heightened arousal. This aroused, keyed-up feeling can motivate us to give aid, but only if the rewards and costs of helping are balanced: Higher costs (such as great effort, personal risk, or possible embarrassment) almost always decrease helping.

In addition to *general* arousal, potential helpers may feel *empathic* arousal. This means that they empathize with the person in need or feel some of the person's pain, fear, or anguish. Empathic arousal also motivates helping—especially when the person in need seems to be similar to ourselves. In fact, feeling a connection to the victim may be one of the most important factors in helping. This, perhaps, is why being in a good mood also increases helping. When we are feeling successful, happy, or fortunate, we may also feel more connected to others (Dovido, 1984).

Question: Is there anything that can be done to encourage prosocial behavior?

There is evidence that people who see others helping are more likely to offer help themselves. For example, motorists were much more likely to stop to help a woman fix a flat tire when they had just passed another woman being helped by someone (Bryan & Test, 1967). Also, persons who give help in one situation tend to perceive themselves as helpful people. This change in self-image encourages them to help in other situations. One more point is that norms of fairness encourage us to help others who have helped us (Dovido, 1984). For all these reasons, helping others not only assists them directly, it encourages others to help too.

Learning Check

1. Psychologists have shown that the dehumanizing qualities of urban living explain most instances of bystander apathy. T or F?
2. Defining an event as an emergency is the first step toward bystander intervention. T or F?
3. People sometimes fail to define an event as an emergency because they are misled by a seeming lack of concern displayed by others. T or F?
4. In laboratory experiments, a large number of potential helpers tends to reduce the likelihood that help will be given. T or F?

Answers: **1.** F **2.** F **3.** T **4.** T

Chapter Summary

- *Attitudes* are learned dispositions made up of a *belief component*, an *emotional component*, and an *action component*.
- Attitudes may be formed by *direct contact*, *interaction with others*, and *child-rearing practices*. Groups also exert pressures on attitudes held by their members. *Peer group influences*, the *mass media*, and *chance conditioning* also appear to be important in attitude formation.
- Attitudes are typically measured by use of techniques such as *open-ended interviews*, *social distance scales*, and *attitude scales*. Attitudes expressed in these ways do not always correspond to actual behavior.
- Attitude change is related to *reference group membership*, to deliberate *persuasion*, and to significant *personal experiences* (which may be engineered through *role playing*).
- The maintenance and change of attitudes are closely related to needs for consistency in thoughts and actions. *Cognitive dissonance theory* explains the dynamics of such needs.
- *Brainwashing* is a form of forced attitude change. It depends on control of the target person's total environment. Three steps in brainwashing are *unfreezing*, *changing*, and *refreezing* attitudes and beliefs.
- Many religious and quasi-religious cults recruit new members with high-pressure indoctrination techniques resembling brainwashing. Such groups attempt to catch people when they are vulnerable. Then they combine isolation, displays of affection, discipline and rituals, intimidation, and escalating commitment to bring about conversion.
- *Prejudice* is a negative attitude held toward members of various *out-groups*. One theory attributes prejudice to *scapegoating*. A second says that prejudices may be held for personal reasons *(personal prejudice)* or simply through adherence to *group norms (group prejudice)*.
- Prejudiced people tend to have *authoritarian* or *dogmatic personalities*, characterized by rigidity, inhibition, intolerance, oversimplification, and *ethnocentrism*.
- *Intergroup conflict* gives rise to hostility and the formation of *social stereotypes*. *Status inequalities* tend to build prejudice. *Equal-status contact* tends to reduce it. Muzafer Sherif and others have emphasized the concept of *superordinate goals* as a key to reducing intergroup conflict, be it racial, religious, ethnic, or national. On a smaller scale, *jigsaw classrooms* (which encourage cooperation through mutual interdependence) have been shown to be an effective way of combating prejudice.
- *Aggression* and violence are serious social problems and the subject of much current research. *Ethological explanations* of aggression attribute it to inherited instincts. *Biological explanations* emphasize brain mechanisms and physical factors related to thresholds for aggression. According to the *frustration-aggression hypothesis*, frustration and aggression are closely linked, especially when *aggressive cues* are present. *Social learning theory* has focused attention on the role of aggressive models in the development of aggressive behavior.
- Four *decision points* that must be passed before a person gives help are: *noticing*, *defining an emergency*, *taking responsibility*, and *selecting a course of action*. Helping is less likely at each point when other potential helpers are present. Helping is encouraged by general arousal, empathic arousal, being in a good mood, low effort or risk, and similarity between the victim and the helper. For several reasons, giving help tends to encourage others to help too.

Chapter 26

Applied Psychology

Chapter Preview

Birdbrains

Imagine yourself lost at sea in a tiny rubber raft, the victim of a boating accident. After 10 hours adrift, you begin to lose all hope of being found. Then, seemingly out of nowhere, a Coast Guard helicopter swoops in and lifts you from the waves. Gratefully, you thank your rescuers. But with a laugh, they insist the real credit belongs to three "birdbrains."

Sound farfetched? In tests, pigeons—who are sharp-eyed and nearly immune to boredom—have been taught to aid search-and-rescue crews. The pigeons are first conditioned in Skinner boxes to peck images of red or yellow rafts, life vests, and life preservers. During rescues, they ride in a chamber under the helicopter, where their pecking is monitored electronically. A buzzer in the cockpit, activated by the pecking, guides pilots to the target (Japenga, 1982; Stark, 1981).

Applied psychology *refers to the use of psychological principles and research methods to solve practical problems—such as finding victims lost at sea. Increasingly, psychology is being used to enhance the quality of life and to improve human performance. And, as we will soon see, the ocean is not the only place where applied psychology can make a life-or-death difference.*

The Towering Inferno *All too often, fires in high-rise buildings lead to needless deaths. Using the elevators, for instance, can be fatal, because they act as chimneys for smoke and poisonous fumes (Keating & Loftus, 1981).*

Question: How can psychology improve the odds for survival?

In the confusion following a fire alarm, many people ignore posted safety instructions. To remedy the situation, psychologists Jack Keating and Elizabeth Loftus created an unusual, life-saving "fire alarm." The best alarm, they found, is a voice *that tells people exactly what to do. After much research, they designed the following message to be broadcast during fires:*

> Female voice: "May I have your attention, please. May I have your attention, please." Male voice: "There has been a fire reported on the 20th floor. While this report is being verified, the building manager would like you to proceed to the stairways and walk down to the 18th floor. Please do not use the elevators, as they may be needed. Please do not use the elevators, but proceed to the stairways." (Loftus, 1979)

As simple as this message seems, it contains three key elements: (1) Research has shown that switching from a female to a male voice (or the reverse) is very attention getting. *(2) During emergencies, people like to feel that some* authority *is in control (the "building manager" in this case). (3) The crucial reminder to avoid the elevators is* repeated, *so that it will be remembered.*

Sea rescues and fire escapes may be dramatic examples of applying psychology, but they are far from unusual. In fields as diverse as industry, sports, and medicine, psychology is being applied to our lives. Let's see how.

Survey Questions What are the major areas of applied psychology? What is the nature of each area? How is psychology applied in business and industry? What have psychologists learned about the effects of our physical and social environments? How do people choose careers?

Resources

Community psychology A specialty that seeks to improve community-wide mental health through direct services, prevention, education, and consultation.

Industrial/organizational psychology A field that focuses on the psychology of work and on behavior within organizations.

Flexitime A work schedule that allows flexible starting and quitting times, centered around a core work period.

Introduction to Applied Psychology

Question: What are the major areas of applied psychology?

The largest area is clinical psychology (see Chapter 1). A closely related specialty is **community psychology.** Instead of focusing on individuals (as clinical psychologists do), community psychologists treat whole neighborhoods or communities as their "clients" (Conyne & Clack, 1981). (Community psychologists have BIG offices!) To promote community mental health, community psychologists typically emphasize prevention, education, and consultation. Often, they target drug abuse, child neglect, unemployment, prejudice, and similar problems for solution. Such efforts, they believe, help prevent mental health problems before they begin.

Beyond clinical areas in psychology, the list of applications grows large. In this chapter we will cover the psychology of work, environmental behavior, education, consumer behavior, health, and sports. To begin, let's see how psychology is applied in business and industry.

Industrial/Organizational Psychology—Psychology at Work

Do you consider work a blessing? Or a curse? Or do you simply agree that it is "better to wear out than to rust out"? Whatever your attitude, the simple fact is that most adults work for a living. From the 1920s until the present, **industrial/organizational psychologists** have studied the problems people face at work. Very

Box 26-1

Flexitime

If you've ever worked "9 to 5," you know that traditional time schedules can be confining. In addition, they doom many workers to a daily battle with rush-hour traffic. To improve worker morale, industrial psychologists have proposed the use of flexible working hours, or **flexitime.** The basic idea is that starting and quitting times are made flexible, as long as employees are present during a core work period (Owen, 1976). For example, employees might be allowed to arrive between 7:30 A.M. and 10:30 A.M., and to depart between 3:30 P.M. and 6:30 P.M.

Is flexitime really an improvement? Studies of two groups of clerical workers suggest that in many cases it is. A switch to flexitime brought a number of benefits, including more job satisfaction, better work-group relations, better relations with supervisors, and less absenteeism (Narayan & Nath, 1982; Orpen, 1981). Although more research is needed, perhaps we can say that it is better, when possible, to bend hours instead of people.

likely, their efforts will affect how you are selected for a job and how you are tested, trained, and evaluated for promotions. A psychologist may even help design your work environment or the machines you use at work.

Industrial/organizational psychologists are employed mostly by government, industry, and businesses. Typically, they work in three major areas: testing and placement (personnel psychology), human relations at work, and industrial engineering (the design of machines and work environments) (Landy & Trumbo, 1980). To get a fuller flavor of what I/O psychologists do, look at Table 26-1. As you can see, their interests are quite varied. As a further illustration, see Box 26-1 for an interesting sample of recent I/O research.

Question: You mentioned that industrial psychologists sometimes help design machines. What does a "shrink for machines" do?!

Table 26-1 Topics of Special Interest to Industrial/Organizational Psychologists

absenteeism	pay schedules
decision making	personnel selection
design of organizations	personnel training
employee stress	productivity
employee turnover	promotion
interviewing	task analysis
job enrichment	task design
job satisfaction	work behavior
labor relations	work environment
machine design	work motivation
management styles	worker evaluations
minority workers	

Engineering psychology (human factors engineering) A specialty concerned with the design of machines and work environments so that they are compatible with human sensory and motor capacities.

Display Any dial, screen, light, or other device used to provide information about a machine's activity to a human operator.

Control Any knob, handle, button, lever, or other device used to alter the activity of a machine.

Personnel psychology Branch of industrial/organizational psychology concerned with testing, selection, placement, and promotion of employees.

Job analysis A detailed description of the skills, knowledge, and activities required by a particular job.

Critical incidents Situations that arise in a job, with which a competent worker must be able to cope.

Biodata Detailed biographical information about a job applicant.

Engineering Psychology

However helpful a machine may be in theory, it is of little value until it can be operated by humans. A poorly designed pocket calculator that causes errors might just as well be a paperweight. An automobile design that blocks large areas of the driver's vision could be deadly. To adapt machines for human use, the **engineering psychologist** (or **human factors engineer**) must make them *compatible* with our sensory and motor capacities (Neff, 1977; Wickens & Kramer, 1985). For example, *displays* must be easy to perceive, *controls* easy to use, and the tendency to make errors must be minimized (see Figure 26-1). Many of the machines we rely on each day were designed, in part, by human factors engineers. Some familiar examples include: push-button telephones, user-friendly computers, home appliances, cameras, airplane controls, and traffic signals. More elaborate machines, such as the United States space shuttle, stretch human capacities to their limits—and require *extensive* human factors engineering.

Personnel Psychology

The mark of maturity, Sigmund Freud said, is a capacity for love and work. While most people gladly embrace love, many would just as soon forget work. Yet the fact is, employed adults spend an average of over 2000 hours a year at their jobs. With so much time at stake, understanding the world of work is clearly a survival skill. Let's explore some additional aspects of industrial/organizational psychology likely to affect your life.

Fig. 26-1 *Human Factors Engineering.* (a) *Early roll indicators in airplanes were perceptually confusing and difficult to read (top). Improved displays are clear even to nonpilots. Which would you prefer if you were flying an airplane in heavy fog?* (b) *Even on a stove, the placement of controls is important. During simulated emergencies, subjects made no errors in reaching for the controls on the top stove. In contrast, they erred 38 percent of the time with the bottom arrangement (Chapanis & Lindenbaum, 1959).* (c) *Sometimes the shape of a control is used to indicate its function, so as to discourage errors. For example, the left control might be used to engage and disengage the gears of an industrial machine, whereas the right control might operate the landing flaps on an airplane.*

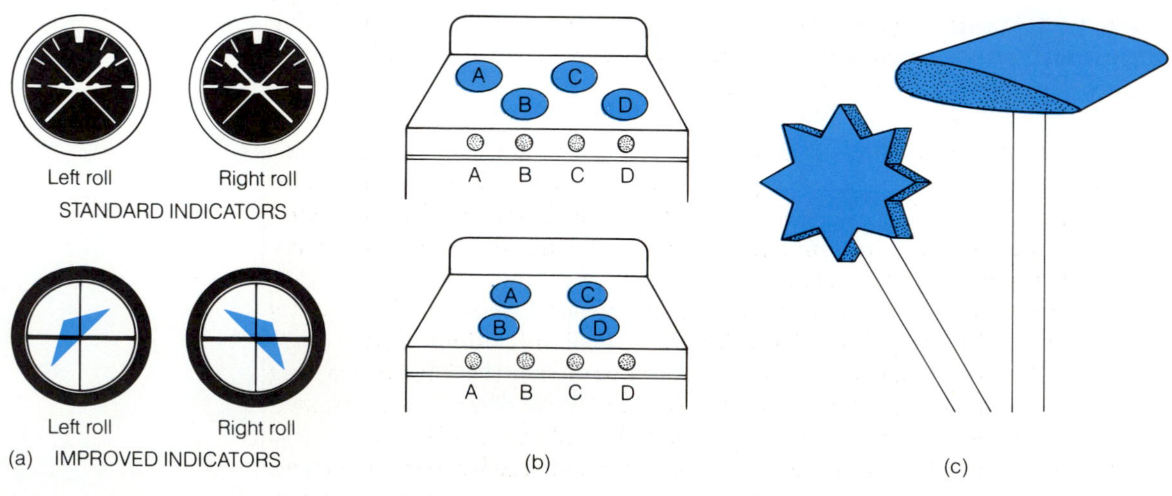

Fig. 26-2 *Analyzing complex skills has also been valuable to the United States Air Force. When million-dollar aircraft and the lives of pilots are at stake, it makes good sense to do as much training and research as possible on the ground. Air force psychologists use flight simulators like the one pictured here to analyze the complex skills needed to fly jet fighters. Skills can then be taught on the ground without risk. The General Electric simulator shown here uses a computer to generate full-color images that respond realistically to a pilot's use of the controls. (Photograph courtesy of General Electric Company)*

At present, the odds are 9 out of 10 that you are, or will be, employed in business or industry. Thus, nearly everyone who holds a job is sooner or later placed under the "psychological microscope" of personnel selection procedures. Clearly, there is value in knowing how selection for hiring and promotion is done.

Question: How do personnel psychologists make employee selections?

Personnel selection begins with a **job analysis** to find out exactly what workers do and what skills or knowledge they need for success in a job (Tenopyr & Oeltjen, 1982). A job analysis may be done by interviewing workers or supervisors, by giving them questionnaires, by observing work, or by identifying **critical incidents.** Critical incidents are situations that an employee *must* be able to cope with if he or she is going to succeed in a particular job. The ability to deal calmly with a mechanical emergency, for instance, might be a critical incident for an airline pilot. Once job requirements are known, psychologists can state what skills, aptitudes, and interests are needed (Fig. 26-2).

Selection Procedures After desirable skills and characteristics are identified, the next step is to learn which job applicants possess them. Currently, the methods most often used for evaluating job candidates are: gathering *biodata*, *interviewing*, giving *standardized psychological tests*, and the *assessment center* approach. Let's see what each entails.

As simple as it may seem, one good way to predict job success is to collect **biodata** (detailed biographical information) from applicants. The premise behind biodata is that past behavior tends to predict future behavior. Thus, by learning in detail about a person's life, it is often possible to say whether the person is suited for a particular type of work (Owens & Shoenfeldt, 1979). Some of the most useful items of biodata are: past athletic interest, academic achievement, scientific interest, extracurricular activities, religious activities, social popularity,

Box 26-2

The Sweet Smell of Success? Not Always

Each year, clothing and cosmetics manufacturers spend huge sums to convince us that their products make us more attractive. Actually, such claims are somewhat justified. You might recall from Chapter 17, for instance, that physically attractive individuals are often given more positive evaluations in interviews—even on traits that have no connection to appearance. Presumably, this effect might even extend to the effects of wearing a pleasant perfume or cologne. But does it? In a recent experiment, *female* interviewers did, in fact, give higher ratings to job applicants who wore pleasant scents. But *males* gave *lower* ratings to persons who wore perfume or cologne (Baron, 1983).

Psychologist Robert Baron, who conducted this experiment, speculates that the male interviewers were more aware of the scents and resented the implied attempt to influence their ratings. Whatever the case, one thing is clear: If possible, you should learn an interviewer's sex beforehand—if you want to avoid making a flagrant, fragrant error, that is.

friction with brothers and sisters, attitudes toward school, and parents' socioeconomic status (Eberhardt & Muchinsky, 1982). Taken together, this information tells quite a lot about personality, interests, and abilities.

The traditional **personal interview** is still one of the most popular ways of selecting candidates for jobs or promotions. However, as we discussed in Chapter 17, interviews are subject to the *halo effect* and similar problems. For this reason, psychologists continue to investigate factors that affect interviews, with an eye toward improving their value. (See Box 26-2.)

Question: What kinds of tests do personnel psychologists use?

In addition to general intelligence and personality tests, like those described in earlier chapters, personnel psychologists frequently administer **vocational interest tests,** such as the *Kuder Occupational Interest Survey* and the *Strong-Campbell Interest Inventory*. Such tests identify interests by requiring a choice among statements like the following:

I would prefer to
a. visit a museum
b. read a good book
c. take a walk outdoors

If you take an interest test and your preferences match those of people who are successful in a given occupation, it is assumed that you, too, would be comfortable doing the work they do.

Aptitude tests are another mainstay of personnel psychology. Such tests rate a person's potential to learn tasks or skills used in various occupations. Tests exist for clerical aptitude, verbal aptitude, mechanical aptitude, artistic, legal, or medical aptitudes, and many others. As an example, tests of clerical aptitude emphasize the capacity to do rapid, precise, and accurate office work. One section of a clerical aptitude test, therefore, might ask a person to mark all numbers and names that are identical in a long list of pairs like those shown here (Schultz, 1979). (Also see Fig. 26-3.)

49837266	49832766
Global Widgets, Inc.	Global Wigets, Inc.
874583725	874583725
Sevanden Corp.	Sevanden Corp.
Perlee Publishing	Perlee Puhlishing

As a college graduate, you will quite likely encounter the **assessment center** approach to personnel selection. Assessment center programs are set up by many large organizations to do in-depth evaluations of job candidates. Assessment centers have become so popular that the list of businesses using them—Ford Motor Company, International Business Machines, Kodak, Exxon, Sears, Bell Telephone, and over 1000 others—reads like a corporate *Who's Who*.

Question: How do assessment centers differ from the selection methods already described?

Assessment centers are used primarily to fill management and executive positions. After applicants have been tested and interviewed at an assessment center, they are placed in simulated work situations for observation and evaluation. For example, in one exercise applicants are given an *in-basket test*. This test consists of a basket full of memos, requests, and problems typical of those faced by executives. The applicant is asked to quickly read all of the materials and to take appropriate action. In another, more stressful test, applicants take part in a *leaderless group discussion* in which they try to solve a realistic business problem (Schultz, 1979). While the group grapples with the problem, "clerks" bring in price changes, information on delayed supplies, and so forth. By observing applicants, it is possible to evaluate leadership skills and, especially, how job candidates cope with stress.

Personal interview Formal or informal questioning of job applicants to learn their qualifications and to gain an impression of their personalities.

Halo effect The tendency of an interviewer to extend a favorable or unfavorable impression to unrelated aspects of an individual's personality.

Vocational interest test A paper-and-pencil test that assesses a person's interests and matches them to interests found among successful workers in various occupations.

Aptitude test A test that rates a person's potential to learn skills required by various occupations.

Assessment center A program set up within an organization to conduct in-depth evaluations of job candidates.

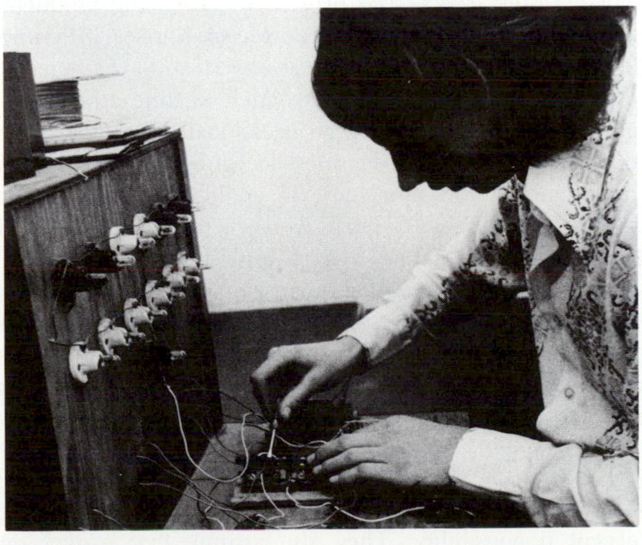

Fig. 26-3 *Not all aptitude tests are of the paper-and-pencil variety. Here, a job applicant takes a mechanical aptitude test.*

Scientific management (Theory X) An approach to managing employees that emphasizes work efficiency.

Work efficiency Maximum output (productivity) at lowest cost.

Psychological efficiency Maintenance of good morale, labor relations, employee satisfaction, and similar aspects of work behavior.

Theory Y A management style that emphasizes human relations at work and that views people as industrious, responsible, and interested in challenging work.

Participative management An approach to management that allows employees at all levels to participate in decision making.

Question: How well does this approach work?

Assessment centers have had success in predicting performance in a variety of jobs, careers, and advanced positions in the military (Borman et al., 1983). One recent study of women, for instance, found that assessment center predictions of management potential were strongly related to career progress 7 years later (Ritchie & Moses, 1983). On the basis of long-range studies, it appears that future success is most clearly predicted by oral communication skills, leadership, energy, resistance to stress, tolerance for uncertainty, need for advancement, and planning skills (Bray et al., 1974; Ritchie & Moses, 1983).

As you will soon learn, psychologists working in business do far more than match people with jobs. Let's see how they also contribute to management and the quality of work.

Theories of Management and Job Satisfaction

At 7 A.M. each morning at a major manufacturing plant, more than 400 assembly line workers, supervisors, and top executives begin their work day talking, joking, and exercising together, all to the beat of amplified music. To say the least, these are unusual working conditions. To understand the rationale behind them, let's consider two basic theories of employee management.

Theory X and Theory Y One of the earliest attempts to improve worker efficiency was made in 1923 by Frederick Taylor, an engineer. To speed up production, Taylor standardized work procedures and emphasized careful planning, control, and orderliness. Today, modern versions of Taylor's approach are called **scientific management** (also known as **Theory X,** for reasons explained shortly). Scientific management uses time-and-motion studies, task analysis, job specialization, assembly lines, pay schedules, and the like, to increase productivity.

Question: It sounds like scientific management treats people as if they were machines. Is that true?

To some extent it is. Managers who adhere to Theory X tend to assume that workers must be coerced or guided into being productive. Many psychologists working in business are concerned, of course, with improving **work efficiency** (defined as maximum output at lowest cost). As a result, they alter conditions they believe will affect workers (such as time schedules, work quotas, bonuses, and so on). Some might even occasionally wish that people would act like well-oiled machines. However, most recognize that **psychological efficiency** is just as important as work efficiency. In addition to achieving high productivity, businesses must be able to retain workers, minimize absenteeism, sustain good morale and labor relations, and so forth if they are to prosper. Management that ignores or mishandles the human element can be very costly.

The term **Theory X** was coined by psychologist Douglas McGregor (1960) as a way to distinguish scientific management from a newer management style. McGregor dubbed this approach, which emphasizes human relations at work, **Theory Y.**

Question: How is this approach different?

Theory Y managers assume that workers enjoy independence and are willing to accept responsibility. They also assume that worker needs and goals can be meshed with the company's goals, and that people are not naturally passive or lazy. In short, Theory Y assumes that people are industrious, creative, and rewarded by challenging work. It appears that, given the proper conditions of freedom and responsibility, many people *will* work hard to gain competence and to use their talents fully.

Many features of Theory Y are illustrated by the Honda plant at Marysville, Ohio. As you probably know, the automobile industry has a long history of labor-management clashes and widespread discontent among workers. In fact, outright sabotage by assembly line workers is not uncommon. To avoid such problems, Honda initiated a series of simple, seemingly successful measures. They include:

Regardless of their position, all employees wear identical white uniforms. This allows workers and supervisors to interact on an equal footing and builds a feeling of teamwork.

To further minimize status differences, all employees hold the title *associate*.

There are no private offices, separate dining halls, or reserved parking for executives.

Employees work alongside company executives, to whom they have easy access.

Every employee has a say in, and responsibility for, quality control and safety.

Departmental meetings are held daily, in which announcements are made, decisions are made, and thoughts are freely shared (Abrams, 1983).

Of the many elements that make Theory Y methods effective, two that stand out are *participative management* and *management by objectives*. In **participative management,** employees at all levels are included in decision making (Fig. 26-4). By taking part in decisions that affect them, employees like those at the Honda factory come to see work as a cooperative effort—not as something imposed on

Fig. 26-4 *Participative management techniques encourage employees at all levels to become involved in decision making. Quite often this arrangement leads to greater job satisfaction.*

Management by objectives A management technique in which employees are given specific goals to meet in their work.

Job satisfaction The degree to which a person is comfortable with or satisfied with his or her work.

Job enrichment A deliberate attempt to make a job more personally rewarding, interesting, or intrinsically motivating.

Environmental psychology The formal study of how environments affect behavior.

them by an authoritarian boss. The resulting benefits include greater productivity, greater job satisfaction, and less job-related stress (Jackson, 1983).

Question: What does management by objectives refer to?

In **management by objectives,** workers are given specific goals to meet, so they can tell if they are doing a good job. Typical objectives include reaching a certain sales figure, making a certain number of items, or reducing waste by a specific percentage. In any case, workers are free to choose (within limits) how they will achieve their goals. As a result, they experience a greater sense of independence and personal meaning in their work.

Job Satisfaction It often makes perfect sense to apply Theory X methods to work. However, doing so without taking worker needs into account can be a case of winning the battle while losing the war. That is, immediate productivity may rise while job satisfaction declines. And, when job satisfaction is low, morale falls and absenteeism skyrockets. There is also a high rate of turnover of employees, leading to high training costs and inefficiency. Understandably, many of the methods used by successful managers tend to improve **job satisfaction.**

Question: Under what conditions is job satisfaction highest?

Basically, job satisfaction comes from a good fit between a person's interests, abilities, needs, and expectations, and his or her work. What, then, do workers consider important? When a sample of American workers was asked to rate the importance of 25 aspects of work, the first 8 choices were:

1. Interesting work
2. Enough help and equipment to get the job done
3. Enough information to get the job done
4. Enough authority to get the job done
5. Good pay
6. Opportunity to develop special abilities
7. Job security
8. Seeing the results of one's work (*Work in America*, 1973)

Undoubtedly, some workers get satisfaction mainly from the money they earn. As you can see, however, most rate other factors higher. To summarize much research, we can say that job satisfaction is highest when workers are: (1) allowed ordinary social contacts with others; (2) allowed to use their own judgment and intelligence; (3) recognized for doing well; (4) given a chance to apply their skills; (5) given relative freedom from close supervision; and (6) given opportunities for promotion and advancement.

Job Enrichment For years the trend in business and industry was to make work more streamlined and efficient and to tie greater pay to greater productivity. However, in recent years far too many jobs have become routine, repetitive, boring, and unfulfilling. It's no wonder that incentives such as bonuses and raises often have little effect on productivity. A better strategy, it would seem, is **job enrichment**—an approach that combines many of the principles just discussed.

Question: How is job enrichment done?

Job enrichment usually involves removing some of the controls and restrictions on employees and giving them greater responsibility, freedom, choice, and authority. Also, instead of performing an isolated part of a larger process, employees may switch to doing a complete cycle of work or completing an entire item or project. Whenever possible, workers are given feedback about their work or progress. This feedback comes to them directly instead of to a supervisor. Workers are encouraged to learn new and more difficult tasks and to learn a broad range of skills.

Job enrichment has been used with great success by large corporations such as IBM, Maytag, Western Electric, Chrysler, and Polaroid. It is usually accompanied by lower production costs, increased job satisfaction, reduced boredom, and less absenteeism (Schultz, 1979).

Although we have only scratched the surface of industrial/organizational psychology, it is time to move on for a look at another applied area of great personal relevance. Before we begin, here's a Learning Check.

Learning Check

1. To gain attention for an emergency announcement, it is better to switch from a male voice to a female voice than it is to do the reverse. T or F?

2. An important element of engineering psychology is making ________________ and ________________ compatible with human use.

3. Identifying critical work incidents is sometimes included in a thorough __________ ________________.

4. Detailed biographical information about a job applicant is referred to as ________________.

5. The Strong-Campbell Inventory is a typical aptitude test. T or F?

6. A leaderless group discussion is most clearly associated with which approach to employee selection?
a. aptitude testing *b.* personal interviews *c.* job analysis *d.* assessment center

7. Theory X, or scientific management, is concerned primarily with improving ________________ __________.

8. Participative management is often a feature of businesses that follow Theory Y. T or F?

9. For the majority of workers, job satisfaction is almost exclusively related to the amount of pay received. T or F?

10. Job enrichment is a direct expression of scientific management principles. T or F?

Answers: **1.** F **2.** displays, controls **3.** job analysis **4.** biodata **5.** F **6.** *d* **7.** work efficiency **8.** T **9.** F **10.** F

Environmental Psychology—Life in the Big City

For the last decade psychologist Terry Daniel has pursued an unusual and very interesting line of research. Using a variety of special analytic techniques, Daniel and his colleagues have helped the United States Forest Service evaluate the psychological effects of harvesting timber from forest lands (Daniel & Boster, 1976). The Forest Service was interested in learning how to harvest timber (especially dead trees) from forests without damaging their appeal. By doing an analysis of

Fig. 26-5 *Various behavioral settings place strong demands on people to act in expected ways.*

Physical environments Natural settings, such as forests and beaches, as well as environments built by humans, such as buildings, ships, cities.

Social environment An environment defined by a group of people and their activities or interrelationships (such as a parade, revival meeting, or sports event).

Behavior setting A smaller area within an environment whose use is well defined, such as a bus depot, waiting room, or lounge.

Territorial behavior Any behavior that tends to define a space as one's own or that protects it from intruders.

Territorial markers Objects and other signals whose placement indicates to others the "ownership" of a particular area.

scenic beauty, Daniel and his colleagues helped guide harvesting plans. Loosely speaking, what they found is that, in the public eye, the ideal forest scene consists of a green meadow, a few young, healthy pine trees, and one or two picturesque, old fallen logs. This description suggests that much thinning of natural forestation can be done without hurting forest aesthetics—at least as far as the general public is concerned.

The work of Terry Daniel, and psychologists like him, falls into an area known as **environmental psychology,** a specialty concerned with how environments influence our behavior. Environmental psychologists are interested both in **physical environments** (natural or constructed) and in **social environments** (such as a dance, business meeting, or party) (Conyne & Clack, 1981). They also give special attention to **behavioral settings** (for example, an office, locker room, church, casino, or classroom). As you have no doubt noticed, various environments and behavioral settings tend to "demand" certain actions (Fig. 26-5). Consider, for example, the difference between a classroom with all seats facing forward and one in which the seats are arranged in a circle. In which classroom would group discussion most likely occur?

Other major interests of environmental psychologists are personal space, territorial behavior (see Box 26-3), stressful environments, architectural design, environmental protection, and many related topics (Table 26-2).

Environmental Influences A major implication of environmental research is that much of our behavior is controlled, in part, by the environment (Conyne & Clack, 1981). A case in point is the seismograph (earthquake detector) housed at a museum in the author's hometown. Even though this instrument is cased in solid concrete, its lure is apparently irresistible—below it are countless shoe marks made by visitors who have kicked the wall to see if the seismograph's needle would move! (It doesn't.) Similarly, psychologists have found that a variety of factors influence the amount of vandalism that occurs in public places.

Box 26-3

Territoriality

In Chapter 24 we noted that powerful norms govern the use of space surrounding each person's body. As we move farther from the body, it becomes apparent that personal space also extends to adjacent areas that we claim as our "territory." For example, in the library **territorial behavior** might include protecting your space with a book, coat, notebook, or other personal belonging (Sommer, 1969). "Saving a place" at a theater or beach also demonstrates the tendency to identify a space as "ours."

Respect for the temporary ownership of space is widespread. It is not unusual for a person to "take over" an entire table or study room by looking annoyed when others intrude. Your own personal territory may include your room, specific seats in many of your classes, or a particular table in the cafeteria or library that "belongs" to you and your friends.

Researchers have found that the more attached you are to an area, the more likely you are to signal your "ownership" with obvious territorial markers, such as decorations, plants, photographs, posters, or even graffiti (Hansen & Altman, 1976). College dorms and business offices are prime places to observe this type of territorial marking.

On the basis of psychological research, many architects now "harden" and "deopportunize" public settings to discourage vandalism and graffiti (Wise, 1982). Some such efforts limit opportunities for vandalism (doorless toilet stalls, tiled walls). Others weaken the lure of potential targets. (Strangely enough, a raised flower bed around signs helps protect them, because people resist trampling the flowers to get to the sign.)

Given the personal impact that environments have, it is important to know how we are affected by stressful or unhealthy environments—a topic we will now consider.

Stressful Environments

Everyone has his or her own list of complaints about living in, or visiting, a large city. Traffic congestion, pollution, crime, and impersonality are urban problems

Table 26-2 Topics of Special Interest to Environmental Psychologists

architectural design	noise
behavioral settings	personal space
cognitive maps	personality and environment
constructed environments	pollution
crowding	privacy
energy conservation	proxemics
environmental stressors	resource management
heat	territoriality
human ecology	urban planning
littering	vandalism
natural environment	

Crowding A subjective feeling of being overstimulated by a loss of privacy or by the nearness of others (especially when social contact with them is unavoidable).

Density The number of people in a given space or, inversely, the amount of space available to each person.

Attentional overload A stressful condition caused when sensory stimulation, information, and social contacts make excessive demands on attention.

that rapidly come to mind. To this list psychologists have added crowding, noise, and overstimulation as major sources of urban stress. Recent psychological research has begun to clarify the impact of each of these conditions on human functioning.

Crowding Overpopulation ranks as one of the most serious problems facing the world today. The world's population is now well over 4 billion, and it will more than double in the next 40 years. Nowhere are the effects of overpopulation more evident than in the teeming cities of many underdeveloped nations. Closer to home, the jammed buses, subways, and living quarters of our own large cities are ample testimony to the stresses of crowding.

Question: Is there any way to assess the effect crowding has on people?

One approach is to study the effects of overcrowding among animals. Although the results of animal experiments cannot be considered conclusive for humans, they point to some disturbing effects.

Question: For example?

In an interesting experiment, John Calhoun (1962) let a group of laboratory rats reproduce without limit in a confined space. Calhoun provided plenty of food, water, and nesting materials for the rats. All the rats lacked was space. At its peak, the colony numbered 80 rats, yet it was housed in a cage designed to comfortably hold about 50. Overcrowding in the cage was heightened by actions of the two most dominant males, who staked out private territory at opposite ends of the cage, gathered harems of 8 to 10 females, and prospered. This situation forced the remaining rats into a small middle area where severe crowding resulted.

Question: What effect did crowding have on the animals?

A high incidence of pathological behavior developed in both males and females. Females abandoned nest building and caring for their young. Pregnancies decreased and infant mortality ran extremely high. Many of the animals became highly aggressive and went on rampaging attacks against others. Sexual behavior was rampant, with some animals displaying hypersexuality, bisexuality, homosexuality, or complete sexual passivity. Many of the animals died, apparently from stress-caused diseases. The connection between these problems and overcrowding is unmistakable.

Question: But does this apply to humans?

Many of the same pathological behaviors can be observed in crowded inner-city ghettos. It is therefore tempting to assume that violence, social disorganization, and declining birthrates as seen in these areas are directly related to crowding. However, the link has not yet been demonstrated with humans. Nutritional, educational, income, and health care disadvantages suffered by those living in the inner city may also be to blame (Freedman, 1975). In fact, many laboratory studies using human subjects have failed to produce any serious ill effects by crowding people into small places. Most likely, this is because *crowding* is a psychological condition that is separated from **density** (the number of people in a given space).

Question: How does crowding differ from density?

Crowding refers to *subjective* feelings of being overstimulated by social inputs or by a loss of privacy. Whether high density is experienced as crowding may depend on relationships among those involved (Fig. 26-6). In an elevator, subway, or prison, high densities may be uncomfortable. In contrast, a musical concert, party, or reunion may be most pleasant at high density levels (Freedman, 1975). Thus, crowding may interact with various situations to intensify existing stresses or pleasures. Researcher Garvin McCain and his colleagues have recently reported that there are substantial increases in death rates among prison inmates and mental hospital patients living in crowded conditions.

Overload One clear cost of high densities and crowding is a condition that psychologist Stanley Milgram calls **attentional overload.** Large cities tend to bombard inhabitants with sensory stimulation, information, and interpersonal contact. The resulting sensory and cognitive overload can be quite stressful (see Box 26-4). Milgram (1970) believes city dwellers learn to prevent overload by engaging in only brief, superficial interpersonal contacts, by ignoring nonessential events, and by adopting cold and unfriendly expressions. In short, many city dwellers may find that a degree of callousness is essential for survival.

Question: Is there any evidence that such strategies are actually adopted?

A fascinating study suggests that they are. In several large American cities and smaller nearby towns, a young child stood on a busy street corner and asked passing strangers for help, saying, "I'm lost. Can you call my house?" About 72

Fig. 26-6 *High densities do not automatically produce feelings of crowding. The nature of the situation and the relationship between crowd members are also important.*

Box 26-4

The High Cost of Noise

How serious are the effects of daily exposure to noise? A study of children attending schools near Los Angeles International Airport suggests that constant noise can be quite damaging. Children from the noisy schools were compared with students of similar background attending schools farther from the airport (Cohen et al., 1980). Testing showed that children attending the noisy schools had higher blood pressure than those from the quieter schools. They were more likely to give up attempts to solve a difficult puzzle. And, they were poorer at proofreading a printed paragraph—a task that requires close attention and concentration.

The greater tendency of children from the noisy schools to give up or become distracted is a serious handicap. It may even indicate a state of "learned helplessness" (described in Chapter 12) caused by daily, uncontrollable blasts of sound. Even if such damage proves to be temporary, it is clear that "noise pollution" is a major source of environmental stress.

percent of those approached in small towns offered to help. Only about 46 percent of those asked for help in the cities aided the child. In some cities (Boston and Philadelphia), only about one-third were willing to help (Takooshian et al., 1977). A decline in sensitivity to the needs of others may yet prove to be one of the more serious costs of overpopulation.

Environmental Problem Solving

While overcrowding ranks high on the list of environmental stresses, it is only one of many problems that press for attention. Other major difficulties center on pollution, the effects of noise, the energy crisis, poor architectural design, and related problems. Although the challenge is large, environmental psychology has begun to provide many solutions. To conclude, let's examine some representative problems.

Problem The way people think about the environment greatly affects behavior. Mental "maps" of various areas, for instance, often guide actions and alter decisions. A case in point is a study recently done in Philadelphia. There, researchers found that an existing school bus route contributed to truancy, because many of its stops were at corners where children were afraid of being attacked and beaten (Conyne & Clack, 1981).

Solution By doing an **environmental assessment,** psychologists can develop a picture of environments as they are perceived by people using them. An assessment often includes such things as charting areas of highest use in buildings, using attitude scales to measure reactions to various environments (such as schools, businesses, parks), and even having people draw a version of their "cognitive map" of a building, campus, or city (Stokols, 1978). In the case of the schoolchildren, residents of the neighborhood were asked to rate how much stress they felt when walking in various areas. The result was a contour map (somewhat like a high and low pressure weather map) that showed the areas of highest perceived stress. This "stress map" was then used to reroute school buses to "low pressure" areas.

Environmental assessment Measurement and analysis of the effects an environment has on the behavior of people within that environment.

Cognitive map A mental image of an area (building, city, country) that guides movement from one location to another.

Architectural psychology Study of the effects buildings have on behavior and the design of buildings using behavioral principles.

Problem Anyonc who has ever lived in a college dorm knows that at times a dorm hall can be quite a "zoo." Most architects undoubtedly aim to create buildings in which people will be comfortable, happy, and healthy. But sometimes they miss the mark regarding human behavior. In one well-known experiment, Baum and Valins (1977) found that students housed in long, narrow, corridor-design dormitories often feel crowded and stressed. The crowded students tended to withdraw from other residents and even made more trips to the campus health center than did those living in less crowded buildings.

Solution **Architectural psychology** is a specialty of growing importance for designing buildings. By studying the effects of existing buildings, psychologists are often able to suggest design changes that solve or avoid problems. For example, Baum and Valins (1979) studied two basic dorm arrangements. One dorm had a long corridor and one central bathroom. As a result, residents were constantly forced into contact with one another. The other dorm consisted of rooms clustered in threes, with each suite sharing a small bathroom. Even though the amount of space available to each student was the same in both dorms, students in the long-corridor dorm reported feeling more crowded. They also made fewer friends in their dorm and showed greater signs of withdrawing from social contact.

Question: What sort of solution does this suggest?

A later experiment showed that small architectural changes can greatly reduce the stress of high-density living. Baum and Davis (1980) compared students living in a long-corridor dorm housing 40 students to those living in an altered long-corridor dorm. In the altered dorm, Baum and Davis divided the hallway in half with unlocked doors and made three center bedrooms into a lounge area (see Fig. 26-7). At the end of the term, students living in the divided dorm reported less stress from crowding. They formed more friendships, and they were more open to social contacts. In comparison, students in the long-corridor dorm felt more crowded, stressed, and unfriendly, and they kept their doors shut much more frequently—presumably because they "vahnted to be alone." Similar improve-

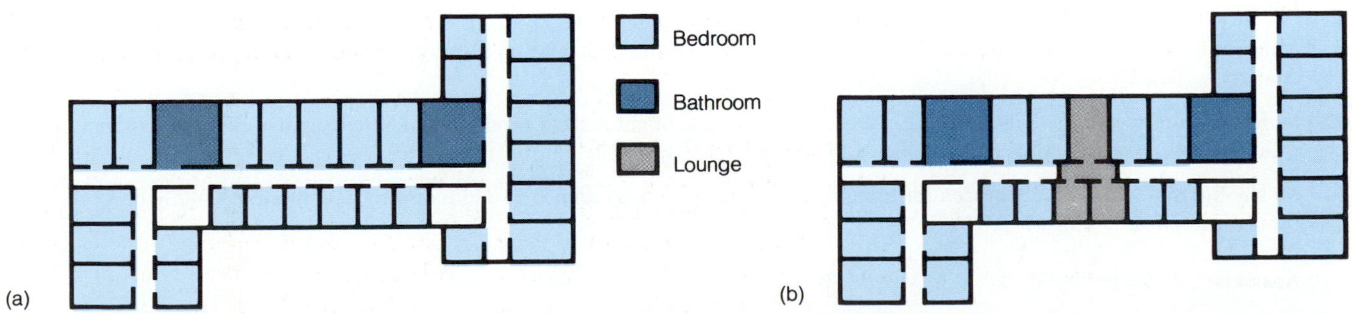

Fig. 26-7 *An architectural solution for crowding. Psychologists divided a dorm hall like that shown in the left diagram* (a) *into two shorter halls separated by unlocked doors and a lounge area* (b). *This simple change minimized unwanted social contacts and greatly reduced feelings of crowding among dorm residents. (Adapted from Baum & Davis, 1980)*

Educational psychology Branch of psychology that seeks to understand how people learn and teachers instruct.

ments have been made by altering the interior designs of businesses, schools, apartment buildings, and mental hospitals.

Problem The rapid worldwide consumption of energy and other resources is one of the most devastating of all social problems. The energy crisis of the early 1980s, whether engineered by oil companies, or not, was a small taste of what may lie in the future. In the face of projected shortages, and the bloated consumption of natural resources by Western nations, what can be done to encourage conservation on a personal level?

Solution Even if you sincerely tried to reduce your use of energy (electricity, for instance), you would probably find it difficult. A major problem is that *feedback* concerning energy use (the monthly bill) arrives long after the temptation to turn up the heat or leave lights burning (see Chapter 8). Recognizing this problem, psychologists have shown that moderately lower energy bills result from simply giving families daily feedback about their use of gas or electricity (Seligman & Darley, 1978).

Even more effective are programs that give monetary rewards for energy conservation (Cone & Hayes, 1980). This is especially true for *master-metered* apartment complexes. In such apartments, families do not receive individual bills for their utilities. Consequently, they have no reason *not* to use gas and electricity. Often they consume about 25 percent more energy than they would in an individually metered apartment (McClelland & Cook, 1980). At this rate of waste, apartment owners can split any savings (from reduced consumption) with tenants and still be ahead.

Conclusion We have had room here only to hint at the creative and highly useful work being done in environmental psychology. While many environmental problems remain, it is encouraging to see that behavioral solutions exist for at least some of them. Surely, creating and maintaining healthy environments is one of the major challenges facing coming generations.

Learning Check

1. Although male rats in Calhoun's crowded animal colony became quite pathological, female rats continued to behave in a relatively normal fashion. T or F?

2. To clearly understand behavior, it is necessary to make a distinction between crowding and ______________ (the number of people in a given space).

3. Milgram believes that many city dwellers prevent attentional overload by limiting themselves to superficial social contacts. T or F?

4. Performing an environmental ______________ might make a good prelude to redesigning college classrooms to make them more comfortable and conducive to learning.

5. So far, the most successful approach for bringing about energy conservation is to add monetary penalties to monthly bills for overconsumption. T or F?

Answers: **1.** F **2.** density **3.** T **4.** assessment **5.** F

Box 26-5

Elements of a Teaching Strategy

Whether it's "breaking in" a new co-worker, instructing a friend in a hobby, or helping a child learn to read, the fact is we all teach at times. The next time you are asked to share your knowledge, how will you do it? One good way to become more effective is to use a specific **teaching strategy.** The example that follows was designed for classroom use, but it applies to many other situations as well (adapted from Thornburg, 1984).

Step 1: Learner preparation Begin by gaining learner's attention and focusing interest on the topic at hand.

Step 2: Stimulus presentation Present instructional stimuli (information, examples, and illustrations) deliberately and clearly.

Step 3: Learner response Allow time for learner to respond to the information presented (by repeating correct responses or asking questions, for example).

Step 4: Reinforcement Give positive reinforcement (praise, encouragement) and feedback ("Yes, that's right," "No, this way," and so forth) to strengthen correct responses.

Step 5: Evaluation Test or assess the learner's progress so that both you and the learner can make adjustments when needed.

Step 6: Spaced review Review periodically to help strengthen responses to key stimuli.

A Panorama of Applied Psychology

We have discussed work and the environment at some length because of their major effects on our lives. To provide a fuller account of the diversity of applied psychology, let's conclude by briefly sampling some additional topics of interest.

Educational Psychology

You have just been asked to teach a class of fourth-graders for a day. What will you do? (Assume that bribery, showing them films, and a field trip to a video arcade are out.) If you ever do try teaching, you might be surprised at how challenging it can be. Effective teachers must understand processes involved in learning, instruction, classroom dynamics, and testing. Fortunately, teachers (and their students) have benefited greatly from the work of educational psychologists (see Box 26-5). Specifically, **educational psychology** seeks to understand how people learn and how teachers instruct (Thornburg, 1984) (Fig. 26-8).

Fig. 26-8 *Educational psychologists are interested in enhancing learning and improving teaching.*

What are the best ways to teach? Is there an optimal teaching style for different age groups, topics, or individuals? These and many related questions lie at the heart of educational psychology (Table 26-3). In addition to studying such questions, educational psychologists design aptitude and achievement tests, evaluate educational programs, and help train teachers at colleges and universities.

Table 26-3 Topics of Special Interest to Educational Psychologists

aptitude testing	language learning
classroom management	learning theory
classroom motivation	moral development
classroom organization	student adjustment
concept learning	student attitudes
curriculum development	student needs
disabled students	teacher attitudes
exceptional students	teaching strategies
gifted students	teaching styles
individualized instruction	test writing
intellectual development	transfer of learning
intelligence testing	

Direct instruction Teaching in which factual information is presented to relatively passive learners by lecture, demonstration, and rote practice.

Open teaching Style of teaching that encourages active student-teacher discussion and interaction.

Consumer psychology Specialty area that focuses on understanding consumer behavior and applying psychology to advertising, marketing, product testing, and the like.

Marketing research A type of public opinion polling used to assess consumer views of products, services, and advertising.

Brand image The image that consumers have of various products, especially with regard to their personal or emotional meanings.

Question: As a student, I've encountered different teaching styles. Do different styles affect classroom learning?

There is little doubt that teachers can greatly affect student interest, motivation, and creativity. But what styles have what effects? To answer this question, psychologists have compared a number of teaching styles. Two of the most basic are direct instruction and open teaching.

In **direct instruction,** factual information is presented by lecture, demonstration, and rote practice. In **open teaching,** active teacher-student discussion is emphasized (Peterson, 1979). And now, the winner: As it turns out, both approaches have advantages. Students of direct instruction do slightly better on achievement tests than do those in open classrooms (Thornburg, 1984). However, students of open teaching do somewhat better on tests of abstract thinking, creativity, and problem solving. They also tend to be more independent, curious, and positive in their attitudes toward school (Peterson, 1979). At present it looks as if a balance of teaching styles goes hand in hand with a balanced education.

Although we have viewed only a small sample of educational research, its value for improving teaching and learning should be apparent. In the next section we will consider how psychology is applied in a very different context—the highly competitive world of consumer affairs.

Consumer Psychology

Whether it's buying a car, toothpaste, a record, or lunch, we are all consumers. **Consumer psychology** is an applied field that focuses on how and why consumers act as they do (Robertson et al., 1984) (see Table 26-4). Consumer psychology is a rapidly growing specialty, especially as applied to business and advertising (Kassarjian, 1982).

Many people give little thought to why they buy what they do. But, in fact, **consumer behavior** can be separated into several steps. These include: deciding to spend, selecting a brand, shopping, making the purchase, and evaluating the product in use (Robertson et al., 1984). At each step, advertising, packaging,

Table 26-4 Topics of Special Interest to Consumer Psychologists

attitude change	marketing research
brand loyalty	marketing strategies
brand recognition	mass media effects
buying habits	opinion leaders
consumer attitudes	opinion polling
consumer complaints	package design
consumer needs	product image
consumer protection	promotional schemes
consumer values	shopping behavior
effects of advertising	subcultural markets
family decision making	

and a host of other factors affect our behavior. To pinpoint such factors, a type of public opinion polling called *marketing research* is done.

In marketing research, people in a representative sample are asked to give their personal impressions of products, services, and advertising. In this way researchers have learned, among other things, that powerful, widely held brand images often develop. A case in point is the images many people have of automobiles, such as: Mercedes-Benz (high status), Corvette (power and sportiness), Buick (conservatism), and so forth (Robertson et al., 1984). Brand images often direct buying behavior and help explain why many people purchase products for their labels as much as for their performance.

In addition to marketing research, consumer psychologists do laboratory testing of products (see Box 26-6); they try to match products to consumer needs; they test public acceptance of new products, brand names,* and packaging; and they devise plans to change buying habits (including designing TV commercials, printed advertisements, premiums, contests, promotional schemes, and the like).

Question: It sounds like consumer psychology is concerned with getting people to buy things they don't need. Is that the case?

It is true that many consumer psychologists use their knowledge to increase sales. However, not all consumer psychology is profit oriented. For instance, principles of consumer behavior may be used to encourage the conservation of gasoline, water, or electricity. Also, many consumer psychologists are interested in protecting and enhancing consumer welfare by persuading people to act in their own best interest. Advertising campaigns concerning auto seat belt use, highway safety, drug abuse prevention, and the like all draw on an understanding of consumer behavior.

As a final example, it was consumer psychologists who documented the large number of commercials on "kidvid" (children's television programs). Each year the average child sees over 20,000 commercials—most of which are for highly sugared cereals and overpriced toys. Related research showed that children under

*The importance of product names is illustrated by the difficulty Chevrolet had in initial attempts to market its *Nova* model in South America. Until the name was changed, consumers shunned the car. The problem? In Spanish, *no va* means "doesn't go"!

Box 26-6

Name that Beer

It is quite common for products to be promoted as "superior," "the best," "unmistakably different," and the like. How well do such claims hold up? In one recent test, three nationally advertised brands of beer were compared. The results are typical of many similar tests: When consumers sampled beer under controlled conditions—where taste was the only cue available—there was no evidence of any noticeable difference in brands (Fowler, 1982).

Although beer lovers would probably disagree, it appears that the labels could be interchanged on many major brands and no one would notice the difference. Minimal differences of this sort are what spur massive, image-conscious advertising campaigns.

Consumerism A social movement whose goal is to enhance consumer knowledge, rights, and welfare.

Behavioral medicine (health psychology) The study of behavioral factors in physical illness and the use of behavioral methods to preserve health and treat disease.

Behavioral risk factors Behaviors that increase the chances of disease or that shorten life expectancy.

Community health campaign A community-wide education project or media campaign that provides information on factors affecting health and what to do about them.

Sports psychology A specialty that combines study of sports skills with clinical techniques to enhance sports performance and the benefits of sports participation.

age 6 are easily victimized because they often cannot distinguish commercials from the program itself (Oskamp, 1984). Such findings have helped advance the cause of **consumerism** (attempts to enhance consumer knowledge, rights, and welfare) for both children and adults.

Behavioral Medicine

Most people agree that health is important—especially their own. Yet, almost half of all deaths in the United States are primarily due to unhealthy behavior or lifestyles. A new specialty called **behavioral medicine** aims to do something about it. Behavioral medicine (also known as **health psychology**) is the study of behavioral factors in physical illness and the use of behavioral methods to preserve health and treat disease (Miller, 1982) (see Table 26-5).

Question: What kinds of behavior are you referring to as unhealthy?

Although some causes of poor health are beyond our control, health psychologists have identified a number of major **behavioral risk factors** that *can* be changed. Each of the following factors greatly increases the chances of disease and early death: cigarette smoking, alcohol abuse, overeating, underexercise, and Type A

Table 26-5 Topics of Special Interest to Health Psychologists

addictions	lifestyle and health
biofeedback	pain management
brain activity and health	personality and disease
chronic illness	psychology of illness
coping patterns	psychosomatic illness
eating disorders	stress effects
emotions and health	stress inoculation
health education	stress reduction
health skills	training health personnel
health systems planning	unhealthful behavior
immune system response	

Box 26-7

Have a Heart

A good example of a community health campaign in action is the Stanford Heart Disease Prevention Program (Meyer et al., 1980). In the Stanford project, a media campaign about risk factors in heart disease—smoking, diet, and exercise—was combined with special group workshops for high-risk individuals. The program's success can be seen in the fact that, after 2 years, the number of smokers had decreased by 17 percent in the test community. Compare this figure to the 12 percent *increase* observed in a similar, untreated community. Such progress may seem modest, but it is, in fact, worthwhile, cost-effective, and highly promising (Miller, 1983).

behavior (Miller, 1983). (For more information on Type A behavior, return to Chapter 13.)

Question: What have health psychologists done to lessen the risks?

Recent attempts to "immunize" youths against pressures to start smoking are a good example of behavioral medicine in action. The smoker who says, "Quitting is easy, I've done it dozens of times," states a basic truth—giving up smoking is very difficult. In fact, only 1 smoker in 10 has long-term success. This observation suggests the value of concentrating on early prevention. In one program, junior-high students were given "standard" information on the unhealthy effects of smoking. Then, to add to the program's impact, the students *role played* ways to resist pressures from peers, adults, and cigarette advertisements. Follow-up checks indicated that students who did the role playing were only half as likely to begin smoking as were students in a control group (Hurd et al., 1980).

In addition to small projects like that described, health psychologists have had some success with **community health campaigns.** These are education projects designed to lessen a combination of major risk factors (see Box 26-7 and Fig. 26-9).

By also specializing in stress management, pain control, the treatment of psychosomatic diseases, and similar applications, psychologists are making a growing contribution to good health.

Sports Psychology

Question: What does psychology have to do with sports?

As almost all serious athletes soon learn, peak performance requires more than physical training—mental and emotional "conditioning" are also important. For this reason, many teams, both professional and amateur, now include psychologists on their staffs (Greenspan, 1983). On any given day, a sports psychologist might teach an athlete how to relax, how to ignore distractions, or ways to cope with emotions. He or she might also provide personal counseling for performance-lowering stresses and conflicts (Rushall, 1975). Other psychologists are interested in studying factors that affect athletic achievement, such as skill learning, the

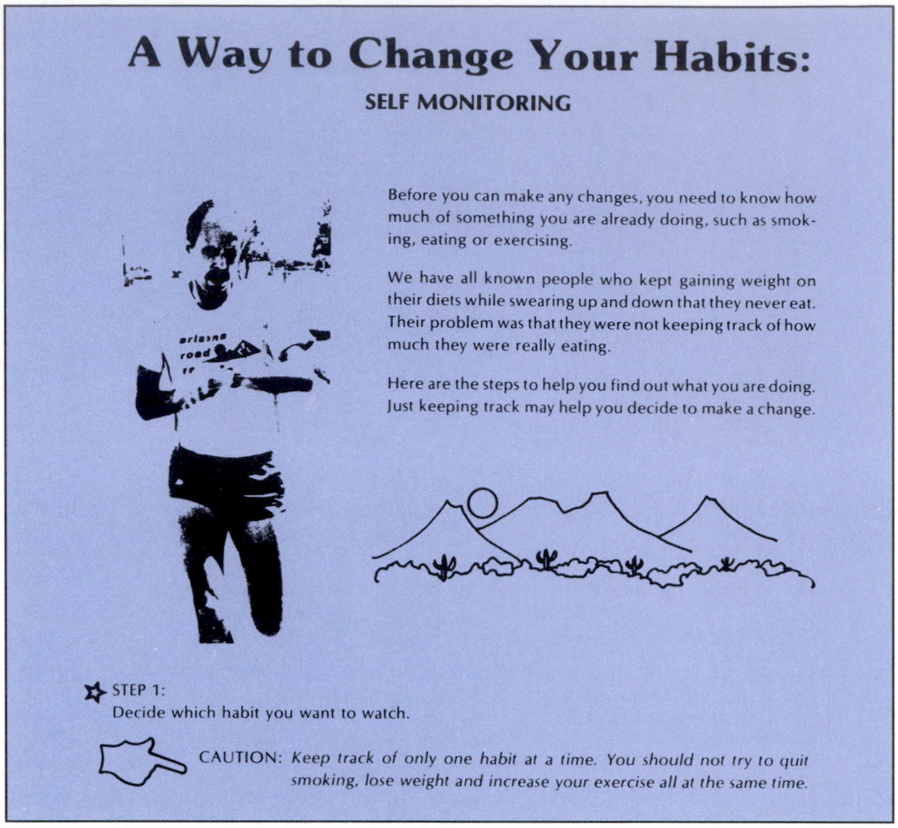

A Way to Change Your Habits:

SELF MONITORING

Before you can make any changes, you need to know how much of something you are already doing, such as smoking, eating or exercising.

We have all known people who kept gaining weight on their diets while swearing up and down that they never eat. Their problem was that they were not keeping track of how much they were really eating.

Here are the steps to help you find out what you are doing. Just keeping track may help you decide to make a change.

STEP 1:
Decide which habit you want to watch.

CAUTION: *Keep track of only one habit at a time. You should not try to quit smoking, lose weight and increase your exercise all at the same time.*

Fig. 26-9 *The page you see reproduced here is from a booklet prepared as part of a public health campaign conducted in southern Arizona. Such campaigns promote health by calling attention to psychological risk factors and by telling what to do about them.* (From Marques et al., 1982)

personality profiles of champion athletes, the effects of spectators, and related topics (Table 26-6). In short, **sports psychologists** seek to understand and improve sports performance and to enhance the benefits of sports participation.

Before the advent of sports psychology, it was debatable whether athletes improved because of "homespun" coaching methods, or in spite of them. For example, in early studies of volleyball and gymnastics, it became apparent that people teaching these sports had very little knowledge of crucial, underlying skills (Salmela, 1974, 1975).

Table 26-6 Topics of Special Interest to Sports Psychologists

achievement motivation	hypnosis
athletic personality	mental practice
athletic task analysis	motor learning
coaching styles	peak performance
competition	positive visualization
control of attention	self-regulation
coping strategies	skill acquisition
emotions and performance	social facilitation
exercise and mental health	stress reduction
goal setting	team cooperation
group (team) dynamics	training procedures

Box 26-8

Taking the Pulse of a Bull's-Eye

It doesn't take much to be off target in the new Olympic sport of marksmanship. The object is to hit a bull's-eye the size of a dime at the end of a 165-foot-long shooting range. Nevertheless, an average of 50 bull's-eyes out of 60 shots is not unusual in international competition (prone position).

What does it take—beyond keen eyes and steady hands—to achieve such accuracy? The answer is surprising: Sports psychologists have found that top marksmen consistently squeeze the trigger *between* heartbeats (see Fig. 26-10). Apparently the tiny tremor induced by the heartbeat is enough to send the shot astray (Pelton, 1983). Without careful psychological study it is doubtful that this element of marksmanship would have been identified. Now that its importance is known, competitors have begun to use various techniques—from relaxation training to biofeedback—to steady and control their heartbeat. In the future the best marksmen may be those who set their sights on mastering their hearts.

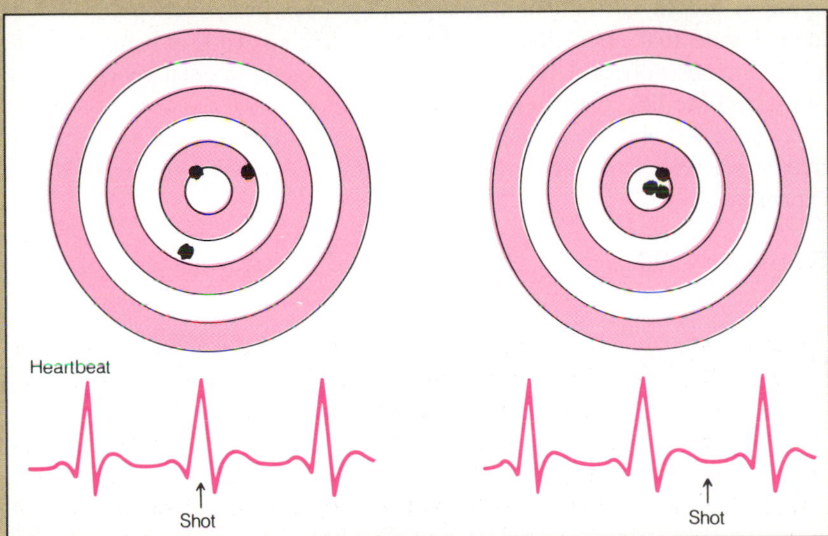

Fig. 26-10 *The target on the left shows what happens when a marksman fires during the heart's contraction. Higher score, as shown by the three shots on the right, is more likely when shots are made between heartbeats. (Adapted from Pelton, 1983)*

Question: How has psychology helped?

A major contribution by psychologists has been their ability to do detailed studies of complex skills (Desharhais, 1975). In a psychological **task analysis,** sports skills are broken into subparts, so that key elements can be identified and taught (see Box 26-8 for an example). Such methods are an extension of techniques first used for job analyses, as described earlier.

Task analysis Breaking a complex task into subparts to identify key skills needed for optimal performance.

Because sports have strong positive or negative effects on participants, they often provide valuable information on human behavior in general. For example, a study of Little League baseball found that children's self-esteem improved significantly after a season of play (Hawkins & Gruber, 1982). Psychologists have also learned that such benefits are most likely to occur when competition, rejection, criticism, and the "one-winner mentality" are minimized. When working with children in sports, they emphasize fair play, intrinsic rewards, self-control of emotions, independence, and self-reliance (Orlick, 1975).

Adults also benefit from sports. For many the payoffs are stress reduction, a better self-image, and improved general health. Researchers have reported, for instance, that distance running is associated with lower levels of tension, anxiety, fatigue, and depression than is found in the nonrunning population (Gondola & Tuckman, 1982; Morgan, 1978).

One of the most interesting topics in sports psychology is the phenomenon of **peak performance.** Many athletes report episodes during which they felt almost as if they were in a trance. The experience has also been called "flow" because the athlete becomes one with his or her performance and flows with it. At such times athletes experience intense concentration, detachment from surroundings, a lack of fatigue and pain, a subjective slowing of time, and feelings of unusual power and control (Browne & Mahoney, 1984). It is at just such times that "personal bests" tend to occur.

A curious aspect of flow is that it cannot be forced to happen. In fact, if a person stops to think about it, the flow state goes away. Psychologists are now trying to identify conditions that encourage peak performance and the unusual mental state that often accompanies it. Promising work is being done to train athletes to use physical relaxation, guided imagery, mental rehearsal, autohypnosis, and the like to attain peak performance.

At present, sports psychology is a very young field and still much more an art than a science (Greenspan, 1983). Nevertheless, interest in the field is rapidly expanding.

Summary Although we have now sampled several major areas of applied psychology, they are by no means the only applied specialties. Others that immediately come to mind are school psychology, military psychology, the psychology of law, and space psychology (a skyrocketing field that is really looking up).

In the Applications section that follows we will discuss the psychology of making vocational choices—a topic that has a great deal of personal impact. But first, a word from your conscience: It's time for a Learning Check.

Learning Check

Match the term on the left with one or more related topics or concepts from the list on the right.

1. ____ Educational psychology
2. ____ Consumer psychology
3. ____ Behavioral medicine
4. ____ Sports psychology

A. Risk factors
B. Teaching strategies
C. Peak performance
D. Marketing research
E. Mental health
F. Brand image
G. Styles of instruction
H. Community campaigns
I. Task analysis

5. Compared with direct instruction, open teaching produces better scores on achievement tests. T or F?

6. List at least three behavioral risk factors identified by health psychologists: ______________________________

____

Answers:

1. B, G **2.** D, F **3.** A, E, H **4.** C, I **5.** F **6.** cigarette smoking, alcohol abuse, overeating, underexercise, Type A behavior

Applications

Vocational Choice and Occupational Survival—Charting Your Course in the World of Work

Within 5 years after first becoming employed, more than half of all college graduates change jobs. Why? Contrary to what might be expected, higher pay is not the prime reason. Needs for recognition and challenge, the desire to do something worthwhile, opportunities to learn, and needs to use skills and abilities are all ranked higher than money by workers (Renwick & Lawler, 1978).

The message in these findings seems to be that work needs to be satisfying on a day-to-day basis. When it's not, many people quickly tire of trading their time and energy for money. Professionals, in particular—such as accountants, nurses, engineers, architects, biologists, and teachers—rate the nature of their work as the greatest source of their job satisfaction (Bird, 1975).

In recognition of the likely importance of work in your life, this final Applications provides a look at how vocational choices are made, and how they can be improved. Let's begin with a short case history.

John's Story John was always an excellent student, but his real love was sports. Being on the track team was, in fact, the high point of his college career. (About 7 feet high, to be exact. John was a high jumper.) After he graduated, John was hired by a large accounting firm at an enviable starting salary. Yet within 2 years, John knew he had made a mistake. Accounting left him dissatisfied, restless, and often bored.

In college John's career choice had seemed highly practical. Now he was miserable. What could he do about it? John decided to take a chance. He quit his job, and after several years of additional education, financial hardship, and personal sacrifice, he accepted his first college coaching position.

Vocational Choice

As John's story illustrates, vocational decisions are neither permanent nor easily undone. Usually, by the time a person has selected a career path, it takes a large amount of effort to change course. Moreover, doing so can be a major risk. (What if John had discovered that he also disliked coaching?) The reality that John faced is illustrated by a survey in which 44 percent of the respondents indicated that, for better or worse, they felt "locked into" their current jobs (Renwick & Lawler, 1978). Clearly, there is value in making good vocational choices and in making them early, if possible.

Career Development John's abrupt change is somewhat unusual. For most people who enter professions, career development tends to flow through four broad phases. These are: (1) the **exploration phase,** during which an initial search for career possibilities is made; (2) the **establishment phase,** during which the person finds a job, enters a career, develops competence, and gains status; (3) the **midcareer phase,** which is a time of high productivity and acceptance by co-workers; and (4) the **later career phase,** when the individual serves as a respected expert, and often, as a "mentor" (role model and guide) for younger workers (Van Maanen & Schein, 1977).

Of the four phases, the two most likely to be of immediate relevance to students are exploration and establishment. Let's probe them in greater depth.

Question: How do most people choose their vocations?

During the exploration phase, most people go through a recognizable series of stages as they choose a vocation (Weiten, 1983).

In the **fantasy stage** children under age 10 simply *imagine* what they want to be when they grow up. The roles they fantasize—such as President, pilot, rock star, rodeo rider, or TV announcer—may be unrealistic, but they do show that children realize they will need to work someday.

During the **tentative stage** (roughly, ages 10 to 18), adolescents begin to form more realistic, if

Applications: Vocational Choice and Occupational Survival, continued

somewhat general, ideas about what they want to do. However, their plans may shift several times during this period and typically remain tentative. Toward the end of high school, many students begin to more fully appreciate the importance of choosing a vocation. They also become aware that there are limits to their options and barriers to certain careers.

After high school, various social and practical pressures lead most people to narrow their range of vocational options. During this **realistic stage** the first steps are taken to find out what particular jobs are like and to prepare for them. At this time many college students use coursework as a way to discover what they are good at and what holds their interest.

By the early twenties, most people begin to carry out their vocational plans. This involves completing necessary training and landing that important first job.

The preceding description implies that most people carefully choose a vocation or career. Actually, there is evidence that vocational choice is often rather haphazard (Janis & Wheeler, 1978). For example, it is not unusual for students to allow a tentative choice of major to determine school coursework. Soon, they find themselves channeled into a particular career path—without really having made a clear decision.

Question: How would a person go about improving the quality of his or her vocational choice?

To begin with, it is worthwhile to recognize that the jobs or careers we are attracted to are influenced by a multitude of factors. Some of the more important influences are: socioeconomic status, intelligence and school achievement, family background, gender, and personal interests (Kaplan & Stein, 1984). As much as these factors may influence your own choice, it is also important to realize that you have the potential for success in a variety of occupations. This is reflected by the fact that the best single predictor of the job category you will enter is your **vocational aspiration,** which is simply what you tell yourself you would like to do.

The world of work is rapidly changing and increasingly complex. In the face of such changes, it is becoming more important to make careful, informed decisions about what kind of work you would like to do. To make sure your vocational choice will be realistic and personally rewarding, you must: (1) gain an accurate understanding of various occupations and (2) get a clear picture of your own interests, needs, and goals.

Question: That seems obvious. But how?

Vocational Counseling The easiest way to improve occupational choice is to consult a **vocational counselor.** Vocational counselors are counseling psychologists who have specialized in the skills and knowledge needed to match people with jobs. A vocational counselor can help you clarify your career goals and can administer interest and aptitude tests to guide your choice. Many colleges now offer vocational counseling at campus **career centers.** These centers also typically store a wealth of information about various jobs and careers. (An introductory discussion of careers in psychology follows this chapter in Appendix A.)

If formal guidance is unavailable, you will have to serve as your own "vocational counselor." A good way to start is to consult the *Occupational Outlook Handbook,* available in most libraries. This book, published yearly by the United States Department of Labor, provides objective information about the outlook for various occupations. The *Handbook* includes job descriptions, information on necessary training, average earnings, and the number of jobs likely to be available in coming years. A simple look at such facts could prevent many students from pursuing overpopulated careers (law, for instance).

Learning about the intangibles that affect job satisfaction may require more initiative. In many occupations the nature of the work is not what it seems from the outside. For instance, medical students are often dismayed when they first begin to realize that disease is ugly and that many medical procedures are distasteful. To find out beforehand what an occupation is like, it is advisable to talk to at least several

Applications: Vocational Choice and Occupational Survival, continued

people in that line of work. Be sure to ask your informants what they dislike about their jobs, as well as their rewards. If possible, you might even spend a day observing people in an occupation that interests you.

After you have selected, prepared for, and begun a career, many challenges remain—far too many, in fact, to discuss here. To conclude, let us briefly consider the challenge of maintaining a healthy attitude at work.

Occupational Survival

Many businesses are now trying to reduce stresses at work by altering management practices and restructuring their organizations. Some also hire psychologists to teach employees to better cope with stress—an approach that seems to have merit. For instance, one recent study found that teaching employees stress inoculation techniques (Chapter 13) and progressive relaxation (Chapter 21) lowered adrenaline levels and depression ratings at work (Ganster et al., 1982).

If an employer does not provide for occupational stress reduction, it may be up to you to ensure your own health by practicing stress coping strategies. Sometimes, it is also possible to carry out a personal program of job enrichment, in order to make work more rewarding. If such strategies fail to keep job satisfaction high and work stresses within bounds, it may be time to consider a change in jobs or even careers.

Making Career Decisions

Another way of improving work adjustment is to examine your approach to making career decisions. Yale University psychologist Irving Janis and writer Dan Wheeler (1978) have described the ways in which people typically deal with work dilemmas, especially those that lead to a change in careers. Their analysis suggests that there are four basic coping styles. See if you recognize yourself in any of the following descriptions.

The Vigilant Style This style is the most effective of the four. It describes individuals who evaluate information objectively and make decisions with a clear understanding of the alternatives. Persons using this style make mental "balance sheets" to weigh possible gains and losses before taking action.

The Complacent Style Persons of this type drift along with a nonchalant attitude toward job decisions. They tend to let chance direct their careers and to take whatever comes along without really making plans.

The Defensive-Avoidant Style These people are fully aware of the risks and opportunities presented by career choices and dilemmas. However, they are uncomfortable making decisions. This leads them to procrastinate, rationalize, and to make excuses for their inaction and indecision.

The Hypervigilant Style People with this style more or less panic when forced to make career decisions. They may collect hundreds of job announcements and brochures, but they become so frantic that making logical decisions is nearly impossible.

These coping styles may seem exaggerated, but they are easy to observe when people are forced to change jobs or make major alterations in career plans. To relate them to yourself, think about how you have handled vocational decisions to date, or decisions about your college career. Of the four, Janis and Wheeler consider only the first, or vigilant style, to be constructive. With this insight you may be able to greatly improve the quality of your career choices.

Conclusion Work, leisure, family, community, environment—all contribute to the quality of our lives. And, as we have seen throughout this text, psychology has much to offer in each of these areas. It is my sincere hope that you have found enough relevance and value in this book to kindle a lifelong interest in psychology. Psychology's future looks exciting. What role will it play in your life?

Applications: Vocational Choice and Occupational Survival, continued

Learning Check

1. Those working in professions generally place greater emphasis on the nature of their work more than on money as the source of job satisfaction. T or F?
2. The establishment phase of career development is a time during which an initial search for career possibilities is made. T or F?
3. Many people go through a fantasy stage and a tentative stage before they become more realistic about choosing a career. T or F?
4. The best single predictor of what occupations college students will enter is their IQ scores. T or F?
5. Stress inoculation techniques have proved capable of lowering stress levels at work. T or F?
6. The vigilant style of making career choices is characterized by panic and illogical decisions. T or F?

Answers: **1.** T **2.** F **3.** T **4.** F **5.** T **6.** F

Chapter Summary

- *Applied psychology* refers to the use of psychological principles and research methods to solve practical problems.
- *Community psychologists* treat entire communities as their "clients" and engage in activities that help promote community-wide mental health.
- *Industrial/organizational psychologists* are interested in the problems people face at work. Typically, they specialize in *personnel psychology*, *human relations* in the work setting, and/or *engineering psychology* (the design of machines and work environments for human use).
- Personnel psychologists try to match people with jobs by combining *job analysis* with a variety of selection procedures, including: gathering *biodata*, *interviewing*, giving *standardized psychological tests* (especially *interest inventories* and *aptitude tests*), and through the *assessment center* approach.
- Two basic approaches to business and industrial management are *scientific management (Theory X)* and *human relations approaches (Theory Y)*. Theory X is most concerned with *work efficiency*, whereas Theory Y emphasizes *psychological efficiency*.
- *Job satisfaction* is not directly related to productivity, but it is linked to absenteeism, morale, employee turnover, and other factors that affect overall business efficiency. Job satisfaction is usually enhanced by Theory Y–oriented *job enrichment*.
- *Environmental psychologists* are interested in the effects of *behavioral settings*, *physical* or *social environments*, and *human territoriality*, among many other major topics.
- Overpopulation is a major world problem, often reflected at an individual level in crowding. Animal experiments indicate that excessive crowding can be unhealthy. However, human research shows that psychological feelings of *crowd-*

ing do not always correspond to *density* (the number of people in a given space). One major consequence of crowding is *attentional overload*.

- A large number of practical problems—from *noise pollution* to architectural design—have come under the scrutiny of environmental psychologists. In many cases effective behavioral solutions to such problems have been found, often as a result of first doing a careful *environmental assessment*.
- *Educational psychologists* seek to understand how people learn and teachers instruct. They are particularly interested in teaching styles, such as *direct instruction* and *open teaching*, and *teaching strategies*.
- Consumer psychologists study *consumer behavior* and serve as consultants to businesses and advertising agencies. Consumer psychologists often do *marketing research* to aid the promotion of various products. Some also do research that helps advance the cause of *consumerism* and consumer welfare.
- *Behavioral medicine*, or *health psychology*, is concerned with psychological factors in physical illness and in behavioral methods for preserving health. Often this is achieved by identifying and removing *behavioral risk factors*, and through *public health campaigns*.
- *Sports psychologists* seek to understand and improve sports performance and to enhance the benefits of sports participation. A careful *task analysis* of sports skills is one of the major tools for improving coaching and performance.
- Four broad periods in career development are the *exploration phase*, the *establishment phase*, the *midcareer phase*, and the *later career phase*. The exploration phase can be further divided into a *fantasy stage*, a *tentative stage*, and a *realistic stage*. *Vocational counseling* can greatly aid career decision making.
- Styles of making career decisions have been classified as *vigilant*, *complacent*, *defensive-avoidant*, and *hypervigilant*. Of these four only the vigilant style is consistently constructive.

Appendix A

Careers in Psychology

Let's say that you have taken the first step toward a career in psychology: Your introductory course has convinced you that you want to learn more about human behavior. The next step is to learn more about careers in psychology—something you can begin doing right here.

First Questions Are you suited to a career in psychology? What kinds of jobs are available to persons with associate, bachelor's, master's, or doctoral degrees in psychology? What is the employment outlook for psychology and related fields? These are questions to ask if you are thinking about majoring in psychology. Although this appendix can only provide preliminary answers, it should help you get started. First, let's see if you are on the right track.

- Do you have a strong interest in human behavior?
- Are you emotionally stable?
- Do you have good communication skills?
- Do you find theories and ideas challenging and stimulating?
- Do your friends regard you as especially sensitive to the feelings of others?
- Have you read popular books on psychology and found them interesting?
- Have discussions in this text matched some of your own insights about human behavior?
- Do you enjoy working with other people?

If most of the preceding statements apply, a career in psychology or a related field may be a good choice for you.

Majoring in Psychology

As a quick survey of your classmates might indicate, the majority of students studying introductory psychology are not psychology majors. More surprising is the fact that the majority of undergraduate psychology majors do not plan to work as psychologists. Most are interested in moving directly into careers and vocations that do not require extended graduate training. Many of today's psychology majors recognize that a psychology degree can be valuable in careers other than psychology. Learning psychology can provide a general knowledge of behavior that aids success in various occupations.

If you think you would like to major in psychology, but you are not interested in graduate training, here are some points to consider:

- Few workers hold one job forever, or even remain in a single line of work for life.
- The nature of work is likely to change greatly in your lifetime, and adaptability will be important.
- A broad education that develops many skills makes a person more vocationally adaptable.
- It is a major myth that every job requires a precise set of skills. Apart from highly technical or specialized jobs, many positions can be filled by persons with differing combinations of skills.
- Specific undergraduate programs do not exist for many mental health professions—making psychology a good undergraduate major leading to later specialized training.
- Job recruiters look primarily for general competence in verbal and written communication, plus social skills and facility in meeting the public.

General Skills For reasons like those listed here, a general education in psychology can lead to a variety of interesting jobs and professions. Even a brief list of "marketable" abilities provided by a psychology degree includes the following: clear, analytic thinking; objectivity and keen observation; an ability to handle data, recognize patterns, and draw conclusions; ability to plan and organize complex activities; ability to communicate clearly, both verbally and in writing; the capacity to comprehend abstract principles and the subtleties of human behavior; ability to critically evaluate evidence; interpersonal skills; and general knowledge relevant to success in many settings.

Again, the point is that even if you do not plan to work as a psychologist, psychology can be a practical undergraduate major.

Education and Options

If you do decide to major in psychology, it is important to be aware of the level of training required for various jobs. While opportunities exist for those with an A.A. or B.A. degree in psychology, many of the most rewarding positions require further education. The discussion that follows should give you some idea of the options at each level.

Associate Degree Level Training in psychology at the associate degree level tends to yield fewer choices than those available to graduates with bachelor's degrees or more advanced training. Even so, all of the jobs listed here are open to persons with a 2-year, A.A. degree.

child care worker	public survey worker
human services worker	recreation aide
mental health assistant	rehabilitation aide
nursing home attendant	senior citizen aide
playground supervisor	teacher's aide
preschool aide	ward attendant
psychiatric technician	youth supervisor

These jobs are only a sample of what is available. People with associate degrees in psychology are qualified to do interviewing, to give and score specific psychological tests, and to communicate the needs of clients to psychologists and other professionals. In general, a person with an associate degree can expect to work directly with clients, but under the supervision of more highly trained professionals.

In some communities specific training programs exist for students interested in working as psychiatric (or psychological) technicians at hospitals or clinics. Often, a year or two of training can lead directly to a job in a local mental health facility. In some cases provisions have been made for "psych tech" trainees to combine classroom study with on-the-job training.

Bachelor's Degree As already mentioned, a bachelor's degree in psychology can be considered preparation for a variety of jobs or occupations. An undergraduate psychology major is also a good prelude to advanced training in several related professions. And, of course, a bachelor's degree is the first step toward a master's or doctoral degree in psychology.

Most of the jobs you see listed here are available to persons with bachelor's degrees in psychology. Some, however, require additional training (becoming a high school teacher, for example). Also, you would be most competitive for many of the listed jobs if you were to combine a psychology major with a minor in another area, such as business (Carducci et al., 1987). In other cases it would be better to make psychology your minor, in combination with a major in a related area (law enforcement and nursing are examples).

advertising agent
art therapist
assistant youth coordinator
biofeedback technician
business management trainee
case worker
child development specialist
child welfare agent
college admissions representative
counselor aide
crisis intervention team member
customer relations
director of day care center
drug counselor
educational salesperson
employment counselor
employment interviewer
family services worker
geriatric technician
group home coordinator
high school psychology teacher
human relations director
job analyst
labor relations specialist
management consultant
marketing researcher
music therapist
occupational therapist
patient service representative
personnel worker
probation/parole officer
psychiatric nurse
public health assistant
public relations specialist
recreational therapist
research assistant
sales representative
social worker
special education teacher
statistical assistant
veteran's adviser

Again, these are only some of the possibilities. As the diversity of the list suggests, it is important to remain flexible when pursuing a psychology major. Plan your education so that you are exposed to psychology's many areas of knowledge, and avoid specializing too soon. To further broaden your employment options, consider taking classes in computer programming, mathematics, statistics, accounting, finance, business, marketing, advertising, education, technical writing, or law enforcement.

Master's Level A master's degree in psychology usually requires from 1 to 2 years of graduate-level training beyond the bachelor's degree. The master's degree usually requires completion of a research thesis and/or a certain number of hours of supervised practical experience in an applied setting. At present the most popular master's-level specialty is counseling psychology. Undoubtedly, this is because a master's degree in counseling is one of the most direct routes to a career as a mental health professional.

Those with a master's degree in counseling psychology may further specialize in marriage and family counseling, vocational or educational counseling, child counseling, or rehabilitation counseling—to name only a few major possibilities. Many counselors are self-employed, but some work for human service agencies, at mental health clinics, and occasionally for the military or large businesses. Recently, counselors have begun to move into new areas such as hospices, child abuse clinics, rape counseling centers, stress clinics, and so on.

Other master's-level specialties, such as human factors engineering, school psychology, psychometrics, clinical psychology, industrial psychology, or general psychology are also offered. But recently, employment opportunities have become more limited for new master's-level psychologists. When positions open in such areas, they are often filled by doctoral-level psychologists. (However, master's-level psychologists with prior work experience often are competitive for such positions.) On the other hand, a master's degree could make you more competitive for all of the jobs listed earlier, at the bachelor's level. It might also help you qualify for higher pay. For such reasons a master's degree in psychology remains valuable, even in areas other than counseling.

Doctoral Level Earning a doctorate in psychology requires commitment. (That's personal commitment, not commitment to a mental hospital—although some doctoral candidates might disagree!) It usually takes at least 3 years of education beyond a bachelor's degree to attain a doctorate (Ph.D., Psy.D., or Ed.D.). More often, a doctorate takes 4 or more years to complete, and some specialties, such as clinical and counseling psychology, require at least 1 more year of internship. (An internship is a closely supervised, on-the-job training experience for professionals entering the field.)

How do the three doctoral degrees differ? The answer may help you decide which would be most appropriate for you if you want to become a psychologist. A Ph.D. is a research degree. As such, it requires completion of a dissertation (an original research contribution to the field). Psychologists holding Ph.D. degrees are active in all areas of psychology, including clinical psychology. However, some psychologists who primarily want to work as therapists now earn a Psy.D. degree (Doctor of Psychology) instead of a Ph.D. This newly created degree allows students in clinical psychology to gain practical experience as a psychotherapist rather than doing a dissertation. The Ed.D. (Doctor of Education) is also typically more applied in orientation than the Ph.D. Coursework for the Ed.D. focuses on the psychology of learning and education.

It is also worth mentioning that in most states a doctoral degree alone does not automatically allow a person to practice psychology. To be legally licensed or certified as a psychologist, a person usually must have a doctorate in psychology, plus at least 1 year of internship, as well as having passed written and oral state licensing exams.

As you can see, becoming a psychologist is a major achievement, reflecting the attainment of a high level of knowledge. Understandably, doctoral-level psychologists have the widest range of work choices. These include settings such as colleges and universities, clinics, rehabilitation centers, government agencies, businesses, industry, the military, and private practice. Also, as you can see in Table A-1, psychologists holding doctoral degrees average several thousand dollars per year greater income in most professional positions.

If you wish to pursue a doctorate in psychology, it is not absolutely necessary to make plans now for attending graduate school—but it helps! Getting admitted to a doctoral program in psychology is as difficult as getting into medical school. The sooner you know what kind of program you would like to enter, the better your chances will be of meeting all of its requirements. To learn more, consult the book *Graduate Study in Psychology*, published by the American Psychological Association. This book is loaded with information to help you plan your graduate education. Be sure to read Appendix D, which gives practical, step-by-step information on how to get accepted to graduate school. (An address for APA publications is given at the end of the present discussion.)

Employment Outlook

The good news is that, overall, jobs for people with psychology degrees are expected to grow faster than average in coming years. However, professional-level jobs (master's and doctorate) will account for a relatively small percentage of total new positions. With projections for a decline in college enrollments, academic positions will be in especially short supply. Even in industrial, clinical, and other applied areas, there will be much competition for positions. However, this should not deter a person who is strongly interested in psychology from pursuing a doctoral-level career. It simply means that it is wise to take steps to make yourself highly employable. These include: (1) Attending an APA-accredited graduate

Table A-1 1982 Median Income for Psychologists

Area	Master's	Doctorate
College faculty	23,000*	29,000*
Educational administration	40,000	40,000
Clinical psychology	26,000	38,000
Counseling psychology	25,000	32,000
Research	32,000	36,000
School psychology	26,000*	27,000*
Applied (I/O) psychology	36,000	45,000

*For a 9 to 10 month academic year.
(Data from Stapp & Fulcher, 1983. Figures are rounded to the nearest thousand dollars.)

school. (2) Gaining work experience while in school (by working as a research assistant, teaching assistant, or even as a volunteer, if necessary). (3) Specializing in additional skills that are in demand, such as computer programming, therapy for special populations (such as the mentally retarded), research in heavily funded areas (such as drug abuse research), and so forth.

Best Bets At all degree levels, applied areas are probably the best bet for employment in the near future. The prospects remain reasonably good for clinical and counseling psychologists, industrial/organizational psychologists, and clinical or psychiatric social workers. Health-related jobs also look good, especially anything associated with senior citizens, as the "graying of America" continues. Two of the fastest growing jobs for the next decade are projected to be employment interviewers and occupational therapists. Both positions are open to bachelor's and master's degree holders.

For further information on careers in psychology, talk with your psychology teacher or visit the campus career center if your school has one. Additional sources of information are listed below.

The Future In addition to the jobs discussed here, there are a number of emerging specialties that are likely to grow rapidly. It shouldn't be long before job titles such as the following become more common: shyness counselor, thanatologist, retirement counselor, jury selection specialist, weight control counselor, stress-reduction counselor, executive recruiter, sleep disorders therapist, and others as yet unnamed. In short, psychology should remain a stimulating and innovative field as the demand for psychological skills and services continues to grow. Perhaps psychology holds a future for you.

Additional Sources of Information

American Psychological Association. *Careers in psychology*. Washington, DC: American Psychological Association, 1980. (Address: 1200 Seventeenth Street N.W., Washington, DC 20036. One copy of this pamphlet will be sent free, on request.)

American Psychological Association. *Graduate study in psychology* (revised annually). Washington, DC: American Psychological Association, 1988. (Address is given above.)

Fretz, B. R., & Stang, D. J. *Preparing for graduate study in psychology: Not for seniors only!* Washington, DC: American Psychological Association, 1980.

Woods, P. J. (Ed.). *Career opportunities for psychologists: Expanding and emerging areas*. Washington, DC: American Psychological Association, 1976.

Woods, P. J. (Ed.). *The psychology major: Training and employment strategies*. Washington, DC: American Psychological Association, 1979.

Appendix B

Statistics*

Statistics from "Heads" to "Tails"

Let's say a friend of yours invites you to try your hand at a "game of chance." He offers to flip a coin and pay you one dollar if the coin comes up "heads." If the coin shows "tails," you must pay him a dollar. He flips the coin, tails—you pay him a dollar. He flips it again: tails. Again: tails. And again: tails. And again: tails.

At this point you are faced with a choice. Should you continue the game in an attempt to recoup your losses? Or should you assume the coin is biased and quit before you really get "skinned"? Taking out a pocket calculator (and the statistics book you carry with you at all times), you compute the odds of obtaining 5 tails in a row from an unbiased coin. The probability is 0.031 (roughly 3 times out of 100).

If the coin really is honest, 5 consecutive tails is a rather rare event. Wisely you decide the coin is probably biased and refuse to play again. (Unless, of course, your "friend" is willing to take tails for the next 5 tosses!)

Perhaps a decision could have been made in this hypothetical example without using statistics. But notice how much clearer the situation becomes when it is expressed statistically.

Statistics in Psychology Psychologists try to extract and summarize useful information from the observations they make. To do so, they use two major types of statistics. The first type, called **descriptive statistics,** summarizes or "boils down" numbers so they become more meaningful and easier to communicate to others. The second type, known as **inferential statistics,** is used for decision making, for generalizing from small samples, and for drawing conclusions. As was the case in the coin-flipping example, psychologists must often base decisions on limited data. Such decisions are greatly aided by inferential statistics.

Descriptive Statistics

Statistical techniques bring greater clarity and precision to psychological thought and research. To see how, let's begin by considering three basic techniques of

*Portions of this appendix were contributed by Danniel Downey, Ph.D.

Table B-1 Raw Scores of Hypnotic Susceptibility

55	86	52	17	61	57	84	51	16	64
22	56	25	38	35	24	54	26	37	38
52	42	59	26	21	55	40	59	25	57
91	27	38	53	19	93	25	39	52	56
66	14	18	63	59	68	12	19	62	45
47	98	88	72	50	49	96	89	71	66
50	44	71	57	90	53	41	72	56	93
57	38	55	49	87	59	36	56	48	70
33	69	50	50	60	35	67	51	50	52
11	73	46	16	67	13	71	47	25	77

Table B-2 Frequency Distribution of Hypnotic Susceptibility Scores

Class Interval	Number of Persons in Class
0-19	10
20-39	20
40-59	40
60-79	20
80-99	10

descriptive statistics: **graphical statistics**, measures of **central tendency**, and measures of **variability.**

Graphical Statistics Table B-1 shows hypothetical scores on a test of hypnotic susceptibility administered to 100 college students.

With such disorganized data, it is difficult to form an overall "picture" of differences in hypnotic susceptibility. But with the use of a **frequency distribution,** large amounts of information can be neatly organized and summarized. A frequency distribution is made by breaking down the entire range of possible scores into *classes* of equal size. Next, the number of scores falling into each class is recorded. In Table B-2 the raw data have been condensed into a frequency distribution. Notice how much clearer the scores of the entire group become.

Frequency distributions are often expressed *graphically* to make them more *visual*. **Histograms,** as these are called, are constructed by labeling frequencies on the *ordinate* (vertical line) and class intervals on the *abscissa* (horizontal line). Next, bars are drawn for each class interval; the height of each bar is determined by the number of scores in each class (see Fig. B-1). An alternate way of graphing scores is the more familiar **frequency polygon** (Fig. B-2). Here points are placed

Fig. B-1 *Frequency histogram of hypnotic susceptibility scores contained in Table B-1.*

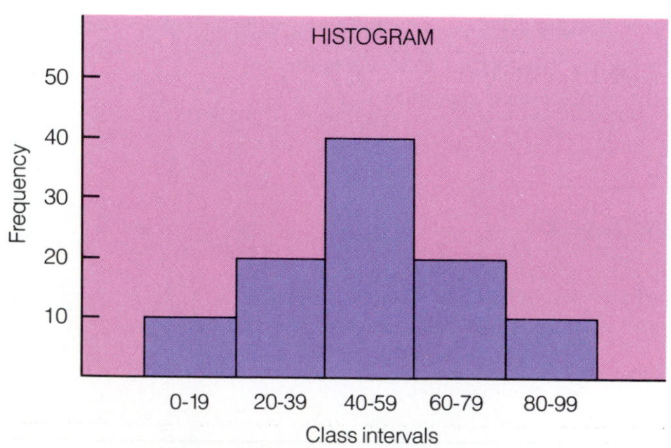

Fig. B-2 *Frequency polygon of hypnotic susceptibility scores contained in Table B-1.*

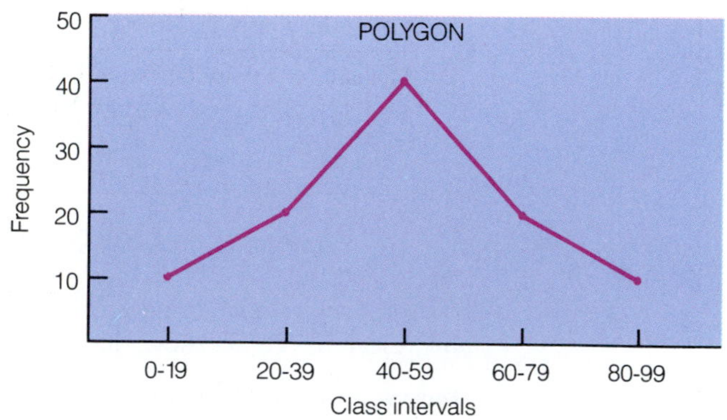

at the center of each class interval to indicate the number of scores. Then, the dots are connected by straight lines.

Measures of Central Tendency A measure of central tendency is simply a number describing a "middle score" around which other scores fall. A familiar measure of central tendency is the mean, or "average." But as we shall see in a moment, there are other types of "averages" that can be used. To illustrate each we need an example: Table B-3 shows the raw data for a hypothetical experiment in which subjects were given a test of memory. Assume that one group was given

Table B-3 Raw Scores on a Memory Test for Subjects Taking Rememberine or a Placebo

Subject	Group 1 Rememberine	Group 2 Placebo
1	65	54
2	67	60
3	73	63
4	65	33
5	58	56
6	55	60
7	70	60
8	69	31
9	60	62
10	68	61
Sum	650	540
Mean	65	54
Median	66	60

$$\text{Mean} = \frac{\Sigma X}{N} \text{ or } \frac{\text{Sum of all scores, X}}{\text{number of scores}}$$

$$\text{Mean Group 1} = \frac{65 + 67 + 73 + 65 + 58 + 55 + 70 + 69 + 60 + 68}{10}$$

$$= \frac{650}{10} = 65$$

$$\text{Mean Group 2} = \frac{54 + 60 + 63 + 33 + 56 + 60 + 60 + 31 + 62 + 61}{10}$$

$$= \frac{540}{10} = 54$$

Median = the middle score or the mean of the two middle scores*

Median Group 1 = 55 58 60 65 [65 67] 68 69 70 73

$$= \frac{65 + 67}{2} = 66$$

Median Group 2 = 31 33 54 56 [60 60] 60 61 62 63

$$= \frac{60 + 60}{2} = 60$$

*□ indicates middle score(s).

a drug purported to improve memory (let's call the drug Rememberine), while a second group received placebos. Is there a difference between memory scores in the two groups? It's difficult to tell without computing an average.

As one type of "average," the **mean** is computed for each group by adding all the scores and then dividing by the total number of scores. Notice in Table B-3 that the means reveal a difference between the two groups.

The mean is sensitive to extremely high or low scores. For this reason it is not always the best measure of central tendency. (Imagine how distorted it would be to calculate average yearly incomes from a small sample of people that happened to include a multimillionaire.) In such cases the *middle score* in a group of scores—called the **median**—is used instead.

The median is found by arranging scores from the highest to the lowest and selecting the score that falls in the middle. Consider for example, the following weights obtained from a small class of college students: 105, 111, 123, 126, 148, 151, 154, 162, 182. The median for the group is 148, the middle score. Of course, if there is an even number of scores, there will be no "middle score." This problem is handled by averaging the two scores that share the middle spot. This procedure yields a single number to serve as the median (see bottom panel of Table B-3).

A final measure of central tendency is the **mode,** which is simply the most frequently occurring score in a group of scores. If you were to take the time to count the scores in Table B-3, you would find that the mode of Group 1 is 65 and the mode of Group 2 is 60. Although the mode is easy to obtain, it can be an unreliable measure, especially in a small group of scores. The mode's advantage is that it gives the score actually obtained by the greatest number of people.

Measures of Variability Let's say a researcher discovers two drugs that lower anxiety in agitated patients. However, let's also assume that one drug consistently lowers anxiety by moderate amounts; whereas the second sometimes lowers it by large amounts, sometimes has no effect, or may even increase anxiety in some patients. Overall, there is no difference in the *average* (mean) amount of anxiety reduction, yet an important difference exists between the two drugs. As this example shows, it is not enough to simply know the average score in a distribution; usually, we would also like to know if scores are grouped closely together or scattered widely.

Measures of *variability* provide a single number that tells how "spread out" scores are. When the scores are widely spread, this number gets larger. When they are close together, it gets smaller. If you look again at the example in Table B-3, you will notice that the scores within each group vary widely. How can we show this fact?

The simplest way would be to use the **range,** which is the difference between the highest and lowest scores. In Group 1 of our experiment, the highest score is 73 and the lowest is 55; thus, the range is 18 (73 minus 55 equals 18). In Group 2, the highest score is 63, and the lowest is 31; this makes the range 32. Scores in Group 2 are more spread than those in Group 1.

A better measure of variability is the **standard deviation.** To obtain the standard deviation, the deviation (or difference) of each score from the mean is found and then squared (multiplied by itself). These squared deviations are then added and averaged (the total is divided by the number of deviations). Taking the square root

Table B-4 Computation of the Standard Deviation

Score		Mean		Deviation (d)	Deviation Squared (d^2)
Group 1 Mean = 65					
65	−	65	=	0	0
67	−	65	=	2	4
73	−	65	=	8	64
65	−	65	=	0	0
58	−	65	=	−7	49
55	−	65	=	−10	100
70	−	65	=	5	25
69	−	65	=	4	16
60	−	65	=	−5	25
68	−	65	=	3	9
					291
Group 2 Mean = 54					
54	−	54	=	0	0
60	−	54	=	6	36
63	−	54	=	9	81
33	−	54	=	−21	441
56	−	54	=	2	4
60	−	54	=	6	36
60	−	54	=	6	36
31	−	54	=	−23	529
62	−	54	=	8	64
61	−	54	=	7	49
					1276

Group 1:

$$SD = \sqrt{\frac{\text{sum of } d^2}{n}} = \sqrt{\frac{291}{10}} = \sqrt{29.1} = 5.4$$

Group 2:

$$SD = \sqrt{\frac{\text{sum of } d^2}{n}} = \sqrt{\frac{1276}{10}} = \sqrt{127.6} = 11.3$$

of this average yields the standard deviation (see Table B-4). Notice again that the variability for Group 1 (5.4) is smaller than that for Group 2 (where the standard deviation is 11.3).

Standard Scores A particular advantage of the standard deviation is that it can be used to "standardize" scores in a way that gives them greater meaning. For example, John and Susan have both taken psychology midterms but in different classes. John earned a score of 118, and Susan scored 110. Who did better? It is impossible to tell without knowing what an average score was on each test, and whether John and Susan scored at the top, middle, or bottom of their classes. We would like to have one number that gives all this information. A number that does this is the **z-score.**

Table B-5 Computation of a z-Score

$$z = \frac{X - \overline{X}}{SD} \text{ or } \frac{\text{score} - \text{mean}}{\text{standard deviation}}$$

$$\text{Susan: } z = \frac{110 - 100}{10} = \frac{+10}{10} = +1.0$$

$$\text{John: } z = \frac{118 - 100}{18} = \frac{+18}{18} = +1.0$$

Original scores are converted to z-scores by subtracting the mean from the score. The resulting number is then divided by the standard deviation for that group of scores. To illustrate, Susan had a score of 110 in a class with a mean of 100 and a standard deviation of 10. Therefore, her z-score is +1.0 (see Table B-5). John's score of 118 came from a class having a mean of 100 and a standard deviation of 18; thus his z-score is also +1.0 (see Table B-5). Originally, it looked as if John did better on his midterm than Susan did, but we now see that, relatively speaking, their scores were equivalent. Compared with other students, each was an equal distance above average.

The Normal Curve

When chance events are recorded, we find that some outcomes have a high probability and occur very often; others have a low probability and occur infrequently; still others have little probability and occur rarely. As a result, the distribution (or tally) of chance events typically resembles a **normal curve** (see Fig. B-3). Most psychological traits or events are determined by the action of a large number of factors. Therefore, like chance events, measures of psychological variables tend to form a normal curve. For example, direct measurement has shown that such characteristics as height, memory span, and intelligence are distributed normally. In other words, many people have average height, memory ability, and intelligence; but as we move above or below average, we find fewer and fewer people.

It is very fortunate that many psychological variables are distributed "normally," because a great deal is known about the normal curve. One property relevant to our discussion is the relationship between the standard deviation and the normal curve; specifically, the standard deviation measures off set proportions of the curve above and below the mean. For example, in Fig. B-4, notice that 68 percent of all cases (IQ scores, memory scores, heights, or whatever) fall between one standard deviation above and below the mean (±1 SD); 95 percent of all cases fall between ±2 SD, and 99 percent of cases can be found between ±3 SD from the mean.

Table B-6 gives a more complete account of the relationship between z-scores and the percentage of cases found in a particular area of the normal curve. Notice, for example, that 93.3 percent of all cases fall below a z-score of +1.5. A z-score of 1.5 on a test (no matter what the original or "raw" score was) would be a good performance, since approximately 93 percent of all scores fall below this mark. Relationships between the standard deviation (or z-scores) and the normal

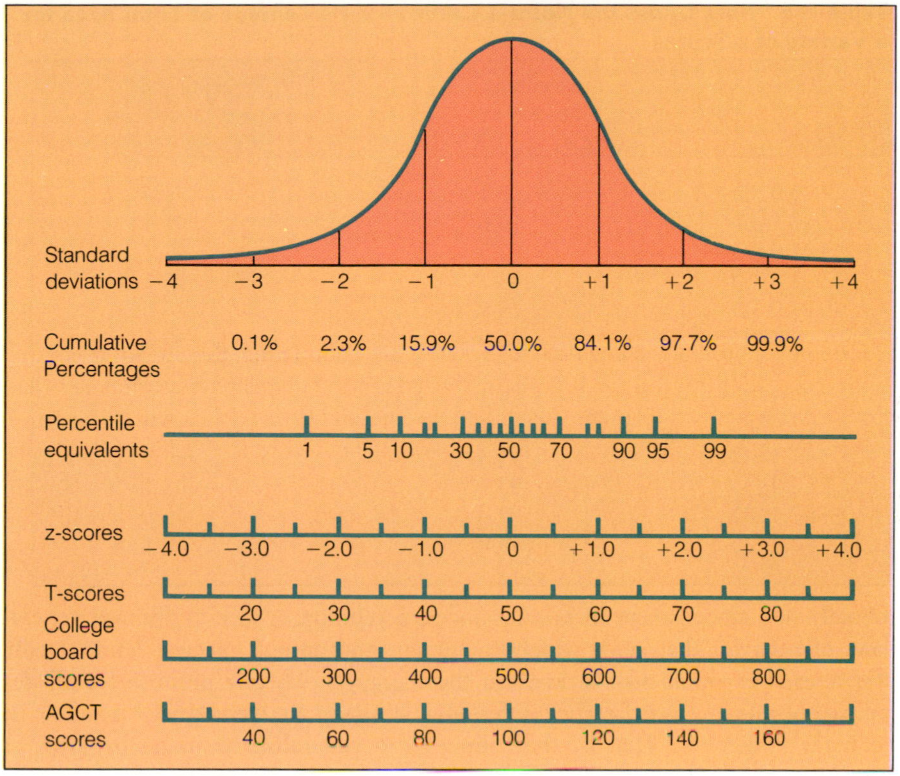

Fig. B-3 *The normal curve. Scales show the relationship of standard deviation, z-scores, and other measures to the curve.*

curve are invariant, making possible useful comparisons between various tests or groups of scores.

Inferential Statistics

Let's say a researcher studies the effects of a new therapy on a small group of depressed individuals. Is he or she interested only in these particular individuals?

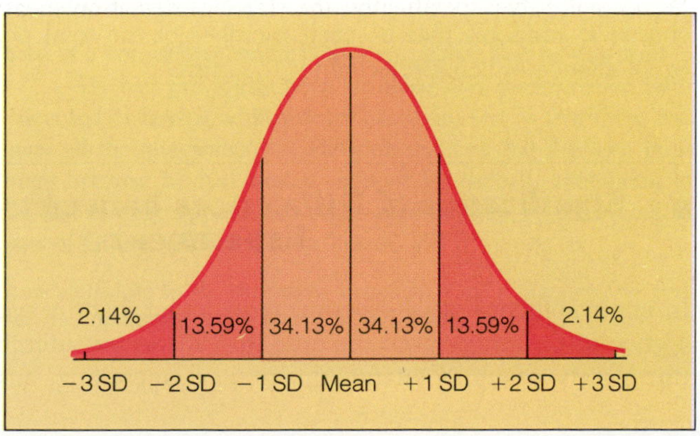

Fig. B-4 *Relationship between standard deviation and the normal curve.*

Table B-6 Area Under the Normal Curve as a Percentage of Total Area for a Variety of z-Scores

z-Score	Percentage of Area to the Left of This Value	Percentage of Area to the Right of This Value
−3.0 SD	00.1	99.9
−2.5 SD	00.6	99.4
−2.0 SD	02.3	97.7
−1.5 SD	06.7	93.3
−1.0 SD	15.9	84.1
−0.5 SD	30.9	69.1
0.0 SD	50.0	50.0
+0.5 SD	69.1	30.9
+1.0 SD	84.1	15.9
+1.5 SD	93.3	06.7
+2.0 SD	97.7	02.3
+2.5 SD	99.4	00.6
+3.0 SD	99.9	00.1

Usually not, since except in rare instances, psychologists seek to discover general laws of behavior that apply widely to human and animal species. Undoubtedly the researcher would like to know if the therapy holds any promise for all depressed people. As stated earlier, **inferential statistics** are techniques that allow us to make inferences. That is, they allow us to generalize from the behavior of small groups of subjects to that of the larger groups they represent.

Samples and Populations In any scientific investigation we would like to observe the entire set, or **population,** of subjects, objects, or events being studied. However, this is usually impossible or impractical. Observing all Catholics, all cancer patients, or all mothers-in-law could be both impractical (since all are large populations) and impossible (since people change denominations, may be unaware of having cancer, and change their status as relatives). In such cases, **samples** or smaller cross sections of a population are selected, and observations of the sample are used to draw conclusions about the entire population.

The major requirement for any sample is that it be **representative.** That is, the sample group must truly reflect the characteristics of the larger population. Referring to our earlier hypothetical study of the effects of a drug on memory, it would be essential that the sample of 20 subjects be representative of the general population. A very important aspect of representative samples is that their members are chosen at **random;** that is, each member of the total population must have an equal chance of being selected for the sample.

Significance of Differences between Groups in an Experiment

In our hypothetical drug experiment we found that the average memory score was higher for the group given the drug than it was for subjects who received no drug (the placebo group). Certainly this result is interesting, but could it have occurred by chance? If two groups were repeatedly tested (with neither receiving any drug), their average memory scores would sometimes differ. How much must two means differ before we can consider the difference "real" (not due to chance)?

Notice that the question is similar to one discussed earlier: How many tails in a row must we obtain when flipping a coin before we can conclude that the coin is biased? In the case of the coin, we noted that obtaining 5 tails in a row is a rather rare event. Thus, it became reasonable to assume the coin was biased. Of course, it is possible to get 5 tails in a row when flipping an honest coin. But since this outcome is unlikely, we have good reason to suspect that something other than chance (a loaded coin, for instance) caused the results. Similar reasoning is used in tests of statistical significance.

Tests of **statistical significance** provide an estimate of how often experimental results could have occurred by chance alone. The results of a test of statistical significance are stated as a probability giving the odds that the observed difference was due to chance. In psychology any experimental result that could have occurred by chance 5 times (or less) out of 100 (in other words, a probability of .05 or less) is considered *significant*. In the memory experiment we have used as an example, the probability is .025 ($p \leq .025$) that the group means would differ as they do by chance alone. This allows us to conclude with some certainty that the drug actually did improve memory scores.

Correlation

Many of the statements that psychologists make about behavior do not result from the use of experimental methods. Rather, they come from keen observations and measurement of existing phenomena. For example, a psychologist might note that the higher a couple's socioeconomic and educational status, the smaller the number of children they are likely to have. Or that grades in high school are related to how well a person is likely to do in college. Or even that as rainfall levels increase within a given metropolitan area, crime rates decline. In these instances we are dealing with the fact that two variables are **co-relating** (varying together in some orderly fashion).

The simplest way of visualizing a correlation is to construct a **scatter diagram.** In a scatter diagram, two measures (grades in high school and grades in college, for instance) are obtained. One measure is indicated by the X axis and the second by the Y axis. The scatter diagram plots the intersection of each pair of measurements as a single point. Many such measurement pairs give pictures like those in Fig. B-5.

Figure B-5 also shows scatter diagrams of three basic kinds of relationships between variables (or measures). Graphs A, B, and C show **positive relationships** of varying strength. As you can see, in a positive relationship, increases in the X measure (or score) are matched by increases in the Y measure (or score). An example would be finding that higher IQ scores (X) are associated with higher college grades (Y). A **zero correlation** (or relationship) is pictured in graph D. This might be the result of comparing subjects' hat sizes (X) to their college grades (Y). Graphs E and F both show a **negative relationship** (or correlation). Notice that as values on one measure increase, those on the second become smaller. An example might be the relationship between amount of alcohol consumed and

Fig. B-5 *Scatter diagrams showing various degrees of relationship for a positive, zero, and negative correlation. (Adapted from Pagano, 1981)*

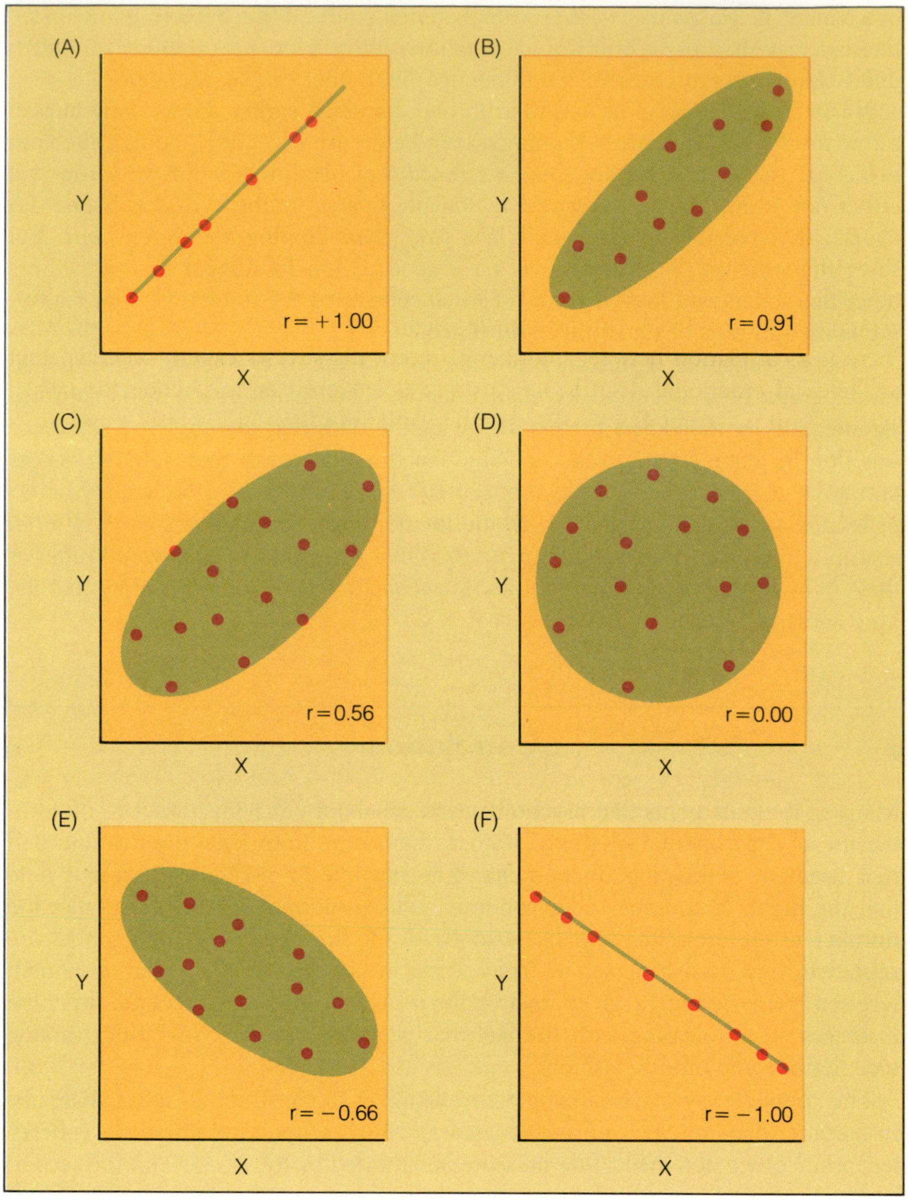

scores on a test of coordination: Higher alcohol levels are correlated with lower coordination scores.

Correlations can also be expressed as a **coefficient of correlation.** This coefficient is simply a number falling somewhere between + 1.00 and −1.00. If the number is zero or close to zero, it indicates a weak or nonexistent relationship. If the correlation is +1.00, a **perfect positive relationship** exists; if it is −1.00, a **perfect negative relationship** has been discovered. The most commonly used correlation coefficient is called the Pearson *r*. Calculation of the Pearson *r* is relatively simple, as shown in Table B-7. (The numbers shown are hypothetical.)

As stated in Chapter 2, correlations in psychology are rarely perfect. Most fall somewhere between zero and plus or minus one. The closer the correlation coefficient is to +1.00 or −1.00, the stronger the relationship. An interesting example of some typical correlations is provided by a study that compared the IQs of adopted children with their biological mothers. At age 4, the children's IQs correlated .28 with their mothers' IQs. By age 7 the correlation was .35, and by age 13 it had grown to .38.

Correlations often provide highly useful information. For instance, it is valuable to know that there is a correlation between cigarette smoking and lung cancer rates. Another example is the fact that higher consumption of alcohol during pregnancy is correlated with lower birth weight and a higher rate of birth defects. There is a correlation between number of recent life stresses experienced and the incidence of emotional disturbance. And so on. More examples could be cited, but the point is, correlations help identify relationships that are worth knowing.

Correlations are particularly valuable for making **predictions.** If we know two measures are correlated, and we know a person's score on one measure, we can predict his or her score on the other. For example, most colleges have formulas

Table B-7 IQ and Grade Point Average for Computing Pearson *r*

Student No.	IQ X	Grade Point Average Y	X Score Squared X^2	Y Score Squared Y^2	X Times Y XY
1	110	1.0	12,100	1.00	110.0
2	112	1.6	12,544	2.56	179.2
3	118	1.2	13,924	1.44	141.6
4	119	2.1	14,161	4.41	249.9
5	122	2.6	14,884	6.76	317.2
6	125	1.8	15,625	3.24	225.0
7	127	2.6	16,124	6.76	330.2
8	130	2.0	16,900	4.00	260.0
9	132	3.2	17,424	10.24	422.4
10	134	2.6	17,956	6.76	348.4
11	136	3.0	18,496	9.00	408.0
12	138	3.6	19,044	12.96	496.8
Total	1503	27.3	189,187	69.13	3488.7

$$r = \frac{\Sigma XY - \dfrac{(\Sigma X)(\Sigma Y)}{N}}{\sqrt{\left[\Sigma X^2 - \dfrac{(\Sigma X)^2}{N}\right]\left[\Sigma Y^2 - \dfrac{(\Sigma Y)^2}{N}\right]}}$$

$$= \frac{3488.7 - \dfrac{1503(27.3)}{12}}{\sqrt{\left[189{,}187 - \dfrac{(1503)^2}{12}\right]\left[69.13 - \dfrac{(27.3)^2}{12}\right]}}$$

$$= \frac{69.375}{81.088} = 0.856 = 0.86$$

(Adapted from Pagano, 1981)

that make use of multiple correlations to decide which prospective students have the best chances for success. Usually the formula includes such "predictors" as high school GPA, teacher ratings, and scores on the Scholastic Aptitude Test (SAT) or some equivalent. Although none of the predictors is perfectly correlated with success in college, together they correlate highly and provide a useful technique for screening applicants.

There is an interesting "trick" you can do with correlations that you may find useful. It works like this: If you *square* the correlation coefficient (multiply *r* by itself), you will get a number telling the **percent of variance** accounted for by the correlation. For example, the correlation between IQ scores and college grade point average is 0.5. Multiplying 0.5 times 0.5 gives 0.25, or 25 percent. This means that 25 percent of the variation in college grades is accounted for by knowing IQ scores. In other words, with a correlation of 0.5, college grades are "squeezed" into an oval like that in graph C, Fig. B-5. IQ scores take away some of the possible variation in corresponding grade point averages. If there were no correlation between IQ and grades, grades would be completely free to vary, as shown in Fig. B-5, graph D.

Along the same line, a correlation of 1.00 or −1.00 means that 100 percent of the variation in the Y measure is accounted for by knowing the X measure: If you know a person's X score, you can tell exactly what the Y score is. An example that comes close to this state of affairs is the high correlation (0.86) between the IQs of identical twins. In any group of identical twins, 74 percent of the variation in the "Y" twins' IQs is accounted for by knowing the IQs of their siblings (the "X's").

Correlation and Causation It is very important to recognize that the existence of a correlation between two measures does not automatically mean that one causes the other: *Correlation does not demonstrate causation.* When a correlation exists, the best we can say is that two variables are related. Of course, this does not mean that it is impossible for two correlated variables to have a cause-effect relationship. Rather, it means that we cannot *conclude* that a causal relationship exists solely on the basis of a correlation. To establish greater confidence in the existence of a causal relationship, we must perform an experiment (see Chapter 2).

Often two correlated variables are related through the influence of a third variable. For example, we might observe that the more hours students devote to studying the better their grades. Although it is tempting to conclude that more studying produces (causes) better grades, it is possible (indeed, it is probable) that grades and the amount of study time are both related to the amount of motivation or interest a student has.

The distinction between having data that indicate causality versus data that indicate a relationship of unknown origin is one that should not be forgotten. Since we rarely run experiments in daily life, the information on which we act is largely correlational. This should make us more humble and more tentative in the confidence with which we make pronouncements about human behavior.

Glossary

Absolute threshold A point indicating the minimum amount of physical energy necessary to produce a sensation.
Accommodation Changes in the shape of the lens of the eye that serve to focus objects at varying distances. Also, modifying old concepts and thinking habits to fit new information or demands (Piaget).
Acetylcholine (uh-SEET-ul-COH-leen) A neurotransmitter substance that is released at synapses and at the neuromuscular junction (point of contact between a neuron and a muscle fiber). Acetylcholine can initiate a nerve impulse or a muscle contraction, depending on its point of release.
Achievement motivation A need for success or the attainment of excellence.
Acromegaly (ak-row-MEG-uh-lee) A condition involving progressive enlargement of the hands, face, and feet due to excessive secretion of growth hormones by the pituitary.
Acuity (ah-CUE-ih-tee) That aspect of visual perception having to do with the sharpness or resolution of images.
Acupuncture (AK-you-punk-chur) The Chinese medical art of relieving pain and treating illness by inserting thin hairlike needles at various points on the body.
Adaptation In general, adjustment to environmental demands. In connection with the senses, a gradual decline in response to a constant stimulus.
Adaptation level An internal or mental medium point that we use to judge amounts.
Addiction Development of physical dependence on a drug such that craving and physical discomfort (withdrawal symptoms) occur in its absence.
Adjustment disorder A combination of emotional, psychological, and physical disturbances caused by identifiable life stresses.
Adrenal glands (ah-DREE-nal) Source of adrenaline, a hormone secreted during emotional arousal. Also, a source of other important hormones.
Adrenaline (ah-DREN-ul-in) A hormone produced by the adrenal glands similar in its effects to sympathetic nervous system activation; produces diffuse activation throughout the body.
Affect Pertaining to emotion or feelings.
Affective disorders A form of psychopathology characterized by mania or severe depression; disorders involving extremes of emotion.
Affective psychosis A loss of contact with reality involving extremes of emotional response, such as mania, depression, or manic-depressive mood swings.
Afferent (AF-er-ent) Carrying or conducting inward, as in nerves or neurons conveying impulses toward the brain or central nervous system; opposite of *efferent*.
Afferent or sensory nerves Incoming sensory fibers.
Affiliation motive The desire to associate with other people.
Ageism A prejudice held on the basis of age; hence, any tendency to discriminate on the basis of age.
Age regression Return of a hypnotized subject to a younger age.
Aggression Any response made with the intention of bringing harm to another person.
Agnosias (ag-NO-zyahs) In perception, disturbances of the meaning of sensory stimuli; hence, an inability to know; for example, an inability to recognize objects or pictures.
Alpha wave A relatively large, slow brain wave pattern indicating a passive state of relaxed awareness.
Altered state of consciousness Any nonordinary mental state, including meditation, hypnosis, and drug-induced states.
Ambivalence (am-BIV-ah-lence) Holding opposite emotions such as love and hate toward some person or object.
Amnesia Loss of memory (partial or complete) for past events.
Amniocentesis (AM-nee-oh-sen-TEE-sus) The extraction and analysis of amniotic fluid from the womb in the early stages of pregnancy; used for the detection of genetic anomalies in the fetus.
Amphetamines Class of drugs acting as central nervous system stimulants. Not known to be physically addictive but may cause strong psychological dependency.
Anal stage In Freud's theory, the second stage of psychosexual development corresponding roughly to the period of toilet training between the second and third year. (See also *genital stage; oral stage; phallic stage.*)
Androgen (AN-dro-jen) Any of a number of male sex hormones.
Androgyny (an-DROJ-ih-nee) The condition of having both male and female behavioral traits or a balance between "masculinity" and "femininity" as they are defined by one's culture.
Anesthesia (an-es-THEE-zyah) Loss of bodily sensations.
Anima (AN-ih-muh) In Jung's theory, an archetype representing femaleness or the female principle within the psyche. (See *archetype.*)
Animus (AN-ih-mus) In Jung's theory, an archetype representing maleness or the male principle within the psyche. (See *archetype.*)
Anorexia nervosa (AN-uh-REX-see-ah ner-VOH-sah) A condition in which a person will eat, but with great reluctance, and typically not enough to sustain normal weight. A serious loss of appetite apparently of psychological origin.
Anosmia (a-NAHZ-me-ah) Loss of the sense of smell, particularly for a specific type of odor.
Anthropomorphic fallacy (AN-thro-po-MORE-fik) The error of attributing human thoughts, feelings, and motives to animals.
Antidepressants Drugs that counteract depression or despondency by elevating the individual's mood.
Antipsychotics (An-tie-sie-KOT-iks) Drugs that alleviate psychotic symptoms, making it easier to treat psychiatric problems.
Anxiety A feeling of painful or apprehensive uneasiness closely related to fear; especially, that characterized by dread or anticipation of some unclear threat.
Anxiety disorders A class of personal disturbances characterized by excessive and chronic anxiety states. Formerly referred to as neurosis.
Aphasias (ah-FAZE-yahs) Speech disturbances resulting from damage to certain areas in the temporal lobe of the brain.

Apnea (ap-NEE-uh) To be without breath; an interruption in breathing.
Approach-avoidance conflict Unpleasant situation in which a person is simultaneously attracted to and repelled by the same goal. (See *conflict*.)
Aptitude test A test that rates a person's potential for learning skills required by various occupations.
Architectural psychology Study of the effects buildings have on behavior; the design of buildings using behavioral principles.
Archetype (AR-keh-type) An original pattern, prototype, or idea on which others are modeled. In Jung's theory, universal primordial images found in the collective unconscious.
Arousal The overall level of excitation or activation present at any given time for a person or animal.
Assessment Evaluation or measurement.
Assimilation In Piaget's theory, the application of existing mental patterns to new situations. (Compare *accommodation*.)
Astigmatism (ah-STIG-mah-tiz-im) A defect in the shape of the cornea, the lens, or the eye as a whole that causes some parts of vision to be out of focus.
Attention Orienting toward or focusing on some stimulus.
Attitude A predisposition having emotional, belief, and behavioral components that determines a person's reaction toward a particular social stimulus.
Attribution The process of mentally ascribing one's own behavior, and that of others, to various causes.
Autism (OT-is-im) A severe disorder of childhood involving mutism, sensory spinouts, sensory blocking, tantrums, lack of awareness of others, echolalia, and other difficulties.
Autokinetic effect (OT-oh-kih-NET-ik) The apparent movement of a stationary pinpoint of light displayed in a dark room; often occurs as a result of suggestion.
Autonomic nervous system (ANS) Division of the peripheral nervous system concerned with involuntary functions of the body.
Aversive conditioning (ah-VER-siv) Use of an unpleasant or painful stimulus to reinforce learning.
Avoidance learning Learning procedure in which the occurrence of a particular response results in postponement or prevention of an unpleasant stimulus.
Axon (AK-sahn) A thin fiber process extending from the cell body of a neuron (nerve cell); normally conducts information away from the cell body.

Babinski reflex Curling and spreading of the toes that occurs when the sole of an infant's foot is stroked.
Bait shyness An unwillingness or hesitation on the part of animals to accept a particular food. Often caused by the presence of a taste aversion. (See *taste aversion*.)
Barbiturates Addictive drugs that depress activity of the central nervous system. Barbiturate intoxication resembles intoxication caused by alcohol.
Behavioral medicine The study of behavioral factors in physical illness and the use of behavioral methods to preserve health and treat disease.
Behaviorism The school of psychology that emphasizes the study of overt, observable behavior.
Behavior modification Application of principles of learning to change or eliminate maladaptive or abnormal behavior.
Beta waves (BAY-tah) Fast, low-voltage activity of a more or less random character recorded on the EEG when an organism is alert and attending to stimuli. (See *EEG*.)
Biased sampling Selection of subjects for an experiment or public opinion poll that gives some subjects a greater chance of being included than others. (See also *randomization*.)
Binocular cues Any cue for depth perception that requires two eyes.
Biodata Detailed biographical information about a job applicant used to predict suitability for various occupations.
Biofeedback A technique allowing a subject to monitor and control his or her own internal bodily functions.
Bipolar disorders Emotional disorders in which a person is manic (excited) or depressed, or swings between mania and depression.
Blind spot A portion of the retina where the optic nerve leaves the eye and therefore there are no visual receptors.
Brain lesion (LEE-zhun) Destruction of brain tissue experimentally, accidentally, or through disease.
Brainstorming A group problem-solving technique in which ideas are offered freely, imaginatively, and without evaluation as to their practicality.
Brainwashing Engineered or forced change in attitudes and beliefs.
Brightness In perception, the relative amount of light reflected from or emanating from the surface of a stimulus or objects.

Caffeine A natural drug with stimulant properties that is found in coffee, tea, and synthetic beverages and medicines.
Carcinogen (kar-SIN-oh-jen) Any cancer-producing substance.
Case study An intensive investigation of the behavior of a single person.
Cataplexy (CAT-ah-plek-see) A sudden loss of all muscle tone and voluntary movement in the body causing complete collapse.
Catatonic (CAT-ih-TAWN-ik) A schizophrenic state marked by alternate periods of stupor and activity, also by mutism and waxy flexibility of the body.
Central nervous system (CNS) The brain and spinal cord.
Character A subjective evaluation of an individual's personality, often as to its desirable and undesirable attributes.
Chemotherapy (KEE-mo-therapy or CHEM-oh-therapy) Use of psychoactive drugs for the treatment of mental disturbances.
Chromosomes (KRO-muh-somz) Threadlike structures ("colored bodies") within the nucleus of each cell that carry the genes. Normal human cells each have 23 pairs of chromosomes.
Circadian rhythms (SUR-kay-dee-an) Cyclical changes in bodily function that vary on a schedule approximating one 24-hour day.
Clairvoyance (klare-VOY-ans) Purported form of extrasensory perception (ESP) in which objects or events are perceived without the aid of normal sensory systems.
Classical conditioning A basic form of learning discovered by Pavlov in which existing (reflex) responses are attached to new stimuli by pairing the new stimuli with stimuli that naturally elicit the response.
Client-centered therapy A form of therapy designed by Rogers in which the client assumes responsibility for solving his or her own problems. The therapist's role is to clarify and assist, not to give advice.
Climacteric (kly-MAK-ter-ik) A period or point during late middle age in males in which a significant change in health, vigor, appearance, or potency takes place. Roughly analogous to *menopause* in women.
Clinical psychologist A psychologist who specializes in treating

psychological and behavioral disturbances or who does research on such disturbances.

Cloning (KLO-ning) The reproduction of an entire plant or organism from a single cell of the original plant or organism.

Closure Gestalt term for the perceptual tendency to complete figures by "closing," or ignoring, small gaps.

Cocaine A crystalline drug derived from coca leaves; used as a central nervous system stimulant and local anesthetic.

Cochlea (KOCK-lee-ah) The snail-shaped organ of hearing in the inner ear containing the ultimate sensory receptors for hearing.

Coding Organizing information for efficient memory storage and retrieval.

Coefficient of correlation (KOE-eh-FISH-ent of KORE-eh-LAY-shun) An index of the degree of relationship between two sets of measures or two variables. Coefficients are expressed as a number ranging from -1.00 to $+1.00$.

Cognition (cog-NISH-un) The process of thinking, knowing, or processing information.

Cognitive (COG-nuh-tiv) Of or pertaining to thinking, knowing, understanding, or the internal processing of information.

Cognitive dissonance (COG-nuh-tiv DIS-uh-nuns) An imbalance between one's thoughts, beliefs, attitudes, or behavior; a tension state that people are motivated to reduce.

Cognitive map Internal images of an area (maze, city, campus, and so forth) that presumably underlie an ability to choose alternate paths to the same goal.

Collective unconscious According to Jung's theory, a portion of the psyche that is common to all people and that contains archetypal images. (See *archetype*.)

Colostrum (kuh-LOSS-trum) The milklike substance secreted by women during the first few days after childbirth. Colostrum is rich in antibodies to disease.

Community psychology A specialty that seeks to improve community-wide mental health through direct services, prevention, education, and consultation.

Comparative psychology The study and comparison of the behavior of different species, especially animals.

Compensation Counteracting a real or imagined weakness by emphasizing desirable traits or seeking to excel in other areas.

Compression In hearing, the squeezing together of air molecules at the front of a sound wave. Collision of the compressed wave front with the auditory apparatus then sets the auditory apparatus in motion.

Compulsion An act the individual feels driven to repeat, often against his or her will.

Concept A generalized idea representing a class of objects or events that are grouped together on the basis of some common feature or property characteristic of each.

Condensation In the Freudian theory of dream interpretation, a tendency to combine images from several sources into a single complex image.

Conditioned emotional response The conditioning of autonomic nervous system response and/or visceral response to a previously nonemotional stimulus.

Conditioned response In classical conditioning, a learned response that becomes attached to the conditioned stimulus.

Conditioned stimulus In classical conditioning, a previously neutral stimulus that acquires the capacity to evoke a response as the result of association with an unconditioned stimulus.

Conditioning The process of learning by association discovered by Pavlov. Also sometimes used to refer to operant learning. (See *classical conditioning* and *operant conditioning*.)

Cones Visual receptors in the eye responsible for color vision and daylight visual acuity. (See *rods*.)

Conflict A mental or behavioral state characterized by clashing or incompatible motives, desires, goals, and so forth. The four most basic conflicts are: approach conflicts, avoidance conflicts, approach-avoidance conflicts, and double approach-avoidance conflicts.

Congenital problems (kon-JEN-ih-tal) A defect acquired during development in the uterus; hence, a problem existing at birth (a "birth defect"). Distinct from a *hereditary* problem (that is, one transmitted by genes).

Conjunctive concept (kon-JUNK-tiv) A concept defined as having one value on one dimension *and* a second value on another dimension (for example, red triangles). (Compare with *disjunctive* and *relational* concepts.)

Connotative meaning (KON-oh-TAY-tiv) The subjective personal or emotional significance of a word or concept apart from its explicit and recognized meaning.

Conscience (KON-chuns) Internalized sense of right and wrong; in Freudian theory, the superego.

Consolidation (kon-sol-ih-DAY-shun) Theoretical process by which material is solidified as a permanent memory in the brain after being learned.

Constructs Explanatory concepts inferred from observable events but not directly observable themselves.

Consumer psychology Specialty area that focuses on understanding consumer behavior; often applied to advertising, marketing, product testing, and the like.

Contact comfort A pleasant and reassuring feeling human and animal infants derive from touching or clinging to something soft and warm, usually the mother.

Contiguity (kon-tih-GEW-ih-tee) In close proximity or contact; very near in time or space.

Continuous reinforcement A schedule of reinforcement in which every response is reinforced.

Control Eliminating, identifying, or equalizing all factors in an experiment that could affect its outcome.

Control group A group in a psychological experiment that is exposed to all experimental conditions except the independent variable. (See *experimental group*.)

Convergence The simultaneous turning inward of the two eyes as they focus on nearby objects.

Convergent thought Thinking directed toward discovery of a single established correct answer; conventional thinking.

Conversion reaction A symptom or disability that appears to be physical but that actually results from anxiety, stress, or emotional conflict.

Cornea (KOR-nee-ah) The clear outer membrane covering the eyeball.

Corpus callosum (KOR-pus cah-LO-sum) A large nerve unit in the middle of the brain connecting the two hemispheres; serves to transfer information from one hemisphere to the other.

Correlation (KOR-eh-LAY-shun) The existence of a consistent (nonrandom) relation between two variables or measure.

Correlational study A nonexperimental study designed to assess the degree of relationship between two or more variables.

Corticalization (KOR-tih-kal-ih-ZAY-shun) The increase in the relative size and importance of the cerebral cortex observed as one ascends the biological scale from lower animals to humans.
Counseling psychologist A psychologist who specializes in the treatment of milder emotional and behavioral disturbances.
Counselor A mental health professional who specializes in adjustment problems not involving serious mental disorder; for example, marriage counselors, occupational counselors, or school counselors.
Cretinism (KREET-un-ism) A form of mental retardation resulting from a malfunction of the thyroid gland.
Critical period A time during which a certain event must occur in an organism's life if development is to occur normally.
CT scan Computed tomography scan; a computer-enhanced X-ray image of the brain.
Culture An ongoing pattern of life characterizing a society at a particular historical period or stage in its development.

Dark adaptation The process by which the eye adapts to conditions of low illumination, principally, by a shift to rod vision. (See *rods.*)
Decibel (DES-ih-bel) A unit used to measure the loudness of sounds; ordinary speech registers around 60 decibels.
Deductive thought A pattern of thought in which the thinker must use a general set of rules to draw a logical conclusion. (Compare with *inductive thought.*)
Defense mechanisms Habitual and unconscious psychological devices used to reduce or avoid anxiety.
Delayed speech A significant delay in the development of speech capacity in early childhood.
Delta waves Large, slow, regular waves of brain activity recorded on the EEG during the deeper stages of sleep.
Delusions False beliefs held against all evidence to the contrary; symptomatic of some psychotic disorders.
Demonology (DEE-mon-OL-oh-gee) In Medieval Europe, that branch of knowledge dealing with the study of demons and the treatment of those "possessed" by demons.
Dendrites (DEN-drites) Branching projections of nerve cell bodies (neurons) that form synapses with other neurons and conduct information toward the cell body. (See *neurons.*)
Denial A defense mechanism used to deny the existence of a problem or an unpleasant reality.
Denotative (DEE-no-TATE-iv) The objective dictionary meaning of a word or concept.
Dependent variable The variable (usually a behavior) that reflects changes in the independent variable. (See *independent variable.*)
Depressant A drug or chemical agent that lowers bodily or nervous system function.
Depressive neurosis (new-ROW-sis) Prolonged and severe depression triggered by a stressful event but representing an overreaction to it.
Depressive psychosis (sie-KOH-sis) A form of psychosis characterized by the deepest possible despondency.
Deprivation In development, the loss or withholding of normal stimulation, nutrition, comfort, love, and so forth. A condition of lacking.
Depth perception The ability to see three-dimensional space and to accurately estimate distances.
Detoxification (de-TOKS-ih-fih-KAY-shun) To remove poison or the effects of poison. In the treatment of alcoholism, the physical withdrawal of the patient from alcohol.
Developmental tasks Any of the countless personal changes that must be made throughout life for optimal development.
Developmental psychologist A psychologist interested in the course of human growth and developmment, from before birth until death.
Difference threshold The smallest change in a physical stimulus that can be detected by an observer.
Digit span test A test of attention and short-term memory. Subjects are asked to recall a series of random digits of varying lengths that has just been read to them.
Discrimination (learning) The ability to detect differences between two or more objects or events; often brought about by reinforcement of responses to one stimulus but not the other.
Dishabituation (DIS-ha-bit-you-AY-shun) A reinstatement of sensory response lost or reduced by the occurrence of habituation. (See *habituation.*)
Disjunctive concept A concept defined by the presence of at least one of a number of features, or a concept defined as having one value on one dimension *or* a different value on another dimension (for example, blue *or* triangular). (Compare with *conjunctive* and *relational* concepts).
Disorganized schizophrenia (SKIT-suh-FREE-nee-ah) A form of psychosis characterized by giddy, obscene, or silly behavior and including a severe disintegration of personality.
Displacement In Freudian theory, the rechanneling of energy from one target or activity to another. Often used as a defense mechanism, as when aggression is displaced on someone or something other than the actual source of frustration.
Dissociative reaction (dih-SOSH-ih-tiv) Unusual disorders including amnesia, fugue, and multiple personality that allow individuals to separate themselves from upsetting thoughts and actions.
Divergent thinking Thinking that produces many ideas or alternatives; creative or unconventional thinking.
DNA (deoxyribonucleic acid) Large and complex chemical molecules found in chromosomes and believed to be the substance of which genes are composed.
Dogmatism (DOG-mah-tizm) An unwarranted positiveness or certainty in matters of opinion.
Dominant gene A gene whose influence will be expressed on every occasion in which it is present. (Compare *recessive gene.*)
Dopamine (DOPE-ah-meen) An important neurotransmitter found in the brain, particularly at sites within the limbic system.
Double-bind communication A message that contradicts itself and places the person who receives it in an unsolvable conflict.
Down syndrome A hereditary abnormality associated with the presence of 47 chromosomes rather than the usual 46 and characterized by a shortened life expectancy, mental retardation, and unusual physical features.
Drive The psychological representation of internal need states; for example, hunger, thirst, and so forth.
Drug interaction The outcome of combining two or more drugs within the body producing effects above and beyond what would be expected from the mere addition of the effects of one to the effects of the other.
Dual personality A form of dissociative disorder in which the person maintains two separate personalities, one of which typically is unaware of the existence of the other.
Dyslexia (dis-LEK-see-ah) An inability to read with understanding,

often caused by a tendency to misread letters (by seeing their mirror images, for instance).

Echolalia (ek-oh-LAY-lee-ah) A tendency, sometimes observed in autistic children, to repeat, or echo back, whatever is said to them.
Eclectic Selected or chosen from many sources.
Educational psychology The psychological study of learning, teaching, and related topics.
EEG (electroencephalogram) Record of the electrical activity of the brain; made by attaching electrodes to the scalp.
Efferent (EF-er-ent) Carrying or conducting outward, as in nerves or neurons conveying impulses away from the brain or central nervous system: opposite of *afferent*.
Ego (EE-go) In Freudian terminology, the portion of personality that is in conscious control of behavior and that reconciles the demands of the id, superego, and external reality.
Egocentric (EE-go-SEN-trik) Unable to take a viewpoint other than one's own.
Eidetic imagery (eye-DET-ik IM-ij-ree) The ability to retain an image long enough to use it as a source of information; basically, a photographic memory.
Ejaculation (EE-jac-you-LAY-shun) The release of sperm and seminal fluid by the male at the time of orgasm.
Electra conflict (ih-LEK-trah) In Freudian theory, a conflict experienced by female children when they become attracted to their fathers and feel themselves to be in competition with their mothers. (See *Oedipus conflict*.)
Electroconvulsive shock (ECS) (ih-LEK-tro-cun-VUL-siv) An electric shock passed directly through the brain, producing a convulsion. ECS can impair memory and produce amnesia in experimental animals. Clinically, it is used in the treatment of severe depression.
Electrode Any needle, wire, metal plate, or saltwater-filled glass tube used to apply electrical current to the body, especially to neural tissue.
Electromagnetic radiation (ih-LEK-tro-mag-NET-ik) Waves of energy produced by electric and magnetic oscillations. Radio waves, light waves, X rays, and gamma rays are all electromagnetic waves differing only in their wavelength.
Empathy (EM-puh-thee) A capacity for taking another's point of view or sharing another's state of consciousness; to feel what another is feeling.
Empirical (im-PIR-ih-cul) Founded on experiment or experience; based on direct observation.
Encoding Changing information into a form that allows it to be stored in memory and manipulated in thought.
Encopresis (en-coh-PREE-sis) An inability to control defecation (elimination of solid wastes); hence, "soiling."
Encounter group A group experience that emphasizes intensely honest interchanges among participants regarding feelings and reactions to one another.
Endocrine system (EN-duh-krin) Bodily system made up of those glands whose secretions pass directly into the bloodstream or lymph system.
Endogenous depression (en-DAHJ-eh-nus) Depression that appears to be produced from within, rather than as a reaction to life events.
Endorphins (en-DOR-funz) A class of brain peptides (proteins) having an apparent link to the control of pain and possibly to psychiatric disturbances.
Engineering psychology A specialty concerned with the design of machines and work environments so that they are compatible with human sensory and motor capabilities.
Engrams (EN-gramz) "Memory traces" or physical changes taking place in the brain; a general term referring to the theoretical basis for learning and memory.
Enkephalins (en-KEF-ah-lins) Recently discovered brain peptides (proteins) having an apparent link to emotional functioning.
Enuresis (EN-you-REE-sis) An inability to control urination, particularly with reference to bed-wetting.
Environmental psychology The formal study of how environments affect behavior.
Episodic drive (ep-ih-SOD-ik) A noncyclical drive state occurring in distinctly separate episodes associated with particular conditions (for example, pain avoidance, specific hungers, sexual motivation).
Episodic memory (ep-ih-SOD-ik) A hypothesized "autobiographical" subpart of memory that records life events or "episodes."
Erogenous zone (eh-ROJ-ih-nus) Any bodily area productive of pleasurable sensations and particularly those areas producing erotic desire when stimulated.
Escape learning Learning to make a response to escape or to terminate an aversive (painful) stimulus. Escape learning is negatively reinforced by termination of the aversive stimulus.
Escapism Reducing discomfort by leaving frustrating situations or by psychologically withdrawing from them.
Estrogen (ES-truh-jen) Any of a number of female sex hormones.
Estrus (ES-trus) Changes in the reproductive organs and sexual drives of animals associated with a desire for mating, particularly used to refer to female animals "in heat."
Ethnocentric (ETH-no-CEN-trik) Placing one's own group or race at the center; that is, tending to reject all other groups but one's own.
Ethologist (ETH-all-oh-jist) A person who studies the natural behavior patterns of animals.
Eugenics (you-GEN-iks) The science that deals with the improvement of an animal species or race.
Exorcism In Medieval Europe, the practice of expelling or driving off an "evil spirit," particularly one residing in the body of an individual who is "possessed."
Experiment A scientific technique whereby all relevant variables are manipulated, measured, or controlled so that cause-effect relationships may be observed. Simple experiments typically involve both an *experimental group* and a *control group*.
Experimental group In a controlled experiment, the group of subjects exposed to the independent variable or experimental manipulation. (See control group.)
Experimental psychologist A psychologist primarily interested in the scientific study of human and animal behavior.
Experimenter effect Changes in subjects' behavior caused by the unintended influence of an experimenter's presence and actions.
Extinction The process of consistently not reinforcing a learned response, leading to a gradual decrease in the frequency with which the response occurs.
Extraneous variables (ex-TRAY-nee-us) Those conditions or factors to be excluded from possible influence on the outcome of a controlled experiment (that is, variables the experimenter is not interested in).

Extrasensory perception The purported ability to perceive events in ways that cannot be explained by known capacities of the sensory organs.
Extrinsic motivation Motivation based on obvious external rewards, obligations, or similar factors, not on the inherent satisfactions of the task or activity.
Extrovert (EK-struh-vert) An individual whose energies and interests are directed outward; a person who seeks social contact or is outgoing. (Compare introvert.)

Factor analysis A statistical technique whereby multiple measures are intercorrelated. Measures that form "clusters" of correlations are assumed to represent some more general underlying factor.
Family therapy Therapeutic technique in which all family members participate, both individually and as a group, to change destructive relationships.
Fantasy A product of the imagination determined mainly by one's motives or feelings. Fantasy may be used as an escape mechanism.
Feedback Knowledge of results or relaying the effect of some action to the person controlling it.
Figure-ground Gestaltist's observation that some aspects of a stimulus pattern appear to stand out as an object (figure) while others appear to stand in the background (ground).
Fixation The tendency to repeat wrong solutions or faulty responses as a consequence of frustration. In Freudian theory, lasting conflicts developed during a particular stage of development as a result of frustration or overindulgence during that stage.
Fixed-action pattern A genetically programmed sequence of movements occurring mechanically and virtually universally in members of a particular species.
Fixed-interval schedule A schedule of reinforcement in which reinforcement is administered following a fixed period of time after the previous reinforcement; for example, every 3 minutes.
Fixed-ratio schedule A schedule of reinforcement in which a predetermined number of responses must be made before reinforcement is delivered; for example, one reinforcement for every five responses.
Flat affect A seemingly total lack of emotional responsiveness.
Fovea (FOE-vee-ah) A small depression in the center of the retina containing the greatest concentration of *cones* and providing the sharpest vision.
Frame of reference A mental and emotional perspective, relative to which events are perceived and evaluated.
Fraternal twins Twins conceived from two separate eggs. Fraternal twins are no more alike genetically than other siblings. (See *identical twins.*)
Free association A technique of *psychoanalysis* in which persons say anything that comes into their minds regardless of how embarrassing or unimportant it may seem.
Free-floating anxiety Feelings of dread or apprehension that cannot be traced to any particular source.
Free will The doctrine that humans are capable of freely making choices or decisions.
Frigidity An abnormal lack of sexual desire.
Frontal lobotomy Surgical destruction of the frontal lobes of the brain, or separation of the frontal lobes from the remainder of the brain.
Frustration An internal emotional state resulting from interference with satisfaction of a motive or blocking of goal-directed behavior.
Fugue (FEWG) A dissociative reaction characterized by taking flight and by a loss of memory for events before or during the act of fleeing.
Functional fixedness Rigidity in problem solving caused by an inability to see novel uses for familiar objects.
Functionalism (FUNK-shun-ul-ism) School of psychology concerned with how behavior and mental abilities help people adapt to their environments.
Functional psychosis A psychosis with no apparent biological basis.

Galvanic skin response (GSR) (gal-VAN-ik) A change in the electrical resistance of the skin associated with arousal or anxiety.
General adaptation syndrome (GAS) Selye's description of a consistent pattern of reactions to prolonged stress occurring in three stages: alarm, resistance, and, finally, exhaustion.
General paresis (pah-REE-sis) An organic psychosis that results when syphilis attacks the brain.
Generalization The transfer of a learned response from one stimulus or set of circumstances to others that are in some way like the original stimulus.
Generalized anxiety disorder Defined as at least 6 months of persistent anxiety.
Genes Areas on the chromosomes that carry hereditary instructions affecting various personal characteristics.
Genital stage The final stage in psychosexual development (according to Freud); typically attained in late adolescence and representing full psychosexual maturity. (See also *anal stage; oral stage; phallic stage.*)
Gerontologist (JER-un-TOL-uh-jist) One who studies the effects of aging.
Gestalt (guh-SHTALT) A German word meaning form or pattern. The school of psychology emphasizing the study of perception, learning, and thinking in whole units, not by analysis into parts.
Gestalt therapy A psychotherapy developed by Perls and others that emphasizes immediate experience and participation of the whole person in any activity.
Goal The object of a motivated and directed sequence of behavior.
Gonads The sex glands—testes in males and ovaries in females.
Grammar The study of classes of words and their functions and relations within sentences.
Graphology (gra-FALL-uh-jee) The legitimate study of handwriting to detect forgeries; also, the discredited notion that personality characteristics are revealed by handwriting.
Group sanctions Any rewards or punishments (real or symbolic) applied to members of a group for adherence to, or deviation from, group norms for acceptable conduct.
Group therapy Any form of psychotherapy taking advantage of the special characteristics of group interaction. Individuals work out personal problems with the guidance of a trained therapist and the help of other group members.
Gustation (gus-TAY-shun) The sense of taste or the act of tasting.

Habituation (ha-bich-oo-WAY-shun) A decrease in the strength of a reflex caused by its repeated elicitation. Also, a decrease in sensory response to repeated presentation of a stimulus.
Hallucinations (ha-loos-un-AY-shuns) Imaginary sensations such as seeing, hearing, or smelling things that don't exist in the real world.
Hallucinogen (ha-lu-SIN-oh-jen) Any substance or drug that causes hallucinations.

Halo effect The tendency to generalize a favorable or unfavorable impression to unrelated details of personality.
Heredity A transmission of physical and psychological characteristics from parents to offspring through genes.
Hermaphroditism (hur-MAF-roh-dite-ism) The condition of having genitals suggestive of both sexes; ambiguous genital sexuality.
Hippocampus A structure in the brain associated with the regulation of emotion and the transfer of information from short-term memory to long-term memory.
Homeostasis (HOE-me-oh-STAY-sis) Steady state of physiological equilibrium maintained by various bodily mechanisms.
Hormone A bodily chemical transported by body fluids that has an effect on physiological functioning or psychological behavior.
Hospitalism A pattern of deep depression observed in institutionalized infants; marked by weeping and sadness and a lack of normal response to other humans.
Hue That property of color represented by its classification into basic categories of red, orange, yellow, green, blue, indigo, and violet or intermediaries of these.
Humanism An approach to psychology that focuses on human experience, problems, potentials, or ideals.
Hydrocephaly (HI-dro-SEF-ah-lee) A type of mental retardation caused by accumulation of cerebrospinal fluid within the brain.
Hyperactivity A behavioral state characterized by short attention span, restless movement, and impaired learning capacity. Sometimes referred to as minimal brain dysfunction (MBD).
Hyperopia (HI-per-OH-pea-ah) A visual defect causing farsightedness.
Hypnogogic images (hip-no-GAH-jik) Unusually vivid mental imagery associated with hypnosis, the period immediately preceding sleep, and other unusual states of consciousness.
Hypnosis An altered state of consciousness characterized by relaxation, focused attention, and increased susceptibility to suggestion.
Hypochondria (HI-po-KON-dree-ah) An excessive preoccupation with minor bodily problems or complaints about illnesses that seem to be imaginary.
Hypoglycemia (HI-po-gly-SEE-me-ah) Below-normal blood sugar level.
Hypothalamus (HI-po-THAL-ah-mus) A small area at the base of the brain that regulates many aspects of motivation and emotion, particularly hunger, thirst, and sexual behavior.
Hypothesis (hi-POTH-eh-sis) The predicted outcome of an experiment or an educated guess about the relationship between variables.
Hysteria (his-TAIR-ee-ah) Wild emotional excitability sometimes associated with the development of apparent physical disabilities (numbness, blindness, and so forth) without known physical cause.

Icon (EYE-con) A mental image or representation.
Id According to Freud, the most primitive part of the personality, which supplies energy and which demands immediate gratification of needs, drives, and desires.
Identical twins Twins who develop from the same egg and who, therefore, have an identical hereditary makeup. (See *fraternal twins.*)
Identification A process in personality development in which a person becomes like an admired adult by incorporating the adult's goals and values into his or her own behavior. Also used as a defense mechanism in adulthood.
Illusion In perception, an unreal or misleading impression presented to vision or other senses; thus, a perception that fails to give a true representation of the stimulus. (Compare with *hallucination.*)
Implicit trial and error In problem solving, the internal elimination (by covert trial and error) of wrong solutions.
Imprinting A rapid and relatively permanent type of learning that occurs within a limited period of time early in life.
Incentive A goal object valued by an individual that can be employed to motivate behavior.
Incentive value The value a goal holds for a person or animal above and beyond its ability to fill a need.
Independent variable In a controlled experiment, the condition under investigation as a potential cause of some change in behavior; the variable manipulated (changed) by the experimenter. (See *dependent variable.*)
Inductive thought A type of thinking in which one is given a series of specific examples and must infer from them a general rule. (Compare with *deductive thought.*)
Industrial psychology The application of psychology to work, especially to personnel selection, human relations, and machine design.
Innate Inborn or hereditary traits.
Insanity Mental disability resulting in an inability to manage one's affairs or to be aware of the consequences of one's actions. Legally, persons declared insane may not be held fully responsible for their actions.
Insight A sudden reorganization of the elements of a problem causing the solution to become self-evident. Also, one's understanding of one's own behavior or motives.
Insomnia A consistent or prolonged inability to sleep; insufficient sleep or poor quality sleep.
Instinct Complex unlearned behaviors that are species-specific and relatively uniform.
Instrumental conditioning Learning brought about when voluntary responses are affected by their consequences, as when an animal learns its way through a maze to get food; specifically, the effects of positve and negative reinforcement, nonreinforcement, and punishment.
Intellectualization A psychological defense mechanism in which anxiety or emotion is removed from a situation by thinking or speaking of the situation in very formal or abstract terms.
Intelligence quotient (IQ) An index of intelligence defined as a person's mental age divided by his or her chronological age and multiplied by 100.
Interference theory The theory of forgetting that holds that previously learned materials interfere with the storage of new material or that the recall of previous learning is prevented by recent learning.
Intermittent reinforcement Reinforcement occurring irregularly or unexpectedly (partial reinforcement).
Intrauterine environment (IN-tra-YOOT-uh-run) The chemical and physical environment existing in the womb before birth.
Intrinsic motivation Motivation that comes from within, rather than from the presence of external rewards; the motivation that derives from enjoyment of a task or activity.
Introspection (IN-tro-SPEK-shun) A psychological technique used to examine one's own conscious experience; self-observation of one's thoughts, feelings, and sensations.
Introvert (IN-truh-vert) An individual who prefers being alone, who withdraws from social contact, or who is self-centered. (Compare *extrovert.*)
Iris Colored circular muscle of the eye that opens and closes to admit more or less light into the eye.

Isolation A psychological defense involving the separation of contradictory feelings or ideas in "logic-tight" compartments.

Just noticeable difference The amount of increase or decrease in a stimulus that can be reliably detected as a change in amount, value, or intensity.

Kinesics (kih-NEE-siks) The study of the meaning of body movements, posture, hand gestures, and facial expressions.

Kinesthesis (KIN-es-THEE-sus) The sense of one's own bodily position, muscle movement, or equilibrium.

Latency (LATE-un-see) In Freudian theory, the period from age 6 until puberty characterized as a quiet interruption of psychosexual development.

Latent learning Learning that occurs without obvious reinforcement and that is not apparent until reinforcement is provided.

Lateralization Refers to the concentration of specific mental functions or abilities on one side of the brain or the other.

Learned helplessness A learned inability to overcome environmental obstacles or to avoid punishment.

Learning In general, any relatively permanent change in behavior that can be attributed to experience but not to such factors as fatigue, maturation, injury, and so forth.

Learning set A readiness for learning a task or mastering a problem established by prior learning of similar tasks or solution of similar problems.

Lens A transparent structure at the front of the eye that focuses images on the retina.

Libido (lih-BEE-doe) In Freudian terminology, the sexual energy involved in the functioning of personality; primarily sexual in nature.

Limbic system A collection of interconnected brain structures whose functions include smell and emotional reactions.

Linguistic determinism Hypothesis proposed by Whorf that the language one speaks shapes one's perception of reality and influences one's thought.

Localization of function The theory that particular psychological functions are represented by particular parts of the brain.

Logotherapy (LO-go-therapy) Therapy that emphasizes the need to find meaning in life.

Long-term memory Memory of events for relatively long periods, usually presumed to be based on permanent storage of information transferred from short-term memory. (See also *short-term memory*.)

Major affective disorders Psychotic disorders marked by lasting extremes of mood or emotion.

Major depression A severe and lasting depression accompanied by the symptoms of psychosis.

Major tranquilizers Drugs that in addition to having tranquilizing properties also serve as antipsychotics by reducing hallucinations, sensory distortions, and delusional thinking. (Compare with *minor tranquilizers*.)

Manic Extremely excited, hyperactive, or irritable.

Manic-depressive psychosis A psychosis in which a persons' moods swing from elation or excitement to deep depression. (See *psychosis*.)

Mantra A flowing word or sound repeated silently to oneself as the focus of attention in meditation.

Masochism (MAS-oh-kizm) Deriving sexual gratification from pain inflicted on oneself by others.

Massed practice Continuous practice without rest periods or interruption, as distinct from distributed practice.

Mass media Major channels of public communication and information flow, such as radio, television, newspapers, magazines.

Masturbation Erotic stimulation of the genitals other than by intercourse, usually resulting in orgasm.

Maternal influences The aggregate of all psychological effects mothers have on their children. (See *paternal influences*.)

Maturation The emergence and development of personal characteristics in an orderly sequence as a result of underlying physical growth.

Meditation A contemplative exercise for the production of relaxation, heightened awareness, or spiritual revelation.

Memory The mental capacity for storing, organizing, and recovering information.

Menarche (MEN-ar-kee) The onset of menstruation; a woman's first period.

Menopause (MEN-oh-paws) In females, the time during middle age when regular monthly menstrual periods end. (See also *climacteric*.)

Mental age An indication of mental ability defined in terms of the average capabilities of individuals at each age; that is, mental ability apart from actual age in years.

Mental retardation The presence of a developmental disability; a formal IQ score below 70; or a significant impairment of adaptive behavior.

Mescaline (MES-kuh-lin) A psychoactive drug derived from the peyote cactus that has properties similar to LSD.

Mesmerize An archaic term for hypnotize.

Metabolism (meh-TAB-oh-lizm) The rate of energy production and expenditure in the body.

Microcephaly (MY-kro-CEF-ah-lee) A type of mental retardation characterized by a very small skull that prevents normal brain development.

Microsleep A momentary shift in brain wave patterns to those of sleep.

Minimal brain dysfunction A condition of brain immaturity believed by some to underlie hyperactivity in children. (See *hyperactivity*.)

Minor tranquilizers Drugs capable of producing relaxation or a reduction of general tension or activation, and those that have an antianxiety property such as Valium. (Compare with *major tranquilizers*.)

MMPI (Minnesota Multiphasic Personality Inventory) The most widely used self-rating personality test.

Mnemonic device (nee-MON-ik or ni-MON-ik) Any technique or strategy to assist remembering.

Model A system of ideas and concepts designed to interrelate known facts and to provide an explanatory system.

Modeling A type of imitation in which an individual mimics behavior performed by another person (the model).

Monocular (mah-NOCK-you-ler) Pertaining to the function of one eye. For example, monocular cues for depth perception are those involving the use of only one eye.

Morphemes (MORE-feems) The smallest meaningful units in a language.

Motive A drive or force within the organism that activates behavior or directs it toward a goal.

Motor neuron An efferent neuron that carries motor commands from the central nervous system to muscles and glands. (See *efferent*; *neurons*.)

Motor program A mental representation or model of a skilled movement; similar in some ways to a computer program.
Motor skills Learned skills having an element of physical dexterity or requiring the coordination of muscular movements.
Multiple personality A rare form of emotional disturbance in which an individual maintains two or more distinct personalities; formally classified as a dissociative reaction.
Myoclonus (MY-ahk-luh-nus) Reflex contractions of muscles, causing a jerking motion.
Myopia (my-OH-pea-ah) A visual defect making it difficult to focus distant objects (nearsightedness).

Narcolepsy (NAR-co-lep-see) A serious sleep disturbance in which the individual suffers uncontrollable sleep attacks, which can occur even when the person is standing or driving.
Natural selection Charles Darwin's theory that evolution favors the survival of those plants and animals best adjusted to the conditions under which they live (survival of the fittest).
Naturalistic observation Observation and recording of naturally occurring behavior that is not manipulated experimentally.
Need In motivational theory, a specific state within the organism that may elicit behavior appropriate to the need (often related to the depletion of essential bodily substances or the disruption of homeostasis).
Negative practice The deliberate repetition of an unwanted response until it becomes aversive or painful.
Negative reinforcement Increasing the probability of a response by terminating or withdrawing an unpleasant stimulus on completion of the response.
Negative transfer A carryover of skills or responses from one task to another when such carryover impairs performance on the second task. (Compare *positive transfer.*)
Neo-Freudians (NEE-oh-Freudians) Personality theorists who accept the broad features of Freud's psychodynamic approach but who have revised his theory to fit their own concepts.
Neonate (NEE-oh-nate) The human newborn.
Nervous system A network of neurons that interconnects sensory receptors and effector organs to produce behavior and conscious experience.
Neurilemma (NEW-rih-LEM-ah) A thin layer of cells wrapped around the axons of some neurons.
Neurons Individual nerve cells that form the basic structure of the nervous system.
Neurosis (new-ROW-sis) A behavior disturbance primarily characterized by excessive anxiety, minor distortions of reality, and subjective discomfort. The term is now considered outdated.
Neuropeptides (NEW-roh-PEP-tides) A newly discovered class of brain chemicals consisting of simple proteins capable of a wide range of effects on moods and behavior.
Neurotransmitter (NEW-roh-transmitter) Any one of a number of chemical substances secreted by neurons, which cross the synapse and alter activity in the receiving neuron.
Night blindness A condition in which vision becomes impaired in low levels of illumination.
Nondirective therapy (See *client-centered therapy.*)
Nonhomeostatic Not subject to the maintenance of homeostatic balance. (See *homeostasis.*)
Nonsense syllable A meaningless syllable usually consisting of a consonant, a vowel, and a consonant; used in experiments on retention and memory.
Noradrenaline (NOR-ah-DREN-ah-lin) A neurotransmitter secreted by neurons of the sympathetic nervous system; also produced at various locations within the brain. Increased noradrenaline output is associated with anger.
Normal curve A bell-shaped curve having known mathematical properties and characterized by a large number of scores in the middle, tapering toward very few extremely high and low scores at either end.
Norms Accepted social rules for behavior to which the individual members of a group tend to conform.
NREM sleep Sleep periods during which there is a minimum of eye movement and little or no dreaming.
Nystagmus (nis-TAG-mus) Involuntary vibration or movement of the eyeball, including tiny oscillations (physiological nystagmus) and larger reflex movements seen in the blind.

Object constancy Tendency to perceive objects in the same way even when one's view of them changes.
Object permanence Recognition that objects continue to exist when they cannot be seen. Very young children appear to believe that objects cease to exist when the objects are out of sight.
Obsessions Recurring irrational or disturbing thoughts a person cannot prevent.
Obsessive-compulsive disorder Extreme preoccupation with certain thoughts and compulsive performance of certain behaviors, both of which occur in ritualistic or unavoidable fashion.
Oedipus conflict (ED-ih-pus) A Freudian concept referring to a boy's sexual attachment to his mother. (See *Electra conflict.*)
Olfaction (ol-FAK-shun) The sense of smell.
Operant conditioning (OP-er-unt) Type of learning that occurs when an organism "operates" on the environment. The consequences of a response affect its probability of recurrence.
Operational definition Definition of a concept or variable that specifies the operations (actions or procedures) used to measure the concept or manipulate the variable.
Optic nerve The large nerve carrying visual impulses from each eye to the brain.
Oral stage The Freudian stage of psychosexual development in which the individual is preoccupied with his or her mouth. (See also *anal stage; genital stage; phallic stage.*)
Organic mental disorder A mental or emotional problem caused by clearly identifiable physiological or genetic factors.
Organismic valuing (or-gan-IS-mik) The process of evaluating events on the basis of spontaneous personal reaction rather than by reference to learned systems of values.
Orgasm A climax and release of sexual excitement.
Orientation response The pattern of changes occurring throughout the body that prepares an organism to receive information from a particular stimulus.
Ovaries Female sex organs that produce hormones and ova (eggs).
Overlearning Practice that is continued beyond the point of mere mastery of memorized material or of a skill.

Palmistry (PALM-is-tree) A false system that claims to be able to identify personality traits or to predict the future by analyzing the lines on the palms of the hand.
Panic disorder Persistently high levels of anxiety coupled with sudden episodes of intense, but unfocused, panic.

Paradoxical sleep A sleep pattern in which the individual produces an EEG record similar to Stage 1 sleep, or even to waking, yet remains behaviorally asleep (and typically dreaming).
Paranoia (pair-ih-NOY-yah) A psychotic state characterized by delusions of persecution or grandeur.
Paranoid schizophrenia (PAIR-ih-noid SKIT-suh-FREE-nee-ah) A psychosis characterized by delusions of persecution or grandeur and accompanied by severe disturbances of thought and emotion. (See *psychosis.*)
Paraprofessional An individual who works in a near-professional capacity under the supervision of a more highly trained person.
Parapsychology (PAIR-ah-sie-COLL-uh-jee) The scientific study of extranormal psychological events; for example, extrasensory perception.
Parasympathetic nervous system (PAIR-ah-sim-pah-THET-ik) The division of the autonomic nervous system associated with production of relaxation, bodily deactivation, and conservation of energy.
Partial reinforcement Reinforcement administered only after a portion of the total responses in a particular situation (also called intermittent reinforcement).
Partial reinforcement effect A greater resistance to extinction observed in responses acquired on a schedule of partial reinforcement (responses rewarded on only a portion of their occurrences).
Paternal influences The aggregate of all psychological effects fathers have on their children. (See *maternal influences.*)
Pedophilia Sex with children; child molesting.
Peer group A group of people of one's own age and of equal or similar background.
Perception The process of meaningfully organizing sensation.
Peripheral nervous system (peh-RIF-er-al) All portions of the nervous system lying outside the brain and spinal cord, including sensory neurons, motor neurons, the spinal nerves, cranial nerves, skeletal nervous system, and autonomic nervous system.
Peripheral vision Vision at the periphery (edges) of the visual field.
Persona (per-SO-nah) In Jung's system, an archetype representing the "mask" or public self presented to others.
Personality An individual's unique and enduring traits and psychological characteristics and the dynamic relationship among them. (See *traits.*)
Personality disorder Disturbances involving maladaptive and long-standing distortions of personality characteristics.
Personality types Systems of personality description employing only a few categories, with each category representing a collection of related traits. (See *traits.*)
Personnel psychology Branch of industrial/organizational psychology concerned with testing, selection, placement, and promotion of employees.
PET scan Positron emission tomography; the colored image of brain areas and their activity produced by the scanning process.
Phallic stage (FAL-ik) The Freudian developmental stage in which the individual is preoccupied with pleasure derived from the genital organs. (See also *anal stage; genital stage; oral stage.*)
Phenomenal field (fi-NOM-un-ul) One's complete field of subjective awareness.
Phenylketonuria (PKU) (FEN-ul-KEET-un-YURE-ee-ah or FEEN-ul-KEET-un-YURE-ee-ah) A metabolic disorder causing the accumulation of phenylalanine in the body and leading to mental retardation.
Phi phenomenon (FIE fi-NOM-uh-non) The apparent movement of two stationary lights caused when they are lighted in quick succession.
Phobia (FOE-bee-ah) An intense and unrealistic fear of some specific object or situation.
Phobic disorder (FOE-bik) A type of anxiety disorder in which irrational fears predominate.
Phonemes (FOE-neems) The basic sounds of a language that can be distinguished from one another.
Phosphene (FOSS-feen) A luminous visual impression caused by activation of the retina by any means, including pressure and electrical stimulation.
Photoreceptors Sensory receptors sensitive to light and specialized for transforming light waves into neural impulses.
Phrenology (freh-NOL-oh-jee) A false system that holds that the shape of the skull indicates mental faculties or personal characteristics.
Physiological psychologist A psychologist who studies the relationship between the nervous system and behavior.
Pica (PIE-kah) A craving for unnatural foods or substances such as chalk, ashes, and so forth.
Pitch Psychological experience of high or low tones corresponding to the physical dimension of frequency.
Placebo (pla-SEE-bo) An inactive substance given in the place of a drug in psychological research or by physicians who wish to treat chronic aches and pains by suggestion.
Placebo effect Changes in behavior due to one's expectations that a drug (or other treatment) will have some effect.
Polygenetic Any physical or behavioral trait influenced by three or more (often many) genes.
Polygraph An instrument for recording several measures of bodily activity simultaneously; commonly used to refer to the records of emotional response made by a "lie detector."
Population An entire defined group, all members of a class or set from which a smaller sample may be drawn. (See *sample.*)
Positive reinforcement Rewards or stimuli that increase the probability of a response they have followed.
Positive transfer The carryover of skills or responses from one task to another when such carryover improves performance on the second task. (Compare *negative transfer.*)
Post-traumatic stress disorder Psychological and emotional disturbance following exposure to stresses outside the range of normal human experience, such as natural disasters and military combat.
Precognition (PREE-kog-nish-un) Literally, knowing beforehand; hence, any foretelling of the future or any prior knowledge of events unknowable by normal means.
Prejudice A negative attitude or prejudgment held against members of a particular group of people. Most often, attitudes held about racial or ethnic groups, but also frequently applied to other groups as well.
Prenatal Events occurring before the birth of a child.
Presbyopia (prez-by-OH-pea-ah) Farsightedness caused by aging.
Pressure In psychological terms, pressure is said to exist when extended vigilance must be maintained, when events must be speeded up, or when a person must work at or near maximum capacity for an extended period.
Primary impotence (IM-pu-tens) In the male, total inability to perform sexually. (See also *secondary impotence.*)
Primary motives Innate motives based on biological needs.
Primary reinforcers Unlearned reinforcers; usually those that satisfy physiological needs.
Primate A member of the family of mammals, including humans, apes, and monkeys.

Proactive inhibition (pro-AK-tiv) Forgetting that occurs when previous learning interferes with more recent learning.
Projection Attributing one's own feelings, shortcomings, or unacceptable impulses to others as a means of defending against anxiety.
Projective tests Psychological tests making use of unstructured stimuli, wherein the subject is presumed to project his or her own thoughts and impulses onto the stimulus.
Proxemics (prox-EM-iks) Systematic study of the human use of space; particularly, interpersonal space in various social settings.
Pseudo-memories (SUE-doe) False memories that a person believes to be true or accurate.
Pseudo-psychologies (SUE-do) False or dubious systems that purport to explain behavior.
Psi events (SEYE events) Paranormal events falling outside the traditional bounds of psychology and science. Includes clairvoyance, telepathy, precognition, psychokinesis, astral projection, out-of-body experiences, and the like.
Psyche (SIE-kee) The mind, mental life, and personality as a whole.
Psychiatrist A medical doctor who has additional training in the diagnosis and treatment of mental illness.
Psychoactive drugs (SIE-co-AK-tiv) Any of a large number of substances (often quite potent) capable of altering sensation, perception, cognition, memory, or other psychological events.
Psychoanalysis (SIE-co-ah-NAL-ih-sis) A Freudian approach to therapy emphasizing free association, dream interpretation, and transference.
Psychoanalyst (SIE-co-AN-ah-list) A mental health professional (usually a medical doctor) trained to practice psychoanalysis.
Psychodrama (SIE-co-DRAH-ma) A technique of psychotherapy in which people act out personal conflicts in the presence of other people who play supporting parts.
Psychodynamic (SIE-co-die-NAM-ik) Pertaining to internal motives, unconscious forces, and other aspects of mental functioning.
Psychokinesis (SIE-co-kih-NEE-sis) The ability to influence physical events by mental activity or the act of exerting mental control over inanimate objects.
Psycholinguist (SIE-co-LING-wist) A psychologist who specializes in the study of language.
Psychologist An individual highly trained in the philosophy, methods, factual knowledge, and theories of psychology; usually has at least a master's degree and frequently a doctorate.
Psychology The scientific study of behavior and conscious experience.
Psychometrics (SIE-co-MET-riks) Specialty that focuses on mental measurement or psychological testing, such as personality and intelligence testing.
Psychopath (SIE-co-path) An individual who appears to make no distinctions between right and wrong and to feel no guilt about destructive or antisocial behavior.
Psychopathology (SIE-co-pah-THOL-ih-jee) Abnormal or maladaptive behavior; literally, mental sickness.
Psychophysics (SIE-co-fiz-iks) The study of the relationship between physical stimuli and the sensations evoked by them in a human observer.
Psychosexual stages (SIE-co-sexual) In Freudian theory, development of the personality according to the following stages: *oral stage, anal stage, phallic stage,* and *genital stage.*
Psychosis (sie-CO-sis) A severe psychological disturbance characterized by withdrawal from reality, by hallucinations and delusions, by disturbed emotions, and often by personality disorganization.
Psychosomatic illnesses (SIE-co-so-MAT-ik) Disorders in which actual physical damage results from psychological stress.
Psychosurgery (SIE-co-surgery) Surgical alterations of the brain designed to bring about certain behavioral or emotional changes; may be performed with traditional surgical instruments or by the removal of brain tissue through use of electrical currents and electrodes.
Psychotherapy (SIE-co-therapy) General term referring to any form of psychological treatment for behavioral disorders; most often used to refer to verbal interaction between the client and a trained mental health professional.
Punishment After a response, the delivery of an event or stimulus that tends to reduce the future probability of that response.
Pupil The dark spot at the front of the eye through which light moves in to reach the retina.
Pupillometrics (PUE-pil-oh-MET-riks) A technique developed by Hess for measuring dilation and constriction of the pupils in response to various stimuli; purportedly a measure of emotional response.

Racism Racial prejudice that has become institutional (that is, reflected in government policy, schools, and so forth) and that is enforced by the existing social power structure.
Random Haphazard and without definite pattern. Random numbers represent a series in which each digit from 0 to 9 has an equal probability of appearing in any particular position.
Randomization The use of random numbers or a random procedure (for example, flipping a coin) to assign subjects to the experimental and control groups in an experiment or a similar situation.
Rarefaction (rare-eh-FAK-shun) In hearing, the spreading or thinning of air molecules between the crests of successive sound waves.
Rational emotive therapy A direct and forceful therapy in which clients learn to abandon irrational and self-defeating behavior and beliefs.
Rationalization Explaining away one's shortcomings in such a way as to avoid responsibility.
Reaction formation A psychological defense mechanism in which an individual controls unconscious anxiety-producing impulses by behaving in exactly the opposite way.
Recall Detailed remembering with a minimum of memory cues.
Recessive gene A gene whose influence will only be expressed when it is paired with a second recessive gene (that is, it cannot be expressed in the presence of a dominant gene). (See *dominant gene.*)
Recitation (RES-ih-TAY-shun) Repeating aloud material that is to be learned as a means for improving memory of the material.
Recognition Memory in which previously learned material is correctly identified as that which has been seen before.
Redintegration (ruh-DIN-tuh-GRAY-shun) The process of inferring or reconstructing an entire complex memory after first observing or remembering only a part of it.
Reference group Any group with which the individual identifies psychologically and uses as a standard for social comparison.
Reflex An automatic response to a stimulus; for example, an eye blink, knee jerk, or dilation of the pupil.
Regression Return to earlier behavior patterns appropriate to a child or younger person, particularly as a response to stress.
Reinforcement Any stimulus that brings about learning or increases the frequency of the response. Often simply a reward.

Reinforcer Any stimulus that reliably increases the frequency or probability of responses it follows.
Relational concept A concept defined by the relationship of one or more dimensions to a second (or other) dimension (for example, "greater than," "above," "equal to"). (Compare with *conjunctive* and *disjunctive* concepts.)
Relearning Learning again something previously learned; used as a measure of memory for prior learning.
Reliability An important characteristic of any test. A test that is reliable gives the same score each time it is administered.
Remission (reh-MISH-un) Disappearance of symptoms of a psychological disorder.
REMs An abbreviation for rapid eye movements characteristic of Stage 1 dream sleep.
REM sleep Rapid-eye-movement sleep corresponding to periods of dreaming.
Replicate To reproduce or repeat, as in duplicating the results of an experiment.
Representative sample A sample of a larger population of subjects or observations that accurately reflects the characteristics of the larger population. Representative samples are frequently achieved by random selection of subjects or observations. (See *randomization* and *sample.*)
Repression Pushing out or barring from consciousness unwanted memories, impulses, or feelings.
Resistance Blocks that occur in psychoanalysis during free association.
Respondent conditioning Another term for classical conditioning. (See *classical conditioning.*)
Response Any muscular action, glandular activity, or other objectively identifiable aspect of behavior.
Retardation Mental capacity significantly below average; traditionally defined as an IQ score below 70.
Retention Storage or memorization of information.
Retina The photosensitive lining at the back of the eye containing rods and cones.
Retrieval Extracting stored information from memory.
Retroactive inhibition (RET-ro-AK-tiv) The interference of new learning with the memory of previously learned material.
Retrograde amnesia (RET-ro-grade) Loss of memory for events that happened before a head injury or other amnesia-producing events.
Rhodopsin (row-DOP-sin) The photosensitive pigment in the rods of the retina. A chemical composed of retinene and opsin that breaks down into retinene and opsin when struck by light.
RNA (ribonucleic acid) A chemical substance similar to DNA and believed to be involved in learning and memory.
Rods Visual receptors in the retina that are responsive to low levels of illumination but that produce only black-white vision. (See *cones.*)
Role Pattern of behavior one is expected to exhibit when occupying a particular position within a group.
Role reversal Taking the role of another person to learn how one's own behavior appears from the other person's perspective.

Sadism (SADE-izm) Deriving erotic satisfaction by the infliction of pain on another; more broadly, love of cruelty.
Sample A subset or portion of a population.
Saturation As applied to colors, saturation refers to colors that are free from the mixture of white, that are very pure, and that represent a concentrated area of the spectrum.
Savings score In testing memory by relearning, the score that is obtained by subtracting the amount of time necessary to remaster material from the amount of time necessary to master it originally.
Scapegoating The act of causing a person or group of people to bear the blame for others or for conditions not of their making; habitual redirection of aggression toward some person or group.
Schedule of reinforcement A rule for determining which response will be reinforced.
Schizophrenia (SKIT-suh-FREE-nee-uh) A form of psychosis characterized by withdrawal from reality, apathy or inappropriate emotion, and, in many cases, delusions and hallucinations.
Schizotypal personality (SKIT-suh-TYPE-al) A serious personality disorder involving withdrawal, odd behavior, and eccentric thought, but lacking the hallucinations and delusions of true schizophrenia.
Scientific method A technique for testing the truth of a proposition through careful measurement and controlled observation.
Secondary elaboration In Freudian dream theory, a tendency to fill in gaps and missing details in the recall or retelling of dreams, thus making dream accounts more logical and organized.
Secondary impotence (IM-pu-tens) In the male, unsatisfactory sexual performance caused by premature ejaculation. (See also *primary impotence.*)
Secondary motives Motives based on learned psychological needs.
Secondary reinforcement A previously neutral stimulus that acquires reinforcement value through association with primary reinforcers. (See also *primary reinforcers.*)
Sedative A drug that tends to calm, tranquilize, or to encourage sleep.
Self-actualization The full development of personal potential, especially emotional potential.
Self-disclosure The process of revealing private thoughts, feelings, and personal history to others.
Self-image Total subjective perception of oneself, including an image of one's body and perceptions of one's personality, capabilities, and so forth.
Semantics The study of meanings in language.
Semantic memory A hypothetical "mental dictionary" of basic facts and knowledge said to be a subpart of long term memory.
Senile dementia Serious mental impairment in old age caused by physical deterioration of the brain.
Sensation The immediate response to stimulation of the sensory receptors and the transduction of environmental or internal events into neural response.
Sensitivity group A group experience consisting of exercises designed to increase self-awareness and sensitivity to others.
Sensory adaptation A reduction in sensory responses to any unchanging form of stimulation.
Sensory memory The first stage in memory storage that holds detailed and literal images of incoming information for a half-second or less.
Sensory neuron An afferent neuron that carries sensory information toward the brain or central nervous system.
Separation anxiety Distress displayed by infants when they are separated from their parents or principal caretakers.
Serial position effect The tendency for the greatest number of memory errors to occur for the middle portions of an ordered list.
Set A predisposition to respond in a certain way.
Set point A theoretical proportion of body fat that tends to be maintained by alterations in hunger and eating.

Sexism Prejudice and discrimination based on gender, particularly that which is reflected in existing social power structures, but also in more subtle attitudes and actions.
Sex roles Learned behavior that fits societal expectations of proper behavior for males and females.
Shaping Gradual molding of responses to a final desired behavior by reinforcing successive approximations of the behavior.
Short-term memory (STM) The retention of information for brief periods without rehearsal, the first step in the creation of permanent memories. (See also *long-term memory*.)
Skin senses The senses of touch, pressure, pain, heat, and cold.
Social comparison Making judgments about ourselves through comparison with others.
Social learning theory An approach that combines learning principles with cognitive processes (perception, thinking, anticipation), plus the effects of observational learning, to explain behavior.
Social influence Changes in a person's behavior induced by the presence or actions of others.
Social motives Learned motives that are acquired as part of growing up in a particular society or culture.
Socialization The process of learning to live in a particular culture by adopting socially acceptable behavior.
Social psychologist A psychologist particularly interested in the effects of other people on individual behavior.
Sociopath Another name for the psychopath or antisocial personality. (See *psychopath*.)
Soma (SO-ma) The body of any living cell, particularly the body of a nerve cell (neuron).
Somatic therapy (so-MAT-ik) Any therapy directly involving bodily processes; for example, drug therapy, electroconvulsive therapy, psychosurgery, and so forth.
Somatoform disorders (so-MAT-oh-form) A class of disturbances characterized by exaggerated bodily complaints (hypochondria) or by the presence of physical disability without apparent cause.
Somesthetic (som-es-THET-ik) Pertaining to sensations produced in the skin, muscles, joints, and viscera.
Somnambulism (som-NAM-bue-lizm) The formal term for sleepwalking.
Spaced practice Learning trials or practice sessions spread over an extended period of time and including a number of rest periods.
Species A classification comprising closely related plants or animals potentially able to breed with one another.
Species-specific behavior Patterned behavior that is exhibited by all normal members of a particular species. (See also *species*.)
Specific hunger A heightened desire for, or consumption of, a particular food item, especially one that remedies a nutritional deficiency.
Spontaneous recovery The sudden reappearance of a learned response after apparent extinction.
Spontaneous remission In psychiatry or clinical psychology, the spontaneous disappearance of psychological symptoms or behavioral disturbances (for example, clients placed on waiting lists sometimes improve at the same rate as those accepted into therapy).
Sports psychology A specialty that combines study of sports skills with clinical techniques to enhance sports performance and the benefits of sports participation.
Status An individual's position in a group or social system.
Stereoscopic vision The seeing of objects as three-dimensional and the perception of space made possible chiefly by the separation of the eyes.
Stereotype An inaccurate or oversimplified image of the traits of individuals who belong to a particular social group.
Stereotyped response A rigid, repetitive, and nonproductive response made mechanically and without regard for its appropriateness.
Stimulant A substance that produces temporary excitation of the body and/or nervous system.
Stimulus Any physical energy that has some effect on an organism and that evokes a response.
Stimulus generalization The tendency to make a learned response to stimuli similar to the stimulus an organism was originally conditioned to respond to.
Stimulus motives Innate needs for stimulation and information.
Stress A condition in which an organism is subjected to external conditions to which it must adjust or adapt.
Stroboscopic movement (strobe-oh-SKOP-ik) An illusion of movement caused by the rapid presentation of a series of photographs or other representations of phases of a continuous movement. More commonly, the illusion of movement created by cartoon animation and by movie films.
Structuralism (STRUK-chur-al-izm) An early school of thought in psychology that tried to analyze sensations and to break down subjective experience into its basic building blocks.
Sublimation (SUB-lih-may-shun) A psychological defense mechanism involving the expression of socially unacceptable impulses in a socially acceptable way; for example, converting greed into a successful business career.
Subliminal (sub-LIM-ih-nal) Perception of a stimulus that is presented below the threshold for conscious recognition.
Superego (super-EE-go) In Freud's theory of personality, the representation of parental values and the rules of society; basically, the unit that acts as the conscience.
Superordinate goals (super-ORD-ih-nate) Goals that exceed or override all others; goals that render other goals relatively less important.
Survey method The use of public polling techniques to answer psychological questions.
Syllogism (SIL-oh-jizm) A logical format for reasoning consisting of a major premise, a minor premise, and a conclusion.
Symbolization In dream imagery, the tendency for images to stand for or suggest something else by reason of similarity, relationship, appearance, or unconscious association.
Sympathetic nervous system A division of the autonomic nervous system responsible for activating the body at times of emotion or stress by speeding up energy consumption and preparing the body for action.
Synapse (SIN-aps) The microscopic space over which nerve impulses travel in the junction of two neurons.
Synesthesia (sin-es-THEE-zyah) Experiencing one sensory modality in terms of another, for example, "seeing" sounds as colors.
Synesthete (sin-es-THEET) A person who regularly experiences synesthesia. (See *synesthesia*.)
Syntax The study of the word order used in the formation of phrases, clauses, and sentences.

Tachistoscope (tuh-KIS-toh-scope) A mechanical device capable of flashing words or pictures on a screen for very short periods of time; used in perceptual testing, especially in studies of subliminal perception.

Taste aversion An active dislike for a particular food frequently when the food is associated with sickness or discomfort. (See *bait shyness.*)
Telepathy (teh-LEP-ah-thee) A purported form of extrasensory perception in which thoughts are transferred from a sender to a receiver without direct contact. (See *extrasensory perception.*)
Telodendria (tel-oh-DEN-dree-ah) A branching network of fibers at the end of the axon in nerve cells that forms multiple synapses with other neurons.
Temperament The physical foundation of personality including such things as prevailing mood, sensitivity, energy levels, and so forth.
Terminal decline A significant decline in mental capacity observed before death and in some cases anticipating the occurrence of death.
Testes The male sex organs, located in the scrotum; the source of sperm and male sex hormones.
Testosterone (tes-TOS-ter-own) Male sex hormone responsible for the development of secondary sexual characteristics.
Thanatologist (THAN-ah-TOL-oh-jist) One who studies death and the process of dying.
Theory A system of ideas and concepts designed to set forth and interrelate concepts and facts in a way that summarizes existing data and predicts future observations.
Timbre (TIM-ber) The psychological aspect of sound that corresponds to the complexity of a tone.
Tinnitus (tin-NYE-tus) A ringing or whistling sensation in the ears due to disease, injury, drugs or unknown causes.
Tip-of-the-tongue phenomenon The experience of feeling that a memory is available but being unable to retrieve it.
Tolerance A condition in drug addiction brought about by the body's ability to withstand increased amounts of the drug. As tolerance develops, the dosage must be increased to produce the same reaction a smaller dosage once produced.
Traits (personality) Enduring attitudes and personal qualities that an individual tends to display in most life situations.
Transactional analysis (TA) A therapeutic technique designed to improve awareness of one's transactions (interchanges) with others.
Transduction Changing one form of energy into another.
Transference Refers to the tendency of a patient to transfer feelings to the therapist that correspond to feelings held toward important figures in the patient's past.
Trepanning (treh-PAN-ing) In modern usage, any surgical procedure in which a hole is bored into the skull. Historically, the chipping or boring of holes in the skull by primitive people as a means of treating mental disturbances.
Trichromatic color theory (TRY-kroe-MAT-ik) Theory of color vision that states that there are three types of cones, each type maximally sensitive to either red, green, or blue.

Unconditioned response In classical conditioning, the unlearned response that is innately elicited by the unconditioned stimulus; usually a reflex response.
Unconditioned stimulus A stimulus innately capable of eliciting a response.
Unconscious (un-KON-shus) That part of a person's mind or personality that contains impulses and desires not directly known to the person.
Unipolar disorder An emotional disorder in which a person experiences extended periods of deep depression but has no history of ever having been manic.

Vacillation (VAS-ih-LAY-shun) Wavering in aim or action, especially in conflict situations.
Validity The ability of a test to measure what it purports to measure.
Variable interval schedule A schedule of reinforcement that varies the time period between reinforcements.
Variable ratio schedule A schedule in which the number of responses required to produce reinforcement varies.
Vestibular senses (ves-TIB-you-ler) Concerned with balance or equilibrium, senses that are produced by the semicircular canals located close to the inner ear.
Vicarious conditioning (vic-CARE-ee-us) The establishment of a conditioned response (often an emotional response) by observing the reactions of another person to a particular stimulus.
Visual acuity The clarity of visual perception.
Vocational interest test A paper-and-pencil test that assesses a person's interests and matches them to interests found among successful workers in various occupations.

White noise An auditory stimulus that is made up of all audible frequencies of sound and that sounds like a hiss or a waterfall.

References

Aarons, L. (1976). Sleep-assisted instruction. *Psychological Bulletin, 83,* 1–40.

Abrams, A. (1983, January 7). Honda Ohio plant transplants Japan methods, harmony. *Los Angeles Times,* Part IV, pp. 1, 2.

Adams, J. A. (1967). *Human memory.* New York: McGraw-Hill.

Adams J. A. (1980). *Learning and memory.* Homewood, IL: Dorsey Press.

Adler, C. S., & Adler, S. M. (1976). Biofeedback—psychotherapy for the treatment of headaches: A 5-year follow-up. *Headache, 16,* 189–191.

Adorno, T. W., Frenkel-Brunswik, E., Levinson, D. J., & Sanford, R. N. (1950). *The authoritarian personality.* New York: Harper.

Ahles, T. A., Blanchard, E. B., & Leventhal, H. (1983). Cognitive control of pain: Attention to the sensory aspects of the cold pressor stimulus. *Cognitive Therapy and Research, 7,* 159–178.

Ainsworth, M. D. S. (1979). Infant-mother attachment. *American Psychologist, 34,* 932–937.

Akerstedt, T., Torsvall, L., & Gillberg, M. (1982). Sleepiness and shift work: Field studies. *Sleep, 5,* S95–S106.

Albert, E. M. (1963). The roles of women: Question of values. In Farber & Wilson (Eds.), *The potential of women.* New York: McGraw-Hill.

Alberti, R., & Emmons, M. (1978). *Your perfect right.* San Luis Obispo, CA: Impact.

Alcock, J. E. (1981). *Parapsychology, science or magic?* New York: Pergamon.

Alevizos, P. N., & Callahan, E. J. (1977). Assessment of psychotic behavior. In A. R. Ciminero, K. S. Calhoun, & H. E. Adams (Eds.), *Handbook of behavioral assessment.* New York: Wiley.

Allen, B. (1979). Winged victory of "Gossamer Albatross." *National Geographic, 156,* pp. 642–651.

Alloy, L. B., Peterson, C., Abramson, L. Y., & Seligman, M. E. (1984). Attributional style and the generality of learned helplessness. *Journal of Personality and Social Psychology, 46,* 681–687.

Allport, G. W. (1958). *The nature of prejudice.* Garden City, NY: Anchor Books, Doubleday.

Allport, G. W. (1961). *Pattern and growth in personality.* New York: Holt, Rinehart & Winston.

Allport, G. W., & Odbert, H. S. (1936). Trait-names: A psycholexical study. *Psychological Monographs,* 221.

Alvino, J., & the Editors of Gifted Children Monthly. (1985). *Parents' Guide to Raising a Gifted Child.* Boston: Little, Brown.

Amabile, T. M. (1983). *The social psychology of creativity.* New York: Springer-Verlag.

Amabile, T. M. (1985). Motivation and creativity: Effects of motivational orientation on creative writers. *Journal of Personality and Social Psychology, 48,* 393–397.

American Medical Association, Department of Mental Health. (1968). The crutch that cripples: Drug dependence, Part I. *Today's Health,* 46(9), pp. 11–12, 70–72.

American Psychiatric Association. (1980). *Diagnostic and statistical manual of mental disorders* (3rd ed.). Washington, DC: Author.

Anand, B. K., & Brobeck, J. R. (1951). Hypothalamic control of food intake in rats and cats. *Yale Journal of Biological Medicine,* 123–140.

Anastasi, A., & Foley, J. P., Jr. (1958). *Differential psychology* (3rd ed.). New York: Macmillan.

Anderson, R. H., Anderson, K., Fleming, D. E., & Kinghorn, E. (1984). A multidimensional test of the attributional reformulation of learned helplessness. *Bulletin of the Psychonomic Society, 22,* 221–213.

Annett, J. (1979). Memory for skill. In M. M. Gruneberg & P. E. Morris (Eds.), *Applied problems in memory.* London: Academic Press.

Apfel, R. E. (1977, November). Resounding facts on hearing loss. *The Science Teacher, 44*(8), 31–34.

Arehart-Treichel, J. (1977, March 26). The science of sleep. *Science News, 111,* 203–208.

Arndt, S., & Berger, D. E. (1978). Cognitive mode and asymmetry in cerebral functioning. *Cortex, 14,* 78–86.

Aronson, E. (1969). Some antecedents of interpersonal attraction. In W. J. Arnold & D. Levine (Eds.). *Nebraska symposium on motivation.* Lincoln: University of Nebraska Press.

Aronson, E. (1972). *The social animal.* San Francisco: Freeman.

Aronson, E. (1980). *The social animal.* San Francisco: Freeman.

Aronson, E., with Blaney, N., Sikes, J., Stephan, C., & Snapp, M. (1979). Busing and racial tension: The jigsaw route to learning and liking. In V. J. Derlega & L. H. Janda (Eds.), *Personal adjustment, selected readings.* Glenview, IL: Scott, Foresman.

Aronson, E., Stephan, C., Sikes, J., Blaney, N., & Snapp, M. (1978). *The jigsaw classroom.* Beverly Hills, CA: Sage.

Asch, S. E. (1956). Studies of independence and conformity: A minority of one against a unanimous majority. *Psychological Monographs,* 70(416).

Asimov, I. (1967). *Is anyone there?* Garden City, NY: Doubleday.

Astronomical Society of the Pacific. (1983). *Astrology and astronomy.* San Francisco: Author.

Athenasiou, R., Shaver, P., & Tavris, C. (1970). Sex. *Psychology Today,* 4(2), pp. 37–52.

Atkinson, R. C., & Shiffrin, R. M. (1971, August). The control of short-term memory. *Scientific American,* pp. 89-90.

Ayllon, T. (1963). Intensive treatment of psychotic behavior by stimulus satiation and food reinforcement. *Behavior Research and Therapy, 1,* 53–61.

Ayllon, T., & Azrin, N. H. (1965). The measurement and reinforcement of behavior of psychotics. *Journal of the Experimental Analysis of Behavior, 8,* 357–383.

Ayllon, T., Haughton, E., & Hughes, H. B. (1965). Interpretation of symptoms: Fact or fiction? *Behavior and Therapy, 3,* 1–7.

Azrin, N. H., Hutchinson, R. R., & McLaughlin, R. (1965). The opportunity for aggression as an operant reinforcer during aversive stimulation. *Journal of Experimental Analysis of Behavior, 8,* 171–180.

Bach, G., & Wyden, P. (1969). *The intimate enemy.* New York: Morrow.

Bachman, J. G., & Johnson, L. D. (1979). The freshmen. *Psychology Today, 13,* pp. 78–87.

Bachrach, L. L. (1984). Asylum and chronically ill psychiatric patients. *American Journal of Psychiatry, 141,* 975–978.

Back, K. W. (1972). The group can comfort but it can't cure. *Psychology Today,* 6(7), pp. 28–35.

Baddeley, A. D. (1976). *The psychology of memory.* New York: Basic Books.

Baddeley, A. D., & Hitch, G. (1974). Working memory. In G. H. Bower (Ed.), *The psychology of learning and motivation,* Vol 8, New York: Academic Press.

Baer, D. M. (1971, October). Let's take another look at punishment. *Psychology Today.*

Ball, G. G., & Grinker, J. A. (1981). Overeating and obesity. In S. J. Mule (Ed.), *Behavior in Excess* (pp. 194–220). New York: Free Press.

Baltes, P. B., & Schaie, K. W. (1974). Aging and I.Q.: The myth of the twilight years. *Psychology Today,* 7(10), pp. 35–40.

Bandura, A. (1965). Vicarious processes: A case of no-trial learning. In L. Berkowitz (Ed.), *Advances in experimental social psychology, Vol.* 2, (pp. 1–55). New York: Academic Press.

Bandura, A. (1971). *Social learning theory.* New York: General Learning Press.

Bandura, A. (1973). *Aggression: A social learning analysis.* Englewood Cliffs, NJ: Prentice-Hall.

Bandura, A. (1977). Self-efficacy: Toward a unifying theory of behavioral change. *Psychological Review, 84,* 191–215.

Bandura, A., & Rosenthal, T. L. (1966). Vicarious classical conditioning as a function of arousal level. *Journal of Personality and Social Psychology,* 3, 54–62.

Bandura, A., Ross, D., & Ross, S. A. (1963). Vicarious reinforcement and imitative learning. *Journal of Abnormal and Social Psychology,* 67, 601–607.

Bandura, A., & Walters, R. (1959). *Adolescent aggression.* New York: Ronald.

Bandura, A., & Walters, R. (1963). Aggression. In H. W. Stevenson (Ed.), *Child psychology.* Chicago: Universtiy of Chicago Press.

Bandura, A., & Walters, R. (1963). *Social learning and personality development.* New York: Holt.

Bank, S. P., & Kahn, M. D. (1982). *The sibling bond.* New York: Basic Books.

Barahal, H. S. (1958). 1000 prefrontal lobotomies: Five to ten year follow-up study. *Psychiatric Quarterly,* 32, 653–678.

Barber, T. X. (1959). Toward a theory of pain: Relief of chronic pain by prefrontal leucotomy, opiates, placebos, and hypnosis. *Psychological Bulletin,* 56, 430–460.

Barber, T. X. (1970). Suggested ("hypnotic") behavior: The trance paradigm versus an alternative paradigm (Report No. 103). Harding, MA: Medfield Foundation.

Barchas, J. D., Elliot, G. R., & Berger, P. A. (1978). Biogenic amine hypothesis of schizophrenia. In L. C. Wynne, R. L. Cromwell, & S. Matthysse (Eds.), *The nature of schizophrenia: New approaches to research and treatment.* New York: Wiley.

Baron, R. A. (1983). "Sweet smell of success"? The impact of pleasant artificial scents on evaluations of job applicants. *Journal of Applied Psychology, 68,* 709–713.

Barron, F. (1958). The psychologv of imagination. *Scientific American, 199*(3), pp. 150–170.

Barrow, G. M., & Smith, P. A. (1979). *Aging, ageism, and society.* St. Paul: West.

Basedow, R. A. (1925). *The Australian aborigine.* Adelaide, Australia: Peerce.

Bassuk, E. L., & Gerson, S. (1978). Deinstitutionalization and mental health services. *Scientific American,* 238(2), pp. 46–53.

Bassuk, E. L., Rubin, L., & Lauriat, A. (1984). Is homelessness a mental health problem? *American Journal of Psychiatry, 141,* 1546–1550.

Baum, A., & Davis, G. E. (1980). Reducing the stress of high-density living: An architectural intervention. *Journal of Personality and Social Psychology,* 38, 471–481.

Baum, A., & Valins, S. (Eds.). (1977). *Human response to crowding: Studies of the effects of residential group size.* Hillsdale NJ: Erlbaum.

Baum, A., & Valins, S. (1979). Architectural mediation of residential density and control: Crowding and the regulation of social contact. *Advances in Experimental and Social Psychology, 12,* 131–175.

Baumrind, D. (1980, July). New directions in socialization research. *American Psychologist,* 35, 639–652.

Beach, F. A. (1975). Behavioral endocrinology: An emerging discipline. *American Scientist, 63,* pp. 178–187.

Beck, A. T. (1985). Cognitive therapy of depression: New perspectives. In P. Clayton (Ed.), *Depression.* New York: Raven.

Beck, A. T., & Greenberg, R. L. (1974). Coping with depression. Institute for Rational Living.

Beck, A. T., Rush, A. J., Shaw, B., & Emery, G. (1979). *Cognitive therapy of depression: A treatment manual.* New York: Gilford Press.

Beck, A. T., & Young, J. E. (1978, September). College blues. *Psychology Today,* pp. 80–92.

Becker, P. (1982). Fear reactions and achievement behavior of students approaching an examination. In H. W. Krohne & L. Laux (Eds.), *Achievement, stress and anxiety* (pp. 275–290). Washington, DC: Hemisphere.

Beebe, B., Gerstman, L., Carson, B., Dolins, M., Zigman, A., Rosensweig, H., Faughey K., & Korman, M. (1982). Rhythmic communication in the mother-infant dyad. In M. Davis (Ed.), *Interaction rhythms, periodicity in communicative behavior.* New York: Human Sciences Press.

Beecher, H. K. (1959). *Measurement of subjective responses: Quantitative effects of drugs.* New York: Oxford University Press.

Been, H., & Sklar, I. (1985). Transference in short-term dynamic psychotherapy. In A. Winston (Ed.), *Short-term dynamic psychotherapy* (pp. 2–18). Washington, DC: American Psychiatric Press.

Beljan, J. R., Rosenblatt, L. S., Hetherington, N. W., Layman, J., Flaim, S. E. T., Dale, G. T., & Holley, D. C. (1972). *Human performance in the aviation environment* (NASA Contract No. 2-6657), Pt. Ia, 253–259.

Bell, A. P., Weinberg, M. S., & Hammersmith, S. K. (1981). *Sexual preference.* Indiana University Press.

Belsky, J., Gilstrap, B., & Rovine, M. (1984). The Pennsylvania infant and family development project, I: Stability and change in mother-infant and father-infant interactions in a family setting at one, three, and nine months. *Child Development,* 55, 692–705.

Belsky, J., Rovine, M., & Taylor, D. G. (1984). The Pennsylvania infant and family development project, III: The origins of individual differences in infant-mother attachment: Maternal and infant contributions. *Child Development*, *55*, 718–728.

Bem, S. L. (1974). The measurement of psychological androgyny. *Journal of Consulting and Clinical Psychology*, *42*, 155–162.

Bem, S. L. (1975a). Sex-role adaptability: One consequence of psychological androgyny. *Journal of Personality and Social Psychology*, *31*, 634–643.

Bem, S. L. (1975b, September). Androgyny vs. the tight little lives of fluffy women and chesty men. *Psychology Today*, pp. 58–62.

Bem, S. L. (1977). Psychological androgyny. In A. G. Sargent (Ed.), *Beyond Sex Roles*. St. Paul: West.

Bem, S. L. (1981). Gender schema theory: A cognitive account of sex typing. *Psychological Review*, *88*, 354–364.

Beneke, W. M., & Harris, M. B. (1972). Teaching self-control of study behavior. *Behavior Research and Therapy*, *10*, 35–41.

Bennett, W., & Gurin, J. (1982). *The dieter's dilemma*. New York: Basic Books.

Benson, H. (1977). Systematic hypertension and the relaxation response. *The New England Journal of Medicine*, *296*, 1152–1156.

Benton, A. L. (1980, February). The neuropsychology of facial recognition. *American Psychologist*, *35*, 176–186.

Bergin, A., & Suinn, R. M. (1975). Individual psychotherapy and behavior therapy. *Annual Review of Psychology*, *26*, 509–556.

Berkowitz, L. (1968). The frustration-aggression hypothesis revisited. In L. Berkowitz (Ed.), *Roots of aggression: A re-examination of the frustration-aggression hypothesis*. New York: Atherton Press.

Berkowitz, L. (1982). Aversive conditions as stimuli to aggression. In L. Berkowitz (Ed.), *Advances in experimental social psychology*, *Vol. 15*. New York: Academic Press.

Berkowitz, L. (1984). Some effects of thoughts on anti- and prosocial influences of media events: A cognitive-neoassociation analysis. *Psychological Bulletin*, *95*, 410–427.

Berlyne, D. (1966). Curiosity and exploration. *Science*, *153*, 25–33.

Berman, L. H. (1982). Family therapy. In L. E. Abt & I. R. Stuart (Eds.), *The newer therapies: A sourcebook*. New York: Van Nostrand Reinhold.

Berne, E. (1961). *Transactional analysis in psychotherapy*. New York: Grove Press.

Berne, E. (1964). *Games people play*. New York: Grove Press.

Berry, P., Groeneweg, G., Gibson, D., & Brown, R. I. (1984). Mental development of adults with Down syndrome. *American Journal of Mental Deficiency*, *89*, 252–256.

Bersheid, E., & Walster, E. (1974a). Physical attractiveness. In L. Berkowitz (Ed.), *Advances in experimental social psychology*, *Vol. 7*. New York: Academic Press.

Bersheid, E., & Walster, E. (1974b). A little bit about love. In T. L. Huston (Ed.), *Foundations of interpersonal attraction*. New York: Academic Press.

Bertsch, G. J. (1976). Punishment of consummatory and instrumental behavior: A review. *Psychological Record*, *26*, 13–31.

Bettelheim, B. (1960). *The informed heart*. New York: Free Press.

Beyerstein, B. (1985, Fall). The myth of alpha consciousness. *The Skeptical Inquirer*, *10*, 42–59.

Bickman, L. (1974, April). Clothes make the person. *Psychology Today*.

Biller, H. B. (1982). Fatherhood: Implications for child and adult development. In B. B. Wolman (Ed.), *Handbook of developmental psychology*. Englewood Cliffs, NJ: Prentice-Hall.

Binder, V. (1976). Behavior modification: Operant approaches to therapy. In V. Binder, A. Binder, & B. Rimland (Eds.), *Modern therapies* (pp. 150–165.). Englewood Cliffs, NJ: Prentice-Hall.

Bird, D. (1975). *The case against college*. New York: David McKay.

Blanchard, E., Andrasik, F., Neff, D., Arena, J., Ahles, T., Jurish, S., Pallmayer, T., Saunders, N., Teders, S., Barron, K., & Rodichok, L. (1982). Biofeedback and relaxation training with three kinds of headache: Treatment effects and their prediction. *Journal of Consulting Clinical Psychology*, *50*, 562–576.

Blanchard, E., McCoy, G., Andrasik, F., Acerra, M., Pallmeyer, T., Gerardi, R., Halpern, M., & Musso, A. (1984). Preliminary results from a controlled evaluation of thermal biofeedback as a treatment for essential hypertension. *Biofeedback & Self-Regulation*, *9*, 471–495.

Blanchard, E. B., & Epstein, L. H. (1978). *A biofeedback primer*. Reading, MA: Addison-Wesley.

Blaske, D. M. (1984). Occupational sex-typing by kindergarten and fourth-grade children. *Psychological Reports*, *54*, 795–801.

Block, J. (1979, September). Socialization influence of personality development in males and females. American Psychological Association Master Lecture, Convention of the American Psychological Association, New York.

Bloom, B. (1985). *Developing talent in young people*. New York: Ballantine.

Bloom, B. L., & Parad, H. J. (1977). Professional activity patterns in community mental health centers. In I. Iscoe, B. L. Bloom, & C. D. Spielberger (Eds.), *Community psychology in transition*. Washington, DC: Hemisphere.

Bloom, L., & Lahey, M. (1978). *Language development and language disorders*. New York: Wiley.

Blumenthal, A. L. (1976). *The process of cognition*. Englewood Cliffs, NJ: Prentice-Hall.

Blumenthal, A. L. (1979). The founding father we never knew. *Contemporary Psychology*, *24*, 547–550.

Bock, F. G. (1980). Cocarcinogenic properties of nicotine. In G. B. Gori & F. G. Bock (Eds.), *Banbury report*. Cold Spring Harbor Laboratory.

Boker, J. R. (1974). Immediate and delayed retention effects of interspersing questions in written instructional passages. *Journal of Educational Psychology*, *66*, 96–98.

Bolles, R. C. (1979). *Learning theory* (2nd ed.). New York: Holt, Rinehart & Winston.

Bolton, R. (1976). Hostility in fantasy: A further test of the hypoglycemia-aggression hypothesis. *Aggressive Behavior*, *2*, 257–274.

Bonnet, M. H., & Moore, S. E. (1982). The threshold of sleep: Perception of sleep as a function of time asleep and auditory threshold. *Sleep*, *5*(3), 267–276.

Bootzin, R. (1973, August). *Stimulus control of insomnia*. Paper presented at the meeting of the American Psychological Association, Montreal.

Borkovec, T. D. (1982). Insomnia. *Journal of Consulting and Clinical Psychology*, *50*, 880–895.

Borman, W. C., Eaton, N. K., Bryan, J. D., & Rosse, R. S. (1983). Validity of army recruiter behavioral assessment. Does the assessor make a difference? *Journal of Applied Psychology*, *68*, 415–419.

Bornstein, M. H. (1975). Qualities of color vision in infancy. *Journal of Experimental Child Psychology*, *19*, 401–419.

Botwinick, J. (1984). *Aging and behavior*. New York: Springer.

Bouchard, T. J., Jr. (1983). Twins—Nature's twice-told tale. *Yearbook of science and the future* (pp. 66–81). Chicago: Encyclopedia Britannica.

Bouchard, T. J., Jr., Heston, L., Eckert, E., Keyes, M., & Resnick, S. (1981). The Minnesota study of twins reared apart: Project description and sample results in the developmental domain. In L. Gedda, P. Parisi, & W. E. Nance (Eds.), *Twin research 3, Part B: Intelligence, personality, and development* (pp. 227–233). New York: Liss.

Bower, B. (1984, October 6). Not popular by reason of insanity. *Science News, 126*(14), pp. 218–219.

Bower, G. H. (1973, October). How to . . . uh . . . remember. *Psychology Today*, pp. 63–70.

Bower, G. H. (1981). Mood and memory. *American Psychologist, 36*, 129–148.

Bower, G. H., & Clark, M. C. (1969). Narrative stories as mediators for serial learning. *Psychonomic Science, 14*, 181–182.

Bower, G. H., & Springston, F. (1970). Pauses as recoding points in letter series. *Journal of Experimental Psychology, 83*, 421–430.

Bowlby, J. (1969). *Attachment and loss, Volume I: Attachment*. New York: Basic Books.

Bowlby, J. (1973). *Attachment and loss, Volume II: Separation and anxiety*. New York: Basic Books.

Brackbill, Y. (1979). Obstetrical medication and infant behavior. In J. D. Osofsky (Ed.), *Handbook of infant development*. New York: Wiley.

Braginsky, B. M., & Braginsky, D. D. (1967). Schizophrenic patients in the psychiatric interview: An experimental study of their effectiveness at manipulation. *Journal of Consulting Psychology, 31*, 543–547.

Bransford, J. D., & McCarrell, N. S. (1977). A sketch of cognitive approach to comprehension: Some thoughts about understanding what it means to comprehend. In P. N. Johnson-Laird & P. C. Wason (Eds.), *Thinking: Readings in cognitive science*. Cambridge: Cambridge University Press.

Bray, D. W., Campbell, R. J., & Grant, D. (1974). *Formative years in business: A long-term study of managerial lives*. New York: Wiley.

Brazelton, T. B., Koslowski, B., & Main, M. (1974). The origins of reciprocity: The early mother-infant interaction. In M. Lewis, & L. A. Rosenblum (Eds.), *The effect of the infant on its caregiver*. New York: Wiley Interscience.

Brazelton, T. B., et al. (1975). Early mother-infant reciprocity. In *Parent-infant interaction* (Ciba Foundation Symposium 33). Amsterdam: Associated Scientific Publishers.

Brecher, E. M. (1975a, March). Marijuana: The health questions. *Consumer Reports, 40*, pp. 143–149.

Breier, A., & Strauss, J. S. (1983, October). Self-control in psychotic disorders. *Archives of General Psychiatry, 40*, 1141.

Bresler, D. E., & Trubo, R. (1979). *Free yourself from pain*. New York: Simon & Schuster.

Brewer, J. S. (1981). Duration of intromission and female orgasm rates. *Medical Aspects of Human Sexuality, 15*(4), 70–71.

Bridges, K. M. B. (1932). Emotional development in early infancy. *Child Development, 3*, 324–334.

Brown, A. S. (1974). Satisfying relationships for elderly and their patterns of disengagement. *Gerontologist, 14*, 258–262.

Brown, B. (1980). Perspectives on social stress. In H. Selye (Ed.), *Selye's guide to stress research, Vol. 1*. New York: Van Nostrand Reinhold.

Brown, R., & Kulik, J. (1977). Flashbulb memories. *Cognition, 5*, 73–99.

Brown, R., & McNeill, D. (1966). The "tip of the tongue" phenomenon. *Journal of Verbal Learning and Verbal Behavior, 5*, 325–337.

Browne, M. A., & Mahoney, M. J. (1984). Sports psychology, *Annual Review of Psychology, 35*, 605–625.

Brownell, K. D. (1982). Obesity: Understanding and treating a serious, prevalent, and refractory disorder. *Journal of Consulting and Clinical Psychology, 50*, 820–840.

Brownell, K. D., Marlatt, G. A., Lichtenstein, E., & Wilson, G. T. (1986). Understanding and preventing relapse. *American Psychologist, 41*, 765–782.

Bruch, H. (1973). *Eating disorders*. New York: Basic Books.

Bruner, J. (1983). *Child's Talk*. New York: Norton.

Bruner, J. S. (1968). *Toward a theory of instruction*. New York: Norton.

Bruner, J. S., et al. (1966). *Studies in cognitive growth*. New York: Wiley.

Bryan, J. H., & Test, M. A. (1967). Models and helping: Naturalistic studies in aiding behavior. *Journal of Personality and Social Psychology, 6*, 400–407.

Bryan, J. H., & Walbek, N. H. (1970). Preaching and practicing generosity: Children's actions and reactions. *Child Development, 41*, 329–353.

Buchwald, A. (1965, June 20). Psyching out. *The Washington Post*.

Buckhout, R. (1974, December). Eyewitness testimony. *Scientific American, 231*, pp. 23–31.

Budzynski, T. H. (1977). Biofeedback strategies in headache treatment. In J. V. Basmajian (Ed.), *Biofeedback: A handbook for clinicians*. Baltimore: Williams & Wilkins.

Burka, J. B., & Yuen, L. M. (1983). *Procrastination*. Menlo Park, CA: Addison-Wesley.

Burns, D. D., & Persons, J. (1982). Hope and hopelessness: A cognitive approach. In L. E. Abt & I. R. Stuart (Eds.), *The newer therapies: A sourcebook* (pp. 33–57). New York: Van Nostrand Reinhold.

Bursten, B. (1973). *The manipulator*. New Haven, CT: Yale University Press.

Burtt, H. E. (1941). An experimental study of early childhood memory: Final report. *Journal of General Psychology, 58*, 435–439.

Bushsbaum, M. S., & Haier, R. J. (1983). Psychopathology: Biological approaches. *Annual Review of Psychology, 34*, 401–430.

Buss, A. H. (1980). *Self-consciousness and social anxiety*. San Francisco: Freeman.

Buss, D. M. (1985). Human mate selection. *American Scientist, 73*, 47–51.

Butler, R. (1954). Curiosity in monkeys. *Scientific American, 190*(18), pp. 70–75.

Butler, R., & Harlow, H. F. (1954). Persistence of visual exploration in monkeys. *Journal of Comparative Physiological Psychology, 47*, 258–263.

Byrne, D. (1971). *The attraction paradigm*. New York: Academic Press.

Cabanac, M., & Duclaux, P. (1970). Obesity: Absence of satiety aversion to sucrose. *Science, 168*, 496–497.

Calhoun, J. B. (1962). A "behavioral sink." In E. L. Bliss (Ed.), *Roots of behavior*. New York: Harper & Row.

Campbell, A., Gurin, G., & Miller, W. E. (1954). *The voter decides*. New York: Harper & Row.

Campbell, J. B., & Hawley, C. W. (1982). Study habits and Eysenck's theory of extraversion–introversion. *Journal of Research in Personality, 16*, 139–146.

Campos, J. J., Hiatt, S., Ramsay, D., Henderson, C., & Svejda, M. (1978). The emergence of fear on the visual cliff. In M. Lewis &

L. A. Rosenblum (Eds.), *The development of affect* (pp.149–182). New York: Plenum Press.

Canadian Government's Commission of Inquiry. (1971). *The non-medical use of drugs*. Baltimore: Penguin.

Cannon, J. T., Liebeskind, J. C., & Frenk, H. Neural and neurochemical mechanisms of pain inhibition. In R. A. Sternbach (Ed.), *The psychology of pain*. New York: Raven Press.

Cannon, W. B. (1932). *The wisdom of the body*. New York: Norton.

Cannon, W. B. (1934). Hunger and thirst. In C. Murchinson (Ed.), *Handbook of general experimental psychology*. Worcester, MA: Clark University Press.

Cannon, W. B. (1942). "Voodoo" death. *American Anthropologist*, *44*, 169–181.

Cannon, W. B., & Washburn, A. L. (1912). An exploration of hunger. *American Journal of Physiology*, 29, 441–454.

Caplan, P. J., MacPherson, G. M., & Tobin, P. (1985). Do sex-related differences in spatial abilities exist? A multilevel critique with new data. *American Psychologist*, *40*, 786–799.

Caplan, P. J., MacPherson, G. M., & Tobin, P. (1986). The magnified molehill and the misplaced focus: Sex-related differences in spatial ability revisited. *American Psychologist*, *41*, 1016–1018.

Carducci, B. J., Deeds, W. C., Jones, J. W., Moretti, D. M., Reed, J. G., Saal, F. E., & Wheat, J. E. (1987). Preparing undergraduate psychology students for careers in business. *Teaching of Psychology*, *14*, 16–20.

Carelli, R. (1982, May 31). Insanity: A legal lever that tips justice scales. *Santa Barbara News Press* (Associated Press news article).

Carew, J. V., Chan, I., & Halfor, C. (1976). *Observing intelligence in young children: Eight case studies*. Englewood Cliffs, NJ: Prentice-Hall.

Carlson, N. R. (1981). *Physiology of behavior (2nd ed.)*. Boston: Allyn and Bacon.

Carmen, R., & Adams, W. R. (1985). *Study skills: A student's guide for survival*. New York: Wiley.

Carr, R. R., & Meyers, E. J. (1980). Marijuana and cocaine: The process of change in drug policy. In The Drug Abuse Council, *The facts about "drug abuse"*. New York: Free Press.

Carson, R. C., Butcher, J. N., & Coleman, J. (1988). *Abnormal psychology and modern life* (8th ed.). Glenview, IL: Scott Foresman.

Carter, W. E. (Ed.) (1980). *Cannabis in Costa Rica: A study of chronic marihuana use*. Philadelphia: Institute for the Study of Human Issues.

Cartwright, R. (1969). In M. Kramer (Ed.), *Dream psychology and the new biology of dreaming*. Springfield, IL: Thomas.

Cartwright, R. D. (1978). Sleep and dreams, Part II. *Annual Review of Psychology*, 29, 223–252.

Cartwright, R. D. (1978, December). Happy endings for our dreams. *Psychology Today*, pp. 66–77.

Case, R. B., Heller, S. S., Case, N. B., Moss, A. J., & The Multicenter Post-Infarction Research Group. (1985). Type A behavior and survival after acute myocardial infarction. *New England Journal of Medicine*, *312*(12).

Casler, L. (1965). The effects of extra tactile stimulation on a group of institutionalized infants. *Genetic Psychology Monographs*, *71*, 137–175.

Cattell, R. B. (1965). *The scientific analysis of personality*. Baltimore: Penguin.

Cattell, R. B. (1973, July). Personality pinned down. *Psychology Today*, pp. 40–46.

Cautela, J. (1973). Covert processes and behavior modification. *The Journal of Nervous and Mental Disease*, *157*, 27–36.

Cautela, J. R., & Bennett, A. K. (1981). Covert conditioning. In R. J. Corsini (Ed.), *Handbook of innovative psychotherapies* (pp. 189–204). New York: Wiley.

Chaikin, A. L., & Derlega, V. J. (1974). *Self-disclosure*. Morristown, NJ: General Learning Press.

Challinor, M. E. (1980, December). *Science 80*, p. 27.

Chance, P. (1982, January). Your child's self-esteem. *Parents*.

Chapanis, A., & Lindenbaum, L. E. (1959). "A reaction time study of four control-display linkages. *Human Factors*, *1*, 1–7.

Check, J. V. P., & Malamuth, N. M. (1983). Sex role stereotyping and reactions to depictions of stranger versus acquaintance rape. *Journal of Personality and Social Psychology*, *45*, 344–356.

Cheek, J., & Buss, A. H. (1979). Scales of shyness, sociability, and self-esteem and correlations among them (cited by Buss, 1980). Unpublished research, University of Texas.

Chess, S., Thomas, A. & Birch, H. G. (1965). *Your child is a person: A psychological approach to parenthood without guilt*. New York: Viking.

Chomsky, N. (1968). *Language and mind*. New York: Harcourt Brace Jovanovich.

Chomsky, N. (1975). *Reflections on language*. New York: Pantheon Books.

Cialdini, R. B., Petty, R. E., & Cacippo, T. J. (1981). Attitude and attitude change. *Annual Review of Psychology*, 32, 357–404.

Cialdini, R. B., Vincent, J. E., Lewis, S. K., Catalan, J., Wheeler, D., & Darby, B. L. (1975). A reciprocal concessions procedure for inducing compliance: The door-in-the-face technique. *Journal of Personality and Social Psychology*, *21*, 206–215.

Clark, K. B. (1965). *Dark ghetto*. New York: Harper & Row.

Clarke-Steward, A., & Koch, J. B. (1983). *Children, development through adolescence*. New York: Wiley.

Cleckley, H. (1964). *The mask of sanity* (4th ed.). St. Louis: Mosby.

Cline, V. B., Croft, R. G., & Courrier, S. (1972). Desensitization of children to television violence. *Journal of Personality and Social Psychology*, *27*, 360–365.

Clore, G. L. (1976). Interpersonal attraction: An overview. In *Contemporary topics in social psychology*. Morristown, NJ: General Learning Press.

Coates, D. L., & Lewis, M. (1984). Early mother-infant interaction and infant cognitive status as predictors of school performance and cognitive behavior in six-year-olds. *Child Development*, *55*, 1219–1230.

Cobb, S. (1976). Social support as a moderator of life stresses. *Psychosomatic Medicine*, *38*, 300–314.

Cofer, C. N. (Ed.). (1975). *The structure of human memory*. San Francisco: Freeman.

Cohen, D. (1974). *Intelligence*. New York: Evans.

Cohen, S., Evans, G. W., Krantz, D. S., & Stokols, D. (1981). Cardiovascular and behavioral effects of community noise. *American Scientist*, *69*, 528–535.

Cohen, S. (1977, September). Internal opioid-like compounds. *Drug Abuse and Alcoholism Newsletter*, *6*(7).

Coleman, J., Butcher, J. N., & Carson, R. C. (1984). *Abnormal psychology and modern life* (7th ed.). Glenview, IL: Scott, Foresman.

Coleman, J. C., & Hammen, C. L. (1974). *Contemporary psychology and effective behavior*. Glenview, IL: Scott, Foresman.

Coleman, J. S., Hersberg, J., & Morris, M. (1977). Identity in adolescence: Present and future self-concepts. *Journal of Youth and Adolescence, 6*(1), 63–75.

Collins, A. M., & Quillian, M. R. (1969). Retrieval time from semantic memory. *Journal of Verbal Learning and Verbal Behavior, 8,* 240–247.

Collins, J. J. (1981). Alcohol use and criminal behavior: An empirical, theoretical, and methodological overview. In J. J. Collins (Ed.), *Drinking and crime: Perspectives on the relationship between alcohol consumption and criminal behavior.* New York: Guilford.

Comfort, A. (1976). *A good age.* New York: Crown.

Comstock, G., Chaffee, S., Katzman, N., McCombs, M., & Roberts, D. (1978). *Television and human behavior.* New York: Columbia University Press.

Condon, W. S., & Sander, L. W. (1974). Neonate movement is synchronized with adult speech: Interactional participation and language acquisition. *Science, 183,* 99–101.

Cone, J. D., & Hayes, S. C. (1980). *Environmental problems/behavioral solutions.* Monterey, CA: Brooks/Cole.

Coni, N., Davison, W., & Webster, S. (1984). *Ageing.* Oxford: Oxford University Press.

Conley, J. J. (1984). Longitudinal consistency of adult personality: Self-reported psychological characteristics across 45 years. *Journal of Personality and Social Psychology, 47,* 1325–1333.

Conte, H. R., Weiner, M. B., & Plutchik, R. (1982). Measuring death anxiety: Conceptual, psychometric, and factor-analytic aspects. *Journal of Personality and Social Psychology, 43,* 775–785.

Conyne, R. K., & Clack, R. J. (1981). *Environmental assessment and design.* New York: Praeger.

Cook, S. W. (1985). Experimenting on social issues. *American Psychologist, 40,* 452–460.

Cooper, J., & Fazio, R. H. (1984). A new look at dissonance theory. *Advances in Experimental Social Psychology, 17,* 226–229.

Coopersmith, S. (1968). Studies in self-esteem. *Scientific American, 218,* pp. 96–106.

Corballis, M. C. (1980, March). Laterality and myth. *American Psychologist, 35,* 284–295.

Coren, S., & Porac, C. (1977, November). Fifty centuries of right-handedness: The historical record. *Science, 198,* 631–632.

Cornsweet, T. N. (1970). *Visual perception.* New York: Academic Press.

Costell, C. G. (1976, March). Electroconvulsive therapy: Is further investigation necessary?" *Canadian Psychiatric Association Journal, 21*(2), 61–67.

Cowles, J. T. (1937). Food tokens as incentives for learning by chimpanzees. *Comparative Psychology Monograph, 14*(5, Whole No. 71).

Cox, F. D. (1984). *Human intimacy.* St. Paul, MN: West Publishing.

Cox, T. (1979). *Stress.* Baltimore: University Park Press.

Coyle, J. T., Price, D. L., & DeLong, M. R. (1983). Alzheimer's disease: A disorder of cortical cholinergic innervation. *Science, 219,* 1184–1190.

Craig, K. (1978). Social modeling influences on pain. In R. A. Sternbach (Ed.), *The psychology of pain.* New York: Raven Press.

Crawley, S. B., & Sherrod, K. B. (1984). Parent-infant play during the first year of life. *Infant Behavior & Development, 7,* 65–75.

Crits-Christoph, P., & Singer, J. L. (1984). An experimental investigation of the use of positive imagery in the treatment of phobias. *Imagination, Cognition and Personality, 3,* 305.

Cronbach, L. (1970). *Essentials of psychological testing* (3rd ed.). New York: Harper & Row.

Culver, B., & Ianna, P. (1979). *The gemini syndrome.* Tucson, AZ: Pachart Publishing.

Cumming, E., & Henry, W. E. (1961). *Growing old: The process of disengagement.* New York: Basic Books.

Cutrona, C. E., & Troutman, B. R. (1986). Social support, infant temperament and parenting self-efficacy: A mediational model of postpartum depression. *Child Development, 57,* 1507–1518.

Daniel, T. C., & Boster, R. S. (1978). Measuring landscape esthetics: The scenic beauty estimation method. *USDA Forestry Service Research Paper, RM-167* (66). Rocky Mt. Forest Range Station, Ft. Collins, CO.

Daniel, T. L., & Esser, J. K. (1980). Intrinsic motivation as influenced by rewards, task interest, and task structure. *Journal of Applied Psychology, 65,* 566–573.

Darley, J. M., & Latane, B. (1968). Bystander intervention in emergencies: Diffusion of responsibility. *Journal of Personality and Social Psychology, 8,* 377–383.

Darwin, C. (1872). *The expression of emotion in man and animals.* Chicago: The University of Chicago Press.

Davis, D. M. (1928). Self-selection of diet by newly weaned infants. *American Journal of Diseases of Children, 36,* 651–679.

Davis, J. M. (1978). Dopamine theory of schizophrenia: A two-factor theory. In L. C. Wynne, R. L. Cromwell, & S. Matthysse (Eds.), *The nature of schizophrenia: New approaches to research and treatment.*

Davis, M., McKay, M., & Eshelman, E. R. (1980). *The relaxation and stress reduction workbook.* Richmond, CA: New Harbinger.

Davis, R. E. (1975). Changing examination answers: An educational myth? *Journal of Medical Education, 50,* 685–687.

Deaux, K. (1985). Sex and gender. *Annual Review of Psychology, 36,* 49–81.

Deaux, K., & Emswiller, T. (1974). Explanation of successful performance on sex-linked tasks: What is skill for the male is luck for the female. *Journal of Personality and Social Psychology, 29,* 80–85.

de Bono, E. (1970). *Lateral thinking: Creativity step by step.* New York: Harper & Row.

DeCharms, R., & Muir, M. S. (1978). Motivation: Social Approaches. *Annual Review of Psychology, 29,* 91–113.

Deese, J. (1978). Thoughts into speech. *American Scientist, 66,* 314–321.

Deese, J., & Hulse, S. J. (1967). *The psychology of learning* (3rd ed.). New York: McGraw Hill.

DeGood, D. E. (1975). Cognitive factors in vascular stress responses. *Psychophysiology, 12,* 399–401.

De Koninck, J., Gagnon, P., & Lallier, S. (1983). Sleep positions in the young adult and their relationship with the subjective quality of sleep. *Sleep, 6*(1), 52–59.

De La Cruz, F. F., & Muller, J. Z. (1983, November–December). Facts about Down syndrome. *Children Today, 12*(6), pp. 2–7.

DeLamater, J., & MacCorquodale, P. (1979). *Premarital sexuality: Attitudes, relationships, behavior.* Madison: University of Wisconsin Press.

Dember, W. N., & Warm, J. S. (1979). *Psychology of perception* (2nd ed.). New York: Holt.

Dement, W. (1960). The effect of dream deprivation. *Science, 131,* 1705–1707.

Dement, W. (1972). *Some must watch while some must sleep.* Stanford, CA: Stanford Alumni Association.

Dement, W., & Kleitman, N. (1957). The relation of eye movements during sleep to dream activity: An objective method for the study of dreaming. *The Journal of Experimental Psychology*, 53(5).

Denning, P. J. (1987). Computer models of aids epidemiology. *American Scientist*, 75, 347–352.

Depue, R. A., & Monroe, S. M. (1978). The unipolar-bipolar distinction in the depressive disorders. *Psychological Bulletin*, 85, 1001–1029.

Deregowski, J. B. (1972, November). Pictorial perception and culture. *Scientific American*, pp. 82–88.

Desharnais, R. (1975). Sports psychology in athletic training: Programs for maximum performance, In B. S. Rushall (Ed.), *The status of psychomotor learning and sports psychology research*. Dartmouth, Nova Scotia: Sport Science Associates.

DeSpelder, L. A., & Strickland, A. L. (1983). *The last dance*. Palo Alto, CA: Mayfield Publishing Co.

Deutsch, D. (1978). Pitch memory: An advantage for the left-handed. *Science*, 199, 559–560.

Deutsch, M., & Collins, M. E. (1951). *Interracial housing*. Minneapolis: University of Minnesota Press.

Diamond, M. (1977). Human sexual development: Biological foundations for social development. In F. A. Beach (Ed.), *Human sexuality in four perspectives* (pp. 22–61). Baltimore: Johns Hopkins University Press.

Dixon, J. (1975, September 30). Jeanne Dixon strikes back at scientists who knock astrology. *National Star*, p. 5.

Dobelle, W. H., Mladejovsky, M. G., & Girvin, J. P. (1974). Artificial vision for the blind: Electrical stimulation of visual cortex offers a hope for a functional prosthesis. *Science*, 183, 440–444.

Dollard, J., et al. (1939). *Frustration and aggression*. New Haven, CT: Yale University Press.

Dollard, J., & Miller, N. E. (1950). *Personality and psychotherapy: An analysis in terms of learning, thinking and culture*. New York: McGraw-Hill.

Donnerstein, E. I., & Linz, D. G. (1986, December). The question of pronography. *Psychology Today*, pp. 56–59.

Dovidio, J. F. (1984). Helping behavior and altruism: An empirical and conceptual overview. In L. Berkowitz (Ed.), *Advances in experimental social psychology*, *Vol. 17*. New York: Academic Press.

Dreyfuss, J. (1985, January 29). Implant liberates the deaf from silence. *Los Angeles Times*, Part V, p. 1.

Driskell, J. L., & Kelly, E. L. A. (1980). A guided notetaking and study skills system for use with university freshmen predicted to fail. *Journal of Reading*, 1, 4–5.

Drowatzky, J. N. (1975). *Motor learning: Principles and practices*. Minneapolis, MN: Burgess.

Drug Abuse Council. (1980). *The facts about "drug abuse."* New York: The Free Press.

DSM-III: Diagnostic and Statistical Manual of Mental Disorders (3rd ed.). 1980. Washington DC: American Psychiatric Association.

Duncker, K. (1945). On problem solving. *Psychological Monographs*, 58(270).

Dunkle, T. (1982). The sound of silence. *Science 82*, pp. 30–33.

Durden-Smith, J., & DeSimone, D. (1984, January). Hidden threads of illness. *Science Digest*, pp. 51–53.

Dutton, D. G., & Aron, A. P. (1974). Some evidence for heightened sexual attraction under conditions of high anxiety. *Journal of Personality and Social Psychology*, 30, 510–517.

Dywan, J., & Bowers, K. S. (1983). The use of hypnosis to enhance recall. *Science*, 222, 184–185.

Ebbinghaus, H. (1885). *Memory: A contribution to experimental psychology*. Translated by H. A. Ruger & C. E. Bussenius, 1913. New York: New York Teacher's College, Columbia University.

Eberhardt, B. J., & Muchinsky, P. M. (1982). An empirical investigation of the factor stability of Owens' biographical questionnaire. *Journal of Applied Psychology*, 67, 138–145.

Edelson, S. M. (1984). Implications of sensory stimulation in self-destructive behavior. *American Journal of Mental Deficiency*, 89, 140–145.

Edwards, K. A., & Marshall, C. (1977). First impressions on tests: Some new findings. *Teaching of Psychology*, 4, 193–195.

Egar, G. (1984). Skilled helping: A problem-management framework for helper training. In D. Larson (Ed.), *Teaching Psychological Skills* (pp. 133–150). Monterey, CA: Brooks/Cole.

Ehara, T. H. (1980, December). On the electronic chess circuit. *Science 80*, pp. 78–79.

Ehrlichman, H., & Weinberger, A. (1978). Lateral eye movements and hemispheric asymmetry: A critical review. *Psychological Bulletin*, 85, 1080–1101.

Ekman, P. (1980). *The face of man: Expressions of universal emotions in a New Guinea village*. New York: Garland STPM Press.

Ekman, P., & Friesen, W. V. (1975). *Unmasking the face*. Englewood Cliffs, NJ: Prentice-Hall.

Ekman, P., Levenson, R. W., & Friesen, W. V. (1983). Autonomic nervous system activity distinguishes among emotions. *Science*, 221, 1208–1210.

Elkind, D. (1981). *The hurried child*. Reading, MA: Addison-Wesley.

Elkind, D. (1984). *All grown up & no place to go*. Reading, MA: Addison-Wesley.

Ellis, A. (1962). *Reason and emotion in psychotherapy*. New York: Lyle Stuart.

Ellis, A. (1973, February). The no cop-out therapy. *Psychology Today*, 7, pp. 56–60, 62.

Ellis, A. (1976). Rational-emotive therapy. In V. Binder, A. Binder, & B. Rimland (Eds.), *Modern therapies* (pp. 21–34). Englewood Cliffs, NJ: Prentice-Hall.

Ellis, A. (1979). The practice of rational-emotive therapy. In A. Ellis & J. Whiteley (Eds.) *Theoretical and empirical foundations of rational-emotive therapy*. Monterey, CA: Brooks/Cole.

Engel, G. (1977, November). Emotional stress and sudden death. *Psychology Today*, p. 144.

Epstein, R., Langa, R. P., & Skinner, B. F. (1981). "Self-awareness" in the pigeon. *Science*, 212, 695–696.

Erdelyi, M. H. (1974). A new look at the new look: Perceptual defense and vigilance. *Psychological Review*, 81, 1–25.

Erdelyi, M. H., & Appelbaum, A. G., (1973). Cognitive masking: The disruptive effect of an emotional stimulus upon the perception of contiguous neutral items. *Bulletin of the Psychonomic Society*, 1, 59–61.

Ericsson, K. A., & Chase, W. G. (1982). Exceptional memory. *American Scientist*, 70, 607–615.

Erikson, E. H. (1963). *Childhood and society* (2nd ed.). New York: Norton.

Eron, L. D. (1987). The development of aggressive behavior from the perspective of a developing behaviorism. *American Psychologist*, 42, 435–442.

Etaugh, C. (1980, April). Effects of nonmaternal care on children. *American Psychologist, 35*, 309–319.

Evarts, E. V. (1979). Brain mechanisms of movement. *Scientific American, 241*(3), pp. 164–179.

Eysenck, H. J. (1957, 1958). *Sense and nonsense in psychology*. Harmondsworth, Middlesex, England: Penguin.

Eysenck, H. J. (1967, June). New ways in psychotherapy. *Psychology Today*, p. 40.

Eysenck, H. J. (1981). *The intelligence controversy*. New York: John Wiley.

Eysenck, H. J. (1983). Stress and personality as contributory factors in the causation of cancer. In F. J. McGuigan, W. E. Sime, & J. M. Wallace (Eds.), *Stress and Tension Control, Vol. 2*. (pp. 35–46). New York: Plenum.

Fantz, R. L. (1963). Pattern vision in newborn infants. *Science, 140*, 296–297.

Fantz, R. L. (1961, May). The origin of form perception. *Scientific American*, p. 71.

Faraday, A. (1972). *Dream power*. New York: Coward.

Farber, B. A. (1983). Introduction: A critical perspective on burnout. In B. A. Farber (Ed.), *Stress and burnout in the human service professions* (pp. 1–22). New York: Pergamon.

Farber, S. L. (1981). *Identical twins reared apart*, New York: Basic Books.

Fast, J. (1970). *Body language*. New York: Evans.

Fehr, L. (1976). J. Piaget and S. Claus: Psychology makes strange bedfellows. *Psychological Reports*, 39, 740–742.

Feldman, D. H., & Bratton, J. S. (1972). Relativity and giftedness: Implications for equality of educational opportunity. *Exceptional Children*, 38, 491–492.

Feldman, R. D. (1982). *Whatever happened to the quiz kids: Perils and profits of growing up gifted*. Chicago: Chicago Review Press.

Ferster, C. B. (1968, February). The autistic child. *Psychology Today*, pp. 35–37, 61.

Ferster, C. B., Nurnberger, J. I., & Levitt, E. B. (1962). The control of eating. *Journal of Mathematics, 1*, 87–109.

Festinger, L. (1954). A theory of social comparison processes. *Human Relations*, 7, 117–140.

Festinger, L. (1957). A *theory of cognitive dissonance*. Stanford, CA: Stanford University Press.

Festinger, L., & Carlsmith, J. M. (1959). Cognitive consequences of forced compliance. *Journal of Abnormal and Social Psychology, 58*, 203–210.

Festinger, L., Schachter, S., & Back, K. (1950). *Social pressures in informal groups: A study of a housing project*. New York: Harper.

Feuerstein, R., Rand, Y., & Hoffman, M. B. (1980). *Instrumental enrichment: An intervention program for cognitive modifiability*. Baltimore: University Park.

Fink, M. (1977). Myths of shock therapy. *American Journal of Psychiatry, 134*, 991–996.

Finkelstein, P., Wenegrat, B., & Yalom, I. (1982). Large group awareness training. *Annual Review of Psychology*, 33, 515–539.

Fishbein, M., & Ajzen, I. (1975). *Belief, attitude, intention, and behavior: An introduction to theory and research*. Reading, MA: Addison-Wesley.

Fisher, K. (1984, December). Berkeley study finds stress is value-laden. *APA Monitor*, pp. 26, 30.

Fisher, S. (1973). *The female orgasm*. New York: Basic Books.

Fitzgerald, L. F., & Osipow, S. H. (1986). An occupational analysis of counseling psychology. *American Psychologist, 41*, 535–544.

Fleming, J. (1974, January). Field report: The state of the apes. *Psychology Today*, p. 46.

Flint, B. M. (1978). *New hope for deprived children*. Toronto: University of Toronto Press.

Foos, P., & Clark, M. C. (1984). *Human Learning*, 2(3).

Foulkes, D., & Schmidt, M. (1983). Temporal sequence and unit composition in dream reports from different stages of sleep. *Sleep*, 6(3), 265–280.

Fouts, R., Fouts, D., & Schoenfield, D. (1984). Sign language conversational interaction between chimpanzees. *Sign Language Studies*, 42, 1–12.

Fowler, R. L. (1982). Detection of differences in beer composition by brand and level of calorie content. *Perceptual and Motor Skills, 55*, 967–970.

Fox, P., & Oakes, W. (1984). Learned helplessness: Noncontingent reinforcement in video game performance produces a decrement in performance on a lexical decision task. *Bulletin of the Psychonomic Society*, 22, 113–166.

Frank, J. D. (1973). The demoralized mind. *Pscyhology Today*, 6(11), pp. 22–31, 100–101.

Frankenburg, W. K., & Dodds, J. B. (1967). The Denver Developmental Screening Test. *The Journal of Pediatrics, 1*, 181–191.

Frankl, F. H. (1977). Current perspectives on ECT: A discussion. *American Journal of Psychiatry, 134*, 1014–1019.

Frankl, V. (1955). *The doctor and the soul*. New York: Knopf.

Franklin, D. (1984). Growing up short. *Science News, 125*(6), pp. 92–94.

Freedman, J. L. (1984). Effect of television violence on aggressiveness. *Psychological Bulletin*, 96, 227–246.

Freedman, J. L., & Fraser, S. C. (1966). Compliance without pressure: The foot-in-the-door technique. *Journal of Personality and Social Psychology*, 4, 195–202.

Freud, S. (1900). *The interpretation of dreams*. London: Hogarth.

Freud, S. (1949). *An outline of psychoanalysis*. New York: Norton.

Friedberg, J. (1977). Shock treatment, brain damage, and memory loss: A neurological perspective. *American Journal of Psychiatry, 134*, 1010–1014.

Friedman, M., & Rosenman, R. (1974). *Type A behavior and your heart*. New York: Knopf.

Friedman, M. I., & Stricker, E. M. (1976). The physiological psychology of hunger: A physiological perspective. *Psychological Review*, 83, 409–431.

Frodi, A. N., Lamb, M. E., Leavitt, L. A., Donovan, W. L., Neff, C., & Sherry, D. (1978). Fathers' and mothers' responses to the faces and cries of normal and premature infants. *Developmental Psychology, 14*, 190–198.

Fuastman, W. O. (1976, November). Aversive control of maladaptive sexual behavior: Past developments and future trends. *Psychology, 13*(4), 53–60.

Fuchs, C., & Rehm, L. (1977). A self-control behavior therapy program for depression. *Journal of Consulting and Clinical Psychology*. 45, 206–215.

Fulgosi, A., & Guilford, J. P. (1968). Short-term incubation in divergent production. *American Journal of Psychology*, 7, 1016–1023.

Fuller, B. (1969). *Utopia or oblivion: The prospects for humanity*. New York: Bantam Matrix.

Furey, E. M. (1982). The effects of alcohol on the fetus. *Exceptional Children*, *49*, 30–34.

Furumoto, L., & Scarborough, E. (1986). Placing women in the history of psychology. *American Psychologist*, *41*, 35–42.

Gagne, R. M., & Fleishman, E. A. (1959). *Psychology and human performance*. New York: Holt, Rinehart & Winston.

Gagnon, J. H. (1977). *Human sexualities*. Glenview, IL: Scott, Foresman.

Galanter, E. (1962). Contemporary psychophysics. In *New directions in psychology, Vol. 1* (pp. 87–156). New York: Holt, Rinehart & Winston.

Galston, A. W., & Slayman, C. L. (1983). Plant sensitivity and sensation. In G. O Abell & B. Singer (Eds.), *Science and the paranormal* (pp. 40–55). New York: Scribner.

Ganster, D. C., Mayes, B. T., Sime, W. E., & Tharp, G. D. (1982). Managing organizational stress: A field experiment. *Journal of Applied Psychology*, *67*, 533–542.

Garcia, J. (1977). Intelligence testing: Quotients, quotas and quackery. In J. L. Martinez (Eds.), *Chicano psychology*. New York: Academic Press.

Garcia, J., Hankins, W. G., & Rusiniak, K. W. (1974). Behavioral regulation of the milieu interne in man and rat. *Science*, *185*, 824–831.

Gardner, H. (1985). *Frames of mind*. New York: Basic Books.

Gardner, M. (1966). Dermo-optical perception: A peek down the nose. *Science*, *151*, 654–657.

Gardner, M. (1977, November/December). A skeptic's view of parapsychology. *The Humanist*.

Gardner, R. A., & Gardner, B. T. (1969). Teaching sign language to a chimpanzee. *Science*, *165*, 664–672.

Gates, A. I. (1958). Recitation as a factor in memorizing. In J. Deese (Eds.), *The psychology of learning* (2nd. ed.). New York: McGraw-Hill.

Gazzaniga, M. S. (1970). *The bisected brain*. New York: Plenum.

Geldard, F. A. (1972). *The human senses* (2nd. ed.). New York: Wiley.

Gerbner, G., & Gross, L. (1976). Living with television: The violent profile. *Journal of Communication*, 26, 173–199.

Gersh, R. D. (1982, June 20). Learning when not to shoot. *Santa Barbara News Press*.

Geschwind, N. (1979, September). Specializations of the human brain. *Scientific American*, *241*, pp. 180–199.

Gibson, E. J., & Walk, R. D. (1960). The "visual cliff." *Scientific American*, 202(4), pp. 67–71.

Gillam, B. (1980). Geometrical illusions. *American Psychologist*, 242, 102–111.

Giniger, S., Dispenzieri, A., & Eisenberg, J. (1983). Age, experience, and performance on speed and skill jobs in an applied setting. *Journal of Applied Psychology*, 68, 469–475.

Ginott, H. G. (1965). *Between parent and child: New solutions to old problems*. New York: Macmillan.

Giovannoni, J. M., & Becerra, R. M. (1979). *Defining child abuse*. New York: The Free Press.

Girodo, M. (1978). *Shy? (You don't have to be!)*. New York: Pocket Books.

Glaser, R. (1977, September/October). Adapting to individual differences. *Social Policy*, pp. 27–33.

Glass, A. L., Holyoak, K. J., & Santa, J. L. (1979). *Cognition*. Reading, MA: Addison-Wesley.

Glass, D. C. (1977). Stress, behavior patterns, and coronary disease. *American Scientist*, *65*, 177–187.

Glass, D. C., & Singer, J. E. (1972). Behavioral aftereffects of unpredictable and uncontrollable aversive events. *American Scientist*, *60*, 457–465.

Glick, D., & Hargreaves, W. A., with Drues, J., & Showstack, J. (1979). *Psychiatric hospital treatment for the 1980s: A controlled study of short versus long hospitalization*. Lexington, MA: Lexington Books.

Goering, P., Wasylenki, D., Lancee, W., & Freeman, S. J. (1984). From hospital to community: Six-month and two-year outcomes for 505 patients. *Journal of Nervous & Mental Disease*, *172*, 667–673.

Goldenson, R. M. (1970b). *The encyclopedia of human behavior, Vol. 2*. Garden City, NY: Doubleday.

Goldiamond, I. (1965). Fluent and non-fluent speech (stuttering): Analysis and operant techniques for control. In L. Krasner & L. P. Ullman (Eds.), *Research in behavior modification*. New York: Holt, Rinehart & Winston.

Goldiamond, I. (1971). Self-control procedures in personal behavior problems. In M. S. Gazzaniga & E. P. Lovejoy (Eds.), *Good reading in psychology*. Englewood Cliffs, NJ: Prentice-Hall.

Goleman, D. (1982, March). Staying up: The rebellion against sleep's gentle tyranny. *Psychology Today*, pp. 24–35.

Gomes-Schwartz, B., Hadley, S. W., & Strupp, H. H. (1978). Individual psychotherapy and behavior therapy. *Annual Review of Psychology*, 29, 435–471.

Gondola, J.C. & Tuckman, B.W. (1982). Psychological mood state in "average" marathon runners. *Perceptual and Motor Skills*, 55, 1295–1300.

Goodglass, H. (1980). Disorders of naming following brain injury. *American Scientist*, *68*, 647–655.

Goodman, G. (1984). SASHAtapes: Expanding options for help-intended communication. In D. Larson (Ed.), *Teaching psychological skills* (pp. 271–286). Monterey, CA: Brooks/Cole.

Gordon, T. (1970). *P.E.T. parent effectiveness training: A tested new way to raise children*. New York: Wyden.

Gottesman, I. I., & Shields, J. (1982). *The schizophrenic puzzle*. New York: Cambridge University Press.

Gottfried, A. W., & Bathurst, K. (1983). Hand preference across time is related to intelligence in young girls, not boys. *Science*, *221*, 1074–1075.

Gough, H. G., Fioravanti, M., & Lazzari, R. (1983). Some implications of self versus ideal-self congruence on the revised adjective check list. *Journal of Personality and Social Psychology*, *44*, 1214–1220.

Gould, J. L., & Gould, C. G. (1981, May). The instinct to learn. *Science 81*.

Gould, R. (1975, February). Growth toward self-tolerance. *Psychology Today*.

Grady, D. (1986, July). Don't get jittery over caffeine. *Discover*, pp. 73–79.

Graubard, P. S., & Rosenberg, H. (1974, March). Little brother is changing you. *Psychology Today*.

Green, H. (Joanne Greenberg). (1964). *I never promised you a rose garden*. New York: Holt, Rinehart & Winston.

Green, J. A., & Shellenberger, R. D. (1986, September). Biofeedback research and the ghost in the box: A reply to Roberts. *American Psychologist*, 1003–1005.

Greenberg, J. (1977, July 30) The brain and emotions: Crossing a new frontier. *Science News*, *112*(5), pp. 74–75.

Greene, D., & Lepper, M. R. (1974, September). How to turn play into work. *Psychology Today*, p. 49.

Greenspan, E. (1983, August 28). Conditioning athlete's minds. *New York Times Magazine*, pp. 32–34.

Gregory, R. L. (1977). *Eye and brain: The psychology of seeing* (3rd ed.). New York: World University Library.

Griffin, D. R. (1984). Animal Thinking. *American Scientist*, *72*, 456–463.

Grinspoon, L., & Bakalar, J. B. (1977). *Cocaine, a drug and its social evolution*. New York: Basic Books.

Grobstein, P., & Chow, K. L. (1975). Perceptive field development and individual experience. *Science*, *190*, 352–358.

Grossman, F. K., Eichler, L. S., & Winicoff, S. A. (1980). *Pregnancy, Birth and Parenthood*. San Francisco: Jossey-Bass.

Grossman, K. E., & Volkmer, H. (1984). Fathers' presence during birth of their infants and paternal involvement. *International Journal of Behavioral Development*, *7*, 157–165.

Grover, S. C. (1983). *The cognitive basis of the intellect: A response to Jensen's "Bias in mental testing."* Calgary, Alberta: University of Calgary.

Guilford, J. P. (1950). Creativity. *American Psychologist*, *5*, 444–454.

Gustavson, C. R., & Garcia, J. (1974, May). Pulling a gag on the wily coyote. *Psychology Today*, pp. 68–72.

Gutek, B. A. (1981, August). Experiences of sexual harassment: Results from a representative survey. Paper presented at the annual convention of the American Psychological Association, Los Angeles, CA.

Haber, R. N. (1969). Eidetic images, with biographical sketches. *Scientific American*, *220*(12), pp. 36–44.

Haber, R. N. (1970, May). How we remember what we see. *Scientific American*, pp. 104–112.

Haber, R. N. (1974). Eidetic images. In *Image object and illusion*. San Francisco: Freeman.

Haber, R. N. (1980). How we perceive depth from flat pictures. *American Scientist*, *68*, 370–380.

Haefele, J. W. (1962). *Creativity and innovation*. New York: Reinhold.

Hall, C. (1966). *The meaning of dreams*. New York: McGraw-Hill.

Hall, C. (1974). What people dream about. In R. L. Woods & H. B. Greenhouse (Eds.), *The new world of dreams: An anthology*. New York: Macmillan.

Hall, E. T. (1966). *The hidden dimension*. Garden City, NY: Doubleday.

Hall, E. T. (1974). *Handbook for proxemic research*. Washington, DC: Social Anthropology and Visual Communication.

Hall, G. S. (1922). *Senescence, the last half of life*. New York: Appleton-Century-Crofts.

Hall, R. G., Sachs, D. P., Hall, S. M., & Benowitz, N. L. (1984). Two-year efficacy and safety of rapid smoking therapy in patients with cardiac and pulmonary disease. *Journal of Consulting and Clinical Psychology*, *52*, 574–581.

Hammer, S., & Hazleton, L. (1984, October). Cocaine and the chemical brain. *Science Digest*, *92*, pp. 58–61, 100–103.

Hansel, C. E. M. (1980). *ESP and parapsychology: A critical reevaluation*. Buffalo, NY: Prometheus.

Hansen, W. B., & Altman, I. (1976). Decorating personal places: A descriptive analysis. *Environmental Behavior*, *8*, pp. 491–505.

Hardy, A. B. (1976). *Agoraphobia: Symptoms, causes, treatment*. Menlo Park, CA: Terrap.

Hardyck, C., Petrinovich, L. F., & Goldman, R. (1976). Left-handedness and cognitive deficit. *Cortex*, *12*, 266–278.

Harlow, H. F. (1966). Learning to love. *American Scientist*, *54*, pp. 244–272.

Harlow, H. F. (1967). The young monkeys. *Psychology Today*, *1*(5), pp. 40–47.

Harlow, H. F., & Harlow, M. K. (1962). Social deprivation in monkeys. *Scientific American*, *207*, pp. 136–146.

Harlow, H. F., & Zimmerman, R. R. (1958). The development of affectional responses in infant monkeys. *Proceedings of the American Philosophical Society*, *102*, 501–509.

Harlow, J. M. (1868). Recovery from the passage of an iron bar through the head. *Massachusetts Medical Society*, *2*, 327ff.

Harper, (1959). *Psychoanalysis and psychotherapy*. Englewood Cliffs, NJ: Prentice-Hall.

Hart, K. J., & Ollendick, T. H. (1985). Prevalence of bulemia in working and university women. *American Journal of Psychiatry*, *142*, 851–854.

Hartmann, E. L. (1973). *The functions of sleep*. New Haven, CT: Yale University Press.

Hartmann, E. L. (1978). *The sleeping pill*. New Haven, CT: Yale University Press.

Hartmann, E. L. (1981). The functions of sleep and memory processing. In W. Fishbein (Ed.), *Sleep, dreams and memory* (pp. 111–124). New York: SP Medical & Scientific Books.

Hass, A. (1983). *Teenage sexuality—A survey of teenage sexual behavior*. New York: Pinnacle Books.

Hatfield, E., Greenberger, D., Traupmann, J., & Lambert, P. (1982). Equity and sexual satisfaction in recently married couples. *Journal of Sex Research*, *18*, 18–32.

Hattie, J. A., Sharpley, C. F., & Rogers, H. J. (1984). Comparative effectiveness of professional and paraprofessional helpers. *Psychological Bulletin*, *95*, 534–541.

Havighurst, R. J. (1961). Successful aging. *Gerontologist*, *1*, 8–13.

Havighurst, R. J. (1976). Choosing a middle path for the use of drugs with hyperactive children. *School Review*, *85*(1), pp. 60–77.

Havighurst, R. J. (1979). *Developmental tasks and education* (4th ed.). New York: McKay.

Hawkins, D.B., & Gruber, J.J. (1982). Little league baseball and players' selfesteem. *Perceptual and Motor Skills*, *55*, 1335–1340.

Haywood, H. C., Meyers, C. E., & Switzby, H. N. (1982). Mental retardation. *Annual Review of Psychology*, *33*, 309–342.

Hayakawa, S. I. (1965). The use and misuse of language. In R. E. Farson (Ed.), *Science and human affairs* (pp. 95–113). Palo Alto, CA: Science and Behavior Books.

Háyes, C. (1951). *The ape in our house*. New York: Harper & Row.

Hayes, J. R. (1978). *Cognitive psychology: Thinking and creating*. Homewood, IL: Dorsey.

Hearst, E. (1969). Psychology across the chess board. In *Readings in Psychology Today* (pp. 16–23). Del Mar, CA: CRM.

Hebb, D. O. (1949). *Organization of behavior*. New York: Wiley.

Hebb, D. O. (1966). *A textbook of psychology* (2nd ed.). Philadelphia: Saunders.

Hebb, D. O. (1974). What psychology is about. *American Psychologist*, *29*, 71–79.

Heiby, E. M. (1983). Assessment of frequency of self-reinforcement. *Journal of Personality and Social Psychology*, *44*, 1304–1307.

Heiman, J. R. (1977). A psychophysiological exploration of sexual arous-

al patterns in females and males. *Psychophysiology, 14*(3), 266–274.
Heinstein, M. I. (1963). Behavioral correlates to breast-bottle regimes under varying parent-infant relationships. *Monographs of the Society for Research in Child Development, 28*(4), 1–61.
Held, R. (1971). Plasticity in sensory-motor systems. In *Contemporary psychology*. San Francisco: Freeman.
Heller, J. (1961). *Catch 22*. New York: Simon & Schuster.
Helson, H. (1964). *Adaptation-level theory*. New York: Harper & Row.
Henderson, N. D. (1982). Human behavior genetics. *Annual Review of Psychology, 33*, 403–440.
Herbert, W., & Greenberg, J. (1983, September 10). Behavior: Sex roles remain. *Science News, 124*, p. 172.
Heron, W. (1957). The pathology of boredom. *Scientific American, 196*, pp. 52–56.
Herrnstein, R. J. (1979). Acquisition, generalization, and discrimination reversal of a natural concept. *Journal of Experimental Psychology: Animal Behavior Processes, 5*, 116–129.
Herron, J. (1980). *Neuropsychology of left-handedness*. New York: Academic Press.
Hess, E. H. (1959). Imprinting. *Science, 130*, 133–141.
Hess, E. H. (1975a). *The tell-tale eye: How your eyes reveal hidden thoughts and emotions*. New York: Van Nostrand Reinhold.
Hess, E. H. (1975b, November). The role of pupil size in communication. *Scientific American*, pp. 110–119.
Heussenstamm, F. K. (1971). Bumper stickers and the cops. *Transaction, 8*, pp. 32–33.
High-risk sex less common. (1987, August). *APA Monitor*, p. 16.
Hilgard, E. R. (1974, November). Weapon against pain—Hypnosis is no mirage. *Psychology Today*.
Hilgard, E. R., & Hilgard J. R. (1983). *Hypnosis in the Relief of Pain*. Los Altos, CA: Kaufmann.
Hite, S. (1976). *The Hite report*. New York: Macmillan.
Hobson, J. A., & McCarley, R. W. (1977). The brain as a dream state generator: An activation-synthesis hypothesis of the dream process. *American Journal of Psychiatry, 134*, 1335–1348.
Hodgson, R., & Miller, P. (1982). *Selfwatching*. New York: Facts on File.
Hoffer, A. (1972). *Description, diagnosis, theory and treatment of schizophrenia*. Karpat.
Hoffman, L. W. (1977). Changes in family roles, socialization, and sex differences. *American Psychologist, 32*, 644–657.
Hoffman, M. L. (1975). Altruistic behavior and the parent-child relationship. *Journal of Personality and Social Psychology, 31*, 937–943.
Holland, M. K. (1975). *Using psychology: Principles of behavior and your life*. Boston: Little, Brown.
Holmes, D. S., Solomon, S., Cappo, B. M., & Greenberg, J. L. (1983). Effects of transcendental meditation versus resting on physiological and subjective arousal. *Journal of Personality and Social Psychology, 44*, 1245–1252.
Holmes, T., & Masuda, M. (1972, April). Psychosomatic syndrome. *Psychology Today*, p. 71.
Holmes, T. H., & Rahe, R. H. (1967). Social readjustment rating scale. *Journal of Psychosomatic Research*.
Honzik, M. P. (1983). Measuring abilities in infancy: Value and limitations. In M. Lewis (Ed.), *Origins of intelligence*. New York: Plenum.
Hopkins, J., Marcus, M., & Campbell, S. B. (1984). Postpartum depression: A critical review. *Psychological Bulletin, 95*, 498–515.
Hopson, J. L. (1986, June). The unraveling of insomnia. *Psychology Today*, pp. 43–49.
Horn, J. M., Loehlin, J. C., & Willerman, L. (1979). Intellectual resemblance among adoptive and biological relatives: The Texas adoption project. *Behavior Genetics, 9*, 177–207.
Horn, J.M., Plomine, R. & Rosenman, R. (1976). Heritability of personality traits in adult male twins. *Behavior Genetics, 6*, 17–30.
Horne, J. A., Brass, C. G., Pettitt, A. N. (1980). Circadian performance differences between morning and evening "types." *Ergonomics, 23*, 29–36.
Horne, J. A., & Staff, L. H. E. (1983). Exercise and sleep: Body-heating effects. *Sleep, 6*, 36–46.
Horowitz, M. J. (1970). *Image formation and cognition*. New York: Appleton-Century-Crofts.
Horwitz, W. A., Kestenbaum, C., Person, E., & Jarvik, L. (1965). Identical twin—"Idiot savants" calendar calculators. *The American Journal of Psychiatry, 121*, 1075–1079.
Hosch, H. M., & Cooper, D. S. (1982). Victimization as a determinant of eyewitness accuracy. *Journal of Applied Psychology, 67*, 649–652.
Houston, J. P. (1985). *Motivation*. New York: Macmillan.
Howard, A., Pion, G. M., Gottfredson, G. D., Flattau, P. E., Oskamp, S., Pfafflin, S. M., Bray, D. W., Burstein, A. G. (1986). The changing face of American psychology. *American Psychologist, 41*, 1311–1327.
Howard, K. I., Kopta, S. M., Krause, M. S., & Orlinksy, D. E. (1986). The dose-effect relationship in psychotherapy. *American Psychologist, 41*, 159–164.
Howitt, D., Craven, G., Iveson, C., Kremer, J., McCabe, J., & Rolph, T. (1977). The misdirected letter. *British Journal of Social and Clinical Psychology, 16*, 285–286.
Hoyenga, K. B., & Hoyenga, K. T. (1984). *Motivational explanations of behavior*. Monterey CA: Brooks/Cole.
Hsia, Y., & Graham, C. H. (1965). Color blindness. In C. H. Graham (Ed.), *Vision and visual perception* (pp. 395–413). New York: Wiley.
Hubel, D. H. (1979, September). The brain. *Scientific American, 241*, pp. 45–53.
Hubel, D. H. (1979b). The visual cortex of normal and deprived monkeys. *American Scientist, 67*, 532–543.
Hubel, D. H., & Wiesel, T. N. (1979). Brain mechanisms of vision. *Scientific American, 241*, pp. 150–162.
Huesmann, L., Eron, L., Klein, L., Brice, P., & Fischer, P. (1983). Mitigating the imitation of aggressive behaviors by changing children's attitudes about media violence. *Journal of Personality and Social Psychology, 44*, 899–910.
Huges, J. (1974). Acquisition of a non-vocal "language" by aphasic children. *Cognition* 3, 41–55.
Humphrey, J. A., Puccio, D., Niswander, G. D., & Casey, T. M. (1972). An analysis of the sequency of selected events in the lives of a suicidal population: A preliminary report. *Journal of Nervous Mental Disorders, 154*, 137–140.
Hunt, M. (1974). *Sexual behavior in the 1970s*. Chicago: Playboy Press.
Hunt, M. (1982). *The universe within*. New York: Simon & Schuster.
Hunter, W. S. (1913). The delayed reaction in animals and children. *Behavior Monographs, 2*.
Hurd, P., Johnson, C. A., Pechacek, T., Bast, L. P., Jacobs, D. R., & Luepker, R. V. (1980). Prevention of smoking in seventh-grade students. *Journal of Behavioral Medicine, 3*, 15–28.
Hurst, M. W., Jenkins, C. D., & Rose, R. M. (1979). The relation of

psychological stress to onset of medical illness. In C. A. Garfield (Ed.), *Stress and survival: The emotional realities of life-threatening illness*. St. Louis: Mosby.

Huston, T. L., & Levinger, G. (1978). Interpersonal attraction and relationships. *Annual Review of Psychology, 29,* 115–156.

Huxley, A. (1965). Human potentialities. In R. E. Farson (Ed.), *Science and human affairs*. Palo Alto, CA: Science and Behavior Books.

Hyde, J. S. (1984). *Understanding human sexuality*. New York: McGraw-Hill.

Hyman, B. T., Van Hoesen, G. W., Damasio, A. R., & Barnes, C. L. (1984). Alzheimer's disease: Cell-specific pathology isolates the hippocampal formation. *Science, 225,* 1168–1170.

Hyman, R. (1977). The case against parapsychology. *The Humanist*, 37, pp. 47–49.

Hyman, R. (1979). Patterns of PSI—Exposed or imposed. *Contemporary Psychology, 24,* 766–767.

Isenberg, P. L., & Schatzberg, A. F. (1976). Psychoanalytic contribution to a theory of depression. In J. O. Cole, A. F. Schatzberg, & S. H. Frazier (Eds.), *Depression: Biology, psychodynamics, and treatment*. New York: Plenum Press.

Iversen, L. L. (1979, September). The chemistry of the brain. *Scientific American, 241*(3), pp. 134–147.

Ivey, A. E., & Galvin, M. (1984). Microcounseling: A metamodel for counseling, therapy, business, and medical interviews. In D. Larson (Ed.), *Teaching psychological skills* (pp. 207–225). Monterey, CA: Brooks/Cole.

Jackson, S. E. (1983). Participation in decision making as a strategy for reducing job-related strain. *Journal of Applied Psychology, 68,* 3–19.

Jacobson, A., Kales, A., Lehmann, D., & Zweizia, J. R. (1965). Somnambulism: All night EEG studies. *Science, 148,* 975–977.

Jacobson, L. E. (1932). The electrophysiology of mental activities. *American Journal of Psychology, 44,* 677–694.

Jacobson, S. W., et al. (1984). Neonatal correlates of prenatal exposure to smoking, caffeine, and alcohol. *Infant Behavior & Development, 7,* 253–265.

Jahn, R. G. (1982). The persistent paradox of psychic phenomena. *Proceedings of the IEEE, 70*(2), 136–166.

Janis, I. L., & Mann, L. (1965). Effectiveness of emotional role-playing in modifying smoking habits and attitudes. *Journal of Experimental Research in Personality, 1,* 84–90.

Janis, I. L., & Mann, L. (1977). *Decision making*. New York: The Free Press.

Janis, I. L., & Wheeler, D. (1978, May). Thinking clearly about career choices. *Psychology Today, 11,* pp. 66–78.

Japenga, A. (1982, May 19). The birds that hunt people. *Los Angeles Times*, Part V, pp. 1,2.

Jarvik, E. M. (1964). Ciba found. In H. Steinberg et al., *Symposium of Animal Pharmacology Drug Action*.

Jellinik, E. M. (1960). *The disease concept of alcoholism*. New Haven: Hill House Press.

Jemmott, J. B., III, & Locke, S. E. (1984). Psychosocial factors, immunologic mediation, and human susceptibility to infectious diseases: How much do we know? *Psychological Bulletin, 95,* 78–108.

Jenkins, J. G., & Dallenbach, K. M. (1924). Oblivescence during sleep and waking. *American Journal of Psychology, 35,* 605–612.

Jensen, M. D., Benson, R. C., & Bobak, I. M. (1981). *Maternity care. The nurse and the family* (2nd ed.). St. Louis: Mosby.

Jerome, L. E. (1975). Astrology: Magic or science? In *Objections to astrology*, Prometheus Books.

John, E. R. (1967). *Mechanisms of memory*. New York: Academic Press.

Johnson, J. J. (1975). Sticking with first responses on multiple-choice exams: For better or for worse? *Teaching of Psychology*, 2(4).

Johnson, L., Naitoh, P., Lubin, A., & Moses, J. Sleep stages and performance. In W. P. Colquhoun (Ed.). *Aspects of human efficiency* (pp. 81–100). London: English University Press.

Johnson, R. E. (1970). Some correlates of extramarital coitus. *Journal of Marriage and Family, 32,* 449–456.

Johnson, S. M., & White, G. (1971). Self-observation as an agent of behavioral change. *Behavior Therapy*, 2, 488–497.

Jones, E. (1953). *The life and work of Sigmund Freud*. New York: Basic Books.

Jones, E. E., & Nisbett, R. E. (1971). The actor and observer: Divergent perceptions of the causes of behavior. In E. E. Jones, D. E. Kanouse, H. H. Kelley, R. E. Nisbett, S. Valins, & B. Weiner (Eds.). *Attribution: Perceiving the causes of behavior*. Morristown, NJ: General Learning Press.

Jones, K. L., & Smith, D. W. (1973). Recognition of the fetal alcohol syndrome in early infancy. *Lancet*, 2, p. 999.

Jones, W. R., & Ellis, N. R. (1962). Inhibitory potential in rotary pursuit acquisition. *Journal of Experimental Psychology, 63,* 534–537.

Jospe, M. (1978). *The placebo effect in healing*. Lexington, MA: Lexington Books.

Jourard, S. M. (1963). *Personal adjustment* (2nd ed.). New York: Macmillan.

Jourard, S. M. (1974). *Healthy personality*. New York: Macmillan.

Judson, A. I., & Cofer, C. N. (1956). Reasoning as an associative process: I. "Direction" in a simple verbal problem. *Psychological Reports*, 2, 469–476.

Julesz, B. (1971). *Foundations of cyclopean perception*. Chicago: University of Chicago Press.

Julesz, B. (1975, April). Experiments in the visual perception of texture. *Scientific American*, 232, pp. 34–43.

Julien, R. M. (1985). *A primer of drug action* (4th ed.). San Francisco: Freeman.

Kagan, J. (1969). *Personality development*. New York: Harcourt Brace Jovanovich.

Kagan, J. (1971). *Change and continuity in infancy*. New York: Wiley.

Kagan, J. (1976). Emergent themes in human development. *American Scientist, 64,* 186–196.

Kagan, J., & Klein, R. E. (1973). Cross-cultural perspectives on early development. *American Psychologist, 28,* 947–961.

Kahneman, D., Slovic, P., & Tversky, A. (1982). *Judgment under uncertainty: Heuristics and Biases*. Cambridge: Cambridge University Press.

Kahneman, D., & Tversky, A. (1972). Subjective probability: A judgment of representativeness. *Cognitive Psychology*, 3, 430–454.

Kahneman, D., & Tversky, A. (1973). On the psychology of prediction. *Psychological Review, 80,* 237–251.

Kales, A., & Kales, J. (1973). Recent advances in the diagnosis and treatment of sleep disorders. In G. Usdin (Ed.), *Sleep research and clinical practice*. New York: Brunner/Mazel.

Kaluger, G., & Kaluger, M. F. (1984). *Human Development*. St. Louis: Times Mirror/Mosby.

Kamin, L. J. (1981). *The intelligence controversy*. New York: Wiley.

Kamiya, J. (1968). Conscious control of brain waves. *Psychology Today, 1*, pp. 57–66.

Kandel, E. R. (1976). *Cellular basis of behavior: An introduction to behavioral neurobiology*. San Francisco: Freeman.

Kanfer, F. H., & Goldfoot, D. A. (1966). Self-control and tolerance of noxious stimulation. *Psychological Reports, 18*, 79–85.

Kaplan, H. S. (1974). *The new sex therapy*. New York: Brunner/Mazel.

Kaplan, M. (1983). The issue of sex bias in DSM-III: Comments on the articles by Spitzer, Williams, and Kass. *American Psychologist, 38*, 802–803.

Kaplan, P. S., & Stein, J. (1984). *Psychology of adjustment*. Belmont, CA: Wadsworth.

Kapleau, P. (1966). *The three pillars of Zen*. New York: Harper & Row.

Karlins, M., Coffman, T. L., & Walters, G. (1969). On the fading of social stereotypes: Studies in three generations of college students. *Journal of Personality and Social Psychology, 13*, 1–16.

Kasamatsu, A., & Hirai, T. (1966). An electroencephalographic study of Zen meditation (Zazen). *Folia Psychiatria et Neurologia Japonica, 20*, 315–336. Reprinted in Tart, *Altered states of consciousness*.

Kastenbaum, R., & Aisenberg R. (1972). *The psychology of death*. New York: Springer.

Kassarjian, H. H. (1982). Consumer psychology. *Annual Review of Psychology, 33*, 619–649.

Katahn, M. (1984). *Beyond diet*. New York: Norton.

Katz, B. J. (1972). Finding psychiatric help can be traumatic itself. *The National Observer*.

Kazdin, A. E. (1975). *Behavior modification in applied settings*. Homewood, IL: Dorsey Press.

Kearney, M. (1984). A comparison of motivation to avoid success in males and females. *Journal of Clinical Psychology, 40*, 1005–1007.

Keating, J. P., & Loftus, E. F. (1981, June). The logic of fire escape. *Psychology Today*, pp. 14–19.

Keefe, F. J. (1982). Behavioral assessment and treatment of chronic pain: Current status and future directions. *Journal of Consulting and Clinical Psychology, 50*, 896–911.

Kelley, H. H. (1950). The warm-cold variable in first impressions of persons. *Journal of Personality, 18*, 431–439.

Kelley, H. H. (1967). Attribution in social psychology. *Nebraska Symposium on Motivation, 15*, 192–238.

Kelley, H. H. (1971). *Attribution in social interaction*. Morristown, NJ: General Learning Press.

Kemeny, A., & Maltzman, I. (1987). *The role of individual differences in mental practice*. Paper presented at the Western Psychological Association Convention, Long Beach, CA.

Kennedy, J. M. (1983). What can we learn about pictures from the blind? *American Scientist, 71*, 19–26.

Kety, S. S. (1979, September). Disorders of the human brain. *Scientific American, 241*, pp. 202–214.

Keys, A., Brozek, J., Henschel, A., Mickelson, O., & Taylor, H. L. (1950). *The biology of human starvation*. Minneapolis: University of Minnesota Press.

Kiell, N. (Ed.). (1973). *The psychology of obesity: Dynamics and treatment*. Springfield, IL: Thomas.

Kihlstrom, J. F. (1985). Hypnosis. *Annual Review of Psychology, 36*, (385–418).

Kimble, G. A. (1961). *Hilgard and Marquis' conditioning and learning* (2nd ed.). New York: Appleton-Century-Crofts.

Kimura, D. (1985, November). Male brain, female brain: The hidden difference. *Psychology Today*, pp. 50–58.

Kinsey, A., Pomeroy, W., & Martin, C. (1948). *Sexual behavior in the human male*. Philadelphia: Saunders.

Kinsey, A., Pomeroy, W., & Martin, C. (1953). *Sexual behavior in the human female*. Philadelphia: Saunders.

Kipnis, D. (1987). Psychology and behavioral technology. *American Psychologist, 42*, 30–36.

Klatzky, R. L. (1980). *Human memory structures and processes*, (2nd ed.). San Francisco: Freeman.

Klaus, M. H., & Kennell, J. H. (1976). *Maternal-infant bonding*. St. Louis: Mosby.

Klaus, M. H., & Kennell, J. H. (1982). *Parent-infant bonding*. St. Louis: Mosby.

Klausmeir, H. J., & Goodwin, W. (1975). *Learning and human abilities* (4th ed.). New York: Harper & Row.

Kleitman, N. (1963). *Sleep and wakefulness* (2nd ed.). Chicago: University of Chicago Press.

Kleitman, N., & Kleitman, E. (1953). Effect of non-24-hour routines of living on oral temperature and heart rate. *Journal of Applied Physiology, 6*, 283–291.

Klienke, C. L. (1978). *Self-perception: The psychology of personal awareness*. San Francisco: Freeman.

Klinnert, M. D. (1984). The regulation of infant behavior by maternal facial expression. *Infant Behavior & Development, 7*, 447–465.

Knapp, M. L. (1978). *Nonverbal communication in human interaction* (2nd ed.) New York: Holt, Rinehart & Winston.

Knox, D. (1984). *Human sexuality*. St. Paul: West.

Kohlberg, L. (1963). The development of children's orientation toward a moral order: 1. Sequence in the development of moral thought. *Vita Humana, 6*, 11–33.

Kohlberg, L. (1969). The cognitive-developmental approach to socialization. In A. Goslin (Ed.). *Handbook of socialization theory and research*. Chicago: Rand McNally.

Kohlberg, L. (1976). Moral stages and moralization: The cognitive-developmental approach. In T. Lickona (Ed.), *Moral development and behavior*. New York: Holt, Rinehart & Winston.

Kohlberg, L. (1981a). *Essays on moral development: Vol. 1. The philosophy of moral development*. San Francisco: Harper.

Kohlberg, L. (1981b). *The meaning and measurement of moral development*. Worcester, MA: Clark University Press.

Kohler, I. (1962). Experiments with goggles. *Scientific American*, Offprint No. 465, pp. 62–72.

Kohler, W. (1925). *The mentality of apes*. New York: Harcourt Brace Jovanovich.

Kopp, C. B., & Parmelee, A. H. (1979). Prenatal and perinatal influences on infant behavior. In J. D. Ofsky (Ed.), *Handbook of infant development*. New York: Wiley.

Korte, C., & Milgram, S. (1970). Acquaintance networks between racial groups. *Journal of Personality and Social Psychology, 15*, 101–108.

Kosslyn, S. M. (1975). Information representation in visual images. *Cognitive Psychology, 7*, 341–370.

Kosslyn, S. M. (1983). *Ghosts in the mind's machine*. New York: Norton.

Kosslyn, S. M., Ball, T. M., & Reiser, B. J. (1978). Visual images preserve metric spatial information: Evidence from studies of image scanning. *Journal of Experimental Psychology: Human Perception and Performance, 4*, 47–60.

Kottler, J. A., & Brown, R. W. (1985). *Introduction to therapeutic counseling*. Monterey: Brooks/Cole.

Koukkou, M., & Lehmann, D. (1968). EEG and memory storage in sleep experiments with humans. *Electroencephalography and Clinical Neurophysiology*, 25, 455–462.

Krebs, D., & Adinolfi, A. A. (1975). Physical attractiveness, social relations, and personality style. *Journal of Personality and Social Psychology*, 31, 245–253.

Krech, D., Rosenzweig, M. R., & Bennett, E. L. (1962). Relations between brain chemistry and problem solving among rats raised in enriched and impoverished environments. *Journal of Comparative and Physiological Psychology*, 55, 801–807.

Krieger, D. T. (1983). Brain peptides: What, where, and why? *Science*, 222, 975–985.

Kripke, D. F., & Simons, R. N. (1976). Average sleep, insomnia, and sleeping pill use. *Sleep Research*, 5, 110.

Kristt, D. A., & Engel, B. T. (1975). Learned control of blood pressure in patients with high blood pressure. *Circulation*, 51, 370–378.

Kruger, L., & Liebeskind, J. C. (Eds.). (1984). *Advances in pain research and therapy*. New York: Raven Press.

Kubler-Ross, E. (1975). *Death: The final stage of growth*. Englewood Cliffs, NJ: Prentice-Hall.

Kulik, J. A., Bangert-Drowns, R. L., & Kulik, C. C. (1984). Effectiveness of coaching for aptitude tests. *Psychological Bulletin*, 95, 179–188.

Kunst-Wilson, W., & Zajonc, R. (1980). Affective discrimination of stimuli that cannot be recognized. *Science*, 207, 557–558.

Labbe, R., Firl, A., Jr., Mufson, E. J., & Stein, D. G. (1983). Fetal brain transplants: Reduction of cognitive deficits in rats with frontal cortex lesions. *Science*, 221, 470–472.

Labovitz, S., & Hagedorn, R. (1971). An analysis of suicide rates among occupational categories. *Social Inquiry*, 41, 67–72.

Lagerspetz, K. (1981). Combining aggression studies in infra-humans and man. In P. F. Brian & D. Benton (Eds.), *Multidisciplinary approaches to aggression research* (pp. 389–400). New York: Elsevier/North-Holland.

Laing, R. D. (1967). *The politics of experience*. New York: Pantheon.

Laing, R. D. (1970). *The divided self*. New York: Pantheon.

Laird, J. D. (1974). Self-attribution of emotion: The effects of expressive behavior on the quality of emotional experience. *Journal of Personality and Social Psychology* 29, 475–486.

Laird, J. D. (1984). The real role of facial response in the experience of emotion. *Journal of Personality and Social Psychology*, 47, 909–917.

Lake, A. (1973). Get thin, stay thin. *McCalls*, *100*(4).

Landis, D. (1980, December). A scan for mental illness. *Discover*, pp. 26–27.

Landy, F. J., & Trumbo, D. A. (1980). *Psychology of work behavior*. Homewood, IL: Dorsey.

Lang, P. J., & Melamed, B. G. (1969) Avoidance conditioning therapy of an infant with chronic ruminative vomiting. *Journal of Abnormal Psychology*, 74, 1–8.

Lappe, F. M. (1971). *Diet for a small planet*. New York: Ballantine.

Last, C. G., Barlow, D. H., & O'Brian, G. T. (1984). Precipitants of agoraphobia: Role of stressful life events. *Psychological Reports*, 54, 567–570.

Latane, L., Nida, S. A., & Wilson, D. W. (1981). The effects of group size on helping behavior. In J. P. Rushton & R. M. Sorrentino (Eds.), *Altruism and helping behavior: Social, personality and developmental perspectives*. Hillsdale, NJ: Erlbaum.

Laurence, J., & Perry, C. (1983). Hypnotically created memory among highly hypnotizable subjects. *Science*, 222, 523–524.

Lazarus, A. H. (1964). The treatment of chronic frigidity by systematic desensitization. In H. J. Eysenck (Ed.), *Experiments in behavior therapy*. New York: Pergamon.

Lazarus, R. S. (1975). A cognitively oriented psychologist looks at feedback. *American Psychologist*, 30, 553–561.

Lazarus, R. S. (1981). The stress and coping paradigm. In C. Eisdorfer, D. Cohen, A. Kleinman, & P. Maxim (Eds.). *Models for clinical psychopathology*. New York: Spectrum.

Lazarus, R. S. (1981, July). Little hassles can be hazardous to health. *Psychology Today*, pp. 58–62.

Lazarus, R. S., DeLongis, A., Folkman, S., & Gruen, R. (1985). Stress and adaptational outcomes. *American Psychologist*, 40, 770–779.

Lazarus, R. S., & Folkman, S. (1984). *Stress, appraisal, and coping*. New York: Springer.

Lee, M., Zimbardo, P. G., & Bertholf, M. (1977, November). Shy murderers. *Psychology Today*.

Lee, T., & Seeman, P. (1980). Elevation of brain neuroleptic/dopamine receptors in schizophrenia. *American Journal of Psychiatry*, 137, 191–197.

Leeper, R. W. (1935). A study of a neglected portion of the field of learning: The development of sensory organization. *Pedagogical Seminary and Journal of Genetic Psychology*, 46, 41–75.

Lefkowitz, M., Blake, R. R., & Mouton, J. S. (1955). Status factors in pedestrian violation of traffic signals. *Journal of Abnormal and Social Psychology*, 51, 704–706.

Le Magnen, J. (1980). The body energy regulation: The role of three brain responses to glucopenia. *Neuroscience and Biobehavioral Reviews*, 4, 65–72.

Lenfant, C., & Schweizer, M. (1985). Contributions of health-related biobehavioral research to the prevention of cardiovascular diseases. *American Psychologist*, 40, 217–220.

Lepper, M. R. (1985). Microcomputers in Education. *American Psychologist*, 40, 1–18.

Lerner, R. M., & Shea, J. A. (1982). Social behavior in adolescence. In B. B. Wolman, G. Stricker, S. J. Ellman, P. Keith-Spiegel, & D. S. Palermo (Eds.), *Handbook of developmental psychology* (pp. 503–525). Englewood Cliffs, NJ: Prentice-Hall.

Lester, D. (1971). Relationship of mental disorder to suicidal behavior. *New York State Journal of Medicine*, 71, 1503–1505.

Lester, D. (1972). *Why people kill themselves: A summary of research on suicidal behavior*. Springfield, IL: Thomas.

Lester, G., & Lester, D. (1971). *Suicide: The gamble with death*. Englewood Cliffs, NJ: Prentice-Hall.

Lettvin, J. Y. (1961). Two remarks on the visual system of the frog. In W. Rosenblith (Ed.), *Sensory communication*. Cambridge, MA: MIT Press.

Leveton, E. (1977). *Psychodrama for the timid clinician*. New York: Springer.

Levin, R. J., & Levin, A. (1975, September). Sexual pleasure: The surprising preference of 100,000 women. *Redbook*, p. 51.

Levin, R. J., & Levin, A. (1975, October). The redbook report on premarital and extramarital sex. *Redbook*, p. 38.

Levine, J. D., Gordon, N. C., & Fields, H. L. (1979). The role of endorphins in placebo analgesia. In J. J. Bonica, J. C. Lielseskind, & D. Albe-Fessard (Eds.), *Advances in pain research and therapy* (Vol. 3). New York: Raven Press.

Levinson, D. J., with Darrow, C. N., Klein, E. B., Levinson, M. H., & McKee, B. (1979). *The seasons of a man's life*. New York: Knopf.

Levitt, R. A. (1977). Recreational drug use and abuse. In D. C. Rimm & J. W. Somervill (Eds.), *Abnormal psychology*. New York: Academic Press.

Levy, J., & Redd, M. (1976). Cerebral organization. *Science*, 337–339.

Lewin, K. (1935). *A dynamic theory of personality*. New York: McGraw-Hill.

Lewin, R. (1974, October 5). The brain through a cat's eyes. *Saturday Review/World*.

Lewis, M., & Brooks-Gunn, J. (1979). *Social cognition and the acquisition of self*. New York: Plenum Press.

Lichtenstein, E. (1982). The smoking problem: A behavioral perspective. *Journal of Consulting and Clinical Psychology*, *50*, 804–819.

Lieberman, D. A. (1979). Behaviorism and the mind: A (limited) call for a return to introspection. *American Psychologist*, *34*, 319–333.

Lieberman, R. P., Fearn, C. H., Derisi, W., Roberts, J., & Carmona, M. (1976). The credit-incentive system: Motivating the participation of patients in a day hospital. *British Journal of Clinical Psychology*, *15*.

Liebert, R. M., Neale, J. M., & Davidson, E. S. (1973). *The early window: Effects of television on children and youth*. Elmsford, NY: Pergamon Press.

Lilly, J. C. (1972). *The center of the cyclone*. New York: Julian Press.

Lindsley, D. B., Bowden, J., & Magoun, H. W. (1949). Effect upon the EEG of acute injury to the brain stem activating system. *EEG and Clinical Neurophysiology*, *1*, 475–486.

Linton, M. (1979, July). I remember it well. *Psychology Today*, pp. 81–86.

Lipinski, E., & Lipinski, B. G. (1970). Motivational factors in psychedelic drug use by male college students. In R. E. Hormon & A. M. Fox (Eds.), *Drug awareness*. New York: Discus Books, Avon.

Lipscomb, D. M. (1974). *Noise: The unwanted sounds*. Chicago: Nelson-Hall.

Loevinger, J., & Knoll, E. (1983). Personality: Stages, traits, and the self. *Annual Review of Psychology*, *34*, 195–222.

Loftus, E. (1977). Shifting human color memory. *Memory & Cognition*, *5*, 696–699.

Loftus, E. (1979). *Eyewitness testimony*. Cambridge, MA: Harvard University Press.

Loftus, E. (1980). *Memory*. Reading MA: Addison-Wesley.

Loftus, E., & Loftus, G. (1980). On the permanence of stored information in the human brain. *American Psychologist*, *35*, 409–420.

Loftus, E., & Monahan, J. (1980). Trial by data: Psychological research as legal evidence. *American Psychologist*, *35*, 270–283.

Loftus, E., & Palmer, J. C. (1974). Reconstruction of automobile destruction: An example of interaction between language and memory. *Journal of Verbal Learning and Verbal Behavior*, *13*, 585–589.

Loftus, E. F. (1979, November). Words that could save your life. *Psychology Today*, pp. 102, 105–106.

Lorenz, K. (1937). Imprinting. *The Auk*, *54*, pp. 245–273.

Lorenz, K. (1962). *King Solomon's ring*. New York: Time.

Lorenz, K. (1966). *On aggression*. Translated by M. Kerr-Wilson. New York: Harcourt Brace Jovanovich.

Lorenz, K. (1974). *The eight deadly sins of civilized man*. Translated by M. Kerr-Wilson. New York: Harcourt Brace Jovanovich.

Los Angeles Times. (1981, September 24). Man tells how rod ran through head, p. 3.

Lovaas, O., & Simmons, J. (1969). Manipulation of self-destruction in three retarded children. *Journal of Applied Behavior Analysis*, *2*, 143–157.

Lowen, A. (1965). *Love and orgasm*. New York: Macmillan.

Luce, G. G. (1965). Current research on sleep and dreams (Health Service Publication No. 1389). Washington, DC: U.S. Department of Health, Education and Welfare.

Luce, G. G. (1971). *Body time: Physiological rhythms and social stress*. New York: Pantheon.

Luce, G. G. (1974). Sleepwalking not related to dreams. In R. L. Woods & H. B. Greenhouse (Eds.). *The new world of dreams*. New York: Macmillan.

Luce, G. G., & Peper, E, (1971, September 12). Mind over body, mind over mind. *The New York Times Magazine*.

Ludwig, A. M. (1966). Altered states of consciousness. *Archives of General Psychiatry*, *15*, 225–233.

Lueptow, L. B. (1980). Social change and sex-role changes in adolescent orientations toward life, work, and achievement: 1964–1975. *Social Psychology Quarterly*, *43*, 48–59.

Luria, A. R. (1968). *The mind of a mnemonist*. New York: Basic Books.

Luthans, F., Paul, R., & Baker, D. (1981). An experimental analysis of the impact of contingent reinforcement on salespersons' performance behavior. *Journal of Applied Psychology*, *66*, 314–323.

Lykken, D. T. (1974). Psychology and the lie detector industry. *American Psychologist*, *29*, 725–739.

Lykken, D. T. (1981). *A tremor in the blood: Uses and abuses of the lie detector*. New York: McGraw-Hill.

Maccoby, E. E., & Jacklin, C. N. (1974). *The psychology of sex differences*. Stanford, CA: Stanford University Press.

MacKinnon, D. W. (1962). The nature and nurture of creative talent. *American Psychologist*, *1*, 484–495.

MacKinnon, D. W. (1968). Selecting students with creative potential. In P. Heist (Ed.), *The creative college student: An unmet challenge*. San Francisco: Jossey-Bass.

Madsen, C. H., Jr., Becher, W. C., Thomas, D. R., Koser, L., & Plager, E. (1968). An analysis of the reinforcing function of "sit down" commands. In R. K. Parker (Ed.), *Readings in educational psychology*. Boston: Allyn & Bacon.

Maier, N. R. F. (1949). *Frustration*. New York: McGraw-Hill.

Main, M., & George, C. (1985). Responses of abused and disadvantaged toddlers to distress and agemates: A study in day care. *Developmental Psychology*, *21*, 407–412.

Malamuth, N. M., & Donnerstein, E. (1982). The effects of aggressive-pornographic mass media stimuli. In L. Berkowitz (Ed.), *Advances in Experimental Social Psychology*, *15* (pp. 103–136). New York: Academic Press.

Malatesta, V. J., Pollack, R. H., Wilbanks, W. A., & Adams, H. E. (1979). *Journal of Sex Research*, *15*, 101.

Malmo, R. B. (1975). *On emotions, needs, and our archaic brain*. New York: Holt, Rinehart & Winston.

Mandell, A. J., Segal, D. S., Kuczenski, R. T., & Knapp, S. (1972, October). The search for the schizococcus. *Psychology Today*, pp. 68–72.

Mandler, G. (1968). Association and organization: Fact, fancies, and theories. In T. R. Dixon & D. L. Horton (Eds.), *Verbal behavior and general behavior theory* (pp. 109–119). Englewood Cliffs, NJ: Prentice-Hall.

Mark, V. H., & Ervin, F. R. (1970). *Violence and the brain.* New York: Harper & Row.

Markman, E. M., Seibert, J. (1976). Classes and collections: Internal organization and resulting holistic properties. *Cognitive Psychology, 8,* 561–577.

Marks, D., & Kammann, R. (1979). *The psychology of the psychic.* Buffalo, NY: Prometheus Books.

Marks, L. (1978). *The unity of the senses: Interrelations among the modalities.* New York: Academic Press.

Markus, H., & Nurius, P. (1986). Possible selves. *American Psychologist, 41,* 954–969.

Marmon, J. (1975). Psychiatrists and their patients, a national study of private office practice. Washington, DC: Joint Information Service of the American Psychiatric Association and the National Association for Mental Health.

Marmor, J. (ed.) (1980). *Homosexual behavior: A modern reappraisal.* New York: Basic Books.

Marques, P., Bradley, J., Shappee, J., & Marques, C. (1982). *Bienestar: Health, well-being and lifestyle choices for Pinal County.* Project West Pinal, University of Arizona Health Sciences Center.

Martin, B. M., Garrity, T. F., & Bowers, F. R. (1975). The influence of recent life experience on the health of college freshman. *Journal of Psychosomatic Research, 19,* 87–98.

Martin, J. A., King, D. R., Maccoby, E. E., & Jacklin, C. N. (1984). Secular trends and individual differences in toilet-training progress. *Journal of Pediatric Psychology, 9,* 457–467.

Marx, J. L. (1983). The two sides of the brain. *Science, 220,* 488–490.

Maslach, C. (1982). *Burnout: The cost of caring.* Englewood Cliffs, NJ: Prentice-Hall.

Maslow, A. H. (1954). *Motivation and personality.* New York: Harper.

Maslow, A. H. (1967). Self-actualization and beyond. In J. F. T. Bugental (Ed.), *Challenges of humanistic psychology.* New York: McGraw-Hill.

Maslow, A. H. (1969). *The psychology of science.* Chicago: Henry Regnery.

Maslow, A. H. (1970). *Motivation and personality* (2nd ed.). New York: Harper & Row.

Maslow, A. H. (1971). *The farther reaches of human nature.* New York: Viking.

Masters, W. H., & Johnson, V. E. (1966). *Human sexual response.* Boston, Little, Brown.

Masters, W. H., & Johnson, V. E. (1970). *The pleasure bond: A new look at sexuality and commitment.* Boston: Little, Brown.

Matheny, A. P. Jr., Wilson, R. S., & Nuss, S. M. (1984). Toddler temperament: Stability across settings and over ages. *Child Development, 55,* 1200–1211.

Matossian, M. K. (1982). Ergot and the Salem witchcraft affair. *American Scientist, 70,* 355–357.

Maupin, E. W. (1965). Individual differences in response to a Zen meditation exercise. *Journal of Consulting Psychology, 29,* 139–145.

Mayer, J. (1968). *Overweight: Causes, cost, and control.* Englewood Cliffs, NJ: Prentice-Hall.

McBurney, D. H., & Collings, V. B. (1984). *Introduction to sensation/perception* (2nd ed.). Englewood Cliffs, NJ: Prentice-Hall.

McCabe, M. S., (1976). Reactive psychoses and schizophrenia with good prognosis. *Archives of General Psychiatry, 33*(5), 571–576.

McCain, G., & Segal, E. M. (1969). *The game of science.* Monterey, CA: Brooks/Cole.

McCardel, J., & Murray, E. J. (1974). Nonspecific factors in weekend encounter groups. *Journal of Consulting Psychology, 42,* 337–345.

McCaul, K. D., & Malott, J. M. (1984). Distraction and coping with pain. *Psychological Bulletin, 95,* 516–533.

McCauley, E., & Ehrhardt, A. A. (1976). Female sexual response: Hormonal and behavioral interactions. *Primary Care, 3,* 455.

McClelland, D. C. (1958). Risk taking in children with high and low need for achievement. In J. W. Atkinson (Ed.), *Motives in fantasy action and society.* New York: Van Nostrand.

McClelland, D. C. (1961). *The achieving society.* New York: Van Nostrand.

McClelland, D. C. (1965). Achievement and entrepreneurship. *Journal of Personality and Social Psychology, 1,* 389–393.

McClelland, D. C. (1973). Testing for competence rather than "intelligence." *American Psychologist, 28,* 1–14.

McClelland, D. C. (1975). *Power, the inner experience.* New York: Irvington.

McClelland, D. C., & Pilon, D. A. (1983). Sources of adult motives in patterns of parent behavior in early childhood. *Journal of Personality and Social Psychology, 44,* 564–574.

McClelland, L., & Cook, S. W. (1980). Promoting energy conservation in master-metered apartments through group financial incentives. *Journal of Applied and Social Psychology, 10,* 20–31.

McFadden, D., & Wightman, F. L. (1983). Audition. *Annual Review of Psychology, 34,* 95–128.

McGaugh, J. L. (1983). Hormonal influences on memory. *Annual Review of Psychology, 34,* 297–323.

McGee, M. G., & Snyder, M. (1975). Attribution and behavior: Two field studies. *Journal of Personality and Social Psychology, 32,* 185–190.

McGinnies, E. (1949). Emotionality and perceptual defense. *Psychological Review, 56,* 244–251.

McGregor, D. (1960). *The human side of enterprise.* New York: McGraw-Hill.

McGuire, W. J. (1969). The nature of attitudes and attitude change. In G. Lindzey & E. Aronson (Eds.), *The handbook of social psychology* (Vol. 3). Reading, MA: Addison-Wesley.

McKean, K. (1982, August). A picture of Hinckley's brain. *Discover,* 3, pp. 78–80.

McKean, K. (1982, December). Anatomy of an air crash. *Discover,* pp. 19–21.

McKean, K. (1984, May). The fine art of reading voters' minds. *Discover,* pp. 66–69.

McKean, K. (1985, April). Of two minds: Selling the right brain. *Discover,* pp. 30–40.

McKellar, P. (1965). The investigation of mental images. In S. A. Barnett & A. McLaren (Eds.), *Penguin science journal.* Harmondsworth, England: Penguin.

McMahon, F. B. (1964). A contingent-item method for constructing a short personality questionnaire. *Journal of Applied Psychology,* 197–200.

McMullan, W. E., & Stocking, J. R. (1978). Conceptualizing creativity in three dimensions. *The Journal of Creative Behavior, 12,* 161–167.

McNett, I. (1982, January). Psy.D. fills demand for practitioners. *APA Psychology Monitor, 13,* pp. 10–11.

Mead, M. (1935). *Sex and temperament in three primitive societies.* New York: Morrow.

Meeker, M. (1978). Measuring creativity from the child's point of view. *The Journal of Creative Behavior, 12,* 52–62.

Mehrabian, A. (1969). Significance of posture and position in the communication of attitude and status relationships. *Psychological Bulletin, 71,* 359–372.

Meichenbaum, D. (1977). *Cognitive behavior modification: An integrative approach.* New York: Plenum Press.

Meichenbaum, D., Henshaw, D., & Himel, N. (1982). Coping with stress as a problem-solving process. In H. W. Krohne & L. Laux (Eds.), *Achievement, stress, and anxiety.* New York: Hemisphere.

Melton, R. F., (1978). Resolution of conflicting claims concerning the effect of behavioral objectives on student learning. *Review of Educational Research, 48,* 291–302.

Meltzoff, A., & Moore, M. K. (1977, October). Imitation of facial and manual gestures by human neonates. *Science,* 75–78.

Melzack, R. (1974). Shutting the gate on pain. *Science year: The world book science annual.* Palo Alto, CA: Field.

Melzack, R., & Dennis, S. G. (1978). Neurophysical foundations of pain. In R. A. Sternbach (Ed.), *The psychology of pain.* New York: Raven Press.

Melzack, R., & Scott, T. H. (1957). The effects of early experience on the response to pain. *Journal of Comparative and Physiological Psychology, 50,* 155–161.

Menninger, K. (1964, April 25). Psychiatrists use dangerous words. *Saturday Evening Post.*

Menzel, E. W. (1978). Cognitive mapping in chimpanzees. In S. H. Hulse, H. Fowler, & W. K. Honig (Eds.), *Cognitive processes in animal behavior.* Hillsdale NJ: Erlbaum.

Meredith, N. (1984, December). The murder epidemic. *Science 84,* pp. 43–48.

Messerer, J., Hunt, E., Meyers, G., & Lerner, J. (1984). Feuerstein's instrumental enrichment: A new approach for activating intellectual potential in learning disabled youth. *Journal of Learning Disabilities, 17,* 322–325.

Meyer, A. J., Nash, J. D., McAlister, A. L., Maccoby, N., & Farquhar, J. W. (1980). Skills training in a cardiovascular health education campaign. *Journal of Consulting and Clinical Psychology, 48,* 129–142.

Meyers, B. J. (1984). Mother-infant bonding: The status of this critical-period hypothesis. *Developmental Review, 4,* 240–274.

Milgram, S. (1963). Behavioral study of obedience. *Journal of Abnormal and Social Psychology, 67,* 371–378.

Milgram, S. (1965). Some conditions of obedience and disobedience to authority. *Human Relations, 18,* 57–76.

Milgram, S. (1967, May). The small-world problem. *Psychology Today,* pp. 61–67.

Milgram, S. (1970). The experience of living in the cities: A psychological analysis. *Science, 167,* 1461–1468.

Milgram, S. (1974). *Obedience to authority: An experimental view.* New York: Harper & Row.

Milgram, S., Bickman, L., & Berkowitz, L. (1969). Note on the drawing power of crowds of different size. *Journal of Personality and Social Psychology, 13,* 79–82.

Miller, G. (1956). The magical number seven, plus or minus two: Some limits on our capacity for processing information. *Psychological Review, 63,* 81–87.

Miller, G. (1964). Language and psychology. In E. H. Lennenberg (Ed.), *New directions in the study of language* (pp. 89–107). Cambridge, MA: MIT Press.

Miller, G. (1977). *Spontaneous apprentices: children and language.* New York: Seabury Press.

Miller, H. L., & Siegal, P. S. (1972). *Loving: A psychological approach.* New York: Wiley.

Miller, L. K. (1976). The design of better communities through the application of behavioral principles. In W. E. Craighead, A. E. Kazdin, & M. J. Mahone (Eds.), *Behavior modification: Principles, issues, and applications.* Boston: Houghton Mifflin.

Miller, N. E. (1941). The frustration-aggression hypothesis. *Psychological Review, 48,* 337–342.

Miller, N. E. (1944). Experimental studies of conflict. In J. McV. Hunt (Ed.), *Personality and the behavior disorders,* Vol. I. (pp. 431–465). New York: Ronald Press.

Miller, N. E. (1969). Learning of visceral and glandular responses. *Science, 163,* 434–445.

Miller, N. E. (1982, May). Understanding psychological man: A state of the science report. *Psychology Today.*

Miller, N. E. (1983). Behavioral medicine: Symbiosis between laboratory and clinic. *Annual Review of Psychology, 34,* 1–31.

Miller, N. E. (1985). The value of behavioral research on animals. *American Psychologist, 40,* 423–440.

Miller, N. E. & Bugelski. R. (1970). The influence of frustration imposed by the in-group on attitudes expressed toward out-groups. In R. I. Evans & R. M. Rozelle (Eds.), *Social psychology in life.* Boston: Allyn & Bacon.

Miller, N. E., & Di Cara, L. V. (1967). Instrumental learning of heart rate changes in curarized rats: Shaping and specificity to discriminative stimulus. *Journal of Comparative and Physiological Psychology, 63,* 12–19.

Miller, N. E., & Dworkin, B. R. (1974). Visceral learning: Recent difficulties with curarized rats and significant problems for human research. In D. A. Obrist et al. (Eds.), *Cardiovascular physiology* (pp. 312–331). Chicago: Aldine.

Miller, W. R., Rosellini, R. A., & Seligman, M. E. P. (1977). In J. D. Maser & M. E. P. Seligman (Eds), *Psychopathology: Experimental models* (pp. 104–120). San Francisco: Freeman.

Milner, B. (1965). Memory disturbance after bilateral hippocampal lesions. In P. Milner & S. Glickman (Eds.), *Cognitive processes and the brain* (pp. 97–111). Princeton, NJ: Van Nostrand.

Mischel, W. (1968). *Personality and assessment.* New York: Wiley.

Mischel, W. (1973). Toward a cognitive social learning reconceptualization of personality. *Psychological Review, 80,* 252–283.

Mitchell-Heggs, N., Kelly, D., & Richardson, A. (1976). Stereotactic limbic leucotomy—A follow-up at 16 months. *British Journal of Psychiatry, 128,* 226–240.

Money, J. (1965). Psychosexual differentiation. In J. Money (Ed.), *Sex research: New developments* (pp. 3–23). New York: Holt, Rinehart & Winston.

Money, J. (1977). Human hermaphroditism. In F. A. Beach (Ed.), *Human sexuality in four perspectives.* Baltimore: Johns Hopkins University Press.

Money, J. (1987). Sin, Sickness, or Status? *American Psychologist, 42,* 384–399.

Money, J., & Ehrhardt, A. (1972). *Man and woman, boy and girl.* Baltimore: Johns Hopkins University Press.

Money, J., & Mathews, D. (1982). Prenatal exposure to virilizing progestins: An adult follow-up study of twelve women. *Archives of Sexual Behavior, 11,* 73–83.

Moore, D. C. (1981). Anorexia nervosa. In S. J. Mule (Ed.), *Behavior in excess*. New York: The Free Press.

Moore-Ede, M. C., Sulzman, F. M., & Fuller, C. A. (1982). *The clocks that time us*. Cambridge, MA: Harvard University Press.

Moreno, J. L. (1953). *Who shall survive?* New York: Beacon.

Morgan, W.P. (1978). The mind of the marathoner. *Psychology Today, 11*(11), pp. 38–49.

Moriarty, T. (1975, April). A nation of willing victims. *Psychology Today*, pp. 43–50.

Moritz, A. P., & Zamchech, N. (1946). Sudden and unexpected deaths of young soldiers. *American Medical Association Archives of Pathology*, 42, 459–494.

Moruzzi, G., & Magoun, H. W. (1949). Brain stem reticular formation and activation of the EEG. *EEG and Clinical Neurophysiology, 1*, 455–473.

Moser, D. (1965, May 7). The nightmare of life with Billy. *Life*.

Moss, H. A., & Susman, E. J. (1980). Longitudinal study of personality development. In O. G. Brim, Jr., & J. Kagan (Eds.), *Constancy and change in human development* (pp. 530–595). Cambridge, MA: Harvard University Press.

Moss, S., & D. C. Butler. (1978). The scientific credibility of ESP. *Perceptual and Motor Skills, 46*.

Moyer, R. S., & Bayer, R. H. (1976). Mental comparison and the symbolic distance effect. *Cognitive Psychology*, 8, 228–246.

Mueller, J. H., & Thompson, W. B. (1984). Test anxiety and distinctiveness of personal information. In H. M. Van Der Ploeg, R. Schwarzer, & C. D. Spielberger (Eds.), *Advances in test anxiety research*, Vol. 3 (pp. 21–37). Hillsdale, NJ: Erlbaum.

Munn, N. L. Fernald, L. D., Jr., & Fernald, P. S. (1969). *Introduction to psychology* (2nd ed.). Boston: Houghton Mifflin.

Murphy, L. B. & Moriarty, A. E. (1976). *Vulnerability, coping and growth*. New Haven, CT: Yale University Press.

Murray, F. S. (1980). Estimation of performance levels by students in introductory psychology. *Teaching of Psychology*, 7, 61–62.

Mussen, P. H., Conger, J. J., & Kagan, J. (1969). *Child development and personality* (3rd ed.). New York: Harper & Row.

Mussen, P. H., Conger, J. J., Kagan, J., & Geiwitz, J. (1979). *Psychological development: A life span approach*. New York: Harper & Row.

Myers, A. (1980). *Experimental psychology*. New York: Van Nostrand.

Nachman, M. (1970). Learned taste and temperature aversions due to lithium chloride sickness after temporal delays. *Journal of Comparative and Physiological Psychology*, 73, 22–30.

Nahas, G. G. (1979b). *Keep off the grass*. Elmsford, NY: Pergamon Press.

Nahas, G. G., & Paton, W. D. M. (1979a). *Marihuana, biological effects*. Elmsford, NY: Pergamon Press.

Naranjo, C. (1970). Present-centeredness: Technique, prescription, and ideal. In J. Fagan & I. L. Shepherd (Eds), *What is Gestalt therapy?* (pp. 63–97). New York: Harper & Row.

Narayanan, V. K., & Nath, R. (1982). A field test of some attitudinal and behavioral consequences of flexitime. *Journal of Applied Psychology*, 67, 214–218.

National Commission on Marihuana and Drug Abuse, R. P. Shafer, Chairman. (1973). *Drug use in America: The problem in perspective*. Washington, DC: U.S. Government Printing Office.

National Institute on Drug Abuse (NIDA). (1976). *Marihuana and health*. Princeton, NJ: Response Analysis Corporation.

Nauta, W. J. H., & Feirtag, M. (1979). The organization of the brain. *Scientific American*, pp. 88–111.

Navran, L. (1967). Communication and adjustment in marriage. *Family Process*, 6, 173–184.

Neff, W. S. (1977). *Work and human behavior* (2nd ed.). Chicago: Aldine.

Nelson, R., & Crutchfield, R. S. (1970). Mathematicians: The creative researcher and the average Ph.D. *Journal of Consulting and Clinical Psychology*, 34, 250–257.

Neufeld, R. W. (1970). The effect of experimentally altered cognitive appraisal on pain tolerance. *Psychonomic Science*, 20(2), 106–107.

Neugarten, B. (1971, December). Grow old along with me! The best is yet to be. *Psychology Today*, p. 45.

Neuringer, A. J. (1970). Superstitious key pecking after three peck-produced reinforcements. *Journal of the Experimental Analysis of Behavior, 13*, 127–134.

Newman, P. R. (1982). The peer group. In B. B. Wolman, G. Stricker, S. J. Ellman, P. Keith-Spiegel, & D. S. Palermo, (Eds.), *Handbook of developmental pscyhology*. Englewood Cliffs, NJ: Prentice-Hall.

Nickerson, R. S., & Adams, M. J. (1979). Long-term memory for a common object. *Cognitive Psychology, 11*, 287–307.

Nicol, S. E., & Gottesman, I. I. (1983). Clues to the genetics and neurobiology of schizophrenia. *American Scientist, 71*, 398–404,

Nomellini, S., & Katz, R. C. (1983). Effects of anger control training on abusive parents. *Cognitive Therapy and Research*, 7, 57–68.

Norris, P. A. (1986, September). On the status of biofeedback and clinical practice. *American Psychologist*, 1009–1010.

Nurnberger, J. I., & Zimmerman, J. (1970). Applied analysis of human behaviors: An alternative to conventional motivational inferences and unconscious determination in therapeutic programming. *Behavior Therapy, 1*, 59–69.

O'Brien, R. M., Figlerski, R. W., Howard, S. R., & Caggiano, J. (1981, August). The effects of multi-year, guaranteed contracts on the performance of pitchers in major league baseball. Paper presented at the annual meeting of the American Psychological Association, Los Angeles, CA.

Olds, J. (1977). *Drives and reinforcements: Behavioral studies of hypothalamic functions*. New York: Raven Press.

Olds, J., & Milner, P. (1954). Positive reinforcement produced by electrical stimulation of septal area and other regions of rat brain. *Journal of Comparative and Physiological Psychology*, 47, 419–427.

Olds, M. E. & Fobes, J. L. (1981). The central basis of motivation: Intracranial self-stimulation studies. *Annual Review of Psychology*, 32, 523–574.

O'Leary, K. D., & Becker, W. C. (1967). Behavior modification of an adjustment class: A token reinforcement program. *Exceptional Children*, 33, 637–642.

Olmstead, B. (1983, February 17). More heavy drinking in colleges. *Los Angeles Times*.

Orlick, T.D. (1975). The sports environment: A capacity to enhance - a capacity to destroy. In B.S. Rushall (Ed.), *The status of psychomotor learning and sport psychology research*. Dartmouth, Nova Scotia: Sport Science Associates.

Orne, M. T. (1982). Perspectives in biofeedback: Ten years ago, today, and . . . In L. White & B. Tursky (Eds.), *Clinical biofeedback: Efficacy and mechanisms* (pp. 422–437). New York: Guilford.

Orne, M. T., & Wilson, S. K. (1978). On the nature of alpha feedback training. In G. E. Schwartz & D. Shapiro (Eds.), *Consciousness and self-regulation* (pp. 359–400). New York: Plenum.

Ornstein, R. E. (1972). *The psychology of consciousness*. San Francisco: Freeman.

Ornstein, R. E., & Galin, D. (1976). Physiological studies of consciousness. In P. Lec, R. E. Ornstein, D. Galin, A. Deichman, & C. Tart (Eds.), *Symposium on consciousness*. New York: Viking Press.

Orpen, C. (1981). Effect of flexible working hours on employee satisfaction and performance: A field experiment. *Journal of Applied Psychology, 66*, 113–115.

Osgood, C. E. (1952). The nature and measurement of meaning. *Psychological Bulletin, 49*, 197–237.

Oskamp, S. (1984). *Applied social psychology*. Englewood Cliffs, NJ: Prentice-Hall.

Oster, G. (1984). Muscle sounds. *Scientific American*, 250(3), pp. 108–114.

Overmier, J. B., & Seligman, M. E. P. (1967). Effects of inescapable shock upon subsequent escape and avoidance learning. *Journal of Comparative and Physiological Psychology, 63*, 23–33.

Overton, D. A. (1985). Contextual stimulus effects of drugs and internal states. In P. D. Balsam & A. Tomie (Eds.), *Context and learning* (pp. 357–384). Hillsdale, NJ: Erlbaum.

Owen, J. D. (1976). Flextime: Some problems and solutions. *Industrial and Labor Relations Review, 29*, 152–160.

Owen, M. T., Easterbrooks, M. A., Chase-Lansdale, L., & Goldberg, W. A. (1984). The relation between maternal employment status and the stability of attachments to mother and to father. *Child Development, 55*, 1894–1901.

Owens, W. A., & Schoenfeldt, L. F. (1979). Toward a classification of persons. *Journal of Applied Psychology Monograph, 64*, 569–607.

Pagano, R. R. (1981). *Understanding statistics*. St. Paul: West.

Pagano, R. R., & Warrenburg, S. (1983) Meditation. In R. J. Davidson, G. E. Schwartz, & D. Shapiro (Eds.), *Consciousness and self-regulation* (pp. 153–210). New York: Plenum.

Page, J. D. (1971). *Psychopathology*. Chicago: Aldine.

Paivio, A. (1969). Mental imagery in associative learning and memory. *Psychological Review, 76*, 241–263.

Palazolli, M. (1978). *Self starvation*. Jason Aronson.

Palkovitz, R. J., & Lore, R. K. (1980). Note taking and note review: Why students fail questions based on lecture material. *Teaching of Psychology, 7*, 159–160.

Palmer, M. H., Lloyd, M. E. & Lloyd, K. E. (1977). An experimental analysis of electricity conservation procedures. *Journal of Applied Behavior Analysis, 10*, 665–671.

Pappenheimer, J. R. (1976, August). The sleep factor. *Scientific American*.

Pardine, P., Napoli, A., Goodman, M., & Schure, M. (1981, August). Physiological correlates of recent life stress experience. Paper presented at the annual convention of the American Psychological Association, Los Angeles, CA.

Parke, R. D., & Asher, S. R. (1983). Social and personality development. *Annual Review of Psychology, 34*, 465–509.

Parke, R. D., & Sawin, D. B. (1977, November). Fathering: It's a major role. *Psychology Today*.

Parkes, C. M. (1979). Grief: The painful reaction to the loss of a loved one. *Monograph, University of California, San Diego*.

Parks, T. E. (1984). Illusory figures: A (mostly) atheoretical review. *Psychological Bulletin, 95*, 282–300.

Parlee, M. B. (1979). Psychology and women. *Journal of Women in Culture and Society, 5*, 121–133.

Parlee, M. B., & the Editors of *Psychology Today* Magazine. (1979, October). The friendship bond. *Psychology Today*.

Parnes, S. J. (1967). *Creative behavior workbook*. New York: Scribners.

Pasachoff, J. (1981). *Contemporary Astronomy* (2nd ed.). New York: Holt, Rinehart & Winston.

Patterson, F. (1978). Conversations with a gorilla. *National Geographic, 154*(4), pp. 438–465.

Patterson, G. R. (1982). *Coercive family process*. Eugene, OR: Castilia Press.

Pavlov, I. P. (1927). *Conditioned reflexes*. Translated by G. V. Anrep. New York: Dover.

Pelham, W. E. (1977). Withdrawal of a stimulant drug and concurrent behavioral intervention in the treatment of a hyperactive child. *Behavior Therapy, 8*, 473–479.

Pellegrino, J. W. (1985, October). Anatomy of analogy. *Psychology Today*, pp. 49–54.

Pelton, T. (1983, May). The shootists. *Science 83*, 4(4), pp. 84–86.

Penfield, W. (1957, April 27). Brain's record of past: A continuous movie film. *Science News Letter*, p. 265.

Penfield, W. (1958). *The excitable cortext in conscious man*. Springfield, IL: Thomas.

Perin, C. T. (1943). A quantitative investigation of the delay of reinforcement gradient. *Journal of Experimental Psychology, 32*, 37–51.

Perkins, D. G., & Perkins, F. M. (1976). *Nailbiting and cuticlebiting: Kicking the habit*. Richardson, TX: Self-Control Press.

Perkoff, G. T. (1980). The meaning of "experimental." In E. S. Valenstein (Ed.), *The psychosurgery debate*. San Francisco: W. H. Freeman.

Perlmutter, F., & Silverman, H. A. (1972). CMHC: A structural anachronism. *Social Work, 17*, 78–84.

Perls, F. (1969). *Gestalt therapy verbatim*. Lafayette, CA: Real People Press.

Persky, H., Lief, H. I., Straus, D., Miller, W. R., & O'Brien, C. P. (1978). Plasma testosterone level and sexual behavior of couples. *Archives of Sexual Behavior, 7*, 157–173.

Peters, W. A. (1971). *A class divided*. Garden City, NY: Doubleday.

Peterson, L. R., & Peterson, M. J. (1959). Short-term retention of individual verbal items. *Journal of Experimental Psychology, 58*, 193–198.

Peterson, P. L. (1979). Direct instruction: Effective for what and for whom? *Educational Leadership, 37*, 46–48.

Phillips, D. (1982). The impact of fictional television stories on U.S. adult fatalities: New evidence on the effect of mass media on violence. *American Journal of Sociology, 87*, 1340–1359.

Phillips, J. L. (1969). *Origins of intellect: Piaget's theory*. San Francisco: Freeman.

Piaget, J. (1951; original French, 1945). *The psychology of intelligence*. New York: Norton.

Piaget, J. (1952). *The origins of intelligence in children*. New York: International University Press.

Pierrel, R., & Sherman, J. G. (1963, February). Train your pet the Barnabus way. *Brown Alumni Monthly*.

Piliavin, I. M., Rodin, J., & Piliavin, J. A. (1969). Good samaritanism: An underground phenomenon? *Journal of Personality and Social Psychology, 13*, 289–299.

Pilkonis, P. A. (1977). The behavioral consequences of shyness. *Journal of Personality, 45*, 596–611.

Pines, M. (1963, May). How three-year-olds teach themselves to read—and love it. *Harper's Magazine*, pp. 58–64.

Pines, M. (1969, July 6). Why some three-year-olds get A's and some get C's. *The New York Times Magazine*, pp. 4–5, 10–17.

Pines, M. (1970, November 29). Infants are smarter than anybody thinks. *The New York Times Magazine*, pp. 32–33, 110, 114–120.

Pines, M. (1980, December). The sinister hand. *Science 80*, pp. 26–27.

Pion, G. (1986, January). Job focus shifts to service, policy. *APA Monitor*, p. 25.

Playboy, (1969). *16*(2), 46.

Plutchik, R. (1980). *Emotion*. New York: Harper & Row.

Polivy, J., & Herman, C. P. (1985). Dieting and Binging. *American Psychologist*, *40*, 193–201.

Potkay, C. R., & Allen, B. P. (1986). *Personality: Theory, research, and applications*. Monterey, CA: Brooks/Cole.

Premack, A. J., & Premack, D. (1972, October). Teaching language to an ape. *Scientific American*, pp. 92–99.

Premack, D. (1970, September). The education of S*A*R*A*H. *Psychology Today*, pp. 54–58.

Premack, D. (1983). Animal cognition. *Annual Review of Psychology*, *34*, 351–362.

Premack, D., & Premack, A. J. (1983). *The mind of an ape*. New York: Norton.

President's Commission on Mental Health. (1978). Report to the President. Washington DC: U.S. Government Printing Office.

Pressley, M., Levine, J. R. Nakamura, G. V., Hope, D. J., Bispo, J. G., & Toye, A. R. (1980). The keyword method of foreign vocabulary learning: An investigation of its generalizability. *Journal of Applied Psychology*, *65*, 635–642.

Pritchard, R. M. (1961). A collimator stabilizing system. *Quarterly Journal of Experimental Psychology*, *13*, 181–183.

Pueschel, S. M., Canning, C. D., Murphy, A., & Zausmer, E. (1978). *Down syndrome: Growing and learning*. Kansas City, MO: Sheed Andrews & McMeel.

Pursch, J. A. (1983, June 12). Cocaine can give you the business. *Los Angeles Times*, Part VII, p. 12.

Rader, P. E., & Hicks, R. A. (1987, April). Jet lag desynchronization and self-assessment of business-related performance. Paper presented at the Western Psychological Association meeting, Long Beach, CA.

Rafaeli, A., & Klimoski, R. J. (1983). Predicting sales success through handwriting analysis: An evaluation of the effects of training and handwriting sample content. *Journal of Applied Psychology*, *68*, 212–217.

Rahe, R. H. (1972). Subjects' recent life changes and their near-future illness reports. *Annals of Clinical Research*, *4*, 250–265.

Randi, J. (1980). *Flim-flam!* New York: Lippincott & Crowell.

Randi, J. (1983). Science and the chimera. In G. O. Abell & B. Singer (Eds.), *Science and the paranormal*. New York: Scribner.

Raven, B. H. (1974). The analysis of power and power preference. In J. T. Tebeschi (Ed.), *Prospectus on social power*. Chicago: Aldine.

Rechtschaffen, A., Gilliland, M. A., Bergmann, B. M., & Winter, J. B. (1983). Physiological correlates of prolonged sleep deprivation in rats. *Science*, *221*, 182–184.

Reif, A. E. (1981). The causes of cancer. *American Scientist*, *69*, 437–447.

Reiser, M. (1985). *Mind, brain, body: Toward a convergence of psychoanalysis*. New York: Basic.

Renwick, P. A., & Lawler, E. E. (1979) What you really want from your job. *Psychology Today*, *11*(12), pp. 53–65.

Rescorla, R. (1980). *Pavlovian second-order conditioning: Studies in associative learning*. MacEachren Lectures, Halsted Press.

Rescorla, R. A. (1987). A Pavlovian analysis of goal-directed behavior. *American Psychologist*, *42*, 119–126.

Resnick, R. B., Kestenbaum, R. S., & Schwartz, K. L. (1977). Acute systemic effects of cocaine in man: A controlled study in intranasal and intravenous routes. *Science*, *195*, 696–698.

Reybowski, J. (1982). Social motivation. *Annual Review of Psychology*, *33*, 123–154.

Rhine, J. B. (1953). *New world of the mind*. New York: Sloane.

Rhine, J. B. (1974). Security versus deception in parapsychology. *Journal of Parapsychology*, *38*, 99–121.

Rhine, J. B. (1977). History of experimental studies. In B. B. Wolman (Ed.), *Handbook of parapsychology*. New York: Van Nostrand Reinhold.

Ricketts, M. S., & Galloway, R. E. (1984). Effects of three different one-hour single-session treatments for test anxiety. *Psychological Reports*, *54*, 113–119.

Rieger, M. G. (1976, October 30). Pain control through hypnosis. *Science News*.

Rimland, B. (1978). Inside the mind of the autistic savant. *Psychology Today*, *12*, pp. 68–80.

Rincover, A., Newsom, C. D., Lovaas, O. I., & Koegel, R. L. (1977). Some motivational properties of sensory stimulation in psychotic children. *Journal of Experimental Child Psychology*, *24*, 312–323.

Ritchie, R. J., & Moses, J. L. (1983). Assessment center correlates of women's advancement into middle management: A 7-year longitudinal analysis. *Journal of Applied Psychology*, *68*, 227–231.

Roach, M. (1985, August). Reflection in a fatal mirror. *Discover*, pp. 76–85.

Roberts, D. F., & Bachen, C. M. (1981). Mass communication effects. *Annual Review of Psychology*, *32*, 307–356.

Robertson, T. S., Zielinski, J., & Ward, S. (1984). *Consumer behavior*. Glenview, IL: Scott, Foresman.

Robinson, F. P. (1941). *Effective behavior*. New York: Harper & Row.

Robinson, H. B., & Robinson, N. M. (1976). Mental retardation. In P. H. Mussen (Ed.), *Carmichael's manual of child psychology*, Vol. 2 (3rd ed.). New York: Wiley.

Robson, P. (1984). Prewalking locomotor movements and their use in predicting standing and walking. *Child Care, Health & Development*, *10*, 317–330.

Rock, I., & Kaufman, L. (1962). The moon illusion II. *Science*, *136*, 1023–1031.

Rodgers, J. E. (1982, July/August). Roots of madness. *Science 82*.

Rodin, J. (1978). Stimulus-bound behavior and biological self-regulation: Feeding, obesity, and external control. In G. E. Schwartz & D. Shapiro (Eds.), *Consciousness and self-regulation* (pp. 215–239). New York: Plenum.

Rodin, J. (1981). Current status of the internal-external hypothesis for obesity: What went wrong? *American Psychologist*, *36*, 361–372.

Rogers, C. R. (1957). The necessary and sufficient conditions of therapeutic personality change. *Journal of Consulting Psychology*, *21*, 95–103.

Rogers, C. R. (1959). A theory of therapy, personality, and interpersonal relationships, as developed in the client-centered framework. In

S. Koch (Ed.), *Psychology: A study of a science*, Vol. 3. New York: McGraw-Hill.

Rogers, C. R. (1961). *On becoming a person: A therapist's view of psychotherapy*. Boston: Houghton Mifflin.

Rogers, C. R. (1962, January 28). Learning to be free. Paper presented at a session on "Conformity and Diversity" in the conference on "Man and Civilization," sponsored by the University of California School of Medicine, San Francisco, CA.

Rogers, C. R. (1980). *A way of being*. Boston: Houghton Mifflin.

Rohsenow, D. J., & Smith, R. E. (1982). Irrational beliefs as predictors of negative affective states. *Motivation and Emotion, 6*, 299–301.

Rokeach, M. (1960). *The open and closed mind*. New York: Basic Books.

Rorer, L. G., & Widiger, T. A. (1983). Personality structure and assessment. *Annual Review of Psychology, 34*, 431–463.

Rosch, E. (1977). Classification of real-world objects: Origins and representations in cognition. In P. N. Johnson-Laird & P. C. Wason (Eds.). *Thinking: Reading in cognitive science*. Cambridge: Cambridge University Press.

Rose, K. J. (1984, February). How animals think. *Science Digest, 89*, pp. 59–61.

Rosen, J. C., & Leitenberg, H. (1982). Bulimia nervosa: Treatment with exposure and response prevention. *Behavior Therapy, 13*, 117–124.

Rosenbaum, M. B. (1979). The changing body image of the adolescent girl. In M. Sugar (Ed.), *Female adolescent development*. New York: Brunner/Mazel.

Rosenberg, J., & Pettinati, H. M. (1984). Differential memory complaints after bilateral and unilateral ECT. *American Journal of Psychiatry, 14*, 1071–1074.

Rosenfeld, P., Giacalone, R. A., & Tedeschi, J. T. (1983). Cognitive dissonance vs. impression management. *Journal of Social Psychology, 120*, 203–211.

Rosenhan, D. L. (1973). On being sane in insane places. *Science, 179*, 250–258.

Rosenman, R. H., Brand, R. J., Jenkins, C. D., Friedman, M., Straus, R., & Wurm, M. (1975). Coronary heart disease in the Western Collaborative Group Study: Final follow-up experience of 8½ years. *Journal of the American Medical Association, 233*, 872–877.

Rosenthal, D., (1963). *The Genain quadruplets*. New York: Basic Books.

Rosenthal, D., & Quinn, O. W. (1977). Quadruplet hallucinations: Phenotypic variations of a schizophrenic genotype. *Archives of General Psychiatry, 34*(7), 817–827.

Rosenthal, R. (1965). Clever Hans: A case study of scientific method. Introduction to *Clever Hans: (The horse of Mr. Von Osten)*, O. Pfungst. New York: Holt, Rinehart & Winston.

Rosenthal, R. (1976). *Experimenter effects in behavioral research*. New York: Appleton-Century-Crofts.

Rosenthal, R. (1973, September). The Pygmalion effect lives. *Psychology Today*, pp. 56–63.

Rosenthal, R. (1976). *Experimenter effects in behavioral research*. New York: Irvington.

Rosenthal, T. L., Linehan, K. S., Kelley, J. E., Rosenthal, R. H., Theobald, D. E., & Davis, A. F. (1978). Group aversion by imaginal, vicarious and shared recipient-observer shocks. *Behavior Research and Therapy, 16*, 421–427.

Rosenthal, T. L., & Rosenthal, R. (1980). The vicious cycle of stress reaction. Memphis, TN: Stress Management Clinic, Department of Psychiatry, University of Tennessee College of Medicine.

Rosenthal, T. L., & Zimmerman, B. J. (1978). *Social learning and cognition*. New York: Academic Press.

Roskies, E., & Lazarus, R. (1980). Coping theory and the teaching of coping skills. In P. Davidson & S. Davidson (Eds.), *Behavioral medicine: Changing health life styles*. New York: Brunner/Mazel.

Ross, L. (1977). The intuitive psychologist and his shortcomings: Distortions in the attribution process. In L. Berkowitz (Eds.), *Advances in experimental social psychology*. New York: Academic Press.

Ross, M., Karniol, R., & Rothstein, M. (1976). Reward contingency and intrinsic motivation in children. *Journal of Personality and Social Psychology, 33*, 442–447.

Rotter, J. B., & Hochreich, D. J. (1975). *Personality*. Glenview, IL: Scott, Foresman.

Rowe, D. C. (1987). Resolving the person-situation debate. *American Psychologist, 42*, 218–227.

Rubenstein, C. (1983, July). The modern art of courtly love. *Psychology Today*.

Rubin, V., & Comitas, L. (Eds.). (1975). *Ganja in Jamaica*. The Hague: Mouton.

Rubin, Z. (1970). Measurement of romantic love. *Journal of Personality and Social Psychology, 16*, 265–273.

Rubin, Z. (1970, December). Jokers wild in the lab. *Psychology Today*.

Rubin, Z. (1973). *Liking and loving: An invitation to social psychology*. New York: Holt.

Rubin, Z. (1975). Disclosing oneself to a stranger: Reciprocity and its limits. *Journal of Experimental and Social Psychology, 11*, 233–260.

Rubinstein, E. A. (1978). Television and the young viewer. *American Scientist, 66*, 685–693.

Ruch, F. L., Zimbardo, P. G. (1971). *Psychology and life* (8th ed.). Glenview, IL: Scott, Foresman.

Rudestam, K. E. (1971). Stockholm and Los Angeles: A cross-cultural study of the communication of suicidal intent. *Journal of Consulting and Clinical Psychology, 36*, 82–90.

Ruff, H. A., & Birch, H. G. (1974). Infant visual fixation: The effect of concentricity, curvilinearity, and number of directions. *Journal of Experimental Child Psychology, 17*, 460–473.

Rushall, B.S. (1975). Applied psychology in Sports. In B.S. Rushall (Ed.), *The status of psychomotor learning and sport psychology research*. Dartmouth, Nova Scotia: Sports Science Associates.

Rushton, N. A. H. (1975, March). Visual pigments and color blindness. *Scientific American*, pp. 64–74.

Saarni, C. (1982). Social and affective functions of nonverbal behavior: Developmental concerns. In R. S. Feldman (Ed.), *Development of nonverbal behavior in children* (pp. 123–148). New York: Springer-Verlag.

Saegert, S., Swap, W., & Zajonc, R. B. (1973). Exposure, context, and interpersonal attraction. *Journal of Personality and Social Psychology, 25*, 234–242.

Salmela, J.H. (1974). An information processing approach to volleyball. *C.V.A. Technical Journal, 1*, 49–62.

Salmela, J.H. (1975). Psycho-motor task demands of artistic gymnastics. In J.H. Salmela (Ed.), *The advanced study of gymnastics: A textbook*. Sundby Publications.

Salmoni, A. W., Schmidt, R. A., & Walter, C. B. (1984). Knowledge of results and motor learning: A review and critical reappraisal. *Psychological Bulletin, 95*, 355–386.

Sanders, G. S., & Simmons, W. L. (1983). Use of hypnosis to enhance eyewitness accuracy: Does it work? *Journal of Applied Psychology, 68,* 70–77.

Santrock, J. W. (1984). *Adolescence.* Dubuque, IA: Brown.

Sarason, I. G. (1975). Test anxiety, attention, and the general problem of anxiety. In C. D. Spielberger & I. G. Sarason (Eds.), *Stress and anxiety,* Vol. 1. Washington, DC: Hemisphere.

Sarason, I. G. (1981). Test anxiety, stress, and social support. *Journal of Personality, 49,* 101–114.

Savage-Rumbaugh, E. S., Rumbaugh, D. M., & Boysen, S. (1980). Do apes use language? *American Scientist, 68,* 49–61.

Saxe, L., Dougherty, D., & Cross, T. (1985). The validity of polygraph testing. *American Psychologist, 40,* 355–366.

Scarr, S., Webber, P. L., Weinberg, R. A., & Wittig, M. A. (1981). Personality resemblance among adolescents and their parents in biologically related and adoptive families. *Journal of Personality and Social Psychology, 40,* 885–898.

Scarr-Salapatek, S. (1971). Race, social class, and I.Q. *Science, 174,* 1223–1228.

Scarr-Salapatek, S., & Weinberg, R. A. (1975, December). When black children grow up in white homes . . . *Psychology Today.*

Schachter, S. (1951). Communication, deviation, and rejection. *Journal of Abnormal and Social Psychology, 46,* 190–207.

Schachter, S. (1959). *Psychology of affiliation.* Stanford, CA: Stanford University Press.

Schachter, S. (1978). Pharmacological and psychological determinants of smoking. In R. E. Thornton (Ed.), *Smoking behavior.* Edinburgh: Churchill Livingston.

Schachter, S., & Rodin, J. (1974). *Obese humans and rats.* Potomac, MD: Earlbaum.

Schachter, S., & Wheeler, L. (1962). Epinephine, chlorpromazine and amusement. *Journal of Abnormal and Social Psychology, 65,* 121–128.

Scheer, R. (1987, August 14). Aids threat to all—How Serious? *Los Angeles Times,* p. 1.

Schein, E. H., Hill, W. F., Lubin, A., & Williams, H. L. (1957). Distinguishing characteristics of collaborators and resistors among American prisoners of war. *Journal of Abnormal and Social Psychology, 55,* 197–201.

Schein, E. H., Schneier, I., & Barker, C. H. (1961). *Coercive persuasion.* New York: Norton.

Schiff, M., Duyme, M., Dumaret, A., Stewart, J., Tomkiewicz, S., & Feingold, J. (1978). Intellectual status of working-class children adopted early into upper-middle-class families. *Science, 200,* 1503–1504.

Schlesier-Stropp, B. (1984). Bulimia: A review of the literature. *Psychological Bulletin, 38,* 247–257.

Schless, A. P. (1977). Life events and illness: A three-year prospective study. *British Journal of Psychiatry, 131,* 26–34.

Schlosberg, H. (1954). Three dimensions of emotion. *Psychological Review, 61,* 81–88.

Schmeidler, G. R. (1977). Methods for controlled research on ESP and PK. In B. B. Wolman (Ed.), *Handbook of parapsychology.* New York: Van Nostrand Reinhold.

Schmidt, J. A. (1976). *Help yourself: A guide to self-change.* Champaign, IL: Research Press.

Schneidman, E. S. (1971). You and death. *Psychology Today,* 5(1), pp. 43–45, 74–80.

Schneidman, E. S., Farherow, N. L., & Cabista, L. (1965). *Some facts about suicide causes and prevention.* Washington, DC: U.S. Government Printing Office.

Schommer, N. (1984, October). Shrinks on the air. *Discover,* pp. 68–70.

Schopler, E. (1978). Changing parental involvement in behavioral treatment. In M. Rutter & E. Schopler (Eds.). *Autism: A reappraisal of concepts and treatment.* New York: Plenum.

Schreiber, F. R. (1973). *Sybil.* Chicago: Regency.

Schuele, J. G., & Wiesenfeld, A. R. (1983). Autonomic response to self-critical thought. *Cognitive Therapy and Research,* 7, 189–194.

Schultz, D. P. (1979). *Psychology in use, an introduction to applied psychology.* New York: Macmillan.

Schulz, R. (1978). *The psychology of death, dying and bereavement.* Reading, MA: Addison-Wesley.

Schuman, M. (1980). The psychophysiological model of meditation and altered states of consciousness: A critical review. In J. M. Davidson & R. C. Davidson (Eds.), *The psychobiology of consciousness.* New York: Plenum.

Schwartz, B. (1984). *Psychology of learning & behavior* (2nd ed.). New York: Norton.

Sclafani, A., & Springer, D. (1976). Dietary obesity in adult rats: Similarities to hypothalamic and human obesity syndromes. *Psysiology and Behavior, 17,* 461–471.

Scott, E. M., & Verney, E. L. (1947). Self-selection and diet: VI. The nature of appetites for B vitamins. *Journal of Nutrition, 34,* 471–480.

Sears, R. R., Maccoby, E. E., & Levin, H. (1957). *Patterns of child rearing.* Evanston, IL: Row, Peterson.

Seiden, R. H. (1966). Campus tragedy: A study of student suicide. *Journal of Abnormal Psychology, 1,* 389–399.

Seixas, F. A. (1981). Alcoholism. In S. J. Mule (Ed.), *Behavior in Excess* (pp. 120–129). New York: The Free Press.

Seligman, C., & Darley, J. M. (1978). Feedback as a means of decreasing residential energy consumption. *Journal of Applied Psychology,* 62, 363–368.

Seligman, M. E. P. (1972). For helplessness: Can we immunize the weak? In *Readings in psychology today* (2nd ed.). Del Mar, CA: CRM.

Seligman, M. E. P. (1974). Submissive death: Giving up on life. *Psychology Today, 7,* pp. 80–85.

Selye, H. (1956, 1976). *The stress of life.* New York: Knopf.

Selye, H. (1976). *Stress in health and disease.* Boston: Butterworth.

Senden, M. V. (1960). *Space and sight.* Translated by P. Heath. Glencoe, IL: Free Press.

Serban, G. (1982). *The tyranny of magical thinking.* New York: Dutton.

Serbin, L. A., & O'Leary, K. D. (1975, December). How nursery schools teach girls to shut up. *Psychology Today,* pp. 57–58, 102–103.

Sexual Medicine Today (1980, April), p. 17.

Shaffer, L.F. (1974). Fear and courage in aerial combat. *Journal of Consulting Psychology, 11,* 137–143.

Shapiro, D. A., & Shapiro, D. (1982). Meta-analysis of comparative therapy outcome studies: A replication and refinement. *Psychological Bulletin,* 92, 581–604.

Shaw, G. A., & Belmore, S. M. (1983). The relationship between imagery and creativity. *Imagination, Cognition, and Personality,* 2, 115–123.

Sheehan, J. G., & Costley, M. S. (1977). A reexamination of the role of heredity in stuttering. *Journal of Speech and Hearing Disorders,* 42, 47–59.

Sheehan, P. W., Grigg, L., & McCann, T. (1984). Memory distortion following exposure to false information in hypnosis. *Journal of Abnormal Psychology*, 93, 259–265.

Sheehy, G. (1976). *Passages: Predictable crises of adult life*. New York: Dutton.

Sheils, M., & Monroe, S. (1976, March 22). A ban on I.Q. tests? *Newsweek*, p. 49.

Shepard, R. N. (1975). Form, formation, and transformation of internal representations. In R. L. Solso (Ed.), *Information processing and cognition: The Loyola Symposium*. Hillsdale, NJ: Erlbaum.

Sherif, M. (1935). A study of some social factors in perception. *Archives of Psychology*, 27,(187).

Sherif, M., Harvey, O. J., White, B. J., Hood, W. R., & Sherif, C. W. (1961). *Intergroup conflict and cooperation: The Robbers Cave experiment*. University of Oklahoma: Institute of Group Relations.

Shiffman, S. M. (1980). Diminished smoking, withdrawal symptoms, and cessation: A cautionary note. In G. B. Gori & F. G. Bock (Eds.), *Banbury report*. Cold Spring Harbor Laboratory.

Shiffrin, R. M. (1970). Forgetting: Trace erosion or retrieval failure? *Science*, *168*, 1601–1603.

Shiffrin, R. M., & Cook, J. R. (1978). Short-term forgetting of item and order information. *Journal of Verbal Learning and Verbal Behavior*, *17*, 189–218.

Shneidman, E. (1987, March). At the point of no return. *Psychology Today*, pp. 54–58.

Shodell, M. (1984). The clouded mind. *Science 84*.

Short, A. B. (1984). Short-term treatment outcome using parents as cotherapists for their own autistic children. *Journal of Child Psychology & Psychiatry*, 25, 443–458.

Shulman, G. I. (1974). Race, sex and violence: A laboratory test of the sexual threat of the black male hypothesis. *American Journal of Sociology*, 79, 1260–1277.

Siegel, O. (1982). Personality development in adolescence. In B. B. Wolman, G. Stricker, S. J. Ellman, P. Keith-Spiegel, & D. S. Palermo (Eds.), *Handbook of developmental psychology* (pp. 537–548). Englewood Cliffs, NJ: Prentice Hall.

Siegel, S., Hearst, E., George, N., & O'Neal, E. (1968). Generalization gradients obtained from individual subjects following classical conditioning. *Journal of Experimental Psychology*, 78, 171–174.

Simon, W., & Gagnon, J. (1973). Psychosexual development. In E. S. Morrison & V. Borosage (Eds.). *Human sexuality: Contemporary perspectives*. Palo Alto, CA: Mayfield.

Singer, M. T. (1979, January). Coming out of the cults. *Psychology Today*, pp. 72–82.

Singer, R. N. (1978). Motor skills and learning strategies. In H. F. O'-Neil, Jr. (Ed.), *Learning strategies*. New York: Academic Press.

Skeels, H. M. (1966). Adult status of children with contrasting early life experiences. *Monograph of the Society for Research in Child Development*, 31(3).

Skinner, B. F. (1938). *The behavior of organisms*. Englewood Cliffs, NJ: Prentice-Hall.

Skinner, B. F. (1971). *Beyond freedom and dignity*. New York: Bantam.

Smith, B. M. (1971). *The polygraph in contemporary psychology*. San Francisco: Freeman.

Smith, M. L., & Glass, G. V. (1977). Meta-analysis of psychotherapy outcome studies. *American Psychologist*, 32, 752–760.

Snow, C. E. (1977). The development of conversation between mothers and babies. *Journal of Child Language*, 4, 1–22.

Snow, C. P. (1961, February). Either-or. *Progressive*, p. 24.

Snow, R. E. (1986). Individual differences and the design of educational programs. *American Psychologist*, *41*, 1029–1039.

Snyder, C. R., & Shenkel, R. J. (1975, March). P. T. Barnum effect. *Psychology Today*, 8, pp. 52–54.

Snyder, S. H. (1972, January). The true speed trip: schizophrenia. *Psychology Today*.

Snyder, S. H., & Childers, S. R. (1979). Opiate receptors and opioid peptides. *Annual Review of Neuroscience*, 2, 35–64.

Solanto, M. V. (1984). Neuropharmacological basis of stimulant drug action in attention deficit disorder with hyperactivity: A review and synthesis. *Psychological Bulletin*, 95, 387–409.

Sommer, R. (1969). *Personal space: The behavioral basis of design*. Englewood Cliffs, NJ: Prentice-Hall.

Sommer, R. (1977, January). Toward a psychology of natural behavior. *APA Monitor*.

Sorce, J. F., Emde, R. N., Campos, J. J., & Klinnert, M. D. (1985). Maternal emotional signaling: Its effect on the visual cliff behavior of 1-year-olds. *Developmental Psychology*, *21*, 195–200.

Spence, J. T. (1984). Masculinity, femininity, and gender-related traits: A conceptual analysis and critique of current research. In B. A. Maker & W. B. Maker (Eds.), *Progress in experimental personality research: Normal personality processes* (Vol. 13). New York: Academic Press.

Sperry, R. W. (1956). The eye and the brain. *Scientific American*, Offprint No. 465, pp. 48–52.

Sperry, R. W. (1968). Hemisphere deconnection and unity in conscious awareness. *American Psychologist*, 23, 723–733.

Spielberger, C. D., Anton, W. D., & Bedell, J. (1976). The nature and treatment of test anxiety. In M. Zuckerman & C. D. Spielberger (Eds.), *Emotions and anxiety: New concepts, methods, and applications* (pp. 317–345). Hillsdale, NJ: Erlbaum.

Spiesman, J. C., Lazarus. R. S., Mordkoff, A. M., & Davidson, L. A. (1964). The experimental reduction of stress based on ego-defense theory. *Journal of Abnormal and Social Psychology*, 68, 367–380.

Spitz, R. A. (1945). Hospitalism: An inquiry into the genesis of psychiatric conditions in early childhood. In *The psychoanalytic study of the child* (Vol. 1, pp. 53–74). New York: International University Press.

Spotts, J. V., & Shontz, F. C. (1980). *Cocaine users*. New York: The Free Press.

Stapp, J., & Fulcher, R. (1983). *Salaries in psychology*. *Washington DC*: American Psychological Association.

Stark, E. (1981, September). Pigeon patrol. *Science 81*, pp. 85–86.

Stark, R., & McEvoy, J. (1970, November). Middle-class violence. *Psychology Today*.

Stefanis, C., Dornbush, R. L., & Fink, M. (1977). *Hashish: A study of long-term use*. New York: Raven Press.

Stein, M. I. (1974). *Stimulating creativity* (Vol. 1). New York: Academic Press.

Steinberg, L. D., Catalano, R., & Dooley, P. (1981). Economic antecedents of child abuse and neglect. *Child Development*, 52, 975–985.

Sterman, M. B. (1977). Effects of sensorimotor EEG feedback training on sleep and clinical manifestations of epilepsy. In J. Beatty & H. Legewie (Eds.), *Biofeedback and behavior*. New York: Plenum.

Stern, C. (1956). Hereditary factors affecting adoption: A study of adoption practices. *Child Welfare League of America*, 2, p. 53.

Stern, D. (1982). Some interactive functions of rhythm changes between

mother and infant. In M. Davis (Ed.), *Interaction rhythms, periodicity in communicative behavior*. New York: Human Sciences Press.
Stern, D., Jaffe, J., Beebe, B., & Bennett, S. (1975). Vocalizing in unison and in alternation: Two modes of communication within the mother-infant dyad. In D. Aronson & Rieber (Eds.), *Developmental psycholinguistics and communication disorders* (pp. 89–100). Annals of the New York Academy of Sciences.
Stern, W. C. (1981). REM sleep and behavioral plasticity: Evidence for involvement of brain catecholamines. In W. Fishbein (Ed.), *Sleep, dreams and memory* (pp. 99–109). New York: SP Medical and Scientific Books.
Sternberg, R. J. (1985a). *Beyond IQ*. Cambridge: Cambridge University Press.
Sternberg, R. J., & Davidson, J. E. (1982, June). The mind of the puzzler. *Psychology Today*.
Stevens, J. O. (1971). *Awareness: Exploring, experimenting, experiencing*. Lafayette, CA: Real People Press.
Stiles, W. B., Shapiro, D. A., & Elliott, R. (1986). Are all psychotherapies equivalent? *American Psychologist, 41*, 165–180.
Stokols, D. (1978). Environmental psychology. *Annual Review of Psychology*, 29, 253–295.
Stoller, F. H. (1967). The long weekend. *Psychology Today, 1*(7), pp. 28–33.
Stoller, F. H. (1972). Marathon groups: Toward a conceptual model. In L. N. Solomon & B. Berzon (Eds.), *New Perspectives on Encounter Groups* (pp. 171–194). San Francisco: Jossey-Bass.
Strange, J. R. (1965). *Abnormal psychology*. New York: McGraw-Hill.
Streissguth, A. P., et al. (1984). Intrauterine alcohol and nicotine exposure: Attention and reaction time in 4-year-old children. *Developmental Psychology, 20*, 533–541.
Stunkard, A. (1980). *Obesity*. Philadelphia: Saunders.
Sue, D., Sue, D. W., & Sue, S. (1981). *Understanding abnormal behavior*. Boston: Houghton Mifflin.
Suefeld, P. (1966). *Social processes*. Dubuque, IA: Brown.
Suefeld, P. (1975, January–February). The benefits of boredom: Sensory deprivation reconsidered. *American Scientist, 63*.
Suinn, R. M. (1970). *Fundamentals of behavior pathology*. New York: Wiley.
Suinn, R. M. (1975). *Fundamentals of behavior pathology* (2nd ed.). New York: Wiley.
Suinn, R. M. (1982). Intervention with Type A behaviors. *Journal of Consulting and Clinical Psychology, 50*, 933–949.
Sully, R. (1983). The work-setting support group: A means of preventing burnout. In B. A. Farber (Ed.), *Stress and burnout in the human service professions* (pp. 188–197). New York: Pergamon.
Swensen, C. H. (1973). *Introduction to interpersonal relations*. Glenview, IL: Scott, Foresman.

Takooshian, H., Haber, S., & Lucido, D. J. (1977, February). Who wouldn't help a lost child? You, maybe. *Psychology Today*, p. 67.
Tanner, J. M. (1973, September). Growing up. *Scientific American*, pp. 34–43.
Tanzer, D., & Block, J. L. (1976). *Why natural childbirth?* New York: Schocken.
Tart, C. T. (1975). *States of consciousness*. New York: Dutton.
Taylor, C. W. (1978). How many types of giftedness can your program tolerate? *The Journal of Creative Behavior, 12*, 39–51.
Taylor, T. E. (1983, March 17). Learning studies of higher cognitive levels in short-term sensory isolation environment. Paper presented at the First International Conference on REST and Self-regulation, Denver, CO.
Ten Danger Signals of Depression. The National Association for Mental Health, Virginia.
Tenopyr, M. L., & Oeltjen, P. D. (1982). Personnel selection and classification. *Annual Review of Psychology*, 33, 581–618.
Tephly, J. B., & Elardo, R. (1984). Mothers and day-care teachers: Young children's perceptions. *British Journal of Developmental Psychology*, 2, 251–256.
Terman, L. M., & Oden, M. (1959). *The gifted group in mid-life: Vol. 5. Genetic studies of genius*. Stanford, CA: Stanford University Press.
Terman, L. M., & Merrill, M. A. (1937; revised ed., 1960). *Stanford-Binet Intelligence Scale*. Boston: Houghton Mifflin.
Terrace, H. S. (1985). In the beginning was the "name." *American Psychologist, 40*, 1011–1028.
Thigpen, C. H., & Cleckley, H. M. (1957). *The three faces of Eve*. New York: McGraw-Hill.
Thomas, A., & Chess, S. (1977). *Temperament and development*. New York: Brunner/Mazel.
Thompson, R. I. (1967). *Foundations of physiological psychology*. New York: Harper & Row.
Thoreau, H. D. (1893). *Walden, or life in the woods*. New York: Houghton Mifflin.
Thornburg, H. D. (1984). *Introduction to educational psychology*. St. Paul, MN: West.
Time (1973, January 8).
Tobin, R. L. (1972). Murder on television and the fourteen-year-old. *Saturday Review, 55*, pp. 39–40.
Tolman, E. C., & Honzik, C. H. (1930). Introduction and removal of reward and maze performance in rats. *University of California Publications in Psychology, 4*, 257–275.
Tolman, E. C., Ritchie, B. F., & Kalish, D. (1946). Studies in spatial learning: II. Place learning versus response learning. *Journal of Experimental Psychology, 36*, 221–229.
Tresemer, D. W. (1977). *Fear of success: An intriguing set of questions*. New York: Plenum.
Triandis, H. C. (1977). *Interpersonal behavior*. Monterey, CA: Brooks/Cole.
Trotter, R. J. (1974, August 3). Obesity and behavior. *Science News*.
Truax, S. R. (1983). Active search, mediation, and the manipulation of cue dimensions: Emotion attribution in the false feedback paradigm. *Motivation and Emotion, 7*, 41–60.
Tryon, R. C. (1929). The genetics of learning ability in rats. *University of California Publications in Psychology, 4*, pp. 71–89.
Turek, I. S., & Hanlon, T. E. (1977). The effectiveness and safety of electroconvulsive therapy (ECT). *Journal of Nervous and Mental Disease, 164*, 419–431.
Turnbull, C. M. (1961). Some observations regarding the experiences and behavior of the Bambuti Pygmies. *American Journal of Psychology, 74*, 304–308.
Tversky, A., & Kahneman, D. (1982). Judgments of and by representativeness. In D. Kahneman, P. Slovic, & A. Tversky, *Judgment under uncertainty: Heuristics and biases* (pp. 84–98). Cambridge: Cambridge University Press.
Tversky, A., & Kahneman, D. (1981). The framing of decisions and the psychology of choice. *Science, 211*, 453–458.
Tzeng, O. J. L., & Wang, W. S. Y. (1983). The first two R's. *American Scientist, 71*, 238–243.

Udry, J. R., & Eckland, B. K. (1984). Benefits of being attractive: Differential payoffs for men and women. *Psychological Reports, 54,* 47–56.

Udry, J. R., & Morris, N. M. (1977). Human sexual behavior at different stages of the menstrual cycle. *Journal of Reproduction and Fertility, 51,* 419.

Ulrich, R. E., Stachnik, T. J., & Stainton, N. R. (1963). Student acceptance of generalized personality interpretations. *Psychological Reports, 131,* 831–834.

Underwood, B. J. (1957). Interference and forgetting. *Psychological Review, 64,* 49–60.

Unger, R. K. (1979). Toward a redefinition of sex and gender. *American Psychologist, 34,* 1085–1094.

U.S. Commission on Civil Rights. (1977). *Window dressing on the set: Women and minorities in television.* Washington, DC: U.S. Government Printing Office.

U.S. National Commission on the Causes and Prevention of Violence (1970). *To establish justice to insure domestic tranquility: The final report.* New York: Praeger.

U.S. News and World Report (1979, May 14). Aptitude test scores: Grumbling gets louder, pp. 76–79.

Valenstein, E. S. (1980). Extent of psychosurgery worldwide. In E. S. Valenstein (Ed.), *The psychosurgery debate.* San Francisco: Freeman.

Valins, S. (1966). Cognitive effects of false heart-rate feedback. *Journal of Personality and Social Psychology, 4,* 400–408.

Valins, S. (1967). Emotionality and information concerning internal reactions. *Journal of Personality and Social Psychology, 6,* 458–463.

Van de Castle, R. L. (1971). *The psychology of dreaming.* Morristown, NJ: General Learning Corporation.

Van Gelder, L., & Carmichael, C. (1975, October). But what about our sons? *Ms Magazine.*

van Lawick-Goodall, J. (1971). *In the shadow of man.* New York: Houghton Mifflin.

Van Maanen, J., & Schein, E. H. (1977). Career development. In J. R. Hackman & J. L. Suttle (Eds.), *Improving life at work.* Santa Monica, CA: Goodyear Publishing Co.

Varley, C. K. (1984). Attention deficit disorder (the hyperactivity syndrome): A review of selected issues. *Journal of Developmental & Behavioral Pediatrics, 5,* 254–258.

Vils, U. (1976, February 26). Alcoholism: Tempest in a shot glass. *Los Angeles Times.*

Vogler, R. E., Weissbach, T. A., Compton, J. V., & Martin, G. T. (1977). Integrated behavior change techniques for problem drinkers in the community. *Journal of Consulting and Clinical Psychology, 45,* 267–279.

Volpicelli, J. R., Ulm, R. R., Altenor, A., & Seligman, M. E. P. (1983). Learned mastery in the rat. *Learning and Motivation, 14,* 204–222.

Waid, W. M., & Orne, M. T. (1982, July/August). The physiological detection of deception. *American Scientist, 70,* 402–409.

Wall, P. D. (1976). In J. J. Bonica & D. Albe-Fessard (Eds.). *Advances in pain research and therapy,* Vol. 1. New York: Raven Press.

Wallach, M. A., & Kogan, N. (1965). *Modes of thinking in young children.* New York: Holt.

Walster, E. (1971). Passionate Love. In B. I. Murstein (Ed.), *Theories of attraction and love.* New York: Springer.

Walster, E., & Walster, G. W. (1978). *A new look at love.* Reading, MA: Addison-Wesley.

Warrenburg, S., & R. Pagano. (1983). Meditation and hemispheric specialization: Absorbed attention in long-term adherence. *Imagination, Cognition and Personality, 2,* 211–229.

Watkins, C. E., Jr., Lopez, F. G., Campbell, V. L., & Himmell, C. D. (1986, May). Counseling psychology and clinical psychology: Some preliminary comparative data. *American Psychologist,* 581–582.

Watson, D. L., & Tharp. R. G. (1981). *Self-directed behavior: Self-modification for personal adjustment* (3rd ed.). Monterey, CA: Brooks/Cole.

Watson, J. B. (1913). Psychology as the behaviorist views it. *Psychological Review, 20,* 158–177.

Watts, B. (1982). Individual differences in circadian activity rhythms and their effects on roommate relationships. *Journal of Personality, 50,* 374–384.

Webb, W. (1975). *Sleep the gentle tyrant.* Englewood Cliffs, NJ: Prentice-Hall.

Webb, W. (1978). Sleep and dreams, Part I. *Annual Review of Psychology, 29,* 223–252.

Webb, W. B., & Agnew, H. W. (1975, July). Are we chronically sleep deprived? *Bulletin of the Psychonomic Society, 6*(1), 47–48.

Wechsler, D. (1958). *The measurement and appraisal of adult intelligence* (4th ed.). Baltimore: Williams & Wilkins.

Wegner, D. M., & Vallacher, R. R. (1977). *Implicit psychology.* New York: Oxford University Press.

Weinberg, M. S., & Williams, C. J. (1974). *Male homosexuals.* New York: Oxford University Press.

Weiner, R. D. (1984). Convulsive therapy: 50 years later. *American Journal of Psychiatry, 14,* 1078–1079.

Weintraub, M. I. (1983). *Hysterical conversion reactions.* New York: SP Medical & Scientific Books.

Weisfeld, G. E., & Beresford, J. M. (1982). Erectness of posture as an indicator of dominance or success in humans. *Motivation and Emotion, 6,* 113–131.

Weiss, J. M. (1972). Psychological factors in stress and disease. *Scientific American, 26,* pp. 104–113.

Weisstein, N. (1975). Psychology constructs the female. In I. S. Cohen (Ed.), *Perspectives on psychology* (pp. 318–331). New York: Praeger.

Weiten, W. (1983). *Psychology applied to modern life: Adjustment in the 80's.* Monterey CA: Brooks/Cole.

Weitzenhoffer, A. M., & Hilgard, E. R. (1959). *Stanford hypnotic susceptibility scales forms A and B.* Palo Alto, CA: Consulting Psychologists Press.

Wells, G. L., & Murray, D. M. (1983). What can psychology say about *Neil v. Biggers* criteria for judging eyewitness accuracy? *Journal of Applied Psychology, 68,* 347–362.

Wertheimer, M. (1959). *Productive thinking.* New York: Harper & Row.

Wexley, K. N. (1984). Personnel training. *Annual Review of Psychology, 35,* 519–551.

Whimbey, A., with Whimbey, L. S. (1980). *Intelligence can be taught.* New York: Dutton.

White, B. L., & Held, R. (1966). Plasticity of sensorimotor development in the human infant. In J. F. Rosenblith & W. Allinsmith (Eds.), *The causes of behavior,* Vol. I (2nd ed.). Boston: Allyn & Bacon.

White, B. L., & Watts, J. C. (1973). *Experience and environment,* Vol. I. Englewood Cliffs, NJ: Prentice-Hall.

Wickens, C. D., & Kramer, A. (1985). Engineering psychology. *Annual Review of Psychology*, *36*, 307–348.

Wickes, I. G. (1958). Treatment of persistent enuresis with the electric buzzer. *Archives of Diseases in Childhood*, *33*, 160–164.

Wilber, R. (1986, March). A drug to fight cocaine. *Science 86*, pp. 42–46.

Wilhelm, J. L. (1976). *The search for superman*. New York: Simon & Schuster.

Williams, B. A. (1984, November 30). U.S. approves implants to aid the totally deaf. *Santa Barbara News Press*, Part C, p. 6.

Williams, B. M. (1974, November). Promise and caution—"Hypnosis is like a scalpel. You wouldn't want it wielded by your janitor." *Psychology Today*.

Williams, G. J., & Money, J. (Eds.). (1980). *Traumatic abuse and neglect of children at home*. Baltimore, MD: Johns Hopkins University Press.

Williams, R. L., et al. (1964). Sleep patterns in young adults: An EEG study. *Electroencephalography and Clinical Neurophysiology*, 376–381.

Williams, R. L., & Long, J. D. (1979). *Toward a self-managed life style*. Boston: Houghton Mifflin.

Wilson, R. R. (1968). Perceptual distinction of height as a function of ascribed academic status. *Journal of Social Psychology*, *74*, 97–102.

Wilson, S., Strong, B., Clarke, L. M., & Thomas, J. (1984). *Human sexuality*. St. Paul, MN: West Publishing Co.

Winget, C., & Kramer, M. (1979). *Dimensions of dreams*. Gainesville: University Presses of Florida.

Winson, J. (1985). *Brain and psyche: the biology of the unconscious*. Garden City, NY: Doubleday.

Wise, E. H., & Haynes, S. N. (1983). Cognitive treatment of test anxiety: Rational restructuring versus attentional training. *Cognitive Therapy and Research*, *7*, 69–78.

Wise, J. (1982, September). A gentle deterrent to vandalism. *Psychology Today*, pp. 31–38.

Wolfe, J. B. (1936). Effectiveness of token rewards for chimpanzees. *Comparative Psychology Monographs 12*(5. Whole No. 60).

Wolpe, J. (1974). *The practice of behavior therapy* (2nd ed.). New York: Pergamon.

Woodmansee, J. J. (1970). The pupil response as a measure of social attitudes. In G. F. Summers (Ed.), *Attitude measurement*. Chicago: Rand McNally.

Woolfolk, R., & Richardson, F. (1978). *Stress, sanity and survival*. New York: Signet.

Work in America. (1973). Special Task Force, Department of Health, Education and Welfare. Cambridge, MA: MIT Press.

Wrightsman, L. S., & Deaux, K. (1981). *Social psychology in the 80s*. Monterey, CA: Brooks/Cole.

Wulbert, M., & Dries, R. (1977). The relative efficacy of methylphenidate (Ritalin) and behavior-modification techniques in the treatment of a hyperactive child. *Journal of Applied Behavior Analysis*, *10*, 21–31.

Yalom, I. D. (1980). *Existential psychotherapy*. New York: Basic Books.

Yule, W., Urbanowicz, M., Lansdown, R., & Millar, I. B. (1984). Teachers' ratings of children's behavior in relation to blood lead levels. *British Journal of Developmental Psychology*, *2*, 295–305.

Zaludek, G. M. (1976, February). How to cope with male menopause. *Science Digest*, pp. 74–79.

Zane, M. D., & Milt, H. (1984). *Your phobia*. Washington, DC: American Psychiatric Press.

Zilbergeld, B. (1983). *The shrinking of America: Myths of psychological change*. Boston: Little Brown.

Zimbardo, P. G. (1974). On the ethics of intervention in human psychological research: With special reference to the Stanford prison experiment. *Cognition*, *2*, 243–256.

Zimbardo, P. G. (1975). *Psychology and life* (9th ed.). Glenview, IL: Scott, Foresman.

Zimbardo, P. G., Haney, C., & Banks, W. C. (1973, April 8). A pirandellian prison. *The New York Times Magazine*.

Zimbardo, P. G., Pilkonis, P. A., & Norwood, R. M. (1978). The social disease called shyness. In *Annual editions, personality and adjustment* 78/79. Guilford, CT: Dushkin.

Zinberg, N. E. (1976, December). The war over marijuana. *Psychology Today*, pp. 92–98.

Zuckerman, M., & Allison, S. (1976). An objective measure of fear of success: Construction and validation. *Journal of Personality*, *40*, 422–430.

Zuckerman, M., Eysenck, S., & Eysenck, H. J. (1978). Sensation seeking in England and America: Cross-cultural, age, and sex comparisons. *Journal of Consulting and Clinical Psychology*, *46*, 139–149.

Zung, W. W. K., & Green, R. H., Jr. (1974). Seasonal variation of suicide and depression. *Archives of General Psychiatry*, *30*, 89–91.

Index

p. 23 Ulrich, R. E., Stachnik, T. J., and Stainton, N. R. Student acceptance of generalized personality interpretations. PSYCHOLOGICAL REPORTS, 1963, 13, 831–834.
p. 29 van Lawick-Goodall, Jane. *In The Shadow of Man*. Houghton Mifflin Co., 1971. World Rights: William Collins Sons & Co. Ltd., London.
Fig. 2-1 © Richard Wood, The Picture Cube.
Fig. 2-2 National Geographic Society Magazine. Photo by Baron Hugo van Lawick.
p. 33 Courtesy of Peter Mueller.
Fig. 2-4 © Jean-Claude Lejeune, Stock Boston.
p. 60 Gazzaniga, M. S. *The Bisected Brain*. Plenum Publishing Co., 1970.
p. 60 Ornstein, R. E. *The Psychology of Consciousness*. W. H. Freeman & Co., 1972.
Fig. 3-15 © Michael Serino, The Picture Cube.
Fig. 4-9 *(left)* © Harvey Eisner, Taurus; *(right)* © David M. Campione, Taurus.
Fig. 4-11 © Jeffry W. Myers, Stock Boston.
Fig. 4-14 © Jon L. Barken, The Picture Cube.
Fig. 4-24 The Bettmann Archive.
Fig. 5-1 Photo by Kevin McMahon.
Fig. 5-4 © E. R. Degginger, Animals, Animals.
Fig. 5-8 © Enrico Ferorelli/DOT.
Fig. 5-16 M. C. Escher "Still Life and Street" © BEELDRECHT, Amsterdam/VAGA, New York Collection Haags Gemeentemuseum—The Hague.
Fig. 5-17 From "Pictorial Perception and Culture" by J. B. Deregowski. Copyright © 1972 by *Scientific American*, Inc. All rights reserved.
Fig. 5-18 The Bettmann Archive.
Fig. 5-20 Baron Wolman
Fig. 5-21 © Dan Francis, Mardan Photography.
Fig. 5-26 Erdelyi, M. H. and A. G. Appelbaum, "Cognitive Masking: The Disruptive Effect of an Emotional Stimulus Upon the Perception of Contiguous Neutral Items." *Bulletin of the Psychonomic Society*. 1973, 1, 59-61.
p. 138 Kapleau, Philip. *The Three Pillars of Zen*, Harper & Row, 1966.
Fig. 6-2 Yale Joel, LIFE Magazine, © Time Inc.
Fig. 6-3 © 1981 Martin M. Rotker, Taurus.
Fig. 6-5 Wide World Photos.
Fig. 6-6 Dan Francis, Mardan Photography.
Fig. 6-7 Dan Francis, Mardan Photography.
Table 6-1 Stanford Hypnotic Scale, adapted from Weitzenhofler and Hilgard. Stanford University Press, 1959.
Fig. 6-8 Spectrum and Continuum of Drugs, Dr. Robert W. Earle, University of California, Irvine.
p. 160 Cartoon courtesy of Chronicle Features.
Fig. 6-9 D. Coon.
Fig. 6-10 Blood Alcohol Content Chart, courtesy of Jozef Cohen.
Table 6-2 Facts About Drugs from *The Resource Book for Drug Abuse Education*. National Education Association, 1969.
Fig. 6-11 "Beware Marijuana" Poster courtesy of Dr. Lester Grinspoon, Harvard Medical School.
p. 167 H. Benson, "Systematic Hypertension and The Relaxation Response." Reprinted by permission from *The New England Journal of Medicine*, Vol. 296, pp. 1152-1156, 1977.
Fig. 7-4 © Dan Francis, Mardan Photography.
Fig. 7-8 Ira Kirschenbaum, Stock, Boston.
Fig. 7-9 Yale Joel, LIFE Magazine, © Time, Inc.
Fig. 7-11 Chimp-O-Mat. Yerkes Regional Primate Research Center, Emory University.
Fig. 7-14 Dan Francis, Mardan Photography.
Fig. 7-15 Loomis Dean, LIFE Magazine, © Time, Inc.
Fig. 7-17 Photos by Barbara Martin, Courtesy of the *Los Angeles Times*, © 1984.
Fig. 7-18 Alain Dejean, Sygma.
Fig. 8-5 "Effects of Punishment on Extinction." Chart from B. F. Skinner, *The Behavior of Organism*, 1938. Permission from Prentice-Hall, Inc.

Fig. 8-6 © Ellis Herwig, The Picture Cube.
p. 218 Cartoon courtesy of Ed Arno and *Science 80*.
Fig. 8-9 Nursery School Children, Dr. Albert Bandura, Stanford University.
p. 221 Cartoon reproduced courtesy of the Edmonton Journal.
Fig. 8-10 Owen Franken, Stock Boston.
Fig. 8-11 Steven Stone, The Picture Cube.
Fig. 9-1 Courtesy of IBM.
Fig. 9-3 Penfield, W. *The Excitable Cortex in Conscious Man*, 1958. Courtesy of Charles C Thomas Publisher, Springfield, Illinois.
Fig. 9-5 © Larry Day.
Fig. 9-10 © Dan Francis, Mardan Photography.
Fig. 9-15 © Animals, Animals.
Fig. 10-2 © Ralph Reinhold, Animals, Animals.
Fig. 10-5 Osgood, C. E. "The Nature and Measurement of Meaning." *Psychological Bulletin*, 49, Copyright, 1952 by The American Psychological Association. Reprinted by permission.
Fig. 10-8 From "Teaching Language to An Ape." by Ann Premack and David Premack. Copyright © 1972 by *Scientific American, Inc. All rights reserved.*
Fig. 10-14 U.S. Patent No. 556,248. From *Absolutely Mad Inventions* by A. E. Brown and H. A. Jeffcott, Jr. Dover, 1970.
Fig. 11-1 © David Austen, Woodfin Camp.
Fig. 11-4 Hyperphagic Rat courtesy of Dr. Neal E. Miller, Rockefeller University.
Fig. 11-5 © Peter Menzel, Stock Boston.
Fig. 11-6 "Monkeys and Locks." Harry F. Harlow, University of Wisconsin Primate Laboratory.
Fig. 11-7 Berlyne, D. E. "Curiosity and Exploration." *Science*, Vol. 153, pp. 25-33, Figure 4, 1 July, 1966, Copyright 1966 by the American Association for the Advancement of Science.
Fig. 11-8 © David F. Hughes, The Picture Cube.
p. 307 Zuckerman, M. *Manual and Research Report for the Sensation-Seeking Scale (SSS)*. Mimeograph, University of Delaware, Newark, Delaware, April, 1972. Reproduced by permission.
Fig. 11-11 © Dan Francis, Mardan Photography.
Fig. 11-13 © Marty Heitner, Taurus.
Figs. 12-1, 12-10 Courtesy of The Record, Hackensack, New Jersey.
Fig. 12-4 © Phillip Jon Bailley, The Picture Cube.
Fig. 12-6 Photo courtesy of the Stoelting Company, Chicago, Illinois.
Fig. 12-7 Bridges, K. M. B. "Emotional Development in Early Infancy." *Child Development*, 3, 324-341. Figure 1, p. 340. Copyright, 1932.
Fig. 12-8 Zoological Society of San Diego.
Fig. 12-9 © Dan Francis, Mardan Photography.
Fig. 12-11 © Laimute Druskis, Taurus.
p. 343 © Dan Francis, Mardan Photography.
p. 344 The Danger Signals of Depression, National Association of Mental Health.
p. 349 Associated Press news article courtesy of the Associated Press.
Table 13-2 Friedman, M. and R. Roseman. *Type A Behavior and Your Heart*, Alfred A. Knopf, Inc. 1974. Reprinted by permission.
Table 13-3 Reprinted with permission from the *Journal of Psychosomatic Research* Vol. 11. T. H. Holmes and R. H. Rahe. "Social Readjustment Rating Scale," 1957, Pergamon Press, Ltd.
p. 352 The Better Half by Barnes, reprinted courtesy of Register and Tribune Syndicate, Inc.
Fig. 13-2 © David Woo, Stock Boston.
Fig. 13-5 © Liane Enkilis, Stock Boston.
Fig. 13-6 © Cary Wolinsky, Stock Boston.
Fig. 13-7 The General Adaptation Syndrome graph from *The Stress of Life* by Hans Selye. Copyright © 1956, 1976 by Hans Selye. Used by permission of McGraw-Hill Book Company.
Fig. 14-1 "Imitation of Facial and Manual Gestures by Human Neonates," by A. N. Meltzoff and M. K. Moore, *Science*, vol. 198, pp. 75-78, Fig. 1, October 7, 1977. Copyright 1977 by The American Association for the Advancement of Science.
Fig. 14-2 From "The Origin of Form Perception." by Robert L. Fantz. Copyright © 1961 by Scientific American, Inc. All rights reserved. Photograph of Fantz's Looking Chamber by David Linton.
p. 381 Huxley, A. "Human Potentialities." in R. E. Farson (ed.) *Science and Human Affairs*. Palo Alto, California: Science and Behavior Books, 1965.

Fig. 14-4 © Michael Grecco, Stock Boston.
Fig. 14-6 © Petit Format/Nestle, Science Source, Photo Researchers.
Fig. 14-7 © A. Glauberman, Photo Researchers.
Fig. 14-8 © Frank Siteman, Taurus.
Fig. 14-11 Jerome Bruner, *Child's Talk, Learning to use Language*, W. W. Norton & Co., 1981. Reprinted by permission.
Fig. 14-12 Nina Leen © 1964 Time Inc.
p. 395 Associated Press newsarticle courtesy of the Associated Press.
Fig. 14-13 © Martin Rogers, Stock Boston.
Fig. 14-14 © Yves Debraine, Black Star.
Fig. 14-15 © Mimi Forsyth, Monkmeyer
p. 403 Hayakawa, S. I. "The Use and Misuse of Language," In R. E. Farson (ed.) *Science and Human Affairs*. Palo Alto, California: Science and Behavior Books, 1965.
Fig. 15-1 © Gabor Demjen, Stock Boston.
Fig. 15-2 From "Growing Up" by J. M. Tanner. Copyright © September, 1973 by *Scientific American*, Inc. All rights reserved.
Fig. 15-3 © Lenore Weber, Taurus.
Fig. 15-4 © Bohdan Hrynewych, Stock Boston.
Fig. 15-5 © Ellis Herwig, The Picture Cube.
Fig. 15-7 © Pam Hasegawa, Taurus.
Fig. 15-8 © Elaine Wicks, O.S.F., Taurus.
p. 429 Ginott, H. *Between Parent and Child*. 1965. Reprinted by permission of Dr. Alice Ginott.
Table 16-1 Terman, L. and M. Merrill, *Stanford-Binet Intelligence Scale*. 1937 (Revised ed. 1960b). Houghton Mifflin Co.
Table 16-2 Wechsler Scale, The Psychological Corporation, 1958.
Fig. 16-1 © Mimi Forsyth, Monkmeyer.
Fig. 16-3 Wide World Photos.
Fig. 16-4 *(left)* © Karen R. Preuss, Taurus; *(middle)* © Dan Francis, Mardan Photography; *right)* © David M. Campione, Taurus.
Fig. 16-5 Special Olympics Photograph courtesy of Priscilla Copass and Steve Neighbors.
Fig. 16-8 Culture Fair Test Sample Items from R. B. Cattell, "Are I.Q. Tests Intelligent?" Reprinted by permission of Dr. R. B. Cattell.
Fig. 17-1 © Gregg Mancusco, Stock Boston.
Fig. 17-2 Cattell, R. B. "Personality Pinned Down." 1973. Reprinted by permission of Dr. R. B. Cattell.
Fig. 17-3 © Alvis Upitis, Black Star.
Fig. 17-4 © Dan Francis, Mardan Photography.
Table 17-2 Reproduced by permission. Copyright 1943, renewed 1970 by the University of Minnesota. Published by the Psychological Corporation, New York, New York. All rights reserved.
Fig. 17-5 © Stacy Pick, Stock Boston.
Fig. 17-6 Woodfin Camp.
p. 471 Art Buchwald quotation courtesy of Art Buchwald, Los Angeles Times.
Fig. 18-1 "All is Vanity," Courtesy of Illusions, Park Ridge, Illinois.
Fig. 18-3 UPI/Bettmann News Photos.
Fig. 18-4 ©Dan Francis, Mardan Photography.
Fig. 18-5 © Terry McKoy, Taurus.
Fig. 18-6 © Frank Siteman, Stock Boston.
Fig. 18-7 © Charles E. Schmidt, Taurus
p. 504 *Catch 22* copyright © 1955, 1961 by Joseph Heller. Reprinted by permission of Simon & Schuster, a division of Gulf and Western Corporation; and by A. M. Heath & Co., Ltd., London
Fig. 19-1 Photographs courtesy of Ulrike Kantor Gallery.
Fig. 19-3 © Laimute Druskis, Taurus.
p. 515 Suinn, Richard M. *Fundamentals of Behavior Pathology*, 2nd ed. Copyright © 1975 by Richard Suinn. Reprinted by permission of John Wiley & Sons, Inc.
Fig. 19-4 © Cary Wolinsky, Stock Boston.
Fig. 19-5 *(left)* UPI/Bettmann News Photos; *(right)* D. Coon.
Fig. 19-6 © Charles Gupton, Stock Boston.
p. 532 *I Never Promised You a Rose Garden* by Hannah Green (Joanne Greenberg). Copyright © 1964 by Hannah Green. Reprinted by permission of Holt, Rinehart and Winston.

Fig. 20-1 Zalesky/Clemmer, Black Star.
Fig. 20-2 The Bettmann Archive.
Fig. 20-3 © Dan Francis, Mardan Photography.
Fig. 20-4 Benyas, Black Star.
p. 540 Suinn, Richard M. *Fundamentals of Behavior Pathology*, 1st ed. Copyright © 1970 by Richard Suinn. Reprinted by permission of John Wiley & Sons, Inc.
Fig. 20-5 © 1975 Jerry Cooke.
Fig. 20-7 Derek Bayes/Courtesy Gottman-Mackey, Life Picture Service.
Fig. 20-8 *(left)* Dennis Brack, Black Star; *(right)* Duke University Hospital.
Fig. 20-9 The Brookhaven Institute.
Fig. 20-10 © Will McIntyre, Photo Researchers.
Fig. 20-11 Jeff Albertson, Stock, Boston.
Fig. 21-1 (a) University Museum of the University of Pennsylvania; (b) courtesy of the New York Public Library; (c) The Bettmann Archive.
Fig. 21-3 Historical Pictures Service, Chicago.
Fig. 21-4 Michael Routgier, Life Magazine © Time, Inc.
p. 576 Stevens. J. O. *Awareness: Exploring, Experimenting. Experiencing.* Real People Press, 1971.
Fig. 21-5 © Bohdan Hrynewych, Stock Boston.
Fig. 22-1 Curt Gunther, Camera 5.
Fig. 22-2 © Peter Menzel, Stock Boston.
Fig. 22-3 Photograph courtesy of Albert Bandura and the American Psychological Association. Copyright 1969 by the American Psychological Association. Reprinted by permission. From the *Journal of Personality and Social Psychology*, 1969, 13, pp. 173–199.
p. 585 Lazarus, Arnold. "The Treatment of Chronic Frigidity by Systematic Desensitization." In *Experiments in Behavior Therapy*. H. J. Eysenck, (ed.). Reprinted by permission of the author. Copyright © 1964 Pergamon Press, Ltd.
Fig. 22-4 Lovaas, O. I. and Simmons, J. Q. Manipulation of Self-destruction in Three Retarded Children." *Journal of Applied Behavior Analysis*, 1969, 2. pp. 143-157. Reprinted by permission.
Fig. 22-5 Token Economy photograph courtesy of Robert Liberman, M.D.
Figs. 23-4, 23-5 Beach, Frank A., ed. *Sex and Behavior*. New York: John Wiley & Sons, Inc., 1965.
Fig. 24-1 © Charles Gupton, Stock Boston.
Fig. 24-2 © Gregg Mancusco, Stock Boston.
Fig. 24-3 © Stacy Pick, Stock Boston.
Fig. 24-4 © Janeart 1983, The Image Bank.
Table 24-1 Zick Rubin. "Measurement of Romantic Love." *Journal of Personality and Social Psychology*. Copyright 1970 by the American Psychological Association. Reprinted by permission.
Box 24-1 From Zick Rubin, *Liking and Loving: An Invitation to Social Psychology*, 1973, Holt, Rinehart and Winston.
Fig. 24-8 © Robert V. Eckert, Stock, Boston.
Fig. 25-1 © C. Kuhn, The Image BankWest.
Fig. 25-2 © Mark Mittelman, Taurus.
Fig. 25-4 Ellis Herwig, The Picture Cube.
Fig. 25-5 Wide World Photos.
Fig. 25-6 © Bill Gallery, Stock Boston.
Fig. 25-7 © Charles Gupton, Stock Boston.
Fig. 25-8 © LeBeck, Black Star.
Table 25-1 M. Karlins, T. L. Coffman and G. Walters. "On the Fading of Social Stereotypes: Studies in Three Generations of College Students." *journal of Personality and Social Psychology*. Copyright 1969 by the American Psychological Association. Reprinted by permission.
p. 665 Adorno, Theodore, E. Frenkel-Brunswik, D. J. Levinson and R. N. Stanford. *The Authoritarian Personality*. Copyright © 1950. Harper & Row.

Fig. 25-9 L. D. Eron. "The development of aggressive behavior from the perspective of a developing behaviorism. Copyright 1987 by the American Psychological Association. Reprinted by permission.
Fig. 26-2 Photograph reproduced courtesy of General Electric.
Fig. 26-3 © David Strickler, Monkmeyer.
Fig. 26-4 © Charles Feil, Stock Boston.
Fig. 26-5 © Steve Hanson, Stock Boston.
Fig. 26-6 © Arthur Grace, Stock Boston.
Fig. 26-8 © Charles Gupton, Stock Boston.
Fig. 26-9 Reproduced courtesy of Paul Marques. Bienestar: Health, Well-Being and Life Style Choices for Pinal County. Project West Pinal, University of Arizona Health Sciences Center. 1982.

Chris	Jim
~~0~~	~~0~~
~~2~~	~~2~~
~~1~~	~~4~~
~~3~~	~~6~~
~~6~~	~~7~~
~~10~~	~~10~~
12	11